Theater of a Thousand Wonders

The great many shrines of New Spain were long-lived sites of shared devotion and contestation across social groups, providing a lasting sense of enchantment, of divine immanence in the present, and a hunger for epiphanies in daily life. This is a story of consolidation and growth during the seventeenth and eighteenth centuries, rather than one of rise and decline in the face of early stages of modernization. Based on research in a wide array of manuscript and printed primary sources, and informed by recent scholarship in art history, religious studies, anthropology, and history, this is the first comprehensive study of shrines and miraculous images in any part of early modern Latin America.

William B. Taylor is Muriel McKevitt Sonne Professor of History, Emeritus at the University of California, Berkeley. Research for this book took him to Spain, Guatemala, various archives and libraries in the United States, and many places in Mexico. It is the culmination of a long-term study of religious life and especially political and cultural power in colonial Latin America. Earlier books include *Magistrates of the Sacred: Priests and Parishioners in Eighteenth-Century Mexico* (1996) and *Shrines and Miraculous Images: Essays on Religious Life in Mexico Before the Reforma* (2010). He is the recipient of several awards, including the Albert J. Beveridge Prize from the American Historical Association.

Cambridge Latin American Studies

General Editors
KRIS LANE, *Tulane University*
MATTHEW RESTALL, *Pennsylvania State University*

Editor Emeritus
HERBERT S. KLEIN, *Columbia University and Stanford University*

Other Books in the Series

102. *Indian and Slave Royalists in the Age of Revolution*, Marcela Echeverri
101. *Indigenous Elites and Creole Identity in Colonial Mexico, 1500–1800*, Peter Villella
100. *Asian Slaves in Colonial Mexico: From Chinos to Indians*, Tatiana Seijas
99. *Black Saint of the Americas: The Life and Afterlife of Martín de Porres*, Celia Cussen
98. *The Economic History of Latin America since Independence*, Third Edition, Victor Bulmer-Thomas
97. *The British Textile Trade in South American in the Nineteenth Century*, Manuel Llorca-Jaña
96. *Warfare and Shamanism in Amazonia*, Carlos Fausto
95. *Rebellion on the Amazon: The Cabanagem, Race, and Popular Culture in the North of Brazil, 1798–1840*, Mark Harris
94. *A History of the Khipu*, Galen Brokaw
93. *Politics, Markets, and Mexico's "London Debt," 1823–1887*, Richard J. Salvucci
92. *The Political Economy of Argentina in the Twentieth Century*, Roberto Cortés Conde
91. *Bankruptcy of Empire: Mexican Silver and the Wars between Spain, Britain, and France, 1760–1810*, Carlos Marichal
90. *Shadows of Empire: The Indian Nobility of Cusco, 1750–1825*, David T. Garrett
89. *Chile: The Making of a Republic, 1830–1865: Politics and Ideas*, Simon Collier
88. *Deference and Defiance in Monterrey: Workers, Paternalism, and Revolution in Mexico, 1890–1950*, Michael Snodgrass
87. *Andrés Bello: Scholarship and Nation-Building in Nineteenth-Century Latin America*, Ivan Jaksic
86. *Between Revolution and the Ballot Box: The Origins of the Argentine Radical Party in the 1890s*, Paula Alonso
85. *Slavery and the Demographic and Economic History of Minas Gerais, Brazil, 1720–1888*, Laird W. Bergad
84. *The Independence of Spanish America*, Jaime E. Rodríguez
83. *The Rise of Capitalism on the Pampas: The Estancias of Buenos Aires, 1785–1870*, Samuel Amaral
82. *A History of Chile, 1808–2002*, Second Edition, Simon Collier and William F. Sater
81. *The Revolutionary Mission: American Enterprise in Latin America, 1900–1945*, Thomas F. O'Brien
80. *The Kingdom of Quito, 1690–1830: The State and Regional Development*, Kenneth J. Andrien
79. *The Cuban Slave Market, 1790–1880*, Laird W. Bergad, Fe Iglesias García, and María del Carmen Barcia
78. *Business Interest Groups in Nineteenth-Century Brazil*, Eugene Ridings
77. *The Economic History of Latin America since Independence*, Second Edition, Victor Bulmer-Thomas
76. *Power and Violence in the Colonial City: Oruro from the Mining Renaissance to the Rebellion of Tupac Amaru (1740–1782)*, Oscar Cornblit
75. *Colombia before Independence: Economy, Society and Politics under Bourbon Rule*, Anthony McFarlane
74. *Politics and Urban Growth in Buenos Aires, 1910–1942*, Richard J. Walter

73. *The Central Republic in Mexico, 1835–1846, "Hombres de Bien" in the Age of Santa Anna*, Michael P. Costeloe
72. *Negotiating Democracy: Politicians and Generals in Uruguay*, Charles Guy Gillespie
71. *Native Society and Disease in Colonial Ecuador*, Suzanne Austin Alchon
70. *The Politics of Memory: Native Historical Interpretation in the Colombian Andes*, Joanne Rappaport
69. *Power and the Ruling Classes in Northeast Brazil, Juazeiro and Petrolina in Transition*, Ronald H. Chilcote
68. *House and Street: The Domestic World of Servants and Masters in Nineteenth-Century Rio de Janeiro*, Sandra Lauderdale Graham
67. *The Demography of Inequality in Brazil*, Charles H. Wood and José Alberto Magno de Carvalho
66. *The Politics of Coalition Rule in Colombia*, Jonathan Hartlyn
65. *South America and the First World War: The Impact of the War on Brazil, Argentina, Peru and Chile*, Bill Albert
64. *Resistance and Integration: Peronism and the Argentine Working Class, 1946–1976*, Daniel James
63. *The Political Economy of Central America since 1920*, Victor Bulmer-Thomas
62. *A Tropical Belle Epoque: Elite Culture and Society in Turn-of-the-Century Rio de Janeiro*, Jeffrey D. Needell
61. *Ambivalent Conquests: Maya and Spaniard in Yucatan, 1517–1570*, Second Edition, Inga Clendinnen
60. *Latin America and the Comintern, 1919–1943*, Manuel Caballero
59. *Roots of Insurgency: Mexican Regions, 1750–1824*, Brian R. Hamnett
58. *The Agrarian Question and the Peasant Movement in Colombia: Struggles of the National Peasant Association, 1967–1981*, Leon Zamosc
57. *Catholic Colonialism: A Parish History of Guatemala, 1524–1821*, Adriaan C. van Oss
56. *Pre-Revolutionary Caracas: Politics, Economy, and Society 1777–1811*, P. Michael McKinley
55. *The Mexican Revolution, Volume 2: Counter-Revolution and Reconstruction*, Alan Knight
54. *The Mexican Revolution, Volume 1: Porfirians, Liberals, and Peasants*, Alan Knight
53. *The Province of Buenos Aires and Argentine Politics, 1912–1943*, Richard J. Walter
52. *Sugar Plantations in the Formation of Brazilian Society: Bahia, 1550–1835*, Stuart B. Schwartz
51. *Tobacco on the Periphery: A Case Study in Cuban Labour History, 1860–1958*, Jean Stubbs
50. *Housing, the State, and the Poor: Policy and Practice in Three Latin American Cities*, Alan Gilbert and Peter M. Ward
49. *Unions and Politics in Mexico: The Case of the Automobile Industry*, Ian Roxborough
48. *Miners, Peasants and Entrepreneurs: Regional Development in the Central Highlands of Peru*, Norman Long and Bryan Roberts
47. *Capitalist Development and the Peasant Economy in Peru*, Adolfo Figueroa
46. *Early Latin America: A History of Colonial Spanish America and Brazil*, James Lockhart and Stuart B. Schwartz
45. *Brazil's State-Owned Enterprises: A Case Study of the State as Entrepreneur*, Thomas J. Trebat
44. *Law and Politics in Aztec Texcoco*, Jerome A. Offner
43. *Juan Vicente Gómez and the Oil Companies in Venezuela, 1908–1935*, B. S. McBeth
42. *Revolution from Without: Yucatán, Mexico, and the United States, 1880–1924*, Gilbert M. Joseph
41. *Demographic Collapse: Indian Peru, 1520–1620*, Noble David Cook
40. *Oil and Politics in Latin America: Nationalist Movements and State Companies*, George Philip
39. *The Struggle for Land: A Political Economy of the Pioneer Frontier in Brazil from 1930 to the Present Day*, J. Foweraker
38. *Caudillo and Peasant in the Mexican Revolution*, D. A. Brading, ed.
37. *Odious Commerce: Britain, Spain and the Abolition of the Cuban Slave Trade*, David Murray
36. *Coffee in Colombia, 1850–1970: An Economic, Social and Political History*, Marco Palacios

35. *A Socioeconomic History of Argentina, 1776–1860*, Jonathan C. Brown
34. *From Dessalines to Duvalier: Race, Colour and National Independence in Haiti*, David Nicholls
33. *Modernization in a Mexican ejido: A Study in Economic Adaptation*, Billie R. DeWalt
32. *Haciendas and Ranchos in the Mexican Bajío, Léon, 1700–1860*, D. A. Brading
31. *Foreign Immigrants in Early Bourbon Mexico, 1700–1760*, Charles F. Nunn
30. *The Merchants of Buenos Aires, 1778–1810: Family and Commerce*, Susan Migden Socolow
29. *Drought and Irrigation in North-east Brazil*, Anthony L. Hall
28. *Coronelismo: The Municipality and Representative Government in Brazil*, Victor Nunes Leal
27. *A History of the Bolivian Labour Movement, 1848–1971*, Guillermo Lora
26. *Land and Labour in Latin America: Essays on the Development of Agrarian Capitalism in the Nineteenth and Twentieth Centuries*, Kenneth Duncan and Ian Rutledge, eds.
25. *Allende's Chile: The Political Economy of the Rise and Fall of the Unidad Popular*, Stefan de Vylder
24. *The Cristero Rebellion: The Mexican People between Church and State, 1926–1929*, Jean A. Meyer
23. *The African Experience in Spanish America, 1502 to the Present Day*, Leslie B. Rout, Jr.
22. *Letters and People of the Spanish Indies: Sixteenth Century*, James Lockhart and Enrique Otte, eds.
21. *Chilean Rural Society from the Spanish Conquest to 1930*, Arnold J. Bauer
20. *Studies in the Colonial History of Spanish America*, Mario Góngora
19. *Politics in Argentina, 1890–1930: The Rise and Fall of Radicalism*, David Rock
18. *Politics, Economics and Society in Argentina in the Revolutionary Period*, Tulio Halperín Donghi
17. *Marriage, Class and Colour in Nineteenth-Century Cuba: A Study of Racial Attitudes and Sexual Values in a Slave Society*, Verena Stolcke
16. *Conflicts and Conspiracies: Brazil and Portugal, 1750–1808*, Kenneth Maxwell
15. *Silver Mining and Society in Colonial Mexico: Zacatecas, 1546–1700*, P. J. Bakewell
14. *A Guide to the Historical Geography of New Spain*, Peter Gerhard
13. *Bolivia: Land, Location and Politics since 1825*, J. Valerie Fifer, Malcolm Deas, Clifford Smith, and John Street
12. *Politics and Trade in Southern Mexico, 1750–1821*, Brian R. Hamnett
11. *Alienation of Church Wealth in Mexico: Social and Economic Aspects of the Liberal Revolution, 1856–1875*, Jan Bazant
10. *Miners and Merchants in Bourbon Mexico, 1763–1810*, D. A. Brading
9. *An Economic History of Colombia, 1845–1930*, W. P. McGreevey
8. *Economic Development of Latin America: Historical Background and Contemporary Problems*, Celso Furtado and Suzette Macedo
7. *Regional Economic Development: The River Basin Approach in Mexico*, David Barkin and Timothy King
6. *The Abolition of the Brazilian Slave Trade: Britain, Brazil and the Slave Trade Question, 1807–1869*, Leslie Bethell
5. *Parties and Political Change in Bolivia, 1880–1952*, Herbert S. Klein
4. *Britain and the Onset of Modernization in Brazil, 1850–1914*, Richard Graham
3. *The Mexican Revolution, 1910–1914: The Diplomacy of Anglo-American Conflict*, P. A. R. Calvert
2. *Church Wealth in Mexico: A Study of the "Juzgado de Capellanias" in the Archbishopric of Mexico 1800–1856*, Michael P. Costeloe
1. *Ideas and Politics of Chilean Independence, 1808–1833*, Simon Collier

Theater of a Thousand Wonders

A History of Miraculous Images and Shrines in New Spain

WILLIAM B. TAYLOR
University of California, Berkeley

CAMBRIDGE
UNIVERSITY PRESS

One Liberty Plaza, 20th Floor, New York, NY 10006, USA

Cambridge University Press is part of the University of Cambridge.

It furthers the University's mission by disseminating knowledge in the pursuit of education, learning, and research at the highest international levels of excellence.

www.cambridge.org
Information on this title: www.cambridge.org/9781107102675

© William B. Taylor 2016

This publication is in copyright. Subject to statutory exception and to the provisions of relevant collective licensing agreements, no reproduction of any part may take place without the written permission of Cambridge University Press.

First published 2016

Printed in the United States of America by Sheridan Books, Inc.

A catalogue record for this publication is available from the British Library.

Library of Congress Cataloging-in-Publication Data
Taylor, William B., author.
Theater of a thousand wonders : a history of miraculous images and shrines in New Spain / William B. Taylor, University of California, Berkeley.
New York : Cambridge University Press, 2016. | Series: Cambridge Latin American studies
LCCN 2016015475 | ISBN 9781107102675
LCSH: Christian shrines – New Spain. | Christian shrines – Mexico. | Mexico – Church history.
LCC BX2320.5.N49 T39 2016 | DDC 263/.04272–dc23
LC record available at https://lccn.loc.gov/2016015475

ISBN 978-1-107-10267-5 Hardback

Cambridge University Press has no responsibility for the persistence or accuracy of URLs for external or third-party Internet Web sites referred to in this publication and does not guarantee that any content on such Web sites is, or will remain, accurate or appropriate.

To Barbara, Karin, and Jill

Contents

List of Figures	*page* xiii
List of Maps	xviii
List of Tables	xix
Preface and Acknowledgments	xxi
Archive Abbreviations	xxv
Introduction	1

Part I Bearings: Historical Patterns and Places of Image Shrines

1	Formative Developments, 1520s–1720s	35
2	Growth, Other Changes, and Continuities in the Late Colonial Period	95
3	Miraculous Images of Christ and the Virgin Mary	170
4	Advocations of the Virgin Mary in the Colonial Period	245

Part II Soundings: Divine Presence, Place, and the Power of Things

5	Making Miracles	309
6	Relics, Images, and Other Numinous Things	361
7	Religious Prints and Their Uses	398
8	Placing the Cross in Colonial Mexico	454
9	Pilgrims, Processions, and Romerías	502
	Conclusion	551

Appendix 1 Colonial Image Shrines 567
Appendix 2 When Shrines Began 592
Appendix 3 Other Saints 604
Index 639

Figures

1.1 Erection of the great Cross of Tlaxcala, depicted in the Lienzo de Tlaxcala. *page* 51
1.2 Juan de Rúa's painting of the tree root figure discovered by Lorenço de Aguilar and his companions in 1611, commissioned by the *comisario* of the Inquisition in Antequera to guard against pious mutilation of the object. Ink rendering by Palma Edith Christian. 56
3.1 Print of the Virgin of Guadalupe from unsigned engraving, 1759. 174
3.2 The shrine compound at Tepeyac, 1757, loose print from engraving by Francisco Sylverio de Sotomayor. 181
3.3 Nuestra Señora del Patrocinio of Tepetlatcingo, loose print from engraving by Baltasar Troncoso y Sotomayor, 1743. 184
3.4 Loose print of "Our Lady of the Immaculate Conception in the miraculous image known as Our Lady of the Angels, venerated in her chapel in the pueblo of Santiago Tlatelolco, for [those who] help in finishing her chapel," from engraving by Manuel Galicia de Villavicencio (active 1753–1788). 186
3.5 Cover print for Br. D. Diego de Ribera, *Amoroso canto que con reverentes afectos* ..., Mexico: Viuda de Bernardo Calderón, 1663, in honor of the Virgin of Remedios's ninth visit to Mexico City. Unsigned. 188
3.6 Print depicting the discovery of the Virgin of Remedios at Totoltepec, collected in Mexico by Francisco de Ajofrín in the mid-1760s. Unsigned, undated. 189
3.7 Print of Our Lady of San Juan de los Lagos from engraving by Joseph Eligio Morales, 1761. 191
3.8 Loose print of "Miraculous Image of Our Lady of Tzapopan" from engraving by Joseph de Andrade (active 1756–1771). 192
3.9 Print of "True portrait of the miraculous image of Our Lady of El Pueblito that is venerated in her shrine on the outskirts of the city

xiv *List of Figures*

3.10 of Querétaro" from engraving by Antonio Onofre Moreno (active 1748–1774). 194

3.10 Print of "True portrait of the miraculous image of Our Lady of Itzmal that is venerated fifteen leagues from Mérida de Yucatán," from unsigned engraving, 1764. 196

3.11 Print of "True portrait of Our Lady of Remedios venerated in the convent of San Francisco of the villa of San Juan Zitáquaro. Blessed and praised be the Immaculate Conception of the Most Blessed and Saintly Virgin Mary. Devoutly sponsored by Father Fray Felipe Velasco," from engraving by Francisco Sylverio de Sotomayor, 1758, and re-engraved by Zapata, 1783. 199

3.12 Print of "True portrait of the Santo Cristo of Amacueca," from unsigned engraving, 1784. 203

3.13 Loose print of the Santo Cristo of Tlacolula, Oaxaca, from unsigned engraving, undated. 206

3.14 "True portrait of the Miraculous Image revered in its chapel in Saltillo [Coahuila]," print from unsigned engraving, 1775. 207

3.15 "Miraculous image of the Holy Christ of Chalma." Loose print from engraving by Francisco Sylverio de Sotomayor, 1761. 208

3.16 Print from unsigned engraving of the Christ of Esquipulas, with Mary and Joseph, based on a copy of the Esquipulas statue in the Church of San Juan de Dios in the city of Colima, Mexico, 1811. 209

3.17 "True portrait of the Santo Cristo of Ixmiquilpan, placed by Archbishop D. Juan de la Serna in the convent of Discalced Carmelites of St. Joseph of Mexico City, where it is to this day." Print from unsigned, undated engraving tipped into a 1724 text. 211

3.18 "True Image of the Lord of Meca [Señor del Sacromonte of Amecameca] venerated in a cave where it is said to have appeared to the Venerable Father Fray Martín de Valencia." Loose print from engraving by Pavia, 1782. 212

3.19 The Deposition of Christ. Loose print from unsigned eighteenth-century engraving. 215

3.20 Unsigned, undated print of Nuestra Señora del Rosario in Juan de Villa Sánchez, OP, 1728. 216

3.21 "True Portrait of the miraculous image of Our Lady of Mercy venerated in the church of the main convent in Mexico City of the Royal and Military Order of Redemptors of Captives." Loose print from engraving by Baltasar Troncoso y Sotomayor, 1759. 217

List of Figures

4.1 Print from unsigned, undated (ca. 1729) woodcut of Mary Immaculate above eagles with serpents in their talons, perched on a nopal cactus, symbols of Mexico City. 249
4.2 Print from unsigned woodcut of the Virgin Mary of the Immaculate Conception with standard symbols of the advocation, 1675. 251
4.3 Print of the Mater Dolorosa from unsigned engraving, 1816. 253
4.4 Two mid-eighteenth-century prints from engravings of Nuestra Señora de la Soledad, Oaxaca. 254
4.5 Print of the Mater Dolorosa from engraving (engraver's name not legible), 1817. 255
4.6 Loose print of Our Lady of Calvary of Metepec, from unsigned eighteenth-century engraving. 256
4.7 Print of Nuestra Señora del Pilar de Zaragoza, from unsigned woodcut, 1674. 260
4.8 Nuestra Señora de Covadonga, print from undated engraving by "García," 1785. 262
4.9 Nuestra Señora de la Cueva Santa. Unsigned print from engraving, 1790. 264
4.10 Print of Juan Bautista Zappa, SJ, holding a replica of the statuette of Our Lady of Loreto, engraving by Baltasar Troncoso, 1754. 269
4.11 Print of the Santa Casa of Loreto from engraving by "Agüera," 1805 270
4.12 Painting of La Divina Pastora by Miguel Cabrera, ca. 1760. 273
4.13 Print of Our Lady of Light from engraving by Tomás Suriá, 1790. 279
4.14 Print of Nuestra Señora del Refugio, from unsigned woodcut, 1773. 281
5.1 Exvoto painting by José Patricio Polo, Huamantla, Puebla, ca. 1741. 317
5.2 Samuel Stradanus engraving of the Virgin of Guadalupe with eight ex-voto depictions of miraculous events, ca. 1620. 320
5.3 The arrival of the Totolapan Christ in Mexico City, 1583. 327
5.4 Print of Spain's Nuestra Señora de Guadalupe, from unsigned woodcut, 1736. 335
7.1 *Patente* or certificate of membership in a confraternity dedicated to the miraculous image of Jesucristo del Despojo (Christ Mortified) of Huamantla, Puebla, 1821. 403
7.2 Print of Nuestra Señora de Bethlén from unsigned woodcut, 1731. 405
7.3 Print of the martyrdom of San Hipólito, from engraving by "Torreblanca, 1812." 406

List of Figures

7.4	The forbidden print of the Cross of Huaquechula, from engraving by "Nava," 1809.	410
7.5	Facing pages of a manuscript booklet of prayers for farm laborers with a small print of the Cinco Señores, Puebla, 1795.	413
7.6	Loose print of Our Lady of Guadalupe found in a shoe worn by a *cajero* (probably a bookkeeper in a merchant house) in Mexico City in 1759.	419
7.7	Print of the miraculous stone cross of Querétaro from engraving (engraver's name not legible), ca. 1760.	421
7.8	Print of the Holy Child of San Juan de la Penitencia from engraving by Manuel Villavicencio, 1818.	422
7.9	Loose print of "Miraculous Image of Nuestra Señora de la Bala" from engraving by Antonio Moreno, 1751.	423
7.10	Print of Our Lady of Guadalupe from an engraving by Tomás Suriá, 1790.	424
7.11	Fine print of the Madonna and Child promoted as a cult object in the mid-eighteenth century, from engraving by José Benito Ortuño, 1760.	425
7.12	Print from unsigned woodcut of Our Lady of Immaculate Conception, with title page, reprinted 1783.	426
7.13	Print from engraving based on Mrs. H. G. Ward's sketch of a display of religious prints and paintings in a modest dwelling at El Bozal, San Luis Potosí, 1820s.	428
7.14	Title page of Theodoro de Almeida, *Tesoro de paciencia* . . ., 1790, with signature by Felipa Luna y Rosales.	429
7.15	Pages 108–109 of Theodoro de Almeida, *Tesoro de paciencia* . . ., 1790, with inscription and signature by Cypriana García Castañiza.	430
7.16	Print in rose-colored ink of Mexico City's miraculous Christ of Atonement (El Cristo de los Desagravios), from unsigned engraving, pasted into a copy of Theodoro de Almeida, *Tesoro de paciencia* . . ., 1790.	431
7.17	Title page and unsigned print from Fernando Martagon, *Devota rogación en forma de novena, para venerar a la rodigiosa imagen del Ssmo Christo de los Desagravios*, Mexico: Zúñiga y Ontiveros, 1772.	435
8.1	Depiction of cosmic order as four quarters supported by celestial trees, Codex Fejervary-Mayer.	459
8.2	The cross and praying friars vanquish native demons in Tlaxcala. Ink drawing, ca. 1585.	462

List of Figures

8.3 The two crosses of Todos Santos Cuchumatán, Guatemala, photograph by Hans Namuth. 465

8.4 A living cross depicted on the cover of an Indian confraternity book from Rancho Santa Bárbara, near Dolores Hidalgo, Gto. in the late eighteenth century. 467

8.5 Anonymous seventeenth-century painting of English pirates attempting to destroy the Cruz de Huatulco in 1587. 472

8.6 Print of the "Prodigious Cross of Tepique," from unsigned, undated engraving. 477

9.1 Print of the pilgrim Fr. Francisco de la Cruz from unsigned engraving, and title page, in *Vida del venerable siervo de Dios Fr. Francisco e la Cruz*, Madrid: Pantaleón Aznar, 1768. 508

9.2 Print of a celebration in Mexico City's great square for the beatification of native son Felipe de Jesús, from engraving by José Montes de Oca, 1801 515

A3.1 Loose print of San José and the Christ Child, on a globe held up by allegorical figures representing the four continents, from unsigned, undated engraving (ca. 1760). 608

A3.2 Loose eighteenth-century print of El Tránsito de Sr. S. Joseph, Refugio de Agonisantes, from unsigned, undated engraving. 609

A3.3 Print of the city of Córdoba's miraculous image of San José, from engraving by Joseph de Nava, 1765. 611

Maps

1.1 Images and shrines discussed in the text. Prepared by Cox Cartographic Limited. *page 36–37*

Tables

3.1	Miraculous images of Christ and the cross (238 total)	*page* 201
3.2	Black Cristos in New Spain	221
6.1	Fragments of the True Cross in New Spain	367
6.2	Thorns from the Crown of Thorns in New Spain	368

Preface and Acknowledgments

This study of sacred images, shrines, and devotion in New Spain began with two puzzles about Mexico's celebrated Virgin of Guadalupe. First, by the late colonial period Guadalupe seemed to be known and revered almost everywhere yet drew few long-distance pilgrims to the shrine at Tepeyac and its precious matrix image; and, second, devotion to Guadalupe continued to grow and prosper when other image shrines are thought to have been in decline, shadowed by early signs of modernization and creeping disenchantment. It became clear to me that these puzzles and the history of devotion to this image and shrine more broadly could best be addressed as part of a larger story of European Catholic Christianity becoming an American religion in which hundreds of celebrated image shrines with followings beyond their immediate vicinity flowed into a deep river of devotion. Finding that few of those shrines declined during the eighteenth and nineteenth centuries led beyond the Virgin of Guadalupe to other questions. How and when did the many shrines develop? Why have so many of them lasted so long? How did devotion to them spread? How did some become more prominent than others? Who were the devotees and what did a particular shrine mean to visitors and to devotees who sought the divine presence through a celebrated image without going to its shrine? How were such images received and used? Who shaped and managed the business and culture of devotion to them?

Reckoning with the disparate record of hundreds of image shrines and related matters of spiritual landscape, material culture, popular devotion, miracles, relics, different advocations, and the economy and politics of the miraculous tends to silence the would-be oracle in me. Local histories of miraculous images converged and overlapped, but they rarely interlocked like pieces of a vast jigsaw puzzle or links in a chain; too many of the places and people involved are too fleetingly glimpsed to be certain how they came together, if at all; detecting something new is not proof that it was transformative at the time; and rules in human affairs have their exceptions. The individual stories of people, places, images, and episodes in colonial records are all suggestive and often engrossing, but, by themselves, they do not go far toward conclusions about the long history of shrines and images. So I have tried to approach the subject and reach conclusions by surrounding what I could learn about places and incidents with a composite picture of many shrines, images, and contexts, and attention to many kinds of devoted and sometimes adversarial participants, together: for instance, not only priests at large but particular prelates, pastors, and missionary preachers who often did not act as one. The aim is synoptic, to keep in mind at the same time many places, people, situations, and contrasting but related developments. Rather than claiming to have grasped the whole picture, I have reached for the "fullness" that art historian Meyer Schapiro sought for the sense of life in a painting or statue – attending to many details and perspectives, together, and accepting that the endeavor will be incomplete.[1] *Theater of a Thousand Wonders* is more about how sacred images were presented and taken in than I imagined it would be, and less about the architecture of devotion and pilgrimage – how the shrines were designed, furnished, and organized for worship, education, and accommodating crowds of visitors. But the architectural history of devotion is an elusive subject even for European shrines before the nineteenth century,[2] and the shrines as found today rarely can be taken as certain guides to what they once were.

The book has a long, opportune history – a little like its subject. It would not have been completed in this form without the support of several institutions and far-flung colleagues and friends. They have my warmest thanks. The Center for Advanced Study in the Behavioral Sciences in Palo Alto, California; Southern Methodist University; and the University of California at Berkeley covered some of the costs of research and two periods of leave from teaching responsibilities that gave me time to take stock and keep going. Since I retired in 2008, a research associate affiliation at Bowdoin College made it possible to continue to follow developments in the fields of religious studies, art history, anthropology, colonial literature, and early modern European and Latin American history as they converge on questions addressed in this book. I am grateful to Guy Saldanha and his colleagues in the Hawthorne-Longfellow Library at Bowdoin for finding many of the materials I needed through interlibrary loan, and to the libraries in the interlibrary loan network that shared their holdings. I am equally indebted to librarians and archivists elsewhere in the United States, Mexico, England, Scotland, and Spain for their knowledge and consideration over the years, especially Michael Hironymous of the Rare Books and Manuscripts department in the Benson Collection at the University of Texas at Austin; Walter Brem and Theresa Salazar of the Bancroft Library of the University of

California at Berkeley; Martha Whittaker of the Sutro Branch of the California State Library in San Francisco; Daniel Slive of the Bridwell Library at Southern Methodist University; Anton duPlessis of the Cushing Library at Texas A&M University; Suzanne Schall of the Zimmerman Library at the University of New Mexico; and colleagues of the Real Academia de la Historia (Madrid), the Archivo General de la Nación (Mexico), the Biblioteca Nacional (Mexico), the John Carter Brown Library, the Center for Creative Photography at the University of Arizona, the Los Angeles County Museum of Art (with special thanks to Ilona Katzew and Megan Knox), the John Paul Getty Research Institute Library, the National Museums Liverpool, the Glasgow University Library, the Kislar Center for Special Collections of the University of Pennsylvania, and the Lilly Library of Indiana University, who arranged for digital photographs of many of the images in these pages and guided me through the permissions process. I am indebted, too, to the priests and sacristans who indulged my questions and sometimes opened the way for research.

Others also did much to make this a fuller study and lift my spirits. With me from the beginning, in every good way, were David Carrasco, Bill Christian, Inga Clendinnen, Brian Connaughton, Susan Deans-Smith, and Ken Mills. In the first years of research, Isabel Estrada Torres gave me invaluable help locating and gathering sources in Mexico City. More recently, the perspectives, generosity, and exemplary work of Ilona Katzew and Jaime Cuadriello have been a great boon. And I remember with gratitude an afternoon tour of the saints in the city of Oaxaca with Ross Parmenter more than forty years ago. The seed was planted there.

Much appreciated leads, suggestions, and sources came from José Adrián Barragán, Martinus Cawley, José Refugio de la Torre Curiel, Jessica Delgado, Ivonne del Valle Wiarco, Jason Dyck, Iván Escamilla González, Michel Estefan Gutiérrez, Raphael Folsom, Luis Gordo Peláez, Kristin Huffine, Jennifer Hughes, Brianna Leavitt-Alcántara, Sean McEnroe, Brian Madigan, Karen Melvin, Kinga Novak, Guilhem Olivier, Felipe Pereda, Rosalba Piazza, Paul Ramírez, Ethelia Ruiz Medrano, Richard Salvucci, Gabriela Sánchez Reyes, Sylvia Sellers-García, Gretchen Starr-LeBeau, Dorothy Tanck de Estrada, Nicole Von Germeten, and Kenneth Ward.

The scholarship of Antonio Rubial García, Roberto Aceves Ávila, David Brading, Louise Burkhart, Cristina Cruz González, Kelly Donahue-Wallace, Denise Fallena Montaño, Rosario Granados Salinas, Jaime Lara, Brian Larkin, Óscar Mazin Gómez, Felipe Pereda, Pierre Ragon, Benjamin T. Smith, Laura Ackerman Smoller, David Tavárez, Elizabeth Wilder Weismann, and others already mentioned have especially enriched my understanding of religious institutions, images, prints, and enchantment in New Spain.

xxiv *Preface and Acknowledgments*

The insights and *respaldo moral* of Lewis Bateman, Thomas A. Brady, Jeffrey Burns, Simon Ditchfield, Lisbeth Haas, William F. Hanks, Walter Hauser, Ana Carolina Ibarra González, Rosemary Joyce, Timothy Matovina, Alicia Mayer González, Álvaro Matute, Óscar Mazín Gómez, Mieko Nishida, Esteban Sánchez de Tagle, Rus Sheptak, Jeffrey Stout, Jorge Traslosheros, and Allen Wells added to the pleasure of the research and my desire to share it. Once again, Nancy D. Mann's editorial skills helped me make good on the desire, and Karin E. Taylor solved every computer and scanning problem. I am indebted, too, to Palma Christian for her expert drawing of the pine root Virgin Mary, and to David Cox of Cox Cartographic Ltd. for the map locating image shrines discussed in the text. As always, the love and forbearance of my family made it all possible.

Chapters 7 and 8 include material that first appeared in the *Catholic Historical Review* and *The Americas: A Quarterly Review of Latin American History*, and are used here by permission.

A note on citations and translations: Since a separate bibliography is not included, published sources are cited in full in the notes at their first use in each chapter. For archives referenced in short form in the notes, see the Archive Abbreviations list in the following section. To reduce the length of the notes, the original Spanish passages quoted in English in the text have been omitted. Should there be a future Spanish edition, the original wording will appear there.

Notes

1. Schapiro was skeptical of claims that seeing a work as a whole was sufficient: "We do not see all of a work [of art] when we see it whole, ... the larger aspects that we call the whole," Meyer Schapiro, *Theory and Philosophy of Art*, New York: George Braziller, 1994, p. 49.
2. Paul Davies and Deborah Howard caution readers that "the architecture of pilgrimage is less well served" in the literature than other aspects of pilgrimage for Europe in the Medieval and Early Modern periods. See their "Introduction" for *Architecture and Pilgrimage, 1000–1500: Southern Europe and Beyond*, ed. Paul Davies, Deborah Howard, and Wendy Pullan, Burlington, VT: Ashgate, 2013, p. 2.

Archive Abbreviations

ACAM	Archivo de la Catedral del Arzobispado de México
AGCA	Archivo General de Centro-América, Guatemala City
AGI	Archivo General de Indias, Seville
AGN	Archivo General de la Nación, Mexico, Mexico City
AHAG	cathedral archive of the Archdiocese of Guadalajara
AHBG	Archivo Histórico de la Basílica de Guadalupe, Mexico City
AHCM	Archivo Histórico de la Ciudad de México
AHJ	Archivo Histórico de Jalisco, Guadalajara
AHM	Archivo Histórico de la Mitra, Archdiocese of Mexico, Mexico City
AJANG	Archivo Judicial de la Audiencia de la Nueva Galicia, Biblioteca Pública del Estado de Jalisco, Guadalajara
Alderman	Rare Books and Manuscripts Division, Alderman Library, University of Virginia
Bancroft	Bancroft Library, University of California, Berkeley
BEJ	Biblioteca del Estado de Jalisco, Guadalajara, Fondos Especiales
BIBM	*Boletín del Instituto Bibliográfico Mexicano* IV and V, publication of early issues of the *Gazeta de México*, 1722, 1728–1742
BNE	Biblioteca Nacional de España, Madrid
BNM	Biblioteca Nacional, Mexico, Mexico City, Fondos Reservados
BPE	Fondos Especiales, Biblioteca Pública del Estado de Jalisco, Guadalajara
CONDUMEX	Centro de Estudios Históricos, Grupo Carso, Fundación Carlos Slim

FHA	microfilms from the Biblioteca Americana José Toribio Medina, Biblioteca Nacional de Chile in the John D. Rockefeller, Jr. Library, Brown University, Providence, RI
Getty	John Paul Getty Research Institute Library, Los Angeles
JCB	The John Carter Brown Library, Providence, RI
LC	Library of Congress, Washington, DC
Newberry	Ayer Collection, The Newberry Library, Chicago
RAH	Real Academia de la Historia, Madrid
SMU Bridwell	Special Collections, Bridwell Library, Southern Methodist University, Dallas, TX
Sutro	The Sutro Library, a branch of the California State Library, San Francisco
TAMU Cushing	Cushing Memorial Library and Archives, Texas A&M University, College Station, TX
TU VEMC	Latin American Library, Tulane University, Viceregal and Ecclesiastical Mexican Collection
UD	University of Dayton Marian Library, Dayton, OH
UND	University of Notre Dame Hesburgh Libraries, South Bend, IN, Harley L. McDevitt Inquisition Collection
UT Benson	The Benson Collection, University of Texas at Austin

Introduction

> [Living tissue] is constantly replacing itself, even when it seems to stay the same. It is not a thing but a performance. — Colin Tudge[1]

Christian shrines — *santuarios* — in New Spain were privileged "places of God," "renowned and miraculous,"[2] that were acclaimed beyond the confines of the local community. Their standing as shrines originated in a "burst of divine presence,"[3] and they remained popular over many years because people believed that extraordinary consolation and favors for the faithful were available there. These shrines typically displayed a statue or painting of Christ or the Virgin Mary that was associated with a founding miracle in which the figure was understood to have come to life in some fashion or suddenly became the site of amazing protection and other wonders. Whether it was in a cathedral, a fine temple, a modest chapel, or on an altar, the shrine was literally a vessel of sacred treasure and place of refuge, meant to welcome, honor, protect, and contain the divine presence that had shown favor there and might do so again as a "theater of a thousand more wonders."[4]

I have written essays and occasional pieces about various shrines, images associated with miracles, and sacred space in colonial Mexico, but working toward a more comprehensive historical account is a different challenge. What is the narrative line for such a subject, where high politics and warfare do not dominate, the secondary literature is sparse, and many particular places stand out? What is gained and lost in proposing patterns over time from the particulars? The chapters in Part I set out the main lines of change and continuity I noticed from the first years of Spanish colonization and Christian evangelization to the founding of most shrines in the seventeenth century and to their consolidation and expansion in the eighteenth century, pieced together from information about roughly 500 shrines and images.[5] (See Map 1.1 for the location of image shrines discussed in the text.) They offer a perspective on change and a foundation for the later chapters, which turn to the material culture of devotion, miracles, pilgrimage, and some particular images and places in time that bend as much as they punctuate a history of how and why some shrine images came to be more widely known and why most of them remained popular.

This introduction describes what the book aims for, and why, at least in my hands, a more or less continuous, chronological treatment of colonial shrines and the people devoted to them blurs at the center as well as at the edges, laced with localized, often loosely related developments. In search of the people behind the patterned tendencies in often opaque or one-sided sources about the history of shrines and images, I looked for dynamic and relational ways to think about locality and familiar categories of place and space, center and periphery, elite and popular, Spaniard and Indian, promotion and devotion. It is tempting to frame the history of shrines in terms of sharp distinctions like these because the written record adopts or implies them.[6] The documentation on shrines is more about place and authority than it is about space or devotees and their activities, but the power of place was more than just a convenient organizing principle for colonial record keepers. When, for example, the pastor of Huitzilopochco (Churubusco) took stones from a ruined temple platform nearby to repair the parish church in the early 1730s, local people protested that in this very place was all the strength of the community.[7]

In colonial-era terms, a shrine was a house of God widely known for signs of divine presence and power, especially an apparition or an image that had become a channel of divine benevolence and judgment.[8] But these shrines are not all the same, and they did not amount to a network of sacred sites, hierarchically organized, with Tepeyac – the shrine of Our Lady of Guadalupe outside Mexico City – at the apex. A few colonial shrines had a broad and growing provincial appeal over many years and are of special interest (see the starred entries in Appendix 1), but most drew their devotees from nearby communities, sometimes not much farther away than the eye could see. Large or small, a shrine's uniqueness depended on its devotees feeling a special relationship to it as a place of intense divine presence. Nevertheless, the outsider's questions need to be asked: Who came and why? What did people do there? What was brought and taken away? Were these Christian shrines rooted in a more distant sacred past? Were they nestled in a sacred landscape, of mysterious, awesome, and orderly power, with numinous physical features such as holy springs, hills, trees, and caves? When and how did colonial shrines develop? How did some shrines grow into places with regional followings? What favored or hindered the spread of a new devotion? The voices of those who knew about these matters as participants are not often registered in their own words in colonial records, so that the researcher must seek them in evidence of what they did.[9] This silence is neither surprising nor especially regrettable, since the participants in just about any event, whether visitors to the shrine of Our Lady of El Pueblito in the eighteenth century or professional athletes in our time, routinely offer up observations and explanations that reduce the complexity of their own actions and traditions to clichés.

A sacred place was more than the shrine, chapel, or altar that enclosed a celebrated image, or the site of a founding miracle associated with it. The place was also the image itself – where the spiritual acted through the material – and it might be present wherever the image was represented and revered.[10] This idea that images as well as shrines were places is important because many devotees never visited the primary shrine of a miraculous image, never saw the matrix image in person. It could be enough to have a cheap printed depiction on a home altar, to visit a painted or sculpted copy in a nearby church or chapel, to have touched a portable copy that passed by on an alms-collecting mission, or even to have the image tattooed on one's body.[11] In the end, it was enough to have Christ, the Virgin Mary or another saint in mind through a particular image, in one's prayers and other acts of devotion. That is, there is a more fluid sense of place and divine presence to reckon with than just the physical location of a shrine or a pilgrim's home.

My principal aim, then, is to understand shrines and sacred images during the colonial period in terms of finding, making, and maintaining a place in the world – in this case, a sheltering place for the spirit and divine favor. Understood this way, the subject carries with it debates about space and place, utopias and heterotopias, sacred and profane, promotion and devotion. I have no grand synthesis of competing views to propose, but in thinking about these distinctions and the longevity of shrines I have looked for people in action, in their surroundings, and what their activities of place making and maintaining might say about them.[12] This sense of place has as much to do with what was understood to happen there, the circulation of people and things, and news and memory of divine presence (not to mention what hindered circulation, and how tradition is established and renewed) as it does with belief in a treasure chest of wonders at a fixed sacred center of the labyrinth of everyday struggles. Places were not so much settings or containers of activity as ongoing creations from accumulating experiences, memories, and meanings. This fluid sense of place was expressed more in auspicious movement at and near the destination than in the journey from home to a distant shrine.

How some sacred places reached regional audiences is also part of the story of spiritual geography. Major shrines such as those dedicated to Our Lady of Guadalupe, Our Lady of Remedios, Our Lady of Zapopan, Our Lady of El Pueblito, Our Lady of Ocotlán, and Our Lady of La Defensa located in and near Mexico City and provincial cities had a concentrated nucleus of devotees, but other regional sites of the sacred like Our Lady of San Juan de los Lagos, Our Lady of Xuquila, the Lord of Chalma, and the Lord of Esquipulas were far from cities. In either case, sometimes the catalysts for growing appeal were groups of evangelizing holy men, especially Franciscans, Jesuits, and Augustinians; or the publication and distribution of cheap prints, novena booklets, and other devotional texts; or alms-collecting missions from a shrine bearing a miniature "portrait"[13] of a celebrated image, along with prints and news of miracles. These and other promotional, regulatory, and commercial activities often contributed mightily, but how enthusiasm spread and how people were moved to action with lasting effects are fundamental, too, and more elusive.

Condensed Presence: Baroque Tapestries of Paradise

Luis de Cisneros, author of the first devotional history of a Mexican shrine, published in 1621, offered a glimpse of what makers, promoters, and devotees of a shrine expressed and hoped to experience: "Every time I see that shrine, a vivid portrait of Glory is laid out before me, a whole firmament, this eighth sphere adorned with stars on a peaceful night."[14] A perennial conviction that a heavenly God is present in the world, watching and listening, especially at a shrine but also in daily life, is an underlying thread of this faith and a great theme in this history. Although this conviction may have been more universally shared in New Spain during the sixteenth and seventeenth centuries, it is still widely held and is as closely associated as ever with images, especially of Christ and the Virgin Mary. Shortly before Spanish and Portuguese colonization in America, a Portuguese Franciscan, João Mendes de Silva (1420–1482), gave theological expression to the waning popular interest in relics – the physical remains of saints – and the growing interest in images of holy persons as channels of divine presence. Known as Blessed Amadeus, Mendes de Silva reported messages from the Virgin Mary that the Immaculate Conception was true and that she would be "bodily present" in her sacred images, as would be evidenced by the miracles she worked through them. Amadeus's mystical revelations in *Apocalypsis Nova* reverberated through religious thought and devotional practice in New Spain. Francisco de Florencia, the American-born Jesuit author of devotional histories of many Mexican shrines and miraculous images in the late seventeenth century, echoed Amadeus's revelations in one of his texts for the shrine of the Virgin of Guadalupe, citing him and writing that "The certain sign that she is present in her images is the miracles that she works through them, ... that Our Lady is visible on the altar of her Shrine in order to grant favors to all."[15]

Not surprisingly, priests were ambivalent about sacred images, "the sight of which causes great devotion,"[16] embracing them as vital to Christian worship, yet alert to their misuse and inappropriate presentation. Throughout the colonial period clerics were at pains to work out in words and regulations the difference between unacceptable worship of idols and welcome veneration of images – a material means to true faith, communion with the divine, and the possibility of miracles. In the spirit of the Council of Trent's principal decree on images, Hermenegildo de Vilaplana, a mid-eighteenth-century Franciscan chronicler and featured preacher in his order's missionary college of Santa Cruz de Querétaro, explained this essential distinction in his history of the miraculous image of Nuestra Señora del Pueblito:

> Sacred images have no power or capacity to work miracles, for they are no more than revered instruments of their Prototypes, without life, without movement, and without any independent operational vitality. But it should not be doubted that, through them, their Originals [the divine and sainted people depicted] who have eternal and glorious life in the company of the Lord may be moved to intercede for special favors.[17]

The aura of a usually benevolent, watchful divine presence perhaps accessible through sacred images, and the striving of image makers to achieve the appearance of life in the image, promoted beliefs, feelings, practices (including pilgrimages to image shrines, processions, recitations of the Rosary, devotion to the cross, and sponsorship of confraternities), and the creation and uses of things and settings that, in combination, have come to be called the Baroque in Catholic Europe and Latin America.[18] It has been an enduring current in the history of Mexican shrines and the material culture of faith there since the late sixteenth century. But the notion of the Baroque in Latin America is contested ground among scholars, and the term itself is anachronistic. Those who embraced Baroque sensibilities during the seventeenth and eighteenth centuries did not call them by this name. Medieval jewelers in France and the Mediterranean had used "baroque" to describe odd, irregular, surprising shapes, but the term's broader application to a style of art came in the mid-eighteenth century, by commentators with little interest in the sources of its popular appeal. Famously, if not first, the term appeared in a short passage of Johann Joachim Winckelmann's treatise on classical Greek art (1755). For Winckelmann, Baroque "taste" favored a style of decoration found especially in the seventeenth century that delighted in a showy profusion of irregular shapes.[19] He preferred "the noble simplicity" and "quiet grandeur" of the ancient Greeks.

Taking a page from Winckelmann, more than a few later historians have regarded "Baroque" as a passing style in the history of high art in Catholic Europe and its dependencies, focused on elaborate surface decoration and melodramatic, three-dimensional special effects, that was tangential to the lives and values of most people of the time and best left to art historians concerned with formalities. Others with an interest in social and cultural history, whether working in the fields of literature, history, art history, or anthropology and sociology, regard the laity as patrons, custodians, consumers, and, in a sense, co-creators and re-creators of Baroque works in the ways they preserved, used, adorned, and sometimes commissioned them. But these scholars, too, disagree on the wellsprings and significance of Baroque culture. For some, it represents superficiality and crude imitation, a disheartening expression of phony or overwrought sentiment, subservient to an oppressive Counter-Reformation ideology that responded defensively to the rise of Protestantism and was "designed solely to extinguish local realities in the service of state power."[20] For some literary historians, Baroque expression centers on satire and *desengaño* (disillusionment) more than the sacred – exposing the counterfeit and hypocritical, the pretenses in public conduct.[21] For other scholars, the Baroque begins with forms of architecture, painting, sculpture, music, and literature made in Catholic Europe during the late sixteenth and seventeenth centuries that aimed to spiritualize the elements of these arts, to create church interiors as a dramatic stage that could *be* the sacred more than symbolize or comment on it.[22] In this sense the Baroque "worked poorly as a colonizing instrument," and became a vehicle for American creativity and self-expression.[23] Following the lead of celebrated Cuban writers José Lezama Lima and Alejo Carpentier, scholars working in this vein (including me) have regarded Baroque expression in general as having a life beyond period artistic conventions. It became a longer-lasting validation of emotional truths, a style of thought and action that is rich in restless, sometimes extravagant improvisation, if not invention, not simply impoverished by pessimism, rote imitation, superficiality, and ideological oppression and repression. Still other commentators suggest that since repression and rule-breaking extravagance were both in play, Baroque expressed a growing alienation of high from low culture, with Baroque sensuality and exuberance representing popular tradition, and impositions in the name of decorum being the pursuit of governors and bishops.[24]

Critiquing or reconciling these differences and their internal contradictions[25] is not my goal, but studying shrines, images, devotees, and local practices during the seventeenth and eighteenth centuries leads me to regard the Baroque as a durable, sometimes flexible expression of longing, faith, social values, political relationships, and engagement with sacred images as objects of devotion, even rapture, as much as meditation, along with a bleak view of original sin, that cut across social groups and regions during the colonial period and beyond.[26] There was always some tension between devout sculptors and painters striving to make sacred images that were amazingly lifelike, and the admonition of church fathers at the Council of Trent and later to refrain from trying to make a painting or statue so lifelike that it would be mistaken for the sacred subject itself, even as they encouraged the use of images.[27] This tension would become greater in the late colonial period, but without often splitting elite devotion from popular devotion.

Baroque, then, is more than a period-specific art style that can be adequately described in secular terms. It is not only about showy, high relief surfaces coated with gold leaf that shimmer in the light, meant to dazzle the viewer with the opulence, grandeur, and power of God and the institutional church. It was at least as much about striving to represent heavenly delights, honor the divine, and coax a purifying contrition and longing for transcendence and union with God in this life and beyond. It was meant to touch the emotions, simulate movement, and release the viewer into a higher realm.[28] This reaching for transcendence and union with God's palpable presence in the world and beyond was famously expressed in the mid-sixteenth century by the Spanish church reformer and mystic Theresa of Avila. In her words, a deeply moving experience of divine presence led to her program of spiritual reform for the Carmelite Order:

It pleased the Lord that I should sometimes see the following vision. I would see beside me, on my left hand, an angel in bodily form ... In his hands I saw a long golden spear and at the end of the iron tip I seemed to see a point of fire. With this he seemed to pierce my heart several times so that it penetrated to my entrails ... He left me completely afire with a great love of God.[29]

Sensing the Unseen

The material culture of devotion and notions of landscape – how, for participants of all kinds, sacred things were recognized, depicted, named, revered, embellished, seen, touched, and otherwise used; and how people viewed their surroundings – are fundamental to the study of shrines, images, and the sense of divine presence in New Spain expressed in Baroque art during and after the colonial period. They thread through this book, often blurring the distinction between the spiritual and the material. Sacred things included printed texts, paintings, statues, fine dresses for statues of the Virgin, figurative votive offerings, church architecture, furnishings, altars, rosary beads, woodcuts, and etchings, but also the more humble ephemera and evanescent expressions of faith such as candles,[30] flowers, ribbons, coveted dust, incense, fireworks, home altars and other household trappings, prayers uttered or silently recited, and movement, especially penitential journeys of faith and supplication, processions, dances, and genuflections. They drew people closer to the sacred. Their uses could compress chronological time, triggering memories and uncanny, providential associations with the past. Occasionally these memories and associations were written down when they were freshest. News in April 1921 that a crucifix had begun to tremble in the parish church of Tlaltenango, Zacatecas and was attracting throngs of visitors reminded the local pastor of religious persecution during the Reform period. He noted in the parish *libro de gobierno* at the time that this numinous figure had been rescued from the old Franciscan convent of Nuestra Señora de Guadalupe outside the city of Zacatecas in the late 1850s by Tlaltenango's future pastor Rafael Herrera after General Jesús González Ortega, a Liberal hero of the civil war of 1858–1861 and governor of Zacatecas in 1859–1860, had ordered it and other religious images there destroyed.[31] That Father Herrera, himself an outspoken Liberal by then, was the steadfast protector of this crucifix suggests that the appeal of sacred images in Mexico continued to reach across battle lines of political ideology and social standing long after Independence.[32]

The meaning of beauty during the colonial period also complicates the distinction between elite and popular art and devotional practices. Beauty was understood to be a perfection of proportion and technique that was pleasing to God, asserting the charisma of the image – the being of the figure represented, the life in it – and inviting divine favor. It was a manifestation of the divine as much as a stimulus toward it. Beauty itself was a kind of miracle, the product of divine inspiration more than the realization of an artist's personal talent. The form was important to the effects, especially for church authorities – the richer the materials and the more polished, exquisite, and seemly the rendering, the more beautiful, perfect, and holy the result.[33] The finery added to the preciousness of the image itself and testified to the generosity and sacrifice of devoted donors. Popular taste in decorative refinements and offerings and the idea that signs of use and embellishment made images more beautiful could, of course, rub against official taste. Favorite local images in their niches might appear ugly and in need of a makeover to church authorities who knew them remotely, not as things full of years of reverent use. But as Alexander Nehamas puts it, "Beauty is the object of love and, for better or worse, love can be provoked by anything."[34] There was general agreement in colonial sources that the measure of beauty was its transformational power, the feelings it evoked, the ineffable sense of life and the divine favors believed to be manifest through chosen religious images if they were honored in the right way. And feelings associated with beauty converged for all concerned on awe, tenderness, tearful rapture, contrition, and a sense of intimate grandeur and wholeness that brought them close to God. These ideas about redemptive beauty strengthened the connection between images and immanence or "inner presence" for colonial Christians.[35] Cayetano Cabrera y Quintero, a creole scholar and priest in Mexico City, in his book about divine intervention in the great epidemic of 1737 repeatedly tacked between "it" (the image) and "s/he" (the divine personage). In attempting to establish what made an image sacred in terms of its appearance, he wrote,

> whether or not it is produced miraculously, arrives as an apparition, or its maker was a saint, it is a holy image if it represents a canonized person. It is holy, whether or not it is miraculous, if it is more or less beautiful and perfect. And even with the most wondrous of images there may be some lack of beauty or imperfection in the art of image making ... It is the saints who are admirable in their images, whether or not they are well and artfully made ... Pay attention not to the maker, but to the work itself.[36]

What counted most was the effect, the reception or actions by faithful viewers, the feelings of love, awe, and anguish. As James Clifton writes, the impact of such images "can be so powerful that they overwhelm a merely aesthetic response."[37] And the effect or experience in Baroque terms involved all the senses, spoken and heard in the poetry of prayer and prayers made visible in votive offerings, in the feel of rosary beads and holy water, in sweet odors of sanctity, in the blaze of candlelight and oil lamps, in the notes of a church organ and voices of the choir that brought sacred texts to mind, and the church bells that punctuated the day from sunrise to evening with calls to devotion and reminders of Christ's sacrifice.[38] Colonial authorities routinely privileged sight when they described religiosity, but sight was more than what met the eye. Religious experience meant meeting the divine presence in every way that suspended the transience of life and the stench and ugliness of evil in the world.[39] Dominican Fray Andrés Ferrero de Caldecebro's description of the ceremonies in St Peter's Basilica in Rome for the beatification of Rose of Lima in 1671 celebrated this multisensory experience of divine, transcendent truth: "All the senses are nourished with surpassing delights, as if in a new Paradise – sight, treated to sumptuous splendors; smell, to fragrant aromas; hearing, to the most delicate consonance of voices; and taste, to harmonious combination."[40] Fray Andrés did not mention touch and movement, but reception meant the sensation of physical contact and motion, too – images caressed, kissed, washed, retouched, decorated, and carried in processions, addressed in the rhythms of music, poetry, and dance.[41] Sacred things, especially statues, could become more beautiful with age and use, the face colored by candle smoke and incense, the paint on feet, hands, and cheeks worn thin by touch. These images were not time capsules, out of devotees' reach. Unlike a fine old toy that has value on the antiques market because it is still in pristine condition and housed in its original (preferably unopened) box, religious images could become more beautiful, more present and alive through the marks of living care and devotion. This was a kind of beauty "not immune to time, but embedded in it."[42]

A Historical Narrative of Mexican Shrines?

The first four chapters and Appendix 3 address Mexican shrines and images in general over time, describing changes as well as some overarching continuities of belief in divine presence and the staying power of many of these places. But what kind of historical survey does this amount to? Is there a defining narrative, such as continuities from precolonial times, dramatic transformations, crystallization of medieval European forms and practices, growing control by the Inquisition over the production and use of images,[43] or the rapid rise to preeminence of the image of Our Lady of Guadalupe and her shrine near Mexico City at Tepeyac? Certainly her image was the most widely recognized and revered, but is there one image at the center of the story, at the apex of a hierarchy of shrines? Or is there a dominant narrative of persistent, widespread "Baroque" sensibility, or of declension and disenchantment, if not desacralization? Or is the narrative line less a chronology of stages and completion than a jumble in soft focus, with many exceptions, broken sequences, and loose ends? Reaching for an ordered story of events in human affairs is almost irresistible. Folklore depends on it, as do biographies and national histories, and ordered narrative is a rhetorical device embraced by historians even when our writings appear more analytical than sequential. Across many cultures, the same questions are asked: What happened? Why? How did it begin? What followed? How did it end? Telling stories about a course of events or a personal or collective past is a way to give them purpose and result, to tell ourselves and others who we are and what we stand for by where we came from. Even when they remain scrupulously faithful to the available primary sources, coherent narratives are bound to be fictions, to express a point of view and perhaps distill some larger truth. Narrative history's most familiar prototype is biography, framing the passage of time in terms of a lifespan.[44] The plotlines vary across cultures and over time, from clash, conquest, resistance, Last Judgment, community, nation, evolution, devolution, transformation, persistence, and syncretism, to cycles of return, revelation, or some other eternal verity, but we often take the trajectory of an individual life of a person or thing serialized in place and time with a beginning, middle, and end, to intersect with, if not stand for, collective experience and destiny.

As historical artifacts – made and recorded then, remembered later – shrines and images have two types of narrative sources. One is proximate narratives, those sequenced accounts of miraculous images and their shrines created during the colonial period. Whether they tell a seamless story or several less complete ones, nearly all are pious histories, crafted by church authorities, or occasionally by laymen, with an eye to the end of time, streamlined and packaged with the added authority and reach of the written word, often printed. They vary in length, theological pretension, erudition, and sources, but all have a culminating direction: they are success stories about a prodigiously opportune place, with providential beginnings, ongoing signs of divine favor, and an appeal to support the devotion and ensure its continuation. To historians of my time, these texts are valuable primary sources, especially when they established a standard, official story and shaped devotion, but the information in them about popular belief, practice, and past experience is not transparent. Many of the printed devotional histories have, indeed, become the defining story of a shrine or image, leaving us to wonder about other stories that were marginal to these authoritative texts or operated outside their logic. The alternative, unofficial, often fragmentary proximate narratives that occasionally turn up usually express local interests without much attention to chronological time. Those that take the form of ex-voto paintings displayed at shrines and in local churches and homes celebrate favors to ancestors, who remain a living presence and an intimate confirmation of divine protection. For example, when Diego Lázaro's maternal grandmother testified in 1644 to the miracles he had experienced at San Miguel del Milagro (Tlaxcala), she brought with her two paintings of the wondrous events that he entrusted to her, telling her to keep them safe.[45]

These different colonial era narratives of shrines and images did not simply clash or glide past each other as elite and popular views. Official versions absorbed the seer's story, sometimes without much revision.[46] In fact, the printed word sometimes celebrated its reliance on the authority of popular opinion. Chroniclers Francisco de Florencia and Cayetano Cabrera y Quintero extolled the *voz pública y fama* (popular reputation) as the best proof of historical truth, more so than *instrumentos públicos* (formal written records) or experimentation.[47] Whether priests meant to privilege the authority of the human voice as the carrier of God's Word by embracing oral tradition in this way is not clear. Perhaps they were just making the best of a situation in which contemporary writings about the tradition were not available.

Another kind of narrative, written by historians long after the fact, has the advantage of some knowledge of what came next, but such farsightedness risks reducing in-the-moment contingencies and confusion to teleological certainties. Evolution – gradual but definite, apparently irreversible movement in some direction, rising or falling, sometimes returning – has been a common conceit of historians. Some version of the modernization/secularization story remains the most familiar kind of evolutionary narrative for Latin American history: decline or privatization of religion and weakening of church institutions in the wake of emergent and eventually triumphant reason, science, technology, and political reform.[48] Whether or not historians openly subscribe to such a dichotomy of tradition and modernity, we are usually more concerned with stages, dates, and changes than with states of being, even though what we find in the historical record is mainly snapshots of activity and experience rather than smoking guns and incontrovertible sequences. As my cherished colleague Robert Brentano once wrote, "that which I found most compelling was change over time."[49] Perhaps especially for colonial histories, there is the temptation to assume more than demonstrate that new ideas and directions of change were transformative from the start. But if historians are looking for changes and displacements, we also have an eye for details that make for inconvenient exceptions – highlighting the uniqueness of every event and turning coherent narratives into halting tendencies with few well-defined turning points.

Along the shore near my home in Maine, ancient arrow points and fragments of other stone tools from submerged fishing camps occasionally wash up, fashioned mostly from pieces of chert brought far downriver from the Moosehead Lake region. Finding one arrow point, I looked for more, passing over other things deposited and reduced by the wind and waves – lobster buoys and bait bags; bits of pottery, brick, and "sea glass"; fishing lures, plastic bottles, shotgun shells, and driftwood with the telltale marks of beavers and chain saws. The arrow points are only a minute fraction of this churning archive. Despite historians' fascination with change, much of the scholarship on shrines, images, and spiritual geography in Mexico since Spanish colonization has emphasized continuities in an enchanted landscape, perhaps because the changes are usually hard to gauge or place securely in time. But like my little assortment of worn and broken stone tools those Mexican devotional practices that suggest continuities from precolonial times are far less than the whole story of religiosity since Spanish colonization, even in "Indian" communities. How to convey a fuller story of both persistence and transformation, while reckoning with a fragmentary record of things, including written things, that usually offer only a bare glimpse of the devotees and their places? This book and my earlier essays approach this question from the sources I could find.

Over the past fifty years or so,[50] what counts as history has grown far beyond public affairs, institutional studies, and doings of leaders to include, in principle, everyone and just about everything. By the 1980s, attention was turning to the passions and practices of daily life, or intimate episodes of neglected as well as famous people, and "problem-centered" monographs were celebrated or lamented as marking the end of narrative history inside the academy.[51] At about the same time, "postmodern" challengers began to dismiss narrative history and historians' claims to objectivity as unreflective or mendacious fabrications that serve power more than truth. In this view, all versions of a particular episode or time become more or less equally valid because they are all unreliable. When consensus emerges among historians, it signals sociological and political forces at work, not a significant advance in knowledge about the past.[52]

One sustained response to this critique and to the vogue of the intimate, the subjective, the marginal, and the quotidian was the mammoth project Pierre Nora imagined and directed in the 1980s and early 1990s on "the history of memory" in France. Nora, too, declared the "disintegration" of narrative history "with its panegyric tendencies" as a "myth underlying the destiny of the nation."[53] He embraced the postmodern critique but without reducing history to an historical sociology of historians' knowledge claims. For Nora, the past was not entirely unknowable, though he declared himself "less interested in events themselves than in the construction of events over time"; less interested in "'what actually happened' than its reuse and misuse."[54] In other words, his focus shifted attention to the afterlife of things, people, and events – how medieval cathedrals have become national treasures and secular places of memory, especially during the period 1870–1918, not who built them and how they were regarded and used in the Middle Ages[55]; what the Tour de France bicycle race has come to symbolize; or how Charlemagne and Descartes have been remembered, not an evaluation of who they were and what they did. France in Nora's hands became "a reality that is entirely symbolic," expressed especially in ritual.[56]

In a less historiographical key, the aim of many historians since the 1960s has been to examine – with precision and, where possible, serial evidence – particular issues or long-term trends, such as land tenure in eighteenth-century Tlaxcala, patterns of suicide in colonial cities, faith practices of women in seventeenth-century Lima, rituals of power during the reign of Philip II, the meaning of "generation" after the Independence Wars, economic and political ramifications of the *consolidación de vales reales*, or what certain Inquisition witchcraft trials tell us about the history of gender. This simultaneous enlargement and fragmentation of the field of study has been a mixed blessing. As François Furet noted, it amounts to a kind of surrender of historians "before the immense indeterminacy of the object of their knowledge: time."[57] His preference was for a more "problem-centered history" that goes beyond the unique event to an "inquiry into a network of meanings" that can be compared and connected, with an emphasis on verification over "narration's particular kind of logic – post hoc, ergo propter hoc."[58]

How can long-running histories of the evanescent, the anonymous, the commonplace, the collective, and the informal be made from the available record which documents only a tiny fraction of people's lives? Historians' bank of sources has grown in response to the challenge, but the results still are mixed. The call for quantifiable serial evidence has been easier to voice than to practice beyond demographic and fiscal matters. Even for questions of demography, taxation, production, and commerce, the sources are often incomplete, bloodless, and otherwise unrevealing compared to the archival and material remains of warfare and high politics. Nevertheless, with French scholars in the lead, many historians beginning in the 1960s turned away from narrative history as *histoire événementielle* and came to regard episodic, elite, religious, and political developments largely as byproducts of the great, slow-moving historical forces of economic organization, demographic change, cultural inclinations, and social structure that needed more concerted attention.[59]

On two fronts, then, critics dismissed narrative history, whether in the form of sweeping developments and turning points in public life or the endless stream of less obviously consequential events, places, and individuals. Yet historians still thirst for facts and whole stories made out of episodes in the conviction that there is an eventful human past to reckon with, that people as various and complex, loving, imaginative, creative, callous, callow, and turbulent as we are came before us and left indelible traces of who they were. However, there is little agreement on what good history – the past translated into words and signs[60] – amounts to. There are still plenty of narrative histories that glide over questions of authorial subjectivity and problematic sources for the sake of a compelling, purposeful story line that somehow explains itself. A visit to the history shelves of a Barnes & Noble bookstore or the list of best-selling history books on Amazon.com is a reminder of the continuing taste for the course of wars and executive decision-making, national histories, and the personalities of public figures. At the same time, university presses continue to publish self-consciously analytical histories that often sacrifice narrative sweep to close, critical scrutiny of what primary sources can be mustered for apparently less momentous subjects or hypotheses.[61]

Furet thought of these two kinds of historical study as poles on a continuum. At one end, narratives order events and other developments into periods of time; at the other end, "problem-oriented" studies analyze a particular issue or place in time. Institutional structures are still of interest (deservedly so), and my own scholarship has leaned toward more analytical, problem-centered history, but like most historians I know, I seek a fuller understanding. The narrative and analytical poles are not necessarily antithetical, but often the subjects and questions asked in problem-centered history are not obviously central to event-filled political narratives. Their documented episodes seem too local or otherwise tangential.[62] "Analytical" history used to pivot on neglected quantifiable sources in series as a way to address new questions and more inclusive approaches to society, culture, and economics over generations and centuries. Then there was a turn toward more personal sources such as diaries, memoirs, Inquisition trials, and oral testimonies. The quantitative approaches have the virtue of treating extended time in a uniform way. The confessional approach promises a more human scale but often addresses a rather arbitrary, usually brief timespan dictated more by the fortuitous availability of sources than by larger questions the author means to address. Either way, for practitioners of "analytical" history the challenges of describing time in narrative have not been their primary concern.

All the narratives about shrines and miraculous images that have been told or can be imagined may be of intrinsic interest depending on what one hopes to learn from them, but some are more adequate than others as representations of the past. Take Putumayo shaman Mutumajoy's conviction that Spaniards forced conquered Indians to build Machu Picchu. His larger truth about the nature of Spanish rule and extraction of wealth in the Andes interrupts more adequate description of when and how Machu Picchu was built.[63] Not to exercise some critical judgment about this, or not to seek out the fullest possible array of written and material traces of experience and memory comes close to denying that the past is accessible at all. The evidence is likely to be in circumstantial traces, but they are not necessarily just the vestiges of power exercised by colonial rulers and institutions.[64]

This book differs from my earlier studies of land tenure, peasant communities, priests in their parishes, and particular shrines and images in its attempt at a more sustained consideration of change and continuity across much of New Spain over a long time, but it shares with those projects an interest in context (local and beyond), comparisons, and connections as a means of analysis – without assuming that a particular context was salient in all places and times or that relationships can be reduced to a single cause or pattern. There are threads of narrative and periodization in these chapters, but chronological narrative is not the only route to meaning in historical study, especially when the episodes about shrines and images by the late seventeenth century seem to echo each other more often than they follow one from another. I am especially concerned with how tradition and transgression, conflict and cooperation, persistence and transformation, promotion, reception, and spontaneous devotion could be in play simultaneously and differently as well as sequentially and similarly among people in different places and times. I have looked for opportunities to arrange evidence in series and sum, to draw upon various places and times, and to ask: What was representative? But a synoptic study of shrines and images is not just a composite of serial evidence. It is also an attempt to discover which contexts were in play in particular, singular situations, how, and why. The answers are not always the same.

Sources

Some of the richest written sources for European shrines are missing for New Spain.[65] Registers of miracles recorded over many years are not there, nor are more than a few long running lists of donations. There is remarkably little documentation on pilgrimages and providential dreams. Direct evidence of the practices of devotees is hard to come by, and only Our Lady of Remedios and Our Lady of Guadalupe in the Valley of Mexico have archives that offer a more or less continuous record of administrative activity. (Unlike other shrines in New Spain, a municipal council managed the Remedios shrine.) These silences can themselves be revealing. Why was there little record-keeping on these matters when the colonial archives are so vast in some other respects? Why weren't miracles, dream visions, and pilgrimages recorded more meticulously? Perhaps it is simply that devotees felt too much for words; as Emily Dickinson wrote, "Had we less to say to those we love, perhaps we should say it oftener."[66]

Under the circumstances, it is better to bring in many shrines and images rather than rely on a few,[67] but there are detailed records and visual depictions that need attention because they seem to tell their own stories and make a larger point. "Evolved" objects (things in use, that show signs of remaking and use), for example, may have been described and remembered in ways that contribute to a biography. Sometimes the changes in the object are clear, but the contexts for them are missing, and we are left to guess what it meant to those who made, remade, and used it.[68] Yet objects themselves – a well-used devotional book with some marginal notes and a print tipped in, or a renowned statuette that was repeatedly restored – sometimes do suggest how they were deployed. And there is ample evidence of images being repeatedly dressed up, cleaned, moved, showing considerable wear and valued as better than new, or sometimes restored or replaced, or mourned and propitiated when they were damaged or destroyed. There is also evidence of ecclesiastical officials exhorting the laity to adorn their images in ways appropriate to their spiritual purposes, not according to the fashions of the day or covered in cheap ribbons and flowers.[69] Handling and dressing images was a common practice in early modern Spain,[70] but in New Spain parishioners' tastes in decoration and the signs of wear they frequently left unretouched became a particular source of friction with authorities; what contributed to the sacredness and beauty of the image for local devotees might render it "gross" and "ridiculous" in the bishop's eyes.[71]

But by themselves such stories of renewal or transformation do not go far toward compensating for the silences in the record. As William Christian reports for Spain, "The vast majority of unusual sensory experiences, many relating to the dead, go unreported ... Some visions are so local they do not reach a wider audience; or they are experienced by an individual who tells no one or only immediate family ... the first line of censorship, the first filter, is that of the seer."[72] Reasoning from an absence of information without much else to go on is a dubious strategy in any case, and perhaps especially so for a history of marvels in New Spain. For example, the fact that fewer apparitions and dream visions were recorded during the seventeenth and eighteenth centuries may not signal a decline in apparition experiences; any accounts of them that began to gain traction were headed to the Inquisition or the bishop's court unless reshaped into a more acceptable story of divine immanence.[73] Under the circumstances, it was better for seers and local devotees to keep the good news to themselves.

Scattered as they are, there are abundant sources for evaluating what was new and consequential about shrines and images, and what did not change much. They include printed and manuscript texts; painted, sculpted, and printed images; reports of spoken words; activities of a variety of administrators, promoters, and lay devotees; and descriptions of gestures, processions, dance, and other kinds of unspoken expression. Key written sources include ready-made narrative shrine histories, of which there are about thirty for twenty-one shrines, most of them published in the seventeenth and eighteenth centuries. These, the many chronicles written by members of the religious orders, and Francisco de Florencia and Juan Antonio de Oviedo's compendium of Marian shrines, *Zodíaco mariano* (1755) are the sources best known to scholars. A related type of source, sometimes published, was the *información jurídica*, an inquiry into the authenticity of a particular miraculous tradition, commissioned by a bishop. *Relaciones geográficas* – district-level survey reports commissioned by the crown – sometimes include information about shrines and miraculous images. Those for 1743 are especially extensive. Most of these snapshots of popular traditions date from the seventeenth century and are fullest for fourteen shrines.[74] Capsule histories for other shrines sometimes were included in the hundreds of novena booklets published during the colonial period, and a generous scattering of miracles for more than one hundred shrines are recounted in these sources and in various other pious texts such as chronicles of the orders and ex-voto paintings. Another plentiful printed source is sermons, of which nearly a thousand were published during the seventeenth and eighteenth centuries. Many centered on Marian themes and some were delivered at shrines or dedicated to a celebrated image, but few spoke directly about those particular shrines and images.

Historians of early modern Europe often lament the scarcity of firsthand documentation about ordinary devotees in comparison to leaders and promoters,[75] but for colonial Mexico there is considerable evidence of devotees and devotional practices to be found. The published devotional histories and the *Zodíaco mariano* compendium have little to say about devotees other than capsule versions of some miracles bestowed upon them, but other sources do describe their behavior: pastoral visit books; episcopal court records concerning processions, fiestas, property disputes, regulation of image making and use, investigations into reported miracles, theft of images, unruly behavior, and inappropriate decorations; Inquisition inquiries, trials, and decrees about devotional practices, questionable writings and utterances, and use of images; *actas de cabildo* records, for both cathedral chapters and town councils of provincial capitals; viceregal decrees and investigations of complaints related to shrines; royal court records of the policing of shrine grounds and commerce, and disputes involving shrine administrators and visitors, priests, and hermits; other kinds of administrative records related to shrines, especially confraternity account books, licensing for alms collections, appointments to offices, and supervision of officeholders; miracle stories; bibliographies of works published in New Spain before 1821; temple inventories and construction records; and modern ethnographic studies of shrines and pilgrimages.

There is also evidence of the production and consumption of devotional materials, especially visual ones, which were fundamental to the devotional experience of Mexican shrines where the focal point of devotion usually was an image especially associated with miracles. These include statues, paintings, prints, found objects, and other images depicted, described, or inventoried in colonial records, or surviving in present-day shrines, churches, and museums. "Mute sermons," the clergy liked to call them,[76] but they were always more than that. There is documentation in administrative and judicial records about home altars; ex-votos left at the shrine, including the anonymous *milagritos* (little metal or wax representations of body parts and sometimes objects of desire) and more personal votive paintings and written testimonials; and other numinous things housed at the shrines or originating there. Material culture of the sacred also includes things taken away from the shrine as more than mementoes, things that were understood to have partaken of the sacred – stubs of candles that had illuminated the image; flowers and ribbons that had touched it; dust that had gathered on the image or in the shrines, sometimes made into tablets stamped with the image to be swallowed in case of illness; and cheap prints. The buildings themselves and the written record of their construction, reconstruction, and maintenance, sometimes including inventories of donations and furnishings, offer another source of information about the living shrine. Some of these sources can be arranged in series to suggest patterns and changes, especially the longer runs of administrative and judicial records licensing the collection of alms for a shrine, regulating image-making, or dealing with abuse of holy images; financial records for individual shrines and confraternities, dedication pages of university theses; donor lists; chronicles and diaries of public events; baptismal records for popular Christian names; and wills with their listings of family images, home altars, printed works, and other religious paraphernalia. Unfortunately, most of these types of records, other than wills, baptismal records, and bibliographies, are available only in broken series for a few shrines.

The mystique and business of image shrines, the spiritual geographies and activities of the faithful who visited them, and the material culture of devotion can sometimes come together in administrative records. For an example of some of the history, patterns, and contingencies to come in later chapters there is the dossier presented to the archbishop's court in 1820 by Father José Rafael Truxillo, pastor of Malinaltenango, on behalf of the shrine of the "sovereign image" of the Lord of Calvary in his rural parish of Coatepec Harinas, south of the city of Toluca and the snow-capped Nevado de Toluca in what is now the Estado de México.[77] Father Truxillo's purpose was to request renewal of a license to collect alms for the shrine that had been granted by an earlier archbishop, in December 1809. Supporting documentation for his request included the 1809 petition, which described the image, its legendary origins, its growing popularity as a destination, and the physical condition of the shrine. It also included the record of collections and expenditures between 1810 and 1815.

Said to date from the late seventeenth century, this crucifix is still famous in the area, with its feast day on the Sunday of Pentecost. It was described in pastor Miguel Mariano de Nava's 1809 petition as

shaped from a rough piece of planking, finished to form a perfect figure of the cross. Its beautifully painted Divine face evokes respect, admiration, devotion, and deep love because it seems as if it is not the work of human hands ... According to tradition ... this Divine Lord was discovered in a certain private chapel belonging to an Indian founder of this town, built for him by local Indians at a place called Calvary on the edge of town. He moved away and did not return to reclaim the image. Brought to light in this way, the people began to worship the Lord in his Calvary chapel, and innumerable wonders followed so that today the chapel is adorned with a great number of exvoto paintings and an equal number of silver votive offerings. Thanks to this Divine Lord's mercy, the chapel is almost a santuario [a shrine, because of its popularity] and many people come from very distant places to worship and offer candles and Masses. During the feast of Pentecost there is a great gathering of all sorts of men and women. They perform their Indian dances, and the events last four or five days. People from the surroundings come with their offerings of alms, wax, and Masses for the Divine Image.

Father Nava went on to mention an ambitious recent building program and the need for more capital:

Thanks to these [divine] favors, the unsuitable old adobe chapel was demolished and a very fine new one of stone and mortar was begun with the appropriate official license. The construction of the shrine remains unfinished, along with the principal altarpiece for the Divine Lord, to the great chagrin of everyone here ... The non-Indians here are very poor. They have donated what they could and the Indians have contributed building materials, lime, etc., and their labor, but all this and the alms collected [locally] for the Divine Lord have not sufficed to cover the costs.

Nava's petition led to a royal license in December 1809 to collect alms for the shrine in neighboring areas for four years. Records submitted with the 1820 petition for renewal of the license show substantial alms collections and construction while the license was in effect, even during the turbulent early years of Mexico's independence wars. From 1810 to 1812, 1,529 pesos were collected. In 1815, after the license expired, the proceeds amounted to 222 pesos, shrinking to 94 pesos from 1816 to 1820 (presumably just alms collected at the shrine). The collection records for 1810 and early 1811 include signed permissions from pastors in each of the parishes the collector visited that give some sense of the promotional territory of this devotion at the time. The area he covered roughly corresponds to the southern and southwestern catchment area of the great regional shrine of Chalma, which is located about ten miles east of Coatepec Amilpas as the crow flies. Over the course of three months in 1810 – March 6 to June 5 – the collector ventured into eighteen parishes, mostly in the Cuernavaca and Cuauhtla districts, in the state of Morelos, and adjoining areas of highland Guerrero. He began by traveling east into the district of Malinalco near the Chalma shrine. From there he headed south to Tetecala, Morelos, about 20 miles from Coatepec Harinas. For the rest of March, April, and early May he visited parishes throughout Morelos, 70 or more miles to the east and south of his shrine, although he skirted Cuernavaca, the largest town and political seat. By May 16 he was in the district of Taxco in northeast Guerrero, about 25 miles south of Coatepec Harinas, where he visited four parishes before returning home. In July he was out collecting again, at Mezicapa just east of the shrine, near Tenancingo. In all, he collected 402 pesos on these excursions.[78]

In 1820, Father Truxillo presented the records of collections and expenditures after 1809 to demonstrate that the shrine's finances had been well managed. The money had been spent on building materials, skilled labor, a pulpit, new doors for the sacristy and choir, gilding the main altarpiece, and a down payment on an organ. It was also invested in rosary beads and prints of the holy image to sell to devotees for additional income. But the shrine church was still unfinished and installments on the organ were in arrears when this new petition was made after a six-year lapse in the license. Although the 1820 petition does not mention Mexico's prolonged independence wars (1810–1821), the endemic dangers of the road during those years must have discouraged many devotees from visiting, as they did for better known shrines such as Lagos and Chalma. Father Truxillo had reason to think he had made a strong case for renewal of the license to collect alms, but he overreached in asking for carte blanche to collect throughout the archdiocese without a fixed term. A new license was granted, but for one year and only in parishes adjacent to Coatepec Harinas.

****

Before venturing into what moved people to action, there is descriptive work to do – to find out how and when many shrines and devotion to particular images came to be; how they were experienced during the colonial period as vital to well-being; how they developed; and how it is that many of them have lasted so long and some became important regional shrines. Along the way I have looked for the "ands" of human experience as well as the "ors" – tradition and transgression, persistence and transformation, promotion and devotion – and whether these were intertwined and simultaneous or mainly sequential. The answers depend on the record of incidents and details and how they are viewed. Some changes over time and the growing prominence of Our Lady of Guadalupe are clear, but there is no one, resounding story beyond the durability of shrines and devotion to images founded in the colonial period, and an undercurrent of Baroque sensibilities in daily life and public rituals based on confidence by people across this society that God is alive in the world, especially in places that are out of this world yet only steps away.

I share with Pierre Nora an interest in historical places and circumstances of memory, but religious shrines and miraculous images are my chosen subject and in Mexico and Guatemala they remained *mediums* of memory more than the deracinated, contested *sites* of memory and nostalgia that Nora turns to for France's contemporary history.[79] As problematic as the evidence is, I am less inclined than Nora to give up on the study of "events themselves" – the shrines and religious images of colonial Mexico as they were known, used, and contested in their time. In reaching for what happened in narratives about encountering God, the local keeps coming up – in the idea of community autonomy, in veneration of ancestors and elders, in claims of timeless customs[80] – complicating if not sweeping past larger patterns of spiritual geography, devotion, and the reforming aims of colonial authorities. In the end, we may not be sure what even the most prominent and articulate actor thought the situation was, yet there is still something to learn about enduring and changing arrangements of institutionalized faith and habits of thought and feeling from the ways people sought their often mysterious ends.

Notes

1. Colin Tudge, *The Tree: A Natural History of What Trees Are, How They Live, and Why They Matter*, New York: Crown, 2006, p. 252.
2. "Célebres y milagrosas," wrote the Spanish Capuchin friar Francisco de Ajofrín who made a point of visiting as many shrines as he could and collecting prints of their miraculous images during his alms-collecting mission to New Spain in the early 1760s. See *Diario del viaje que hizo a la América en el siglo XVIII el P. Fray Francisco de Ajofrín*, 2 vols., Mexico: Instituto Cultural Hispano Mexicano, 1964.
3. *La pastoral de santuarios en México*, Mexico: Comisión Episcopal de Evangelización y Catequesis, 1988, p. 17.
4. "teatro de otras mil maravillas," Manuel de Loaizaga, OFM, *Historia de la milagrosíssima Imagen de Nuestra Señora de Occotlan que se venera extramuros de la ciudad de Tlaxcala . . .*, reimpreso, Mexico: Vda. de D. Joseph Hogal, 1750, p. 88.
5. See Appendix 1. In addition to the 498 colonial shrines listed there, I have in mind another twenty or so images associated with miracles that appear only once in the sources I consulted.
6. Some leading scholars have done this. For example, *Diálogos con el territorio: Simbolizaciones sobre el espacio en las culturas indígenas de México*, ed. Alicia Barabás, 4 vols., Mexico: INAH, 2003–2004, especially her essay "Ethnoterritorialidad sagrada en Oaxaca," I, 37–125. Conceptually, these volumes draw on Victor Turner's views about center and periphery, communitas, and a hierarchy of shrines.
7. Joseph Navarro de Vargas, "Padrón del pueblo de San Mateo Huitzilopochco, inventario de su iglesia y directorio de sus obvenciones parroquiales," *Anales del Museo Nacional de Arqueología, Historia, y Etnología*, época 3: 1 (1909), 559.
8. The meaning of "shrine" for colonial Mexico is discussed further in Appendix 1.
9. For religious studies, this approach is related to phenomenology – "the investigation of that which is observable" for clues to perceptions, values, and intentions. In effect, meaning resides in use. See "Phenomenology of Religion," in *The Harper Collins Dictionary of Religion*, ed. Jonathan Z. Smith, San Francisco: Harper, 1995, pp. 897–898, and Victor Turner's work on "lived experience," by which he meant the ways rituals are sites of "reflexive (re)production of culture," *Victor Turner and Contemporary Cultural Performance*, ed. Graham St. John, New York and Oxford: Berghahn Books, 2008, pp. 3–4.
10. This inclination to regard the image as the shrine is implicit in the colonial record. An explicit but more recent example is the Christ of Otatitlán, known as the "Señor Santuario." See José Velasco Toro, "Vamos al Santuario del Señor de Otatitlán. Expresión numinosa de un ámbito regional," in *Santuario y región: Imágenes del Cristo negro de Otatitlán*, ed. José Velasco Toro, Jalapa: Universidad Veracruzana, 1997, p. 184; also Rubén Córdoba Olivares, "Señor Santuario: Hacedor de vida," in the same volume, pp. 359–402.
11. Tattooed images from the colonial period are poorly documented and little studied, but an article by Désirée Moreno Silva makes a promising start. In one of her cases, dating from 1750, Nicolás Sarabia, a thirty-seven-year-old "español" weaver, had the Christ of Chalma tattooed on his chest. In testimony he mentioned that in a knife fight he had been stabbed in that exact spot and attributed his recovery from the wound to the protection of this miraculous image. Sarabia's body was covered with a farrago of

Introduction 23

obscene images, the devil, and depictions of saints that authorities would have regarded as far from fitting for a model Christian and not rising above the level of superstition. See Moreno Silva, "Devociones a flor de piel: La imagen sagrada y el tatuaje en la Nueva España del siglo de las luces," in *La imagen sagrada y sacralizada: XXVIII Coloquio Internacional de Historia del Arte*, ed. Peter Krieger, Mexico: UNAM, 2011, I, 191.

12. For a spirited call for studies of culture as mutable and transitory, see Stephen Greenblatt, ed., *Cultural Mobility: A Manifesto*, Cambridge, UK and New York: Cambridge University Press, 2010.

13. Francisco Javier Clavijero, "Breve noticia sobre la prodigiosa y renombrada imagen de Nuestra Señora de Guadalupe" (1782), in *Testimonios históricos guadalupanos*, ed. Ernesto de la Torre Villar and Ramiro Navarro de Anda, Mexico: Fondo de Cultura Económica, 1982, p. 590.

14. "Condensed presence" comes from Emily Dickinson: "To the faithful, absence is condensed presence," *Letters*, ed. Thomas H. Johnson and Theodora Ward, 3 vols., Cambridge, MA: Harvard University Press, 1958, letter #587, to Susan Norcross Dickinson; "tapestries of paradise" is from poem #278 in *The Complete Poems of Emily Dickinson*, ed. Thomas H. Johnson, London: Faber and Faber, 1970, p. 128. Luis de Cisneros's celestial image of the shrine experience is from *Historia del principio, y origen progressos venidas a México y milagros de la Santa Ymagen de nuestra Señora de los Remedios . . .*, Mexico: Iuan Blanco de Alcaçar, 1621, fol. 48r.

15. Francisco de Florencia, *Las novenas del santuario de Nuestra Señora de Guadalupe de México, que se apareció en la manta de Juan Diego*, Madrid: Imprenta de Lorenzo de San Martín, 1785, pp. 8–9. In his introduction to this passage, Florencia mentioned Amadeus directly. See also, D. A. Brading, *Mexican Phoenix. Our Lady of Guadalupe: Image and Tradition Across Five Centuries*, Cambridge, UK and New York: Cambridge University Press, 2001, pp. 4–5, and Martha Reta Hernández, "Manuel de Arellano," in *Sacred Spain: Art and Belief in the Spanish World*, ed. Ronda Kasl, Indianapolis: Indianapolis Museum of Art, 2009, p. 226.

According to Robert Bartlett, *Why Can the Dead Do Such Great Things? Saints and Worshippers from the Martyrs to the Reformation*, Princeton: Princeton University Press, 2013, p. 501, there was a notable increase in the number of miraculous images of the Virgin Mary in Europe from the early fourteenth century.

16. Antonio Tello, *Crónica miscelánea de la Sancta Provincia de Xalisco, libro IV*, preliminary study and notes by Fr. Luis del Refugio de Palacio, Guadalajara: Edit. Font, 1955, p. 73.

17. Hermenegildo de Vilaplana, *Historia de la milagrosa imagen de Nuestra Señora del Pueblito . . .*, 2nd ed., Mexico: Imprenta de la Bibliotheca Mexicana, 1765, p. 57. The relevant Trent decree was issued in the twenty-fifth session, December 4, 1563, *Canons and Decrees of the Council of Trent: Original Text in English*, trans. H. J. Schroeder, OP, St. Louis and London: B. Herder Book Co., 1941, pp. 215–217. Other priests framed the distinction differently, seeming to allow some agency to the image itself. In his sermon for the miraculous image of the Señor de Tziritzíquaro, preached at the shrine in 1745, Fray Manuel Ignacio Frías, OSA, wrote of "the original" (Christ in the flesh) and "la imagen" (this image of him): "Are they two Christs in one or one Christ duplicated? This sacred image went out from its temple to bring health to its people, and with it, invisible, went Christ, who is its sovereign original, to give health,"

Soberano maestro de orthographia, Christo Señor Nuestro Crucificado, venerado en su Milagrosa Imagen del Señor de Tziritziquaro . . ., Mexico: La Imprenta Real del Superior Gobierno, y del Nuevo Rezado de Doña María de Rivera, 1745, p. 18.

18. See, for example, Xavier Bray, "The Sacred Made Real: Spanish Painting and Sculpture, 1600–1700," in *The Sacred Made Real*, ed. Xavier Bray, London: National Gallery, 2009, pp. 15–40. For a different historical view of Baroque that regards the style as the project of absolutist Catholic monarchies engaged in the rise of nation states and therefore confined to a small window of time, see Carl Friedrich, *The Age of the Baroque, 1610–1660*, New York: Harper & Row, 1962, especially pp. 39–43.

19. "This style in decoration got the epithet of *Barroque* taste, derived from a word signifying pearls and teeth of unequal size," quoted from the first English translation of Winckelmann by Henry Fuseli, *Reflections on the Painting and Sculpture of the Greeks*, London: A Millar, 1765, pp. 122–123. As Michael Baxandall cautioned, the ornate (*ornato*) and decorative carried a different, more positive meaning in the sixteenth and seventeenth centuries than Winckelmann and his intellectual heirs have supposed: "anything additional to clarity and correctness was the ornato . . . Quintilian [often quoted by Renaissance authors] lists the general qualities of ornateness: piquancy, richness, liveliness, charm, and finish," *Painting and Experience in Fifteenth-Century Italy: A Primer in the Social History of Pictorial Style*, Oxford: Clarendon Press, 1972, p. 131.

20. José Antonio Maravall's *La cultura del barroco: Análisis de una estructura histórica*, Barcelona: Edit. Ariel, 1975 (English translation, University of Minnesota Press, 1986) is the pioneering text in this vein. Timothy Reiss, "American Baroque Histories and Geographies from Sigüenza y Góngora to Balbuena to Balboa, Carpentier, and Lezama," in *Baroque New Worlds: Representation, Transculturation, Counterconquest*, ed. Lois Parkinson Zamora and Monika Kaup, Durham: Duke University Press, 2010, pp. 394–414 describes this line of interpretation in the writings of Irving Leonard, among others. The quotation is from Lois Parkinson Zamora and Monika Kaup, "Introduction: Baroque, New World Baroque, Neobaroque," in *Baroque New Worlds*, p. 3, describing the perspective of Mexican novelist Rosario Castellanos.

21. See, for example, Rolena Adorno, *Colonial Latin American Literature: A Very Short Introduction*, New York: Oxford University Press, 2011, pp. 77–80, especially p. 80. Adorno regards the convergence of three cultures ("the immigrant European, the indigenous American, and the transplanted African") as the distinctive feature of Latin American Baroque, but what was the distinctive expression of this convergence? Her emphasis is on the theme of *desengaño*.

22. Kenneth Clark, *Civilisation: A Personal View*, New York: Harper & Row, 1969, p. 238.

23. Parkinson Zamora and Kaup, "Introduction," p. 3.

24. E.g., Roberto S. Goizueta, *Christ Our Companion: Toward a Theological Aesthetics of Liberation*, Maryknoll, NY: Orbis Books, 2009, p. 68. Antonio Rubial García takes another approach to the distinction and tension between high and low religious culture, emphasizing the difference between literacy and orality. He notes how the formal texts of the seventeenth and early eighteenth centuries adhered to "the world of rhetoric," with its formal presentation of documents, testimony, and reports and were a world apart from "the absence of criticism and the great credulity that were distinguishing features of the oral world," "Invención de prodigios. La literatura hierofánica novohispana," *Historias* 69 (enero–abril 2008), 130. However, as Rubial

suggests, the written texts were intended to purify popular devotion and offer moral instruction rather than undermine it. The written texts for shrines usually appealed to oral tradition for authority and the partisans of Rubial's literate and oral "realms" both shared devotions, religious sensibilities, and a fundamental belief in divine presence.

Art historian Esther Pasztory extends the argument in favor of the hegemonic power of writing by positing that "the widespread use of writing fundamentally changes the role of things and puts them in a secondary position," quoted from her website at www.columbia.edu/~ep9/ accessed July 25, 2015. Colonial religious images in their various forms do not fit comfortably with this position either.

25. How, for example, to reconcile the idea of oppressive state power overrunning local traditions with abundant evidence of local economic, political, and cultural activity that escaped centralized surveillance, censure, and control?
26. For a study of popular "Baroque" Catholicism in Southwest Germany during and after the Reformation (especially after 1650) that also emphasizes religious practices and clerical-lay relations, see Marc R. Forster, *Catholic Revival in the Age of the Baroque: Religious Identity in Southwest Germany, 1550–1750*, Cambridge, UK and New York: Cambridge University Press, 2001.
27. Cited in Bray, "The Sacred Made Real," p. 40, from Council of Trent, 25th session, 1563. See also John W. O'Malley, *Trent: What Happened at the Council*, Cambridge, MA: Harvard University Press, 2013, p. 273.
28. Altarpieces of the time were approvingly described as "curioso" – not just strange, but surprising, thrilling – much as a lightning bolt symbolized a memorable sermon, in the words of Isidro Félix de Espinosa, OFM, writing in the 1740s about the Franciscan colleges of Propaganda Fide in Mexico, *Crónica de los colegios de Propaganda Fide de la Nueva Espana* [1746], ed. Lino Gómez Canedo, Washington: Academy of American Franciscan History, 1964, p. 291.
29. *The Life of Saint Theresa of Avila*, trans. E. Allison Peers, London: Sheed and Ward, 1979, pp. 192–193.
30. On the symbolism and use of candles, see Yrjo Hirn, *The Sacred Shrine: A Study of the Poetry and Art of the Catholic Church*, Boston: Beacon Press, 1957, p. 97.
31. Parish archive of Tlaltenango, Zacatecas, libro de gobierno, entry 46 (1921). The parish priest noted that Christ's movements had been observed especially on Tuesdays and Fridays, 6:00–8:00 a.m. and 5:00–7:00 p.m., and that many people were coming on pilgrimages to venerate the image.
32. For Father Herrera's political views in 1860, see his pamphlet, *Contestación del cura de Tlaltenango a las observaciones que su Illmo. Prelado hizo a los escritos sobre la paz mexicana*, Mexico: Tip. de Manuel Castro, 1860, and Brian Connaughton's pointed discussion of them in *Dimensiones de la identidad patriótica: Religión, política, y regiones en México. Siglo XIX*, Mexico: Miguel Ángel Porrúa, 2001, chapter 9.
33. The lavish wardrobe for statues of the Virgin Mary is a good example. At the silver-mining center of Real del Monte (Hidalgo), 422 silver pesos were spent on one new dress for the Virgin of the Rosary venerated there in the 1750s, JCB B760 A973i, *relación de méritos* of Dr. Joseph Rodríguez Díaz.
34. Alexander Nehamas, *Only a Promise of Happiness*, Princeton: Princeton University Press, 2007, p. 99.

35. On "inner presence" and Italian painting in the sixteenth and seventeen centuries, see Klaus Krüger, "Authenticity and Fiction: On the Pictorial Construction of Inner Presence in Early Modern Italy," in *Image and Imagination of the Religious Self in Late Medieval and Early Modern Europe*, ed. Reindert Falkenburg, Walter S. Melion, and Todd M. Richardson, Turnhout: Brepols Publishers, 2007, pp. 37–69.
36. Cayetano Cabrera y Quintero, *Escudo de armas de México: Celestial protección de esta nobilíssima ciudad, de la Nueva España, y de casi todo el Nuevo Mundo* . . ., Mexico: Vda. de Joseph Bernardo de Hogal, 1746, pp. 287–288. Florencia, *Las novenas del santuario*, pp. 7–8 speaks of going to Tepeyac "con fin de visitar a la Santísima Virgen en su celestial Imagen," and that "la Señora estaba visible en el Altar de su Santuario para hacer Mercedes a todos."
37. James Clifton, "Introduction," in *The Body of Christ in the Art of Europe and New Spain, 1150–1800*, ed. James Clifton, Munich and New York: Prestel, 1997, p. 11. In this passage Clifton quotes Gridley McKim-Smith's remark that Spanish and New Spanish sculpted figures of Virgin and Christ crucified rarely were to be found in museum collections in the United States, observing that they are so naturalistic, uncomfortably intimate, and insistently religious as to overwhelm museumgoers' expectation of a more detached aesthetic encounter.
38. From his childhood in Yahualica, Jalisco in the years just before the Revolution of 1910, Mexican novelist Agustín Yáñez knew well this kind of somatic devotion regulated by the church bells. Here he describes how time was marked there not by the clock but by the tolling of the bells:

    el tiempo eclesiástico rige la existencia. Los toques de alba y las llamadas a misas fijan el espacio de la mañana; las llamadas a las conferencias; los toques de las doce; de las tres de la tarde [marking Christ's three hours on the cross]; las llamadas al Rosario; el toque de la oración; los dobles de ánimas a las ocho de la noche; y antiguamente el toque de queda marcan el curso fiel del día.

    Quoted in Higinio Vásquez Santa Ana, *Cristos célebres de México*, Mexico: n.p., 1950, p. 70.
39. See William B. Taylor, *Shrines & Miraculous Images: Religious Life in Mexico Before the Reforma*, Albuquerque: University of New Mexico Press, 2010, pp. 20, 211–212.
40. Quoted in Elisa Vargaslugo, "Recordando a Francisco de la Maza," *Anales del Instituto de Investigaciones Estéticas* 84 (2004), 201–202: "todos los sentidos se apacentaban en generosas delicias, como en un nuevo Paraíso: de lúcidos resplandores la vista, de fragrantes aromas el olfato, de suavísimas consonancias de voces el oído, de armónica composición el gusto."

    Music has been an understudied dimension of this synesthesia of devotion in colonial Latin America, but musicologists recently have turned to the subject in ways that put them in conversation with the same kinds of sources, contexts, and issues of locality and power more familiar to historians and art historians. See especially *Music and Urban Society in Colonial Latin America*, ed. Geoffrey Baker and Tess Knighton, Cambridge, UK and New York: Cambridge University Press, 2011; *Devotional Music in the Iberian World, 1450–1800: The Villancico and Related Genres*, ed. Tess Knighton and Álvaro Torrente, Aldershot, England: Ashgate, 2007, and Drew Edward Davies, "Finding 'Local Content' in the Music of New Spain," *Early Music America* 19: 2 (2013), 60–64.

41. Going beyond an emphasis on the pictorial arts, Gerardus Van der Leeuw attempted to bring all of these expressions of beauty and holiness together in *Sacred and Profane Beauty: The Holy in Art*, trans. David E. Green, New York: Holt, Rinehart and Winston, 1963. But his approach was mainly to treat dance, procession, music, poetry, drama, architecture, pictorial arts, and theological aesthetics as separate forms.
42. Mark Doty, *Still Life with Oysters and Lemon*, Boston: Beacon Press, 2001, p. 40. In *The Nature of Order*, vols. 1 and 4, Berkeley: Center for Environmental Structure, 2002–2004, architect Christopher Alexander explores the idea that beauty gives the impression of life – as "living centers" that "materialize feeling"; and his interest in "the forms of things in terms of their impact on us" invites a focus on reception.
43. This plotline has yet to be closely studied, but it has been proposed, most recently by Charlene Villaseñor Black in "Inquisitorial Practices Past and Present: Artistic Censorship, the Virgin Mary, and St. Anne," in *Art, Piety, and Destruction in the Christian West, 1500–1700*, ed. Virginia Chieffo Raguin, Burlington, VT: Ashgate, 2010, pp. 173–200, especially pp. 177, 178, 184.
44. François Furet, *In the Workshop of History*, Chicago: University of Chicago Press, 1982, p. 54. Another prototype for narrative history with some bearing on the history of colonial shrines was the course of a day, from morning to night and back again, writ large. See Chapter 2. For the place of this metaphor in the mythology and historical narratives of ancient Mesoamerica, see Michel Graulich, *Myths of Ancient Mexico*, trans. Bernard R. Ortiz de Montellano and Thelma Ortiz de Montellano, Norman: University of Oklahoma Press, 1997, p. 265.
45. Francisco de Florencia, *Narración de la maravillosa aparición que hizo el archángel San Miguel a Diego Lázaro ...*, Sevilla: Impr. de las Siete Revueltas, 1692, pp. 96–99.
46. Evidently, Diego Lázaro's story that he had been transported by the Archangel Michael to a place where a spring of healing waters miraculously issued forth from dry ground was reiterated by witnesses in the formal investigations that followed and were later incorporated into Florencia's text. The founding story of Our Lady of Tulantongo underwent more substantial revision as the shrine gained popularity and the founder became controversial. See Taylor, *Shrines & Miraculous Images*, pp. 15–16.
47. Cabrera y Quintero appealed to oral tradition as a higher kind of proof that preceded written versions, *Escudo de armas*, pp. 317–318. In Chapter 2 of his text about the Virgin of Remedios, *La milagrosa invención de un tesoro escondido*, Mexico: Vda. de Juan de Ribera, 1685, Francisco de Florencia declared that "tenemos por ciertas sólo con fe humana," after saying in Chapter 1 that "los milagros de esta Imagen son vozes que la publican." In other works Florencia frequently invoked tradition as evidence of miracles (e.g. "según antiquíssima tradición," in *Zodíaco mariano ...*, Mexico: Colegio de San Ildefonso, 1755, p. 89; "es tradición," in *Estrella del norte de México. Historia de la milagrosa imagen de María Santísima de Guadalupe*, Guadalajara: J. Cabrera, 1895, pp. 146, 151).
48. For example, Pilar Gonzalbo Aizpurú, "Auge y ocaso de la fiesta. Las fiestas en la Nueva España. Júbilo y piedad, programación y espontaneidad," in *Fiesta y celebración: Discurso y espacio novohispanos*, ed. María Águeda Méndez, Mexico: El Colegio de México, 2009, p. 72, "extirpar las devociones populares ajenas a la liturgia y sospechosas de vana observancia." There was a deepening tension between the idea of the autonomous individual on one hand and collective expression and collective identity on the other

in the late eighteenth century, but (relying almost exclusively on the writings of a leading Spanish public intellectual of the 1790s and 1800s, Gaspar Melchor de Jovellanos) Gonzalbo goes further to suggest not only that the reform program meant to eliminate popular traditions from religious devotions and replace religious spectacles with popular amusements (*diversiones*), it succeeded, p. 72. Even though "religious fiestas did not disappear, they lost their importance as benchmarks of daily life" (*hitos de la vida cotidiana*), reduced to "symbols that were no longer a spur to community rejoicing" (*un carácter simbólico que ya no era estímulo para el gozo comunitario*), pp. 72–73. There is little in Gonzalbo's essay to support the suggestion of such a sea change at this time from a religious to a secular "world" except in the opinions of those who promoted the idea.

49. Robert Brentano, *A New World in a Small Place: Church and Religion in the Diocese of Rieti, 1188–1378*, Berkeley: University of California Press, 1994, p. 5. For a challenging and well-developed line of interpretation that recognizes a great transition from premodern to modern, but insists on "the continuing influence of the distant past in the present" (medieval Western Christianity, in particular), see Brad S. Gregory, *The Unintended Reformation: How a Religious Revolution Secularized Society*, Cambridge, MA: Harvard University Press, 2012.
50. Pierre Nora finds clearer chronological shifts in French historiography, marked by "stages of disillusionment" crises in French history – 1918, 1929, 1945, 1962, 1968. See Pierre Nora, "The Era of Commemoration," in *Realms of Memory: Rethinking the French Past*, ed. Pierre Nora, New York: Columbia University Press, 1996–1998, III, 609–637, and I, xxii.
51. Furet, *In the Workshop of History*, p. 56. On the debate over narrative history after 1979, see Lawrence Stone, "The Revival of Narrative: Reflections on a New Old History" [1979], in his collected essays, *The Past and the Present*, Boston and London: Routledge & Kegan Paul, 1981, Eric Hobsbawm, "The Revival of Narrative: Some Comments," *Past & Present* 86: 1 (1980), 3–8, Hobsbawm's *Interesting Times: A Twentieth-Century Life*, New York: Random House, 2003, pp. 282–297, and the collection of essays on this topic published during the last third of the twentieth century, edited and introduced by Geoffrey Roberts, *The History and Narrative Reader*, London: Routledge, 2001.
52. The literature on these changes and debates about narrative and historical study is vast. Convenient points of entry from vantage points in 1979, 1988, and 2004 are Stone, "The Revival of Narrative," pp. 74–96; Peter Novick, *That Noble Dream: The "Objectivity Question" and the American Historical Profession*, Cambridge, UK and New York: Cambridge University Press, 1988; and John Brewer, "History and Telling Stories," in *A Sentimental Murder: Love and Madness in the Eighteenth Century*, New York: Farrar, Straus, and Giroux, 2004, pp. 280–293. For a valuable, if incomplete and perhaps overconfident, survey of the state of play in historical study and the question of narrative, there is Allan Megill's *Historical Knowledge, Historical Error: A Contemporary Guide to Practice*, Chicago: University of Chicago Press, 2007.
53. Pierre Nora, "The Era of Commemoration," in *Realms of Memory: Rethinking the French Past*, ed. Pierre Nora, New York: Columbia University Press, 1996, III, 609, 633.
54. Nora, "Preface" to *Realms of Memory*, I, xxii.
55. André Vauchez, "The Cathedral," in *Realms of Memory*, ed. Nora, II, 37–68.
56. Nora, "Preface" to *Realms of Memory*, I, xviii.

57. Furet, *In the Workshop*, p. 56.
58. Furet, *In the Workshop*, p. 56.
59. For example, Michel Vovelle, *Ideologies and Mentalities*, Oxford: Polity, 1990, chapter 5 on popular religion.
60. Greg Dening, *Performances*, Melbourne: Melbourne University Press, 1996, p. xv.
61. Gordon S. Wood briefly addresses this separation in history writing in the U.S. in "In Defense of Academic History Writing," *Perspectives on History* (newsletter of the American Historical Association), April 2010, pp. 19–20. See also Stone, *Revival*, for a more optimistic view of professional historians as writers of narrative history in the late 1970s. While their books may not find a place on the Barnes & Noble bookstore shelves, more than a few "analytical" historians bring narrative into their studies or write full-fledged narrative histories, including Wood himself.
62. As E. H. Gombrich suggests, "Unlike scientists, who have had many reasons since the time of Archimedes for shouting Eureka!, we humanists have been less fortunate, and that for the obvious reason that the events we try to explain tend to be immensely complex and can never be reduced to one easily formulated law, which we may describe as the cause of the event," in *The Essential Gombrich*, ed. Richard Woodfield, London: Phaidon Press, 1966, p. 355.
63. Michael Taussig, "Violence and Resistance in the Americas: The Legacy of Conquest," in *Violence, Resistance, and Survival in the Americas: Native Americans and the Legacy of Conquest*, ed. William B. Taylor and Franklin Pease G.Y., Washington: Smithsonian Institution Press, 1994, pp. 270–276.
64. For an example of the view that the written record speaks to little more than colonial rulers and their institutions, see Walter Mignolo, *The Darker Side of the Renaissance: Literacy, Territoriality, and Colonization*, Ann Arbor: University of Michigan Press, 1995.
65. Writing in the early seventeenth century, Juan de Torquemada, OFM said he had examined a "Libro de las Memorias Antiguas de el Convento" for Tlatelolco that recorded Indian donations, *Monarquía Indiana*, Mexico: Porrúa, 1986 (facsimile of 1723 edition), III, 217–218.
66. *Emily Dickinson, Selected Letters*, ed. Thomas H. Johnson, Cambridge, MA: Harvard University Press, 1971, p. 314, letter #962, January 14, 1885.
67. For examples of local shrines and miraculous images that are virtually unknown historically, but richly described ethnographically from interviews and participant-observation, see Vania Salles and José Manuel Valenzuela, *En muchos lugares y todos los días: Vírgenes, santos, y niños Dios. Mística y religiosidad popular en Xochimilco*, Mexico: El Colegio de México, 1997, and Bibiana Ugalde Mendoza, *Xitaces con sentimiento y tradición: Historia del culto a la cruz verde de Tequisquiapan en la voz de un pueblo creyente*, Querétaro: Hear Taller Gráfico, 1997.
68. A few religious prints are easier to follow in this way than celebrated paintings or statues by well-known artists, or most of the arresting ex-voto paintings. For a case in point, see William B. Taylor, *Marvels & Miracles in Late Colonial Mexico: Three Texts in Context*, Albuquerque: University of New Mexico Press, 2011, pp. 71–136. For other examples, Taylor, *Shrines & Miraculous Images*, pp. 49–51 (the Cross of Huaquechula in 1809) and pp. 50–52 (the Virgin of Cancuc in 1743), and Paul Ramírez and William B. Taylor, "Out of Tlatelolco's Ruins: Patronage, Devotion, and Natural

Disaster at the Shrine of Our Lady of the Angels, 1745–1781," *Hispanic American Historical Review* 93: 1 (February 2013), pp. 33–65 for prints of the image of Nuestra Señora de los Ángeles beginning in the 1770s.

69. *Colección de las ordenanzas, que para el gobierno de el obispado de Michoacán hicieron y promulgaron . . .*, Mexico: Reimpresa de D.F. de Zúñiga y Ontiveros, 1776, pp. 145–146.

70. See Susan Verdi Webster, "Shameless Beauty and Worldly Splendor: On the Spanish Practice of Adoring the Virgin," in *The Miraculous Image in the Late Middle Ages and Renaissance*, ed. Erik Thunø and Gerhard Wolf, Rome: "l'Erma" di Bretschneider, 2004, pp. 249–274.

71. For example, Bancroft MSS 72/57m box 3 folder 20, directive from the Archbishop of Guatemala dated April 20, 1768. Pedro Pitarch discusses the "cult" of "ugly" statues of saints that show signs of wear in Tzeltal communities of highland Chiapas in "Conjeturas sobre la identidad de los santos tzeltales," in *De la mano do lo sacro. Santos y demonios en el mundo maya*, ed. Mario Humberto Ruz, Mexico: UNAM, 2006, pp. 67–90. For an example of a community refusing to allow their old images to be restored or replaced, see Gerardo Lara Cisneros, *El cristianismo en el espejo indígena: Religiosidad en el occidente de Sierra Gorda, siglo XVIII*, Mexico: INAH/CONACULTA, 2002, p. 132, Xichú, 1768.

72. William A. Christian, Jr., "Afterword: Islands in the Sea: The Public and Private Distribution of Knowledge of Religious Visions," *Visual Resources* 25: 1–2 (March–June 2009), 161–162. Christian also reports visions of Christ and God the Father that were muffled in official records or described there as Marian apparitions. I am grateful to the author for this information in a personal communication, March 23, 2010.

73. For example, the claim by Francisco Diego, an Indian of Atenco in the district of Metepec, that the Virgin of Guadalupe appeared to him and promised him money to spend on the poor was immediately investigated and suppressed by the archbishop's court, Archivo Histórico del Arzobispado de México, box for 1728, exp. 11.

74. *Investigaciones jurídicas* exist or are mentioned for La Conquistadora, Puebla 1582 (1584?); 1614, La Piedad; 1639, 1650, Cruz de Piedra, Querétaro; 1641, 1653, Nuestra Señora de Zapopan, authorized but not completed; 1643–1644 and 1675, San Miguel del Milagro (perhaps also in 1632); 1649, El Pueblito, not completed; 1649, Nuestra Señora de la Laguna, Yucatán; 1650, Tix, Yucatán; 1666, 1723, Nuestra Señora de Guadalupe; 1668, Nuestra Señora de San Juan de los Lagos, said to be the second investigation (1634 mention of a *visita* to investigate), 1734; 1670, Nuestra Señora de Talpa (in a 1732 copy); 1689, Cristo Renovado de Santa Teresa; 1739, Nuestra Señora de la Salud, Pátzcuaro; 1754–1755, Nuestra Señora de Ocotlán, Tlaxcala.

A few formal inquiries into particular miracles not connected to a shrine also exist: for the *panecitos* of Santa Teresa in Mexico City, 1681–1686; the Divina Pastora in Veracruz, 1744–1754; the 1769 Picazo case; and an investigation into the marvelous cure of a nun associated with the Virgin of Guadalupe, in the Sutro Library collection, BT660.G8 1864 Rare Bk. Luis de Cisneros's devotional history of the shrine of Nuestra Señora de los Remedios in 1621 might be regarded as an extended brief for an *investigación jurídica*.

75. For example, Eamon Duffy's comment in his remarkable study of sixteenth-century Morebath, "We are forever shut out from all but the surface of Morebath's religion ... only the barest outline" is visible, *The Voices of Morebath: Reformation and Rebellion in an English Village*, New Haven: Yale University Press, 2003, p. 65.
76. Pictures as a substitute for books was an old idea, recorded in twelfth-century Europe, if not earlier, Bartlett, *Why Can the Dead Do Such Great Things?*, p. 495.
77. AHM, Archdiocese of Mexico, box for 1820.
78. The collector's itinerary, tracked by the dates of permission to collect signed by pastors in the parishes he visited: March 6, Malinalco; March 13, Tetecala; March 21, Tepalcingo; March 28, Xantetelco; April 3, Oaxtepec; April 9, Cuauhtla; April 13, Tlayacapan; April 24, Yautepec; April 27, Xiutepec; May 3, Xochitepec; undated, possibly May 5, Yxcatepec; May 8, Tlaquiltenango; May 10, Amacuzac; May 16, Acuitlapan; May 20, Acamixtla; May 27, Teitipac; May 28, Pipichahuazco.
79. In addition to the three stout volumes of translated essays from the Nora project published by Columbia University (1996–1998), the University of Chicago Press has produced another four volumes of the essays (2001–2010) under the title *Rethinking France: Les Lieux de Mémoire*. Lourdes is conspicuously absent from these volumes, perhaps because it does not fit the secularizing currents of nineteenth- and twentieth-century French culture that frame the project, changing mediums of memory – *milieux de mémoire* – into fragmentary, peripheral places of memory – *lieux de mémoire*. Only Philippe Boutry's remarkable essay, "The Village Church," in vol. 3 of the Chicago set (pp. 47–75) considers sites of living religious memory. Boutry's touchstone is the shrine-church to the canonized nineteenth-century parish priest Jean-Marie-Baptiste Vianney at Ars. For the most part, and for better reasons than would apply to Mexico, French scholarship holds to a sharp transition from religious state and society to secular republican culture in France from the eighteenth to the nineteenth centuries, as Nora implies. See, for example, Philippe Boutry, Jacques LeGoff, and others, *Histoire de la France religieuse. Tomo 2: Du roi Très Chrétien à la laïcité républicaine (XVIIIe-XIXe siècle)*, Paris: Seuil, 1991.
80. More than a few traditions said to have been practiced "from time immemorial" (*de tiempo inmemorial*) were only a generation or so old – beyond the eye-witness recollection of any living member of the community – and were rooted in Spanish municipal liberties as much as precolonial American pride of place. On the medieval tradition of municipal political autonomy in Castile and its extension to America, see Helen Nader, *Liberty in Absolutist Spain: The Hapsburg Sale of Towns, 1516–1700*, Baltimore: The Johns Hopkins Press, 1990, pp. 72, 81, 92.

PART I

Bearings

Historical Patterns and Places of Image Shrines

I
Formative Developments, 1520s–1720s

Catholic Christianity and its imagery broke in on Mesoamerica suddenly in the 1520s and has been a pivot point of living and dying there ever since. But there is no simple story of an early formative stage and late decline in the history of Christian image shrines in New Spain. They began in the sixteenth century, haltingly; and with many shrines eventually scattered over a vast, broken terrain, local histories of Christian practice were bound to depart from models and prescriptions in Rome, Madrid, Mexico City, or less remote capitals and style centers.[1] The weight of the European past and present in the development of Christianity and religious practices in New Spain was great, and diffusion from Catholic Europe lends some coherence to the history of image shrines, whether following European trends or working against them. But Europe, too, is a moving target, neither uniform nor fixed and finished in its religious culture. What, then, can be said with some confidence about the impact of European beliefs and practices on the development of those shrines? What changed where and when?

This chapter tracks their early development, during the sixteenth and seventeenth centuries. Most image shrines and the full range of their distinguishing features took shape later than might be expected, mainly during a "long" seventeenth century from the 1580s to the 1720s that amounted to the formative period. Chapter 2 continues into the eighteenth century, suggesting that the late colonial period was less a time of decline for shrines and enchantment than one of consolidation and growth. (See Map 1.1 for the image shrines discussed in the text.) The substantial, if gradual, developments in the seventeenth and eighteenth centuries lead to consideration of long-term continuities from precolonial times on in the second part of Chapter 2, and the leading role of Marian and Christocentric shrines and images in Chapters 3 and 4.

Sixteenth-Century Beginnings: European Roots and Branches

Scholarship about nearly all aspects of religion in New Spain has centered on the sixteenth century rather than taking in the full sweep of the colonial

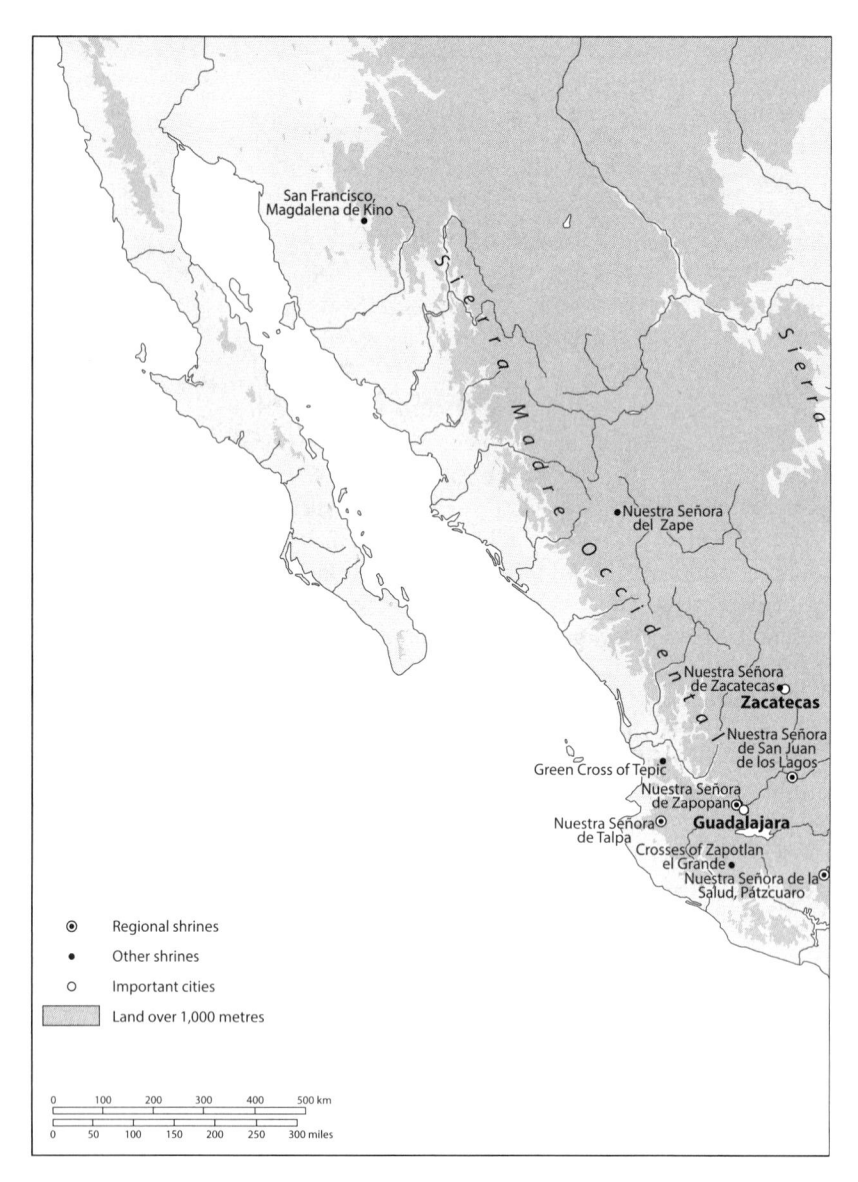

36   Part I Bearings: Historical Patterns and Places of Image Shrines

Map 1.1 Images and shrines discussed in the text. Prepared by Cox Cartographic Limited.

period. Lines of interpretation have varied but the effect has been to treat the early years of colonization as formative for religion in the same ways that colonial institutions, imperial practices, economic activities, and labor systems were largely established then. One line of interpretation advanced

Map 1.1 (cont.)

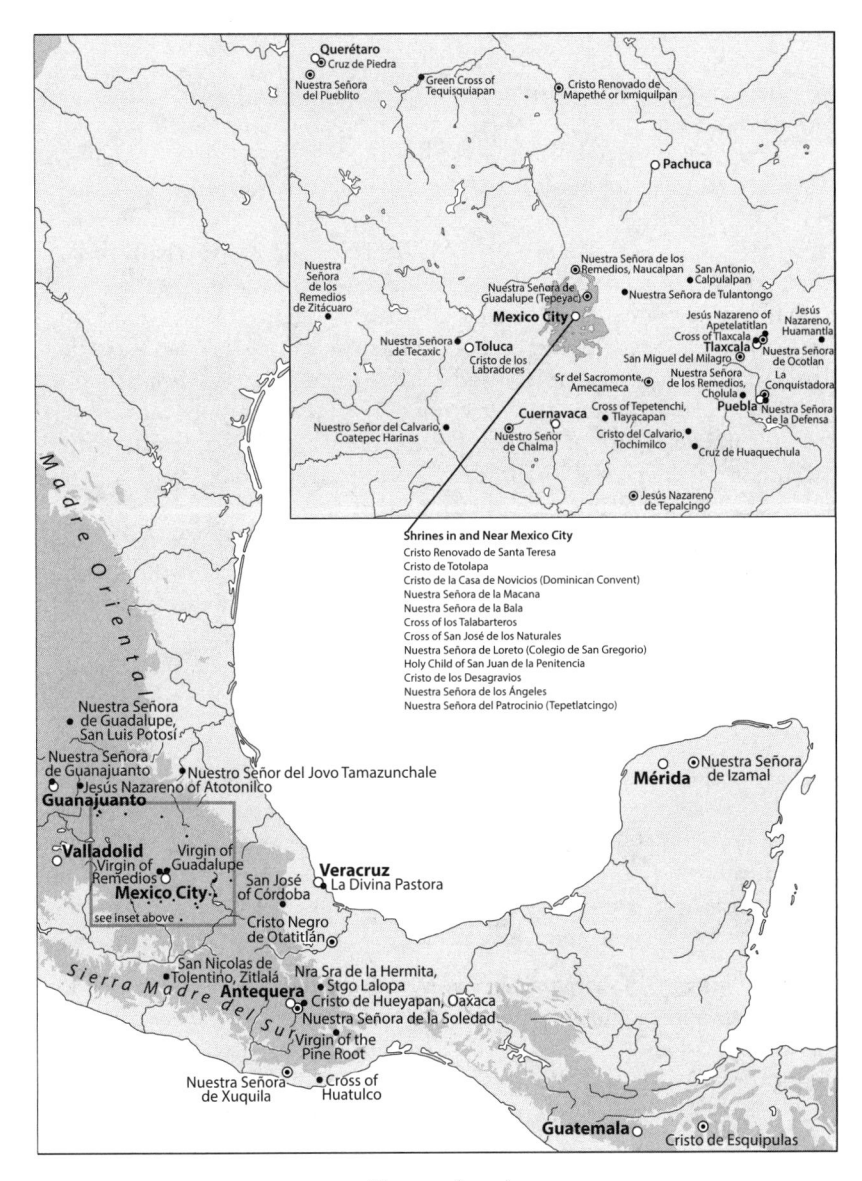

by an earlier generation of historians, art historians, Hispanist literary scholars, and anthropologists that still has currency proposes that the basic features of Iberian culture introduced during "the conquest period" were more or less fixed and predominant by the 1570s. French Hispanist

Robert Ricard put it this way in his landmark 1933 study of early Christian evangelization, which he called *The Spiritual Conquest of Mexico*: "[I]n the religious domain, as in the others, the sixteenth century was the important period, the period in which Mexico was created, and of which the rest of her history has been only the almost inevitable development."[2] A generation after Ricard, art historian George Kubler wrote starkly of removal and replacement: "Conquest was followed at once by massive European substitutions of useful and symbolic behavior for native traditions ... wholesale destruction of the native American civilizations."[3]

Framing a comparative theory of early modern colonization, Louis Hartz, political scientist and proponent of the idea of American exceptionalism, posited that a special kind of "fragment society" implanted by Spanish immigrants came to characterize New Spain, chipped off the social and cultural rock face of medieval Iberia in the early sixteenth century. Because it was "detached from the whole of it and hurled outward onto new soil, it loses the stimulus toward change that the whole provides. It lapses into a kind of immobility."[4] As Hartz implied, and George Foster, a leading social anthropologist with one foot in Spain and the other in Mexico, argued more vigorously, this incompletely Europeanized colonial culture "crystallized" before the end of the sixteenth century.[5] It became fixed, Foster suggested, through a screening process of introductions formalized by Spanish authorities, carried by immigrants, and selectively adopted in America:

The basic outlines of the new colonial cultures took shape at a rapid rate. Once they became comparatively well integrated and offered preliminary answers to the most pressing problems of settlers, their forms became more rigid: they may be said to have crystallized ... These stabilizing cultures were then less receptive to change and less prone to accept new elements from the parent culture which had been left behind or rejected in the initial movement.[6]

If the history of colonial religion and shrines mainly amounted to a crystallization of European ways and things that were then selectively transferred and adopted during the sixteenth century, two matters call for clarification. What was medieval or not medieval about Christianity in New Spain? And was Tridentine Catholicism in New Spain (in the aftermath of reforms set out by the Council of Trent, 1546–1563) a sharp break from medieval Christianity in Iberia? There are obvious problems with treating medieval and Tridentine or Counter-Reformation religion as separate or fundamentally different. They are sweeping terms, in practice overlapping, fluid, and loose fitting. Without a host of qualifications about place and time, "medieval" is too open and sprawling a category to hold much analytical value, especially if coupled with crystallization. And "Tridentine" seems too neat, assuming that the canons and decrees of the

Council of Trent were the blueprint for a transformation of organized Christian faith in opposition to Protestant reforms. Nor are medieval and Tridentine readily separable as successive phases of Catholic orthodoxy in the sixteenth and seventeenth centuries. Reform movements were underway among Christians in the West before Luther, and Catholic reforms continued long after the Council of Trent; and currents of reform coexisted, mixed and adapted more than following in sequence or always in opposition.[7]

Nevertheless, both medieval and Tridentine have a bearing on this colonial history. Much about Christian institutions, practices, and beliefs that developed in New Spain was already well established in Iberia and the rest of European Christendom before Spaniards began to colonize mainland America in the early sixteenth century, including dioceses, parishes, the cult of saints and their intercessory powers, relics, Marian devotion, purgatory, indulgences, lay confraternities, pious hermits, liturgical practices, miracles, animated materiality – including divine immanence associated with images – and the presence of evil in the guise of Satan and his minions. European historians find an "eruption" of images in the fourteenth and fifteenth centuries that were associated with supernatural occurrences and in other respects were taken to be a living presence, sometimes dangerously alive.[8] Already in the fifteenth century, Iberian Christians were expected to have religious images in their homes,[9] and animated images, especially of the Virgin Mary, were beginning to displace apparition stories and the mystique of bone relics as the most compelling signs of divine presence.[10] Sixteenth-century shrines dedicated to celebrated images of the Virgin Mary with regional appeal included Our Lady of Montserrat (Catalonia), Our Lady of Aranzazú (part of the Basque region), Our Lady of the Pillar at Zaragoza (Aragon), Our Lady of Valvanera (La Rioja), Our Lady of Peña de Francia (on the border between Castile and Portugal), the Virgin of Guadalupe (Castile), and Our Lady of La Cabeza (northern Andalusia).[11]

Much as sacred images would be deployed in the New World, statues of Christ, Mary, and other saints had been regarded as essential aids in the evangelization of Muslims and Jews in Granada during the late fifteenth century.[12] A bright thread running from the mystique of sacred images in late medieval Europe to images in the evangelization of New Spain before and after the Council of Trent was the activity of the mendicant orders. Three orders coming out of the mendicant movement in the thirteenth century – Franciscans, Dominicans, and Augustinians – were favored by the crown for the work of converting and ministering to native Christians in New Spain during the sixteenth century, but Observant Franciscans were especially valued for their zeal, austerity, and support for the crown's claim to divine right in American colonization. To early Franciscans in New

Spain, the Spanish king was a charismatic ruler, the messiah-emperor, and Fernando Cortés was "the Moses of the New World."[13]

Franciscans and Augustinians in particular contributed to the air of the marvelous in New Spain in the beginning. Franciscans traditionally looked to miracles and revelation as the great source of God's truths. Whether it was St. Francis's comrade St. Bonaventure recommending the vital power of the affections and "divine illumination" or William of Ockham a century later concluding that the truths of God are known by revelation alone, Franciscans were alert to signs of divine will in the world. Francis himself was renowned for experiencing visions and apparitions of God and Christ, as well as receiving the stigmata and being an agent of wondrous healings and exorcisms.[14] And stories of Christ, Mary, St. Francis, and angels appearing to worthy friars are recorded in early hagiographical texts of the order.[15] Other early Franciscan friars also had the healing touch, which was regarded as an outward sign that they were the chosen of God. With this reputation in mind, Pope Nicholas V (1447–1455) reputedly exclaimed, "If we were to canonize all the Franciscans who work miracles, there would be no time to do anything else."[16] Franciscans were among the ardent Marianists of fifteenth- and sixteenth-century Europe, especially promoting the doctrine of Mary's Immaculate Conception, which was formalized by the general Council of Basel in 1439 as "a pious doctrine to be approved, held, and professed by all Catholics," if not canonically binding. One of their number, Pope Sixtus IV (1471–1484), authorized the feast of the Immaculate Conception with its own special Mass and office. Presenting the faithful with a nurturing, domestic Mary – the loving mother – Franciscan Marianism became a distinguishing feature of the order's evangelizing program in New Spain during the sixteenth century. While sixteenth-century Franciscans were ambivalent about image shrines, the hospitals they founded in many indigenous communities each had a chapel dedicated to Mary Immaculate that featured a statue or painting of her.

In spite of their shared traditions, the several branches of Franciscans were in flux during the fifteenth century, reflecting a long history of reformist doctrinal and institutional debates within the order and the Church more generally. There was a long-standing rift between Observants, who were determined to hew to the Rule of St. Francis and follow lives of strict discipline and poverty, and their more institutional brethren, the Conventuals, who accepted that Franciscan houses and provinces could hold property in common.[17] In Spain, the division between Observants and Conventuals was resolved in favor of the Observants, which made for a particular kind of evangelical urgency among Franciscans in America during the sixteenth century, a time when Observants were especially receptive to a strain of millenarianism within the Franciscan tradition that was well suited to the Spanish crown's colonizing ambitions.[18] Several generations of Franciscans in America were moved to follow the example of the "Apostolic Twelve" and heed the call to "hurry down now to the active life" of conversion, pastoral care, and spiritual purification before the imminent Day of Judgment.[19]

Before the Council of Trent (1545–1563), but after Martin Luther posted his ninety-five theses in 1517 and opened the great confessional struggles of the sixteenth century, another religious order, the Society of Jesus, was established that would be woven into the fabric of Catholic life and religious politics in Spanish and Portuguese America by the early seventeenth century. The spirituality of the Jesuit "soldiers of Christ" centered on rigorous intellectual inquiry in which images were employed to stir contemplation, contrition, and love that led toward communion with the divine presence.[20] Like the Franciscans, Jesuits were ardent Marianists. These two orders were sometimes rivals in preaching and evangelizing, but more often than not they shared enthusiasm for the same Marian advocations and promoted the same image shrines. Together, they were the chief publicists of shrines and miraculous images in the seventeenth and eighteenth centuries. Without their shared interest, some of the more prominent image shrines and Marian advocations might have been only locally known.

Even though there was no significant Protestant challenge in Spanish America, the confessional upheavals of the sixteenth century and the Council of Trent's response to them were inevitably felt in New Spain from the time Philip II circulated the Tridentine canons and decrees soon after they were ratified by the pope in 1564. The Council of Trent provided greater clarity on the doctrines of transubstantiation and justification by works as well as faith, a standardized liturgy of the Mass in the Roman Missal, and a mandate for more powerful popes and bishops and a better educated, more disciplined clergy, but it was far from a prescription for sweeping reform or a revolution in faith and practice.[21] The main focus of the Trent decrees was social disciplining – of both the clergy and laity – and institution building, but even there the decrees were more about correcting abuses and defending traditional practices than transforming the Church as an institution or body of believers.[22] For the most part, bishops were left to establish what "Tridentine" Catholicism would amount to in their jurisdictions. So there were bound to be many and various Catholic reforms in the sixteenth century, both in the context of the Council of Trent's decrees and beyond. In New Spain, bishops were inclined to endorse long-standing European traditions more than institute major reforms, but this, too, was in the spirit of Trent as a response to Protestant challenges – for example, emphasis on the cult of saints and relics, purgatory, and indulgences to redeem souls in purgatory. Among other traditions the bishops reaffirmed were processions and festive splendor, anticipation of miracles, belief in Satan's insinuation into daily affairs, the doctrine of works, the use of Latin in the liturgy, and confraternities. While the Council of Trent had little to say about shrines, images, or the Virgin Mary in defending the cult of saints and relics against deniers who dismissed them as idolatrous, the councilors declared that "due honor and veneration [are] to be given to images of Christ, the Virgin Mary and other saints" and that shrines were founded to honor the memory of the saints.[23] By their actions, most American bishops agreed.

The Spanish crown's power of *patronato* in the New World – especially the right to appoint priests to ecclesiastical benefices, which reduced the direct role of the papacy in the colonies – shaped how the Tridentine decrees were received. The crown could embrace the Council of Trent's focus on greater episcopal authority while advancing its own political interests in selecting bishops who were judged to be royal allies. While the crown favored mendicants as pastors as well as evangelizers among native subjects in the beginning, and mendicants continued to have a freer hand and a larger pastoral role in New Spain than in Spain, Philip II (1556–1598) and his successors invoked the Council of Trent as they began to rein in their special privileges in America, especially the dispensation that allowed friars to serve as pastors and administer sacraments to the laity. From the 1570s, royal decrees used Trent to justify replacing mendicant pastors with diocesan parish priests, a process that took place by stages late into the eighteenth century.

While images of Christ on the cross and in other guises were increasingly featured in Catholic Europe after the Council of Trent, as illustrations of the theology in the Savior's life story and his salvific suffering, the Virgin Mary, too, was in the forefront of Counter-Reformation imagery, politics, and mystique. Whether in Italy, Germany, France, or Spain, new, reputedly miraculous images of Mary were heralded and confraternities were established to sponsor them and support shrines to honor and protect them.[24] It was not unusual for new Marian devotions to overshadow, if not displace, local devotions to a favorite saint.[25] And reported miracles of the Virgin became an effective source of popular support and a way to consolidate political and spiritual boundaries against the challenge of Protestant princes and Muslim rivals in the Mediterranean basin.[26] Imminent threats to Catholic Christianity from both quarters brought out the martial side of Marian devotion. Our Lady of the Rosary after the Battle of Lepanto in 1571 is the famous case, but Mary's prominence in the sixteenth century was not just a matter of looming large in battle. There was always her long-standing appeal as the loving, nurturing mother who might relieve suffering in the world and gain personal favors for her followers, as the Franciscans and the Jesuits, especially, encouraged devotees to believe. These contrasting representations of Mary were fluid and responsive to local circumstances, as Bridget Heal demonstrated in her study of Marian devotion in the contested spiritual landscape of Germany during the sixteenth and early seventeenth centuries.[27] Heal highlights two urban centers where Catholicism held on during the confessional struggles, both of them under Jesuit influence. In Augsburg, where the Protestant challenge was greater, Catholics embraced the Blessed Mary as the warrior Virgin; but in Cologne, where the Protestant challenge was less immediate, Mary as the nurturing mother was ascendant. As Heal puts it, "traditional manifestations of Marian veneration persisted."[28]

As if these complications of a medieval heritage and Counter-Reformation were not enough, the idea of *Spain* in America is blunted by the fact that Spain hardly existed as a polity and culture during the early years of mainland colonization, beyond a common monarch and his ministers and courts issuing laws, establishing political institutions, and rendering judgment. Although most of the early immigrants were Castilians and Spanish – *castellano* – would become the common language of empire, virtually every part of Iberia, with different languages and traditions, was represented among colonial bishops, governors, and other public figures, as well as ordinary immigrants. And the various Spains were themselves moving targets. In the course of 300 years, different generations and classes of immigrants from different parts of Spain brought their own changing religious sensibilities and devotional preferences.

The 1520s to 1570s amounted to the beginning of image shrines in New Spain, but not yet the formative stage. Statues and paintings of Christ, the Blessed Mary, and other saints were found almost everywhere during the sixteenth century,[29] miracles were in the air, and several shrines dedicated to wonder-working images are documented, but the connection between images and enchantment was not yet strong. There were many chapels dedicated to particular saints, with paintings or statues of them on display, but few of the images were objects of veneration in and of themselves, and fewer yet were publicized in print or registers of miracles on site, as they already were in Spain. Enchantment and divine intervention were favorite themes in early colonial church chronicles and annals before the 1580s, but those texts are nearly silent about miraculous images or the infrastructure to support devotion to them. Enchantment in those early years of colonization was expressed especially in apparitions of divine beings, lost souls, and demons at work in the world, or marvelous healings and other surprising events associated with saintly friars and hermits. Late sixteenth- and early seventeenth-century Franciscan chronicles, including Gerónimo de Mendieta's *Historia eclesiástica indiana* (mainly written in the 1580s and 1590s), the Oroz Codex (1584–1586), and Antonio Tello's *Crónica miscelánea* (second quarter of the seventeenth century), recounted visions of Christ in the elevated Host during Mass; a sick Indian girl of Juchipila, Zacatecas, recovering from a grave illness when the Virgin Mary visited her; Indians receiving communion from the Virgin or saints; souls returning to animate moribund Indians in order to receive last rites; an Indian woman (the Virgin Mary?) appearing to an Indian rowing his canoe in Lake Xochimilco during the great epidemic in 1576 to warn sinners to repent; and the saintly Fr. Juan de Gracia learning the hour of his death in a visit from St. Augustine, who assured him of his salvation.[30] Demons were also a presence in early apparition stories. The Dominican chronicler Alonso Franco described a lifeless Indian from Tepetlaoxtoc, near Mexico City, in 1541 coming back to life long enough to confess and take communion. In Franco's telling, the pious Indian informed his confessor, "when my soul left my body, abominable demons took possession of it. With terrible bellowing, they took it."[31]

These same early mendicant chroniclers were nearly silent about cult images,[32] as were leading diocesan authorities in Mexico City even though some of them were early supporters of the Virgin of Guadalupe and the Virgin of Remedios. The sixteenth-century synods in New Spain had little to say directly about images, miraculous or otherwise. The first synod, in 1555, passed over images except to order that no paintings were to be made unless the painter and his work had been examined beforehand, while the second synod in 1565 presumably had images in mind in its provision that no church furnishings (*ornamentos*, which would have included religious images) were to be acquired without a license.[33] The third synod, in 1585, was the most consequential, the one that effectively brought the Council of Trent to Mexican shores in its many provisions for the organization of the Church and ceremonial life. In addition to the authority of bishops and their delegates, it addressed indulgences, processions, relics, veneration of saints, and correction of particular abuses but there was no mention of shrines, and little about images. The only attention to images in the synod's proceedings was a petition of Pedro Martínez, inspector of paintings, for religious images not to be made and sold unless they had been inspected and found to be suitably decorous, and that sculpted images should be crafted from wood rather than maize by-products (*caña de maíz*).[34]

In Spain, by contrast, more than a dozen regional image shrines already were well developed and celebrated in print after the advent of movable type in the late fifteenth century led to a "communications revolution" during the early modern period;[35] and episcopal authorities, the crown, and the Inquisition after Cardinal Jiménez de Cisneros's tenure as inquisitor general (1495–1517) had become deeply suspicious of reported apparitions and their seers.[36] The prominence of apparition stories over cult images in sixteenth-century New Spain may mainly reflect American circumstances – Franciscan interest in apparitions and widespread worries about native idolatry among early bishops and evangelizers.[37] But the striking shift toward cult images in America by the turn of the seventeenth century followed developments in Catholic Europe.

Judging by the small number of celebrated images and their shrines that are securely dated in the sixteenth century – Appendix 2 identifies twenty-two possibilities, and only a few definitely documented before the 1580s – they emerged only gradually. Their origin stories were not yet elaborated and fixed in writing: no devotional history about any of the early image shrines in New Spain was published before 1621, and few *informaciones jurídicas* seem to have been undertaken to authenticate providential beginnings. Several of the distinguishing features of later shrines and miraculous images can be seen in the earliest examples. They were representations of Christ or the Virgin Mary, several of which echoed Mary's role as a celestial warrior in the Spanish Reconquista. They were said to have protected and enabled Spaniards in military and spiritual conquests of the native kingdoms in central Mexico (La Conquistadora of Puebla, Our Lady of Remedios at Naucalpan and Cholula, and Our Lady of Zacatecas), and one, Our Lady of Guanajuato, boasted a Spanish Reconquista history of its own. (See also the discussion of San Miguel and Santiago in Appendix 3.) But in other respects these early examples represent a narrow slice of what Marian shrines would become. The first cult images were introduced by peninsular Spaniards or developed under their direction. This would be less true in the seventeenth century. Diocesan officials were leading promoters of the early shrines, as they would be later, but the Franciscans and Dominicans were not ardent sponsors in the beginning, and the Jesuits were not yet present. The earliest recorded origin stories from the sixteenth century lacked much of what would come to be representative. Before the 1590s, they did not yet mention native seers visited by the Virgin Mary – Juan Diego and the Virgin of Guadalupe, Juan Ceteutli and the Virgin of Remedios, or Juan Diego and the Virgin of Ocotlán.[38] And few of the cult images in the beginning were said to have come to life or to have had supernatural origins. Our Lady of Remedios may have protected the Spaniards in retreat during the Noche Triste by throwing dust in the eyes of native attackers, but the celebrated Christs and crosses were not yet bleeding, twitching, or groaning, and the Virgins were not yet said to weep or change expression.[39] Another distinction of the earliest likely image shrines is that they were located in or near colonial cities – Mexico City, Puebla, Tlaxcala, Querétaro, Guanajuato, and Zacatecas.[40] Mexico City by 1580 already was promoted as capital of the sacred, as well as seat of the viceroyalty and archdiocese, through its association with the Virgin of

Guadalupe, the Virgin of Remedios, a reputedly numinous Christ brought to the city by resident Augustinians from the Indian community of Totolapan, the Cristo de los Siete Velos (said to be a gift from Charles V), and the monumental wooden cross at the chapel of San José de los Naturales.[41] Tlaxcala had the Virgin of Ocotlán nearby, plus its own great wooden cross, erected by Cortés and the native lords; Querétaro had its prodigious stone cross; Guanajuato had Our Lady of Guanajuato; Zacatecas had Our Lady of Zacatecas; and Puebla had La Conquistadora and Nuestra Señora del Pópulo.[42]

Most of the images just mentioned and others listed in Appendix 2 probably were in place before the 1580s, but whether they were regarded as prodigious images or had many followers then is less certain. Their sixteenth-century beginnings are expressed in traditions recorded retrospectively and smoothed into a providential narrative line. Of the possible early shrines, Our Lady of Guadalupe at Tepeyac and Our Lady of Remedios are the most securely documented. Although their appeal and sponsorship differed, they were intertwined from the beginning with support from political and ecclesiastical leaders in Mexico City.

Pious writings by 1648 famously presented the origins of the image and cult of Our Lady of Guadalupe in terms of apparitions of the Virgin and miraculous imprinting of her image on the cloak of her Indian seer, Juan Diego, in 1531. But the earliest documented references to the shrine and image cluster in the 1550s, not the 1530s.[43] Edmundo O'Gorman and others conclude that it was then, in 1555, that the famous image on cloth was made, and promoted by Archbishop Alonso de Montúfar. O'Gorman suggests that it was painted by a native artist, Marcos de Aquino, for the recently constructed chapel at Tepeyac.[44] By that time news had spread that a rancher or shepherd (*ganadero*) had regained his health by going to the chapel; and "the devotion of the people began to grow," as Viceroy Martín Enríquez put it twenty years later.[45] The next year, Fr. Francisco Bustamante, OFM, provincial of his order's Province of the Holy Gospel, objected to the manner of devotion of "the people of this city" to the Virgin of Guadalupe at Tepeyac as a bad example for neophyte Indians[46] – evidence that popular devotion in the city was widespread enough to cause concern. After this flurry of recorded activity in 1555–1556, the documentary trail becomes fainter, but devotion to Guadalupe evidently continued to grow. Scattered references in the 1560s include a note written in 1561 by Antonio Valeriano, the celebrated Latinist and Nahua nobleman from Azcapotzalco, on behalf of the officials of his community, complaining that five local Indians had been working without pay on "the temple of the Virgin Mary which is commonly known as Guadalope."[47] For 1564, Nahua annals apparently completed in the 1590s recorded penitential processions from the city to Tepeyac: "Many people were whipping themselves, and so they did at Lent when they walked in procession and in the feast where the Spaniards were whipping themselves in Tepeyac."[48] Those penitential visits were not always voluntary: in 1568 Archbishop Montúfar sent a Portuguese merchant accused of heresy to the chapel of Guadalupe on three successive Fridays to do penance and pay the chaplain there to say Masses for souls in purgatory.[49] By 1570 a sponsoring confraternity was established, with perhaps 400 members,[50] and a Jeronymite friar was dispatched from the convent-shrine of Our Lady of Guadalupe in Extremadura in 1574 to stake a claim on revenues collected at Tepeyac. He described the shrine as very poor and unadorned, but his presence was a sign that the image was now known as Guadalupe and that the alms collected were substantial enough to draw the attention of claimants in Spain.[51] Although there seems not to have been great interest in the shrine by the city council in the 1570s and 1580s, Archbishop Montúfar's successor, Pedro Moya de Contreras (1573–1591), looked favorably on it and in 1576 helped to secure new papal indulgences for devotees.[52]

For the shrine and image of Our Lady of Remedios, Luis de Cisneros published in 1621 what became the standard origin story and early history. Basing his version in part on paintings displayed at the shrine, Cisneros described how the statue was left on the hill of Totoltepec during the Spaniards' retreat from Tenochtitlan during the Noche Triste in 1520 and found by a local Indian noble, Juan Ce Cuautli Tovar, around 1540. A different, earlier origin story was recorded in the minutes of Mexico City's municipal council in 1579, after the city was granted patronato privileges at the shrine and entrusted with the care of the image. This alternate version highlighted Cortés and the Spaniards with him as both beneficiaries of the Virgin's protection and sponsors of the first chapel. No pious Indian protagonists or lost statue were mentioned. Again, the Spaniards in retreat from Tenochtitlan carried this little statue with them and at the hill of Totoltepec the Virgin appeared to them and the tide of battle turned in their favor. In gratitude, Cortés and others resolved to build a chapel to the Virgin there.[53] Presumably it was this chapel dating from the 1520s that the city council agreed to rebuild in 1574.

Like the cult of the Virgin of Guadalupe at Tepeyac, organized devotion to Our Lady of Remedios in this image seems to have begun in the 1550s, later than either of the two recorded founding stories proposed.[54] Perhaps Archbishop Montúfar encouraged the devotion then, as he did devotion to the Virgin of Guadalupe. In any case, following the designation of the city council as official patron of the shrine in a royal cedula of April 30, 1574, the chapel on the site was rebuilt at the council's expense and in 1576 the Virgin of Remedios made her first of many ceremonial visits to the capital. In 1579, a confraternity led by council members was established to secure the shrine's financial future and support the devotion.

At least four other pre-1580s Marian image shrines are likely, if less certain than these two. By the early seventeenth century, Franciscan chronicler Juan de Torquemada could describe Puebla's La Conquistadora as "outstanding" (*resplandece*) for the miracles associated with it. But for evidence of devotion in the sixteenth century, we must rely on an 1804 publication of what is represented as a 1582 inquiry to establish that this statuette was the one given by Cortés to his trusted Tlaxcalan captain Don Gonzalo Alxotecatlcocomitzi of Atlihuetzian after the conquest of Tenochtitlan.[55] The 1804 publication seems to be the second edition of a text first published in 1666, but I have not located a copy of the 1666 edition or references to it before 1804.[56] If the 1804 publication is a faithful copy of a 1582 record of inquiry, it would be the earliest example by half a century or more of a formal *información jurídica* for a miraculous image. Denise Fallena, in her full study of La Conquistadora, suggests that it may well have been the creation of Franciscans in Tlaxcala during the 1630s who sought to legitimate and promote the devotion in the face of growing interest in the Valley of Mexico's Virgin of Remedios, with its similar reputation for assisting in the Conquest and being placed by Cortés in the Aztecs' Templo Mayor.[57] Most of this possible información jurídica amounts to depositions by three Tlaxcalan elders dated August 29 to September 1, 1582. All three claimed to have known Cortés and Don Gonzalo, and they swore that this was the image Cortés gave him in 1521. They said Don Gonzalo had kept it for three years, taking it with him to celebrations and dances until the Franciscans arrived in 1524, at which time he turned the statuette over to them. The witnesses had not seen the image in many years, but they understood that it was in the Franciscan convent in Puebla. They were asked only to testify to the provenance of the statuette assumed now to be in Puebla. They were silent about the devotion itself, but if the depositions are authentic and date from 1582, they signal an early stage of promotion of the image in the Franciscans' convent church in Puebla. The 1804 publication also includes copies of two documents from the 1630s that added to the promotional campaign in Puebla at that time: the first is a 1631 petition by the guardian of the Franciscan convent in Puebla requesting certification of this statuette as the one given to Don Gonzalo; the second, dated May 22, 1632, states that the city government of Puebla would sponsor the annual fiesta and novena (the nine-day round of prayers and Masses that renewed the bond between the faithful and a saint, Christ, or other devotion, especially in times of crisis) for La Conquistadora.[58]

In the turbulent frontier areas north of central Mexico, the traditional origins of Nuestra Señora de Guanajuato and Nuestra Señora de los Zacatecas fit into the story of conquest and evangelization attached to Our Lady of Remedios at Totoltepec and La Conquistadora in Puebla during the sixteenth century. For Nuestra Señora de Guanajuato, there is a twist that connected this statue directly to the Spanish Reconquista. As the *Zodíaco mariano* recounts, soon after the opening of the great silver mines in Guanajuato and Zacatecas in the mid-sixteenth century, Philip II sent to Guanajuato a statue of the Blessed Mary that had been hidden from the Moors before the Reconquista in a cave near the settlement of Santa Fe outside Granada. This statue was placed in the chapel of Guanajuato's hospital for Christian Indians. Both this origin story and the history of endemic warfare with Chichimecs during the sixteenth century fit the pattern of the Blessed Mary as warrior Virgin in support of the Spaniards' righteous Christian crusade. Unfortunately, explicit accounts of the image's history and popular devotion that have come to light date only from the eighteenth century.[59] Nuestra Señora de los Zacatecas, for whom the city of Zacatecas was named in 1585,[60] was connected to military conquest in the vicinity, celebrated well into the eighteenth century every September 8 (Mary's birthday) to mark the date Zacatecas warriors surrendered to unarmed Spaniards.[61] Whether there was an early following for this particular image and whether the first Spanish settlers brought it there is not clear, but eighteenth-century residents of Zacatecas certainly thought it dated from the conquest period. In the early eighteenth century the Conde de la Laguna had a chapel built on the site of the first "chapel of the conquistadores" where he placed "the sainted image that the conquistador, D. Diego Ibarra, brought."[62]

Other image shrines that may have begun in the mid-sixteenth century were not so clearly warrior Virgins, although they were associated with evangelization of native peoples, which the mendicants framed as "spiritual conquest." The most famous regional shrine in Yucatán, to Our Lady of Izamal, described in a printed devotional text by Fr. Bernardo de Lizana, OFM, in 1633, is a case in point. It was said to date from the pastoral work of Diego de Landa, OFM, in Izamal during the 1550s and 1560s. Lizana was forthright about his providential purpose in writing the book:

My history is only directed toward giving a clear and true account of the miracles and marvels that the King of Heaven, God, and Our Lord, all powerful and immense, has worked and does work every day through his most holy Mother by means of devotion to this image of her that this celebrated convent of Itzamal fortunately possesses.

The first miracle was the portentous arrival of the statue of Mary in the time of spiritual combat against the devil's grip on native piety and the many idols and pagan sites of worship in the hills near Izamal. Lizana's account of the early history of this image of the Virgin points directly to Izamal's status as an ancient sacred center and negotiations with the Franciscans reflecting its importance to Mayas in the area.[63] To Lizana, Mary was "the hand of God," and thanks to her "our enemies have been reduced to nothing ... she has cast out that infernal serpent and has raised ... the hearts of these natives to adore God's only begotten son and our lord."[64] Landa, he wrote, told the local people that if they wanted their settlement located next to the *cue* (temple) where they had worshiped a false god, they would have to provide him with money to purchase an image of the Virgin Mary for the new church there. As Landa was returning from Guatemala with two statues of Mary – one for the Franciscan convent in Mérida and the other for Izamal – a remarkable sign of divine presence and favor appeared: in a driving rainstorm the statues of Mary remained completely dry. Landa did not mention this story in his own writings, but the presence of the statue of Mary at Izamal by the 1560s seems certain. It would have been one of many introduced and revered by the first generation of Spaniards in Yucatán, and soon by Mayas as well.[65]

Another well-known colonial image shrine, to Nuestra Señora de Ocotlán above the city of Tlaxcala, also has uncertain, but possibly early beginnings. A Marian shrine at the site was mentioned by local chronicler Diego Muñoz Camargo in 1588 or 1589, but what kind of Christianized devotion may have preceded it and what providential stories of origin may have been told then are unclear. Rodrigo Martínez Baracs's study of this site and image treats the 1580s as the time when the celebrated image known as the Virgin of Ocotlán was placed in a chapel there and the devotion began to grow, but he also suggests that a "dualistic cult" may have developed as early as the 1530s or 1540s, with the encouragement of Franciscan evangelizers. The friars' goal, he suggests, was to replace worship of the Tlaxcalan divine pair, Xochiquetzal and Camaxtle, with a new divine pair, the Virgin Mary and Christ, but the result was more a combination than replacement. Martínez Baracs infers that a chapel and image of the Virgin Mary would have been placed there and probably suppressed by diocesan authorities in 1553 out of concern about unseemly veneration of images by Indian neophytes. If he is right about these early developments at Ocotlán, this Franciscan promotion of an image shrine happened half a century before Franciscans showed interest in promoting other image shrines, such as the Guadalupe shrine at Tepeyac and the Remedios shrine at Totoltepec.[66]

Several crosses also commanded special attention before 1580, perhaps encouraged by early mendicants, but, again, there is little to go on. Two

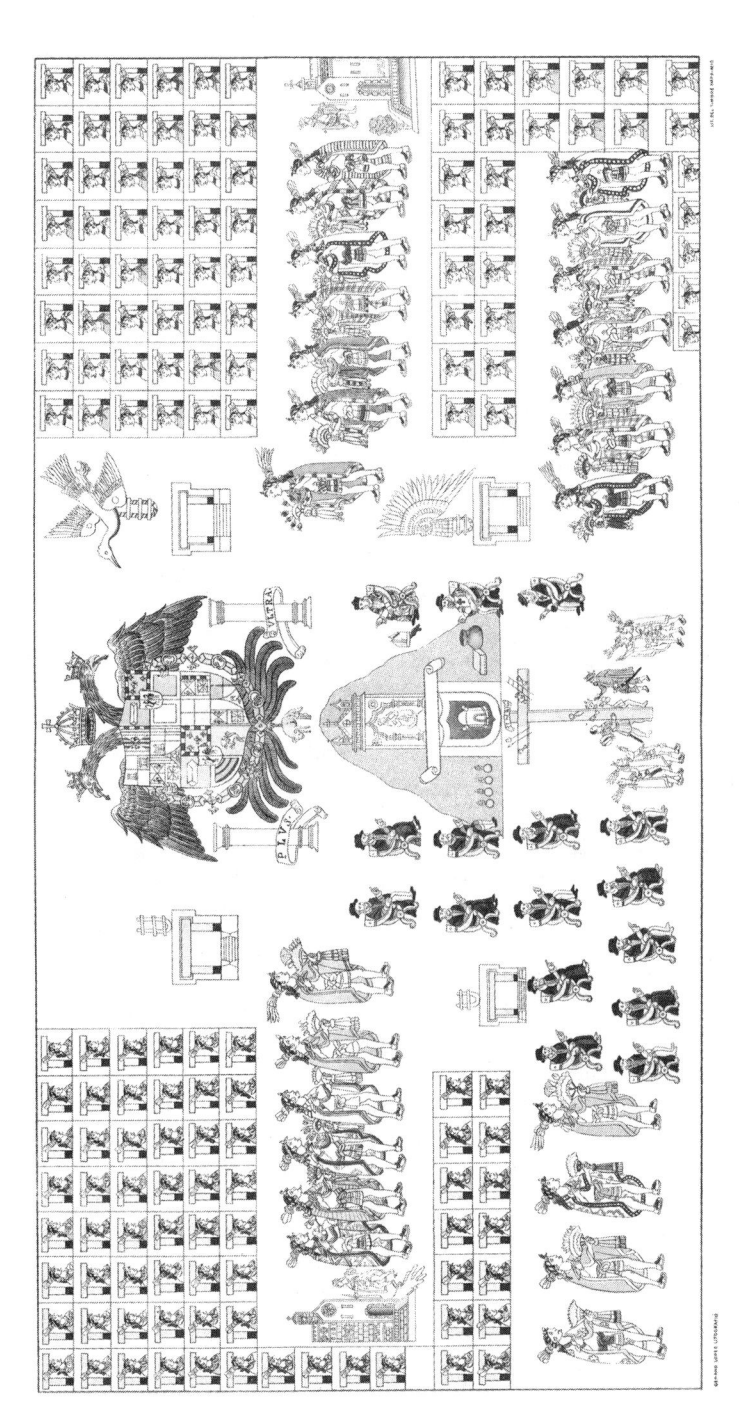

Figure 1.1 This famous image from the Lienzo de Tlaxcala treated the erection of the great cross as a foundational story for the Tlaxcalans' place in the colonial story. In the lower center Spanish authorities and native lords join in ceremonial union under the sign of the Hapsburg emperor and the Pillars of Hercules, above a hill surmounted by a chapel dedicated to the Virgin Mary. Below the hill a native lord and a Spanish leader, perhaps Cortés, erect the great wooden cross and remark on it while other lords watch. Published in Alfredo Chavero, *Antigüedades mexicanas: Homenaje a Cristóbal Colón*, Mexico: Junta Colombina de Mexico, 1892, II, plate 29. Courtesy of the Getty Research Center.

great wooden crosses erected in the 1520s in Mexico City and Tlaxcala under the direction of early Franciscan friars, and Cortés himself in the case of Tlaxcala, drew special attention from local Indian neophytes, echoing the importance of great trees in the cosmic landscape and the idea that natural features and objects contained or could attract divine presence. Copies of the Lienzo de Tlaxcala, originally painted in the 1550s at the behest of the native town council, appear to show Cortés and a native lord erecting this cross, which, according to Torquemada (ca. 1615), Tlaxcalans called *Tonacaquihuitl* or "wood that nourishes our life," but it did not endure as a shrine site.

Also in the 1520s a huge cross, "taller than any tower in Mexico," was erected in the patio of the first Indian chapel in Mexico City, San José de los Naturales.[67] It was made from an ancient tree harvested in the woods of Chapultepec, the royal retreat where Moctezuma kept his collection of animals. Torquemada again, citing native elders, reported that "the Mexicans regarded it as a deified thing; in the time of their heathendom, they cleaned and pruned it often and with the greatest care." This cross apparently was still considered precious when it fell over during a storm in 1571. Torquemada says that splinters from it were widely distributed as relics, but the cross itself was gone. A more durable cross, the *cruz de piedra* of Querétaro, became a revered cult image in the Franciscan church of the Colegio de la Santa Cruz during the seventeenth and eighteenth centuries. It may well date from the 1550s, but its origin and reverence for it before the 1630s are obscure.[68]

Most of the institutions of the Catholic Church and many of its devotional practices were in place in New Spain by 1580. Two synods of prelates had met to begin to standardize religious life and, whether imported or locally made, images of the saints and Christ seemed to be everywhere. Given the emergence of several image shrines and the widely held conviction that any sacred image might invite divine presence and protection, the way was open for a boom in cult images and shrines. But unlike some other aspects of colonial life – such as the institutional structure of viceroyalties, audiencias, district governorships, treasuries, municipal councils, dioceses, parishes, and the Inquisition, or laws meant to govern the operation of these institutions, property rights, labor systems, and the legal standing of Spaniards, "Indians," and other social groups – it was not yet clear what miraculous images and their shrines could be.

Image Shrines in a Long Seventeenth Century

Four centuries on, the 1600s in New Spain can seem like a time of motion but little movement, except perhaps in reverse. The historical highlights from that time have amounted to minor scandals, autos da fé, urban riots, bickerings over protocol, and quirky characters, but no decisive conquests and few unforgettable leaders making transformative decisions. By contrast, Europe was undergoing momentous developments. In philosophy, natural science, and commerce, there were early signs of what modernity and an urge to dominate nature would come to mean, but the overshadowing events of the time were filled with misery and terror. The Thirty Years War (1618–1648), rooted in confessional struggles and dynastic ambitions, was one of the most destructive, prolonged conflicts in European history, compounded by civil wars, early frosts, severe winters, droughts, floods, and short growing seasons.[69] Deprivation and destruction led to waves of migration and sudden death. The Thirty Years War was not fought on Spanish soil, but the Spanish crown emerged from the Peace of Westphalia in 1648 diminished on the international stage, weakened internally by regional revolts, piracy, and chronic financial crisis at home, to which it responded with more taxes, fortress-building and other costly military expenditures, and spasms of mostly short-lived repression. The accumulated effects have been described from contemporary Spanish sources, revenue data, and population figures as an embattled state and economic depression – a "general crisis" for Europe in general, and Spain and New Spain in particular. There were similarities, and Catholic Europe's exalted Baroque religiosity of the time was on display in New Spain, but America was not Europe. Even the similarities and direct connections played out in somewhat different ways, as they would also for the history of image shrines.

Adjustments to embattled, diminished circumstances were not hard to find in New Spain, but the notion of a prolonged economic depression applies better to Spain and its relationship to the American colonies.[70] Sectors of the colonial economy that counted most to Spaniards and the Spanish monarchy were in decline during the first half of the seventeenth century, especially the flow of precious metals and high value dyestuffs. And revenue from royal taxes such as the tribute continued to shrink until the Indian population began to recover in the late seventeenth century. Exports from Spain to America also declined, including mercury, textiles, shoes, pottery, hardware, religious art, jewelry, and wax and wine for liturgical uses. Some other sectors of the colonial economy also declined, but there was new production for domestic markets. Silver mining, with its multiplier effects, began to recover only after 1650,[71] but regional economies and local production were adjusting earlier to meet local needs, which discouraged imports; and overall the population grew modestly after the 1620s from natural increase of the creole and *casta* groups, Iberian immigration, and African slavery once mining and plantation agriculture began to recover. More Spaniards moved to America during the seventeenth century than during the sixteenth or eighteenth centuries, including groups of artisans from Castilian towns, such as weavers of Brihuega in the Province of Guadalajara who settled in the city of Puebla and *obraje* centers elsewhere that produced basic textiles for local uses.[72] Private landed estates – *haciendas* – were formed, less as a throwback to beleaguered, more or less self-contained medieval manors with a large residential population of landless laborers than as sites of comparatively small-scale production for regional markets and provincial cities in need of meat, hides, wool, grains, pulque, and draft animals, employing seasonal labor in addition to a small core of permanent residents. The seventeenth century also witnessed some territorial expansion into the far north with missions, mines, presidios, and small towns. There was new construction, especially in provincial capitals and Mexico City (which became a two-story central city by the end of the seventeenth century).[73] Convents were built in the major cities, some on a grand scale, and new churches both in the cities and smaller settlements almost everywhere. The weakened state and lethargy of the Spanish imperial bureaucracy, tax farming, and sale of minor political offices made it difficult to counter regional production that amounted to import substitution. In short, the seventeenth century was not a time of robust prosperity in New Spain, but by most measures it was not a general crisis, either, and fairly widespread economic and demographic growth was underway by the 1680s.[74]

While the weakened Spanish state and administrative inertia loosened the bonds with Spain and contributed to growing creole Spanish and local affiliations, Spain and Spaniards remained a shaping presence in America. In addition to the immigration from Spain, and from Portugal during the 1580s to 1640 when the Iberian crowns were joined, many of the leading public officials including viceroys, bishops, audiencia judges, district governors, inquisitors, cathedral chapter members, and even pastors in the most desirable parish benefices still were peninsular Spaniards, and the regular clergy included other Europeans and *peninsulares* as well as American-born Spaniards.

Formative Developments

From the 1580s to the 1720s most of the many long-lived colonial shrines were founded and the full range of practices associated with them developed. The direction of change became clear during what Nathan Mitchell calls "a crucial quarter century, from roughly 1585 to 1610," when European Catholicism, on the defensive in Counter-Reformation mode, shifted toward a more "proactive community of renewal ready to reinvent itself."[75] Not exactly a reinvention, but part of the turn in religious practice, was mounting interest in sacred images, shrines, and enchantment in everyday life whether in the use of images in prayer and worship (promoted especially by Jesuits, Franciscans, bishops, and the new Oratorian communities of diocesan priests) or in the abundance of emotion-laden church art produced in America that "created figures and images that are real, tangible, human and 'naturalistic.'"[76]

For New Spain, the direct effects of the Council of Trent and the decisive movement for renewal in the Catholic Church were not much felt until after the publication of the decrees of the Third Synod of prelates meeting in Mexico City in 1585; and these decrees of the Council of Trent and the Mexican synod shed little light on policies about sacred images. Trent's mixed messages of encouragement and restriction, representation and presence in the short decree on sacred images issued in the twenty-fifth session (1563) echoed through the subsequent history of cult images and shrines in New Spain, but amounted to less than a revolution in faith and practice.[77] True to form, the prelates at Trent stressed the role of bishops "and others who hold the office of teaching" to instruct and correct the faithful in "the legitimate use of images."[78] Figures of Christ, the Virgin Mary, and other saints were to be kept especially in the churches and "shall not be painted and adorned with a seductive charm." "Honor and veneration" was due to sacred images, but without attributing "any divinity or virtue" to them: "The honor which is shown them refers to the prototypes they represent, so that by means of the images, ... we adore Christ and venerate the saints whose likeness they bear." But there was a rub. Trent also presented images as something more than didactic symbols. Images invited love of God that might, in turn, invite the divine presence and lead to miracles; but the council stipulated that "no new miracles be accepted and no relics recognized unless they have been investigated and approved by the same bishop." The stage was set for a mixture of promotion, suspicion, and regulation by colonial authorities on one hand, and local devotion that spilled beyond official control on the other. Especially, church officials and the crown attempted to identify and eliminate independent operators.

What the Introduction describes as Baroque Catholicism turned on the idea of *mirabilia* – wonder, astonishment, the feeling of being in the presence of God, where spiritual union was sought by the privileged, the bold or, less conspicuously, anonymous believers through prayers and works; where souls in purgatory communicated with the living; where miracles might happen in daily life. In this kind of charged spirituality, the atmospherics of faith, including imagery, were employed to excite and amaze, to induce joy but also anxiety and fear, since the yearning for communion could be diverted into superstition and heresy by the devil's wiles and the permanent stain of original sin. Human flesh was corrupt, while divine flesh was exalted in painted and sculpted images that might suddenly come to life. In both Spain and New Spain, this long seventeenth

56   Part I Bearings: Historical Patterns and Places of Image Shrines

century was a time not only of visionaries and image shrines, but also of willful mortification of the flesh, witch hunts, exorcisms, a prolonged spike in Inquisition trials for feigned sanctity,[79] and some formal inquiries that were meant both to promote and to filter news of divine intervention and exalted piety.

Along with its main targets – heretics, blasphemers, Jews, false mystics, witches, incontinent priests, and banned books – the Mexican Inquisition (f. 1571) occasionally netted evidence of the growing fascination with images as touchstones of divine presence across social groups and regions. An early record of this kind concerns markings on a pine tree root that were immediately recognized and embraced as a figure of the Virgin Mary by the casta men who found it in rural Oaxaca in 1611.[80] Their discovery came to the attention of the Inquisition's agent (*comisario*) in Antequera (Oaxaca), Lic. Cristóbal Barroso de Palacios, choirmaster of the cathedral church

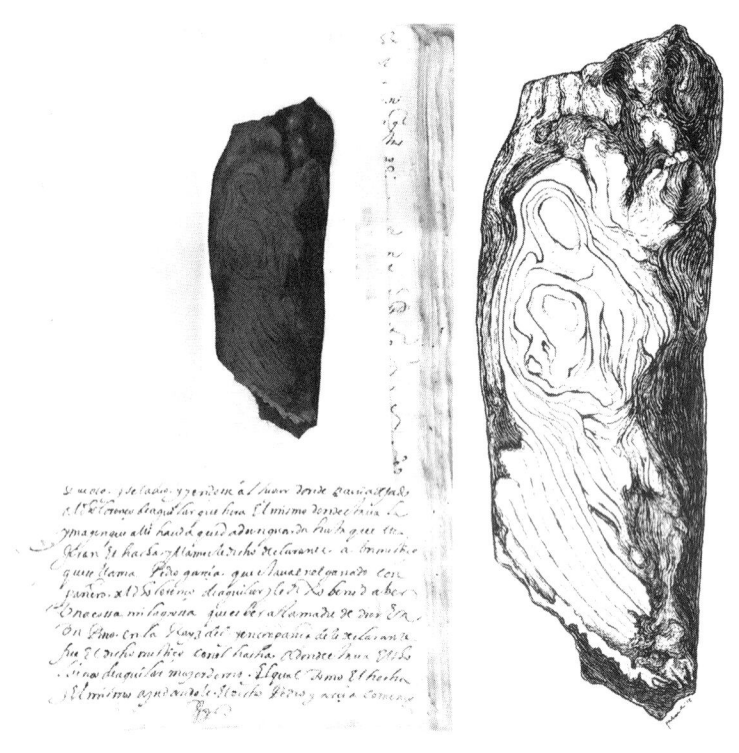

Figure 1.2 Juan de Rúa's painting of the tree root figure discovered by Lorenço de Aguilar and his companions in 1611, commissioned by the *comisario* of the Inquisition in Antequera to guard against pious mutilation of the object. From AGN Inquisición 455 exp. 23. Courtesy of the Archivo General de la Nación, Mexico. Ink rendering by Palma Edith Christian.

there, on September 7 when Vizente Gonsales, a local shoemaker, appeared before him "to unburden his conscience." Gonsales reported that Lorenço de Aguilar, a free mulato from Tehuantepec, had approached him about gilding an object he had found on the exposed root of a pine tree. Comisario Barroso directed Gonsales to bring Aguilar and the object to him, which he did later that day. Barroso took possession of the item and described it as a piece of pitch pine about five and a half inches long, three inches wide, and the thickness of a small finger, on which the grain of the wood "formed a figure, like an image." Two days later he deposed Aguilar and his *compadre*, Joan Pacheco. Then on December 7 three more men, including Aguilar's son, Miguel, were deposed. Shortly thereafter the comisario shipped the object to the offices of the Inquisition in Mexico City, along with his written record of the depositions and a painting of the piece of wood by Juan de Rúa, a master painter (*maestro de pinzel*) then living in Antequera,[81] in order to guard against damage en route through "pious removal as relics of pieces of the wood on which the image is sculpted, leaving it defective and affecting the image."[82]

While the testimony of the five witnesses varied in a few details, they agreed about the circumstances of the discovery and what they had found. All of them, along with two Zapotec Indians from Tehuantepec who were not summoned to testify,[83] had been moving a herd of cattle belonging to the alcalde mayor of Tehuantepec to market in the city of Puebla. Lorenço de Aguilar, about forty years old, was the *mayordomo* in charge of the herd. His younger companions included his son, compadres Joan Pacheco (like Aguilar and his son, identified as a *mulato libre*) and Pedro García (identified as a thirty-one-year-old mestizo from Jalapa), Mateo García (age twenty-three), and the two Zapotecs, named Pedro Hernandes and Mateo Hernandes. On August 13, two days before the feast of the Assumption of Mary, the men stopped for a midday siesta near the little settlement of San Francisco Nictepeque in the district of Quiechapa, midway between Nejapa and the Valley of Oaxaca. Joan Pacheco and Miguel de Aguilar found shade under the tallest pine tree on the brow of a prominent hill. Sitting on an exposed root of the tree, Pacheco noticed a distinctive pattern traced by the wood's grain. It looked to him like an image of the Virgin Mary. He called Miguel to come see. Both testified that they were excited by the discovery, but neither one thought to mention it to the others at the time. Instead, they went about their work for the rest of the afternoon. That evening Pacheco described the image to his compadre and mayordomo, Lorenço de Aguilar. In his testimony, Aguilar said his heart began to race when he heard the news, and he took his son and Pacheco to task for not telling him earlier in the day. He spent a sleepless night, wondering whether it was real or not, whether it was an act of God or made by human hands. At first light he and the others set out to find the hill and tree. When they reached the tree he could see the figure of the Mother of God on an exposed section of root about three feet long. Both ends of the root were charred, but the image, in the middle section, was undamaged. Aguilar testified that he knelt down before it, as did the others who were with him. Then he ordered Pedro García and Joan Pacheco to go into the Indian settlement and find an axe so they could cut out the section with the image. They returned with an Indian carpenter who helped García reverently cut out the section of the root and trimmed it.

All signs in the record of testimony suggest that the herders were sincere devotees of the Virgin Mary and judged the figure they found on the pine root to be an image of her, a precious sign from God. Pedro García and Miguel de Aguilar kissed the object reverently when the comisario asked them to identify it under oath; and, according to the scribe, Lorenço de Aguilar was distraught when the object was confiscated, "for he is deeply devoted to the said image." The comisario kept his opinions to himself, but his actions suggest some ambivalence about the discoverers, if not the discovery. That he placed the object in a box for safekeeping, allowed the witnesses to kiss it after they testified, and took steps to protect it from pious mutilation en route to Mexico City do not seem to be the acts of a skeptic. But in moving quickly to take charge of the object and sending it to the Inquisition after deposing the witnesses, he seemed to be wary of the intentions of Aguilar and his companions. Did he wonder whether these men were worthy seers and whether they were presumptuous in declaring the image to be, as Lorenço de Aguilar put it, "a miracle thanks to the mercy of God"?[84] Did their social standing impeach the authenticity of the object itself? Why had he learned about the object from a local artisan who was approached by Lorenço de Aguilar to gild it, rather than from Aguilar himself or one of his companions? Joan Pacheco's wordy, obsequious testimony did not help the herders' credibility. If his first thought was, as he claimed, to hurry to the *comisario* with news of his discovery, why hadn't he done so? And why did he gloss over the fact that he did not tell the mayordomo about it until that evening? Comisario Barroso must have wondered whether he would even have heard about this object if the local artisan had not come forward. Might Aguilar and his men have been planning to use the image to promote themselves as seers and sorcerers or establish a shrine independent of Church authority? Whatever their intentions and whatever the comisario surmised, this Lady of the pine tree was soon lost to her devotees and to history. We know only that the packet sent by the comisario must have reached its destination in Mexico City. His written report with Rúa's painting was filed in the Inquisition's archive, but there is no sign of administrative or judicial action on the standing of this artifact as a divine image even with all its portentous signs – discovered by pious herders shortly before the feast of Mary's assumption to heaven, located in a high place in the tallest tree, and unmarked by the fire that damaged the rest of the exposed root. The object itself disappears from the written record at this point.

In late-sixteenth-century Europe, with the encouragement of the clergy and backing of confraternities of laymen under their direction, miraculous images, especially figures of the Virgin Mary and Christ that were said to show signs of life, became increasingly popular.[85] The number of new image shrines began to increase about 1580, peaking in Spain and Italy in the seventeenth and early eighteenth centuries.[86] Image shrines in Europe at this time usually were encouraged more than grudgingly permitted by the bishops, even though the bishops were likely to express reservations about excesses of exuberance and superstition that could lead to idolatry. This was a time when church authorities sought, as Jonathan Seitz puts it, "to limit access to the supernatural to specifically authorized groups working in specifically authorized contexts."[87] Hermits and reputed visionaries, prophets, mystics, witches, shamans, and other spiritual free agents were brought before the Inquisition and episcopal courts in record numbers and dealt with more severely than they would be in the eighteenth century.[88] Apparition stories gave way to miraculous images.[89] As objects sited in a cathedral, parish church, convent, or shrine licensed by the bishop, miraculous images were more manageable than the visionary who claimed to have been instructed by Christ or the Virgin Mary in ways that might challenge orthodoxy and ecclesiastical authority. As William Christian notes for the moving crucifixes celebrated in Italy during the sixteenth century and increasingly popular in Spain and New Spain in the seventeenth century, these miracles of animation reinforced church authority more than threatened it, "for their context was totally within the acceptable language of the well-rehearsed forms of Christ's Passion."[90]

As miraculous image shrines grew in fame and number in Catholic Europe, the material culture of devotion associated with them became part of devotional life in America, if sometimes inflected differently. Formal investigations of miracle stories for shrine images occasionally were recorded in writing, and ex-voto paintings that graphically attested to individual miracles mounted up in various shrines, along with more anonymous votive offerings and brandea (anything associated with a sacred body and thought to enjoy its prophylactic and healing favor[91]), such as *milagritos* (wax and silver body parts left there to memorialize a favor granted or prayed for), *medidas* (ribbons cut to the exact size of the sacred image and usually touched to it, that were treated as numinous mementoes), and other things acquired at a shrine. Devotional histories of at least eight Spanish shrines with miracle stories, six of them image shrines, were published in the sixteenth century, and others followed during the seventeenth century.[92] The first pass at a compendium of important regional shrines in Spain appeared in the early 1570s, followed by a more ambitious collection of miracle stories by a Spanish Jesuit, Alonso de Andrade in 1623–1624, a treasury of leading Marian shrines of Catalonia by Narcís Camós, OP, in 1651–1653, and German Jesuit Wilhelm Gumppenberg's *Atlas Marianus*, a monumental project to survey Marian shrines worldwide, proposed in 1649 and begun in 1652, with the first two "books" published in 1657 and the whole work completed in 1672.[93] Novena booklets, another kind of devotional text, became popular at about the same time, and a few years later were introduced in America.

The foremost changes in the history of sacred images and shrines in New Spain during this long seventeenth century were the large number and variety of new shrines to celebrated images of the Virgin Mary and Christ and the growth of a group of them into significant regional devotions. Images of Mary still attracted much of the attention, but, increasingly, crucifixes and other depictions of Christ's Passion became shrine images. Of the Marian and Christocentric shrines that can be dated with some confidence, two-thirds began between 1580 and 1700.[94] They were less concentrated in and near colonial cities than they had been in the sixteenth century, although Mexico City and provincial cities and towns including Puebla, Antequera, San Cristóbal de las Casas, Veracruz, Querétaro, Pátzcuaro, Campeche, Mérida, Valladolid (Yucatán), and Toluca boasted new shrines as well.[95] Mexico City in particular deepened its claim as capital of the sacred, not only through ongoing association with the Virgin of Guadalupe and the Virgin of Remedios, but with the addition of several dozen other reputedly miraculous images located in or near the center city.[96] A Spanish Capuchin friar, Francisco de Ajofrín, visiting Mexico City in the mid-eighteenth century, found a veritable city of shrines there: "In this city there are famous shrines, mostly devoted to miraculous images of Christ and his most chaste Mother, and not a few devoted to particular saints. Because there is a multitude of them, to write the history of all of them would be a difficult assignment."[97]

But most new image shrines emerged in rural areas near smaller settlements, whether Indian parish towns and villages or colonial ranching, farming, and mining settlements throughout the territory of modern Mexico. Augustinian chronicler Juan de Grijalva (1624) observed that colonial Indians in central Mexico had become deeply attached to their favorite Christian images: "An Indian who is unwilling to spend even two reales on clothing and food gladly spends a thousand on an image. This being so, their living quarters may amount to a single room that serves as kitchen, dormitory, and living space, but they add on another, larger room for an oratory."[98] Central Mexico – the modern states of Mexico, Hidalgo, Morelos, and Tlaxcala – was well represented with new shrines, but now western Mexico and the south were prominent, too, with ten shrines recorded in the territory of modern Michoacán and eight in Jalisco. In the south new shrines are mentioned in rural areas of Oaxaca (6), Chiapas (4), Veracruz (2), and Yucatán (9).

A dozen or so shrines stood out from the rest in the seventeenth century for their regional followings. The Virgin of Guadalupe was especially favored in and near the Valley of Mexico, still the most densely populated area of the viceroyalty, and pockets of devotion and secondary shrines to Guadalupe developed in north-central Mexico when painted copies of the image were placed in the provincial cities of San Luis Potosí and Querétaro. Our Lady of Remedios was famous in Mexico City and developed a following in rural districts near the shrine site, but did not become one of the greatest regional shrines then or later. Other seventeenth-century shrines that gained a following beyond their immediate area include Our Lady of San Juan de los Lagos on the fringe of the Bajío in eastern Jalisco, Our Lady of Zapopan outside the city of Guadalajara, Our Lady of Ocotlán near the city of Tlaxcala, Our Lady of Soledad in and near Antequera, Our Lady of El Pueblito and the Cruz de Piedra in the vicinity of the city of Querétaro, the Lord of Chalma in the district of Malinalco (Estado de México), San Miguel del Milagro in rural Tlaxcala, Nuestra Señora de la Soledad in the city of Antequera, Our Lady of Izamal in rural Yucatán, and perhaps La Conquistadora in Puebla. Most of these budding regional shrines were associated with a provincial city and were promoted first by local Spaniards before reaching into settlements of Indians and castas. La Conquistadora apparently has a different story, starting as a devotion among Tlaxcalan elites who allied with Cortés in the conquest of the Mexicas and Tenochtitlan, then becoming a patroness of the city of Puebla in the care of resident Franciscans by the early seventeenth century. Izamal was different again, originating as a local Maya shrine before reaching a growing constituency in and beyond the provincial capital of Mérida later in the seventeenth century. When Bernardo de Lizana's evangelistic text about miracles worked by the Virgin of Izamal was published in 1633,[99] the devotion was concentrated among Mayas living nearby and rested on a triumphalist story of conversion to Christianity and epic struggle with the devil for the souls of local Mayas. Fifteen years after Lizana's text appeared, a calamity turned devotion to Our Lady of Izamal in a new direction. An epidemic struck Mérida, and officials there called for the statue to be brought to rescue the city. After the epidemic passed, it was returned to Izamal, but what had been a local Maya devotion gained a lasting regional fame among Spaniards and castas, too.[100]

Along with Jesuits and bishops, the Franciscans and Augustinians became leading supporters and promoters of miraculous images and image shrines. In a turn from their reluctance to support the shrine of Our Lady of Guadalupe in the mid-sixteenth century, Franciscans administered or were closely associated with at least sixteen prominent seventeenth-century image shrines in central Mexico: La Conquistadora of Puebla, Our Lady of Tulantongo near Texcoco, Our Lady of Tecaxic outside Toluca, the Cruz de Piedra in Querétaro, Our Lady of El Pueblito outside Querétaro, Our Lady of Ocotlán outside the city of Tlaxcala, Our Lady of los Ángeles at Tlatelolco, Our Lady of La Redonda in Mexico City, the Christ of the Labradores in Toluca, the Christ of Tacuba outside Mexico City, Our Lady of La Macana at Tlalnepantla and Mexico City, and altars and chapels to Spanish miraculous Marian images of Cueva Santa, Aranzazú, Pilar de Zaragoza, Balvanera, and Desamparados in Mexico City.[101] Augustinians were especially associated with the shrines to miraculous images of the crucified Christ at Chalma and El Cardonal, and the Christ of Totolapa, which they moved to Mexico City.[102]

As image shrines grew in number and became well established during the seventeenth century, the institutions, devotional aids, and written record of activities and reputation mounted up. Confraternities (*cofradías, congregaciones,* and *hermandades*) licensed by the Church hierarchy were a key feature, established to sponsor and oversee liturgical events and special devotions at the shrines, as well as provide special benefits for members. They lent cash and draft animals to community members in times of need; confraternities that owned livestock typically grazed them on community lands; and the prestige of service as a confraternity officer reinforced and sometimes reordered local society. Some confraternities, especially in cities, amounted to elite clubs, but many were founded in Indian communities and among non-Indians, with more open membership.[103] The seventeenth century was the great growth period for confraternities in general, with few of the restrictions and pressures to reduce them that would come in the late eighteenth century. A sense of how numerous confraternities of all kinds were in Mexico City by the 1660s comes from a list of those participating in the funeral procession there for King Philip V in 1666. Members of sixteen cofradías for *pardos, negros,* mulatos, and Filipinos participated, along with representatives of eighty-seven Indian cofradías and twenty-two of the leading cofradías for Spaniards, plus members of the Archicofradía del Santísimo Sacramento y Caridad.[104]

The rich material culture of image shrines comes into full view during this period – public processions bearing the revered image; the annual gatherings and *romerías* (short pilgrimages); the novena observances; the array of votive offerings, including milagritos, medidas, lavish consumption of candlewax, some painted ex-votos depicting a miraculous event commissioned by a grateful recipient of divine favor; the published sermons, novena booklets, prayers, and several devotional histories of particular shrines; the first pass at an anthology of Marian shrines, by Francisco de Florencia, SJ, in the late seventeenth century (completed by

Juan Antonio de Oviedo for publication in 1755); records of pastoral visit inspections of shrines; and *informaciones jurídicas*.

There were many advocations and local representations of the Virgin Mary. The warrior Virgin, represented in several of the best-known early cult images of the Blessed Mary, was not forgotten thanks to seventeenth-century publications and new battles, especially in northern New Spain. There was the statue of Nuestra Señora del Zape in a Jesuit mission church mutilated in the Tepehuan rebellion of 1616, then replaced with an image that was said to work many wonders for local devotees; Mary as la Conquistadora in New Mexico after the Pueblo Revolt in the 1680s; and Nuestra Señora de la Macana, a statue reputedly grazed by a native war club (*macana*) during the Pueblo Revolt and renamed to commemorate the event and the statue's surprising survival. But most shrine images of Mary were representations of the Immaculate Conception, the Mater Dolorosa, the Assumption, and the Rosary that acquired local names and fame. They appealed especially to the Blessed Mary's love, compassion, grief, and motherhood, and her role as mediatrix.[105]

All these developments were in line with practices in Spain, where image shrines matured earlier and cult figures of Christ and Mary as Mater Dolorosa were growing in number and popularity from the 1590s. But there were differences that go beyond timing. In particular, bone relics in New Spain did not have the hold that they did in Spain and other parts of Catholic Europe; many origin stories for image shrines in New Spain were different from the "pastoral cycle" stories of Spanish Marian cult images that had been hidden and providentially rediscovered during the Reconquista (see Chapter 5); and *libros de milagros* – registers of many miracles kept in some Spanish and other Europe shrines – were rarely kept in New Spain.[106]

Temporal Patterns

Some of these developments can be roughly tracked together, chronologically, across the early (1580s–1620s), middle (1630s–1670s), and late (1680s–1720s) years of this extended seventeenth century. From the 1580s to 1620s more miraculous images with different origin stories and attributes are documented, along with growing episcopal and mendicant interest in promoting them, but cult images and shrines to shelter them had not yet become a central feature of religious practice in New Spain. Although the third synod of prelates in 1585 was silent about miraculous images and shrines, there were other signs of growing interest and support for image shrines. The Tacuba Franciscans' bid for assignment to the nearby shrine of the Virgin of Remedios in 1589, soon followed by their association with various image shrines was a striking change from the order's reluctance to promote the earliest shrine images.[107] From the

1590s, chroniclers of the orders began to include in their accounts celebrated images, their signs of life, and other miracles. For example, in 1596 Agustín Dávila Padilla, OP, recounted how a statue of Santa Catalina de Sena spoke on many occasions to an exemplary friar, Jordán de Santa Catalina, who was in the habit of weeping while he knelt in prayer before the image in the Dominicans' great convent in Antequera (Oaxaca).[108]

For Our Lady of Guadalupe, it is clear from the minutes of cathedral chapter meetings in Mexico City from 1600 to 1612 that archdiocesan authorities oversaw the development of the shrine at Tepeyac. They planned and supervised construction of a new shrine church on the site from August 1600, with the viceroy placing the cornerstone on February 16, 1601, in public ceremonies on which the cathedral spent 800 silver pesos.[109] The canons ordered an inspection of the shrine in 1607, elected one of their own, Alonso López Cárdenas, as general administrator, and in October 1612 staged a grand reception there in honor of the newly arrived viceroy, the Marqués de Guadalcázar.[110] The cathedral clergy also commissioned a golden statue of the Virgin Mary that became a local attraction, if not a cult image. It was presented to the public in a procession on the feast of the Assumption in 1610 and again in 1612 at the request of the viceroy.[111] But the minutes of the cathedral chapter from the 1580s to the 1620s also indicate that the cult of saints still overshadowed the mystique of particular images. San Hipólito Mártir, San Marcos, San Sebastián, San Nicolás Tolentino, San Pedro, San Juan de Dios, San Gregorio Taumaturgo, Santa Teresa, and prospective American saints Gregorio López and Felipe de Jesús all commanded the cathedral clergy's attention in their chapter meetings, but of the budding shrine images, only Our Lady of Guadalupe and Our Lady of Remedios did.

At about the same time, the earliest shrines in the Valley of Mexico, Puebla, and Tlaxcala were showing signs of institutional growth and promotion beyond their local Spanish base. Paintings displayed in the Remedios shrine outside Mexico City from the 1580s or 1590s introduced an Indian seer and scenes of divine favor to appeal to Indian and casta devotees. Similar works meant to recognize and attract Indian interest in the Virgin of Guadalupe at Tepeyac may also date from this time, although the record is less clear.[112] The prestige of at least two of the earliest shrines was enhanced by their association with exemplary hermits, Gregorio López at the Remedios shrine and Sebastián de Aparicio for La Conquistadora in Puebla.[113]

Publication of Mercedarian Luis de Cisneros's devotional history of the image-shrine of Our Lady of Remedios in 1621, and the great floods in Mexico City from 1629 to 1634, in which the image of Nuestra Señora de Guadalupe made its only excursion beyond Tepeyac, opened a phase of more active development, when many new shrines were established in nearly every part of the viceroyalty and some crossed ethnic lines to achieve regional fame.[114] In 1635, a royal chronicler of the Indies, Tomás Tamayo de Vargas, for the first time asked American informants about image shrines: "What images are venerated with the most signal devotion and what miracles have been verified?"[115] Perhaps in response to this query, a "historical" report for Yucatán in 1639 by Francisco de Cárdenas Valencia, OFM, mentioned eight image shrines that had achieved a following by that time, and included a famous miracle or type of miracle for most of them – the Cristo de San Román of Campeche, which was famous for amazing healings; Nuestra Señora de Izamal with its display of ex-votos that testified to many miracles for devotees; an image of the Spanish Virgin of Guadalupe in her chapel in Mérida that was processed in times of hunger, epidemic, and drought; Nuestra Señora de la Soledad, with its confraternity of Spaniards in the Franciscan church in Mérida; a miraculous statue of Mary Immaculate from Spain in the parish church of Valladolid; Nuestra Señora de Calatayud, a statue of Mary Immaculate that had favored devotees with "thousands of favors"; and Tabi's miraculous statue of Mary Immaculate.[116]

It was in the middle phase of the seventeenth century that many colonial image shrines began to leave a paper trail. By the 1680s, the shrines were a widespread feature of New Spain's sacred landscape. Published histories were becoming more common, including those for the Virgin of Izamal, the Virgin of Cosamaloapan, Our Lady of Remedios, Our Lady of Guadalupe, Our Lady of San Juan de los Lagos, Our Lady of Zapopan, San Miguel del Milagro, and the Cristo Renovado de Santa Teresa. The mounting written record testifies both to the presence of miraculous images and shrines and to campaigns to promote and regulate them. In some cases, such as the brief report in 1647 that an infant Jesus in a family oratory in Acayucan, Veracruz had perspired,[117] records were mainly about information gathering and surveillance, but image shrines also appeared more often in chronicles of the mendicants, and not just Franciscan ones. For example, Francisco de Burgoa, chronicler of the Dominican province of San Hipólito Mártir centered on Oaxaca, singled out a miraculous crucifix in the chapel of the village of Hueyapan, near the city of Antequera, that had perspired profusely and had begun to work miracles for visitors.[118] Several other images and shrines were documented more formally in informaciones jurídicas. Nominally, these proceedings were authentications and could be used to suppress frauds and bogus rumors, but in the mid-seventeenth century they were more likely to be cursory administrative inquiries intended to confirm diocesan authority and promote the devotion. In the case of the Virgin of Guadalupe, they were part of a campaign to gain papal recognition for the image's miraculous origin and apparitions associated with it. Depending on how investigations and briefs for miracles, miraculous images, and shrines are counted, between sixteen and twenty-two informaciones jurídicas were undertaken during the colonial period, fifteen of them for ten shrines, concentrated in the years 1639 to 1670 and all but five of the twenty-two taking place during the long seventeenth century. The concentration of new confraternities in the seventeenth century that sponsored Masses, feast days, and other ritual activities at the shrines is another sign of new activity and growth.[119]

Diocesan pastoral visit records – the daybooks of canonically-mandated inspection tours of parishes made by bishops or their delegates – also brought to light new shrines and numinous images at this time. Unfortunately, few of these pastoral visit records survive for the seventeenth century, but two from the 1640s – Juan de Palafox's *visita* through his Diocese of Puebla in stages from 1643 to 1646, and Juan de Mañozca's visita for the Archdiocese of Mexico in 1646 – provide a glimpse into promotion and oversight by diocesan authorities. Palafox visited the chapel of San Miguel del Milagro, where the archangel Michael was believed to have recently appeared to an Indian visionary and taken him to a spring of miraculous healing waters, and issued an order that the site be developed as a *santuario* (shrine). He also gave a boost to the already important shrine of Nuestra Señora de Ocotlán, near the city of Tlaxcala, by visiting the church and praying the Rosary there; and he visited the shrine to an image of the Virgin Mary in the remote town of Cosamaloapan, Veracruz in 1643 and apparently encouraged publication that year of a devotional history about the image.[120] In his visita, Archbishop Mañozca supported the growing popularity of miraculous images, but his concerns seem to have been more administrative, licensing alms collectors and correcting superstitions. At Zinacantepec, Mañozca found the people of Amanalco in a state of agitation, convinced that their small statue of the Virgin Mary sometimes wandered away. He noted that he calmed them down and had the image put back in the village church.[121] At the same time, this archbishop gained notoriety in Mexico City for having transferred to the cathedral grounds one of the old stone crosses depicting the instruments of Christ's Passion he had seen during his visit to Tepeapulco, Hidalgo.

It is usually uncertain just when and how a select group of image shrines began to develop a wider following and whether this development was largely a product of promotion by ecclesiastical authorities, economic circumstances, a local event that struck a chord of latent devotion, or some combination. The growth of the shrine of Nuestra Señora de San Juan de los Lagos into a major regional shrine is best documented for the late eighteenth century because it was closely connected to the fortunes of the annual fair that burgeoned there as the silver mines of Zacatecas and Guanajuato revived and trade north into Durango, Chihuahua, and New Mexico followed, but feelers far to the south as early as the 1640s for what was then a new image shrine to the Virgin of San Juan de los Lagos are documented in the pastoral visit report of Archbishop Mañozca to the parish of Tlayacapan, Morelos in 1646. There the archbishop found alms collectors from the Lagos shrine collecting for construction of a new church. He had previously given them permission to collect in his territory even though Lagos was in the Diocese of Guadalajara, but now he took exception to the collectors' practice of persuading local Indians that the stubs of candles burned in the presence of the little statue of the Lagos Virgin they brought with them could cure illnesses and work other wonders. Worried about the superstitious fervor encouraged by the alms collectors, he revoked their license to collect in his jurisdiction and ordered them to take their image back to Lagos.[122] For the most part, however, alms-collecting missions were not closely monitored at this time, as they would be at the end of the colonial period. They were one of the ways some shrine images, such as the Virgin of Guadalupe and the Lord of Chalma, as well as the Virgin of San Juan de los Lagos, extended their reputation and influence beyond a local following.

By comparison, the program of promotion for the Virgin of Guadalupe at this time is notable, as is the direct role of the cathedral clergy in managing shrine affairs at Tepeyac. By 1637 the cathedral's interests in the shrine were expressed as much in financial as in spiritual terms. Cathedral officials were overseeing the financial records, recording and encouraging endowment of Masses and other *obras pías*, authorizing alms-collecting excursions, and serving as the administrators of the shrine's properties and rents. In the name of quality control, the cathedral's *juez administrador* of the shrine's properties moved to restrict the lucrative production and sale of medidas by private vendors. The cathedral also built in more accountability through independent oversight of the shrine administration. The vicar general, who served as the shrine's general administrator, underwent an audit of accounts in 1637, and again in 1638 and 1640 the financial records were inspected for irregularities. Then in 1641 the cathedral chapter called for a review of administrative practices at the shrine to determine whether reforms were needed; and in 1650 a full-fledged inspection of shrine operations was made by an appointed *juez visitador y protector de la hermita*, Dr. Pedro de Barriento, cantor of the cathedral, who was named chaplain of the shrine at the same time.[123]

For shrines with a growing but more localized audience the interplay of local interest and official oversight must have had many permutations. In one scenario, local people resisted an attempt by episcopal authorities to take control of an image that had shown signs of life, and accepted a more limited official presence of priests. According to Francisco de Burgoa, the Dominican chronicler of Oaxaca in the third quarter of the seventeenth century, when news spread that the crucifix in the chapel of Hueyapan had perspired and was working other wonders, the bishop called for the image to be removed to a suitable location in the cathedral city. "Indians" of Hueyapan banded together in public protest and set about building "a very pretty chapel" in their community. Apparently writing as events were unfolding, Burgoa described how priests and laity from the city had begun to visit the chapel for novenas and special prayer meetings and noted that the healing miracles were continuing and improvements to the shrine were being made.[124]

Nearly all of these mid-seventeenth-century developments bear the marks of official supervision and tacit approval, if not promotion, but it is usually difficult to tell whether ecclesiastical authorities were leading or following the establishment and growth of devotion to particular images. In the case of Nuestra Señora de Tulantongo, on the fringe of the Valley of Mexico near Texcoco, an independent-minded local seer, Antonio de Gandía, was the prime mover and thorn in the side of local Franciscans. In 1656, they complained to the viceroy that Gandía, whom they described as a mestizo beggar out for personal gain, claimed to have received a special favor from the Virgin Mary fourteen years before. While praying before a crude, worm-eaten painting of the Madonna and Child on wooden boards that belonged to a local Indian, he heard a woman's voice say that she would restore his sight after he built her a chapel by the well in his yard. As news of the apparition spread, many Indians from nearby Texcoco went to visit Gandía and the painting and contribute to the promised chapel. Now, said the Franciscans, the little shrine was thriving, and Gandía, his sight restored, refused to allow them to supervise his activities and participate in shrine affairs beyond celebrating Mass there. They added that during a recent pastoral visit the archbishop's delegate had ordered Gandía to submit a financial report to the Franciscan guardian at Texcoco every six months and turn over to him the collections not spent on routine expenses. But Gandía had not complied, and now bogus copycat miracles were cropping up in the district. The Franciscans wanted to assign one of their own to reside at the shrine and supervise its spiritual and financial affairs. The viceroy's office warned Gandía to follow orders and avoid excesses, but it did not specify the orders or excesses. In the long run, however, the Franciscan ministers would have their way, as Gandía drifted out of the judicial record and into legend. A fine new church was dedicated in 1676, and during his pastoral visit in 1683 Archbishop Aguiar y Seixas ordered that a Franciscan pastor-administrator fluent in Nahuatl be placed there "in order to inflame this devotion." When Franciscan chronicler Agustín de Vetancurt published his *Teatro mexicano* in 1697, a Franciscan pastor was in residence and the shrine continued to receive many visitors thanks to its reputation for cures and other divine favors. By the 1740s the legend of Our Lady of Tulantongo was reduced to a proper founding miracle and history of devotion: Gandía had become a virtuous Indian who, when he washed his face in the well water and opened his eyes to sight "more than two hundred years ago," saw the decrepit image of the Madonna and Child restored to fine condition.[125]

The shrine of Nuestra Señora de Tecaxic, situated on stony ground at the foot of a hill outside the city of Toluca, is documented from more than one vantage point near its beginning in the mid-seventeenth century and can serve as an example that blurs neat distinctions between official promotion and popular devotion, or resistance and collaboration in its genesis, development, and longevity. For its earliest years, this shrine is known mainly through the official chronicle composed in the late 1670s by Fr. Juan de Mendoza, OFM, and published in 1684: *Relación de el santuario de Tecaxique, en que está colocada la milagrosa Imagen de Nuestra Señora de los Ángeles* ... Mendoza's work resulted from a commission by the Franciscans' provincial *comisario general* to investigate the origin of this sacred image of the Virgin Mary and her wonders, "so that [they] ... would be known, for the greater glory of God, the honor of his Most Holy Mother, and the affectionate devotion of the faithful."[126] Mendoza added that he sought "simple and true information about what was known," and that he had "complied with the rules of a true Historian."

Most of the thirty-six pages of Mendoza's text concern marvels associated with the image, beginning with an origin story of early devotion at a chapel and subsequent neglect, providential signs, and gratifying revival.[127] The site had been home to a substantial Indian settlement in the pastoral care of the Franciscan convent of Toluca, but at some unspecified time in the past, the local population had been devastated by an epidemic and the chapel and its painting of Our Lady of the Assumption on rough native cloth had been abandoned. Then around 1640[128] Pedro Millán Hidalgo, "an honorable man," a trader from the Valley of Toluca, passed the site of the chapel at night in his travels to and from the city of Toluca and heard heavenly music there, especially on Tuesdays and Saturdays. When he approached the ruins to see who was singing, there was no one in sight. Some nights he also saw the place from a distance illuminated in a resplendent halo, but when he approached, the site was in darkness. He poked around in the dark but found only the painting of the Virgin, still in remarkably good condition. From then on, every Saturday he would light a candle before the painting and fervently commend himself to Her Majesty. According to Mendoza, word of the marvel spread throughout the valley and other visitors saw the lights, heard the music, and brought candles for the altar. And stories of miracles for devotees began to circulate. Fr. Joseph Gutierres, a virtuous friar from the Toluca convent, was assigned to the decrepit chapel. He organized special services there on August 15, the day of the Assumption of Mary, and with the help of devotees and neighbors from nearby farms began to gather building materials for a new chapel. It was not yet finished by the time Fr. Gutierres was transferred to other duties in 1651, but there was a continual outpouring of devotion, money, building materials, food, and Indian laborers so that by the time Mendoza wrote, he could celebrate "this very ample, very beautiful shrine, well furnished with everything needed in the sacristy, all of which derives from offerings made to this Lady."

In other words, Mendoza's little book dates from the early decades of the devotion's authorized history, when memories of revival were fresh and there was a major push to develop the site with a fitting architectural monument. By the time his *relación* appeared in print, some 221 people lived nearby, most of them Otomí, Mazahua, and Nahuatl speakers.[129] Mendoza's informants either knew the seer Pedro Millán, knew someone who knew him, or claimed to have witnessed the heavenly sound and light show. Mendoza's key informant was María Fuentes. She provided eight of his miracle stories of apparitions, cures, and other signs of divine presence. Born in Toluca, Señora Fuentes was widowed and serving on a rural estate near the shrine at the time her testimony was taken in 1676. More to the point, she was Pedro Millán's niece and an ardent devotee of Nuestra Señora de Tecaxic, eager to tell her stories. As a child she had listened to her uncle's account of the wonders of Tecaxic and had accompanied her father and siblings to the site to experience the divine presence herself. In particular, one night when her family stayed in the ruined chapel six young men appeared, making beautiful music. Two of them were dressed in blue cloaks, two in bright red cloaks the color of cochineal, and the other two in white cloaks embroidered in the style of Indians from Xaltocan. Near dawn the men mysteriously disappeared, and one of her brothers told her that the two in front had their feet off the ground like the angels in the painting [of Nuestra Señora de Tecaxic]. Her father decided to move to the site and serve the Virgin. She recalled him saying that one morning when he had slept in, a woman's voice called out to him and he quickly arose and gathered other construction workers to begin the day's labor, convinced that the Most Holy Virgin was gently admonishing him for his laziness.

Mendoza assured readers that "there are a great many marvels happening all the time, it being virtually impossible to mention them all." To María Fuentes's list he added six more cases of resuscitation, recovery from paralysis, and survival in near-fatal accidents and lightning strikes, but at the top and bottom of his list of providential signs were unexpected gifts of construction materials and food for the builders. From Mendoza's *relación* and the short treatment of the Tecaxic shrine in Agustín de Vetancurt, OFM's *Teatro mexicano* of 1698 (which may well have been based on Mendoza's text), it might seem that this blossoming devotion beginning in the 1640s and construction of the new church after 1651 developed with little official Church involvement.[130] Administrative and financial accounts for the shrine of Tecaxic from the 1650s and 1660s, and a 1696 inventory of endowments record a somewhat different, more reciprocal story.[131] The cathedral chapter of the Archdiocese of Mexico proposed to monitor the shrine and its providential story as early as 1650. In the minutes of the chapter meeting on December 22 that year news of a miraculous image in a shrine at Tecaxic was noted and the canons ordered "an investigation of the discovery of this Holy Image and the miracles associated with it" and proceeded to name an investigator. The shrine attracted unnamed small donors and volunteer workers, especially during the periodic fiestas, but evidence of possessions, income, and expenditures for the shrine between 1657 and 1663 indicates that the Franciscans and a small number of individual benefactors who donated larger sums were key players in its early development. The collection boxes at the shrine produced a total of 338 pesos 4 reales from anonymous donors during these years, especially between July and December, when the principal feasts were held and more people visited the shrine, but larger donations by named individuals identified as *españoles* and *indios* totaled 494 pesos 6 reales, and the Franciscans in Toluca alone accounted for more than 35 percent of this amount. The largest source of cash income during these years (707 pesos) was from *demandas* – Franciscan-managed alm-collecting missions to neighboring districts in the modern states of México, Hidalgo, and Morelos. In other words, there was a promotional campaign led by the Franciscans and some individual devotees in the city and valley of Toluca. Other important donations were made in kind rather than cash. They included building materials, grain, and a fine new organ for the church valued at 700 pesos given by the native *gobernador* of Metepec, Don Francisco Mathías, who also donated precious silver implements for the altar. The expenses in the 1650s and 1660s included some purchases of finery for the Mass, furnishings for the church interior, and maintenance work, but mainly they covered construction costs, especially building materials and the wages of day laborers and artisans.[132]

The process of developing the shrine at Tecaxic and securing its future continued into the late seventeenth century and beyond. By the mid-1690s more of the shrine's expenses, now including memorial Masses performed by the resident chaplain and other priests, as well as supplies of wax and oil, were covered by income from endowments and annual gifts.[133] The shrine continued to grow and prosper in the eighteenth century, with new endowments listed in a 1723 inventory and completion of a more substantial shrine church in 1731.[134] Reports in 1743 and 1757 noted growing popularity of the shrine among residents of the city of Toluca and surrounding jurisdictions, and a few additional endowments.[135] Other than as donors of some income-producing lands, Indian devotees were not listed among those who endowed Masses, but they reportedly paid for various special Masses and made gifts of candle wax and incense. Mendoza's booklet was republished in 1761, and the archbishop found the shrine in good order when he went there during his pastoral visit in 1775. At that time, there were ten obra pía endowments, plus lands donated by Indians.[136]

The last decades of the long seventeenth century, 1680–1720, saw the popularity of shrines and miraculous images grow and established patterns and institutional support deepen. More shrines had confraternities and endowments that supported the ceremonial life of the shrine, sponsored full time chaplains, and undertook construction projects on a grander scale. More miracles, activated images, and images discovered in nature were reported. Bishops continued to encourage local image shrines in their jurisdictions, and actively promoted, even sponsored, some with a wider following. Archbishop Aguiar y Seixas (1680–1698) stood out in this regard. A little-noticed side of this fiercely ascetic, moralizing, misogynistic prelate was his interest in charitable institutions including hospitals and schools, his regard for shrines, and his promotion of church construction, including the great shrine church at Tepeyac, completed in 1709. Aguiar was one of the few seventeenth-century bishops to personally undertake his pastoral visit to all parts of the Archdiocese of Mexico (in three trips between 1683 and 1688), and he used the occasion to visit local shrines and encourage support for them. He was also a key figure in popularizing the Cristo Renovado de Santa Teresa in the newly finished Carmelite convent church of Santa Teresa, which he dedicated in 1684. When bishops supported a shrine, the papal indulgences,[137] gifts, and licenses for publication of devotional literature flowed, lay organizations prospered, and alms-collecting missions were encouraged; but there was also more oversight and regulation, as when the archbishop intervened to forbid the annual fiesta for the miraculous stone cross of Querétaro in 1694 because of unruly behavior and damages the previous year.[138] The published devotional histories bishops authorized gave added exposure to the shrines they favored, and tended to fix their version of the shrine's origin story and its representative miracles.[139] Formal investigations of the miracles of shrine images were occasionally undertaken at a bishop's request, but not as often as they had been in midcentury.

Near the end of the seventeenth century when regional shrines grew in reach and importance, an ardent creole devotee and publicist, Francisco de Florencia, SJ, spread the good news in an unprecedented outpouring of published devotional histories: for Our Lady of Guadalupe, Our Lady of Remedios, San Miguel del Milagro, the Lord of Chalma, Our Lady of San Juan de los Lagos, Our Lady of Zapopan, Our Lady of Loreto in the Jesuits' Casa Profesa in Mexico City and their church of Espíritu Santo in Puebla, and the Cruz Verde of Tepic. He also left an unfinished anthology of Marian shrines in New Spain with short histories, legends, and selected miracles, evidently inspired by fellow Jesuit Wilhelm Gumppenberg's global *Atlas Marianus*.[140] Florencia's pious labors were a high point for the Jesuits' role in publicizing and promoting shrines in New Spain during the seventeenth century, mainly through their writings, teaching, and revival missions. He was the most conspicuous Jesuit author and authority on miraculous images and shrines, but not the only one.

Jesuits had been ardent Marianists going back to St. Ignatius of Loyola's vision of the Virgin Mary and the infant Jesus at the shrine of Our Lady of Montserrat shortly before he composed the *Spiritual Exercises* in the 1520s; and in the 1570s his follower Peter Canisius, SJ, had urged Catholics to revere the Virgin and honor her both at home and in public as a symbol of the Church Triumphant. The Jesuits' prestige and scholarly reputation in New Spain led the archbishop of Mexico to appoint Joan Sánchez, SJ, to inspect the Virgin of Guadalupe's shrine at Tepeyac in 1607, while other Jesuits routinely served as evaluators and censors of published sermons and devotional texts during the seventeenth and eighteenth centuries; and their network of colleges, churches, frontier missions, and preaching missions in and near cities made them unusually effective disseminators of the devotions they championed.[141] Seventeenth-century Jesuits in New Spain identified especially with Italy's Virgin of Loreto at Ancona, one of the few shrines administered by the order. As early as 1615 they established a major confraternity (*congregación*) in her name in the Casa Profesa in Mexico City, and by the late 1680s six chapels and altars dedicated to Our Lady of Loreto and five replicas of the Virgin's Holy House could be found in western, central, and southern Mexico, mostly in Jesuit establishments. But it was after 1675 with the arrival and missionary work of two young Italian Jesuits, Juan Bautista Zappa and Juan María Salvatierra, that devotion to the Virgin of Loreto took off. Jesuits in New Spain were also closely associated in the seventeenth century with the Mater Dolorosa and some locally renowned miraculous images in their churches and colleges in Mexico City, including Santa María la Mayor, Our Lady of Dolores in the Colegio Máximo de San Pedro y San Pablo, and Our Lady of Xalmolonga. But, in the spirit of Florencia's embrace of many miraculous images, Jesuits in New Spain had a hand in promoting most of the leading regional shrines and image devotions of the time no matter who was in charge. For example, in 1660 Mateo de la Cruz, a Jesuit from Puebla, authored a booklet designed to introduce a popular readership to the image, apparitions, and miracles of the Virgin of Guadalupe, based on Miguel Sánchez's more discursive text of 1648.[142] And the Jesuits did not try to monopolize their special association with the Virgin of Loreto and the Mater Dolorosa.[143]

This growing interest in image shrines in the last decades of the long seventeenth century was distinguished as well by other new or increasingly popular devotional aids and artifacts of faith. In addition to more published devotional histories and sermons, novena booklets for nine-day observances at image shrines or for particular saints became common. These pocket guides printed for the occasion contained instructions and special prayers for each day of devotions. The novena booklets for miraculous images sometimes also included a thumbnail history with the providential origin story, a few representative miracles, and a print of the celebrated image. Whether in novena booklets or as single sheets, more prints depicting miraculous images were in circulation, thanks in part to the use of engraved metal plates that stood up to larger print runs and made for more detailed images. This was also a time when more full-size "true copies" (*fieles copias*) of some shrine images were produced and disseminated, especially of the Virgin of Guadalupe. Also at this time more paintings depicting the origin stories of miraculous images were produced, both to spread religious values and to proclaim a providential social and political heritage.[144] Ex-voto paintings of prodigious favors displayed in shrines were not unknown earlier, but, judging by those that survive, they were becoming more popular as personal yet public testimonies of faith and sources of inspiration for viewers, as were votive milagritos and medidas.[145]

The shrine of the Cristo Renovado de Santa Teresa in the church of the discalced Carmelites in Mexico City is a good example of how these kinds of devotional materials contributed to the growth of an image shrine. This crucifix rose to become "the greatest of all the capital's many miraculous images," according to a visitor in the 1760s.[146] In the 1680s Archbishop Aguiar y Seixas commissioned a leading Oratorian priest and academic, Dr. Alonso Alberto de Velasco, to report on a formal investigation to authenticate the image's celebrated self-restoration and other miracles. His findings were completed in 1685 and published in 1688 as *Renovación por sí misma de la Soberana Imagen de Christo Señor Nuestro Cruvcificado, Que llaman Ytzimiquilpan* ... In 1699, again with official encouragement and sponsorship, Dr. Velasco published the first of many editions of his devotional history of the image and shrine, revised for a general readership from the more juridical *Renovación por sí misma*. Also printed in 1699 was a novena booklet for the Cristo Renovado composed by Velasco. It, too, would go through other editions during the eighteenth century. Several different prints of this crucifix on its altar in the Carmelite nuns' church were included in each of the seven colonial-era editions of Velasco's devotional history, and other prints of this Christ were sold as single sheets or given out by alms collectors. Another, shorter book about the Cristo Renovado for a popular audience was written by Domingo de Quiroga, SJ, and published in 1724,[147] followed by publication in 1731 of a sermon in the Cristo Renovado's honor by Manuel de Folgar, one of the capital's leading preachers.[148] And from the 1730s, fine, large paintings of this self-restoring crucified Christ by leading Mexico City artists were commissioned, three by José de Ibarra and others by Miguel Cabrera, José de Páez (see cover image), and Francisco Antonio Vallejo. Sacred images like these paintings and prints, wrote Velasco, were "for the instruction and learning of the unintelligent; for permanent recollection of the Sovereign Mysteries of Our Redemption and the examples of the saints; and to stimulate in us tender feelings of devotion that are nurtured more by what is seen than by what is heard."[149]

Conclusion

Two Franciscan chronicles that open and close the seventeenth century mark the striking rise and development of image shrines in New Spain's sacred geography. Both authors embraced the materiality of faith, but in different ways that expressed their time. Fr. Juan de Torquemada's monumental *Monarquía Indiana*, first published in 1615 but at least twenty years in the making, is filled with the Franciscans' palpable sense of divine presence in the world, manifested in apparitions, miracles of protection and healing, and the power of relics, all posed against the ever-present subversions by Satan.[150] Above all, Christian crosses populate Torquemada's narrative – planted just about everywhere in the Mesoamerican landscape, on mountaintops, in towns, and homes, wherever pagan temples and idols were found or had been – to signify the protective presence of Christianity, the true religion, and the promise of life everlasting. Torquemada marveled at native peoples' eagerness to embrace the Christian cross as object and sign, and their willingness to forsake treasured idols and put crosses in their place. Torquemada was well aware of the abundance of images of Christ, the Virgin Mary, and other saints in New Spain. He mentioned them especially in descriptions of solemn processions in Mexico City during Semana Santa in 1609, in which 230 elaborate gilded platforms supporting statues of Christ, Mary, and other saints were carried through the streets. For Corpus Christi, he added, all the portable platforms bearing images from Mexico City and Tlatelolco were assembled. In passing, he mentioned the shrine to Our Lady of Remedios, and in another text he mentioned the miraculous image of La Conquistadora in Puebla.[151] But otherwise he had little to say about miraculous images and shrines. The only one featured in the *Monarquía Indiana* was the Cruz de Huatulco, famed for withstanding an attempt by English pirates to destroy it in 1587. Slivers from this cross quickly became prized as protective talismans, much like slivers of the True Cross, he added.

Fellow Franciscan Fr. Agustín de Vetancurt offered a strikingly different picture of divine presence in the world in his 1698 chronicle *Teatro mexicano: descripcion breve de los sucesos ejemplares de la Nueva-España en el Nuevo Mundo Occidental de las Indias*. His chronicle was rooted more in Mexico City and the order's central Mexico Province of the Holy Gospel, and he was an unabashed booster of his native city, swelling with pride at the thought of its greatness: "wishing to single out everything great about

Mexico City would require writing whole volumes because [this city] exceeds many in Christendom and stands shoulder to shoulder with the best in the world. It is among the greatest cities in His Majesty's Crown."[152] But even in his embrace of the capital, Vetancurt had much to say about cult images and shrines across central Mexico. Early in his chronicle, he promised a "catalogue of the images" associated with Franciscan establishments in the Province of the Holy Gospel.[153] He delivered less than a full inventory, but did include thumbnail descriptions of twenty-eight image shrines in the care of his Franciscan brethren, plus several pages of text about the two most famous shrine images associated with Mexico City: Our Lady of Guadalupe and Our Lady of Remedios.[154] Image shrines had by then become fixtures in the devotional landscape.

The composite history of growing interest in image shrines during the long seventeenth century outlined in this chapter contains a stubborn paradox. While miraculous images became extremely popular and often were actively promoted by Church officials, this was also a time when ecclesiastical authorities were deeply concerned about idolatry, both present and prospective. With Satan ever threatening to seduce feeble souls, especially through idols and false gods,[155] encouraging image shrines would seem to be a risky move, but the power of the image in Catholic Christianity, especially at this time, trumped the risks. The paradox lived in Palafox's and Aguiar y Seixas's mixture of somber, regalist austerity; enthusiasm for image shrines; and sense of a palpable double-edged enchantment in which evil and goodness, Satan and Christ, were fully present in the world. Witchcraft trials, idolatry inquests, wandering souls, and visions of purgatory were as much a part of the enchantment of this world as self-restoring crucifixes and weeping Madonnas.

Notes

1. On early cities as style centers, see Paul Wheatley, *Pivot of the Four Quarters: A Preliminary Enquiry into the Origins of the Character of the Ancient Chinese City*, Chicago: Aldine, 1971, chapter 2.
2. Robert Ricard, *The Spiritual Conquest of Mexico: An Essay on the Apostolate and the Evangelizing Methods of the Mendicant Orders of New Spain, 1523–1572*, trans. Lesley B. Simpson, Berkeley: University of California Press, 1964, p. 295.
3. George Kubler, *The Shape of Time: Remarks on the History of Things*, New Haven: Yale University Press, 1962, p. 107.
4. Louis Hartz, *The Founding of New Societies: Studies in the History of the United States, Latin America, South Africa, Canada, and Australia*, New York: Harcourt, Brace & World, 1964, p. 3.
5. George Foster, *Culture and Conquest: Latin America's Spanish Heritage*, New York: Wenner-Gren Foundation, Viking Fund Publications, 1960, especially pp. 232–233.

Formative Developments, 1520s–1720s 77

6. Medievalists Luis Weckmann and Amy Remensnyder have advanced similar views about Marian devotion and cultural practices more broadly in New Spain, as a streamlined, crystallized version of particular medieval Iberian ways. Weckmann's quest to "discover the medieval roots of Mexican culture" in colonial era sources is developed in *The Medieval Heritage of Mexico*, trans. Frances M. López-Morillas, New York: Fordham University Press, 1992, p. 3. Remensnyder focuses on the Virgin Mary in New Spain as crusader-warrior, which she regards as a durable extension of medieval Reconquista beliefs and practices, *La Conquistadora: The Virgin Mary at War and Peace in the Old and New Worlds*, Oxford and New York: Oxford University Press, 2014. Reacting against the idea that "Mary embodied boundless maternal love" and little more, she argues that the Blessed Virgin was "a particularly effective agent in the conversion of Jews, Muslims, and native peoples of the Americas," with the accent on conquest and military domination, pp. 1, 8. In Remensnyder's Iberian medieval legacy, the Blessed Mary was La Conquistadora.

> [T]he medieval Mary would linger in many corners of the new worlds of the Early Modern Spanish empire, her active powers perhaps tempered by the changing religious climate, but certainly not effaced. Like the Spaniards who colonized the lands across the Atlantic, Mary took the medieval past with her into the New World. Otherwise, she would not have gained the title in sixteenth-century New Spain of La Conquistadora, the name that would cause such bitter controversy in New Mexico five hundred years after Columbus first made landfall on a Caribbean island.   p. 222

That this was a fixed and focused outlook is posited on pages 21 and 68: "[C]oncepts of crusade and reconquest were crystallizing"; "[B]y the beginning of the fifteenth century, the Marian past had impressed itself as heavily on the contours of Iberia's human history as on its geography."

7. An underlying assumption in Weckmann's *Medieval Heritage* is that cultural patterns, including music, were transferred intact from Spain to Mexico and changed little thereafter: "The music of Spain, and the instruments used to produce it at the end of the medieval period, were transplanted unchanged to the Indies by conquistadors and missionaries," p. 550. Recent work by musicologists makes the transfer less predictable, noting that devotional music in the colonial period, including *villancicos*, did indeed follow European models and was slow to change, but because it was written for local performance, it put down local roots expressing local sensibilities. As Drew Edward Davies puts it, "[M]usic in a European aesthetic may contain local topicality," if not obvious local content, "Finding 'Local Content' in the Music of New Spain," *Early Music America* 19: 2 (2013), 60–64. See also the essays in *Music and Urban Society in Colonial Latin America*, ed. Geoffrey Baker and Tess Knighton, Cambridge, UK and New York: Cambridge University Press, 2011 and *Devotional Music in the Iberian World, 1450–1800: The Villancico and Related Genres*, ed. Tess Knighton and Alvaro Torrente, Aldershot, England: Ashgate, 2007.

8. See especially Caroline Walker Bynum, *Christian Materiality: An Essay on Religion in Late Medieval Europe*, New York: Zone Books, 2011, and Richard Trexler, "Florentine Religious Exerience: The Sacred Images," *Renaissance Studies* 19 (1972), 7–41.

9. For Castile, in 1478 Hernando de Talavera, archbishop of Granada (and confessor to Queen Isabella), joined with the archbishop of Sevilla to order that all Christians have

images of holy personages in their homes, David Nirenberg, *Aesthetic Theology and Its Enemies. Judaism in Christian Painting, Poetry, and Politics*, Lebanon, NH: University Press of New England/Brandeis University Press, 2015, p. 42.

10. William A. Christian, Jr., *Local Religion in Sixteenth-Century Spain*, Princeton: Princeton University Press, 1981, p. 91; Robert Bartlett, *Why Can the Dead Do Such Great Things? Saints and Worshippers from the Martyrs to the Reformation*, Princeton: Princeton University Press, 2013, p. 498.

11. Christian, *Local Religion*, p. 122. A more comprehensive list of regional shrines was made in the third quarter of the sixteenth century by the future royal chronicler Esteban de Garibay y Zamalloa. He listed seventeen shrines, including ten dedicated to images of the Virgin Mary, three to images of Christ and the Cross, one sudarium, one bleeding Host, one image of Santiago, and one image of Santo Domingo. Of the thirteen identified by religious affiliation, five were associated with the diocesan clergy, three with the Benedictines, two with the Dominicans, one with the Franciscans, one with the Jeronymites, and one with the Augustinians, *Los XL libros del compendio historial de las c(h?)ronicas y universal historia de todos los reynos de España*, 1st ed., Amberes: Plantino, 1570–1572. I consulted the 1628 Barcelona edition published by Sebastián de Cormellas, vol. 1 libro 3, chapter 10, pp. 65–66.

12. Felipe Pereda, *Las imágenes de la discordia: Política y poética de la imagen sagrada en la España del 400*, Madrid: Marcial Pons, 2007, p. 372.

13. John L. Phelan, *The Millennial Kingdom of the Franciscans in the New World*, Berkeley: University of California Press, 2nd ed., 1970, pp. 29–38.

14. See *St. Francis of Assisi, Writings and Early Biographies: English Omnibus of the Sources for the Life of St. Francis*, ed. Marion A. Habig, Chicago: Franciscan Herald Press, 1973, especially "Lives of St. Francis" by Thomas of Celano, pp. 177–612, and "Lives of St. Francis" by St. Bonaventure, pp. 613–851.

15. For a sampling, see *The Little Flowers of Saint Francis*, ed. Raphael Brown, Garden City, NY: Doubleday, 1958, pp. 48–52, 55, 60, 70, 78, 83, 151, 160, 163, 186, 237, 252, 305–307.

16. Juan Papió, *El Colegio Seminario del Arcángel San Miguel de Escournalbou …*, Barcelona: Imprenta de los Padres Carmelitas, 1765, p. 373.

17. John Moorman, *A History of the Franciscan Order from Its Origins to the Year 1517*, Oxford: Oxford University Press, 1968.

18. A common emphasis in treating the Franciscans in New Spain, to which Phelan contributed, has been to regard the millenarian thread as if it were dominant in a timeless way, as if Mendieta can stand for Franciscan thought generally during the early modern period. Other influential currents of Franciscan thought and practice among Observant Franciscans, especially the thought of Duns Scotus, focused less on the imminent end of the world and final Judgment.

19. Other Catholic reformers before Trent included rigorously ascetic Francisco Jiménez de Cisneros, OFM, Archbishop of Toledo, Inquisitor General, and, from 1495 to his death in 1517, principal adviser to Isabella and Ferdinand and regent for their grandson, Prince Charles. Jiménez de Cisneros pressed the Observant reforms in his order; purged hundreds of lax clerics and monastics; promoted biblical scholarship and better education for priests; supported the distribution of key texts to standardize liturgical and devotional practices, especially the missal and breviary; weeded out corruption among

Inquisition officials; and promoted forced baptism and mass conversion of remaining Muslims and Jews in Castile, Christian expansion into North Africa and the New World, and the rights of indigenous peoples. See Carlos Eire, "The Reformation," in *The Blackwell Companion to Catholicism*, ed. James J. Buckley, Frederick Christian Bauerschmidt, and Trent Pomplun, Oxford and Malden, MA: Blackwell, 2007, p. 71, and Erika Rummel, *Jiménez de Cisneros: On the Threshold of Spain's Golden Age*, Tempe: Arizona Center for Medieval and Renaissance Studies, 1999, chapter 3. In some of these initiatives, he evidently enjoyed papal permission and encouragement (Rummel, *Jiménez de Cisneros*, p. 23).

For a recent study of Franciscans in New Spain during the sixteenth century, including an ongoing tension between their traditional eremetic spirituality and the evangelizing mission, and a "creolizing" of Franciscan personnel in the New World, see Steven E. Turley, *Franciscan Spirituality and Mission in New Spain, 1524–1599: Conflict Beneath the Sycamore Tree*, Burlington, VT: Ashgate, 2014, especially pp. 184–188.

20. Erik Thunø, "From Neglected to Sacred Space: Miraculous Images and Their Early Modern Shrines," in *La imagen sagrada y sacralizada*, ed. Peter Krieger, Mexico: UNAM, 2011, I, 255–263.
21. As John O'Malley writes, the sketchy coverage of most theological and devotional matters in the Trent decrees meant that "Trent was ... pervasively influential, but ... it was not Catholicism. Nor did it intend to be." The impact of directions signaled in the Trent decrees was realized locally and depended on what a particular bishop and leaders around him made of them as they worked to consolidate Roman Catholicism, and sometimes depended, too, on the response of the laity. John W. O'Malley, *Trent: What Happened at the Council*, Cambridge, MA: Harvard University Press, 2013, especially p. 274; Eamon Duffy, "The Staying Power of Christianity," *New York Review of Books*, June 20, 2013, pp. 69–71.
22. Eire, "The Reformation," p. 65; Christian, *Local Religion*, p. 179.
23. *Canons and Decrees of the Council of Trent: Original Text in English*, trans. H. J. Schroeder, OP, St. Louis and London: B. Herder Book Co., 1941, p. 215. Carina Johnson suggests that the Trent decree affirming veneration of images was "a crucial turning point" in the history of images (and, by extension, image shrines) in Catholic practice and "new understandings of idolatry and culture," "Idolatrous Cultures and the Practice of Religion," *Journal of the History of Ideas* 67: 4 (2006), 617. On idolatry as about more than images, see the discussion in Chapter 2 and Sabine MacCormack, "Gods, Demons, and Idols in the Andes," *Journal of the History of Ideas* 67: 4 (2006), 623–647.
24. Nicholas Terpstra, *Lay Confraternities and Civic Religion in Renaissance Bologna*, Cambridge, UK: Cambridge University Press, 1995 and "Confraternities and Local Cults: Civic Religion between Class and Politics in Renaissance Bologna," in *Civic Ritual and Drama in Late Medieval and Renaissance Europe*, ed. Alexandra F. Johnson and Wil Hüsken, Amsterdam: Rodopi, 1997, pp. 143–174; Thunø, "From Neglected to Sacred Space"; Christian, *Local Religion*; Richard Trexler, *Public Life in Renaissance Florence*, Ithaca: Cornell University Press, 1991; Bridget Heal, *The Cult of the Virgin Mary in Early Modern Germany: Protestant and Catholic Piety, 1500–1648*, Cambridge, UK and New York: Cambridge University Press, 2007. On confraternities in Spain at this time, see Maureen Flynn, "Baroque Piety and Spanish Confraternities," in *Confraternities*

and *Catholic Reform in Italy, France, and Spain*, ed. John Patrick Donnelly and Michael W. Maher, Kirksville, MO: Truman State University Press, 1999, pp. 233–246.
25. Marie-Hélène Froeschlé-Chopard, "Espace et sacré au XVIIIe siècle," in *Lieux sacrés, lieux de culte, sanctuaires*, ed. André Vauchez, Rome: EFR, 2000, pp. 297–316.
26. Froeschlé-Chopard, "Espace et sacré."
27. Heal, *The Cult of the Virgin Mary in Early Modern Germany*.
28. Heal, *The Cult of the Virgin Mary in Early Modern Germany*, p. 306.
29. Juan de Grijalva, OSA, for example, spoke of many images, many chapels before 1592, *Crónica de la Orden de N.P.S. Agustín en las provincias de la Nueva España en cuatro edades desde el año 1533 hasta el de 1592*, Mexico: Porrúa, 1985, p. 162.
30. Gerónimo de Mendieta, OFM, drawing upon the earlier chronicle of Motolinía, recounted apparitions in *Historia eclesiástica indiana*, Mexico: CONACULTA, 1997, I, chapters 24–28. The Oroz Codex included most of the same apparitions, visions, and prophesies, Pedro Oroz, *The Oroz Codex*, ed. and trans. Angélico Chávez, Washington: Academy of American Franciscan History, 1972, pp. 98, 162–164, 168, 187–192, 216–217, 248–252, 255–256, 268–269, 302–306. A mid-seventeenth-century chronicle for the Franciscan province of Xalisco by Antonio Tello, OFM, recounted the apparitions to the sick girl in Juchipila and Fr. Juan de Gracia in *Crónica miscelánea de la sancta provincia de Xalisco*, libro III, Guadalajara: Edit. Font, 1942, pp. 78–79, 475. Javier Otaola, "Visiones y apariciones en el siglo XVI: Una aproximación al lenguaje simbólico," in *Serie Historia Novohispana*, Mexico: Instituto de Investigaciones Históricas, UNAM, No. 72 (2004), pp. 297–311 suggests that "el número de apariciones que los indios comunicaban a los frailes era enorme."
31. Robert H. Jackson, *Conflict and Conversion: The Augustinian War on and Beyond the Chichimeca Frontier*, Leiden: Brill NV, 2013, chapter 1, especially p. 6. Jackson notes that a mural in the Dominican convent of Tetela del Volcán, apparently dating to the late sixteenth century, may represent this miracle.
32. An exception is the Augustinian chronicler Juan de Grijalva. In addition to apparitions, he mentioned two cases of images associated with miracles: the Santo Niño de Cebu in Manila and Our Lady of Remedios, Grijalva, *Crónica*, pp. 258, 188.
33. Francisco Antonio de Lorenzana, *Concilios provinciales primero y segundo ...*, Mexico: Joseph Antonio de Hogal, 1769, pp. 91–94, 200.
34. *Manuscritos el Concilio Tercero Provincial Mexicano (1585)*, ed. and introduction by Alberto Carrillo Cázares, Zamora: El Colegio de Michoacán, 2006, I, 189–190, 193.
35. On the "communications revolution" in printed material that gradually followed the introduction of movable type in the late fifteenth century, see Elizabeth Eisenstein, *The Printing Press as Agent of Change: Communications and Cultural Transformations in Early Modern Europe*, 2 vols., Cambridge, UK and New York: Cambridge University Press, 1979.
36. William A. Christian, Jr., *Apparitions in Late Medieval and Renaissance Spain*, Princeton: Princeton University Press, 1981, p. 150. Sixteenth-century ecclesiastical authorities in Spain also regarded most hermits as idlers and cheats. Hermits seemed to find a warmer welcome in New Spain, especially in the late sixteenth century, although the first synod (1555) was concerned enough to declare that hermits had to be licensed, Lorenzana, *Concilios provinciales*, pp. 92–94.

Cardinal Cisneros was a major figure in Catholic reforms at the beginning of the sixteenth century, but as inquisitor general he was not inclined to act decisively against visionaries, Rummel, *Jiménez de Cisneros*, pp. 42–45, Eire, "The Reformation," p. 71. Thereafter, Spanish authorities regarded apparitions and dream visions with disapproval, if not hostility. See Enrique Fernandez-Rivera, "Dream," in *Lexikon of the Hispanic Baroque*, ed. Evonne Levy and Kenneth Mills, Austin: University of Texas Press, 2014, p. 99: "[T]he Church and the Crown strongly persecuted those who publicized revelatory or prophetic dreams, not only because they opened a door to all kinds of heresies ... Having lost the otherworldly cachet, dreams were reduced to a sphere of existence of obscure origins but clearly not divine."

37. Franciscans were wary of miraculous images at the beginning. Among the friars, Augustinians were more conspicuous early promoters of miraculous images and image shrines, judging by the removal of a renowned crucifix from their *doctrina* of Totolapan to the mother convent in Mexico City in 1583. See the discussion of the Cristo de Totolapan in Chapter 5 and early seventeenth-century Augustinian chronicler Juan de Grijalva's observations about miraculous images before 1592, including Our Lady of Remedios, the Santo Niño de Cebu of the Philippines, and various crosses, *Crónica*, pp. 188, 231, 258, 269. On Augustinians and miraculous crosses, see also Chapter 8.

38. Rosario Inés Granados Salinas notes that paintings dating from the 1590s in the shrine church of Our Lady of Remedios at Naucalpan depict Juan Ceteutli and his discovery of the statue of Mary beneath a large maguey, "Fervent Faith. Devotion, Aesthetics, and Society in the Cult of Our Lady of Remedios (Mexico, 1520–1811)," Ph.D. dissertation, Harvard University, 2012, pp. 101–109. This may be the earliest recorded case.

39. Little evidence has yet come to light that cult images in the sixteenth century were considered to have had origins that defied the laws of nature. If the Nican Mopohua is, in fact, a sixteenth-century text, the Virgin of Guadalupe would be an exception, but Magnus Lundberg notes that early references to the cult of the Virgin of Guadalupe in the cathedral records did not make this claim. *Actas de cabildo* of the cathedral chapter from 1570 do suggest a close relationship between the cathedral and the chapel dedicated to Guadalupe that had been constructed at Tepeyac in the 1550s, Lundberg, *Unification and Conflict: The Church Politics of Alonso de Montúfar OP, Archbishop of Mexico, 1554–1572*, Uppsala: Swedish Institute of Missionary Research, 2002, p. 219.

40. The pattern of early image shrines closely associated with cities is explored for Puebla and Tlaxcala by Rosa Denise Fallena Montaño in "La imagen de María: Simbolización de conquista y fundación en los valles de Puebla-Tlaxcala: La Conquistadora de Puebla, la Virgin Asunción de Tlaxcala y Nuestra Señora de los Remedios de Cholula," Ph.D. dissertation, Instituto de Investigaciones Estéticas, UNAM, 2013, p. 8 and *passim*.

41. "Furta sacra" – removing a coveted image from its home parish – such as the transfer of the Totolapa crucifix to Mexico City, was unusual in New Spain. Another late-sixteenth-century case was the removal of most of the cross of Huatulco, Oaxaca to the cathedral church in Antequera. However, removal of reputedly miraculous images from homes and villages to the parish church was more common.

42. A different image of Our Lady of Remedios, atop the great pyramid of Cholula near the city of Puebla, has a conquest origin story, too, but it seems to have been a late sixteenth- or early seventeenth-century development. The first chapel was constructed in 1594. See Fallena Montaño, "La imagen de María," chapter 4. Early rural shrines

include the Cristo del Sacromonte of Amecameca (Estado de México), Nuestra Señora de Izamal (Yucatán), and Nuestra Señora de la Asunción of Xalostotitlán (Jalisco).

43. Still unsettled is the date of the Nican Mopohua, a retrospective text in Nahuatl published in 1649 as the work of the diocesan priest Luis Lasso de la Vega, describing the famous apparitions. Some scholars believe it was written by Antonio Valeriano in the 1540s or at least before 1572. Stafford Poole discounts the likelihood of Valeriano's authorship, but acknowledges that the text under Lasso's name seems to mix Nahuatl phrasing from earlier periods and may, at least in part, reflect traditions that circulated orally before 1649, *Our Lady of Guadalupe: The Origins and Sources of a Mexican National Symbol, 1531–1797*, Tucson: University of Arizona Press, 1995, pp. 111–118. Another brief account in Nahuatl on a Marian apparition associated with Tepeyac known as "Inin huei tlamahuiçoltzin" (This is the great marvel) adds to the possibility of an emerging apparition tradition at Tepeyac in the late sixteenth century. Lundberg comments,

> As in the case with the Nican Mopohua, there is no consensus among scholars on the origins and date of this manuscript. According to Louise Burkhart, the manuscript could be linguistically and palaeographically dated to the late sixteenth or early seventeenth century, while Stafford Poole dates it to the eighteenth century. The basic story of the apparition and the transformation of the flowers as told by Lasso de la Vega is found in the manuscript, but the text does not indicate any date and the Indian is unnamed, and nor is the archbishop, to whom he presents the cloak. Therefore, Louise Burkhart argues that the story was probably a part of an emergent legend, where only later the Indian was named as Juan Diego, the archbishop was named as Zumárraga, and the year of the apparition became 1531. (*Unification and Conflict*, p. 204)

44. Edmundo O'Gorman, *Destierro de sombras: Luz en el origen de la imagen y culto de Nuestra Señora de Guadalupe del Tepeyac*, Mexico: UNAM, 1986, p. 86.
45. *Cartas de Indias*, Madrid: M.G. Hernández, 1877, p. 310.
46. O'Gorman, *Destierro de sombras*, pp. 83–91; de la Torre Villar and Navarro de Anda, eds., *Testimonios históricos guadalupanos*, pp. 36–141.
47. Lundberg, *Unification and Conflict*, p. 216.
48. Lundberg, *Unification and Conflict*, p. 217, citing the "Histoire méxicane depuis 1222 jusqu' en 1594" (Bibliothèque nationale de France). Miles Phillips, an English sailor held in Mexico from 1568 to 1582 also left the impression that it was "Spaniards" who were the main devotees at Tepeyac. Spaniards, he wrote, had built the church and "Whensoeuver any Spaniards passé by this church, although they be on hourse backe, they will alight, and come into the church, and kneele before the image, and pray to our Lady to defend them from all euil," in Richard Hakluyt, *The Principal Navigations, Voiages, Traffiques and Discoueries of the English Nation . . . {1598}*, London: J. M. Dent, 1907, VI, 314–315.
49. Lundberg, *Unification and Conflict*, p. 216.
50. Viceroy Martín Enríquez's letter of September 12, 1575, *Cartas de Indias*, p. 310.
51. Two letters about this matter by Fr. Diego de Santa María, dated December 12, 1574 and March 24, 1575, are in the Archivo de Indias, Audiencia de Mexico 69 and 283. I thank Kenneth Mills for sharing his transcriptions. In one of the letters Santa María writes that "concurre mucha gente" (many people go there). See also Poole, *Our Lady of Guadalupe*, pp. 71–73.

52. Poole describes Moya's support for more indulgences and concludes that he "had a special concern for the chapel at Guadalupe," *Our Lady of Guadalupe*, p. 76.
53. AHM num. de inventario 1066 exp. 68 1579. This version of the origin of the Remedios shrine was echoed in a 1616 poetic text by Ángel de Betancur, as Granados Salinas has shown, "Fervent Faith," pp. 184–185 and Appendix 3.
54. The early history of the Remedios image and shrine is discussed in Chapters 1 and 2 of Granados Salinas, "Fervent Faith." She suspects that this little figure of Mary was made in Spain as a representation of Our Lady of the Assumption and that the child in her arms was added by a Mexican maker around 1550 when the devotion was becoming popular.
55. *Información jurídica recibida en el año de 1582 con la que se acredita que la Imagen de María Santísima baxo la advocación de Conquistadora que se venera en su capilla del convento de Religiosos Observantes de San Francisco de la ciudad de la Puebla de los Ángeles es la misma que el conquistador Hernando Cortés endonó al gran capitán Gonzalo Alxotecatlcocomitzi, indio del pueblo de Atlihuetzian de la Feligresía de San Dionysio, en jurisdicción de Tlaxcalan* ..., Puebla: Oficina de D. Pedro de la Rosa, 1804.
56. The 1804 publication includes a 1666 *aprobación* by the audiencia judge Lic. Juan Manuel Sotomayor and a license to publish from Fr. Martin de Castillo.
57. Fallena Montaño, "La imagen de María," p. 121. The record of "informaciones sobre la virgen conquistadora del convento de Puebla" noted in the inventory of papers in the Franciscan convent archive of Tlaxcala may suggest the authenticity of the depositions as published in 1804, BN Fondo Franciscano, doc. 3907, fols. 29–51. Relying on secondary sources, Remensnyder offers a discussion of this image and devotion in early colonial context, *La Conquistadora*, pp. 311–316.
58. And in 1639 the city council of Puebla declared La Conquistadora to be the patroness of the city, Fallena Montaño, "La imagen de María," p. 111.
59. Among the standard sources for the tradition of Nuestra Señora de Guanajuato are Francisco de Florencia and Juan Antonio de Oviedo, *Zodíaco mariano* ..., Mexico: Colegio de San Ildefonso, 1755, pp. 282–286; *Rasgo breve de la grandeza guanajuateña* ..., Puebla: Impr. del Real Colegio de San Ignacio, 1767; and Manuel Rangel Camacho, *IV centenario de Nuestra Señora de Guanajuato*, Cuernavaca: Manuel Quesada Brandi, 1968.
60. José de Rivera Bernárdez, *Compendio de las cosas más notables contenidas en los libros del cabildo de esta ciudad de Nuestra Señora de los Zacatecas desde el año de su descubrimiento 1546 hasta 1730*, Mexico: Academia Mexicana de la Historia, 1945, p. 12.
61. Joaquín de Vayas, OSA, *Sermón panegyrico, que en la fiesta anual que acostumbra celebrar la muy ilustre, opulenta, y leal ciudad de Nuestra Señora de los Zacatecas, en memoria de su conquista a la natividad gloriosa de la Santíssima Virgen María Nuestra Señora* ..., Mexico: Impr. de F. de Rivera Calderón, 1721; Br. Joseph Mariano de Bezanilla y Mier, *Breve noticia histórica del Santuario de la Bufa de Zacatecas* ..., Mexico: Zúñiga y Ontiveros, 1797, p. 2.
62. Bezanilla, *Breve noticia*, p. 2. As Pbro. Miguel Flores Solís suggests, the earliest image of the Virgin Mary in Zacatecas is sometimes confused with Nuestra Señora del Patrocinio, with her shrine on the hill above the town, the Cerro de la Bufa. Both images were known at various times as Nuestra Señora de la Concepción, la Conquistadora, and Nuestra Señora de los Remedios, *Nuestra Señora de los Remedios*, Mexico: Edit. Jus, 1972, p. 23.
63. See also Amara Solari, *Maya Ideologies of the Sacred: The Transfiguration of Space in Colonial Yucatan*, Austin: University of Texas Press, 2013, pp. 149–150. Linda K. Williams,

"Modalities of Representation: Symbol and Narrative in 16th-Century Murals at the Convent of Izamal, Yucatán," *Colonial Latin American Review* 22: 1 (April 2013), 98–126 finds the late sixteenth-century murals in the passageway from the church to the cloister at Izamal to be in this spirit of evangelization, recognizing the ancient sacrality of Izamal, now reconsecrated through the presence of the Virgin Mary. It features a figure of Mary Immaculate and includes a struggle in which demons seem to be under attack while friars gather fruit from a large tree.

64. Bernardo de Lizana, *Devocionario de Nuestra Señora de Izamal, y conquista de Yucatán*, ed. René Acuña, Mexico: UNAM, 1995, pp. 85, 86, 89.

65. Lizana, *Devocionario*, p. 89 on images of Mary in Yucatán introduced by Spaniards, and the image of Izamal revered by Indians and Spaniards throughout the province.

66. Rodrigo Martínez Baracs acknowledges that evidence of a Marian cult image at Ocotlán was not recorded in written records for Tlaxcala before 1570, *La secuencia tlaxcalteca: Orígenes del culto a Nuestra Señora de Ocotlán*, Mexico: INAH, 2000, p. 53.

67. Fr. Agustín de Vetancurt, OFM, *Teatro mexicano. Descripción breve de los sucesos ejemplares históricos y religiosos del Nuevo Mundo de las Indias; Crónica de la Provincia del Santo Evangelio de México* [1698], Mexico: Porrúa, 1982, facsimile edition, part. 4 trat. 2 ("de los sucesos religiosos"), p. 41; Juan de Torquemada, OFM, *Monarquía Indiana*, Mexico: Porrúa, 1986, I, 303 (libro 3, cap. 26).

68. This cross is discussed in Chapter 8. Some early crucifixes and other figures of Christ became cult images by the late sixteenth century and are mentioned in the next section of this chapter on "the long seventeenth century." The Cristo de los Siete Velos in Mexico City has a rich legendary tradition connected to the founding of a confraternity and chapel of "los Caballeros de la Cruz" by Cortés and some of the earliest settlers of Mexico City in 1526. In one account, the crucifix associated with the confraternity and chapel was there when the confraternity was founded; in another, it was a gift from Charles V; and in a third, it was sent to the confraternity by Pope Paul III (1534–1549), along with a sliver of the True Cross and other relics, Higinio Vásquez Santa Ana, *Cristos célebres de México*, Mexico: n.p., 1950, entry #1; *Constituciones de la muy ilustre Archicofradía de ciudadanos de la Santa Veracruz ...*, Mexico: Impr. del ciudadano A. Valdés, 1824. However, this crucifix is made from corn pith paste and stalks, a precolonial Mesoamerican type of construction, Derek Burdette, "*Caritas* and the Christ of the Seven Veils: The Cult Statue as Confraternal Charity during Mexico City's Smallpox Outbreak of 1779," paper presented at the 2010 Congress of the Latin American Studies Association, Toronto, Canada, p. 5. It may well date from the sixteenth century, but probably not from the inception of the confraternity, and it was not imported from Europe. Its history as a cult object in the sixteenth century remains obscure.

Another crucifix that may have become a cult image by 1580 was the Señor de Nextongo of Azcapotzalco. According to Vásquez Santa Ana, a chapel at the site had a crucifix by the late 1560s, and by the 1590s it was taken in procession to nearby towns. Vásquez Santa Ana does not cite his sources for this early history or elaborate on the uses of the image before the 1590s, *Cristos célebres*, entry #18. Yet another crucifix, in the "chapel of relics" of the cathedral in Mexico City, was known as the Cristo de los Conquistadores, but whether this was a sixteenth-century devotion is not clear,

Vicente de Paula Andrade, *Mes histórico del la Preciosa Sangre*, Mexico: Tipografía de "Artes Gráficas", 1908, pp. 6–7.

69. In *Global Crisis: War, Climate Change and Catastrophe in the Seventeenth Century*, New Haven: Yale University Press, 2013, Geoffrey Parker posits that this "little ice age" (roughly from 1350 to 1850) brought a "general crisis" worldwide, with similar economic, social, and political disruption, but he is uncertain whether New Spain was swept up in the full effects of the climate change experienced in Europe and China. If Spain experienced greater, more prolonged social hardships at the time, he suggests it was because of the heavier tax burden on farmers and laborers there and the lower population density in New Spain, p. 49. Specific and cumulative effects of this "Little Ice Age" of cooling temperatures and more extreme weather are still far from clear, although there seems to be broad agreement that cooling occurred. For recent work on the problem of the Little Ice Age, including a contribution that questions whether there was, in fact, widespread cooling even in Eurasia, see Morgan Kelly and Cormac Ó Gráda, "The Waning of the Little Ice Age: Climate Change in Early Modern Europe," *Journal of Interdisciplinary History* 44: 3 (Winter 2014), 301–325, followed by commentary from Sam White, Ulf Büntgen, Lena Hellmann, and Jan de Vries, pp. 326–377.

70. The classic study for New Spain, from which later scholars have sometimes inferred a general economic depression during the seventeenth century is Woodrow Borah, *New Spain's Century of Depression*, Berkeley and Los Angeles: University of California Press, Ibero-Americana Series XXXV, 1951. Borah's study concentrates on the last third of the sixteenth century and the first third of the seventeenth century, and posits wide-ranging effects of declining numbers of Indian tribute payers and laborers. It is more a pioneering invitation to further research than a full study of colonial economic activity.

71. Enrique Tandeter, "The Mining Industry," in *The Cambridge Economic History of Latin America*, ed. Victor Bulmer-Thomas, John H. Coatsworth, and Roberto Cortés Conde, Cambridge, UK and New York: Cambridge University Press, 2006, I, 320.

72. Ida Altman, *Transatlantic Ties in the Spanish Empire: Brihuega, Spain and Puebla, Mexico, 1650–1620*, Stanford: Stanford University Press, 2000. Richard J. Salvucci suggests that Puebla's obrajes generally were in retreat during the seventeenth century, but that textile enterprises in and near Mexico City were growing, especially from 1640 to 1679, *Textiles and Capitalism in Mexico: An Economic History of the Obrajes, 1539–1840*, Princeton: Princeton University Press, 1987, p. 138.

Estimates of Spanish immigration to America during the colonial period are spotty, but Nicolás Sánchez-Albornoz's summary suggests that roughly 200,000 Spaniards came to America in the first half of the seventeenth century alone, compared to about 240,000 for the entire sixteenth century and fewer than 100,000 during the eighteenth century, *La población de América latina desde los tiempos precolombinos al año 2025*, 2nd ed., Madrid: Alianza Editorial, 1994, p. 77, and *The Population of Latin America: A History*, Berkeley: University of California Press, 1974, pp. 124–125, 137. John Elliott puts the emigration figure at about 450,000 in the seventeenth century, more than the number of emigrants for the sixteenth and eighteenth centuries combined, *Spain and Its World, 1500–1700: Selected Essays*, New Haven: Yale University Press, 1989, p. 11. These figures suggest that Spanish America became an unusually attractive destination for peninsular Spaniards in this time of putative depression. More of the fewer immigrants from Spain during the eighteenth century were people of rank and privilege – elite civil servants, merchants, high clergy, and military officers. See Mark A. Burkholder, *Spaniards in the Colonial Empire: Creoles vs. Peninsulars?*, Malden, MA: Wiley-Blackwell, 2012.

73. On Mexico City becoming a two-storey central city in the seventeenth century, see Francisco de la Maza, *La ciudad de México en el siglo XVII*, Mexico: Fondo de Cultura Económica, 1968.

74. See Ramón Serrera Contreras, *La América de los Habsburgos (1519–1700)*. Sevilla: Universidad de Sevilla, 2011, chapter 10, "Siglo de crisis o de autoidentidad en Indias"; Richard L. Garner and Spiro E. Stefanou, *Economic Growth and Change in Bourbon Mexico; Transferring Wealth and Power from the Old to the New World*, Gainesville: University Press of Florida, 1993; Pedro Pérez Herrero, "Regional Conformation in Mexico, 1700–1850: Models and Hypotheses," in *Mexico's Regions: Comparative History and Development*, ed. Eric Van Young, San Diego: UCSD Center for U.S.-Mexican Studies, 1992, pp. 118–144.

75. Nathan D. Mitchell, *The Mystery of the Rosary: Marian Devotion and the Reinvention of Catholicism*, New York and London: New York University Press, 2009, p. 2 and *passim*.

76. Mitchell, *Mystery of the Rosary*, pp. 29, 38, 41. Mitchell singles out Caravaggio's paintings and the 1582 treatise *Discorso intorno alle immagini sacre e profane* by Archbishop of Bologna Gabriele Paleotti as markers in this process of Catholic renewal and the development of Baroque art.

77. *Canons and Decrees of the Council of Trent*, pp. 215–217 (twenty-fifth session, December 1563).

78. As Jonathan Seitz put it in his study of Venice, "by the later sixteenth century, the establishment of new institutions such as the Society of Jesus and the Congregations of the Index and the Inquisition in the wake of the Council of Trent … show the leadership of the Catholic Church increasingly emphasizing correction over accommodation," *Witchcraft and Inquisition in Early Modern Venice*, Cambridge, UK and New York: Cambridge University Press, 2011, p. 4.

79. For Spain and moves to eliminate independent operators in the spiritual realm, see Andrew W. Keitt, *Inventing the Sacred: Imposture, Inquisition, and the Boundaries of the Supernatural in Golden Age Spain*, Leiden: Brill, 2005; for New Spain, Nora E. Jaffary, *False Mystics: Deviant Orthodoxy in Colonial Mexico*, Lincoln: University of Nebraska Press, 2004.

80. AGN Inquisición 455 exp. 23, fols. 243r–251r.

81. According to Manuel Romero de Terreros, Juan de Rúa was born in the province of Ávalos in western Mexico in 1565 (which is confirmed by Rúa's testimony in this Inquisition record that he was 47 in 1612), descended on his mother's side from the Tarascan king Caltzontzin. He was a student of Andrés de Concha and became a distinguished painter in his own right. He settled in Puebla and lived "for a time" in Antequera, producing painted altarpieces in and near both cities, including the altarpiece at Etla (Valley of Oaxaca) and paintings of the life of the Virgin at Cuauhtinchan (Puebla). He drew up a will in Puebla in 1637 and presumably died shortly thereafter, "El pintor Alonso López de Herrera," *Anales del Instituto de Investigaciones Estéticas* 34: (1965), 6.

82. AGN Inquisición 455, fol. 250r.

83. The treatment of race and ethnicity in this record deserves comment. Pedro García is not mentioned without being called a *mestiço*; Joan Pacheco, Lorenço de Aguilar and Miguel de Aguilar also are identified more than once by race and status as *mulatos libres*; and the Indian actors are left anonymous. Neither of the Zapotec Indian herders was called to testify, and no one could remember the name of the Indian carpenter living near the site of the special pine tree, even though he had an important part in the story – supplying the axe, helping Pedro García cut the image from the tree root, and trimming it to Lorenço de Aguilar's satisfaction.
84. AGN Inquisición 455, fol. 246v.
85. See, for example, Christian, *Local Religion*, chapter 6; Heal, *Cult of the Virgin Mary in Early Modern Germany*, p. 304; Philip Soergel, *Wondrous in His Saints: Counter-Reformation Propaganda in Bavaria*, Berkeley: University of California Press, 1993; Erik H. C. Erik Midelfort, *A History of Madness in Sixteenth-Century Germany*, Stanford: Stanford University Press, 1999; Jean Michel Sallmann, *Naples et ses saints à l'âge baroque, 1540–1750*, Paris: Presses Universitaires de France, 1994; Froeschlé-Chopard, "Espace et sacré"; and Jane Garnett and Gervase Rosser, *Spectacular Miracles: Transforming Images in Italy from the Renaissance to the Present*, London: Reaktion Books, 2013, pp. 16–17.
86. Christian, *Local Religion*, chapters 3, 6, *Apparitions*, chapter 3; Sallmann, *Naples et ses saints*, pp. 8, 137 (Mendicants in Italy were especially interested).
87. Seitz, *Witchcraft and Inquisition*, p. 6.
88. Sallmann, *Naples et ses saints*, p. 178.
89. In Narcís Camós's mid-seventeenth century compendium of 182 Marian shrines in Catalonia, 111 of the 137 for which he recorded an origin miracle were providential discoveries of the image. Only fourteen legendary beginnings involved apparitions of the Virgin Mary, Camós, *Jardín de María, plantado en el principado de Cataluña*, Barcelona: Joseph Bró, 1772, and Christian, *Apparitions*, pp. 14–16, 21.
90. William A. Christian, Jr., *Moving Crucifixes in Modern Spain*, Princeton: Princeton University Press, 1992, p. 6.
91. Michael J. Walsh, *Dictionary of Catholic Devotions*, New York: HarperCollins, 1993, p. 49. Brandea, could be "anything ... which might have gained virtue by its proximity to the body of the saint." In the Middle Ages brandea meant especially cloth or paper lowered into a saint's tomb, but it could also mean a piece of the tomb, or dust gathered at the site or candle stubs or faded flowers from the altar that had touched or been close to the relic.
92. Christian, *Local Religion*, p. 102: for St. Isidore of León in the Archdiocese of Sevilla, 1525; Our Lady of Montserrat, 1536; Our Lady of Peña de Francia, 1544; the Christ of Burgos, 1554; Our Lady of Guadalupe, 1575; Santiago de Compostela, 1575; the Niño de la Guardia, Toledo, 1583; and Our Lady of Puig, 1591.
93. On Gumppenberg's project as a Jesuit endeavor, see Olivier Christin, "La mundialización de María. Topografías sagradas y circulación de las imágenes," *Relaciones. Estudios de Historia y Sociedad* 139 (verano 2014), 305–333.
94. See Appendix 2. Of the 206 datable shrines, fewer than 22 (perhaps half this number) were established in the sixteenth century before the 1580s; 139 began between the 1580s and 1700; and 46 began between 1700 and 1820.
95. See Appendix 2. Three miraculous images gained fame in Toluca in the seventeenth century; two in Querétaro; three in Pátzcuaro; seven in Puebla; two in Antequera; one in Veracruz; two in Campeche; and four in Mérida and Valladolid, Yucatán.

88 Part I Bearings: Historical Patterns and Places of Image Shrines

96. See Appendix 2 for a list of forty-six local shrines in Mexico City that evidently began in the seventeenth century. Most of the examples of miraculous images transferred to Mexico City date from this long seventeenth century: the Christ of Totolapa, Cristo Renovado de Santa Teresa, Cruz de Mañozca from Tepeapulco, Hidalgo (which the archbishop may have regarded more as a curio than as a miraculous cross), Nuestra Señora de Xalmolonga, Nuestra Señora de la Bala, Nuestra Señora de la Macana, and the Señor de la Cuevita (removed to Ixtapalapa from Etla Oaxaca). The Virgin of La Macana and the Señor de la Cuevita may have reached Mexico City later.
97. Francisco de Ajofrín, *Diario del viaje que hizo a la América en el siglo XVIII el P. Fray Francisco de Ajofrín*, 2 vols., Mexico: Instituto Cultural Hispano Mexicano, 1964, I, 120. For a detailed account of images deployed for protection in Mexico City during the 1737 epidemic, see Cayetano Cabrera y Quintero, *Escudo de armas de Mexico: Celestial protección de esta nobilíssima ciudad, de la Nueva España, y de casi todo el Nuevo Mundo . . .*, Mexico: Vda. de Joseph Bernardo de Hogal, 1746.
98. Grijalva, *Crónica*, p. 162.
99. Lizana, *Devocionario*, p. 57.
100. Florencia and Oviedo, *Zodíaco mariano*, pp. 6–11.
101. This shift in the Franciscans' interest in image shrines coincided with their more prominent role in administering sacred sites and hospitality for pilgrims, most famously at the Holy Land sites in and near Jerusalem, Annabel Jane Wharton, *Selling Jerusalem: Relics, Replicas, Theme Parks*, Chicago: University of Chicago Press, 2006, chapter 3, especially p. 109.

    Not all the orders in public service participated wholeheartedly in the growing popularity of sacred images. For example, a dispute over images developed in the 1620s among members of the hospitallers of San Hipólito in Mexico City. In 1626, Fr. Pedro López, leader of the community, ordered his fellow brothers not to keep more than one poor image and no devotional books about saints and images. Another brother, Fr. Pedro de Vera, appealed to the Inquisition to order López to grant licenses permitting other brothers to have the images and devotional books they wanted, including Cristos and crosses, AGN Inquisición 356 exp. 130, no verdict.
102. Antonio Rubial García, et al., *La iglesia en el México colonial*, Mexico: UNAM, 2013, pp. 358–367.
103. The founding of a confraternity for the shrine of Santo Domingo Soriano in the Indian headtown of Villa Alta, Oaxaca around 1640 is documented in AGN Clero Regular y Secular 188 exp. 12. In this case, the first benefactor was the district alcalde mayor.
104. Rubial García, et al., *La iglesia en el México colonial*, p. 369.
105. See Chapters 3 and 4 for more on representations of the Virgin Mary. For La Conquistadora of New Mexico, Remensnyder, *La Conquistadora*, chapter 10. For Nuestra Señora del Zape and Charlotte M. Gradie, *The Tepehuan Revolt of 1616: Militarism, Evangelism, and Colonialism in Seventeenth Century Nueva Vizcaya*, Salt Lake City: University of Utah Press, 2005, and Andrés Pérez de Ribas, *History of the Triumphs of Our Holy Faith Amongst the Most Barbarous and Fierce Peoples of the New World* [1645], ed. Daniel T. Reff, trans. Daniel T. Reff, Maureen Ahern, and Richard K. Danford, Tucson: University of Arizona Press, 1999, pp. 631–635. Native rebels took the image, shot it with arrows, hung it by the neck in church, cut off its head and hands, and threw it in a well, Florencia and Oviedo, *Zodíaco*

mariano, pp. 321–325. The captain ordered a new image and it turned out to be a beautiful one. The rebellion soon ended, Indians became devotees, and by 1755 the site was an important shrine for Nueva Vizcaya. For Nuestra Señora de la Macana during and after the Pueblo Revolt of 1680, see Felipe Montalvo, OFM, *Novena de la Puríssima Madre de Dios ... Nuestra Señora de la Macana ...*, Mexico: Herederos de Da. María de Rivera, 1755, and Ilona Katzew, "The Virgin of the Macana: Emblem of a Franciscan Predicament in New Spain," *Colonial Latin America Review* 12: 2 (2003), 172, quoting Agustín de Vetancurt on a paralyzed daughter of the captain governor of New Mexico in 1674 who "entrusted herself" to an image of Our Lady of the Sacristy of Toledo, was suddenly cured, and claimed the Virgin told her to tell people "that this province will soon be destroyed for the lack of reverence that it shows my priests ... that they mend their ways, should they not want to experience punishment." In Montalvo's telling, during the 1680 rebellion a native chief struck this image on the head with a *macana* – an obsidian-studded club – but inflicted little damage. "However, lest this execrable misdeed go unpunished, the devil himself became his executioner by hanging him from a tree on that miserable battlefield." The image was moved to the Franciscan convent of Tlalnepantla before 1745 and eventually to the order's Convento Grande in Mexico City.

106. Points made in this paragraph are developed further in Chapters 7 and 8. Also for the mystique of activated images, Tello, *Crónica miscelánea*, libro III, cap. 241 described the "cruz de Sayula" at a crossroads in town that was seen by many to shake on May 3, 1632 (the Day of the Invention of the Cross), and Antonio de Robles, *Diario de sucesos notables (1665–1703)*, Mexico: Porrúa, 1946, I, 284 mentioned a print of Christ washing the feet of St. Augustine that perspired on June 15, 1680, in the novitiates' chapel of the Augustinian convent in Mexico City.
107. Negotiations over Franciscans as administrators of the shrine are mentioned in AHM *actas de cabildo* for January 3, 1589; also Jesús García Gutiérrez, *Datos históricos sobre la venerable imagen de Nuestra Señora de los Remedios de México*, 2nd ed., Mixcoac: Edición Ant-Val, 1940, p. 19.
108. Agustín Dávila Padilla, *Historia de la fundación y discurso de la Provincia de Santiago de México de la Orden de Predicadores ...*, 2nd ed., Brussels: Juan de Meerbeque, 1625, pp. 627–628.
109. ACAM, minutes of the cathedral chapter meetings, August 29, 1600, and February 16, 1601.
110. ACAM, minutes of the cathedral chapter meetings, January 16, 1607, February 28, 1608, and October 26, 1612.
111. Crafted by silversmith Luis de Vargas, this "imagen de oro de Nuestra Señora" is the subject of the cathedral chapter minutes in ACAM for February 5, 1610, February 12, 1610, July 10, 1610, August 12, 1610, August 31, 1610, and October 16, 1612. It was not the cathedral's only statue of the Virgin Mary made of precious metals. An image known as Nuestra Señora de la Plata was commissioned from two Indian silversmiths in 1610, AGN General de Parte 5 exp. 839, fol. 177v.
112. The 1606 painted copy of the Guadalupe image depicts the cloth as well as the image.
113. For the prestige gained by images and shrines associated with celebrated hermits, see Francisco Losa, *Vida del siervo de Dios Gregorio López*, Madrid: Juan de Aritzia,

1727, p. 73, and Fallena Montaño, "La imagen de María," p. 106 for Sebastián de Aparicio and La Conquistadora, and p. 244 for Juan Bautista and Nuestra Señora de la Defensa of Puebla. Antonio Rubial García has written key works on hermits in the spiritual landscape, including shrines: *Profetisas y solitarios. Espacios y mensajes de una religión dirigida por ermitaños y beatas laicos en las ciudades de Nueva España*, Mexico: UNAM/Fondo de Cultura Económica, 2006, and "Imágenes y ermitaños: Un ciclo hierofánico ignorado por la historiografía," *Anuario de Estudios Americanos* 66: 2 (2009), 213–239.

The información jurídica concerning La Conquistadora that allegedly dated from 1582 (but may well be a Franciscan confection some years later) and represented the little statue as a gift from Cortés to a Tlaxcalan lord who remained a loyal ally during the Spanish Conquest also seems to have attracted Tlaxcalan devotion to the image once it was transferred to the Franciscan convent church in Puebla.

114. The development of shrines in various parts of the viceroyalty between the 1620s and 1670s merits closer study. In western Mexico, for example, the 1606–1616 *relaciones* of *visitas de oidores* did not mention shrines or miraculous images, *Sociedades en construcción: La Nueva Galicia según las visitas de oidores, 1606–1616*, ed. Jean-Pierre Berthe, Thomas Calvo, and Águeda Jiménez Pelayo, Mexico: Universidad de Guadalajara, 2000; but Antonio Tello, OFM's chronicle for the order's province of Xalisco completed in the 1640s and cited elsewhere in this book mentions various images and shrines.
115. Weckmann, *Medieval Heritage*, p. 293.
116. Francisco Cárdenas Valencia, *Relación historial eclesiástica de la Provincia de Yucatán de la Nueva España, escrita el año de 1639*, Mexico: Porrúa, 1937, pp. 90–91.
117. AGN Bienes Nacionales 420 exp. 19 bis.
118. Francisco de Burgoa, *Geográfica descripción de la parte septentrional del Polo Ártico de la América {1674}*, Oaxaca: Instituto Oaxaqueño de las Culturas, 1997, fol. 248v. Burgoa also described a miracle in which a consecrated host had kept a chapel of the Dominican convent in Antequera from collapsing until it could be removed (fol. 138). On the other hand, his chapter on the doctrina of Xuquila (fols. 299v–303r), the site of a famous image of the Virgin Mary and shrine in the eighteenth century, does not mention them at all.
119. On the growing number of cofradías in the seventeenth century, María Dolores Palomo Infante, "Antécédents historiques des organisations: les confrères indigènes au Chiapas," *Anthropologica* 44 (2002), 237–246, and Margarita Loera, "Una historia de larga duración en el valle de Toluca. La lucha por el origen étnico, la territorialidad y la autonomía política en Calimaya y sus pueblos sujetos," *Historias* 63 (enero–abril 2007), 37–60.
120. Juan de Palafox y Mendoza, *Relación de la visita eclesiástica del obispo de Puebla (1643–1646)*, ed. Bernardo García Mártinez, Puebla: Secretaría de Cultura, Gobierno del Estado, 1997, p. 75.
121. Magnus Lundberg, "Relación de la visita pastoral del arzobispado de México de Juan de Mañozca y Zamora, 1646," *Historia Mexicana* 58: 2 (2008), 879, 884.
122. Lundberg, "Relación de la visita pastoral," p. 884.
123. Cathedral archive, minutes of cathedral chapter meetings on July 14, 1737; July 15, 1737; October 9, 1737; April 30, 1738; April 17, 1740; and March 12, 1741.

124. Burgoa, *Geográfica descripción*, fol. 248v.
125. The beginnings of the shrine at Tulantongo are documented from the Franciscans' perspective in 1656 in AGN Indios 20 exp. 200, fols. 151–153. For Archbishop Aguiar y Seixas's pastoral visit to Tulantongo, Archivo Histórico del Arzobispado de México, filed with other pastoral visit records, fols. 39–40, November 17, 1683. Vetancurt mentions the dedication of the new church in 1676, the Franciscan pastor in residence, and popularity of the shrine in the 1690s in *Teatro mexicano*, p. 134, para. 87. For the shrine's origin story as told in the mid-eighteenth century, *Relaciones geográficas del Arzobispado de México. 1743*, ed. Francisco de Solano, Madrid: C.S.I.C., 1988, II, 460–461, and José Antonio de Villaseñor y Sánchez, *Theatro Americano: Descripción general de los reynos y provincias de la Nueva España, y sus jurisdicciones ...*, México: Vda. de J.B. de Hogal, 1746, I, chapter 34, 156–157.
126. The *comisario general* was Fray Juan de Luzuriaga, himself the author of a devotional history for an image shrine – the first of its kind for the miraculous statue and shrine of Nuestra Señora de Aranzazú, in his Basque homeland, published in Mexico in 1686, then in Spain at Madrid and Donostia (San Sebastián) in 1690. Several times Luzuriaga's narrative treats 1676 and 1683 as the present.
127. Cristina Cruz González, "Mexican Instauration: Devotion and Transformation in New Spain," *Religion and the Arts* 18 (2014), 87–113.
128. Mendoza says it was more than forty years before he composed his chronicle, and one witness in 1676 said the first new providential signs occurred thirty-four years earlier, *Relación de el santuario de Tecaxique, en que está colocada la milagrosa Imagen de Nuestra Señora de los Ángeles ...*, Mexico: J. de Ribera, 1684, fols. 1v, 11v. The cathedral chapter in Mexico apparently did not have news of a miraculous image at Tecaxic ("Tajxique") until late 1650, judging by the cathedral chapter minutes for December 22, 1650, "la qual pretendían los religiosos de San Diego y oy la poseían los de la observancia de San Francisco." The cathedral chapter proceeded to order an investigation of "el descubrimiento desta Santa Ymagen y milagros que obraba."
129. The 1683–1685 portion of Aguiar y Seixas's pastoral visits is in AHM. He visited Tecaxic on April 10, 1685. Vetancurt in 1696 noted many visitors to the shrine, but reported that only a few more than twenty people resided at the site, *Teatro mexicano*, 2nd num., p. 89. The "Otomí" refer to themselves as *Hñähñú, Hñähño, Hñotho, Hñähü, Hñätho, Yųhų, Yųhmų, Ñųhų, Ñotho,* or *Ñañhų* depending on which dialect of the language they speak.
130. Louise Burkhart, *Before Guadalupe: The Virgin Mary in Early Colonial Nahuatl Literature*, Albany: Institute for Mesoamerican Studies, University at Albany, 2001, p. 129, summarizes the view of Serge Gruzinski in "Indian Confraternities, Brotherhoods, and Mayordomías in Central New Spain. A List of Questions for the Historian and the Anthropologist," in *The Indian Community of Colonial Mexico*, ed. Arij Ouweneel and Simon Miller, Amsterdam: Centre for Latin American Research and Documentation, 1990, p. 209.

Vetancurt says that two Franciscans were assigned to Tecaxic "porque con las limosnas de los bienhechores de aquel Valle, se hizieron celdas y casas de novenas, y se continúa la fábrica de su Templo, a cuenta de distintas Provincias agradecidos a sus beneficios; los Naturales la celebran con danzas que vienen en quadrillas ofreciendo de sus sementeras ...," *Teatro mexicano*, 2nd num., p. 134.

131. Cristina Cruz González comes to a similar conclusion by a different route, comparing the story of Tecaxic's famously well preserved painting of the Virgin of the Assumption to a similar story for the shrine image of Nuestra Señora de los Ángeles at Tlatelolco. She concludes that "(in)corruptibility had a double effect: it delineated [the] divine and sanctioned official intervention," "Mexican Instauration," p. 109.

132. These early account records are found in BN Archivo Franciscano MS 1107, "Hermita de Nuesta Señora de los Ángeles. Libro de memorias inventariales." The 1653 inventory of "ornamentos y demás cosas del culto divino" on the first leaf of this manuscript shows that the shrine was already well stocked with fine garments and silver utensils for the Mass.

133. For the 1696 *visita de archivos* that lists endowments and gifts at Tecaxic, see BN Archivo Franciscano doc. 1394.

134. For the 1723 list of *obras pías*, BN Archivo Franciscano doc. 1394 fol. 53. Another inventory of 1725 also listed a substantial little library of religious literature, totaling 123 volumes, BN Archivo Franciscano doc. 1499. The dedication of the "beautiful" new shrine church, measuring 60 varas long and 12 varas wide, on October 7, 1731 is mentioned in the *Gazeta de México* for December 1731, published in Nicolás León, *Bibliografía mexicana del siglo XVIII (Boletín del Instituto Bibliográfico Mexicano,* num. 4), Mexico: J.I. Guerrero y Cía, 1903 [Hereafter BIBM 4], p. 294. According to the reporter, it took four years and five months to construct.

135. Relaciones geográficas del Arzobispado de México. 1743, II, 504; obras pías and lands in 1757 are listed in BN Archivo Franciscano, doc. 1389.

136. BN Archivo Franciscano, doc. 1499 (1773).

137. An example of an early seventeenth-century papal indulgence granted for the Santo Cristo in the Augustinian church of Puebla "and all crucifixes and crosses that may touch it" is reprinted in Ajofrín, *Diario* [1964 ed.], I, 15–16.

138. AGN General de Parte 17 exps. 34, 35.

139. How origin stories and iconic miracles became standardized is rarely traceable since the process depended on endless repetition and circulation more than official action. But the printed text, officially sanctioned, could be decisive. In effect, the printed word was the loudest voice, with near-scriptural authority especially when it came with official approval. It had permanence as a source of exact repetition and a check against variation. In a rare early-nineteenth-century reference, the Carmelite nuns of Mexico City clearly understood this authority of the printed text when they gave copies of Velasco's devotional history of the Cristo Renovado de Santa Teresa to priests who were to preach sermons during the annual celebrations for this miraculous Cristo so they would get the story right, Bancroft XF1232 B975 untitled tract "1a" by Carlos María Bustamante, dated December 7, 1831. Bustamante referred to "la relación del prodigio que impresa circulan las monjas anualmente a los predicadores para que se arreglen a ella en la función anual."

140. The *Zodíaco mariano* was revised and edited by the distinguished early-eighteenth-century Jesuit, Juan Antonio de Oviedo and published in 1755. José Mariano Beristáin de Souza (1756–1817), listed a manuscript history of the Cristo Renovado de Santa Teresa by Florencia in the collections of the Universidad de México, *Biblioteca Hispano Americana Septentrional, o catálogo y noticias de los literatos . . ., 1521–1825* [1st ed., 3 vols., 1816–1821], 3rd ed., Mexico: Ediciones Fuente Cultural, 1947, II, 274.

Formative Developments, 1520s–1720s 93

141. Clara Bargellini, "Painting for Export in Mexico City in the Seventeenth and Eighteenth Centuries," in *Art in Spain and the Hispanic World: Essays in Honor of Jonathan Brown*, ed. Sarah Schroth, London: Paul Holberton, 2010, pp. 284–303.
142. Mateo de la Cruz's *Relación de la milagrosa aparición de la santa imagen de la Virgin de Guadalupe de México, sacada de la historia que compuso el Br. Miguel Sánchez por el P. Mateo de la Cruz* is more than a mere digest of Sánchez's book. The text is included in *Testimonos históricos guadalupanos*, ed. Ernesto de la Torre Villar and Ramiro Navarro de Anda, Mexico: Fondo de Cultura Económica, 2005, pp. 267–281.
143. Jesuits were Marianists, but their interest in devotional images always was wider, including images of Christ (and the cult of the sacred heart of Jesus) and saints (especially Ignatius of Loyola and other Jesuit saints). Some Jesuits, even some engaged in pastoral duties in frontier missions, did not mention images at all in their letters and chronicles; e.g. Johann Jakob Baegert, *Observations in Lower California*, Berkeley: University of California Press, 1952. And they were especially famous devotees and promoters of relics. See Chapter 6 below and Jeffrey Chipps Smith, "Salvaging Saints: The Rescue and Display of Relics in Munich During the Early Catholic Reformation," in *Art, Piety, and Destruction in the Christian West, 1500–1700*, ed. Virginia Chieffo Raguin, Burlington, VT: Ashgate, 2010, pp. 23–43.
144. With the support of the Museo Nacional de Arte, the Consejo Nacional para la Cultura y las Artes, the Instituto Nacional de Bellas Artes, Banamex, and the Universidad Nacional Autónoma de México, Jaime Cuadriello and his colleagues brought this subject to light in the landmark series of exhibitions of historical paintings called "Los Pinceles de la Historia," mounted in Mexico City beginning in 1999. The catalogues and essays published for these exhibitions are significant scholarly contributions in their own right. For the long seventeenth century, see especially Cuadriello's "El origen del reino y la configuración de su empresa: Episodios y alegorías de triunfo y fundación" and "Tierra de prodigios: La ventura como destino," in *Los pinceles de la historia: El origen del Reino de la Nueva España, 1680–1750*, Mexico: Museo Nacional de Arte, 1999, pp. 50–107, 180–227. This volume reproduces twenty-six paintings for eleven miraculous images. Of those that can be dated with some confidence, at least twelve of them for the images of the Cross of Huatulco, Nuestra Señora de Ocotlán, San Miguel del Milagro, and Nuestra Señora de los Remedios date from this last phase of the long seventeenth century, 1680s–1720s (as may the historical paintings for Querétaro's stone cross and Zacatecas's Nuestra Señora de los Zacatecas).
145. See Chapters 5 and 6.
146. Ajofrín, *Diario* [1964 ed.], I, 120.
147. Domingo de Quiroga, *Pequeño ramillete: Breve compendio histórico místico moral de la milagrosíssima renovación de la imagen de N.S. Jesuchristo* ..., Mexico: Herederos de la Viuda de Miguel de Rivera, 1724.
148. Antonio Manuel de Folgar, *La mayor fortuna de la América* ..., Mexico: Francisco de Rivera Calderón, 1731. Dr. Folgar would later become a canon in collegiate church of Our Lady of Guadalupe at Tepeyac.
149. Alonso Alberto de Velasco, *Exaltación de la divina misericordia en la milagrosa renovación de la soberana imagen de Christo Señor crucificado* ..., Mexico: Herederos de Joseph de Jáuregui, 1790, p. 1.

150. A native Spaniard, probably born in the late 1550s, Torquemada went to New Spain as a child and studied Nahuatl and theology in the Franciscan convent in Mexico City. He was ordained in 1579, moved to the convent of Santiago Tlatelolco several years later, and became *guardián* (warden) there in 1600. Later he served as *guardián* at Zacatlán (Puebla) and Tlaxcala. He became chronicler of his Franciscan province in 1610, served as provincial of the order in New Spain from 1614 to 1617, and died in 1624.
151. For Remedios, Torquemada, *Monarquía Indiana*, libro IV, cap. lxxii, p. 370; for La Conquistadora, Juan de Torquemada, *Vida y milagros del sancto confessor de Christo F. Sebastián de Aparicio ...*, Mexico: Imprenta de Diego López Dávalos, 1602, p. 128.
152. Torquemada, *Monarquia Indiana*, 2nd num., p. 45.
153. Vetancurt, *Teatro mexicano*, 2nd num., p. 83.
154. Vetancurt, *Teatro mexicano*, 2nd num., especially pp. 127–135, but also pp. 41, 69, 83, 109–111. Vetancurt's approach to cataloguing cult images and shrines was different from Francisco de Florencia's more ambitious project to survey the most important Marian shrines in New Spain. As a Jesuit, Florencia (and Juan Antonio de Oviedo, who completed the project sixty years later) featured images associated with his order, but these are in addition to many others he learned about. Except for Our Lady of Remedios and Our Lady of Guadalupe, Vetancurt limited his coverage to miraculous images and shrines associated with the Franciscans in Mexico City and the Province of the Holy Gospel and, unlike Florencia and Oviedo, he includes some miraculous images of Christ.

    Two Augustinian chronicles for the province of San Nicolás de Tolentino de Michoacán, completed a century apart in 1644 and the 1740s, also are different in their treatment of image shrines. Diego Basalenque's *Historia de la Provincia de San Nicolás de Tolentino de Michoacán del Orden de N.P.S. Agustín* [1644], ed. José Bravo Ugarte, Mexico: Editorial Jus, 1963 recounts a number of miracles associated with exemplary friars of the province, but mentions only one miraculous image, Jacona's cross found in a guava tree. Mathías de Escobar, OSA's *América thebaida ...* [ca. 1748], Morelia: Balsal Editores, 1970, which he began to write in 1729, attends to exemplary friars, but also presents eleven miraculous images in the vicinity of Lake Chapala: ten crucifixes and one statuette of the Virgin Mary. Both authors served as pastors of rural *doctrinas* in Michoacán, so the difference in their coverage of miraculous images would seem to have little to do with an urban versus a rural perspective.
155. As Félix Báez Jorge puts it, "una de las grandes preocupaciones de virreyes, arzobispos e inquisidores de la Nueva Espana fue el renacimiento – fresh outbreaks – de la idolatría," *La parentela de María: Cultos marianos, sincretismo e identidades nacionales en Latinoamérica*, Xalapa: Universidad Veracruzana, 1994, pp. 42–43.

    On the prominence of Satan and demons in colonial religiosity, see, for example, Kenneth Mills, "Demonios within and without: Hieronymites and the Devil in the Early Modern Hispanic World," in *Angels, Demons, and the New World*, ed. Fernando Cervantes and Andrew Redden, Cambridge, UK and New York: Cambridge University Press, 2013, pp. 40–68.

2

Growth, Other Changes, and Continuities in the Late Colonial Period

It would not be surprising to find that image shrines in New Spain declined during the eighteenth century, as they did in much of Catholic Europe, diminished by Enlightenment skepticism and individualism, government intervention to maximize tax revenue, minimize administrative costs, promote devotional sobriety and private soul searching, and a campaign to moderate costly and provocative public exuberance.[1] In a way this would seem to have happened. Fewer new shrines and confraternities were established in the eighteenth century than during the long seventeenth century; some reputedly miraculous images and incipient shrines were suppressed; restrictions on alms collecting for local devotions of all kinds, including shrine images, were put forward by the 1790s; and priests who spoke of miracles increasingly felt obliged to assure authorities that they were not naïve seekers of supernatural signs.[2] But decline, disenchantment, and rise of the spiritually "buffered self" pale in comparison to the many signs of vitality, official encouragement, mounting wealth, and popularity of image shrines, or the frequent news of miracles in the late colonial period.[3]

The impact of Spain and Europe on the history of image shrines in America was felt directly but not uniformly during the eighteenth century, and not always in expected ways. Confessional crusades that pitted Protestants against Catholics had declined by 1700, replaced by the challenges of a growing conviction among educated classes that the universe was governed by natural laws more than by the omnipresent hand and will of God. But Spanish Bourbon administrators endorsed a paler version of the continental Enlightenment that did not question the existence of God as creator and mover of the universe or tolerate unfettered critical thinking. Their reforms were more instrumental, designed to apply secular, scientific procedures to policy and administration in order to strengthen the monarchy, spur material progress, maximize revenues, and burnish a mystique of absolutist order and royal benevolence without banishing the divine from human affairs. Catholicism remained the official religion of the Spanish kingdoms, although ecclesiastical authority was challenged in various ways.[4] Royal administrators and regalist bishops were inclined to try to limit the priesthood to spiritual matters narrowly defined and to favor a less showy, more restrained public piety.[5] Compared to the seventeenth century, there was less talk of "the two majesties" – the paternal monarchy and the maternal "madre iglesia" as co-sovereigns – and less scope for pastors to manage the social and cultural lives of parishioners.

By mid-century, the appointment of regalist, reform-minded bishops contributed to mixed messages about sacred images, fewer new confraternities to support devotion to them, more rules, closer surveillance of irreverent or otherwise improper public celebrations, and better record keeping.[6] But if reform affected the prosperity and popularity of image shrines, this was more evident in Europe than in New Spain.[7] And even in Europe the signs of disenchantment seem to have been clearer, if still incomplete, in France, Germany, the Low Countries, and England than they were in Spain, Italy, and Portugal. Even though news of images coming to life was recorded less often in Europe after the 1710s, and diocesan priests expressed more skepticism about miracles and the efficacy of images,[8] official moves against popular devotion to shrine images were less systematic than the occasional sweeping decrees against superstition may suggest.[9] In Spain, as in New Spain, bishops continued to grant indulgences for donations to shrines and devotions before images, and they enabled a boomlet in publication of devotional booklets and inexpensive prints depicting miraculous images.[10] If the eighty-five Marian shrines and miracles associated with them in Spain described in Juan de Villafañe, SJ's thick 1726/1740 compendium are an indication, image shrines continued to prosper there.[11] Even so, a growing rift between a more restrained religiosity, coupled with more conspicuous skepticism of public officials and polite society on one hand, and popular traditions of faith on the other runs deeper in the European record after the 1740s than in New Spain. Most of New Spain's image shrines may have lost the wholehearted support they enjoyed in the seventeenth century from prelates like Juan de Palafox y Mendoza and Francisco de Aguiar y Seixas, but late-eighteenth-century bishops did not target the cult of images except indirectly, by calling for decorous sacred images in rural churches and chapels and imposing some restrictions on processions with images and collection of alms beyond the vicinity of a shrine. In some measure, the continuing appeal of shrines and several new Marian advocations depended on greater "laicization" of devotions that had once been the special projects of religious orders (especially the Jesuits and Franciscans who had promoted Our Lady of Loreto, Our Lady of La Luz, and Our Lady of Refugio) in much the same way that Marian congregations founded by Jesuits in France and Belgium were more popular than ever after the Jesuit order was suppressed in 1773.[12]

In the later eighteenth century, Spain was drawn into recurring European wars with American theaters: the War of Austrian Succession and Jenkins's Ear (1739–1746), the Seven Years' War (1756–1763), and ongoing struggles with Britain and France after 1789, which resulted not only in French occupation of Portugal and then Spain from 1807 to 1814 but also in more piracy and interdiction of Spain's transatlantic trade. The immediate result was increasing costs to the royal treasury, debts, and pressure on the Bourbon administration to raise taxes and generate other revenue in the American colonies.[13] Shrines were affected to some extent by the reforms meant to channel more church wealth into the royal treasury and reduce expenditures on religious rituals, but the aggressive taxing policies of the Spanish Bourbons had a greater impact on trade, mining, rural estates, and chaplaincies (especially with the "consolidación de vales" conversion of many chaplaincy endowments after 1805). For image shrines, a more striking effect of the eighteenth-century wars in Europe was more interest in the Blessed Mary as warrior-protectress. In Mexico City, the Virgin of Guadalupe, the Virgin of Remedios, and regional peninsular advocations, such as Our Lady of Covadonga sponsored by wealthy immigrant merchants and military officers, came to new prominence and were frequently invoked in this way after the 1740s.[14]

Consolidation and Expansion in the Eighteenth Century

More than restrictions and disenchantment, the later eighteenth century was a time of consolidation and expansion for many shrines. If the eighteenth century can be regarded as a new information age, the information disseminated amounted to more than records of surveillance and administration commissioned by the royal government. Many new publications were in circulation, produced by print shops in Mexico City and several provincial cities as well as imported from Europe. In Mexico City, the number of religious publications rose steadily after the late seventeenth century: on average 13 publications annually for 1601–1684, 36 for 1685–1717, and 45 for 1745–1767. Even more such publications were issued in the capital thereafter: 120 a year for 1768–1794 and 133 a year for 1795–1812.[15] Devotional books, pamphlets, novena booklets, and broadsides were prominent among them, as well as hundreds of thousands, if not millions, of printed depictions of images of saints, advocations of Mary and Christ, and miraculous images that circulated throughout New Spain.

Few of the shrines that began during the long seventeenth century fell out of favor. Even the occasional origin stories of renewal in which forgotten shrines regained their fame and following when the sacred images they sheltered came to life or began to work wonders for devotees attest to image shrines being on the rise in the eighteenth century.[16] While most image shrines remained local, many developed a financial base and institutions – especially during the 1730s and 1760s – that contributed to their longevity. For example, administrators of Tepalcingo's wonder-working Christ could draw upon alms gathered at the shrine and in collection tours, a well-funded *cofradía*, and endowments that covered much of the cost of a fine new shrine church built between 1759 and 1782 to accommodate "the multitude of people who gather there especially on the third Friday of Lent to venerate the aforesaid sacred image."[17] The variety and number of objects in the inventories of the later eighteenth century attest to the shrines' importance in the cultural landscape, among them, new churches, paintings, statues, paraphernalia of religious ritual, and *casas de novenarios* (lodgings for devotees who visited during novena observances) at the shrine sites; fine painted, sculpted, and engraved copies of celebrated matrix images; altars and chapels dedicated to them elsewhere; devotional literature, brandea, *milagritos*, and more ex-voto paintings of thanksgiving for personal and collective favors. Beginning in the 1740s, reports and surveys commissioned by the crown generated more systematic information about shrines: the 1743 *relaciones geográficas* submitted by district governors in central Mexico, as well as Antonio Villaseñor y Sánchez's wide-ranging survey, *Theatro Americano: Descripción general de los reynos, y provincias de la Nueva-España ...* published in 1746, which contained an extensive, if idiosyncratic inventory of image shrines. Nine years later, the more comprehensive survey of Marian shrines in New Spain that had been started in the late seventeenth century by Francisco de Florencia was completed by his fellow Jesuit Juan Antonio de Oviedo and published as the *Zodíaco Mariano*.

Another sign of consolidation and growth in the late colonial period was how many shrines gained a wider regional following. Devotion to Our Lady of Guadalupe and her shrine at Tepeyac grew dramatically between 1709 and the 1760s, but at least twenty-three other image shrines attracted or retained regional followings during the late eighteenth century, especially in the center, west, and south: Nuestra Señora de San Juan de los Lagos (Jalisco); Nuestra Señora de Zapopan (Jalisco); Nuestra Señora de Talpa (Jalisco); the Green Cross of Tepic (Nayarit), Nuestra Señora de la Salud (Pátzcuaro, Michoacán); Nuestra Señora del Socorro (Morelia, Michoacán); the stone cross of Querétaro; Nuestra Señora del Pueblito (Querétaro); the Señor de Chalma (Edo. de México); Nuestra Señora de Tecaxic (Edo. de México); Nuestra Señora de los Remedios (Naucalpan, Valley of Mexico); the Cristo del Sacromonte (Amecameca, Estado de México); Jesús Nazareno of Tepalcingo (Morelos); San Miguel del Milagro (Tlaxcala); Nuestra Señora de Ocotlán (Tlaxcala); La Conquistadora and Nuestra Señora de la Defensa (Puebla); the Señor de Otatitlán (Veracruz); Nuestra Señora de Xuquila (Oaxaca); Nuestra Señora de la Soledad (Oaxaca); Nuestra Señora de Izamal (Yucatán); the Señor de Esquipulas (Guatemala); and the shrine of Nuestra Señora de Guadalupe in San Luis

Potosí. Especially striking is the growth of several of these shrines in the center and west from little-known local centers in the late seventeenth century into regional shrines with fine new churches, sodalities, endowed Masses, and ambitious promotional programs by the 1750s. They include the shrines of the Christ of Tepalcingo (Morelos), Our Lady of Talpa (Jalisco), the Green Cross of Tepic (Nayarit), Our Lady of La Salud (Pátzcuaro, Michoacán), and the Christ of the Sacromonte at Amecameca (Estado de México). The eighteenth century also produced an unusual kind of shrine and spiritual retreat – a virtual theme park of piety – at the Santuario de Jesús Nazareno of Atotonilco, north of San Miguel de Allende, Guanajuato (see Chapter 3).

The shrine of Our Lady of San Juan de los Lagos in the Altos region of eastern Jalisco is better documented than most, and it stands out as unusually popular in the later eighteenth century, along with the shrines of the Virgin of Guadalupe, the Lord of Chalma, and the Lord of Esquipulas. Staffed by diocesan chaplains, the Lagos shrine was prominent in the late seventeenth century; indeed, Francisco de Florencia, writing in the 1680s, thought it reached a wider audience than did Our Lady of Guadalupe.[18] But there are clear signs that it became even more popular from the 1740s. The *Theatro Americano* described "a miraculous image of Our Lady the Virgin Mary that is the solace of that region and much greater distances, so that it is frequently visited in *romerías*; and even though its population is small, innumerable people come to the annual feast day celebrations from throughout the kingdom."[19] And Juan Antonio de Oviedo observed in 1755 a striking increase in the importance of this shrine since Francisco de Florencia's time.[20] Construction on the large, fine shrine church at the site today, begun in 1732, was completed in 1769 except for the bell towers, which were dedicated in 1790. Other building projects there date from the same time, including new lodgings for the growing number of visitors started in 1769 and finished in 1775.[21] The number of visitors to San Juan de los Lagos during the commercial fair and annual feast day celebrations in early December apparently grew from about 10,000 in 1736 to 35,000 in 1792, five years before royal permission for the annual fair was formally given.[22] Publication of twenty-four devotional texts for this miraculous image of the Virgin Mary between 1750 and 1805, including sermons, histories with miracle stories, and novena booklets, also suggests the growing appeal of this image.[23]

The concentration of these new publications between 1751 and 1757 (six) and between 1790 and 1805 (nine) parallels the mounting administrative record for the shrine and annual commercial fair and feast of the Immaculate Conception.[24] Disagreement developed over how the plaza in front of the shrine church would be used during the festivities and fair, a sore point well into the 1790s. Solutions were proposed, decreed, and revisited in 1751, 1757–1758, 1761, 1778, 1779, 1781, 1792, and 1796, but turnover of officials and the shifting, competing interests of commerce, public safety, royal jurisdiction and revenue, ecclesiastical authority, and decorum in public festivities precluded a lasting resolution. Chaplains of the shrine in the 1750s had complained to the Audiencia of Guadalajara that the alcalde mayor allowed vendors of all kinds to overrun the plaza during the trade fair so that on the feast day of December 8 the customary procession with the image through the plaza was impeded and the fireworks display that went with it had to be moved elsewhere. In 1757, the chaplain petitioned for renewal of the decree issued by the *audiencia* and captain general on November 2, 1751 that limited any temporary booths, shops, and food stalls to the edges of the plaza in order to leave room for the procession and other religious ceremonies. The fiscal of the audiencia agreed, and the captain general issued a decree to this effect on December 22, 1757. The decree was repeated on September 16, 1758 after the chaplain complained that the problem persisted, "resulting in the complete loss of the ceremony's splendor." The issue of the plaza surfaced again the next year at the beginning of the fair, but this time it was the alcalde mayor who complained, of the increasing difficulty and cost of managing the crowds and the demands of commerce to provision so many people. His point was that the fees paid by vendors in the plaza were needed to defray the costs of maintaining order during the trade fair and fiesta.

While still calling for room in the plaza for the procession and fireworks on December 8, the audiencia shifted its position on the issue in 1778, coming down on the side of revenues and public order. The alcalde mayor was instructed on November 23 to designate spaces for stalls in the plaza and use the permit fees to pay for a militia detachment from Guadalajara to help police the crowds. He reported back immediately that vendors were now complaining that the fireworks were a fire hazard, which prompted a new decree from the president of the audiencia invoking the importance of maximizing revenue from the *alcabala* tax and ordering that the fireworks display be moved, "even if it has to be at some distance from the church."[25] After the festivities, the alcalde mayor reported that nineteen shops in the plaza had paid a total of 593 pesos 4 reales in fees and taxes and that the fireworks had been moved to the cemetery on another side of the church. The chaplain of the shrine praised the alcalde mayor for his "zeal and care" in trying to allow the procession in the plaza but complained that the plaza was too crowded with shops and stalls for the ceremony to take place. He asked to be empowered to supervise the plaza next time so that the procession could be staged there. The alcalde mayor objected that this was an infringement on the crown's jurisdiction and his authority as the district governor. In 1779, the audiencia fiscal noted that the plaza issue was still a sore point – *asunto de perpetua discordia* – and that the audiencia's decree permitting the procession in the plaza had not been implemented. He recommended that the decree should be reissued, but that public order and the alcabala revenues be protected and the alcalde mayor oversee the use of the plaza and collect the fees from vendors there. He also suggested that perhaps the food stalls – but not other vendors – could be located outside the plaza. The administrative records following the fair and fiesta in 1779 include an accounting of the cost of bringing militia troops from Guadalajara to keep the peace: one officer, one sergeant, two grenadier corporals, two fusilier corporals, and fifteen armed militiamen at a cost of 100 pesos, plus maintenance expenses apparently amounting to 52 pesos 4 reales.[26] By 1792, plans were well underway for construction of permanent stalls in the plaza that would cover the costs of policing the fair, but authorities in Mexico City noted two problems: the plaza was small and would be overwhelmed by the proposed installations and the "immense crowds" that would gather there; and property owners on the plaza would lose their view and preferential place, which they had enjoyed from time immemorial.[27] The celebrated designer, mapmaker, and lieutenant colonel of the corps of engineers, Miguel Constanzó, offered a compromise solution that may have finally resolved the problem to the satisfaction of the parties.[28] He suggested that the stalls, to be made of stone and mortar rather than wood, be erected not in the little plaza facing the shrine church façade, but in the largely unoccupied space facing the side entrance, on the east. The last decree, a royal cedula dated November 20, 1796 in Mexico City, referred to the "well-known usefulness of this fair" and endorsed Costanzó's proposal to place the market next to the side entrance of the shrine church. The merchant guild (*consulado*) of Guadalajara was to pay the construction costs. Other public works projects, including a permanent customs house, bridges, and road repairs, would be covered by a market tax.[29]

As others have noted, diocesan priests played a greater role in the operation of image shrines during the eighteenth century.[30] Bishops and the diocesan clergy had long been players in the development of shrines, most notably for the Virgin of Guadalupe, the Virgin of Remedios at Totoltepec (Naucalpan), San Miguel del Milagro (Tlaxcala), the Cristo Renovado de Santa Teresa in Mexico City, Our Lady of La Defensa (Puebla), Our Lady of La Soledad (Oaxaca), Our Lady of San Juan de los Lagos, Our Lady of Ocotlan (Tlaxcala), Our Lady of la Salud (Pátzcuaro), and Our Lady of Talpa (Jalisco). And in the eighteenth century, some diocesan chaplains took over shrines that had been administered by the orders, such as the Lord of the Sacromonte at Amecameca. But this change was not as decisive as the wholesale transfer of *doctrinas* or proto-parishes from mendicant to diocesan pastors. Some seventeenth-century shrines that came into their own during the eighteenth century, such as Our Lady of

Talpa in Jalisco and Our Lady of la Salud in Michoacán, were administered by diocesan chaplains from the beginning, but the orders, especially Jesuits and Franciscans, remained leading promoters, and the Franciscans continued to serve as chaplains and administrators of various shrines in the late eighteenth century.[31] Both orders had their own "new style" of piety that turned especially to Marian images and advocations as allies in the spiritual revival missions they conducted to awaken contrition among sinners and invigorate the anxious quest for personal salvation. In this focus on personal salvation and personal piety, the revival missions of the Jesuits and Franciscans were compatible with the devotional reforms of "Jansenist" bishops, but they were likely to part company with the bishops on the value of lavish public spectacles of enchantment and miracle-working images.

Until the Society of Jesus was expelled from Spanish America in 1767, Jesuit preachers, teachers, and administrators were leaders in the spiritual life and religious politics of eighteenth-century New Spain. Admired for their learning and intellectual rigor, envied for their wealth and influence as confessors and teachers to the rich and influential, and roundly criticized for their defense of probabilism and their privileged position as a virtual state within a state, they also remained at the forefront of the promotion of miraculous images and shrines.[32] Jesuits claimed few famous miraculous images as their own,[33] but Jesuit-inspired devotions to Our Lady of Refuge, Our Lady of Loreto (with a concentration of images and shrines in the Valley of Mexico and northern missions[34]), and Our Lady of Light flourished in the eighteenth century, and Jesuit authors published an array of devotional texts about many miraculous images, including the very popular *Zodíaco Mariano* (1755).[35] As these examples suggest, Jesuits were ardent Marianists. Juan Antonio de Oviedo, SJ, coauthor of the *Zodíaco Mariano*, put it memorably in his earlier Marian text of 1739: her life was like a nourishing river "that delights, waters, and fertilizes the farflung field of the Church."[36]

But there was more to Jesuit interest in sacred images and shrines than devotion to the Virgin Mary. Their association with the Sacred Heart of Jesus beginning in the 1730s is well known,[37] and in the late seventeenth century Florencia devoted whole books and book-length manuscripts to the Cristo Renovado de Santa Teresa (Mapethé) and San Miguel del Milagro, as well as several pages to the green cross of Tepic in his book about the Marian shrines of San Juan de los Lagos and Zapopan. Among less well-known Jesuit publications about miracles and images is a booklet intended to publicize an *información jurídica* about statues of Jesuit saints and providential lightning strikes in the cathedral of Puebla in July 1747. Printed in September of that year, this report is an instructive example of Jesuits' didactic interest in images and enchantment that celebrated a devotion largely forgotten but providentially rekindled. As the booklet recounts, in 1699 the Jesuit provincial requested the bishop of Puebla's permission to establish a chapel in the cathedral dedicated to his order's founder, St. Ignatius, and two other Jesuit heroes, St. Francis Xavier and St. Francis Borgia. Three "magnificent" altars to them were dedicated in the chapel in 1706 following a grand procession with the statues of these saints. For a time, the chapel enjoyed great popularity, but the devotion eventually was almost forgotten and the chapel was used for storage. Then, according to the anonymous author of the booklet, God in his wisdom, who "sent St. Ignatius into the world as a lightning bolt and celestial flame that would illuminate and light the fire of divine love throughout the world ... wished to [re]kindle the devotion of the faithful for His great servant and his two main followers."[38] And to "alert the people to the lack of reverence they were showing the images in the chapel [of St. Ignatius],"[39] lightning bolts repeatedly struck the cathedral and entered this chapel, injuring no one but leaving scorch marks on the three altars. People marveled at the three lightning bolts that struck the chapel in this way in July 1747, and the cathedral chapter quickly resolved that every July 30 and 31 the statue of St. Ignatius would be placed on the main altar of the cathedral for high Mass after being carried in procession through the building as a commemorative act of thanksgiving.[40]

Franciscans, who had often acted in concert with Jesuits to promote devotions to particular images and shrines, took up the cause of other Jesuit favorites after the order's expulsion – Our Lady of Refuge, Our Lady of Light, and Our Lady of Loreto. Next to the Jesuits, they were the most prolific authors and patrons of devotional texts and prints of shrine images, and their interest ranged even more widely, including altars and shrines to miraculous Spanish images of Mary such as Covadonga, Balvanera, Pilar de Zaragoza, and Aranzazú. The Spanish advocation of Nuestra Señora de la Cueva Santa was a Franciscan favorite, fueled by the preaching missions of their Propaganda Fide colleges based in Querétaro, Zacatecas, Pachuca, and Mexico City. And the Franciscans seem to have focused even more on celebrated sacred images, shrines, and preaching missions when they lost nearly all their remaining pastoral assignments after 1749.

About forty new image shrines and reports of animated and wonder-working images, most with origin stories similar to those of their seventeenth-century predecessors, are known for the eighteenth century.[41] Most of these new image shrines were dedicated to figures of Christ (56 percent compared to 40 percent for images of the Virgin Mary) including the Holy Child, and many were located in the west, the Bajío, and the north, on or near commercial routes to flourishing silver mining centers in Guanajuato, Zacatecas, San Luis Potosí, Durango, and Chihuahua.[42] But the new shrines represent only about a third the number that began in the long seventeenth century, and few new image shrines are recorded for Mexico City and vicinity after the 1730s, thanks apparently to the popularity and concerted promotion there of Nuestra Señora de Guadalupe and Nuestra Señora de los Remedios by archbishops, viceroys, and the city council.

Only two of the new shrines soon developed into regional centers at the time: Nuestra Señora de la Salud in Pátzcuaro, Michoacán, and Nuestro Señor de Otatitlán in southern Veracruz. As described in the *Zodíaco Mariano*, the statue of Nuestra Señora de la Salud, made in the sixteenth century in a traditional Mesoamerican way largely from maize by-products, was a Franciscan hospital shrine statue that gained local fame for visiting sick patients and bringing consolation and recovery. Then in 1690 the Virgin's face reportedly perspired when craftsmen commissioned by the bishop to shorten the statue began their examination. During this restoration work, the statue gave off a wonderfully sweet odor and the craftsmen found to their surprise that the figure was undamaged by insects despite its age. The next year it was taken out on a first alms-collecting mission, and after the drought of 1692 it began to gain a wider following. But the watershed came with the great epidemic of 1737 when Nuestra Señora de la Salud was proclaimed patroness and protectress of the city of Pátzcuaro. In 1739, there was a formal inquiry into her miracles and in 1742 Pedro Sarmiento, SJ, published the first edition of a short devotional history and novena booklet.[43] A convent of Dominican nuns was founded at the shrine in 1750 and more publications followed, including reprints of Sarmiento's text in 1765, 1796, and 1802. Novena booklets to Nuestra Señora de la Salud published in the provincial cities of Puebla (1767) and Guadalajara (1817) suggest how far the devotion may have reached, but alms-collecting missions with a small replica of the statue during the second half of the eighteenth century were the primary source of the shrine's revenue and the devotion's expansion.[44]

The miraculous black Christ of Otatitlán, Veracruz was not favored in its early years with so many publications, but it, too, gained regional fame by the mid-eighteenth century that continued to grow thereafter. The earliest word of a local image shrine at Otatitlán seems to come from a personal prayer written in 1709 by Manuel del Barrio y Sedano to the Santo Cristo de Otatitlán for good health and the strength "to serve the Indians, black slaves, and mulatos."[45] By the 1740s, it was a significant shrine with a sponsoring sodality and fine church. Villaseñor y Sánchez's survey of jurisdictions in the viceroyalty, commissioned by the crown in 1741 and published in 1746, described the image as "most miraculous" and the church as a fine, respectable temple.[46] And the following year the first novena booklet devoted to the Christ of Otatitlán appeared in print.[47] By the 1790s, the manuscript record for this shrine swelled with administrative papers about finances, a jurisdictional dispute, and, especially, slow progress toward completion of a new and larger church to accommodate the crowds of devout visitors on feast days.[48] Sponsors of the devotion complained that the construction was slowed by restrictions on alms-collection tours, but collections at the shrine in 1808 were impressive: 2,769 pesos, plus 15 pounds 6 ounces in silver milagritos. People were said to gather there "from all over."[49] Funds on hand at that time to support the building project totaled 11,553 pesos.[50]

Late colonial bishops were alert to what they considered popular excesses and superstitions, so it is no surprise that eruptions of local devotion and fresh rumors of miracle-working images of Christ and the Virgin Mary were ongoing concerns.[51] Nevertheless, in less dramatic ways they supported the mystique of shrines and sacred images. Indulgences – papal remissions of sin solicited and published by bishops – remained a popular inducement to support particular devotions, including image shrines. An extensive calendar of indulgences still in effect for churches in Mexico City compiled by Fr. José de Ávila, OFM, in 1787 included dispensations for special devotions to Our Lady of Guadalupe, the Cristo Renovado de Santa Teresa, Our Lady of los Ángeles, and several Spanish Marian image shrines with chapels in New Spain.[52]

Bishops and their representatives also granted licenses for the growing volume of printed matter meant to promote image shrines – devotional histories, novena booklets, sermons, and prints of sacred images. News of miracles would have spread mainly by word of mouth and religious texts, but some circulated in the biweekly *Gazeta de México*, published in Mexico City from 1784 to the end of the colonial period, and were recorded in personal journals of the time, such as José Gómez's "Diario de México." His entry for February 1783 reads, "in Mexico City, on the old façade of the church of San Felipe Neri there were two images of San Juan: San Juan Bautista and San Juan Evangelista. These two saints began to work miracles. The images were repaired and many people have gathered there with candles and wax and silver milagritos."[53]

But if the later eighteenth century was a time of growth and consolidation, why were fewer new shrines and reputedly numinous images reported then? Local circumstances inevitably come into play, and conclusive evidence for why something apparently did not happen is always elusive. For Mexico City and vicinity the answer is more straightforward than elsewhere. With the fame and aggressive promotion of the Virgin of Guadalupe and Our Lady of Remedios by viceroys, archbishops, and the city council, and acceptance of the Virgin of Guadalupe throughout the viceroyalty after papal endorsement in 1754, there was little room for robust growth of the other shrines that had helped make Mexico City a capital of the sacred in the seventeenth century. In fact, several of the most conspicuous cases of suppression of newly renowned images and sites took place in greater Mexico City after the epidemic of 1737 passed and the Virgin of Guadalupe was recognized as the great protectress of the city, among them the shrines of Nuestra Señora de los Ángeles and Nuestra Señora del Patrocinio at Nativitas Tepetlatcingo.

Since local shrines are poorly documented for the most part and local affiliations were strong in many small towns and villages, it may well be that more impromptu image shrines in family and neighborhood chapels date from the eighteenth century but were not officially recorded unless they became controversial or were moved to the parish church. (For example, the case of the Señor del Jovo discussed later in this chapter.) It could also be that with so many shrines with district-level appeal continuing from the long seventeenth century, with several dozen developing into regional shrines during the eighteenth century, there was less room for new shrines to grow and generate a written record. In either case, a decline in formal recognition of new shrines had less to do with disenchantment than with devotees recognizing that it was best to keep the good news local, rather than risk losing a numinous image to colonial authorities, as the neighborhood women of Tlamacazapa learned when their precious Lady in a kernel of corn was confiscated by the Inquisition in Mexico City in 1774. If the caretakers of a reputedly numinous image hoped to benefit financially from popular interest in it, they would need to spread the word and, ultimately, gain the approval of colonial authorities. That outcome was more likely in the seventeenth century. In the eighteenth century, the result might be approval, as it was for Tepalcingo; suppression, as for Huaquechula and temporarily for Nuestra Señora de los Ángeles; or discouragement of wider district and regional activity, as at Nativitas Tepetlatcingo.[54]

One image that failed to gain official recognition as miraculous after it was duly investigated was an infant Jesus belonging to Mexico City's contemplative nuns of the Order of the Immaculate Conception. The case was opened on February 2, 1756 when the prioress of the convent and church of San Bernardo Abad approached the archbishop for an evaluation of reported miracles associated with their statue of the Holy Child. Her hope, as she put it a few days later, was that the circumstances of the image's arrival in 1740 would be declared a true miracle, "granting us your blessing and license to place an inscription about this prodigy next to the statue, as Your Highness sees fit."[55] Her original intention, she said, was not to publicize the matter; however, many of those involved in the events of 1740 were still alive and wanted to testify so that it would be remembered. Furthermore, the devotion was already growing spontaneously. "Pious persons" had donated a silver pedestal and fine clothes for the statue, and miraculous healings had been reported. Sick people were clamoring for a visit from this wondrous image, and already its divine presence had extinguished fires in two houses near the convent.[56] The prioress did not mention that official recognition of the Holy Child's providential appearance and association with personal favors would no doubt serve to benefit the convent's ongoing building projects. (Work on the church and convent eventually was completed in 1777.)

The prioress presented the archbishop's lead attorney (*promotor fiscal*) with her summary of the Holy Child's appearance in 1740, along with a transcript of sworn testimony by eleven witnesses who had some connection to the origin story. According to tradition, she wrote, in the early evening of January 31 some neighborhood boys playing in the churchyard noticed a small figure, the size of a baby six or seven months old, skipping along the cornices of the church façade and over the doorway. Thinking it was a goblin, they chased after it, throwing stones. The figure disappeared, but they found it half hidden in the dirt of the street drain, stained up to its thighs. Andrés, a black slave of D. Ignacio Coronado Pipino rushed up to the boys thinking that the figure they had been chasing was now a dead or injured child. Moved by compassion, he called his fellow slave Joseph to help rescue the Holy Child from the boys' torments. Joseph picked up the figure by one arm and found it warm to the touch, as if it were flesh. But to his astonishment, the figure he had seen running and pulsing with life was now transformed into wood. Reverently, he took it to his master who in turn brought it to the nuns.

The witnesses, all men, included a priest, eight creole Spanish artisans and shopkeepers from the neighborhood, a mulato cobbler, and a free black servant of the superintendent of the royal mint. They confirmed the prioress's story and added minor details and variations about where the statue was found and how many times the infant had appeared on the façade of the church. Some of the witnesses acknowledged that they had not actually seen the apparitions. One witness, D. Christóval Cervantes, a creole tobacconist whose deceased son had chased the Holy Child, averred that the statue was not likely to have been stolen and abandoned in the street because it still wore its clothing and jewelry. The archbishop's attorney took the case to heart but would later observe that the evidence was weak. Nine of the eleven witnesses provided only hearsay testimony, and most were no more than children in 1740. Only Román Lorenzo de Arellano, a mulato cobbler, had been among the boys who chased "the goblin," and he acknowledged that he did not get a good look at the statue because Joseph already was walking away with it when he arrived.

The promotor fiscal did note that devotees were appealing to this Holy Child in time of need and that "many distinguished people" were among the faithful who asked that it be brought to their homes. He recommended that the black slave Joseph, who everyone said saw the hubbub and picked up the statue, be deposed if he was still living, along with the nun who had served as sacristan in 1740, and any of the other nuns who knew whether the statue had belonged to the convent before 1740. He added that two expert painters and two sculptors should be engaged to examine the statue.[57] The file lacks the testimony of Joseph and the nuns, but it ends with an evaluation by two celebrated painters, José de Ibarra and Miguel Cabrera, that apparently sealed the outcome of the investigation. It was a far cry from the enthusiastic report Cabrera penned for the image of the Virgin of Guadalupe at Tepeyac that same year. Ibarra noted on June 6, 1756, that they had undressed the figure and found nothing remarkable about it. It was not the work of a known master, nor was it of the highest quality.[58] It was made of ordinary wood, and the painting to simulate flesh was merely adequate. "I find nothing about it that could be considered supernatural," he concluded. "With fifty years' experience, I find nothing more to say."

Policing the Numinous: Church, State, and the Changing Political Economy of Shrines

The most obvious reason why fewer new shrines were recognized and recorded in the eighteenth century is government policies and regulation, but when and where official promotion or restriction was decisive needs to be established one shrine at a time. Cases of suppression were rare and far outnumbered by official acts in favor of miraculous images or temporizing about the inevitability of vulgar superstitions.

Minor ecclesiastical officials (themselves crown appointees, and perhaps more alert to regalist intentions) acted upon official skepticism with closer scrutiny of miraculous images, but not often with outright incredulity. Take the mixed messages in the letter to the court of the Inquisition on January 26, 1790 by Fr. Mariano José Casasola, OFM, *comisario* (local agent) of the Inquisition for Toluca. Casasola wrote that "even the most sophisticated people of this place, including many priests" believed that the city's celebrated black Christ on the Cross housed in the cemetery chapel of the parish church, known as the Señor de la Vera Cruz o de los Labradores, grew hair on its head and chest. From time to time, he reported, the hair was clipped – harvested as relics – and was said to grow back. On Wednesday of Holy Week the image customarily was taken down from its niche and rubbed with wine, which was also treated as a relic. "I am told that the farmers who obtain a little of the wine in small vials sprinkle it on their crops to ward off drought and freezes." Casasola distanced himself from these certainties of faith – "In the fifteen years I have lived in Toluca, I have never seen evidence of real hair growing" on the statue. But he acknowledged that "this holy image is very miraculous and its marvels are visible, especially in times of drought and threat of frost." Now he remembered that the Inquisition had once ordered an inspection of the image to determine whether the Christ's hair was growing; if not, whoever was spreading news of "apocryphal miracles" was to be told to desist. According to Casasola, certain respectable outsiders (*forasteros decentes*) were again spreading the legend of the hirsute Christ, so he decided it was time to seek the court's advice.[59]

Six days later, the *inquisidor fiscal* responded that this was, indeed, a matter that concerned the Inquisition. Recently, a rumor had circulated among "certain members of the orders" that a statue of Our Lady of Loreto opened and closed its eyes; and another rumor had it that a statue of the Holy Child was growing fingernails and hair. Both were false and the Inquisition had ordered the images withdrawn from public view. The watchword, wrote the court's *fiscal*, was "in matters where there could be most pernicious consequences, it is best to proceed with prudence and circumspection befitting the nature of the claim." The court ordered an inspection to determine whether the hair was glued onto the statue's head and chest. The comisario was also to search for documents that might shed light on the tradition of this image, including the archive of the Franciscan convent and the records of pastoral visits. Although the record ends here, any inspection would have noted that this was a longstanding tradition; and clearly the 1790 investigation did not lead to suppression of the devotion since the Señor de la Santa Vera Cruz is still renowned for its favors to devotees in the vicinity of Toluca.[60]

Occasionally, a late colonial state official deliberately provoked villagers and their priests over local religious practices and church properties. In a complaint to the viceroy in 1793, the exasperated parish priest of Villa Alta, Oaxaca, Juan Pío Alvarez, spelled out a long list of grievances against the royal governor for the district, Bernardo Bonavía. Usually complaints of this kind were brief and specific – the governor had usurped control over a local cofradía or had not allowed a customary procession with sacred images through the streets to mark Corpus Christi festivities. But in this case, the elderly pastor, who had invested many years of service in Villa Alta, went on at length about Governor Bonavía's various moves to aggrandize authority, interfere with the liturgy, disparage the faith, and denigrate the pastor's place of respect in the community. Villa Alta was not widely known for shrines to miraculous images, but one of the pastor's complaints was that the governor no longer allowed alms collections for the upkeep, furnishing, and ceremonies honoring the miraculous image of Our Lady of Remedios in her chapel in the Analco neighborhood. And the house donated by Doña Andrea del Tojo of Santo Domingo Roayaga to support veneration of a statue of Christ in the parish church no longer produced any income because tenants let part of the building go to ruin and the subdelegado illegally granted ownership to one of them. Furthermore, the erstwhile owner would not allow the Christ to be made available in the anteroom of the house during Holy Week or taken out in the customary processions, leaving the parishioners to find another house where the statue could be kept until it was processed. Then the governor interrupted the traditional all-parish gathering to build covered arches for the great Corpus Christi procession, leading the people of San Juan Yetrecobi to refuse to participate in the construction. The pastor had to borrow some 250 woven mats from a local dignitary, but even that was not enough to cover the part of the route unattended by the insolent people of Yetrecobi. The result, said the pastor, was an indecent procession, lacking proper respect for the presence of God. Furthermore, the subdelegado no longer allowed local residents to display the traditional lights in their homes on the eve of the annual feast of the Virgin of Remedios, even in the parish house. Father Pío claimed he had personally paid for all the annual feasts of the Blessed Virgin and other saints, including the feast of the patron saint over the past seven years, yet the subdelegado would not allow him the customary service of two boys from San Cristóbal Lachirio as apprentice sacristans. On top of all these provocations, the parish church no longer had its cantors from the Analco neighborhood, a customary service dating from the sixteenth century. The governor had simply relieved them of their duty. In Father Pío's estimation, he was destroying all that the pastor had long nurtured. "All of the natives' fervent devotion in sacred things is growing cold."[61]

In this new era of investigation and regulation, "moderation," "decorum," "propriety" (*decencia*), and "fixed rules" became watchwords of the church hierarchy as well as Bourbon administrators. The new rules were not frontal assaults on shrines and miraculous images, but official moves to purify devotion and "remedy abuses" inevitably affected the public presentation of sacred images. The pastoral visits of Archbishop Manuel José Rubio y Salinas (1748–1765) marked a new emphasis on the proper appearance of images. Visiting Atlatlahuca above the Valley of Mexico in 1759, he ordered the parish priest to either remove or reclothe a statue of the Santo Cristo de la Piedad that he described as "ridiculously dressed." At Chalco, he issued a more general instruction to pastors: "take special care that the Holy Images have the qualities necessary for public veneration. If you discover that some lack the appropriate *decencia* and circumstances, either remove them or make them presentable."[62] In the same spirit, the Inquisition issued an edict in 1767 on the appearance and presentation of sacred images, apparently prompted by a royal decree earlier that year against the "profane" uses of religious images, such as decorating buttons and domestic utensils with depictions of Christ and the saints. Religious images, declared the Inquisition, should be made with "true and decorous propriety" to evoke "piety, devotion, and reverence for their sacred models"; and they should "be located in a dignified, religious way in places suited to the sacred purpose." The proper authorities were to police the presentation of images in order "to avoid anything that invites derision and mockery of the Saints, their Images, or their Sacred Relics."[63] Archbishop Rubio y Salinas's successor, Francisco Antonio de Lorenzana y Butrón (1766–1772), the high-flying future primate of Toledo, devoted less attention to images in his pastoral visit, but he, too, urged the public to act with "decorum, dignity, and uniformity" in their devotional habits and to set superstitions aside.[64] The synod of prelates convened by Lorenzana in 1771 addressed religious images more directly, at the urging of the crown's representative. He recommended a resolution that would "take away from the Indians the deformed images they keep in their churches and public and private chapels," and the prelates included a provision to remove paintings of the Virgin Mary and female saints that depicted them with low necklines or fashionable dresses that they never would have worn, or in provocative poses and adorned with worldly finery.[65] But they did not go as far as the Jansenist bishop of Pistoia, Italy, Scipio Ricci, did in 1786. In his program "to cleanse the Church of ignorance and superstition," Ricci openly campaigned against "false beliefs in the supposed power of particular images." Bishops and pastors in New Spain either had more faith in the power of sacred images or they already knew what Scipio would learn the hard way when his campaign met open hostility from lay devotees and the clergy in his diocese.[66] In practice, it was better to respect local traditions than invite righteous indignation by tampering with revered images as long as parishioners attended and sponsored regular Masses, did their Easter duty, kept their consecrated churches in good order, paid their clerical fees, and treated the clergy with respect.

But image presentation was not just a matter of pragmatic priests bending to stubborn parishioners. It was not unknown for villagers in central Mexico near the end of the colonial period to request new images of the kind the authorities found more acceptable. In 1798, the *gobernador* and community of Mexicalcingo on the edge of Mexico City petitioned the Juzgado de Indios for permission to use funds from their community treasury to remodel two statues that were "highly irregular in their construction, inappropriate in ways that cause derision . . . It is essential that they be remade because they are very ugly and horrendous." The town elders also asked for permission to purchase a proper litter for carrying the statues in procession. Their petition ended with the words, "We wish our House of God to be presentable."[67]

Confraternities (cofradías) were one of the main targets of reform after the 1760s. Generally, the administration of cofradía affairs during the long seventeenth century rested with the clergy, and often the smaller confraternities in rural communities operated without formal constitutions. Most were governed more by local custom and informal arrangements than by formal rules until the Spanish reformers set out to expand royal authority and manage corporate wealth more closely. Then cofradías in the Archdiocese of Mexico came under the watchful eye of long-serving Archbishop Alonso Núñez de Haro y Peralta (1772–1800). During his pastoral visits, he inquired into whether local cofradías and other sodalities were properly licensed and their accounts were in good order. Few new licensed cofradías were established after the 1770s, and in 1786 the crown's interest in reducing the influence of priests in public finances and politics, including cofradías, became more pronounced in the ordinance for establishment of intendancies. Article 13 called for royal district judges (not priests) to preside over elections in Indian pueblos, and article 31 called for all communities to report in detail to the intendants (not to their parish priest) on their community properties. Priests were conspicuously missing from the provisions for these activities. The question then arose whether community properties included those attached to cofradías. In 1789, the subdelegado of Santa María del Oro in the Diocese of Guadalajara judged that they did. He ordered the pastors in his district to turn over to him all the local cofradía records. The bishop questioned the subdelegado's authority to inspect the cofradías, which he regarded as "the patrimony of that church."

The issue was now directly engaged: cofradías were being redefined as community corporations, under the nominal authority of the crown. Priests were losing their authority to preside over cofradía meetings; cofradía lands, livestock, and cash increasingly were treated as property of the community; and royal officials used their new authority in cofradía affairs to intervene in spending decisions and ritual practices. These changes were more sweeping in Spain than in New Spain, where the crown was more concerned with the administration of cofradía wealth than with managing religious ritual or reducing the number of confraternities.[68] Fewer were disbanded in New Spain for lack of proper titles and formal constitutions than is sometimes thought, and those attached to image shrines seem to have been less vulnerable to appropriation for community purposes in times of crisis than the larger cofradías and congregaciones to the Blessed Sacrament and patron saints.[69] The main effect may have been new restrictions on the ability of shrine cofradías to collect alms in the public streets.[70]

Closer regulation of alms collecting was one of the notable late-colonial changes in royal policy and practice that could affect image shrines. Licensed by the bishop or his delegate (the *juez provisor*), communities and confraternities, including Indian pueblos, had sent out alms collectors (*demandantes*) to support devotion to a favored image since the late sixteenth century, often carrying with them a small replica.[71] Licenses from the cathedral for these pious excursions seem to have been granted routinely and without close supervision during the long seventeenth century and up to the early 1780s.⁷² A time limit of six months or a year usually was specified, but the territory that collectors could traverse was ample, often the whole diocese or a radius of twenty leagues (about 50 miles) from the shrine. From the 1750s to the early 1780s, licenses continued to be granted with few exceptions and restrictions, including the archbishop's permission for alms to be collected for San Miguel del Milagro from the neighboring diocese of Puebla (1752) and for the Cristo de Totolapa throughout the archdiocese and without time limit (1759),⁷³ but there were signs of change. One shrine image came to be favored over others: after papal recognition in 1754 of the apparitions of the Virgin of Guadalupe and her image at Tepeyac, alms-collecting licenses for this shrine became especially liberal, and royal governors actively promoted them. As early as 1756, royal authorities granted a priest permission to collect alms for Our Lady of Guadalupe throughout the viceroyalty.⁷⁴

The political reforms of the 1780s, especially the creation of the intendancy system, set the stage for a more active state role in licensing and regulating *demandas*. The ordinance to establish the intendancy governorships in New Spain set out in minute detail most of the principal duties of the office, including the intendants' role as vice-patrons of the church.⁷⁵ Reflecting the perennial financial straits of the Spanish state and ongoing wars in Europe that threatened Spain's political existence, the ordinance concentrated on the intendants' special responsibilities for defense and tax collection. Government management of natural resources, public finances, promotion of commerce and industry, and public works projects was emphasized, along with efficiency and accountability in administration and tax collection. True to form, the intendants' tax-collecting duties as vice-patrons of the church were specified as never before. The ordinance also made clear that their authority extended to confirming the elections of lay religious officeholders and, in cooperation with church officials, supervising confraternity finances, which opened wider the contentious issue of whether cofradía properties belonged to the church or the community. Indirectly, the 1786 ordinance invited more state intervention in alms collecting by instructing intendants to undertake a campaign against vagabonds, loafers, and professional beggars.⁷⁶ An early sign that demandas could become an issue arose later in 1786 when an application for a license on behalf of the chapel of the Cerrito at Tepeyac where the Virgin was believed to have appeared to Juan Diego was denied because of abuses. The audiencia judged that the alms collectors for the chapel were enriching themselves rather than collecting for the devotions they claimed to represent.⁷⁷

Into this opening provided by the intendancy ordinance stepped Viceroy Conde de Revillagigedo II, who was no great friend of image shrines. In a circular to intendants of May 21, 1790, he denounced abuses that resulted from the traditionally relaxed approach to licensing and monitoring itinerant alms collectors.[78] The year before, Revillagigedo had taken up the issue of cofradía properties as community property (*bienes de comunidad*) that would lead to closer royal management. Now he moved to extend royal authority over alms collecting for image devotions, shrine building, and cofradías involved in these activities. The result was not only a wave of petitions from 1790 to the early 1800s by communities for licenses to collect for their celebrated images but also confusion and tension in Mexico City's corridors of power. Before 1790, royal officials had rarely passed judgment on the licensing of demandas (as they could have done under their power of *patronato*). The licensing, such as it was, had been left to the bishops. Now when the archbishop and his provisor dispensed licenses in the customary way, the audiencia court was likely to cancel them or limit solicitations to the local community or the parish.[79]

The governor and community of San Bernardino Contla, Tlaxcala would discover that the Audiencia of Mexico took Revillagigedo's directive seriously when they requested a license to collect alms throughout the Diocese of Puebla for the miraculous statue of Jesús Nazareno in the church of San Pablo Apetelatitlan in November 1790. They had prepared the way for their application by enlisting the support of the parish priest, who pledged to oversee the collections "vigilantly," and the subdelegado's lieutenant for the district who enthused about the beautiful image and the many devotees in the vicinity whose prayers were answered with "a thousand marvels." The lieutenant added that the collections were vital to maintaining the church and the devotion. But the audiencia's attorney for civil matters was unmoved. His only concern was whether there was a cofradía or *hermandad* established in support of this image and, if so, whether it had the proper licenses. Discovering that there was no cofradía and the cult was supported by donations from devotees in the vicinity, he recommended that it was not advisable to grant the license, and on December 15 the viceroy concurred.[80]

When alms-collecting petitions came before the audiencia in the 1790s, as they did in the Contla case, the judges usually asked whether formal licenses had been obtained for construction and cofradía sponsorship. Whether or not episcopal permission had been granted in the past, often the petitioners were unable to present written licenses and titles, a convenient reason for the audiencia to decline to grant or renew collection permits. But even during the 1790s, the audiencia and viceroy were not free agents in this licensing matter. The archbishop still had a voice, and if a case was appealed to the Consejo de Indias in Spain, there was no certainty that the audiencia's judgment would stand. Take the case of Tochimilco, Puebla, in 1795. That year the parish priest petitioned the court for permission to collect alms "by means of a demanda ... for the greater honor and glory of God," and to complete construction of a temple dedicated to the miraculous image of the crucified Christ of the Calvary. The priest explained that the temple was nearly done but that the alms given by local residents and visitors fell short of what was needed to complete the work. The court's attorney responded by calling upon the priest to produce for inspection the building permits, account books for the construction, and information about who was supervising the project and what was needed to finish it. The priest responded that no one alive knew when the construction began "because everyone agrees it is very old, from the time when the Franciscans served as pastors," so he had not been able to find written records to establish whether it had been begun with formal licenses.[81] Construction had ceased for many years until native son Br. Juan Gonzales de la Zarza, the parish priest of Huitzuco, retired to his hometown and revived the project at his own expense. Since the costs were borne by him personally, no account records were kept. After Gonzales de la Zarza's death, don Juan Ventura de Tapia became the manager of the building project, but there were no records from that time either, the priest explained, because expenses always far exceeded the meager income. He emphasized that only another 2,000 pesos were needed to finish the job.[82] The audiencia's attorney responded on September 30 that the priest's report simply established that the project had never been properly licensed, that there were notable irregularities in the disbursement of funds, and apparently no request had been made to the archbishop to establish a branch of the parish church (*ayuda de parroquia*) there.[83]

In his response of October 21, Archbishop Núñez de Haro y Peralta, then twenty-three years into his tenure and not known for challenging regalist initiatives, supported both the construction of the temple of the Cristo del Calvario and the proposed demanda. He began by stating that he had gone to this pueblo during his pastoral visit in 1783 and found the building in question in very good condition and the licenses for celebrating Mass were in good order, although the vessels and other provisions for a proper Mass were lacking. He had personally urged the priest to finish the project. He also noted that neither he nor his predecessor, Cardinal Lorenzana, had inspected building permits for this temple because no one alive could recall when the building was begun. He explained away any need for a formal written designation of the temple as an ayuda de parroquia "because in reality it is nothing more than what in Spain we would call an *hermita* (small chapel) and what here is called a *capilla pública* (public chapel)." Cloaking himself in the authority of long experience and several pastoral visits, the archbishop claimed that in former times licenses for capillas públicas had rarely been required, and since this one was nearly finished and the people of this community and the surroundings were deeply devoted to this image of Christ, he had no objection to the viceroy issuing the requested license to collect alms as long as it was only in the parish and nearby places.

The audiencia's attorney read the archbishop's letter in his own way, as he had the parish priest's. It proved once again, he wrote, that a royal license for construction of the chapel had not been obtained. But he was loath to simply flout the archbishop. In consideration of the benefits of this chapel to parishioners in this outlying area, he recommended suspending the order for its demolition. But he also advised against issuing a license to collect alms. Viceroy Marqués de Branciforte concurred on March 27, 1796. Usually the viceroy's judgment would have ended the matter, but this parish priest was more determined than many. In a lengthy brief to the audiencia dated May 14, 1796, he argued that there were strong reasons (*gravíssimos fundamentos*) to believe that the chapel had been built with the necessary license even though a written document could not be found: almost every parish church in New Spain, he wrote, had a licensed chapel devoted to the sacrifice of Christ on Mt. Calvary constructed soon after, or sometimes before, the parish church. Archives are notoriously incomplete, he added, as papers have "gone astray," been destroyed in fires, and otherwise lost. Furthermore, local Indians were the patrons and administrators of the cult of this prodigious image – "they are owners of it all, not only the image, but the chapel." The pastor's argument here seems to be that Indians enjoyed special privileges in religious matters, as they did in legal affairs. The fiscal was still unmoved, noting again, on May 14, 1796, that there was no royal license for the construction. Unless the priest presented such a license, the petition for permission to collect alms would be denied, he wrote, but the construction of the temple could continue by other means. With the archbishop's support, the parish priest appealed directly to the crown. The following year, a royal cedula dated June 10 in Madrid reached the viceroy. Citing the pastor's brief favorably and referring twice to the archbishop's 1795 report, the king ordered that an alms-collecting license be granted for the territory of the parish. In the last lines of the case file, the fiscal advised the viceroy to instruct the pastor to name a collector, as the royal edict prescribed, and specified that the collector must keep "an exact account of income and expenses" until the temple was finished.[84]

The change in licensing alms collections must have slowed building programs at other local shrines and kept them from reaching a wider audience, but if the underlying motives were religious skepticism or determination to reform popular religiosity, they were well concealed; rather, the new restrictions and judicial opinions were framed narrowly in terms of "eradicating the abuses and misconduct of the alms collectors" and "their repeated attempts to collect on the basis of various specious means and reasons."[85] Most district officials and high courts had more pressing concerns. Administrative records from the first decade of the nineteenth century incidentally recorded that alms-collecting missions continued, whether licensed or not. For example, the 1807–1809 account book for a *pulque*-producing estate near the modern boundary between the modern states of Tlaxcala and Hidalgo noted that various demandantes had passed through, collecting alms for the miraculous images of San Antonio of Calpulalpan, San Francisco of San Martín Texmelucan, the Christ of Huamantla, Nuestra Señora de la Defensa of Puebla, souls in purgatory and Nuestra Señora de los Dolores of Atlaugatepec, San Juan de Dios of Texcoco, San Juan de Dios of Puebla, San Roque of Puebla, the Blessed Sacrament of Tlaxco, the "holy places" of Cholula, the convent churches of Cholula, Huaquechula, and Churubusco, and the church of Totimehuacan.[86]

Intendant Flon and the Politics of Enchantment

Although royal officials in New Spain under the Bourbons generally regarded the priesthood and lavish religious ceremonies as targets of reform, they were not all of one mind about religion and the church. Even successive viceroys in the late eighteenth century, the Conde de Revillagigedo II (1789–1794) and the Marqués de Branciforte (1794–1798), differed in this regard. Revillagigedo made news by ordering that all religious images, including Our Lady of Guadalupe, be removed from the viceregal palace in Mexico City, and fed the gossip mill when he failed to attend religious events where a viceroy's presence was customary, including the December 12 festivities at Tepeyac in 1791.[87] Branciforte was partial to French fashions and did not favor alms-collecting missions for just any image,[88] but he and his wife made their enthusiasm for shrines and public piety in and near the capital well known. During the fourteen months from September 1794 to October 1795, one or both of them attended festivities at the shrines of Remedios, Guadalupe, and San Juan de la Penitencia and served as the guests of honor at the *fiestas titulares* of five leading churches in the city. The *virreina* also presented a "rich vestment" to the miraculous painting of Nuestra Señora de los Ángeles at Tlatelolco and made news by visiting the shrine of Guadalupe in a rainstorm.[89]

Nevertheless, by the mid-eighteenth century, skeptical royal officials in the colonies were more likely than before to make disparaging comments about faith in miraculous images and to thwart parish priests when the opportunity arose. And occasionally an official held sacred rituals up to public ridicule. In 1732–1733, the recently appointed alcalde mayor of Atlixco, Puebla, D. Diego Hernández, a twenty-one-year-old Castilian, was reported to the Inquisition for making fun of priests and sacred images. According to witnesses and his own evasive confession, he and a group of young friends decided to pay a visit to a hilltop chapel above the town of Atlixco for food and fun during the octave of the feast of St. Michael, to whom the chapel was dedicated, doing things that demeaned the image of St. Michael and the solemnity and majesty of the occasion. His friends, including several women, carried him in a "ridiculous" procession around the churchyard on the platform used to carry the saint, using the chapel's censer to envelop him in holy smoke. Then they entered the chapel, where Hernández and two of his friends put on the chaplain's vestments and pretended to celebrate Mass. Hernández ascended to the pulpit and began to preach a nonsensical sermon. He and his friends also went into the cemetery and picked up offerings Indians had placed on the graves of their ancestors.[90]

Hernández begged the court's pardon, blaming his own immaturity and lack of sound judgment on that occasion. He denied doing anything equally outrageous on earlier occasions in the village of Axocopan or in pueblos near Acapulco, maintaining that he was only having a little fun there at the expense of local church officials by ascending the pulpit or when he was dressing up in a clerical collar and going inside several Indian homes to see the offerings on their home altars. He assured the court that he had acted lightheartedly, albeit improperly, just to pass the time "in an innocent way," and had said nothing "against the saints or hallowed traditions" nor intended to "malign anything sacred." It was a religious feast day in Atlixco, he admitted, but he assured the judges that most local Indians had left by the time he and his friends reached the chapel so that only a few mestizo and mulato families had witnessed their frivolities.

The Inquisition judges were not amused, especially since Hernández had had his irreverent fun in the presence of Indians, who they judged to be "not very well rooted in the faith and true manner of worship that is owed to God and his saints."[91] The inquisitors warned him that "God is very jealous of his honor and worship, especially since the alcalde mayor is the most preeminent secular leader in this jurisdiction,"[92] but they were also wary of a confrontation with higher royal authorities if they excommunicated the young governor, incarcerated him, or called for his removal. They decided to suspend the case for the time being and instruct the local comisario of the Inquisition to reprimand Hernández and his friends and warn them of serious consequences if they did such things again.[93] Even later, at the height of the Bourbon reforms near the end of the eighteenth century, such mockery was the kind of self-indulgence that ambitious royal functionaries avoided. Other late colonial royal governors may well have shared alcalde mayor Hernández's anticlerical irreverence, but most were more circumspect about how they presented themselves in public. As for Hernández, he would not be among those later chosen for higher colonial office or other special preferment from the crown.

A more suggestive case of religious skepticism and sometime anticlericalism by a late colonial governor that aroused the suspicion of ecclesiastical courts but in the end did not stunt his career in New Spain is the trajectory of Don Manuel Flon. A colonel in the royal army from Pamplona, Flon first served in New Spain as interim governor of Nueva Vizcaya, headquartered in Durango before accepting appointment as intendant of Puebla in 1786 at the age of forty. He came to the attention of the Inquisition during the journey south to his new post at Puebla. Stopping to rest at the Hacienda del Arroyo Zarco in southern Durango, Flon struck up a conversation with the manager of the estate, Don Alfonso Ramón de Barturen, about Barturen's "Christian custom" of going into the fields with a priest during the rainy season to conjure hailstorms away from his crops. According to Barturen, Flon let out a derisive laugh and told him this was superstitious nonsense. Storms, continued Flon, were natural events and could not be made to disappear by means of incantations. He proceeded to unpack some metal rods and an electricity device to make his case. Barturen said he detected in Flon's manner a certain aversion to priests. At the same time, Don Nicolás Mijares Solórzano, parish priest of Sombrerete, also voiced his concern to the Inquisition about Flon's apparent anticlericalism. During a visit to Sombrerete, Flon went on about the scandalous conduct of priests he had seen in Havana and elsewhere, breaking their vow of chastity with impunity. If he had the power, Flon said, he would require all priests to marry. That way they would be more domesticated and dutiful. Mijares said he politely reminded Flon that in the eyes of God chastity was preferable to the married state, but Flon insisted on his point. Mijares said he was not certain Flon held impious beliefs – this just seemed to be his manner of speaking – and added that Flon, in his capacity as interim governor of Nueva Vizcaya, had been even-handed in his treatment of priests. After the judges determined that no previous complaints against Flon had been registered in the Inquisition's archives, they opened a file, one that would grow with fresh entries in 1793, 1794, 1799, and 1805.

Famously overbearing, opinionated, and protective of royal authority, Flon was a decisive leader during his long tenure as intendant of Puebla (1787–1811).[94] His particular interest in public works including bridges, roads, street lighting, and civic buildings did double duty in moral terms as a program to put vagrants and other idlers to work. But before long he was at odds with the city fathers and cathedral clergy over church matters. In 1790, he undermined the city council's plans to stage a lavish civic celebration marking the beatification of Sebastián de Aparicio, the revered sixteenth-century holy man and hermit whose relics were displayed in Puebla's Franciscan church. He limited publicity about the celebrations as a way to support the audiencia's order that the celebrations be modest and cost no more than 2,000 pesos.[95] Then between 1793 and 1799

Intendant Flon was embroiled in a series of disputes with Puebla clergymen over the limits of his authority as vice-patron of the Church. He attempted to prevent parish priests from appointing their lay assistants (fiscales) and to invite litigation over whether the assistants should be chosen by eligible voters during the annual election of community officers each January, as he prescribed for Tehuacán in 1793.[96] He also insisted on special ceremonial honors for himself as intendant in cathedral events, and when a dispute ensued there, he stopped attending Mass. Not coincidentally, in 1793 and 1794 his Inquisition made fresh inquiries into any "suspicious and scandalous assertions and acts" he might have made. The Inquisition judged in 1794 that Flon had been "less than edifying in his behavior," but left it at that for the time being.

Flon remained a staunch defender of royal interests over clerical traditions, but by 1797 he seems to have muffled his personal opinions about miracles, images, and priests and was making common cause with regalist bishops when he could. That year, taking his cue from the viceroy, Flon rose to champion decorous displays of faith and endorse the bishop's effort to end the popular practice of carrying images of Christ and the saints in processions from town to town. This practice, Flon wrote, took Indians away from home and work in unsupervised crowds where they committed all sorts of stupidities including irreverence and abuse of sacred images.[97] In 1799, Flon's conduct again received a secret evaluation by the Inquisition. The principal informant found him "muy mudado" – much changed, more Christian in his demeanor. In the last notation, dated May 20, 1805, the Inquisition's legal adviser recommended that the file be deactivated – "archivado" – concluding that "much has been asserted and little proved." Flon was judged "bold and not very devout," but there was no good reason to regard him as a threat to "the purity of our Holy Faith."

A legal dispute that surfaced at Tamazunchale in the Huasteca region of southeastern San Luis Potosí between 1803 and 1805 over possession and decorous veneration of the Señor del Jovo – Our Lord of the Hog Plum Tree – can serve to illustrate these late colonial patterns of ongoing enchantment, the power of images, the fraught relationship between Church and Crown at several levels under the later Bourbons, and their shared interest in managing the contagiousness of the sacred. The chief protagonists were the parish priest, Br. Lucas Antonio Rosado, backed by judicial officers of the archdiocese in Mexico City, and Don Alonso Peña, an Indian noble residing in the community, who received a more sympathetic hearing of his side of the story from the royal audiencia, also in Mexico City. Peña had recently been appointed the subdelegado's lieutenant for the Tamazunchale area and is best known in Mexican history as the father of Francisco Peña, who led a local rebellion against Spanish rule in 1812.[98]

No one on the opposing sides and none of the colonial authorities in Mexico City who decided the legal case openly doubted that the Señor del Jovo was a "Cristo aparecido" – a divine apparition rather than the work of human hands – and that some devotees had been marvelously healed in its presence. Everyone involved also agreed on how the crucifix had been discovered and enhanced. José Zais or Saens, an itinerant ironmonger from Huejutla, had noticed the figure in the branches of a hog plum tree around 1800. A local creole Spanish farmer, José Vicente Coronel, cut the knobbly cross out of the tree for Zais, who placed it in a small building for protection. Before long Zais moved away, leaving the cross behind. The building was converted into a chicken coop and in 1802 was about to be burned down by its owner when Alonso Peña recovered the rustic crucifix and sent it to Don José Melo Basconcelos, a carpenter in neighboring Xilitla, to enhance the figure of Christ without adding any material. Peña had begun to build a chapel for the Cristo aparecido adjacent to his home but had not yet completed it in late 1803 when the dispute over possession reached the courts. Meanwhile, he had placed the figure in a separate room of his house, where devotees left flowers, candles, and silver and wax milagritos. Peña had a concession to sell cane alcohol from his home as well as in the town plaza, and part of the parish priest's complaint was that a private home where alcohol was dispensed and people were likely to behave impiously was not a suitable place for a precious religious image, even if it was kept in a separate room.

The court proceedings began in December 1803 with Pastor Rosado complaining to the provisor (the archbishop's judge) that Peña was collecting alms for the Cristo without license or supervision, that he had started building a chapel with coerced labor while the pastor was out of town and without his permission, and that members of the public were visiting the room in Peña's home-tavern where the Cristo was kept and leaving behind votive offerings of various kinds. The provisor responded in February 1804 with an order that construction at the chapel site cease, that the Cristo be moved to "a respectable location," and that the pastor conduct an inquiry into his own charges and report on the merits of the apparition story and the reputed miracles. Pastor Rosado proceeded to call four witnesses, including Peña, whose testimony was limited to the wondrous healings. Rosado's star witness was José Vicente Coronel, the farmer who had cut the tree for Saiz and was later discredited as the pastor's crony and an unreliable witness. Coronel played down Peña's role in the development of the devotion, testifying that various residents had contributed money to have the Cristo enhanced by Basconcelos, that Don José María Salazar had taken the image to Xilitla for the restoration work and brought it back at his own expense, and that Peña was still collecting alms. He added that Indians of the town were constructing the chapel, while Peña kept the Cristo at home where liquor was consumed. Coronel added that he had heard of many healing miracles associated with this image, both in Xilitla while the image was being refinished there and in Tamazunchale. The other two creole Spanish witnesses, the town scribe, D. José Remigio Melo, and another farmer, Juan José Villasana, mainly testified that they had contributed money to refinish the image and purchase embellishments for it and that inebriated Indians habitually entered the room in Peña's house to kiss this figure of the Lord. Both spoke enthusiastically about miracles associated with the image. "All who come with offerings attain what they ask the Lord for."

The pastor's report led the provisor to order the chapel construction and alms collections suspended and the figure removed to the parish church. Peña objected, replying in writing that the chapel had been left unfinished two years before because he did not have the money to continue construction; that he did not collect alms, only some money for Masses, which went directly to the priests; and that the image should be left in place because it was his personal property. He had salvaged the neglected object and paid to have it refined and placed in a separate room of his house that was a respectable place to honor the Cristo.

Irritated, the ecclesiastical court's lead attorney urged the provisor to ask the viceroy to intervene and see that the image was taken away from Peña. The provisor did so on August 18, 1804, but the case was far from over. Peña refused to give up the image and wrote to the viceroy on January 22, 1805, asking for clarification. The provisor again ordered Peña to give up the Cristo and stop collecting alms, but agreed on March 18 to pass the case to the viceroy for his consideration and assistance in implementing the provisor's order. The case went to the audiencia, and on March 31 the legal counsel to that court recommended that any construction on the chapel be suspended (a moot point since there had been no building activity for two years) but that Peña not be required to give up the image until its ownership was established. The viceroy agreed on May 7, giving Peña an opening to present his side, which he did with three witnesses and a new deposition of his own. His first witness, Fr. José Herrera, the Augustinian pastor of Xilitla, testified that Peña had, indeed, paid for the restoration work by Basconcelos with money he sent with Herrera's nephew, José María Salazar, and that he, Father Herrera, had celebrated Masses to the Señor del Jovo that Peña also paid for. Salazar backed up his uncle's testimony, saying that he gave Basconcelos seventeen pesos from Peña for the restoration work. Basconcelos, the carver, came forward with testimony that contradicted Pastor Rosado and Coronel. He had done the work in Xilitla, he said, because Pastor Rosado would not let him do it in Tamazunchale, and he had received the seventeen pesos sent by Peña in the care of Salazar. Part of that money went to Father Herrera for gold leaf, silver, paints, and other supplies he ordered from Mexico City. Everyone in and around Xilitla was devoted to the Señor del Jovo, he added, but Peña was the sponsor and paid the costs, in addition to another twelve pesos for the decorated platform used to carry the image. Pastor Rosado's claim that Saiz had paid Basconcelos to work on the image was, he said, false.

Peña's deposition was particularly damaging to Pastor Rosado's argument because he submitted in evidence a written petition made by the pastor to the archbishop back in July 1802 supporting Peña's efforts to build a chapel for the Señor del Jovo. In that petition, Rosado had requested permission for construction of such a chapel "to the Crucified Lord known as the Señor del Jovo" because so many people came to Sunday Mass in the village church that his predecessors had had to set up an indecent outdoor altar to serve the overflow crowd. The new chapel would make it possible to celebrate the additional Mass under cover "and with the reverent attention that the Holy Mass ought to receive." Peña's lawyer used this document to build a case that the pastor later turned against the lieutenant and was using this litigation to deprive Peña of the sacred image as an act of revenge. He claimed that Rosado had not previously objected to Peña's keeping the image in his home as the centerpiece of a private chapel while encouraging him to build a larger chapel for the public Mass. The chapel was the pastor's pet project, not Peña's, he argued; Peña clearly was the image's sponsor; and those residents who contributed to its embellishment and helped in other ways did so freely, and their contributions did not add up to more than 10 percent of what Peña had given. Peña's lawyer concluded with a soaring rebuke of Pastor Rosado for acting out of personal animosity rather than "holy zeal" (*zelo santo*) and bringing forward his toadies (*adictos suyos*) as witnesses in his "sordid scheme" (*torpe arbitrio*). The audiencia's chief counsel largely agreed, advising the audiencia judges that there was no good reason to deprive Peña of his personal rights to the image. Peña had sponsored the devotion largely on his own, and the pastor had acted out of malice. But the audiencia's counsel also recommended some restrictions to check and privatize popular devotion, hem in Peña's ability to promote the cultus as he wished, and offer a face-saving bone to a weakened ecclesiastical court. Peña could keep the image but not collect alms to promote popular devotion, and he could not move ahead with construction of the chapel to the Señor del Jovo "without the necessary licenses of this superior authority and those of the archbishop." The audiencia endorsed these recommendations on October 17, 1805. The case was closed, but not popular interest in images like the Señor del Jovo.

Continuities: New and Old

Threading through the changes described in these first two chapters are deep and lasting continuities, some of which are taken up in the chapters of Part II. Spanish colonization, itself, was a source of new continuities rather than simply displacing local precolonial traditions and practices. Descendants of the native population remained the majority during the colonial period, but Spaniards and their Christianity came to stay, replenished and modified by waves of immigration and a growing population of American-born Spaniards and Hispanophone groups of mixed European, African, and indigenous peoples. Once the watershed of political authority over a region was crossed, Catholicism became one of the great continuities, with its holy days, sacraments, liturgy, sacred images, ecclesiastical institutions, and lay confraternities devoted to the Eucharist, souls in purgatory, the specter of final judgment, saints, and image shrines.[99] Catholic faith became important to collective and personal identity, though the political and cultural unity it provided did not necessarily transcend the local.

The mystique of sacred images and supernatural presence in the world – the immanence not only of Christ, the saints, and angels but also of Satan – was an enduring feature of the Catholic legacy, appealing across classes and traditions. This enchantment of sacred images did not wane even as the Enlightenment impulse to dominate nature and apply scientific principles gained traction in political discourse, public works, and medical practice toward the end of the colonial period.[100] This was so even in mundane ways – in the ubiquitous home altars or in the practice of the late-eighteenth-century pharmacist who carried a statue of the baby Jesus in his medical kit for house calls to women in labor.[101] It was what his clients expected.

But despite their longevity, most image shrines remained local centers. The devotees who visited came from the immediate vicinity or could reach the shrine in a few days. Celebrated images themselves also traveled, in processions on special feast days and emergencies, to the homes and hospitals of the sick and injured, and to the fields in springtime where devotees prayed for rain and a good harvest. Sometimes they, or portable copies of them, traveled farther afield in alms-collecting missions and visits to other communities or shrines and their saints.

On closer inspection, these colonial continuities were neither uniformly distributed nor simply continuous. There was much local and regional variation. Not only were most image shrines known mainly in their locality, but neighboring communities could be devoted to different shrines with more regional reach. The kinds of miracles associated with a particular shrine image might depend on its location or the local constituency: maritime miracles were usually associated with coastal shrines, and narrow escapes from runaway horses and rampaging bulls were common in ranching areas. There were fewer image shrines in the north, and more shrines to images of Christ and crosses were to be found in Otomí communities and Augustinian doctrinas. Shrines were located in cities as well as remote places. Officials in Mexico City aspired to make their city the capital of the sacred as well as the seat of political authority and wealth, with dozens of image shrines, several of which were eventually promoted as regional and universal shrines.[102] Puebla was something of a rival, with a number of reputedly miraculous images of its own and a reputation as the home of saintly women and some men. The smaller city of Querétaro also claimed to be an especially sacred city but was more in the shadow of Mexico City. It had two well-known shrines of its own, Nuestra Señora del Pueblito and the Cruz de Piedra, and other miraculous images, two of which were copies of shrine images from Mexico City, the Virgin of Guadalupe and the Cristo Renovado of Santa Teresa. And the tradition of bringing Nuestra Señora del Pueblito into the city from its nearby shrine followed the example of the *visitas* of the Virgin of Remedios to Mexico City. The variations and complexities also included temporal rhythms – cyclical, incidental, and cumulative. An image and its shrine were likely to attract more attention and more visitors during crises, in the spring and Easter season or around the image's annual feast day. Activity in the intervals often waned, although by the eighteenth century there was more activity at some regional shrines throughout the year.

Personal, family, and community devotions to one image or another often overlapped. Home altars usually displayed images of several saints and miraculous statues and paintings; and patron saints of a community or personal favorites occasionally changed. Devotees of the Virgin of Guadalupe often were also devotees of Our Lady of Remedios, including two of the most conspicuous seventeenth-century *guadalupanos*, Miguel Sánchez and Francisco de Florencia.[103] Mexico City's celebrated eighteenth-century painter, Miguel Cabrera, was an ardent guadalupano, but he also painted other miraculous images with the same loving care. Juan de Mendoza Ayala, author of the canonical text about the Virgin of Tecaxic (1672) delivered and published sermons in honor of the Virgin of Guadalupe (also in 1672), Santa María la Redonda (1679), and the miraculous apparition of Our Lady of Aranzazú (1685). The examples seem endless.

The other side of the coin of continuity is the staying power of precolonial Mesoamerican principles, practices, and ritual knowledge. This is a fundamental matter of ongoing scholarly debate. Modern practices and folklore described by ethnographers often are treated as undisturbed continuations of precolonial ways,[104] but it has proven difficult to match precolonial and colonial practices and contexts with much precision. Furthermore, ancient Mesoamerica was a vast, mountainous territory peopled in thousands of settlements. There were contacts and mutual influences among them, but many communities were not closely connected across regions and generations. David Tavárez's metaphor of archipelagos of faith for indigenous practices and cosmologies perpetuated by local elites in rural Oaxaca during the colonial period is especially suggestive. For now, generalizations about precolonial continuities in colonial circumstances are difficult to establish with certainty, yet irresistible.

Such generalizations have been a compelling part of the cultural politics of Mexico especially since the Revolution of 1910. After the Revolution, as the academic fields of anthropology and history developed, governmental institutions officially incorporated Indians – now *indígenas*, in the language of political authority – into the nation's history as protagonists; not just victims or mere symbols, but as a living presence to be honored, if not necessarily empowered and otherwise encouraged. Especially since the 1930s and 1940s, with official valorization of the indigenous past and establishment of the Instituto Nacional de Antropología de Historia (INAH) and the Instituto Nacional Indigenista (INI), it has been accepted practice among many anthropologists, historians, and art historians in Mexico and elsewhere to infer colonial patterns of thought and action by connecting ethnographies of present-day "indigenous" communities with precolonial patterns, referring to archaeological, pictorial, and early colonial narrative sources.[105] The ethnographic record in rural central Mexico provides many examples of fertility deities associated with particular figures of Christ or Mary, such as Xmalana Tiyat, "dueño de las tierras de cultivo" in the Sierra Totonaca of Veracruz, is associated with a local image of the entombed Christ (the Santo Entierro).[106] Tacitly, at least, the apparent similarities across time are understood to preserve the core of an ancient Mesoamerican "cosmovision" or worldview that could absorb elements of Christianity into its system and give old gods new names and new divinities old meanings.[107]

The underlying principle in this Mesoamerican cosmovision – if one can be specified for diverse communities of indigenous heritage – is a monistic spirituality coursing through the cosmos, in which the spiritual and material were inseparable. Powerful tutelary spirits that sowed misfortune as well as favor were alive in nature, traced on high in the cyclical movement of the sun, moon, stars, and planets, as well as on and below the earth's surface. Their spirit and will was manifest in natural events such as thunder, sunlight, night, lightning, earthquakes, wind, rain, floods, hail, drought, fire, and cloud formations, and in the majestic sweep of calendrical time. Animals, trees, plants, and geographic features, as well as people and their ancestors, pulsed and joined in the same divine life force. In this conception of cosmic order, the sacred dwelled in place: prominent local landscape features such as mountains, hills, unusual rocks, caves, springs, and wells were favored for temples and for fertility and propitiatory rites. They were dwelling places of revered ancestors as well as the gods in their many manifestations.

It is tempting to see this continuity as undisturbed, to emphasize precolonial origins of contemporary practices without considering the centuries in between, as do the recent essays from a major collective research project on landscape, concepts of territory, sacred space, and natural shrines in indigenous Mexico (Proyecto Nacional Etnográfico de las Regiones Indígenas de México en el Nuevo Milenio).[108] The most familiar bridging of ancient and contemporary through the colonial period for the history of shrines and images is that which takes the Virgin of Guadalupe at Tepeyac to be an Aztec mother goddess, Tonantzin, in Christian guise, a proposition that is repeated so often it has become self-evident.[109] Like most hills and mountaintops in central Mexico, Tepeyac was a precolonial ceremonial site, but it remains uncertain whether this site was dedicated solely to a mother goddess that was later equated with a colonial-era image of the Virgin Mary, whether Tepeyac was much visited by supplicants beyond the immediate vicinity in precolonial times, and even whether Tonantzin was a particular mother goddess.[110]

A common form of this monistic spirituality, occasionally glimpsed in precolonial and colonial images and much studied by ethnographers,[111] is *tonalismo*, the belief in an animal companion a person acquired at birth (*tonal*), identified by a local shaman, reader of signs and calendars. During the colonial period, ritual calendars of 260 days apparently were still in wide use for this purpose, among others.[112] Some individuals and family lines, especially those associated with powerful animals, were regarded as having special powers and knowledge of the spirit world. Usually called *naguales*, they were believed to transform themselves into their animal counterpart and exercise superhuman powers in that state, including casting spells and curses. These shape shifters were consulted, feared, and respected; and rival naguales could become lightning rods for factional disputes in a community.[113] Naguales involved in local factional disputes were likely to attract the attention of royal and ecclesiastical officials as threats to the colonial order and the church and to be identified as witches and evildoers (*brujos* and *hechiceros*) by colonial officials and local adversaries.[114]

Other less conspicuous ritual specialists, usually not community officeholders or native lords, remained in many, perhaps most late colonial "Indian" communities and were tolerated by colonial authorities. Drawing upon some variant of the ritual calendar, they, too, were regarded as masters of esoteric knowledge with oracular powers and occult ways of communicating with spiritual forces. Some of the male *maestros de enseñanza* became trusted lay assistants (fiscales) to the parish priest and exercised their shamanic role without challenging the priest's authority or antagonizing potential adversaries in the community. Judging by the scant record of them in episcopal court archives, few were controversial enough to be reported and investigated. They were better known in colonial records as part-time healers (*curanderos* and *curanderas*) and soothsayers (*agoreros*), practicing a tolerable white magic in a world of disease and disorder, rather than as dangerous spiritual specialists covertly tracing their knowledge and authority deep into precolonial times. They were enlisted by their neighbors in times of trouble and transition to parse omens and natural phenomena (such as a bird's call or a solar eclipse), to find lost objects, predict the future, and make offerings of food, drink, blood, and incense in order to propitiate divine powers in nature and appeal for rains, a good harvest, a successful hunt, or a cure for illness.

But these local ritual leaders were still a worry to colonial authorities. Writing in the late 1570s, Fr. Diego Durán, OP, a veteran pastor fluent in Nahuatl, was convinced that while the Nahuas of central Mexico had largely forgotten their innumerable gods and no longer practiced human sacrifice, they still had a great affinity for "idolatries," and there were still traditional oracles steeped in "their old dogmas" (*su vieja ley*) who were instructing a new generation of shamans to read calendar signs, practice prescribed rituals, and recount local myth-histories.[115] In more remote areas of southern and central Mexico far from major colonial cities and administrative centers, where Catholic priests did not reside, indigenous spiritual specialists had a more conspicuous place in public life. Or at least the concerted efforts by colonial officials to find and punish "idolatrous" spiritual specialists in those places during the middle and late seventeenth century brought to the surface a more oppositional "epistemological dissent" against the dogma of Catholic priests than was usual in central Mexico.[116]

Idolatry in Mind

Images – sculpted, painted, or made of more perishable materials – were an integral part of precolonial life and steeped in rituals that expressed Mesoamericans' convictions about the universe and charted their place in it. Not surprisingly, the near universal interest in sacred images in New Spain was repeatedly invigorated and unsettled by worries on the part of colonial authorities over Mesoamericans' fascination with images and their skill in making them. Those official worries produced a copious written record of treatises, regulations, investigations, and trials about native "idolatry" that probed precolonial connections. But this record is a minefield of sweeping and value-laden commentary that says more about the investigators and judges than it does about local practices and historical continuities. Nevertheless, something can be learned from these records about the power and politics of sacred images during the colonial period and beyond.

As an analytical category, "idolatry" dissolves on inspection. In the mind of the beholder-commentator, idolatry – and false religion more broadly – is someone else's practice. Protestants from the beginning of the Reformation regarded Catholic Christians as idolaters for their attachment to sacred images. In turn, Catholic authorities throughout the colonial period worried that native converts were wedded to the worship of idols, whether the effigies were pagan or Christian. Human shape shifters (naguales and *ixiptlas*) and anthropomorphic images of divine beings were familiar in Mesoamerica before the arrival of Europeans, famously represented in great stone carvings and ritual books. And the abundance of ceramic figurines found in the remains of precolonial and early colonial house sites suggests widely shared and continuing use of effigies in daily life at home. Just what those uses were is not certain, although there is general agreement that they may have been associated with health, curing, and protection through divine intervention, much like images of saints and offerings on home altars during the colonial period. It seems fair to say that precolonial deities and images were more than emblems or personifications of "natural" forces. They were those forces, represented in figures that often incorporated human and animal forms. And they carried the premise that powerful dualities of creation and destruction were located in the same manifestation of divine power.[117] Christian views of Christ, Mary, and the saints involved judgment and punishment, but they were more about protection and salvation, and focused on the human form and the humanity of these holy personages. Female divinity was associated with fertility in both belief systems (and purity, if to a lesser extent in Mesoamerica), but the most common representation of divine females in Mesoamerica attached them literally, not just figuratively, to the sacred food plant maize as much as to motherhood. The maize stalk and paste figures of Mary, Christ, and some saints made in the sixteenth and seventeenth centuries are colonial creations rich in these multiple meanings that may not have challenged Christian teachings, but were not limited to them either.

Not surprisingly, "idolatry" came to have a core – but not exclusive – meaning in colonial religious and judicial practice as set out in the third commandment: idols were graven images treated as gods.[118] As a result of accepting this notion of idolatry as graven images from the indigenous past, colonial Indians often willingly gave up ancient effigies for the ones their Catholic pastors offered – crosses and statues and paintings of Christ, Mary, and the saints that were presented to them as more than teaching aids. They, too, might come to life and provide favors as potential vehicles of divine presence. Church officials worried about Indians' regard for Christian images as a new idolatry: asked to report on religious images in his parish in 1680, the pastor of Arantzan, Michoacán, dutifully submitted his list and editorialized about how "the people here adore the images of

Our Lord, the Most Holy Virgin, and the saints in a literal-minded, superstitious way that becomes idolatry. They prefer images and crosses to the Most Holy Sacrament of the Eucharist because they can't see what it contains; they worship and are moved by what they see."[119]

But, as Durán's worry about "idolatries" in the 1570s suggests, there was more to colonial notions of idolatry than worship of effigies. Idolatry came to stand for any kind of improper worship, important or trivial – sorcery, witchcraft, superstitious beliefs and practices, heresy, blasphemy, paganism, idol worship, and even memories of the precolonial, pre-Christian past.[120] The Third Synod of prelates meeting in 1585 made explicit the early bishops' conviction that "the vomit of idolatry" meant improper native worship of any kind when they included in the same breath graven images, "superstitions," native dances, songs about the pre-Christian past, sorcery, spells, divination, and love potions.[121] Idolatry in this broad sense was a perennial concern of colonial authorities in Indian districts, even in the last years of Spanish rule when unsanctioned religious practices were more often treated as superstitions – venial sins – than as heresy, apostasy, or obdurate paganism. "Idolatry" inevitably stirred anxiety about the devil at large, subverting the Christian journey toward eternal salvation. And the devil remained ever-present as the dark side of enchantment, blamed for a host of misdeeds, from blasphemy to rape, robbery, and murder, as well as idolatry.[122]

Strictly speaking, the term should have been reserved for religious practices of pagans before the coming of Christianity, a sin of ignorance to be overcome by conversion rather than punishment. However, Indians were regarded in colonial law as perpetual minors and not usually Christians in the fullest sense, and "idolatry" appears often in colonial legal records as a loaded term for rites and beliefs of Indians and *castas* that were beyond the bounds of acceptable Christian practice.[123] With a note of exasperation, pastors and their superiors spoke of fighting an "invisible war" on behalf of wretched parishioners who were easily deceived by the devil and, willfully or not, corrupted the true and pure faith.[124] And as David Tavárez observes, "colonial idolatry emerged as a coherent [if sprawling] category only when both native and ecclesiastical minds willed it into existence."[125] For native Christians, accusations and prosecutions of idolatry in both the narrow and broad senses proved to be a convenient way to marginalize rivals and eccentrics.[126] Especially if there were effigies involved, accusations of idolatry were an effective political weapon among colonial Indians as well as against them in the courts. The search for hidden pagan idols never ended.

Case records from central and southern Mexico can illustrate the uses of "idolatry," and these records show that in the eighteenth century fewer reports of idolatry led to full-blown investigations or trials.[127] But early or late, most of the investigations ended where they began, with a preliminary report filed in a judicial archive. This official response suggests why the longstanding worries about idolatry did not much affect the widespread enthusiasm for image shrines, even when Bourbon reforms of religious institutions and practices were underway after the 1720s.

In 1585, Bishop of Chiapas Fray Pedro de Feria, OP, sent an exasperated report to the king denouncing Juan Atonal and his son, prominent native leaders of the settlement of Chiapa de Indios (modern Chiapa de Corzo, Chiapas), as idolaters and heretics, and complaining of the favor and influence the two enjoyed with the district governor (*corregidor*) and the high court (audiencia) of Guatemala.[128] Bishop Feria mentioned that Atonal had an idol at home that he worshiped "day and night," but his "idolatry" extended much farther than this. Feria claimed that, despite having been baptized and taken communion, Atonal disparaged Christianity and its priests,[129] advised Indians to seek forgiveness by looking up to the heavens rather than consulting Catholic priests,[130] and joined with twelve other native men calling themselves the Twelve Apostles to form a heretical confraternity in nearby Suchiapa to practice secret rituals at night in hilltop caves. According to the bishop, they included two young women, calling them Santa María and María Magdalena, and all fifteen collaborators claimed to be transformed into gods and goddesses during the ceremonies.[131] In the guise of goddesses, the women reputedly brought rain and good crops to those who worshiped them. Now that their subversions were spreading to other communities, they were a "cancer" on the whole region.

These were serious matters and Bishop Feria assured the king that he had tried to move quickly and decisively against Atonal's group. First he ordered a preliminary investigation of the cave sites and took depositions from the natives who made the accusations during his pastoral visit in late 1584.[132] After fresh offerings (*sacrificios*) were discovered in the caves, the bishop obtained a writ from the synod of prelates then meeting in Mexico City that instructed the corregidor to arrest Atonal and his group.[133] Following the arrests, the bishop ordered a full investigation by a veteran missionary, Fr. Pedro Barrientos. But the idolatry issue was quickly sidetracked by a jurisdictional dispute between the bishop and the Audiencia of Guatemala, from which Atonal and his son procured a *provisión de amparo* ordering colonial governors in Chiapas not to detain the suspects until the bishop petitioned the high court for an arrest warrant. To Bishop Feria's consternation, Atonal and his followers were released by the corregidor. As the bishop put it, "They returned to their homes very pleased, laughing at ecclesiastical justice ..., saying aloud that it [the colonial system of justice] was all a fraud except for the corregidor and the king, and that the bishops and friars had deceived the people with their churches and laws."[134]

The bishop scoffed at the audiencia's argument that Indians were still new to the faith and should be forgiven their errant ways.[135] Feria was convinced that Atonal was a deliberate apostate, not an innocent neophyte. He had been baptized forty years earlier and had confessed and taken communion for the past thirty years. Feria's report provides a clue to why the corregidor and the audiencia may have excused Atonal's behavior. Atonal was widely regarded locally as a trusted, even saintly ally of Spanish colonists and governors, one who had served the crown well for many years. Forty years later, charges of idolatry might have trumped the jurisdictional dispute, but in 1585 the king and his Council of the Indies evidently decided not to take up either part of the bishop's complaint.[136] His report was filed in what became the Patronato section of the Archivo General de Indias in Seville, without administrative action. And two years later, Juan Atonal received formal confirmation from the Audiencia of Guatemala as the *cacique* (chief) of Chiapa de los Indios.[137]

From the 1580s to the 1640s, there was a notable increase both in the Inquisition's surveillance of improper religious behavior and in episcopal interest in Indian "idolatry" in the broad sense.[138] While extirpation campaigns in New Spain were not as conspicuous and sustained as they were in Peru and Bolivia, several parish priests in central Mexico composed treatises on the subject and inquiries were made.[139] But this activity was on the wane by 1660, when Fray Francisco de Medina, pastor and prior of the Augustinian convent in Huauchinango, Hidalgo, received a letter written in Nahuatl from Don Juan Francisco, fiscal mayor (a local Indian notable and the pastor's lay assistant) of the village of Aiohuizcuauhtla denouncing a young man named Gregorio Juan for idolatry and witchcraft. Worried about subversion of Christianity on his watch and suspecting demonic intervention, Father Medina moved quickly to call in witnesses and detain and depose Gregorio Juan. He sent the record of this initial investigation to the archbishop's court, but there is no evidence that the case was taken up there. That initial investigation is all we have to go on.[140]

According to Don Juan Francisco's letter, Gregorio Juan had recently moved to Aiohuizcuauhtla and caused a commotion among people there, claiming that he was God Almighty who created the heavens and earth, that he was aided by the Twelve Apostles, and that he would protect from all harm those who worshipped him. "He said that he had come to the aforementioned village to be recognized as God and that in doing so the people would be freed from the illnesses they were suffering." Furthermore, Don Juan Francisco claimed, Gregorio Juan declared that five local unbelievers would die, and if others did not believe he would punish them with fire, burning the village to the ground.

The eight Indian witnesses from Aiohuizcuauhtla who were summoned by the prior told corroborating stories, but their versions differed in ways that blur Don Juan Francisco's stark description of a prophet of salvation and doom come to town. No one seems to have doubted that powerful spirits could materialize and work their will in the world through chosen intermediaries. The witnesses included eight Indians from Aiohuizcuauhtla who had either witnessed or participated in several healing ceremonies Gregorio Juan performed there, plus Gregorio Juan's father, from the village of San Agustín, also in the district of Huauchinango. Both the participants and the spectators told basically the same story of Gregorio Juan performing three healing rituals at the homes of Clemente (the "mandón" or designated leader of the village) and Marcos Juan, but only some of the local witnesses said Gregorio Juan claimed to be God.

The first witness, Miguel Juan, who had reported the suspicious acts to Don Juan Francisco, lived near Marcos Juan and observed at a distance the rites Gregorio Juan and others performed in Marcos Juan's yard one night. He and the second witness, also named Miguel Juan (both were said to be between twenty-five and thirty years old), reported they were together when they heard loud noises at about nine at night and went to see what was going on. They saw "a sort of tabernacle" or enclosure made of a wooden frame draped with white *tilmas* (cloaks or blankets). Gregorio Juan was inside the enclosure speaking in Nahuatl and Totonac in the cadence of a Catholic priest's sermon, saying that he was the true God, accompanied by the Twelve Apostles. Outside the enclosure, two couples – Marcos Juan and his wife, Christina Constanzia, and Juan Diego and his wife – knelt in prayer, and Juan Diego was beating on a *teponaxtli* (a hollowed out log drum). Other people were present, including the village leader Clemente, who participated in the ceremony, and Pablo, who did not.[141] Gregorio Juan demanded contributions from those present[142] and told the spectators that the ceremonies were to determine whether the three or four village youngsters then sick with measles would die (one of them apparently was a son of Marcos Juan).

The third local witness, Juana María, fifty, said that Clemente had summoned her to his home to see what Gregorio Juan was doing. There she saw Gregorio Juan, Marcos Juan "el Viejo," his wife Magdalena María, and Clemente and his wife around the enclosure. Gregorio Juan stood up and entered the enclosure and incensed it with copal. Then Juan Diego entered the enclosure playing the teponaxtli and singing. Everyone else remained silent, kneeling in prayer. Then she heard a voice that she thought was Gregorio Juan's say that he was very angry because the people did not want to obey him and he would take revenge – that Miguel Juan, Bernardo, and Clemente Agustín would die because they did not follow him. Clemente Agustín, sixty, testified next, but being nearly deaf and blind, he could add little information.

The fifth and sixth local witnesses were Diego Juan, forty-eight, and his wife Isabel Ana, who had been summoned by Clemente to participate in

Gregorio Juan's curing ceremonies for his sick wife.[143] Diego Juan was, he said, enlisted to play the teponaxtli and sing. They added some details about the ceremonies, such as Gregorio Juan extinguishing the pitch pine torches that illuminated the enclosure when he said his god was arriving and requiring everyone to lower their eyes. They said Gregorio Juan carried a gourd of water into the enclosure with him, made some noise inside, and gave the water to the sick woman saying he had prepared and refined the potion for her to drink. According to Isabel Ana, Clemente's wife recovered after taking the potion. Both Diego Juan and Isabel Ana testified that Gregorio Juan also claimed to be God Almighty, as did the seventh and eighth witnesses, Marcos Juan "el Viejo" and his wife Christina Constanzia. But Marcos Juan and Christina Constanzia made it clear that what was of interest to them was his claim to healing powers. Marcos Juan said Gregorio Juan had arrived in this time of growing "great illness," and Christina Constanzia said she understood that Gregorio Juan came "only to cure the sick."

Last to testify were Gregorio Juan's father, Bernabé Gregorio, and Gregorio Juan, himself. Bernabé Gregorio had come to Aiohuizcuauhtla when he learned of his son's arrest. He found Gregorio Juan in the village jail, roughed up by his captors. Then he, too, was arrested. The testimony of father and son substantially coincided, but perhaps not because they had coordinated their stories ahead of time. There had been tension between father and son long before they were reunited in jail, and there is one glaring discrepancy in their testimony: Bernabé Gregorio said his son had, indeed, declared himself to be God Almighty at the end of a curing ceremony in their home village of San Agustín. Gregorio Juan admitted only that that he had access to a tutelary god who enabled him to cure the sick. Briefly, father and son testified that when Gregorio Juan was thirteen or fourteen he had run away from home and settled in Polcalintla in the neighboring district of Xalpantepec where his brother Juan de la Cruz was living. Bernabé Gregorio had brought his son home several times, but Gregorio Juan had kept returning to Polcalintla, where he came under the influence of a local farmer and shaman, Pedro, who taught him curing rites and exposed him to an apparition that the father understood to be a goat. Recently, Gregorio Juan had returned to his home village briefly and organized two curing ceremonies inside an improvised enclosure of tilmas, where he said he met two gods: one a goat and the other a star, who warned that a great epidemic was imminent. Father and son had argued over this and Gregorio Juan left for Aiohuizcuauhtla with two Indian girls named Clara and María. Before long, Bernabé Gregorio heard that his son had been arrested.

Gregorio Juan's lengthy deposition filled in some details about his estrangement from his parents, his association with the shaman in

Polcalintla, and the curing ceremonies he conducted at Aiohuizcuauhtla. In the charged circumstances of his deposition, Gregorio Juan did not mention boasting that he was God Almighty. Instead he insisted that he had been a good Christian who tried to resist the threats and blandishments of the shaman. But he admitted that he was drawn to the older man's healing powers and had learned from him how to summon his tutelary god. He described how the shaman, Pedro, had taken him to a remote place where he taught him to cure the sick with various powders, as his god instructed. Gregorio Juan said Pedro took him to a cave and threatened to whip him to death if he did not follow his lead and obey his god. Eventually, Gregorio Juan then agreed to become the sorcerer's apprentice and learn the ceremonies. Pedro would enter the enclosure of tilmas and after saying "Come here, goat," would beckon Gregorio Juan to follow him. Inside a small boy with blue skin, a white face, and saffron-colored hair was seated. The boy told him "you must serve me" and said he would teach Gregorio Juan "many great things" to cure the sick. Gregorio Juan testified that he hesitated again because he was a Christian and wanted to return to his parents' house but gave in after the blue-skinned boy mixed powders in water and instructed him to give the potion to the sick, saying, "I will be at your side no matter where you are. I am the true priest." The blue boy ordered Gregorio Juan not to confess to the Catholic priests any longer. When Gregorio Juan told his brother about all this a few days later, the brother became angry and confronted Pedro, asking why he was teaching Gregorio Juan "such bad things." Gregorio Juan said he briefly returned to his parents' home in San Agustín, where he performed the curing ceremonies and the blue boy appeared to him as before. After the first ceremony, his mother berated him as his brother had, so in the next ceremony he told the blue boy that he could no longer serve him. The boy threatened him and disappeared. Gregorio Juan performed the ritual again a few days later for a sick child named Pedro. Bernabé Gregorio was present this time. They argued and Gregorio Juan left home again, this time to settle in Aiohuizcuauhtla, where he began performing his curing rites, first at the home of Marcos Juan, who asked him to cure his sick son, Melchor. The blue boy appeared as usual and gave Gregorio Juan the powders to mix in water for Melchor. He performed a second ceremony for chief Clemente to cure his sick wife. This time Gregorio Juan requested fried eggs, tortillas, and other things for the blue boy inside the enclosure, who again appeared and prepared the powders. Then, said Gregorio Juan, other Indians in the village objected to these ceremonies and arrested him. They also arrested his father when he came looking for him.

The record ends on March 8, 1660 with the witnesses and Gregorio Juan confirming their testimony as recorded. No action by the archiepiscopal court is noted in the record, even though there were loose ends to resolve in what might have been regarded as a clear and present threat to Christianity. Conspicuously absent from the original group of witnesses was Clemente, the village chief, who had invited Gregorio Juan on at least two occasions to perform curing rites for his wife that were said to have succeeded in restoring her health. And there were inconsistencies in the testimony to be reconciled and missing information about several witnesses.

Why was this case centering on apparitions by a numinous blue boy with healing secrets not regarded by colonial authorities as an imminent threat to the Christian community, as it might have been fifteen or twenty years before?[144] We cannot know for certain, but the record itself is suggestive. No written record has come to light to indicate that Gregorio Juan's activities in Aiohuizcuauhtla touched off a wider nativist, anti-Christian, anticolonial movement in the district of Huauchinango or elsewhere. The loud dissension within the village of Aiohuizcuauhtla suggests that young Gregorio Juan was not in a position to lead a pagan revivalist movement if that was his intention. The testimony of Marcos Juan "el Viejo," Christina Constanzia, and Ana Isabel suggests that they were more interested in Gregorio Juan's possible healing powers than in his claims to be God Almighty or his threats to visit sickness and ruin upon those who did not follow him. Surprisingly, none of the witnesses, not even the fiscal mayor, mentioned the devil even though the summoning of a "goat" invited the association. The main concerns of both villagers and priest seem to have been instrumental – recovery from acute illness, local politics, and proper Christian conduct. Church leaders and colonial officials may have concluded that this was a local dispute touched off by a deluded newcomer rather than an emerging threat to Christianity and colonial order. Gregorio Juan may well have been released from the village jail into his father's custody before long and not heard from again in the public record, chastened by the rough treatment and wary of another encounter with ecclesiastical justice.

Idolatry investigations and some notable trials continued in the late seventeenth century and a few spectacular cases went to trial and led to executions, especially in northern Oaxaca, 1691–1706, but during the eighteenth century they were less frequent and less often resulted in a thundering denouement. What was regarded as Indian idolatry in the early seventeenth century was more often considered superstitious witchcraft or ignorant folkways and treated as a venial sin during the last century of colonial rule. It no longer warranted much of the court's time. Archbishop Rubio y Salinas's directive about judicial review of witchcraft accusations issued on June 15, 1754 pointed the way; it would have been out of place a century earlier. After observing that many cases against Indians for *maleficio* (casting spells and curses, often associated with pacts with the devil) and otherwise improper religious practices were pending in his tribunal, most of them frivolous and harmful to the accused, and that only a single accusation of maleficio processed by his *provisorato* in recent years had proved to be substantial enough to justify a trial, the archbishop ordered his pastors not to make arrests on the basis of simple accusations of witchcraft and idolatry. Only if the pastor discovered strong evidence of guilt was he to proceed to interrogate collateral witnesses, and then only in secret. The archbishop went on to outline how an investigation and trial was to proceed. Among other things, the suspect was not to be arrested until the *provisor de indios* (the archbishop's vicar general for Indian affairs) had given his authorization, and the investigations were to include detailed medical evidence and evaluation by experts. This more discretionary way of proceeding would, he thought, reduce the number of false accusations that sprang from personal enmities and local political rivalries.[145]

Still, idolatry equated with *gentilismo* ("heathendom") remained a political and devotional issue, especially when Archbishop Lorenzana convened the Fourth Synod of New Spain's prelates in 1771. The prelates attending the synod had idolatry in mind in their campaign to reform worship. In a sweeping gesture early in their deliberations, they expressed their intention "to erase everything that is a reminder of heathendom" and make Indians into model Christians in order "to ensure peace, security, and success of both the church and the state."[146] Native celebrations (*mitotes*), mountaintop ceremonies, exotic dances, traditional songs in which ancient history and impieties were recounted all had to go, along with any "other signs of idolatry."[147] And there were ancient effigies and indigenous beliefs and practices still to be found in central Mexico, even in and near the capital. In 1803, the vicar general advised the attorney general for the Real Audiencia that the pastor of Santa Ana Xilotzingo in the parish of Tlalnepantla had undertaken a campaign of idol smashing "with happy results." The idol worship had come to his attention when some Indian wives refused to obey their husbands' and in-laws' demand that they pay homage to certain idols. The pastor was convinced that "almost all of the community was possessed by the abominable offense of idolatry." With the vicar general's guidance, various parishioners had been interrogated and expeditions had been made to more than twenty-five mountain caves in the vicinity, where "innumerable idols, dolls, and ridiculous figures (*monos*)" were confiscated. To the priests' pleasant surprise, parishioners readily "abjured their idolatry, confessed their errors, and gave signs of true repentance, giving up even their ceremonial musical instruments," and "with the greatest humility and respect complied with the salutary spiritual penitence that was applied according to the Church's spirit of leniency because of the Indians' rusticity and ignorance."[148]

Occasionally a fuller, more formal investigation of suspected idolatry was undertaken by a bishop's court in the late colonial period, but without the high drama and urgency of earlier times. In one instance from 1817 to 1819, the pastor of San Lorenzo Huitzizilapan near Toluca surprised a group of Indians dancing reverently around a collection of clay figures and images of Christ, crosses, and saints, which he took to be a "superstitious or idolatrous" practice.[149] Blind Domingo Francisco was the apparent organizer of the event, which included at least seventeen other participants, including the local churchwarden (fiscal), his assistant, and a former gobernador of the community. Those who could be found were arrested and the pastor denounced them to the archbishop's court. The case wore on for more than a year, including an investigation by the district *juez eclesiástico*, a formal interrogatory and testimony, and eventual review in the *provisorato de indios*. In the end, the archbishop's chief counsel (promotor fiscal) ruled that Domingo Francisco had organized this improvised, one-time ceremony, that only one Indian had danced, and that there had been no music. He was persuaded that a stranger in Mexico City had misled Domingo Francisco into thinking that his sight could be restored if he staged a ceremony with food offerings and little figures he could buy in the capital and invoked Macquetla Xhant, which the promotor fiscal judged not to be a pagan god but an image of Christ's Divine Face (*el Divino Rostro*) on a nearby mountain revered by the people of Huitzizilapan. He concluded that Domingo Francisco was a sincere Christian who, despite his ignorance, limited understanding (*incapacidad*), and superstitious habit of invoking spirits, believed in only the one true God, did not regard the figures he bought in Mexico City as gods, and knew his catechism. In effect, Domingo Francisco was taken at his word. Congratulating themselves on the Church's magnanimity, albeit glossing over the hardship of a year's incarceration up to that point, the promotor fiscal and the archbishop absolved them all of the crimes of heresy and idolatry. Domingo Francisco was ordered to attend Mass for fifteen days in a row and make a profession of faith in church before witnesses after being "examined and instructed in Christian doctrine."[150]

There was not one fixed definition of "idolatry" or well-marked chronology in how ecclesiastical courts pursued idolaters after the mid-sixteenth century, just a halting decline in the seriousness and frequency of the charge. But there *is* a familiar thread in the welter of meanings and official responses to idolatry by the mid-seventeenth century: ritual activities that did not pose an imminent threat to colonial authority were not likely to be treated as endangering Christianity or requiring a decisive response. Idolatry in the broad sense remained an issue in good part because there was more at stake than effigies and false beliefs.

Colonial Processes of Continuity and Change

While these old and new continuities are striking, to focus mainly on one set or the other leaves the impression that change in the colonial period was either sweeping or superficial, that the new or the old either replaced or succeeded in fending off the other, or that the two largely glided along separate tracks without much interaction. On the replacement side, some writers still assert that "with the arrival of the Europeans, cultures and powers collided, cosmologies clashed – specifically, the Amerindian cosmologies were systematically obliterated."[151] In this view, the carry-overs that can be documented are treated as the flotsam of a shipwreck rather than deeper continuities. On the survival side, the emphasis has been either on precolonial cosmovisions expressed in particular practices described recently by ethnographers, with little attention to the centuries of adjustments in between, or on studies of architecture, visual arts, and liturgical practices during the first years of Spanish colonization that find striking similarities between Mesoamerican and Spanish forms, beliefs, and practices – similarities that early evangelizers used to facilitate acceptance of Christianity without necessarily undermining core precolonial principles about the place of humans in the cosmic order.[152] Emphasizing continuities from precolonial times leaves much unexplained about colonial practices and Christianity after the early years, such as the burials in Querétaro studied by Daniel Valencia Cruz and Juan Carlos Saint-Charles Zetina. They examined 178 eighteenth-century gravesites on the grounds of the San Francisco church and the Capilla de los Naturales (between 81 percent and 97 percent of them classified as Indian burials) and found that the bodies at the San Francisco site were buried facing west toward the setting sun where Christ would appear during his Second Coming. Many were buried in a religious habit, with their hands crossed on their chest, some with ankles crossed in imitation of the crucified Christ. Valencia and Saint-Charles Zetina relate these burials to two Indian wills from Querétaro in 1608, one of which called for the body to be taken in procession by members of the testator's Blessed Sacrament confraternity to the Capilla de los Indios for burial next to the altar of Our Lady; the other will, made by an Indian noblewoman (*cacica*), called for her burial in the San Francisco church in a Franciscan habit.[153]

There seems to be a consensus now that something more complex and various in faith and devotional practices than largely undisturbed continuities or sweeping spiritual conquest was going on in most places and times, but just what the complexities were and how they relate to ongoing enchantment in the world and the power of images in the meeting of Spaniards and Indians remains elusive. In addition to coerced substitution and survival through resistance, near isolation, or subversive substitution,[154] the various processes of combination that scholars have proposed – usually metaphorically or in passing – include addition, subtraction, mixture, hybridization, fusion, syncretism, conjugation, asymmetrical exchange, convergence, reconstitution, and accommodation.[155] These ways of describing change are only loosely connected to recorded experience in many particular places during the colonial period (to the extent that the written and material record expresses actual experience of faith in action); and as David Tavárez observes, despite some broad Mesoamerican similarities in ritual practices, calendars, and manifestations of divinity, there was no centralized state religion and priesthood before Spanish colonization, no unified religious field.[156] In any case, a balance sheet of traits and practices with European or Mesoamerican roots will not go far toward a description of what changed and did not change. How to conceive of Mesoamerican traditions continuing is a perennial question that cannot be resolved here, but a few qualifications and clarifications about similarities, exchanges, exuberant understandings, and misunderstandings may help to convey a sense of process in the development of image shrines described in these first two chapters.

The fundamental similarities were a shared interest in effigies and the conviction that divine energy suffused the material universe. These similarities were deep and lasting, amounting to a shared sense of divine presence in and through visible images, landscapes, and soundscapes.[157] In both Mesoamerican and Hispanic cultures, images could be actualizations of divine presence, not only symbols or representations.[158] Many other similarities have been noted, too, including apparitions; prophecies; astrology; white magic; divinatory practices; the sanctifying power of ritual; tutelary spirits; ancestor veneration; the human body as a sacred vessel of transcendence (either made in the image of God or endowed with cosmic life, in which bloodletting was a holy act of renewal, bodily remains were revered as relics, and the heart was the wellspring of vitality and feeling); the equivalence of certain saints and Mesoamerican deities (such as the Mater Dolorosa and Cihuacoatl, the Virgin of Guadalupe and Tonantzin, St. Anne and Toci, and Christ Entombed and divine male manifestations of fertility and agriculture); the sanctity of elevated places such as hills and mountains, caves, springs, and sacred trees as potent symbols for the cycle of death and rebirth; cities that reproduce cosmological order and concentrate sacred power; ritual journeys and processions to holy places; and a common sense of dwelling in a world of suffering and despair.[159]

These similarities and theological common ground made room for nominal acceptance and compliance. After all, Catholic priests, including Jesuits who were among the chief promoters of image shrines, shared with Mesoamerican Christians a conviction that the divine was present in all things. But similarities often sprang from different understandings and different uses and entailed translations of Christian theology and practices that amounted to exchanges, accommodations, and misunderstandings. Apparently the translations were more compatible across class and ethnic divides for colonial image shrines, but even here it is not often clear how native agency played into Christianization for most shrines. Even though colonial subjugation was a fact, communities with precolonial histories and their leaders in the heartland of Mesoamerica were not likely to see the new shrines either as alien impositions by imperial officials or as undisturbed continuities. They had more than a passing interest in what was new to them about Christianity as they came to know it, especially access to the power of God and routes of divine communication through the saints and images of the great Christ, Son of God, and his divine mother, the Virgin Mary.

Colonial officials sometimes saw grave differences between European and Mesoamerican traditions that scholars now see as similarities, such as bloodletting and bone relics, and some authorities remained suspicious that Indians were poised to "resume their old way of life."[160] But these differences narrowed and blended as Baroque religiosity developed during the long seventeenth century, engaging all the senses and drawing out a state of high emotion, whether of exaltation or anguish.[161] As with medieval Christian reliquaries, the sacred energy of an effigy in precolonial Mesoamerica could be enhanced by inserting precious stones associated with a divine being or ashes and bones of the totemic ancestor it represented into a recess in the figure. Deities in precolonial Mesoamerica sometimes were represented as part human, and the annual cycle of rituals that involved effigies blended with Christian practices in the colonial period to honor cosmic creation, and appeal for divine protection and fertility, and prepare for war and sacrifice.[162]

In the heartland of Mesoamerica from central Mexico to the Maya regions of Yucatan, Chiapas, and Guatemala, engagement with Christianity was sustained and taken seriously. William Hanks's study of Yucatec Maya and Spanish discourse production as a central aspect of incorporation into the colonial order suggests that both continuation and transformation took place, with Christian concepts adopted and reinterpreted in Maya terms. This was not merely the appearance of Christianity or a restatement of Christian terms from Spanish into Maya, but adoption and reworking of Christian concepts in a "new version of the native language" for sacred expression, practiced by local shamans.[163] When this kind of epistemological work was expressed in more public ways, it was likely to embrace and revise Christian doctrine at the same time, as in the *Book of Chilam Balam of Tizimin*, where the Maya leaders acknowledged that the Lord Dios – the Christian God – was coming, but they would know when: "They ask to be sprinkled {blessed and baptized} at a propitious time of their choosing."[164] God was Maya, as Hanks puts it.[165]

Mesoamerican and Iberian Christian spirituality converged also on death and death rituals in ways that both promoted Christianization and contributed to confusion. Ancestor veneration in Mesoamerica made the Catholic idea of purgatory and remission of the sins of deceased relatives compelling to colonial Indian Christians.[166] Most communities sponsored a special confraternity dedicated to souls in purgatory; they were receptive to the idea that ancestral spirits were present among them in the form of unquiet souls trapped in purgatory and seeking help from the living; indulgences were popular among them; and their wills, like those of other ethnic groups, provided for Masses for the souls of departed relatives as well as the soul of the testator.[167] But whether an immortal "soul" was clearly understood in Christian terms as unique to humans and separate from the body is unclear and as yet little studied.[168] When Christianized Indians were encouraged to speak of *teyolia* – which Alfredo López Austin identifies in precolonial terms as an "animistic entity" seated in the heart that went to the world of the dead – as the Christian soul in questions of salvation and damnation, was the old meaning of the word simply replaced?[169]

With the hallucinogenic cactus bud peyote, indigenous sacred knowledge and occult power moved in a different direction. Here, folk Christian practices guided by Indian curanderos and agoreros served clients across ethnic and social backgrounds, both urban and rural. Inquisition records for activities of ritual specialists understood to have the "oficio" or calling and knowledge of peyote tend to highlight urban clients and their practical and personal reasons for seeking out peyote clairvoyants: finding lost or stolen property, predicting the future, healing or preventing illness, and love magic.[170] Mulato and mestizo curanderos, including women, appear quite often among the seventeenth- and eighteenth-century peyote specialists in towns and cities, though Indian curanderos, including women, were the most often mentioned. Not only did their clientele include non-Indians, their rituals included Christian references, instruments, and practices. Before it was swallowed by the seer, the peyote might be ground up in holy water and placed on a table with candles and a cross or prescribed for use only after the *peyotero* prayed three credos before a statue of the infant Jesus, wearing clean clothes in a freshly swept room "as if it were the Blessed Sacrament."[171] When the divine materialized in human form in a peyotero's dream vision, it was likely to be as a *mancebo*, a young man dressed in white, reminiscent of the angels in shrine image origin stories who arrived bearing beautiful statues of Mary or Christ and then mysteriously disappeared.[172] Another hallucinogen, *ololiuhqui* or morning glory seeds, was commonly called "the mother of god" and taken in ceremonies where the cross was displayed and rosaries were prayed.[173]

But the approximations that drew Mesoamericans to Christian images and invited acceptance and conflation also were sources of misunderstandings, both minor and fundamental, that church officials rarely seemed to fathom and could not easily control or erase by exhortation and persuasion. The meaning of an image of Christ or a saint could be embodied as much in its raw material as in the figure and the teachings of the clergy. In the case of the sixteenth-century crucifix of Mexicalcingo in the Valley of Mexico, its substance – largely peeled maize stalks, a thick paste consisting of ground maize pith, orchid-bulb glue, and carpenter's paste, with the torso wrapped around a sheaf of papers with the story of Christ's Passion written on them in alphabetical Nahuatl script and local tax records – connected Christ's life and miraculous resurrection to the life cycle and regeneration of the sacred food plant, maize, and to this community.[174] Similarly, the story of the miraculous Cruz de Piedra of Querétaro – sweet-smelling stones of an unusual color and form that fitted together in the form of a cross were discovered at the very time they were needed to complete the conquest and conversion of local natives – drew attention to the stones themselves, much as the makers of the monumental Aztec "calendar stone" left intact a ragged edge of the unusually large, flat stone on which it was carved (rather than trimming it off to form a perfect circle).

Other images of saints and Christ also could signify locally in ways that might differ from the universal meanings presented in doctrinal writings or by colonial evangelizers. The association of St. Jerome and Santiago with powerful animals in European paintings and prints – the lion for Jerome and the horse for Santiago – made these saints especially appealing Christian saints in Mesoamerican settings where the well-being and power of animal counterparts was understood to shape an individual's or family's destiny (*tonalismo*). Writing in the 1850s, Guillermo Prieto noted that a kind of dependent relationship akin to tonalismo existed between the image of a saint and the saint's Indian devotees: "superstition reaches an extreme where the wellbeing of a devotee depends on the condition of the image so that when the devotee becomes ill, the *santo* is inspected for the smallest blemish caused by insects or time, and repaired."[175] While not extensively documented in colonial records, home altars could serve as more than a stage for displaying holy images of saints and Christ. When set up on a table (a furnishing of European origin), they have been described as the cosmos in miniature – with the four corners of the table representing the cardinal directions and the surface serving as the sacred center, or fifth direction.[176] The "mesa" – table-altar – also could serve as sacred center of the microcosmos of the home, with the corners of the house representing the cardinal directions where, as Mercedes Guadarrama Olivera describes for contemporary mountain Totonac communities in Veracruz, offerings were buried during construction.[177] And while the human body was understood to be a living vessel of divine presence in both traditions, humans merged more completely with natural forms and forces for Mesoamericans.[178] Mountains also could signify differently. They were frightening, dangerous places, places of spirits in both traditions, but they were less about isolation and herding livestock in Mesoamerica, less about a radical distinction between nature and divinity. Their caves were storehouses of wealth teeming with life, opening to the underworld and fundamental to community identity in central and southern Mexico. Suggestively, the generic, place-centered term in Nahuatl for local communities grouped into polities was *altepetl* – water and mountain.

The shared interest in astronomy and astrology also could be invested with different meanings. In Mesoamerican traditions, the appearance and disappearance of Venus on the horizon in eight-day cycles became a majestic expression of death and the anxious anticipation of renewal, its cycles standing for "the seed that dies and germinates, the bones that fertilize the earth," its disappearance not only a cosmic death but also "the spark of life ... a forerunner of the sun" in its return. For early Christianity, Venus as the brightest star in the morning sky carried a different kind of fraught ambivalence that was best muffled. Venus as Lucifer, "bringer of light," might be taken to signify Christ's Second Coming, but the name became firmly attached to the devil before his fall from grace, a sign of temptation and impending evil.[179]

Such exuberant Mesoamerican understandings of becoming Christian illustrate the underlying monistic principle of Mesoamericans' religiosity that continued to influence their acceptance of Christian images and the idea of being Christian during the colonial period.[180] Unlike the sharp dualisms of Christian monotheism, such as Christ and the devil, God and nature, heaven and earth, heaven and hell, Mesoamerican dualities were integral to divinity. The sacred penetrated every aspect of the fragile material world and daily life, overpowering people, bringing hunger and destruction as well as bounty. Stone, wood, clay, incense, plants, and seeds were not simply inert materials; they, like the human body, were alive with the sacred and possibly responsive to the entreaties of people and their efforts to harmonize with cosmic order.[181] When this basic difference occasionally surfaced in the written record, it could leave a novice Spanish pastor or ecclesiastical court investigator bemused. As one extirpator remarked in his report following a search for graven images among Indians in the parish of Atlixco, Puebla, around 1677, local people practiced "idolatry" not by worshiping idols as he understood the term but by seeming to worship water in a jar: "Apparently they would bring to the

Growth, Other Changes, and Continuities in the Late Colonial Period 145

bank of the stream a cart covered with branches and flowers with a vessel filled with water, burning copal to incense the water, which was 'their idol whom they all worshiped as their god.'"[182] In this monistic religiosity where opposites mixed, the devil was of perennial interest, to be propitiated for his superhuman powers and not simply rejected as the evil enemy.

Conclusion

In the later eighteenth century, there were fewer new shrines and cofradías, some notorious cases of suppression, and, after 1790, restrictions on alms-collecting missions and processions with images, but there was no widespread decline of image shrines. In Mexico City, even with much official support for the Virgin of Guadalupe at Tepeyac at the expense of other shrines from the 1740s, some shrines that had been eclipsed regained lost ground by the 1780s, especially the Cristo Renovado de Santa Teresa, Nuestra Señora de los Ángeles, and Nuestra Señora de Loreto. Except for lending their support to the official cult of the Virgin of Guadalupe, late colonial bishops rarely were unabashed advocates of image shrines, as many had been in the seventeenth century, but few of them challenged the growing popularity of image shrines. They meant to weed out bogus miracle claims and cooperate with royal governors in making shrine activities less costly and more respectable, but they backed away from their own decrees regulating the appearance and display of sacred images when popular opposition seemed likely. They also granted indulgences for image devotions and licensed the rapidly growing supply of devotional books, leaflets, and allowed prints that fed the popularity of image shrines and miracles, rarely exercising their authority to prohibit and censor them.[183]

Despite the vaunted aim of a "second conquest" of America by Spain under the Bourbons, and some more sweeping attempts to manage public devotions, these developments in the late colonial history of image shrines in New Spain separate New Spain from Spain and Europe more than the long, formative seventeenth century had done, and as surely as did the deepening of creole patriotism. There were fewer new shrines and stricter regulation of confraternities, alms collecting, and the presentation of sacred images, but there was also a pattern of colonial officials temporizing in the name of public tranquility. Even in Mexico City where the Virgin of Guadalupe and the Virgin of Remedios were officially favored, other image shrines were popular. In short, there were more shrines in the eighteenth century, regional shrines were growing, and in many parts of the viceroyalty they still appealed to a cross-section of social groups.

Threading through the changes and tensions accompanying the advent of Catholic Christianity as New Spain's state religion and the development of image shrines was the force of customary ideas and practices that usually went without saying or appeared in the written record wrapped in the timeless verity of "de tiempo inmemorial."[184] Many seemingly timeless truths, including early colonial beginnings for many image shrines, proved not to be so old. It was enough that they were beyond the personal experience of anyone alive. But they were not simply "invented traditions" in the sense Eric Hobsbawm and Terence Ranger had in mind for modern nationalism framed and promoted by political elites in the nineteenth and twentieth centuries. Marshall Sahlins's counterphrase "inventiveness" of tradition – renewal and transformation within and across places and ethnic groups – comes closer to capturing how changes and continuities went together for image shrines and religious practices. Colonial officials and other elites were by turns repressive and forgiving, usually unable to impose their will across whole regions, and the purpose in practice was more to alter and adjust in order to incorporate and govern than to destroy the existing order.[185]

Among colonial Indians in the heartland of New Spain, responses to the all-or-nothing rhetoric of conversion to Christianity took many forms, but they infrequently amounted to open resistance carried to a bitter or triumphant end. Acceptance of Christianity was not usually understood by Mesoamericans as a sharp break with the past or being lost between worlds, and practices that Catholic priests would have called idolatrous usually were not performed openly as public rejections of Christianity. They were mostly undertaken at home, at night, or in mountain caves by small groups acting for the community.[186] Alan Sandstrom described this kind of evasive or covert dissent in a Nahua village of northern Veracruz in the 1980s: "the Indians consciously avoid revealing anything about their religion to outsiders and they do so in a typically Nahua way. Should a schoolmaster happen upon a ritual, no attempt would be made to cover up the proceedings or eject the unwanted visitor. The people hid ritual activity passively, simply by never revealing where or when a given ritual is held."[187] The potential of the rhetoric of conversion and idolatry to guide official action after the mid-sixteenth century was lessened both by the limits of colonial rule in this time and place and by an unwritten compact among priests and the laity. For their part, colonial subjects, whatever their ethnic identity, swore allegiance to pastors and the king as God-given fathers. Priests and royal governors might complain of their subjects' excessive liberty and childish behavior, but veteran pastors and prelates were likely to let pass devotional practices and speech that did not openly reject Christianity, question their authority, or begin to spread. Laws against idolatry, however defined, were seldom enforced to the letter even during the height of extirpation investigations in the seventeenth century. As Rosalba Piazza observes in her forthcoming study of people caught in the web of idolatry investigations and trials in southern Mexico, "in evaluating the results of Christian evangelization, those in power found in obedience to the colonial order not only their principal criterion, but [in the end] their only one."[188] They were not in a position to require much more than nominal obedience.

Notes

1. An example of this line of interpretation is Serge Gruzinski's *Images at War: Mexico from Columbus to Blade Runner (1492–2019)*, Durham: Duke University Press, 2001, which posits peak interest in miraculous images and shrines at the beginning of the eighteenth century, followed by a steep decline due to repression and "constant attacks" by colonial authorities. Baroque devotions "gave way to a sneering rejection and cold repression instituted by bureaucrats who lacked the humanist gaze that had tempered the violence of the priests during the sixteenth century," p. 209. For a recent study of religious practice in Mexico City that questions the extent and momentum of religious reform and disenchantment, see Brian Larkin, *The Very Nature of God: Baroque Catholicism and Religious Reform in Bourbon Mexico City*, Albuquerque: University of New Mexico Press, 2010.
2. For example, José Antonio Alcocer, OFM's avowal to his superiors, "I am no credulous miracle hunter" ("Yo, Señor mío, no soy milagrero"), *Carta apologética a favor del título de madre santísima de la luz que goza la reyna del cielo . . .*, Mexico: Zúñiga y Ontiveros, 1790, p. 118.
3. Two recent doctoral dissertations on particular shrines and images that carry into the eighteenth century make notable contributions to this history: Rosa Denise Fallena Montaño, "La imagen de María: Simbolización de conquista y fundación en los valles de Puebla-Tlaxcala: La Conquistadora de Puebla, la Virgin Asunción de Tlaxcala y Nuestra Señora de los Remedios de Cholula," Instituto de Investigaciones Estéticas, UNAM, 2013; and Rosario Inés Granados Salinas, "Fervent Faith. Devotion, Aesthetics, and Society in the Cult of Our Lady of Remedios (Mexico, 1520–1811)," Ph.D. dissertation, Harvard University, 2012.

    For the Enlightenment "buffered self" – in which the individual is seen as "distinct from the 'outer' world . . . [and] begins to find the idea of spirits, moral forces, causal power with a purposive bent, close to incomprehensible" – see Charles Taylor, *A Secular Age*, Cambridge, MA: Harvard University Press, 2007, p. 539.
4. William B. Taylor, *Magistrates of the Sacred: Priests and Parishioners in Eighteenth-Century Mexico*, Stanford: Stanford University Press, 1996, chapter 1.
5. William Callahan, *Church, Politics, and Society in Spain, 1750–1874*, Cambridge, MA: Harvard University Press, 1984, *passim*. That religious tolerance and political freedom were not part of the official package would have been abundantly clear to any Francophile, atheist, religious relativist, or agnostic who witnessed the Inquisition's *auto da fé* in Mexico City on August 9, 1795. There, three French freethinkers were paraded through the streets. Two had committed suicide in the cells of the Holy Office and were represented in effigy, along with their mortal remains. One was impenitent to the end. His remains were burned. The second repented before killing himself. His remains were buried intact. The third, a cook in the household of Viceroy Revillagigedo,

was made to wear a *coroza*, the cone-shaped headgear of a repentant heretic, and a sign identifying him as a Freemason. He was sentenced to three years of presidio labor in Africa and perpetual exile on the island of Guadaloupe. A fourth Frenchman in this auto da fé was gagged as a sign of his blasphemy, Bancroft M-M 105 José Gómez, "Diario de México," pp. 685–686.
6. More bishops appointed to American dioceses after 1750 were *peninsulares* than before. The figures in Mark A. Burkholder, *Spaniards in the Colonial Empire: Creoles vs. Peninsulars?*, Malden, MA: Wiley-Blackwell, 2012, pp. 52, 103, 131 indicate that from 1687 to 1750 42 percent of bishops were American-born. That proportion dropped to 27 percent from 1751 to 1808, when close to three-fourths of the bishops were born and raised in Spain.
7. Monique Scheer, "From Majesty to Mystery: Change in the Meanings of Black Madonnas from the Sixteenth to Nineteenth Centuries," *American Historical Review* 107: 5 (December 2002), 1434.
8. William A. Christian, Jr., *Divine Presence in Spain and Western Europe, 1500–1960*, Budapest–New York: Central European University Press, 2012, pp. 49, 76–77, 80.
9. Scheer, "From Majesty to Mystery," p. 1434.
10. Javier Portús and Jesusa Vega, *La estampa religiosa en la España del Antiguo Régimen*, Madrid: Fundación Universitaria Española, 1998, pp. 141, 158.
11. Juan de Villafañe, *Compendio histórico en que se da noticia de las milagrosas y devotas imágenes de la reyna de cielos y tierra, María Santíssima que se veneran en los más célebres santuarios de España*, Salamanca: Impr. de Eugenio de Honorato, 1726, and Madrid: Manuel Fernández, 1740. Several new Marian devotions from Italy and Spain were introduced with considerable success in New Spain by Jesuits and Franciscans, especially Nuestra Señora de la Luz, Nuestra Señora del Refugio, and La Divina Pastora. See Chapter 4.
12. Louis Chatellier, *The Europe of the Devout: The Catholic Reformation and the Formation of a New Society*, trans. Jean Birrell, Cambridge, UK and New York: Cambridge University Press, 1989, p. 175.
13. Carlos Marichal and Marcello Carmagnani, "Mexico: From Colonial Fiscal Regime to Liberal Financial Order, 1750–1912," in *Transferring Wealth and Power from the Old World to the New World: Monetary and Fiscal Institutions in the 17th through the 19th Centuries*, ed. Michael D. Bordo and Roberto Cortés-Conde, Cambridge, UK and New York: Cambridge University Press, 2001, p. 287. Under the motto "evitar gastos a mi Real Erario" (to avoid expenditures by my Royal Treasury), the public works and welfare programs promoted by the crown were to be financed from American revenues not taxes collected for remittance to Spain.

How the history of many particular shrines, and shrines in general, may have been shaped by the economic and demographic history of New Spain in the eighteenth century is beyond my reach. The revival of silver mining in Guanajuato and Zacatecas, along with population growth and migration in the Bajío and north, which promoted long distance trade, was reflected in the burgeoning trade fair and shrine at San Juan de los Lagos in the late eighteenth century, but how other shrines may have been affected is less obvious, especially if the recent scholarship in economic history is correct that the colonial economy was growing only in nominal terms after the 1740s and more of the wealth generated was siphoned off to Spain in tax remittances, Carlos Marichal, "Money, Taxes, and Finance," in *The Cambridge Economic History of Latin America*

Growth, Other Changes, and Continuities in the Late Colonial Period 149

{*CEHLA*}, ed. Victor Bulmer-Thomas, John Coatsworth, and Robert Cortés Conde, Cambridge, UK and New York: Cambridge University Press, 2006, I, 433–436; Enrique Tandeter, "The Mining Industry," in *The Cambridge Economic History of Latin America*, ed. Victor Bulmer-Thomas, John H. Coatsworth, and Roberto Cortés Conde, Cambridge and New York: Cambridge University Press, 2006, I, 433, 436; and Richard L. Garner and Spiro E. Stefanou, *Economic Growth and Change in Bourbon Mexico*, Gainesville: University Press of Florida, 1993, especially pp. 5, 11, 17, 35, and 257. On population growth, see Nicolás Sánchez-Albornoz, *La población de América latina desde los tiempos precolombinos al año 2025*, nueva edición revisada, Madrid: Alianza Editorial, 1994, pp. 86, 104. The great work on Spain's commercial empire in the eighteenth century is the four volumes by Stanley J. Stein and Barbara H. Stein published between 2000 and 2014 (The Johns Hopkins University Press): *Silver, Trade and War: Spain and America in the Making of Early Modern Europe; Apogee of Empire: Spain and New Spain in the Age of Charles III, 1759–1789; Edge of Crisis: War and Trade in the Spanish Atlantic, 1789–1808*; and *Crisis in an Atlantic Empire: Spain and New Spain, 1808–1810*. Also essential is Josep M. Delgado Ribas's, *Dinámicas imperiales (1650–1796). España, América y Europa en el cambio institucional del sistema colonial español*, Barcelona: Edicions Bellaterra, 2007.

14. See Chapter 4 for more on peninsular advocations of the Virgin Mary. On warrior Virgins, see also Chapter 3 and Amy Remensnyder, *La Conquistadora: The Virgin Mary at War and Peace in the Old and New Worlds*, Oxford, UK, and New York: Oxford University Press, 2014, *passim*. Antonio Rubial García notices that the declining imperial prowess of Spain during the eighteenth century was accompanied by a shift in triumphalist discourse in the direction of greater interest in the apocalyptic symbolism of Mary Immaculate in combat with the devil, "Dos santos sin aureola. Las imágenes de Duns Scoto y la Madre Ágreda en la propaganda inmaculista franciscana," in *La imagen sagrada y sacralizada. XXVIII Coloquio Internacional de Historia del Arte*, ed. Peter Krieger, Mexico: UNAM, 2011, II, 563.

15. Figures based on entries in José Toribio Medina, *La imprenta en México (1539–1821)*, facsimile edition, 8 vols., Mexico: UNAM, 1989–1990. For Guadalajara, Roberto Aceves Ávila tracks and analyzes the devotional literature published in Guadalajara from 1793 to 1821 in his fully documented, unpublished paper, "Un acercamiento a la piedad novogalaica a través de los los impresos religiosos de Guadalajara del período colonial (1793–1821)." My thanks to the author for sharing this paper in advance of publication.

16. For the seventeenth century, "founding" stories of renewal are associated with the Virgin of Tecaxic in the Valley of Toluca and the Cristo Renovado of Ixmiquilpan (at Mapethé), Hidalgo. I know of eight similar origin stories of neglect and revival that date from the eighteenth century: Nuestra Señora de los Ángeles at Tlatelolco, Nuestra Señora de Tzocuilac of Cholula, Nuestra Señora de los Dolores of Acatzingo, the Señor de la Humildad y Paciencia del Monasterio de Regina Coeli, Mexico City, Nuestra Señora de la Soledad in the Recogimiento de Bethlehen, Mexico City, Nuestra Señora de la Soledad of Guadalajara, Nuestra Señora del Rayo, Guadalajara, and Nuestra Señora del Carmen of Tlalpujahua. Cristina Cruz González highlights two of these "instauration" origin stories (Tecaxic and Nuestra Señora de los Ángeles) in "Mexican Instauration: Devotion and Transformation in New Spain," *Religion and the Arts* 18

(2014), 87–113. A somewhat different story of providential revival is associated with the chapel to St. Ignatius of Loyola and St. Francis Xavier in Puebla's cathedral described later in this chapter.
17. William B. Taylor, *Shrines & Miraculous Images: Religious Life in Mexico Before the Reforma*, Albuquerque: University of New Mexico Press, 2010, pp. 196–201 and note 117 on p. 197.
18. Francisco de Florencia, *Origen del célebre santuario de Nuestra Señora de San Juan del Obispado de Guadalajara* ... [1694], reprint, Mexico: Zúñiga y Ontiveros, 1787, pp. 116–119. Florencia observed that 2,000–3,000 devotees visited the shrine of the Virgin of San Juan during its *fiesta principal* and that they came from Mexico City, Puebla, San Luis Potosí, Zacatecas, Guanajuato, Guadalajara, Sombrerete, "etc., y de todas las partes de los reynos de Nueva España y Galicia," whereas for the shrines of Guadalupe and Remedios near Mexico City "apenas acuden a estas fiestas algunas personas de afuera." He added that the alms collectors for the San Juan de los Lagos shrine were unrivaled in their success.
19. José Antonio de Villaseñor y Sánchez, *Theatro Americano: Descripción general de los reynos y provincias de la Nueva España, y sus jurisdicciones* ..., México: Vda. de J.B. de Hogal, 1746, II, 253. The chaplain of the San Juan de los Lagos shrine made a similar comment in 1758, noting the "numeroso concurso que de todas partes viene a esta plausible celebridad," AGN Alcabalas 105 exp. 1, fol. 73r.
20. Francisco de Florencia and Juan Antonio de Oviedo, *Zodíaco mariano* ..., Mexico: Colegio de San Ildefonso, 1755, p. 321; *Rasgo breve de la grandeza guanajuateña* ..., Puebla: Impr. del Real Colegio de San Ignacio, p. 321. The Spanish Capuchin traveler–alms collector Francisco de Ajofrín wrote in the mid-1760s of this "exceedingly famous shrine" ("famosísimo santuario"), *Diario del viaje que hizo a la América en el siglo XVIII el P. Fray Francisco de Ajofrín*, 2 vols., Mexico: Instituto Cultural Hispano Mexicano, 1964, I, 220.
21. Remberto Hernández Padilla, *San Juan de los Lagos frente a su historia*, Guadalajara: Edit. Egida, 2001, pp. 44, 240.
22. Hernández Padilla, *San Juan de los Lagos*, pp. 266–268.
23. The publications between 1751 and 1805 are listed in Medina, *La imprenta en México*, vol. V, 164 (1751), 218 (1754), 345 (1755), 271 (1756), 294 (1757), 299 (1757), 472 (1763), 555 (1766); vol. VI, 116 (1773), 140 (1774), 238 (1777), 378 (1786), 468 (1787), 479 (1787), 552 (1790), 607 (1792), 659 (1794); vol. VII, 51 (1796), 94 (1798), 123 (1800), 250 (1801), 319 (1804), 348 (1805). By comparison, Medina lists two publications for this shrine during the first half of the eighteenth century: vol. III, 535 (1717) and vol. IV, 18–19 (1718). Surprisingly, Medina, *La imprenta en Guadalajara de México (1793–1821)*, Santiago de Chile: Imprenta Elzeviriana, 1904 does not record publications for this shrine and image.
24. AGN Alcabalas 105 exps. 1, 8; AGN Alcabalas 463 exp. 84 (1779).
25. AGN Alcabalas 105, fol. 44.
26. AGN Alcabalas 105, fols. 102ff, eighteen days of travel and maintenance for the *tropa* at twenty reales per man. It is not clear whether the twenty reales were per day or for the eighteen days. I assume it was for the whole period. AGN Alcabalas 463 exp. 84 concerns the need to contract more guards in 1779 for the fiestas de San Juan de los Lagos.

27. AGN Alcabalas 105, fols. 436v–439r.
28. AGN Alcabalas 105, fols. 443r–444r.
29. AGN Alcabalas 105, fols. 447ff. The last record in the file is a notation that this cedula was received by the consulado on January 4, 1799.
30. For example, Antonio Rubial García, et al., *La iglesia en el México colonial*, Mexico: UNAM, 2013, pp. 362–367, 489.
31. A different impression is offered in Rubial García, et al., *La iglesia en el México colonial*, pp. 362–367, 488–498, which centers attention for the eighteenth century on shrines with chaplains who were diocesan priests. Only one shrine administered by an order is discussed – Chalma. "Various" shrines are said to have been secularized in the eighteenth century, but only Amecameca is mentioned. There were others – including Tecaxic and Tepetlatcingo – but not many.
32. Probabilism proposes that between laws that forbid or do not forbid an action there can be varying degrees of uncertainty about whether a prohibition does or does not exist. In such cases of uncertainty, "it is permissible to follow a solidly probable opinion in favor of liberty," *New Advent Catholic Encyclopedia* online (newadvent.org), entry for "probabilism."
33. Those few celebrated Jesuit images included Nuestra Señora del Zape in Durango, ten in Jesuit houses of Mexico City and Tepotzotlán mentioned in *Zodíaco mariano*, the painting of Nuestra Señora de la Luz in León, Guanajuato, and several images and Holy Houses of Nuestra Señora de Loreto.
34. See Chapter 4. While the first *congregación* to Our Lady of Loreto dated from 1615 in Mexico City, this devotion was especially evident from the 1720s.
35. Francisco Javier Lazcano considered the *Zodíaco mariano* to be a prime reason for the popularity of the Virgin of Guadalupe after the 1750s, *Vida exemplar y virtudes heroicas del venerable padre Juan Antonio de Oviedo de la Compañía de Jesús*, Mexico: Colegio de San Ildefonso, 1760, p. 342.
36. Juan Antonio de Oviedo, *Vida de Nuestra Señora, repartida en quince principales mysterios, meditados en los quince días primeros de agosto*, Mexico: Siete Revueltas, 1739.
37. For New Spain, see especially Lauren G. Kilroy-Ewbank, "Holy Organ or Unholy Idol? Forming a History of the Sacred Heart in New Spain," *Colonial Latin American Review* 23: 3 (2014), 320–359.
38. Brown University, Medina microfilms, FHA-M 29 exp. 10, "Relación de los rayos que … cayeron en la Capilla que en la Santa Iglesia Cathedral de la Puebla de los Ángeles está dedicado al glorioso Patriarca San Ignacio de Loyola …"
39. Brown Medina microfilm, FHA-M 29 exp. 10.
40. Not surprisingly, Juan Antonio de Oviedo, coauthor of the *Zodíaco mariano*, was there on November 8, 1747 to certify that the information in this publication was faithful to the información jurídica.
41. See Chapter 4.
42. See Appendix 2.
43. Pedro Sarmiento, *Breve noticia del origen y maravillas de la milagrosa imagen de nuestra Señora de la Salud …*, Mexico: María de Rivera, 1742. Between Sarmiento's text and the *Zodíaco mariano*, Nuestra Señora de la Salud gained a reputation for repeated signs of life and working some unusual miracles in the presence of devotees.
44. In recognition of its argument that it was vital to the well-being of a farflung constituency and had little income other than alms collected in tours with the *peregrina*

image, the shrine of Nuestra Señora de la Salud was one of the few to receive a license after 1790 to collect alms over a wide area. The license was granted in 1799 for the whole Diocese of Michoacán, with the enthusiastic endorsement of Michoacan's intendant: "dicha soverana ymagen es el apoyo de las necesidades en bastante estensión de leguas, la devoción es notoria, podría minorarse o del todo resgriarse sin la visita de tan soverana ymagen, lo que sería el maior mal de los males," AGN Clero Regular y Secular 27 exp. 7, fol. 108.

45. AGN Inquisición 741, fols. 317r–318v. According to Stanislaw Iwaniszewski, a land dispute record of 1711 mentions a crucified Christ venerated in Otatitlán, "Cotidianidad y cosmología: La representación social del espacio en Otatitlán," in *Santuario y región: Imágenes del Cristo negro de Otatitlán*, ed. José Velasco Toro, Jalapa: Universidad Veracruzana, 1997, pp. 221, 223.

46. *Theatro Americano*, p. 375. Villaseñor y Sánchez went on at length about the legendary origin of the image, as described in the cofradía archive: more than a hundred years before, a local Indian harvested the trunk of a cedar tree that he hoped would be made into a statue of the Virgin Mary. One day two "beautiful and gallant young men" arrived and offered their services as sculptors. The Indian set them up in a hut with the piece of wood and paid them in advance. The next day, he went to see how they were doing and found the prodigious effigy of Christ crucified, perfectly done. The money was there, too, but the sculptors had disappeared. They must have been angels, mused Villaseñor y Sánchez.

47. *Novena de Christo Nuestro amantísimo redentos con el título del Santísimo Christo de Otatitlan en el obispado de Oaxaca,* CONDUMEX, Misceláneas Novenas, Puebla, No. 7, folleto 5.

48. At least one chapel in another community, Orizaba, was dedicated to the Christ of Otatitlán by the 1760s, Ajofrín, *Diario* [1964 ed.], II, 26.

49. AGN Templos y Conventos 18 exp. 4, fols. 198–202.

50. Collections at the shrine in 1808 are listed in AGN Templos y Conventos 18 exp. 4 fol. 212. The vagaries of the construction project after 1793 are documented in AGN Indios 69 exps. 419, 421, 423, 433, 437; AGN Indios 70 exp. 28; AGN Ilustraciones nos. 3150–5156; and AGN Templos y Conventos 18 exp. 4. By 1809 the shrine's considerable wealth was coveted by the subdelegado of the district, headquartered in Cosamaloapan. He set off a violent protest (*motín*) that year when he moved to transfer the shrine's savings from the care of the parish priest at Otatitlán to someone of his choosing at Cosamaloapan. Apparently he succeeded in seizing 5,000 pesos by sending in an armed guard in the dead of night to do the job, AGN Templos y Conventos 26 exp. 4 and AGN Indios 100 exp. 77.

51. Rubial, *La iglesia en el México colonial*, p. 489. Examples I discuss elsewhere in this book and in earlier essays include the Cruz de Huaquechula, the kernel of corn of Tlamacazapa, the trembling cross of Tepetenchi, the Lord of the hog plum tree of Tamazunchale, the Divina Pastora in Veracruz, and the natural crucifix of Teccistlan, Jalisco.

52. José de Ávila, *Colección de noticias de muchas de las indulgencias plenarias y perpetuas que pueden ganar todos los fieles de Christo . . .*, Mexico: Zúñiga y Ontiveros, 1787. See also Ajofrín, *Diario* [1964 ed.], I, 15–16, 48.

53. Gómez, "Diario de México," Bancroft M-M 105, p. 230.

54. Taylor, *Shrines & Miraculous Images*, pp. 49–51, 196–202; William B. Taylor, *Marvels & Miracles in Late Colonial Mexico: Three Texts in Context*, Albuquerque: University of

New Mexico Press, 2011, pp. 71–136; and Paul Ramírez and William B. Taylor, "Out of Tlatelolco's Ruins: Patronage, Devotion, and Natural Disaster at the Shrine of Our Lady of the Angels," *Hispanic American Historical Review* 93: 1 (February 2013), 33–66.

55. AGN Templos y Conventos caja 59 exp. 11, fol. 341.
56. AGN Templos y Conventos caja 59 exp. 11, fol. 323.
57. AGN Templos y Conventos caja 59 exp. 11, fol. 343.
58. The figure was described as "one inch short of three-quarters of a vara tall, made of varnished wood with its sandals and short blond hair also of wood. The left arm was lowered slightly, with the right arm half raised as if to make a blessing with the index and middle fingers. The back and chest had various marks like varnished splinters. The legs were a different color, as if they had been submerged in dirty water or mud."
59. AGN Inquisición 1365 exp. 16.
60. Apparently, the chapel to the Señor de la Veracruz was under construction in December 1733 and in the care of Franciscans who served the parish. The cofradía sponsoring the project and the devotion eventually came under the direction of diocesan priests who declined to pay customary dues to the Franciscans. In response, the Franciscans questioned whether the proper permits for construction of the chapel had ever been obtained. For a time, beginning on December 30, 1796, the chapel was closed, according to Gustavo G. Velásquez in a blog titled "El Señor de la Santa Veracruz," posted on the Gobierno del Estado de México website: "Inicio-Estado-Identidad Mexiquense-Mitos y Leyendas-Virgenes y Milagros." Velásquez suggests that the struggle between the Franciscans and diocesan priests in 1796 arose also because the chapel was recently completed and the cofradía members wanted to have the crucifix moved there from the parish church. However, the 1790 Inquisition record is clear that the crucifix was in the chapel at that time and does not suggest that it had been moved there recently or that the chapel was unfinished.
61. AGN Clero Regular y Secular 188 exp. 12, 1793 (fol. 213 for the quotation). The viceroy's advisers commissioned an independent review of Father Pío's charges, but they were slow to intervene. In the end, they did not reject the pastor's many complaints, but they found his judgments of the crown's appointed governor intemperate, not in keeping with the prudence and circumspection of a loving pastor. A final note in the file by the *fiscal de lo civil*, dated September 3, 1803, reported that the pastor had died by then and the subdelegado was no longer serving in Villa Alta. He ordered the case file "archived."
62. AHM L10A/7–8, Rubio y Salinas pastoral visit books, fols. 13r–v, 86r–87r.
63. AGN Inquisición 1113 exp. 6. A set of compliance letters from parish priests to their bishops in central and southern Mexico and Guatemala raised questions about the scope of this decree that add a few details about local practices. One priest in Antequera wrote on August 18, 1768 to ask whether he was supposed to police "various people," mainly women, who called attention to themselves in public by wearing gold or silver crosses and reliquaries. The priest of San Juan Coxutepeque, Guatemala inquired of his archbishop on April 10, 1768 whether he should try to remove all the ridiculous and otherwise defective religious images from the church there when all of them seemed defective and ridiculous to him. Other examples of authorities concerned about "imperfect" and "ugly" religious images are not hard to find in late eighteenth-century records. For yet another example, AGN Inquisición 1318 exp. 5, 1793, in

which the pastor of Zapotiltic, Jalisco denounced the scandalously malformed and ugly images of Christ and the saints that were displayed in public.
64. AHM L10/A/10, Archbishop Lorenzana's pastoral visit record, "decoro, decencia, uniformar."
65. Bancroft M-M 69, 70, I, 131v, and decree 3–21-7 of the fourth Concilio Provincial. The decrees of this synod failed to gain the approval of the papacy or the Spanish crown, but they reflect the thinking and to some extent the policies of prelates and royal officials in New Spain at the time.
66. Jane Garnett and Gervase Rosser, *Spectacular Miracles: Transforming Images in Italy from the Renaissance to the Present*, London: Reaktion Books, 2013, pp. 51–52.
67. AGN Civil 1457 exp. 13.
68. David Carbajal López, "La reforma de las cofradías en el siglo XVIII: Nueva España y Sevilla en comparación," *Estudios de Historia Novohispana* 48 (January–June 2013), 10, 12–13, 30 comments that in Spain the crown effectively dissolved *cofradías gremiales* and many others that lacked royal or ecclesiastical licenses, whereas in New Spain the process was more gradual and less complete, and the clergy remained a leading presence in cofradía affairs.
69. Carbajal López finds that few confraternities in New Spain were substantially reformed and concludes that the purpose of the reforms was to reorganize rather than eliminate, "La reforma de las cofradías," pp. 15, 23.
70. Carbajal López, "La reforma de las cofradías," p. 27.
71. For example, the *Libro de los guardianes y gobernadores de Cuauhtinchan (1519–1640)*, ed. Constantino Medina Lima, Mexico: CIESAS, 1995, p. 63 notes for 1588 that a *macehual* was collecting alms for "la Virgen de la Cofradía," with the permission of the Archdiocese of Mexico's provisor. In this instance, the local fiscal had him arrested when he entered the town.
72. The written record for licensing demandas and keeping accounts during this period is incomplete, but I have not yet found cases of requests denied. Local authorities sometimes objected to alms collectors visiting their communities (for example, AGN Inquisición 546 exp. 5, ff 430–444, 1705, Autlán, Jalisco), and occasionally an individual was arrested for failing to present a license (e.g., Yanhuitlan in 1699, AGN Inquisición 373 exp. 17, fols. 170–177, arrest of Juan Antonio de Jesús María, español, as a liar and cheat – *embustero* – caught collecting for an image of Nuestra Señora de la Consolación without a license), but licenses seem to have been granted routinely for acceptable devotions, whether during pastoral visits or by special petition. The licenses usually specified a time limit (of six months or a year); and if territorial limits were specified, they were generous, often for the entire diocese. For example, for the shrine of Our Lady of Remedios in 1639, AHACM num. de inventario 3898; Atoiaque, province of [Z]acatlan, 1646, AGN Inquisición 461 exp. 18, fols. 460–461; AGN General de Parte 17 exp. 149, 1695, for the church of Nuestra Señora del Pilar de Zaragoza in Mexico City; AGN Civil 1384 exp. 11 for the Cristo Renovado de Santa Teresa in the 1720s; Tulane VEMC leg. 70 exp. 45, 1722, Nuestra Señora de Tulantongo; AGN General de Parte 29 exp. 50, 1732, for an image of Jesús Nazareno in the city of Puebla; for Nuestra Señora de San Juan de los Lagos, 1736, 1743, 1756–1764, Pedro M. Márquez, *Historia de Nuestra Señora de San Juan de los Lagos, Jal.*, 5th ed., San Juan de los Lagos: Imprenta "Alborada," 1966, pp. 145ff and AGN

General de Parte 27 exp. 15; Archbishop Aguiar y Seixas's pastoral visit in 1685 to Meztitlán, Tzoquisoquipa, and Capulhuac, and his 1687 visit to Tepecoacuilco. The two parts of Aguiar y Seixas's visita record are in LC Monday Collection roll 10 and AHM. Florencia and Oviedo, *Zodíaco mariano* (1690s/1755) mentions alms-collecting missions for Nuestra Señora de la Salud of Pátzcuaro (pp. 264–268), Nuestra Señora de Zapopan (pp. 289–291), and Nuestra Señora de Ocotlán (pp. 219, 225).

73. For San Miguel del Milagro, pastoral visit record of November 24, 1752, AHM L10 A/7, fol. 112; for Totolapa 1759 pastoral visit record, AHM L10 A/8.
74. AGN General de Parte 41 exp. 133, 1756 blanket license.
75. *Real ordenanza para el establecimiento é instrucción de intendentes de exército y provincial en el reino de la Nueva España*, Madrid: n.p., 1786.
76. "corregir y castigar los ociosos y malentretenidos ... no se consientan vagamundos ... mendigos de profesión."
77. AGN Civil 1762 exp. 16, 1786–1787.
78. Revillagigedo acted in response to a letter from the alcalde ordinario of the Villa de Córdoba seeking instructions on how to deal with the many alms collectors coming into his district, Raffaele Moro Romero, "¿Una práctica poco visible? La demanda de limosnas 'indígena' en la Nueva España del siglo XVIII (Arzobispado de México)," *Estudios de Historia Novohispana* 46 (enero–junio 2012), 121–123. Revillagigedo's successor, the Marqués de Branciforte summarized the issue in similar terms in a letter to the king ("... el abuso con que a pretexto de qualquiera imagen de Dios, la Virgen o sus santos tratavan de asegurar su subsistencia muchos yndividuos que de otra manera carecían de destino o entretenimiento ... vajo el velo de culto, adorno de capillas o altares occurían a la curia eclesiástica de donde obtenían en multitud las licencias para colectación de limosnas." The result was, he said, "infinitas gentes vagas"), but he was uncertain about the extent of his and the audiencia's authority in the matter and sought the king's advice, AGN Correspondencia de Virreyes 179 ff 61r–64v, dated November 20, 179_. (The fourth numeral in the year is hidden in the bound seam of the volume, but probably is 4 or 5.)

Moro Romero (p. 124) suggests that this "new attitude of the government" toward demandas, as seen in Revillagigedo's directive and the spike in judicial cases involving policing of alms collection for image shrines and denial of demandas licenses, was brought on by a growing number of itinerant collectors following the subsistence crisis of 1785–1786. Whether there were many more alms-collecting missions at this time is an open question. Licensed or not, short-range collections had been common long before 1785 or 1790, as the author of the instruction to Jesuit hacienda administrators made clear earlier in the eighteenth century when he wrote of "la multitud de demandas que piden los indios para las imágenes de sus pueblos," in *Instrucciones a los hermanos jesuitas administradores de haciendas*, ed. François Chevalier, Mexico: UNAM, 1950, p. 250. Chevalier judges that these *instrucciones* were written during the second quarter of the eighteenth century, "or slightly later." Research into alms-collecting missions from Indian pueblos in the late colonial period includes Moro Romero's essay and Edward W. Osowski, *Indigenous Miracles: Nahua Authority in Colonial Mexico*, Tucson: University of Arizona Press, 2010, chapter 3, and appendix A, Table A.1 of Osowski's doctoral dissertation, "Saints of the Republic: Nahua Religious Obligations in Central Mexico, 1692–1810," Pennsylvania State University, 2002, pp. 357–362.

79. For demandas petitions that were considered, rejected, modified, or sometimes approved on advice from the audiencia's fiscal between 1790 and 1809, AGN Clero Regular y Secular 19 fol. 298 (no expediente number visible); AGN Clero Regular y Secular 22 exp 15; AGN Clero Regular y Secular 27 exp. 2, 3, 4, 6, 7, 9, and 12; AGN Clero Regular y Secular 116 exp. 3, 4, 5, 13, and 16; AGN Clero Regular y Secular 151 exp. 4, 5, 6, 7, and 10; AGN Clero Regular y Secular 155 exp. 3, 7, and 12; AGN Clero Regular y Secular 179 exp. 10; AGN Clero Regular y Secular 181 exp. 5, 6, 6bis, and 7; AGN General de Parte 77 exp. 185; AGN Cultos Religiosos 1 exp. 5. Typically, petitions were denied in the name of "eliminating abuses and disorder resulting from the collection of alms," AGN Clero Regular y Secular 151 exp. 7 case of Tulantongo 1795, or "mala versación" by collectors; AGN Clero Regular y Secular 151 exp. 5 case of Tlaquiltenango 1795, or "jamás se cortará el abuso de la questura de limosnas en los pueblos si no se cierra la puerta a los repetidos ocursos con que los demandantes la solicitan valiéndose de distintos y especiosos medios"; AGN Clero Regular y Secular 151 exp. 7 case of San Agustín Coaguayutla, 1795.

80. AGN Civil 1557 exp. 8.
81. AGN Clero Regular y Secular 151 exp. 10, fol. 193.
82. AGN Clero Regular y Secular 151 exp. 10, fol. 193, September 12, 1795, signed B. Rafael Antonio Sánchez Yruegas.
83. AGN Clero Regular y Secular 151 exp. 10, fol. 195.
84. AGN Clero Regular y Secular 151 exp. 10, fol. 210.
85. AGN Clero Regular y Secular 151 exp. 5 Tlaquilentango, 1795; AGN Clero Regular y Secular 151 exp. 7, San Agustín Coaguayutla, 1796.
86. Bancroft MSS 87/191m, and José Gómez, *Diario curioso y cuaderno de las cosas memorables ... 1789–1794*, ed. Ignacio González-Polo, Mexico: UNAM, 1986, pp. 12, 14, 44, 82, 88, 110.
87. Gómez, *Diario curioso*, pp. 12, 14, 44, 110.
88. AGN Correspondencia de Virreyes 179 fols. 61–64.
89. These events are chronicled by José Gómez in the manuscript copy of his "Diario de México" in the Bancroft M-M 105, entries for 1794 dated September 1, November 28, and November 30; and for 1795 dated February 2, June 24, July 2, August 15, and October 4, 11, and 12.
90. Bancroft MSS 72/57m. The traditional feast of St. Michael is September 29, but perhaps the Orthodox feast in early November was celebrated here, as well, so that the octave to the saint when Hernández visited the chapel overlapped, or fell close to, the feast of All Souls when offerings would have been placed on gravesites.
91. Bancroft Library MSS 72/57m, fols. 123–124.
92. Bancroft MSS 72/57m, fol. 92r.
93. Bancroft MSS 72/57m, fols. 123–124, *auto* of December 14, 1733.
94. Rafael D. García Pérez, *Reforma y resistencia: Manuel de Flon y la Intendencia de Puebla*, Mexico: Editorial Porrúa, 2000. This was the same Manuel Flon who, in his mid-sixties, perished in the Battle of Calderón in 1811 while leading royalist troops against Miguel Hidalgo's insurgents.
95. Montserrat Balí Boadella, "Una ciudad en busca de un santo: Fray Sebastián de Aparicio y la ciudad de Puebla de los Ángeles," in *La imagen sagrada y sacralizada: XXVIII Coloquio Internacional de Historia del Arte*, ed. Peter Krieger, Mexico: UNAM, 2011, II, 592.

96. AGN Clero Regular y Secular 195 exp. 6.
97. AHM Fondo Catedral Colonia, 1796, "Representación del Yllmo. Sr. Obispo de Puebla sobre excesos en el tránsito de las Ymágenes de los pueblos de Yndios a las caveceras por su concurrencia en las proceciones," fol. 72. Flon's letter is dated June 1, 1797.
98. Father Rosado also seems to have been an insurgent leader in the early stages of Mexico's independence movement. Whether or not this dispute over the Señor del Jovo contributed to their political leanings, both Rosado and the Peña family had reason to feel less than vindicated by the affair.
99. For the ongoing importance of ecclesiastical institutions, see especially Óscar Mazin Gómez, *El cabildo catedral de Valladolid de Michoacán*, Zamora: El Colegio de Michoacán, 1996, and *Entre dos majestades: El obispo y la Iglesia del Gran Michoacán ante las reformas borbónicas, 1758–1722*, Zamora: El Colegio de Michoacán, 1987.
100. In Europe during the eighteenth century, too, the demise of enchantment can be exaggerated. On ongoing magical thinking, see, for example, H. C. Erik Midelfort, *Exorcism and Enlightenment: Johann Joseph Gassner and the Demons of Eighteenth-Century Germany*, New Haven: Yale University Press, 2005. Pope Benedict XIV (1740–1758) was especially receptive to reports of the miraculous and famously facilitated new canonizations.
101. For an example from 1774 to 1797, see AHACM num. de inventario 3902 exp. 48.
102. See Appendix 1. Also Juan de Viera, *Compendiosa narración de la ciudad de México*, Mexico/Buenos Aires: Editorial Guaranía, 1952, p. 50, "dezir en fin el numeroso venerable conjunto de imágenes milagrosas que en todas las parroquias se veneran fuera cassi imposible"; and Ignacio Carrillo y Pérez, *Pensil americano florido en el rigor del invierno, la imagen de María Santísima de Guadalupe*..., Mexico: Zúñiga y Ontiveros, 1797, pp. ii–iii, "Y siendo una de las cosas que más engrandecen a esta capital los célebres Santuarios con que Dios la ha singularizado, sirven de corona a la enunciada obra la historia de ellos, en que el Lector piadoso hallará sobrados motivos de alabanza a la omnipotencia divina, que a manos llenas la ha enriquecido con tan portentosas Imágenes. La que adoramos en Tepeyac, aparecida y estampada en la grosera capa de un Indio, se lleva con primacía las atenciones devotas de los Mexicanos, sin que por esto dexen de tributar los más reverentes cultos a las otras Imágenes que con la Guadalupana forman los sagrados muros en que la Imperial México funda su ser, su conservación y sus aumentos."
103. See, for example, Miguel Sánchez's *Novenas de la Virgen María Madre de Dios: para sus dos devotíssimos santuarios de los Remedios y Guadalupe*..., Mexico: Viuda de Bernardo Calderón, 1665, and Florencia's devotional histories for both shrines, *La milagrosa invención de un tesoro escondido*... (1685, for Remedios), and *Estrella del norte de México* (1688, for Guadalupe).
104. The ethnographic literature is vast. For a taste in English, see Timothy J. Knab, *The Dialogue of Earth and Sky: Dreams, Souls, Curing, and the Modern Aztec Underworld*, Tucson: University of Arizona Press, 2004, pp. 98–99 on life-giving trees of earth and stone in the underground realm, Tlalocan; James M. Taggart, *Nahuatl Myth and Social Structure*, Austin: University of Texas Press, 1983 on folklore and cosmology; and Alan R. Sandstrom, *Corn Is Our Blood: Culture and Ethnic Identity in a Contemporary Aztec*

Indian Village, Norman: University of Oklahoma Press, 1991, p. 229, sacred places and the earth spirit in a Nahua cosmos that is "firmly rooted in the pre-Hispanic past."

105. Institutes such as INAH (Instituto Nacional de Antropología e Historia, founded in 1939, eventually with thirty-one regional centers), ENAH (the Escuela Nacional de Antropología e Historia, which began in the Departamento de Antropología of the Escuela de Ciencias Biológicas of the Instituto Politécnico Nacional, incorporated into INAH under its current name in 1946), and INI (Instituto Nacional Indigenista, formally established in 1948, but with its roots in the Primer Congreso Indigenista Interamericano convened in 1940 by President Cárdenas. INI was replaced in 2003 by the Comisión Nacional para el Desarrollo de los Pueblos Indígenas).

106. Mercedes Guadarrama Olivera, "El espacio y el tiempo sagrados en tres comunidades totonacas de la Sierra de Papantla," in *Procesos rurales e historia regional (sierra y costa totonacas de Veracruz)*, ed. Victoria Chenaut, Mexico: CIESAS, 1996, pp. 183–205.

107. See Alfredo López Austin, "Cosmovision," in *Oxford Encyclopedia of Mesoamerican Cultures*, ed. David Carrasco, New York: Oxford University Press, 2001, I, 268–274. On "cosmovision" as a watchword among Mexican scholars for an enduring Mesoamerican religious system, see, for example, the essays in *Peregrinaciones ayer y hoy: Arqueología y antropología de las religiones*, ed. Patricia Fournier, Carlos Mondragón, and Walburga Wiesheu, Mexico: El Colegio de México, 2012, especially pp. 119–123, "se trata de una visión estructurada en la cual los antiguos mesoamericanos combinaban de manera coherente sus nociones sobre el medio ambiente en que vivían y sobre el cosmos en que situaban la vida del hombre," p. 122 (Sergio Sánchez Vázquez, "Peregrinaciones, espacios sagrados y santuarios: El ámbito nacional, regional y local en la cosmovisión otomiana del Valle del Mezquital," in *Peregrinaciones ayer y hoy*, ed. Fournier, Mondragón, and Wiesheu, pp. 119–153).

Félix Báez Jorge's approach to a more theoretical and historical understanding of indigenous religiosity in Mexico (including *La parentela de María: Cultos marianos, sincretismo e identidades nacionales en Latinoamérica*, Xalapa: Universidad Veracruzana, 1994, and *Entre los naguales y los santos: Religión popular y ejercicio clerical en el México indígena*, Xalapa: Universidad Veracruzana, 1998) has inspired others to consider long-term continuities across the colonial period and beyond. Báez Jorge envisions a complex "syncretic" field – "like a luxuriant jungle" in which "an array of trees, plants, and animals introduced from different places intermix in a multiplicity of microsystems united by a complex, vitalizing and transforming force" (*Parentela*, p. 17). Syncretism in his studies comes down to the reconstitution of a native worldview and practices – "the ancient autochthonous cosmovision" – including especially "the new consecration of the natural surroundings." He does not explore these overarching ideas closely for any particular place during the colonial period. Rather, the historical approach relies especially on upstreaming from modern ethnographic work – for example, his hypothesis about modern pilgrimage patterns reproducing precolonial patterns and the continuation of "antecedent prehispanic cultic practices" in contemporary shrines, *Entre los naguales*, pp. 63, 68, 69–70.

Several recent research seminars and symposia in ethnography and history have sought to apply to particular places Báez Jorge's vision of a dynamic, performative syncretism in native terms, but the results so far are inconclusive. For example, the essays in *Religiosidad popular y cosmovisiones indígenas en la historia de Mexico* (coordinated by Johanna Broda, Mexico: INAH, 2009) warmly salute Báez Jorge on syncretism and popular religiosity, but they mainly connect Broda's scholarship on precolonial cosmovision to ethnographic observation and description in contemporary communities, tacking back and forth between the present and the precolonial past, and skipping over the centuries in between. For similar procedures and results see also Guadarrama Olivera, "El espacio"; Alejandro Robles García, "El Nevado de Toluca: 'Ombligo' del mar y de todo el mundo," and Catherine Good Eshelman, "Oztotempan: El ombligo del mundo," in *La montaña y el paisaje ritual*, ed. Johanna Broda, Stanislaw Iwaniszewski, and Arturo Montero, Mexico: CONACULTA/INAH, pp. 149–159, 375–394; and *Cosmovisión mesoamericana y ritualidad agrícola: Estudios interdisciplinarios y regionales*, ed. Johanna Broda and Alejandra Gámez, Puebla: BUAP, 2009. More open-ended and perhaps more promising for historical study is Alfredo López Austin's invitation to consider how the sense of particular concepts – more than an undisturbed cosmovision – could continue in the course of the dislocations and transformations of Spanish colonization, and Inga Clendinnen's less theological emphasis on "ways to the sacred." See her *The Cost of Courage in Aztec Society: Essays on Mesoamerican Society and Culture*, Cambridge, UK and New York: Cambridge University Press, 2010, chapter 4.

108. In four volumes coordinated by Alicia Barabás, *Diálogos con el territorio*, Mexico: INAH, 2003–2004; for example, "casos muy interesantes de santuarios de matriz prehispánica con presencia contemporánea," Elio Masferrer Kan, on the state of Puebla, 2: 75; writing about the Maya lowlands, Ella F. Quintal concludes that "el modelo prehispánico sobrevive basicamente a través de una multiplicidad de prácticas rituales familiares y colectivas asociadas al monte, la milpa, el solar, y el pueblos," 1: 350; also 4: 105–162 (especially 116–120), "Espacios y tiempos rituales en el Valle del Mezquital." A recent monograph in this vein from a religious studies perspective posits that modern Maya cosmology, especially quadripartite signs, including natural crosses that come to life, hearken back to Classic period Maya beliefs and practices, Miguel Ángel Astor Aguilera, *The Maya World of Communicating Objects, Quadripartite Crosses, Trees and Stones*, Albuquerque: University of New Mexico Press, 2011.

109. For example, Gregory A. Cajete, "Guadalupe: An Indigenous Mythic Education Perspective," in *Religion as Art: Guadalupe, Orishas, and Sufi*, ed. Steven Loza, Albuquerque: University of New Mexico Press, 2009, pp. 143–158, and the critique by Stafford Poole in the same volume, "Our Lady of Guadalupe in Historical Perspective," pp. 58–69.

110. Poole, "Our Lady of Guadalupe in Historical Perspective," p. 65.

111. For example, the recent five-volume collective work of Mexican anthropologists, *Los sueños y los días: Chamanismo y nahualismo en el Mexico actual*, Mexico: INAH, 2013–2014. Three of these volumes on different regions were assembled and edited by Miguel A. Bartolomé and Alicia Barabás.

112. Elizabeth Hill Boone highlights the similarity of Mesoamerican ritual calendars before the Spanish Conquest and "a common divinatory ideology that was widely shared throughout central and southern Mexico" in *Cycles of Time and Meaning in the Mexican Books of Fate*, Austin: University of Texas Press, 2007. David Tavárez discusses the ninety-nine ritual calendar booklets of northern Zapotec specialists

160   Part I Bearings: Historical Patterns and Places of Image Shrines

that surfaced in the Villa Alta district at the beginning of the eighteenth century during an extirpation campaign by the Bishop of Oaxaca, *The Invisible War: Indigenous Devotions, Discipline, and Dissent in Colonial Mexico*, Stanford: Stanford University Press, 2011, pp. 145–156.

113. For example, Ixmiquilpan, 1624 in AGN Inquisición 303 fols. 69–71. The parish priest reported that there were other examples of Indians claiming to have been bewitched and *hechiceros* transforming themselves into animals and killing people. Other ecclesiastical court investigations of local Indian shamans include AHM caja 1691–1769, 1691 Calimaya; AGN Inquisición 789 exp. 31 Sacala, Campeche 1721; AHM caja 1728 exp. 11 1728 San Matheo Atenco, Metepec; AHM caja for 1745, Calimaya; AHM caja 1754–1755, Toluca; AGN Criminal 120 exp. 25, 1769 Huizquilucan; AHM caja 1779 Tlalnepantla 1803. And there are the narrative accounts by seventeenth-century extirpators, including Ruiz de Alarcón, Ponce, Serna, Navarro de Vargas, and Balsalobre. Gonzalo de Balsalobre's text is not cited elsewhere in this book. It can be consulted in a version accompanied by relevant Inquisition records, edited by Heinrich Berlin, *Idolatría y superstición entre los indios de Oaxaca*, Mexico: Ediciones Toledo, 1988.

114. For an example of a local Spaniard accusing six Indians of Calimaya of witchcraft and conjuring hailstorms ("maleficio, conjurador de granizos"), see the complaint of Esteban Cayetano Pérez before the parish priest of Tenango del Valle in 1745, AHM caja 1745.

115. Diego Durán, *Historia de las Indias de Nueva España e islas de Tierra Firme*, Cien de México series, Mexico: CONACULTA, 1995, II, 224–225 (Tratado Tercero, "Epístola").

116. See Tavárez, *Invisible War*, especially chapters 4–6. Also for idolatry investigations and trials triggered by fractious local politics in Oaxaca in the late seventeenth and early eighteenth centuries, the forthcoming book by Rosalba Piazza, *La conciencia oscura de los naturales: Procesos de idolatría de Oaxaca, siglos XVI–XVIII*, Mexico: El Colegio de México.

117. Michel Graulich, *Myths of Ancient Mexico*, trans. Bernard R. Ortiz de Montellano and Thelma Ortiz de Montellano, Norman: University of Oklahoma Press, 1997, *passim*. Among others, there is Alfredo López's Austin's classic *Hombre-dios: Religión y política en el mundo náhuatl*, Mexico: UNAM, 1973.

118. "You shall have no other gods before me. You shall not make for yourself a graven image, or any likeness of anything that is in heaven above, or that is in the earth beneath, or that is in the water under the earth; you shall not bow down to them or serve them; for I the Lord your God am a jealous God, visiting the iniquity of the fathers upon the children to the third and the fourth generation of those who hate me, but showing steadfast love to thousands of those who love me and keep my commandments," Exodus 20:3–6, Deuteronomy 4:4–21. From the beginning, ecclesiastical chroniclers viewed native effigies as idols; for example Durán, *Historia de las Indias*, III, 90.

119. Alberto Carrillo Cázares, *Michoacán en el otoño del siglo XVII*, Zamora: El Colegio de Michoacán, 1993, p. 339.

120. On native medicine regarded as witchcraft and the work of the devil, see Osvaldo F. Pardo, "Angels, Demons, and Plants in Colonial Mexico," in *Spiritual Encounters: Interactions between Christianity and Native Religions in Colonial America*, ed.

Nicholas Griffiths and Fernando Cervantes, Lincoln: University of Nebraska Press, 1999, pp. 163–184, especially p. 173. Jacinto de la Serna had idolatry in this broad sense in mind when he described offerings to fire and Christian images by Indian villages near Toluca in the 1620s: "celebran a el fuego, ofresciéndole comida, y bediba, haziéndole la salva a el Sancto a su modo idolátrico, derramando delante del fuego o de la imagen del Sancto un poco del pulque, o del vino," "Manual de ministros de indios para el conocimieno de sus idolatrías, y extirpación de ellas," in *Colección de documentos inéditos para la historia de España*, Madrid: Academia de la Historia, 1892, 104, 69.

121. *Concilio III provincial mexicano celebrado el año de 1585* . . ., ed. Mariano Galván Rivera, Mexico: Eugenio Maillefert y Compañía, 1859, libro I título 1 and libro V títulos 4, 6. The *relaciones geográficas* from the Archdiocese of Mexico and the Diocese of Oaxaca in the 1570s described dances, feasts, sacrificial offerings, and other religious rites from particular places in the same sweeping terms and, pointedly, as the work of the devil. See especially vol. 6 for the Archdiocese of Mexico. This is not to say that official concern about graven images was diverted by this sweeping notion of idolatry as improper worship. For example, in Book 2 of the Florentine Codex, Sahagún and his informants emphasize images of the gods and refer repeatedly to sacrificial ceremonies "before the image" (e.g., *General History of the Things of New Spain: Florentine Codex*, ed. and trans. Arthur J. O. Anderson and Charles E. Dibble, Santa Fe, NM: School of American Research and Salt Lake City, University of Utah Press, 1950–1982, Book 2, p. 17, feast of Xiuhtecutli).

122. Criminal trials are sprinkled with explanations of the kind: "el diablo le había engañado" (Centro de Documentación del Castillo de Chapultepec, INAH Library, Museo de Antropología, Serie Oaxaca, microfilm roll 8, Archivo colonial de Teposcolula, exp. 299, murder trial of Francisco Nicolás) and "por su suma desgracia o aconcejado por el demonio," AGN Criminal 184 fols. 408–, trial of José Ramón Monroy, mulato, for rape and murder.

123. Kenneth R. Mills, *Idolatry and Its Enemies: Colonial Andean Religion and Extirpation, 1640–1750*, Princeton: Princeton University Press, 1997, pp. 3, 7, 10, 34, 196–197; John Chuchiak, "Toward a Regional Definition of Idolatry: Reexamining Idolatry Trials in the 'Relaciones de Méritos' and Their Role in Defining the Concept of 'Idolatría' in Colonial Yucatán, 1570–1780," *Journal of Early Modern History* 6: 2 (2002), 140–167.

124. Tavárez, *Invisible War*, p. 276. The term is drawn from the Sola de Vega Inquisition cases referring to the "enemigo común," AGN Inquisición 456 exps.16, 18.

125. David Tavárez, "Ideology as an Ontological Question: Native Consciousness and Juridical Proof in Colonial Mexico," *Journal of Early Modern History* 6: 2 (2002), 114.

126. For an example of accusations of idolatry and witchcraft as a political weapon, see Carlos Paredes Martínez, *El Hospitalito de Irapuato: La cofradía de Tarascos de Nuestra Señora de la Misericordia. Documentos para su historia*, Irapuato: Ayuntamiento de Irapuato, 2009, doc. 12, fol. 191v.

127. Other cases include AHM caja for 1745, Calimaya, 1745; AHM L10A/8 1759–60 pastoral visit record, Tlaquiltenango; JCB B760 relación de méritos y servicios for Nicolás de Castilla; AGN Criminal 120 exp. 25 Huizquilucan 1769; AGN Bienes Nacionales 638 exp. 84 Huizquilucan 1795; AGN Inquisición 1255 Misantla 1784; CONDUMEX, fondo XVI-1 carpeta 10 Col. Enrique A. Cervantes, 1796 near

Tecamachalco; AGN Historia 413 San Gabriel Chilac, Puebla 1801–1802; AHM caja 1779 Tlalnepantla 1803.
128. When a formal court of the Inquisition was established in New Spain in 1571, Indians were exempted from its jurisdiction. The bishops' ecclesiastical courts for Indian affairs – the *provisoratos de indios* – retained nominal jurisdiction over Indian religious matters, but without the latitude exercised earlier by episcopal inquisitors, most notoriously by Fray Diego de Landa in Yucatán in 1562. Exercising inquisitorial jurisdiction, Landa reportedly tortured some 4,500 Mayas after idols were discovered in a cave near Mani. He evidently took the discovery and confessions of idol worship personally as a betrayal of his love and trust in baptized Mayas, Inga Clendinnen, *Ambivalent Conquests: Maya and Spaniard in Yucatan, 1517–1570*, Cambridge, UK and New York: Cambridge University Press, 1987, pp. 73–76. Feria's complaint came a generation after the torture and deaths set in motion by Landa.
129. "They disparage the faith" ("hacen burla de la fe").
130. In Feria's words, Atonal assured people that "para alcanzar perdón de los pecados basta mirar al cielo y que no era menester otra cosa."
131. "They transformed themselves into gods and goddesses" ("se convertían en dioses y diosas").
132. In an article about strategic cooperation between native elites and colonial rulers in sixteenth-century Mexico, Amos Megged found that Atonal had made enemies in Chiapa de Indios going back to the 1540s and recruited laborers for the local encomendero's sugar mill, "Accommodation and Resistance of Elites in Transition: The Case of Chiapa in Early Colonial Mesoamerica," *Hispanic American Historical Review* 71: 3 (August 1991), 477–500.
133. Kevin Gosner, "Caciques and Conversion: Juan Atonal and the Struggle for Legitimacy in Post-Conquest Chiapas," *The Americas* 49: 2 (October 1992), 117–118. For a published transcription of the bishop's *relación*, see Pedro de Feria, *Revelación sobre la reincidencia en sus idolatrías*, Guatemala: Linkgua Digital, 2010. The original manuscript is in the Archivo General de Indias (AGI), Patronato 183 núm. 1, ramo 11. Gosner's thorough discussion of the content of Bishop Feria's *relación* is directed toward understanding how indigenous elites worked to maintain their privileged places in local society when Spanish rule became inevitable. His thesis is that Maya elites such as Atonal and his Twelve Apostles were working to "reassert the supernatural foundations of their legitimacy" (p. 123).
134. AGI Patronato 183 n. 1, r. 11.
135. As Gosner notes, "Caciques and Conversion," p. 119, the audiencia invoked a papal bull issued by Gregory XIII calling for leniency and absolution of new Christians accused of heresy or idolatry.
136. Perhaps still influenced by the Yucatán debacle described in Clendinnen, which ushered in the creation of the Holy Office of the Inquisition without jurisdiction over Indian religiosity.
137. Dolores Aramoni Calderón, "Don Juan Atonal, cacique de Chiapa de la Real Corona," *Liminar. Estudios Sociales y Humanísticos* 2: 2 (julio–diciembre 2004), 131–142.
138. With surges in 1610–1630 and the 1640s, Solange Alberro charts this pattern for the Mexican Inquisition in *Inquisición y sociedad en México, 1571–1700*, Mexico: Fondo de

Growth, Other Changes, and Continuities in the Late Colonial Period 163

Cultura Económica, 1988, pp. 148–151, 168–171. The number of actual trials – about fifteen a year – was not unusual compared to most Inquisitions in the Spanish kingdoms.

139. Taylor, *Magistrates of the Sacred*, pp. 63–66, and especially Tavárez, *Invisible War*.

140. Roughly 200 years later, this record was removed from the ecclesiastical archive by Mexican civil authorities and filed with other church records in the Bienes Nacionales section of the Archivo General de la Nación, box 1285 exp. 19, fourteen folio sheets. For more on the setting for this case, see Serge Gruzinski, *Man-Gods of the Mexican Highlands: Indian Power and Colonial Society, 1520–1800*, trans. Eileen Corrigan, Stanford: Stanford University Press, 1989, pp. 63–88. Especially for Gregorio Juan's lengthy deposition, Gruzinski offers a full description as summarized by the scribe and translator, which he reorders and shapes to elaborate on his "hypothesis of the paranoid personality" and glimpse the "initiation of a[n Amerindian] shaman." Young Gregorio Juan evidently aspired to the charisma of a shaman and prophet in Max Weber's terms – set apart as a person of exceptional powers and superhuman qualities – but we have this documentation because he was not widely accepted in Aiohuizcuahtla or at home in those terms.

It is tempting, but risky, to treat this record as an unmediated ethnographic nugget from a remote past. Since it is the product of a preliminary, local investigation rather than a formal trial, the witnesses responded to a general prompting by Fr. Medina, not a detailed list of leading questions that called for brief answers. Unlike most tightly scripted episcopal and Inquisition trial records that put the words in witnesses' mouths, the testimony about what Gregorio Juan said and did varies somewhat from witness to witness, offering an unusual opportunity to compare them and speculate about the differences. My immediate purpose here is to highlight the nature of the documentation and ask (1) why the accusation was brought to the prior of Huauchinango and (2) why the preliminary inquiry did not lead to a formal investigation and trial in the archbishop's court.

141. These two witnesses said that several young women who seemed to be between fourteen and twenty years old were also present. The first Miguel Juan said there were four of them, and they were inside Marcos Juan's house. The second Miguel Juan said there were two, and they were kneeling with the others outside the enclosure.

142. The first Miguel Juan said he donated a shirt, Clemente gave his wife's petticoat, and Pablo gave a pair of trousers.

143. Diego Juan mentioned two occasions, both at Clemente's house; Isabel Ana mentioned three, the two at Clemente's house and one at the house of Marcos Juan "el Viejo."

144. Apparitions of any kind generally were treated with more suspicion in the seventeenth century than they had been earlier when the Franciscans, in particular, collected and promoted apparition stories. But another example of a mid-seventeenth-century apparition story that was not prosecuted is described in Taylor, *Shrines & Miraculous Images*, pp. 27–28.

145. AHM caja 1794. The serious injuries ("graves perjuicios and daños") caused by false accusations that the archbishop had in mind went beyond the financial hardships of imprisonment and embargo of property. As Don Juan Nicolás, an Indian noble of San Martín Quautlalpan in the district of Tlalmanalco said in his complaint against the

Indian alcalde of his community, when the alcalde called him a witch (*hechicero*) it robbed him of his good reputation ("quitarle el crédito") with the people who knew him, both Indians and Spaniards, AGN Criminal 1 exp. 7. Archbishop Rubio y Salinas made the point in other words, writing of the "contemptible reputation attributed to them" by such accusations, with the accusers gaining the satisfaction of their revenge ("despreciable opinión les atribuye . . . quedando éstos entre pequeñas ocasiones satisfechos de su benganza").

146. *IV Concilio Provincial* 1–1-4; Bancroft M-M 69–70, fols. 200v–201r, in the special session of the synod devoted to Indian idolatry, the prelates focused on the Santiaguitos dance and singing, which a Franciscan provincial had been told was a lament over their defeat in the Conquest, and which the parish priest of Otumba said referred to the sainted apostle as arrogant or haughty.

147. *IV Concilio Provincial* 1–1-4 p. 6. Lorenzana was a catalyst, probably *the* catalyst, for this focus of the synod. In much the same language used by the assembly of prelates in 1771, his edict of February 11, 1769 called for "desterrar idolatrías, supersticiones y otros abusos de los Indios" with a focus on "heathen" customs, especially dances and singing.

148. AHM formerly caja 1779. The year before, the parish priest of San Gabriel Chilac in the district of Tehuacán, Puebla found the audiencia less receptive to his charge that parishioners there were rebellious pagans, "the most superstitious in all America." The district governor and the audiencia concluded that the people of San Gabriel "certainly display a haughtiness that should be moderated or suppressed" ("tienen un orgullo digno de moderarse o suprimirse") but that the pastor's own arrogance was also part of the problem. Their solution was to remove the pastor, AGN Historia 413.

Also with less happy results and apparently no action by higher ecclesiastical courts, the Franciscan pastor of the Indian community attached to the shrine of Nuestra Señora del Pueblito outside the city of Querétaro reported to the Inquisition in 1817 that his predecessor had neglected his duties during the turbulent times of the independence wars and now he found it impossible "to weed out the innumerable superstitions that are more deeply rooted than faith in Jesus Christ" ("desterrar inumerables supersticiones que tienen mas intimamente arraigadas que la fe de jesuchristo"). In particular, there was "a growing superstitious cult among them to a Holy Cross they call 'the cross of justice.' They hold nighttime meetings several times a week, attended by people from various pueblos, followers of this superstitious congregation founded in a chapel in Indian Patricio García's house." The pastor described in some detail one of the "bamboozles" or tricks (*faramayas*) of this cult. When Patricio's father-in-law became ill, Patricio went to his house with a tallow candle, among other things. He lit the candle and separated the wick into two halves. As the candle wax melted the halves of the wick formed a cross, which was taken as a great marvel. Since these charges were made against Indians, the Inquisition did not have jurisdiction in the case. Whether or not the case was forwarded to the archbishop's court is not recorded, AGN Inquisición 1465 exp. 7, fols. 85–87.

149. This case is reminiscent of another idolatry investigation in the Toluca valley in 1755 that also did not go to trial. The son of the owner of the Hacienda de Nuestra Señora de Guadalupe Tlachaloya reportedly discovered a group of Indian laborers on the estate

gathered in the flower-bedecked family chapel of Juan de la Cruz for a feast surrounded by clay animal and human figurines, some of them on horseback, AHM, caja labeled 1754–1755.
150. My thanks to Ethelia Ruiz Medrano for sharing her notes and photocopy of this case record from the Newberry Library.
151. Ángel F. Méndez Montoya, "Latin America," in *The Blackwell Companion to Catholicism*, ed. James Buckley, Frederick Christian Bauerschmidt, and Trent Pomplun, Malden, MA: Wiley-Blackwell, 2010, pp. 173–188, echoes Kubler's view of wholesale destruction and European substitutions.
152. Several Anglophone scholars working on colonial architecture, the visual arts, theater, and liturgy in the sixteenth century have found inspiration for this approach in James Lockhart's observation that "existing Nahua patterns were what made the quick apparent success of Spanish modes possible," *The Nahuas after the Conquest: A Social and Cultural History of the Indians of Central Mexico, Sixteenth Through Eighteenth Centuries*, Stanford: Stanford University Press, 1992, p. 203. See Samuel Y. Edgerton, *Theaters of Conversion: Religious Architecture and Indian Artisans in Colonial Mexico*, Albuquerque: University of New Mexico Press, 2001; Eleanor Wake, *Framing the Sacred: The Indian Churches of Early Colonial Mexico*, Norman: University of Oklahoma Press, 2010; Jaime Lara, *City, Temple, Stage: Eschatalogical Architecture and Liturgical Theatrics in New Spain*, South Bend: University of Notre Dame Press, 2004 and *Christian Texts for Aztecs: Art and Liturgy in Colonial Mexico*, South Bend: University of Notre Dame Press, 2008; and Osvaldo F. Pardo, *The Origins of Mexican Catholicism: Nahua Rituals and Christian Sacraments in Sixteenth-Century Mexico*, Ann Arbor: University of Michigan Press, 2006. In the same vein, see Robert H. Jackson's *Visualizing the Miraculous, Visualizing the Sacred: Evangelization and the "Cultural War" in Sixteenth-Century Mexico*, Newcastle upon Tyne: Cambridge Scholars Publishing, 2014.
153. "La población indígena de la Ciudad de Querétaro en el siglo XVIII," in *Episodios novohispanos de la historia Otomí*, ed. Rosa Brambila, et al., Toluca: Instituto Mexiquense de Cultura, 2002, pp. 47–92.
154. Subversive substitution remains a popular theory, especially for Mexico's most famous image shrine, Our Lady of Guadalupe at Tepeyac: the hill of Tepeyac, which housed a precolonial ceremonial site to a mother goddess Tonantzin, "Our Precious Mother," lived on as the great shrine of Our Lady of Guadalupe with a predominately Indian following in the sixteenth century.
155. Peter Burke, *Cultural Hybridity*, Cambridge, UK: Polity, 2009, p. 17; on "conjugation," Gisela von Wobeser, "Mitos y realidades sobre el origen del culto a la Virgen de Guadalupe," *Revista Grafía* 10: 1 (January–June 2013), 148–160. I discuss syncretism and congruence in *Magistrates of the Sacred*, chapter 3.
156. Tavárez, *Invisible War*, p. 271 for archipelagoes of faith. On reaching for cross-cultural patterns of the local and the central in premodern societies, see Edward Shils, "Center and Periphery," in his *Center and Periphery: Essays in Macrosociology*, Chicago: University of Chicago Press, 1975, pp. 3–16. On p. 10 Shils notes that "for the most part, the mass of the population in premodern societies have been far removed from the immediate impact of the central value system. They have possessed their own value systems, which are occasionally and fragmentarily articulated with the central value system."

157. Examples of early friars seeing signs in nature: Gerónimo de Mendieta, OFM, *Historia eclesiástica indiana*, Mexico: CONACULTA, 1997, II, 304, and Pedro Oroz, *The Oroz Codex*, ed. and trans. Angélico Chávez, Washington: Academy of American Franciscan History, 1972, p. 125 recounted a St. Francis-like story of birds gathering in a tree outside Martín de Valencia's cave at Amecameca when he went outside, and disappearing after he died; and Antonio Tello, OFM, recounted the apparitions to the sick girl in Juchipila and Fr. Juan de Gracia in *Crónica miscelánea de la sancta provincia de Xalisco*, libro III, Guadalajara: Edit. Font, 1942, p. 9 included the story of trees and flowers suddenly bursting into bloom as a sign of God's pleasure when friars from Tzintzuntzan preached the Gospel at Valle de Banderas. Bernardino de Sahagún exhorted Nahua sculptors to give life to the materials they used: "What is carved should be like the original, and have life, for whatever may be the subject which is to be made. The form of it should resemble the original and the life of the original ... Take great care to penetrate what the animal you wish to imitate is like, and how its character and appearance can best be shown," quoted in Elizabeth Wilder Weismann, *Mexico in Sculpture, 1521–1821*, Cambridge, MA: Harvard University Press, 1950, p. 33.

158. Diana Taylor, *The Archive and the Repertoire: Performing Cultural Memory in the Americas*, Durham: Duke University Press, 2003, pp. 106–107.

159. See especially Guilhem Olivier, "Indios y españoles frente a prácticas adivinatorias y presagios durante la conquista de México," *Estudios de Cultura Nahuatl* 37: 1 (2006), 169–192; Alfredo López Austin, *The Human Body and Ideology: Concepts of the Ancient Nahuas*, trans. Thelma Ortiz de Montellano and Bernardo Ortiz de Montellano, Salt Lake City: University of Utah Press, 1988, I, 190; and Guadarrama Olivera, "El espacio," p. 190 for the equivalence of a local figure of Christ Entombed and Xmalana, "dueño de las tierras de cultivo" in the Sierra Totonaca.

European Christians also were deeply interested in astrology and calendars, scanning the majestic passage of the sun, stars, and planets and the phases of the moon for their bearing on human affairs and agricultural cycles. See, for example, Keith Thomas, *Religion and the Decline of Magic: Studies in Popular Beliefs in Sixteenth- and Seventeenth-Century England*, Oxford: Oxford University Press, 1971, pp. 333, 578. On cities of the sacred, Diana L. Eck, "The City as a Sacred Center," in *The City as a Sacred Center: Essays on Six Asian Contexts*, ed. Bardwell Smith and Holly Baker Reynolds, Leiden: E.J. Brill, 1987, p. 2. Eck considers cities as expressions of "moral order": "Their primary self-image is that they reproduce the cosmological order on a human scale ... centers of the world-ordering rites and ceremonies of the gods, or of the kings."

160. For a late colonial example of a parish priest near Mexico City expressing himself in these terms, see AGN Clero Regular y Secular 156 exp. 5, Tepetlaostoc, 1759.

161. On the "intense interest" of Mesoamerican peoples in transcendant experience that engages all the senses, see Stephen Houston and Karl Taube, "An Archeology of the Senses: Perception and Cultural Expression in Ancient Mesoamerica," *Cambridge Archaeological Journal* 10: 2 (2000), 261–294.

162. Henry B. Nicholson, "Religion in Pre-Hispanic Central Mexico," in *Handbook of Middle American Indians*, Austin: University of Texas Press, 1971, 10, 395–446, especially p. 408.

163. William F. Hanks, *Converting Words: Maya in the Age of the Cross*, Berkeley: University of California Press, 2010, pp. 157–158, 363–364, Mayas "had learned the new religion ... internalizing the religion's meaning structures and ways of speaking, translating meaning."
164. Quoted by David Carrasco, "Jaguar Christians in the Contact Zone: Concealed Narratives in the Histories of Religions in the Americas," in *Beyond Primitivism: Indigenous Religious Traditions and Modernity*, ed. Jacob K. Olupona, New York: Routledge, 2004, p. 129.
165. Hanks, *Converting Words*, p. 368. Hanks turns the idols-behind-altars interpretation on its head while affirming Mayas' agency as new Christians in Maya ways. Instead of positing that what appeared to be Christian was only superficially so, Hanks finds that colonial Maya language was deeply influenced by Christian concepts: "The new language spread faster and penetrated deeper and more tenaciously into Maya culture than any other aspect of reducción," p. xiv. In the same spirit, see Louise M. Burkhart, *Aztecs on Stage: Religious Theater in Colonial Mexico*, Norman: University of Oklahoma Press, 2009, and her earlier four volumes on Nahuatl theater, with Barry D. Sell, Norman: University of Oklahoma Press, 2001–2009.
166. On ancestor veneration in the European Christian tradition, see Robert W. Shaffern, *The Penitents' Treasury: Indulgences in Latin Christendom, 1175–1375*, Scranton: University of Scranton Press, 2007.
167. For the case of Indian witnesses from Irapuato testifying in the late colonial period to the sacrifices their ancestors made to establish a confraternity for their beloved image of Our Lady of Mercy and the well-being of the souls of those who came after, see Paredes Martínez, *El Hospitalito de Irapuato*. For early Nahuatl testaments as a source of information about Christian devotions, see Caterina Pizzigoni, *The Life Within: Local Indigenous Society in Mexico's Toluca Valley, 1650–1800*, Stanford: Stanford University Press, 2012, chapter 6.
168. Leon-Portilla notes that "Nahuatl religion did not imply a doctrine of salvation," but, adds Graulich, "both Spanish and Indian writers in the sixteenth century often wrote of a reward or a punishment after death, and very different sources mention it, so that Christian influence does not seem to have been a determining factor," quoted and glossed in *Myths of Ancient Mexico*, pp. 257–258. For Andean peoples, Gabriela Ramos suggests that if the Christian concept of the soul was widely adopted, it did not happen quickly, *Death and Conversion in the Andes: Lima and Cuzco, 1532–1670*, South Bend: University of Notre Dame, 2010, p. 219.
169. López Austin, *The Human Body and Ideology*, I, 229–231.
170. For a few of the cases of non-Indians consulting Indian peyoteros in the seventeenth and early eighteenth centuries, see AGN Inquisición 510 exps. 112, 284, and fols. 548–550; and AGN Inquisición 356 segunda parte fols. 83r, 314, 360.
171. AGN Inquisición 317 exp. 21, AGN Inquisición 339 exp. 34.
172. For example, AGN Inquisición 486 exp. 229.
173. For example, AGN Inquisición 826 exp. 8, 1729 San Pedro Piedra Gorda, Zacatecas. For visions induced by ingesting the plant *panquitzi*, see the case of Domingo de San Juan, "indio idólatra" of Calimaya in 1691, AHAM caja "1691–1769."
174. William B. Taylor, "Cristos de Caña," in *Oxford Encyclopedia of Mesoamerican Cultures*, ed. David Carrasco, New York: Oxford University Press, 2001, I, 286–287.

175. Guillermo Prieto, *Viajes de orden suprema, año de 1853*, 54 y 55, 3rd ed., Mexico: Editorial Patria, 1970, p. 376.
176. *Mesas and Cosmologies in Mesoamerica*, ed. Douglas Sharon and James E. Brady, San Diego: Museum of Man, paper #42, 2003. The *mesa* adorned with candles and a cross could be used as a ritual stage for peyote ceremonies, e.g., Gonzalo Aguirre Beltrán, *Medicina y magia. El proceso de aculturación en la estructura colonial*, Mexico: INI, 1963, pp. 147–148.
177. Guadarrama Olivera, "El espacio," p. 191.
178. On the human body as sacred vessel of cosmic powers in precolonial Mesoamerica, see David Carrasco, *Religions of Mesoamerica: Cosmovision and Ceremonial Centers*, San Francisco: Harper & Row, 1990, p. 66, and López Austin, *The Human Body and Ideology*. A suggestive example is Elizabeth Boone's reading of the Mixtec Codex Vienna, in which the divine figure/culture hero Nine Wind proceeds to create life on earth following "a conference" with twelve anthropomorphic stones and plants, *Stories in Red and Black: Pictorial Histories of the Aztecs and Mixtecs*, Austin: University of Texas Press, 2000, p. 94. The traditional Christian conception of the human body as sacred comes from Genesis 1:27–28, "So God created man in his own image ..."
179. On Venus in Mesoamerican traditions, see Graulich, *Myths of Ancient Mexico*, p. 269.
180. López Austin goes further in identifying enduring "cosmic principles" that were alien to Christianity: (1) Mesoamerican polytheism and (2) the need in Mesoamerica for participation of people in the epic cosmic struggle to save the fragile earth from complete and final destruction. See his essays in *De hombres y dioses*, ed. Xavier Noguez and Alfredo López Austin, Mexico: El Colegio de Michoacán and El Colegio Mexiquense, 1997, pp. 209–227 and 229–254, and his article "Cosmovisión," 268–274. Christian monotheism was presented to Mesoamericans peopled with many divine mediators – saints and saintly individuals – associated with wonders that made acceptance of the remote one true God congruent with their theology. And Christians, too, participated in the world's renewal, albeit more as supplicants than agents. Unlike precolonial Mesoamericans, they, including colonial Indians in their wills, accepted the finality of an eventual judgment day.
181. See Taylor, *Magistrates of the Sacred*, pp. 49–51, 550.
182. Ethelia Ruiz Medrano, "The Lords of the Land: The Historical Context of the Mapa de Cuauhtinchan No. 2," in *City, Cave and Eagle's Nest: An Interpretive Journey Through the Mapa de Cuauhtinchan No. 2*, ed. Davíd Carrasco and Scott Sessions, Albuquerque: University of New Mexico Press, 2007, p. 106. The text cited in Ruiz Medrano's essay is by Diego Jaime Ricardo Villavicencio, *Luz y método de confesar idólatras, y destierro de idolatrías ...*, Puebla: Diego Fernández de León, 1692.
183. Bishops promoting as well as seeking to regulate and limit the reach of image shrines and particular devotions appear throughout this book. For further discussion of the example of Nuestra Señora de la Luz, see William B. Taylor, *Shrines and Miraculous Images in Mexico before the Reforma*, Albuquerque: University of New Mexico Press, 2010, pp. 52–57 and Lenice Rivera Hernández, "La novísima imagen de la Madre Santísima de la Luz. Origen, programa, sistema y función de una devoción jesuítica, 1717–1732," licenciatura thesis, Facultad de Filosofía y Letras, Universidad Nacional Autónoma de México, 2010.

184. See William A. Christian, Jr., "Catholicisms," in *Local Religion in Colonial Mexico*, ed. Martin Nesvig, Albuquerque: University of New Mexico Press, 2006, p. 262 on customs largely invisible to historians.
185. For Sahlins, culture is not just imposed; rather that "people [also] want culture." See Marshall Sahlins, "Two or Three Things I Know about Culture," *Journal of the Royal Anthropological Institute* 5 (1999), 399–421.
186. de la Serna, "Manual de ministros de indios," p. 37. Serna also implied that Catholic priests encouraged local shamanism by presenting themselves as supershamans, claiming that they were regarded as "predicadores hechiceros que encantan a los hechiceros con la sabiduría de su doctrina."
187. Alan R. Sandstrom, *Corn is Our Blood: Culture and Ethnic Identity in a Contemporary Aztec Indian Village*, Norman: University of Oklahoma Press, 1991, p. 231.
188. Piazza, *La conciencia oscura* (p. 201 of the book manuscript. Quoted with permission of the author). Much new thinking about idolatry in colonial Spanish America begins with Mills's *Idolatry and Its Enemies*, and extends to Tavárez's *Invisible War* and Piazza's forthcoming study of the politics of idolatry.

3
Miraculous Images of Christ and the Virgin Mary

Figures of Christ and the Virgin Mary, renowned for miracles and showered with votive offerings and heartfelt thanks, account for nearly all shrine images in New Spain. This chapter surveys these celebrated figures of Christ and Mary in a more focused way than do the first two chapters, as both a subject in its own right and another context for the themes developed in Part II, where particular shrines and images serve as examples or sources of a suggestive incident or facet of devotion and enchantment. Here, figures of Christ and Mary are discussed in relationship to each other, as well as separately, in order to highlight similarities, differences, and connections that establish how both became and remained central to the history of image shrines. Shrines to figures of Mary and Christ bore similarities and close associations, but there were three striking differences. In both New Spain and Europe, more Marian shrines achieved regional fame. The other two differences distinguish New Spain from Spain: the rise of the Virgin of Guadalupe to singular fame in New Spain during the late seventeenth and eighteenth centuries (notably without eclipsing the local and regional popularity of hundreds of other shrine images) and the prominence of dark Christs in New Spain and dark Madonnas in Europe.

Images of the Blessed Mary

As Robert Orsi writes, "It is impossible to tell a simple story about the Virgin Mary. She cannot be held in place by a single attribute – sorrow or delight, purity or compassion – or held accountable for a single social consequence – liberation or oppression, solidarity or fracture."[1] Mary is barely glimpsed in the Bible, a largely undefined figure, yet, as Mother of God[2] and Mother of the Church, she came to occupy a singular place in Catholic devotions, the source of endless fascination and veneration. Unlike other saints, the Virgin Mary commanded a special, higher devotion, or *hyperdulia*, that in practice shaded toward *latria* – the worship owed only to God.[3] Forever young and, in the eyes of adoring devotees, beautiful, she was represented in different guises that extended out from her part in the virginal conception of Jesus and the promise of salvation. She was Queen of Heaven; divine mother of the Son of God and also loving human mother, grieving yet merciful; modest virgin, meek and sweet, but also a warrior against enemies of the true faith; spotless mirror of purity; the closed gate and enclosed garden, protected in her perfection and protecting her faithful children; a great river, source of abundance; ladder to Heaven; patron of religious orders; and, above all, for many the all-purpose divine advocate and intercessor, typically represented with her hands pressed together in prayer and supplication.[4]

These and other Marian attributes and symbolic associations were in play in New Spain. In his *Mes mariano*, a devotional text published in Mexico City in 1760, José Joaquín de Ortega y San Antonio listed thirty-one attributes of Mary, one for each day of the month, many of them associated with nature's bounty (*los dones de naturaleza*), beauty, sweet smells, and containers: aurora, staff of authority, mirror, daisy, tree, rose, magnet, ark, Galeed (witness to the covenant of peace, as at Galeed), resin, rainbow, earth, flame, eagle, spade, moon, stairway, ship, aroma, sweetness, gold, manna, image, tuberose (aromatic flowering plant), vessel, shrine, tower, star, column, grapevine, and sea.[5] Some of Mary's many attributes often were invoked in the same breath, as a gestalt more than a congeries of separate qualities. In one of his sermons, the popular mid-eighteenth-century preacher Dr. Andrés de Arce y Miranda invoked Mary as the tree of life, manna of the saints, mother of hope and fear, and especially as sweetness and love, protector, and great intercessor for the unfortunate.[6]

In and beyond the sixteenth century, Spaniards of all social stations and regions brought with them to America an ardent devotion to the Blessed Mary.[7] She became the principal patron saint of Spanish state enterprises and Queen of America. As the opening section of the great compendium of early colonial law, the *Recopilación de leyes de los reynos de las Indias* (1681), declared, she was the "patron and protector throughout our kingdoms."[8] And during the formative period of New Spain's image shrines, animated, wonder-working figures of the Virgin Mary stood out as the most numerous and widely known. During the eighteenth century, the Virgin Mary in New Spain, as in Europe, was especially the merciful mother through whom all graces passed,[9] but her many other attributes and advocations were not forgotten, and they could signify somewhat differently in particular settings and times, whether in Europe, the New World, or elsewhere. For New Spain, she was the warrior queen especially in the sixteenth century, during what for Spaniards was the political and spiritual conquest of Mesoamerica – as La Conquistadora and Nuestra Señora de la Defensa of Puebla, Nuestra Señora de los Remedios of Totoltepec and Cholula, and Nuestra Señora de Guanajuato; or, in the early seventeenth century, Nuestra Señora del Pueblito. But she was also available later and elsewhere in martial guise as defender of the faith and the faithful – in the unfinished conquests of northern New Spain during the seventeenth and eighteenth centuries, especially in New Mexico after the Pueblo Revolt as the Conquistadora and Nuestra Señora de la Macana, and during the eighteenth century as protector of the Spanish fleets and navy in the Atlantic, and Spanish armies at war in Europe.

Place and time entered into the identity and popularity of particular representations and miraculous images of Mary. Some advocations introduced in the eighteenth century were popular in one region and not in others; for example, Nuestra Señora del Refugio had devotees in the Bajío and north, but was less often mentioned in the center and south except for Puebla. And shrine images of Mary Immaculate often became known by their location more than by their advocation – the Virgin of San Juan de los Lagos or the Virgin of Zapopan, for example.[10] This was especially true of the Marian shrines located outside major cities. (See Appendix 1 for examples.) On the other hand, every important city had at least one reputedly miraculous image of Mary as patron saint, giving that image a larger local base of followers and sometimes considerable regional fame – for instance, Our Lady of Guadalupe and Our Lady of Remedios for Mexico City, the Virgin of La Soledad for Antequera, the Virgin of El Pueblito for Querétaro, the Virgin of Zapopan for Guadalajara, the Virgin of Ocotlán for Tlaxcala, the Virgin of La Defensa and La Conquistadora for Puebla, Our Lady of El Patrocinio for Zacatecas, and Our Lady of Guanajuato. As all-purpose protector and advocate, the Virgin Mary in a particular image could also take on a specialist role in times of crisis or if the image's home base was particularly prone to drought, flood, frosts, lightning, an illness, witchcraft, or raids by hostile neighbors.

Many of the older miraculous images of the Blessed Mary in New Spain were diminutive, which made them more portable and perhaps more approachable.[11] Otherwise, the mystique of most of the miraculous Marian images resembled that of their counterparts in Europe. When an image of Mary reportedly showed signs of life, she was likely to weep, perspire, blush, or flash her eyes. Occasionally, a bright star was noted in the sky when the image was carried in procession, in at least one case leaving its mark on the Virgin's forehead. The most anticipated providential sign of the Virgin Mary's living presence was that the statue or painting remained unblemished, especially the face and hands, in spite of exposure to the elements and generations of handling. In a few instances, a blemished image of Mary in New Spain became more precious. The nick on the face of Nuestra Señora de la Macana (Virgin of the War Club, which survived the Pueblo Revolt in New Mexico) and the bullet lodged in the base of Nuestra Señora de la Bala (Our Lady of the Bullet; see Figure 7.9 in Chapter 7) were treated as marks of her divine presence and will that transformed the identity of the image. When ecclesiastical officials ordered restoration of a celebrated image in poor condition, it was done in secret or closely supervised. The written plan for restoring the Virgin of Remedios and the Christ Child in her arms in 1758 stipulated "[1] that the restoration be carried out with the greatest veneration by an appropriate sculptor; [2] that two members of the city council and two members of the cathedral chapter be present; [3] that prelates of the religious orders and other persons of distinction be present; and [4] that the governors of this viceregal court and neighboring communities be invited to attend." Not specified here, but often required, were devotional exercises by the sculptor or painter before the work was undertaken.[12]

Our Lady of Guadalupe

Reading the history of image shrines back from the present, it is tempting to notice little more than Our Lady of Guadalupe and her shrine at Tepeyac just northeast of the colonial center of Mexico City as the timeless essence of Marian devotion and the Mecca of Mexico. A parish priest in the Chinantec area of Oaxaca introducing the Virgin Mary to his flock in the early nineteenth century did just that. After referring to the Blessed Mary as Mother of God, full of grace, and the true, endlessly benevolent mother of all sinners, all mankind, he turned to Guadalupe as her Mexican face and perpetual presence:

My children, there are so many things I would like to tell you now about the many and great marvels that the Mother of God has done for the benefit of people. This is to say that that powerful woman, full of grace from the first moment of her conception, merited being chosen among all women to be the mother of God and also the mother of all sinners, a title that has obliged her to act on various occasions for the benefit of all mankind as their true Mother. But as this subject is so vast I will speak to you on this occasion only about the apparition of Our Lady of Guadalupe on the edge of Mexico City, ... deigning to appear among us.[13]

For nearly three centuries now, this image has been the great symbol of Mexican identity, providential unity, and collective pride. By the mid-eighteenth century she had become the center of attention, if there was *a* center, but there was always more to this history than one center, and Guadalupan devotion resists sharp and timeless definition. She has represented many things to different people. Perspectives from Mexico City are the most familiar, but they are only part of this story.

It is not surprising that scholars and devotees have been drawn to the sixteenth-century origins of this image and shrine in spite of the meager historical record for those years.[14] Or perhaps it is especially because the record is meager that the legendary beginnings are recounted so decisively

AL HECHIZO DE LAS ALMAS,
AL CENTRO DE LOS AFECTOS,
AL IMAN DE LOS CORAZONES,
AL MAS RICO THESORO DE LAS
INDIAS,
A LA CONOCIDA, VENERADA, Y GLORIFICADA
POR TODAS LAS NACIONES,
NUESTRA MADRE, Y SEÑORA
MARIA SANTISSIMA
EN SU MILAGROSA, Y FLORIDA
IMAGEN
DE GUADALUPE.

SE-

Figure 3.1 "To the charmer of souls, the center of feelings, the magnet of hearts, the richest treasure of the Indies, well known, venerated and glorified by all nations, our mother and lady Most Holy Mary in her miraculous and flower-laden image of Guadalupe." The Latin banner reads "He has not done thus for any other nation," from Psalm 147, which was especially associated with Our Lady of Guadalupe in the 1754 papal bull that recognized the apparitions at Tepeyac and the image as miraculous. Published in Andrés de la Santíssima Trinidad, *La venerada y glorificada en todas las naciones, por haverse aparecido en estos reynos* . . ., Mexico: Bibliotheca Mexicana, 1759. Courtesy of the Bancroft Library, University of California, Berkeley.

and embraced so fervently: the Virgin Mary appears at the hill of Tepeyac to a devout Indian seer, Juan Diego, in early December 1531, instructing him to tell the bishop that a church should be built for her there; Juan Diego communicates with a doubting Bishop Juan de Zumárraga who wants proof; and, finally, following another encounter between the Virgin and Juan Diego, proof is presented in the form of the Virgin's likeness miraculously impressed on his coarse cloak, an indelible sign of her presence, protecting all, but especially the downtrodden native population. Belief in the apparition story, first circulated in print in 1648, was greatly enhanced by papal validation in 1754. But for the sixteenth century, silences abound: Zumárraga (bishop, 1530–1548) did not mention these stirring events of 1531 in any of his surviving records; the image is not documented before the 1550s, at the earliest; no painted, printed, or sculpted copies of the image have come to light before the early seventeenth century; Juan Diego is first mentioned in writing in 1648; and there were no special December celebrations in honor of Our Lady of Guadalupe until the second half of the seventeenth century. What can be said with more certainty is that in the 1550s a small shrine devoted to the Virgin Mary in an image on cloth known as Our Lady of Guadalupe had been built and promoted by Archbishop Alonso de Montúfar, OP (1551–1572).[15] By the 1570s, a confraternity with some 400 members backed the shrine and sponsored dowries for orphan girls, which became a traditional pious work of the shrine.[16] By then the chapel at Tepeyac was a popular destination of residents of Mexico City and nearby *pueblos de indios*,[17] and before long Tepeyac was used as the official reception site for new viceroys and other dignitaries making their ceremonial entrance into Mexico City.[18]

There are more records for developments in the seventeenth century, but the nature of these sources – mainly a patchwork of administrative documents, paintings, and hagiographical writings by elite clergymen in the capital – leaves room for debate that cannot be resolved here. An interpretation favored during the past forty years is some variant of a creole patriotism thesis in which American-born Spanish elites embraced or perhaps even invented the apparitions story and Juan Diego as a symbol of their American identity, in tension with Spain and peninsular Spaniards, who enjoyed special privileges in America; and, for the creole priesthood, the apparitions of Guadalupe inspired renewed evangelizing missions among Indians as imperfect Christians still seduced by the devil. Miguel Sánchez's book *Imagen de la Virgen María* (1648), about the apparitions and their providential significance, is taken by many scholars as a clarion call of this creole identity.[19] Creole patriotism certainly is evident in the devotional histories, published sermons, and some of the pictorial record of the late seventeenth century, but dwelling on it obscures both the thirst for divine protection across ethnic groups and classes, and the prominent role in the development of the shrine and devotion to the image of prelates, cathedral canons, viceroys, judges, and dignitaries who were either born in Spain or identified as Spaniards in America.[20]

In any case, Mexico City and the vicinity of the Valley of Mexico were the focal point of the growing official and popular interest in the matrix image and shrine of Guadalupe during the seventeenth century. From the early 1600s the cathedral chapter and archbishop oversaw the administration of the shrine at Tepeyac – organizing the lavish receptions for incoming viceroys and archbishops, appointing the shrine administrators from among their number, accounting for construction projects, shrine properties, alms collections, and festivities.[21] Archbishop Juan Pérez de la Serna (1613–1627) took a special interest in the shrine and Guadalupan devotion during the 1610s and 1620s and, unlike Archbishop Montúfar, he had an administrative infrastructure to work with and a new church already under construction, albeit haltingly.[22] Pérez de la Serna himself was officially received at Tepeyac in September 1613, and early in his tenure arranged for alms-collecting missions to distant places including Acapulco on the Pacific Coast and the Diocese of Valladolid (greater Michoacán), as well as closer to home, to help finance the construction.[23] The engraving by Samuel Stradanus that depicts the Virgin of Guadalupe and eight miracles dates from this period and would have been useful in promoting the building project and devotion.[24] (See Figure 5.2 in Chapter 5.) By the time the church was finished in 1622 there were other indications of the shrine's local popularity and increasing wealth, including bequests, chaplaincies, real estate in Mexico City and the vicinity of the shrine, growing alms collections, and the beginnings of a successful trade in brandea, especially *medidas*.[25]

From the 1610s, the shrine traced a pattern of growth, but it was not yet a smooth or steep trajectory. There must have been many devotees, but mostly from the city and nearby districts. Even in the city, Guadalupe was not the overshadowing official patroness she would become in the later eighteenth century: she was not mentioned as a protector in the floods of 1607 and 1608, nor did the minutes of the city council include her among the patrons of the city in 1628–1630.[26] These silences may bear little relationship to popular devotion since, unlike the shrine and image of the Virgin of Remedios, which was managed by the city government through a confraternity of city councilors and well documented in the *ayuntamiento* archive, the image shrine at Tepeyac was managed by the archdiocesan officials.

A defining event in the development of the shrine and devotion to the image during the seventeenth century was the great flood in Mexico City from 1629 to 1634. Those years were a time of both crisis and promise for the shrine. Revenues shrank, the church was in a dilapidated state, and few devotees ventured there, especially after the celebrated image was removed to the city and became famous for eventually rolling back the floodwaters. That the image would not leave the shrine at Tepeyac again after it was returned in 1634 was part of its mystique and fed a growing demand for fine, full-size copies by leading artists of the late seventeenth and eighteenth centuries. Increased revenue and expenditures, more active management by the cathedral clergy, and the installation of a "sumptuous" new altar in 1637[27] suggest that the shrine had a loyal following before as well as after the publication of Miguel Sánchez's *Imagen de la Virgen María* and Luis Lasso de la Vega's *Huei tlamahuiçoltica* in 1648 and 1649 respectively, which became the standard versions of the story of apparitions to Juan Diego at Tepeyac and are generally regarded as marking the major turning point in the popularity of the image and shrine. These books and several others that followed in the 1660s and 1680s cemented the tradition,[28] directed more attention to Indian devotion,[29] contributed to the campaign for papal recognition of the apparitions undertaken in the 1660s, and helped establish the Virgin of Guadalupe more formally as one of the city's divine guardians, especially during floods. Signs of mounting interest and promotion included more alms-collecting missions to distant places; a novena booklet in 1665 (possibly the first novena booklet published in Mexico, it was devoted to Guadalupe and Remedios);[30] the formal inquiry of 1666 into miracles associated with Guadalupe; construction of a hillside chapel in 1667 – the Capilla del Cerrito – above the shrine at the site of the Virgin's first apparition and where December 12 observances were held until this date replaced the traditional two weeks of festivities in November, one week for Spaniards and *castas*, and one week for Indians;[31] a chapel to the Virgin of Guadalupe in the Mexico City cathedral, completed in 1671; and published sermons on the apparition theme beginning in the 1660s. By the late 1660s, Guadalupe was a favorite patroness of candidates for advanced degrees in the royal university of Mexico;[32] a major new confraternity (*congregación*) was established at the shrine in 1674 and received special papal indulgences the next year;[33] and construction of the great paved thoroughfare from the city, lined with monuments to the fifteen mysteries of the Rosary, began in 1675.[34] As Fr. Isidro de la Asunción, a Spanish Carmelite sent to inspect the work of his order's Province of San Alberto in New Spain, observed in 1673, the Virgin of Guadalupe was now regarded as "the most prodigious image of the Virgin in New Spain" and known in many copies, but he found the shrine church "neither sumptuous nor rich, . . . capacious enough but not very large and without any side chapels."[35]

Devotion to the Virgin Mary in the image of Guadalupe was also spreading beyond the Valley of Mexico, thanks in part to the far-flung alms-collecting missions and proselytizing by pastors educated in Mexico

City. Witness the first regional shrine, at San Luis Potosí, established in 1656 for a painted copy of the image said to date from 1624; a chapel to Guadalupe in the Indian community of Zacoalco, Jalisco in 1658; reports that a copy of the image was working miracles in Antequera in 1665; a license to construct a chapel in the Indian community of Tepemajalco (Valley of Toluca) in 1674; the fine church to Our Lady of Guadalupe in Querétaro, under construction in 1674 and completed in 1680; a *beaterio* (community house for lay sisters) in Guadalajara devoted to Guadalupe founded by the bishop in 1677; chapels to the Virgin of Guadalupe at the shrine of Chalma in 1683 and Tlaxcala in 1686; raffles to support the cult at Valladolid in 1693; and a painted copy at San Francisco de los Conchos, Chihuahua that reportedly perspired in 1695.[36]

From the 1690s to the 1720s devotion to Our Lady of Guadalupe deepened in institutional ways and in everyday practice. More Guadalupan sermons were delivered and published; more novenas were observed, often guided by published booklets of prayers and a program of events; and more painted and printed copies of the image were commissioned and circulated. The outstanding development was construction of a great new shrine church, begun in 1694 and completed in 1709.[37] Its formal dedication in 1722 was marked by the debut of a monumental gold-plated, solid silver tabernacle for the image, which weighed 3,257 *marcos* (or about 1,620 pounds) and cost a breathtaking 52,119 pesos.[38] This celebrated building project led to another grand plan, to establish a prestigious self-governing college of canons (*colegiata*) at the shrine, which required, in turn, that the community surrounding the shrine be elevated from a mere pueblo to the status of a *villa*. It would take four decades from the initial 1707 proposal for the colegiata to be established,[39] but, together, the notoriety of the new church and royal encouragement for the colegiata helped stir enthusiasm for bicentennial celebrations in 1731 in Mexico City and a fresh bid, beginning in 1722, for papal recognition of the apparitions. By 1729 there were also annual December 12 festivities in honor of Guadalupe in most Mexico City churches.[40]

During the 1730s the shrine and image gained a powerful advocate in Archbishop-Viceroy Juan Antonio de Vizarrón y Eguiarreta (archbishop, 1731–1747; viceroy, 1734–1740). Received at the shrine upon his arrival from Spain, and present for the bicentennial festivities, he had a personal attachment to the shrine and image evident in his 1735 donation of a sumptuous Italian vestment embroidered with gold and silk threads, valued at 3,000 pesos.[41] Vizarrón's name is inseparable from the designation of Guadalupe as official patroness of the city and viceroyalty during the great epidemic in Mexico City in 1737 and establishment of the colegiata, but in neither case was he leading alone. The colegiata project had been in progress for many years, with the encouragement of papal bulls, royal cedulas, inquiries, and instructions.[42] Vizarrón himself was instructed in a royal cedula of March 8, 1735 to "finalize" the colegiata. How Guadalupe emerged as the great official protector of the city and viceroyalty during the epidemic of 1737 has a twist that places the city council in a leading role, again complicating the picture of Vizarrón and canons of the cathedral as the guiding lights. When the epidemic was first noted in the minutes of the cathedral chapter meetings on January 22, the canons voted to donate 2,000 pesos for disaster relief, but did not mention Our Lady of Guadalupe.[43] The next day, January 23, the municipal council of the city discussed whether to establish and sponsor an annual fiesta in early January to the Virgin of Guadalupe as the singular protector of the whole kingdom, and voted to petition the viceroy for permission to bring the Virgin of Guadalupe to the cathedral for special prayers of supplication.[44] On January 26 the cathedral canons took note of the ayuntamiento's initiative and approved a novena at the shrine to begin on January 28 "so that ... the scourge of her most Holy son that is being felt in this epidemic may be stayed."[45] The next day Archbishop-Viceroy Vizarrón declined to authorize the removal of the image from the shrine to the cathedral, but urged the city government to participate in the novena at Tepeyac, referring to Guadalupe as an "indispensable refuge born in New Spain, in this capital city, which venerates her as its north star," invoking the title of Florencia's popular devotional history of the image and shrine. He promised to attend the first and last days of the novena. The ayuntamiento agreed, and voted unanimously on February 11 to have Guadalupe named *patrona general* of the city, to sponsor a fiesta to her at Tepeyac every December 12, and to canvas all the dioceses and cities in the kingdom of New Spain for their support and oath of allegiance to her as universal patron. On February 16 the city councilors sought the approval of the viceroy to send a contingent of priests to Rome to request this special designation as patrona.[46] Thereafter, both the municipal council and the cathedral chapter voted unanimously, by secret ballot on March 28 and April 2 respectively, to urge Vizarrón to initiate the process of making Our Lady of Guadalupe the official patrona of the city and viceroyalty.[47]

Vizarrón moved ahead with alacrity, leading a *gran jura de patronato* (ceremonial oath of allegiance) in the cathedral on May 26.[48] Within eighteen months at least fifteen cities and towns had held similar oaths of allegiance to the Virgin of Guadalupe as patroness of the viceroyalty.[49] Another jura de patronato was ordered by the archbishop in 1746 to confirm universal allegiance to the Virgin of Guadalupe, followed by new oaths of allegiance in many towns and cities in 1747 to mark the tenth anniversary of the first oaths.[50] By the time Vizarrón died in early 1747, the stage was set for the final step to secure Guadalupe's formal elevation: the approval of the Congregation of Rites in Rome and papal recognition of the apparitions and the Virgin of Guadalupe as patron of New Spain, with December 12 as the appointed feast day with its own office of worship. This came in Benedict XIV's bull *Non fecit taliter omni nationi* of May 25, 1754, which was made widely known in New Spain in 1756.[51] The bull opened a floodgate of promotion and popular rejoicing, including new oaths of allegiance and lavish festivities in communities throughout the viceroyalty.

Other signs of maturing interest in and institutionalized devotion to Our Lady of Guadalupe, both at Tepeyac and elsewhere in New Spain during the middle and late eighteenth century, especially after 1756, include publication and circulation of more novena booklets, sermons (many of which were now delivered in towns and cities other than Mexico City), publication and reprintings of at least seven different booklets of devotional exercises for Guadalupan devotees on the twelfth of every month, prints, new and reprinted devotional histories, endorsement by the distinguished artist Miguel Cabrera in his book *Maravilla americana* (1756), many new churches and chapels devoted to Guadalupe, growing numbers of university theses dedicated to her, open-ended licenses to collect alms for the shrine, and publication of the first tourist booklet for a Mexican shrine in 1794.[52] Guadalupe is mentioned incidentally in many late colonial records, and tens of thousands of homes and churches, perhaps more, displayed a painting or print of the image. After 1756 many more rural estates and other places were named or renamed for her; Guadalupe became a widely popular baptismal name for infant girls and boys of all social groups;[53] and her guiding hand was reported more often in healing miracles, rescues, and other prodigious blessings.[54] At the shrine, properties, endowments, and Masses continued to grow in number and value, producing a base of annual income, excluding alms, of at least 26,790 pesos by 1746.[55]

As Fr. Miguel Tadeo de Guevara put it in the title of his sermon at Tepeyac on December 12, 1780, Guadalupe had made a visit without goodbyes, a "visita sin despedida."[56] She had come to stay, now as a patrona for all purposes. But exclusive, universal appeal and unremitting growth are not simply the story. Guadalupe was more popular in some places than others, and her continuous presence and growing prominence happened within the context of development of hundreds of other Marian and Christocentric image shrines that also came to stay. Generally speaking, as Guadalupan devotion grew, so did devotion to these other images and shrines, although most remained more localized in their appeal. And limits to Guadalupan devotion can be tracked in various ways. She continued to be especially popular in Mexico City and the Valley of Mexico, but other colonial cities developed a special relationship to her, including San Luis Potosí, Querétaro, Puebla, Valladolid, Guadalajara, and Antequera. So, too,

Figure 3.2 Proud depiction of the shrine compound at Tepeyac by Mexico City engraver Francisco Sylverio [de Sotomayor] in 1757, shortly after festivities throughout New Spain celebrated the papal bull *Non fecit taliter omni nationi*. In addition to depicting the landscape, this loose print marks

did towns and villages in modern Morelos and the Estado de México, which surround the Valley of Mexico, although it is surprising how rarely Guadalupe was mentioned in the 1743 *relaciones geográficas* for the Archdiocese of Mexico. Less surprising were the disappointing results of an imperial plan in 1756 to legislate universal devotion to Guadalupe and provide a steady stream of income for the shrine at Tepeyac by ordering that all wills drawn up in New Spain include a provision for the shrine of Guadalupe at Tepeyac.[57] Thirty years later, the canons at Tepeyac complained that this requirement of testamentary donations had been ignored. They petitioned for the royal directive to be republished and implemented with a network of specially appointed collectors working on commission. Guadalupan devotion was energetically promoted in Indian pueblos by pastors and missionaries during the eighteenth century, especially during Archbishop Lorenzana's tenure (1776–1771),[58] but the results were best in Nahua and Otomi-speaking regions of central Mexico, and even there some pueblos balked at the expense and trouble of mobilizing community resources for an annual fiesta in the parish seat.[59] More *cofradías* were established to sponsor local devotions to Guadalupe in pueblos de indios, but they came and went judging by those that were registered in the pastoral visit reports from Aguiar y Seixas in the 1690s to Lizana y Beaumont at the end of the eighteenth century. In the end, the catchment area of practiced belief in divine presence through the Guadalupan image was far greater than the attraction of the Tepeyac shrine.

In and Beyond the Shadow of Our Lady of Guadalupe

The greatest concentration of colonial image shrines was in Mexico City and nearby towns of the Valley of Mexico. As many as fifty-five Marian images and forty-seven images of Christ made news for working wonders during the seventeenth and eighteenth centuries (see Appendix 1). But as

Caption for Figure 3.2 (cont.)

the sites of the apparitions to Juan Diego and Bishop Zumárraga, the "magnificent" church completed in 1709, the new Capilla del Cerrito and pathway, the plaza and "magnificent" fountain, the old church, the abbot's house, and the causeway to Mexico City and one of the Rosary monuments lining it. There would be additions before long: a new high altar chapel (*camarín*) in the church, begun in 1778; the eye-catching Capilla del Pocito (1777–1791) marking the location of the Virgin's fourth appearance to Juan Diego; and the convent of Capuchin nuns (1780–1787; planned since 1731) next to the church. Print collected by Capuchin friar Diego de Ajofrín during his alms-collecting mission to New Spain in the 1760s. Courtesy of the Real Academia de la Historia, Madrid.

Guadalupe gained unrivalled prominence in the Valley of Mexico during the eighteenth century, few new image shrines were reported there, few of the existing shrines became more popular and prosperous, and several prominent ones would be largely forgotten by the early twentieth century, notably the Cristo Renovado de Santa Teresa and Nuestra Señora de la Bala.

Most image shrines in and very near Mexico City remained local neighborhood or community devotions although Nuestra Señora de los Ángeles of Tlatelolco, Nuestra Señora de la Piedad, and the Cristo Renovado de Santa Teresa drew citywide attention during the 1730s and 1740s, and were marshaled as protectors during the epidemic. But by the early 1740s the archbishop and civil authorities in the city were actively promoting Guadalupe at the expense of other shrine images in the vicinity, with the partial exception of Our Lady of Remedios. The little shrine of the Virgin of Nativitas Tepetlatcingo gained a presence and following in the city during the early 1740s shortly after the epidemic subsided thanks in large measure to promotion by its busy Franciscan pastor, Francisco Antonio de la Rosa Figueroa, but in 1745 his Franciscan superiors removed him from pastoral work, and the budding devotion to Our Lady of Tepetlatcingo was reduced again to its home village and locality.[60]

The shrine of Nuestra Señora de los Ángeles in Tlatelolco, the Aztec twin city that remained an important Nahua neighborhood between Mexico City and Tepeyac, presents an unusual example of a miracle image with a local following that attracted wide interest in the 1740s, and then was suppressed by diocesan officials in 1745, only to regain its standing among image shrines in and near the city during the last third of the eighteenth century. Legend places the beginning of devotion in 1580, when a painting of Our Lady of the Assumption floated by the home of a native lord during a flood. Although the canvas was damaged beyond repair, the lord adored the image and had an artist copy it onto an adobe wall facing the entrance of his neighborhood chapel. It remained one of the many neighborhood chapels with a local following until 1745, when word spread that the face and hands were still in perfect condition or had miraculously restored themselves to perfection in spite of exposure to the weather and saline soil. The chapel began to attract boisterous crowds and there were reports of licentious behavior. The archbishop's vicar general ordered the chapel closed and the image covered with wet mats so that erstwhile devotees would "realize the renovation of the Holy Image was not miraculous, but the work of nature." But local interest in the image and site continued, with some support from Tlatelolco's Franciscans. Then in 1776, shortly after the chapel was transferred to the secular parish of Santa Ana, two developments brought the image back to citywide prominence. In February a prosperous Spanish master tailor from the city center, José de Haro, visited the locked, run-down chapel and, out of curiosity, asked to

Figure 3.3 A print of Nuestra Señora del Patrocinio of Tepetlatcingo, in an edition of 3,000–4,000 copies commissioned by Fr. Francisco de la Rosa Figueroa and sponsored by Don Francisco Unsueta in 1743 at the height of the statue's popularity in Mexico City. The caption notes that Archbishop Vizarrón granted 40 days indulgence to all who say a prayer to God for the well-being of his Militant Church and give alms for rebuilding the ruined church and convent at Tepetlatcingo or who pray three Ave Marias before the miraculous statue there. Engraving by Baltasar Troncoso y Sotomayor. BNM Archivo Franciscano caja 109 doc, 1494. Courtesy of the Biblioteca Nacional de México.

see the image inside it. The mats were removed and he found the face and hands of the Virgin still in fine condition. With Haro's sponsorship and his appeals to archiepiscopal authorities and relentless promotion, the chapel was rebuilt and reopened, the image restored, rich furnishings acquired, and Masses celebrated. When a major earthquake and aftershocks shook the city and much of central Mexico in April and May, leading people sought refuge at their favorite shrines. Many *capitalinos* who may have been fleeing to Tepeyac gathered at the shrine of Our Lady of los Ángeles on the way and became devotees. From then into the nineteenth century the shrine counted archbishops, cathedral priests, political leaders, and other city elites among its benefactors as it gained a heterogeneous group of urban devotees with a strong local, mainly Indian nucleus.[61]

The image and shrine of Our Lady of Remedios at Totoltepec is the outstanding case of a Valley of Mexico image shrine that was limited but not eclipsed by the Virgin of Guadalupe's popularity and official promotion during the eighteenth century. Both were among the earliest image shrines in New Spain, apparently developing in the 1550s.[62] The wooden statuette of the Remedios image was understood to have been carried by retreating Spaniards during the Noche Triste of 1520 and to have helped turn back the pursuing Aztec warriors at the hill of Totoltepec, near Naucalpan. But the image and its small chapel there were more than a triumphalist Spanish shrine. Indian communities in the vicinity were drawn to it, setting up a counterpoint between local Indian devotion and a close connection to the Spanish colonial capital of Mexico City that was institutionalized in 1574 when the city council became the official patron and caretaker of the shrine, agreeing to underwrite construction of a new chapel and assume sponsorship, which included appointing the chaplains. In 1576, the little statue made the first of its ceremonial visits to the city.

During the seventeenth century, the shrine and cult of Remedios may have been more prominent, at least in Mexico City, and more prosperous than the Guadalupe shrine. A petition by Dominican friars in Mexico City to be allowed to send six of their number to the Remedios shrine in 1621 declared "one finds in this shrine greater devotion and attachment than in any other."[63] The city council's deliberations in the seventeenth century devoted considerable attention to Remedios affairs, but the image and shrine of Guadalupe are hardly mentioned except in connection with roads and other public works, and receptions of new viceroys at Tepeyac. By contrast, the cathedral chapter, which was more involved with administration and promotion of the Guadalupe shrine, often mentioned the Remedios image and shrine in the minutes of its meetings, especially between 1621 and 1644. The late-seventeenth-century commentators emphasized the complementarity of the Virgin of Guadalupe and the Virgin of Remedios. For example, Baltasar Medina, the Dieguino

186　　　*Part I Bearings: Historical Patterns and Places of Image Shrines*

Figure 3.4 Print of "Our Lady of the Immaculate Conception in the miraculous image known as Our Lady of the Angels, venerated in her chapel in the pueblo of Santiago

Franciscan chronicler whose major work was published in 1682, referred to Guadalupe as the "master spigot" (*llave maestra*) to turn off heavenly waters and Remedios as the master spigot to open them. They were two in one, protecting the city: "both ladies were really just one, dedicated to protecting Mexico City."[64] Or, as Mexico's great Marianist and devotee of both advocations, Francisco de Florencia, SJ, put it a few years later, "When the Virgin of Remedios comes to Mexico, Mary of Guadalupe comes, too, different in its image but the same in the original."[65] But Carmelite friar Isidro de la Asunción, writing in the 1670s, still considered the Remedios shrine to be the richer and finer of the two: "the church [of Remedios] is more sumptuous in grandeur, rich furnishings, and attractiveness than [the church of] Guadalupe."[66]

At the end of the seventeenth century, roughly as many confraternities to Remedios as to Guadalupe were recorded in the pastoral visit books of Archbishop Aguiar y Seixas (1682–1698), and Archbishop-Viceroy Juan de Ortega y Montañes (archbishop 1700–1708; interim viceroy 1696 and 1701–1702) made it clear that he was devoted to both images.[67] They continued to be treated as complementary advocations of the Blessed Mary, and devotees of one advocation still were often devotees of both, but the balance of popularity and promotion shifted decisively toward the Virgin of Guadalupe during the eighteenth century. Guadalupe was mentioned and invoked more often in all kinds of sources, published and unpublished, devotion became widespread, and the balance of wealth in bequests, donations, and property tipped strongly toward Guadalupe and Tepeyac. Remedios still enjoyed a great public following in the city, especially when natural disasters struck; her visits to the city for novenas in times of trouble were becoming more frequent and often longer than the prescribed eleven days, to the point that in the late eighteenth century she was visiting almost every year, and sometimes more than once in a year. But the leading sponsors of the devotion were a narrower slice of urban society, mainly wealthy peninsular and Hispanophile families, including members of the city council who had long led the city's confraternity dedicated to

---

Caption for Figure 3.4 (cont.)

Tlatelolco, for [those who] help in finishing her chapel." Engraving by Manuel [Galicia de] Villavicencio (active 1753–1788). Loose print collected by Francisco de Ajofrín in the mid-1760s. Ajofrín wrote below the image that the chapel was in the jurisdiction of the Observant Franciscan College of Tlatelolco. This was one of more than half a dozen different prints of this shrine image published in the late eighteenth century, mostly after 1776, to promote the devotion and the shrine. Courtesy of the Real Academia de la Historia, Madrid.

AMOROSO CANTO,[6]

QVE CON REVERENTES AFECTOS, CONTINVANDO
su devocion escrive *el Bachiller Don Diego de Ribera, Presbytero*. A la Novena venida, que hizo à esta Nobilissima Ciudad de Mexico, la Milagrosa Imagen de Nuestra Señora de los REMEDIOS; Para que con su intercession consiguiese, como siempre remedio à las dolencias, que le ocasiona la falta de aguas.

DEDICALO AFECTVOSO, Y CONSAGRALO RENDIDO,
Al Señor Don Martin de San Martin, Cavallero de la Orden de Santiago, Contador de los Reales Tributos, y Azogues de este Reyno, y Corregidor actual de esta Nobilissima Ciudad.

Con licencia. *En Mexico*, por la Viuda de Bernardo Calderon, año de 1663.

Figure 3.5 Cover print for a devotional text prepared by Br. D. Diego de Ribera in honor of the Virgin of Remedios's ninth visit to Mexico City, in 1663. This unsigned print depicts the Remedios Madonna and Christ Child statuette on their pedestal in the center, above the eagle and serpent symbolizing Mexico City, with four miracles attributed to the Virgin depicted in the corners. Courtesy of the John Carter Brown Library.

Miraculous Images of Christ and the Virgin Mary 189

Figure 3.6 This undated, unsigned print collected in Mexico by Francisco de Ajofrín in the mid-1760s offers a standard eighteenth-century depiction and account of the appearance of the statuette of Our Lady of Remedios to an Indian cacique in 1540. The caption declares that the archbishop grants 40 days indulgence to those who give alms. Courtesy of the Real Academia de la Historia, Madrid.

Remedios; and the disasters and dangers that drew her in were increasingly Spain's military troubles in Europe.

Shrines elsewhere in the viceroyalty that began to develop a regional base in the seventeenth century, such as Our Lady of San Juan de los Lagos in eastern Jalisco, Our Lady of Zapopan near Guadalajara, Our Lady of Remedios of Zitácuaro, Our Lady of Izamal in Yucatán, and Our Lady of El Pueblito outside the city of Querétaro, continued to grow in importance during the eighteenth century, little diverted, and perhaps even enhanced, by the rise of the Virgin of Guadalupe from the 1730s to the 1750s.[68] Like many others, four of these shrines were closely associated with Franciscans: El Pueblito, Zapopan, Zitácuaro, and Izamal. And most of the emerging Marian shrines were dedicated to images of Mary Immaculate and associated with a provincial city.

The exceptional popularity of the image shrine of Our Lady of San Juan de los Lagos in the late eighteenth century is considered in Chapter 2. Here it is enough to add that most devotional and promotional publications for this image and shrine – novena booklets, prints, devotional histories, sermons, and prayers – were published between 1751 and 1820, and nineteen of the twenty-four publications during these years appeared from 1754 to 1800, which were also peak years for comparable publications devoted to Our Lady of Guadalupe.

The colonial history of the image shrine of Our Lady of Zapopan, located about 7 miles west of Guadalajara, resembled that of Our Lady of Remedios in the Valley of Mexico more than the major rural shrine of Our Lady of San Juan de los Lagos with which it was often paired as the two great shrines of Nueva Galicia.[69] Like Lagos, the Zapopan shrine developed in the seventeenth century and reached new heights of popularity, promotion, and prosperity during the eighteenth century; but like Remedios, it came to be associated with a major colonial city in tension with an Indian settlement at the shrine, Franciscan missions in the province, and local commercial interests that favored keeping the image at home.

Tradition has it that the small statue of the Virgin of Zapopan was given to Indians from Xalostotitlan in the Altos de Jalisco by their first pastor when they resettled at Zapopan in 1541. Little is known about the devotion before the 1640s, when the bishop of Guadalajara encouraged construction of a new church and called for an inquiry into reports of many miracles associated with this image.[70] The image became more popular in the late seventeenth century thanks in part to alms-collecting missions, perhaps with the original image rather than a replica, in the diocese.[71] A grand shrine church, planned under Bishop Juan de Santiago y León Garabito (1678–1694), was the goal, but it would take several generations to complete.[72] The image reportedly was taken for a ceremonial visit to the

Figure 3.7 Eighteenth-century print of Our Lady of San Juan de los Lagos from an engraving by Joseph [Eligio] Morales, 1761, published in *Novena en honra de la milagrosíssima Imagen de ... Nuestra Señora de San Juan*, Mexico: Zúñiga y Ontiveros, 1761. The caption advises readers that the archbishop of Mexico and the bishop of Puebla grant forty days indulgence to those who pray a Hail Mary before the image and pray to God for the exaltation of Our Holy Faith. Courtesy of the Sutro Branch of the California State Library, San Francisco.

192 Part I Bearings: Historical Patterns and Places of Image Shrines

Milagrosa Imagen de Nª Sª de Tzapopan.

Figure 3.8 "Miraculous Image of Our Lady of Tzapopan," published by Bibliotheca Mexicana, engraved by Joseph de Andrade (active 1756–1771). Loose print collected by Francisco de Ajofrín in the 1760s. Courtesy of the Real Academia de la Historia, Madrid.

cathedral in Guadalajara before 1663,[73] but devotion was not yet concentrated in the city. That would begin to change during the epidemic of 1693 when the bishop declared the Virgin of Zapopan the city's patron saint against rampant illness and other public calamities.[74] Although the Indian town council of Zapopan resisted attempts to arrange an annual visit by their Virgin to the churches of the city, those visits became more common. The bond to the city was well established by 1721, when the statue again visited the cathedral during another epidemic. It was also in the city in September 1731, when a fire broke out in the public market (the Portal de la Fruta). According to the news item in the *Gazeta de México* for October 1731, people there prayed to the Virgin of Zapopan and the damage was much less extensive than it might have been.[75]

Finally completed and dedicated in September 1729, thanks especially to generous sponsors in Guadalajara,[76] the imposing new shrine church of Zapopan raised the profile of the image both in the city and surrounding communities.[77] Developments in the 1730s further solidified the association of the image with the city. Lightning strikes in Guadalajara frequently resulted in deaths as well as property damage and fires, but belief spread in the early eighteenth century that there was never a death or serious damage from lightning when the Zapopan image was present.[78] Then on June 27, 1734, a great lightning storm hit the city and people clamored for the image to be brought in procession to the cathedral and other churches of Guadalajara. The bishop agreed, and declared her the patron saint against lightning strikes.[79] From then on the Virgin of Zapopan made annual visits to churches in the city, for up to four months at a time.[80] In an exception that apparently hardened the rule, Bishop Juan Gómez de Parada (1735–1751) responded to complaints from Indians of Zapopan by ordering that the image visit only the cathedral and the church of Santa Teresa. A little girl died in a lightning storm that year, and the tradition of the Virgin's longer visits was revived. The shrine remained popular in the late eighteenth century and was promoted with papal indulgences, novena booklets, prints, and other devotional materials.

Development in the eighteenth century of the shrine and statue of Nuestra Señora del Pueblito, about 6 miles north of the provincial city of Querétaro at the Otomí settlement of San Francisco Galisteo, was inspired by the relationship between Mexico City and Our Lady of Remedios. Indeed, in 1741 the city council of Querétaro made its intentions clear in this respect when they petitioned the cofradía of the Remedios shrine (led by members of the ayuntamiento of Mexico City) for permission to model the organization, stages, and sequence of ceremonies for visits to their city by the Pueblito image on those prescribed for Remedios's periodic trips to Mexico City.[81] The main difference was the continuing authority of the Franciscans at El Pueblito, which both extended the

Figure 3.9 "True portrait of the miraculous image of Our Lady of El Pueblito that is venerated in her shrine on the outskirts of the city of Querétaro." Print from engraving by Antonio Onofre Moreno (active 1748–1774), published in Hermenegildo de Vilaplana, *Novena de la milagrosa imagen de Nuestra Señora del Pueblito . . .*, Mexico: Bibliotheca Mexicana, 1761. Courtesy of the Sutro Branch of the California State Library, San Francisco.

shrine's importance beyond the city of Querétaro and the vicinity of the shrine, and limited the municipal council's and diocesan officials' discretion in managing when and how the visits took place. The history of this image and shrine are said to have begun in 1632, when a Franciscan maker of religious images, Fr. Sebastián Gallegos, gave the Franciscan pastor of San Francisco Galisteo one of his small statues of Mary Immaculate. A late colonial preacher, José Francisco de la Rocha Manrique de Lara, would observe that this statue of the Virgin was most holy even though its appearance was not unusually beautiful and it was not especially well made. Its divine beauty had more to do with the devotion the Virgin engendered through this image, overcoming idolatry that had continued among the local Indians for more than a century before the statue was placed there.[82] Seventeenth-century documentation about the Virgin of El Pueblito is scarce, but the statue apparently became famous for showing signs of life as early as 1648, repeatedly perspiring, weeping, flashing its eyes, and working miracles of healing and protection.[83] Another seventeenth-century benchmark of local devotion was establishment of a cofradía by Indian villagers of Galisteo in 1682,[84] but the cofradía established in the city of Querétaro in 1686 was more decisive – the first clear sign of the emerging identification of the image with the city.

The most sustained growth of the Pueblito devotion took place during the eighteenth century, thanks especially to this association with the city and regular visits by the image for novenas in times of drought, epidemic, and other calamities after the visits were formalized by the crown in 1733 with written rules.[85] Two years later a larger and more substantial chapel for the Virgin at the El Pueblito site was completed with the help of the city council, local Indians, and a bequest from a leading citizen of the city, Captain Don Pedro de Urtiaga.[86] Popular interest was also fueled by reports in the 1730s and 1740s that the statue was showing signs of life and that a star had appeared on the Virgin's forehead.[87] Meanwhile, the Franciscans continued to claim a share of the fame of this miraculous image, naming her patrona of their province in 1745.[88] The 1760s were perhaps the apogee of the Pueblito Virgin's popularity in the city during the colonial period, with an outpouring of publications including novena booklets, two editions of Hermenegildo de Vilaplana's devotional history, and news of scores of miracles including cures, narrow escapes, mining bonanzas, and relief from drought and disease, culminating in the widely publicized miracle of a Franciscan friar, Andrés Picazo, surviving certain death at the hands of an assassin when he invoked the Virgin of El Pueblito.[89] The image continued to be taken to the city often for novenas in times of trouble to the end of the colonial period and was regarded as the great protectress of the city during the Independence period.[90]

V.R. de la Milagrosa Imagen de N.Sra de Jzmal que
se venera quinze leguas de Merida de Yucatan.
A devoció del S. Conde de Miraflores D.Santigo Calderon, Coron.

Figure 3.10 "True portrait of the miraculous image of Our Lady of Itzmal that is venerated fifteen leagues from Mérida de Yucatán. This engraving was sponsored by the Conde de Miraflores. D. Santiago Calderón, colonel, devotee of this advocation of the Virgin." Unsigned and undated, this print was published in *Novena de la Santissima Virgen de Ytzmal*..., Mexico: Zúñiga y Ontiveros, 1764. Courtesy of the Sutro Branch of the California State Library, San Francisco.

The Virgin of Izamal, identified in Chapter 1 as one of the provincial shrines emerging in the early seventeenth century, came to have wider appeal after its first, brief trip to the capital of Mérida in 1648, summoned by the city council during the epidemic then afflicting the city.[91] Izamal's history as a regional shrine deepened and broadened during the eighteenth century, when Our Lady of Izamal was designated Reina y Patrona de Yucatán,[92] and made three more visits to Mérida in times of sickness and drought, in 1730, 1744, and 1769. These trips were said to be for novenas, but in each case the image remained in the city longer – twenty-two days in 1730, twenty-six days in 1744, and fifty days in 1769 – in a pattern reminiscent of Our Lady of Remedios's more frequent, longer visits to Mexico City in the eighteenth century.[93] Reports from that time added that at least twice during public presentations of the Virgin of Izamal, providential signs appeared in the sky. Near the end of the novena in Mérida in 1730, as the epidemic was coming to an end, a brilliant cross was formed by a white cloud and lasted a remarkably long time; and during a procession in Izamal on the annual feast day an exceptionally bright, "most beautiful" star appeared, as bright as the star that guided the Magi to the Christ Child.[94]

Many more localized Marian shrines also continued to prosper during the late colonial period. The image shrine of Nuestra Señora de los Remedios of Zitácuaro, Michoacán, for example, followed the trajectory of the shrine of the Virgin of San Juan de los Lagos, if on a smaller scale and somewhat later. Both statuettes apparently dated from the sixteenth century, gained notoriety in the seventeenth century, and enjoyed greater popularity in the eighteenth century that was little affected by the boom in devotion to the Virgin of Guadalupe. Both towns developed into commercial centers with periodic trade fairs. Zitácuaro's Virgin was well known by the 1630s, prompting Franciscan chronicler Alonso de la Rea (writing in 1639) to devote a chapter to her shrine as "one of the main shrines in this province ... reporting miracles every day."[95] Referring to the image only as the Virgin of Zitácuaro, without reference to a particular Marian advocation, de la Rea reported that the image had been brought from Spain in 1543 by the *encomendero* of Taximaroa and deposited in Zitácuaro after a mule carrying the statuette stopped in front of the pueblo's church and could not be moved. De la Rea mentioned that the original church – "poor and needy" – had been replaced thanks to the generosity of Manuel de Santa Cruz, who made a fortune in the silver mines of Sultepec after attending a novena for the Virgin in Zitácuaro and being directed to the vein of silver by an unknown Indian. According to de la Rea, people were now visiting the shrine from "all around." The church was rebuilt in the 1650s, and the pueblo began to celebrate the feast of the Immaculate Conception with this image in 1665, sponsored by a designated cofradía.[96] Judging by early eighteenth-century inventories of jewels and other precious items, the shrine continued to grow, at least modestly, and was attracting visitors from Sultepec, Taximaroa, and other settlements in the vicinity, perhaps as far away as the city of Valladolid. A third building campaign, in the 1750s, was led by Franciscan pastor Fr. Felipe Velasco who wrote and published an illustrated novena booklet (Figure 3.11) that was reprinted several times. In 1759, Zitácuaro became a diocesan parish, without much change in the fortunes of the shrine. The image was still identified with the Immaculate Conception, although the Christ Child in her hands was not typical of representations of this advocation, and the image was also known as Nuestra Señora de los Remedios, as it is today. Construction on another new church began in 1807, but was not completed until 1840, when the commercial fair of Zitácuaro became more important.[97]

The colonial prints of celebrated images included in this section offer a glimpse of how the Virgin Mary was represented to devout viewers. There was remarkably little variety in the basic depictions of her. She was the standing Madonna holding her child, the grieving mother, or alone on a crescent moon in a pose that was widely understood to depict Mary Immaculate, but served for other advocations as well; forever young and lovely (unlike her husband, Joseph, who could be depicted as old, young, or in middle age, with or without carpentry tools). Other than the grieving mother, these figures were distinguished from each other mainly by an added attribute, such as a string of rosary beads, or the insignia of the Mercedarians, or a scapular for Our Lady of Carmen. As Rosario Granados Salinas suggests, the similarity of the depictions of different advocations of the Virgin was purposeful. It was a way to emphasize their unity, that they all represented one person, the Blessed Mary herself.[98]

Miraculous Images of Christ

Miraculous images of the Virgin Mary and the shrines dedicated to them in New Spain have received most of the attention of hagiographers and historians since the seventeenth century. Less has been written about celebrated images of Christ, but they were as numerous as the more publicized figures of the Blessed Mary and, unlike those in Spain, most of them are still remembered and revered as miraculous.[99] Writing in the early 1620s, Augustinian chronicler Juan de Grijalva declared that images of Christ were unusually popular in New Spain: "there are more Christs [here] than in all of Europe. I am not stretching the truth; all who have seen for themselves say the same thing."[100] Whether or not Grijalva exaggerated, shrine images of Christ became prominent in the seventeenth century, and during the eighteenth century more of the new image shrines

Figure 3.11 "True portrait of Our Lady of Remedios venerated in the convent of San Francisco of the villa of San Juan Zitáquaro. Blessed and praised be the Immaculate Conception of the Most Blessed and Saintly Virgin Mary. Devoutly sponsored by Father Fray Felipe Velasco. Engraved by [Francisco] Sylverio [de Sotomayor], 1758, re-engraved by Zapata." Published in Felipe Velasco, *Novena para celebrar el Mysterio de la Imaculada Concepción de María...*, reimpreso, Mexico: Zúñiga y Ontiveros, 1783. Courtesy of the Lilly Library, Indiana University.

honored figures of Christ than Mary. Writing in the late 1750s, Francisco Javier Lazcano, SJ, hoped for "another great work of history worthy of the Christian world's acclamation [comparable to Florencia and Oviedo's Marian compendium *Zodiaco Mariano*] that describes in detail the prodigious crosses and miraculous images of Jesus Christ, Our Lord, that make this kingdom famous in innumerable magnificent shrines throughout its vast dioceses. This kingdom is no less favored by the Son of God, Jesus Christ, Our Lord in his infinite mercy than by the most beloved Mother of a God who is her son."[101]

The special veneration of particular Christ figures and crosses in New Spain took hold in some distinctive ways, but for the most part it followed developments in European Christianity during the late Middle Ages and early modern period. In scripture and practice, Christ was represented in several ways, including stages and layers of meaning in his life, as Son of God, light of the world, redeemer, and Satan's great adversary. He was the infant Jesus; the transfigured young and merciful Messiah who preached, taught, and worked miracles; the mocked and scourged figure, presented to the public ("Ecce Homo") and condemned to death; the Nazarene Christ (Christ as the Man of Sorrows) bearing his cross up the road to Calvary; the crucified Christ, sacrificed to save humankind; the dead Christ brought down from the cross and laid in the sepulcher; the resurrected Christ; and the cool Pantocrator, ruler of the universe, seated in majesty and judgment. During the first centuries of Christianity, he was represented as youthful, kindly, and approachable. Early on, the cross became a universal symbol of Christ's protection and the redemption for his followers. Later, as protector of the Roman Empire and Christian kingdoms, he became a more forbidding, more mature and regal figure. Christ as judge was still the favored representation in the eleventh and twelfth centuries, but by the fourteenth century, with the institutionalization of the Corpus Christi feast and paintings depicting the instruments of the Passion, he was more the man on the way to his crucifixion, the Lamb of God, regal mainly in his heroic suffering, more human, gentler.[102] In the early fifteenth-century devotional classic *The Imitation of Christ* by Thomas à Kempis, which went through many editions in European languages before 1800 (and at least one in Nahuatl), most of these representations of Christ come into play, but with the emphasis less on judgment and punishment than on Christ as a model of the spiritual life of self-abnegation and service to others.[103] Echoing Mark 8:34 ("If any man would come after me, let him deny himself and take up his cross and follow me"), Kempis instructed his readers to "follow in the footsteps of Christ": follow his example of travail, self-denial, abasement, discipline, obedience, humility, and solitude.[104]

In both Spain and New Spain, the marked development of shrines featuring images of Christ after the 1580s depended on the promotion of

Table 3.1 *Miraculous images of Christ and the Cross (238 total)*

Image	Number	% of total
Crucifix	163	68.5
Cross	23	9.7
The Nazarene	17	7.1
Holy Child	15	6.3
Ecce Homo	11	4.6
Christ at the column	3	1.3
Sudarium painting	3	1.3
Entombed Christ	2	.84
Christ of the ascension	1	.47

Eucharistic devotion and other Christ-centered observances by Church authorities, in response to the challenges of Protestantism.[105] There was a new focus on Christ's Passion and Corpus Christi and Semana Santa observances, and the church bells that punctuated the soundscape every afternoon at three to remind those in earshot of the "agonies that Christ suffered on the Cross."[106] The preaching orders that were so prominent in the Hispanic world of this time – the mendicants first, soon joined by the Jesuits – promoted Semana Santa rites and brotherhoods of the cross and the Blessed Sacrament to sponsor them and orchestrate the popular processions of flagellants leading up to Easter Sunday.[107] In many of the images of this time in Spain and New Spain, Christ was alive on the cross, often blood-soaked, in agony, but the message conveyed in the published sermons and devotional literature was less about judgment and punishment than about mercy and redemption.[108] And in the eighteenth century, when more new shrines to images of Christ than to Mary were established, it was common to find figures of the crucified Christ described in similar terms, as kind (*amable*) and most beautiful. In the 1743 *relación geográfica* for Querétaro, for example, the city's miraculous Cristo de San Benito was celebrated for its "tender and attractive presence" and "the prodigious favors worked by His mercy."[109]

As in Spain, most of New Spain's enshrined figures of Christ were crucifixes – more than two-thirds – and an additional 15 percent depicted other stages of the Passion (Christ as the Man of Sorrows; the Ecce Homo; Christ at the column; the sudarium or imprint of Christ's face on Veronica's veil; descent from the Cross; Christ entombed; and the ascension to heaven). Most of the crucifixes were life size, human yet majestic and usually alone. Some were embellished with a golden sunburst attached to the head of the figure, but the body was not elaborately attired, unlike so many images of the Virgin Mary. It was naked except for a loincloth or skirtlike wrap called a *sudario*, as if it were Christ's shroud, that was sometimes fitted out in dark red velvet or white silk with a fancy tie on the figure's hip, embroidered with gold or silver thread. This is not to say all these New World crucified Christs were otherwise the same. Some were dark in color; some had lithe, youthful bodies that seemed to float on the cross; others were gaunt figures or hung heavy on the cross in contorted positions, disfigured by horrible bleeding wounds that coagulated in dark blotches to emphasize suffering and the offering of Christ's precious, life-giving blood.[110] In some crucifixes the thorns of the mock crown dig deep into Christ's forehead, dripping blood. Still others from the late colonial period, at least in prints representing them, portray an idealized human form, athletic, muscular, and graceful even in its agony, barely marked by the wounds, transcending the moment.[111] The many devotional prints of shrine images of Christ produced in the eighteenth century – several of them reproduced in this chapter – illustrate these variations, even different prints of the same sculpted image, but they also share a spare solemnity that is not always found in the Marian figures and prints other than representations of the Mater Dolorosa. The background in these conventional prints of miraculous crucifixes is plain and somber, relieved mainly by the urns of flowers at the bottom that represent Christ's Resurrection and the mystery of everlasting life originating in his death.

Echoing Christ's resurrection, there were many more figures of Christ crucified than of the Virgin Mary that reputedly restored themselves to fine condition.[112] Self-restored crucifixes are not mentioned in Mary Lee Nolan and Sidney Nolan's survey of Christian shrines in Europe,[113] but given this compelling connection to the resurrection it would be surprising if there were no forerunners in Spain. More distinctively New World – distinguished both from celebrated Spanish Christ figures and from American Marys – was the number of miraculous crucified Christs – about one in ten – that were said to be natural images formed in trees. They were considered natural apparitions, *of* nature, not just found in natural settings (see list below). As particular as these natural crucifixes and crosses may have been to New Spain, they are not so far removed from trees as a traditional Old World Christian symbol – the tree of Jesse, the tree of life, wood as the material of the True Cross – and sites of miracles that would seem to draw attention to the life cycle of all living things as well as the life of Christ.

Crucifixes and crosses "of nature" in New Spain and early nineteenth-century Mexico include

1 Señor del Cerezo, Pachuca, Hidalgo
2 Cruz de Maye, Ixmiquilpan, Hidalgo
3 Señor del Encino, Aguascalientes

Figure 3.12 "True portrait of the Santo Cristo of Amacueca," in its chapel next to the Franciscan convent church, district of Sayula, Jalisco. This unsigned print served as the frontispiece for *Novena en honra de la milagrosísima imagen del Santo Cristo de Amacueca...*, reprinted in 1784 in Mexico City by Zúñiga y Ontiveros. This *cristo de caña* was said to have been made in Pátzcuaro in the sixteenth century. It was mentioned as a wonder worker in the mid-seventeenth century, and by the eighteenth century chroniclers described the shrine as "sumptuous" and attributed many miracles to the image, including relief from drought. Courtesy of the John Carter Brown Library.

4 Señor de Ocote, Tapalpa, Jalisco
5 Cristo Crucificado de ramas de huizache, Tamazula, Jalisco
6 Señor del Encino, Yahualica, Jalisco
7 Señor del Ocote, Atemajac, Jalisco

8   Señor del Encino, San María Lagos, Jalisco
9   Señor del Mesquite, Zacoalco, Jalisco
10 Señor del Mezquitito, Belén del Refugio, Jalisco
11 Señor del Huaje, Jocotepec, Jalisco
12 Cruz Verde, near Tepic, Nayarit
13 Cristo Crucificado, Almoloyan, Colima
14 Crucifixo de raíces, temple of the Virgin of Guadalupe, Valladolid, Michoacán
15 Señor de Jacona, Michoacán
16 Señor de Tupátaro, Michoacán
17 Señor del Socorro, Salvatierra, Guanajuato
18 Cruz de Piedra, Querétaro
19 Cruces negros, barrio Santiago, Querétaro
20 Señor del Saucito, San Luis Potosí
21 Señor del Jovo, Tamazunchale, San Luis Potosí
22 Señor del Espino, Jojutla, Morelos
23 Two crosses found inside a zapote, sixteenth-century Cuernavaca
24 Natural cross of Ecatepec, Valley of Mexico
25 Señor Crucificado de Ylita, Puebla
26 Cristo de las Ampollas, Yucatán

The Holy Child was another staple of Christian iconography, venerated long before Spanish colonization of America, and a popular shrine image in eighteenth-century Aragón, if not throughout Spain.[114] He was a familiar figure in New Spain as well, although not so often as a shrine image (perhaps one in sixteen of the shrine images of Christ). Although the infant figure was not directly connected to the Passion, and none of the colonial images I know of was said to have restored itself to pristine condition, the birth of Christ was taken to mean a renewal of the world. In one of the early seventeenth-century sermons by the Spanish priest Cristóbal de Avendaño that circulated in America, Christ's birth "renewed everything; everything old came to an end and was made anew; the whole world became new once Christ was born."[115] In Spain, miraculous images of the Holy Child were renowned as wandering healers, sometimes called "the nurse" (el enfermero). Curing blindness was a specialty there, as it was in New Spain.[116] Unlike the celebrated Niño de Atocha of Plateros, near Fresnillo, Zacatecas, which became one of Mexico's most popular images and shrines by the 1830s, none of the colonial figures was widely known. Several of them, however, were represented in ways that were familiar in Spain and would make the Niño de Atocha easily recognizable in the nineteenth century. Wearing one of a collection of little hats, they were said to mysteriously disappear from their altars at night to work wonders in distant places.[117] As a wanderer or pilgrim, the Santo Niño of the San Juan de la Penitencia convent in Mexico City reportedly wore out his tiny shoes. The colonial images of the Santo Niño were popular in cities, including Mexico City, Valladolid, and Toluca, especially in nunneries, but none became a well-publicized shrine figure before the eighteenth century.[118] The Holy Child of San Juan de la Penitencia, said to have eased an epidemic in Mexico City in 1813, gained a wider audience after a print and lengthy sermon by José María Barrientos were published in 1818 (see Figure 7.8 in Chapter 7). According to Barrientos, this Holy Child worked its greatest miracles in the late sixteenth century after a period of neglect, "like Christ himself." It came to life during an earthquake in 1598, changing posture as if to hold up the church walls, which somehow remained standing. At the same time, its deformed face changed into one of great beauty. Barrientos added that the image had perspired many times and the water in which it was bathed had proven to be a healing tonic. Accounts of its marvelous cures "would doubtless fill a thick volume."

For most miracle-working images of Christ in New Spain, the followers were concentrated in a parish or cluster of nearby communities – that is, in smaller, scattered communities more than urban areas, other than the city of Querétaro with at least nine celebrated images of Christ in the mid-eighteenth century,[119] and Mexico City, which boasted at least seventeen wonder working crucifixes at different times and more numinous images of the Holy Child than any other community. Celebrated crucifixes were scattered throughout the viceroyalty, but there were several regional concentrations. All but two of the natural crucifixes were located in provincial towns and villages, mostly in central and western Mexico (see list, p. x). The self-restoring crucifixes were concentrated in central Mexico – Mexico City with three, the Valley of Toluca with two, Hidalgo with one and the reputation of another (the Cristo Renovado of Mapethé, which was removed to Mexico City and became known as the Cristo Renovado de Santa Teresa or Cristo de Ixmiquilpan), and one each for Puebla and Jalisco. And nearly a quarter of the miraculous figures of the Nazarene were located in the modern state of Morelos. Regional patterns in the Christocentric devotions also varied somewhat over time for the shrines that can be dated (see Appendix 2). In the sixteenth century, seven of the new shrines to images of Christ were located in central Mexico, especially Mexico City. In the seventeenth century, the new shrines were more widely distributed across regions: ten in Mexico City; three others in central Mexico; ten in the western states of Jalisco, Michoacán, Nayarit, and Guerrero; four in Querétaro and the north; and seven in the south. In the eighteenth century, fewer new shrines to Christ images were located in Mexico City (three), and there was now a notable concentration in the west, the Bajío region of north-central Mexico, and the north.

Figure 3.13 Loose, unsigned print of the Santo Cristo of Tlacolula, Oaxaca collected by Francisco de Ajofrín. Also known as the Señor de las Batallas, this crucifix had become "a magnificent cult" and was "visited by devotees from throughout the province of Oaxaca," according to Ajofrín in the 1760s. It was a common practice for bishops to encourage the market in devotional prints by granting indulgences to devotees who offered prayers before them. Here the bishop of Oaxaca grants 40 days indulgence to those who pray a credo, appealing, in the presence of this print "which has touched the original image," for "peace and concord among Christian princes." Courtesy of the Real Academia de la Historia, Madrid.

V.R. de la Milagrosa Img. que se venera en su Capilla en el Saltillo.

Figure 3.14 "True portrait of the Miraculous Image revered in its chapel in Saltillo [Coahuila]," unsigned print used as frontispiece for *Novena a Christo Señor Nuestro Crucificado, cuya portentosa imagen se venera en su capilla contigua a la Parroquia de la Villa de Saltillo*, by Pedro Joseph Quintín de Arispe, Mexico: Jáuregui, 1775. Also known as the Santo Cristo, this was another *cristo de caña*. It was said to have been brought to Saltillo in 1607 by a Spanish founder of the community. This was one of the few colonial cities or *villas* identified primarily with a miraculous Christ as the divine patron. Courtesy of the Getty Research Center.

MILAGROSA IMAGEN DEL STO. XPTO. DE CHALMA.
Cerca de Mexico, Santuario Celeberrimo.
Sylverio ex. a. 1761.   En las escalerillas.   N. 1193.

Figure 3.15 "Miraculous image of the Holy Christ of Chalma." Loose print from engraving by Francisco Sylverio de Sotomayor, 1761, collected by Francisco de Ajofrín. Ajofrín has written in the caption that "this most famous shrine is near Mexico City." Courtesy of the Real Academia de la Historia, Madrid.

Few major regional shrines featured a celebrated figure of Christ during the colonial period. The Señor de Chalma and the Señor de Esquipulas stand out, but the Cristo Renovado de Santa Teresa and the Christ of the Sacromonte at Amecameca also deserve mention. They are treated elsewhere in the book, so a brief description here is enough to keep their distinctiveness in mind.

Comments of observers in the eighteenth century suggest that Chalma was the most popular rural shrine in central Mexico, singled out as a place visited by devotees from "distant lands."[120] Perched in the western mountains of the modern Estado de México, about 60 miles from Mexico City, Chalma's miraculous black Christ became a focal point for evangelization of Otomí, Mazahua, and Nahua Indians from the Archdiocese of Mexico and the Diocese of Michoacán during the late seventeenth century. It was reputed to be a "cristo aparecido" that mysteriously materialized at the site where an ancient idol was worshiped, rather than an image that had long been in place before it showed signs of divine presence and will. The shrine was administered by as many as twenty Augustinian friars at a time, and in the seventeenth century its iconic miracles involved Christ in perpetual combat against idols and Satan. Its core constituency remained Indian villagers from parts of central Mexico, but the shrine also became a haven for hermits. Once it gained official standing as a royal shrine in the 1770s, it attracted more devotees from Mexico City, including at least one viceroy and several audiencia judges,[121] as well as non-Indian townspeople

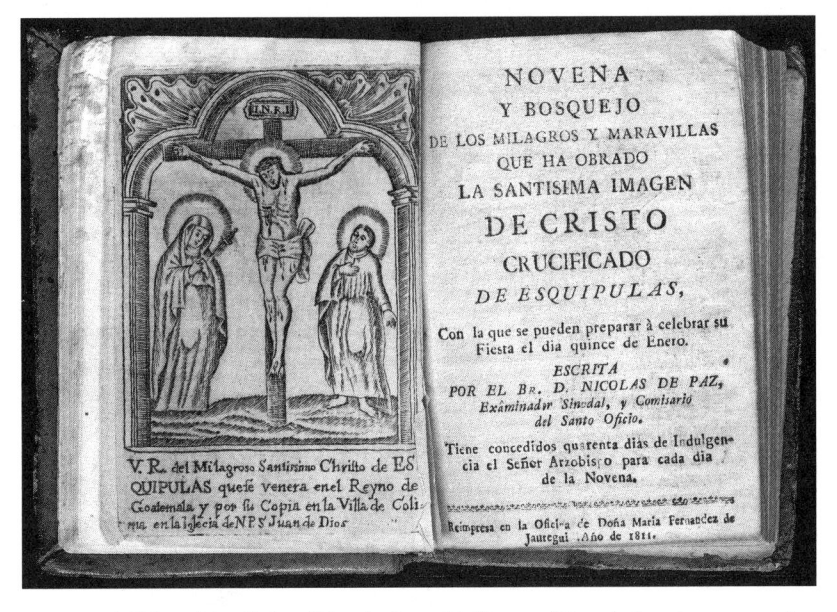

Figure 3.16 Print of the Christ of Esquipulas, with Mary and Joseph, based on a copy of the Esquipulas statue in the Church of San Juan de Dios in the city of Colima, Mexico, from Br. Nicolás de Paz, *Novena y bosquejo de los milagros y maravillas que ha obrado la santísima imagen de Christo Crucificado de Esquipulas* ... reprinted in Mexico City by Jáuregui, 1811. Courtesy of the Cushing Memorial Library and Archives, Texas A&M University.

from the Valley of Toluca and nearby districts in the modern state of Morelos, even after the original image had been destroyed in a fire.[122]

Located in the rural eastern highlands of Guatemala, the Christ of Esquipulas, a figure apparently dating from the 1590s, developed an extensive following in Central America and parts of southern Mexico, in the city of Tabasco's church of San Juan Bautista, and in the Chiapas towns of Tila and Tapachula. It also reached beyond its regional base in two ways that were different from the outreach of the Chalma shrine. Judging by miracle stories recounted in the mid-eighteenth century, it attracted Caribbean travelers and sailors who had made vows to the Cristo. In the eighteenth century its fame also jumped from Guatemala and southern Mexico far to the north. One dynamic Spanish Franciscan missioner in the early eighteenth century seems to have been central to this unusual geographical pattern. Antonio Margil de Jesús served in Guatemala and other parts of Central America and Yucatán from the 1680s to the early 1700s, including the city of Guatemala (Antigua), where the Lord of Esquipulas was a patron saint, before being assigned to found a new Franciscan *colegio apostólico* in Zacatecas (1707) for the training of missionaries to serve in Nueva Galicia and the northern frontier. He also continued his own missionary work in Nayarit (1712–1716), Coahuila, Nuevo León, and Texas (1716–1722). The presence of pockets of devotion to the Christ of Esquipulas in central and northern Mexico reflects his presence and influence. Margil de Jesús served twice in the missionary college of Querétaro, where a celebrated copy of the Esquipulas Christ was revered during the eighteenth century. Other crucifixes called the Lord of Esquipulas were revered in or near places in western and northern Mexico where he went or where Franciscans who trained with him served – in Colima (in the church of San Juan de Dios), Jalisco (in at least eight communities), Michoacán (in four communities), Moroleón (in Guanajuato), Durango (in the temple of San Juan de Dios), and eventually New Mexico (in the shrine of Chimayó).[123]

The Cristo Renovado de Santa Teresa in Mexico City's church of the Carmelite nuns followed a different kind of bifurcated path to regional notoriety.[124] This *cristo de caña* crucifix (fashioned mostly from the sacred food plant, maize) apparently was brought to the lead mines of Mapethé, near Ixmiquilpan, Hidalgo, by a Spanish settler in the mid-sixteenth century. According to tradition, the image and its chapel were abandoned before long, until in 1621 the Christ came alive during a great storm and restored itself to fine condition. Marvelous healings of local people and an abundant crop of maize followed. By 1623 it had been removed to Mexico City on the archbishop's orders, to the newly founded Carmelite convent church of Santa Teresa. During the late seventeenth century, the Carmelite church had become a major shrine in the city, especially after an epidemic

Miraculous Images of Christ and the Virgin Mary 211

VERDADERO RETRATO DEL S. XPTO. DE IXMIQVILPAN,
COLOCADO, POR EL ILL.ᵐᵒ Sᴿ. ARÇOBISPO D. IVAN DE LA SERNA;
EN EL CONVENTO DE CARMELITAS DESCALZAS DEL Sᴱ. S.
JOSEPH DE MEXICO, DONDE ESTA OI.

Figure 3.17 "True portrait of the Santo Cristo of Ixmiquilpan, placed by Archbishop D. Juan de la Serna in the convent of Discalced Carmelites of St. Joseph of Mexico City, where it is to this day." Print from unsigned engraving tipped into a copy of the 1724 edition of Velasco's devotional history of the statue, *Exaltación de la divina misericordia*. Of the various eighteenth-century prints of this statue, this one shows a particularly muscular Christ. Other than the stigmata, the body is little marked by his agony. Courtesy of the Bancroft Library, University of California, Berkeley.

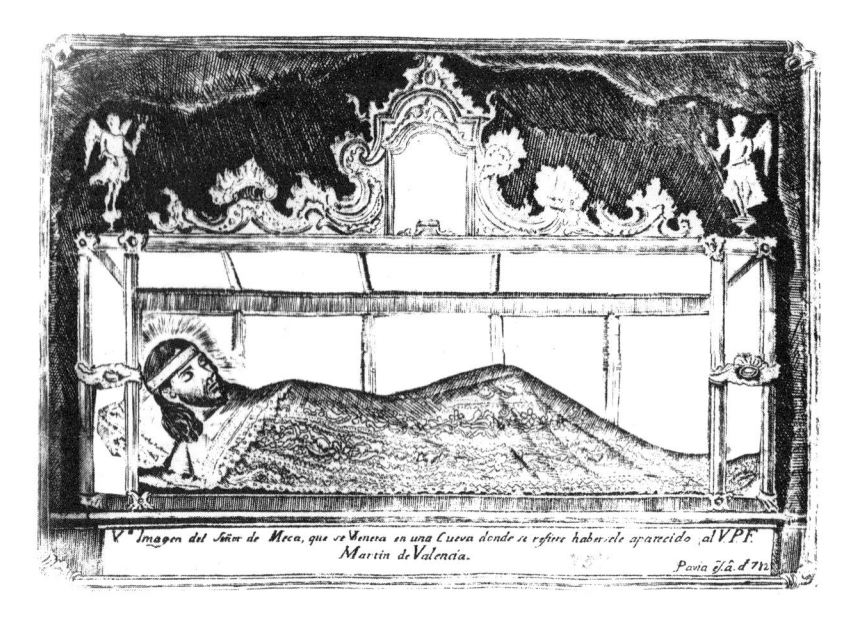

Figure 3.18 Señor del Sacromonte of Amecameca. "True Image of the Lord of Meca venerated in a cave where it is said to have appeared to the Venerable Father Fray Martín de Valencia." Print from engraving by Pavia, 1782, in AGN Inquisición 1360 fol. 357. Courtesy of the Archivo General de la Nación, Mexico.

in 1697. By some accounts it was the most important, the most visited, and the most efficacious image shrine in the city in the eighteenth century, generating an array of published prints, a pious history, novena booklets, and other devotional materials. From the early eighteenth century, the first editions of Alonso Alberto de Velasco's *Exaltación de la Divina Misericordia en la milagrosa renovación...* (1699, 1724), in particular, stirred interest in the image and the story of self-restoration in the town of Mapethé and surrounding Otomí settlements and mining camps. Devotees in the district of Ixmiquilpan unsuccessfully appealed for repatriation of the miraculous crucifix, but ultimately the site of the miracle of self-restoration was as important as the relic itself. By the 1760s, Mapethé was a popular shrine site with its own fine church and altars, attracting Otomí villagers and a network of migrants who had gone to the Bajío region, as well as devotees from other mining towns in Hidalgo. The devotion apparently reached its zenith at both shrines during the second half of the eighteenth century.

The shrine of the Sacromonte at Amecameca, 38 miles southeast of Mexico City at the foot of Mt. Popocatépetl, developed a multiracial, regional following in nearby districts of the Estado de Mexico, the Valley of Mexico, Morelos, Tlaxcala, and Puebla during the seventeenth and eighteenth centuries. Paradoxically, this is also the least documented period in its history. The site and its association with Martín de Valencia, the revered leader of the "Apostolic Twelve" Franciscans who proselytized in central Mexico during the first years of Spanish colonization, attracted considerable hagiographical interest in the sixteenth century, and there is a substantial paper trail for the nineteenth and twentieth centuries, when the site drew pilgrims from as far away as eastern Querétaro and San Luis Potosí.[125] The saintly Valencia was famous for using a small hillside cave at Amecameca as a refuge for rigorous spiritual exercises and meditations on the Passion of Christ. After his death in 1534, Franciscans, and then the first Dominican pastor there in the 1580s, Juan Paz, and local native lords revered Valencia as a Saint-Francis-like figure and made his cave retreat into a shrine for his relics and a kind of New World Holy Sepulchre.[126] Near the end of the sixteenth century, Franciscan chronicler Gerónimo de Mendieta observed that the cave was secured with locked doors and Indian guards. Every Friday a priest ascended the hill to celebrate Mass at the shrine in memory of Christ's Passion, "as the saintly Fr. Martín did with his prayers and tears and harsh penances." Mendieta added, "Indians visit the site all the time, especially on that day [Friday], as do Spaniards in the vicinity and travelers on the road to and from Puebla."[127] Several other early chronicles mention that a recumbent figure of Christ was laid in a coffin-shaped box across from the altar. This would presumably be the Señor del Sacromonte, the entombed figure of Christ. When and how this Christ became the featured, wonder-working artifact at the shrine, famous for arriving providentially on a mule that would not be moved, is not clear, but by the late eighteenth century the site had a variety of other attractions to offer its visitors, too, including a fine arched stone entrance with a figure of Christ, a chapel of Our Lady of Guadalupe, the hilltop shrine, the old Dominican church of Our Lady of the Assumption, processions of the Cristo to and from the church, and a lively marketplace, as well as Valencia's relics, with the majestic, smoking, snow-capped cone of Popocatépetl as backdrop. By the 1830s a retreat house and stations of the cross were added.[128]

The santuario de Jesús Nazareno de Atotonilco, near San Miguel Allende, Guanajuato, founded in the eighteenth century, was also designed as a destination with various attractions for pious visitors. Perhaps it should be included among the leading shrines of the late colonial period, but it is not clear either that this Cristo was the main attraction then or that large numbers of people were drawn there from beyond the vicinity of San Miguel, even though alms-collecting missions were sent to the city of Guanajuato, among other places in the region. Development of this shrine was largely the work of Father Luis Felipe Neri de Álfaro, a leading Oratorian priest who was inspired by a vision of Christ telling him to build a religious retreat at the site of mineral springs near San Miguel that had become a haven for robbers. From 1740 to the 1770s, a compound containing *casas de ejercicios espirituales* (retreat houses), the springs of healing waters, and six chapels with didactic paintings and inscriptions took shape. The main chapel featured a sculpture of the Nazarene Christ, modeled on the figure in Father Luis Felipe's apparition. In the early years, memory of this saintly priest apparently was as much or more the focus of devotion as the Cristo and the other attractions.

Son of God, Son of Mary

While often there are good reasons to distinguish images of Christ from images of Mary as objects of devotion – and I will do so again below – the distinction can be carried too far. The histories of Mary and Christ obviously are intertwined. Think of one and the other comes to mind and into play. They were linked in the great Christian feasts and processions, especially at Christmas and during the Easter season; and representations of Mary usually referred to her motherhood and to Christ – the Immaculate Conception; the Madonna and Child; and the Mater Dolorosa coupled with the Pietà, the Crucifixion, and the Entombment of Christ, meeting on the plane of suffering and sacrifice. They appear together in the venerated painting of the Deposition of Christ in the Dominican convent in Mexico City (Figure 3.19), in the shrine image of Nuestra Señora de la Piedad on the outskirts of the city, and especially in the many shrines and sacred images of the Madonna and Child. (See Figures 3.20–3.21.)

In most prodigious shrine images of the Madonna and Child, the two figures were inseparable, but occasionally the Christ Child came to stand alone and overshadow the companion figure of Mary as an object of special devotion. The outstanding case is the Santo Niño de Atocha, outside Fresnillo, Zacatecas, which was initially paired with the Madonna as a copy of the Spanish sacred image of Our Lady of Atocha. The first evidence that this Holy Child was celebrated in its own right comes from the 1810s. By the 1830s it was extremely popular in northern and western Mexico, with a published literature and many printed, painted, and sculpted copies in circulation, and it remains one of the most popular shrine images in Mexico. It is unclear how many of the other twenty-three shrine images of the Niño Jesús in Appendix 1 had originally been paired with a figure of the Madonna and how many were freestanding images from the beginning, perhaps made for a nativity scene.[129] But with celebrated images of the Madonna and Child there was sometimes suspicion that the revered child had been stolen and a "foundling" substituted. For example, in 1797 there was an investigation into rumors that the original Christ Child associated with the statue of Our Lady of Remedios at Totoltepec had been replaced and was now in the hands of an apothecary in Mexico City, who used it when

Figure 3.19 The Deposition of Christ — Mary cradling the lifeless body of her son, the Son of God — surrounded by the Santos Varones, the holy men who helped her remove Christ's body from the cross and prepare him for burial. Eighteenth-century engraved print of a painting venerated in the Dominican convent of Mexico City's Chapel of the Deceased Christ (Espiración). Loose print from unsigned eighteenth-century engraving made in the Calle de la Portería de la Profesa. The caption is a prayer to the Santos Varones for the favor of their aid in spiritual and temporal matters. Courtesy of the Getty Research Center.

Figure 3.20 Print of Nuestra Señora del Rosario from an unsigned, undated woodcut published in Juan de Villa Sánchez, OP, *Sermón que en la solemnidad del capítulo provincial de la Provincia angelopolitana de San Miguel . . .*, Mexico: J.B. de Hogal, 1728. Courtesy of the Bancroft Library, University of California, Berkeley.

he was called to assist in birthings and other cures. The investigators inspected the apothecary's statue of the Holy Child and concluded that it was not the Remedios Child.[130]

In some shrines dedicated to a figure of Mary or Christ, a complementary image of the other one also was revered as miraculous. For example, at the shrine for Nuestra Señora de la Bala on the northern outskirts of Mexico City in the church of San Lázaro, a miraculous crucifix known as the Señor del Balazo was present in the eighteenth century, so named because an

Miraculous Images of Christ and the Virgin Mary 217

V.^{ro} R.^{to} de la milagrosa Imagen de N.ª S.ª de la Merced, que se venera en la Iglesia de su Convento grande de Mexico, del Real, y Militar Orden de Redentores de Captivos.

Figure 3.21 "True Portrait of the miraculous image of Our Lady of Mercy venerated in the church of the main convent in Mexico City of the Royal and Military Order of Redemptors of Captives." Loose print from engraving by Baltasar Troncoso y Sotomayor, 1759, collected by Francisco de Ajofrín. This representation of the Mercedarians' founder and patron saint is unusual in depicting her with the infant Jesus. Courtesy of the Real Academia de la Historia, Madrid.

errant bullet had penetrated the church door and lodged in the figure's left leg.[131] Miraculous figures of both Christ and Mary in Puebla's Hospital de San Pedro were celebrated in Pedro Delgado Loria's 1721 sermon *Septena de la Soledad de María Sanctíssima y Entierro de Christo cuyas devotas imágenes se veneran en su Iglesia del Hospital Real del Señor San Pedro de la Ciudad de Puebla de los Ángeles.*[132]

The mystique of shrine images of Christ and Mary were similar in some basic ways, too. They were renowned for most of the same kinds of miracles of protection and well-being. Pregnant women were more likely to seek out a prodigious image of the Blessed Mary, but the differences in how, when, and why shrine images were invoked varied more by local and regional circumstances than by whether the miraculous image depicted Mary or Christ. Their origin stories were similar in some ways, too: both images of Mary and Christ resisted being moved from a chosen place; or they were brought or made by unknown young men dressed in white who mysteriously disappeared without a trace; or their location was signaled by celestial music or lights; or images already in place spontaneously came to life or worked miracles of healing and protection. Reported acts of mistreatment of sacred images were rare, but they were as likely to be images of Mary as of Christ. (The main difference is that statues of Christ and male saints were more likely to be whipped by their abusers.) Confraternities devoted to Mary and Christ, along with the Blessed Sacrament and souls in purgatory, were the most common kinds, whether in Indian or predominately Spanish and casta parishes; and it was unusual for a Marian or Christocentric confraternity to prosper at the expense of the other. These similarities and the popularity of Christocentric shrines may seem surprising since Christ as the Son of God could be considered a more remote, even forbidding figure, rarely depicted in a posture of supplication, and especially associated with suffering, sacrifice, death, and judgment. Blood-soaked images of Christ on the cross, alive or dead, may have been approached with more trepidation than were images of a smiling Mary with her hands pressed together in prayer and intercession,[133] yet there were about as many Christ-centered as Marian shrines. In spite of suffering, the prodigious images of Christ, like the Marian images, were called and revered as "santos" – not abstractions or symbols, but real – figures of redemption and protection. In them, the divine was present and active in that place.[134] They were beloved patrons, trusted to respond to local cares and wants; and both were associated with fertility, family, the trials of life, and transcendence more than defeat and death.

Within this base of similarities and connections, there were some striking differences in the devotional histories of shrine images of Mary and Christ. Any sacred image might perspire and move its eyes, but otherwise images of Christ and Mary were renowned for showing different signs of life that simulated their distinct, gendered roles in the story of Christianity.

True to Christ's agony, sacrifice, and resurrection, when crucifixes came to life they groaned (though rarely spoke), trembled, twitched, spurted blood, grew hair, and sometimes restored themselves to fine condition. Not surprisingly, miraculous images of the Holy Child were more likely to cry than twitch or groan, but their tears were sometimes bloody, foretelling Christ's martyrdom. Images of Mary reportedly wept, blushed, and changed posture. Unlike the Christs, Marian images were famous for remaining in fine condition despite age and exposure, recalling the Blessed Mary's perpetual virginity and purity.[135]

Marian shrine figures were more likely to be transported beyond their local communities, whether it was to a nearby city in need of protection or in "peregrina" (pilgrim) copies carried on alms-collecting missions. Most of the prodigious Christs were processed locally during the Easter season, Corpus Christi, and the feast days of the Invention and Exaltation of the Cross, but traveled less often outside their home communities. Many early colonial Marian figures that became shrine images were smaller and more portable than the frequently life-size figures of Christ, but more importantly they were the chosen patron saints of cities, either drawing nearby shrine images into the city, or extending the fame of an urban-based image into the countryside. The great regional shrine of Our Lady of San Juan de los Lagos was not located near a city, but its trade fairs drew merchants and devotees from cities in the Bajío, as well as Guadalajara, and Mexico City.

With the denser networks of communications and centralized authority of urban Marian shrines, it is not surprising that they produced more administrative and devotional records, including promotional and apologetic publications such as the *Zodíaco Mariano* (1755). Images and advocations of the Virgin Mary were also the first choice as patrons of academic theses presented in the Real y Pontificia Universidad de México from the 1660s to the 1800s, commemorated in single-sheet announcements with a print of her image.[136] Thanks to this written record and the urban and regional appeal of the many Marian images, they and their shrines attracted the attention of more authors during the colonial period, as they still do. Most image shrines to a figure of Christ were popular in their locality, often a rural district, and rarely generated an abundant paper trail unless they became controversial. Most were too large to transport long distances, and rarely were reproduced in diminutive *peregrina* images for alms-collecting missions. The local focus of shrine images of Christ was also expressed in the number that were found growing in tree branches and roots nearby.[137]

Black Christs, White Madonnas

The most striking difference between shrine images of Christ and the Virgin Mary in New Spain reverses a European pattern: there were more wondrous dark or "black" images of Christ in New Spain and many more dark or "black" images of the Virgin Mary in Spain and Western Europe. For Europe, just a few miraculous black Christs have been identified: the monumental crucifix in the Wawel Cathedral of Cracow, Poland, that reputedly spoke to young queen and future saint Jadwiga in 1384; the metal Cristo Negro de Cáceres, Spain; the black Christs of Lucca and Licata, Italy; and three French Christs, in Paris's Notre Dame cathedral, Saint-Flour, and Bastia on the island of Corsica. In New Spain, by comparison, more than twenty black Christs enjoyed a measure of fame. They were to be found throughout the viceroyalty, from Chihuahua and Durango in the north to Yucatán, Chiapas, and Guatemala in the south, somewhat concentrated in central Mexico, especially in Indian districts of modern Hidalgo (see Table 3.2). Two of these American black Christs had followings well beyond the vicinity of their shrines: the Christ of Chalma, in the mountains of the Estado de México near Malinalco, which drew visitors from Indian districts in Hidalgo, Morelos, Querétaro, and the Valley of Mexico, as well as Mexico City and pueblos de indios nearby; and the Christ of Esquipulas, with its shrine situated in the district of Chiquimula in eastern Guatemala. Fewer devotees from districts in modern Mexico visited the Esquipulas shrine, but during the eighteenth century cherished copies of this crucified Christ were to be found in churches and family chapels from Tabasco to the Bajío, western Mexico, and New Mexico, and at least eighteen editions of novena booklets for the Cristo Negro de Esquipulas were published in Mexico City and Puebla, mainly from 1778 to 1797.[138]

All of these black Cristos recall scenes of the Passion – twenty-three crucifixes, one Christ Entombed, and one Jesús Nazareno.[139] I have not found references to black or dark figures of the Holy Child, much less one that was the focus of an image shrine. About a third of these dark figures (eight of twenty-five), plus various crosses, including the Cruz Verde of Tequisquiapan, Querétaro, were said to have been found formed in a living tree: El Señor del Encino of Aguascalientes; the Señor del Cerezo of Pachuca, Hidalgo; the Señor del Jovo of Tamazunchale, San Luis Potosí; the Cristo de las Ampollas of Mérida; the Señor del Huaje of Jocotepec, Jalisco; the Señor de Jojutla, Morelos; the crucifix of the Dieguino convent of Nuestra Señora de Guadalupe in Valladolid; and the Cristo of Jacona, Michoacán in a guava tree.[140]

The fact that many of the colonial black Cristos come from Indian districts has invited explanations that focus on possible indigenous, precolonial symbolism. For example, the black Christs in central Mexico are thought by some scholars to be associated especially with Tezcatlipoca in central Mexico and Ek-Chuah in Maya Yucatan and Guatemala because a leading feature of these divinities was their black coloring, and black also is often associated with the regalia of native shamans.[141] Or colonial

Table 3.2 *Black Cristos in New Spain**

Location	Name
Chihuahua	Señor de Mapimí
Durango	Jesús Nazareno, Nombre de Dios
Zacatecas	Señor de Guerreros, Santuario de Nuestra Señora de Guadalupe
Aguascalientes	Señor del Encino, Templo del Señor del Encino, city of Aguascalientes
Jalisco	Señor de los Rayos, Temastián
	Señor de Huaje, Jocotepec (Teccistlan)
Michoacán	Cristo de Jacona
Guanajuato	Señor del Hospital, Salamanca
Hidalgo	Señor del Cerezo, Pachuca
	Señor del Buena Viaje, Orizabita
	Cristo Negro de la Villa de Tezontepec
Estado de Mexico	Señor de Santa Maria de Ahuacatlan, Valle de Bravo
	Señor del Sacromonte, Amecameca
	**Señor de Chalma, near Malinanco
Mexico City and vicinity	Señor del Veneno, cathedral church in Mexico City
	Cristo de Mizquic, Valley of Mexico
Puebla	Señor de la Paz, San Pablo Anicano
	Señor de Ylita, Teteles, Pue.
	Señor de Tlacotepec
Veracruz	Señor de Otatitlán
Oaxaca	Señor de la Capilla, Villa de Tezoatlan
Chiapas	**Señor de Tila
Campeche	Cristo Negro, Barrio de San San Román church, city of Campeche
Yucatán	**Cristo de las Ampollas, Mérida cathedral
Guatemala	Cristo Negro de Esquipulas

* Other black Christs in several parts of Mexico have been mentioned in ethnographic studies, but not yet identified as shrine images in the colonial period. For Yucatán, Barabas I, 328–333 mentions five others: the Santo Cristo de Sitilpech, the Santo Cristo de la Expectación of Citilcum, the Santo Cristo de la Transfiguración of Chumayel, the Santo Cristo of Ichmul, and the Santísima Cruz Tun Tres Personas of Xocen. Other secondary sources mention the Señor de Villaseca (Guanajuato, Gto), the Cristo de Moroleón (Guanajuato), the Cristo de Carácuaro (Michoacán), the Cristo de Colotlipa (Guerrero), the Cristo de la Capilla de la Santísima Trinidad (Taxco, Guerrero), the Señor de la Piedad (Oaxaca), the Cristo Negro de San Nicolás Ayotla (Teotitlán del Camino, Oaxaca), and the Cristo del Buen Viaje (Veracruz).

** These were lighter images, but still known as black Christs. Two others, the Divino Pastor of Sauceda, Durango and the Señor del Tizonazo, Durango apparently were not colonial shrine images.

Indians are thought to have identified more readily with the suffering of a Christ who was dark skinned, like them. Historical evidence is lacking, but it is plausible that at least some black Christs were understood in terms of precolonial knowledge and memory. Ethnographers often find devotees in traditional communities where indigenous languages are still spoken connecting their Christs to local beliefs and practices that seem to have historical roots reaching into the precolonial past.[142] A more developed, if still speculative version of precolonial continuity and native agency in the meaning of these distinctive black Christs during the colonial period has been proposed by art historian Jeannette Favrot Peterson.[143] Her touchstone for "the ways in which blackness was observed and ideologically deployed" is the Lord of Chalma, an image that signifies as black even though a lighter colored wooden image replaced the original dark cristo de caña after that image was destroyed in a fire during the seventeenth or eighteenth century.[144] For Peterson, Chalma's blackness means a "cooptation of the Christian God by local constituencies." "[B]lackness made it possible to return to a pre-Christian state," while incorporating aspects of a more dualistic Christian outlook.[145]

Anthropologist-geographer Miles Richardson brought a different eye and a different line of interpretation to the black Christs of Spanish America. Focusing on the Señor de los Milagros of Buga, Colombia, and Guatemala's Christ of Esquipulas, he dismissed the idea that these images are dark because Indians prefer images that look like them or represent a hybrid of precolonial and Christian symbolism. Instead, he suggested that they are black because they are passional figures, foretelling or representing Christ's death on Good Friday, before his resurrection. For Richardson, their color signifies the solemn mourning rituals of Semana Santa, the fading of light into darkness. Black, then, is the color of death, mourning, and anxious anticipation of resurrection.[146]

Richardson's sharp focus on a less racialized or ethnic interpretation deserves consideration. Black did and does stand in for death, decay, and mourning in Christian practice. It is the color of Semana Santa before Easter Sunday. And there were at least two colonial figures of Christ on the Cross in pueblos de indios described as dark with age, decay, and death that turned light in color when they were miraculously restored to their original state: the Cristo Renovado of Mapethé, Hidalgo, and the Señor de Tila in Chiapas. In the first volume of the landmark *Los pinceles de la historia* series on visualization of history in Mexico, Jaime Cuadriello included a set of four late-eighteenth-century paintings from the shrine at Mapethé that depict the miracle of Christ's self-restoration. In the first painting a decrepit black Christ hangs limp on the cross, dark with age, deterioration, and sorrow. In the second painting, the black figure floats free of the cross, witnessed by a group of men. In the third, the Christ figure has been marvelously restored to fine condition, pale white, eyes closed, and reattached to the cross. The body is unmarked, but lifeless. In the fourth painting, Christ's eyes are open and his complexion is pale, but there is a rosy hue. His wounds are visible, fresh, and dripping blood. He is alive, suffering and dying in a way that foretells the Resurrection and promise of eternal life.[147]

Were the few famous European black Christs understood in racialized terms in the seventeenth and eighteenth centuries? The meager secondary literature has little to say on the subject, but Monique Scheer's emphasis on dark coloration as a sign of antiquity in European sacred images (discussed below) and Richardson's symbolism of Semana Santa would seem to be a promising place to begin. Both Peterson and Richardson doubt that black Christs were dark from many years of handling and exposure to the smoke of incense and candles, but Carlos Navarrete, longtime student of the Cristo Negro of Esquipulas, reported that restorers of the image in 2005 concluded that its dark color was caused by impurities accumulating on the surface of the statue over the years, especially from habitually rubbing the statue with linseed oil.[148] Navarrete is quick to add that the truth of why Christs in Mexico, Guatemala, and elsewhere are black is determined more by tradition than by disinterested scholarly inquiry: "beliefs grow with time, based on what people feel and wish to see."[149] Darkened with age might then carry the additional meaning of darkened by the touch and care of ancestral devotees.

Any high-flying explanation for the many black Christs in New Spain will be brought down to earth by particular cases, local considerations, and inconclusive evidence. And what can be said with much confidence about black Christs and white Madonnas together in either New Spain or early modern Europe is complicated by still other considerations that add to the risk of exaggeration. First, a large majority of figures of both Christ and the Virgin Mary in New Spain were light skinned rather than black or very dark, and the black Christs generally have angular facial features that look more European than native American. Second, not all the black Christs in Mexico belonged to Indian communities or attracted mainly Indian devotees. There is the Cristo del Veneno from the Dominican convent of Porta Coeli in Mexico City, later moved to the cathedral, with its origin story about the figure turning black as a warning to the archbishop not to drink a poisoned beverage prepared for him; and there were black Christs in the Bajío region, such as the Cristo de Salamanca that appealed to a diverse population. And third, pueblos de indios evidently were no less interested in their light-skinned Christs. Take the figure of Jesús Nazareno beloved as a great miracle worker in the parish of San Pablo Apetelatitlan, Tlaxcala. It was described in the 1790s by a district official as "a most marvelous pallid image that commands the greatest veneration and respect for its beauty and the perfection of its adorable and attractive face. The people of that town turn to it, brimming with faith and confidence in all their troubles."[150]

Not only were dark images of Mary few in number, in one case, the Virgin of Loreto, a black European Virgin was rendered white in America by its Jesuit promoters. In the late seventeenth century they evidently decided she should be white rather than "the blackened color of the original at Loreto," so that "this image would not be less esteemed by ordinary folk whose preferences are sometimes more governed by appearances, color."[151] The scarcity of dark images of the Virgin in America makes a striking contrast to Europe, where at least 167 black or very dark images of the Virgin Mary were venerated,[152] including some of the most famous Marian images of late medieval and early modern times: Our Lady of Czestochowa in Poland, Our Lady of Loreto in Italy and beyond, the Virgin of Rocamadour in France, and Our Lady of Guadalupe, Our Lady of Montserrat, and Our Lady of the Pillar of Zaragoza in Spain. In their survey of black images of the Virgin Mary in Europe, Leonard W. Moss and Stephen C. Cappannari suggested that many of them originated in the Middle Ages as "Christian borrowings from earlier pagan art forms" that depicted dark Greek, Roman, or more localized goddesses of the land.[153] But did devotees of dark Virgins in the early modern period think of them as former earth goddesses, regal and remote? And is there a connection to honored figures of the Virgin Mary in New Spain?

That there were few renowned dark Virgins in New Spain is distinctive and perhaps surprising not only because dark Virgins were familiar in Spain and other parts of Europe in the fifteenth and sixteenth centuries, but also because their darkness often has been regarded as a universal symbol in agricultural societies of regeneration of life, the color of rich, fertile soil. The most famous image of the Virgin Mary in New Spain, the Virgin of Guadalupe at Tepeyac, has been treated in these terms, as a dark Virgin in a long line of earth mothers stretching back to medieval Europe and Mesoamerican goddesses.[154] If so, why was the Mexican Guadalupe not described as dark from the early years of the devotion in the sixteenth and seventeenth centuries? Why was the earliest known copy of the Guadalupe image, dated 1606, depicted with fair skin? And why weren't many dark images of Mary revered in the farming communities of rural New Spain? No one answer is likely to satisfy, but in this time and place Mary's marvelous virgin motherhood may have been a more compelling marker of her association with fertility than the color of her skin. And to evangelizers and colonial devotees versed in the fundamentals of Catholic Christianity, there was a compelling symbolic association between Mary and whiteness. White signified purity and virtue, especially Mary's virginity even in motherhood. Unlike deteriorated and miraculously restored figures of the wounded Christ, figures of the Virgin Mary famously expressed a lasting perfection, resisting the ravages of time and use. This was not a barren whiteness; like Christ's resurrection, it signified glorious abundance of eternal life. The bond between purity and abundance was established early, and it endured.[155]

But the racial connotations of skin color eventually intersected with the appearance and appeal of religious images. Mexico's Nuestra Señora de Guadalupe is the prime example of an image of Mary that came to be known as "la morena," dark like a native woman. But who regarded the Mexican Guadalupe this way and when are questions that have yet to be adequately answered. The earliest recorded mention of this association seems to have been in a sermon delivered by Juan de Mendoza Ayala, OFM, on December 12, 1672, and published in 1673:

> This holy image of Guadalupe was made to resemble the heathen natives of this land. It is expressed in her face, which is of a toned-down color, brown similar to theirs. The same is true of her manner of dress. She clothed herself in their fashion so that when the heathens see her made in their likeness and dressed as they dress, they will fall in love with her and convert.[156]

Guadalupe's dark complexion and Indian appearance did not become automatic until after Nicolás de Segura, SJ's sermon in 1741:[157]

> Who would deny that this most benign Mother appeared with the avowed intention of resembling in every way the natives of the country, valuing the Indian so highly that she seems to have affected their appearance in every way: in the *tilma* or cloak of Juan Diego on which her image was painted; in her humble and shy posture and the tilt of her head; in the pleasing separation of her hair, which is black and thick; and in the distinct olive-colored complexion of the face and hands; in the full-length tunic from her neck and shoulders to her feet, and the flowing robe from head to foot in the manner of a shawl – all of these signs and indications by which she shows her wish to have appeared in every way like Indian nobles of this America.

Judging by the enthusiastic promotion of the Guadalupan devotion by church dignitaries, such as Archbishop Francisco Antonio de Lorenzana in the late 1760s and parish priests trained in Mexico City after the great epidemic of 1737, Indian tributaries were then encouraged more than ever to identify with this image and shrine in a new evangelization by their bishops, pastors, and missionary preachers. They were drawn to her name and image in large numbers, but whether or not they and others identified with Guadalupe especially in racial terms is not often clear. Monique Scheer's study of black Madonnas in Europe (especially Germany) during the early modern period offers an interpretation of their identity as black from another perspective. She posits that by the eighteenth century, as race came into fashion in European discourse about the world's peoples,[158] race became a factor in the identity of European black Virgins like the Virgin of Czestochowa or the Virgin of Loreto, but in a secondary way, as one among several associations.[159] The darkness of a sacred image was still significant mainly as a marker of antiquity and authenticity, she suggests.[160] Dark coloring was taken as a sign of both great age and divine beauty, as Jesuit authors emphasized by quoting the scriptural passage from the Song of Solomon, "I am black, but comely."[161] For Mexican Marys, signs of great age and discovery of a long lost image generally were less important than signs of her purity and virtue, which were understood to be essential aspects of Mary's beauty and power. Notions of race came to be intertwined with Christian genealogies in Iberian families and "purity" of blood during the sixteenth and seventeenth centuries,[162] but, as Scheer's study and the case of New Spain's Virgin of Guadalupe seem to suggest, race apparently did not much enter the discourse and popular expressions of Christianity in ways that shaped the meaning of color for images of Christ and Mary until the eighteenth century.[163]

In the case of the Christs and crosses, their darkness tended to draw attention to the material from which they were formed. The mystique of roughly one-third of these celebrated crucifixes and crosses was that they were *of* nature, extracted from the trunk, branches, and roots of trees, which were regarded as divine, living matter.[164] This union of nature and spirit may be a more direct and lasting connection to precolonial notions of enchantment than a conflation of the black crucifixes with particular Mesoamerican deities or an association with the shamanic powers of native rulers. Modern ethnographic studies of some Nahua communities see a connection between black Christs or the Virgin of Guadalupe and precolonial divine beings, but whether or which colonial Indian Christians saw black Christs and the Virgin of Guadalupe this way remains unclear.[165] And the idea that colonial Indians identified with a black Christ on the Cross because he was of their color and suffered as they did may be a compelling metaphor of our time more than an established fact with a long history.

Conclusion

New Spain was not especially or uniquely "the land of Mary" in its image shrines. While there were hundreds of celebrated Marian shrines and different advocations with their distinctive imagery, figures of Christ also were at the center of popular faith in divine presence. Yet far less has been written about the Christs and their shrines. Many printed depictions of them circulated, but other devotional materials and manuscript records are harder to come by, and the secondary literature about them is accordingly thin. Marian shrines had Florencia and Oviedo's *Zodíaco mariano*, and dozens of devotional histories for particular shrines were published during the seventeenth and eighteenth centuries. But only two of the Christocentric shrines and devotions received comparable attention from pious historians and administrators during the colonial period: the Señor de Chalma in the Estado de México and the Cristo Renovado de Santa Teresa in Mexico City.[166]

Were the hundreds of sites of numinous images of Christ less important to their devotees than the Marian places? Evidently not, but few of the Cristos with a wider following were located in colonial cities where authors resided or were trained, and printers and leading painters and sculptors were based. The celebrated miraculous Cristos were mostly located in small towns and rural sites, and they were of their place in ways that could not often be said of the famous Marian images, sometimes growing in the trunk or limbs of a nearby tree, emerging directly from the land. So, some of the differences between Christocentric and Marian shrines in New Spain can be tracked along these lines of urban and rural, regional and local, center and periphery, Spain and America, but the differences that stood out at the time were connected to the meaning of Christ and Mary in Catholic theology. Mary was the mother of the Son of God. She was the favored intermediary to him, idealized for her womanly virtues of modesty, gentleness, propriety, steadfastness, and love, often depicted in a posture of prayer and supplication, appealing to God for mercy and relief on behalf of her devoted children in Christ. When images of Mary came to life, she was usually weeping, or she remained in perfect condition in the midst of decay – signs of her compassion and perpetual purity. The celebrated Christs, usually depicted on or with the Cross, were the Word incarnate, truly God and truly man. Blood, suffering, and sacrifice were the main themes. Unlike animated figures of Mary, when the Cristos came to life, they trembled, groaned, and oozed blood. Recalling the Resurrection, they were more likely to restore themselves to fine condition than to remain in pristine condition. They were also less likely to speak or engage a seer in conversation.

Contrasts between the figures of Mary and Christ were not so stark in other respects. The miraculous Christ figures were not just forbidding embodiments of death, defeat, and the prospect of divine judgment while the Marys could be other than kindly mothers coaxing compassion and mercy from an angry God. Christ and Mary were often intertwined in the iconography of shrine images. Mary's presence nearly always implied the presence of Christ, and many figures of Christ are shown with Mary – Mary holding the infant Jesus, in depictions of the Holy Family, and as the Mater Dolorosa grieving for Him at the Crucifixion. As shrine images, they seem to have been honored, used, and cared for in ways that were more alike than different. They were "santos," as devotees called them – precious, visceral manifestations of Christ's or Mary's divine presence and power right there, in that place, associated with fertility, family, the tribulations of life, and the possibility of transcendence. But they were also fragile. They could bruise, bleed, or break like human flesh and bone. They required protection as much as providing protection, evoking compassion as much as showing compassion.

Notes

1. Robert Orsi, "The Many Names of the Mother of God," in *Divine Mirrors: The Virgin Mary in the Visual Arts*, ed. Melissa Katz, New York: Oxford University Press, 2001, pp. 3–18.
2. Her title of theotokos – God-bearer – was affirmed as early as 431 at the Council of Ephesus, Robert L. Wilken, *The First Thousand Years: A Global History of Christianity*, New Haven: Yale University Press, 2012, p. 139.
3. Geoffrey Ashe, *The Virgin*, London: Routledge & Kegan Paul, 1976, p. 197.
4. For an introduction to the many symbols, advocations, and representations of the Virgin Mary, see Mirella Levi D'Ancona, *The Iconography of the Immaculate Conception in the Middle Ages and Early Renaissance*, New York: College Art Association of America, 1957; Ashe, *The Virgin*; Hilda C. Graaf, *Mary: A History of Doctrine and Devotion*, 2 vols., New York: Sheed and Ward, vol. 1 in 1963, vol. 2 in 1965; and Marina Warner, *Alone of All Her Sex: The Myth and the Cult of the Virgin Mary*, New York: Knopf, 1976.
5. José Joaquín de Ortega y San Antonio, *Mes mariano, o lección mensal ...*, Mexico: Bibliotheca Mexicana, 1760: aurora, vara, espejo, margarita, árbol, rosa, imán, arca, Galaad, resina, arco iris, tierra, incendio, águila, pala, luna, escala, nave, aroma, dulzura, oro, manna, imagen, nardo, vaso, santuario, torre, estrella, columna, vid, mar.
6. Andrés de Arce y Miranda, *Sermones varios del doctor d. Andrés de Arce y Miranda*, tomo segundo, Mexico: Bibliotheca Mexicana, 1755. See the first seven sermons in vol. II on the Blessed Mary as "semejante sin semejante," especially pp. 45, 64, 90, and 139. On associations of sacred trees with the Virgin Mary and pre-colonial goddesses, see Patrizia Granziera, "The Worship of Mary in Mexico: Sacred Trees, Christian Crosses, and the Body of the Goddess," *Toronto Journal of Theology* 28: 1 (2012), 43–60.
7. For Iberians and the Virgin Mary, see William A. Christian, Jr., *Local Religion in Sixteenth-Century Spain*, Princeton: Princeton University Press, 1981; Linda Hall, *Mary, Mother and Warrior: The Virgin in Spain and the Americas*, Austin: University of Texas Press, 2004, chapter 2; and Amy Remensnyder, *La Conquistadora: The Virgin Mary at War and Peace in the Old and New Worlds*, Oxford, UK, and New York: Oxford University Press, 2014.
8. *Recopilación de leyes de los reynos de las Indias*, 1-1-24.
9. Graaf, *Mary*, II, 74–77, notes the popularity of texts by Ludovico Antonio Muratori and, especially, St. Alphonsus Liguori's *Glories of Mary* (apparently first published in 1760) as evidence of the growing emphasis on Mary the merciful in the later years of the eighteenth century.
10. To list all the instances of a particular advocation of Mary known in the late colonial period mainly or only by their place name would require several pages. For the Diocese

of Guadalajara, I counted fifteen examples in volume 1 of Enrique Orozco's *Iconografía mariana de la Arquidiócesis de Guadalajara*, Guadalajara: n.p., 1954.

11. Elizabeth Wilder Weismann, *Mexico in Sculpture, 1521–1821*, Cambridge, MA: Harvard University Press, 1950, p. 173.

12. AHCM num. de inventario 3896, *libro de cabildo* of the cofradía dated July 2, 1758. Retouching or restoring treasured images was a delicate matter and could cause a fracas if mishandled, as it did in the Barrio de la Alameda in Mexico City in September 1782, Bancroft M-M 105, José Gómez, "Diario de México," p. 211, September 2, 1782. Sometimes church officials had repairs done at night in order to avoid gossip and a crowd of angry onlookers.

13. This quotation comes from an early nineteenth-century parish priest's primer of useful phrases and sentences in Chinantec and Spanish, University of Virginia Special Collections MSS 10784 box 1.

14. For a large sampling of the vast secondary literature about the Virgin of Guadalupe, see *Nuevos testimonios históricos guadalupanos*, ed. Ernesto de la Torre Villar and Ramiro Navarro de Anda, 2 vols., Mexico: Fondo de Cultura Económica, 2007.

15. Magnus Lundberg, *Unification and Conflict: The Church Politics of Alonso de Montúfar OP, Archbishop of Mexico, 1554–1572*, Uppsala: Swedish Institute of Missionary Research, 2002, p. 219.

16. AHBG Sección Obras Pías caja 394 exp. 50 for the cofradía and caja 394 exp. 48 for the dowries.

17. Viceroy Enríquez's letter to the king, September 12, 1575, and letters of Fr. Diego de Santa María in AGI Audiencia de México 69 (December 12, 1574) and Audiencia de México 283 (March 24, 1575). My thanks to Kenneth Mills for sharing his copies of these letters.

18. ACAM, chapter minutes of September 15, 1786 and January 9, 1796.

19. For a review of some of the literature that centers attention on creole patriotism, see Cornelius Conover, "Reassessing the Rise of Mexico's Virgin of Guadalupe, 1650s-1780s," *Mexican Studies/Estudios Mexicanos* 27: 2 (summer 2011), 251–279. Conover questions the creole patriotism explanation for popularity of the Virgin of Guadalupe in the seventeenth century, although he acknowledges that creole consciousness "figures prominently in Guadalupan sermons," p. 255. Turning to the minutes of the city council of Mexico City and the cathedral chapter, and the *efemérides* of Gregorio Guijo and Antonio Robles, he tracks the interest of peninsular elites, plus Indian devotion, and notes that there were other miraculous image shrines in Mexico City at the time. In other words, the appeal of the Virgin of Guadalupe as wonder-worker was not limited to creole Spaniards.

20. Indians as Guadalupan devotees became a special focus of treatise writers and proselytizers in the seventeenth century, beginning with Miguel Sánchez's *Imagen de la Virgen María Madre de Dios de Guadalupe, milagrosamente aparecida en la Ciudad de México ...*, Mexico: Vda. de Bernardo Calderón, 1648 and Diego Lasso de la Vega's *Nican mopohua* (1649) as part of a campaign of spiritual renewal. That Indians in and near the city were actively involved in building the devotion during the second half of the seventeenth century is exemplified in the bitter dispute in 1679 between the Indian cofradía of the settlement at Tepeyac and Spanish devotees in Mexico City over rights to collect alms for Guadalupe in the city. AGN Acervo 49, caja 174.

21. AHBG, the archive of the Basilica of Guadalupe, is rich in financial and administrative records for the shrine from the beginning of the seventeenth century. *Censos* were recorded and collected in Sección Donaciones, for example caja 375 exp. 4, 1607; appointment of cathedral chapter members as *administrador general de la hermita* appear in chapter meeting minutes as early as 1608 with the election of Canon Alonso López Cárdenas; records of construction projects are in Sección Obras de la Iglesia, e.g. caja 378 exp. 25 for 1611.

22. A new church on the site had been planned since early 1601, with the first stone scheduled to be laid on September 10 of that year, ACAM, chapter minutes for February 16, 1601. Construction was still in the early stages in 1609, AHBG Sección Obras de la Iglesia caja 378 exp. 25.

23. AHBG Sección Limosnas caja 378 exps. 6, 48, alms collections for "las obras de la iglesia." Dr. Diego de Cisneros, medical professor of the Real Universidad de México, wrote in his 1618 treatise on the location of Mexico City that construction on the new church was well advanced "thanks to the singular devotion and infinite care of the most Illustrious Don Juan de la Serna, Archbishop of this city," *Sitio, naturaleza y propiedades de la Ciudad de México . . .*, Mexico: J. Blanco de Alcaçar, 1618, fol. 109r. As I suggest elsewhere, devotees of Guadalupe or any other celebrated image of Mary or Christ rarely favored only that one devotion. Pérez de la Serna, for example, was also instrumental in bringing the Cristo Renovado de Ixmiquilpan to Mexico City.

24. Jeanette Favrot Peterson, "A Wonder-Working Guadalupe in the Seventeenth Century," in *Religion in New Spain*, ed. Susan Schroeder and Stafford Poole, Albuquerque: University of New Mexico Press, 2007, pp. 125–156. Mariano Fernández Echeverría y Veitia (1779) wrote that he had seen an *información de milagros* approved by Pérez de la Serna in October 1614, UT Benson manuscripts TxU-A Discursos Académicos y Papeles sobre Puebla, pp. 85–86.

25. William B. Taylor, *Magistrates of the Sacred: Priests and Parishioners in Eighteenth-Century Mexico*, Stanford: Stanford University Press, 1996, p. 679 note 97 on medidas vendor Joseph Ferrer in 1620s. Ferrer was still the principal medidas vendor in the late 1650s and early 1660s, and evidently had enjoyed a lucrative business career. When his license to sell medidas at the shrine was revoked by the new pastor in 1657, Ferrer complained to the archiepiscopal court and demonstrated that he had paid an annual fee of 100 pesos and 50 pesos worth of medidas for the privilege and was a generous benefactor of the shrine, having commissioned a large painting depicting the apparitions. His license was renewed on September 17, 1663, AGN Acervo 49 Secretaría Arzobispal caja 140 folder 3. For more on the development of the Tepeyac shrine at several stages in the seventeenth century, see "Mexico's Virgin of Guadalupe in the Seventeenth Century: Hagiography and Beyond," in Taylor, *Shrines & Miraculous Images in Mexico Before the Reforma*, Albuquerque: University of New Mexico Press, 2010, chapter 3.

26. Bancroft M-M 272, fol. 19r. In 1608, San Gregorio thaumaturgo was the patron saint against flood, mentioned in the city council minutes of September 3, 1607 in AHCM, and ACAM cathedral chapter minutes of March 26, 1609. The Montesclaros papers of the archive of the Duque del Infantado, Madrid, exp. 82 record the archbishop recalling the flood of 1608 but without mentioning the Virgin of Guadalupe. Guadalupe was still not mentioned among the "abogados" (advocates) of the city in the city council minutes for 1628–1630.

27. Efraín Castro Morales, "El santuario de Guadalupe de México en el siglo XVII," in *Retablo barroco a la memoria de Francisco de la Maza*, Mexico: UNAM, 1974, p. 75 mentions the new altar of 1637.
28. Publication of the last of these influential early devotional histories of Guadalupe in 1688, Francisco de Florencia's *Estrella del norte de México. Historia de la milagrosa imagen de María Santísima de Guadalupe*, Guadalajara: J. Cabrera, 1895, represented a substantial investment by the shrine administration: 1,917 pesos 2 reales and an additional 300 pesos for a press run of 1,000 copies, AGN Bienes Nacionales 457 exp. 3.
29. Indian devotion at the shrine was more visible by the 1650s, thanks in part to an initiative of "spiritual reconquest" by the cathedral clergy. On May 11, 1657 the archbishop mentioned that Indians and other people were going to the shrine to receive the sacraments, AGN Acervo 49 caja 140 folder 23.
30. Miguel Sánchez, *Novenas de la Virgen María Madre de Dios para sus devotíssimos santuarios de los Remedios y Guadalupe . . .*, Mexico: Viuda de Bernardo Calderón, 1665.
31. See Taylor, *Shrines & Miraculous Images*, chapter 3. On December 22, 1650 the minutes of the cathedral chapter (ACAM) recorded that they had declared Guadalupe "la amparadora y protectora desta Ciudad." In the minutes of December 11, 1665 canon Dr. Francisco de Siles proposed a feast day for the apparition on December 12 as part of the presentation to the papacy for recognition of the image and miracle. As reported in the minutes of February 26, 1669, the presentation had been reviewed in Rome by the cardinals of the Congregation of Rites. They agreed that special prayers could be made to the Virgin of Guadalupe on December 12, but they did not recommend granting a special feast day and office. In the same meeting of the cathedral chapter, Francisco de Florencia (who was serving as the Mexican Jesuits' *procurador general* to Rome) was authorized to obtain the official documentation in this matter.
32. The Virgin of Guadalupe was patroness of an academic thesis as early as 1651, but she was more often found in this role after 1660: before the 1650s, 0; 1650s, 2; 1660s, 7; 1670s, 7; 1680s, 12; 1690s, 9.
33. AHBG Sección Congregación de Nuestra Señora de Guadalupe, caja 69 exp 2; AHBG Sección Cofradías caja 391 exp 33. There were more indulgences in the 1680s. See AHM caja 1684 for three papal indulgences and Archbishop Aguiar y Seixas's license to publish them on October 30, 1685.
34. Antonio de Robles, *Diario de sucesos notables (1665–1703)*, Mexico: Porrúa, 1946, I, 189.
35. Fr. Isidro de la Asunción, *Itinerario a Indias (1673–1678)*, Mexico: CONDUMEX, 1992, pp. 103–104.
36. For Zacoalco, AGN Acervo 49 caja 140 folder 22; for Tepemajalco, AGN Indios 25 exps. 23 and 76; for Antequera, Florencia, *Estrella*, chapter 26, pp. 146–149; for Querétaro, AHM caja 1674; for Guadalajara, José Ignacio Dávila Garibi, *El culto guadalupano en lo que fue la Nueva Galicia*, Mexico: Librería "San Ignacio de Loyola," 1948, p. 32; for Chalma, José Olivares, OSA's sermon, *Oración panegyrica . . . milagrosa efigie de Christo Crucificado . . .*, Mexico: Viuda de B. Calderón, 1683; for Tlaxcala, Rodrigo Martínez Baracs, *La secuencia tlaxcalteca: Orígenes del culto a Nuestra Señora de Ocotlán*, Mexico: INAH, 2000, pp. 28–29; for Valladolid, AGN Bienes Nacionales 457 exp. 1; for Conchos, Chih., Lauro López Beltrán, *La guadalupana que sudó tres veces en San Francisco de Conchos, Chih.*, Chih: Edit. Camino, 1989.

232   Part I Bearings: Historical Patterns and Places of Image Shrines

37. See David A. Brading, *Mexican Phoenix: Our Lady of Guadalupe: Image and Tradition Across Five Centuries*, Cambridge, UK and New York: Cambridge University Press, 2001, p. 119.
38. *Gazeta de México*, issue for May 1722, published in Nicolás León, *Bibliografía mexicana del siglo XVIII (Boletín del Instituto Bibliográfico Mexicano*, num. 5), Mexico: J.I. Guerrero y Cía, 1905 [Hereafter BIBM 5], p. 995.
39. For the long history of the founding of the Colegiata at Tepeyac – from the first initiatives and donations in 1708, to the endowments totalling 160,000 pesos from Andrés de Palencia and Pedro Ruiz de Castañeda in 1714, to the authorizing papal bull of February 9, 1725 (renewed on August 18, 1729, August 30, 1730, and January 9, 1731), to the royal cedulas elevating the settlement at Tepeyac to the status of *villa*, to the final stages of authorization and establishment in 1748 and 1750, see Paulino Castañeda Delgado and Isabel Arenas Frutos, *Un portuense en México: Don Juan Antonio Vizarrón, arzobispo y virrey*, El Puerto de Santa María (Spain): n.p., 1998, pp. 159–167. For more on the history of the Colegiata, see Ignacio Carrillo y Pérez, "La Real Colegiata," in *Nuevos testimonios guadalupanos*, ed. de la Torre Villar and Navarro de Anda, II, 182–203.
40. The run up to bicentennial celebrations of the apparitions at Tepeyac and the great image-relic began in 1722 with authorization of a second "averiguación" and petition for papal recognition. The investigation was undertaken the next year with two witnesses: the great Franciscan missioner, Antonio Margil de Jesús, and Dr. Rodrigo García Flores de Valdés, dean of the cathedral. In 1729, the archbishop ordered that December 12 be celebrated "with great solemnity" in all the churches of Mexico City to commemorate the 198th anniversary of the apparitions, as a rehearsal for the great Mass and sermon at the shrine in 1731 attended by all the dignitaries of the capital and "innumerable pueblo." It is worth noting that there had not been centennial observances in 1631, another indication that the apparition accounts given in Miguel Sánchez's and Lasso de la Vega's texts were not yet fully formed, or at least not yet widely recognized before they published in 1648 and 1649. See Fortino Vera, *Informaciones sobre la milagrosa aparición de la Santísima Virgen de Guadalupe recibidas en 1666, 1723*, Amecameca: Colegio Católico, 1889. The December 1731 issue of the *Gazeta de México* in BIBM 4, pp. 291–292, and the December 14, 1731 entry in the city council's *actas de cabildo* in AHCM describe some of the solemn festivities.
41. "rico ornamento entero bordado de oro y seda en Italia," *Gazeta de México*, August 1735 issue, in BIBM 4, p. 557.
42. See, for example, the proposal and deliberations in the Council of the Indies recorded in February and March 1717, AGI México leg. 2531. The administrative groundwork for establishing the Colegiata, including papal bulls and licenses of 1725, 1729, 1730, and 1731, is summarized in Castañeda Delgado and Arenas Frutos, *Un portuense en México*, pp. 159–167.
43. ACAM, chapter minutes for January 22, 1737.
44. *Guía de las actas de cabildo de la Ciudad de México* . . ., Mexico: Departamento del Distrito Federal, 1970–1988, V, 333. In their deliberations the city councilors agreed that there should be a novena to the Virgin of Guadalupe, but they were divided on whether it should be held at the shrine or in the cathedral, AHCM num. de inventario 62A, January 23, 1737.

45. ACAM, chapter minutes, January 26, 1737.
46. AHCM actas de cabildo January 27, 1737 and February 11, 1737, *Guía de las actas de cabildo*, V, 337.
47. *Guía de las actas de cabildo*, V, 343, February 16, 1737; AHCM actas de cabildo, April 2, 1737.
48. These events are recorded in issues of the *Gazeta de México* for 1737 (BIBM 4) and the *actas de cabildo* for both the cathedral chapter and ayuntamiento of the city, and various published sermons.
49. Cities taking the oath in 1737–1738 include San Miguel el Grande, Zamora, Durango, Puebla, Valladolid, Guadalajara, Antequera, Guatemala, Guanajuato, Aguascalientes, Querétaro, Toluca, Villa de Carrión, Cholula, San Luis Potosí, and Tlaxcala. In 1746, merchants of Guadalajara declared Guadalupe their patrona.
50. The oaths of the 1730s and 1740s were accompanied by more published sermons. The most ambitious account of the mobilizing of miraculous images against the epidemic of 1737 and the election of the Virgin of Guadalupe as patrona of the city and viceroyalty is *Escudo de armas de México: Celestial protección de esta nobilíssima ciudad, de la Nueva España, y casi todo el Nuevo Mundo*, Mexico: Vda. de Joseph Bernardo de Hogal, 1746, by Cayetano Cabrera y Quintero, a diocesan priest and protégé of Archbishop Vizarrón. See Brading, *Mexican Phoenix*, chapter 6, for more on Cabrera's writings and their place in the presentation of the case before the papal court.
51. Brading, *Mexican Phoenix*, pp. 132–139. Copies of the bull reached Veracruz in August 1756 and were published in Mexico City on September 19. Celebrations throughout the viceroyalty began in December 1756.
52. José Francisco Valdés, *Salutación a María Santísima de Guadalupe. Práctica devota para venerarla en su santuario, quando se le hace la visita*, Mexico: Zúñiga y Ontiveros, 1794 Digest 33 for the 1794 booklet. *Día doce* booklets searched in WorldCat. For a blanket alms-collecting license "por todas las ciudades y lugares de este reino," AGN General de Parte 41 exp. 133.

   Publications listed in Medina, *La imprenta en México*, for the Virgin of Guadalupe increased in number throughout the eighteenth century: eleven for 1601–1684; eighteen for 1685–1717 (especially after 1690); twenty-one for 1718–1744 (of which thirteen date from 1737 to 1744); forty for 1745–1767; forty-seven for 1768–1794; and forty-two for 1795–1812. For university theses dedicated to Guadalupe the numbers charted by decade from the *Catálogo de ilustraciones. Archivo General de la Nación*, 14 vols., Mexico: Archivo General de la Nación, 1979–1982, reached unprecedented levels during the eighteenth century, especially after 1750: 1720s, fifteen; 1730s, nine; 1740s, sixteen; 1750s–1810, more than twenty each decade except for the 1780s with thirty-seven theses.
53. From a survey of baptismal names in eighteenth-century parish registers for six parishes in Jalisco (Zacoalco, Acatlán, Arandas, Tonalá, Tlajomulco, and the sagrario parish in Guadalajara), one in central Mexico (Tenango del Valle), and one in Oaxaca (Mitla), two patterns were especially strong: Guadalupe became a much more popular name for both girls and boys after the 1750s, and non-Indians were about three times more likely to be given the name Guadalupe than were Indians.
54. Taylor, *Shrines and Miraculous Images*, pp. 118, 119, 244.
55. Castañeda Delgado and Arenas Frutos, *Un portuense en México*, pp. 159–167.

234   Part I Bearings: Historical Patterns and Places of Image Shrines

56. Or as Joseph Manuel Ruiz y Cervantes wrote in 1791, Guadalupe was "the flower that does not wilt" ("la flor que no se marchita"), *Memorias de la portentosa imagen de Nuestra Señora de Xuquila* . . ., Mexico: Zúñiga y Ontiveros, 1791, p. 5.
57. AGI México legajo 2531, September 7, 1756 order from the Council of the Indies, "se sirva mandar que en los testamentos que se otorgaren en la Nueva España, se exprese forzosa el santuario y simulacro de aquella santa imagen." On the 1786 complaint and proposal, Tulane VEMC leg. 50 exp. 11, September 5, 1786.
58. On the use of Indians and the Virgin of Guadalupe as symbols of local pride for creole artists in the eighteenth century, see Jaime Cuadriello's illustrated essay, "Tierra de prodigios: La ventura como destino," in *El origen del Reino de la Nueva España*, vol. 1 of the series "Los pinceles de la historia," Mexico: Museo Nacional de Arte, 1999, pp. 180–227.
59. Examples of resistance include AGN CRS 156 exp. 5, 1758, Tepetlaostoc; AGN CRS 136 exp. 8 1817, Acatlán in the district of Tulancingo, Hidalgo; AGN CRS 204 exp 9 1760, Tejupilco Indians celebrated December 12, but objected to the parish priest requiring them to attend and help fund the oath of allegiance in the head town. It is telling that when the colegiata designated six *sala capitular* chairs for native language specialists in 1778 to meet the needs of the shrine's Indian constituency, four were for the Nahuatl language, one for Otomí, and one for Mazahua. There were none for Purépecha, Zapotec, Mixtec, Maya, or the many other languages spoken in New Spain.
60. For more on the shrine of Nativitas Tepetlatcingo and its prime mover in Mexico City, see William B. Taylor, *Marvels & Miracles in Late Colonial Mexico: Three Texts in Context*, Albuquerque: University of New Mexico Press, 2011, pp. 71–136.
61. For more on the shrine of Nuestra Señora de los Ángeles in the eighteenth century, see Paul Ramírez and William B. Taylor, "Out of Tlatelolco's Ruins: Patronage, Devotion, and Natural Disaster at the Shrine of Our Lady of the Angels, 1745–1781," *Hispanic American Historical Review* 93: 1 (2013), 33–65.
62. See Chapter 1 on the beginnings of the Remedios shrine. The first, modest chapel at Totoltepec may have been constructed in 1528, as mentioned in the city council's *acta de cabildo* of July 31, 1528, AHCM.
63. City council *acta de cabildo* of January 8, 1621, AHCM.
64. Baltasar de Medina, *Crónica de la Provincia de San Diego de México*, 2nd ed., Mexico: Editorial Academia Literaria, 1977, fols. 122v–124r. Florencia was a Marianist as well as ardent *guadalupano*. He celebrated both images. See *Las novenas del santuario de Nuestra Señora de Guadalupe*, Mexico: 1785. Unnumbered p. 1, *Estrella,* p. 189 "Dos providencias al parecer opuestas, en las que por ser uno su Original, no pueden estar encontradas. ¡Bendito sea Dios, que puso en tan dos buenas manos nuestro remedio!"; pp. 188–189 "han sido casi igualmente el empleo de la piedad generosa de los devotos mexicanos; el uno más librado de joyas de oro y piedrería; el otro de plata de la iglesia. Bien se puede poner en utrum a cual de los dos ha tributado más dádivas la devoción."
65. Florencia, *Estrella,* p. 189. Since the 1810s, the secondary literature about Guadalupe usually has set up a sharp antagonism between Remedios as *gachupín* Virgin and Guadalupe as Indian Virgin, the patriotic emblem of Mexico's providential destiny. I am suggesting that there was not such a sharp distinction in the colonial period. See my essay "Guadalupe, Remedios, and Cultural Politics of the Independence Period," in *Shrines & Miraculous Images*, chapter 5. For a full, nuanced treatment of the image and

devotion to Our Lady of Remedios in the colonial period, see Rosario Inés Granados Salinas, "Fervent Faith. Devotion, Aesthetics, and Society in the Cult of Our Lady of Remedios (Mexico, 1520–1811)," Ph.D. dissertation, Harvard University, 2012.
66. de la Asunción, *Itinerario a Indias (1673–1678)*, p. 103.
67. *Instrucción reservada al Conde de Moctezuma*, ed. Norman F. Martin, Mexico: Edit. Jus, 1965, pp. 15, 160.
68. These are just three of about twenty cases from central, western, and southern Mexico, Nuestra Señora de Ocotlán and San Miguel in Tlaxcala and Nuestra Señora de la Soledad in Antequera being especially notable. See Chapter 2 for an enumeration.
69. See Francisco de Florencia's *Origen de los dos célebres santuarios de la Nueva Galicia* ..., Mexico: Juan Joseph Guillena Carrascoso, 1694, Mexico: Biblioteca Mexicana, 1757, and Mexico: Zúñiga y Ontiveros, 1766.
70. The inquiry apparently began in 1641 and was presented in 1653. A second inquiry was undertaken in 1663, Luis Sandoval Godoy, *Reina de Jalisco: Historia y costumbrismo en torno a la imagen de Nuestra Señora de Zapopan*, 2nd ed., Guadalajara: n.p., 1984, p. 18. Writing in the 1640s, Antonio Tello noted that "many miracles" had been worked by God through the Virgin of Zapopan ("por quien ha hecho Dios muchos milagros"), *Crónica miscelánea de la Sancta Provincia de Xalisco*, libro III, Guadalajara: Edit. Font, 1942, p. 27.
71. Francisco de Florencia and Juan Antonio de Oviedo, *Zodíaco mariano* ..., Mexico: Colegio de San Ildefonso, 1755, pp. 289–293, undated, says the image was taken to "algunos lugares del obispado para solicitar limosnas." Sandoval, *Reina de Jalisco*, p. 26 says these missions, undertaken during the seventeenth century up to 1730 reached as far as Sinaloa and Zacatecas. In his professional resumé of 1770 the parish priest of Hostotipaquillo said he had gone on "pilgrimage" with the image to collect alms during the 1750s and covered 300 leagues in all, roughly 750 miles, Archivo Arzobispal de Guadalajara, file of 1770 *relaciones de méritos y servicios*.
72. Sandoval, *Reina de Jalisco*, p. 22.
73. Florencia and Oviedo, *Zodíaco mariano*, p. 295.
74. Sandoval, *Reina de Jalisco*, p. 50.
75. *Gazeta de México* for October 1731, BIBM 4, p. 283.
76. Sandoval, *Reina de Jalisco*, p. 29, Florencia and Oviedo, *Zodíaco mariano*, pp. 288–302. The bell towers were not finished until the 1750s.
77. That the image shrine at Zapopan remained popular with people from surrounding districts is suggested by José Antonio Villaseñor y Sánchez's comment in 1746 about the devotion "que con fervor se venera en sus distritos" and the "many people" who visited the shrine ("muchas personas en romerías"), *Theatro Americano: Descripción general de los reynos y provincias de la Nueva España, y sus jurisdicciones* . . ., Vda. de J. B. de Hogal, p. 238.
78. Florencia and Oviedo, *Zodíaco mariano*, pp. 300–302.
79. Florencia and Oviedo, *Zodíaco mariano*, pp. 300–302.
80. On the visits of the Virgin of Zapopan to Guadalajara, see Armando González Escoto, *Biografía de una tradición: Las visitas de Nuestra Señora de Zapopan a la ciudad de Guadalajara, 1734–1999*, Guadalajara: Universidad del Valle de Atemajac, 1999.
81. AHCM *actas de cabildo*, June 2, 1741 (fol. 38r–v). In other ways the sacred geography of the city of Querétaro took cues from Mexico City. Like the capital city, albeit on

a smaller scale, Queretano authors prided themselves on coming from a city of prodigious images – at least fifteen with their own separate chapels in the eighteenth century. Two of the images revered as miracle workers were copies of images associated with Mexico City: Our Lady of Guadalupe (with its own fine church in Querétaro), and a copy of the Cristo Renovado de Santa Teresa in Querétaro's Carmelite convent. Creole pride of place in Querétaro as sacred center of many churches, convents, and prodigious images runs through the published tracts by native sons and residents in the eighteenth century. See, for example, Francisco Antonio Navarrete, SJ, *Relación peregrina de la agua corriente, que para beber, y vivir goza la muy noble, leal, y florida ciudad de Santiago de Querétaro*, Mexico: José Bernardo de Hogal, 1739, p. 24 on its many churches and convents as providential landmarks: "una ciudad tan poblada de padrones, y monumentos de la Religión y de la christiana piedad ... es tan Christiana, devota y piadosa ... merece del Omnipotente los muchos beneficios que experimenta por la soberana interposición de tantas imágenes milagrosas que la mano liberal del Altíssimo la ha franqueado para su refugio, amparo y defensa."

82. José Francisco de la Rocha Manrique de Lara, *La amada del Señor: Sermón panegírico de la inmaculada Concepción ...*, Mexico: Zúñiga y Ontiveros, 1797, wrote of the image as an "artífice no extraordinario."

83. Hermenegildo de Vilaplana wrote that he had read a text in the archive of the Franciscan province of San Pedro y San Pablo de Michoacán by the first pastor, Fr. Nicolás de Zamora, that recounted activations in 1648, *Histórico y sagrado novenario de la milagrosa imagen de Nuestra Señora del Pueblito ...*, Mexico: Bibliotheca Mexicana, 1765, p. 40.

84. Vicente Acosta and Cesáreo Munguía, *La milagrosa imagen de Nuestra Señora del Pueblito*, 2nd ed., Mexico: Edit. Jus, 1962, p. 13. Other important secondary sources for the history of this advocation and shrine image are Cristina Cruz González, "The Circulation of Flemish Prints in Mexican Missions & the Creation of a New Visual Narrative, 1630–1800," *Boletín: The Journal of the California Mission Studies Association* 25: 1 (2008), 5–34, Ignacio R. Frías y Camacho, *Semblanza y realidad a través de la Santísima Virgen del Pueblito*, Querétaro: n.p., 1997 (revision of 1923 ed.), and Esteban López Frías, *El Pueblito: sus calles y su gente*, Querétaro: H. Ayuntamiento de Corregidora, 2000.

85. Luis Mario Schneider, *Cristos, santos, y vírgenes: Santuarios y devociones de México*, Mexico: Grupo Editorial Planeta, pp. 310–311.

86. Joseph Manuel Rodríguez, *Relación jurídica de la libertad de la muerte intentada contra la persona del R.P. Fr. Andrés Picazo ... por intercesión de Nuestra Señora en su prodigiosa imagen del Pueblito ...*, Mexico: Zúñiga y Ontiveros, 1769. Chapter 17 is an "apéndice succinto en que se da razón del origen de la Santa Imagen de Nuestra Señora del Pueblito y progresos de su culto," pp. 27–30.

87. Vilaplana, *Histórico y sagrado novenario*, 2nd ed., 1765.

88. *Gazeta de México*, November 28, 1801 refers to a November 7 chapter meeting and elections the Franciscan province that noted the image of Pueblito had been "patrona principal de la Provincia y sus capítulos" since 1745.

89. Rodríguez, *Relación jurídica*, was published in 1769, the year of the miracle.

90. See, for instance, issues of the *Gazeta de México* for November 25, 1797 and July 23, 1803 describing the Virgin's continuing visits to the city of Querétaro for novenas in times of epidemic and drought.

91. Stella María González Cicero, *Nuestra Señora de Izamal, reina y patrona de Yucatán*, Mérida: Pro-Historia Peninsular, A.C., 1999, pp. 54–57. The city fathers apparently also gave thanks to the Virgin of Izamal for protecting Mérida and Izamal from pirate raids in 1688, Florencia and Oviedo, *Zodíaco mariano*, pp. 20–21.
92. González Cicero, *Nuestra Señora de Izamal*, p. 59.
93. The three eighteenth-century visits of Our Lady of Izamal to Mérida are commemorated on stone plaques set into the walls of a house on the plaza of Izamal, Gabriel Ferrer de Mediolea, *Izamal, monografía histórica*, Mérida: Editoral "Ayer y Hoy," 1940, p. 20.
94. *Novena de la Santíssima Virgen de Ytzamal* . . ., Mexico: Zúñiga y Ontiveros, 1764, n.p., and Florencia and Oviedo, *Zodíaco mariano*, p. 21.
95. *Crónica de la orden de N. Seráfico P.S. Francisco, Provincia de San Pedro y San Pablo de Mechoacán en la Nueva España* [composed in 1639], following the first edition, Mexico: Viuda de Bernardo Calderón, 1643, Mexico: Barbedillo, 1883, pp. 228–233.
96. Moisés Guzmán Pérez, *Nuestra Señora de los Remedios de San Juan Zitácuaro: Historia y tradición de un culto mariano*, Morelia: Universidad Michoacana, 1999, pp. 30–34.
97. For this and more about the shrine of the Virgin of Zitácuaro, see Guzmán Pérez, *Nuestra Señora de los Remedios de San Juan Zitácuaro*, pp. 30–61.
98. Granados Salinas, "Fervent Faith," p. 93.
99. Christian, *Local Religion*, p. 204 notes that most of the shrine images of Christ celebrated in Early Modern Spain have been forgotten.
100. Juan de Grijalva, OSA, *Crónica de la Orden de N.P.S. Agustín en las provincias de la Nueva España en cuatro edades desde el año 1533 hasta el de 1592*, Mexico: Porrúa, 1985, p. 225.
101. Francisco Javier Lazcano, *Vida ejemplar y virtudes heroicas del venerable padre Juan Antonio de Oviedo de la Compañía de Jesús*, Mexico: Colegio de San Ildefonso, 1760, p. 341.
102. Federico Zeri, *Behind the Image: The Art of Reading Paintings*, trans. Nina Rootes, New York: St. Martin's Press, pp. 15–22; David Nirenberg, "The Historical Body of Christ," in *The Body of Christ in the Art of Europe and New Spain, 1150–1800*, ed. James Clifton, Munich and New York: Prestel, 1997, pp. 19–20. For a somewhat different chronology in which the human Christ came to the fore earlier, see Rachel Fulton, *From Judgment to Passion: Devotion to Christ and the Virgin Mary, 800–1200*, New York: Columbia University Press, 2002.
103. For a study of early editions of Kempis's *Imitation of Christ* and how the book was understood by St. Ignatius of Loyola and early Jesuits, among others, see Maximilian von Habsburg, *Catholic and Protestant Translations of the Imitatio Christi, 1425–1650: From Late Medieval Class to Early Modern Bestseller*, Burlington, VT: Ashgate, 2011.
104. Thomas à Kempis, *The Imitation of Christ*, Harmondsworth, UK: Penguin Books, 2013, pp. 45, 84.
105. For Spain, see Christian, *Local Religion*, p. 182.
106. Florencia and Oviedo, *Zodíaco mariano*, p. 274.
107. According to the *Constituciones de la muy ilustre Archicofradía de ciudadanos de la Santa Veracruz* . . ., Mexico: Valdés, 1824, this confraternity of the Holy Cross began in 1523 and led to others in Coyoacán, Tlalmanalco, Córdoba, Puebla, Veracruz, and "finally to almost all the cities and even the towns (*villas*) of this America."
108. On iconographic changes, see Nelly Sigaut, "El árbol de la vida en el convento de Meztitlán," *Relaciones. Estudios de Historia y Sociedad* 47 (1991), 7–28. Christian, *Local*

238 Part I Bearings: Historical Patterns and Places of Image Shrines

Religion, p. 222 suggests that depictions of the cross and crucifixion signified judgment especially, and that the Christ Child was associated with innocent victims of plague, and future sacrifice. Perhaps this was less true in New Spain, and even in Spain by the eighteenth century.

109. *Relaciones geográficas del Arzobispado de México, 1743*, ed. Francisco de Solano, Madrid: C.S.I.C., 1988, I, 258.

110. On Christ's blood and purification (cleansing sins), and sacraments depicted as a fountain of his flowing blood, see Sigaut, "El árbol de la vida," and her references to Old Testament passages in Ezekiel 36:25 and Exodus 24:8.

111. Printed depictions of the Cristo Renovado of Santa Teresa over the course of the eighteenth century display some of this variation. See Taylor, *Shrines & Miraculous Images*, chapter 2.

112. Colonial *cristos* and *cruces* "renovados" include the Cristo de Hueyapan, Oaxaca; the Señor de Tila, Chiapas; the Cristo Renovado of Ixmiquilpan or Santa Teresa (Mapethé, Hidalgo and Mexico City); the Señor de Singuilucan, Hidalgo; the green cross of Tepic; the Cristo of the church of San Juan de Dios, Toluca; the Señor de los Labradores of Toluca that grew hair; the Señor del Huerto, Atlacomulco, Edo. de México; the Señor de Tecamachalco, Pue.; a niño Jesús of Atlixco, Pue.; the Cristo de Amacueca, Jalisco; and in Mexico City, the Señor Crucifixo of the church of San Juan de Dios, the Ecce Homo of the Balvanera church, the Cristo de la Condesa del Valle, and, again, the Cristo Renovado de Santa Teresa (the common name of Cristo Renovado de Ixmiquilpan once it was moved to the capital).

113. Mary Lee Nolan and Sidney Nolan, *Christian Pilgrimage in Modern Western Europe*, Chapel Hill: University of North Carolina Press, 1989.

114. Of the 104 Aragonese shrine images mentioned in Roque Alberto Faci's *Reyno de Christo y dote de Maria Santissima* . . . [1739], facsimile edition published in Zaragoza in 1979 by the Diputación General de Aragón, thirteen were figures of the Holy Child – that is, one in eight.

115. Christóval de Avendaño, *Sermones para las festividades de Christo nuestro Señor*, Madrid: Vda. de I. Gonçalez, 1634, fol. 60v.

116. Occasionally the direct connection to a Spanish precedent is documented, as in the novena booklet for one of the legendary Spanish figures of the Holy Child, known as "el enfermero," from the Puerto de Santa María in Andalusia that was reprinted in Mexico City in 1776 by Zúñiga y Ontiveros: *Novena de la milagros imagen de el Niño Jesús Peregrino el Enfermero que se venera en la Santa Caridad y RR.MM. Capuchinas Descalzas del Puerto de Santa María* . . . .

117. The late colonial figures with hats and worn shoes were the Santo Niño de la Penitencia and the Santo Niño of the Santa Cruz Acatlán parish, both in Mexico City, AGN Bienes Nacionales 1172 exp. 4, and José María Barrientos, *Sermón del Santo Niño llamado de San Juan* . . ., Mexico: Valdés, 1818.

118. See Appendix 1.

119. Miraculous Christs and crosses in the city of Querétaro: the Cruz de Piedra, Franciscan College of Santa Cruz; Santo Cristo de San Benito; Jesús Nazareno de los Terceros; Ecce Homo de la Huertecilla; Ecce Homo in the Capuchin convent; Santo Cristo de los Trabajos; Señor de Santa Teresa; Niño Jesús de bulto; Señor del Mesquite; also a Santo Cristo de marfil. See Joseph María Zelaá e Hidalgo, *Glorias de Querétaro y sus adiciones*,

Miraculous Images of Christ and the Virgin Mary 239

introduced by Jaime Septién, Querétaro: Gobierno Constitucional del Estado, 2009, pp. 311–331, Navarrete, *Relación peregrina de la agua corriente, que para beber, y vivir goza la muy noble, leal, y florida ciudad de Santiago de Querétaro*, pp. 4–23, and *Relaciones geográficas del Arzobispado de México*. 1743, II, 252–273. The most celebrated were the Santo Cristo de San Benito, the Ecce Homo de la Huertecilla, and the Cristo de los Trabajos.

120. *Relaciones geográficas* . . . 1743, I, 169. Cuadriello makes the point that Florencia's book sparked greater interest in the image and led the Augustinians to bring the Christ down from its cave to the first santuario in 1683, "Los pinceles de la historia," I, 219. The key work on Florencia's writings is Jason Dyck, "The Sacred Historian's Craft: Francisco de Florencia and Creole Identity in Seventeenth-Century New Spain," Ph.D. dissertation, University of Toronto, 2012, pp. 241–255.

121. Juan Antonio Rivera, *Diario curioso del capellán del Hospital de Jesús Nazareno de México*, Mexico: Vargas Rea, 1953, II, 7 records the visit to Chalma of the viceroy and two audiencia judges in January 1786.

122. The date of the destruction of the original image is uncertain. The substitute image was said to incorporate the ashes of the original figure.

123. At least nineteen dark Christs called the Señor de Esquipulas or other dark Christs apparently modeled after the Guatemala image were identified in the territory of modern Mexico during the eighteenth and early nineteenth centuries. Publication of at least ten editions in Mexico between 1778 and 1817 (eight in Mexico City, one in Puebla, and one in Guadalajara) of a novena booklet for the Christ of Esquipulas by José de Paz no doubt aided the spread of this devotion. Paz elaborated on a number of striking miracle stories in his *Novena y bosquejo de los milagros y maravillas que ha obrado la santísima imagen de Christo Crucificado de Esquipulas* . . . reprinted in Mexico City by Jáuregui, 1793.

124. For more on the development of devotion to the Cristo Renovado de Santa Teresa and Ixmiquilpan, William B. Taylor, "Two Shrines of the Cristo Renovado: Religion and Peasant Politics in Late Colonial Mexico," *American Historical Review* 110: 4 (October 2005), 945–974.

125. Fortino Hipólito Vera, *Santuario del Sacromonte; o lo que se ha escrito sobre él desde el siglo XVI hasta el presente*, Amecameca: Tip. del "Colegio Católico," 1881, pp. 19–24, based on "Una romería," *El Espectador de México*, tomo IV, num. 14 (March 3, 1852), p. 330. According to this 1852 account, the crowds were twice as large as before and most of the pilgrims were Indians.

126. Spanish chronicles celebrating Martín de Valencia include Gerónimo de Mendieta, OFM, *Historia eclesiástica indiana*, Mexico: CONACULTA, 1997, II, 262–306; Pedro Oroz, *The Oroz Codex*, ed. and trans. Angélico Chávez, Washington: Academy of American Franciscan History, 1972, pp. 125–129; and Juan de Torquemada, OFM, *Monarquía Indiana*, Mexico: Porrúa, 1986 (facsimile of 1723 edition), III, 418–423. Edward Osowski sets them alongside Chimalpahin's view from an elite native perspective, in *Indigenous Miracles: Nahua Authority in Colonial Mexico*, Tucson: University of Arizona Press, 2010, chapter 1. See also Hipólito Vera's collection of sources, *Santuario del Sacromonte*, Pierre Ragon, "La colonización de lo sagrado: La historia del Sacromonte de Amecameca," *Relaciones. Estudios de Historia y Sociedad* 75 (1998), 281–300, his *Les saints et les images du Mexique (XVIe-XVIII siècle)*, Paris:

L'Harmattan, 2003, pp. 61–67, and Brian C. Wilson, "Tepeyac and Plymouth Rock: Pilgrimage and Nationalism in Mexico and the United States," in *The Future of Religion: Toward a Reconciled Society*, ed. Michael R. Ott, Leiden: Brill, 2007, pp. 129–146 (132–136 for Amecameca), stressing precolonial connections. The sixteenth century continues to receive most of the attention.

127. Mendieta, *Historia eclesiástica*, II, 305–306.
128. Fortino Hipólito Vera, *Itinerario parroquial del arzobispado de Mexico y reseña histórica, geográfica y estadística de las parroquias del mismo* . . ., Amecameca: Tip. del "Colegio Católico," 1880, p. 90.
129. See Appendix 1. Originally, they may have been freestanding Nativity figures.
130. AHCM num. de inventario 3902 exp. 48.
131. Nuestra Señora de la Bala as the northern "bastion" (*baluarte*) of Marian shrines guarding Mexico City was mentioned in Cabrera y Quintero, *Escudo de armas*[1746], p. 145 para. 301. Nuestro Señor del Balazo was mentioned in a news item in the *Gazeta de México* for October 19, 1738, BIBM 4, p. 797 noting that the event with the bullet occurred over forty-six years before, or before 1692. The providential story of the Christ was embellished in Vicente de Paula Andrade's *Mes histórico de la Preciosa Sangre*, Mexico: Tipografía de "Artes Graficas," 1908, pp. 7–8: the bullet was fired during the 1692 uprising in Mexico City and Christ's leg was said to have swelled where it was hit.
132. Pedro Delgado Loria, *Septena de la Soledad de María Sanctíssima y Entierro de Christo cuyas devotas imágenes se veneran en su Iglesia del Hospital Real del Señor San Pedro de la Ciudad de Puebla de los Ángeles*, Puebla: Vda. de Miguel de Ortega, 1721. Among other examples of miraculous images of Christ and Mary joined in the same shrine: the Cristo del Encino and Nuestra Señora de la Raíz of Jacona, Michoacán; the crucifix and Mater Dolorosa of Tziritícuaro, Michoacán; the Mary Immaculate and Christ crucified of the Hospital de Jesús, Mexico City; the Cristo de la Salud and Nuestra Señora de la Salud of the church of the Santíssima Trinidad, Mexico City; the Santo Niño de la Penitencia and Nuestra Señora del Socorro in the convent church of La Penitencia, Mexico City; Nuestra Señora de la Balvanera and the Cristo Renovado de la Balvanera in Mexico City; Nuestra Señora de la Merced and the Ecce Homo of the Mercedarian church in Mexico City; and the Ecce Homo and copy of the Virgin of Guadalupe in the convent church of San Bernardo in Mexico City.
133. Andrés Miguel Pérez de Velasco, *El ayudante de cura* . . ., Puebla: Colegio Real de San Ignacio, 1766, pp. 76–77 urged pastors to recognize the authenticity of Indian devotion with the example of an individual who approached an image of Christ with such holy fear that he dared not touch it, as if that would be an audacious act ("Si este Indio despues de tantas genuflexiones, tantas y tan expresivas demostraciones de Devoción, le llega con tanto miedo a la Imagen, o no se atreve a llegar la mano, porque le parece osadía el tocar la Imagen de Jesu-Christo").
134. For discussion of the Christ of Totolapa's status as a "santo," see Jennifer Scheper Hughes, *Biography of a Mexican Crucifix: Lived Religion and Local Faith from the Conquest to the Present*, New York: Oxford University Press, 2010, chapter 7, especially pp. 171–174. Isabel Hernández, "El Catolicismo popular en San Mateo Atenco," in *Historia de la religión en Mesoamérica y áreas afines*, ed. Barbro Dahlgren de Jordán, Mexico: UNAM, 1987, p. 220, also mentioned images of Christ as "santos" in this community in the Valley of Toluca.

135. While most self-restoring images were crucifixes, several were figures of the Virgin Mary: Nuestra Señora del Rayo in the convent church of Jesús María in Guadalajara; Nuestra Señora de Talpa, Jalisco; Nuestra Señora de Tulantongo, Estado de México; and Nuestra Señora de Acazingo, Puebla.

136. The single sheets announcing the completion and defense of a university thesis usually included a printed depiction of the author's choice of patron saint/godparent (*padrino*). Many are recorded and illustrated in the AGN's published *Catálogo de ilustraciones, Archivo General de la Nación*, 14 vols., Mexico: Archivo General de la Nación, 1979–1982.

137. Marian images "of" nature were rare. An early seventeenth-century example is discussed in Chapter 1.

138. Editions published in Mexico City: 1778, 1784, 1785, 1788, 1791, 1793, 1794, 1795, and 1807; in Puebla, 1790 and 1797. There was a Guadalajara edition in 1817.

139. Several other dark Christs that may or may not date from the colonial period depict him entombed.

140. For the long, late colonial political history of a competition between this dark crucifix and another one found in a mesquite in the 1720s, see Taylor, *Magistrates of the Sacred*, pp. 271–272. Everett Gee Jackson described the Christ of Jocotepec from his visit to the town in 1926 as "an interesting piece of primitive sculpture. Obviously some Indian had noticed that the form of a tree root with two branches above and one below had something in common with the form of a man's body. He had imagined just how to carve it here and there to bring about a closer resemblance, and then he painted it black and attached it to a crude cross," *Burros and Paintbrushes*, College Station: Texas A&M Press, 1985 p. 75. For the Virgin of Guadalupe in Valladolid (Morelia), see Francisco de Ajofrín, *Diario del viaje que hizo a la América en el siglo XVIII el P. Fray Francisco de Ajofrín*, 2 vols., Mexico: Instituto Cultural Hispano Mexicano, 1964, I, 153, 155.

141. For example, Fernando López Aguilar and Patricia Fournier, "Peregrinaciones otomíes. Vínculos locales y regionales en el Valle del Mezquital," in *Peregrinaciones ayer y hoy: Arqueología y antropología de las religiones*, coords. Patricia Fournier, Carlos Mondragón, and Walburga Wiesheu, Mexico: El Colegio de México, 2012, p. 103. See also José de la Cruz Pacheco Rojas and Rebeca Treviño Montemayor, *Religiosidad y cultura popular en el Camino Real de Tierra Adentro. Tres ensayos socio-anthropológicos*, Durango: Gobierno del Estado, 2010, pp. 19–20, "se destaca su importancia como figura sagrada que se funde con las deidades y los antiguos ritos mesoamericanos"; Angélica Galicia Gordillo and Sergio Sánchez Vásquez, *Cristos y cruces en la cosmovisión otomí de Ixmiquilpan, Hidalgo*, Pachuca: Universidad Autónoma del Estado de Hidalgo, 2002, and Carlos Navarrete Cáceres, *En la diáspora de una devoción: Acercamientos al estudio del Cristo Negro de Esquipulas*, Mexico: UNAM, 2015, p. 105.

142. For example, see Timothy J. Knab, *The Dialogue of Earth and Sky: Dreams, Souls, Curing, and the Modern Aztec Underworld*, Tucson: University of Arizona Press, 2004, p. 73, black Christs as trees from the earth, and pp. 98–99 a tree in the center of the underworld supports the surface of the earth. José Velasco Toro, *De la historia al mito: Mentalidad y culto en el Santuario de Otatitlán*, Veracruz: Instituto Veracruzano de Cultura, 2000, p. 87, reports that Mixtecs, Zapotecs, and Mazatecs believe they descend from trees.

242   Part I Bearings: Historical Patterns and Places of Image Shrines

143. Jeanette Favrot Peterson, "Perceiving Blackness, Envisioning Power: Chalma and Black Christs in Colonial Mexico," in *Seeing Across Cultures in the Early Modern World*, ed. Dana Leibsohn and Jeanette Favrot Peterson, Farnham: Ashgate, 2012, pp. 49–71.
144. Peterson, "Perceiving Blackness," p. 50.
145. Peterson, "Perceiving Blackness," pp. 49, 63. Peterson acknowledges that there were a "plurality of visual codes in circulation in colonial Mexico" ("Renaissance: A Kaleidoscopic View from the Spanish Americas," in *Renaissance Theory*, ed. James Elkins and Robert Williams, New York: Routledge, 2008, pp. 321–332, 329), but posits the precolonial cosmovision connection in this article.
146. Miles Richardson, "Clarifying the Dark in Black Christs: The Play of Icon, Narrative, and Experience in the Construction of Presence," *Yearbook of the Conference of Latin Americanist Geographers*, 21 (1995), 107–120.
147. These paintings are reproduced in *Los pinceles de la historia*," I, 222–223. For the change in color of the Señor de Tila from dark to light in 1694, which was treated as a miraculous *renovación*, see Navarrete, *En la diáspora*, p. 110. There were other kinds of miracles suggesting the same kind of transformation; for example, black candles turning white, Florencia and Oviedo, *Zodíaco mariano*, p. 294.
148. For Navarrete's discussion of how the Christs of Esquipulas and Tila came to be dark, see *En la diáspora*, pp. 106–110. In effect, Navarrete endorses the opinion of an earlier historian and priest of the shrine of Esquipulas, Juan Paz Solórzano, *Historia del Señor de Esquipulas, de su santuario . . .*, Guatemala: Imp. Arenales, 1916.
149. Navarrete, *En la diáspora*, p. 108. "El color verdadero lo imponen la tradición, las creencias que aumentan al correr el tiempo, lo que la gente siente y quiere ver."
150. AGN Civil 1557 exp. 8 fols. 3–4.
151. Luisa Elena Alcalá, "La problemática de las copias de vírgenes negras.La recepción de Loreto en Nueva España," in *La imagen sagrada y sacralizada: Coloquio Internacional de Historia del Arte*, ed. Peter Krieger, Mexico: UNAM, 2011, I, 103, quoting Miguel Venegas, SJ, "Y para que esta [imagen] no se disminuyesse en la estimación de la Plebe, que a veces govierna sus afectos más por la apariencia de los colores que por la realidad de la más perfecta hermosura, paresció conveniente que a esta sagrada Ymagen no se le diesse el color denegrido de la original de Loreto."

Any sharp contrast here between Europe and America, even for Loreto, has to be qualified. The complexion of European images of Loreto sometimes was rendered white. See for example, Lucio Massari's painting from the 1620s reproduced in Klaus Krüger, "Authenticity and Fiction: On the Pictorial Construction of Inner Presence in Early Modern Italy," in *Image and Imagination of the Religious Self in Late Medieval and Early Modern Europe*, ed. Reindert Falkenburg, Walter S. Melion, and Todd M. Richardson, Turnhout: Brepols Publishers, 2007, p. 51. And there was at least one black Virgin of Loreto in late colonial Mexico City, in the church of Nuestra Señora del Pilar (La Enseñanza), although it may have been made in Europe, according to Clara Bargellini, "Jesuit Devotions and Retablos in New Spain," in *The Jesuits: Cultures, Sciences, and the Arts, 1540–1773*, ed. John W. O'Malley et al., Toronto: University of Toronto Press, 1999, p. 685.
152. Nolan and Nolan, *Christian Pilgrimage in Modern Western Europe*, pp. 202, 204.
153. Leonard W. Moss and Stephen C. Cappanari, "In Quest of the Black Virgin: She Is Black Because She Is Black," in *Mother Worship: Theme & Variation*, ed.

James J. Preston, Chapel Hill: University of North Carolina Press, 1982, pp. 53–74, especially pp. 65, 68, 71.

154. For example, this is the approach of Malgorzata Oleszkiewicz-Peralba, *The Black Madonna in Latin America and Europe: Tradition and Transformation*, Albuquerque: University of New Mexico Press, 2009: "My book examines the phenomenon of the Black Madonna, a fluid syncretic blend of the Virgin Mary and ancient Mother Goddesses from Eurasian, Native American, and African cultures who is worshipped and adored by millions of people around the world," p. 9. The great Earth Mother is described across religious traditions in Mircea Eliade, *Patterns in Comparative Religion*, trans. Rosemary Sheed, London and New York: Sheed & Ward, 1958, pp. 2, 91, 133, 239–264.

   The Virgin of Xuquila, another miraculous image celebrated for its darkness, had a very different story from that of the Virgin of Guadalupe or mother earth figures. According to Ruiz y Cervantes, *Memoria*, pp. 14–15, this light-skinned Virgin of Xuquila was blackened in a fire in the 1630s that destroyed the first shrine to the image in Amialtepec (Oaxaca). Except for the change in skin color, the little statue was unchanged.

155. To the pastors, at least, whiteness may also have represented conversion, the triumph of Christianity, of light over the darkness of paganism and idolatry, as Jeanette Favrot Peterson suggests, *Visualizing Guadalupe: From Black Madonna to Queen of the Americas*, Austin: University of Texas Press, 2014, p. 17.

156. Quoted in Francisco de la Maza, *El guadalupanismo mexicano*, Mexico: Fondo de Cultural Económica, 1981,, pp. 128–135. Apparently the only copy of this sermon in a public collection is in the Biblioteca Nacional de México, *Sermón que en el dia de la Aparición de la Imagen Santa de Guadalupe, doze de diziembre del Año de 1672 predicó el P. Fr. Ioan de Mendoza Commissario Visitador de la Orden Tercera de Penitencia, en el Convento de N. Padre S. Francisco de México*, Mexico: Francisco Rodríguez Lupercio, 1673.

157. Quoted in Taylor, *Shrines and Miraculous Images*, pp. 125–126. Other Guadalupan sermons published in the late seventeenth century did not make the connection to the image's Indian appearance. For example, the sermon of José Herrera Suárez, OP, published the same year as Mendoza's sermon, referred to her "surpassing beauty" (peregrina hermosura) but made no mention of skin color, *Sermón que predicó el r.p. lector regente f. Joseph de Herrera, del Orden de Predicadores, en la solemne fiesta, que se celebró este año de 1672 . . .*, Mexico: Viuda de B. Calderón, 1673, fols. 2–3.

158. Monique Scheer, "From Majesty to Mystery: Change in the Meanings of Black Madonnas from the Sixteenth to Nineteenth Centuries," *American Historical Review* 107: 5 (December 2002), 1412–1440, highlights Linnaeus's system of classification (1735), dividing humanity into four groups, black, white, red, and yellow, and Friedrich Blumenbach's five races (1779), including the Caucasian or white race, the Mongolian or yellow race, the Malayan or brown race (including Southeast Asians and Pacific Islanders), the Ethiopian or black race, and the American or red race.

159. For this point Scheer relies mainly on Gumppenberg's treatment of close to 1,200 Marian pilgrimage centers worldwide in the *Atlas Marianus*, "From Majesty to Mystery," p. 1433.

160. Scheer, "From Majesty to Mystery," p. 1430.

161. Scheer, "From Majesty to Mystery," p. 1430ff; Song of Solomon 1:5 "I am black, but comely, O ye daughters of Jerusalem."
162. María Elena Martínez, *Genealogical Fictions: Limpieza de Sangre, Religion, and Gender in Colonial Mexico*, Stanford: Stanford University Press, 2008, p. 198.
163. Martínez, *Genealogical Fictions*, p. 198. Martínez tracks the intertwining roots of religion and race in Spain and Spanish America during the sixteenth and seventeenth centuries while recognizing that they were not formulated in political tracts, *limpieza de sangre* validations, and artwork until the eighteenth century.
164. For example, the small crucifix in the shrine of Our Lady of Guadalupe in Valladolid described by Joaquín Osuna in 1756 as "la Imagen de un Crucifixo como de una bara que se halló naturalmente esculpido dentro de un grande tronco que estaba en una Hacienda llamada de las Rosas, de quien tomó su título," *Peregrinación christiana por el camino real de la celeste Jerusalén*, Mexico: Bibliotheca Mexicana, 1756, paragraph 3 no. 7.
165. For example, Alan R. Sandstrom's studies of a Nahua community in the southern Huasteca treats devotion to Guadalupe as "a 'Christianized' version of Tontantsi," a native mother goddess worshiped there since precolonial times, "The Tonantsi Cult of the Eastern Nahua," in *Mother Worship: Theme & Variations*, ed. James J. Preston, Chapel Hill: University of North Carolina Press, 1982, pp. 25–50, especially 26, 48, and *Corn is Our Blood: Culture and Ethnic Identity in a Contemporary Aztec Indian Village*, Norman: University of Oklahoma Press, 1991, chapter 6. Ethnographers have been less inclined to consider the possibility that influence and congruence might run also in the opposite direction – that the modern cult of Tonantsi in some Nahua communities may owe more to the colonial cult of the Virgin of Guadalupe, reframed in terms of local knowledge of female divinity, than to a particular native goddess reframed as Guadalupe. Whether the term *tonantzin* – our precious mother – referred to a distinct precolonial goddess or was a generic term for divine motherhood used by Nahuatl speakers in the colonial period for the Virgin of Guadalupe and other images of Mary remains a subject of discussion and debate. The terms we use in English and other European languages – goddess and deity, etc. – may be too thing-like to adequately represent Mesoamerican conceptions of divinity and enchantment.
166. Surprisingly, the shrines for Esquipulas and the Sacromonte of Amecameca did not receive comparable attention in publications.

4
Advocations of the Virgin Mary in the Colonial Period

Marian shrine images are discussed in the preceding chapters mainly in terms of their place identities (Our Lady of Xuquila, etc.), but the advocations they depicted also informed how they were understood.[1] For example, shrine images of Mary Immaculate such as La Purísima of Tecamachalco (Puebla) and Buctoz (Yucatán) continued to be identified by this advocation, and devotees of Our Lady of Guadalupe at Tepeyac often referred to her as "la Purísima."[2] Many images of the Blessed Mary were similar in pose and appearance so that an image of the Virgin might change advocation without much difficulty, but each advocation had a distinguishing feature, usually a symbol or setting, whether it was rosary beads, a candle, a scapular, a sword pointed at her heart, a crescent moon beneath her feet, or a backdrop of billowing clouds and cherubs or a fire-breathing monster. Different advocations traced different histories in New Spain, appealing to particular devotees and promoters, and being honored on different feast days that reminded devotees of the advocation's special attributes.

Advocations, then, are another dimension of the complex interplay of image and presence that often centered on a shrine image and sometimes defined it. Some advocations initially were associated with one of the religious orders – the Immaculate Conception with Franciscans; the Mater Dolorosa and Loreto with Jesuits; Our Lady of the Rosary with Dominicans – but became more widely known, promoted, and venerated.[3] Others associated with an order, such as Our Lady of Carmen and the Carmelites or Our Lady of Mercy and the Mercedarians remained closely identified with that order and a more restricted audience. Some regional Spanish advocations in America preserved their peninsular identities in America; for example, the advocations of Pilar de Zaragoza, Aranzazú, Montserrat, and Covadonga appealed mainly to immigrant families from Aragón, the Basque provinces, Catalonia, and Asturias, respectively. But they could have other significance, too. Our Lady of Covadonga, for instance, was associated with the Dominicans as well as the Asturias homeland, and her role as divine warrior came to the fore in the eighteenth century as Spain's entanglements in European politics led to more international warfare. Another regional Spanish advocation, Our Lady of Cueva Santa, was less attached to immigrants from her home region of Valencia. She became popular across the city of Querétaro and reached audiences elsewhere through revival missions led by Querétaro's Franciscans. The distinctive images of several new advocations in the eighteenth century with European origins, especially Nuestra Señora del Refugio and Nuestra Señora de la Luz, were successfully promoted by missionaries and became very popular in parts of central and northern New Spain without being reduced to a single enshrined painting or statue that had reputedly come to life. The image of another new advocation, the Divina Pastora, gained notoriety in a less managed way in the streets and homes of the port city of Veracruz but did not attract regional interest the way Nuestra Señora del Refugio and Nuestra Señora de la Luz did. The second part of this chapter considers these Spanish and Italian advocations and copies of their images that had an Old World identity yet gained a following in New Spain during the late colonial period: both time-honored advocations associated with regional shrines in Spain, which had limited appeal and new ones that attracted wider interest.

The first part of the chapter introduces the two most popular Marian advocations that were closely associated with miraculous images and developed into regional shrines: Our Lady of the Immaculate Conception and the Mater Dolorosa. Their identity as advocations was preserved and embraced in ways that made particular images of them unusually appealing representations of the Blessed Mary, evoking powerful feelings of love and contrition understood to invite divine favor. Images of the grieving and merciful Mater Dolorosa gained great popularity in the seventeenth century when Christocentric devotions were coming to the fore and were especially renowned for miracles, but from the beginning Mary Immaculate had a special resonance, too, closely associated with healing and innocence. Embraced as more than an unapproachable icon of purity, physical beauty, and majesty, she was often depicted as an angelic, welcoming figure of more ordinary appearance.[4] Another leading advocation, Our Lady of the Rosary, receives less attention here because none of her many images became the treasured figure of a major shrine. This is puzzling since nearly every church served by the Dominicans had a chapel or altar displaying an image of Our Lady of the Rosary holding a string of beads that recalled Mary's apparition to the order's founder in which she taught him to pray the Rosary, and the Rosary was a fundamental devotion in early modern Spain and the colonies. Perhaps the more limited regional charisma of these figures has to do with the fact that Dominicans were less inclined than other orders to promote image shrines, aiming to elicit religious emotion more through litanies and awe-inspiring church interiors than through reputedly numinous figures. It may also be that most representations of the Virgin of the Rosary were so standardized in their placid immobility as to seem interchangeable, more an emblem than an individualized, living presence (see Figure 3.20 in Chapter 3). In practice, the desire for miracles associated with the Rosary seems to have focused on the beads and the prayerful faith they stood for more than on the Lady who inspired them. For example, the *Gazeta de México* reported in January 1735 that when a lightning bolt struck the main house of the Hacienda San Francisco Xavier del Ojo de Agua in the district of Salvatierra, Guanajuato, everyone was killed except a child who wore a string of rosary beads. The reporter noted that a similar event had occurred at Erongarícuaro, Michoacán, on May 1, 1722, when three Indian men were killed by a lightning strike. Only their companion who wore rosary beads was spared.[5]

Two Leading Advocations

Our Lady of the Immaculate Conception

Holy Mary of the Immaculate Conception was the most familiar representation of the Mother of God in America, often invoked as the indispensable intercessor to her son at the Last Judgment,[6] and the representation of many famous shrine images known by their local place names in New Spain. Although the feast of the Immaculate Conception, December 8, was not established by the papacy as a Holy Day of Obligation until 1708 and the doctrine was not canonically binding until 1854, a feast day of the Immaculate Conception had been authorized by the papacy in 1476, with its own special Mass and office. The belief was popular in Iberia by the sixteenth century, especially after Queen Isabella adopted this advocation of the Virgin in the late fifteenth century as a symbol of unity.[7] The Spanish crown declared December 8 the patronal feast day in 1615, and papal recognition of Mary Immaculate as protector of Spain and Spanish dominions in 1662 and Queen of America in 1727 also legitimated the devotion and boosted its appeal.[8] By then, Mary Immaculate was well established as the most familiar representation of the Virgin Mary in Spanish territories. The doctrine of the Immaculate Conception was complex, involving both the proposition that Mary was free from all stain of original sin from the moment of her conception in the womb of her mother, St. Anne, and the proposition that Christ was conceived in her womb without sin through the action of the Holy Spirit. Both aspects of the doctrine were widely accepted, but Mary's immaculate conception remained controversial, countered especially by the Dominicans, who followed the reasoning of their "angelic doctor," Thomas Aquinas, that the Blessed Virgin could not have been redeemed by Christ unless she had been born in sin. Rather than offering a robust endorsement and elaboration of the doctrine, the Council of Trent decrees made only a brief reference to the controversy in canon 23, to the effect that no person escapes sin entirely "except by a special privilege of God, as the Church holds in regard to the Blessed Virgin." Not surprisingly, popular understanding of the Immaculate Conception skirted the theological debate over whether Mary was free from all stain of original sin and centered attention on the divine conception of Christ in her womb.

The standard depiction of Mary Immaculate beginning in the early seventeenth century as a young woman in flowing robes, her hands pressed together in prayer, a crescent moon beneath her feet and a halo of stars and sunlight encircling her head and body – was rich in symbolic associations that were understood and accepted irrespective of theological disagreement over the doctrine.[9] Inspired by the pregnant woman "clothed with the sun, with the moon under her feet, and over her head a crown of twelve stars" in *The Revelation to John*, chapter 12,[10] they highlighted qualities of the Blessed Mary that made the guise of the Immaculate Conception a compelling and timeless depiction of her loving presence and intercessory powers, and her reconciliation of opposites. Frequently, the images of Mary Immaculate included a dragon beneath her feet, another reworking of the Revelation 12 text, to represent Christ's triumph over Satan. As Dr. Andrés de Arce y Miranda, renowned preacher and canon of the cathedral of Puebla, explained the iconography of the pregnant Virgin in 1755, the twelve stars stand for the twelve apostles and illumination of the night sky; the moon in its mutability stands for the transience of worldly things amid darkness, in contrast to the church's constancy; that Mary stands on the moon shows her steadfast resolve and disdain for worldly possessions; and that she stands in a posture of prayer and is clothed in the sun represents Christ, the Sun of Justice in her womb, and the mediation of opposites (such as sun and moon, darkness and light), through her loving, protective intercession.[11]

Franciscans, who played a central role in the early evangelization and pastoral work among native peoples during the sixteenth century, were leading advocates of the doctrine of Immaculate Conception and source of statues and paintings depicting this advocation from the early years of Spanish colonization. They promoted the image and devotion everywhere they evangelized. Later, along with the Jesuits – who became leading preachers, teachers, and evangelists in colonial cities and on mission frontiers – they carried the devotion north.[12] Mary Immaculate became a veritable logo for the Franciscan presence in New Spain. Hospitals as models of Christian charity, both as hospitality to travelers and havens for the sick and injured, were a basic feature of the Franciscan evangelization, and nearly all of the many hospital chapels they established were dedicated to her. She was an equally familiar

AL ILL.MO. V. SEÑOR DEAN, Y CAVILDO SEDE-
Vacāte de la Sāta Iglefia Metropolítana de Mexico.

Figure 4.1 Print from unsigned, undated woodcut of Mary Immaculate above symbols of Mexico City: eagles with serpents in their talons, perched on a nopal cactus. The papal tiara and angels holding the keys of St. Peter indicate her association with heavenly authority. Published in Antonio Díaz del Castillo, *Sermón panegírico de dedicación de la iglesia con el título de el glorioso apostol San Bartholomé* ... Mexico: Herederos de la Viuda de M. de Rivera, 1729. Courtesy of the Bancroft Library, University of California, Berkeley.

figure and object of devotion in urban churches, convents, and private homes. Beyond depicting the Virgin standing in prayer enveloped by a sunburst, there was more flexibility and variation in representations of Mary Immaculate than was true for most other iconic images of Marian advocations such as Our Lady of Loreto and Our Lady of Light, discussed later in this chapter, where the original representation was fixed by the belief that it had been made by the hand of St. Luke or derived from a heavenly apparition. Occasionally, as in Figure 4.1, Mary Immaculate was depicted in an American setting, here surrounded by symbols of Mexico City as the seat of worldly authority: the nopal cactus surmounted by eagles with serpents in their talons – ancient symbol of Aztec Tenochtitlan and the viceregal capital of Mexico City. That there are two eagles rather than one may refer to the double eagle on the Hapsburg coat of arms.

Usually she was standing on the crescent moon, her head framed by a halo of stars. The array of additional symbols and tableaux ranged from the complex and elaborate in several seventeenth-century oil paintings – as in those by Baltasar de Echave Ibía before 1637 (possibly 1622) and Basilio de Salazar in 1637 – to just a few basic signs of the Blessed Mary's holiness and her connection to the great drama of salvation. Even the elaborate paintings by Echave Ibía and Salazar did not match the evocative range of symbolic references in late medieval European images of Mary Immaculate. Indeed, a leading student of medieval iconography of the Immaculate Conception used Echave Ibía's painting as her example of the reduced, standardized iconography of Renaissance and Baroque depictions of this advocation of the Virgin Mary.[13]

Not surprisingly, the iconography of the Immaculate Conception as it was displayed in the sixteenth and seventeenth centuries emphasized the conception of Christ in the womb of the Blessed Virgin and her role as mediatrix in the apocalyptic drama of judgment and salvation. The Litany of the Blessed Virgin Mary (also known as the Litany of Loreto), which was widely adopted after it gained papal approval in 1587, does not neglect Mary's purity (referring to her seven times as "virgin"), but its symbols emphasize Christ's prophecies, the struggle for redemption, and Mary's position as mother of God and queen (referring to her thirteen times as mother and twelve times as queen). The Marian symbols drawn directly from the litany to represent Mary Immaculate include the morning star (lighting the way for Christ as sun; also "the star of the sea by which we sail"), the gates of heaven, the house of gold and ivory tower (representing the riches of paradise), the tower of David (the impregnable fortress), the mystical rose (purity), the ark of the covenant, and the mirror of justice (spotless and pure). Three other symbols are displayed in many of the conventional images of Mary Immaculate: Jacob's ladder to heaven (from the *Book of Genesis*) and the cedar tree and the palm tree, from Psalm 92, emblems of God, his chosen people, and life everlasting.[14] Most rudimentary prints of Mary Immaculate that elaborate on the figure modeled on the woman of Revelation 12 include some of these symbols of her purity and role as intercessor. In Figure 4.2, Mary is shown with the sun and moon, the halo of stars, Jacob's ladder, the spotless mirror, the gate of heaven, the morning star, the fountain of everlasting water, and the cedar and palm trees.

Figure 4.2 Late seventeenth-century print from unsigned, undated woodcut of Mary Immaculate with standard symbols of the advocation, published in José Díaz Chamorro, *Sermón que predicó... en la solemne fiesta de la puríssima concepción...*, Puebla: Viuda de I. de Borja y Gandia, 1675. Courtesy of the Bancroft Library, University of California, Berkeley.

Mater Dolorosa

"There is no church without an altar dedicated to Our Lady of Sorrows, no house without prayers every Friday and a candle lit from noon until three in memory of the three hours that Our Redeemer was on the Cross," wrote Matías de la Mota Padilla, a diocesan priest and chronicler, from Guadalajara in 1742.[15] Mota Padilla exaggerated, but one of the strongest threads of continuity across the history of devotion to saints and their images during the colonial period was this perennial, near universal appeal of the Mater Dolorosa – whether as Nuestra Señora de los Dolores with a sword or seven swords piercing her heart, Nuestra Señora de la Soledad (Mary alone and desolate following the death of Jesus, usually wearing a black robe and head covering), or the Pietà – the Blessed Mary cradling her dead son, the Son of God.[16] The essential truth of Mota Padilla's observation runs through the written record in all directions – in church inventories, pastoral visit reports, liturgical practices, petitions, devotional books, sermons, and prints.[17] In far-off New Mexico, early nineteenth-century inventories list more images of Our Lady of Sorrows than of other advocations of Mary.[18] Every parish needed at least one statue of the Mater Dolorosa for solemn processions during the Easter season, on the Friday before Palm Sunday, Good Friday (in the Calvary procession), and Holy Saturday processions of women with a statue of the Blessed Virgin draped in mourning;[19] many homes and churches had their own images, usually a painting or at least an inexpensive print on display; pastors and the laity frequently expressed their special devotion to her;[20] and confraternities dedicated to the Mater Dolorosa were numerous, exceeded in the Archdiocese of Mexico only by those dedicated to the Blessed Sacrament, souls in purgatory, and the rosary.

This appeal built on a long history in Europe that gained institutional expression in the thirteenth century when the Servites of Mary adopted the Mater Dolorosa as their special advocation. She seems to have gained wide popularity later in Spain than in Italy, but was well established there by the 1570s and popular in New Spain by the end of the sixteenth century.[21]

Jesuits were leading promoters of the Mater Dolorosa, constructing altars and chapels to her in their churches, publishing sermons in her honor, promoting devotions on the last Friday of every month, and introducing the third order of Servites to New Spain in the late seventeenth century.[22] But the devotion was always more than a Jesuit specialty. The papacy and the Spanish crown were prominent sponsors in the seventeenth and eighteenth centuries; Franciscans, Augustinians, bishops, and diocesan priests were devotees and promoters; and some of the most celebrated churches and chapels to the Mater Dolorosa were

Figure 4.3 The Mater Dolorosa was increasingly humanized in the representations of her suffering from the fifteenth century on. This half-length portrait print from the late colonial period emphasizes Mary's anguish by drawing attention to her face and hands. Print from unsigned, undated engraving published in Pedro Curruchaga, *Devoción a Nuestra Señora de los Dolores* . . ., Mexico: Benavente, 1816. Courtesy of the Lilly Library, Indiana University.

the work of Dominicans, especially the church and shrine of Nuestra Señora de la Soledad in Antequera (dedicated in 1686), although even this church and devotion also depended in the beginning on crucial support from a prebend of the cathedral chapter, Jesuits, and the Augustinian Recollect nuns. Some of the institutions supporting the cult of the Mater Dolorosa seem to have been initiatives of the laity; for instance, the painter's guild in Mexico City adopted her as their patron saint in the last third of the seventeenth century, and images of her were reportedly used in curing ceremonies.[23]

254 Part I Bearings: Historical Patterns and Places of Image Shrines

SOBERANA SEÑORA

Figure 4.4 Two prints from engravings of Antequera's miraculous Nuestra Señora de la Soledad. The variation here is in the Virgin's dress, pedestal, and position of the hands rather than the basic form. Both prints represent themselves as "a true portrait" or "as she is." The print on the left was collected by Francisco de Ajofrín in the early 1760s. Courtesy of the Real Academia de la Historia, Madrid. The print on the right was published in Gerónymo Morales Sigala, *Sermón que en el día de la espectación de María Santíssima nuestra señora con el nombre y título de la Soledad* ..., Mexico: Colegio de San Ildefonso, 1756. Courtesy of the Bancroft Library, University of California, Berkeley.

The appeal of the Mater Dolorosa and her prominence in church teachings and the liturgy stems from her central place in Semana Santa observances, and especially in her modeling of "true suffering" (*verdadero dolor*) and modesty – the kind of empathetic anguish that could elicit a wholehearted confession of sins, bringing the contrite penitent closer to union with God and the possibility of a "good death."[24] She was closely associated with the sacrament of penitence.[25] It is no surprise, then, that images of the Mater Dolorosa were especially revered, whether they appeared alone or in tableaux of the Pietà and the entombment of Christ (see Figure 4.6). As Francisco Antonio Navarrete, SJ put it in 1739, "No image of Our Lady of Dolores can help but be miraculous."[26] Her appeal was universal, but it had special meaning for women, who in medieval Europe had been encouraged to identify with Christ's suffering

Advocations of the Virgin Mary in the Colonial Period 255

MATER DOLOROSA

Figure 4.5 Engraved print of the Mater Dolorosa published in a pocket size devotional text, *Consuelos a María Santísima en su penosa soledad*, Mexico: Mariano Ontiveros, 1817. The sword aimed at her heart is a standard symbol of this advocation of the Virgin Mary and her grief. She is modestly dressed and her head covered in full-length, "biblical" attire. Author's copy.

on the cross[27] and look to the Mater Dolorosa for protection during pregnancies and the rigors of childbirth.[28]

The distinctive features of Mater Dolorosa images were the sword aimed at her heart, her mourning cloak, and signs of weeping, often with her head drooping and hands clasped. Figures 4.3 and 4.5 illustrate two standard

Figure 4.6 Loose print from an undated, unsigned eighteenth-century engraving produced in the Calle de la Profesa, Mexico City, of a painting known as the miraculous Virgin of the Calvary from Metepec (Estado de México), depicting Our Lady of Sorrows with the "santos varones" – Nicodemus and Joseph of Arimathea – and assistants who came forward to help the Virgin prepare the body of Jesus for burial. This print was sponsored as an expression of faith by "Xilacatzi," perhaps Don Juan Ximénez Xilacatzi. Courtesy of the Getty Research Center.

depictions of the weeping Mater Dolorosa, one a full-length depiction with the sword poised above her heart, her posture expressing vulnerability and grief. Such full-length representations also emphasize the timeless modesty of her attire. Figure 4.3 is a more intimate depiction that became popular in Europe by the sixteenth century and was familiar in Spanish America during the seventeenth and eighteenth centuries. It is a half-length portrait that draws attention to the Virgin's drooping head, her anguished expression, and her clasped hands in a way meant to move the viewer to cleansing tears.[29]

Depictions of and devotions to the sorrowing mother were frequently seen in Mexico during the sixteenth century: the base of the atrium cross at Acolman; the seven sorrows of the Virgin on one of the corner chapels in the atrium at Calpan, Puebla, near Huejotzingo; murals of Christ's Passion on convent walls; early statuettes crafted from maize stalks and pith; or some of the earliest confraternities in Mexico City and Guadalajara.[30] Late sixteenth-century Franciscan chronicler Gerónimo de Mendieta also mentioned a popular confraternity to Dolores in the capital and a procession on Good Friday that featured her statue, with over 770 penitents scourging themselves and wearing the insignia of the sorrowing mother.[31] His Franciscan compatriot and near contemporary Juan de Torquemada described a Maundy Thursday "Procesión de la Soledad" in which two dozen maidens dressed in black marched, "as they were taught to do by the evangelizers."[32] The written and pictorial evidence of Dolores's presence in official and popular piety was even greater and more varied during the seventeenth and eighteenth centuries, suggesting further growth, institutional development, and popular appeal.[33] Thanks especially to the efforts of Jesuits and occasional initiatives by the Spanish crown and bishops, public devotion to the Mater Dolorosa grew and deepened through the creation of new chapels, altars, and many paintings and prints during the second half of the seventeenth century. In the eighteenth century, it was expressed in yet more publications, including novena booklets and a great many prints.[34] The devotion also became more institutionalized at that time, with the founding and development of confraternities and endowments to sponsor Masses and other observances, devotions on the eighteenth of every month, and licensed alms-collecting missions in most of the dioceses of New Spain.

Reports of miracles were always part of the Dolores story. Sometimes her statues came to life, as Antonio de Robles reported in his journal in October 1702 when news reached Mexico City of an image of the Mater Dolorosa in Mérida, Yucatán that perspired off and on for three hours, in tandem with another image of the Virgin Mary elsewhere in Yucatán.[35] But the most common miracle stories follow from her intercession in times of mortal danger, whether in drought, earthquakes, epidemics, or a difficult birthing.[36] Cayetano Cabrera y Quintero recounted in his *Escudo de armas de México* (1746) the special favor Br. Ignacio Santoyo of Mexico City believed he had received from the Mater Dolorosa during the great epidemic of 1737. When the epidemic struck, all the other chaplains serving the Hospital Real de los Indios succumbed, leaving Santoyo to carry on alone. Troubled and fearing for his life in the midst of "the multitude of sick people," he "took refuge" in "Most Holy Mary venerated in this image of the Sorrows in the chapel of the women's retreat house called Bethlehem" and promised her a special Mass. Seven more times the "furnace of the deathly illness" flared, yet Santoyo was spared again and again, "immune to the flames of the fever, bathed in the fresh and welcoming breeze of Mary's sea of grace."[37]

The chronology of devotion to two favored images of the Mater Dolorosa from Jalisco illustrates the pattern of early presence and lasting interest. Devotion to Nuestra Señora de la Soledad and the Santo Entierro de Cristo (the entombed Christ, a central figure in Good Friday observances) in Guadalajara was recorded in the founding of an elite confraternity in the Hospital de San Miguel in 1589, the main purpose of which was to sponsor a solemn procession with these two images on Viernes de Dolores, the Friday before Palm Sunday. The statue of Dolores was described as made from maize stalks and a paste made from maize pith in Pátzcuaro earlier in the sixteenth century. The image was moved several times and eventually placed in its own *santuario* next to the cathedral, which was dedicated in the mid-1670s. This image of the Mater Dolorosa came to be known as *la milagrosa*[38] and was chosen patroness of the city by royal decree in the 1770s.[39] Devotion to Nuestra Señora de los Dolores at Santa Cruz de las Flores centered on a statue in the hospital founded by Franciscans there in the sixteenth century. A confraternity to support the devotion was established then and a separate, larger chapel was under construction in the late seventeenth century, completed in 1692. The image and shrine remained popular into the late eighteenth century, at least until diocesan pastors replaced the Franciscans.[40]

A growing popular tradition of home altars to the Dolores advocation displayed outdoors during special supplications in times of crisis is documented in official decrees by a late colonial bishop and a viceroy, albeit to different purposes. On March 10, 1769, Puebla's Bishop Francisco Fabián y Fuero called for an end to the practice of public display of improvised altars in residential doorways and public places "even if they have images, altars, and decorations dedicated to the Most Holy Virgin of Sorrows."[41] But in 1785, Viceroy Bernardo de Gálvez openly encouraged open-air altars to Dolores in a plea for divine intervention during months of near starvation that year after torrential rains and a killing frost destroyed much of the maize crop. The viceroy himself set the example, having such an altar constructed on one of the balconies of the viceregal palace. Soon improvised altars to Dolores appeared at the entrances of homes elsewhere in the city.[42]

Spanish Regional Shrines and Devotions in New Spain

Spain's most famous wonder-working images and advocations of the Virgin Mary (and one celebrated crucifix, the Christ of Burgos) also have a place in the history of popular devotion to shrine images in New Spain, especially during the eighteenth century. Chapels to them were built or rebuilt then, sponsored by confraternities, and made known in an unprecedented number of published sermons and novena booklets. This growing popularity and promotion was centered in Mexico City and several provincial cities, particularly Puebla and Guadalajara. For the most part, the devotees were either wealthy overseas Spaniards from the region associated with a particular image or members of one of the mendicant orders.

Chapels and devotions to the Marian images of Montserrat, Aranzazú, Pilar de Zaragoza, and Balvanera all were established in Mexico City and occasionally elsewhere in New Spain during the seventeenth century.[43] Montserrat, the great Catalan shrine image, had a small chapel and shrine near the Salto del Agua fountain in Mexico City, dedicated in 1589 or 1590.[44] Perhaps this was the chapel in the native *tlaxilacalli* (residential subunit) of Tequixquipan, in the *parcialidad* of San Juan that Chimalpahin mentioned several times in his annals between 1589 and 1595 as housing an image of the Virgin of Montserrat.[45] Our Lady of Aranzazú had her own confraternity of Mexican Basques in the Franciscan Convento Grande in 1671; her chapel there was completed in 1688.[46] Curiously, the first edition of the standard devotional history of the Spanish Basque shrine to Aranzazú was published in Mexico City rather than Spain, in 1686. Its author, Juan de Luzuriaga, was a Basque Franciscan who had been sent to Mexico in 1680.[47] Devotion to the Aragonese Virgin of Pilar de Zaragoza was centered in the Franciscan Convento Grande in Mexico City by the 1670s, with the chronicler Agustín de Vetancurt, OFM as an especially enthusiastic promoter.[48] An altar dedicated to her was placed in this church before the end of the seventeenth century, sponsored by a local Aragonese immigrant, and by 1691 a sponsoring confraternity had been founded.[49] By the 1690s, the city of Puebla also had a chapel dedicated to this Virgin in the *sagrario* (parish church attached to the cathedral) that was famous for "innumerable miracles."[50] Our Lady of Balvanera, a Marian image shrine in La Rioja, in the northern borderlands of Castile just south of the Basque province of Álava, was venerated both in the Mexico City convent of La Balvanera and in the convent of Santa Inés in Puebla. A sermon for her annual feast in Puebla was published in 1680, and several Mexican paintings of the statue date from the late seventeenth century, one by Juan Correa.[51]

With the eighteenth century came more sustained efforts at promotion and signs of devotion. Replicas of the original statues in Spain and

Figure 4.7 Print of Nuestra Señora del Pilar de Zaragoza, from an unsigned woodcut in Agustín de Vetancurt's *Sermón a la Aparición de la milagrosa Imagen de N. Señora del Pilar de Zaragoza ...*, Mexico: Francisco Rodríguez Lupercio, 1674. Courtesy of the Bancroft Library, University of California, Berkeley.

paintings featuring them were commissioned more often than in the past, along with construction of fine altars in their honor, and a few temples and chapels. Publications included sermons dedicated to them, American printings of their devotional histories, dozens of novena booklets to guide devotees through nine-day rounds of public worship directed to them, and many devotional prints of varying quality.[52] The 1750s to the 1770s account for nearly two-thirds of the prints of European Marian images published in New Spain between 1600 and 1820 included by Manuel Romero de Terreros in his study of colonial-era prints.[53]

These devotions to images of the Virgin Mary from regional shrines in Spain were provincial in the sense that the sponsors and leading devotees in Mexican cities usually were natives of the home region – Aragonese devotees of Pilar de Zaragoza, etc. But in America, this provincialism could be more inclusive than it might have been at home. Our Lady of Aranzazú in Mexico City and Guadalajara is a prime example. As Juan Javier Pescador has written, Our Lady of Aranzazú was more popular among the network of Basques in America than in the Basque-speaking provinces of northern Spain at the time.[54] Basques from the provinces of Álava, Navarra, Guipúzcoa, and Biskaia, and their descendants born in America, banded together to establish the confraternity of Our Lady of Aranzazú in Mexico City in 1671, and another confraternity and fine little temple to her adjoining the Franciscan convent in Guadalajara in the 1770s[55] – a panethnic collaboration that was still to come in Spain.

Several famous Spanish images of the Virgin Mary were promoted in New World evangelization initiatives during the late seventeenth and eighteenth centuries. Nuestra Señora del Pilar de Zaragoza – "the Column of Faith," who reputedly appeared to the Apostle St. James when he preached the gospel to pagans in the Roman province of Hispania – was a natural choice for queen of a new spiritual and temporal conquest in America. In his 1674 sermon in the Franciscan Convento Grande in Mexico City, Vetancurt, who had embraced his order's mission to convert heathens throughout the world, regarded this image of the Virgin as the *madre común* of all nations. Although Pedro de San Francisco's 1739 sermon also highlighted Nuestra Señora del Pilar's association with spiritual conquest, especially with the Augustinians' sacrifices in the Philippines,[56] the evangelizing promise of this devotion was not much pursued in eighteenth-century America. Nuestra Señora del Pilar was adopted by some Spanish military units in America as their patroness,[57] but mainly she attracted wealthy immigrant Aragonese devotees, who endowed Masses, sponsored chapels and altars, and paid for publication of religious tracts dedicated to her.

Two Spanish Marian devotions – Our Lady of Covadonga and Our Lady of the Cueva Santa – came to have a public following in Mexico City only during the eighteenth century and responded as much to the politics and reforms of the time as to the devotion of immigrants from their home regions. Devotion to Our Lady of Covadonga was closely associated with the Dominicans and evidently began in the capital city in 1732 or 1733 when a group of immigrants from Asturias in northwestern Spain requested permission to stage an annual celebration on her feast day, the second Sunday of November, in the convent church of La Balvanera.[58] During the next few years, Asturians in Mexico City formed a confraternity to Our Lady of Covadonga, and the Dominicans allowed them to place an

Figure 4.8 Nuestra Señora de Covadonga, print from undated engraving by "García," published in *Constituciones de la congregacion de Nuestra Señora con el titulado de Covadonga*, Mexico: Herederos de Joseph de Jáuregui, 1785. Author's copy.

altar to her in their great convent church. By 1785, a *congregación* – a larger, more important sodality – was constituted along the same lines as the Spanish confraternity in order to "assure its perpetuity" and mobilize collection of donations to rebuild the recently damaged Spanish shrine.[59] Sermons in honor of the Virgin of Covadonga, usually delivered by Dominican friars, were published in Mexico City in 1736, 1748, 1758, 1774, 1805, 1807, 1808, 1809, and 1816.

Our Lady of Covadonga had long been a symbol of the early Reconquista as well as Asturian patriotism – her alternate name was Nuestra Señora de las Batallas, commemorating what was believed to be the first military victory of Christians against Muslim forces at Covadonga around 722. Hidden in a cave, the statue of Mary aided the legendary Christian king, Pelayo, in the battle. As one international war involving Spain followed another in the eighteenth century, devotion to Our Lady of Covadonga in Mexico City came to have a strong martial character. The early years of the documented Mexican devotion coincided with the War of the Austrian Succession in the 1740s, and by 1792, during Spain's European wars in the wake of the French Revolution, the congregación was conducting an annual celebration of Our Lady of Covadonga as "Patroness and Restorer of Spanish Liberty," with members of the company of Grenadiers of the Royal Infantry Regiment in Mexico City among the leading participants. In this context, this new title seems to have stuck, for in the feast day sermon of 1806 referred to her again as "The Spaniards' renowned liberator." But despite the appeal to peninsular nationalism, the devotees still seem to have been mainly Asturians. The 192 sponsors of the publication of this sermon were all male Asturians living in Mexico City, nine of them priests. Nevertheless, some copies of the statue of Our Lady of Covadonga may well have found their way to other places and gained local followings unrelated to Spanish patriotism and providential military exploits. For example, near the turn of the nineteenth century, Don Juan Cosio Argüeyes gave his statue of the Covadonga Virgin to the community of Tenancingo, where he resided. When he went out with the statue in 1805 to collect alms in the neighboring parish of Ocuilan, the pastor there seized the statue and chased Argüeyes out of town as an interloper.[60]

Of the dozen or so Spanish image devotions with a public presence in New Spain during the late colonial period,[61] none had a more unusual trajectory than Nuestra Señora de la Cueva Santa (see Figure 4.9). Promoted by Franciscan missionary preachers, this advocation was the least connected to peninsular regional or martial patriotism, and it proved compatible with the kind of traditional spirituality centered on private devotions and individual salvation favored by ecclesiastical reformers in the eighteenth century. Unlike other Spanish devotions, the Cueva Santa was popular in the provincial city of Querétaro as well as in the viceregal capital. This favorite advocation in the province of Valencia originated in the mountains of Castellón near the beginning of the sixteenth century when a young shepherd reportedly discovered the image in a cave. Spring water from the site became renowned for its healing properties, and by the end of the sixteenth century the shrine and image were acclaimed for cures and seasonable rainfall and a good harvest. The image comes into view in the written record for New Spain late, in 1741, with a published novena

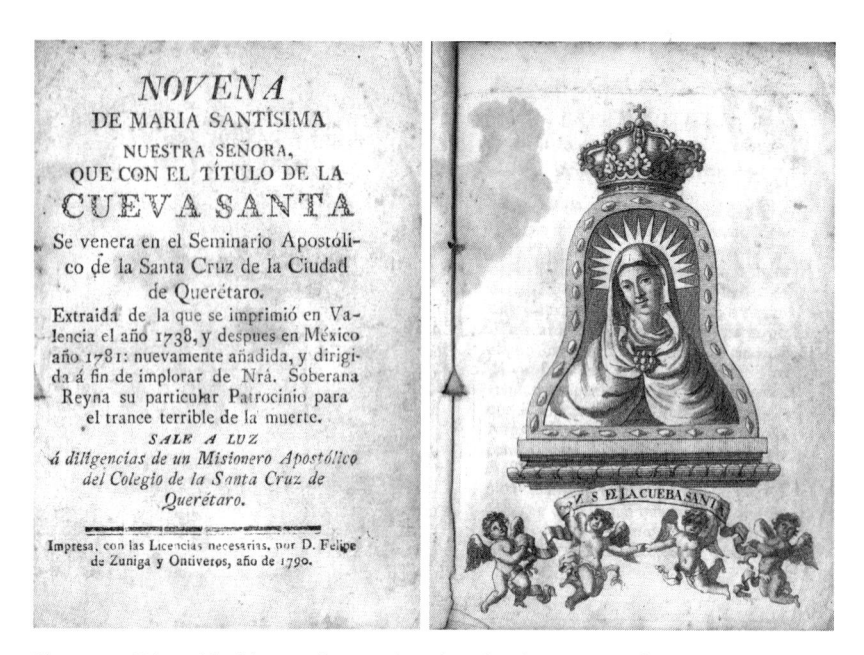

Figure 4.9 Print with title page from unsigned, undated engraving of Nuestra Señora de la Cueva Santa published in *Novena de María Santísima Nuestra Señora, que con el titulo de la Cueva Santa* ..., Mexico: Zúñiga y Ontiveros, 1790. Courtesy of the Kislar Center for Special Collections, University of Pennsylvania.

booklet sponsored by a Conceptionist nun in Mexico City. Thereafter, it was promoted vigorously in print as escort on the journey to a "good death," because this "Most Merciful Mother of Sinners and Universal Remedy for Spiritual and Physical Ills ... is our chosen protector to guide us in the terrible act of dying," coaxing a full and cleansing confession of sins from her devotees.[62] At least fourteen more novena booklets to her were printed or reprinted in a steady stream between 1749 and 1820 (eight of them from 1790 to 1820) as introductions to the devotion and guides to spiritual exercises for the individual believer in the last days of life.[63] Some of these devotional booklets were commissioned in Querétaro by the Franciscan Missionary College of the Holy Cross, which remained a center of devotion to Our Lady of the Cueva Santa through the end of the colonial period. Interest in the devotion in Mexico City accompanied the arrival of Camillian Missionaries of the Good Death in 1755. Founded in 1586 by Camillus de Lellis whose canonization in 1746 drew new attention to this strict and demanding order, the Camillians ministered to the sick and poor, focusing on spiritual preparations for death. Not surprisingly, their hospital in the capital became a center of devotion to the Virgin of the

Cueva Santa even though it seems not to have been actively promoted by viceregal authorities.[64]

The exception to this growing interest in and promotion of the great Spanish miracle images of Mary toward the end of the colonial period is Extremadura's Virgin of Guadalupe, which may have been the most prominent of all during the first years of Spanish colonization. Hernán Cortés was a devotee, and it is sometimes suggested that the original image revered in the shrine of the Virgin of Guadalupe at Tepeyac was a replica of the Extremaduran statuette of the Madonna and Child. There is some evidence that devotees of the Extremaduran Guadalupe wished to promote the image in New Spain and took a proprietary interest in the shrine at Tepeyac: Fr. Diego de Santa María, procurator of the monastery of Nuestra Señora de Guadalupe in San Juan, Puerto Rico, was dispatched to Mexico City in 1574 to look after the interests of the mother shrine in New Spain[65] and was followed by fellow Jeronymite Diego de Ocaña, indefatigable alms collector, painter, and promoter of the Extremaduran image and shrine in South America who went to Mexico City and pressed authorities there to further the devotion. That the Spanish Guadalupe was out of favor after 1754 when the Vatican officially recognized the apparitions of the Mexican Guadalupe in 1531 is understandable, but the near silence after Ocaña's time is puzzling. Perhaps the seventeenth-century developments outlined in Chapter 3 indicate that *capitalinos* had embraced the Guadalupe of Tepeyac story at the expense of the Spanish devotion. Surely, some later peninsular viceroys, oidores, and archbishops would have known the Extremaduran Guadalupe and perhaps been devotees, but they seem not to have made a public point of it.

The Christ of Burgos, the only celebrated Spanish crucifix with a substantial, following in New Spain,[66] traced the familiar pattern of development of Spanish Marian devotions: it was sited in a few cities of New Spain and came to notice mainly in the eighteenth century. In this case, Augustinians and "montañeses" (immigrants from the Santander region of northern Spain, also known as Cantabria, including the city of Burgos) were the principal sponsors and devotees of this late medieval articulated figure of the crucified Christ, revered in the Augustinian church of Burgos and in several other Spanish cities by the late sixteenth century.[67] Mexico City, again, seems to have been the main site of the devotion in New Spain.[68] Perhaps the earliest reference to a Mexican cult of the Christ of Burgos was an altar with a painting of this crucifix under construction in 1700 in the Augustinians' convent church in Mexico City.[69] The Franciscans also had a chapel and sponsoring confraternity for the Christ of Burgos in their main convent church there by 1780.[70] Other devotions to the Christ of Burgos were reported on the southern fringes of the Valley of Mexico: in the Augustinian church of San Juan Bautista Culhuacan in

1797, with its own principal confraternity (*archicofradía*), and in the Carmelite church of San Ángel with its monumental painting of the Christ of Burgos, Saint Theresa of Ávila, and Saint Thomas Aquinas, completed by Miguel Cabrera in 1764.[71] The city of Guanajuato boasted an altar to the Christ of Burgos in its Templo de San Diego, dating from the reign of Charles III (1759–1788), and there was a late colonial chapel to the Christ of Burgos in nearby León.[72] Most Mexican images of the Christ of Burgos were painted rather than sculpted, but the Christ of Burgos in the city of Puebla was an outstanding exception. Sponsored again by local Augustinians, a "sumptuous altarpiece" in their church was dedicated to this sculpted image of the crucifixion in 1737.[73] This particular figure was famous in the mid-eighteenth century for showing signs of life – the Christ's beard and hair were said to grow.[74]

New and Growing Evangelical Devotions in the Late Colonial Period

Four other Marian advocations introduced from Europe are notable for their development in New Spain during the eighteenth century. Miracles were associated with particular depictions of them, but the Virgin Mary was present in the advocation generally more than through one or a few images that were regarded as perenially numinous.[75] All four advocations were adopted by at least one of the religious orders in their revival missions (five if Nuestra Señora de la Cueva Santa is included here). Three – Nuestra Señora de la Luz, the Divina Pastora, and Nuestra Señora del Refugio – were new devotions in the eighteenth century. The fourth, Nuestra Señora de Loreto, was introduced into New Spain in the early seventeenth century and rose to prominence after the 1670s.

Our Lady of Loreto

One of the many image devotions that came into their own in Mexico during the late seventeenth century and remained popular into the nineteenth century was Our Lady of Loreto. Like Our Lady of the Rosary, Mary Immaculate, and Our Lady of Sorrows, Loreto was already well established as a Marian advocation in Europe before Spanish colonization in America. The statue of a small, dark Madonna and Child enveloped in a conical robe, Our Lady of Loreto is associated with one of the most famous relics in the Christian tradition: devotees believed that the Virgin's original home in Nazareth had been miraculously transported to a safe haven in the 1290s, first to a site in Croatia, then to Loreto, near the Italian seaport of Ancona on the Adriatic. By the fifteenth century, if not before, the house and statue were famous devotional objects. In 1469, an imposing church built over the

Holy House was completed and in 1510 Loreto received formal papal recognition as a pilgrimage site. Members of the Society of Jesus became particular devotees and propagators of this advocation of the Virgin Mary, and in 1554 they were assigned pastoral care of the shrine. By 1577, a leading Jesuit, Peter Canisius, would describe Loreto as the most important pilgrimage site of the time.[76]

The Virgin of Loreto had a shorter, later history in New Spain than the Immaculate Conception or Mater Dolorosa advocations. The image and devotion were introduced and promoted chiefly by Jesuits, who were not present until 1572.[77] It is not clear when the Loreto devotion was introduced, but there is some evidence that it was present during the 1610s. A confraternity was established in the Jesuits' Casa Profesa in Mexico City by 1615, five years after this church and novices' residence were established; around 1634 there was an altar to the Virgin of Loreto in the church of the Jesuit Colegio de Espíritu Santo in Puebla; and a hospital dedicated to her was under construction in the port city of Veracruz in 1632.[78] Most of the evidence of growing devotion to Our Lady of Loreto comes after 1670, suggesting both growing interest and more concerted promotion of public devotion then. According to Francisco de Florencia – the Florida-born Jesuit Marianist author and publicist who visited the Loreto shrine in Italy and published a history of the devotion in the late 1680s – seven chapels and altars dedicated to Our Lady of Loreto and five replicas of the Holy House were spread across western, central, and southern Mexico, mostly in Jesuit establishments.[79] Five of these twelve centers were located in or near Mexico City. Presumably all of them displayed replicas of the statue of the Madonna and Child from the shrine in Italy. Replicas of the Holy House were in the churches of the Jesuit Colleges of San Gregorio in Mexico City and Tepotzotlán on the northeast fringe of the Valley of Mexico, both apparently dedicated in 1680;[80] in the Jesuit college in Mérida, Yucatán; in the city of Puebla next to the parish church of San José; and in the town of San Agustín de las Cuevas administered by Dominicans on the edge of the Valley of Mexico south of the city.[81] Altars and chapels to the Virgin of Loreto had been erected by then in the cathedral in Guatemala, in the Jesuit Casa Profesa and Colegio de San Pedro y San Pablo in Mexico City, in the Jesuit Colegio del Espíritu Santo in Puebla, in the Dominican convent church in Puebla, in the Jesuit church of Pátzcuaro, Michoacán, and in the convent church of the Conceptionist nuns of La Encarnación in Mexico City. Florencia wrote that the chapels in Pátzcuaro and the Casa Profesa in Mexico City had the added distinction of displaying a star from the ceiling of the original Holy House in Italy and that the replica in the Colegio de San Gregorio had become one of the most popular shrines in Mexico City.[82]

If we can trust the pious histories of the time, especially the *Vida y virtudes del V.P. Juan Bautista Zappa de la Compañía de Jesús* by Miguel Venegas, SJ,[83] two young Italian Jesuit missionaries, Juan Bautista Zappa (1651–1694) and Juan María Salvatierra (1648–1717), spurred the growing devotion in Mexico City and elsewhere, especially in towns and Jesuit missions of northern New Spain, after they arrived in 1675.[84] Zappa brought with him the exact dimensions of the Santa Casa to reproduce in the New World and commissioned a Jesuit companion from Italy to bring a copy of the Virgin's head and the Christ Child that had touched the original statue[85] (see Figure 4.10).

Whether sculpted or painted, images of Our Lady of Loreto varied little in appearance. Occasionally, she was shown with her Holy House, but her basic form was fixed by the tradition that the original image at the Holy House in Loreto had been made by St. Luke under divine guidance. It would have been unseemly if not sacrilegious to alter such perfection. Here was the kindly Mary Queen of Heaven and mediatrix, with flowing hair under a distinctive imperial crown, presenting her infant son-king who holds the world globe in one hand and raises the other hand in a gesture of blessing. Mary is planted in a stationary pose, and both figures are enveloped in a triangular garment that falls in straight, vertical folds. Her hands and body are hidden from view.

As with the advocations of the Virgin of the Rosary and Our Lady of Sorrows, no one Loretan image or site became the main shrine, the center from which the devotion spread and to which all devotees naturally turned; and while the Jesuits were identified with this advocation, they were also involved with many other Marian shrines, images, and advocations. Their association with Loreto was not foundational to the order, like those of the Mercedarians with Our Lady of La Merced, the Carmelites with Our Lady of El Carmen, or even the Dominicans with Our Lady of the Rosary. And the Jesuits were not alone as propagators of Loretan devotion. Dominicans and diocesan priests were among the seventeenth-century devotees and advocates, and the cathedral of Mexico and a Dominican church in Puebla were among the early sites of popular devotion. Especially in Mexico City, the Colegio de San Gregorio's image of Loreto – the image Zappa ordered from Italy – became a protective mother for *capitalinos* at large before 1767, carried in processions of supplication to the cathedral for novenas at the onset of epidemics in 1727 and 1737.[86] The image of Loreto in the city of Puebla also continued to appeal to a wide audience, if we can believe Dominican sermonizer Fr. Juan Villa Sánchez in 1746 that the Virgin of Loreto was among "the five most celebrated images" there.[87] Healing miracles and safe births associated with images of Loreto were reported,[88] and confraternities, shrines, and chapels were established in provincial towns

Figure 4.10 Print from a mid-eighteenth-century engraving by Baltasar Troncoso of Juan Bautista Zappa, SJ holding a replica of the statuette of Our Lady of Loreto, published in Miguel Venegas, *Vida y virtudes del V.P. Juan Bautista Zappa*, Barcelona: Pablo Nadal, 1754. Courtesy of The John Carter Brown Library.

including Omitlan (Hidalgo), Españita in the parish of Hueyotlipa (Tlaxcala), and San Miguel El Grande (Guanajuato).[89] Although the devotion was growing, the fact that few confraternities dedicated to Loreto were listed in parishes of the Archdiocese of Mexico in pastoral visit records for the 1680s, 1717, the 1750s, 1766–1768, and 1774 suggests that it was not one of the most widely popular devotions. Still,

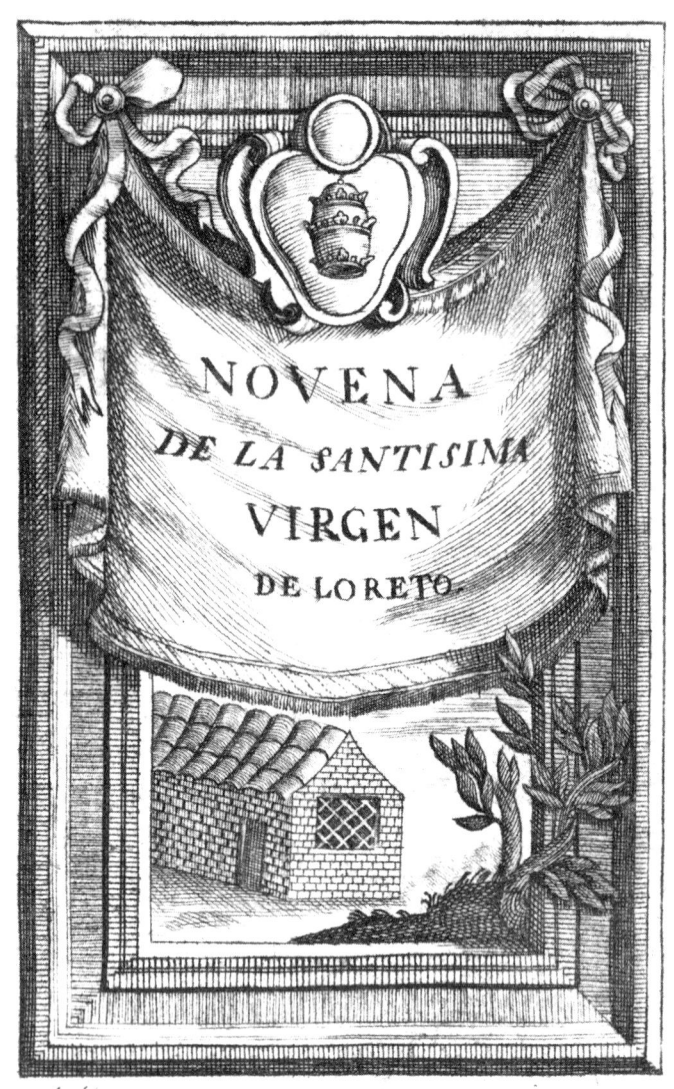

Figure 4.11 Print depicting the Santa Casa de Loreto from an engraving by "Agüera," published in Juan Croiset, SJ, *Novena a la Virgen Santísima de Loreto* ..., printed in Valencia, Spain in 1805, based on a Mexican edition by María Fernández de Jáuregui, 1805. Courtesy of the Lilly Library, Indiana University.

after the Jesuit expulsion devotion to Our Lady of Loreto continued in the places where it had already gained a following, promoted by other orders and lay groups, with regular novena observances in Mexico City documented in a string of novena booklets and devotional guides (one prepared by a Franciscan) that were published in the late eighteenth century.[90]

The enduring strength of popular devotion to Our Lady of Loreto in Mexico City beyond Jesuit orchestration is suggested by the travels and travail of the Colegio de San Gregorio's statue after the Jesuits were expelled in 1767. The college's church was soon shuttered and some of its portable treasures provisionally dispersed for use elsewhere, including Father Zappa's celebrated statue. It went to the convent church of the Conceptionist nuns of La Encarnación, also in Mexico City, who displayed it on an altar that was already dedicated to the Virgin of Loreto. The transfer of the image to the Conceptionists was provisional, and authorities sent other mixed signals about religious activities at San Gregorio. By royal cedula in 1770, a group of chaplains versed in native languages were to continue preaching and confessing there, attend to "the little seminary," and "look after the cult of Our Lady of Loreto." In 1772, Indians from the neighborhood of the college, having enlisted the support of the governors of the two great Indian districts of the city, San Juan and Santiago, and Indian officials from other nearby communities, petitioned for the return of the image and its temporary placement in the Church of Corpus Christi attached to the convent and Colegio de Nuestra Señora de Guadalupe for Indian noble girls and women. Viceroy Bucareli denied their request on July 22, 1773, leaving the statue with the Conceptionist nuns for the time being. But he recognized the ardent devotion of the Indian neighbors, which was evident not only in their petition, but in the Virgin's fine jewels and clothing, the silver throne, silver votive offerings, gold chalices, and "many depictions of miracles, crutches, and other signs of favor and thanks that adorn the chapel walls" of the old shrine, which "was visited on a daily basis by aristocratic families as well as the plebe."[91] Acknowledging the "profound sadness" caused by the image's absence, he ordered the nuns not to restrict the Indians' access to the image in their customary ways, including kissing the altar and placing candles next to it. He warned the nuns that they could not claim ownership of the image by right of possession or any other legal reasoning, since sacred images in principle belonged to the king by way of the Real Patronato. Indian officials continued to petition for its return, and they pressed viceregal officials during the 1770s and early 1780s to reestablish a *colegio seminario* for Indians at San Gregorio.[92] A 1791 application for the woman who led devotion to "la portentosa ymagen de Nuestra Señora de Loreto del Colegio Seminario de San Gregorio" to collect alms in support of the cult suggests either that the image had been returned to the San Gregorio church by then or, more likely, that the Indian devotees had organized their own devotions in the Encarnación church.[93] By 1805 the funds to build a new church in the San Gregorio neighborhood dedicated to Loreto had been collected, mostly with 25,000 pesos from the estate of Don Juan de Castañiza (who was also a major benefactor of the shrine of the Virgin of Guadalupe at Tepeyac), administered by his son-in-law, the Conde de Bassocco, and 9,000 pesos from Don Francisco Beña, an hacendado in Querétaro.[94] Construction began the next year and was completed in 1819, with Father Zappa's statue of the Virgin of Loreto back in place on the main altar.

La Divina Pastora

Devotion to the Divina Pastora (the Virgin as Good Shepherdess) in the port city of Veracruz goes back to Sevilla in 1703 with a painting depicting a recent vision of the Virgin as Shepherdess of Souls by the Capuchin missionary friar, Isidoro de Sevilla.[95] The image became popular in Andalucía during the eighteenth century, especially in the port of Cádiz, gateway to the Indies, and Fray Isidoro himself founded brotherhoods dedicated to the image in Sevilla and Cádiz.[96] The Divina Pastora was mainly a Spanish devotion, but it was carried to Venezuela in 1706 by Spanish Capuchin missionaries and took root especially in Barquisimeto and the Estado Lara, where she became the patron saint.[97] The port of Veracruz in 1744 apparently was the first site of the devotion in New Spain and was important enough by the early 1750s for Oviedo to include a paragraph about it in the *Zodíaco mariano* (1755).[98] How many prints and painted or sculpted copies circulated in New Spain during the eighteenth century is unknown. Several fine late eighteenth-century paintings of the Divina Pastora by leading Mexican artists Miguel Cabrera and José de Páez can be found in the Museo de América in Madrid, the Museo Nacional del Virreinato at Tepotzotlán, and the Los Angeles County Museum of Art (see Figure 4.12), but they may have been private commissions for wealthy peninsular or creole patrons and not displayed in public.[99] A sixteen-page prayer booklet dedicated to the Virgin Mary that contains verses to the Divina Pastora was republished at least fourteen times in Mexico City and Puebla between 1765 and 1819, suggesting some popular devotion and promotion beyond Veracruz.[100]

Thanks to the first Veracruz devotees' efforts to organize popular devotion and gain official approval, as it began to prosper, the inevitable disputes over who should manage the devotion and how during the first years are quite well documented in this case. Spontaneous devotion, rumor, high hopes, tetchy egos, clashes among leading devotees, interventions by public officials on both sides of the Atlantic, an emerging legend, and timely institutionalization are all there in the dossier compiled for the

Figure 4.12 Miguel Cabrera's painting of La Divina Pastora, ca. 1760. Oil on copper, tortoiseshell and bone frame. It is a bucolic scene in which sheep are eating roses under the watchful eye of the Virgin Shepherdess, with Leviathan lurking in the background, emblematic of the devil and sin. Courtesy of the Museum Associates/Los Angeles County Museum of Art.

Consejo de Indias in Sevilla between 1750 and 1753. The file contains thirteen "tiras" or separate records arranged in chronological order that document the formalities of licensing the devotion in 1744, depositions in 1747 by the makers of a celebrated statue of the Divina Pastora, a petition and witness testimony brought forward by one of the rival devotees in 1748, reports and certifications by the chaplain of the new shrine and the district *juez eclesiástico* in 1749 and 1752, instructions issued by the Consejo de Indias in 1750, a long summary report by the Governor of Veracruz, Don Diego de Peñaloza, in 1753, and the Consejo's final judgment later that year.[101] Governor Peñaloza ended his report in January 1753 with a ringing endorsement of the devotion, recommending that the construction be carried to completion as "a new diamond in the royal crown, ... destined to terrify the enemies of our Holy Faith, hammer of heresies." The cult would prosper again because the people of Veracruz looked on it as their own: "born in their own land, the leading citizens regard it as a special jewel, sent from heaven for their well-being; and because of its many miracles it is sought out and adored by outsiders who find it a comfort."

This celebrated statue has a documented history, no legendary beginning from the mists of time. Pasqual Campos, a young Indian from Campeche, had purchased a cheap print of the Divina Pastora from a stall in the plaza of Veracruz and started the devotion with the help of some other boys and his employer, Don Juan de Nava. Campos hired the sculptor and paid for the statue with alms he collected after the devotion centered on the print began to grow. He persuaded each of eight leading families – "algunas casas conocidas de esta ciudad" – to host the print of the Divina Pastora on a different holy day; a rosary procession would go out that night from the host family's house, and when the rosary ended, the print was welcomed into the home of another family. Before a confraternity was officially licensed in 1751, Campos organized an informal brotherhood with the permission of the parish priest. He was careful to notify leading churchmen of his plans and to seek their support.

In Oviedo's telling, however, the devotion amounted to a spontaneous children's crusade that was largely nameless and faceless. Nava and his son are mentioned, but not by name; and Pasqual Campos and his principal ally, Father Antonio Basilio Berdejo, are not mentioned at all. Whether or not Nava was his source, Oviedo either knew nothing about Campos and the record of the long-running dispute among Campos, Nava, and others over management of the devotion or found them unedifying.[102]

> A young boy was given a print of the Most Holy Virgin as Divine Shepherdess ... This innocent child had it framed and called upon other children about his age to join him. They sometimes took it out in processions, singing the rosary through the streets. Later he kept asking his father for a finer image and eventually they had a most beautiful sculptured image made, with which devotion to the Divine Shepherdess began to grow among the adults who began to participate often in the rosary procession. And in order to have a yet more appropriate devotion and veneration of this Holy Image, there is now a beautiful chapel under construction to house it.[103]

In his essay about Marian devotion and "dechristianization" in Spain during the eighteenth century, Joel Saigneux framed the Divina Pastora devotion in a way that invites comparison to the events in Veracruz.[104] Describing a dialectic that pitted church leaders imbued with a Christian Enlightenment against popular religiosity, Saugnieux highlighted efforts by regalist priests with Jansenist sympathies and their allies at court to "root out abuses, errors, and superstitions," particularly the cult of saints, including the Virgin Mary. But, in what Saugnieux called a "dechristianization," popular practices expressing lay hopes and fears in a time of crisis periodically swamped the Church hierarchy's attempts at supervision. This dialectic was unresolved in the eighteenth century, with little interaction between leaders and laity except for the work of some missionary preachers who encouraged, and to some extent facilitated, the lay movements. The new Spanish cult of the Divina Pastora promoted by discalced Franciscan friars (Capuchinos) was his prime example.[105]

Whether or not Saigneux was right about Spain, his sharp distinction between high and low religion mediated by the revivalist efforts of missionary friars does not altogether fit the story of the Divina Pastora in Veracruz. The devotion there reportedly did begin in a spontaneous way with popular enthusiasm for the Divina Pastora, but it would not have gotten far without the enduring interest and moral and political support of some local elites and various churchmen, from the bishop, to the parish priest and juez eclesiástico, to the chaplain of the devotion, to the Dominican prior who gave his consent for the Rosary processions, the Augustinians who temporarily hosted the image and Rosary procession, and the Franciscan devotees who celebrated the first miracle of healing for one of their own. Equally important to the success of the cult – and more surprising – was the timely support of Governor Peñaloza and the Consejo de Indias in 1753. Later intendants and councilors probably would not have been as receptive to a new devotion like this, but the beginnings of the Divina Pastora in Veracruz suggest that the modernizing aims, "Jansenist" sobriety, and anticlerical tendencies of subsequent Bourbon reformers did not simply translate into agnostic skepticism about divine intervention in the world or rigid restrictions on the cult of saints and public expressions of faith.

This case highlights contingencies and individual agencies that cast doubt on atemporal, categorical generalizations about how cults develop. The popular devotion among local people who were not peninsulares or missionary priests was impressive, but it was not self-sustaining. Judging by the decline in alms collections and the stalled building project in the late 1740s and early 1750s, popular ardor could wane. The creation of a fully licensed *cofradía* in 1750–1751 by prominent citizens, including priests,[106] helped to stabilize the devotion's finances, but the efforts of Campos and Berdejo and the good offices of other priests, including the juez eclesiástico of the city and the bishop, were crucial to its success. Whether or not

Campos was as important as he and his supporters led the governor and the Consejo de Indias to believe, he was the cult's original voice and public face. No one he dealt with, from the bishop, to the governor, to officials in Madrid, to the priests and leading laymen of the city (including his rivals) seems to have doubted his sincerity, selfless devotion, honesty, and integrity. And he was indefatigable; he was not the first *indio* to take ship to Spain seeking the king's favor in some urgent matter (usually family preferment, a land dispute, or a special public work[107]), but he was unusual in making the trip as a lone commoner, effectively without corporate backing. Campos did have the firm support and loyalty of Father Berdejo, which almost from the beginning provided Campos with added respectability and political sense. If we can believe Governor Peñaloza's report and Berdejo's testimony, Campos and Berdejo were admired for rising above the unedifying opportunism of others who, for a time, were also prominent in the development of the cult.

The support of more exalted figures, such as the juez eclesiástico, the bishop, and Governor Peñaloza, is treated matter-of-factly in the record, but in retrospect their participation was not inevitable either. Domingo Pantaleón Álvarez de Abreu, who served as Bishop of Tlaxcala (Puebla) throughout the early years of the cult's history in Veracruz (1743–1763), sympathized with efforts at spiritual revival and veneration of saints and images, including promotion of Nuestra Señora de Ocotlán, the Immaculate Conception, Puebla's famous nun, Sor María Anna Águeda de San Ignacio, and an especially fine, icon-like engraving of a sweet Madonna and Child (he granted forty days' indulgence to those who prayed a Salve Regina in its presence).[108] It is unlikely that his successor, Francisco Fabián y Fuero (1765–1773), the unbending regalist reformer and ally of Archbishop Lorenzana (1766–1771), would have looked so kindly on an exuberant new public devotion in his diocese. And Governor Peñaloza's fulsome support for the new devotion was unusual even in the 1750s; it would have been rare, indeed, for a Bourbon provincial governor thirty or forty years later to take the lead as he did.

Place was another important contingency. At first glance, Veracruz would seem an unlikely hotspot for a new devotion like this. Unlike the provincial cities of Puebla, Querétaro, Valladolid, or Guadalajara, Veracruz was not famous for the piety of its people or shrines to miraculous images; and, as New Spain's only important Atlantic port, it was the gateway for everything new from Europe, including, at this time, a more emphatic privatization of piety and Enlightenment skepticism about divine intervention and the cult of saints.[109] But skepticism was not yet in vogue in the 1740s, and decline of public faith arguably did not run deep in popular practice even in the nineteenth century. Perhaps more importantly, the city's very exposure to novelty might also have led Veracruz authorities to perceive public piety as a bulwark against social and religious peril. Strangers came and went through the port, and there was the nagging fear that such an open and vulnerable place was a haven of irreligion and in danger of being overrun by Spain's Protestant enemies. Stories circulated about people in the heart of the port city who lived beyond the reach of priests and Christian practice. A news item published in the *Gazeta de México* on November 13, 1792, recounted that a gravely ill man named Joseph Ortega confessed to a priest in the district of Igualapan, Oaxaca, that he had never been baptized. Ortega avowed "with serene simplicity that he did not know his age, where he was from, or who his parents were." He had been raised in Veracruz by "a negress who seemed to be a heathen, for she lacked both name and religion ... He never saw her cross herself, pray, attend Mass, confess, take communion or engage in any other Christian act." The sense of external danger would also have been keenly felt in Veracruz during the 1740s, as the War of Jenkins's Ear (1739–1748), folded into the European War of Austrian Succession (1740–1748), threatened Spanish American ports with attacks by English and Dutch privateers, and led to the sacking of Porto Belo and a massive assault on Cartagena, Colombia, in 1741.

Still, the sense of danger does not really explain the flowering of devotion to the Divina Pastora. Campos, Berdejo, and their fellow devotees could just as well have directed their faith and affection to one of the existing devotions to Our Lady of the Rosary in the city or breathed new life into the local shrines of Nuestra Señora de la Escalera or El Señor de la Antigua Veracruz or Our Lady of Loreto.[110] Even in this well-documented case, other than a boy's enthusiasm we have no way to know for sure why they chose the Divina Pastora, or why this particular devotion introduced from Spain in the eighteenth century apparently did not spread to other parts of Mexico except among elite families.

Nuestra Señora de la Luz

According to the tradition recounted in a long devotional text published in Italy in 1733 and republished in Mexico in Spanish translation in 1737 when devotion to the image of Nuestra Señora de la Luz/Our Lady of Light was spreading there, the original painting was made in Palermo, Sicily, around 1722 for an Italian Jesuit, Antonio Genovesi, in need of a new image of Mary that would rekindle the faith of indifferent Catholics.[111] He asked a nun known for her visionary gifts to seek direction from the Blessed Mary. The nun reported that Mary visited her, radiantly beautiful, just as she wanted to be represented, and gave detailed instructions for a tableau, including graphic depiction of a sinner being saved from falling into the gaping maw of a fire-breathing demonic monster.[112] On the second try, a painting was completed to the Blessed Mary's satisfaction and used by Father Genovesi in his itinerant, wonder-working mission. In 1732, the painting was brought to Mexico, where Jesuit houses and colleges vied for it. Lots were drawn and the honor went to the new hospice in the Villa de León, Guanajuato.[113] Before long, the devotion took off and copies were commissioned, first in Mexico City, where an altar was dedicated to this advocation of Mary in the church of Porta-Coeli that year.[114] In 1734, the Dominicans commissioned a large painted copy for their church in the capital, and highly ornamented altars dedicated to Nuestra Señora de la Luz were installed in several Jesuit churches and colleges there in 1735 and 1739.

The devotion spread mainly to places in central, western, and northern New Spain where Jesuits and Franciscans led spiritual revivals. In addition to the images in León and Mexico City, celebrated painted and sculpted copies and altars were placed in the Jesuit church of the city of Zacatecas in 1750; in several churches of Puebla by the 1750s; in the Franciscans' convent church in Pachuca, Hidalgo; in the Castrense Chapel of Santa Fe, New Mexico in 1761; and at Salvatierra, Guanajuato, in 1785.[115] Elsewhere confraternities were established in Our Lady of Light's honor, several university theses were dedicated to her in the 1740s and 1760s, and at least twenty-one publications and various prints were published in Mexico City and Puebla between 1732 and 1821, with a cluster in the 1760s. Then the presses were silent until 1790, after which at least seven more devotional publications appeared before 1821.[116] Missions and altars dedicated to Nuestra Señora de la Luz became a feature of Franciscan frontier evangelization in the eighteenth century, from Texas (1756) to the Sierra Gorda of Querétaro (1760s), Chihuahua, and Alta California (1770s). The Santa Fe and Salvatierra paintings were famously associated with great favors to devotees and souls in purgatory.

The standard representation of the image in New Spain from 1732 to the 1750s was faithful to the painting sent to the Villa de León. The Blessed Mary, with her left knee bent as if about to step out of the frame, holds the Christ Child in her left arm. He has taken two flaming hearts, representing penitential souls, from a basket brimming with other hearts, held up to him by a kneeling angel. Cherubs surround Mary, beneath her feet and above; two of them in a sunburst around her head hold up a starry golden crown. With her right hand, Mary grasps the arm of a soul in danger of falling into the fiery abyss of Leviathan's mouth. Most of the early paintings for churches were larger than life size, accentuating the drama of the scene. Nuestra Señora de la Luz is directly related to the longstanding devotional interest in souls trapped in purgatory, for which there were confraternities in many Mexican communities by the eighteenth century, but the name "Our Lady of *Light*" draws attention back to the Christ Child, who is also an

Advocations of the Virgin Mary in the Colonial Period 279

Figure 4.13 Print of Our Lady of Light from engraving by Tomás Suriá, 1790, in José Antonio Alcocer, *Carta apologética a favor del título de Madre Santísima de la Luz* ..., Mexico: Zúñiga y Ontiveros, 1790. The fire-breathing monster is back in the lower left corner, as it was before the late 1760s. Author's copy.

active figure in this scene. The usual explanation of the name was that light stood for Christ – "I am the light of the world."[117]

In the years just before the expulsion of the Jesuits from New Spain in 1767, a controversy arose over Our Lady of Light that altered the image for a while and accounts for the lull in publications and other promotional activity during the 1770s and 1780s. The objection to the image was that it seemed to suggest one could receive salvation directly from the Virgin and that naïve or disingenuous devotees might conclude that the Mother of God would pull devotees out of hell's fire no matter what their transgressions, rather than leading them toward a more virtuous life and thereby lessening the likelihood of eternal damnation. Evidently this was a serious controversy, and some paintings of the time omitted the fire-breathing Leviathan. At the Fourth Synod of Mexican prelates in 1771, the case against graphic depiction of hell in images of Our Lady of Light was discussed. The issue, as it was framed for the synod, was whether to "erase the dragon in order to avoid the error of thinking that the Most Holy Virgin rescued condemned sinners from Hell."[118] On the archbishop's strong recommendation, the synod agreed to prohibit new paintings of the image and to "secretly" blot out the "dragon" in existing works. Perhaps because the proposed decrees of the synod were never confirmed by the papacy,[119] Our Lady of Light in its original depiction would make a comeback, but the immediate effect was that many prints showing the fiery jaws of hell were destroyed and at least some paintings were removed from church walls or the Leviathan was painted out. In the painting of Our Lady of Light that still hangs in the former Jesuit church of La Profesa in Mexico City the Leviathan has been covered over with black paint.[120]

A rehabilitation of the image and devotion that began in the late 1780s responded to popular interest and Franciscan promotion, with Fray José Antonio Alcocer in the lead. In his treatise on Our Lady of Light published in 1790 with the approval of the viceroy and various church dignitaries, Alcocer defended the devotion and the original representation.[121] The Blessed Mary herself devised the original painting, he noted. For good measure, he argued that the image clearly shows the Virgin preventing the soul from falling into the inferno, not pulling him out. There was no doctrinal error in this at all, he concluded (see Figure 4.14). The iconography of the painting brought from Italy in 1732 had finally won the day, and most images made or displayed thereafter show the fire-breathing monster of hell in graphic detail.[122]

Nuestra Señora del Refugio de Pecadores

The advocation of Nuestra Señora del Refugio bears comparison to Nuestra Señora de la Cueva Santa and Nuestra Señora de la Luz in that it was

> DIA QUATRO
> DE CADA MES,
> EN OBSEQUIO, Y CULTO
> DE LA REYNA DE CIELO, Y TIERRA
> MARIA SANTISSIMA,
> EN SU ADMIRABLE TITULO
> DEL REFUGIO,
> Devocion muy util, y provechofa
> para los miferables pecadores.
> DISPUESTA
> *Por un Religiofo del Colegio de Pro-*
> *paganda Fide de nueftra Señora de*
> *Guadalupe de la Ciudad de Zacatecas.*
>
> Reimpreffo en Mexico, en la Imprenta de la Bibliotheca Mexicana del Lic. D. Jofeph de Jauregui, Calle de San Bernardo, Año de 1773.

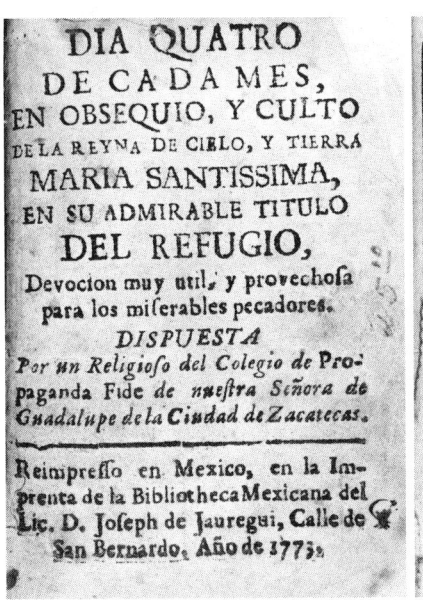

Figure 4.14 Title page and print from woodcut of Nuestra Señora del Refugio in a small devotional booklet produced for spiritual missions of the Franciscan Colegio de Propaganda Fide at Zacatecas, 1773 printing. Courtesy of the Lilly Library, Indiana University. This booklet was first printed in 1766, and reprinted in 1773, 1776, 1790, 1794, 1802, 1803, 1804, and 1820.

introduced to New Spain in the mid-eighteenth century and became a focal point for spiritual revival missions by visiting Jesuit and Franciscan preachers that were compatible with ecclesiastical reformers' emphasis on personal sin, contrition, and the Good Death. Like the Virgin of the Cueva Santa, Nuestra Señora del Refugio was the "mother of sinners" and refuge of troubled souls (*el consuelo de los afligidos*), anticipating the rigors of purgatory and passage beyond. Like Nuestra Señora de la Luz (but unlike Nuestra Señora de la Cueva Santa), Nuestra Señora del Refugio was not attached to a particular shrine or regional ethnicity in Spain; and her Italian origins centered on a painted image more than on a particular place.[123] This devotion is said to have had its beginnings in 1719 when Antonio Baldinucci, a Jesuit preacher in southern Italy commissioned a copy of a painting of the Madonna and Child known as Nuestra Señora de la Encina (from the town of Poggio Prato), which he carried with him in his preaching missions and called Nuestra Señora del Refugio de Pecadores. Baldinucci's painting became famous for touching the hearts of sinners and working marvelous cures, and by the 1740s Jesuit missionaries carried copies of it with them to their missions in other parts of the world.

The Virgin of El Refugio became unusually popular in the territory of modern Mexico, particularly in the west, north-center, and north, where many late eighteenth- and nineteenth-century paintings of her are still found in churches and private collections. It was less popular in the center and south, except for Mexico City and the city of Puebla. Most of the churches, altars, and settlements dedicated to the Refugio advocation are concentrated in Zacatecas, Aguascalientes, San Luis Potosí, Jalisco, Michoacán, Guanajuato, and the far north.[124]

Jesuits introduced this devotion in their frontier missions and spiritual revivals in towns and cities of the Bajío and farther north shortly before the order was expelled in 1767, but other pastors and preachers, especially Franciscan missionary preachers, became advocates, too. One Franciscan chronicler for the order's missionary college in Zacatecas (the Colegio de Propaganda Fide de Nuestra Señora de Guadalupe de la Ciudad de Zacatecas) told a providential story of a particular Jesuit image of Nuestra Señora del Refugio that became the patroness of the Franciscans' preaching missions in the north: in the early 1740s Juan José Giuca, an Italian Jesuit, brought a beautiful copy of the painting of Nuestra Señora del Refugio to the city of Puebla. There, in 1744, when he was praying before the image, the voice of the Holy Spirit instructed him to take it to the Franciscan missionary college in Zacatecas to aid in their evangelical missions.[125] By 1746, Zacatecas Franciscans gladly received the painting and adopted her as their patroness. Fr. José María Guadalupe Alcivia and other missionary preachers at the college rolled up the painting and took it with them on their missions, apparently with great success – with "innumerable conversions" and abundant alms collected.[126] Juan Antonio Oviedo offered a less providential and perhaps more reliable account from a Jesuit perspective in his additions to Florencia's *Zodíaco mariano* (1755), close in time to the explosive growth of the devotion as he described it. In his account, Father Baldinucci died in 1717, leaving behind a painting of the Virgin that had been his companion and guide in his successful preaching missions. The painting was ceremoniously crowned that year by Cardinal Albani in Baldinucci's hometown of Frascati, with the words Refugiam pecatorum inscribed below it; hence her new title, refuge of sinners, Nuestra Señora del Refugio de Pecadores. Father Giuca carried a print of the image to New Spain in 1719 and spread the devotion in his travels, especially in Puebla. New prints were made to meet the clamor of interest, and Cardinal Juan Baptista Salerno sent a beautiful painted copy of the original canvas to the Jesuit college at Tepotzotlán. In 1741, a humble devotee had a painted copy of this celebrated copy made and displayed it in his home on the outskirts of Puebla. People began to visit this image and leave votive offerings, crutches, and ex-voto paintings. A chapel dedicated to Nuestra Señora del Refugio was built in Puebla in 1746 to display the painting, and the devotion took off from there.[127] Yet another, larger chapel was built, more than sixty niches with images of Nuestra Señora del Refugio sprang up in the city, and, in Oviedo's estimation, nearly every house and hovel there had a painting or cheap print of the image. He judged that the devotion had spread throughout the Diocese of Puebla. In his telling, Father Alcivia of the Franciscan missionary college in Zacatecas visited Puebla and took a painted copy of the Refugio image back to Zacatecas. In a letter of May 25, 1746, Father Alcivia wrote that over the previous nine months when he took the image of Nuestra Señora del Refugio on his preaching tours the results had been amazing, attracting thousands of penitents and achieving "innumerable" conversions of sinners. Writing in 1788, José Antonio Alcocer, Franciscan chronicler of the apostolic college at Zacatecas (who figured so prominently as a defender of devotion to Nuestra Señora de la Luz in the 1790s), seemed to agree with Oviedo. He was more interested in the popularity of the Refugio devotion promoted by his fellow Franciscan missionaries than in a reputed providential intervention by the Holy Ghost. He was noncommittal about the story of Father Giuca carrying the image to Zacatecas under divine injunction: "I have heard here in the College about the strange way that Father Alcivia obtained this image, but since there is not a shred of evidence that it happened, I refrain from mentioning it."[128]

However, the image reached the Franciscan missionaries in Zacatecas, popular devotion spread rapidly from the time they adopted this representation of Mary, famed for touching the hearts and purses of sinners and facilitating miraculous cures.[129] From 1761 to 1803 nine novena booklets and other devotional materials for Refugio were printed in Mexico City, most of them either sponsored by the Franciscans in Zacatecas or for novenas in the Church of the Espíritu Santo in Mexico City, where a celebrated painting of the image of Nuestra Señora del Refugio was displayed on the altar dedicated to San Hipólito Mártir.[130] Alcocer described in 1788 the elaborate staging of the missionaries' arrival in town with the image of Refugio:

Notice is sent to the parish priest of the place, informing him of the day and hour of her arrival so that a procession that is long enough to pray part of a rosary can be organized. This procession centers on the most holy image of Nuestra Señora del Refugio, who, of course, steals the hearts of the inhabitants along the way. In the church, the Litany is sung or prayed and, after a brief exhortation by one of the missionaries, the crowd is dismissed with the announcement that lessons will be preached in the streets that evening shortly before the Angelus hour. Throughout the Mission, the image of Nuestra Señora del Refugio remains prominently displayed on the high altar of the main church. The commotion among the settlements of the area from just this entrance of the Most Holy Virgin is noteworthy. From that instant, sinning ceases among many of the people and they begin to fill themselves seriously with the important matter of salvation.[131]

Conclusion

The Marian advocations closely associated with their European roots that are discussed in this chapter traced somewhat different histories in New Spain, but not mainly because they had specialized uses in the way that particular saints were believed to respond to deafness or lightning strikes, or another kind of malady, danger, or want. On the contrary, the Virgin Mary in her many guises was the great mediatrix for all seasons and reasons. Representations of Mary Immaculate and the Mater Dolorosa were introduced from the beginning and became the most familiar advocations, shaping expectations about purity and compassion for many individual shrine images of Mary. Others, including Nuestra Señora del Refugio, Nuestra Señora de la Luz, and La Divina Pastora, arrived later, in the eighteenth century, in ways that accentuated Mary's role in spiritual revival movements introduced from Europe. Sometimes European-made images were individualized as great wonder workers and became known by a local name among their New World devotees, such as Nuestra Señora de Tecaxic or Nuestra Señora de Guanajuato. Other images of Mary retained their European identities and appealed mainly to immigrants from their region of origin in Spain (such as Nuestra Señora de Aranzazú) or to a broader peninsular patriotism (such as Nuestra Señora del Pilar de Zaragoza); or, like Nuestra Señora de Covadonga, they attracted mainly local and late interest in New Spain. Nuestra Señora de la Cueva Santa was different again. Thanks to Franciscan missionary preachers from Querétaro's Colegio de Propaganda Fide, she reached an audience in central and north central Mexico beyond New World immigrants from her home region in the mountains of northern Valencia. Most of these images and advocations initially were promoted by a religious order and remained closely identified with that order, usually Franciscans or Jesuits. Our Lady of Loreto, coming from a particular shrine in Italy, associated with an even more famous icon, the Holy House of Loreto, and promoted first by Jesuits, would seem to be a good example, but Our Lady of Loreto and the Holy House transcended these particular associations and were adopted and transmitted more widely both before and after the expulsion of the Jesuits.

Despite these differences, three similarities among most of these Marian advocations distinguish them from many of New Spain's regional Marian shrines presented in earlier chapters. First, most of the Marian centers of devotion with European connections, at least in their origin stories, were located in a few cities. Mexico City was the site for most of them, sometimes the only important one. Even with Nuestra Señora de Loreto, which was more widely known, depicted, and venerated than most, about half of the centers of devotion were located in or near the capital city. Other devotions of this kind connected Mexico City to a second provincial city and sometimes a third – Puebla for Nuestra Señora de Loreto; Puebla and Zacatecas for Nuestra Señora del Refugio; León and Guanajuato for Nuestra Señora de la Luz; Querétaro for Nuestra Señora de la Cueva Santa; and Guadalajara for Nuestra Señora de Aranzazú.

Second, while the promotional side of the history of these advocations and images with strong European associations in the eighteenth century stands out in the written record and may, in fact, be the main story of their development, the Jesuits' Nuestra Señora de la Luz clearly struck a chord in communities of central Mexico and the Bajío, where devotees were drawn to the dramatic juxtaposition of danger and redemption in María de la Luz's sweet visage hovering above the firebreathing Leviathan poised to swallow lost souls. They would dedicate altars to her, name their daughters after her, and, with the Franciscan promoters after 1767, insist on the monster. And the Divina Pastora was an even more grassroots, self-generating devotion. This popular eighteenth-century Spanish advocation was not actively promoted at the beginning by any of the religious orders in New Spain, as it had been by Capuchin Franciscans in Venezuela early in the eighteenth century.[132] Instead, devotion to the Divina Pastora seems to have begun as a more spontaneous local development, mainly in and near the port city of Veracruz, eventually attracting some interest from Jesuits and diocesan officials. The image was originally Spanish, but it was not so perceived by its early plebeian devotees.

The most striking pattern in this colonial history of these Marian advocations is the timing of their newfound fame. Most of the recorded activity and formative development – construction of altars and temples, development of confraternities, and publications – happened in the eighteenth century, especially after the 1740s. This seems paradoxical at first glance. More Spaniards came to America during the seventeenth century than later (or than earlier, for that matter), and the late eighteenth century has been regarded as a time of decline for traditional devotional practices, including most shrines and image devotions, under the pressure of Bourbon modernizers and clerical reformers emphasizing a less adorned, more private, contemplative piety. But here, again, the eighteenth century appears to have been a time of consolidation, if not expansion, more than decline or retrenchment for shrines and enchantment. The new prominence of Spanish devotional images was situational in a particular way. Although there were fewer peninsular immigrants in the eighteenth century, many of them had less interest in becoming American and were better positioned as merchants, elite bureaucrats, high clergy, and concessionaires to make their fortune in New Spain and express their personal piety in good works and devotions that were dearest to them, which often meant a favorite Marian image and shrine from their peninsular homeland. Perhaps also because of the international wars into which Spain was drawn in the eighteenth century, these immigrants were more self-consciously patriotic in provincial and proto-national Spanish ways. But even more important to the development of some of these devotions (especially the new ones – Nuestra Señora de la Cueva Santa, Nuestra Señora de la Luz, and Nuestra Señora del Refugio), their immigrant and institutional promoters among the Jesuits and Franciscans had their own "new style" of piety that turned to these Marian images and advocations as aids in the spiritual revival missions they undertook to open the hearts of sinners and advance the campaign for a good death and personal salvation.

Notes

1. Not discussed here are other well-known advocations of the Blessed Mary – Our Lady of Carmen, Our Lady of Mercy, Our Lady of the Assumption (Nuestra Señora de la Asunción, of which Our Lady of Santa María la Redonda and Our Lady of Tzocuilac were celebrated examples that became shrine images in their own right), Our Lady of Purification (Nuestra Señora de la Candelaria, the Blessed Mary at the presentation of the Christ Child in the temple), Our Lady of the Anunciation (Nuestra Señora de la Anunciación, often conflated with Mary Immaculate although the iconography of the famous statue of the Anunciation in Sevilla is somewhat different, with Mary looking down at a book held in her hands), Our Lady of Expectation (Nuestra Señora de la Expectación, the Blessed Mary as expectant mother), and Our Lady of Succor (Nuestra Señora del Socorro, depicted as a Madonna and Child, often conflated with Nuestra Señora de los Remedios and Nuestra Señora del Patrocinio, all of which were popular devotions in early modern Spain). A few others, such as Nuestra Señora del Tránsito, were regarded as variations on a universal devotion, in this case the Mater Dolorosa. All of these advocations were known in New Spain, especially in paintings and statues displayed in some of the larger churches and homes of the aristocracy, and a few became cult images in their own right, especially of Nuestra Señora de la Candelaria and Nuestra Señora de los Remedios.
2. Other examples of local shrine images of Mary Immaculate remembered by this advocation: Nuestra Señora de la Purísima Concepción de Capuchinas (Mexico City), the celebrated image in the chapel of the Congregación de la Purísima of the Jesuits' Colegio Máximo (Mexico City), and the Purísima Concepción of Cuauhtitlán (Estado de México), Mazatán (Chiapas), and Monterrey (Nuevo León). For a late seventeenth-century example of the Virgin of Guadalupe identified as La Purísima, there is the will of Francisco de Fuentes, parish priest of Yahualica, who invoked the Virgin of Guadalupe as his special advocate: "... por mi abogada a la puríssima Virgen de Guadalupe Señora nuestra concebida sin la culpa original desde el primer ynstante de su ser," AGN Templos y Conventos 95 exp. 3, 1692.

3. Our Lady of Mercy was closely associated with the Mercedarians, and Our Lady of Carmen with the Carmelites. Neither was as widely adopted beyond the order as the four advocations discussed in this chapter. On the enthusiasm of diocesan clergy for Our Lady of the Rosary in the sixteenth and seventeenth centuries, see Nathan D. Mitchell, *The Mystery of the Rosary: Marian Devotion and the Reinvention of Catholicism*, New York and London: New York University Press, 2009.
4. Elizabeth Wilder Weismann, *Mexico in Sculpture, 1521–1821*, Cambridge, MA: Harvard University Press, 1950, pp. 154–155.
5. *Gazeta de México*, January 1735, BIBM 4, p. 559.
6. For example, in the will of Francisco de Fuentes, pastor of Yahualica, in 1692, AGN Templos y Conventos 95 exp. 2.
7. Miri Rubin, *Mother of God: A History of the Virgin Mary*, New Haven: Yale University Press, 2009, p. 380.
8. José Toribio Medina, *La imprenta en México*, edición facsimilar, Mexico: UNAM, 1989, IV, 192–193.
9. Francisco Pacheco's *Arte de la pintura* (apparently written in the 1630s and first published in 1649) set out in some detail how Mary Immaculate should be represented: "she was in the guise of the mysterious Woman of the Apocalypse, clothed with the sun, crowned with stars and with a crescent moon at her feet as described in the *Book of Revelation*," Alfonso Rodríguez G. de Ceballos, "The Art of Devotion: Seventeenth-Century Spanish Painting and Sculpture in Its Religious Context," in *The Sacred Made Real: Spanish Painting and Sculpture, 1600–1700*, ed. Xavier Bray, London: National Gallery, 2009, p. 53.
10. Jaime Cuadriello probes the theology and "codification" of iconography of Mary Immaculate during the seventeenth century in "The Theopolitical Visualization of the Virgin of the Immaculate Conception: Intentionality and Socialization of Images," in *Sacred Spain: Art and Belief in the Spanish World*, ed. Ronda Kasl, New Haven: Yale University Press, 2009, pp. 121–145.
11. Andrés de Arce y Miranda, *Sermones varios del doctor d. Andrés de Arce y Miranda*, tomo segundo, Mexico: Bibliotheca Mexicana, 1755, pp. 20, 22.
12. By the early seventeenth century, the Franciscans again were key promoters of lay organizations devoted to the Immaculate Conception, establishing branches of the Third Order of St. Francis to sponsor the feast and the devotion. For early records of the Third Order organization founded in the Franciscans' Convento Grande in Mexico City in 1615, see Bancroft MSS 87/156m. This was a large sodality-like organization that had both male and female members and officeholders.
13. Mirella Levi D'Ancona, *The Iconography of the Immaculate Conception in the Middle Ages and Early Renaissance*, New York: College Art Association of America, 1957, p. 72 (fig. 52). Echave Ibía's painting depicts Mary in the guise of the haloed woman of the Apocalypse in Revelation 12 encircled by the sun and moon (Christ and Mary), the dove of the Holy Ghost, the spotless mirror (symbol of Mary's purity), Jacob's ladder to heaven, the gates of heaven, the white lily (Mary's purity), the white, thornless rose that grows in paradise, the fountain of living water (Christ), David's tower (symbol of an impregnable fortress), the morning star (as lighting the way for Christ the sun of justice), and the cedar and palm of Psalm 92 ("They flourish in the courts of our God ... They will remain vital and green. They will declare, 'The Lord is just! He is my rock!'"). The siren

Echave painted below Mary, rather than the dragon or angels, would have been outside the usual symbolism, although not unknown elsewhere.

Levi D'Ancona was mainly interested in describing the array of symbolic associations for Mary Immaculate in European art before 1500, many of them drawn from the Litany of the Virgin and the Votive Office of the Conception. They ranged from Jacob's ladder, to the fountain of living water, the olive tree, the fig tree, the palm tree, the cedar tree, the tree of Jesse, Noah's ark, the ark of the Covenant, the unicorn, the dragon as Lucifer, the pelican, the bear, Moses and the burning bush, Gideon and his fleece, Aaron and his rod, the tower of David, the holy city, the enclosed garden, Ezquiel pointing to the closed gate, the spotless mirror, the sun, the crescent moon, the twelve stars, the morning star, the white lily, the white and thornless rose, and more.

14. These symbols of the Immaculate Conception were presented to the public in various settings. See, for example, Chimalpahin's description in Nahuatl of a Good Friday procession in 1613, as translated by James Lockhart, Susan Schroeder, and Doris Namala:

the sign and the announcement of [God's] purely taking on the form of flesh and being born, called the Immaculate Conception, to which belong the sun, the moon, and the great star that comes out close to dawn, when the gate of our lord God's temple is closing, as a ladder to heaven; the palm tree, the olive tree, the cypress; the mirror; the Spanish flower from a broad-leafed water plant, the lily; the rose; the enclosure for a field of green plants, a garden entirely enclosed; a spring or fountain, fully enclosed; they brought out all this and other things that speak symbolically of the royal maiden of the Conception.

Don Domingo de San Antón Muñón Chimalpahin Quauhtlehuanitzin, *Annals of His Time*, ed. and trans. James Lockhart, Susan Schroeder, and Doris Namala, Stanford: Stanford University, 2006, p. 247.

15. Quoted in Francisco de Icaza Dufour, *El altar de Dolores. Una tradición mexicana*, Mexico: Miguel Ángel Porrúa, 1998, p. 66, from Mota Padilla's *Historia de la conquista del Reino de la Nueva Galicia en la América Septentrional* (1742; first published in 1748), Guadalajara: Universidad de Guadalajara, 1973, p. 409.

16. All three appellations stood for the sorrowing Blessed Mary. Sometimes "Dolores" and "Soledad" were used in the same breath, as Puebla's Bishop Fabián y Fuero did in a decree of March 23, 1766, regulating Semana Santa processions with figures of Nuestra Señora de la Soledad in which he affirmed his allegiance to "el Mysterio amoroso de los Dolores de la Virgen." Representations of Dolores and Soledad are sometimes difficult to distinguish and mix the attire that usually distinguishes them from each other.

17. Personal prayers and petitions are the least institutionalized expression and the least likely to be recorded in writing, but when they were recorded, the Mater Dolorosa often was invoked. For example, when the Indian *gobernador* of San Juan Atlistaca (district of Tlapa, Guerrero) petitioned for release from prison in Chilapa during a dispute with his community's parish priest in 1797, he beseeched the viceroy in the name of the Mater Dolorosa: "por no tener amparo más que el de María Santíssima que es mi Señora de los Dolores" ("I have no protector other than Most Holy Mary; that is, my Lady of Sorrows"), TU VEMC leg. 68 exp. 9.

18. Larry Frank, *A Land So Remote: Religious Art of New Mexico*, Santa Fe: Red Crane Books, 2001, *passim*.
19. For a description of Holy Week processions including the Mater Dolorosa, see Ilarione da Bergamo, *Daily Life in Colonial Mexico: The Journey of Friar Ilarione da Bergamo, 1761–1768*, ed. Robert Ryall Miller and William J. Orr, Norman: University of Oklahoma Press, pp. 184–187.
20. For example, in the competition for vacant parishes in the Archdiocese of Mexico in 1762, more pastors declared their special devotion to the Mater Dolorosa than to any advocation other than Our Lady of Guadalupe. They include Br. Joseph Antonio Ximenes Frías, recently ordained; Br. Nicolás Ximenes, then serving as the parish priest of San Andrés Epasoyucan; Dr. Fermín Aurelio de Tagle, not then in pastoral service; Br. Juan Miguel Tinoco, who had served as a substitute pastor in Pachuca; Lic. Antonio Domingo Thello y Barbero, who had served as an assistant pastor in Atotonilco el Grande; Br. Ignacio Ramón Moreno, who had served in Tequisquiapan, Querétaro; and Br. Tiburcio de Salazar, parish priest of Real de San Pedro Escanela, JCB file of resumés of aspirants in the 1762 competition, B760 A973i.
21. William A. Christian, Jr., *Local Religion in Sixteenth-Century Spain*, Princeton: Princeton University Press, 1981, p. 150. Agustín Dávila Padilla, *Historia de la fundación y discurso de la Provincia de Santiago de México de la orden de Predicadores* . . . [1596], 2nd ed., Bruselas: En casa de Francisco Vivien, 1648, pp. 555–558 described a late sixteenth-century penitential procession in Antequera with images of Our Lady of Solitude and Our Lady of the Rosary clothed in "mantos de luto que provocavan a grande sentimiento."
22. De Icaza Dufour, *El altar de Dolores*, pp. 65–67; Clara Bargellini, "Jesuit Devotions and Retablos in New Spain," in *The Jesuits: Cultures, Sciences, and the Arts, 1540–1773*, ed. John W. O'Malley et al., Toronto: University of Toronto, 1999, I, 680–698; Francisco de Florencia and Antonio de Oviedo, *Zodíaco mariano* . . ., Mexico: Colegio de San Ildefonso, 1755, pp. 326–327, especially chapels to Dolores in the Candelaria barrio and the chapel of their Colegio de San Francisco Borja in the city of Guatemala. Florencia or Oviedo – both of them Jesuits – claimed that the Jesuit order was largely responsible for the propagation of devotion to the Mater Dolorosa, with their image in the Colegio Máximo in Mexico City as the matrix image, *Zodíaco mariano*, p. 99. Nuestra Señora de Cosamaloapan, another image of the Mater Dolorosa, was also featured by Florencia and Oviedo in the *Zodíaco mariano*, pp. 40–42. Yet another particular image of the Mater Dolorosa by another name revered for healing miracles and promoted by Jesuits was Nuestra Señora de la Salud in the Mexico City church of the Santíssima Trinidad, initially sponsored by local physicians, Cayetano Cabrera y Quintero, *Escudo de armas de México: Celestial protección de esta nobilíssima ciudad, de la Nueva España y de casi todo el Nuevo Mundo* . . ., Mexico: Vda. de D. Joseph Bernardo de Hogal, 1746, p. 153. For spiritual exercises focused on the Virgin of Dolores and prayers on the last Friday of every month in the Jesuit college of Querétaro, see the pocket books by Bernardino Therán, *Camino seguro para el Cielo, descubierto con los dolorosos pasos que nuestro Redemptor Jesu-Christo y su Dolorosísima Madre anduvieron en en su Sagrada Pasión*, and *Día de Dolores viernes último de cada mes* . . ., both published in Mexico by Biblioteca Mexicana, 1754, 1756. But some famously miraculous images of the Mater Dolorosa owed little, if anything, to Jesuit interest; for instance, Nuestra Señora de las

290   *Part I Bearings: Historical Patterns and Places of Image Shrines*

Lágrimas, an image based at the shrine of Nuestra Señora de los Remedios of Totoltepec that was especially popular among nuns in Mexico City before the Remedios statuette gained its lasting fame, Luis de Cisneros, *Historia de el principio, y origen progressos venidas a México y milagros de la Santa Ymagen de nuestra Señora de los Remedios* . . ., Mexico: Iuan Blanco de Alcaçar, 1621, f. 49r.

23. For example, AGN Inquisición 1053 exp. 7 fols. 420v–423r, a denunciation of Juan Miguel Escandón for curing with candle stubs, holy water, cane alcohol, and an image of the Virgen de Dolores, San Bartolomé Capuluac, May 1769.

24. See, for example, José Antonio de Mora, *Alientos a la verdadera confianza* . . ., Mexico: Herederos de la Vda. de M. de Rivera, 1724; Louise Burkhart, *Before Guadalupe: The Virgin Mary in Early Colonial Nahuatl Literature*, Albany: Institute for Mesoamerican Studies, University at Albany, 2001, p. 87.

25. The often reprinted and revised standard moral theology text of the eighteenth century, *Promptuario de la theología moral, muy útil para todos los que se han de exponer de confessores y para la debida administración del Santo Sacramento de la Penitencia*, Madrid: Herederos de Don Joseph Horta, 1751, by Fr. Francisco Lárraga, OP, described the exalted meaning of *dolor* in terms that parallel representations of the "disposition" of the Mater Dolorosa:

el dolor es detestación del pecado cometido: y como el pecado nos aparta de Dios, no sólo como Autor de la naturaleza, sino como Autor de la gracia, se infiere que el dolor ha de ser sobrenatural. También este dolor ha de ser sobrenatural como disposición: lo uno por las razones dichas, y lo otro, porque es disposición para la gracia. (p. 26)

26. Francisco Antonio Navarrete, *Relación peregrina de la agua corriente . . . Querétaro* . . ., Mexico: Joseph Bernardo de Hogal, 1739, p. 18. For an especially fine painting of Our Lady of Sorrows by Cristóbal de Villalpando, ca. 1690, said to be a painted copy of a famously miraculous statue in Madrid, see *Sacred Spain: Art and Belief in the Spanish World*, ed. Ronda Kasl, New Haven: Yale University Press, 2009, p. 220.

It is no surprise that Liberal reformers in Mexico in the mid-nineteenth century and later had a less exalted view of melodramatic representations of the Mater Dolorosa's suffering, for example, Guillermo Prieto's rebuke about "esas Dolorosas que comen ácido, todas gestas y despropósitos" ("those Ladies of Sorrow that look as if they had swallowed acid, all epic and ridiculous"), *Viajes de orden suprema: años de 1853, 54, y 55*, Mexico: Editorial Patria, 1970, p. 72.

27. Joanna E. Ziegler, "Introduction," in *Performance and Transformation: New Approaches to Late Medieval Spirituality*, ed. Mary A. Suydam and Joanna E. Ziegler, New York: St. Martin's Press, 1999, pp. xvii–xviii. Ziegler here builds on work by Caroline Walker Bynum.

28. Brianna Leavitt-Alcántara, "Practicing Faith: Laywomen and Religion in Central America, 1750–1870," Ph.D. dissertation, University of California, Berkeley, 2009, pp. 85, 102, 140. On p. 85, Leavitt-Alcántara includes a pointed statement by a Dominican chronicler for the province of Chiapas and Guatemala at the turn of the eighteenth century, Francisco Antonio Ximénez:

Cierta mujer, hallándose preñada y que había pasado el tiempo regular de la preñez pues había ya cumplido los once meses, hallándose sumamente afligida se fue a velar y encomendar a la Virgen Santísima de los Dolores. Y tomando unas flores secas y un poco de sebo de las candelas que los devotos encienden a la santa se fue a su casa y con gran fe coció las flores y bebió de aquel agua y se untó el vientre con aquel sebo y sobreviniéndole a la media noche los dolores del parto, arrojó una sarta de huevos y un sapo y quedó buena y sana.

Historia de la provincial de San Vicente de Chiapa y Guatemala de la orden de Predicadores [1700–1703], Guatemala: Sociedad de Geografía e Historia de Guatemala, 1971, p. 187. For a Mexican example of Indian women devoted to the Virgin of Dolores during pregnancy, see "Our Lady in the Kernel of Corn," in William B. Taylor, *Marvels & Miracles in Late Colonial Mexico: Three Texts in Context*, Albuquerque: University of New Mexico Press, 2011, pp. 53–70.

29. "Compunctive worship" James Elkins calls it in *Pictures and Tears: A History of People Who Have Cried in Front of Paintings*, New York and London: Routledge, 2001, chapter 9 ("Weeping, Watching the Madonna Weep"), p. 154.
30. Burkhart, *Before Guadalupe*, p. 87; Luis Enrique Orozco, *Iconografía mariana de la Arquidiócesis de Guadalajara*, Guadalajara: Imprenta de J. Vera, 1953, I, 51–62, 179–188.
31. Gerónimo de Mendieta, OFM, *Historia eclesiástica indiana*, Mexico: CONACULTA, 1997, 2, chapter 20.
32. Juan de Torquemada, OFM, *Monarquía Indiana*, Mexico: Porrúa, 1986 (facsimile of 1723 edition), libro XVII cap. 7, pp. 226–227.
33. The following colonial images, chapels, and churches to the Mater Dolorosa became famous beyond their immediate vicinity, at least for a time: Nuestra Señora de la Soledad of Antequera (Oaxaca); Nuestra Señora de la Soledad of the city of Puebla; Nuestra Señora de los Dolores of Acazingo, Puebla; Nuestra Señora de la Soledad of Jerez, Zacatecas; Nuestra Señora de los Dolores de Soriano of Colón, Querétaro; Nuestra Señora de los Dolores of Dolores Hidalgo, Guanajuato; Nuestra Señora de los Dolores of Tlaquepaque, Jalisco; Nuestra Señora de los Dolores of Guadalajara; Nuestra Señora de la Soledad de Capuchinas, Guadalajara; Nuestra Señora de la Soledad of Guadalajara's Hospital de San Miguel; Nuestra Señora de la Soledad of Zapopan, Jalisco; Nuestra Señora de la Soledad of Santa Cruz de las Flores, Jalisco; Nuestra Señora de la Soledad of Ayó el Chico, Jalisco; Nuestra Señora de la Piedad, Mexico, DF; Nuestra Señora de las Angustias, Mexico City; Nuestra Señora del Socorro of the convent church of San Juan de la Penitencia, Mexico City; Nuestra Señora de los Dolores of the Colegio Máximo de San Pedro y San Pablo, Mexico City; María Santísima de la Soledad of Teziuitlan y Atempa, Puebla; Nuestra Señora de los Dolores del Calvario of Tenancingo, Estado de México; Nuestra Señora de los Dolores of Xaltocan, Estado de México; Nuestra Señora de los Dolores of Huauhtla, Morelos; Nuestra Señora de la Soledad of Atlixco, Puebla; Nuestra Señora de los Dolores of Tolcayuca, Hidalgo; Nuestra Señora de los Dolores of San Pedro de los Pozos, San Luis Potosí; Nuestra Señora de los Dolores of Mérida, Yucatán; Nuestra Señora de los Dolores of Barrio Candelaria, Guatemala City; Nuestra Señora de los Dolores of the Jesuit colegio chapel of San Francisco Borja, Guatemala City.
34. For one of those prints of the Mater Dolorosa in action, see Chapter 5.
35. Antonio de Robles, *Diario de sucesos notables (1665–1703)*, Mexico: Porrúa, 1946, II, 234. Another statue of the Mater Dolorosa reportedly turned to face the figure of Christ on the Cross during an earthquake in Antigua, Guatemala in March, 1751, *Relación del admirable y portentoso movimiento que se notó en varias Imágenes de la siempre Virgen María*

Nuestra Señora de los Dolores en la Ciudad de Santiago Capital del Reyno de Goatemala . . ., Guatemala: Impr. de Sebastián de Arébalo, 1751.

36. Examples include Robles, Diario de sucesos, I, 124–125 reporting in May 1673 that in August 1672 a raging fire in a bakery facing the plaza in Madrid had been quenched with little loss of life by "the intercession of the image of Nuestra Señora de la Soledad" which was brought to the scene from its church; in Puebla in May 1784 the bishop sponsored a novena to "the miraculous Image of María Santíssima de la Soledad" in the Carmelite convent during the epidemic of pox that year, *Gazeta de México* number 9 for May 5, 1784; and *Gazeta de México* number 12 for June 4, 1796 reported copious rains at Huautla, Morelos after the parish's statue of the Nuestra Señora de los Dolores was processed to the parched fields outside of town. An array of favors attributed to Nuestra Señora de la Soledad in the city of Antequera, Oaxaca, are documented in ex-votos discussed and illustrated in Elin Luque Agraz, *El arte de dar gracias: Los exvotos pictóricos de la Virgen de la Soledad de Oaxaca*, Mexico: Centro de Cultura Casa Lamm, 2007.
37. Cabrera y Quintero, *Escudo de armas de México*, p. 202.
38. For example, in the *Gazeta de México,* October 28, 1797.
39. Orozco, *Iconografía mariana*, I, 51–62.
40. Orozco, *Iconografía mariana*, I, 179–188. Some images and chapels to Dolores trace later, rather dramatic histories that are more like those of many Mexican shrines dedicated to miracle-working images. The statue of the Virgen de los Dolores de Soriano in Colón, Querétaro has a peripatetic history like some other Mexican shrine images. The statue was imported from Spain for a new Dominican mission at Zimapán, Hidalgo. Within a few years, the mission was moved further into the Sierra Gorda and the image was transferred to the mining community of Maconí. That mission was destroyed by fire and the statue was moved again to another church in the Sierra Gorda. In the late 1770s, it was moved to a new mission at Bucareli, then to the Mission of Santo Domingo de Soriano (near Colón), when news of miracles began to attract many visitors. Jorge Ruiz Martínez, *Apuntes históricos acerca de la venerada imagen de Nuestra Señora de los Dolores de Soriano*, Mexico: Editorial Jus, 1967.
41. CONDUMEX, Col. Puebla, Edictos del Obispo Fabián y Fuero, edicto no. LIII. While Fabián y Fuero was a stickler for restricting what he regarded as unseemly public displays of faith, he had made a point of declaring his support for devotion to the Mater Dolorosa in an earlier decree of March 22, 1766, edicto no. XVII.
42. De Icaza Dufour, *El altar de Dolores*, pp. 87–90. Icaza sees this as the beginning of a popular custom in Mexico, along with the Nativity displays (*nacimientos navideños*) at Christmas and family altars for the All Souls observances in November.
43. Other than Nuestra Señora de Montserrat and Nuestra Señora de Guadalupe, the earliest move to promote a regional Spanish miracle image in New Spain seems to have been Nuestra Señora de Atocha. A devotional history of this Castilian image published in Valladolid in 1604 was reprinted in Mexico four years later, but popular devotion seems not to have become widespread although a novena booklet to her was published in Mexico City in 1796, sponsored by an anonymous devotee, Fr. Juan de Escajedo, *Historia de la Ymagen Milagrosa de Nuestra Señora de Atocha, Patrona de la Real Villa de Madrid*, enlarged from 1604 texts by Fr. Francisco de Pereda, Mexico: n.p., 1608, and *Devota novena en obsequio y culto de María Santísima Señora Nuestra, que con el*

título de Atocha ..., Mexico: Imprenta Madrileña del Br. Don Joseph Fernández Jáuregui, 1796. Nuestra Señora del Milagro of the Villa de Cocentayna was also promoted in Spanish America during the seventeenth century. See the royal cedula of 1662, authorizing the collection of alms for this shrine throughout the Indies, AGN Reales Cédulas Originales 7 exp. 76, fol. 140.

Other regional Marian devotions in Spain were not unknown in New Spain, but they are poorly documented and were probably popular mainly among immigrants from their homeland. These include Nuestra Señora del Sagrario (Toledo and Madrid), Nuestra Señora de los Urdiales (Cantabria), Nuestra Señora del Pópulo (Cádiz), Nuestra Señora del Socorro (Huelva, Palma de Mallorca), and Nuestra Señora del Tránsito (Zamora, Madrid).

44. Francisco Sedano, *Apéndices a la obra Noticias de México*, Mexico: Barbedillo, 1880, II, 47. A sermon for the anniversary of the apparition of the Virgin of Montserrat was published in 1672, Fr. Francisco de los Rios, *Sermón en la festividad a la Aparición Milagrosa de la Imagen de María Santíssima ... de Monserrate ...*, Mexico: Viuda de Bernardo Calderón, 1672. And a late seventeenth-century Mexican painting of her is in the Philadelphia Museum of Art.

45. Chimalpahin, *Annals of His Time*, pp. 33 (1589), 47 (1594), and 53 (1595).

46. Juan Javier Pescador, *The New World Inside a Basque Village: The Oiartzun Valley and Its Atlantic Emigrants, 1550–1800*, Reno and Las Vegas: University of Nevada Press, 2004, p. 115; Robles, *Diario de sucesos*, II, 38, 170. A sermon for the anniversary of the apparition of the Virgin of Aranzazú was published in Mexico City in 1685, Fr. Juan de Mendoza Ayala, *Sermón de la milagrosa aparición de la Imagen Santa de Aranzazú*, Mexico: Vda. de Francisco Rodríguez Lupercio, 1685; and a late seventeenth-century painting of her by Villalpando, published in *The Arts in Latin America, 1492–1820*, ed. Suzanne Stratton-Pruitt, Philadelphia: Philadelphia Museum of Art, 2006, p. 374. On cofradías devoted to the Virgin of Aranzazú, see the essay by Amaya Garritz Ruiz, "Nuestra Señora de Aranzazú en la Nueva España," in *Las huellas de Aranzazú en América*, ed. Óscar Álvarez Gila, Idoia Arrieta, and San Sebastián, Guipúzcoa: Eusko Ikaskuntza, 2004, pp. 69–87.

47. Fr. Juan de Luzuriaga, *Paranympho celeste. Historia de la Mystica Zarza, Milagrosa Imagen, y prodigioso Santuario ...*, Mexico: Herederos de la Viuda de Bernardo Calderón, 1686. This first edition was followed by two 1690 editions printed in Spain.

48. Agustín de Vetancurt, *Sermón a la Aparición de la milagrosa Imagen de N. Señora del Pilar de Zaragoza ...*, Mexico: Francisco Rodríguez Lupercio, 1674. Other published sermons from the late seventeenth century include Fr. Alonso de Ávila, *Sermón ... a la apparición {sic} milagrosa de Nuestra Señora del Pilar de Zaragoza ...*, Mexico: Francisco Rodríguez Lupercio, 1679; Fr. Juan Calderón, *España illustrada con la mysteriosa luz de N. Señora del Pilar de Zaragoza ...*, Mexico: Francisco Rodríguez Lupercio, 1682; and José Gómez de la Parra, *Idea evangélica, que en elogio de la milagros imagen de Nuestra Señora del Pilar de Zaragoza ...*, Puebla: D. Fernández de León, 1691.

49. Gómez de la Parra, *Idea evangélica*, fol. 2r.

50. Gómez de la Parra, *Idea evangélica*, fol. 28v. One miracle for an Aragonese is described in this source, a man wounded by Chichimecs who appealed to Nuestra Señora del Pilar and was healed. He went on to endow Masses in Puebla in her honor before his death in 1603.

51. The Correa painting is in the Museo Franz Mayer in Mexico City; a painting by Juan González is in the Museo de América in Madrid. Antonio Delgado y Buenrosto's *Panegírico sagrado al nacimiento de la Virgen María N.S. delineado en su milagrosíssima imagen de Valvanera* . . ., preached in Puebla's convent church of Santa Inés in 1674, was published in Sevilla by T. López de Haro in 1680.
52. Novena booklets were a rather new genre of devotional literature in New Spain during the eighteenth century. Novenas, *triduos*, and other rounds of devotions were practiced from the early years of Christianity, but Alexander VII (1655–1667) was the first pope to grant indulgences to those who completed a prescribed novena. His encouragement of novenas may have touched off the vogue of these published booklets containing the schedule of devotions and prescribed prayers. Some also include a thumbnail history of the cult and a few miracles associated with it. I have not been able to establish whether these novena booklets were as popular in Europe as they became in New Spain during the eighteenth century.
53. Manuel Romero de Terreros, *Grabados y grabadores en la Nueva España*, Mexico: Ediciones Arte Mexicano, 1948, *passim*.
54. Pescador, *The New World Inside a Basque Village*, pp. 115–116. The reach of the confraternity of Aranzazú in Mexico City was unusual, counting 3,087 members during the eighteenth century, Elisa Luque Alcaide, "Recursos de la Cofradía de Aranzazú de México ante la corona (1729–1763)," *Revista de Indias*, LVI, núm 206 (1996), 206.
55. Other chapels and cofradías to this image of the Virgin Mary were established in the late eighteenth century in Puebla (1788), Veracruz, Zacatecas, San Luis Potosí, and possibly Sombrerete. See Garritz Ruiz, "Nuestra Señora de Aranzazú en la Nueva España," pp. 82–85. The devotion in San Luis Potosí may date from the early eighteenth century, while the chapel dedicated to her there was the later work of Manuel Tolsá and Francisco Eduardo Tresguerras. According to Luzuriaga, *Paranympho*, libro 2, capítulo ix, devotion in Veracruz and Zacatecas from the early eighteenth century centered on the Franciscan convent churches. On colonial confraternities dedicated to her in Mexico City, Guadalajara (1775), Puebla (1788), and possibly Sombrerete, Zacatecas, see the Garritz article again, p. 75.

For the Aranzazú mission of the Jesuits at Cocómora, Chihuahua, see Clara Bargellini, *Misiones y presidios de Chihuahua*, Chihuahua: Gobierno del Estado de Chihuahua, 1997. Another Spanish Marian devotion, to Nuestra Señora de los Desamparados of Valencia, was closely associated with the Franciscan college of San Fernando in Mexico City, founded by peninsular friars in the early eighteenth century. For eighteenth-century devotional texts to her published in Mexico, see Medina, La imprenta en México, V, 372 (1759), 578 (1767); and VI, 51 (1770), 173 (1775), and 301 (1780).
56. Pedro de San Francisco, *La Reyna de la América* . . ., Mexico: Joseph Bernardo de Hogal, 1739, sermon delivered in the church of the Augustinians' Hospicio de San Nicolás Tolentino.
57. For example, *Gazeta de México,* October 18, 1785, celebration in cathedral sponsored by the Mexico City royal regiment.
58. A fire swept through the shrine in 1777. Information about the Spanish shrine and early Mexican devotion is drawn from *Constituciones de la Congregación de Nuestra Señora con el título de Covadonga, defensora, y restauradora de la libertad española, fundada baxo la Real*

Protección por los naturales y originarios del Principado de Asturias, y Obispado de Oviedo . . ., Mexico: Herederos del Lic. D. Joseph de Jáuregui, 1785, 83 numbered pages. Seven Asturian men, all *dones*, were listed as founders of the Mexican devotion in the 1730s.

59. *Constituciones . . . Covadonga*, pp. 45–83. These pages amount to a separate publication, "Noticia de la antigüedad y situación del santuario de Santa María de Cobadonga." It includes both an account of the 1777 fire and the royal license of March 10, 1778 to collect alms for the rebuilding project throughout Spanish America. In each American diocese, a resident of the capital city was to be appointed to oversee the alms collection and submit an annual account.

60. AGN Bienes Nacionales 760 exp. 15.

61. Still other Spanish images are mentioned in colonial sources, but few developed into broad-based devotions during the eighteenth century: the Mexico City cathedral – that great storehouse of sacred things – had chapels in the seventeenth century dedicated to Nuestra Señora de las Angustias (Granada), Nuestra Señora de la Fuente (Osma), and Nuestra Señora de la Antigua (Sevilla). The dean of the cathedral in Valladolid (Morelia) actively supported a chapel to María Santíssima de los Urdiales there in the 1780s. A novena booklet was published in Puebla 1786 for María Santíssima del Madroñal (near Brihuega in the Province of Guadalajara, from which several generations of weavers emigrated in the seventeenth century). Paintings, devotional literature, and prints of other Spanish Marian images circulated during the eighteenth century: Nuestra Señora del Cortijo (venerated in Soto de los Cameros, near the city of León in northern Spain); Nuestra Señora del Sagrario of Toledo was favored by the Spanish military commander during the conquest of Nayarit in 1722 (he named the incorporated province Nuevo Reino de Toledo); Nuestra Señora del Brezo near Villafría de la Peña, Province of Palencia (northern Spain, southwest of Santander), with a devotional history of the shrine published in Mexico City in 1807; Nuestra Señora de la Peña de Francia (mountain shrine in southern Salamanca province); Nuestra Señora de la Candelaria of Tenerife, Canarias, with a novena booklet published in Puebla in 1750; a bachelor's thesis by don Francisco de la Cruz y Sarabia in 1708 dedicated to Nuestra Señora de Begoña (Asturias, northern Spain), and an eighteenth-century painting on hide in New Mexico modeled on a published print of her (Asturias, northern Spain); Nuestra Señora de los Dolores in the Carmelite church of Calatayud y Huesca (province of Zaragoza, Aragón); Nuestra Señora de El Henar (Cuéllar, Segovia); Nuestra Señora de Fuensanta (Murcia, southeastern Spain). Immigrants from the home region sponsored most of these publications. The printing establishment of the Zúñiga y Ontiveros family stocked devotional publications for several other Spanish advocations of the Virgin including, in 1808, one for Nuestra Señora del Socorro of Valencia.

Some of the imported devotions to miraculous images depended heavily on a particular devotee and failed to attract much of a following. The Virgin of la Cabeza de Sierra Morena (Andalusia) was made known by a devout priest who sponsored the reprinting in Mexico in 1753 of the standard devotional history and novena booklet originally published in Madrid in 1677, but there is little to suggest that the devotion became popular thereafter. A devotion to the late medieval statue of Nuestra Señora de la Soterraña de Nieva with its shrine near Segovia, had a somewhat different trajectory. It was the inspiration of Fr. José Cabezas, a Dominican living in Mexico City in the 1740s who authored a *Historia prodigiosa . . .* based on the accepted Spanish authorities and published in Mexico City in 1748 by María de Ribera, in order to spread the good news and offer a personal testimony of faith and gratitude for a narrow escape from English corsairs in his journey to the New World. He also produced and had published a novena booklet to the same advocation that year. The cult he meant to promote may have withered after his death, but this image of the Virgin Mary apparently gained something of a following beyond ethnic Castilians in New Spain as a special protector against lightning strikes and earthquakes. The novena booklet was reprinted in Puebla and Mexico City at least seven times by 1784, and prints from a fine etching of Nuestra Señora de Soterraña by Ortuño (active between 1750 and 1808) circulated. Inexpensive prints depicting Nuestra Señora de los Desamparados (Valencia) and touting the "singular miracles" happening every day that were associated with her image also circulated before 1766; a novena booklet was printed in 1796; and a replica of the Spanish statue was placed in the Franciscan missionary college of San Fernando in Mexico City in 1796; but it is not clear who the devotees were.

62. Domingo Antonio Chiva, *Compendio histórico y novena de María Santísima Nuestra Señora, que con la advocación de la Cueva Santa se venera en el Seminario de la Santa Cruz de la ciudad de Querétaro* ..., Mexico: Joseph de Jáuregui, 1792, p. 71.

63. The 1807 reprinting from the Jáuregui printshop in Mexico City includes two illustrations, one a crude engraved print of Our Lady of the Cueva Santa with lettering at the bottom extolling her ability to elicit heartfelt contrition. This reprinting is not listed in WorldCat, but a copy was recently advertised by Librería Urbe in Mexico City.

64. For the 1805 petition by a brother of the Camillian hospitalers (Pasqual Hernández, a native of Murcia) for permission to collect alms for the cult of Nuestra Señora de la Cueva Santa, see AGN Indiferente Virreinal caja 5388 exp. 8. The petition was denied, as were many other petitions to collect alms for religious causes in New Spain after 1790.

65. Stafford Poole, *Our Lady of Guadalupe: The Origins and Sources of a Mexican National Symbol, 1531–1797*, Tucson: University of Arizona Press, 1995, p. 229.

66. Another Spanish Christ – the Niño Jesús known as "El Enfermero" (the nurse), venerated in the Capuchin nuns' infirmary in Puerto de Santa María, had a novena published in Mexico in 1776 at the behest of "a devotee of the Blessed Souls in Purgatory" in 1776 (noted in Medina, *La imprenta en México*, vol. 6, item no. 5875). I have seen no evidence that it was a well-known or popular devotion in New Spain.

67. The moving parts and bladder from which animal blood could be squirted through the wound in Christ's side were hidden inside the leather skin of this sculpture. They are described by Felipe Pereda, "Images Made of Flesh: The Christ of Burgos and the Conversion of a Jewish Bishop in Early Modern Iberia." My thanks to the author for sharing this paper.

68. An outlier is Ciudad Jiménez, a military garrison and town in southeastern Chihuahua. Apparently the church to the Christ of Burgos built there between 1804 and 1824 depended on the devotion and promotion by the settlement's late colonial chaplain, Pbro. Rafael Nevárez Solórzano, a Spanish immigrant who served from 1785 to the early 1820s. To my knowledge, Ciudad Jiménez is the only town in Mexico dedicated to the Christ of Burgos. A parish dedicated to the Christ of Burgos is located northwest of the city of San Luis Potosí, famous for its Señor del Saucito.

69. Robles, *Diario de sucesos notables*, III, 113, entry for October 15, 1700. A sculpted Christ of Burgos was known and celebrated in the Augustinian church of Lima, Peru as early as 1593, Pereda, "Images Made of Flesh." Pereda suggests that the cult of the Christ of Burgos was slow to spread to the New World because the Augustinian intellectual elite discouraged circulation of reproductions.
70. José Gómez, "Diario de México," Bancroft M-M 105 fol. 59r, entry for February 25, 1780. Gómez noted that this chapel to the Christ of Burgos "es de los Montañeses." For a published sermon from this period dedicated to the Christ of Burgos in the name of "los Montañeses," see Fr. Juan Agustín Morfi, *La nobleza y piedad de los Montañeses demonstrada por el Smo Cristo de Burgos*, Mexico: Joseph de Jáuregui, 1775.
71. This *archicofradía* is documented in AGN Bienes Nacionales 873 exp. 30, 1797. For the Cristo de Burgos in San Ángel, Lázaro Gila Medina, "Un cuadro inédito de Miguel Cabrera: El Cristo de Burgos de la iglesia del Carmen del ex-convento de San Ángel, en México, D.F.," *Anales del Museo de América* 12 (2004), 205–216. Gila Medina reported that the canvas covers twenty square meters.
72. The Guanajuato devotions are mentioned in *Gazeta de México*, August 21, 1787, which noted that a novena in this time of drought ended on August 8.
73. This early reference to the Christ of Burgos in Puebla is in the July 28, 1737 issue of the *Gazeta de México*, BIBM 4, p. 708. The dedication took place at the beginning of June.
74. *Una visión del México del Siglo de las Luces: La codificación de Joaquín Antonio de Basarás, 1763*, ed. Ilona Katzew, Mexico: Landucci, 2006, p. 165.
75. There were bound to be exceptions since every image potentially invited divine presence and favor. The Virgin of Merced in Mexico City during the eighteenth century is an example. This advocation of Mary was at the center of the Mercedarian order's legendary beginning in the early thirteenth century, appearing to Pedro Nolasco and exhorting him to establish an order of priests to ransom captive Christians. Wherever Mercedarians went – and they were established in the leading cities of New Spain – images of Our Lady of la Merced and altars to her were likely to be found. As one Mexican Mercedarian, Fr. Agustín de Andrada, put it in 1706, she was "my mother, . . . being the principal founder and governess of the Mercedarians," in his manuscript "Panal místico. Compendio de las grandezas del celeste, real, y militar orden de Nuestra Señora de la Merced, Redempción de Cautivos Cristianos," John Carter Brown Library Codex Sp 76. The image of Our Lady of La Merced in the Mercedarians' main convent church (*convento grande*) was singled out as a great miracle worker and focal point of devotion. In the May 1737 entry, the *Gazeta de México* described the lavish celebrations for the debut of the church's main altar devoted to "the miraculous image of Our Lady of La Merced" (apparently sponsored by D. Domingo del Campo y Murga, the gunpowder monopolist, at a cost of 50,000 pesos), BIBM 4, p. 694. Nine years later, José Antonio de Villaseñor y Sánchez in the supplement to his *Theatro Americano* described the image as not only "exquisite and beautifully adorned," but "singularly appealing to devotees because in their tribulations and illnesses God has granted through her intercession many favors in miraculous circumstances," Ramón María Serrera Contreras, *Suplemento al Theatro Americano: la ciudad de México en 1755*, Sevilla: Escuela de Estudios Hispanoamericanos, 1980, p. 128. And inexpensive prints of this image advertising her wonder-working fame were in circulation by the 1760s, if not before. Francisco de Ajofrín included one in the journal of his travels that advertised

"the most miraculous image of Our Lady of la Merced, 'La Peregrina' ["the pilgrim" traveling copy] that is venerated in the choir of the Convento Grande in the city of Mexico," *Diario del viaje que hizo a la América en el siglo XVIII el P. Fray Francisco de Ajofrín*, 2 vols., Mexico: Instituto Cultural Hispano Mexicano, 1964, I, 155.

The Carmelites identified themselves and the founding of their order with a special advocation of the Virgin Mary, Nuestra Señora del Carmen. Mary in this guise was believed to have appeared in a cloud to the Old Testament prophets Elijah and Elisha on Mt. Carmel in Palestine, and later, in the thirteenth century, she appeared to St. Simon Stock, superior general of the Carmelite order and presented him with her scapular, promising to liberate from purgatory the souls of those who wore the scapular during their lifetime. Both Our Lady of La Merced and Our Lady of El Carmen were closely associated with their orders, but Merced gained popularity in New Spain beyond the Mercedarian order (as the reports of miracles suggest), while Carmen was more popular in Spain than America, as patroness of sailors and the Spanish Armada. Her popular appeal in New Spain apparently was mainly among sailors and fishermen, and concentrated along the Gulf Coast from Ciudad del Carmen (Campeche) to Veracruz beginning in the mid-seventeenth century. An exception was the miraculous image of El Carmen in Puebla mentioned in the *Zodíaco mariano*, pp. 156–159. The painted image was said to have come to life and spoken to Puebla's visionary nun María de Jesús, and subsequently was associated with many miraculous healings. Booklets were published in Mexico City to promote novenas to Our Lady of El Carmen in the late eighteenth century, and she was occasionally invoked during the Independence period as a protectress and advocate in wartime.

76. Bridget Heal, *The Cult of the Virgin Mary in Early Modern Germany: Protestant and Catholic Piety, 1500–1648*, Cambridge, UK and New York: Cambridge University Press, 2007, p. 157. Jesuit enthusiasm for Our Lady of Loreto and the Holy House was plain by the 1590s, in Orazio Torsellini, *Lauretanae historiae. Libri quinque*, Rome: Apud Aloysium Zannettum, 1597 (first Spanish translation, *Historia lauretana en que se cuentan las translaciones, Milagros y sucessos de la Santa Casa de N. Señora de Loreto*, Madrid: Madrigal, 1603), and reaffirmed in Wilhelm von Gumppenberg, SJ's *Atlas Marianus* ..., first published in 1655. Gumppenberg visited the shrine in 1632 and was himself responsible for the erection of seventeen replicas of the Holy House in Bavaria before his death in 1675.

77. For a compelling global perspective on devotion to Our Lady of Loreto and the Holy House that features the Americas as well as Europe, see Karin Vélez's 2008 doctoral dissertation in history at Princeton University, "Resolved to Fly: The Virgin of Loreto, the Jesuits, and the Miracle of Portable Catholicism in the Seventeenth-Century Atlantic World."

78. *The Jesuits: Cultures, Sciences, the Arts*, ed. John W. O'Malley, Toronto: University of Toronto Press, 2006, I, 683–684 for the Casa Profesa; Francisco de Florencia, *La casa peregrina, solar ilustre, en que nació la Reya de los Ángeles* ..., Mexico: Vda. de Bernardo Calderón, 1689, fol. 83r (for Puebla); AGN Hospitales 3 exp.12 (for the hospital in Veracruz).

79. Florencia, *La casa peregrina*, fols. 83–84.

80. Luisa Elena Alcalá, "Blanqueando la Loreto mexicana," in *La imagen religiosa en la monarquía hispánica: Usos y espacios*, ed. María Cruz de Carlos, et al., Madrid: Casa de

Velásquez, 2008, pp. 171–193. Robles, *Diario de sucesos*, II, 120 says a "nueva casita de Nuestra Señora de Loreto" at San Gregorio was dedicated on May 12, 1686. Perhaps this was this the same Holy House Alcalá dates to 1680.

81. According to Fr. Luis del Refugio de Palacio, at one time there was also a replica of the house in the Jesuit church in Guadalajara, Antonio Tello, *Crónica miscelánea de la Sancta Provincia de Xalisco, libro IV*, preliminary study and notes by Fr. Luis del Refugio de Palacio, Guadalajara: Edit. Font, 1955, p. 199. The shrine of Nuestra Señora de los Remedios in the Valley of Mexico also had a Loretan connection. Late colonial inventories of the shrine's possessions included "relics" of the House of Loreto, AHACM número de inventario 3903 exp. 97, 1814.

82. Florencia, *La casa peregrina*, fols. 103v–104v Florencia noted also that an altar to Loreto was under construction in Puebla – presumably in the Jesuit church of Espíritu Santo – and that it displayed a miracle-working relic from the Virgin's bedroom.

83. Barcelona: Pablo Nadal, 1754.

84. Florencia and Oviedo, *Zodíaco mariano*, pp. 107–109 indicated that Salvatierra initiated the construction of the Santa Casa at the Colegio de San Gregorio and treated Zappa as promoter of the developing *culto* at Tepotzotlán. Florencia and Oviedo contrast the two young Jesuits as missionaries – Salvatierra as the frontier missionary and Zappa as the urban missionary engaged more in spiritual revivals in towns and cities in central Mexico.

85. Alcalá, "Blanqueando la Loreto mexicana." Alcalá suggests that these figures brought for Zappa were the first European images of Loreto in Mexico that had touched the original. They were surely not the first images of Loreto in Mexico, but, as Alcalá shows, Jesuit sponsors made a striking change by whitening the dark faces of the Virgin and Christ Child at San Gregorio.

86. 1728: Bartolomé Felipe de Ittá y Parra, *Consejera de la salud. María Santíssima en su Soberana Imagen de Loreto que venera en esta Corte Mexicana* ..., Mexico: n.p., 1728, and Francisco Javier Alegre, *Historia de la Compañía de Jesús en Nueva España* ..., Mexico: Impr. de J. M. Lara, 1841, II, 233, 261–267. According to Cabrera y Quintero, *Escudo de armas de México*, p. 98, a novena dedicated to the Holy House at the San Gregorio college drew 20,000 participants. A prodigious amount of candle wax was burned and processions were mounted on this occasion in order to purify the city.

87. Juan de Villa Sánchez and Francisco Javier de la Peña, *Puebla sagrada y profana. Informe dado a su muy ilustre Ayuntamiento el año de 1746*, Puebla: J. M. Campos, 1835, p. 34.

88. See, for example, Florencia and Oviedo, *Zodíaco mariano*, pp. 107–109.

89. De Villa Sánchez and de la Peña, *Puebla sagrada*, pp. 34ff; report on cofradía funds at Omitlan in 1749, AGN Clero Regular y Secular 154 exp. 6. The shrine at Españita was one of the few known by another name – the soon politically incorrect Nuestra Señora de España. It is documented in a prolonged alms-collection petition in 1816, AGN Clero Regular y Secular 181 exp. 11 and discussed in rewarding detail in Jaime Cuadriello's "La Virgen como territorio: Los títulos primordiales de Santa María Nueva España," *Colonial Latin American Review* 19: 1 (2010), 69–113, and "Santa María Nueva España: El reino de un pueblo," in *Españita y Altlihuetzia*, Mario Ramírez Rancaño, Jaime Cuadriello, and Guillermo Alberto Xelhuantzi Ramírez, Tlaxcala: Colegio de Historia de Tlaxcala, 2004, pp. 119–199. Unfortunately, the origins of Loretan devotion at Españita are obscure, and it is unclear even whether Jesuits were directly involved in

its development before their expulsion. Franciscans were the pastors there before secularization in the mid-seventeenth century, and Tlaxcalan towns generally were closely connected to the provincial center of Puebla, where Dominicans as well as Jesuits were among the Loretan devotees from the seventeenth century. For San Miguel, see AGN General de Parte 32 exp. 151, 1737.

90. Novena booklets were published in 1769, 1774, 1782, 1783, 1803, 1805, and 1817; new and old devotional texts including a 1784 reprinting of Florencia's devotional text, "Meditaciones de los principales mysterios ...," an 1802 reprint of "Esclavitud nobilíssima consagrada al culto de la Ssma Virgen María de Loreto venerada en su capilla del Colegio de San Gregorio de la Compañía de Jesús," which was first published in 1724, and a devotional guide by Domingo Francisco de Villa Señor, OFM, *Devoción práctica para exercitarse* ..., Puebla: Colegio Real de San Ignacio, 1765, reprinted in Mexico City in 1797 by the printing office of Br. D. Joseph Fernández Jáuregui. For the financial records of the *congregación* from 1767 to 1776, see AGN Obras Pías, vol. 3 exp 3. Substantial bequests in the late colonial period are recorded in AGN Colegios 24 exps. 1, 3–5, 20–22, 24, and 27, AGN Bienes Nacionales 1596 exp. 23, and AGN Consolidación 1 exp. 4.

91. AGN Templos y Conventos 6 exp. 2, fols. 47–63.

92. E.g. AGN Templos y Conventos 6 exp. 2 fol. 62, September 12, 1778; and Bancroft MSS 86/130m, 1,801 copies of cedulas issued by the viceroy from 1771 to 1797 related to the affairs of Br. Julián Cirilo de Galicia y Castilla, an ordained priest from a Tlaxcalan noble family who died in Puebla in 1790. One of the cedulas, dated November 25, 1780, cites a letter from Viceroy Bucareli of August 27, 1778 referring to a cedula of November 5, 1774 that called for establishment of a seminary for the sons of Indian nobles and commoners at San Gregorio, to be renamed San Carlos. Another cedula from July 20, 1797 noted that a clause in Galicia y Castilla's will of 1789 bequeathed his books to the Colegio de San Gregorio, to be renamed San Carlos, for the education of Indians of the Diocese of Puebla and the Archdiocese of Mexico, and asked about the current state of the Colegio de San Gregorio and why it had not yet been reestablished. Another cedula of December 6, 1774 ordered that the church at the Colegio de San Gregorio be refurbished with altars and paraphernalia from the chapels of the former Jesuit Colegio de San Pedro y San Pablo and the proceeds from chaplaincies there to go to support two or three priests versed in Indian languages to preach and confess Indians there and maintain the cult of the Virgin of Loreto. The reopening of the Colegio de San Gregorio was postponed until the funds to support it were complete.

93. Unfortunately, the documentation in AGN Clero Regular y Secular 22 exp. 15 does not establish whether the image had been returned to the San Gregorio neighborhood before then. The petition for the female administrator (*mayordoma*) to collect alms was approved by the archbishop but rejected by the viceroy on the advice of his *fiscal de lo civil*, who argued that women should not be out collecting alms in faraway places and that devotion to Nuestra Señora de Loreto was flourishing so that such special collections were not necessary, fol. 249v–250r.

94. AGN Consolidación 1 exp. 4.

95. See Isidoro de Sevilla, *La pastora coronada: idea discursiva y predicable en que se propone María Santíssima Nuestra Señora, pastora universal de todas las criaturas, venerada en su imagen de la pastora; tratase del origen, principio y excelencias de la devoción de la corona de la*

hermandad que a esta pastora divina han fundado los Capuchinos en esta ciudad de Sevilla, Sevilla: Francisco de Leefdael, 1705. According to the website "La Pasión Digital," Fr. Isidoro de Sevilla's vision in the Sevilla's Capuchin convent on June 24, 1703 was rendered on canvas by Miguel Alonso de Tovar and displayed in a Rosary procession there for the first time on September 8, 1703. The first sculpted image was processed in Sevilla in October 1705, www.lapasion.org/directoria/item.php?categoria_id= 39&item=393.

96. Additional information about the early history of the devotion in Andalucía is available in Sebastián de Ubrique, "Origen y desarrollo de la devoción de la Divina Pastora en los pueblos de España y América," in *Crónica oficial del Congreso Mariano Hispano-Americano de Sevilla, mayo 1929*, Madrid: Sáez Hnos., 1930, pp. 812–823. Ubrique suggests that the devotion grew after 1729 when Felipe V moved his court to Seville and the royal family made public their special devotion to the Divina Pastora.

97. The Capuchins also founded a mission dedicated to the Divina Pastora in the Valle de Cutacuas (Province of Cumaná, in the modern state of Sucre, Venezuela) in 1751, but the two missionaries assigned there died within two months of each other, supposedly poisoned, and the mission was abandoned in 1754, "Relación de las conversiones de Capuchinos aragoneses de la provincial de Cumaná ... (1780)," in *Relaciones históricas de las misiones de padres capuchinos de Venezuela: siglos XVII y XVIII*, Madrid: Librería General de Victoriano Suárez, 1928, pp. 242–243. The image and devotion attracted some interest elsewhere in Latin America, including Colombia and several places directly linked to the Atlantic trade – Havana, Buenos Aires, and the merchants of Tucumán and Salta, Ubrique, "Origen y desarrollo," pp. 818–819. And several Spanish ships plying Atlantic waters in the eighteenth century were named La Divina Pastora. American-made paintings of the Divina Pastora have also been identified in Quito and the southern Andes at Cuzco and Potosí, Lisa Duffy-Zeballos, "'And My Sheep Know Me': Colonial Transformations in the Divina Pastora de las Almas in the Art of the New World," in *Art in Spain and the Hispanic World: Essays in Honor of Jonathan Brown*, ed. Sarah Schroth, London: Paul Hoberton and the Center for Spain in America, 2010, pp. 413–436. In several Andean paintings Duffy-Zeballos finds an Americanizing "transformation" of imagery (with more emphasis on the flock of sheep, American landscapes, and native dress), and "a process of mestizaje in the representation of her features," pp. 421, 433. The paintings and prints in New Spain I have seen closely follow Isidoro de Sevilla's vision and Tovar's painting.

98. Florencia and Oviedo, *Zodíaco mariano*, p. 208.

99. Ilona Katzew has located other paintings of the Divina Pastora in Querétaro's church of Santa Rosa de Viterbo and Santa Barbara, California. Personal communication. Bernard Fontana identified eighteenth-century paintings in the Mission San Xavier del Bac (Arizona), the Puríssima Concepción Mission in San Antonio, Texas, and two statues in the Valley of Oaxaca at Xoxocotlán and Santa María Coyotepec. New Mexico *santeros* began to depict the image in the 1820s, Bernard L. Fontana and Edward McCain, *A Gift of Angels: The Art of Mission San Xavier del Bac*, Tucson: University of Arizona Press, 2010, p. 115. Ubrique, "Origen y desarrollo," pp. 819–820, mentions two oil paintings of the Divina Pastora from Mexico in the Capuchin convent of Sevilla. A painting of the Divina Pastora by the late eighteenth-century Mexican painter José de Páez is in the collection of the Museo de América in Madrid (Concepción García Saiz,

La pintura colonial en el Museo de América. La escuela mexicana, Madrid: Ministerio de Cultura, 1980, I, 94–96). Susan Deans-Smith kindly shared a reference from the Mexican Inquisition records to prints of the Divina Pastora imported by the merchant Pedro Muguerza, resident in Mexico City (September 19, 1795, AGN Inquisición 1264).

100. Antonio Llinaz de Jesús María, *Devoción a María Santíssima Nuestra Señora . . . al fin van añadidos los versos de Nuestra Madre la Divina Pastora*. Listings in WorldCat include a Puebla edition in 1776 and Mexico City editions in 1765, 1766, 1773, 1779, 1787, 1796, 1807, 1810, 1816, 1818, and 1819. Other editions may have appeared in 1772 and 1780.

101. AGI Audiencia de México 716.

102. If Oviedo knew about Campos, it is surprising that he did not capitalize on the story of a humble Indian who was also an exemplary Christian leading the way, which had become a theme of spiritual revival movements in New Spain during the eighteenth century.

103. Florencia and Oviedo, *Zodíaco mariano*, p. 208.

104. "Ilustración católica y religiosidad popular: El culto mariano en la España del siglo XVIII," in *La época de Fernando VI*, Textos y Estudios del Siglo XVIII, no. 9, Oviedo: Universidad de Oviedo, 1981, pp. 275–295.

105. Spanish Capuchins did adopt the Divina Pastora as their special patroness and introduced the devotion in their missions, both in Spain and overseas. See Ubrique, "Origen y desarrollo," pp. 812–823. That there were no Capuchin missionaries in Mexico before the twentieth century helps account for the more spontaneous, scattered, lay-centered devotion here. Capuchin nuns were established in a convent next to the shrine of Our Lady of Guadalupe at Tepeyac in the late eighteenth century. I do not know whether they were devotees of the Divina Pastora.

106. Peñaloza's report, AGI México 716, tira 9, fols. 8v–9r.

107. Tlaxcalan lords were especially so inclined, and the occasional village elders from Oaxaca and an Ópata chief turned up at the royal court or the offices of the Consejo de Indias, seeking the king's support in a land dispute, an appointment to office, or the establishment of a special school.

108. Published in José Joaquín de Ortega y San Antonio, *Mes mariano, o lección mensal . . .*, Mexico: Bibliotheca Mexicana, 1760.

109. Pamela Voekel, *Alone Before God: The Religious Origins of Modernity in Mexico*, Durham: Duke University Press, 2002, chapters 4 and 5.

110. On Nuestra Señora de la Escalera, see Florencia and Oviedo, *Zodíaco mariano*, pp. 207–208; on El Señor de la Antigua Veracruz, see Higinio Vásquez Santa Ana, *Cristos célebres de México*, Mexico: n.p., 1950, pp. 56–59; and on interest in the Virgin of Loreto there in the 1740s, see AGN Indiferente Virreinal caja 5837 exp. 55, 1744–1745 libro de cuentas for the Convento Hospital de Mujeres de Nuestra Señora de Loreto.

111. Antonio Genovesi, *La devoción de María Madre Santíssima de la Luz, distribuida en tres partes por un sacerdote de la Compañía de Jesús*, trans. Lucas Rincón, SJ, 2 vols., México: Imprenta Real del Superior Gobierno y del Nuevo Rezado, de Doña María de Rivera, 1737–1738. A 1732 Mexico City publication first announced the new devotion. (It is mentioned in *Gazeta de México* for March 1732, BIBM 4, p. 313, and cited in Medina, *La imprenta en México*, entry no. 3251.)

112. Leviathan is a monstrous image of Satan, into whose gaping mouth the damned will disappear at the Last Judgment. This fire-breathing monster is depicted in European art from the ninth century on. The iconography here follows scriptural references to hell's doorstep: Job 3:8, "May those who curse days curse that day, those who are ready to rouse Leviathan"; Job 41:5 "Who can open the doors of his face?" Together they suggest that Leviathan's gaping mouth was a one-way entrance to damnation and the pit of hell. The nightmarish monster in Our Lady of Light follows medieval Christian depictions of the entrance to Hell quite closely: "The Mouth of Hell was traditionally represented as the mouth of a huge and malevolent beast, which dragged sinners into its maw ... Leviathan's jaws are open and flame gushes out," Robert Hughes, *Heaven and Hell in Western Art*, London: Weidenfeld and Nicolson, 1968, pp. 175, 178.

113. Why the treasured original would have been exported from Italy is one of many unanswered questions in the streamlined legendary account in *La devoción de María Madre Santísima de la Luz*.

114. According to an early novena booklet dedicated to Our Lady of Light, for which the title page of the copy I consulted unfortunately is missing, the cult was growing in Mexico City, "que el dia de oy hai en varias iglesias pinceles de ellas." It singles out the images in the church of Porta Coeli (1732) and the Dominican monastery (1734), Sutro BX 2161.5.I4 N68 exp. 4.

115. By the 1780s, the devotion was evident in images and confraternities in various communities, not only where Jesuits and Franciscans were active promoters of it. I have not made a systematic search, but late colonial records and secondary works mention other paintings and sculpted images as personal possessions and in the parish of Santa María de la Redonda (Mexico City), Tepotzotlán (DF), the city of Guanajuato, Pachuca (Hidalgo), Yautepec and Tlaltizapán (Morelos), Tochimilco (Puebla), several parishes of the city of Puebla, Alta California missions, Jesuit missions in Chihuahua, Sonora, Baja California, Durango, and Mérida (Yucatán). A number of ships plying Atlantic waters were named after her in the late eighteenth century.

116. These figures for devotional publications dedicated to Our Lady of Light are based on a survey of Medina, *La imprenta en México*. For an example of an early 1760s print, see Ajofrín, *Diario del viaje*, I, 156.

117. Matthew 5:14; John 9:6. Light is a fundamental metaphor in Christianity and the most common votive offerings were candles.

118. Bancroft M-M 69, 70, vol. 1, fols. 46–47.

119. Bancroft M-M 69–70, vol. 1, fol. 46ff. A valuable secondary source on Our Lady of Light, Norman Neuerburg's "La Madre Santísima de la Luz," *The Journal of San Diego History* 41: 2 (Spring 1995) [unpaginated version consulted online at www.sandiegohistory.org/journal/95spring/laluz.htm], suggests that the debate in the synod ended without resolution, but does not elaborate.

120. The campaign to blot out the image of the monster continued off and on into the early 1780s. During his pastoral visit to parishes in the modern state of Morelos in 1778, Archbishop Ildefonso Núñez de Haro y Peralta ordered the "dragon" to be painted over in two paintings of Our Lady of Light in Yautepec and one in Tlaltizapán, AHM L10/20 1770, fols. 191v–212r. And José Gómez recorded in his diary on August 24, 1781 that the large painting of Our Lady of Light that had been displayed in the Jesuit church of the Colegio de San Pedro y San Pedro was moved to a side altar in the

Sagrario church attached to the cathedral. He noted that on August 26 of that year, the "dragon" had been removed "on higher orders" (*por superior mandato*), presumably by Archbishop Haro y Peralta. Bancroft M-M 105, "Diario de México," pp. 170–171.

121. Alcocer, *Carta apologética a favor del título de Madre Santísima de la Luz que goza la reyna del cielo* . . ., México: Zúñiga y Ontiveros, 1790.

122. There are exceptions. Examples of nineteenth-century paintings without the fire-breathing monster are in the parish church of San Agustín in Tlalpan, DF (*Catálogo Nacional de Monumentos Históricos. Muebles: Tlapan*, México: INAH, Dirección de Monumentos Históricos, 1988, p. 48) and the shrine to Our Lady of Light in Lagos de Moreno, Jalisco (Orozco, *Iconografía mariana*, I, 411). An undated lavishly illustrated publication from the late nineteenth century shows Our Lady of Light with a fiery man in the lower left corner, but not as an anthropomorphized furnace of Hell, *Galería Americana: A Collection of Religious Pictures*, México: Casa de J. Michaud, n.d., second plate.

123. And sometimes the two devotions intersected, as they did for José Antonio Alcocer, OFM, who wrote both a spirited defense of the devotion to Our Lady of La Luz, the *Carta apologética a favor del título de Madre Santísima de la Luz,* and a history of his Colegio de Propaganda Fide de Nuestra Señora de Guadalupe de la Ciudad de Zacatecas that featured Our Lady of El Refugio, *Bosquejo de la historia del Colegio de Nuestra Señora de Guadalupe y sus misiones, año de 1788*, Mexico: Porrúa, 1958, pp. 185–188.

124. For the many churches and altars dedicated to Nuestra Señora del Refugio in Aguascalientes, see Manuel Muñoz Díaz, *Fiestas populares en la región de Aguascalientes*, Aguascalientes: Universidad Autónoma de Aguascalientes, 1996, pp. 247–259.

125. Antonio de Oviedo, SJ, offered a different and possibly more reliable account of the early images of Refugio in Puebla, Zacatecas, and Mexico City in his enlargement of Florencia and Oviedo, *Zodíaco mariano*, pp. 187–197.

126. José Francisco Sotomayor, *Historia del Apostólico Colegio de Nuestra Señora de Guadalupe de Zacatecas desde su fundación hasta nuestros días*, 2nd ed., Zacatecas: Impr. de "La Rosa," 1889, I, 144–145, 161–167, 212; José Antonio Alcocer, *Bosquejo de la historia del Colegio de Nuestra Señora de Guadalupe y sus misiones, año de 1788*, Mexico: Editorial Porrúa, 1958, pp. 185–188, 192, 196. The *Zodíaco mariano* appeared too early in the development of the cult of Nuestra Señora del Refugio to describe its growth in detail, but Oviedo featured Father Giuca's celebrated image and the popularity it was stirring in both Puebla and Zacatecas, and the many miraculous cures associated with it. He also mentioned that great numbers of prints of the Virgin of Refugio were circulating, themselves treated as devotional objects, and that the painting on the main altar of the Franciscan college church in Zacatecas was surrounded by silver votive offerings of little bodies, feet, and heads, pp. 187–197. One of the miracles Oviedo recounted concerned a Franciscan from the Zacatecas college who took a painted replica, given to him by another Jesuit, on his return to Spain. His ship was attacked on the high seas by seven enemy ships, but when he put the painting on the ship's prow the enemies were routed.

127. According to Oviedo, the votive offerings then were so numerous that the chapel could not contain them, and at least forty candles regularly were lit before the image.

128. Alcocer, *Bosquejo de la historia del Colegio de Nuestra Señora de Guadalupe y sus misiones, año de 1788*, p. 186.
129. Alcocer claimed that devotion to Nuestra Señora del Refugio continued to grow at the time he wrote, 1788. Sotomayor, *Historia del Apostólico Colegio*, p. 175 has an example of a cure in 1776 and on pp. 210–211 mentions the great collection of wax and silver coins in the city of Guanajuato in 1806.
130. In nineteenth-century Mexico City, Nuestra Señora del Refugio was linked to devotion to the Santo Niño Cautivo, a statue of the Christ Child in the cathedral. Both were known as "refugio de pecadores" and "refugio de almas" (refuge of sinners and souls). This particular Santo Niño apparently was made by the famous Sevillano sculptor Juan Martínez Montañes in the early seventeenth century and ransomed from Turkish forces in Algiers in 1622 before reaching Mexico City. The first mention I have found of the Santo Niño Cautivo in a public devotional setting is in a procession in Mexico City in 1795 (published in the December 28, 1795 issue of the *Gazeta de México*, which briefly recounts the legendary rescue as described on the base of the statue). The earliest *novena* booklets devoted to the Santo Niño Cautivo were published in 1832, 1834 [1833?], and 1845; the first *triduo* booklet was published in 1845, to "appease" him (*desagraviarlo*), sponsored by the female devotee who had underwritten the novena booklet in 1833 when a great cholera epidemic swept through the city and much of Mexico, *Triduo doloroso dedicado al Santo Niño Cautivo* . . ., Mexico: Luis Abadiano y Valdés, 1845. The *triduo* booklet speaks of "this amazing [*portentosa*] image" and its ransom and includes prayers to placate an angry God and appeal for "succor in all my spiritual and temporal needs." In recent years there has been something of a resurgence of interest in the Santo Niño Cautivo, now the resort of families of kidnapped individuals, prisoners, and parents of unruly children.
131. Jesuits had been carrying out similar revival missions in central Mexico from at least the 1660s. For an example with some description of the activities of such a mission in the vicinity of San Miguel el Grande (San Miguel de Allende) and Celaya, see AGN Jesuitas II-4, exp. 19.
132. Capuchins in the provincial capital of Barquisimeto were especially successful in promoting devotion to the Divina Pastora. She is still the patroness of the city and region.

PART II

Soundings

Divine Presence, Place, and the Power of Things

5

Making Miracles

The hold of miracles on the imagination and devotional practices of Catholic Christians is at the heart of the history of shrines, "prodigious" images, and divine presence in the early modern period. But miracles are an elusive subject, perhaps especially for New Spain. Colonial-era writings confidently regarded them as acts of God that defy natural laws,[1] but obviously historians can know with any certainty only that people have believed such events happened and might happen again.[2] Even for belief the record usually is terse, and miracles are a moving target: accepted knowledge of the laws of nature, standards of verification, and mainstream thought about diabolism changed, rendering some events once considered miracles curiosities of nature or demonic deceptions. Nevertheless, there are some constants in official and popular expectations for miracles, especially that many of the colonial accounts echoed miracles worked by Christ and treated in the Gospels as parables of salvation: sight for the blind, hearing and voice for the deaf and mute, healthy limbs for the lame, sudden healing of the mortally ill, resuscitations of the recently deceased, escapes from mortal danger on land and sea, and exorcisms.[3] The healings, exorcisms, calming of waters, multiplication of loaves and fishes, and the rest relieved pain, suffering, and want in this world, but they also stood for something more glorious – spiritual purification and enlightenment, a good death, and the prospect of a soul's salvation. As Jesus said when he healed the blind man in John 9, "I am the light of the world." Often the depiction of miraculous images of Christ and the Blessed Mary conveyed this transcendent meaning. Take the radiance surrounding the image of the Virgin of Guadalupe or, on the cover of this book, José de Páez's painted "portrait" of the miraculous Christ of Ixmiquilpan (ca. 1770), bathed from above in a heavenly light that focuses the viewer's attention squarely on the figure and sacrifice.

Within this shared understanding, there were bound to be disagreements and reservations. Priests knew to teach the salvific promise of Christ's miracles, while parishioners were more likely to think first of pressing problems in the here and now. Christ's miracles also had more to do with cleansing sin and exorcising the diabolical than did most colonial miracle stories that, like their Old World counterparts, were more often about the hand of God breaking in on daily life to bring relief from misfortune. Church authorities warned against routine calls for miracles that tempted God. St. Augustine's understanding of miracles echoes through the official record for New Spain: "God, then, who made the visible heaven and earth, does not disdain to perform visible miracles in heaven and on earth. He does this in order to inspire the soul, hitherto given up to things visible, to worship Him, the Invisible. But where and when He does this depends upon an immutable plan belonging to Himself alone."[4] Or as veteran Jesuit missionary and administrator Andrés Pérez de Ribas put it in the early 1640s, true miracles were rare: "we should not look for extraordinary and miraculous [means], which God dispenses when and as it pleases Him."[5]

While the full repertoire of New Testament miracles may well have been anticipated at many of colonial Mexico's image shrines, and some experiences were so universal that similar miracle stories about them were bound to be told everywhere – epidemics, intestinal complaints, broken bones, infected wounds, paralysis, blindness, deafness, droughts, floods, lightning strikes, hailstorms, infestations of locusts, runaway horses, or the devil – a shrine might also be known for a particular type of miracle event, much as some saints were known as specialized advocates. For instance, Our Lady of the Rosary and El Señor de los Rayos of Temastián, Jalisco, protected against lightning strikes. Some specialties were closely related to local geography and livelihoods: shrines in or near ports and coastal towns, such as the Christ of San Román in Campeche, were best known for saving ships from fearsome storms at sea, fishermen from drowning, and people from attacks by crocodiles; with shrines in ranching areas like Aguascalientes, devotees were saved from fatal accidents involving cattle, runaway horses, and poisonous snakes (although miracles for riders and victims of rabid dogs could be reported just about anywhere); and Our Lady of Guanajuato in New Spain's great silver mining region frequently was invoked in mine accidents. Some rural shrines, such as Chalma, disproportionately featured stories of Indians being blessed by divine grace, no doubt because most people living in the vicinity and visiting the site from more distant places were Indians.[6] And miracle stories for the shrine of the Virgin of San Juan de los Lagos, Jalisco, located along the main corridor of travel and trade to northern New Spain, featured a larger number of mulatos and mestizos because more people classified as castas either lived nearby or passed through town during the trade fairs. Not surprisingly, Nuestra Señora de San Juan also was renowned for protecting traders and merchants from highway robbers.

Other specialties less obviously reflected local circumstances. Some were directed toward a particular audience or served devotional programs initiated by clergy near the shrine. Or so it would seem from pious chronicles, which are often the only written record of miracle stories for a shrine. For example, the unusual stories in Dominican friar Manuel Antonio Moxica's early eighteenth-century devotional booklet for the miraculous Christ housed in the chapel of his order's residence for novices (*casa de novicios*) in Mexico City were directed to the novices themselves more than to a wider public.[7] After mentioning supernatural signs and favors associated with the image – mysterious Indians delivering the statue, then disappearing without a trace; balls of fire hovering over the novices' chapel; some of the usual healings and rescues; and amazing feats performed by resident friars – Moxica settled on eleven stories warning novices of the perils of forsaking divine favor by leaving the order.[8] In most of these stories, former novices met a violent end soon after leaving "the loving presence of the Santo Cristo." One turned to a life of crime and was executed; several others were attacked and killed "before they had time to say the name of Jesus"; another was thrown from a horse and died of his injuries. Moxica sets these grim, cautionary tales alongside one more hopeful story of divine intervention, brotherly compassion, and a ray of hope for redemption:

A young novice was afflicted by the Devil with many thoughts ..., one of which was to give up the habit ... Once he returned to the world he was so afflicted and upset that he swallowed mercury chloride and tried to slit his own throat. But God would not let him die. Not only did He open the eyes of his soul, but also of his body to see that he was surrounded by Dominican friars ... They took him to their convent where they cured him with love and later bade him a forthright farewell.

Other specialties of miraculous images were directed toward the general public, but stressed salvation more than relief from the woes of the world. The *Zodíaco mariano* includes an unusual number of redemptive stories – of sight restored to the blind and devotees raised from the dead as a coming into the light, Christ's truth, and salvation. In this, the authors followed the example of earlier chroniclers, including Franciscan friar Bernardo de Lizana in his *Devocionario de Nuestra Señora de Izamal y conquista espiritual de Yucatán*, published in 1633. Lizana's devotional text highlighted cures for blindness, deafness, and paralysis that reiterated the Gospel parables.[9] According to other devotional texts published in the seventeenth and eighteenth centuries, Our Lady of Zapopan was especially known for her apparitions warning devotees of impending death so they could prepare for confession and communion. And eighteenth-century Dominicans and Franciscans promoted the Virgin Mary in the guise of Nuestra Señora del Refugio as especially efficacious in combatting the Devil.[10]

But definite patterns in local miracle stories usually are complicated by exceptions or a countervailing tendency. For instance, coastal towns and some highland shrines closely connected to Atlantic travelers (such as the Black Christ of Esquipulas in Guatemala and the Christ of San Román in Campeche) were indeed likely to be known for maritime miracles. However, some highland image shrines with less obvious connections to the sea also were known for maritime miracles – for example, Nuestra Señora de la Soledad of Antequera, Oaxaca and Nuestra Señora de los Remedios in the Valley of Mexico. Their association with the sea depended more on the presence of seagoing travelers and the Virgin Mary's reputation for aquatic miracles of all kinds, whether rainmaking, escapes from drowning in a river or well, relief from floods, or quelling storms at sea.

Sources and Problems of Description and Interpretation

Much of the discussion of miracles in this chapter is based on 1,176 miracle stories, testimonials, reports, investigations, and legal proceedings gathered from a scattering of written and pictorial sources. This is not a small number, but it is by no means exhaustive or necessarily representative, and it pales in comparison to the European record, where 12,000 miracle stories and more were recorded for a single shrine in Germany during the seventeenth and eighteenth centuries.[11] Many events regarded locally as miracles were not recorded individually or included in the published devotional texts that account for most of the stories recorded in the colonial period.[12] The difficulty of tracking the reception of miracles in the colonial period stems in part from the term "miracle" and how its use shaped the written record. To church authorities it was a weighty legal term, reserved for supernatural events deemed by bishops and their superiors in Rome to be the fruit of divine intervention. The term was not to be used liberally for every kind of fortunate outcome or misfortune; to do otherwise was to court official derision as superstitious or as a scheming false prophet. Most of the miracle stories for New Spain that circulated widely were chosen, shaped, and published by church authorities. Dr. Manuel de Escalante captured this function of the written and pictorial record in 1684: "Without this book, the miracle would be lost, as if it had never happened."[13] And as Kenneth Woodward suggests, no matter how many are collected and how detailed the record of them may be, most of the surviving miracle stories are lessons more than case histories.[14]

Since ecclesiastical officials considered identifying miracles to be a legal matter, it is curious that reports of supernatural events were not more often investigated in a way that would document how they were initially described and came to be written down, depicted, and disseminated.[15] No doubt, attempting to investigate every case would have overwhelmed the episcopal courts, but only a few dozen full-fledged investigations and episcopal certifications of miracles, known as *informaciones jurídicas*, seem to have been undertaken and completed, and most were confirmation hearings rather than probing investigations.[16] The published novena booklets, chronicles, and devotional histories licensed by diocesan authorities that popularized miracle stories and were meant to fix memory rarely included more than a handful of examples of great good fortune or just punishment.[17] The remembering would be highly selective. Most of the stories in this devotional literature are not much more than early modern tweets – reduced to two or three lines, usually undated, and often without naming the devotee.

Even more striking than so few informaciones jurídicas in the episcopal court records is the near absence of *libros de milagros* (running registers of marvels kept shrines) and the failure of most published histories of shrines to devote much space to marvelous events associated with the prodigious image. William Christian notes that registers of miracles were being kept at some shrines in Western Europe as early as the thirteenth century and were more common by the fifteenth century; the libros de milagros recorded at the shrine of Nuestra Señora de Guadalupe in Extremadura are perhaps the best known. Published histories, too, were in circulation in Spain by the time America was colonized,[18] but none of the shrine histories for New Spain that began to be published a century later described miracles in the way Pedro de Burgos did in his book about the Catalonian shrine of Nuestra Señora de Montserrat, first published in Barcelona in 1536. Burgos devoted nearly 500 printed pages to 325 numbered miracle stories for this image and shrine, covering the full range of familiar miracles, most of them mirroring the wonders worked by Christ, with healings and protection predominating.[19] Although there was nothing for shrines in New Spain comparable to the European registers of miracles, some attempts apparently were made by local chaplains to start them. At the shrine of the Virgin of San Juan de los Lagos in the mid-eighteenth century, there was said to be a list of more than 300 miracles; and for the shrine of Nuestra Señora de la Salud at Pátzcuaro in 1742, Pedro Sarmiento, SJ, reportedly compiled a "book" of miracles.[20]

Colonial-era authors of shrine histories – many of them Franciscans and Jesuits[21] – were well aware of this void in the record and sometimes used it to explain why they presented so few miracle stories to document the power and favor of divine presence. Their explanations ranged from inattentive and overworked shrine chaplains, and prejudices of peninsular chroniclers who doubted that miracles could occur in America, to pronouncements that the miracles were common knowledge and did not need to be written down, and that there were too many of them to even attempt a compilation. The image itself was the greatest miracle; all other benefits paled in comparison. Franciscan friar Francisco de Cárdenas Valencia, writing about Yucatán's Virgin of Izamal in 1639, offered a more considered version of the "common knowledge" explanation: the fact that visitors to the shrine had heard the stories and seen the many votive offerings, there "has removed whatever reason there may have been to undertake formal investigations or advertise them in print."[22] That many of the colonial miracles did not occur at or near the shrine also would have made it difficult for a chaplain to keep track of the particulars of individual cases.

But the main reason for so few reports of miracle stories may well be that church authorities discouraged them in order to keep religious enthusiasm and shrine devotions within bounds, in the spirit of the Council of Trent decrees against indiscriminate saint-making and loose talk about miracles.[23] Mexico's first bishop, Fray Juan de Zumárraga, OFM, reportedly declared that God did not need more miracles since so many were already recorded in the Bible. Writing in the 1580s or 1590s, Franciscan evangelizer Gerónimo de Mendieta added that God needed miracles only for conversion, and the natives had already accepted Christianity. Paraphrasing St. Paul, he declared, "miracles are for infidels and unbelievers, not for the faithful."[24] Their intentions in confining miracle stories were pastoral as well as political. As Fray Juan de Mendoza, OFM, put it in the first chronicle of the shrine of Tecaxic (1684), he wanted to provide "true news in a simple form that would further the devotion."[25] New World bishops worried that excessive interest in miracles and the sacraments bred superstition and encouraged the devil, so that unrestrained exuberance and stubborn ignorance came to be regarded as a greater threat to the true faith than knowing infidelity and apostasy.[26]

Considering that the *Zodíaco mariano* – the only published compilation of more than a few dozen miracle stories for New Spain – accounts for about 20 percent of stories gathered for this chapter, it deserves a few words about how the authors muffled the biblical emphasis on Satan, focused attention on the miraculous image in its shrine, and appealed especially to a literate, creole Spanish audience. In the tradition of Wilhelm Gumppenberg SJ's global survey of Marian shrines, *Atlas Marianus* (first edition, Ingolstad, 1657), the scope of the *Zodíaco mariano* was limited to Marian shrines, and it, too, was the work of Jesuits, both of them American Spaniards. Francisco de Florencia (d. 1695), who served as emissary to Rome for the Jesuit provinces of the Indies and authored more than a dozen devotional texts and histories of miraculous images and their shrines in New Spain, conceived the project.[27] His unfinished manuscript was amended and enlarged by Juan Antonio de Oviedo (d. 1757), a leading Jesuit administrator, noted author of sermons, and Marian devotee. On the subject of miracles, the authors of the *Zodíaco mariano* warned readers that they were barely scratching the surface of all the prodigious favors associated with famous Mexican images, and then proceeded to include 287 thumbnail miracle stories for eighty-four shrines.[28] These stories display nearly the full range of miracles circulating in print and pictures at the time. Personal and collective healings and narrow escapes from hopeless predicaments predominate, as they do in the larger assortment of miracle stories, but Florencia and Oviedo also gave special attention to founding miracles – usually the first sign of divine presence and will associated with a particular sacred image, most often the image coming to life in some way. With few exceptions, they presented these founding miracles in greater detail than the personal favors, drawing attention to the shrines and their locations as much as to the miraculous images.

Comparing miracle stories in the *Zodíaco mariano* to the texts Florencia and Oviedo drew upon for a particular shrine, especially when one published account seems to have been their source, is a way to consider how they shaped their presentation for particular audiences and religious sensibilities. For the shrine image of Nuestra Señora de los Remedios from Zitácuaro, Michoacán, the *Zodíaco mariano* used the six miracle stories in a 1643 chronicle by Alonso de la Rea, OFM.[29] The two paralyzed women, the knife wound suffered by a Spanish man in a fight, the construction workers who escaped harm when the roof of the church collapsed, and the merchant and niece who invoked Nuestra Señora de los Remedios when their ship nearly sank in a storm all are faithfully repeated, but they omitted the revival of a black slave's moribund infant. Did Florencia and/or Oviedo doubt this last miracle? Was it inadvertently left out? Perhaps, but this omission fits a pattern of downplaying miracles associated with castas. For Nuestra Señora de Izamal, the *Zodíaco mariano*'s main source of miracle stories was Lizana's devotional primer begun in 1623 or 1624 and published in 1633. Most of Lizana's seventeen miracle stories follow miracles worked by Christ – healing the paralyzed, sight to the blind, hearing and speech to the deaf and mute, rescues on the water. Nine of the miracle stories feature Indian beneficiaries, although none of them is identified by name; Lizana praises the Indian peoples of Yucatán for their great faith in Christ and their frequent visits to the shrine. Seven stories feature Spaniards, and one features a black slave. The *Zodíaco mariano* included Lizana's miracle stories (except for one in which an Indian woman recovered from a stomachache) but added five others that shift attention to elite Spaniards and great favors for devotees in the Spanish provincial capital of Mérida. And where Lizana emphasized struggles to keep the faith that gained Mary's favor, the *Zodíaco mariano* emphasizes tender acts of personal and collective devotion to her through this image. The last new miracle draws attention back to the image as place: according to a Jesuit eyewitness, when the image was taken out of the shrine in procession for the annual feast day celebrations, a beautiful star appeared above it, as bright as the morning star. Oviedo or Florencia interpreted this marvel as similar to the star that guided the Magi to the Christ Child, in this case bringing devotees to this prodigious image of Christ's mother wherever she might be.

For the Virgin of Guadalupe, the *Zodíaco mariano* included fifteen miracle stories, down from the thirty-five in Florencia's devotional history of the *guadalupana, La estrella del norte de México*, published in 1688. Did Florencia himself reduce the number in order to bring the Guadalupan miracles into line with the number of miracles included in the *Zodíaco mariano* for other shrines? Was Oviedo, rather than Florencia, responsible for editing the original list? From the published text alone we cannot be certain, although Oviedo certainly added at least two miracles that are dated after Florencia's death: relief from the great epidemic of 1737, and discovery of a silver nugget resembling the Virgin of Guadalupe in a Guanajuato mine. Dropped or downplayed from the miracles presented in the *Estrella del norte de México* are exorcisms, other references to Satan, and miracles worked through brandea rather than the image itself. Most of the iconic miracles depicted in paintings in the shrine at Tepeyac and in Stradanus's engraving from the 1610s were retained. Overall, the *Zodíaco mariano* turned attention away from minor healings, personal accidents, and demonic possession toward collective protection, miracles involving water, supernatural signs of Mary's ongoing presence at Tepeyac, and the mystique of the image itself as impossible to copy exactly.

The most beguiling, although not the most abundant or necessarily revealing, miracle stories from the colonial period are recorded in ex-voto paintings placed at shrines by grateful donors.[30] The paintings depict events that were understood to depend on divine intervention – mostly scenes of recovery from illness, accident, and natural disaster – and a selection of them was likely to be displayed on the walls of shrines, near the miraculous image they addressed and honored. At first glance, these graphic depictions seem to take us into the moment in the way a wire service photo on the front page of a newspaper can. People, places, and dates are named, but in fact these paintings are quite stylized, following certain conventions of depiction and subject more than specifying an actual event. They are a form of piety from the Middle Ages that apparently bloomed with new vigor in Italy in the sixteenth century and spread through much of Catholic Europe before declining there toward the end of the eighteenth century and reviving in the late nineteenth century, and then being largely superseded after the early twentieth century.[31] The form had a longer life in New Spain and Mexico, but the conventions of representations of miraculous cures, rescues, exorcisms, and the rest in the ex-voto paintings that survive from the colonial period are much the same as those in their European predecessors. No doubt, the formulaic depictions were what

Making Miracles 317

Figure 5.1 José Patricio Polo, ex-voto painting, Huamantla, Puebla, ca. 1741. Photograph by Elizabeth Wilder Weismann. Courtesy of the Nettie Lee Benson Latin American Collection, University of Texas Libraries, University of Texas at Austin.

people expected and recognized as authentic. But which people? Who made the choices? Was it the painter (who rarely was the donor)? The donor? The parish priest or shrine chaplain who chose which paintings to display and how to display them, and may have been consulted before the painter began his work? Have the museums and private collectors now in possession of many of these paintings tended to value and preserve some kinds of examples and dismiss others?

For only a few surviving colonial ex-voto paintings can we answer these questions directly. In one example from the mid-eighteenth century, described by Elizabeth Wilder Weismann, the artist was also the patron. It is a painted canvas, stretched to 17″ × 23″, depicting a horse that has fallen on top of its rider inside a bare drawing room (Figure 5.1). Next to the horse and rider is a woman with her hands clasped in supplication. Above these figures are clouds at the upper corners containing images of the Virgin of the Rosary and Jesús Nazareno. The caption at the bottom of the painting states that on the day of San Lorenzo, 1741,[32] at Huamantla (Tlaxcala), Joseph Patricio Polo entered the patio of his home on horseback, whereupon the horse took fright and bolted through the doorway into the drawing room, where it slipped and fell on top of the rider. When Polo invoked the sweet name of Jesus and Our Lady of the Rosary, the horse suddenly calmed down and he escaped serious injury.[33] Weismann determined that Joseph Patricio Polo was a provincial painter by trade, born in Huamantla. His father, Bernardino Polo, a mestizo son of unmarried parents, was also a painter in Huamantla. Bernardino married a *castiza* from Cholula in 1696, and Joseph Patricio probably was born within a few years since he married Josefa de la Encarnación Aguilar in 1722. Weismann concludes that the painting dates from 1741, and, unless Joseph Patricio's father was still alive in 1741 to paint the scene of his son's accident, the ex-voto was painted by Joseph Patricio Polo himself, and the woman praying for his safety is his wife, Encarnación. The painting would have fulfilled Joseph Patricio's vow to Mary and Christ, and was probably displayed in the Huamantla church near these images of Christ on the road to Calvary and Our Lady of the Rosary.

Like this example, the standard ex-voto painting in Europe and America was divided into two or three registers: the divine patron depicted at the top of the painting; the miracle scene depicted in the middle register; and, often, a brief written description and declaration of gratitude for divine intervention along the bottom of the painting. Most of the colonial-era ex-voto paintings feature people of privilege, but about a quarter (and more in published chronicles) depict members of the *plebe*, like María de Viscarra of the city of Guanajuato who was eating cactus apples at home and swallowed a spine, which stuck in her throat. "She motioned for a print of Our Lady of El Pueblito, which she kept on a small altar, kissed it reverently, and coughed up the spine."[34] In content and form, colonial ex-voto paintings were much like the better-known Mexican "retablos" and ex-votos of the nineteenth and twentieth centuries that usually are painted on small, mass-produced tin sheets. But there were differences. Fewer in number and mainly done by trained painters, the colonial ex-votos varied in size from about the dimensions of a sheet of writing paper to large framed paintings, and most were painted on stretched canvas or wooden boards called *tablas* or "tablets," rather than sheets of metal.

Comparatively few colonial tablas are known, and the group of 133 considered here from published sources no doubt is incomplete. Several seventeenth- and eighteenth-century chronicles and administrative records mention "tablets of miracles" on church walls, "many little canvases," and "a great number of retablos," and some of the devotional histories of miraculous images clearly drew their short accounts of particular miracle stories from ex-voto paintings.[35] The first published shrine history (1621), Luis de Cisneros's *Historia del principio* . . . for the shrine of Nuestra Señora de los Remedios at Totoltepec in the Valley of Mexico, described 15 paintings of miracles and alluded to as many as 100 others depicting miraculous healings and another 200 depicting survivals from accidents that were displayed in the shrine at that time.[36] Still, there would seem to have been far fewer of these early ex-voto paintings than are known for the nineteenth century and the first half of the twentieth. Of those that have been published, the earliest dates from 1651, for the miraculous image of Our Lady of Tulantongo.[37] Another thirty-seven examples date from the late seventeenth century. Most (ninety-five, or more than two-thirds[38]) date from the eighteenth and early nineteenth centuries and were commissioned by and depict mainly dons and doñas, priests, nuns, government functionaries, merchants, estate owners, and high-status artisans.

While there is reason to doubt that these colonial ex-voto paintings simply stand for the many miracle stories that were not recorded, some tendencies in them are notable as part of the larger story. Besides being produced by artists with some formal training and featuring elite individuals, most of the beneficiaries in these paintings were men – eighteen men to four women in the seventeenth-century examples, sixty-two men to thirty-one women in the eighteenth-century examples, which is close to the 1.58 to 1 male-to-female ratio in the larger group of miracle stories. By a wide margin most of the miracles reported in these ex-voto paintings were either marvelous recoveries from hopeless illness and disability or protection and survival from grave accidents. Accidents outnumber the healings, by fourteen to nine in the seventeenth-century group, and sixty-eight to forty-six in the eighteenth-century group. Few were exorcisms (three) or minatory miracles in which the divine presence warned or punished an unworthy sinner (three).

The specialties of different shrines are reflected in some of these miracle paintings – runaway horses and aquatic miracles (in storms at sea, in devotees swept downriver and nearly drowned, in falls into wells, in bringing rain) for Nuestra Señora de los Remedios. The Virgin of Guadalupe was distinguished by the wide range of miracle events attributed to her mediation, but in capsule form the eight miracles depicted in Samuel Stradanus's engraving from the 1610s illustrate familiar patterns: more men than women (here seven men and one woman); seven elite protagonists and one Indian sacristan; four accidents and three recoveries from acute illness (Figure 5.2). But a few ex-voto paintings refer to miracles that were not likely to find their way into the canon of published miracle stories, such as finding a lost animal or regaining one's personal honor.

How the ex-voto paintings were received over time is even less certain than the reception of most religious prints, but the words written on them provide a clue. Aside from recognizable portraits of the donor in the larger, more accomplished ex-voto paintings, what could make even the most formulaic and rudimentary depiction of a miracle scene intimate and compelling to viewers were the names, places, and dates recorded on them.

Figure 5.2 Print from Samuel Stradanus engraving of the Virgin of Guadalupe with eight ex-voto depictions of miraculous events, ca. 1620. Courtesy of the Metropolitan Museum of Art, New York City.

These details of who, where, when, and the celestial patron announced that the wonders were worked right there – especially for local people: friends, relatives, neighbors, and ancestors of the viewer. The power and meaning of these paintings was not in their numbers, which were small as votive offerings went, but as both what Pierre Bourdieu called a "pre-diction," a calling into presence like that performed in the miraculous image itself,[39] and an exchange between grateful devotees and this protective divine presence.

While colonial ex-voto paintings on display would not have documented more than a small fraction of the marvels and miracles that were public knowledge in one way or another during the seventeenth and eighteenth centuries, there was a more abundant type of graphic votive offering: *milagritos*, little wax and silver figures and body parts placed on or near the honored image as tokens of devotion, desire, and thanks. Like the ex-voto paintings, milagritos were not uniquely American. Virtually identical tokens of faith and thanks, in similarly large numbers, are mentioned at European Christian shrines from the late Middle Ages, and they were increasingly popular in Mediterranean Europe in the early modern period, at least until the late eighteenth century. They appear often in seventeenth-century Italian sources. For example, at the tomb of Andrea Avellino in Naples between 1613 and 1619, 359 silver milagritos and 1,230 wax milagritos were inventoried; and the shrine of San Paolo Maggiore in 1647 reportedly was covered in silver milagritos, a veritable grotto of shimmering light, with some 10,000 more added between 1649 and 1656.[40]

It is not clear whether milagritos were common votive offerings in New Spain during the sixteenth century, but they were frequently mentioned by the second decade of the seventeenth century. One of the miracle paintings depicted in Figure 5.2 shows small replica legs and heads as votive offerings. More pointedly, Luis de Cisneros's devotional history of Nuestra Señora de los Remedios (1621) described the altar on which the miraculous statuette was displayed as "covered with silver feet, hands, heads, chests, and eyes" that sparkled in the light.[41] These are not isolated examples. In 1639, Franciscan friar Francisco Cárdenas Valencia noticed wax bodies, arms, legs, and heads displayed alongside the Christ of San Román and Our Lady of Izamal in Yucatán;[42] in 1645 Dominican Fr. Alonso Franco described the altar dedicated to Santo Domingo de Soriano in his order's headquarters church in Mexico City as covered with innumerable "wax figures ... legs, arms, heads, eyes, and full-length men and women";[43] the first history of the shrine of Our Lady of Tecaxic near Toluca, published in 1684, mentioned "figures of wax – eyes, bodies, feet, hands";[44] and Florencia and Oviedo frequently mentioned milagritos in their survey of notable Marian shrines of New Spain.[45] Incidental mention of milagritos can be found just about everywhere miraculous images appear in eighteenth-century records – in an inventory of the shrine to the Cristo Renovado at Mapethé, Hidalgo in 1748 that included a wooden box containing "various little wax bodies"[46]; in an inventory of the new Divina Pastora chapel in Veracruz, displaying "silver milagritos of various sizes, with their little ribbons";[47] in Archbishop Rubio y Salinas's pastoral visit to the church of the Rosary in Querétaro, where he found "little silver body parts and other valuables";[48] and little silver legs pinned to the girdle of the crucified Christ in the Real del Monte parish church in 1804; and covering the statue of the Señor del Calvario of Coatepec Harinas in 1820.[49] The chronicler of the shrine of Nuestra Señora de Xuquila in Oaxaca in 1791 mentioned that about 2,000 wax milagritos came in every year and some 482 silver figures were inventoried between 1765 and 1785.[50]

Each milagrito was a personal testimonial of faith and good fortune, but displayed together and sometimes arranged in artful designs, especially in the shape of a heart, they must have appeared as a long-running record of favor bestowed on a whole community of devotees. Unfortunately, they are mute to us – anonymous, wordless witnesses to stories of suffering, hope, and recovery that moved devotees to visit the shrine with these offerings or send them with someone else.[51] Even less often inventoried or described in any detail than milagritos are the most ephemeral, and doubtless the most common, offerings of thanks and hope – the countless candles, flowers, locks of hair, umbilical cords, crutches,[52] food, and prayers uttered and gestures made at the shrine, on the road, and at home.

There are many remarks in colonial chronicles and reports about miracles galore, especially after the early seventeenth century, when devotees of the Virgin Mary and Christ, in particular shrine images, regarded themselves as especially favored. Even Torquemada, who had observed in his *Monarquía Indiana* (1615) that few incontrovertible miracles comparable to the Gospel stories had happened in New Spain during the sixteenth century, went on to say that scores of amazing cures, rescues, and quenched fires were associated with slivers of the great wooden cross erected at Tlaxcala in 1519. "Of these kinds, the number of miracles that God has worked through this Holy Relic is almost infinite."[53] While few chronicles and reports of the seventeenth and eighteenth centuries included more than several miracle stories, they were likely to say that many more miracle stories could be told. Here are a few suggestive examples. Cárdenas Valencia, writing about Yucatán in 1639, recounted a dozen or so miracles associated with celebrated images, but noted that many more had not been recorded "for lack of interest."[54] For Our Lady of Izamal he noted that the miracles attributed to her were "many and great, the blind person finding sight, the dumb speech, the paralyzed movement, the sick health, and even the deceased have returned to life."[55] Miguel Sánchez, whose *Imagen de la*

Virgen María (1648) was the key text in the developing cult of Our Lady of Guadalupe, wrote about miracles mostly in generalities and grandly proclaimed that she is the "protectress of the poor, the medicine of the sick, the source of relief for the afflicted, intercessor for the troubled, the pride of the city of Mexico, [and] the glory of all the faithful who live in that New World."[56] Luis Becerra Tanco, one of Sánchez's successor chroniclers of devotion to Nuestra Señora de Guadalupe in the mid-seventeenth century, excused himself from elaborating on the many miracles associated with this image: "they are not written down here because a large volume would be needed, and the image itself is its greatest wonder."[57] Writing in the early 1650s, Antonio Tello, the Franciscan chronicler of his order's activities in Nueva Galicia, mentioned various miraculous images and alluded to illnesses cured, injuries healed, fires quenched, exorcisms, providential rains, storms calmed, and protection against bats, but offered few examples.[58]

Some images were closely associated with a particular kind of miracle. Francisco de Florencia wrote in the 1680s that the shrine to San Miguel del Milagro in Tlaxcala was known for curing blindness, "las tinieblas de la ceguera," as he put it, with "tinieblas" signifying both darkness and benighted ignorance. Curing the blind was like conversion to Christianity: a journey from darkness to light. The eighteenth-century record yields even more of these passing references to many miracles for "bodily needs" and "spiritual remedies" – foiling the devil; suddenly curing the ill and injured; protecting people from harm in earthquakes, epidemics, storms at sea, floods, and famines; and enabling an imminent good death and opening the possibility of salvation. These sources again are short on particular cases.[59] As Franciscan Manuel de Loaizaga noted in recounting more than four dozen miracle stories associated with the Virgin of Ocotlán, "these are only a few of the many ... for I find myself in the middle of a flood [of them] with no other recourse than to drown."[60] Or as a Jesuit chronicler of the province of Zacatecas wrote more prosaically in 1737, "I leave out many other miracles of this Lady which, even though fellow priests wise with age have recounted them to me, I do not find authorized, and others are omitted because the lack of interest by our ancestors denies us even the most limited record of them."[61]

Origin Stories

For at least 137 of the shrines listed in Appendix 1, founding miracles were recorded in writing during the colonial period, a third of them (46) collected in the *Zodíaco mariano*. They are likely to be a more representative group than the other miracle stories, but representative of what? Are they representative of origin stories that actually date from the beginning of a shrine's history? Of a suitably providential tradition devised after a shrine and its image became famous, perhaps replacing or amending an ambiguous or less resounding origin story? In some cases, a group of supernatural signs were treated together as founding miracles, and it is usually far from clear when they may have become part of the shrine's lore.[62] And what of the 300+ shrines for which I found no record of an origin story? Did they have one that was widely accepted at the time?

Most founding miracles were not written down near the time they are said to have occurred, so whether they represent an older oral tradition, a later creation, or a substitution is an open question. As Luis de Cisneros conceded for the shrine of Nuestra Señora de los Remedios in 1621, "its beginning and origin are not known with certainty" so that "it has become famous through its fabulous miracles."[63] And early versions of first signs were likely to be modified and streamlined over time. Our Lady of Tulantongo in a village near the old native city of Texcoco, described in Chapter 1, is one example of a founding history "improved" as the tradition grew.

In many founding miracles of medieval and early modern European Catholic shrines there is a supernatural event that signals the discovery or active presence of the divine in a sacred image. Handsome young strangers dressed in white offer the image to its chosen recipient and then mysteriously disappear; a riderless mule bearing the image stops in a particular location and will not budge; livestock are drawn to the location of a hidden image; radiant light comes from such a place; heavenly music sounds or church bells ring spontaneously; a heavenly apparition is reported, later to be depicted in a painting or statue and revered as if it were the original apparition; the outlines of a figure of Christ or a saint appear in a tree or rock, or on a wall; an image suddenly becomes heavy or light; an apparition speaks in the presence of its image; sacred images, crosses, or consecrated communion wafers resist desecration or bleed when struck; a sign appears in the sky, sometimes a glowing cross, ball of fire, or shower of blood. Images spontaneously come to life – self-restoring, trembling, perspiring, groaning (especially statues of Christ), bleeding, crying, speaking (rarely), growing hair, becoming bigger, relocating, moving their eyes, head, or limbs, changing expression, posture, or complexion, taking a bullet to protect a devotee. Or an image survives a fire or earthquake that destroys everything around it, or resists an attack by enemies and is marked with some surprisingly minor damage; or it somehow remains in perfect condition over many years (especially statues and paintings of the Virgin Mary).

While founding miracles in colonial Mexico include examples of nearly all the familiar European ones,[64] there were differences. Of the three basic types of founding miracles for European image shrines[65] – (1) holiness tried and triumphant (in which an image or sacred material resisted desecration and destruction);[66] (2) holiness lost and found (such as images of Mary hidden from infidels that were discovered thanks to a supernatural sign); and (3) the holiness of an image in place suddenly revealed (through an apparition, activation, or other sign of divine presence and favor) – the third prevailed in Mexico, while the second was more common in Spain, and the first was found mostly in parts of Germany. As they had in Europe, images often appeared in mysterious ways in New Spain (in at least 26 of the 137 stories), or occasionally (in six or seven cases) were commissioned later to commemorate an apparition in the flesh, in which the Virgin Mary or another saint, or less often Christ, appeared in human form and conveyed messages to the seers of the divine figure. And in at least fifty-six other cases in New Spain, an image already in place in the parish church or private chapel began to move or show other signs of life. Some images were found on hilltops, in caves, or near springs or another prominent feature of the landscape, as they were in Spain, but since more than half the cases in New Spain (eighty-two) involved prodigious images already in place in a church or chapel, rural landscapes were less often an essential part of this New World story. An even more distinctive pattern in this Mexican sample is that when images were found in nature (at least twenty-nine cases, of which four or a few more fit the Spanish "shepherd's cycle" pattern of a long-hidden image of the Virgin Mary being found by a shepherd looking for a lost animal that was drawn to the site[67]), over half of them (sixteen) were *of* nature, growing in the trunk, limbs, bark, or roots of trees. Such natural images were not unknown in Spain and other parts of Europe,[68] but they were less common there.

Colonial Developments

Beyond cycles of crisis accompanied by eruptions of grace, the array of reported miracles, their distribution over time, and their beneficiaries may not have changed much during the colonial period. Nevertheless, some significant changes in reporting did occur that fall roughly into three periods outlined in Chapters 1 and 2: the 1520s to the 1570s; a long seventeenth century, from 1580 to 1730; and the 1730s to the 1810s.

Miracle stories during the first generations of Spanish colonization, from the 1520s to the 1570s, stand apart in several respects. First, the written record is less abundant and most of the examples (sixty or so) postdate the events they describe, often by twenty years or more.[69] Since mendicant chroniclers of "the spiritual conquest" (including Franciscans Gerónimo de Mendieta, Pedro de Oroz, Juan de Torquemada, and Dominican Agustín Dávila Padilla[70]) recorded most of these early stories, it is no surprise that many of them feature evangelizing friars and pious Indians. This is not to say that these early stories are without other significance both for that time and in comparison to miracle stories later, but they are selective and we cannot be sure what is missing. The sixteenth-century miracle stories feature supernatural signs in nature[71] and apparitions and visions of Mary, Christ, and the saints prevail;[72] combat and conquest, with some cases of the Virgin Mary coming to the aid of her Christian soldiers against native enemies in thrall to the devil; and wonders associated with saintly friars or their relics. Only rarely was a statue or painting treated as a medium or channel of sacred exchange between Christian supplicants and the divine presence. Our Lady of Guadalupe and Our Lady of Remedios are the outstanding exceptions.[73]

The Oroz Codex, a compilation of Franciscan texts written down by Fray Pedro de Oroz in the 1580s, has an aura of enchantment that is typical of early Franciscan accounts of evangelization and Christian devotion in central Mexico. From the beginning the mendicant orders made use of statues and paintings in their pastoral work, but the miracles recounted by Oroz do not mention them. Rather, the enchantment and miracles in his chronicle mostly take the form of apparitions and visions[74] – of the Virgin Mary, the Christ Child, St. Francis, St. Clare, the devil, troubled or tutelary spirits of deceased relatives and confessors, frequently a heavenly radiance that emanated from a sacred place, sometimes a consecrated Host. In one case the radiance uttered instructions; in another it bestowed upon a friar the gift of fluency in Nahuatl. True to the time and the Franciscans' leading part in the early years of evangelization, most of the seers were Indian neophytes (eleven cases) and Franciscan ministers whose visions involved struggles with the devil (three cases). The apparitions and other miracles for Indians were more benign – finding the Christ Child placed in one's arms; receiving the advice of Christ or a deceased friar; and heavenly priests coming to a sick woman to administer last rites. An underlying theme of most of the Indian miracles in the Oroz Codex is a desire for timely confession and a good death. Perhaps the most evocative apparition miracle in this source describes a beautiful woman dressed in native finery appearing to an Indian in his canoe on Lake Xochimilco during the great epidemic of 1576. She spoke to him "familiarly about secret matters regarding his soul" and told him to tell the Franciscan guardian at Xochimilco to "tell the people to mend their ways."[75]

To be sure, sacred images may have been more important than early mendicant chroniclers and other hagiographical and devotional sources allowed. A glimpse of the fervor a celebrated image might attract, as well as the politics of miracles and images in the late sixteenth century, comes from a judicial inquiry into the transfer of a celebrated crucifix by Augustinians from their *doctrina* of Totolapan (Morelos) to Mexico City on the Thursday before Palm Sunday, March 22, 1583. The statue's arrival met with an outpouring of celebration and hope; ailing and handicapped

Figure 5.3 The arrival of the Totolapan Christ in Mexico City was recorded as a notable event of 1583 by Nahua as well as Spanish chroniclers. In the Codex Aubin on the left-hand page (fol. 63v) it is mentioned in writing for Friday, March 22 as the second of five events that year, and depicted as a crucifix and a church (the church of "Sant Pablo"). Chimalpahin also mentioned the event in his annals for 1583 (*Annals of His Time*, p. 29). Photograph and permission to publish courtesy of the British Museum.

people flocked to its temporary quarters in the Augustinian Colegio de San Pablo to pray for a healing miracle. A grand procession with the image was staged the following Thursday, during Holy Week, with crowds along the route weeping and moaning. At the request of the archbishop's vicar general, the Inquisition moved quickly in early April to investigate rumors of miracles associated with the crucifix.[76] The vicar general said he suspected that opportunistic Augustinians and some other people, especially "insignificant women thirsty for novelty," were spreading unsubstantiated stories and whipping up popular frenzy in order to collect alms and gain notoriety. Apparently, a first deposition was taken the next day, March 23, by the rector of the Augustinian college, Fr. Pedro de Agurto, from Catalina Martín, an illiterate widow from the Barrio San Martín. She came to him in the company of several other women to declare that she had been afflicted with dropsy and unable to walk, but when she prayed before the crucifix and the rector allowed her to kiss the Christ's feet she was suddenly "sound and well." On April 6 and 8, the vicar general consulted two physicians, who declared that Catalina seemed to have made a surprising recovery. Meanwhile, the Inquisition issued an order that no one spread news of any miracles until a qualified judge looked into the matter.[77] Into

May the Inquisition summoned various Augustinians who claimed they had witnessed or heard about sudden cures in the presence of the crucifix, including Ana Joco, an *india* of Culhuacan whose left arm had been paralyzed, as well as Catalina Martín. Several Augustinians also testified that the crucifix itself had shown signs of life during the grand procession on Holy Thursday, seeming to grow larger, whiter, and brighter, as if it had "become human flesh." The court was wary of this outpouring of sanctity and fervor. The judges ordered on June 3 that the crucifix be transferred "without any fanfare or public commotion" to a conspicuous place in the Augustinians' convent church, and they called for "silence and discretion" about any purported miracles.

The reception of the Cristo de Totolapan in 1583 documents public interest in a miraculous image that is not mentioned in the familiar narrative sources of miracle stories from the sixteenth century, thanks at least in part to reticence by the ecclesiastical courts in the capital to encourage the clamor for miracles. In this respect, the case sits on the cusp of an important transition in the history of miracles and miracle-working images in New Spain. In its verdict, the court had been of two minds about the events of March and April 1583, investigating but not readily affirming reports of miraculous cures and the crucifix coming to life: restricting news of these miracles, but not dismissing their possibility nor removing the Christ of Totolapan from public view. The judges seem to have been shaken by the stir the arrival of this statue caused more than by doubts about the power of images. Fifty years later, church leaders were less reluctant to endorse news of miracles associated with images. By then, wonder-working images were embraced by the church hierarchy as well as lay followers, and frequently celebrated in print.[78] Apparitions in the flesh and miracles without reference to images were rarely mentioned except in in-house chronicles of the religious orders, which continued to celebrate the charisma of their local proto-saints and missionary heroes, and even these chronicles now included more accounts of prodigious images and activations.

Over 350 of the 487 seventeenth-century miracle stories tallied here were associated with particular images of Christ and the saints. Cures (242) and accidents, rescues, and protection (142) predominated, as they always did, and men and boys still were favored over women and girls by about six to four, but these miracles represent a fuller range of personal and collective favors than the smaller sixteenth-century group, running the gamut of the New Testament models and beyond, with relatively few exorcisms and "castigos piadosos" or warning and punishment miracles among them (perhaps thirty in the seventeenth and early eighteenth centuries, nearly half of them from the *Zodíaco mariano*), in contrast to the many miracles of punishment recorded for medieval Europe.[79] They also spanned the social spectrum rather than being almost exclusively about Spanish elites and Indian villagers and nobles.

Luis de Cisneros's devotional history of Nuestra Señora de los Remedios published in Mexico City in 1621 is a benchmark in this shift toward miraculous images. While this was the first book of its kind in New Spain, it was organized along the lines of Spanish shrine histories published in the sixteenth century. As in the Spanish models, miracles were a major theme of Cisneros's book, although he described fewer individual miracles. In one forty-eight-page section he presented miracles and "cosas extraordinarias." There he recounted the founding story at length plus fifteen individual miracles, divided into five type sets of three miracles each. (The symbolism of threes would not have been lost on his readers.) In addition, he interspersed allusions to "a great many mortal injuries" healed, special visits of this statuette of the Virgin to Mexico City for vigils when the spring and summer rains were late in coming, and countless votive offerings, especially paintings of miraculous occurrences, milagritos, and jewels. In his opening chapter entitled "On the Certainty of the Miracles worked by Our Lady Through Her Holy Image," Cisneros explained his method:

I include here all the cases that have come to my notice, some (although few) because I have found them in written sources, others that are painted in her house, others that are from the shared tradition that everyone knows and speaks of, and, finally, others that have been told to me by those who experienced them or were eyewitnesses, and there are some witnesses to the many [miracles] worked by the Virgin in her house, of whom I have also availed myself. And as I said at the beginning, this is enough without further investigation because Mary does not need to do great deeds since everything about her is a marvel of nature and divine grace, as St. John put it when he said he had seen a celestial marvel ... not only of nature but of divine grace.[80]

In the decades after Cisneros wrote, the record of miracles in general, especially miracles associated with images, continued to grow. Most still came from chronicles and provincial histories written by mendicants and Jesuits, but there were other sources, too, and the array of miracles approached the variety to be found for many European shrines. Three accounts of miracles for Yucatán date from the 1630s, and nearly all of the prodigious events in them were associated with images. In addition to Lizana's *devocionario*, with its selection of seventeen miracles for the shrine of Nuestra Señora de Izamal that highlights Indian beneficiaries, there is Francisco Cárdenas Valencia's *Relación historial eclesiástica* (1639), which accounted for at least ten miracles associated with the Cristo de San Román, Nuestra Señora de Izamal, and Nuestra Señora de Calatamul; and Dr. Pedro Sánchez de Aguilar, OFM's *Informe contra indolorum cultores del Obispado de*

Yucatán of 1639, which reported that two images of the Virgin Mary perspired.[81] The shift from apparitions to miracles centered on images is evident, too, in the chronicles of Fr. Alonso de la Rea for the Franciscans' Michoacán province in 1639 and Fr. Antonio Tello's *Crónica miscelánea* of the 1640s and 1650s for the Province of Xalisco, although they described in passing only a few particular miracles to go along with their general comments about many cures and other wonders associated with celebrated images that could be recounted.[82] And there was Alonso Franco's 1645 chronicle for the Dominican Province of Santiago, which was presented as a sequel to Agustín Dávila Padilla's *Historia de la fundación y discurso de la Provincia de Santiago de México*, published in 1596. Both texts included a selection of miracle stories, but Dávila Padilla's eighteen stories mostly relate to evangelization – apparitions of the Virgin Mary and the devil to missionaries and neophytes, "marvelous conversions," timely confessions for a good death, and friars who survived Indian attacks. He included two apparitions in the flesh of Virgin Mary and St. Catherine of Siena near images of them, but otherwise excluded images. Franco paid tribute to his heroic Dominican predecessors in the Spiritual Conquest, and some of the forty-two individual miracles he mentioned involved their relics, but he focused more on Mexico City as an enchanted city of miraculous images. He included several warning miracles to novices of the order in case they were tempted to forsake the protection of their miraculous crucifix, plus seventeen miracles for the image and shrine of Nuestra Señora de la Piedad, dated to 1602–1610.[83] He also alluded to many other miracles worked by Nuestra Señora de Guadalupe and the prodigious images of Nuestra Señora del Rosario and Santo Domingo Soriano in the Dominicans' great convent church in the capital city. Five of the miracles for Nuestra Señora de la Piedad were described individually. They range from a near-fatal accident involving a young girl to a fabulous rescue at sea, a riding accident, a child who somehow escaped her kidnappers, and a woman who prayed to the Virgin for milk to nurse her baby and suddenly found her breasts full.

By mid-century Mexico City, the Virgin of Guadalupe, and wonders worked in her shrine at Tepeyac took center stage among the authorized texts about shrines and miraculous images. The first three of her "evangelists," Miguel Sánchez, Luis Lasso de la Vega, and Luis Becerra Tanco, published devotional-historical texts about her image that include the celebrated apparitions and miracles worked for her devotees. All three authors assured readers that there had been many miracles, but they were sparing with details. Sánchez recounted seven miracle stories, four of which overlapped with the eight events depicted in Stradanus's engraving, which, in turn, apparently reprised stories depicted in paintings at the shrine (see Figure 5.2). His other three miracle stories, about Indian beneficiaries and collective favors, again were depicted in paintings at the shrine: the famous recovery of an Indian dancer who was wounded by an arrow during a mock battle honoring the Virgin of Guadalupe; the sparing of Indians from the epidemic of 1544; and the Virgin's intervention against flooding of the city between 1629 and 1634.[84] The second Guadalupan text, Luis Lasso de la Vega's *Huei tlamahuizotlica* (1649), included all eight of the miracles in the Stradanus engraving and the two added by Sánchez that favored Indians. His own additions were an Indian lord whose prayers for forgiveness for his people were answered, and a young woman who was cured of dropsy. Becerra Tanco was content to assure readers that the Virgin of Guadalupe and painted copies of her image that had touched the cloak of Juan Diego worked many marvels every day, most notably saving Mexico City from the great flood of 1629.[85]

The 1680s and 1690s witnessed a second shift for miraculous images that developed into regional shrines. By then, individual reports, ex-voto paintings, prints, and lay reports and records of various kinds were becoming common, along with more devotional histories and other texts about celebrated images that mentioned miracles or narrated a selection of edifying miracles.[86] More ex-voto paintings were commissioned by Indians and non-elite creoles and *castas*; more "true copies" (*fieles copias*) of miraculous paintings and statues came to be displayed in other churches, sometimes hundreds of miles from the original; and many more prints of shrine images were in circulation. Copies of all kinds could have their own charisma, and some of them were also associated with miracles, such as the painted copy of Our Lady of Guadalupe at San Francisco Conchos, Chihuahua, which perspired three times in 1695;[87] the print of San Ignacio that perspired in the Jesuit church at Parras, Chihuahua, in 1748; or the prints on home altars that were believed to have protected family members from misfortune.

Some reported miracles led to full-fledged *informaciones jurídicas*, including one for the Cristo Renovado de Ixmiquilpan (Santa Teresa or Mapethé),[88] but now there were investigations on a smaller scale, too, at the request of grateful beneficiaries of individual rescues and recoveries. For example, on May 20, 1686, María de Álfaro requested permission to have a painting done of the providential recovery of her toddler son Joseph from a horrible accident. She reported that the accident happened just as a procession with the miraculous statue of Santa María de la Redonda was passing by her home and she rushed out with the boy, pleading with a Franciscan friar in the procession to take the boy in his arms and touch him to the statue. The friar did so and the boy quickly recovered. She now wanted a formal información taken to verify the boy's sudden recovery and authorize the painting she proposed to commission.[89]

One of the new devotional histories during the late seventeenth-century transition was Pedro Salgado de Somoza's *Breve noticia* for the image of

Nuestra Señora de la Defensa of Puebla, first published in 1683, with the founding story and three cures of non-Indian men, all of them associated with brandea from the shrine, either flowers that had touched the image or water used to clean it. Others include Mendoza's little 1684 book for the shrine of Our Lady of Tecaxic, near Toluca, which recounts a founding miracle of celestial signs at the site of an abandoned chapel, and a total of twenty miracles with the usual distribution of eight males to five females, cures and accidents that favored Indian devotees, plus the mysterious appearance of urgently needed building materials and meat for the construction workers that seemed to replenish itself.[90] The first edition of Alonso Alberto de Velasco's devotional history of the Cristo Renovado, *Exaltación de la divina misericordia en la milagrosa renovación de la soberana imagen de Christo Señor Nuestro Crucificado*... (1699), described the founding miracle at length and added a selection of personal and collective favors.[91] A text about the miraculous Cruz de Piedra of Querétaro by Fr. Francisco Xavier de Santa Gertrudis that may have been composed in the 1680s was published in 1722 from a 1717 manuscript version, with a selection of ten miracle cures, narrow escapes, and signs of life in the cross itself.[92]

Between 1684 and 1695, Francisco de Florencia, SJ, the fourth of Guadalupe's literary "evangelists," authored not only his Guadalupan text, *La estrella del norte de México* (1688), but also devotional histories for Nuestra Señora de los Remedios (1685), Nuestra Señora de Loreto (1689), Nuestro Señor de Chalma (1689), San Miguel del Milagro (1692), Nuestra Señora de Zapopan, and Nuestra Señora de San Juan de los Lagos (1694). Unpublished at his death were a history of the Cristo Renovado de Santa Teresa and his compendium of miraculous images of the Virgin Mary, the *Zodíaco mariano*. In these texts, Florencia's treatment of miracles naturally varied somewhat according to the particular shrine and image. For Chalma, most were conversion miracles, with the great Lord of Chalma in perpetual combat against idols and the devil.[93] For the Virgin of Remedios, beyond the legendary founding miracles that made her "the defender of the Spaniards, the advocate of the Indians, and the Conqueror of Mexico," as Florencia put it, his miracle stories centered on her relationship with Mexico City and occasional visits to the city as "patroness of rains and the weather." For the shrine of San Miguel del Milagro, Florencia's account highlights supernatural cures of blindness, thanks to spring water and soil from the site of the archangel's apparitions.

Along with these differences among shrines, Florencia retraced the familiar pattern linking most seventeenth-century miracle stories to images, assuring readers that the number of manifest marvels was almost endless,[94] and then describing a few of them individually (five exemplary rescue miracles for Chalma; and for Remedios, three maritime miracles, three equestrian miracles, a lamp in the church that miraculously continued to burn brightly long after its oil would have run out, and an assortment of nine others, apparently drawn from Cisneros).[95] Florencia's treatment of miracles for San Miguel del Milagro was different. He not only alluded to "so many miracles that it is impossible to refer to them all," but also included short accounts of forty-one, ranging far beyond the shrine's fame for curing blindness and the expected attention to favored Tlaxcalan devotees. The difference turns on the fact that he had testimony of witnesses from three *informaciones jurídicas* to draw upon; he might well have included more miracle stories for the other shrines if he had had them at hand.[96]

Mainly after 1730, miracle stories associated with images found their way into some published sermons,[97] unusual texts like Cayetano Cabrera y Quintero's weighty volume about the great epidemic of 1737 in Mexico City, and celebratory civic narratives such as Francisco Antonio Navarrete, SJ's paean to the city of Querétaro's new water system in 1739 in which he paused to ponder three nearly disastrous accidents during the construction that he called *sucesos raros* – perhaps not miracles, but certainly signs of good fortune.[98] Similar incidents were reported in the *Gazeta de México* (miraculous escapes from lightning strikes in the Bajío region in 1732 and 1735, thanks to Nuestra Señora del Pueblito and the Rosary[99]); in the set of *relaciones geográficas* for the Arzobispado de Mexico commissioned in 1743; in José Antonio Villaseñor y Sánchez's *Theatro Americano: descripción general de los reynos y provincias de la Nueva España* ... (1746); and in Antonio de Alcedo's *Diccionario geográfico histórico de las Indias Occidentales o América* (1786–1789).[100] More investigations of individual marvels were undertaken in the eighteenth century, reflecting a growing empirical spirit, but also the concern of Bourbon civil and ecclesiastical administrators to police the boundaries of enchantment and acceptable public activities. Sometimes ecclesiastical investigations of particular events were undertaken because the protagonist was especially well known or the case was a sensational one, like the attempted murder of Fr. Andrés Picazo, OFM, while he was praying before an image of Nuestra Señora del Pueblito in 1769. The assailant attempted to shoot him in the back, but his blunderbuss misfired; then he succeeded in firing a shot containing five balls, but all missed their mark; then he grabbed a pistol and shot Picazo in the face at point blank range, blinding him and burning the upper part of his face. Next he beat the friar with the spent firearm before firing another loaded gun, again missing his target. Finally, he stabbed Picazo repeatedly with a knife. According to the published inquiry, approved by Archbishop Lorenzana, the fact that the friar survived this serial assault must have been the result of supernatural intervention.[101] Other reputed miracles investigated were of a more prosaic kind, like the 1755 inquiry into the sudden recovery from an unspecified illness of a young nun, Madre

Nicolasa Jacinta de San José, of the Dominican convent of Santa Catarina in Puebla, when an image of the Virgin of Guadalupe was applied to her body on Guadalupe's feast day, December 12.[102]

Novena and *triduo* booklets, with their programs for special nine-day and three-day devotions of prayer, petition, and thanksgiving, often to a particular advocation of Mary or Christ, were a new and increasingly popular form of published devotional literature for New Spain in the late seventeenth and early eighteenth centuries, and they remained a popular form of devotional expression and promotion long after Independence.[103] With one exception, the early Mexican novena booklets, dedicated to individual saints and based on Spanish models, appeared in the 1680s and 1690s.[104] All were small, pocket size booklets that included a title page, a dedication, *advertencias* (instructions to the faithful on how to observe the period of devotion), and prayers and acts of contrition for each of the nine days. Sometimes the booklets contained little else.[105] Judging by the standard catalogues of early printed matter from Spain and Spanish America,[106] novena booklets became especially popular in New Spain, with more of them published in Mexico City and Puebla than in Spain or other parts of America during the eighteenth century.[107]

The contents of the Mexican novena booklets were more varied than those of their Spanish counterparts and distinctive in at least one other respect. When a Spanish novena booklet included more than the *advertencias* and daily acts of contrition and prayers, it was usually a print of the image and short instructions and lessons added to the daily entries. In this respect, they seem more devotional than promotional. The novena booklet for the Spanish Virgin of Guadalupe in Figure 5.4, for example, included a print and ten short insertions beginning with a hortatory *considere* ("Consider this:"). Some of these short instructions and lessons contained incidental information about the history and founding story of the image, as well as something particular about its fame as an advocate for devotees. In addition to a print, the later eighteenth-century Mexican novena booklets were more likely to include a thumbnail history of the image and shrine and a few exemplary miracle stories at the beginning, designed to interest a wider public in an as-yet little-known image and shrine, as much as to provide devotees with a script for the nine-day round of devotions. Fr. Joachin Camacho put the purpose clearly enough in his *Novena y breve relación del origen de la Milagrosa Imagen de nuestra Señora de Consolación*: "to further the cult ... and bring to everyone's notice the rich treasure of such a prodigious image, since for many years it has been almost hidden from view and neglected by most (except for some residents of Mexico City)."[108]

Usually the first novena booklet published for a shrine image became a canonical text, reprinted over and over again with few, if any, changes.

NOVENA
A MARIA SANTISSIMA
MADRE DE DIOS,
Y PERPETUA VIRGEN,
EN
SU MILAGROSISIMA IMAGEN
SANTA MARIA
DE GUADALUPE,

ESCRITA
POR F. FRANCISCO DE S. JOSEPH,
indigno esclavo suyo, hijo de su
Santa Casa.

Con licencia, en Madrid, año de 1736.

Figure 5.4 (a) Title page; (b) Print of Spain's Nuestra Señora de Guadalupe, from unsigned woodcut, in Francisco de San Joseph, *Novena a María Santíssima Madre de Dios, y perpetua virgen . . .*, Madrid: n.p., 1736. Author's copy.

But, again, there were some exceptions for New Spain. Camacho's pre-1753 booklet for the image of Nuestra Señora de Consolación housed in his Recollect Franciscan convent church of San Cosmé on the outskirts of Mexico City was comparatively long at fifty-four printed pages, of which twenty-two pages were devoted to the founding miracle story, broken down into nine separate *maravillas*.[109] This miraculous statue had belonged to a woman whose daughter fell into a well and, to all appearances, drowned. The woman rushed to the edge of the well with the statue and the waters mysteriously rose up to the top and the child was pulled out of the water and revived. In the process, the statue of Mary changed posture, extending her right shoulder and arm down, as if to lift the child, "as a perpetual reminder" of the miraculous rescue.[110] Various churches vied to have the statue assigned to them, but the San Cosmé church, located near the site of the miracle, was providentially chosen by lots. Camacho alluded to "countless" miracles, but presented only phases of the founding story as examples. Another novena booklet for this image and shrine by Pedro de Jesús María Priego Velarde, OFM, was published in 1769. Priego enlarged upon Camacho's text, especially in his presentation of miracles, by situating the founding miracle in the late sixteenth century and adding an activation of the image in 1675, providential rains after the statue was carried in procession around the convent cloister in 1769, and the sudden recovery of a distinguished, mortally ill devotee, also dated 1769. And he assured readers that many other people felt they owed their lives to Nuestra Señora de Consolación.[111]

Some novena booklets published in New Spain were even longer and offered readers more miracle stories. The *Novena del milagroso SS. Christo de Esquipulas que se venera en el reyno de Guatemala* ... (ca. 1740), first published in Mexico in 1778 and republished there before the end of the colonial period, devoted twenty-eight of its forty-eight pages to twenty-four miracles worked by this famous Guatemalan Cristo.[112] Nearly all the stories involved men and boys, but they ranged from leading peninsular and creole Spanish captains, nobles, and priests to sailors, Indian villagers, and others without the honorific "don" attached to their name. The stories in this booklet are longer than in most, and one is an unusual sunlit fable about instant wealth rather than a New Testament-style story with a moral lesson about salvation. According to the author, in 1603 Juan García, a poor creole servant born in Havana and living in Mexico City, undertook a pilgrimage on foot to the shrine of Esquipulas. He reached the shrine without even a *real* to buy a piece of ribbon to take the measure of the Cristo as a token for his wife. Dejected, he began the return journey with only three stones from the river near the shrine in his pocket. When his wife asked him what relics of the Holy Christ of Esquipulas he had brought back, he broke into tears and said that all he had were the three stones. But when he unwrapped the stones, they found gold nuggets.

In the mounting array of eighteenth-century texts about miracles in New Spain, one was especially unusual. Fr. Francisco de la Rosa Figueroa's account of marvels associated with Nuestra Señora del Patrocinio in the Franciscan doctrina of Nativitas Tepetlatcingo beyond the southern outskirts of Mexico City that occurred during his two pastoral assignments there between 1739 and 1745 includes more than the usual few exemplary signs of divine will, and many of them are far from biblical in content. The thirty-five events de la Rosa called miracles included gifts of building materials, recovery of a lost animal, and an answered prayer for the closing of a gambling parlor. He was not enthusiastic about the faith of his Indian parishioners, and the supernatural boons he recounted for them were half-miracles – sick Indians survived a typhus epidemic but some of their children died; a man survived a fall but suffered debilitating injuries; a pregnant woman survived a dangerous delivery but died soon after at the hands of ignorant Indian midwives. Equally unusual, de la Rosa repeatedly placed himself at the center of the story, as if he were the person most favored by Nuestra Señora del Patrocinio because he was her most faithful devotee. Not surprisingly, de la Rosa's text, completed at the end of his life in the 1770s after most of the Franciscans' doctrinas had become diocesan parishes, was never published or apparently even circulated in manuscript by fellow Franciscans. But his text sprang from his order's eighteenth-century circumstances, not just his own eccentricities and personal sense of mission. His adulthood coincided with a difficult time for the Franciscans, when their historic missions of pastoral service in proto-parishes (*doctrinas*) and evangelization among new Christians were in decline. Hankering after the halcyon days of "spiritual conquest" in the sixteenth century, de la Rosa was born too late, and he was not chosen to be among the few, mostly European, missionaries sent to the Franciscans' last missionary frontiers in the Sierra Gorda and the far north. Nativitas Tepetlatcingo became his time and place of transcendence and reward in pastoral service and communion with the Blessed Virgin.

The eighteenth-century miracle stories from these disparate sources were not much different from earlier accounts. Images still came to life and conveyed messages, phenomenal cures and rescues occurred, pregnant women survived difficult deliveries, natural disasters were averted or passed with surprisingly little loss of life, and a scattering of other boons were taken to be supernatural, or at least superhuman, in origin. Stories of divine disapproval and reprisal were more common, but not by much in comparison to the stories in Spanish miracle collections of the time.[113] Some of the boons now were surprisingly commonplace, such as finding employment or recovering a lost animal. Men and boys still outnumbered women and girls in the miracle stories by about six to four, and while these fruits of divine favor were showered on a broad spectrum of society, Spanish elites and Indians still predominated (partly because older miracle stories had become canonical). As in the seventeenth century, the accounts of miracles typically were presented in small groups, along with a sweeping comment about there being too many to include more.[114]

The individual miracles from paintings and written texts examined for this chapter, whether for the seventeenth century (487) or the eighteenth century (437), probably do not add up to a random sample for any particular time, but the sources of information for the eighteenth century are more varied, and the circulation of news about miracles was less inhibited and more widespread then despite the efforts of ecclesiastical and civil courts to curate and edit them. Perhaps those efforts were largely desultory because the idea that true miracles ended when Christ was crucified and resurrected was no longer so much in fashion among theologians; or perhaps the authorities were just less able to control popular devotion.

Some eighteenth-century texts about shrines and miracles departed from seventeenth-century norms by including more miracle stories and introducing or enlarging upon particular types of miracles. Loaizaga's *Historia de la milagrosíssima imagen de Nuestra Señora de Occotlán* [sic] ... (1745, 1750) is an example.[115] Rather than the handful of miracle stories usually found in older shrine histories, Loaizaga recounted fifty-two, mostly from the cities of Puebla and Tlaxcala, and nearby towns. The majority of his stories departed from New Testament models and apparently dated from near the time he wrote, rather than being canonical, timeless stories. He included ambiguous miracles of warning and preparation for a good death that were unusual before the eighteenth century. Several of them revolved around the rumor that no one had died in the presence of this image of the Virgin. In one case, an Indian robber and devotee of Nuestra Señora de Ocotlán, who had taken refuge in the shrine, tried to commit suicide by jumping from the tower but suffered no injuries; then he fell off a wall and again survived, as if the Virgin would not let him die in her house before confessing and repenting his sins. Another Indian miscreant who was determined to go to hell threw himself from the dome above the Virgin's dressing room (*camarín*) and also survived. In a third eerie miracle story, Tomás de Anaya promised to serve the Virgin for a year as an itinerant alms collector. He died during his journey, at Huauchinango, and his family was not informed. One night his ghost-spirit appeared to his brother, pleading with him to pay a debt to the chief alms collector so he could be freed from purgatory. His brother did not pay the debt, and soon thereafter when he was on the road Death came for him, too. He pleaded to die at home so he could first make amends. His wish was granted. Influenced by Loaizaga's book, another Franciscan chronicler of the Virgin of Ocotlán, Fr. Vicente del Niño Jesús Suárez de Peredo, writing in the 1790s, presented readers with an even edgier Virgin of Ocotlán, who became angry and dried up the spring of healing waters at the shrine. He added the story of another robber who jumped from the tower, but this time the unfortunate man died on the spot.[116]

A twist beginning in the 1730s that would become a deep current in Mexican miracle stories thereafter was growing interest in miracles of Our Lady of Guadalupe, no doubt boosted by bicentennial celebrations in 1731 of the now canonical apparitions to Juan Diego, and her fame in saving Mexico City from devastation during the great epidemic of 1737. Stories of Guadalupe's miracles circulated in a wide variety of printed sources, including Cabrera y Quintero's *Escudo de armas de México*, reprintings of the seventeenth-century devotional histories of the image and shrine, new sermons, novena booklets, testimonials, paintings, sculpted copies of her image, and cheap prints. But even during the 1740s and later, miracles associated with other shrine images gained recognition, too, and were published, investigated, refined, and broadcast beyond their localities.

Conclusion by Comparison

Mention of miraculous occurrences was a commonplace in colonial Mexico's historical record, but actual descriptions of miracles usually were very short and scripted in standard ways, whether they came from church authorities or the laity. And much of what remains of the material culture of the miraculous occurrences from that time lacks evidence of the personal associations and actual uses that gave it meaning. Milagritos, medidas, and abbreviated miracle stories written down in the colonial period can set the imagination dancing, but perhaps in the wrong directions. Even basic questions – when and why particular miracle stories were collected; where they came from; how and by whom they were framed, received, retold, and otherwise used; and what is representative or distinctive about them – often are beyond the reach of an inductive approach. We are dealing with stories, occasional detailed judicial inquiries, and scattered, edited evidence of acts and utterances, not samples. Most of the recorded stories are timeless and faceless. Some can be placed in time and circumstance, but for the most part we can only guess at how they might stand in for all that is left unrecorded. Still, the silences sometimes are instructive. They invite questions about a history of censorship, generations of editorial discretion, and intentional neglect that can shed some light on colonial politics and the exercise of power;[117] and it would be a mistake to assume that minimal stories from a familiar repertoire were not what people expected, wanted, and confidently recounted, without much nuance, unless perhaps the event happened to them personally or to someone they knew well.

Despite the many silences for most shrines, some developments described in this chapter mark a common history of the miracles in New Spain that goes beyond tightly scripted storytelling and unique local experience. Combining different sources – loose ends and all – and drawing also upon miracle stories and shrines from early modern Europe, especially Spain, several conclusions can be hazarded about what was distinctive for the miracles in New Spain. Two historical trends stand out. Images were always important to Christian devotion in New Spain, introduced everywhere by early European evangelizers and colonists and welcomed by native peoples, especially in the center and south; but there was a shift during the long seventeenth century (1580s–1710s) from divine apparitions, in the flesh so to speak, to sacred images as the principal medium for miracles. Then during the eighteenth century a wider array of narrative sources both secular and ecclesiastical proclaimed (or occasionally doubted) the latest news of miracle-working statues and paintings. Both developments suggest that while ideas about divine presence in the world changed, disenchantment had not divided or alienated whole classes of people in New Spain. If anything, interest in miracles was widespread and growing.

Broad similarities and differences between miracle stories associated with images in Europe and New Spain also invite comment. Catholic Europe experienced a similar transition from apparitions to miraculous images – especially images of the Virgin Mary and Christ – but earlier, in the fifteenth and sixteenth centuries, and the composition and publication of devotional histories for image shrines was well established in Europe before the first imprint of this kind appeared in New Spain in 1621. Much the same array of miracle events is found on both sides of the Atlantic, with New Testament miracles serving as template, and rapid recoveries from life-threatening illnesses and mortal wounds predominating. Many founding miracles for shrines on both sides of the Atlantic centered on the activation of images or were associated with hilltops, mountains, caves, and springs; and the signs that preceded apparitions and discoveries of images in the countryside often were similar, especially celestial music or a heavenly radiance. These similarities are unsurprising given the prominent role of Spanish friars, Jesuits, and bishops in New Spain as in Spain, in promoting the mystique of miraculous images, framing miracle stories in writing, and overseeing shrines; the circulation in New Spain of Spanish texts about the miracles of celebrated Spanish images (such as Our Lady of the Cueva Santa); and the publication of more than a few Mexican miracle accounts first in Spain or in quick succession both in Spain and in Mexico City or Puebla.[118] However, some of the similarities in the miracle stories complicate the idea that European models were transferred more or less intact. Many of the similarities expressed more widely shared, if not universal, human hopes and experiences – yearning for abundance, comfort, health, security, and meaning in life – that do not necessarily amount to a radical departure from the local precontact cosmologies.

There are also patterns of development in the miraculous occurrences that distinguish New Spain from Spain and other parts of Europe. While historians of early modern Europe sometimes speak of the sixteenth and seventeenth centuries as "the golden age" of miracles and of demonic possession and exorcism,[119] in New Spain there seems to have been a rise (at least in reporting) of miracle accounts during the seventeenth century, but little evidence of widespread decline thereafter, and no dramatic rise or fall in the number of exorcisms recounted in miracle stories over the colonial period. Do these differences reflect reality? It is hard to say. Perhaps exorcisms were proportionately more common than the published miracle stories and votive offerings indicate,[120] but if so, their stories would have to have been neglected by chroniclers more or less uniformly throughout the colonial period, which seems unlikely.

Differences between the founding miracles in New Spain and Europe are particularly striking, in ways that complicate the separation of the natural from the supernatural taught by Christian texts. The various kinds of activations of images and other signs of divine will associated with the beginnings of European shrines can be found in New Spain (with the apparent exception of bleeding Hosts, which became famous origin relics in some German shrines), but Spain's signature "shepherd cycle" origin stories of miraculous discovery of long-lost images were rarely found here. In these stories, statues of the Virgin Mary lost or hidden in the countryside by Christians during the Muslim conquest and rule in Iberia after 711 came to light centuries later when a Christian shepherd found one of his stray animals, usually a bull or ox, drawn to the site.[121] Statues of Mary lost and found in wartime were not unknown in Mexico. The statuette of the Virgin of Remedios was believed – at least by the early seventeenth century – to have led the remnants of Cortés's band to safety on the night of the Noche Triste debacle in 1520 before being lost in the confusion of retreat near the hill of Totoltepec, to be discovered twenty years later under a large agave plant by a local Indian notable; and the statue of Our Lady of Guanajuato was understood to be a Spanish image with a Reconquista pastoral cycle history – lost and found during the Middle Ages – before it was brought to New Spain. But such stories were rare in New Spain. By contrast, one of the signature founding stories of discovery of sacred images in New Spain was for crucifixes that were *of* nature as well as found in the countryside – growing in tree trunks, limbs or roots, and bleeding, moaning, or becoming too hard to cut or too heavy to budge from their site. In the Spanish shepherd cycle stories, culture (the Virgin Mary) might be said to have tamed nature, while in found images of Christ in the American stories, the line between nature and culture blurred, with nature *in* culture; at once generative, nurturing, and destructive.

Some differences depended more on a combination of post-Tridentine reforms, and the particular colonial histories and reasons of state of New World Christianity, than on pre-Columbian conceptions of the sacred. But Mexican miracles associated with images played out in some surprising ways, given the potential fit between New Spain's reputation for colonization by conquest and the martial themes of many Spanish stories (Reconquista settings, warrior Virgins, and captivity miracles). Several sixteenth-century central Mexico shrines fit the Spanish pattern, as do several more for northern New Spain in the seventeenth century,[122] but in general Mexican miracles were less fraught with political and social danger. Instead, most sixteenth- and seventeenth-century origin stories for shrines in New Spain were variations on the theme of providential evangelization. Miracles usually protected the righteous. Other than the devil lurking in the wings, enemies of the faith were rarely in sight. Why not? The obvious reason is that the main challenge for Spanish Christians in Mesoamerica was incorporation – conversion and religious education of the indigenous population. There was determined native resistance in parts of the north and pockets elsewhere at different times, but Christianity was nominally accepted and often embraced by colonial "Indians" from the densely settled agricultural and administrative communities in western, central, and southern Mexico, as well as non-Indians. An angry God and militant Virgin Mary, St. James, and St. Michael were not unknown in the heartland of New Spain, especially during the sixteenth century, and in parts of the north and south later; but the Spanish shrine origin stories rooted in Reconquest and Counter-Reformation struggles against invading Muslim infidels and Protestant apostates were out of phase with the dominant New World story told by early religious chroniclers. Granted, mendicant and Jesuit evangelizers and pastors tended to gloss over the disappointments or treat them as evidence of native ignorance and weakness that called for renewed dedication to the mission. But the greater beneficence and prominence of natural origins in the American stories did not result only from a rosy historical perspective of most official chroniclers, or from reasons of state. Indigenous Christians were drawn to Mary as benevolent mother and wonder worker, and to living images of Christ and protective saints that sprang from *their* soil, that belonged to them and their place.[123]

The lack of libros de milagros and other large collections of miracle stories for image shrines in New Spain is another striking difference from the European record. It is likely that this was a tacit policy of Catholic reformers that could be applied more decisively in a new colony than in Europe. Both ecclesiastical and civil authorities were worried about excesses of popular faith that could undermine their authority or encourage idolatry, and they were in a position to manage the formal written record. European authorities, by contrast, were up against a very long tradition of collecting hundreds and thousands of miracle stories, going back at least to Gregory of Tours in fifth-century Gaul, and preserved in – among many other texts – the *Cántigas de Santa María* and *Codex Calixtinus* from thirteenth-century Spain, the register of miracles for the shrine of Sainte Foy at Conques in eleventh-century France, the fifteenth- and sixteenth-century miracle books of the shrine of Nuestra Señora de Guadalupe of Extremadura, Pedro de Burgos's history of the Catalan shrine of Nuestra Señora de Montserrat published in 1536, Gumpennberg's *Atlas Marianus*, and Juan de Villafañe's *Compendio histórico* of 85 Marian shrines and more than 900 miracles published first in 1724. Moreover, while early modern bishops in Europe, like their American counterparts, were concerned about overexuberant devotees and unauthorized religious practices, they had good reasons to endorse the compilations as a riposte to Protestant and Muslim iconoclasm – hardly a consideration in early Spanish America.

The judicial files compiled by colonial authorities to monitor and shape religious practices offer some less processed glimpses of enchantment expressed in rumors of miracles than are found in published sources. The 1583 investigation of the reception of the Christ of Totolapan in Mexico City shows both that miracles were anticipated by all kinds of Christians there at the time and that miracles were becoming more closely associated with sacred images than a reading of the early chronicles suggests. The Totolapan investigation had the effect of endorsing miraculous images even as it discouraged the circulation of unproven miracle stories.[124] Furthermore, the judicial files and array of records of the miracles that survive from the eighteenth century suggest that wary officials had less power to manage the miraculous occurrences than their institutions of surveillance make it seem. The famous case of the reconstituted *panecitos* of Santa Teresa, which occupied archdiocesan authorities and the Inquisition off and on for more than ten years in the late seventeenth century, ended with the verdict that Doña María Poblete had perpetrated a hoax; but that verdict did not kill popular belief in the miraculous powers of the little loaves she dispensed (see Chapter 6). To all appearances, the court's ruling was long forgotten in the late eighteenth century when a shrine chronicler recommended the panecitos miracles in print, trusting in popular opinion, as he put it – the *voz pública y fama*. His book was published with the approval of the archbishop's censors, who also seem to have been unaware that the reconstitution of the panecitos had been judged a hoax.[125]

Church officials were not of one mind about the miracle stories that mounted up during the colonial period, but for the most part they acquiesced and even enshrined some of them for local and regional audiences; and many priests shared with the laity a culture of faith in miracles, even as some undoubtedly shared the skepticism of the occasional outspoken district governors and judges, especially in the late eighteenth century. Popular interest in miracles continued to be deeply ingrained in colonial society, crisscrossing social groups. The ex-voto paintings from the colonial period mainly expressed elite piety, but the thousands upon thousands of milagritos and the blaze of candlelight displayed in Mexican shrines were silent witnesses to a pervasive belief in communication with the divine and prayers offered and believed answered. The Cristo de Totolapa verdict in 1583 attempted to restrict the dissemination of miracle stories, but like so many colonial sources, it did not call into question the possibility that any sacred image *could* be a site of divine favor and retribution. That there were so few investigations of miracle stories may well attest to this common faith, and to political pragmatism on the part of authorities, more than to their lack of interest or will. If nothing more, the thin but ever-present record of marvels and miracles in New Spain evinces what colonial authors from Torquemada on called the miracle of faith – the enduring power of longing, grief, and hope to sense divine presence and possibility of miracles. How that faith was transmitted and acted upon in

Christian terms could change, but, as colonial artifacts of the miraculous occurrences suggest, by the early seventeenth century it had settled on images and personal and collective offerings, including the shrines that devotees constructed to honor them.

Notes

1. Colonial-era writings accepted this thumbnail definition of miracles in other words. For example, in Hermenegildo Vilaplana's estimation "toda obra milagrosa excede y supera todo el orden y las facultades todas de la naturaleza criada" ("Miraculous acts exceed and completely surpass the order and capacity of created nature."), *Histórico y sagrado novenario de la milagrosa imagen de Nuestra Señora del Pueblito* . . ., 2nd ed., Mexico: Imprenta de la Bibliotheca Mexicana, 1765, pp. 56–57. In writing this chapter I had in mind Kenneth Woodward's more elaborate, cross-cultural definition:

   A miracle is an unusual or extraordinary event that is in principle perceivable by others, that finds no reasonable explanation in ordinary human abilities or in other known forces that operate in the world of time and space, and that is the result of a special act of God or the gods or of human beings transformed by efforts of their own through asceticism and meditation.

   The Book of Miracles: The Meaning of the Miracle Stories in Christianity, Judaism, Buddhism, Hinduism, Islam, New York: Simon & Schuster, 2000, p. 28. A yet broader conception in which miracles do not violate the laws of nature was not expressed in colonial sources. For a brief discussion of this conception in modern parlance, see David Basinger, "What Is a Miracle?" and Robert Larner, "The Meanings of Miracle," in *The Cambridge Companion to Miracles*, ed. Graham H. Twelftree, Cambridge, UK and New York: Cambridge University Press, 2011, pp. 19–35 and 36–53.
2. For a stimulating attempt to bridge the gap between belief and science, which recognizes "the continued vibrancy of belief in the healing power of holy figures," see Robert A. Scott, *Miracle Cures: Saints, Pilgrimage, and the Healing Powers of Belief*, Berkeley: University of California Press, 2010.
3. For instance, Luke 7: "the blind receive their sight, the lame walk, lepers are cleansed, and the deaf hear, the dead are raised up." Mark 1:32–34 makes a blanket statement about many cures worked by Christ: "those whom he cured, who were variously afflicted, were many." On exorcisms in the Gospels, see Mark 1:34, 6:13, and 7:21, and 16:17–18 (cited by Pérez de Ribas when he wrote that exorcisms undertaken by Jesuits in northern Mexico were "as in the New Testament"); Luke 8:35, 9. On calming the waters, Mark 5:37, 39 ("And a great storm of wind arose, and the waves beat into the boat . . . And he awoke and rebuked the wind, and said to the sea, 'Peace! Be still!' And the wind ceased, and there was a great calm"). On Christ giving the apostles the power and authority to exorcise and to cure disease, Luke 9:1. On Christ's healing touch, Mark 3:10, 5:23, 5:25–28, Luke 13:10–13, Mark 7:21 (bestowing sight), Luke 11:14 (a deaf and dumb man recovers his speech); raising the dead, Luke 8:49; overcoming metaphorical blindness and deafness, Luke 10:23–24.
4. St. Augustine, *The City of God Against the Pagans*, ed. and trans. R. W. Dyson, Cambridge, UK and New York: Cambridge University Press, 1998, pp. 410–411.

5. Andrés Pérez de Ribas, *History of the Triumphs of Our Holy Faith Amongst the Most Barbarous and Fierce Peoples of the New World* [1645], ed. Daniel T. Reff, trans. Daniel T. Reff, Maureen Ahern, and Richard K. Danford, Tucson: University of Arizona Press, 1999, p. 144. Beyond warning that miracles were rare, Pérez de Ribas's larger point was that God was more likely to help those who help themselves with their God-given abilities. Only once did Christ walk on water, and when St. Peter tried to do so Christ rescued him by extending a hand, not by commanding the waters. "Therefore, the Lord sustained Saint Peter with His hand, thereby teaching us that when we have human means available, we should not look for extraordinary and miraculous ones."
6. Devotional literature for the shrines of Tecaxic, Guadalupe at Tepeyac and Nuestra Señora de Ocotlán in Tlaxcala also highlighted miracles for Indians.
7. I have consulted copies of the 1799 printing of Moxica's booklet (*Tesoro escondido en el delicioso campo, ameno huerto, florida vergel, y fragrante pensil del noviciado de los frayles predicadores de esta Provincia de Santiago de Mexico*, reimpreso, Mexico: J. Fernández Jáuregui, 1799). Moxica's stories warning novices of the perils of leaving the order begin at p. 56. An earlier, perhaps first, edition of this work dates from 1712 according to Cayetano Cabrera y Quintero, *Escudo de armas de México: Celestial protección de esta nobilíssima ciudad, de la Nueva España, y de casi todo el Nuevo Mundo*, Mexico: Vda. de Joseph Bernardo de Hogal, 1746, p. 179. Moxica drew three of the minatory stories from Alonso Franco, *Segunda parte de la historia de la provincia de Santiago de México, Orden de Predicadores en la Nueva España* [1645], Mexico: Museo Nacional, 1900, pp. 527–531; see discussion below.
8. An example of a rare supernatural warning (perhaps written down well after the cult began) that was more common in Europe by the eighteenth century is the first miracle story of Our Lady of La Macana in New Mexico, set in 1686 and recounted in Mexico City by Fr. Felipe Montalvo, OFM, in 1755. In it, Mary cured a sick child, the daughter of the provincial captain general, who was devoted to her in the guise of a local statue of Our Lady of the Sacristy of Toledo. Mary spoke to the child, telling her to sound a warning that the province would soon be destroyed for disregarding her priests unless the people mended their ways, Ilona Katzew, "The Virgin of the Macana: Emblem of a Franciscan Predicament in New Spain," *Colonial Latin American Review* 12: 2 (2003), 172.
9. Facsimile edition of Bernardo de Lizana, *Devocionario de Nuestra Señora de Izamal, y conquista de Yucatán*, ed. René Acuña, Mexico: UNAM, 1995. Miracles are treated in the second part of this chronicle. For the shrines of San Miguel del Milagro and Tulantongo, the signature miracles also were blind devotees who recovered their sight.
10. On Nuestra Señora del Refugio, see Chapter 4.
11. David Freedberg, *The Power of Images: Studies in the History and Theory of Response*, Chicago: University of Chicago, 1989, p. 148.
12. A thousand plus stories is only the tip of this mountain of enchantment, as I suggest below. For example, Fr. Joseph Joaquín Granados, a Franciscan pastor and author claimed that Sebastián Aparicio worked some 599 miracles in Puebla, *Tardes americanas: gobierno gentil y católico: breve y particular noticia de toda la historia Indiana ... trabajadas por un indio y un español*, Mexico: Felipe de Zúñiga y Ontiveros, 1778, pp. 352–353.
13. Quoted from Manuel de Escalante's *sentir* – short preface – for Juan Luzuriaga's *Paranympho celeste. Historia de la Mystica Zarza, Milagrosa Imagen, y prodigioso Santuario ...*, Mexico: Herederos de la Vda. de Bernardo Calderón, 1686, n.p.

14. Woodward, *The Book of Miracles*, p. 26.
15. Two of the better documented cases of inquiries into miracles near the time they were said to have occurred are translated and discussed in William B. Taylor, *Marvels & Miracles in Late Colonial Mexico: Three Texts in Context*, Albuquerque: University of New Mexico Press, 2011, pp. 9–67.
16. *Informaciones jurídicas*, formal investigations of celebrated religious images and their miracles, may have begun as early as 1582, but were more often undertaken by the mid-seventeenth century. It is hard to be certain since original manuscript records survive in few cases. We have either published versions redacted for promotional purposes or references to early informaciones by writers later in the colonial period. The earliest, for La Conquistadora of Puebla in 1582, is known from an 1804 reprinting of a 1666 publication. Florencia referred to the 1582 información in the late seventeenth century (or his editor Oviedo did in 1755) in *Zodíaco mariano* . . ., Mexico: Colegio de San Ildefonso, 1755, p. 153. Later in this chapter I discuss the manuscript record of an Inquisition investigation for the Christ of Totolapa, brought to Mexico City in 1583. Echeverría y Veitia mentioned in the mid-eighteenth century that he had perused a 1614 información for the shrine of Nuestra Señora de la Piedad on the outskirts of Mexico City. Florencia copied portions of investigations for the shrine of San Miguel del Milagro, Tlaxcala done in 1632, 1643–1644, and 1675 in his devotional history of the shrine published in 1692. Investigations are mentioned or excerpted by Florencia for Nuestra Señora de San Juan de los Lagos in 1634, 1668, and 1693 in his 1694 devotional history of the shrine. Informaciones for the Cruz de Piedra of Querétaro in 1639 and 1650 were noted in a 1722 publication, *Cruz de piedra, imán de la devoción, venerada en el Collegio de missioneros de la ciudad de Santiago Querétaro. Descripción panegyrica de su prodigioso origen y portentosos milagros*, Mexico: J.F. de Ortega y Bonilla, by Francisco Xavier de Santa Gertrudis, OFM. For the image shrine of Nuestra Señora de Zapopan, informaciones in 1641, 1653, and 1663 were mentioned or used by Florencia. Bishop Palafox apparently commissioned an investigation of the Virgin of Cosamaloapan in 1641 or 1642 and a partial account was published in 1643, according to the *Zodíaco mariano*, p. 201. Also, according to the *Zodíaco mariano*, formal informaciones were undertaken for miracles of Nuestra Señora de la Laguna, Campeche in 1649, La Purísima in the Jesuit Colegio Máximo in Mexico City in 1649, Nuestra Señora del Pueblito in 1648, and Nuestra Señora de Tix, Yucatán in 1650, pp. 22, 25–30, 102–103, 149–150. The 1666 records for the Virgin of Guadalupe amounted to an investigation for apologetic purposes. A 1670 investigation for the Virgin of Talpa has been cited in a 1732 copy. Alonso Alberto de Velasco's first text on the Cristo Renovado de Santa Teresa, *Renovación por sí misma* . . ., Mexico: Viuda de Francisco Rodríguez Lupercio, 1688, took the form of an información jurídica. Another account presented as a juridical report treated Nuestra Señora de la Salud in 1737. Other eighteenth-century *relaciones jurídicas* about particular miracles include the Picazo case presented in Joseph Manuel Rodríguez, *Relación jurídica de la libertad de la muerte intentada contra la persona del R.P. Fr. Andrés Picazo . . . por intercesión de Nuestra Señora en su prodigiosa imagen del Pueblito* . . ., Mexico: Zúñiga y Ontiveros, 1769, the 1755 recovery of Madre Nicolasa Jacinta de San José of the Dominican convent of Santa Catarina in Puebla, known in an 1864 manuscript copy, Sutro BT660.G8 1864 Rare Bk, and the Señor del Jovo of Tamazunchale in 1805.

Early histories like Cisneros's *Historia* for the shrine and image of Remedios (1621), Lizana's *Devocionario* for Izamal (1633) and Fr. Juan de Mendoza, *Relación de el santuario de Tecaxique, en que está colocada la milagrosa Imagen de Nuestra Señora de los Ángeles . . .*, Mexico: J. de Ribera, 1684, and Manuel de Loaizaga's devotional history and novena for the Virgin of Ocotlán (1754, 1755) may also have been regarded at the time as products of formal inquiries into the history and miracles of their shrines. The most probing independent investigation of reputed miracles was the famous panecitos de Santa Teresa case involving María de Poblete, 1674 discussed in Chapter 6. Others in the eighteenth century include the cross of Huaquechula, the Virgin in a kernel of corn, the Divina Pastora of Veracruz, and the *niño aparecido* of the San Bernardo convent in Mexico City.

When I began the research, I imagined there would be a section in episcopal archives devoted to individual reports of miracles and judicial investigation of them. Initiatives that could have led to such a wealth of documentation are occasionally recorded, but apparently were not pursued systematically. For example, in 1667 the chaplain of the Hospital de la Limpia Concepción de Nuestra Señora in Mexico City (the Hospital de Jesús founded by Cortés) wrote to the vicar general of the Archdiocese of Mexico to report that a fire had been miraculously extinguished with a print of his hospital's famous Christ. He asked for a formal investigation "so that such a manifest and great miracle will be remembered." The vicar general responded by authorizing the chaplain to present a report and bring forward witnesses to be examined by the court, but there is no record in the file to indicate that an independent investigation was carried out, AGN Indiferente Virreinal, "clero regular y secular," caja 6005, exp. 95, one folio.

17. Carmelite friar Lorenzo del Santísimo Sacramento attempted a more comprehensive compilation of the healing miracles of the Señor de los Desconsolados of Tehuacán (Puebla), including short descriptions of twenty-seven events, *El común bienhechor para todos es el Señor de los desconsolados*, Mexico: Imprenta Nueva de la Bibliotheca Mexicana, 1755, pp. 39–46. As he explained, "not all of these marvels would be officially classified as miracles, but they are, as our faith leads us to believe, particular prodigious events worked by the Lord to demonstrate that he is the great Benefactor of All" ("aunque todas estas marabillas no se califiquen por milagros, pero son particulares prodigios que ha hecho el Señor, como cree nuestra piedad, para manifestarse Bienhechor Común").

Many of the miracle stories in the sixteenth- and seventeenth-century chronicles of the religious orders have to do with the special gifts of saintly members rather than images and shrines, so they are not given close attention in this chapter.

18. William A. Christian, Jr., *Apparitions in Late Medieval and Renaissance Spain*, Princeton: Princeton University Press, 1981, p. 5.
19. Pedro de Burgos, *Libro de la historia y milagros hechos a invocación de nuestra Señora de Montserrat*, Barcelona: Claudi Bornat, 1556, fols. 33–269. The 1536 edition was published in Barcelona by Pedro Monpezat.
20. Florencia and Oviedo, *Zodíaco mariano*, pp. 62, 270. Neither has been used and cited in the scholarly literature and I have not located them. Some other chronicles of the orders seem to have drawn on collections of miracle stories that are no longer extant, or to have drawn mainly upon paintings displayed in the shrines. Francisco Javier Alegre's *Historia de la Compañía de Jesús en Nueva España . . .*, Mexico: J. M. Lara, 1841, compiled in the mid-eighteenth century dated most of his twenty-six miracle stories for images of San Ignacio, San Francisco Xavier, and San Francisco Borja in Mexico to 1595–1612; he

would seem to have had access to an early seventeenth-century compilation. Provincial archives for other religious orders may also have gathered miracle accounts that their chroniclers could consult and use. The Carmelites of the Province of San Alberto, for example, kept *libros de cosas notables* including miracles: Celaya, Archivo Histórico de la Provincia de San Alberto de México de los Carmelitas Descalzos (AHPCD), microfilm in the CONDUMEX library and archive, Mexico City: AHPCD carpeta 1477, roll 21; carpeta 1509 roll 23; carpetas 1731 and 1735, roll 45. My thanks to Karen Melvin for sharing these references to the Carmelite records.

21. Jesuits were famous scholars, chroniclers, and compilers of enchantment, both in Europe and New Spain, but Franciscans were at least as prominent in celebrating and promoting the miraculous.
22. Francisco Cárdenas Valencia, *Relación historial eclesiástica de la Provincia de Yucatán de la Nueva España, escrita el año de 1639*, Mexico: Porrúa, 1937, pp. 105–106.
23. Pedro Pablo Patiño, *Disertación crítico-theo-filosófica sobre la conservación de la santa imagen de Nuestra Señora de los Ángeles*, Mexico: Zúñiga y Ontiveros, 1801, p. 3 refers to the Council of Trent decree that new miracles required the approval of the bishop. Mexico's first bishop, Fray Juan de Zumárraga, OFM, reportedly declared that God had no need for more miracles since so many were recorded in the Bible: "Ya no quiere el Redentor del Mundo que se hagan milagros, porque no son menester, pues está nuestra Santa Fe tan fundada por millares de milagros como tenemos en el Testamento Viejo y Nuevo," cited in Francisco de la Maza, *El guadalupanismo mexicano*, Mexico: Fondo de Cultural Económica, 1981, p. 13.
24. Gerónimo de Mendieta, *Historia eclesiástica indiana*, Mexico: CONACULTA, 1997, II, 297.
25. Mendieta, *Historia eclesiástica indiana*, II, 297. Fr. Mendoza, *Relación ... Tecaxique*, unnumbered front matter, dated December 8, 1683.
26. See, for example, Bartolomé de Alva's *Confesionario mayor* for Nahuatl speakers in 1634:

   many things which you still carry on and are engaged in, in a very dark and gloomy night of ignorance, about which the rest of the Christians, your neighbors the Spaniards, are astonished, amazed, and appalled, particularly seeing how weak, miserable, and ill-fated are your faith and works, that it seems that until now it has not taken root in your hearts.

   A Guide to Confession Large and Small in the Mexican Language, 1634, ed. and trans. Barry D. Sell and John Frederick Schwaller, Norman: University of Oklahoma Press, 1999, p. 60.
27. On Florencia and his texts, see Jason Dyck, "The Sacred Historian's Craft: Francisco de Florencia and Creole Identity in Seventeenth-Century New Spain," Ph.D. dissertation, University of Toronto, 2012.
28. Although Oviedo marked some of his additions in the *Zodíaco mariano* with an asterisk, it is not always clear which miracle stories were contributed by Florencia in the late seventeenth century and which by Oviedo half a century later.
29. Alonso de la Rea, *Crónica de la Orden de N. Seráfico P.S. Francisco, Provincia de San Pedro y San Pablo de Mechoacán en la Nueva España ... año de 1639* (1st ed., Mexico: Vda. de Bernardo Calderón, 1643), Mexico: Imprenta de J.R. Barbedillo, 1882, pp. 228–233.
30. Unlike ex-votos, *promesas* were votive offerings appealing for divine intervention and favor rather than giving thanks for a favor granted.

31. On early Italian ex-voto paintings, Angelo Turchini, ed., *Pittura "popolare": Ex voto dipinti della Bergamasca*, Villa d'Almè: Edizioni Capelli, 1983, and Angelo Turchini, ed., *Lo straordinario e il quotidiano: Ex voto, santuario, religione popolare nel Bresciano*, Brescia: Grafo edizioni, 1980. While a few surviving ex-voto paintings for Spanish shrines predate the sixteenth century, this kind of votive offering apparently did not become widely popular there until the seventeenth century. See especially José Cobos Ruiz de Adana and Francisco Luque-Romero Albornoz, *Ex-votos de Córdoba*, Córdoba: Diputación Provincial de Córdoba/Fundación Machado, 1990; Salvador Rodríguez Becerra and José María Vásquez Soto, *Exvotos de Andalucía: Milagros y promesas en la religiosidad popular*, Sevilla: Argantino, Ediciones Andaluzas, 1980; and Fina Parés, "Los exvotos pintados en Cataluña," in *La religiosidad popular. 3, Hermandades, romerías y santuarios*, ed. León Carlos Álvarez Santaló and María Jesús Buxó Rey, Barcelona: Ed. Anthropos, 1989, pp. 423–445.

32. The third numeral in the date is no longer legible, but Weismann makes the case that it is a "4."

33. "An Exvoto by José Patricio Polo – 1741," *Anales del Instituto de Investigaciones Estéticas* X: num. 37 (1968), 45–47.

34. Vilaplana, *Histórico y sagrado novenario*, p. 83, story likely taken from an ex-voto painting, as Cisneros and Florencia often did in recording miracle stories in their devotional histories of miraculous Marian images in the seventeenth century. Gloria Giffords, *Folk Retablos*, Tucson: University of Arizona Press, 1974, p. 121, provides an example of one of the more painterly ex-votos on canvas commissioned by a grateful family of modest means. The three registers show the Christ of Chalma, the Blessed Sacrament, and San Antonio de Padua at the top; a rural scene including a field of maguey plants and parents in Indian dress with two children inside a collapsed building, and a third child with hands clasped in prayer outside the building across the middle; and in the legend at the bottom,

> On August 3, 1797 Faustina María of the town of Teolollucca was sick in bed, with two of her children sleeping beside her. Another son, a little older, told her to hurry out of the house, that it was about to collapse. Just as he left, the building collapsed on the sick woman. She instantly invoked the Blessed Sacrament, San Antonio, and the Lord of Chalma, and emerged alive.

35. For example, Florencia and Oviedo, *Zodíaco mariano*, pp. 43, 194 mention "muchos lienzos pequeños" and, at Dolores Acazingo, "many" ex-voto paintings for the late seventeenth century (when Florencia wrote) or mid-eighteenth century (when Oviedo amended the text). After assuring readers in his chronicle *América thebaida* (1729) that Our Lady of Charo (Michoacán) had worked many miracles, Fr. Matías de Escobar, OSA, noted that "algunos están pintados en las tablas del tabernáculo," *América thebaida: Vitas patrum de los religiosos hermitaños de N.P. San Agustín de la provincia de San Nicolás Toletino de Mechoacán* [1729], Morelia: Balsal Editores, 1970, p. 431. Later in the eighteenth century and into the 1810s, José Manuel Ruiz y Cervantes, *Memorias de la portentosa imagen de Nuestra Señora de Xuquila . . .*, Mexico: Zúñiga y Ontiveros, 1791, p. 38 noticed "little paintings" in the Oaxaca shrine of Our Lady of Xuquila. Viceroy Bucareli referred to "tablas de milagros" on the walls near the altar of Nuestra Señora de Loreto in the chapel of the Colegio de San Gregorio in Mexico City in the 1770s, AGN Templos y Conventos 6 exp. 2. The shrine of the Señor del Calvario of Coatepec

Harinas, Estado de México in 1820 was said to host "gran número de retablos," AHM caja 1820. In his *Estrella del norte de México. Historia de la milagrosa imagen de María Santísima de Guadalupe*, Guadalajara: J. Cabrera, 1895, Florencia evidently drew many of the examples of miracles associated with the Virgin of Guadalupe from ex-voto paintings displayed in the shrine, as did Villaplana for the Pueblito shrine near Querétaro in the 1740s; and Vicente Suárez de Peredo, writing about the shrine of Our Lady of Ocotlán (Tlaxcala) in the 1790s, noticed that many "cuadritos" depicting miracles had been added since Manuel de Loaizaga wrote about miracles there in the 1740s, *La estrella más hermosa, o aparición de la Santísima Virgen de Ocotlán en la noble ciudad de Tlaxcalan*, Puebla: Impr. del Comercio, 1813, pp. 26ff.

36. Luis de Cisneros, *Historia de el principio y origen, progressos, venidas a México, y milagros de la Santa Imagen de nuestra Señora de los Remedios* . . ., Mexico: Juan Blanco de Alcáçar, 1621, fol. 44.
37. The Tulantongo ex-voto painting is reproduced in Elín Luque Agraz, *El arte de dar gracias: Los exvotos pictóricos de la Virgen de la Soledad de Oaxaca*, Mexico: Casa Lamm, 2007.
38. This number does not include the forty-four events of healing, protection, and punishment depicted in a panel of thirty-six painted cells in the parish church of Españita, Tlaxcala that may be based on ex-voto paintings dating from the eighteenth century. The panel carries a notation that it was "retouched" in 1881, but it appears to be more than a light restoration. A nineteenth-century pastor with lessons to teach seems to have edited and shaped at least some of the contents of the panel. Punishment miracles are rare among the surviving colonial ex-voto paintings donated by the faithful (which is not surprising – Who would go to the trouble and expense of advertising that s/he or a relative suffered death or disability as divine retribution for a broken promise or other sin?). Yet, sixteen of the forty-four miracles depicted in the Españita panel were incidents of divine retribution for misdeeds. The panel also contains another four editorial comments exhorting parishioner-viewers to repent and reform, which is even less likely to be found in an early ex-voto painting: "¡Fieles, tomad de aquí un provechoso ejemplo!"; "¡Dios castigue la incredulidad!"; "Aprended de aquí a servirla con la mejor voluntad"; and "Fieles, ¡Ved aquí cuanto puede la fe!" *El origen del reino de la Nueva España, 1680–1750*, "Los pinceles de la historia" series, Mexico: Museo Nacional de Arte, 1999, I, 216–217.
39. Pierre Bourdieu, *Language and Symbolic Power*, ed. John B. Thompson, trans. Gino Raymond and Matthew Adamson, Cambridge, MA: Harvard University Press, 1991, pp. 128, 134, 222. For a fine discussion of ex-votos and their people at several image shrines in contemporary Mexico, see Frank Graziano, *Miraculous Images and Votive Offerings in Mexico*, Oxford and New York: Oxford University Press, 2016.
40. Jean Michel Sallmann, *Naples et ses saints à l'âge baroque, 1540–1750*, Paris: Presses Universitaires de France, 1994, pp. 345–346.
41. Cisneros, *Historia de el principio*, fol. 48r "todo el retablo cargado de pies, manos, cabezas, pechos, ojos de plata."
42. Cárdenas Valencia, *Relación historial*, pp. 92, 105.
43. Alonso Franco y Ortega, *Segunda parte de la Crónica de los Dominicos en México* [1645], Mexico: Imprenta del Museo Nacional, 1983, p. 551.
44. Mendoza, *Relación . . . Tecaxique*, fol. 6. In a metaphorical mood, Mendoza added that "the stones of which the walls of this Shrine are made cry out her marvels."

Making Miracles 351

45. Florencia and Oviedo, *Zodíaco mariano*, pp. 24, 9, 15, 21, 29, 31, 34, 38, 41, 161, 191. The shrine of Nuestra Señora del Refugio in Puebla was singled out for its "innumerables votos" spilling beyond the wall dedicated to them.
46. AGN Civil 1384 exp. 11.
47. AGI México 716, fol. 229.
48. Archbishop Rubio y Salinas pastoral visit to the Dominican *colegio* in the city of Querétaro, January 2, 1753, AHM L10A/7–8, fol. 196.
49. AGN Criminal 31 exp. 6 for the Real del Monte Cristo; AGN Criminal 21 exp. 11 for the Señor de Cerezo; AHM caja 1820 for the Señor del Calvario.
50. Ruiz y Cervantes, *Memorias de . . . Nuestra Señora de Xuquila*, pp. 50–51.
51. Unfortunately, no colonial chronicler who mentioned milagritos lavished the attention on these objects and their donors that Eileen Oktavec did for the shrine of the miraculous image of San Francisco at Magdalena de Kino, Sonora in the 1970s. See her *Answered Prayers: Miracles and Milagros Along the Border*, Tucson: University of Arizona Press, 1995.
52. More unusual miracle relics occasionally were reported. According to Mendoza, *Relación . . . Tecaxique*, fols. 15–16, Gabriel de Guadarrama, a resident of Toluca, made an unusual gift to Nuestra Señora de Tecaxic after he survived a lightning strike by praying to this advocation of Our Lady. Displayed in the shrine was the dagger he had worn in his belt that day, the tip of which had melted into the shape of an apple.
53. Juan de Torquemada, OFM, *Monarquía Indiana*, Mexico: Porrúa, 1986, III, 206 (libro 16 cap. 27).
54. Cárdenas Valencia, *Relación historial*, p. 92.
55. Cárdenas Valencia, *Relación historial*, pp. 105–106.
56. Miguel Sánchez, "Imagen de la Virgen María Madre de Dios de Guadalupe," in *Testimonios históricos guadalupanos*, ed. de la Torre Villar and Ramiro Navarro de Anda, Mexico: Fondo de Cultura Económica, 1982, p. 260.
57. Luis Becerra Tanco, "Nuestra Señora de Guadalupe y origen de su milagrosa imagen," in *Testimonios históricos guadalupanos*, ed. Villar and de Anda, p. 333.
58. The list of seventeenth-century religious chronicles that mention miracles and miraculous images could go on. Alonso de la Rea, the Franciscan chronicler of the Michoacán province described six miracles and assured his readers in 1639 that "otros muchos milagros pudiera referir," *Crónica de la orden de N. Seráfico P.S. Francisco*, p. 239. Alonso Franco, OP, in his 1645 chronicle for central Mexico, *Segunda parte*, mentioned a few miracles individually, but alluded to many more, as did Francisco de Burgoa in 1674 for the miraculous crucifix of Hueyapan in the Valley of Oaxaca, *Geográfica descripción de la parte septentrional del Polo Ártico de la América* [1674], Oaxaca: Instituto Oaxaqueño de las Culturas, 1997, fol. 248v.
59. Escobar, *América thebaida*, pp. 424–431; Juan de Magallanes, *Novena de la santa imagen del Santo Christo . . . de San Miguel de Chalma*, first edition 1731, other editions 1777, 1778, 1788, 1800. The reports in the 1743 *relaciones geográficas* for the Archdiocese of Mexico frequently mention miraculous images and prodigious healings, relief from epidemics, auspicious rainfall, protection from fatal accidents, but nearly all are general comments rather than particular instances, *Relaciones geográficas del Arzobispado de México, 1743*, ed. Francisco de Solano, 2 vols., Madrid: C.S.I.C., 1988. The same is true of Cabrera y Quintero's monumental chronicle of the miraculous images and the great epidemic of 1736–1738 in Mexico City. Vilaplana's *Histórico y sagrado novenario*

for the shrine of Nuestra Señora del Pueblito is unusual in describing forty-one specific miracles, as well as alluding to many more.
60. Manuel Loaizaga, *Historia de la milagrosíssima imagen de Nuestra Señora de Occotlan* [1750], Tlaxcala: Instituto Tlaxcalteca de la Cultura, 2008, p. 83.
61. José de Arlegui, *Crónica de la provincia de N.S.P.S. Francisco de Zacatecas*, Mexico: J. Bernardo de Hogal, 1737, p. 63.
62. The Virgin of Ocotlán (Tlaxcala), for example, was credited in Loaizaga's account, *Historia de la milagrosíssima imagen de Nuestra Señora de Occotlan,* with various activations, as well as remaining incorrupt after two centuries. He treated them ahistorically, as collective evidence of the renewal of a first sign of divine favor. Nuestra Señora del Pueblito reportedly came to life many times, including perspiring twenty-two times, crying, flushing, and showing a star on her forehead three times (1734, 1736, 1743), Vilaplana, *Histórico y sagrado novenario*, pp. 62–65.
63. Cisneros, *Historia de el principio*, fol. 18v.
64. Using information about 3,126 European shrines, Mary Lee Nolan and Sidney Nolan describe seven types of origin stories, *Christian Pilgrimage in Modern Western Europe*, Chapel Hill: University of North Carolina Press, 1989, pp. 216–290. At least a few examples of nearly all of their types can be found in America, but the distribution was substantially different.
65. Philip M. Soergel, *Wondrous in His Saints: Counter-Reformation Propaganda in Bavaria*, Berkeley: University of California Press, 1993, chapter 5.
66. The examples of holiness tried and triumphant are scarce for New Spain. They include several wooden crosses on or near the west coast of Oaxaca and Jalisco in the sixteenth century that resisted the efforts of Protestant pirates to desecrate them.
67. The imported statue of Nuestra Señora de Guanajuato was said to have been hidden in a cave during the Muslim occupation of Iberia and rediscovered after the Reconquista, Florencia and Oviedo, *Zodíaco mariano*, p. 283; Our Lady of Remedios was lost during the Noche Triste at Totoltepec and providentially found by a native nobleman twenty-one years later, Rosario Inés Granados Salinas, "Fervent Faith. Devotion, Aesthetics, and Society in the Cult of Our Lady of Remedios (Mexico, 1520–1811)," Ph.D. dissertation, Harvard University, 2012, p. 4; tradition in Huixquilucan, Estado de México, has it that when a shepherd whistled for his animals, the whistle was returned. He followed the sound to the site of a marvelous cross with two candles burning before it, H. R. Harvey, "Pilgrimage and Shrine: Religious Practices Among the Otomi of Huixquilucan, Mexico," in *Pilgrimage in Latin America*, ed. N. Ross Crumrine and Alan Morinis, Westport, CT: Greenwood Press, 1991, pp. 95–96; Nuestra Señora de Zetuna of Yucatán was said to have been found by a cenote one night after phantom noises and bells were heard in the village church, Florencia and Oviedo, *Zodíaco mariano*, pp. 23–24, Cárdenas Valencia, *Relación historial*, p. 100; and the legend of the statue of Nuestra Señora de los Dolores of Soriano, Querétaro, revolved around an Indian girl looking after family animals who encountered another little girl who came to play with her. Her parents later found the statue at the site of the apparition, Jorge Ruiz Martínez, *Apuntes históricos acerca de la venerada imagen de Nuestra Señora de los Dolores de Soriano*, Mexico: Editorial Jus, 1967, p. 48. The Virgin of Tecaxic was found abandoned in her ruined chapel after celestial lights and music guided Pedro Millán there, Mendoza, *Relación . . . Tecaxique*, fols. 6r–8v.

68. For example, the Christ of the Oak depicted in an eighteenth-century painting in the church of San Mateo, Cáceres, Spain, reproduced in Luisa Elena Alcalá, "The Image of the Devout Indian: The Codification of a Colonial Idea," in *Contested Visions in the Spanish Colonial World*, ed. Ilona Katzew, Los Angeles and New Haven: Los Angeles County Museum of Art and Yale University Press, 2011, p. 229.
69. Torquemada, *Monarquía Indiana*, III, 390, 202: many wonders but few clear miracles, which he attributed to more peaceful reception of Christianity in the New World, the gentle nature of the native Americans, and the evangelizers in America not being as saintly as Christ's apostles. Torquemada's retrospective treatment of the sixteenth century is filled with providential signs, especially visions of heavenly lights and parable stories of the devil, priests, and lost souls, and a communion wafer flying through the air into the mouth of an Indian woman at Tzintzuntzan.
70. John L. Phelan, *The Millennial Kingdom of the Franciscans in the New World*, 2nd ed., Berkeley: University of California Press, 1970, p. 51, wrote that Mendieta was perplexed by an absence of miracles in America. The many supernatural signs Mendieta included in his *Historia eclesiástica indiana* were less stunning than Christ walking on water or turning water into wine, but he clearly regarded them as providential and worth recording.
71. The most common sign was an unearthly, resplendent light (*claridad*) marking a sacred site. Another was a storm that rained blood on many communities in the district of Valladolid, Yucatán, which its Franciscan chronicler regarded as a sign of God's displeasure with Indian idolatry. Dr. Pedro Sánchez de Aguilar, "Informe contra indolarum cultores del Obispado de Yucatan (1639)," in *Tratado de las idolatrías, supersticiones, dioses, ritos, hechicerías y otras costumbres gentílicas de las razas aborígenes de México*, Mexico: Ediciones Fuente Cultural, 1953, 2, 270.
72. See Louise M. Burkhart, "'Here Is Another Marvel': Marian Miracle Narratives in a Nahuatl Manuscript," in *Spiritual Encounters: Interactions between Christianity and Native Religions in Colonial America*, ed. Nicholas Griffiths and Fernando Cervantes, Lincoln: University of Nebraska Press, 1999, pp. 91–115 for early miracles in Nahuatl: eight of ten concern Mary, six of these eight were apparitions. Burkhart regards these stories as Nahua redactions of medieval European stories more than pastoral translations into Nahuatl by the friars.
73. On early miracles at Tepeyac and Totoltepec, see William B. Taylor, *Shrines & Miraculous Images: Religious Life in Mexico Before the Reforma*, Albuquerque: University of New Mexico Press, 2011, chapter 5 and literature cited there.
74. Pedro Oroz, *The Oroz Codex*, ed. and trans. Angélico Chávez, Washington: Academy of American Franciscan History, 1972, did not make a clear distinction between apparitions and visions as God-given signs in the form of vivid mental images. Perhaps many were dream visions, although the colonial record is largely silent about dreams even in terms of shamanistic practices and what were regarded as false or demonic visions induced by peyote and other forbidden drugs. The importance of dream interpretation in the healer's art and calling in contemporary Guatemala is explored in Rosalba Piazza, *El cuerpo colonial: Medicina y tradiciones del cuidado entre los maya-k'iche' de Totonicapán, Guatemala*, Guatemala: Avancsco, 2012. For a fascinating study of Muslim dream interpretation and the legitimacy and semi-institutionalized power of dream visions in contemporary Egypt, see Amira Mittermaier, *Dreams that Matter: Egyptian Landscapes of the Imagination*, Berkeley: University of California Press, 2011.

75. Oroz, *The Oroz Codex*, p. 101.
76. AGN Inquisición 133 exp. 23, fols. 246–293. On the early story of the Cristo de Totolapan from the perspective of Totolapan rather than Mexico City, see Javier Otaola Montagne, "El caso del Cristo de Totolapan. Interpretaciones y reinterpretaciones de un milagro," *Estudios de Historia Novohispana* 38 (enero–junio 2008), 19–38, and Jennifer Scheper Hughes, *Biography of a Mexican Crucifix: Lived Religion and Local Faith from the Conquest to the Present*, New York: Oxford University Press, 2010, chapter 3.
77. Catalina Martín had a relapse and died in May as the investigation was winding down, but this setback apparently did not affect the court's ruling on June 3. At least, it was not mentioned there, AGN Inquisición 133 exp. 23, fol. 293.
78. Miracle stories during the transitional years between 1580 and 1630 point in both directions. Several miraculous images and their shrines began or became regionally famous then, including Our Lady of Guadalupe, Our Lady of Remedios, and Nuestra Señora de la Piedad in the Valley of Mexico and Nuestra Señora de la Defensa and La Conquistadora in Puebla, and miracle stories about them mounted up, but none of the miracle healings in northern New Spain attributed to the beatified Ignatius of Loyola by Jesuit sources in 1602, 1612, and 1618 was described as associated with a particular image of him. AGN Jesuitas I-37 exps. 3–4 describe four miracle cures worked for non-Indian women and children who beseeched Beato Ignacio, 1602, 1612, and 1618. Alegre's *Historia* was compiled in the mid-eighteenth century, but eighteen of his twenty-six miracle stories worked with images of San Ignacio, San Francisco Javier, and San Francisco Borja dated from 1595 to 1612, with a concentration in 1610–1612. Alegre dated the other six miracles to 1613–1737.

    Most of the chroniclers of enchantment of the time, including Mendieta, Dávila Padilla, and Torquemada, either did not mention miraculous images or, as in Torquemada's case, mentioned just two in his *Monarquía Indiana*, the Cross of Huatulco and the first cross of Tlaxcala; and in Dávila Padilla's case, the Virgin Mary and Santa Catarina appeared where images of them were on display. Nahuatl sources from the time that seem to be elite native redactions of stories learned from mendicant and Jesuit teachers center again on apparitions in association with cures and foiling of the devil, Burkhart, "'Here is Another Marvel'." Another native elite source, Chimalpahin's *Annals* (covering the years 1589–1615), includes miracles worked by saints with no mention of images, and two miracles of retribution from 1613 in which a native woman and a Spanish couple were punished for disrespecting a cross, *Annals of His Time*, ed. James Lockhart, Susan Schroeder, and Doris Namala, Stanford, CA: Stanford University Press, 2006, pp. 69, 151–155. Judging from Chimalpahin, Lockhart suggests that Nahuas began to associate saints' images with miracles around 1600, *The Nahuas after the Conquest: A Social and Cultural History of the Indians of Central Mexico, Sixteenth through Eighteenth Centuries*, Stanford: Stanford University Press, 1992, pp. 244–245.
79. Robert Bartlett, *Why Can the Dead Do Such Great Things? Saints and Worshippers from the Martyrs to the Reformation*, Princeton, NJ: Princeton University Press, 2013, p. 344. Bartlett relies on figures for nonhealing medieval miracles compiled by Pierre-André Sigal for France in the eleventh and twelfth centuries. Of a group of 2,048 miracle stories, nearly a quarter (470) were punishments, exceeded only by reported apparitions.

80. Cisneros, *Historia de el principio*, fol. 135r.
81. The third miracle in Sánchez de Aguilar's text was a warning sign – he claimed that it rained blood in many villages in the jurisdiction of Valladolid, which he took as God's displeasure with Indian idolatry, in *Tratado de las idolatrías*, II, 270.
82. The treatment of miraculous images in Antonio Tello, *Crónica miscelánea de la Sancta Provincia de Xalisco, libro IV*, preliminary study and notes by Fr. Luis del Refugio de Palacio, Guadalajara: Edit. Font, 1955 illustrates this change, as does de la Rea, *Crónica de la orden de N. Seráfico P.S. Francisco*, pp. 234–239. Francisco de Burgoa's *Palestra historial de virtudes y exemplares apostólicos* [1670], Oaxaca: Instituto Oaxaqueño de las Culturas, 1997, and *Geográfica descripción de la parte septentrional del Polo Ártico de la América* [1674], Oaxaca: Instituto Oaxaqueño de las Culturas, 1997 for the Dominican province of Santiago de México in Oaxaca looked back in time more than ahead in treating miracles, giving pride of place to struggles with the devil without the intervention of images, but he does draw attention to one miraculous statue, the crucifix of Hueyapan, as a living image that had perspired profusely from head to foot and "son grandes los socorros que hallan lisiados, enfermos, y afligidos que todo el año acuden a su piedad," *Geográfica descripción*, fols. 248v, 261v. The *Palestra historial* does not highlight the miraculous except to describe a prodigious event in 1608 in which the consecrated Host prevented a chapel in the Dominican monastery in Antequera from falling in until it could be removed.

    Several other seventeenth- and even eighteenth-century chronicles, especially the in-house provincial chronicles for orders on the frontlines of missionary work, also echoed the early evangelization narratives and their miracle stories, with few image miracles and an emphasis on old themes of diabolism and saintly priests and their relics. Andrés Pérez de Ribas SJ's *History of the Triumphs of Our Holy Faith* is mainly about expulsion of demons, martyred missionaries, and their numinous relics. The same can be said about Diego Basalenque, OSA's *Historia de la Provincia de San Nicolás de Tolentino de Michoacán del Orden de N.P.S. Agustín* [1644], ed. José Bravo Ugarte, Mexico: Editorial Jus, 1963 which pitted the devil against the cross. Basalenque did include one miraculous image, the Cruz de Jacona, found in a guayabo tree, p. 185. And discalced Franciscan Baltasar Medina's *Crónica de la Santa Provincia de San Diego de México*, 2nd ed., Mexico: Editorial Academia Literaria, 1977 noted a few miracles associated with the images of Our Lady of Remedios and Our Lady of Cosamaloapan, but his twenty-one miracles of healing and rescue were attributed to venerable friars of the province and their relics, pp. 31, 54–57, 91ff, 101ff, 111ff. Matías de Escobar, OSA's *América thebaida* included some discussion of healing miracles worked by Our Lady of Zapopan and miraculous crosses, but his treatment of miracles centered on visions, signs (black candles turning white; a jar of water spilling of its own accord), and Paul Bunyanesque tales of heroic friars riding crocodiles and bringing forth blood from tortillas as a lesson to colonial governors who abused Indian subjects.
83. Franco, *Segunda parte*, pp. 454–456, also included a portentous sign in the sky and heavenly voices.
84. Villar and de Anda, *Testimonios históricos guadalupanos*, pp. 245–260.
85. Villar and de Anda, *Testimonios históricos guadalupanos*, pp. 282ff, 333. To recount them all would require a very long book, Becerra Tanco assured his readers.
86. In addition to the many publications for the Virgin of Guadalupe (including Ignacio Carrillo y Pérez, *Pensil Americano florido en el rigor del invierno, la imagen de*

María Santísima de Guadalupe . . ., Mexico: Zúñiga y Ontiveros, 1797), other devotional histories for image shrines followed during the eighteenth century, including Ruiz y Cervantes's *Memorias de . . . Nuestra Señora de Xuquila*, Vilaplana's *Histórico y sagrado novenario*, Loaizaga's *Historia de la milagrosíssima imagen de Nuestra Señora de Ocotlán*, Fr. Lorenzo del Santísimo Sacramento's *El común bienhechor: El Señor de los Desconsolados* [of Tehuacan de las Granadas], and Moxica, OP, *Tesoro escondido en el delicioso campo* . . . (shrine of the Santo Cristo de la casa de novicios). Oviedo completed and published Florencia's *Zodíaco mariano*, and most of the seventeenth-century shrine histories were also reprinted.

87. Lauro López Beltrán, *La guadalupana que sudó tres veces en San Francisco de Conchos, Chih.*, Chih: Edit. Camino, 1989; AGN Archivo Histórico de Hacienda, leg. 1999 exp. 5.
88. de Velasco, *Renovación por sí misma*.
89. AGN Indiferente Virreinal caja 3427 exp. 25, 1685–1686.
90. Mendoza, *Relación . . . Tecaxique*, fols. 11–15, does not mention ex-voto paintings at the shrine as a source of miracle stories, and seems to have relied mainly on the testimony of local devotees who claimed to be eyewitnesses or relatives of the first protagonists. His main source, María Fuentes, had many stories to tell, including elaborations on the founding story, her own experiences of celestial lights at the site, an apparition of Indian angels making beautiful music, the voice of the Virgin heard by her father there, candles that remained lit long after they should have burned out, the miraculous painting of the Virgin becoming exceedingly heavy when Franciscans tried to move it to Toluca, and various marvelous cures and rescues.
91. See Taylor, *Shrines and Miraculous Images*, chapter 2.
92. Francisco Xavier de Santa Gertrudis, *Cruz de piedra, imán de la devoción, venerada en el Collegio de missioneros de la ciudad de Santiago Querétaro. Descripción panegyrica de su prodigioso origen y portentosos milagros*, Mexico: J.F. de Ortega y Bonilla, 1722.
93. As José Adrián Barragán Álvarez suggested in a personal communication, Florencia wrote about Chalma especially as a promoter. Writing his devotional history of the Chalma shrine a century later, Joaquín Sardo, OP, borrowed much from Florencia, but he was writing about a well-established cultus that boasted a fine church, endowments, and official standing as a royal shrine. Chalma was ready for its historian. In his treatment of miracles associated with the Christ of Chalma and the celebrated hermit, Bartolomé de Jesús María, Sardo largely followed Florencia and several other sources, but he added a miracle of warning and punishment that one might expect to find in an established eighteenth-century shrine with property to protect: a man who stole a silver candlestick from the temple was killed and eaten by wolves as he tried to make his escape, Sardo, *Relación histórica y moral de la protentosa imagen . . . Chalma* [1810], facsimile ed., Mexico: Biblioteca Enciclopédica de México, 1979, pp. 66–67.
94. After describing one miracle for Loreto, he wrote, "I leave it there because I need to move on from the miracles of Our Lady of Loreto and if I were to recount all those that have been written down, I would never be done" ("los dexo porque quiero acabar aqui los Milagros de la Señora Lauretana, y fuera nunca acabar, referir los muchos, que andan escritos"), Florencia, *La casa peregrina, solar ilustre, en que nació la Reya de los Ángeles . . .*, Mexico: Herederos de la viuda de B. Calderón, 1689, fol. 104v.
95. In all, the *Zodíaco mariano* includes 297 miracles for 84 shrines over 150 years, with an emphasis on activations and other founding miracles.

96. Florencia also included more than the usual handful of miracle stories in his histories of the shrines of Guadalupe and Remedios, but still did not approach the hundreds of miracles recounted in the sixteenth-century published history of the Spanish shrine of Montserrat.
97. Most published sermons did not describe particular miracles, but see José María Barrientos, *Sermón del Santo Niño Jesús llamado de San Juan* ..., Mexico: A. Valdés, 1818. Barrientos assured his audience that there were enough maravillas "to fill a thick volume." He described several in which the image of the Santo Niño de la Penitencia perspired, traveled on its own, and saved devotees from epidemics in 1737–1738 and 1813.
98. Francisco Antonio Navarrete, *Relación peregrina de la agua corriente, que para beber, y vivir goza la muy noble, leal, y florida ciudad de Santiago de Querétaro* ..., Mexico: Joseph Bernardo de Hogal, 1739. The 1803 patriotic text for Querétaro by Joseph María Zelaá e Hidalgo, including Carlos de Sigüenza y Góngora's *Glorias de Querétaro*, is suffused with the sacred, but does not include individual miracles, *Glorias de Querétaro y sus adiciones*, introduced by Jaime Septién, Querétaro: Gobierno Constitucional del Estado, 2009.
99. November 1732 and January 1735 issues of the *Gazeta de México*, BIBM 4, pp. 347, 559. By 1794 a miracle report in the *Gazeta de México* (of October 21 that year) expressed some reservation without challenging the possibility of miracles in the material world: on October 2 Anastasia de Paz, "a little Indian girl" of nine, fell into a ditch and over a spillway and water wheel with a forty foot vertical drop at a silver mine and mill near Ixtepeji, Oaxaca. She survived with only minor injuries. The reporter stated that this could have "happened naturally" – a stroke of unusual good fortune – but noted that the girl had invoked St. Anthony of Padua as she fell so he concluded that "we can piously believe that the Saint chose to add this to the many marvels he has worked for those who appeal to him."
100. *Relaciones geográficas del Arzobispado de México, 1743*, 2 vols. There are many references to prodigious healings, cures, and stemming of floods, and epidemics in these reports, but most are general comments. Activated images receive more individual attention; see I, 39, 46, 147, 260. Alcedo's work, *Diccionario geográfico de las Indias Occidentales o América*, was republished in four volumes by Ediciones Atlas of Madrid in 1967.
101. Joseph Manuel Rodríguez, OFM, *Relación jurídica de la libertad de la muerte intentada contra la persona del R.P. Andrés Picazo* ..., Mexico: Zúñiga y Ontiveros, 1769. Another investigation of an extraordinary event that earned episcopal approval and publication concerned repeated lightning strikes in the chapel of the Puebla cathedral dedicated to St. Ignatius of Loyola, Juan Antonio de Oviedo, *Relación de los rayos que ... cayeron en la capilla que en la Santa Iglesia cathedral de la puebla está dedicada al glorioso San Ignacio*, Mexico: n.p., 1747.
102. There is an 1864 manuscript copy of this 1755 inquiry in the Sutro Library BT660.G8 1864 Rare Bk.
103. The first papal indulgence for a novena of public devotions for special graces may have been granted by Pope Alexander VII in the 1650s or 1660s. This indulgence apparently encouraged both more public novena observances and publication of these separate booklets containing prayers, acts of contrition, and other material in Spain and Manila in the 1660s and 1670s. The earliest may be Joseph Millán de

Poblete and Miguel Poblete, *Relación del novenario y rogativa que se hizo en la Sancta Iglesia Cathedral de Manila al glorioso archangel San Miguel*, Manila: n.p., 1663. Other booklets published in Barcelona, Madrid, Mallorca, and Valencia followed in 1669, 1671, and 1675. These early novena booklets before 1700 mostly were dedicated to particular saints and advocations of the Virgin Mary rather than to shrine images. Programs of contrition and prayer for novenas had been included in longer "vida y milagros" texts devoted to different saints that were published in Spain earlier in the seventeenth century, but not yet as separate texts.

104. The second Mexican novena booklet dedicated to a shrine image may have been Alonso Alberto Velasco's for the Cristo Renovado de Santa Teresa, *Novena en honra de N.S. Jesu-Christo crucificado* ... Mexico: Doña María de Benavides, 1699. The first, published in 1665, was dedicated to the Virgin Mary in her shrines of Guadalupe and Remedios, Miguel Sánchez, *Novenas de la Virgen María Madre de Dios para sus devotíssimos santuarios de los Remedios y Guadalupe* ..., Mexico: Viuda de Bernardo Calderón, 1665.

105. For example, *Novenario de alabanzas, en honrra de la gloriosa Santa Paula* ..., Mexico: Francisco de Rivera Calderón, 1715, 4″ × 5 7/8″.

106. My sources for this observation are WorldCat, José Toribio Medina, *La imprenta en México (1539–1821)*, facsimile edition, 8 vols., Mexico: UNAM, 1989–1990, and Antonio Palau y Dulcet, *Manual de librero hispano-ameriano: Inventario bibliográfico de la producción científica y literaria de España y de la América Latina desde la invención de la imprenta hasta nuestro días, con el valor comercial de todos los artículos descritos*, 2nd ed., 35 vols., Barcelona: Librería Palau, 1948–1987.

107. As Carmen Castañeda noted, novena booklets were a staple of printers in New Spain in the late eighteenth century: "A finales del siglo XVIII las imprentas de la ciudad de México, Puebla, y Guadalajara producían sobre todo libros devotos, entre los que sobresalían las novenas," "Libros como mercancías y objetos culturales en la feria de San Juan de los Lagos, México, 1804," *Estudios del Hombre* 20: 1 (2005), 96–97.

108. Joachin Camacho, *Novena y breve relación del origen de la Milagrosa Imagen de nuestra Señora de Consolación*, reimpresa, Mexico: Imprenta del Nuevo Rezado de Doña María de Rivera, 1753, second page (unnumbered) of the "breve relación" section.

109. Camacho cited two Franciscan chronicles for his account of the founding miracle: Balthassar de Medina (*Chronica de la Santa Provincia de San Diego*) and Agustín de Vetancurt (*Teatro mexicano*).

110. Other statues reputedly changed posture in earthquakes and remained fixed in the new position as a sign of their protection; for example, in and near Mexico City, the niño de San Juan de la Penitencia, and San Francisco del Milagro in the Franciscans' *convento grande*, Francisco de Ajofrín, *Diario del viaje que hizo a la América en el siglo XVIII el P. Fray Francisco de Ajofrín*, 2 vols., Mexico: Instituto Cultural Hispano Mexicano, 1964, I, 46.

111. Pedro de Jesús María Priego Velarde, *Relación histórica novenario, y descripción de el culto de María Santíssima en su imagen de consolación, que se venera en el convento de recoletos Franciscanos llamado vulgarmente de San Cosmé*, Mexico: Bibliotheca Mexicana, 1769, "inumerables son las personas que viven persuadidas deber a María Santíssima de la Consolación sus vidas[,] casi infinitas."

Triduo booklets were less likely to include miracle stories, but see *Religioso triduo consagrado a Jesús del Claustro que se venera en Tacuba* [1836], Mexico: Impr.

Making Miracles 359

de M. Murguía y cia., 1854, which quotes the caption on an old, much deteriorated ex-voto painting: "In 1730, the great bell of San Gabriel Tlacopan fell on the Indian Juan Valero. The Indians there invoked the Señor del Claustro and found him uninjured."

112. This anonymous novena booklet published by the Zúñiga y Ontiveros shop in 1778 was based on (or perhaps was the basis for) a smaller, fifteen-page booklet published in Cádiz the same year by Antonio de Alcántara.

113. For example, in Catalan Juan Papió's *El Colegio Seminario del Arcángel San Miguel de Escornalbou* . . ., Barcelona: Imprenta de los Padres Carmelitas, 1765, an entire book (Libro III "de casos raros de las misiones") was given over to miracles of divine punishment for an array of spiritual and moral misdeeds.

114. For example, Juan de Magallanes, *Novena de la santa imagen del Santo Christo . . . de San Miguel de Chalma,* many editions from 1750 to 1816, the first apparently in 1731: "los milagros en fin, que ha hecho son muchos, algunos de ellos, vea el curioso en el Padre Florencia, otros espero en su Magestad saldrán a luz. Pero aunque grandes los que en necesidades corporales han experimentado sus devotos, los que hace para remedio de las almas son continuos." Or, waxing lyrical, Cabrera y Quintero wrote in 1746 that Nuestra Señora de la Fuente – Our Lady of the Spring – "is flooding Mexico City with miracles," *Escudo de armas,* p. 163. The *relaciones geográficas* for the Arzobispado de Mexico prepared by or for royal district governors in 1743 frequently mention that miracles were taking place at image shrines (e.g., I, 260), but other than the activation of several images, only one miracle is specified: in *Relaciones geográficas del Arzobispado de México, 1743,* I, 269, the Mater Dolorosa in the Querétaro convent of Santa Clara was said to have restored hearing and speech to a deaf woman so she could confess before dying.

115. Manuel de Loaizaga, *Historia de la milagrosissima imagen de Nuestra Señora de Occotlan* [1745].

116. Suárez de Peredo, *La estrella más hermosa, o aparición de la Santísima Virgen de Ocotlán en la noble ciudad de Tlaxcalan,* pp. 26ff; *Historia de la Santísima Virgen María, que con el título de Ocotlam . . .* Mexico: Zúñiga y Ontiveros, 1823, p. 66.

117. At the end of the colonial period, ecclesiastical officials may have tried to move more emphatically against rumors of miracles, but without much success. In an 1816–1817 case of a petition from an Indian principal in the district of Hueypoxtla (Estado de México) for permission to collect alms for a statue of the infant Jesus belonging to his family, the archbishop's *promotor fiscal* declared that permission should not be granted and the image should be placed in the parish church under the pastor's watchful eye. To do otherwise, he said, was to "foment belief in miracles that have not been approved and give rise to unfortunate abuses especially among rustic folk" ("fomenta[r] de esta manera la creencia de milagros que no están calificados y da[r] lugar a fatales abusos, principalmente entre la gente rústica"), AGN Civil 2059 exp. 2.

118. Domingo Antonio Chiva, *Compendio histórico y novena de María Santísima Nuestra Señora, que on la advocación de la Cueva Santa se venera en el Seminario de la Santa Cruz de la ciudad de Querétaro . . .,* Mexico: Joseph de Jáuregui, 1792 and Valencia: B. Monfort, 1795. (The text of the novena was based on Chiva's text published in Valencia in 1754.)

119. On a golden age of miracles in seventeenth-century Europe, see Craig Harline, *Miracles at the Jesus Oak: Histories of the Supernatural in Reformation Europe,* New York:

Doubleday, 2003, pp. 4–5. On the early modern period as the "golden age" of demonic possession and exorcism, see Peter Marshall's review of *The Devil Within* by Brian P. Levack in *The Times Literary Supplement*, July 26, 2013, p. 7.

120. De la Rosa's unpublished inventory of miracles and marvels for Nuestra Señora del Patrocinio of Tepetlatcingo in the 1740s, for example, includes a few more exorcisms than the typical group of miracles published in devotional histories and novenas, Taylor, *Marvels and Miracles*, part III.

121. Christian, *Apparitions*, chapter 1 and pp. 208–209; William A. Christian, Jr., *Local Religion in Sixteenth-Century Spain*, Princeton: Princeton University Press, 1981, pp. 75–91. As Christian notes, miraculous discoveries of statues of the Virgin Mary and shepherd cycle origin stories are on full display in Narcís Camós's compendium of Marian shrines in Catalonia, *Jardín de María, plantado en el principado de Cataluña*, printed in Gerona by Joseph Bro in 1772. Of the 137 founding legends recounted by Camós, 111 (81 percent) were miraculous discoveries of images. The theology behind the shepherd cycle founding miracles would seem to be found in Cántiga #144 (*Songs of Holy Mary of Alfonso X, the Wise*, trans. Kathleen Kulp-Hill, Tempe, AZ: Arizona Center for Medieval and Renaissance Studies, 2000, p. 177) in which the Virgin Mary saved a good man in Plasencia from an attack by a bull: "It is only right that the beasts have great fear of the Mother of that Lord who has power over all things."

122. Puebla's Nuestra Señora de la Defensa and La Conquistadora, Cholula's and Totoltepec's Nuestra Señora de los Remedios, Nuestra Señora de Guanajuato, Nuestra Señora de Zacatecas, Nuestra Señora de Zape, Nuestra Señora de la Macana, and La Conquistadora of New Mexico stand out.

123. On the Blessed Mary's love and benevolence in early colonial native sources, see Burkhart, "'Here is Another Marvel'," and the writings of Don Domingo de San Antón Muñón Chimalpahin Quauhtlehuanitzin: *Annals of His Time*, p. 247, and *Codex Chimalpahin*, ed. and trans. Arthur J. O. Anderson and Susan Schroeder, Norman: University of Oklahoma Press, 1997, II, 141, 143, 153, 155.

124. Even during the long seventeenth century, when ecclesiastical officials were especially inclined to join in the enthusiasm for miraculous images, they were wary of random claims by individuals that images had come to life. For example, AGN Inquisición 452 exp. 56, 1603, testimony against Isidro Suárez's claim that a painting of Our Lady had perspired; and AGN Inquisición 796 exp. 9, 1722, proceedings against a married couple in Texcoco for claiming that their statue of Nuestra Señora del Carmen had perspired seven times and worked other miracles (records remitted that year to the Inquisition).

125. Patiño, *Disertación crítico-theo-filosófica sobre la conservación de la Santa Imagen de Nuestra Señora de los Ángeles ...*, pp. 118–122.

6

Relics, Images, and Other Numinous Things

Since Christianity's early years the mystique of divine presence has found expression in sacred things. Beyond the ever-present portability of the consecrated Host, relics come to mind immediately, especially the remains of saints. As Annabel Wharton puts it, the bodies and possessions of saints offer "reassurance that the past retains its authority ... A relic is a sign of previous power, real or imagined. It promises to put that power back to work."[1] Why popular cults and pilgrimages celebrating bone relics did not become more important in New Spain even though thousands of certified remains of saints were brought from Europe is something of a mystery, given the veneration of ancestors and the importance attached to their remains and living presence by precolonial and colonial Mesoamericans, as well as Spaniards' interest in ancestry and recognized relics. Native Mesoamericans would seem to have been predisposed to see Christian relics as numinous things since the bones of totemic ancestors were regarded as sources of regeneration, protection, and legitimacy, if not as the very bones of the gods.[2] Guilhem Olivier's study of sacred bundles containing bones of the ancestors appearing in precolonial and early colonial depictions of processions and migrations suggests that bones as relics were handled in a manner that would have made Christian relics comprehensible and compelling. As Olivier puts it, these sacred bundles served as "the memory constituting the cohesion of their collective identity at the boundary between the founding myths and the specific migration history of each group."[3] But few Christian bone relics were made readily available for public adoration,[4] and none was promoted or spontaneously arose as a pilgrimage site. The Third Synod of prelates meeting in 1585 put it bluntly: "[D]o not expose relics of the saints to public veneration."[5] Granted, colonial laws often bowed to customary practices, and officials learned to make their peace with popular enthusiasms, but bone relics were not often available to the American public in the way images were. Things of the saints and saintly were always treasured, but during the seventeenth and eighteenth centuries they ceded pride of place as relics to images in the material culture of divine immanence.

Primary Relics

Traditionally, the bones, and sometimes the uncorrupted flesh and internal organs, of saints were the prized "first-class" relics of medieval churches and shrines.[6] As the seventh General Council of Nicaea famously decreed in 787, every church needs such a bone relic in its altar for consecration. Saints' bodies were the great transmitters of divine presence and the legitimacy of medieval kings and princes in Europe, long before paintings and statues of them and of Christ and the Virgin Mary became popular as more than teaching aids and symbols during the fourteenth and fifteenth centuries. So many local saints were recognized that their bones were available, although still scarce and private possession restricted.[7] The active trade in bone relics, their public display, and incidents of pious theft suggest how intense and durable the interest in them was.[8] And even at the end of the Middle Ages the remains of canonized saints were not simply replaced by images as ways to the sacred, especially when they continued to reinforce providential localism or their veneration was modeled by a pious monarch such as Philip II of Spain, who reportedly had collected 7,422 relics in the Escorial at the time of his death in 1598.[9]

In New Spain, especially during the sixteenth century, bone relics were an important policy matter for church leaders. Judging by the decrees of the Third Synod in 1585, the prelates in attendance were more concerned with them than they were with painted and sculpted images. They were especially concerned that relics be properly housed and venerated, and mentioned images only in one brief passage stipulating that they not be painted in churches without the bishop's approval and that sculpted images should be appropriately attired.[10] Even though devotion to Christian bone relics in New Spain lacked the popularity it had achieved in Europe, many bone relics certified in Rome were imported throughout the colonial period, from Bishop Zumárraga's request for a special shipment in 1527[11] to bequests and celebrations for newly arrived bones in the late eighteenth century.[12] The most desirable relics of the apostles and early martyrs and doctors of the church were rare in the Americas, but there was no shortage of lesser holy bones – the catacombs of Rome and the "11,000 virgins" of Saint Ursula in Cologne still offered an ample supply.

In the sixteenth and early seventeenth centuries, Franciscans, Dominicans, Jesuits, Carmelites, and bishops were great collectors of bone relics.[13] The Mexican Franciscans' representative in Rome secured the aid of Pope Gregory XIII (1572–1585) in amassing a box of bones of some twenty saints, plus relics of the forty martyrs of Sebaste, which were sent to the order's Convento Grande in Mexico City in February 1582.[14] Agustín de Vetancurt, late seventeenth-century chronicler of the Franciscan province of the Holy Gospel in central Mexico, reported that the Convento

Grande then boasted bone fragments of some fifty saints, including the first apostles and evangelists, St. Anthony of Padua, *el beato* Felipe de Jesús, San Cristóbal, San Martín Obispo, Santa Anastasia, and the heads of two of the 11,000 virgins, among others.[15] The Franciscans in the cities of Puebla and Tlaxcala were similarly fortunate, claiming one of Felipe de Jesús's kneecaps; half a finger of San Nicolás de Tolentino; unspecified bones of Santa Bárbara, San Sebastián, San Damián, and at least eighteen others; and the incorrupt body of Venerable Sebastián de Aparicio, Puebla's prime candidate for beatification.[16] On a smaller scale, Franciscans in other convent churches also collected relics. In the late seventeenth century, the discalced Franciscans of San Diego in Mexico City had relics of the inevitable 11,000 virgins, plus bone fragments of San Lorenzo and San Alejo.[17]

Mexican Dominicans in Rome and Germany on other business also gathered relics for the New World. Thanks to the largesse of Pius V (1566–1572), Fr. Hernando de Paz, member of the governing council of the order's Province of Santiago, managed to send "two chests [*cofres*] of relics," and Fr. Domingo de la Cruz returned from an audience with the Holy Roman Emperor in Germany with two small boxes of relics of the 11,000 virgins.[18] The Dominicans in Mexico City also recorded a tooth of their founder, Santo Domingo de Guzmán.[19] And many cloisters and churches of the religious orders in colonial cities near the end of the colonial period kept a treasure trove of little-seen relics. For example, several Carmelite churches in the seventeenth century organized whole chapels and altars around assortments of relics, and the novices' compound of the Dominicans in Mexico reportedly had several "small chests filled with relics."[20]

In Mexico, Jesuits seem to have been the greatest collectors of certified relics, especially of martyrs' bones. They were responsible for the largest shipments of relics to New Spain in the late sixteenth and early seventeenth centuries, and wherever Jesuits were found in numbers there was likely to be an important collection of bone relics, as at Valladolid (Morelia) by the mid-seventeenth century.[21] Francisco Javier Alegre's chronicle of Jesuit activities in New Spain, composed in the 1760s, recounted how a great number of relics imported by Jesuits in 1575 were scattered on the coast of Veracruz when the ship ran aground in a storm. Coastal people gathered them up for themselves, but a few days later, when a deadly epidemic struck their families, they returned all the relics, which were sent on to Mexico City and received with great veneration even though their authentication papers had been lost. The Mexican Jesuits reported the accident to Rome, requesting new authentications and more relics – 214 in all – which arrived safely in late 1577 or early 1578.[22] A few years later, a papal brief recorded that Father Pedro Chirinos, SJ, was canvassing Roman churches and Vatican officials for bone relics for hospital chapels spread across central

Mexico at Oaxtepec in Morelos, San Roche in Puebla, Santa María de Belem in Perote, Santa María de la Consolación in Acapulco, and the Hospital de San Hipólito in Mexico City. Chirinos's efforts yielded a harvest of bones of at least sixty-four martyred saints, gifted by the pope and officials of the Roman churches of San Lorenzo and San Pancracio.[23]

A survey of the collections of certified relics in New Spain is beyond my reach, but it is noteworthy that other orders and religious groups participated (including the Carmelites in Puebla and Congregation of Guadalupe in Querétaro[24]), as well as cathedral chapters, some parish priests, and laymen, and that while most bone relics arrived from Europe in the sixteenth and seventeenth centuries, there were still celebrated additions into the late eighteenth century, such as a finger of San Juan Nepomuceno acquired by the convent church of La Enseñanza in Mexico City, which was honored in ceremonies attended by the archbishop on July 7, 1782.[25] A skeleton certified to be that of Santa Veneranda (a second-century martyr from the catacombs of Rome[26]) was much anticipated and lavishly received by citizens of the provincial city of Aguascalientes in 1801. According to a news item in the January 30, 1787, issue of the *Gazeta de México*, her remains, shipped from Rome, had reached Guadalajara on December 1, 1786, on their way to Aguascalientes. The relics were on view in the cathedral in Guadalajara for four days, followed by short stays in the schools and convents of nuns in the city before they were to begin the last leg of their journey. But apparently they did not reach Aguascalientes for fourteen years. In the March 10, 1801, issue, the *Gazeta de México* reported that there was great popular rejoicing in Aguascalientes over the recent arrival of the saint's body and the promise of heavenly favor through her intercession. A grand procession to her final destination in the town's Santuario de Nuestra Señora de Guadalupe was staged, with buildings along the route decorated with beautiful hangings and arches spanning the streets.[27] The saint's body was placed in an urn on an imposing altar of faux marble with gold accents built for the purpose under the direction of Don Gerónimo Antonio Gil, a celebrated engraver from the Academy of San Carlos in Mexico City. Since Gil died in 1798, the altar would have been constructed before then, perhaps as early as 1787, in anticipation of the relics' arrival. The reporter in 1801 conveyed only the dimmest sense of this long delay, perhaps to obscure a pious theft by one of the leading families of the region. In his telling, the relics had been brought from Rome in 1786 for Dr. Don Vicente Flórez Alatorre, a canon of the cathedral of Guadalajara. After he died, they were moved to the private chapel of another priest, D. Ignacio Rincón Gallardo, a member of the rich and powerful Rincón Gallardo family, holders of the vast Ciénega de Mata entailment in rural Aguascalientes. Now, in 1801, wrote the reporter, the heirs of Father Flórez had decided to give the relics to the town of Aguascalientes.

Secondary Relics

A second class of relics – anything the holy person had touched or worn, or that came from a shrine housing the remains of a celebrated saint – were less common but still coveted, especially by the religious orders in the early colonial period. The Franciscan *Oroz Codex* of 1585 proudly listed several high-value relics of this kind in the treasury of the order's Convento Grande in Mexico City: a piece of the veil of Santa Lucía and a piece of the tunic of San Luis Obispo.[28] Other relics of the Franciscans in central Mexico included a portion of St. Augustine's miter, pieces of the corded sashes of San Francisco Solano and San Pedro Regalado, a vial of blood from the wound in St. Francis's side, and a dish in which the wounds of St. Francis had been washed.[29] A list of relics introduced by the Jesuits in the 1570s included a garment worn by the Virgin Mary, another worn by her husband, St. Joseph, and a third worn by her mother, St. Anne.[30] Also in the late sixteenth century the Carmelite convent of Puebla treasured two of the coins paid by Emperor Constantine's mother, Santa Elena, to ransom the True Cross, and a large piece of the handkerchief used by the Virgin Mary to wipe her tears when Christ was crucified.[31] No doubt a longer list of such relics could be assembled, but two patterns for New Spain are clear: few were inventoried, and, with two exceptions, they are rarely mentioned in the record of popular devotion.

At the shrine of Our Lady of Remedios, a belt reportedly given to the Indian seer Juan Ceteutli by the Virgin Mary to cure his illness when she appeared to him in 1541 was celebrated in the early seventeenth century as the source of miraculous cures. Augustinian chronicler Juan de Grijalva (1624) was convinced that this wonder-working relic not only was a gift from the Virgin, it had originally belonged to St. Augustine, himself.[32] The belt seems to have been largely forgotten by the eighteenth century. Mariano Fernández Echeverría y Veitia mentioned in his 1779 text that the belt was in the care of the mayordomo of the archicofradía of Nuestra Señora de los Remedios in Mexico City and was taken to the sick in the capital city who asked for it,[33] but the silence of other late colonial chroniclers and the administrative record of the shrine kept by the ayuntamiento suggest that it had become a minor relic, known only to a few.

The most common and coveted relics of this kind in New Spain were from the Lignum Crucis – pieces of wood from the True Cross, on which Christ was crucified – and thorns from the Crown of Thorns with which his persecutors mocked him. Although relics of the True Cross were prized above other secondary relics as "the Tree of Life where our redemption and wellbeing was achieved,"[34] none in New Spain compared in fame and following to Spain's most famous cross relics, which became pilgrimage shrines in their own right: the noble fragment in the monastery of Santo Toribio de Liébana in Cantabria (which was reputed to be the largest authenticated piece of the True Cross), and the Cruz de Caravaca in Murcia. These two relics were regarded (at least by Spaniards) as among Christendom's five "sacred portals," offering perpetual indulgences to visitors.[35] And while many more Spanish confraternities and churches boasted a sliver of the True Cross, New Spain also claimed at least twenty-five certified pieces and five thorns from Christ's Crown of Thorns. Except for the splinter of the True Cross in the parish church of Pachuca, these treasures belonged to churches in the cities of Mexico, Puebla, and Valladolid. Mexico City alone claimed sixteen or seventeen of the twenty-five or twenty-six True Cross relics reported.[36] Franciscan and Jesuit establishments were the principal keepers of these precious splinters and thorns, with seven and four respectively (see Tables 6.1 and 6.2).

None of these secondary relics of Christ was routinely displayed or otherwise available to the public as a Mexican shrine's principal attraction, with the possible exception of the one in Pachuca at the end of the colonial period. It was presented more often for public veneration and carried in processions, its prestige apparently shared by the parish church and the Franciscan convent church and college in Pachuca. When it was acquired and how it was venerated before the 1780s are not clear. Perhaps it was one of the Jesuits' relics that were distributed to different churches after the order was expelled from New Spain in 1767.[37] In any event, the earliest dated references I have located come from the *Gazeta de México* in 1784, 1785, and 1786. The May 19, 1784 issue of the *Gazeta* mentioned that various religious observances in Pachuca sponsored by its citizens had been undertaken during the current epidemic of a pneumonia-like illness, including a solemn procession of their Lignum Crucis, reportedly the largest in New Spain, to the Franciscan college for a special novena, followed by another procession to take the relic back to the parish church. The May 3, 1785 issue announced a special Mass and sermon for the "Santo Lignum Crucis," followed by a procession, during a period of drought. And the issue for May 30, 1786 mentioned a special Mass and procession in Pachuca of the treasured Lignum Crucis and a statue of San José during the great epidemic that year. The procession returned the Lignum Crucis to the parish church from the Franciscan college, where it had been displayed since May 3, the day of the feast of the Invention of the True Cross. Eleven years later, the July 22, 1797 issue reported that the Pachuca area was experiencing extreme drought. High Mass was celebrated in the parish church on May 3 before a large crowd, with the Lignum Crucis displayed on the main altar between statues of San José and the miraculous Christ of the Cherry Tree (Señor del Cerezo). After Mass the pastor kissed the relic and it was left there all day for public adoration. Then at 5:00 p.m. the statues and Lignum Crucis were processed from the parish church to the Franciscan

Table 6.1 *Fragments of the True Cross in New Spain*

Location	Date	Source
	Mexico City (13 or 14)	
Cathedral (2)	16th c, 18th c	Weckmann, p. 255; Sánchez Reyes, p. 306; Cabrera y Quintero, p. 163
Franciscan Convento Grande (2)	late 16th c	Oroz Codex, p. 96; Torquemada I, 96; Vetancurt, p. 47
Franciscan convento de San Diego	1682	Medina, fols. 28v–29v
Dominican convent	1598	Dávila Padilla, pp. 501–504
Augustinian convent	1573	Dávila Padilla, p. 35
Carmelite convent		Sánchez Reyes, pp. 302–303
Jesuit Colegio de S. Ildefonso	1578?; 18th c	Viera, p. 61
Conceptionist convent Archicofradía de la Santa Veracruz	16th c	Constitutions of the archicofradía (1824)
*Ayuntamiento minutes noted receipt of a piece of the True Cross	1663	acta de Cabildo, December 14, 1663
	Puebla (city) (4)	
Cathedral	18th c	Veytia, p. 101
Franciscan convento (2)	Late 17th c	Vetancurt, p. 51
Carmelite convento (Chapel of Our Lady of los Remedios)	Early 17th c	González Dávila, p. 73; Veytia, p. 438, Sánchez Reyes, p. 221
	Valladolid (2)	
Cathedral	1595	AGN Indiferente General caja 5437 exp. 033
Jesuit Church	17th c	González Dávila, p. 109
	Pachuca (1)	
Parish Church	18th c	Gazeta de Mexico, 1784, 1786, 1797; AGN CRS 125 exps. 2–4; Tulane VEMC leg. 66 exp. 13

* It is not clear whether this is one of those already listed. Two pieces of the True Cross in reliquaries are housed in the Museo Nacional del Virreinato. Their origins, too, are obscure, Sánchez Reyes, "Relicarios novohispanos," p. 303.

college, the convent of San Juan de Dios, and the chapels of the Señor del Tránsito and the Santa Veracruz, while the marchers and spectators recited the litany of the saints. At the Franciscan college all the friars assembled at the main entrance in full regalia to receive the relic and carry its litter on

Table 6.2 *Thorns from the Crown of Thorns in New Spain*

Location	Date	Source
	Mexico City	
Jesuit Casa Profesa	1578	Alegre I, 126
Jesuit Colegio de San Pedro y San Pablo	16th c?	Weckmann, p. 254
Franciscan Convento Grande	17th c	Vetancurt, p. 47
Dominican convent	16th c?	Weckmann, p. 254
Augustinian convent	1650	Guijo I, 100; Sánchez Reyes, p. 312
	Puebla	
Poor Clares convent	16th c?	Weckmann, p. 254

their shoulders into the church for another Mass and more ceremonies. Providentially, a great rainstorm soon followed, wrote the reporter.

Pachuca's piece of the True Cross was at the center of an 1807 controversy that suggests the unusual civic interest in it. On the date of the annual feast of the Adoration of the True Cross, September 14, the parish priest, Luis Violet y Ugarte, did not follow the custom of displaying the relic for public veneration. Rumors had spread during the previous two weeks that it had been tampered with, and a noisy crowd gathered at the church clamoring to see it. Only when the priest finally displayed it was calm restored. The priest fired off an angry complaint to the viceroy that a drunken rebellion had occurred during which his sacristan had been attacked, fueled by rumors spread by his enemy the *subdelegado* (the royal governor for the district) that the priest was removing bits of the relic for his own use. Whether or not these were false rumors, the subdelegado had, in fact, come forward during the uproar and called upon Violet y Ugarte to bring out the relic. When he refused, the subdelegado insisted, telling the priest that this was the only way to quiet the crowd. The protesters dispersed when the subdelegado promised them he would take the relic to the Franciscan *guardián* of the college in Pachuca the next morning for an inspection. The case dragged on in the audiencia court for nearly a year, with Father Violet y Ugarte adding his complaints to the record, insisting that the subdelegado was behind the whole affair and the leaders of the crowd were his cronies. The *fiscal* – legal adviser to the court – was not convinced. He noted that the priest had invited the protests by not displaying the relic in the first place. The subdelegado, he added, could not have been responsible for the diminished relic or the clumsy attempt to repair it with wax, which many people noticed. He recommended that the investigation continue, but now with an eye to establishing the priest's culpability. Soon thereafter, in June 1808, Violet y Ugarte's attorney noted that the archbishop had gone to Pachuca on his pastoral visit and smoothed out the animosity between the two and that the priest now wished to drop his complaint against the subdelegado. A few weeks later the audiencia agreed to suspend the proceedings because of the antagonists' "sincere desire for peace." The last record in the file, dated October 20, 1808, registered the audiencia's continuing displeasure with the "frivolous and malicious" charges the priest had brought, but apparently did not pursue the matter further.[38]

Despite the strong suspicion that the pastor of Pachuca had been harvesting bits of his church's Lignum Crucis, most certified fragments would have been too small and precious to be used up in the magical ways sometimes suffered by pieces of celebrated local crosses like the Cruz de Huatulco or the great wooden crosses erected by the early Franciscan evangelizers at Tlaxcala and the chapel of San José de los Naturales in Mexico City; being cast into a roiling sea to quiet a storm or into a fire to quench the flames, or ground up in medicinal potions. True Cross fragments were typically kept out of public view except for processions on the feast of Corpus Christi, or the feast days of the Invention and Exaltation of the True Cross, or in an emergency.[39] Nevertheless, stories circulated about the numinous qualities of other relics of the True Cross. Gil González Dávila in his chronicle of the early history of the Church in the Spanish Empire (much of it written in the 1590s; published in 1648) singled out an instance involving the piece of the True Cross belonging to the convent of the Discalced Carmelites in Puebla told to him by Fr. Juan de Jesús María in Madrid in March 1644. He said that when some miniscule bits were added to a bowl of the purest holy water a ribbon of blood-red color trailed after them until the entire contents turned red. When a sick patient was about to sip some of it, it turned crystal clear again, which was regarded as another miracle, although not a healing one.[40]

A third class of relics – anything closely associated with a certified relic, usually by touch, or inspired by a saint – were still less common, but not unknown. For example, the Franciscans in Mexico City in the late sixteenth century prized their stone chips from Christ's manger and the Holy Sepulchre. And a Dominican mission to Rome in 1570 yielded, among other things, an Agnus Dei – a disc of wax stamped with an image of Christ as the Lamb of God, molded from a paschal candle that had been blessed by the pope.[41] Generally, though, such relics were introduced less often, or at least were not much promoted. More popular were "mystical brandea": things recommended by a saint that might enjoy the saint's protective presence. These included devotional scapulars and medals depicting, or dedicated to, a saint; rosary beads; the cord and habit of a revered Franciscan;[42] "cedulitas," tiny pieces of rice paper with a printed image of a saint that dissolved in the mouth and were regarded by the faithful as powerful medicine; copies of a tracing of one of the Virgin Mary's feet that was said to have been delivered to a pope by an angel; and replicas of nails from the True Cross that had touched the original nails in Rome.[43]

While medals, rosary beads, and devotional scapulars associated with instructions delivered by apparitions of the Virgin Mary (especially those distributed by the Carmelites) were the most common mystical brandea, the most celebrated for their association with miracles may have been *panecitos*, hard little unleavened cakes or molded clay from the site of a shrine, stamped with the image of the saint or Christ. Bits of these breads were ground into powder, mixed with holy water, and administered to patients suffering from fevers and intestinal complaints. The favorite panecitos were associated with San Nicolás de Tolentino (the Augustinian saint who was said to have been instructed by the Virgin Mary to eat a morsel of one of his charity breads when he was ill), and especially those of Santa Teresa, made by Carmelite nuns following a secret recipe of their patron saint.[44]

In a famous seventeenth-century case, panecitos of Santa Teresa became numinous relics in their own right. In 1648, Doña María de Poblete, sister of Dr. Juan de Poblete, dean of the cathedral chapter in Mexico City, ground up one of the nuns' panecitos and mixed the powders in a jar of water for her sick husband. Not only did her husband recover, but she reported that what appeared to be the same panecito bobbed to the surface of the water, solid and complete.[45] With Doña María preparing the medicinal waters, the apparent miracle of the reconstituted panecitos happened again and again (although not when Doña María was being closely observed). Word spread about these marvelous little cakes, reminiscent of Christ's multiplication of the loaves and the Resurrection. Leading citizens of the capital clamored for them, and for more than thirty years panecitos baked by the Carmelite nuns of Mexico City and Puebla kept rising to the top of the jar and were treated as relics without serious doubts raised about whether they were truly reconstituted by faith and the saint's favor or a ruse perpetrated by Doña María.[46] In 1674, at the request of the Carmelites, her brother and other members of the cathedral chapter undertook an investigation of the purported miracles. Twenty-four witnesses came forward to affirm these apparition-style miracles, although few of them said they saw the reconstituted cakes rise from the bottom of the jar. All but two of these witnesses were diocesan priests or Carmelite friars. The opening summary by Fray Juan de la Ascención, procurator of the Carmelite Province of San Alberto, described some of the reconstituted cakes as incorrupt – a sure sign of their sanctity – and several witnesses spoke of theirs as "relics."[47] Br. Francisco de Herrera, a longtime family friend of the Pobletes, was one of the witnesses who spoke glowingly about his now venerable panecito relic, given to him by Doña María twenty-six years before. He seemed to regard it as a talisman. When it began to crumble a bit, he put a piece of dried chile on it and there was no further deterioration, he reported; and thanks to the relic he, like others, "continues to enjoy great happiness and good fortune in his labors, dangers, and illnesses, entrusting himself with true faith to the said most glorious saint for her intercession."[48] Three years after this investigation Archbishop Payo Enríquez de Rivera, OSA, endorsed the miracle of the reconstituted panecitos in a decree of October 9, 1677, "in order to promote the devotion and cult of the glorious Santa Teresa de Jesús."[49] But soon after this archbishop's death in 1680 another, more probing and skeptical inquiry by the Inquisition into the miracles of the panecitos of Doña María was undertaken, albeit slowly, from 1681 to 1686. Doña María's death in 1686 ended the investigation and probably spared her a summons before the court and public humiliation.

Despite damning testimony and the Inquisition's eventual conclusion that Doña María had been surreptitiously dropping whole panecitos into the jar after mixing in the powders, belief in the miracle of the reconstituted panecitos persisted in Mexico City, with the tacit acceptance of archdiocesan authorities.[50] Even a century later, in 1801, Fr. Pedro Pablo Patiño, OFM, devoted more than three pages of his treatise on the miraculous image of Nuestra Señora de los Ángeles at Tlatelolco to Doña María's miraculous panecitos without a hint of irony or reservation.[51] Instead, he affirmed "the reality of this ongoing miracle." Popular belief in Doña María's *panecitos de Santa Teresa* as miraculous objects long after the Inquisition assembled a full case against their authenticity is as much a testament to the power of the printed word to reinforce popular knowledge and memory as it is to stubborn faith. Juan Barrera's *Noticia auténtica de las maravillas que ha obrado Dios con los panecillos de Santa Teresa ...*, published in 1675, the archbishop's printed endorsement of the miracle in 1677, and sermons by Isidro Sariñana y Cuenca and Antonio Núñez de Miranda published in 1678 were the reference points for pious authors like Patiño many years later.[52] The unpublished judgment of the Inquisition in 1686 was overlooked by them, if not forgotten.

Local Relics

The research of Antonio Rubial García and Gabriela Sánchez Reyes into Mexico's colonial religious history and material culture suggests that the paradox of limited interest in canonical relics is more apparent than real. In her study of the architecture of relics in New Spain, Sánchez Reyes shows in abundant detail that many bone relics were, in fact, visible, if not readily accessible, in church altars, chapels, and reliquaries of several kinds displayed mostly in cathedrals and churches of the Carmelites, Jesuits, Franciscans, and Dominicans.[53] More to the point, in New Spain other bones and belongings did attract popular attention as virtual relics, sometimes with the encouragement of church leaders.[54] These were the remains and brandea (anything associated with a sacred body and thought to enjoy its prophylactic and healing favor[55]) of locally esteemed but not officially recognized holy men and women, especially those whose bodies proved to be incorrupt, sweet smelling, or associated with marvelous healings. Some holy men and women were so famous in their own time as the epitome of Christian virtues and self-abnegation that they were treated as living relics. Their touch could cure, and their bodies, clothing, and other effects were treated as numinous. People wanted to kiss their feet and touch their clothing. After death, their body parts and garments were treated as relics, especially if they gave off the fresh, sweet odors of sanctity. Even the bodies of some bishops, viceroys, or other benefactors and figures of authority, including a beloved physician, were treated as relics.[56]

Rubial writes of "a profusion of cults of these relics on the part of Indians and Spaniards," especially during the sixteenth and seventeenth centuries,[57] and regards this interest in the materiality of local holy men and women from the early seventeenth century as an expression of budding creole elite nationalism that then rippled through colonial society and culture.[58] Interest in relics of local holy men and women seems to have peaked during the late seventeenth and early eighteenth centuries after three venerables from Peru, Spain's other American viceroyalty of the time – Rose of Lima, Toribio de Mogrovejo, and Francisco Solano – were beatified in quick succession during the 1660s and 1670s. New Spain's two beatified holy men, Felipe de Jesús and Sebastián de Aparicio (a sixteenth-century Spanish immigrant who became an ascetic Franciscan brother late in life, beloved by many who met him on alms-collecting missions in the Diocese of Puebla and the reputed medium for a great many healing miracles, beatified in 1789) enjoyed local fame in Mexico City and Puebla, respectively; however, they did not compare to the broad appeal of St. Rose of Lima, nor did they quench the thirst for homegrown sanctification of place through local heroes even in these two cities, much less elsewhere.[59] Felipe de Jesús, one of the Franciscan brothers martyred in Japan in 1597, was New Spain's one native-born saint-in-the-making. Although called "San Felipe" from the time of his beatification in 1627, he was not canonized until 1862.

If there was less than a profusion of near-saints and their relics, at least scores of early evangelizers and martyred members of the missionary orders, famously pious nuns, several bishops, and a scattering of virtuous lay men and women were celebrated as saintly by ecclesiastical chroniclers, and their bones and belongings were coveted locally as sacred matter.[60] Juan de Torquemada, for example, chronicled in his *Monarquía Indiana* (published in 1615) the appeal of both the persons and relics of several of his most distinguished brethren from the first generation of evangelizers. Toribio de Benavente – "Motolinia" ("the poor one"), the beloved, indefatigable Franciscan missionary of the first generation in central Mexico – was extolled by Torquemada for his "saintly reputation," and scraps of fabric cut from the habit in which he was buried were treasured as relics, but the chronicler reserved pride of place for two other founding Franciscans: Martín de Valencia, who led the first group of his order's missionaries – "the Apostolic Twelve" – and Juan de Zumárraga, Mexico's first bishop. Late in life Valencia retreated to a hilltop cave near Amecameca, and after death his remains were treasured, especially by local *indios*. After his body went missing, a local "Indian" man came forward with belongings of the good friar that he had hidden away – his rope scourge, a coarse tunic, and two chasubles he had used to celebrate Mass. Torquemada assured readers that when these relics were displayed by the Franciscans and Indians at Amecameca, it was with great reverence and solemnity.[61] With Zumárraga, veneration of the man and his relics seems to have been less immediate but not less fervent, at least among some priests. Torquemada centered his treatment of Zumárraga's relics around the exhumation of the bishop's body during a construction project in Mexico City's cathedral, about thirty-five years after his death, that is, around 1583. A canon of the cathedral present at the excavation did not miss the chance to collect some relics from the bishop's remains (*su Santo Cuerpo*). He took a finger and a plain gold ring set with a small emerald, "very pleased with what he considered very great and estimable relics." Before long the canon noticed that the stone began to sweat and continued to do so, which Torquemada took to be a sign that "God wished to show them the esteem which that sainted body deserved."[62]

In the seventeenth and early eighteenth centuries, the city of Puebla was especially renowned for its "living relics" – holy men and women who sanctified the city with their presence and heroic virtues, and the hundreds, if not thousands, of marvelous healings and other wonders reported to result from their presence in the flesh or by means of their relics. Swelling with civic pride, Joachin Antonio de Villalobos, SJ, declared in his 1734 biography of the city's charismatic cathedral canon Dr. Miguel Nieto de Almirón that Puebla surpassed all other cities of New Spain in the number of heroic spirits who had followed the way of Christian perfection and deserved to be honored.[63] Devotional biographies of at least sixteen of these wonder-working *poblano* spiritual heroes were written (and, with one exception, published) before the 1760s, including eight nuns, one laywoman, two Jesuits, three lay brothers, and two diocesan priests.[64] People clamoring for relics during the funeral of one of these saintly poblanos, Sister María Anna Águeda de San Ignacio, attracted the notice of her biographer in 1758. Nuns and others surged forward to kiss her hands, touch her body with their rosary beads, and take some keepsake that had belonged to her. They removed the blood-spotted *corporal* (cloth used in the liturgy of the Eucharist) that covered her face. They also took the palm frond, crown, and flowers that had adorned her body. As the chronicler put it, prudence gave way to frenzied piety and devotion.[65] Later in the eighteenth century, bits of paper with the signature of a reputed visionary nun in Puebla were carried in little bags by her followers, and scraps of her letters were dissolved in beverages and administered to the sick "as relics."[66]

One of the seventeenth-century provincial chronicles that emphasized the healing and salvific wonders worked through a select group of American members of the Dominican order, and their numinous remains is Dominican Fr. Alonso Franco's *Historia de la Provincia de Santiago de México, Orden de Predicadores en la Nueva España*, completed in 1645, but mostly written in the 1610s and 1620s. Among many marvels, he recounts the virtuous lives and spiritual fervor of three saintly compatriots who were closely connected to marvelous healings and other signs of divine protection, either in life or through their relics: Fr. Domingo de la Anunciación, Fr. Hernando Cortesero, and Fr. Pedro de Galarza. Domingo de la Anunciación is described by Franco as a great promoter of the Rosary prayers, the string of beads used to count them, and the image of the Virgin Mary holding a string of beads. His faith in the efficacy of the Rosary was so great that many miraculous healings, narrow escapes, exorcisms, and resurrections followed from his prayers and the acts of devotion by soldiers, Indians, women, and children who followed his example and wore the beads he gave them. Franco recounted sixteen miracles of the kind, but assured readers there were many more. Calling Cortesero "the saint," Franco noted various signs of divine favor bestowed upon him, including his prescience about lost possessions and future events; but he extolled especially Cortesero's singular devotion to the cross, and miracles worked by God through the little crosses he made and gave to one and all. (In Franco's estimation, everyone in the city of Puebla wanted one of his little crosses or asked him to bless the crosses they had.) Franco recounts an assortment of protective or healing marvels of Cortesero's crosses, including several kinds of divine favor that were especially associated with them – putting out fires and protecting women in childbirth. The marvels continued after Cortesero's death by means of his incorrupt and integral body (a man reportedly failed in his attempt to cut off one of the body's arms as a separate relic, finding that it was like trying to cut through stone) and clothing he had worn. Father Galarza's many healing miracles, as Franco writes of them, all took place in Mexico City by means of his relics and prayers that invoked his aid – especially two of his fingers, which were cut off before burial, and scraps of his clothing and pieces of his shoes.[67]

Many of the vignettes in these pious chronicles read like airbrushed obituaries meant to inspire fellow members of the order to new heights of piety more than to memorialize spiritual heroes for a wider audience.[68] How these men and women were received in their lifetimes and remembered later outside the tight circle of clergymen and nuns is less certain. Clearly, some priests – nearly all of whom were identified as Spaniards, whether born in Spain or America – including bishops and other church leaders, encouraged colonial Indians to regard the remains of Mexico's near-saints as numinous. Dr. Jacinto de la Serna, a prominent priest in Mexico City and pastor of the cathedral's parish church in the early seventeenth century, recalled that when he served as the pastor of Tenancingo (near Tenango del Valle in the Valley of Toluca) an Indian woman named Agustina came to him in great distress, bleeding profusely from the mouth, seeking to confess before she died. Serna had with him a bone of the saintly sixteenth-century hermit Gregorio López, a bit of which he ground up and mixed into water for the woman, "exhorting her to entrust herself to that saint, and appeal to him to free her from the illness she was suffering." The next day she regurgitated an assortment of vile things with which she had been bewitched, and soon recovered.[69] This is an arresting story, but it is usually impossible to know how such stories were viewed by a lay audience, especially Indians, since most of the examples come from pious histories of the chroniclers of the orders. For example, the great history of the early Jesuit missions in northwestern Mexico by Andrés Pérez de Ribas, SJ, completed in 1645, paid considerable attention to the martyrdom of Father Julio Pascual and Manuel Martínez in 1632 at the hands of Guazápare Indians in Sonora and the loving rescue of their remains by the Chínipa people whom Father Pascual had evangelized. According to Pérez de Ribas, the Chínipas were disconsolate when Father Marcos Gómez ordered the remains of the martyred priests disinterred and moved to the Jesuit center at Conicari for safekeeping.[70] However, sweeping skepticism about this kind of statement would be a mistake because there *are* clear cases of pastors who were long revered by their parishioners as ancestral saints. For example, Lorenzo de Horta, pastor of Tlatlauqui in the Sierra de Puebla from 1605 to 1640, was long remembered as the great benefactor of the parish. Horta went on to become a member of the cathedral chapter in Puebla and was buried there, but his star remained brightest in Tlatlauqui. When his body was exhumed in 1820, parishioners of Tlatlauqui welcomed three of his teeth as treasured relics.[71]

Martyred missionaries might quickly gain this standing of virtual sainthood, but we know too little about their hagiographical trajectory. Pérez de Ribas mentioned only two likely candidates for this kind of veneration among his various Jesuit martyrs in the northern missions during the early seventeenth century, and neither case is straightforward.

Pérez de Ribas's main example of a beloved martyr was Father Gonzalo de Tapia, killed in Sinaloa in 1594. At several points in his history, Pérez de Ribas extolled at length the saintly Tapia's saintly aims, heroism and evangelical labors as founder of the Jesuits' Sinaloa mission.[72] Whether his remains were venerated as relics beyond the circle of fellow Jesuit missionaries becomes less clear as Pérez de Ribas elaborated on their disposition.[73] Before long, he wrote, Tapia's body was moved to the church of the Jesuit college in Sinaloa. The head was recovered by "friendly Indians" who found it "dyed with red ocher and used as a drinking vessel" by his executioners. Eventually, the remains were taken to the Jesuit college in Mexico City, "where it is guarded in equal reverence in a decent place."[74] Pérez de Ribas insisted that in his discussion of Tapia's remains he was not speaking of relics:

> I am not speaking here of public veneration by the faithful of the relics of saints, which (as is known) requires the approval of Christ's Supreme Vicar. He alone declares and certifies for the Catholic Church those who should be venerated as saints and implored for favors and intercession with God. I am not speaking here of that [type of] veneration, which to date has not been shown Father Gonzalo de Tapia or the remains of his body. I am speaking instead of the personal veneration taught by the Doctors [of the Church] that each individual can show toward him who, with good and prudent reasoning, the individual judges to have been of distinguished sanctity.[75]

Tapia's fellow Jesuits effectively privatized his remains. His bones came to be treasured by the Jesuits in Mexico City far from the wider audience near the site of his missionary labors and martyrdom. In death Tapia was revered in his home parish in the Spanish city of León more in the way accorded to a saint than he was in New Spain. According to Pérez de Ribas, portraits of him were hung in one of the chapels of León's parish church and in the Jesuit church there. For some years after his death, people of the parish requested a relic, and when it finally arrived a welcoming throng gathered at the city limits, including "all of our priests at the Jesuit college in León, as well as the most eminent people of the city, both ecclesiastical and secular, who all wanted to honor their blessed compatriot."[76]

Hermits, including solitary caretakers of shrines, were other possible paragons of Christian virtue in New Spain whose beings and belongings might be regarded as relics. But few of them, even of those attached to a major shrine, were as widely known and revered as Puebla's bevy of spiritual heroes or some exemplary missionary friars came to be.[77] In good part their limited fame was, like the declining public appeal of bone relics of canonized saints in Europe by the sixteenth century, a product of the time more than a development peculiar to New Spain. The independent hermits and anchorites who had been celebrated as saintly in the tenth to twelfth centuries gave way to members of the monastic and mendicant orders who practiced their asceticism and solitude in community. Hermits made something of a comeback in Spain during the sixteenth and early seventeenth centuries as shrine keepers and alms collectors, especially as economic conditions worsened toward the end of the sixteenth century.[78] But even during this modest revival, there was always a strong current of suspicion about their furtive, unsupervised way of life, and only a few of them in Spain and America gained lasting fame as virtual saints. One of those few was the restless Spanish ascetic Gregorio López (1542–1596) who took up residence near the shrine of Nuestra Señora de los Remedios at Totoltepec in the Valley of Mexico for about two years in the late 1570s and enjoyed the admiration and favor of Archbishop Moya de Contreras.[79] More typical was the Inquisition's treatment of other would-be hermits at the Remedios shrine when it became a celebrated site in the late sixteenth century. Among the aspiring hermits there in the mid-1570s were Hernando Moreno de Navarrete, a forty-year-old musician and weaver by trade from the Andalusian town of Baeza, along with "his woman" María de la Cueva from Salamanca (known as María la Comendadora), and Ana de Ayala, a thirty-eight-year-old widow from Goa. Their new life of service to the Virgin ended abruptly when Moreno was charged with inventing miracles and pretending to be a priest.[80]

Mexico's Third Synod in 1585 expressed concerns about vagrants and beggars generally and decreed that solitary hermits should be forbidden, implying, as its European counterparts had ordered, that respectable hermits ought to be members of an established order and live in community. This view was reinforced by viceregal and episcopal campaigns against vagrancy.[81] Nevertheless, for a time, especially in the sixteenth and early seventeenth centuries, New Spain seemed a more welcoming home to Spanish hermits than Spain itself,[82] and several of the most revered ascetics date from that time: Martín de Valencia, Juan González, and Sebastián de Aparicio, as well as Gregorio López, all of them deceased before 1600. A few celebrated hermits who blessed places with their presence, most of them native Spaniards, were also found in the seventeenth century in Tlaxcala, Puebla, San Luis Potosí, and, above all, in what may have been the most visited long-distance pilgrimage site of the time, the shrine of Our Lord of Chalma, near Malinalco in the Estado de México;[83] but by then most of the solitary spiritual heroes were frontier missionaries, some of them martyred in their calling.[84]

Celebrated hermits by no means disappeared in the eighteenth century, but they were fewer, less often celebrated by chroniclers, and more likely to be in the cross hairs of the ecclesiastical courts' sights as subversives or parasites. For example, the bishop of Chiapas received a report in 1708 about a *ladino* (non-Indian) hermit preaching to Indians near Zinacantán, spreading false stories about an image of the Virgin Mary that gave off rays of light. The parish priest of Chamula discovered the man ensconced in the hollow trunk of an ancient oak tree, ran him off, and had the trunk cut down and burned.[85] Hermits were also stirring controversy by going far afield to collect alms. In 1726 Chalma hermit Diego de Vargas's travels in Tlaxcala on an alms-collecting tour led to a complaint by the chaplain of the shrine of Nuestra Señora de Ocotlán that Vargas was poaching on his territory without a license, and in 1746 Manuel Joseph de San Silvestre, a hermit for the Loreto shrine in Peñacastillo, Santander, was found to be collecting alms without a license.[86] The Fourth Synod of prelates, meeting in Mexico City in 1771, summed up the late colonial dim view of hermits in a way that readers of José Joaquín Fernández de Lizardi and his picaresque protagonist, the *periquillo sarniento*, would have savored: "for the most part they are not like the ancient anchorites; rather, they are loafers and beggars at shrines who hide in the shade of a false piety and devotion to secure for themselves a sweet life of leisure from the alms they collect."[87]

Holy water, bells, and splinters of the celebrated local crosses mentioned earlier could also be treated as secondary relics and brandea – numinous through blessing, physical contact, function, and reputation for miracles.[88] According to Motolinía in the mid-sixteenth century, the Indians "were very devoted to the water that was blessed on Sundays, and there are so many that seek to have it in their home, for their sick, for instance, that each day necessitates special care in the blessing of the baptismal font; ... there are so many jars and containers that even if they give just a little bit to everyone, many refills of water are necessary."[89] In the 1760s, a native shaman in the remote district of Xichú (in the mountainous Sierra Gorda of eastern Guanajuato, near the Querétaro border), who called himself the Old Christ (Cristo Viejo), celebrated a mock Mass with a tortilla and *pulque* and distributed his bath water to followers as a sacramental drink. Local priests regarded this practice as sacrilegious, but it was also a kind of homage to Christian contagion of the sacred by touch.[90] Bells as relics drew more scrutiny from colonial authorities worried about devotional exuberance spilling over into idolatry. Viceregal and diocesan officials of Oaxaca in 1777 mainly found it curious that Zapotec peoples from the vicinity of Ixtepeji would carry their village bells long distances to be blessed by the pastoral visitor as a means of warding off damage to their cactus fields from hailstorms.[91] But in 1796 when prospectors discovered a cave near the pueblo of Magdalena Huecholan (district of Tepeaca, Puebla) where local Indians had decorated a bell with colored silk ribbons, cotton strips, and banners and surrounded it with candles and incense burners, the viceroy moved quickly to investigate "these excesses into which some Indians poorly indoctrinated in the Catholic Religion have fallen."[92]

Images as Relics

During the seventeenth and eighteenth centuries, celebrated images of Christ and Mary often were referred to as holy "relics" – the most heavily promoted and, for many, the most potent of all earthly vessels of divine presence and favor in New Spain (see Chapter 3).[93] For example, in his deposition in support of special royal recognition for the shrine of the Christ of Chalma, Don Josef Ángel de Cuevas Aguirre y Avendaño, senior member of the municipal council of Mexico City, spoke of Indian pilgrims to the shrine "bringing with them their prints and venerating them as relics, carrying them along the roads, raised high, showing in this way that they come to visit and adore that sacred image of Christ Crucified and his shrine."[94] I am suggesting that the common use of "relic" for images in colonial discourse was not an empty expression, but conveyed the sense that any image might attract divine presence and favor and become a relic in the broad sense of divine presence expressed in sacred things. By the seventeenth century, Church officials regarded images as the primary relics for popular devotion and allowed them to travel in much the same ways that bone relics from medieval shrines traveled.[95] Only in the consecrated Host was the divine as conspicuously present to most colonial Catholics. These sacred images were also called *santos* – somewhat confusingly, as Christ and his virginal mother were more than saints in the usual sense. But "santo" in popular parlance meant an image of a holy person revered as a living presence. It was no contradiction or redundancy, then, to find images of Christ called santos and Santo Cristo.[96] Images of saints other than Mary attracted followings for special purposes (such as recovering lost objects, protection from lightning strikes, or curing diseases of the eyes) or as patron saints of a community, a trade, or an individual.[97] But images of Christ and Mary were more compelling, at least in part because Christ and Mary were understood to have ascended bodily to Heaven, so there were no first-class relics and few satisfying secondary relics to be had.[98] Other than apparitions, statues and paintings of them were the main vehicles of their presence.

Sacred images carried an aura of mystery that was both officially encouraged and often enthusiastically embraced in enduring ways by devotees of all kinds. Physical beauty – an ineffable perfection of form thought to be beyond human talent alone to create[99] – was an ingredient, but in the reciprocity of faith, any image that evoked contrition and awe was deemed beautiful. In the late sixteenth-century chronicler Dávila Padilla's telling, for example, the Virgin Mary appeared to Fr. Thomas de San Juan "more resplendent than the sun, accompanied by a host of angels ... when he contemplated her with great fervor."[100] As James Elkins puts it, "devotional images require devotion: that is the bottom line."[101] Devotion also meant honoring the image as the representation of the holy person with votive offerings such as candles, ex-votos, and embellishments such as fresh, sweet-smelling flowers, incense, and fine clothing.

As a result, image relics generated a trove of brandea far greater than for the bones and other remains of saints and the saintly. They include medidas,[102] oil and soot from the lamps in the shrine, soil from the shrine precinct, stubs of votive candles that had illuminated the sacred image,[103] flowers from its altar, the water with which it was cleaned,[104] and just about anything that came in contact with the image, from rosary beads to painted "portraits" of the image, prints, medals, *escudos* (badges), and scapulars, to the hands and lips of the faithful.[105] Some secondary relics and brandea were unique to particular shrine images, such as grass cuttings from the miraculously self-restoring Green Cross of Tepic, or white earth from the bare spot in this cross that was said to replenish itself; the wine with which the statue of the Cristo de los Labradores in Toluca was anointed every Holy Wednesday; or a strand of the hair that was widely believed to grow from this Cristo's head and chest.[106] The clothing and detachable parts of a santo were borrowed as if they were charged with the power of the santo, as when an indio from San Pedro de la Cañada, Querétaro, borrowed San Miguel's *bastón* – his staff of authority – to use in a ritual dance, or when sponsors of processions in Antequera during the 1690s customarily borrowed garments from statues of the Virgin Mary in the city as cloaks for orphan girls who participated in the spectacle.[107]

Because they encouraged veneration of images and the possibility that the faithful could be healed, protected, and propelled toward a good death and heavenly repose by their faith in Christ and the saints through images, church leaders were also perennially concerned about abuses – inappropriate representations, literal-minded beliefs about material rewards in the here and now, and other unacceptable practices.[108] These concerns became a legislative and administrative drumbeat in the eighteenth century, especially from the 1740s. Bishops and viceregal officials of the time more often expressed the need for "decencia" (pious good taste) in the presentation of images in churches, processions, and at home. They called for more information about the circulation of images, especially reputedly miraculous images, and fitfully tried to police what they judged to be excesses and irreverent uses, to bring popular images into the care of pastors in their parish churches and restrict their movement beyond. How different this was from the less discriminating enthusiasm for images and miracles of most seventeenth-century prelates. The principle for inspection and regulation of images in the late colonial period was laid out in an edict of the Mexican Inquisition in 1767: images were to be made and displayed with "true and decorous propriety" in order to evoke "feelings of devotion and reverence for their Sacred Originals" and were to be "placed with worshipful decency in locations befitting their sacred purpose."[109] "Decency" and "decorum" were the watchwords. Periodically, bishops called for reports and inspections by pastors to identify and remove indecent and "misshapen"[110] images and practices, as well as to transfer popular images from homes and the outdoors into the parish church. However, for the most part, clerical leaders drew back from inciting protest and dismay over images.

Elsewhere I have described how vital images could be to the well-being of Christians of all classes in seventeenth- and eighteenth-century New Spain. The "pious" theft of Calpulalpan's treasured statue of San Antonio de Padua during the Independence War is a striking example. In late June 1812, a company of royalist soldiers, including a detachment of Tlaxcalan nobles, drove insurgents and their local supporters from this town in the mountains that drop down to the Valley of Mexico about fifty miles east of Mexico City. To celebrate their victory, the royalist commander granted his troops one hour to pillage the town. In the spirit of calculated mayhem they and Aztec lords had once directed against each other, the Tlaxcalans asked for something that would cut deeper into the well-being of the community of Calpulalpan than random looting. They wanted the miraculous statue of San Antonio from the parish church. The royalist commander granted their wish, and for nearly two months Calpulalpan was bereft of its palladium. We know of this event because the elders of Calpulalpan immediately appealed to the viceroy to help them recover their saint. The viceroy ordered the Tlaxcalans to relinquish the statue to the Franciscans in Texcoco and directed the Franciscans there to send a pastor to Calpulalpan as soon as possible. The friar assigned to Calpulalpan soon reported that he had arrived to a warm welcome by townspeople whose only lament was that he had not brought with him their beloved santo. He pointedly requested that the statue be returned, and the viceroy responded the following day with an order for restitution, which was quickly done.[111]

The mystique of images made them almost universally indispensable to individuals, families, and communities. Popular attachment usually outran official promotion. Not surprisingly, friction between priests and devotees increased as the late colonial initiatives for a more decorous faith led to calls to censor and remove "gross" and "ridiculous" images.[112] Even though the devotion to images usually was institutionalized in shrines and supervised by chaplains, pastors, and bishops, priests came and went while the images themselves and the communities that cared for them remained. Priests who restored, reclothed, removed, or relocated an image without local support risked lawsuits and sometimes open rebellion.[113] The signs of use and wear were part of what could make an image sacred to devotees. Their ancestors had cleaned and clothed it, worn away or discolored its surface with countless kisses and caresses, and accidentally nicked and bumped it in processions that were understood to disperse and recharge its sacred energy. Ygnacio de Barzena, assistant pastor of Real del Cardonal (Hidalgo) in 1802, understood the risks of displacing or "improving" a cherished local image. In a letter to members of the cathedral chapter in Mexico City about a homely crucifix recently removed from the main altar at Mapethé, he wrote:

> There is no doubt, sirs, that this Holy Effigy is quite old and not in the least pleasing to the eyes of those who ponder only its physical appearance and not the Image of Our Redeemer, which is what it represents. But the Indians from throughout the jurisdiction, and even strangers, all of whom sustain the shrine, have been vexed ever since it was stripped from the altar. And in my opinion they will not be pacified and the disputes that occur regularly every year during the feast of the patron saint will not cease until the statue is put back in its place.[114]

Sometimes the legends attached to an image warned of dire consequences for appropriating it, even if the actor was a high official motivated by righteous piety. In the early nineteenth century, a legend circulated among people of Orizaba, Veracruz, about a viceroy returning to Spain who was so taken with the beauty of the community's miraculous statue of the Christ Child and the devotion it inspired in him when he passed through town that he could not resist taking it with him despite the anguished pleas and laments of local people for "the image to which they were so devout and in which they placed their trust in their times of need and affliction." But then the viceroy became seriously ill, and one of his chaplains suggested to him that the clamor of the poor souls of Orizaba apparently had been heard in heaven. Once the viceroy returned the image he recovered and continued on his way. "The image is still there [in Orizaba] and the people's veneration and devotion continues as before."[115]

While either promotion by priests or spontaneous popular enthusiasm against the wishes of colonial officials may seem to stand out in the story of a particular image,[116] official promotion and fervent devotion usually went together. But only occasionally does the written record show just how promotion and deep local attachment to images combined even in protest and litigation. The written contract between a Dominican alms collector from Ecuador, Fr. Joseph de Jesús María Herrera Campuzano, and the community of Tepoztlán, Morelos, in 1759 provides a striking example.[117] Father Herrera had been visiting towns and villages under Dominican pastoral care in central and southern Mexico on a mission to collect donations for a new nunnery and church in his home province. To stir the faithful and elicit donations, he carried with him a fine little Ecuadoran statue of Our Lady of the Rosary.[118] At Tepoztlán, Fr. Herrera made a bargain in writing with the community. Responding, he said, "to their fervent tears, love, and Catholic zeal for this singular relic and image of Our Lady of the Rosary," he agreed in writing on May 7 to leave the statue with the community "until the Day of Universal Judgment, with the oral permission of my beloved and venerated province" in exchange for a donation in perpetuity of one *real* weekly. He assured the people of Tepoztlán that they would "be rewarded in the Kingdom of Heaven" for their devotion to Our Lady of the Rosary.

Six months later Father Herrera decided to reclaim the statue, but the people of Tepoztlán would not give it back. What he had hailed as their "Catholic zeal" was now, to his mind, "the Indians' disobedience and resistance." Viceregal authorities responded to Herrera's appeal for the return of the statue with a decree of December 18, ordering the people of Tepoztlán to relinquish the statue and their pastor to send it to the district seat of Cuernavaca. Representatives of Tepoztlán agreed to obey the decree if their claim to the statue, based on the written agreement signed by Fr. Herrera in May 1759 was considered before a final disposition of the statue was made. But when the statue was on the road to Cuernavaca, local people intercepted the carriers and took it back to Tepoztlán. With Herrera now complaining about "Indian rebellion," local leaders appealed to the archbishop on December 23 to intervene. Evidently with the consent of the viceroy, the archbishop quickly decreed that the matter be left in abeyance until he visited the area. On January 25, 1760, the archbishop reported to the viceroy from Yautepec, on the road between Cuernavaca and Tepoztlán, that he had listened to both parties and succeeded in persuading the people of Tepoztlán to turn over the statue to Herrera "even though they had solid reasons" to claim the image and though Herrera "had acted in bad faith" in the written agreement since he knew that the statue was not his to lease. The archbishop judged that Herrera had brought on this scandal, playing on the Tepoztecans' love for the image and raising false hopes. Accordingly, he ordered that Herrera cease collecting alms in the Archdiocese of Mexico and return all the money he had collected in Tepoztlán. Even though the Tepoztecans were held blameless, they lost what they wanted most.

Conclusion

Divine presence was understood to reveal itself in material ways – in the physical being and touch of the human – yet transcend human existence. Relics in the broad sense of transcendent matter located the sacred in place and beyond time. Accordingly, to the extent that Americans were devoted to bone relics and belongings of Christian heroes, their attention was drawn more to local holy men and women than to the imported relics of European saints. But even these local relics lacked the staying power, official recognition, and regional appeal of the santos that were so familiar a part of family devotions and community identity. While image shrines were growing in wealth and fame in the eighteenth century, bone relics and pious biographies as a whole were fading from view after about 1750, and none of the bone relics or local near-saints approached the popularity of such image shrines as those of the Virgin of Guadalupe, the Lord of Chalma, the Christ of Esquipulas, and Our Lady of San Juan de los Lagos. With few native saints, a dearth of choice Old World relics, native traditions that produced effigies and anticipated apparitions, and Catholic Christianity everywhere emphasizing images in devotional practice, miraculous images and the surfeit of copies and brandea that grew up around them became a leading story of institutionalized faith in Mexican history.

Notes

1. Annabel Jane Wharton, *Selling Jerusalem: Relics, Replicas, Theme Parks*, Chicago: University of Chicago Press, 2006, p. 9.
2. Alfredo López Austin, *Tamoanchan, Tlalocan: Places of Mist*, Niwot: University Press of Colorado, 1997, especially pp. 246 and 255 for bones as a source of regeneration ("Jill Furst argued for the importance of bones as a source of regeneration. Gillespie claims that possessing the predecessor's bones was necessary in order to succeed to power"; "Of course the relics might be the remains of the gods themselves, their bones or their ashes. A source says that Tezcatlipoca entered Popo and from there he sent his femur to the people of Tezcoco. Another source says the faithful kept Quetzalcoatl's ashes in a bag.").
3. Guilhem Olivier, "Sacred Bundles, Arrows, and New Fire: Foundation and Power in the Mapa de Cuauhtinchán No. 2," in *Cave, City, and Eagle's Nest: An Interpretive Journey Through the Mapa de Cuauhtinchán No. 2*, ed. David Carrasco and Scott Sessions, Albuquerque: University of New Mexico Press, 2007, pp. 281–313.
4. Sometimes bone relics were displayed in church altarpieces – visible but not within reach of the public. For a well-documented discussion of such retables of relics, see Gabriela Sánchez Reyes, "Retablos-relicario en la Nueva España," in *Congreso Internacional del Barroco Iberoamericano. Territorio, arte, espacio y sociedad*, Sevilla: Universidad Pablo de Olavide, Ediciones Giralda, 2001, tomo I, pp. 731–746 and, especially, her master's thesis in art history, "Relicarios novohispanos a través de una muestra de los siglos XVI al XVIII," Facultad de Filosofía y Letras, UNAM, 2001.
5. *Concilio III provincial mexicano*, título XVIII parag. vi, p. 324. Many of the decrees of this synod responded to written *memoriales* or petitions by individuals and groups, mostly clerics. Oddly, this emphatic directive about relics was not the subject of any of the forty-four memoriales received by the synod. For the memoriales, see *Manuscritos del Concilio Tercero Provincial Mexicano (1585)*, ed. and intro. Alberto Carrillo Cázares, Zamora: El Colegio de Michoacán, 2006, I, LXVIII–LXXIII, 149–222.
6. On tombs of saints as centers of veneration "throughout Christendom" in the Middle Ages, see Robert Bartlett, *Why Can the Dead Do Such Great Things? Saints and Worshippers from the Martyrs to the Reformation*, Princeton: Princeton University Press, 2013, chapter 8.

On three classes of relics, *Dictionary of Catholic Devotions*, ed. Michael Walsh, San Francisco: HarperSanFrancisco, 1993, pp. 214–217.
7. Jane Garnett and Gervase Rosser, *Spectacular Miracles. Transforming Images in Italy from the Renaissance to the Present*, London: Reaktion Books, 2013, p. 49: "after the twelfth century the number of relics in private hands was strictly limited and their veneration was likewise restrained."
8. See Patrick Geary, *Furta Sacra: Thefts of Relics in the Central Middle Ages*, Princeton: Princeton University Press, 1991, and his essay, "Sacred Commodities: The Circulation of Medieval Relics," in *The Social Life of Things*, ed. Arjun Appadurai, Cambridge, UK and New York: Cambridge University Press, 1986, pp. 169–192.
9. William A. Christian, Jr., *Local Religion in Sixteenth-Century Spain*, Princeton: Princeton University Press, 1981, p. 126; Miguel Luque Taleván, "De santos franciscanos y donaciones. La religiosidad barroca y el culto a las reliquias en el orden hispano-indiano," in *El Mediterráneo y América. Actas del XI Congreso Internacional de la Asociación Española de Americanistas*, ed. Juan José Sánchez Baena and Lucía Provencio Garrigós, Murcia: Asociación Española de Americanistas, 2006, I, 697.
10. On relics, *Concilio III provincial mexicano: celebrado en México el año de 1585 ...*, ed. Mariano Galván Rivera, Mexico: Eugenio Maillefert y Compañía, 1859, título XVIII parag. viii, p. 325; on images, título XVIII parags. viii and ix, pp. 325–326.
11. Luis Weckmann, *The Medieval Heritage of Mexico*, trans. Frances M. López-Morillas, New York: Fordham University Press, 1992, p. 255. Antonio Rubial García followed suit, speaking of "an infinity of bones, objects, and even complete corpses arrived from Europe" in "Icons of Devotion: The Appropriation and Use of Saints in New Spain," in *Local Religion in Colonial Mexico*, ed. and trans., Martin A. Nesvig, Albuquerque: University of New Mexico Press, 2006, p. 49. Bone relics are also discussed in Pierre Ragon, *Les saints et les images du Mexique (XVIe–XVIIIe siècle)*, Paris: L'Harmattan, 2003, pp. 238–248.
12. Almost always the first-class relics in New Spain were bones. A rare example of another body part is the claim of the parish church of Santa Veracruz in Mexico City to have part of the intestines of San Francisco Xavier, Cayetano Cabrera y Quintero, *Escudo de armas de Mexico: Celestial protección de esta nobilíssima ciudad, de la Nueva España, y de casi todo el Nuevo Mundo ...*, Mexico: Vda. de Joseph Bernardo de Hogal, 1746, pp. 171–174.
13. Before long, urban nunneries began to amass collections of bone relics.
14. Fr. Agustín de Vetancurt, *Teatro mexicano. Descripción breve de los sucesos ejemplares históricos y religiosos del Nuevo Mundo de las Indias; Crónica de la Provincia del Santo Evangelio de México* [1698], Mexico: Porrúa, 1982, facsimile edition, 2nd enum. p. 109; Juan de Torquemada, OFM, *Monarquía Indiana*, Mexico: Porrúa, 1986, I, 96.
15. Weckmann, *Medieval Heritage*, p. 255; Vetancurt, *Teatro mexicano*, pp. 47–51. The Discalced Franciscans of the Province of San Diego, also based in Mexico, also boasted an assortment of first-class relics in the late seventeenth century, including an elbow bone of San Lorenzo, a bone of one of the Franciscan martyrs in Japan, a head of one of the 11,000 virgins, and "many relics of saints gathered in Italy," Baltasar de Medina, *Crónica de la Santa Provincia de San Diego de México* [1682], 2nd ed., Mexico: Editorial Academia Literaria, 1977, fols. 28v–29v.
16. Vetancurt, *Teatro mexicano*, pp. 51, 54–55.

17. Medina, *Crónica de la Santa Provincia de San Diego de México* [1682], fols. 18v–19r, chapter 10.
18. Definidor del Capítulo General, described in Agustín Dávila Padilla, *Historia de la fundación y discurso de la Provincia de Santiago de México de la orden de Predicadores . . .* [1596], "second ed.," Bruselas: En casa de Francisco Vivien, 1648, pp. 160–161, 499.
19. Sánchez Reyes, "Relicarios novohispanos," p. 42.
20. Sánchez Reyes, "Relicarios novohispanos," part II; Manuel Antonio Moxica, *Tesoro escondido en el delicioso campo, ameno huerto florida vergel, y fragrante pensil del noviciado de los frayles predicadores de esta Provincia de Santiago de México*, reimpreso, Mexico: Fernández Jáuregui, 1799, p. 45. Substantial collections of first-class relics are still on display in some convent museums, such as the Museo de Arte Religioso de Santa Mónica in the city of Puebla, formerly a convent of Augustinian Recollect nuns.
21. Gil González Dávila, *Teatro eclesiástico de la primitiva Iglesia de las Indias Occidentales*, facsimile edition, Chimalistac, Mexico: CONDUMEX, 1982, p. 73; Mariano Fernández de Echeverría y Veytia, *Historia de la fundación de la ciudad de la Puebla de los Ángeles en la Nueva España. Su descripción y presente estado* [ca. 1781], Puebla: Imprenta Labor, 1941, pp. 438–448.
22. Franciso Javier Alegre, *Historia de la Compañía de Jesús en Nueva Espana que estaba escribiendo el Padre Francisco Javier Alegre . . .*, Mexico: Imprenta de J. M. Lara, 1842, I, 125–126. According to Weckmann, Jesuits had been bringing relics to the New World since the 1560s. Father Pedro Martínez, an early Jesuit missionary to Florida and Virginia martyred in 1565, carried with him a box of relics that reportedly calmed the fury of the sea and saved the governor of Florida's fleet. "According to Father Bartolomé Martínez's account, the Indians tried to open it and immediately fell dead as a divine punishment," *Medieval Heritage*, pp. 256–257.
23. AGN Tierras 3097 exp. 2, fols. 17r–23v. Later Jesuits in Mexico continued to tap their connections in Rome for more relics – for example, the celebrations in Mexico City in 1668 for the relics recently sent by Pope Gregory XIII, described in Beatriz Mariscal Hay, ed., *Carta del padre Pedro de Morales de la Compañía de Jesús: para el muy reverendo Padre Everardo Mercuriano, general de la misma Compañía, en que se da relación de la festividad de las sanctas reliquias que nuestro muy santo Padre Gregorio XIII les embió*, Mexico: El Colegio de México, 2000.
24. González Dávila, *Teatro eclesiástico*, p. 109, Carlos de Sigüenza y Góngora, *Glorias de Querétaro . . .*, with additions by José María Zeláa, Mexico: Zúñiga y Ontiveros, 1803, p. 178. The Congregation of Guadalupe in Querétaro had a small but select collection of relics gathered mostly in the early eighteenth century, including a piece of the skull of St. Peter, bones of the Virgin's parents (San Joaquín and Santa Ana), a bone of the martyr San Florián, and a piece of Juan Diego's *tilma*.
25. José Gómez, "Diario de México," Bancroft M-M 105, 204. The cathedral collections tended to mount up over time through private gifts; for example, the donations to the cathedral in Mexico City of a bone relic of the martyr-saint San Gelacio in 1664 by a Dominican friar, and of San Nicolás de Bari in 1682 by Don Pedro Martínez de Torrentera and his wife Doña Beatriz Tello de Sandoval, AHM Fondo Catedral, caja 5. Weckmann comments on the large number of relics in the Mexico City cathedral's chapel of Santo Cristo, *Medieval Heritage*, p. 255.

26. The relics of Santa Veneranda are generally understood to belong to the church of Mortara, Italy. Although her relics in Aguascalientes were not entirely forgotten, I have found few references to, or special observances for, them after the mid-nineteenth century.
27. *Gazeta de México*, March 10, 1801, pp. 240–250.
28. Pedro Oroz, *Descripción de la Provincia Franciscana del Santo Evangelio de México, hecha en año de 1585*, Mexico: Imprenta Mexicana de J. Aguilar Reyes, 1947, p. 96.
29. Vetancurt, *Teatro mexicano*, 2nd enumeration, pp. 47, 51.
30. Alegre, *Historia de la Compañía de Jesús en Nueva España*, I, 125–126.
31. González Dávila, *Teatro eclesiástico*, p. 73.
32. Juan de Grijalva, *Crónica de la Orden de N.P.S. Agustín en las provincias de la Nueva España* ... [1624], Mexico: Edit. Porrúa, 1985, pp. 186–187. Grijalva criticized his Mercedarian contemporary, Luis de Cisneros, who authored the first chronicle of the miraculous image of Nuestra Señora de los Remedios and the Totoltepec shrine (1621), *Historia de el principio y origen, progressos, venidas a México, y milagros de la Santa Imagen de nuestra Señora de los Remedios* ..., Mexico: Juan Blanco de Alcáçar, 1621, for only mentioning the belt in passing and failing to recognize that it was a relic of St. Augustine.
33. Mariano Fernández de Echeverría y Veitia, *Baluartes de México. Descripción histórica de las cuatro milagrosas imágenes de Nuestra Señora, que se veneran en la muy noble, leal, e imperial ciudad de México* ... Mexico: Valdés, 1820, p. 83.
34. Medina, *Crónica de la Santa Provincia de San Diego de México* [1682], fol. 28v.
35. The other three heavenly "portals" were Rome, Jerusalem, and Santiago de Compostela.
36. Don Domingo de San Antón Muñón Chimalpahin Quauhtlehuanitzin mentioned a sliver of the True Cross from Tlatelolco in a penitential procession in 1604, *Annals of His Time*, ed. and trans. James Lockhart, Susan Schroeder, and Doris Namala, Stanford, CA: Stanford University, 2006, p. 83: "They brought out ... a cross of Soledad, a [processional?] cross, and a decorated cross. And the true cross, a cross with a relic of the true cross, went standing on a carrying platform, [they] went sheltering it under a canopy." I cannot account for this relic otherwise and have not included it in Table 6.1.
37. It is not listed among the Jesuit *temporalidades* dispersed after the expulsion of the order. See Delia Pezzat Arzave, *Catálogos de Documentos de Arte, 31: Archivo General de la Nación, Temporalidades*, Mexico: UNAM/IIE, 2006.
38. Litigation surrounding the pastor's initial complaint is in AGN Clero Regular y Secular 125 exps. 2–4. The subsequent record is in TU VEMC leg. 66 exp. 13.
39. Pachuca's piece of the Ligno Crucis traditionally was displayed on the day of the Exaltation of the Cross, AGN Clero Regular y Secular 125, exps. 2–4.
40. González Dávila, *Teatro eclesiástico*, p. 73.
41. Dávila Padilla, *Historia de la fundación*, p. 499.
42. Gerónimo de Mendieta, OFM, recounted a late-sixteenth-century tradition that the cord and habit of the Franciscans had revived a dead person and aided Indian women in childbirth, *Historia eclesiástica indiana*, Mexico: CONACULTA, 1997, libro III, chapter 56, pp. 501–504.
43. On medals of the Virgin and indulgences to promote them, see AGN Inquisición 1103 exp. 2, 1777. On scapulars, Dionisio Victoria Moreno, *Los Carmelitas Descalzas y la*

conquista espiritual de México: 1585–1612, Mexico: Editorial Porrúa, 1966, pp. 195–198. Sánchez Reyes documents two examples of tracings of the Virgin's feet, and two examples of nails that touched the originals in Rome found in the cathedral of Puebla and the church of Santo Domingo there, "Relicarios novohispanos," pp. 81, 315. For *cedulitas*, José Antonio Pérez de León, *Modo de aplicar las milagrosas cedulitas de María Inmaculada a los enfermos y parturientas . . .*, reimpreso, Mexico: Oficina de Valdés, 1814.

44. For *panecitos de San Nicolás*, AGN Inquisición 278 exp. 7 fols. 254–257, 1614, Celaya, and Joseph Salvá, *Universal patrocinio del glorioso P.S. Nicolás de Tolentino, del Order de N. Gran P.S. Augustín: antidoto celestial, vinculado en los panecitos del santo . . .*, Palma: Emprenta de la Viuda Frau, 1735. For *panecitos de Santa Teresa*, Manuel Ramos Medina, *Místicas y descalzas: Fundaciones feminias carmelitas en la Nueva España*, Mexico: CONDUMEX, 1997, p. 139. During the first half of the seventeenth century, Carmelite nuns of Puebla baked their panecitos for the October 15 feast of Santa Teresa, Martha Lilia Tenorio, *De panes y sermones: El milagro de los "panecitos" de Santa Teresa*, Mexico: El Colegio de México, 2002, p. 11. "Panes de San Diego" are mentioned in discalced Franciscan Baltasar Medina's *Crónica de la Santa Provincia de San Diego de México*, fols. 101v–103r. Among the miracles associated with the venerable Fray Marcos Sánchez Salmerón were his *panes de San Diego*, which were said to remain fresh and incorruptible for many years.

Other *panecitos* were associated with miraculous images and their shrines, such as *panecillos* of the Señor de Chalma and the Virgin of Guadalupe that were dissolved in wine and administered to the sick. See Noemí Quezada, "Dioses, santos y demonios en la curación colonial," in comp. Barbro Dahlgren de Jordán, *III Coloquio de Historia de la Religión en Mesoamerica y Áreas Afines*, Mexico: UNAM, 1993, p. 117, drawing upon a 1798 Inquisition case from Amecameca. The *panecillos* of the shrine of Ocotlán (Tlaxcala) were made with water from the sacred spring at the site, and some were carried by the shrine's alms collector in his travels, Manuel Loaizaga, *Historia de la milagrosíssima imagen de Nuestra Señora de Occotlan* [1750], Tlaxcala: Instituto Tlaxcalteca de la Cultura, 2008, p. 70. *Panecitos* associated with shrine images were more often made of edible clay gathered at the shrine site. The most celebrated of these clay tablets were from Guatemala's shrine of the Lord of Esquipulas. See Judith Green and Anita Jones, *Los Panecitos Benditos, Clay Eating in Oaxaca*, San Diego: Museum of Man, 1968, which describes *panecitos* from Esquipulas as models for locally-produced tablets in Oaxaca that were used to treat stomach complaints, heart problems, blindness, and the travail of childbirth.

45. Two studies of this celebrated case appeared in 2001 and 2002: Tenorio's book cited in note 44 and Antonio Rubial García and María de Jesús Díaz Nava, " 'La santa es una bellaca y nos hace muchas burlas': El caso de los panecitos de Santa Teresa en la sociedad novohispana del siglo XVII," *Estudios de Historia Novohispana* 24 (enero-junio 2001), 53–75.

46. News of the *panecitos* in the house of the Pobletes was received enthusiastically by Bishop of Puebla Juan de Palafox y Mendoza, but doubts apparently were raised in the early years. Archbishop Juan de Mañozca y Zamora (1645–1650) was cool to the reported miracle, and Carmelite Fr. Joan de San Joseph of the Colegio de San Ángel expressed doubts in 1659 although there was no formal investigation at the time,

Rubial and Díaz Nava, "La santa es una bellaca," pp. 57–59. Br. Francisco de Herrera testified to Palafox's enthusiasm for the miracle, trusting the word of Dean Poblete, AGN Inquisición 1515 exp. 1, fol. 73.
47. AGN Inquisición 1515 exp. 1, fol. 3v.
48. AGN Inquisición 1515 exp. 1, fol. 77.
49. AGN Inquisición 1515 exp. 1, fols. 185–186.
50. The annual "fiesta del panecito de Santa Teresa en el Carmen" in Mexico City that began in 1678 after Payo de Rivera's decree apparently ended in 1686 after the death of Doña María de Poblete. Antonio de Robles, *Diario de sucesos notables (1665–1703)*, Mexico: Porrúa, 1946, noted the fiesta in his entry for January 2, 1678, but did not mention after noting Doña María's death in his December 2, 1686 entry, II, 130–131. However, the archbishop's office did not publicize the hoax or censor later publications that mentioned the miracles, such as Vetancurt's *Teatro mexicano*, published in 1698.
51. Pedro Pablo Patiño, *Disertación crítico-theo-filosófica sobre la conservación de la Santa Imagen de Nuestra Señora de los Ángeles...*, Mexico: Mariano Joseph Zúñiga y Ontiveros, 1801, pp. 118–122.
52. Juan Barrera, *Noticia auténtica de las maravillas que ha obrado Dios con los panecillos de Santa Teresa...*, Salamanca: En la imprenta de Lucas Pérez, 1675; Sariñana, *Sermón que a la declaración del milagro de los panecitos de Santa Teresa...*, Mexico: Calderón, 1678; and Antonio Núñez de Miranda, *Sermón de Santa Teresa de Iesus en la fiesta que su muy Observante Convento de San Joseph de Carmelitas Descalzas... por authéntica declaración del Milagro...*, Mexico: Vda. de Bernardo Calderón, 1678.
53. Sánchez Reyes, "Relicarios novohispanos."
54. An example of a seventeenth-century bishop encouraging veneration of local religious heroes is Archbishop Francisco Manso y Zúñiga (1627–1634) promoting beatification for Gregorio López, González Dávila, *Teatro eclesiástico*, pp. 46–59.
55. *Dictionary of Catholic Devotions*, ed. Walsh, p. 49: brandea was "anything... which might have gained virtue by its proximity to the body of the saint." In the Middle Ages, brandea meant especially cloth or paper lowered into a saint's tomb, but it could also mean a piece of the tomb, or dust gathered at the site or candle stubs or faded flowers from the altar that had touched or been close to the relic.
56. For the mystique of the hearts of two bishops of Puebla, see Antonio Rubial García, "Cuerpos milagrosos: Creación y culto de las reliquias novohispanas," *Estudios de Historia Novohispana* 18 (1998), 22, and Miruna Achim, "Mysteries of the Heart: The Gift of Bishop Fernández de Santa Cruz to the Nuns of Santa Mónica," *Colonial Latin American Review* 14: 1 (2005), 83–102. The reputation of deceased Juan José de Escalona y Calatayud, former bishop of Michoacán (1729–1737), grew when it was discovered that some of his internal organs had not decayed, Rubial, "Cuerpos milagrosos," p. 28. In his late eighteenth-century Mexico City *diario*, José Gómez provides examples of unusually charitable and saintly laymen in positions of public trust who were treated as living relics or whose things were treasured in that way after they died. Gómez describes the solemn procession to the shrine of Our Lady of Guadalupe and burial of the body of pious Viceroy Antonio María Bucareli y Urzúa (1771–1779) on April 9, 1779. His heart was given to the Capuchin nuns; most of his intestines passed to the parish church attached to the cathedral, with the rest of his remains going to a chapel in the Oratorio of San Felipe Neri. The saintly were not always priests, nuns,

and brothers. José Gómez also describes the outpouring of emotion and devout touching that went on for the burial of Dr. Juan de la Peña, Mexico City's *protomédico*, in his entry for January 20, 1789: "known as 'the saint,' his remains were taken to the Royal University and buried on the 21st in the cathedral chapel of Nuestra Señora de la Antigua. A great throng attended, pressing forward to see the body . . . and kiss his feet and clothing. Mexico City was deserted as the people went to attend his burial, as if he were a viceroy. The body was dressed in a gorget [a magistrate's ruff], with a dress sword, boots, and ceremonial cane." A notation, apparently by Carlos María Bustamante, adds that "the saintliness of this man was astonishing, especially his virtue of humility and self-abnegation . . . . He was an excellent physician who accepted as payment only what was required to feed himself and his mule," Bancroft M-M 105, pp. 89, 91, 112, 374.

57. Among Rubial García's principal publications on the subject are "Cuerpos milagrosos," pp. 13–30; *Profetisas y solitarios: Espacios y mensajes de una religión dirigida por ermitaños y beatas laicos en las ciudades de Nueva España*, Mexico: UNAM/Fondo de Cultura Económica, 2006, especially pp. 108–117; and "Imágenes y ermitaños: Un ciclo hierofánico ignorado por la historiografía," *Anuario de Estudios Americanos* 66: 2 (julio-diciembre 2009), 213–239.

58. Rubial García, "Cuerpos milagrosos," p. 17, and *La santidad controvertida, passim.*

59. On San Felipe de Jesús's limited appeal beyond Mexico City, see Appendix 3. On the Franciscan campaign for the beatification of Sebastián de Aparicio in the eighteenth century that recast him in prints and paintings as a frontier missionary, see Julie Shean, "*Models of Virtue: Images and Saint-Making in Colonial Puebla (1640–1800)*," Ph.D. dissertation, Institute of Fine Arts, New York University, 2007.

60. In "Cuerpos milagrosos," Rubial identifies more than a dozen examples, and his publications about hermits identify several more. He speaks of close to 100 near-saints by popular acclaim, but does not elaborate. Many of them presumably would come from the official chronicles of the various religious orders published during the colonial period, including Franciscan Dieguino Baltasar de Medina's *Crónica de la Santa Provincia de San Diego de México*, especially book 3, chapters 3–5, 10–11, and 13 which extols the virtues, relics, and miracles of the venerable Fr. Marcos Sánchez Salmerón, Fr. Juan Baptista, and Fr. Pedro de Valderrama. Antonio Tello, OFM's mid-seventeenth-century *Crónica miscelánea de la Sancta Provincia de Xalisco* uses the term "santo" freely when referring to early evangelizers of his order in western Mexico. He attributes to them various revelations and healing miracles and notes that their bones were treated as relics, Libro III, 6, 30, 21, 79–80, and Libro IV, 10, 17, 29. Andrés Pérez de Ribas's history of Jesuit missions on the northern frontier in the early seventeenth century mentions the relicized bodies of several martyred missionaries, *History of the Triumphs of Our Holy Faith amongst the Most Barbarous and Fierce Peoples of the New World* [1645], ed. Daniel T. Reff, trans. Daniel T. Reff, Maureen Ahern, and Richard K. Danford, Tucson: University of Arizona Press, 1999, pp. 309–310. Rosalva Loreto López discusses special interest in the bones of Madre María de Jesús, a candidate for beatification from Puebla who died in 1637. Her bones were exhumed at least three times (in 1685, 1736, and 1752) and found to exude a sweet-smelling liquid, "Las pruebas del milagro en el proceso de beatificación de la Madre María de Jesús en los siglos XVIII y XIX," in *Memoria del I Coloquio Historia de*

la Iglesia en el siglo XIX, ed. Manuel Ramos Medina, Mexico: CONDUMEX, 1998, pp. 351–367.
61. Torquemada, *Monarquía Indiana*, III, 422–424, and Mendieta, *Historia eclesiástica*, libro V primera parte, chapters 13, 16. For more on Valencia's relics and the shrine at Amecameca, see Rubial García, "Cuerpos milagrosos," pp. 13–14; Pierre Ragon, "La colonización de lo sagrado: La historia del Sacromonte de Amecameca," *Relaciones* XIX: #75 (1998), 281–300; and Edward Osowski, *Indigenous Miracles: Nahua Authority in Colonial Mexico*, Tucson: University of Arizona Press, 2010, pp. 34–37, and "Passion Miracles and Indigenous Historical Memory in New Spain," *Hispanic American Historical Review* 88: 4 (November 2008), 607–638.
62. Torquemada, *Monarquía Indiana*, III, 459. Two later Franciscans were also treated as saints and proposed to the Congregation of Rites for sainthood: Antonio Llinás and Antonio Margil de Jesús. See Rubial, "Cuerpos milagrosos," p. 2; and Gómez, "Diario de México," Bancroft M-M101, fol. 53r "el día 10 de febrero de 1778 el sepulcro o sea atahud a donde están los huesos venerables del P. Antonio Margil de Jesús está colocado en la antesacristía de San Francisco de México ... sus virtudes están aprobadas y para su solemne canonización se espera comprobados dos milagros lo menos."
63. Quoted and paraphrased by Michael Destefano in "Miracles and Monasticism in Mid-Colonial Puebla, 1600–1750: Charismatic Religion in a Conservative Society," Ph.D. dissertation, University of Florida, 1977, p. 42. For the clamor for relics of Puebla's legendary *china poblana*, Catarina de San Juan, see Rubial, "Cuerpos milagrosos," pp. 21–22.
64. This number does not include Bishop Juan de Palafox y Mendoza. These published devotional biographies provide the material for Michael Destefano's "Miracles and Monasticism in Mid-Colonial Puebla." For a discussion of the healings, see his chapter 7, pp. 215–276.
65. Joseph Bellido, SJ, *Vida de la V.M.R.M. María Águeda de San Ignacio*, Mexico: Imprenta de la Bibliotheca Mexicana, 1758, pp. 147–148.
66. "Muchas personas llebaban sus firmas en bolsitas y los pedazos de sus cartas las hechaban en las bebidas que daban a los enfermos como reliquias," 1797 Inquisition file against María Michaela de San Joseph, nun of the convent of La Santísima Trinidad, for simulating visions, revelations, and miracles, and suspected apostasy, Bancroft MSS 96/95m vol. 19.
67. Alonso Franco, *Segunda parte de la Historia de la Provincia de Santiago de Mexico, Orden de Predicadores en la Nueva España* [1645], Mexico: Imprenta del Museo Nacional, 1900, pp. 33–38, 246–262, 329–332. Most of such rosters of an order's local ancestral heroes were composed in the seventeenth century, but they appear as early as Mendieta's late sixteenth-century *Historia eclesiástica*, which sketches in glowing terms the lives of scores of his predecessors, including martyrs and others associated with miracles or a few like Martín de Valencia, leader of the famous Apostolic Twelve Franciscan friars, who arrived in 1523 and whose relics were especially in demand, libro V, chapters 1–16. Mendieta identified a few other early missionaries or martyrs whose bones, upon exhumation, were sweet smelling: libros III, IV for Valencia, libro V for others, and p. 466 for the sweet-smelling bones of a martyr. Most of the so-called "menologies" date from the seventeenth century. Jesuit biographies of the kind are especially elaborate, including Pérez de Ribas, *Triumphs of Our Holy Faith* and Francisco de Florencia,

Menologio de los varones más señalados en perfección religiosa de la provincia de la Compañía de Jesús de Nueva España, Mexico: n.p., 1747, whose glowing accounts of many of their exemplary predecessors occasionally mention that they merited beatification and their relics were coveted. But there were also similar accounts in the eighteenth century, viz. Alegre's chronicle of Jesuit activities written in the 1760s, and Isidro Félix de Espinoza's *Crónica de los colegios de Propaganda Fide de la Nueva España* [1746], ed. Lino Gómez Canedo, Washington, DC: Academy of American Franciscan History, 1964, which extolled the virtues of various missionaries of the Franciscan colleges of Propaganda Fide in New Spain, especially Antonio Llinás. See libro II chapter xx ("algunas cosas bien raras que se notaron en en V.P. en el tiempo que se mantuvo en el colegio"), libro III chapter 6 ("frutos maravillosos que logró el V.P. en varias missiones, y raros sucessos con que mosstró el Señor la eficacia de su doctrina"), chapter xiv ("favores muy especiales que recibió el V.P. de la mano divina y de la Madre de Dios por el misterio de su Concepción Puríssima"), chapter xxii ("algunas maravillas que obró el Señor por las oraciones de su siervo"), libro IV chapter ii (compendiosa vida, virtudes y feliz muerte del V.P. F. Miguel Fontcuberta, predicador apostólico), and chapter xiv ("muerte dichosa del V.P. con circunstancias raras, y cómo se celebraron su exequias").

68. Pérez de Ribas was explicit about his intended in-house audience. As Daniel Reff writes, "Pérez de Ribas states that he wrote his history for fellow Jesuits, particularly novices and members of the Society of Jesus who were ignorant of the challenges missionaries face in the New World," preface to *History of the Triumphs of Our Holy Faith*, p. 4.
69. Jacinto de la Serna, "Manual de ministros de indios para el conocimiento de sus idolatrías, y extirpación de ellas," in *Colección de documentos inéditos para la historia de España*, Madrid: Academia de la Historia, 1892, 104: 57–58.
70. Pérez de Ribas, *History of the Triumphs of Our Holy Faith*, pp. 309–310.
71. *Diario de un cura de pueblo y relación de los señores curas que han servido la parroquia de Nuestra Señora de la Asunción de Tlatlauqui, escrita por el señor cura Don Ramón Vargas López*, ed. Ernesto de la Torre Villar, Mexico; UNAM/INAH/Secretaría de Cultura de Puebla/Universidad de las Américas, 2006, pp. 71–81, 121.
72. Pérez de Ribas, *History of the Triumphs of Our Holy Faith*, p. 194.
73. Pérez de Ribas, *History of the Triumphs of Our Holy Faith*, chapters. 3–8, and 36–39.
74. Pérez de Ribas, *History of the Triumphs of Our Holy Faith*, pp. 200–201.
75. Pérez de Ribas, *History of the Triumphs of Our Holy Faith*, p. 200.
76. Pérez de Ribas, *History of the Triumphs of Our Holy Faith*, p. 201.
77. Antonio Rubial García makes a persuasive case for the importance of hermits in the religious life of New Spain, which was largely neglected before he studied them. See his *Profetisas y solitarios*; with Pedro Ángeles Jiménez, "Fray Sebastián de Aparicio. Hagiografía e historia, vida e imagen," in *Los pinceles de la historia: El origen del reino de la Nueva España, 1680–1750*, Mexico: Museo Nacional del Arte, 1999, pp. 247–260; and "Imágenes y ermitaños. Un ciclo hierofánico ignorado por la historiografía," *Anuario de Estudios Americanos* 66: 2 (julio–diciembre 2009), 213–239. These are landmark studies, but there is a tendency to exaggerate the numbers and influence of hermits as spiritual leaders and sources of relics. What does it mean to say that "numerous lay and religious men and women" hermits were "a constant presence … throughout space and time" in New Spain? (*Profetisas y solitarios*, p. 15, and "Imágenes

y ermitaños," p. 224.) Drawing mainly on published hagiographical works, Rubial García discusses roughly 15–20 colonial hermits (some of whom did not retreat from society or lead particularly ascetic lives), only a few of them enjoying lasting fame and nomination for beatification. I can add half a dozen other renowned solitary or shrine-based devouts, but they do not change the secondary, albeit significant, place of hermits in Mexico's history of numinous persons and things.

78. Christian, *Local Religion*, p. 109. Hermits generally were more common and esteemed in Catalonia than in Castile.
79. Francisco Miranda Godínez, *Dos cultos fundantes: Los Remedios y Guadalupe, 1521–1649, historia documental*, Zamora: El Colegio de Michoacán, 2001, p. 168.
80. AGN Inquisición 117 exp. 7, 1575. Because of his apparent naivete, Moreno got off rather lightly even though he was judged a heretic. Along with a stern warning he was fined 100 gold pesos and faced the humiliation of appearing in an auto da fé.
81. See, for example, Norman Martin, *Los vagabundos en la Nueva España: Siglo XVI*, Mexico: Editorial Jus, 1957.
82. Antonio Rubial García, "Los venerables de la Nueva España; Gregorio López, Juan de Palafox, y fray Antonio Margil," in *Los pinceles de la historia: El origen del reino de la Nueva España, 1680–1750*, Mexico: Museo Nacional del Arte, 1999, p. 232. See also Ragon, *Les saints et les images*, pp. 131–146.
83. Sources for the best-known hermits of the sixteenth and seventeenth centuries include Rubial, *Profetisas y solitarios* and his articles "Un ciclo," "Imágenes y ermitaños," and "Los venerables"; Rafael Montejano y Aguiñaga, *Santa María de Guadalupe en San Luis Potosí: Su culto, su santuario, su calzada y sus santuarios*, Mexico: Ediciones Paulinas, 1982, p. 49 (for Juan Barragán Cano, who lived in the "desierto" near San Luis Potosí for thirty-seven years in the early seventeenth century); Torquemada, *Monarquía Indiana*, III, 56, 75, 219, 239, 494; González Dávila, *Teatro eclesiástico*, pp. 46–59, 72–73 (for Gregorio López and Sebastián de Aparicio); Pedro Salgado de Somoza, *Breve noticia de la devotísima imagen de Nuestra Señora de la Defensa*... [1686], Puebla: Ediciones Palafox, 1946 (for Juan Baptista de Jesús in the 1620s); and Ana Laura Cué, "Juan González: Ermitaño y confesor," in *Los pinceles de la historia: El origen del reino de la Nueva España, 1680–1750*, Mexico: Museo Nacional del Arte, 1999, pp. 261–266.

The line of celebrated hermits at Chalma in the seventeenth century included the mestizo muleteer, Bartolomé de Torres; Carlos de Santa Rosa, a diocesan priest; Pedro Suárez de Escobar, OSA; Bartolomé de Jesús María, OSA; Carlos de Santa Rosa; and Doña Marina de Escobar, a blind nun. Sources include CONDUMEX, Col. Enrique R. Cervantes, Fondo XVI-1-carp. 4, doc. 72; Weckmann, *Medieval Heritage*, p. 247; Gonzalo Obregón, "El real convento y santuario de San Miguel de Chalma," in *Estudios históricos Americanos: Homenaje a Silvio Zavala*, Mexico: El Colegio de México, 1953, pp. 109–182; and Robles, *Diario de sucesos*, I, 274.
84. Jesuit chroniclers praised the hermit-like solitude of their frontier missionary pairs and their stoical self-abnegation and anticipation of the martyr's death (Pérez de Ribas, *History of the Triumphs of Our Holy Faith*, p. 322), but Jesuits did not promote their heroes as hermits, and none of the hermits at shrines of New Spain studied to date was a Jesuit.

There was always the suspicion that hermits who had not proven their personal separation from the world as a member in good standing of a religious order were feigning sanctity and had ulterior motives. For example, Ana María de Morales, who settled at the shrine of Our Lady of Remedios at Tepepan in the Valley of Mexico, was investigated in 1683–1689 for false sanctity and doubtful claims of having witnessed apparitions, Bancroft MSS 96/95m.

Relying on early chronicles of several leading colonial shrines, Rubial proposes that hermits were more present and prominent in the founding stories of shrines, most of which began in the seventeenth century, than is usually supposed, "Imágenes y ermitaños," 219–239. But his six cases (including Antonio Gandía, who had little of the hermit about him) are a small group considering the number of image shrines in New Spain.

85. UT Benson G19-36, fol. 91r. In the same record, Dominican pastors at Chamula complained in 1711 that some of their parishioners were visiting a hermit in Zinacantán. He was arrested and sent to Mexico City, fol. 93r.
86. AGN Inquisición 826 exp. 52; AGN Templos y Conventos 9 exp. 2.
87. Bancroft M-M 70, p. 205. Don Calixto Avencerraje, a native of Granada, Spain, was one of the few late colonial hermits lauded as exemplary. The *Gazeta de México* for December 6, 1785, reported his death at Tepeyac, praising his last seven years of self-abnegation as a hermit in the hills above the shrine of Our Lady of Guadalupe and, especially, the thirty-seven years he had devoted to collecting alms for construction of the Capilla del Pocito.
88. See Destefano, "Miracles and Monasticism," pp. 221–222. The Cruz de Huatulco is discussed in Chapter 8 and in "Información de la Santa Cruz de Guatulco hecha en el año de 1610 por el Dr. D. Antonio Cervantes," CONDUMEX Carmelite microfilms, roll 7 no. 670. Other Mexican wooden crosses eventually mined for fragments include the great cross of the chapel of San José de los Naturales in Mexico City mentioned above (Solange Alberro, *El águila y la cruz. Orígenes religiosos en la conciencia criolla. México, siglos XVI-XVII*, Mexico: Fondo de Cultura Económica, 2000, pp. 60, 62; Vetancurt, *Teatro mexicano*, p. 41) and the found crucifix of Jocotepec, Jalisco in the 1720s, "Autos pertenecientes a la cofradía del Santo Cristo de la Espiración del pueblo de Jocotepec," Guadalajara cathedral archive, box of unclassified cofradía records.
89. Quoted in Delia Annunziata Cosentino, *Las joyas de Zinacantepec: Arte colonial en el monasterio de San Miguel*, Zinacantepec, Mexico: El Colegio Mexiquense, 2003, p. 39.
90. Felipe Castro Gutiérrez, "Resistencia étnica y mesianismo en Xichú, 1769," in *Sierra Gorda: Pasado y Presente. Coloquio en homenaje a Lino Gómez Canedo*, Querétaro: Fondo Editorial de Querétaro, 1991, pp. 127–136.
91. AGN Reales Cédulas Originales 126 exp. 137.
92. CONDUMEX, Col. Enrique A. Cervantes, Fondo XVI-1, carpeta 10, 1796–1797.
93. The Council of Trent (1546–1563) and New Spain's synods in 1555, 1585, and 1771 all endorsed the cult of images while expressing concern over proper depiction and display. To the prelates of the Council of Trent and implicitly to colonial priests, "greatness is derived from all holy images," both in moving people to love God and cultivate piety, and serving as conduits for divine favor through the mediation of the saints, *Canons and Decrees of the Council of Trent: Original Text in English*, trans. H. J. Schroeder, OP, trans., St. Louis and London: B. Herder Book Co., 1941, pp. 215–217. Later bishops frequently encouraged image shrines by offering indulgences to devotees and, by the mid-seventeenth century, using their pastoral visits as an

opportunity to promote confraternities to sponsor miraculous images that had gained a local following. Whether for didactic purposes or as cult objects, there must have been an extraordinary colonial commerce in religious paintings and statues. Clara Bargellini estimates that 5,000–6,000 religious paintings produced in Mexico City were "exported" to the Jesuits' missions in northern Mexico during the seventeenth and eighteenth centuries, "Painting for Export in Mexico City in the Seventeenth and Eighteenth Centuries," in *Art in Spain and the Hispanic World: Essays in Honor of Jonathan Brown*, ed. Sarah Schroth, London: Paul Hoberton and the Center for Spain in America, 2010, pp. 285–301. Adding to this number the paintings sent to the Franciscans' northern missions and *doctrinas*, she estimates that 15,000–20,000 were sent north. What might be the total if all the many churches and homes with religious art in the center and south were included?

94. TU VEMC leg. 41 exp. 2.
95. On the travels of bone relics from medieval shrines for ritual purposes and alms collection, see Bartlett, *Why Can the Dead Do Such Great Things?* p. 298.
96. Caterina Pizzigoni, *The Life Within: Local Indigenous Society in Mexico's Toluca Valley, 1650–1800*, Stanford, CA: Stanford University Press, 2012, p. 45, notes that "Santo Cristo" was a common expression in late colonial Nahuatl testaments, referring to statues of Christ, and that holy images of all kinds were usually called "santos" rather than statues or paintings in these records.
97. Pierre Ragon, "Los santos patronos de las ciudades del México central (siglos XVI y XVII)," *Historia Mexicana* LII: 3 (2002), 371, 377–378; and Dorothy Tanck de Estrada, *Atlas ilustrado de los pueblos de indios. Nueva España, 1800*, Mexico: Banamex, 2005.
98. Nevertheless, claims were made to possess some ephemeral remains that had been separated from the body in life such as Christ's foreskin, fingernail clippings, and bloodstained garments, or the Virgin's tears or drops of her milk. The perpetual longing for the body and presence of Christ was manifest in the Mass and the doctrine of transubstantiation.
99. Sentir (opinion) published in the front matter to José Jiménez de Villaseñor, OP, *Sermón panegyrico en la célebre fiesta* ..., Mexico: Herederos de J.J. Guillena Carrascoso, 1712, the statue of Nuestra Señora de la Plata, "no es de Humana mano, sino de la Diestra de Dios." On beauty as perfection, consider *Relaciones geográficas del Arzobispado de México. 1743*, ed. Francisco de Solano, Madrid: C.S.I.C., 1988, I, 251–252, describing the image of Our Lady of Guadalupe in Querétaro's church of Guadalupe: "con partes tan proporcionadas que la hacen perfectísima," and 262, "imágenes de la más perfecta escultura y de hermosos pinceles ... de más pulido artificio." Our Lady of Guadalupe at Tepeyac and Our Lady of Los Remedios at Totoltepec are two examples of miraculous images that were regarded as impossible to copy faithfully. In the case of Remedios, its mystique of irreproducibility stemmed from the belief that the image frequently changed expression, Cisneros, *Historia de el principio*, fol. 47r.
100. Dávila Padilla, *Historia de la fundación* [1596], pp. 376–378.
101. James Elkins, *Pictures and Tears: A History of People Who Have Cried in Front of Paintings*, New York and London: Routledge, 2001, p. 158.
102. On medidas, see William B. Taylor, *Shrines & Miraculous Images: Religious Life in Mexico Before the Reforma*, Albuquerque: University of New Mexico Press, 2010, pp. 152, 196,

and especially Gabriela Sánchez Reyes, "Para el aumento del culto y la devoción: Noticias sobre la venta de medidas de algunas imágenes virreinales de México," *Boletín de Monumentos Históricos*, tercera época, núm. 29 (sept–dic 2013), 72–93. Trade in medidas would have reached beyond purchases by visitors to the shrine. In 1765 the chaplain of the shrine of Nuestra Señora de San Juan de los Lagos sent an official of the Audiencia of Nueva Galicia in Guadalajara six "medidas of Our Lady that have touched the original image," AGN Alcabalas 105 exp. 1, fol. 53.

103. Beeswax candles were particularly potent symbols of Christ and the immortal soul ("I am the light of the world. Whosoever follows me will never walk in darkness, but will have the light of life," John 8:12) and a favorite votive offering and type of brandea. As Yrjö Hirn put it, "wax candles are considered specially suited for use at the Sacrament . . . . [M]anufactured from a pure material, not of man's making . . . the sexless bees have given the wax a kind of virginal character . . . as something spotless and pure," *The Sacred Shrine. A Study of the Poetry and Art of the Catholic Church* [1909], Boston: Beacon Press, 1957, p. 97.

In his pastoral visit of 1646, Archbishop Juan de Mañozca y Zamora criticized alms collectors from the shrine of San Juan de los Lagos for spreading superstitious rumors among Indians in the district of Cuernavaca that stubs of candles that had been burned in the presence of the miraculous statue of Our Lady of San Juan de los Lagos worked miracles and cured all sorts of illnesses when devotees uttered certain prayers, Magnus Lundberg, "Relación de la visita pastoral del arzobispado de México de Juan de Mañozca y Zamora, 1646," *Historia Mexicana* LVIII: 2 (2008), p. 879.

104. For instance, the water in which the famous statue of the Christ Child of San Juan de la Penitencia in Mexico City had been washed was believed to have medicinal value. See José María Barrientos, *Sermón del Santo Niño Jesús llamado de San Juan . . .*, Mexico: Alejandro Valdés, 1818, p. 14.

105. For example, at the shrine of Our Lady of Xuquila, José Manuel Ruiz y Cervantes mentioned that "innumerable" rosaries, badges, medals, scapulars, ribbons, *milagritos*, candles, and flowers were dispensed, *Memorias de la portentosa imagen de Nuestra Señora de Xuquila*, Mexico: Zúñiga y Ontiveros, 1791, p. 42. Painted copies that had touched a famous shrine image had special cachet. For a written certification that various painted copies, including one by Miguel Cabrera, and "relics" touched the "Divine Simulacrum" of Our Lady of Guadalupe on March 21, 1768, see "Testimonio de estar tocada a su original el lienzo de María Santísima de Guadalupe que está en el antepecho del coro," Archivo Histórico del Arzobispado de Mexico, "caja 1768."

106. The Green Cross of Tepic is discussed in Chapter 8. For Toluca's Cristo de los Labradores, AGN Inquisición 1365 exp. 16.

107. The parish priests in both cases were outraged. In the case of the bastón, the pastor regarded this tampering with the saint's image to be a sacrilege, TU VEMC leg. 8 exp. 25, 1795. The sponsors in Antequera said they clothed the young orphans in the Virgin's garments so that would "salir compuestas y adornadas," but the priest called the practice a profanation, AGN Inquisición 684 exp. 8, 1692.

108. These concerns echoed the Council of Trent's decree in the twenty-fifth session, "on the invocation, veneration, and relics of saints, and on sacred images," in which "the legitimate use of images" was recommended, with "due honor and veneration." "All lasciviousness [is to be] avoided, so that images shall not be painted and adorned with

a seductive charm" or "perverted ... into boisterous festivities and drunkenness ... with no sense of decency," *Canons and Decrees of the Council of Trent*, pp. 215–217.
109. AGN Inquisición 1113 exp. 6.
110. "deformes," Bancroft M-M 69, 70 vol. I, fol. 131r.
111. AGN Cofradías y Archicofradías 14 exp. 7, fols. 199–234. Ancestral sacred images are still regarded as essential to well-being by many Mexican communities today. At least several times a year, Mexican newspapers report the recovery by grateful villagers of statues and paintings stolen from their chapels and churches, often at considerable personal and collective expense. See, for example, the story published in *La Jornada*, June 8, 2010, p. 31, about a crucifix and a painting of the Virgin Mary stolen from the community of El Sauz, Hidalgo, and "ransomed" from an art dealer by local people for 35,000 pesos. The images were, they said, "the symbol of our faith, ... our little santo."
112. For a 1767–1768 dossier documenting efforts by prelates and parish priests to implement the Inquisition's orders on the misuse of images, see Bancroft MSS 72/57m, box 3, folder 20.
113. Other cases include 1748 Xaltocan, an uprising when the parish priest tried to move the community's santos to the new parish church, AGI México 704, AGI Indiferente General 244, AGN Reales Cédulas Originales 71 exp. 8; 1776 Teotihuacan, the parish priest imprisoning various members of the *pueblo de indios* for refusing to allow their image of the Nuestra Señora del Rosario to be taken out in procession, AGN Indios 65 exp. 109; 1785–1786 Cuauhtitlán, an uprising in dispute with the parish priest over his sale of an image of the Virgin Mary of the Immaculate Conception, AGN Clero Regular y Secular 102, AGN Civil 159 exp. 3, Gómez "Diario de México," Bancroft M-M 105, pp. 255–256; and 1799 San Miguel de Atlautla, Indians rising up against the parish priest for selling an old side altar from the local church, AGN Criminal 157 fols. 93–132.
114. AGN Bienes Nacionales 1047 exp. 13, informe of June 6, 1802.
115. As told in Antonio de Alcedo, *Diccionario geográfico de las Indias Occidentales o América*, Madrid: Atlas, 1967, III, 64–65.
116. An example of promoters leading the way is Our Lady of Ancona, described in Chapter 4. An example of a self-starting local devotion that grew to become a worry to ecclesiastical authorities is the Cruz de Huaquechula, mentioned in Taylor, *Shrines and Miraculous Images*, pp. 49–51.
117. AGN Bienes Nacionales 223 exp. 89, 1759–1760, 22 unnumbered folio pages.
118. Evidently, this was not the only instance of a celebrated image from Ecuador carried by friars on long-distance alms-collecting missions during the eighteenth century. Jeffrey Schrader describes another statue of the Virgin Mary taken by Mercedarians of Quito on tour that eventually came to rest in Cádiz, Spain: Charles V "supposedly dispatched a statue to Quito, which resided with a Mercedarian community until the eighteenth century. The custodians of the image then sent it on lengthy journeys in South America to assist in gathering funds for the improvement of its church. Because of its peripatetic career, the statue became known as 'la peregrina de Quito' and ultimately ventured across the Atlantic to Cádiz, where it stayed until its destruction in the Spanish Civil War," "The House of Austria as a Source of Miraculous Images in Latin America," in *Art in Spain and the Hispanic World*, ed. Schroth, London: Paul Hoberton and the Center for Spain in America, 2010, p. 383.

7
Religious Prints and Their Uses

Material culture presents a paradox. As John Glassie writes, it is "culture made material," yet "culture is immaterial. Culture is pattern in mind, inward, invisible and shifting."[1] Material remains usually amount to scraps and tracks, or objects largely separated from their earlier contexts, their significance inferred more than established. Emily Dickinson recognized the problem in her untitled poem #344:

> This was the Town she passed
> There where she rested last
> Then stepped more fast
> The little tracks close prest
> Then not so swift
> Slow, slow as feet did weary grow
>
> Then stopped, no other track!
> Wait! Look! Her little Book
> The leaf at love turned back
> Her very Hat
> And this worn shoe just fits the track
> Here though fled.[2]

"Here though fled" is the story of most vernacular objects historians come across. It remains a problem for the study of early modern Catholic Europe and America even though recent art historians, anthropologists, and historians have applied their talents to the study of various religious images as material culture and self-definition. Sensuous religious practices in Catholic Christianity make the connections between images and devotion especially compelling, but insights into their production, promotion, and regulation have been easier to come by than understanding their audience and reception. There is no easy resolution of Glassie's paradox. In a 1989 book that turned European art history decisively toward the power of all kinds of images – how they were received and used, as well as made and promoted – and challenged the idea of a sea change in the sixteenth century from cult images to the cult of art, David Freedberg declared that "the history of art is subsumed by the history of images," by the relationships between images and people in history.[3] Freedberg called attention to images usually overlooked by art historians – especially shrine images and things associated with them that devotees took to be a living embodiment of what they represented and where they came from. But his inquiry into "the efficacy of pictures" slighted actual responses to and uses of those images in their places and times in favor of psychological theories about response.[4]

In addition to the immediate problems of reckoning with objects separated from their physical and temporal contexts, we have often lost the common knowledge, skills, and appetites that patrons, makers, and consumers in the past brought to them.[5] But for historians, the disciplinary problem has been less a matter of thin contexts than an inclination to treat images and other objects from the past as symbols or illustrations of conclusions and developments already reached in other ways.[6] One promising approach to Freedberg's call for attention to the power of images through response centers on Joanna Ziegler's "evolved images" – paintings and statues that show signs of wear, remodeling, and decoration, or were believed to have come to life, shedding tears, perspiring, bleeding, and changing posture.[7] Among art historians, Robert Maniura has worked to blur the distinction between art objects and cult objects by focusing on responses to celebrated shrine images in Catholic Europe and acts of devotion by visitors to them. His study of the shrine image of Our Lady of Czestochowa draws particular attention to the blemish on this famous icon's face as a source of strong feelings and the conviction that the Blessed Mary is present among devotees who visit the shrine.[8] But, again, actual responses and evidence of use in the past remain elusive.[9]

Approaching Early Modern Religious Prints

Compared to some celebrated paintings and statues, evidence of the use of particular religious prints is hard to find, and prints are often not documented in ways that would demonstrate whether they were valued for their signs of age and earlier use. Scattered as the documentation may be, prints still offer a distinctive window onto the power of images. They circulated more widely than paintings and statues as recognizable depictions of a holy personage or scene;[10] most were monochrome,[11] schematic, small and portable, more perishable than statues and paintings, and (because mechanically reproduced) not likely to be mentioned as "singular copies" of a celebrated image or the holy person depicted;[12] and few were described in written records as exquisite artifacts or noted approvingly for their imperfections. Nevertheless, mass production and the didactic uses intended by their promoters[13] did not necessarily strip them of evocative power. For many who kept them, prints were still "sweet magnets of hearts" and a sacred presence in their own right, thanks at least in part to the respect conferred upon printed matter and the circumstances in which many of them were acquired and used.[14]

Scholarship on early modern European prints has treated them mainly as commodities – produced, marketed, and acquired for particular purposes – and charted the development of prints as aesthetic objects. Famous Renaissance engravers and discerning collectors have received attention, as have the pedagogical function of prints and the rise of specialized print-making shops in Italy, the Low Countries, and Germany during the mid-sixteenth century in response to growing demand.[15] And, as Peter Parshall notes, even cheap prints were discretionary purchases that lent a certain gravitas and gentility to the surroundings they accented.[16] Scholars have paid some attention to reception of prints as authentic and true depictions even when they amounted to the bare outline of a figure, but mostly in secular terms, considering them as examples of political and social criticism. The mystique and uses of religious prints have attracted less attention. An exception is *La estampa religiosa en la España del Antiguo Régimen* by Javier Portús and Jesusa Vega, which features religious images in its study of production, dissemination, and censorship of prints in early modern Spain.[17] Portús and Vega identify seven historical patterns that apply to New Spain as well: (1) Local printmakers could not meet the growing demand for printed matter in the sixteenth and seventeenth centuries, which led to immigration of foreign printers and engravers, especially from Flanders, and to work being farmed out to other parts of Europe. (2) As production grew considerably during the eighteenth century, Spanish and American printers and printmakers did most of the work. (3) The great regional shrines dedicated to miraculous images commissioned many of the religious prints that were in circulation, but local shrines also commissioned prints of their treasured images for sale to visitors and distribution by alms collectors and shopkeepers. (4) Especially during the eighteenth century, episcopal and papal indulgences were granted and advertised on religious prints to promote particular shrine images, saints, and advocations of Mary and Christ. (5) Lay confraternities established to sponsor shrine images commissioned prints and exercised some (sometimes considerable) independence from ecclesiastical oversight. (6) For the most part, there was little systematic regulation of printed images by the Inquisition and other ecclesiastical courts.[18] And (7) prints were mostly used in private settings, often on home altars as devotional objects and a source of protection in times and places plagued by danger and disease (which is to say, perennially and just about everywhere in the early modern Catholic world).[19]

For centuries before Iberian colonization of America, Christian theologians wrote about religious images of all kinds having three purposes: to instruct the uneducated; as an aid to remembering the tenets of the faith; and to encourage an emotional bond.[20] This three-part formulation remained the official view of the function of religious images in colonial Mexico. For example, it was expressed in the same terms by Alonso Alberto de Velasco in 1698 on the opening page of his devotional history of the miraculous Cristo Renovado de Santa Teresa, and each of the seven late colonial editions of this book included a print depicting the prodigious crucifix. Sacred images were, wrote Velasco, "for the instruction and learning of the unintelligent; for permanent recollection of the Sovereign Mysteries of Our Redemption and the examples of the saints; and to stimulate in us tender feelings of devotion that are nurtured more by what is seen than by what is heard."[21] Other late colonial priests reduced this formula to the idea that images could stand in for words or at least augment them in propagating the faith. To Mexico City's celebrated theology professor Dr. Juan José Eguiara y Eguren in 1731, images were "mute sermons"; and to Antonio de Paredes, SJ, they were "eloquent orators that elicit piety."[22]

Not surprisingly, the revenue-producing possibilities of making and regulating sacred images went without saying in this standard formulation, but also missing is a fourth devotional purpose that was widely shared in practice by priests and laity of all classes in the New World as well as Catholic Europe by the seventeenth century: to enable humans to approach divine presence alive in the world. This purpose was, I think, left unstated by authorities because of their scruples about inadvertently encouraging "idolatry" – the confusion of images of sanctity with sanctity itself. Another late colonial priest, Pedro Pablo Patiño, OFM, was thinking about the delicate balance between encouraging the use of images and discouraging idolatrous worship of them when he wrote, "we revere images with a relative devotion because of the excellence of their original [the sainted person depicted]."[23] For Patiño and other ecclesiastical authorities it was the reception of the images – "el honor que se les da" – that invited divine favor, not the images as if they were, themselves, the divine presence. The following pages aim to suggest how these understandings of some sacred prints played out in practice and expressed connections between culture and object, and image and immanence.

The Business of Religious Prints

Until the late eighteenth century, colonial printers and printmakers were concentrated in Mexico City and the city of Puebla.[24] Their prints were made from incised wood blocks or engraved copper plates, and most were distributed as single-sheet images. In a 1768 survey for Mexico City, thirteen printing operations were identified, eight of them shops with roller presses that specialized in producing printed images from engraved plates. The printing business was competitive, and nearly all the shops were located in high-traffic areas in the city center, near the cathedral. Larger printing operations, such as the Zúñiga y Ontiveros family enterprise, sometimes advertised their wares in the late eighteenth-century weekly newspaper, *Gazeta de México*, and took the unusual step of hanging out banners to identify their place of business.[25] Some printers operated a retail store attached to their workshop or a stall in the main plaza of the city where they sold their books, devotional booklets, and prints, plus a small assortment of imported printed matter.[26]

Religious prints were also included in a variety of devotional publications, including prayer booklets and single sheets of prayers; booklets designed to guide the faithful through special devotions dedicated to a particular image or advocation, especially for the popular nine-day novenas; published sermons; shrine histories; and folio size *patentes* or certificates of confraternity membership (see Figure 7.1).[27] Confraternities straddled the line between the Catholic Church as a professional institution and individual communicants, and they deserve more attention in terms of the material culture of religion than I can give them. Their members were promoters and audience at the same time, commissioning altarpieces, paintings, statues, processional paraphernalia, prints, patentes, devotional texts, printed broadsides announcing special feast day events, *medidas*, and medals; and organizing novenas and processions as well as serving as burial societies and social organizations. Their activities usually revolved around an advocation of Christ or the Virgin Mary, or a celebrated shrine image.

Many more prints date from the 1700s than from earlier years, both as single sheets and as images made for published texts. Roughly 28 percent of all publications by Mexico City printers between 1801 and 1819 included one or more prints,[28] and the number of prints produced and circulated in the late colonial period must have run to several million. The shrine of Our Lady of Remedios on the outskirts of the Valley of Mexico alone counted 97,531 prints of Our Lady on hand in 1818.[29] And for the annual celebration at this shrine in 1806, the sponsors anticipated dispensing about 3,800 prints and 100 novena booklets, suggesting a smaller market for the illustrated manuals. Even for lesser shrines in provincial towns, thousands of copies of prints circulated. In his 1755 sermon honoring the Señor de los Desconsolados of Tehuacán de las Granadas, Carmelite friar Lorenzo del Santísimo Sacramento estimated that more than 4,000 prints depicting this miraculous image of Christ had been distributed in the Diocese of Puebla.[30]

Figure 7.1 *Patente* or certificate of membership in a confraternity dedicated to the miraculous image of Jesucristo del Despojo (Christ Mortified) of Huamantla, Puebla, 1821. The certificate lists various indulgences granted to members as well as other privileges and duties. The engraved image's caption declares it to be a "true portrait" of the miraculous statue. Author's copy.

Novena booklets typically included a print of the holy personage or advocation to which the observances were dedicated;[31] the published sermons rarely did, even when they were dedicated to a sacred image. The difference suggests something about how ecclesiastical sponsors of these publications viewed their intended audiences and the function of images. Novena booklets were produced for special public observances over the course of nine days. The target audience for novena booklets was the observant laity, and the booklets would have been available at the shrine or church where the observances were to take place. The prints included in them were visual aids for these spiritual exercises, meant to enrich and sacralize the printed words they accompanied.[32] The sermons were a different kind of devotional literature, almost always published months or years after they were delivered. They were expansive verbal displays of erudition and literary ingenuity meant for the delectation and edification of a more select audience of fellow priests and lay connoisseurs. For this discerning audience their soaring rhetoric made visual aids unnecessary.

Although the texts of novenas and devotional histories for a particular miraculous image often were reprinted many times over a century or more without revision, the prints that accompanied them or were published as loose sheets frequently were different. Why was the miraculous image of Nuestra Señora de los Ángeles at her shrine in Tlatelolco not far from the center of Mexico City depicted in at least nine different engravings between 1777 and 1810? No doubt, part of the answer is that engraved plates eventually wore out and needed to be replaced, but in this case and others, the more important consideration is that prints were the favorite way to promote a devotion and 1777–1810 was the period of most intense promotion of this shrine. Images of different sizes, refinement, and subject matter were needed there for different purposes – for a devotional history, novena booklets, prayers, and single sheet prints made to be distributed by alms collectors or that would appeal to different classes of people in and near the capital city.[33]

By the second half of the eighteenth century most prints were made from copperplate engravings.[34] They were somewhat more expensive to produce than prints from woodcuts, but there were advantages. A woodcut might yield 500 copies before signs of wear made the block unusable,[35] while a metal engraving was good for 4,000 copies or more.[36] And in the hands of a skilled engraver even small, rather ordinary metal engravings had a more detailed, finished, and convincing three-dimensional appearance than most colonial woodcuts did (compare Figures 7.2 and 7.3).

Prints differed in other ways, too. They varied in size, quality of paper, embellishments, the skill and reputation of the engraver, and their emotional appeal. These differences were reflected in who acquired them and at what price. The 1818 record of prints available for the shrine of Our

MODO DE HAZER ESTA Novena.

VA fundada la Novena de N. Señora de Bethlen en memoria, y veneracion de las nueve Feſtividades mas celebres de MARIA Santiſſima, en las nueve Alabanzas, ó Renombres, que la dà la Igleſia en la Oracion, ò Antiphona: *Salve Regina*, y en nueve Elogios de ſu Letania Lauretana, que acomodandoſe à los nueve Myſterios, finalizan en el *Salus infirmorum*, por eſtàr colocada Nueſtra Señora en el Convento de el Hofpital de los

Figure 7.2 Title page and woodcut print from a booklet of prayers and other observances for a novena in honor of Nuestra Señora de Bethlén that took place in the church of the hospital order of San Juan de Dios, Mexico City, 1731. Author's copy.

Lady of Los Remedios divided the inventory into nine grades by the size of the print, the quality of paper and image, and any embellishments. The most expensive were described as *dorados*, apparently accented in gold leaf. Prices ranged from one-eighth real, to one-half real, to one real, and up to two reales for "fine prints" (*estampas finas*). One-half real prints were the most common. They were the ones given out in exchange for a one-half real donation (hence the term *medio de limosna* that was applied to them).[37]

Since the production and circulation of religious prints reflected promotion as well as demand, the supply side of the story can sometimes explain early patterns of consumption and the relationships between promoters and users. News of an Italian image of the Virgin Mary that came to life in 1796 offers an example of promotion leading demand. As reported in the *Gazeta de México* on December 17, 1796, the Mater Dolorosa in a painting hanging in the Cathedral of Ancona (providentially near the famous shrine of the Holy House of Loreto) opened and closed her eyes repeatedly just before a virulent epidemic began to subside. The published report announced that an account of this miracle recently translated from Italian and published in Madrid had just been reprinted in Mexico City. Six

Figure 7.3 Print of the martyrdom of San Hipólito, from a small engraving (measuring 2 3/8" × 3 5/8"), facing the title page of *Método de ofrecer el Santísimo Rosario de María Santísima por intersección del esclarecido mártir Señor S. Hipólito*, Mexico: Mariano Ontiveros, 1818. Author's copy.

months later, in the May 20, 1797 issue, the *Gazeta* reported that a print of the image of the Virgin of Ancona on high-quality stock[38] was now available, underwritten by an anonymous devotee who wished to "foment devotion to this Sovereign Lady by all the faithful." Publication of the print included an indulgence from the Archbishop of Mexico granting eighty days remission for each Hail Mary prayed in her name. "And," added the report, "so that the sale of prints is not limited to this capital city, a supply has been sent to the print shops of Puebla and Guadalajara, as well as shops in Oaxaca, Zacatecas, Veracruz, and Guanajuato." Booksellers, flea market vendors, and the offices of the *Gazeta de México* and *El Diario de México* were also retailers of religious prints.

Francisco de Florencia, SJ, author of devotional texts about shrines and miraculous images in the late seventeenth century, clearly described the purpose of religious prints in recounting that a devotee of the miraculous image of Nuestra Señora de la Fuente in Mexico City "had an engraved plate made and distributed a great many prints in order to extend the devotion."[39] How prints circulated and where they went is harder to establish, but occasionally can be tracked in financial records, judicial cases, inventories, wills, and narrative sources. Cities (especially the production and administrative centers of Mexico City and Puebla), image shrines, churches where special festivities took place, and printers and shopkeepers who traded in religious literature and images were the main hubs of circulation. The spokes or carriers included traveling alms collectors, priests,[40] shrine visitors, urban shoppers, regional and long-distance traders, printers and booksellers who took their wares to regional fairs,[41] peddlers,[42] and other travelers. Prints usually were found near their place of origin, but they were portable and could end up far away, in a box of personal valuables or on a table or wall at home for family worship, at a workplace such as a textile or tobacco factory or tailor's or tanner's workshop, in a priest's quarters, in a traveler's luggage for protection and prayer, or at the meeting place of a confraternity. Most would have circulated within well-traveled local and regional routes – for example, the print of the Christ of Petatlán in its shrine on the Costa Grande of northern Guerrero that was displayed on a home altar in Azoyú in the Costa Chica area of southern Guerrero more than 100 miles away; or the print of Our Lady of Zapopan near Guadalajara that turned up in the shoe of a man incarcerated in Guanajuato. But sometimes prints traveled great distances. Francisco de Ajofrín's collection of prints from shrines he visited went back to Spain with him as keepsakes and perhaps devotional aids. New Mexico in the eighteenth century provides examples of how circulation of religious prints from distant places shaped popular devotion. Prints of celebrated shrine images from central and western Mexico and even Guatemala, such as Our Lady of Guadalupe, Santa María de la Redonda, Our Lady of El Pueblito, and the Lord of Esquipulas, served as models there for locally produced statues and paintings that were celebrated devotional images in their own right.[43]

How far did regulations, surveillance, and enforcement by ecclesiastical courts determine the production and distribution of printed matter? The question invites more guesswork than certainty. Freedom of expression was far from a hallowed right in this society, but it seems fair to say that there was little systematic oversight of printmaking during the colonial period, even though the Inquisition was responsible for censoring inappropriate prints and episcopal courts were also involved in policing the suitability of religious images, including prints.[44] Printers and printmakers were not organized into guilds, and little of what they produced seems to have been screened by officials in advance.[45] Published sermons, chronicles of the religious orders, and shrine histories were vetted by learned colleagues and licensed by the bishop, but most eighteenth-century novena booklets, other short devotional texts, and single-sheet religious prints do not mention licenses, although prints and booklets of prayers had begun to advertise indulgences granted by the bishop, suggesting prior approval of some sort.[46] And the Mexican Inquisition of the eighteenth century paid more attention to imported reading matter and the Index of prohibited books (which had become an instrument to screen out suspect political literature as much as doubtful theological treatises and propositions) than it did to local devotional publications.[47] When ecclesiastical judges and royal officials attempted to impose their will, they usually did so after the fact, removing unacceptable images rather than acting in proscriptive ways.

The Council of Trent decrees from the 1560s were the standard source cited for religious images by ecclesiastical officials, but the Tridentine directives were terse and general about the images themselves. The Council's prelates were more intent on affirming a place for images in Christian devotion without encouraging idolatry[48] than they were on defining what a proper image should be. Images of Christ and the saints, they decreed, should not be "unusual" unless approved by the bishop, and they should certainly not "be painted and adorned with a seductive charm."[49] Carlo Borromeo, a leading figure in the deliberations at Trent whose *Instructiones fabricate et supellectilis ecclesiasticae* was known in New Spain, elaborated a bit. Makers of images should not depart from established rules, and they should avoid unusual depictions that are in any way profane, obscene, ugly, or otherwise ridiculous. Above all, sacred images should be decorous and harmonious in their attire, expressing the dignity and saintliness of their model.[50]

This was still not much for post-Trent judges to go on. In effect, an ecclesiastical judge in New Spain was expected to know a bad image when he saw one and, for the most part, the judges were reluctant to declare particular images ugly or unacceptably crude and indecorous as long as they were treated with proper respect and did not cause a scandal.[51] Inappropriate images were pursued selectively rather than in sweeping campaigns, even though late colonial church leaders occasionally called for reports on the appearance and use of religious images in preparation for a more concerted effort to weed out unseemly images. Especially with prints, colonial judges were more inclined to center their investigation on images that violated sound theology or seemed to criticize authorities and pose a threat to public order.[52] Prints depicting individuals who had not been beatified or canonized were banned when they came to the Inquisition's attention.[53] An unusual 1791 print of a hybrid saint, part Santo Domingo and part San Francisco, that apparently was meant to celebrate the similarities and solidarity of Franciscans and Dominicans, was banned, as was another print of Santo Domingo in 1755 that seemed to make excessive claims for his virtues, as if he were God.[54]

Occasionally a print was suppressed because it misrepresented a matrix image that had become more popular than authorities were willing to allow. In 1810, prints of an image known as the Cross of Huaquechula were ordered to be confiscated because they claimed to depict an actual prodigious cross – a crudely painted cross discovered on a small boulder in a nearby river – when, in fact, they reproduced the image on a silver disk that had been made to cover the painted cross (Figure 7.4). The spurt of popular interest in this cross, concluded the Bishop of Puebla, did not honor a genuine apparition and had nothing miraculous about it. He judged it to be little more than a promotional scheme hatched by local people; and as quickly and quietly as possible he had the shrine suppressed and the prints recalled.[55]

Even if these cases of surveillance and enforcement were unusual, the possibility of an investigation and prosecution in an ecclesiastical court would have served as a warning and contributed to self-censorship. Judging by the few cases involving prints that were prosecuted (other than *desacatos* – acts of disrespect toward, and misuse of, religious images – which were less about the print than about the abuser), even in the late eighteenth century when ecclesiastical courts were more interested in policing images and many new religious prints were in wide circulation, church teachings about images may well have been accepted without much question.

In the late colonial period, ecclesiastical and civil authorities probably influenced devotional practices and the use of prints more directly and decisively by selective promotion than by regulation and prosecution. For example, during the seventeenth century and much of the eighteenth century, shrine administrators were allowed to send out alms-collecting missions in which the collectors exchanged cheap prints of the shrine image for donations. Usually they were allowed to travel wherever they wished to within their home diocese, and sometimes beyond. But beginning in the 1790s, permission to send alms-collecting missions beyond the local parish boundaries was routinely denied,[56] with a conspicuous exception – print-bearing alms collectors for the shrine of Our Lady of Guadalupe at Tepeyac were allowed to travel widely as part of a campaign by royal and ecclesiastical officials to promote this image and shrine as the epitome of patriotic devotion.

Figure 7.4 The forbidden print of the Cross of Huaquechula. The caption identifies the image as "a true portrait of the miraculous cross venerated in its shrine in the town of Huaquechula," AGN Clero Regular y Secular 215 exp. 29. Courtesy of the Archivo General de la Nación, Mexico.

Audience and the Mystique of Religious Prints

When Josef Mariano, an Indian farmer from Tezoquipan in the parish of Panotla, Tlaxcala, hid a small, handmade booklet of prayers and pictures under the altar cloth before Mass on Holy Wednesday in 1793, he set in motion an investigation that offers a rare glimpse of (1) a peddler of inexpensive prints, sketches, and prayers who sometimes customized his wares to meet the particular demands of the local market, (2) one of his customers, and (3) the transaction between them. The parish priest, Úrbano Antonio Díaz de las Cuevas, noticed the booklet, found it highly suspect, and inquired into who had put it there. Before long, Josef Mariano admitted that the booklet was his and that he had purchased it in the *baratillo* – flea market – in the central square of the city of Puebla. His admission led to the maker-vendor, a self-styled creole Spaniard named José Manjarres, and to suspicions that Manjarres was spreading superstitions and mixing the sacred and profane in ways that sullied the cult of saints and the efforts of the clergy to make good Christians of ignorant Indians. He and Josef Mariano were arrested and processed by the bishop's court until Manjarres was sent on to the Inquisition in Mexico City for further interrogation. The material evidence and record of the proceedings in Tlaxcala, Puebla, and Mexico City were filed in the archive of the Inquisition.[57]

Manjarres testified that he frequented the baratillo and church grounds in the city of Puebla to sell cheap devotional literature and other printed matter, mainly to villagers (*gente rústica*) visiting the city – printed novena booklets, prayers, prints of Christ and the saints, handwritten love poems, instructions for learning to count, and the like.[58] Sometimes he created booklets of prayers and incantations to the saints to meet the special needs of peasant laborers who came by. These handmade booklets might incorporate small religious prints he had acquired, apparently from the shop of a local printer and bookseller, Pedro de la Rosa, in the Portal de las Flores.[59] The booklet Josef Mariano purchased for the considerable sum of six *reales* (after bargaining Manjarres down from eight reales) contains twelve small leaves, 1½″ ("two fingers") wide and 2″ ("three fingers") tall, with twelve short texts. It has no prints, only simple pen drawings of farm implements, a crescent moon, a guitar, a pair of stocks and chains, a judicial dais, a skull and crossed bones, and a bell. Manjarres titled this booklet, as he did the three others written in his hand that the court confiscated, "little book of magic for all the labor, struggle, and effort in plowing, reaping, escaping, and playing [the guitar]." Each page of brief text includes a crude sketch and amounts to an appeal to a saint for special favor in the affairs of daily life in the fields and community. Saints associated with agriculture are invoked – San Isidro Labrador and San Félix Papa[60] – and the appeals are for light work, quick feet, and an abundant harvest. For example, one page with a sketch of a scythe appeals to San Isidro for a good harvest "and with the scythe may I reap more than anyone else." Another invocation calls upon Samson, the Old Testament strongman and Israelite judge, for the power to make light work of chopping wood in the mountains. While most of the prayer-appeals and images concern good fortune in farming,

Manjarres also included prayers for learning to play the guitar and especially for protection if pursued or imprisoned. One prayer with a sketch of a crescent moon calls upon the Virgin Mary for protection in clandestine travel: "O Sovereign Mother of mine, light my mind so I can travel at night, give me light." Another called upon the "sovereign and just judge" to "free me from imprisonment if the authorities pursue me, [make me] invincible." And with a sketch of stocks and chains, he added the words "in order to escape imprisonment with ingenuity." Below the sketch of a guitar he wrote, "In order to play with skill and artfulness."

The parish priest and two experts for the Inquisition found the booklets full of superstitious humbug (*patrañas*), if not worse. Why, they asked, did Manjarres write on the first page "First God" (*Primero Dios*)? Did he mean that God was only the first of various gods? Why was the booklet called "little book of magic" (*librito de magia*)? Was this evidence of a pact with the devil? Why did no prayers accompany the sketches of the guitar and the stocks? Why did Manjarres include a six-year expiration date? Why did he draw a skull and a bell on the last page? They were convinced that the maker of these booklets needed correction and punishment. The bishop's counselor, the *promotor fiscal*, suspected more sinister *mala creencia* (by which he meant "beliefs contrary to our religion"), arguing that Manjarres's cunning and his ability to read and write portended something more calculated and serious than money-grubbing and self-indulgence.

The other three handmade booklets of pictures and prayers for villagers in Manjarres's inventory are very similar in layout and content, with prayers for favor in the fields and protection in risky situations, but they also contain four little religious prints each.[61] Two of the booklets include the same four prints: the Holy Family in flight in Egypt, with a prayer for traveling at night; and three others, without accompanying text, words, are of the *Cinco Señores* (the Christ Child, Mary, Joseph, Joachim, and Anne), the Trinity, and Christ crucified with Mary and Joseph shown grieving below the cross. The last booklet has a different set of four prints: one of the Holy Family with the dove of the Holy Spirit above them, with a prayer for an easy and prosperous harvest; another of the Blessed Sacrament (depicted in a sunburst monstrance with two angels praying), with a prayer for traveling safely at night; the third, Christ tied to the column, with a prayer for escape from imprisonment; and the fourth, Veronica's veil, with a prayer for gathering firewood. These booklets with prints would have been more costly to produce (since Manjarres would have purchased the prints) and presumably more impressive to potential buyers than the entirely handwritten one purchased by Josef Mariano, since the printed images conferred authority and might be especially favored by the divine presence. But Manjarres advised Josef Mariano that the booklets would be efficacious

Figure 7.5 Facing pages of one of José Manjarres's booklets for farm laborers with a tiny engraved print of the Cinco Señores – the Christ child with Mary, Joseph, and Mary's parents Anne and Joachim – on the left and Manjarres's drawing of a scythe with the following handwritten words on the right: *santos de mi devosion que en el segar sea lijero con la jos que les gane a todos* ("saints to whom I am devoted: may reaping with the scythe be easy and may I harvest more than anyone else"), Bancroft Library MSS 96/95 m vol. 17 exp. 4, booklet labeled Lib°. 3°. Courtesy of the Bancroft Library, University of California, Berkeley.

only if he used them while reciting prayers to the Holy Trinity and the Virgin Mary.

Clearly, José Manjarres saw cheap prints, crude drawings, and practical prayers as a profitable way to tap into the faith and everyday concerns of nearby villagers who were not likely to be customers for the more conventional printed material he stocked. Perhaps he shared their faith. He had been making such booklets before he met Josef Mariano – two of the confiscated booklets were dated 1791, two years before this investigation – and his business sense is evident in a stipulation he included in each of the booklets that is not found in published devotional guides of the time: on the first page he announced that the booklet had an expiration period of six years. That is, those who valued these booklets would then need to purchase new ones. Under oath, Josef Mariano remembers Manjarres telling him that the booklet's power would run out in six years; Manjarres denied this and swore that the expiration date was there because booklets handled by Indians would be in tatters by then and no longer suitable for use as devotional aids. We are left to wonder about his intentions and candor before the court.

Manjarres surfaces in this record as a rather disarming flea market rogue, more than a little like José Joaquín Fernández de Lizardi's fictional *periquillo sarniento*. Asked about his occupation, Manjarres said he had trained as a barber in his youth but had not practiced the trade for many years. Instead, he lived as a freewheeling peddler of a small miscellany of written and printed matter, and admitted that he was generally otherwise occupied in a local tavern on Sundays, Mondays, and Tuesdays. In the muted boasts, prevarications, and outright lies that mark his several depositions,[62] in his broken promises to reform,[63] and in his groveling apologies he presented himself as a disreputable and self-serving, but largely inconsequential, blowhard and cheat – very much what the parish priest of Panotla and ecclesiastical judges in Puebla and Mexico City seemed to expect from a derelict denizen of flea markets. When caught out in his lies, Manjarres freely admitted them as stains on his character: he would admit that he had, indeed, lied in his first deposition about spending his meager earnings in support of his family. He assured the court that of course he did not believe his little books of prayers could achieve the promised effects – it was all just a little white magic to meet the demands of gullible peasants and separate them from their savings, not a pact with the devil. And he was not above poking fun at himself as he elaborated on his business activities. His customers were not, he said, always resigned when his booklets failed to produce the promised results. One dissatisfied customer even confronted him in public and demanded his money back.

Perhaps Manjarres was just the immoral, if now contrite, picaro he seemed to be. At least he gave a convincing performance in the role that deflected more serious charges of apostasy, fomenting superstitions that undermined the Christian faith of his unlettered customers and their communities, or a tacit pact with the devil. He had plausible, if Delphic, explanations for the doubtful features of the booklets the censors had singled out. He said he had written "Primero Dios" on the first page to suggest not that there were other gods, but that there was only one God. Calling the booklets "libro de magia" was confusing, he admitted. He should have made it clearer that this was white magic, not black magic. The moon, he said, was just an allusion to the Virgin Mary, making no mention of lighting the way for a nighttime escape, which was the point of the accompanying prayer. He left prayers off the pages showing the stocks and guitar because he did not know of a saint especially associated with either one. The skull and bell were a reminder of human mortality and divine judgment, not a reference to the superstition that when San Antonio Abad rang a bell the person who heard it would die in three days (which Manjarres professed not to have heard of).

Manjarres's explanations carried some weight because his booklets did not directly challenge church doctrine or openly invoke the Devil.

Although he had not confessed in at least three years (which was his explanation for why he had not previously admitted to misleading his Indian customers with the booklets), he assured the court he was not an apostate. His lies under oath, he said, were just meant to emphasize that fact by making his actions seem less significant and less frequent than they were. He freely admitted to charging exorbitant prices for his wares. But, then, high prices were what his customers demanded. He found that they thought they were getting something better when they paid more. When he offered to sell an item for one real, they would say that they wanted something that was more valuable – worth, say, eight or twelve reales. So he raised his price on the same kind of item the next time. The parish priest and the Inquisition's *fiscal* (legal adviser) judged him to be a *pícaro embustero* (lying scoundrel, swindler) and *zángano* (idler) who might well infect others with his vices and lead rustic villagers astray, but the inquisitors were not convinced that he was a serious danger to the Christian community.

Invoking the poverty of his family and the fact that Josef Mariano had already been released by the bishop's court in Puebla, Manjarres groveled again for the court's indulgence and pardon as a miserable sinner and prodigal son. In the end, the Inquisition judged him to be a contemptible cheat who had confused and corrupted ignorant Indians for personal gain. He had skated near the edge of *mala creencia*, but was not an apostate or heretic, not knowingly in league with the devil. After a formal audience before the judges in which he was given a good scare and warned of the dire consequences of any future offense, Manjarres was assigned to three months' confinement in the Franciscans' Apostolic College of San Fernando. He was to do labor service in the kitchen or elsewhere at the college guardian's pleasure, receive spiritual instruction from one of the friars, pray daily, and confess and take communion every two weeks. He is last glimpsed in a note to the court from the guardian on the day of his release, February 17, 1794. The guardian reported that Manjarres had completed his prescribed period of confinement and work in the convent's garden. He had confessed and taken communion every two weeks, prayed the Rosary daily, and followed his spiritual director's instructions, "fulfilling his duties willingly and patiently." Manjarres was fortunate to be living in the late 1700s, when the Inquisition had more urgent matters to consider than the mind, faith, and religious practices of a small-time swindler.

At the same time that Manjarres entered the Inquisition cells in Mexico City in June 1793, Josef Mariano was released into the temporary custody of his parish priest for instruction in the faith.[64] At that point Josef Mariano disappears from view. Beyond the hope for heavenly favor in his everyday life, his thoughts and actions are harder to discern in the written record than are Manjarres's. The written prayers in the booklet he purchased evidently were not what mattered to him except perhaps as a kind of ineffable communication with divine providence. He was illiterate and had hesitated to buy the booklet for that reason. Manjarres pressed it on him, assuring him that the booklet was still powerful even if he couldn't read it, as long as he recited the Apostles' Creed and prayed some Hail Marys. If he really was persuaded by this assurance, he must have regarded the booklet mainly as a talisman, not so different from wearing a scapular or a string of rosary beads, as he himself noted. The parish priest was concerned that Josef Mariano also relied on the booklet to favor him in disputes and fights with others in the community, and to escape detection and imprisonment.[65] The prayers for traveling at night and the depiction of stocks and chains point in this direction.

But why did Josef Mariano risk public humiliation and prosecution by placing his booklet under the altar cloth? His initial statement seemed off the point – "[He did it] because it contains prayers and he thought it was the equivalent of a Rosary." Perhaps he thought the booklet could be infused with divine presence there on the altar during Mass, much as the wafer and wine became the body and blood of Christ. But after his imprisonment stretched beyond a month, he came forward with a different explanation: he had done it to test the supernatural power of the object as white magic. "[I did it] to determine if it was just and good, in which case it would still be there [after the Mass], and if it was bad, it would disappear. I did not want to use it until my doubt about this was satisfied." An activation? A pious test? Even this extraordinary local record of production and reception leaves much to the imagination.

Among the stated and unstated purposes of religious images, how they were understood to project transformative power comes closest to their wider audience. Prints of a particular woodcut or engraving were available in hundreds or thousands of virtually identical, inexpensive copies, but most were more than throwaway items or mere souvenirs. They were kept and used as devotional objects that could protect and prompt feelings of awe, contrition, and delight. To some they were veritable relics, much as prints of a saint given to devotees by the keeper of a celebrated statue or painting, which when they make an offering are still called "relics of the saint."[66] For example, there was the burgeoning devotion to the Virgin Mary as Divine Shepherdess (La Divina Pastora) in the port city of Veracruz in the 1740s which began with a group of boys attaching a print of her to a silk banner and carrying it aloft through the streets of the city at night while chanting the Rosary (see Chapter 4).[67] A print might be understood to have the same sort of protective power as a splinter of the True Cross or other relic. For example, in Mexico City's Barrio del Rastro (near the chapel of San Lucas, southeast of the Zócalo) during June 1667, a fire reportedly was extinguished when someone picked up a stone, wrapped it in a print of the statue of Jesús Nazareno from the Hospital de la Limpia Concepción (the famous "Hospital de Jesús" founded by Cortés), and threw it into the flames.[68]

The mystique of images, including prints, was too deeply rooted in popular religiosity to be ignored even by indifferent or doubting officials. In 1785 a print of Our Lady of Sorrows figured in this way during a moment of political drama and tetchy egos in the town of Molango, Hidalgo. According to the parish priest in his denunciation to the Inquisition, the peninsular district governor, D. José de Arteaga y Achútegui, committed sacrilegious outrages there during Holy Week. On a whim, Governor Arteaga had violated a local man's right to temporary asylum in the parish church merely because the church bells had not been tolled to mark the governor's own arrival in town after dark on Holy Wednesday. The priest's explanation to the governor that the congregation was in the middle of the Tenebrae service at the time – the somber rite in the evening before Maundy Thursday of extinguishing the stand of candles set before the congregation, accompanied by prayers and lamentations to commemorate the Crucifixion – only added to the governor's anger, and he sputtered that "this was no more than Holy Wednesday of All Devils, and the next day 'such and such' Holy Thursday." (The priest assured the Inquisitors that he was leaving out the term Arteaga used for Holy Thursday "so as not to offend Your Lordships' pious ears.") When the governor was about to whip the wretched man he had pulled out of the church, the people – *gente de razón* and Indians alike – begged him to stop:

> Everyone, all at once, fell to their knees and implored him not to do it. He was still unmoved so they held up before him a print of Our Lady of Sorrows and earnestly begged him in the name of that Lady to contain himself. His response was to treat the image with contempt, poking it three times with his blunderbuss and shouting that only if the image spoke to him would he accede to their request.[69]

The Mater Dolorosa (see Chapter 4) had a special place in the mystique of religious images no matter how crude and common the depiction of her. She was one of the most popular subjects for religious prints, so it was not surprising that her image (see Figures 4.3–4.5) was at hand in the Molango crowd. The print's presence as more than a symbol or cheap illustration was dismissed by the governor in a way that perversely mirrored the ideal relationship between Catholic devotee and the object of devotion (here, the Virgin Mary depicted in the print), hoping for a moment of divine presence and protection, with the aid of the image.

Despite the circulation of so many religious prints in the eighteenth century, the Inquisition investigated comparatively few cases of their abuse even though such acts would have been widely condemned. Although the Inquisition archive in Mexico City has lost some of its records since the end of the colonial period,[70] the Holy Office pioneered systematic recordkeeping – conducting, recording, and filing many preliminary investigations of suspicious conduct as well as actual trials, and storing small artifacts as well as written records. Its archive is the best single source we have to document the policing of misbehavior with images.[71] Of the 101 cases of *desacato de imágenes* tracked in a preliminary survey, the objects of abuse overwhelmingly were paintings and statues, and most of the few abuses of prints dated from the second half of the eighteenth century, when production and distribution of devotional prints peaked.[72] With respect to prints, the abusers were men and boys, with peninsular Spaniards prominent among them. The most common charge was that they lined their shoes with religious prints, or defecated on a print, or used it as toilet paper, all of which were understood to be a kind of superstitious idolatry (Figure 7.6).[73]

It seems unlikely that the reason few cases of abuse of prints were reported was that such acts were routinely condoned; there were cases in which public disrespect for religious prints stirred pious indignation and action, as they did at Molango or more famously, if perhaps apocryphally, in the case of Mariano Matamoros, the parish priest of Jantetelco, Morelos, who joined the struggle for Mexican independence in 1811 after his housekeeper told him she had seen a royalist soldier wipe himself with a print of the Virgin of Guadalupe.[74]

Far more common than scandalous disrespect was the treatment of prints as portals to communication with divine presence. Occasionally a print was reported to come alive. For example, in 1748 eight leading citizens of Parras, Coahuila testified to seeing a print of the face of Christ perspire on the day a new altar to the Holy Trinity was dedicated in the church of the Jesuits' college. This print had a special place in local lore because the first Jesuits to settle there in 1694 had brought it with them and celebrated the first Mass before it in a nearby cave to mark the beginning of their spiritual mission among unconverted Indians of the region.[75] The most common expression of the mystique of prints was the conviction that they were a medium of divine protection and healing. As Luis Becerra Tanco, one of the celebrated chroniclers of Our Lady of Guadalupe, wrote in 1666, "it will not come as news that the Most Holy Virgin may work miracles with any printed depiction of her."[76] Fray Lorenzo del Santísimo Sacramento assured his readers in 1755 that prints of Tehuacán de las Granadas's Señor de los Desconsolados had cured many people stricken with illness, including a nun with a heart ailment and another woman whose tremors completely disappeared with the aid of a print.[77]

Of the many examples of wonder-working prints, some were clearly promoted by church officials. A novena booklet dedicated to "the prodigious image of Our Lady of Soterraña de Nieva" (a favorite image of the Madonna and Child in the Castilian province of Segovia that was promoted

Figure 7.6 Print of Our Lady of Guadalupe found in a shoe worn by a *cajero* (probably a bookkeeper in a merchant house) in Mexico City in 1759. The print shows tears at the top and bottom, and is soiled on the back where it was folded. AGN Inquisición 928 exp. 9. Courtesy of the Archivo General de la Nación, Mexico.

in Mexico during the late colonial period), reprinted in 1818, proudly declared on the title page that "she is the most special protection against lightning bolts for those who carry her print or medal. And there is a pious tradition that where she is found, lightning will not strike within fifty paces."[78] Francisco de la Rosa Figueroa, OFM, pastor of the village of Tepetlatzingo near Mexico City in 1743, was convinced that the prints he commissioned of the local statue of Nuestra Señora del Patrocinio were instruments of miraculous healing and protection (see Figure 3.3 in Chapter 3).[79] Twelve of the thirty-five cures and rescues he described as the work of the Virgin involved the prints. At the end of his chronicle of praise for this image of the Virgin Mary, completed in 1776, he wrote that he kept in his cell one last copy of the print that had recently worked two more wondrous cures: one in which a young woman recovered from a life-threatening seizure when she prayed to the Virgin and the print was placed on her stomach; the other in which a chick pea that a small boy had stuffed up his nose and that had caused a serious infection popped out when the print was placed on his head.[80]

Prints of miraculous images and shrines with more localized appeal attracted devotees in other ways that were familiar in Spain as well as America during the eighteenth century. One way in which value was added to prints of miraculous images was by physical contact with the matrix image and the shrine site, much like third-class relics. Figure 7.7 is an example from the shrine prints collected by Spanish Capuchin Fr. Francisco de Ajofrín during his travels in Mexico in the 1760s. At the shrine of the Cruz de Piedra (the stone cross) of Querétaro he touched his print to the original cross and wrote at the top, "tocada a su sagrado original."

The sacred aura of other prints stemmed from depicting the altered state of a celebrated painting or statue that had either changed appearance or displayed a blemish that testified to a brush with divine providence. One example of a print depicting a statue that was famous for having changed posture is Figure 7.8, the Holy Child of San Juan de la Penitencia. According to tradition, during an earthquake in 1598 the infant looked up and raised his right arm, preventing a wall of the church from collapsing on worshipers inside.[81]

An example of a print depicting a providential blemish is Figure 7.9, Nuestra Señora de la Bala (Our Lady of the Bullet). The bullet hole at the feet of the small statue of the Virgin Mary was said to date from an attempt by a jealous husband to shoot his pious wife. When she held up the statue to protect herself, the Virgin took the bullet and saved the woman's life.[82]

Other prints established their mystique by being "a true portrait" or "the most like" the miraculous painting or statue depicted, or inviting divine presence because they were works of great skill and beauty.

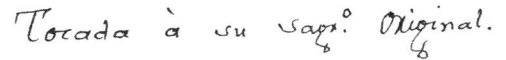

Figure 7.7 Francisco de Ajofrín's copy of a loose print of the miraculous stone cross of Querétaro. He wrote above the print that it had touched the original image. Courtesy of the Real Academia de la Historia, Madrid.

Figure 7.1 is one of several examples reproduced here that claimed to be "true portraits." The engraved image of the Virgin of Guadalupe in Figure 7.10, made by Tomás Suriá in 1790 and reproduced in at least two late colonial texts,[83] asserts the grander claim that it is closer than

Figure 7.8 The Holy Child of San Juan de la Penitencia in his new pose after the earthquake of 1598. Engraving by Manuel Villavicencio, published in José María Barrientos, *Sermón del Santo Niño llamado de San Juan* . . ., Mexico: Valdés, 1818. Courtesy of the Bancroft Library, University of California, Berkeley.

others to being an exact copy of the matrix image, implying that it invited the Virgin's presence more than others could.

There is also the fine eighteenth-century engraving of the Madonna and Child shown in Figure 7.11, which was treated as an original object of devotion in itself. Its caption announces that the Archbishop of Mexico grants an indulgence of forty days to those who pray a Hail Mary in its presence.

Figure 7.9 "Miraculous Image of Nuestra Señora de la Bala [Our Lady of the Bullet]. It is one of the four main [Marian shrines] that surround and protect Mexico City. [Print] paid for by members of her sodality. 1751." Loose print from engraving by Antonio Onofre Moreno, collected by Francisco de Ajofrín. In the print the bullet is lodged just above the crescent moon at the Virgin's feet. Courtesy of the Real Academia de la Historia, Madrid.

N. S. DE GUADALUPE DE MEXICO.
La mas semejante a su Original.

Figure 7.10 Print of Our Lady of Guadalupe from an engraving by Tomás Suriá in 1790 that claims to be "the most like the original" ("La más semejante a su Original"), published in Joseph Ignacio Bartolache, *Manifiesto satisfactorio anunciado en la Gazeta de México (Tom. 1 Núm. 53). Opúsculo Guadalupano*, Mexico: Zúñiga y Ontiveros, 1790 facing p. 1. Author's copy.

Figure 7.11 Fine print of the Madonna and Child that was promoted as a cult object in the mid-eighteenth century. Engraved by José Benito Ortuño and published in José Joaquín de Ortega, *Mes mariano o lección mensal* . . ., Mexico: Bibliotheca Mexicana, 1760. Courtesy of The Bancroft Library, University of California, Berkeley.

AVE MARIA PURISIMA.
SIN PECADO CONCEBIDA.

*SILVOS
DEL PASTOR DIVINO*,
con que los Padres Misioneros del Colegio de Nró. P. S. Francisco del Real, y Minas de Pachuca, llaman à los pecadores à la Mision, y à penitencia.

Y OTRAS CANCIONES DEVOTAS,

en honor de la Purisima Concepcion de la Madre de Dios, y de Christo Crucificado.

Reimpresos en México, en la Imprenta de los Herederos del Lic. D. José de Jauregui, Calle de San Bernardo. Año de 1783.

Figure 7.12 (a) Title page; (b) Print of Mary Immaculate from a well-worn woodcut block in a little pamphlet of twenty-eight printed pages of prayers in the form of songs and verses, *Ave María Purísima. Sin pecado concebida. Silvos del Pastor Divino* ..., Mexico: reprinted by Herederos del Lic. D. José de Jáuregui, 1783. The title page's overleaf states that the Archbishop of Mexico grants forty days indulgence to those who sing its couplets to the Immaculate Conception. The last two pages mention additional indulgences. Author's copy.

More than anything, the mystique of a print depended on how it was received, especially how it was used and remembered as part of a transcendent devotional experience. Prints in novena booklets might carry this kind of meaning for a devotee. The little sheaf of sewn pages containing prayers and songs dedicated to the Marian advocation of the Immaculate Conception with its print from a worn woodcut reproduced in Figure 7.12 dates from a late colonial event in which the faith of promoters and laity converged in prayer, sermons, and spiritual lessons to coax feelings of deep remorse and "change hearts," culminating in confession, communion, and sometimes miraculous healings.[84] This copy, a 1783 reprint, would have been distributed by friars from the Franciscan missionary college at Pachuca, Hidalgo, at the beginning of one of their week-long spiritual revivals conducted at the invitation of parishes in central Mexico.[85] The opening line on the title page recalls the words exchanged at the beginning of a confession: "Ave María Purísima" (Hail purest Mary) says the confessor;

"sin pecado concebida" (conceived without sin) replies the penitent, completing the phrase.[86] The rest of the lengthy title page announces the program of spiritual renewal that is about to begin: "The Divine Shepherd's Whistle, with which the Missionary fathers of the College of Our Father St. Francis at the mines of Pachuca call sinners to this Mission and penitence." It was just such a series of revival meetings led by another group of itinerant Franciscan missionaries in Cuernavaca in the 1730s that Francisco de la Rosa Figueroa said "startled my spirit" and moved him toward the calling of a friar. How this particular print and booklet were used afterward we can only guess, but the purpose of these preaching, prayer, and sacramental missions of the Franciscans and Jesuits was made clear by Fr. Isidro Félix de Espinosa in his early eighteenth-century history of New Spain's *colegios de propaganda fide*. The preaching of the gospel in these missions was meant to be "like a lightning bolt, overwhelming even the most perverse sinners, ... transforming [the preacher's] words into sighs and his ardor into sobs. Dumbfounded by such an extraordinary display, the audience will anticipate some unimagined mystery to present itself."[87]

Religious prints were familiar objects in daily life and personal devotion in Mexico during the eighteenth century, but not many survive, and the most common of them are now among the scarcest. As the saying goes, *todo por servir se acaba* – everything well used is used up. Perhaps the most familiar vernacular use of prints and other religious images was on home altars. Much like altars in churches, home altars created an intimate sanctuary for prayer, where images of Christ, Mary, and saints were displayed and embellished with offerings and decorations. In exchange, family members counted on protection and favor from Christ and the saints they honored. During the sixteenth and seventeenth centuries, home altars usually displayed a few small statues and paintings flanked by votive candles and flowers, perhaps displayed on a table.[88] A 1643 Inquisition decree suggests not only that home altars and private chapels were common, but also that they could be quite elaborate sites of devotion. The Inquisitors noted that people of all kinds in Mexico City and other cities had them in their homes, where they burned candles, set up Nativity scenes, and honored the Virgin Mary and the saints. The judges were especially concerned about home altars where portraits of deceased individuals not officially recognized as saints were displayed and unruly drinking, eating, and dancing took place.[89] By the eighteenth century, home altars displayed prints of holy people as well as paintings and statues, and were regarded as common everywhere. Francisco de Ajofrín, the Capuchin friar mentioned earlier who visited much of central and southern Mexico on an extended alms-collecting mission in the 1760s, commented about the furnishings he noticed in rural Indian dwellings: "their houses are

INTERIOR OF AN INDIAN HUT, EL BOZAL.

Figure 7.13 Print from Mrs. H. G. Ward's sketch of a display of religious prints and paintings in a modest dwelling at El Bozal, San Luis Potosí in the 1820s, published in H. G. Ward, *Mexico*, 2nd ed., London: Henry Colburn, 1829, II, facing p. 261. Author's copy. Mrs. Ward's picture would have made a fitting illustration for Francisco de Ajofrín's travel account from the 1760s.

exceedingly basic huts or hovels without more treasures or embellishments than a few religious prints and an image of Christ."[90] And a 1799 description of Indian life claimed that "in every house" there was a family chapel with religious images.[91]

Small prints were well suited to the intimacy of the home altar, one of which, belonging to Josef de Ávila, a mulato from the Costa Chica community of San Miguel Azoyú in southern Guerrero, was described in an 1787 investigation of his devotional practices. The display of prints was arranged around a cherished statue of the Holy Child that Ávila kept at home as a family treasure. The Santo Niño was placed in the front room "in a little bag on a small shelf against a cloth draped on the wall, behind a table that serves as an altar with various paper saints around it." The prints depicted the Christ of Petatlán,[92] Santa Rita, Our Lady of the Snows, Our Lady of Carmen, "and others."[93]

The prints on José de Ávila's home altar or on the wall of the humble dwelling sketched by Mrs. H. G. Ward in the 1820s (Figure 7.13) may well all have been loose sheets to begin with, but it was not uncommon for prints to be removed from novena booklets and other devotional texts for

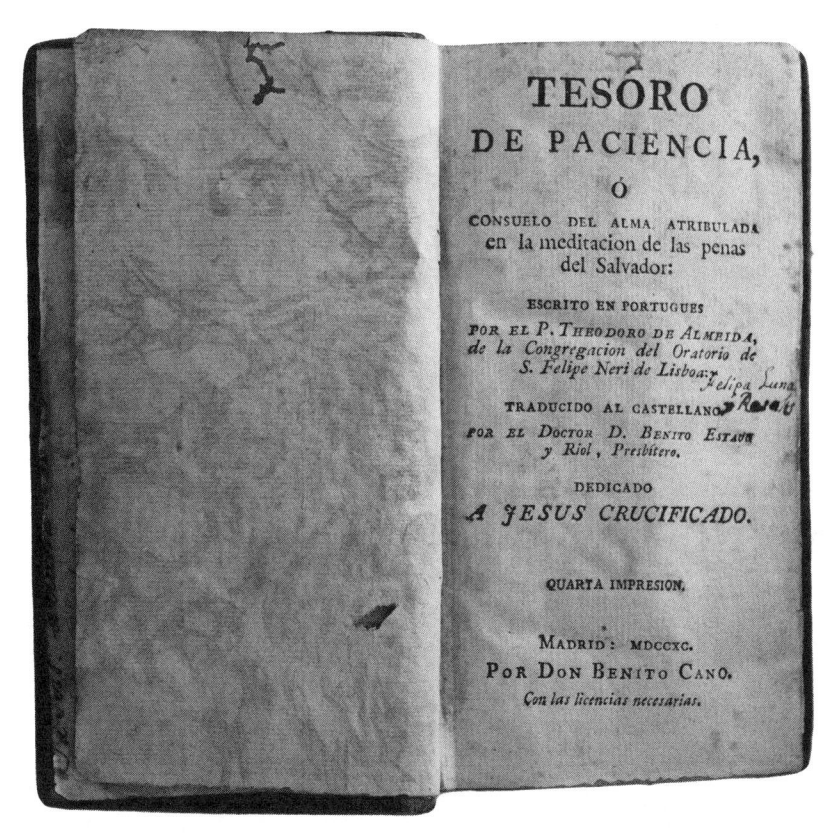

Figure 7.14 Title page of Theodoro de Almeida, *Tesoro de Paciencia . . .*, Madrid: Don Benito Cano, 1790, with Felipa Luna y Rosales's name inscribed. Author's copy.

more public display and veneration on home altars.[94] The devotional books from which they were removed became evolved objects of a kind, but sometimes a devotional book changed by addition rather than subtraction, either with underlinings and marginal notes or with prints, pressed flowers, handwritten prayers, and other things inserted into them.[95] Some books with additions effectively tell their own stories and serve as evidence of some larger historical development. An example is the copy of a pocket size devotional text, *Tesoro de paciencia, o consuelo del alma atribulada en la meditación de las penas del Salvador* ("Treasury of Patience, or consolation for the troubled soul by means of meditation on the suffering of Our Savior") by the Portuguese Oratorian priest Theodoro de Almeida, shown in Figures 7.14, 7.15, and 7.16. Published in Madrid in 1790 and probably unbound when it was shipped to Mexico, the book now has a scuffed, but sturdy calfskin binding. The label on the spine has come off, the boards are

Figure 7.15 Pages 108–109 of this copy of the *Tesoro de paciencia* with Cypriana García Castañiza's inscription, "Del uso de la ha. Cypriana Garcia Castañiza. Me encomendara a Dios." Author's copy.

worn at the corners, and the endpapers recycle the draft of a letter, possibly to a confessor. Apparently, the book first belonged to Felipa Luna y Rosales of Mexico City, whose name is written in cursive letters on the title page (Figure 7.14).

On p. 108 there is an undated note in the hand of another early nineteenth-century owner who identified herself as *hermana* (sister), probably a *beata* or lay sister: "Belonging to Sister Cypriana García Castañiza. May I be commended to God" (Figure 7.15).[96] Cypriana wrote these words on the pages that begin a major section of soliloquies on the penitent's afflicted soul in the presence of God that were meant, writes the author, "to aid the soul in unburdening its oppressed heart before God." The first soliloquy begins, "Oh, my good God, save me for I perish by the moment; I find myself drowning in this terrible storm."[97] What better place to identify herself and appeal for God's mercy?

Facing the first page of the text, someone – Felipa Luna or Cypriana García would seem to be the likely choices – has pasted in a small print in

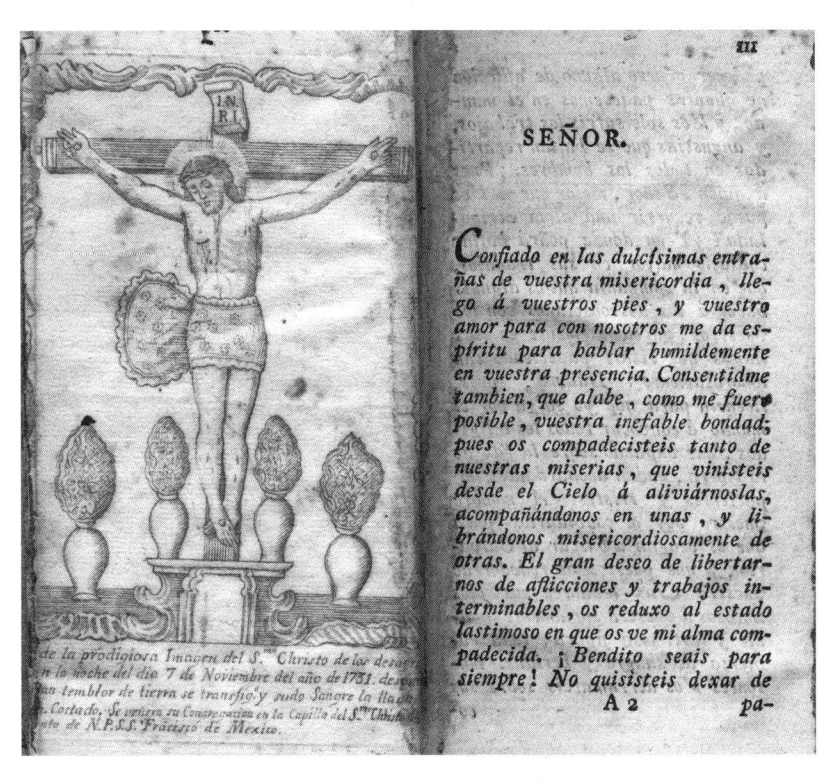

Figure 7.16 A small, unsigned print in rose-colored ink of Mexico City's miraculous Christ of Forgiveness (El Cristo de los Desagravios) pasted into this copy of the *Tesoro de paciencia*. Residue of the paste can be seen along the inside edge of the print and the facing page of text. Even though a few letters in the caption at the bottom of the print were lost when the print was trimmed to the size of the book's pages, the sense of the caption is clear: "Depiction of the prodigious image of the Most Holy Christ of Atonement that, following an earthquake on the night of November 7, 1731, was transformed and sweated blood from the wound in its side. It is venerated by its Congregation in the Chapel of the Most Holy Christ of the convent of Our Most Holy Father St. Francis in Mexico City." The engraving for this print would have been made after 1780 when the crucifix was placed in the chapel of the Christ of Burgos. Author's copy.

rose-colored ink of a crucified Christ, the "prodigiosa Imagen del Smo Christo de los Desagravios" in the Franciscan church in Mexico City (Figure 7.16).

I can only guess at the family background, social station, and relationship, if any, between these two women. Were they members of the same family, perhaps of different generations? Was one or were both members of a *beaterio* or other supervised living arrangement for laywomen under religious instruction?[98] Considering the large number of primary school classes operating in New Spain during the late eighteenth century, rudimentary literacy for women living in corporate communities or under the care of charitable institutions was not unusual, but a book of this content and length would have reached only a more select audience of women from urban beaterios or well-to-do families who would likely have been tutored in reading and writing. Unlike printed images on loose sheets with runs of 5,000 copies or more, or even novena booklets, imported books like this one were expensive and circulated in small numbers, perhaps a few score. Since neither of the owners of this copy of the *Tesoro de paciencia* identified herself as a *doña* (a woman of distinction) and one refers to herself as "Hermana," they may have lived in one of the various shelters for pious women in the capital, but it is also possible that they were laywomen from privileged families who led largely secluded lives at home.

Almeida's text is itself an essential part of this story. During the late eighteenth century, Catholic reformers in Mexico actively promoted a more personal, private, austere piety for the laity over the showy and expensive public practices of Baroque religiosity, whether in the fabulous ornamentation of Puebla's Rosary chapel,[99] or lavish Corpus Christi decorations and processions in virtually every parish.[100] The idea was that a more interiorized, disciplined spiritual life would better merit salvation and honor the saints and Christ by imitating their Christian virtues, rather than looking for divine intercession and relief in everyday life. During the last third of the eighteenth century, Almeida's writings were among the guides for this devotional reform in New Spain.[101] His aims were old ones – to reconcile reason and faith, passions and the intellect – and were grounded in a long-standing Oratorian emphasis on penance and the Eucharist to conquer the forces of evil through devotion to Christ,[102] but he addressed them in an Enlightenment spirit, emphasizing a rigorous piety that was at once intellectualized, sober, and practical. He sought to harmonize faith and scientific knowledge of the world,[103] and when he wrote metaphorically of the heart, he meant reason, not emotion. Almeida was a founding member of the Portuguese Academia das Sciencias de Lisboa and an avid popularizer of the physical sciences, as well as the author of a novel, essays on philosophy and theology, poetry, collections of sermons, and devotional texts about the afflictions suffered by the Blessed Mary as well as Christ. His focus was on perfecting the soul, living righteously, like Christ, even in a sinful world. Miracles, saints, images, and processions were of little interest to him.

The print pasted into the book is from a different current of piety closer to the hearts of seventeenth-century Mexican Oratorians like Archbishop Francisco Aguiar y Seixas (1682–1698) and Dr. Alonso Alberto de Velasco, prefect of the Oratorian community in Mexico

City, bishop-designate of Manila in 1699, author of a pious history of the celebrated Cristo Renovado de Santa Teresa, and a leading figure in the campaign for the canonization of native son Felipe de Jesús.[104] Velasco's Rosary manual and his devotional history of the Cristo Renovado were repeatedly reprinted during the eighteenth and nineteenth centuries, and other Oratorians went on composing and publishing booklets of prayers and programs for public novena observances.

The print depicts a miraculous crucifix that had belonged to the noble family of the Condes del Valle de Orizaba, who lived in the palace known as the House of Tiles, a downtown Mexico City landmark. During an earthquake on the night of November 7, 1731, the crucifix was said to have come to life, according to twenty-seven eyewitnesses, most of them Spaniards and priests. They swore that Christ's face turned pallid and then flushed in the space of a few hours, and that the wound in his side oozed a liquid, either blood or perspiration.[105] News of this activation caused an immediate clamor at the Conde de Orizaba's door, and the archbishop's attorney general (*provisor*) decided to have the image moved across the street to the altar in the Chapel of San Joseph of the Franciscans' mother church. There, too, excited crowds gathered to see this living, suffering Christ.[106] The Conde de Orizaba pressed for an investigation of the reputed miracle, the eyewitnesses were brought forward, and the provisor ordered a thorough examination by medical experts of the cloth used to wipe away the liquid from the statue's wound to determine whether it was blood or perspiration rather than water.[107] In 1734, the provisor and *vicario general* of the archdiocese published a decree affirming that this was a true miracle: the Christ had in fact shed blood that night in 1731.[108] By June 1735 an altarpiece dedicated to the Cristo de los Desagravios was in place in the Franciscans' chapel of San Joseph.[109] And in 1780, a still grander altarpiece was inaugurated for this miraculous Cristo in the same convent's chapel of the Señor de Burgos, named for a famously miraculous Spanish crucifix and sponsored by Mexico City's Cantabrian immigrants.[110] The Cristo de los Desagravios remained there until the Franciscans were removed from the convent and church during the Wars of Reform in the 1860s.[111]

According to its caption, this print depicts a "prodigious image" of the crucified Christ that bled from the wound in its side. It represents a public testimonial of faith in God's presence in the world, and holds out the promise of yet other divine favors in the here and now at the statue's altar. In contrast, the *Tesoro de paciencia* is a text of the reformed piety, instructing the believer in inward "mental prayer or inner approaches to God" ("oración mental o trato interior de Dios") that would set the soul free. It called for disciplined, sustained meditation on the torment and death of Christ as the model of forbearance in the face of extreme hardship, and the source of consolation and divine mercy. Almeida's focus was on perfecting the soul, living righteously, like Christ, even in a sinful world. How did these countercurrents of a more austere, rational piety exemplified by Almeida's text and recommended by "Jansenist" religious reformers on the one hand and Baroque expressions of faith, including miracles, activation of images, and lavish churches and public rituals, on the other meet in the late eighteenth century? If we can believe the more flamboyant religious reformers of the time, old ways of devotion collided with the new crusade against ignorance, superstition, and waste. How, then, should we interpret the pasting in of the print of the miraculous crucifix, so prominently displayed at the beginning of the text? Was this a kind of dissent against reforms that were meant to scrub piety clean of unrestrained joy and the comforting assurance of divine presence and favor in the world? Or was it another in a long line of everyday acts of piety that accepted the new without giving up the old? My guess is that the person who inserted this print regarded doing so as a natural expression of her faith, and that we distort the thinking of many practicing Catholics in this time and place by accepting the idea that a book like the *Tesoro de paciencia* was part of an unprecedented assault on Baroque spiritual practices, or even that reformers who did think in such stark terms represent reformers of the time in general.

The Conde de Orizaba's Franciscan neighbors had long been known for staging annual penitential processions devoted to Christ's Passion that combined personal acts of contrition, including flagellation, with public display of local crucifixes and expressions of collective grief.[112] The practice of carrying crucifixes in processions from their great convent church in Mexico City was so ingrained in popular tradition that it continued during Corpus Christi observances even after 1752, when the archbishop issued instructions that only the consecrated Host could be displayed in public that day.[113] And there is good reason to think that right at the Mexico City Franciscans' altar of the Cristo de los Desagravios in the chapel of the Cristo de Burgos Felipa or Cypriana would have found a kindred spirit in one of the leading reformers of the time, Fr. Fernando Martagon, OFM. Martagon (1740–1804) is regarded as a voice of reformed piety in Mexico City from the 1770s to the early 1810s; his popular books of devotional exercises, like Almeida's *Tesoro de paciencia*, were designed to guide devotees toward atonement for their sins (*los santos desagravios*) through personal identification with the suffering of Christ and the sorrows of Mary.[114] But Martagon was also closely associated with the Cristo de los Desagravios in the Franciscans' chapel of the Cristo de Burgos, serving as chaplain there; sponsoring a new side altar, completed in 1780, that was dedicated to the Cristo de los Desagravios; and publishing a novena booklet for "the prodigious image of the Most Holy Cristo de los Desagravios" that included a print of the Cristo as the frontispiece.[115] Martagon, too, seems to have embraced

> DEVOTA ROGACION
> EN FORMA DE NOVENA,
> PARA VENERAR
> A LA PRODIGIOSA IMAGEN
> **DEL SSmô. CHRISTO**
> DE LOS DESAGRAVIOS,
> A fin de impetrar fu fingulariffimo Patrocinio en la converfion de los pecadores, y en la tribulacion de los temblores de tierra.
> CON UNA BREVE NOTICIA
> DE SU MILAGROSA TRANSFIGURACION,
> Y SUDOR DE SU SANTISSIMO COSTADO.
> *Hecha por el P. F. FERNANDO MARTAGON de la Regular Obfervancia de N. S. P. S. Francifco, Predicador Conventual en fu Convento de Mexico, Director de la Congregacion de Propaganda Fide, y Santos Defagravios de Chrifto N. Sr. è indigniffimo Efclavo de la mifma Santiffima Imagen.*
> DALA A LUZ EL MUY NOBLE Sr.
> DON JOSEF DIEGO SUAREZ
> Peredo, Hurtado de Mendoza, y Malo, Conde del Valle de Orizaba, y Vis-Conde de S. Miguel: à quien la dedica el Author.
>
> Con licencia en México, por D. Felipe de Zúñiga Calle de la Palma, año de 1772.

Figure 7.17 Title page and print from Fr. Fernando Martagon's novena booklet for the Cristo de los Desagravios, Mexico: Zúñiga y Ontiveros, 1772. Courtesy of the Getty Research Center.

a more restrained, disciplined, personal faith without rejecting the idea of enchantment in the world.

Conclusion

As Josef Mariano's parish priest commented, "This was not the first time such an Indian would put his complete trust in the possession of a little book of the kind, which he treasures as if it were a reliquary."[116] The "little books of magic," the well-used copy of the *Tesoro de la paciencia*, the incident at Molango, and other cases of prints in use suggest that the mystique of images was a defining feature of religiosity in colonial Mexico. But prints were not just like paintings or statues in this regard. Though more perishable and less evocative, they were also more portable and ubiquitous – mechanically reproduced in large numbers, they were inexpensive, available to almost anyone. And even the cheapest prints were rarely dismissed as debased or inauthentic. As ordinary as they may appear, anything in print still had authority. Printed depictions of holy figures went beyond written words, joining sight to sounds of praise and prayer and the sensation of touch to coax feelings of love, contrition, and hope. And though officials may well have regarded most prints as visual aids to devotion more than as devotional images in themselves, like celebrated statues and paintings some were said to have come to life; others were carried in processions as if they were relics; and many were displayed on home altars or tipped into devotional texts. Echoing through this chapter are Francisco Antonio Navarrete's words about the Mater Dolorosa: "no image of Our Lady of Dolores can help but be miraculous."

More than searching out other, better documented examples of objects in use, the most telling clue to understanding the potency of printed religious images and the meaning of reception may be the everyday name for the most common kind of religious print: a *medio de limosna* (a half-real alms print). This name connects image to offering and penance, making the exchange of money and print a religious transaction more than an act of selling and buying, or celebration of the printmaker.[117] This exalted sense of exchange was promoted by shrine administrators and alms collectors, and evidently was widely accepted by those who acquired the prints, as both a blessing and a sacrifice with moral and spiritual weight. It was meant to be a celestial conversation, an exchange of gifts that affirmed a bond of mutual fidelity, affection, and favor between the donor and the holy person depicted in the print.

Notes

1. John Glassie, *Material Culture*, Bloomington: Indiana University Press, 1999, p. 41. Art historian George Kubler chose to speak of "the history of things" instead of material culture because of the latter wording's "bristling ugliness" and its use to make an artificial distinction between "mental culture" and artifacts, *The Shape of Time: Remarks on the History of Things*, New Haven: Yale University Press, 1962, p. 9. Glassie does not make such a distinction when he speaks of material culture. Kubler's meaning of "the history of things" is much the same as the usual sense of material culture: "all materials [handled or] worked by human hands under the guidance of connected ideas developed in temporal sequence," *The Shape of Time*, p. 9.
2. Thomas H. Johnson, ed., *The Complete Poems of Emily Dickinson*, London: Faber, 1975, poem #344, ca. 1862.
3. David Freedberg, *The Power of Images: Studies in the History and Theory of Response*, Chicago: University of Chicago Press, 1989, p. xix. Art historian Esther Pasztory goes a step beyond Freedberg to declare that the history of art is subsumed by the history of all kinds of objects, *Thinking with Things: Toward a New Vision of Art*, Austin: University of Texas Press, 2005. A key work addressing the enchantment of images before the Renaissance is Hans Belting's *Likeness and Presence: A History of the Image Before the Era of Art*, Chicago: University of Chicago Press, 1994.

   Michael Baxandall's *Painting and Experience in Fifteenth-Century Italy: A Primer in the Social History of Pictorial Style*, Oxford: Clarendon Press, 1972 is rightly celebrated for

opening the way to a more audience-centered social history of art and visual representation. And historical archaeologists have long recognized this challenge, but in stressing the priority of the sited object, they have rarely deepened the context by investigating the array of other kinds of records for Christian objects in early modern Europe and the Americas.
4. Freedberg's chapters on consecration of things and of things taken to and from pilgrimage shrines come closest to establishing response, but Elizabeth Coatsworth pointed out the risk of carefree conclusions about how objects were received without direct evidence of how they were used and valued:

A man's life or a woman's after a hundred years is usually summed up by little more than an old daguerreotype, a few letters stiffly written, breaking along the folds, or the mute witness of the objects they perhaps cherished: 'these were my grandmother's earrings. This was my great-grandfather's desk.' Yet perhaps the grandmother never cared for the earrings; perhaps the great grandfather preferred to write at a table (as I am writing now) in the kitchen.

Maine Ways, New York: MacMillan, 1947, p. 211.
5. Ludmilla Jordanova, *The Look of the Past: Visual Culture and Material Evidence in Historical Practice*, Cambridge, UK and New York: Cambridge University Press, 2012, p. 33. Jordanova treats audience in chapter 4 and prints on pp. 164–166. See also William B. Taylor, *Shrines & Miraculous Images: Religious Life in Mexico Before the Reforma*, Albuquerque: University of New Mexico Press, 2010, chapter 1.
6. Francis Haskell, *History and Its Images: Art and the Interpretation of the Past*, New Haven: Yale University Press, 1993, pp. 2–10. Another historian's approach to painted images and drawings that pays more attention to the artist's reception of objects depicted than to audience response and questions of beauty is Timothy Brook's *Vermeer's Hat: The Seventeenth Century and the Dawn of the Global World*, New York, Berlin and London: Bloomsbury Press, 2008:

[W]e see a seventeenth-century goblet and think: That is what a seventeenth-century goblet looks like, and isn't it remarkably like/unlike (choose one) goblets today? We tend not to think [as Brooks proposes to do]: What is a goblet doing there? Who made it? Where did it come from? Why did the artist choose to include it instead of something else, a teacup, say, or a glass jar? (pp. 8–9)

7. Joanna Ziegler, "The Medieval Virgin as Object: Art or Anthropology?" *Historical Reflections/Réflexions Historiques* 16: 2–3 (summer–fall 1989), 251–264. In related work, historian Richard Trexler considered the decoration of religious images in Renaissance Italy as acts of beautification and devotion, "Being and Non-Being: Parameters of the Miraculous in the Traditional Religious Image," in *The Miraculous Image in the Late Middle Ages and Renaissance*, ed. Erik Thunø and Gerhard Wolf, Rome: "L'Erma" di Bretschneider, 2004, pp. 15–27.
8. Robert Maniura, *Pilgrimage to Images in the Fifteenth Century: The Origins of the Cult of Our Lady of Czestochowa*, Woodbridge: Boydell and Brewer, 2004. See also his "Voting with Their Feet: Art, Pilgrimage and Ratings in the Renaissance," in *Revaluing Renaissance Art*, ed. Gabriele Neher and Rupert Shepherd, Aldershot, England and Brookfield, VT: Ashgate, 2000, pp. 187–200; "The Images and Miracles of Santa Maria delle Carceri," in *The Miraculous Image in the Late Middle Ages and Renaissance*, pp. 81–95 (which addresses

response through a group of sixty-five miracle stories); and *Presence: The Inherence of the Prototype within Images and Other Objects*, ed. Robert Maniura and Rupert Shepherd, Aldershot, England and Brookfield, VT: Ashgate, 2006 for further reflections about reception centered on belief in divine immanence. Pamela M. Jones, *Altarpieces and Their Viewers in the Churches of Rome from Caravaggio to Guido Peni*, Burlington, VT: Ashgate, 2008 centers attention on historical reception, but her approach is indirect as well, positing hypothetical responses based on "horizons of expectation" gleaned from moralizing messages in sermons, the liturgy, and paintings, and does not address notions of beauty and the miraculous.

9. A journal that seeks to bridge the various academic and public groups interested in the power of religious images was established in England in 2005, *Material Religion: The Journal of Objects, Art, and Belief*. As the editors explain in the first issue, the subject is "material forms and their uses in religious practices," or "what material culture can tell ... about the lived experience of religion." Recent issues have been devoted to museums, visual culture, gendering religious objects, and selected approaches to ritual materials in several religious traditions and parts of the world. Anthropology has been the journal's home base. Latin America, historical contexts, and reception have not received much attention in its pages to date.

10. Even the sketchiest images of, say, Our Lady of Sorrows, Our Lady of Carmen, or Our Lady of the Rosary were readily identifiable in a symbol: the sword aimed at the heart of the grieving Mother; the Carmelites' scapular; and the string of rosary beads in the Virgin's hand. Sometimes advocations of Mary could be identified by how they were dressed. For Our Lady of Loreto, it was the cone-shaped garment that enveloped her figure and the Christ child.

11. The limited use of color and other embellishments in most colonial religious prints removes one of the most evocative aspects of other kinds of religious images. But color, too, has not been much studied in terms of the audience. John Gage, a leading scholar in the field of color and meaning in the history of art, wrote in 1999 that "perhaps the least developed area in the history of colour is indeed the area of spectator-response," *Color and Meaning: Art, Science, and Symbolism*, Berkeley: University of California Press, 1999, p. 54. See also Michael Taussig, *What Color Is the Sacred?* Chicago: University of Chicago Press, 2009, and Michel Pastoureau's several color histories, especially *Black. The History of a Color*, Princeton: Princeton University Press, 2008.

12. Cayetano Cabrera y Quintero wrote of "singular" copies of matrix images in *Escudo de armas de México: Celestial protección de esta nobilíssima ciudad, de la Nueva España, y de casi todo el Nuevo Mundo . . .*, Mexico: Vda. de Joseph Bernardo de Hogal, 1746, p. 199.

13. Most prints were meant to "fix" a devotional image, belief, or biblical passage in the minds of the faithful. Not surprisingly, the Spanish verb "estampar" (to imprint), from which estampa derives, was commonly used in this context, as in "La devoción de la Virgen Santísima y su Rosario quedó estampada en los corazones de todos," AGN Jesuitas II-4 exp. 19, fol. 4. Clara Bargellini finds an early example, from around 1600, of Jesuits in Mexico City distributing prints of saints at the church of their College of San Pedro y San Pablo for this purpose, "Engraving," in *Lexikon of the Hispanic Baroque: Transatlantic Exchange and Transformation*, ed. Evonne Levy and Kenneth Mills, Austin: University of Texas Press, 2013, p. 121.

14. For an extensive checklist of colonial era woodcuts and engravings, see W. Michael Mathes, "Registries of Woodcuts and Copper Engravings in New Spain: 1544–1821," n.p., CD-rom, 2003.
15. For example, Peter Parshall, "Prints as Objects of Consumption in Early Modern Europe," *Journal of Medieval and Early Modern Studies* 28: 1 (winter 1998), 19–36; David Landau and Peter Parshall, *The Renaissance Print, 1470–1550*, New Haven: Yale University Press, 1994; Peter Parshall and others, *Origins of European Printmaking: Fifteenth-Century Woodcuts and Their Public*, New Haven: Yale University Press, 2005; and William B. MacGregor, "The Authority of Prints: An Early Modern Perspective," *Art History* 22: 3 (September 1999), 389–420. For a related article on colonial Mexico, Kelly Donahue-Wallace, "Picturing Prints in Early Modern New Spain," *The Americas* 64: 3 (January 2008), 325–349, which treats religious prints depicted in clerical portraits and the famous *casta* paintings mainly as markers of social standing.
16. Parshall, "Prints as Objects," p. 20.
17. Javier Portús and Jesusa Vega, *La estampa religiosa en la España del Antiguo Régimen*, Madrid: Fundación Universitaria Española, 1998.
18. The terminations of the Inquisition in the second decade of the nineteenth century were followed by a veritable flood of new and more various imagery, which suggests that even desultory policing by the courts served to slow circulation of subversive or otherwise unacceptable prints. Of course, the courts were not an independent variable at the time. The steep decline of royal political power in Spain after 1808, the end of Spanish rule in Mexico beginning in 1810, and the first struggles over freedom of the press may be more to the point.
19. For these patterns, see Portús and Vega, *La estampa religiosa*, pp. 159, 214, 253, and 255.
20. As Michael Baxandall put it, Christian images were meant to "tell a story in a clear way for the simple; in a . . . memorable way for the forgetful; and with full use of all the emotional resources of the senses of sight," *Painting and Experience*, p. 41. Baxandall was summarizing a passage from John of Genoa's late thirteenth-century *Catholicon* as a convenient reference point for the three purposes: images as a means of instruction and learning for "simple people"; images as visual aids to remembering the mysteries of the faith; and images serving to excite feelings of tenderness, devotion, and contrition.
21. Alonso Alberto de Velasco, *Exaltación de la Divina Misericordia en la milagrosa renovación de la soberana imagen de Christo . . .*, Mexico: Reimpresa en la Oficina de los Herederos del Lic. D. Joseph de Jáuregui, 1790, p. 1.
22. Eguiara's borrowed pithy phrase comes from his aprobación for Antonio Manuel de Folgar's sermon, *La mayor fortuna de la América, nacida de gozar un Santo Christo renovado . . .*, Mexico: Francisco de Rivera Calderón, in 1731. The Paredes quotation comes from his 1747 sermon, *La authéntica del patronato, . . . a la Santíssima Virgen María Señora Nuestra en su imagen marabillosa de Guadalupe*, Mexico: María de Rivera, 1748. A century earlier the same view of images and spectacles occurred to Puebla's Bishop Juan de Palafox y Mendoza when he wrote about instructing Indians: "por los ojos entra la fe a estos pobres naturales," quoted in Sor Cristina de la Cruz de Arteaga y Falguera, *Una mitra sobre dos mundos: la de don Juan de Palafox y Mendoza, Obispo de Puebla de los Ángeles y de Osma*, Puebla: Gobierno del Estado, 1992, p. 17.

23. Pablo Patiño, *Disertación crítica-theo-filosófica sobre la conservación de la santa imagen de Nuestra Señora de los Ángeles* ..., Mexico: Mariano Joseph de Zúñiga y Ontiveros, 1801, numbered p. 1.
24. During the last years of the colonial period Mexico City printers produced roughly five times as many works as did printers in Puebla. See Dorothy Tanck de Estrada, "Imágenes infantiles en los años de la Insurgencia. El grabado popular, la educación y la cultura política de los niños," *Historia Mexicana* LIX: 1 (2009), 228. By the late eighteenth century some printed material was also produced in several other cities, especially Guadalajara and Antequera.

    The outstanding recent work on colonial printmakers and prints is Kelly Donahue-Wallace's doctoral dissertation, "Prints and Printmakers in Viceregal Mexico City," University of New Mexico, 2000 and several articles by her based on additional research, especially "Publishing Prints in Eighteenth-Century Mexico," *Print Quarterly* XXIII: 2 (2006), 134–154. Her work informs what I write here about production, but she does not attempt a close study of religious prints. She does discuss prints of St. Josaphat that protested the expulsion of the Jesuits in 1767 in "*La casada imperfecta*: A Woman, a Print, and the Inquisition," *Mexican Studies/Estudios Mexicanos* 18: 2 (summer 2002), 231–250. She has also published an article about two portraits of local holy people – "Saintly Beauty and the Printed Portrait," *Aurora: The Journal of the History of Art* 8 (2007), 1–14; and her dissertation includes a brief discussion of how late colonial printers continued to cater to the Baroque tastes of their popular audience even as neoclassical forms and a more contemplative piety came to be favored by elites. A still-useful older treatment is Manuel Romero de Terreros, *Grabados y grabadores en la Nueva España*, Mexico: Ediciones Arte Mexicano, 1948. On print culture and religion in New Spain, see also Pierre Ragon, "Imprentas coloniales e historia de las devociones en México (siglos XVII y XVIII)," *Revista Europea de Información y Documentación sobre América Latina* 8: 9 (1998), 33–42.
25. Donahue-Wallace, "Prints and Printmakers in Viceregal Mexico City," p. 174.
26. AGN Inquisición 1103 exp. 4 and 1181 exp. 7, documents for 1775–1779 the "tienda pública de devocionarios" run by Manuel Antonio Valdés for the Zúñiga y Ontiveros printing house. It includes a list of works sold in the store, including novena booklets for the Mexican shrines of Nuestra Señora de Talpa (Jalisco), Nuestra Señora de San Juan de los Lagos (Jalisco), and Nuestra Señora del Pueblito (Querétaro).
27. Small religious prints were incorporated into two other common kinds of documents produced in the colonial period. Those who purchased a *bula de la Santa Cruzada* received a certificate that usually displayed a small printed image of a saint. These certificates were striking visual documents since they were stamped with several imposing seals of the ecclesiastical offices that approved publication of the *bula*, giving the document an aura of official authenticity. A *bula* usually came with an indulgence or dispensation of some kind; for example, the certificate confirming the 1784–1785 *bula* published for New Spain, "Sumario de la Bula de la Santa Cruzada, por la qual ha concedido ... el uso de huevos y lacticinios en tiempo de Quaresma ... Provincias de Nueva España MDCCLXXXIV y MDCCLXXXV." Small religious prints also appeared on broadsides announcing the public defense of a university thesis. The saint or advocation or miraculous image of the Virgin Mary or Christ depicted had been chosen by the candidate as his celestial benefactor.

28. Tanck, "Imágenes infantiles," p. 228. For publications from Puebla during the same period, Tanck calculates that 31 percent included at least one print.
29. AHCM num. de inventario 3895 exp. 2. For another example, Joseph Manuel Ruiz y Cervantes claimed in 1791 that in the Diocese of Antequera virtually "everyone in our towns has at least a paper print" of Nuestra Señora de Xuquila, *Memorias de la portentosa imagen de Nuestra Señora de Xuquila* ..., Mexico: Zúñiga y Ontiveros, 1791, chapter 6.
30. Lorenzo del Santísimo Sacramento, *El común bienhechor para todos es el Señor de los desconsolados* ..., Mexico: Imprenta Nueva de la Bibliotheca Mexicana, 1755, pp. 45–46.
31. Most novena booklets were devoted to individual saints, often the lesser known who were regarded as specialist intercessors or personal patrons, such as San Bonifacio, Santa Heduvige, Beato Juan Francisco Regis, San Estanislao Kostka, Santa Quiteria, Santa Catalina de Suecia, Santa Ines de Monte Pulquiano, and Santa Lidubina. The Getty Research Institute Library's collections include three nonce volumes containing forty-two Mexican novena booklets from the eighteenth century that give a sense of the range of subjects, including shrine images, and the prints (usually woodcuts) that accompanied them: "Novenas, 1715–1776" (BX 2170.N7), "Novenas, 1720–1771" (BX2170. N7 N7 1720), and "Varias novenas, 1754–1807" (BX2170.N7 V37 1754).
32. As Antonio Rubial García suggests in "Invención de prodigios. La literatura hierofánica novohispana," *Historias* 69 (enero–abril 2008), 121.
33. Another example of an unchanging text with a new print for the various editions is Alonso Alberto de Velasco's *Exaltación de la Divina Misericordia* (seven editions between 1699 and 1820).

Some fine prints were used for gifts to officials and distinguished citizens. For example, in 1765 the chaplain of the shrine of Nuestra Señora de San Juan de los Lagos sent prints and little cakes with an image of the Virgin stamped on them to members of the Audiencia in Guadalajara and received back a note of thanks: "todos muy agradecidos," AGN Alcabalas 105 exp. 1 fol. 56.
34. Copperplate engravings were introduced in the early seventeenth century, but did not become the most common source of prints in Mexico City until the 1730s.
35. It was more common to find prints from an engraving used in several publications, but for an example of a crude woodcut of Our Lady of Guadalupe used several times, see William B. Taylor, *Our Lady of Guadalupe and Friends: The Virgin Mary in Colonial Mexico City*, Berkeley: Morrison Library Inaugural Address Series, 1999.
36. In 1776, de la Rosa recollected that 3,000 or 4,000 prints were made in 1743 from Troncoso's engraving. He thought that if the plate were found, more prints could be made from it.
37. The Getty Research Center's collection of forty-nine Mexican religious prints, 1700–1830, is unusual in that most are of the common, inexpensive "de a medio" single-sheet kind that generally do not survive, or at least are rarely found in research libraries and other public collections. Another collection of 103 religious prints in the special collections of the Instituto Nacional de Antropología e Historia's library in the National Museum of Anthropology also includes examples of small, mass-produced prints of shrine images from the eighteenth and early nineteenth centuries, Colección Antigua 811. My thanks to Paul Ramírez and Karen Melvin for sharing their photographs of prints from these collections.

38. "papel fino de marquilla" – fine paper of a particular size known as *marquilla*, measuring about 16" × 23". The cachet of a European imprint might give an extra boost to a local devotion. Francisco de Florencia (or perhaps it was his eighteenth-century collaborator Juan Antonio de Oviedo) was convinced that devotion to Puebla's Nuestra Señora de la Defensa was enjoying greater popularity, thanks to a supply of fine prints of the statue imported from Flanders ("una hermossísima lámina de Flandes") and a medal struck in Rome, *Zodíaco mariano* . . ., Mexico: Colegio de San Ildefonso, 1755, p. 176.

Prints imported from Europe remained important in eighteenth-century New Spain. Many were secular in subject matter, but others were of saints and a small number depicted famous shrine images in Spain, such as Nuestra Señora de Aranzazú and Nuestra Señora del Pilar de Zaragoza. Other than some fine prints of Our Lady of Guadalupe, few of the prints imported from Europe depicted New World shrine images. Susan Deans-Smith pointed out this continuing importance of European religious prints in Mexico in a personal communication based on her research into Inquisition activity monitoring imported literature. Juan Martín Manchola, for example, imported 34,100 prints of various saints in 1810. And the manifest for merchant Pedro Mugüerza's smaller shipment of books, maps, and prints in 1795 indicates that he imported 494 religious prints. Among them were ten of the Crucifixion, ten of the Ecce Homo, ten of Jesús Nazareno, eighteen of the infant Jesus, eight of Veronica's veil, one of the Holy Family, eighteen of Mary Immaculate, twenty-eight of the Mater Dolorosa, two of Nuestra Señora del Pilar, eight of Santa María de la Cabeza, eight of Nuestra Señora del Carmen, sixteen of Nuestra Señora de la Merced, eight of Nuestra Señora de la Misericordia, ten of the Divina Pastora, six of Nuestra Señora de Guadalupe, eight of "Our Lady," eight of the Virgin Mary and San Antonio, three of María Magdalena, one hundred of San Luis Gonzaga, four of San Pedro Alcántara, eight of Santa Casilda, four of Santa Bárbara, eight of San Isidro, and eight of San Roque, AGN Inquisición 1264. How choices were made about what and how many printed images to import deserves study.

39. Florencia and Oviedo, *Zodíaco mariano*, p. 94. Promotion through the distribution of prints was an old story in New Spain. Alonso Franco, a seventeenth-century Dominican chronicler, noted that the Archbishop of Mexico's office in 1614 ordered that the recent miracles of the image of Nuestra Señora de la Piedad, housed in a Dominican convent on the outskirts of Mexico City, be preached and published, and that prints describing several miracles be distributed, *Segunda parte de la Historia de la Provincia de Santiago de México, Orden de Predicadores en la Nueva España* [1645], ed. José María de Agreda y Sánchez, Mexico: Imprenta del Museo Nacional, 1900, p. 109.

40. An example of Franciscan friars from one of the missionary colleges distributing prints and devotional booklets containing prints during their revival missions is mentioned below and illustrated in Figure 3.11. Parish priests also distributed prints on their own. For example, Domingo Joseph de la Mota, the pastor of Yautepec, Morelos wrote in his professional resumé in the early 1760s that "to attract and appease the natives he distributed a quantity of catechisms, other printed materials, prints, rosaries, and devotional books," collection of resumés from the 1762 competition for vacant parishes in the Archdiocese of Mexico, JCB B760 A973i. The priest who traveled as an alms collector for the shrine of Nuestra Señora de San Juan de los Lagos from 1756 to 1764 was said to have carried "gran número de panecitos, rosarios, estampas de Nuestra

Religious Prints and Their Uses 443

Señora de San Juan, novenas, y un impreso llamado Esclavitud a María Santíssima," Pedro M. Márquez, *Historia de Nuestra Señora de San Juan de los Lagos, Jal.*, 5th ed., San Juan de los Lagos: Imprenta "Alborada," 1966, following p. 145.

Clara Bargellini adds to an understanding of how religious paintings circulated from Mexico City to the north, thanks to Jesuit missionaries in her "Painting for Export in Mexico City in the Seventeenth and Eighteenth Centuries," in *Art in Spain and the Hispanic World: Essays in Honor of Jonathan Brown*, ed. Sarah Schroth, London: Paul Hoberton and Center for Spain in America, 2010, pp. 285–301.

41. Evidence of the commercial activities of Mexico City booksellers outside the city is spotty, but there is the inventory of printed matter taken by José María Berrueco from his store in the capital to the annual fair at the shrine of San Juan de los Lagos in 1804, in Carmen Castañeda, "Libros como mercancías y objetos culturales en la feria de San Juan de los Lagos, México, 1804," *Estudios del Hombre* 20: 1 (2005), 87–103. His wares included nearly 2,000 books of different sizes and subjects, both secular and devotional, and more than 1,000 other printed works, including 660 "assorted" novena booklets.

42. Small-time peddlers may have been important distributors of religious prints, although not as important as alms collectors. References to them are rare and, in my research, always incidental. For example, in the 1804 criminal record that charged José Antonio Morán with the murder of Antonio Gervasio, Indian of Jocotán, on the road from Guadalajara to Cuquío, Jalisco shortly before Easter, the victim's traveling companion was identified as Antonio Abad, Indian of Colotlán. Abad testified that he was going to Jocotán from Guadalajara in hopes of selling the "seven dozen small prints" he carried with him. For his part, Antonio Gervasio was carrying a supply of wax for Holy Week observances in his hometown, BPE AJANG, bundle of criminal records labeled "1800–1805."

43. Along with their Franciscan pastors, settlers and traders who had traveled south on business would have brought these prints back to New Mexico. Claire Farago mentions the circulation of prints from northern Mexico to New Mexico in the eighteenth and nineteenth centuries that served as models for locally made statues or paintings in "Prints and the Pauper: Artifice, Religion, and Free Enterprise in Popular Sacred Art," in *Art and Faith in Mexico: The Nineteenth-Century Retablo Tradition*, ed. Elizabeth Netto Calil Zarur and Charles Muir Lovell, Albuquerque: University of New Mexico Press, pp. 47–55. Kelly Donahue-Wallace discusses hide paintings made in New Mexico during the eighteenth century that were modeled on prints of miraculous images from central and western Mexico, "The Print Sources of New Mexican Colonial Hide Paintings," *Anales del Instituto de Investigaciones Estéticas* 68 (1996), 43–69.

For close study of a European print that became the model for the shrine image of Nuestra Señora del Pueblito near the city of Querétaro, see Cristina Cruz González, "Landscapes of Conversion: Franciscan Politics and Sacred Objects in Late Colonial Mexico," Ph.D. dissertation in Art History, University of Chicago, 2009.

44. See AGN Inquisición 389 exp. 3, "cartas acordadas por inquisidores generales sobre expurgatorio de libros prohibidos, estampas, medallas . . ." 1771–1640. The Mexican Inquisition received orders to be on the alert for unacceptable prints that had been circulating in Spain; e.g., AGN Inquisición 390 exp. 4 (1641–1651), fol. 56, edict forbidding some prints by "de Bry" (presumably Theodor de Bry) and AGN Edictos de la Inquisición, vol. IV, fol. 20, recalling a book about the life of Madre Sor Martina de

los Ángeles, a nun from Zaragoza, Spain, and all prints depicting her because she was not yet beatified.

45. Donahue-Wallace considers the question of censorship in "Prints and Printmakers in Viceregal Mexico City," Introduction and chapter 3, and "Publishing Prints in Eighteenth-Century Mexico," pp. 152–153.

46. Many of the devotional booklets were reprintings, which suggests that the text had met the test of time without objection from ecclesiastical authorities.

47. This is not to say that the Inquisition took little interest in local texts that might be heterodox. See *Catálogo de textos marginados novohispanos: Siglos XVIII y XIX*, ed. María Águeda Méndez and others, Mexico: Archivo General de la Nación/El Colegio de México/Universidad Nacional Autónoma de México, 1992.

48. "... due honor and veneration is to be given them; not, however, that any divinity or virtue is believed to be in them by reason of which they are to be venerated, or that something is to be asked of them, or that trust is to be placed in images, as was done of old by the Gentiles who placed their hopes in idols; but because the honor which is shown them is referred to the prototypes which they represent," 25th session, "on the invocation, veneration, and relics of saints, and on sacred images," *Canons and Decrees of the Council of Trent: Original Text in English*, trans. H. J. Schroeder, OP, St. Louis and London: B. Herder Book Co., 1941, pp. 215–216.

49. *Canons and Decrees of the Council of Trent*, pp. 216–217.

50. Carlos Borromeo, *Instrucciones de la fábrica y del ajuar eclesiásticos*, ed. and trans. Bulmaro Reyes Coria, Mexico: UNAM, 1985. Periodically, the Inquisition and bishops issued decrees calling for the removal of images that did not meet these criteria, but I have found little to suggest that they were widely enforced.

51. Ecclesiastical judges routinely cautioned local officials not to be too eager to enforce sweeping directives against unseemly images. Better to condone a vulgar practice, if necessary, than chance a rebellion was the message; e.g., Bancroft MSS 72/57m, box 3, folder, 20, file of compliance letters from parishes in Mexico and Guatemala, 1767–1768. The judges were more likely to order that a statue be clothed in a more decorous way than to order it removed, destroyed, or reconditioned.

52. A rare example of the latter – two 1768 prints of San Josaphat that indirectly protested the expulsion of the Jesuits – is discussed by Kelly Donahue-Wallace in "La casada imperfecta." Church authorities regarded another late colonial print circulating in Chiapas in 1743 as even more dangerous, and they moved to collect and destroy all known copies. The print depicting a Madonna and Child was said to be "the Virgin of Cancuc," associated with the Tzeltal Rebellion that had convulsed the highlands of Chiapas in 1712. Dutch traders operating on the coast of Laguna de Términos, Campeche, and Tabasco apparently distributed the prints in Tabasco and Campeche. Authorities in Chiapas were worried that the print was meant to incite Indians in their region to rise up again, AGN Inquisición 801 exp. 9, fols. 108–114. I have not found a copy of this print in the archive of the Inquisition or elsewhere.

53. For example, prints of an as yet unrecognized Saint Simon in 1615, AGN Inquisición 311 exp. 2A, of Puebla's Catarina de San Juan in 1691, and of a pious Spanish woman in 1716, AGN Inquisición Edictos I fol. 20, and Antonio Rubial García, "Cuerpos milagrosos: Creación y culto de las reliquias novohispanas," *Estudios de Historia Novohispana* 18 (1998), 23.

54. AGN Inquisición 699 exp. 7; AGN Inquisición 933 exp. 3.
55. The administrative record leading to the demolition of the shrine is filed in AGN Clero Regular y Secular 215 exp. 29. There is a copy of the bishop's April 16, 1810 edict that pilgrimages to Huaquechula cease and all "relics" depicting the cross be turned over to one's parish priest in CONDUMEX, Col. Enrique R. Cervantes, Fondo XVI-1 Colección Enrique A. Cervantes 1810 GON, A. No. 33163-C.
56. On alms collections for image devotions by Indian *demandantes*, see Raffaele Moro Romero, "¿Una práctica poco visible? La demanda de limosnas 'indígena' en la Nueva España del siglo XVIII (Arzobispado de México)," *Estudios de Historia Novohispana* 46 (enero-junio 2012), 115–172. He does not discuss the dissemination of prints.
57. The Bancroft Library acquired this case record in 1996: 96/95m vol. 17, exp. 4. My thanks to Paul Ramírez for bringing it to my attention and sharing his impressions.
58. The wares confiscated from Manjarres at the time of his arrest in 1793 included three homemade booklets of prayers for peasant farmers; a four-page printed testament of Louis XVI in 1792, translated into Spanish and reprinted in Puebla; a printed broadside of verses praising the glory of Most Holy Mary; a one-page printed table of instructions for learning to count; a small novena booklet with a woodcut dedicated to Mary Immaculate, reprinted in Puebla by Pedro de la Rosa's printshop in 1792; and three quarto size pages of love poems, each with four ten-line stanzas and one of five lines, in Manjarres's hand. Another item, a printed *calendario manual y guía de forasteros* for Madrid in 1787, is not included in the Inquisition file.
59. Manjarres was not asked where he had acquired the little woodcut prints used in his homemade prayer booklets, but Rosa is mentioned in this case record, several of Rosa's publications were in Manjarres's inventory when he was arrested, and Rosa had been asked by Manjarres to serve as a cosigner for bail when he was arrested the first time in 1791 or 1792 for peddling superstitious literature. Rosa declined to cosign.
60. Usually depicted behind a yoke of oxen with an angel guiding the plow, San Isidro Labrador was a favorite saint of farmers in Europe and Ibero-America. San Félix Papa was particularly famous among farmers in Puebla after he was credited with protecting the wheat crops around Atlixco from worm infestations and hail damage in the late sixteenth century. See Appendix 3. Manjarres testified he had tried to sell Josef Mariano and other Indians a printed novena booklet to Nuestra Señora de Soterraña with prayers to the Virgin for only one real, but they were not interested because it did not contain prayers to any saints associated with farming.
61. There is also some variation in the farm implements depicted, and librito #2 has a drawing of a serpent on the title page (presumably a symbol of the dangers to be overcome by the prayers and pictures in the booklet).
62. Was he forty-six years old or forty-two? Did the transaction take place on the Tuesday or Wednesday of Holy Week? How many of these booklets did he make? Just one, as he initially claimed? Eight or ten, as he eventually admitted? Many more? Did he scheme and cheat in order to support his poor wife and four young children? Or was drinking his main goal? Had it been only three years since he last confessed? Was he repentant? Did he have religious convictions? Did he stand for anything at all?
63. Including escaping from the episcopal jail in Tlaxcala, hiding out in Mexico City, and continuing to make the booklets after he assured authorities he would stop.

64. Josef Mariano had spent nearly three months in Tlaxcala's ecclesiastical jail. The bishop's counsel thought he should be sent to a monastery for an unspecified term of instruction, but his recommendation was overruled by the provisor, and Josef Mariano was sent home. Bancroft MSS 96/95m, vol. 17, exp. 4, fol. 29.
65. In his informe to the bishop on April 13, 1793, the priest wrote that Indians in the district often fought during the major religious feasts, "hitting each other hard with their fists to prove who was stronger, with the victor claiming the praise of the spectators." The fighting was bad enough, he concluded, but it also led to betting on the outcome. Bancroft MSS 96/95m vol. 17 exp. 4, fol. 17r–v.
66. See, for example, Guido Munch Galindo, *Etnología del istmo veracruzano*, Mexico: UNAM, 1983, p. 120: "El día 12 empieza a llegar gran cantidad de gente a casa del mayordomo, a dejar una limosna, a cambio se les entregan las reliquias del santo, es decir, una estampa y flores perfumadas."
67. AGI México 716. As the devotion spread and became more official, with a confraternity and elite sponsorship, the print as the main devotional object was overshadowed by a fine statue that the lead boy, Pascual Campos, commissioned; see Chapter 4.
68. AGN Indiferente Virreinal caja 6005, clero regular y secular, exp. 095. I thank Gabriela Sánchez Reyes for this reference. The more common material reported in this kind of quotidian fire-quenching miracle was a splinter of the True Cross.
69. AGN Inquisición 1213 exp. 18.
70. In AGN Inquisición. These stray records include case files removed for the nineteenth-century historian Vicente Riva Palacio that were eventually returned to the archive as the "Lote Riva Palacio." Other Inquisition records removed from the archive in Mexico City during the nineteenth century or later are now in the Huntington Library (San Marino, California), the Bancroft Library of the University of California at Berkeley, the Gilcrease Museum in Tulsa, Oklahoma, and several public collections in Mexico City. A scattering of Mexican Inquisition records are also to be found in other public collections in the United States, including the Monday Collection in the Library of Congress, the University of Texas, Austin, the American Jewish Historical Society in New York City, and the University of Notre Dame. Still others probably remain in private hands in Mexico and elsewhere.
71. Less frequently documented in colonial records were the cases of images accidentally damaged that led to a penitential response. See for example, the seventeenth-century Nahuatl annals edited, transcribed, and translated by Camilla Townsend, *Here in This Year: Seventeenth-Century Nahuatl Annals of the Tlaxcala-Puebla Valley*, Stanford: Stanford University Press, 2010, p. 99: "1645. Here in this year they [accidentally] broke into pieces [images of] San Juan and Santo Cristo at Centepec, on Monday, the 11th day of the month of December. Penances were performed."
72. The earliest case I located of provocative behavior with a print dates from 1615. Ana de Aranda, an elderly peninsular tavern keeper, was accused of throwing down her print of an as yet unrecognized Saint Simon and cursing the officers of the Inquisition who came to confiscate it, AGN Inquisición 311 exp. 2A.
73. Cases of treading on a religious print placed inside one's shoe include 1759, a peninsular shopkeeper (*cajero*) with a print of Our Lady of Guadalupe, torn and soiled along the folds, which he claimed was there in his shoe for protection; 1772, a prisoner in the Guanajuato jail found to have prints of Christ and Nuestra Señora de Zapopan in his

shoes; and 1798, a man was found with a print of St. Joseph in one of his shoes. Of course, lining one's shoes with this kind of paper – virtually all religious images were printed on comparatively durable, high rag content paper – might be a practical decision meant to extend the life of a pair of shoes more than a sacrilegious desire to trample on the Virgin Mary. However, the Inquisition was inclined to suspect sacrilegious motives, AGN Inquisición 1096 exp. 9. Other cases of abuse of prints: AGN Inquisición 854 fols. 428–434 (1734), 928 exp. 7 (1759), 1373 exp. 22 (1795), and 1314 exp. 25 (1798): In 1795, a textile sweatshop worker (*obrajero*) in Tacuba, adjacent to Mexico City, was accused of using a print of the Virgin of Guadalupe as a paper towel to clean windows. In 1734, a peninsular trader was found to have a print of Nuestra Señora del Carmen crumpled up in the pocket of his riding coat. Hearsay had it that the print was stained with excrement – a charge that was not proven to the Inquisition's satisfaction. The trader claimed he kept the print in his coat for protection on the road. More scandalous was the act of an eleven- or twelve-year-old creole boy in Toluca who defecated on a print of the Ecce Homo, Toluca in 1711, AGN Inquisición 751 primera parte exp. 11. And in 1797 D. Manuel de Hoyo, a peninsular immigrant, was brought before the Inquisition for "having the temerity to say that he defecated on a print of Our Lady of Guadalupe" and for denying the apparition of Our Lady of Guadalupe, saying it was "painted on a piece of maguey fiber cloth by the Spaniards who came to conquer this kingdom, and that the Friar [Servando Teresa de Mier] had been right to preach against the widely accepted belief," AGN Inquisición 1379 exp. 13.

74. José Manuel Villalpando César, "Virgen insurgente: Nuestra Señora de Guadalupe en la Independencia de México, 12 de diciembre de 1794 – 12 de diciembre de 1824," *Memorias de la Academia Mexicana de la Historia* XL (1997), 65, citing Carlos María Bustamante.

75. AGN Archivo Histórico de Hacienda leg. 1999 exp. 5. Another case of a print or small painting on copper of Christ perspiring is mentioned by Antonio de Robles on June 15, 1680 in his journal of public events in Mexico City: "este día estando el provincial de San Agustín diciendo misa en la capilla del Noviciado de su convento, sudó una lámina de Cristo Señor Nuestro lavando los pies a San Agustín," *Diario de sucesos notables (1665–1703)*, Mexico: Porrúa, 1946, I, 284.

76. Luis Becerra Tanco, "Origen milagroso del Santuario de Nuestra Señora de Guadalupe," in *Testimonos históricos guadalupanos*, ed. Ernesto de la Torre Villar and Ramiro Navarro de Anda, Mexico: Fondo de Cultura Económica, 2005, p. 333.

77. del Santísimo Sacramento, El común bienhechor, p. 46.

78. *Novena a la prodigiosa Imagen de Nuestra Señora de la Soterraña de Nieva. Especialísima defensora de Rayos y Centellas y con especialidad para los que traen consigo su Estampa o Medalla. Y hay piadosa tradicción {sic} que donde estuviere esta Santísima Imagen en cincuenta pasos de circunferencia no caerá Rayo ni Centella*, Mexico: Mariano Ontiveros, 1818.

79. For an early seventeenth-century marvelous recovery from a life-threatening illness that was attributed to Ignatius of Loyola through a print depicting him, see AGN Jesuitas I-37, exp. 4, fol. 32, case of María Rodríguez, Valle de Puana, district of Nombre de Dios, Durango, 1618. In his 1745 history of the shrine of Nuestra Señora de Ocotlán, Tlaxcala, Manuel de Loaizaga described three miraculous healings with printed images, *Historia de la milagrosíssima imagen de Nuestra Señora de Occotlan* [1750], Tlaxcala: Instituto Tlaxcalteca de la Cultura, 2008, miracles #5, 32, 37.

De la Rosa's faith in the healing power of prints of sacred images is not an isolated case for the eighteenth century. In his devotional text for the Señor de los Desconsolados in Tehuacan de las Granadas, Puebla in 1755, Carmelite Fr. Lorenzo del Santísimo Sacramento noted that "more than 4,000 [prints] have been distributed in the Diocese of Puebla ... [and] people have been cured with the aforementioned prints," *El común bienhechor*, n.p.

80. William B. Taylor, *Marvels & Miracles in Late Colonial Mexico: Three Texts in Context*, Albuquerque: University of New Mexico Press, 2011, pp. 75–77. De la Rosa's narrative is one of the few texts that describe in considerable detail the relationship between a printed image and the circumstances of its making and use.

81. The story of this miracle was told in various colonial sources. See, for example, Fr. Agustín de Vetancurt, *Teatro mexicano. Descripción breve de los sucesos ejemplares históricos y religiosos del Nuevo Mundo de las Indias; Crónica de la Provincia del Santo Evangelio de México* [1698], facsimile edition, 2nd enumeration, Mexico: Porrúa, 1982, p. 110. For a similar case in which the Mexico City convent of San Francisco's statue of San Francisco del Milagro changed posture and saved the church from destruction in a 1711 earthquake, *Diario del viaje que hizo a la América en el siglo XVIII el P. Fray Francisco de Ajofrín*, 2 vols., Mexico: Instituto Cultural Hispano Mexicano, 1964, I, 46.

82. Story recounted in Cabrera y Quintero, *Escudo de armas de México*, pp. 154–156. Other examples of damage to an image that added to its evocative power are Nuestra Señora de la Macana, a statue of the Virgin Mary that survived New Mexico's great Pueblo Revolt in 1680, and Nuestra Señora de Xuquila in Oaxaca. For Nuestra Señora de la Macana, a native warrior attacked the statue with a *macana*, a club studded with obsidian blades, but inflicted only superficial damage to the Virgin's face, leaving a small "scar" on her forehead. According to her chronicler, the mark was later filled and painted over, but always became visible again. A macana was placed in her hands to recall her miraculous survival with only minor damage, evidence of her engagement in battle and eventual defeat of the Indian revolt. The statue was moved by Franciscans to their convent church in Tlalnepantla in the Valley of Mexico and then to the Convento Grande de San Francisco in Mexico City in 1754 when their proto-parish of Tlalnepantla was transferred to diocesan authorities. See Ilona Katzew, "The Virgin of the Macana: Emblem of a Franciscan Predicament in New Spain," *Colonial Latin American Review* 12: 2 (2003), 171–198. For Nuestra Señora de Xuquila, a fire destroyed the shrine soon after it was dedicated in 1633. The statue of the Virgin survived, but was blackened and with "llagas sacratísimas" (most sacred wounds), Ruiz y Cervantes, *Memorias ... Nuestra Señora de Xuquila*, chapter 2.

83. Joseph Ignacio Bartolache, *Manifiesto satisfactorio anunciado en la Gazeta de México (Tom. 1 Núm. 53). Opúsculo Guadalupano*, Mexico: Zúñiga y Ontiveros, 1790, facing p. 1; and Ignacio Carrillo y Pérez, *Pensil Americano florido en el rigor del invierno, o aparición de la milagrosa imagen de Guadalupe*, Mexico: Zúñiga y Ontiveros, 1797, facing p. 1.

84. While these late colonial Franciscan revival missions (*misiones de la doctrina Christiana*) were more elaborately orchestrated, traveling missions by Jesuits and Franciscans were familiar events from the mid-seventeenth century, if not earlier. A pious testimonial about Jesuit revival missions in Querétaro and Puebla between 1663 and 1676 survives in AGN Jesuitas II-4 exp. 19, "Breve relación de algunos casos memorables y raros que

se a dignado nuestro Señor obrar por medio del ministerio sancto de las doctrinas y misiones ... a hecho en algunas ciudades, pueblos, y estancias de la Nueva España desde el año de 63 hasta él de 76," 32pp. The accent in these particular missions was on restoring the peace and sanctity of the family – reconciling married couples, moving unmarried couples to seek the sacrament of marriage, leading abusive parents to repent mistreating their children – and getting many to confess for the first time in years. The "mission" at Celaya lasted thirteen days and included twenty-three sermons, six of them for public acts of contrition in which penitents processed through the streets. Here, too, the Virgin Mary was featured in the devotional exercises: "la devoción de la Virgen Ssma y su rosario quedó estampada en los corazones de todos."

85. Sometimes the missionary friars stayed longer. In one late eighteenth-century revival mission to the parish of Mazatepec (Morelos), friars from the Pachuca college stayed for three months, AGN Clero Regular y Secular 192 exp. 3.

86. Or as a respectful salutation that recognized a priest's authority and the interlocutor's obeisance, as in the testimony of Gabriel de Santiago that "venía el padre d. Gregorio a caballo aprisa y olló que dijo 'Ave María Santíssima,' y el gobernador respondió 'en gracia concebida,' quitándose el sombrero," AGN Clero Regular y Secular 192 exps. 11-12.

87. Isidro Félix de Espinosa, *Crónica de los colegios de Propaganda Fide de la Nueva Espana* [1746], ed. Lino Gómez Canedo, Washington: Academy of American Franciscan History, 1964, p. 291.

88. For two early examples of images kept at home, *Información juridical recibida en el año de 1582 con la que se acredita que la Imagen de María Santíssima baxo la advocación de Conquistadora que se venera en su capilla ...*, Puebla: Oficina de D. Pedro de la Rosa, 1804, deposition of the first witness, Diego de Soto; and AGN Inquisición 471 exp. 78, which describes the home altar of the mayordomo of a textile sweatshop (*obraje*), 1606.

89. Inquisition edict of December 5, 1643 forbidding private *oratorios* in homes displaying portraits of deceased persons who "murieron con opinión de virtud," AGN Inquisición Edictos, vol. 1, fol. 71. For a similar post-1625 Inquisition decree against private display of images of unrecognized saintly persons with purported relics, lit with candles or lamps, see AGN Inquisición, vol. 1, fol. 69. Another decree of the kind was issued in 1691, specifically against images of Juan de Palafox and Catarina de San Juan being venerated on illuminated altars as if they were saints, AGN Inquisición Edictos, vol. 1, fol. 15. The logic behind this ban (and, incidentally, a clue to the popularity of altars for All Souls observances) was explained in Francisco Lárraga, *Promptuario de la theología moral ...*, 32nd printing, Madrid: Herederos de Don Joseph Horta, 1751, p. 224:

se divide la adoración en pública y privada. Las adoraciones públicas se deben a los Santos Canonizados, y Beatificados, a sus Imágenes y Reliquias, aprobadas por el Ordinario. Adoración privada se puede dar a qualquiera que haya muerto en opinión de Santo; pero no sería lícito erigirle Altar, ni llevar su Imagen en procesión, ni aun retratarle con rayos y resplandores.

90. Ajofrín, *Diario* [1964 ed.], II, 164.

91. An *oratorio* or *santocal*, University of Texas, Benson Library, Mexican Manuscripts G273, 1799. There are also eighteenth-century descriptions of elite families in Mexico City assembling lavish outdoor altars in front of their homes during special religious celebrations. See, for example, "Coloquio entre sophronio y leonido sobre

materias políticas, y de estado ...," Bancroft M-M 67, 1775 manuscript, pp. 71–76, and the displays described by Carlos María Bustamante for the "visit" of Our Lady of Remedios to Mexico City in September 1810, *Memoria principal de la piedad y lealtad del pueblo de México*, Mexico: n.p., 1810, pp. 24–29.

92. The regional shrine of the miraculous Christ of Petatlán was located in the Costa Grande area about a hundred miles north of Azoyú.

93. AGN Inquisición 1223 exp. 14, 1787–1791.

94. Many devotional texts, especially novena booklets, from eighteenth-century Mexico that are found in research libraries and on the antiquarian book market lack the prints of sacred images that were part of the original publication. No doubt some were removed for other reasons, but my guess is that many found their way onto home altar displays.

95. An example of a print tipped into a printed book in the eighteenth century was included in the Swann Auction Galleries catalogue for "The Latin Americana Library of Dr. W. Michael Mathes" auction (Sale 2364) on November 6, 2014: lot 351, a print of Our Lady of Guadalupe, also by Ortuño in 1763, in a copy of Florencia and Oviedo's Zodíaco mariano.

96. "Del uso de la ha. [hermana] Cypriana García Castañiza. Me encomendara a Dios." A still later addition, tipped into the book between pages 10 and 11, is a handwritten prayer for the moment of death in the spirit of Almeida's printed text, signed by Felicitas Galarza and dated October 11, 1896.

97. Theodoro de Almeida, *Tesoro de paciencia, o consuelo del alma atribulada en la meditación de las penas del Salvador*, 4th printing, Madrid: Don Benito Cano, 1790, pp. 108, 111.

98. Several kinds of semicloistered living arrangements were to be found in Mexico City in the late eighteenth century, including beaterios or congregations of pious women who lived together in order to practice their devotions in community but did not take irrevocable religious vows; *recogimientos* of former prostitutes and female convicts sentenced to a term of reclusion and instruction; orphanages for girls; and voluntary *recogimientos* or sheltered associations for "poor but virtuous women," "chaste young Spanish women" ("doncellas españolas honestas"), or pious widows. See Susan M. Socolow, *The Women of Colonial Latin America*, Cambridge, UK and New York: Cambridge University Press, 2000, pp. 106–107, and Josefina Muriel, *Los recogimientos de mujeres: Respuesta a una problemática social novohispana*, Mexico: UNAM, 1974, *passim*.

99. For a brief discussion of this famous seventeenth-century Rosary chapel, known locally as "the eighth wonder of the world," see *Colonial Latin America: A Documentary History*, eds. Kenneth Mills, William B. Taylor, and Sandra Lauderdale Graham, Wilmington, DE: Scholarly Resources, 2002, pp. 269–271.

100. As J. Michelle Molina cautions, an emphasis on personal, interior piety was far from new to the late eighteenth century, *To Overcome Oneself: The Jesuit Ethic and Spirit of Global Expansion, 1520–1767*, Berkeley: University of California Press, 2013, pp. 202–203. Her case in point is the practice of the Jesuits' Spiritual Exercises, coming forward from the sixteenth century. The Oratorians' attention to personal devotions and the sacrament of penance for clerical members and lay affiliates alike as a complement to their practices as a group would be another case dating from the religious reforms of the sixteenth century. However, the promotion of personal piety for lay Catholics at the expense of "Baroque" devotional practices in the late

Religious Prints and Their Uses 451

eighteenth century was understood by its most enthusiastic proponents as a new, more sweeping campaign.

101. A glimpse of Almeida's published works in commerce in New Spain at the beginning of the nineteenth century is the stock of books José María Berrueco took with him to the annual fair at San Juan de los Lagos (Jalisco) in 1804. His inventory included two sets of six volumes of Almeida's writings and a copy of his *Gemidos de la Madre de Dios afligida y consuelo de sus devotos con diferentes obsequios ofrecidos a la misma señora considerada en sus Dolores y angustias*, Castañeda, "Libros como mercancías," pp. 87–116.

102. Felipe Neri, "The Apostle of Rome," was famous for founding a society of secular clergy in Rome in the 1550s. Known as the Congregation of the Oratory, or Oratorians, members lived in community and met regularly for readings, discussion, and prayer, often with interested laymen. After Neri was canonized in 1622, autonomous Oratorian communities were established in scores of Catholic centers, including Mexico City by the late 1650s. The Mexico City Oratorians received formal recognition as a Congregation by papal decree in 1701 and prospered during the eighteenth century in spite of losing their church in an earthquake in 1768 and having to relocate to the ex-Jesuit Casa Profesa on terms set by the crown that diminished their independence. Many prominent creoles in the capital were affiliated with this congregation of the Oratory. For a chronicle of the Oratorian congregation in Mexico City published in 1736, see Julián Gutiérrez Dávila, *Memorias históricas de la congregación de el Oratorio de la Ciudad de México*, 3 vols. in one, Mexico: María de Ribera, 1736. A study of the Oratorians in Mexico City by Benjamin Reed is in progress. His 2011 paper, "Devotion to Saint Philip Neri in Mexico City, 1659–1821: Religion, Politics, Spirituality and Identity," has been posted on the Internet at www.laii.unm.edu/podcasts/2011-04-29_benjamin-reed.php

103. For an appraisal of Almeida's practical spirituality in eighteenth-century context, see P. Fernando Azevedo, SJ, "A Piety of the Enlightenment: The Spirituality of Truth of Teodoro de Almeida," *Didaskalia* 5 (1975), 105–130.

104. Miguel Sánchez and Luis Becerra Tanco, two prominent Mexican Oratorians of the mid-seventeenth century, were leading publicists of the miraculous Virgin of Guadalupe.

At the end of the seventeenth century, Archbishop Aguiar y Seixas, also an Oratorian, actively promoted shrines to miraculous images and the confraternities that supported them, including the project for construction of a great new church for the Virgin of Guadalupe at Tepeyac. Velasco worked with Aguiar y Seixas to publicize and promote the tradition of the Cristo Renovado de Santa Teresa. He also authored a popular novena booklet for this miraculous image. Velasco's nomination for and decision not to accept appointment as bishop of Manila in 1699 is recorded in AHBG Serie Documentos Pontificios caja 406 exp. 5.

105. AGN Bienes Nacionales vol. 1157, exp. 1, 1731–1747.

106. As reported in the *Gazeta de México* for November 1731. The reporter wisely was noncommittal about whether a supernatural event had taken place, BIBM 4, pp. 284–285.

107. AGN Bienes Nacionales 1157 exp. 1, fol. 36r–v.

108. *Gazeta de México* for April 1734, BIBM 4, p. 456.

109. *Gazeta de México* for June 1735, BIBM 4, pp. 544–545.

110. Bancroft M-M 105, manuscript copy of José Gómez, "Diario de México," p. 121, February 25, 1780. The Christ of Burgos was venerated in replicas displayed in several eighteenth-century Mexican churches. I am not certain whether or not the chapel in question was the old one of San Joseph now rededicated to the Christ of Burgos. *Noticias de Mexico, recogidas por D. Francisco Sedano, vecino de esta ciudad desde el año de 1756 ... [compiled in 1800]*, Mexico: Impr. de J.R. Barbedillo y Cia., 1880, I, 207 seems to suggest that the chapel of San Joseph was repurposed as the chapel of the Señor de Burgos "of native Montañeses in the atrium of our father St. Francis" rather than being an entirely new one.

111. The miraculous Christ was then moved to the church of Jesús Nazareno (adjoining the hospital founded by Fernando Cortés in the sixteenth century), along with the cloth relic. According to the 1922 edition of *Terry's Guide to Mexico* (Boston: Houghton Mifflin, 1922, p. 348), there was an inscription next to the glass-encased Cristo to the effect that:

> "At 9 p.m. on the seventeenth of November 1732, during a fearsome earthquake, the figure became transformed; that it bled so copiously from the wound in its side a sheet was necessary to catch the flow, and when this sheet [still preserved] was opened it was found to be covered with small red crosses. This occurrence is duly recorded in the church records and sworn to by the clerics who lived at that period."

The stone inscription in Spanish mentioned by Terry, with the same mistaken date – 1732 instead of 1731 – can now be seen in the room housing the archive of the cathedral chapter in Mexico City's cathedral complex on the Zócalo.

112. For example, the October 1731 issue of the *Gazeta de México* reported that on October 16 "an edifying procession to complete the annual holy exercises for the atonement of Christ Our Lord went out from the main convent of Our Father St. Francis" ("salió del Convento Grande de Nuestro Padre San Francisco edificativa procesión con que anualmente se termina el ejercicio Santo de los desagravios de Christo Nuestro Señor"), BIBM 4, p. 279.

113. BNM Archivo Franciscano caja 142 doc. 1736 fol. 1r.

114. Brian Larkin, *The Very Nature of God: Baroque Catholicism and Religious Reform in Bourbon Mexico City*, Albuquerque: University of New Mexico Press, 2010, p. 162 describes Martagon as a reformer in these terms, using as his example the author's *Exercicios espirituales para desagraviar a María Santísima Nuestra Señora de los Dolores*, published in Mexico City in 1799 and reprinted in 1802 and 1807. In the same vein of piety is Martagon's better known *Manual de exercicios espirituales para practicar los santos desagravios de Christo Señor Nuestro*, published by Zúñiga y Ontiveros in Mexico City in 1770 and reprinted at least ten times between 1781 and 1810. Martagon was not the first author published in Mexico to offer spiritual exercises focused on Christ's passion and atonement for the sins of mankind. See Francisco de Soria, *Manual de exercicios, para los desagravios de Christo Señor Nuestro ...*, first published in Puebla in 1686, and reprinted in Mexico City and Puebla at least eighteen times between 1697 and 1793. Thomas à Kempis, *The Imitation of Christ*, Harmondsworth, UK: Penguin Books, 2013 also circulated in various editions during the colonial period.

115. Fernando Martagon, *Devota rogación en forma de novena para venerar a la prodigiosa imagen del Ssmo Christo de los desagravios: a fine de impetrar su singularissimo patrocinio en la*

conversion de los pecadores ..., Mexico: Zúñiga y Ontiveros, 1772. The title page of the 1782 edition of the *Manual de exercicios espirituales para practicar los santos desagravios de Christo Señor Nuestro* published by Zúñiga y Ontiveros identifies Martagon as "primer Capellán del Santísimo Christo de Burgos de Señores Montañeses." Martagon's father paid for this printing of the manual. For the side chapel, see Bancroft M-M 105, manuscript copy of José Gómez, "Diario de México," p. 121, February 25, 1780.

116. Bancroft MSS 96/95m vol. 17 exp. 4, fol. 17r.
117. On giving as a religious transaction in Christianity going back to late antiquity, see Peter Brown, *Through the Eye of a Needle. Wealth, the Fall of Rome and the Making of Christianity in the West, 350–550 A.D.*, Princeton: Princeton University Press, 2012, p. xxv. This idea helps to place consumers into Michael Baxandall's producer-centered thought about images in a market setting and his interest in the "intention" of pictures:

> In the economists' market what the producer is compensated by is money: money goes one way, goods or services the other. But in the relation between painters and cultures the currency is much more diverse than just money; it includes such things as approval, intellectual nurture and, later, reassurance, provocation and irritation of stimulating kinds, the articulation of ideas, vernacular visual skills, friendship and – very important indeed – a history of one's activity and a heredity, as well as sometimes money acting both as a token of some of these and a means to continuing performance.

Patterns of Intention: On the Historical Explanation of Pictures, New Haven: Yale University Press, 1985, p. 48.

The great challenge for the historical study of devotional prints remains contextual and synoptic: to recognize that production, promotion, and consumption in more connected ways because production, promotion, and consumption were not mutually exclusive activities. Producers and promoters often were consumers, as well as influencing consumption by others. Confraternity members devoted to a miraculous image or a special advocation of Mary or Christ were leading consumers as well as promoters, and they were not alone. Bishops, parish priests, ecclesiastical judges, members of the orders – Franciscans and Jesuits especially – and other members of the clergy used prints to arouse spiritual fervor in novenas and other devotional rites even as some of them embraced a more private, austere piety of the Word promoted by peninsular authorities in the eighteenth century. A related challenge is to keep developments in Spain (not to mention Catholic Europe more generally) and New Spain in play together. That most of the patterns of production, distribution, and use were similar, and many of the Mexican images had European origins are facts to be reckoned with, and not just in terms of whether a practice or devotion was imposed, otherwise transferred intact, or conceived on American soil. Even if Spanish America and Brazil are the main subject, it is a mistake to slight Spain and Europe, as if the transatlantic connections were either too obvious to need attention or of little consequence for local American practices.

8
Placing the Cross in Colonial Mexico

In 1960, the May 3 feast of the Invention of the Holy Cross was officially removed from the liturgical calendar in order to focus devotion to the Holy Cross on September 14, the day of the Exaltation of the Cross. But for many Mexicans this favorite feast day was a lifeline to well-being here and now and the promise of salvation hereafter. It was an essential practice, not a vestigial one.[1] Communities all over Mexico, especially rural towns and villages, observe May 3, decorating their special crosses in public and private places, attending Mass, and celebrating with food, drink, fireworks, music, and dancing.[2] Workers in the building trades were conspicuous dissenters in 1960; virtually every construction site in Mexico must have its protective cross, which is decorated and honored on May 3.[3] To steer clear of a prolonged dispute over popular traditions of faith, Mexican bishops successfully appealed to Rome for May 3 to remain a major feast there.

May 3, then, is still widely celebrated in Mexico, as well as in El Salvador and various communities in Spain, as it was during the colonial period. References to outdoor festivities on May 3 abound in early church chronicles, cathedral chapter minutes, parish archives, and civil and religious regulations and court records, especially for the seventeenth and eighteenth centuries. In Valladolid (now Morelia, Michoacán), celebrations in 1629 included a mock battle of Moors and Christians that concluded with the Christians wresting the cross from the infidels. During the festivities that year, a stone cross on the house of one of the cathedral dignitaries was damaged, leading to an inquiry into possible sacrilegious intentions.[4] This mixing of sacred and profane evidently was common, and a worry to authorities. May 3 processions with family and community crosses to hilltop Calvaries were also a common practice then. Mass was celebrated on the spot, followed by the usual festivities. Spirited gatherings mixing sorrow and joy in the presence of the cross were a concern of the Inquisition in March 1691 when it prohibited celebrations in the streets of Mexico City on the grounds that some crosses were placed in "indecent locations, and the celebrations with Mass, sermon, and processions were mixed up with farces, bullfights, and masquerades on the pretext of honoring the cross," which "results in serious scandal in the Christian Republic."[5]

References to May 3 observances outside the cities are sketchy, but they usually mention fertility rites and Calvary processions to nearby hilltops and caves.[6] Recent ethnographic descriptions elaborate on the association of the cross with nourishment and sacrifice and suggest some historical patterns of worship that invite further study.[7] Here I draw from Octavio Hernández Espejo's description of the feast of the Holy Cross in San Francisco Ozomatlán, Guerrero.[8] The festivities there from May 1 to 3 center on offerings to crosses located on the hilltop of Tepehuizco. On May 1 household and neighborhood crosses are taken up and planted, with food offerings piled high to form an altar. The faithful sing and pray on their knees, and the crosses are decorated with chains of flowers and bread. At about 3:00 a.m. hot chocolate and bread from the comestible altar are shared; shortly before dawn, mole and tamales are served; and at sunrise, the fruit and the first offering of flowers are distributed. Then the people come down from the hill and place their crosses at the town entrance. At noon they reassemble to pray a rosary and process to the church with a dancer dressed as *el tecuán* (an ocelot, the "man-eater") running and jumping in the lead. Then come the shepherdesses singing and other women praying, followed by the crosses and the band. On May 3 the dancing and drama continue, with the tecuán again the focal point. Eventually he is "killed," which Hernández Espejo thinks is not so much the victory of culture over nature as an offering to the jaguar deity and an ancient fertility rite. His informants, however, seem more inclined to focus on the crosses and explain the offerings to them as an appeal "to God Our Lord to bring us a good harvest, for the rainy season is anticipated."

What has made the May 3 feast of the Holy Cross so vital in Mexico? Part of the answer is rooted in the long-standing importance of crosses and crucifixes as both liturgical symbols and objects of devotion in religious practice. The history of figures of Christ and the cross as objects of special devotion as well as the great symbol of Christianity is a vast subject. This chapter is limited to colonial-era crosses. Particular crosses as objects of devotion and features in the landscape are another way to think about the early meeting of indigenous peoples and European Catholics, but crosses are not just about those encounters in the sixteenth century. They were a conspicuous feature of the landscape throughout the colonial period, to the extent that some communities – Cuernavaca for one – became known as "the town of crosses."[9] And they remain so. As Gilberto Giménez observed at Chalma, "the town is surrounded by hills and picturesque bluffs, all of them crowned with crosses."[10] In central and southern Mexico, these crosses in high places sometimes have formed networks of sacred sites visited by the faithful throughout the year, but especially during Holy Week and in early May.[11] Singly and together, crosses are still prominent in the Mexican landscape, bearing the imprint of colonial practices, and more.

Two especially strong patterns emerge in the devotional history of Mexican crosses described here. One is the deep appeal of more than a few particular crosses, especially natural crosses, as alive with the sacred for many kinds of people. The other is the localized setting of miraculous crosses. Their association with divine presence was inseparable from their location and protection of people living there. They were nestled in a sacred landscape that could usually be taken in with the naked eye, and their providential appeal usually did not travel far.[12]

Transatlantic Contexts

Spanish, indigenous, and colonial threads are woven into the early May 3 celebrations and complicate the meaning of colonial crosses in particular Mexican places. The Spanish, and more broadly European, features of devotion to the cross are often obscured by fascination with indigenous understandings and use of crosses before the arrival of Europeans. The cross was the universal, ever-present symbol of Christianity and a potent weapon in believers' arsenal against misfortune and diabolical deception. It was signed and displayed to mark Christian territory and appeal for divine favor; in exorcisms as the instrument of God's love and power in the perpetual struggle with Satan;[13] and to mark gravesites and places where a sudden death occurred, as a kind of memorial prayer or blessing. It was placed on or near churches (many of which had a cruciform floor plan), carried in processions, used in rituals for the dead and dying,[14] signed in sworn testimony, adopted by military orders as their insignia, and presented to the laity in paintings and devotional texts as emblematic of Christ's exemplary sacrifice to redeem humanity, bridging death and eternal life. According to Felipe Pereda's study of images and the evangelization of Muslims and Jews in southern Spain during the fifteenth century, the cross in the upraised hand of a missionary became the great symbol of the evangelizing enterprise there before it took on that meaning in America.[15] Steeped in the lore of Emperor Constantine's vision of a resplendent cross in the heavens as he went into battle at Milvia and others appearing during the Reconquista,[16] early modern Spaniards looked for signs of the cross in their wars and overseas colonization, and they found them.[17]

Pereda no doubt is right that the cross in Spain was mainly a liturgical symbol, presiding over the altar at Mass and in processions, and that crosses as cult objects were unusual. But they were not unknown. The survey of miraculous images of Christ and crosses for the Kingdom of Aragón by the

Carmelite friar Roque Alberto Faci, published in 1739, identified three prodigious crosses. One miraculously appeared on top of an oak tree on the outskirts of the Villa de Aynsa during the Reconquista. Another, venerated at Castelnon, whistled when lightning was about to strike, and was invoked to ward off storms. The third was a wooden cross in the Conceptionist convent of Miedes. The Virgin Mary was said to have given this legendary cross to one of the nuns, who presented it to her abbess when she was deathly ill. The abbess recovered and the good news spread. According to Faci, "it is said that many and singular favors have been done by this cross." His example is an exorcism.[18]

That Spaniards in America were open to the idea of particular crosses as cult objects from the beginning, even though the cross was mainly a liturgical sign, is suggested by the early seventeenth-century Franciscan chronicler and native Spaniard, Juan de Torquemada, who described one from Columbus's second voyage to the island of Española: "He ordered a cross to be made from a sturdy tree in the city of Concepción de la Vega. This cross has everywhere been greatly venerated. Its relics have been much in demand by the faithful for it is widely believed to have worked miracles, and that with its wood many sick people have been cured."[19] For early Spanish missionaries the cross was also emblematic of evangelization and martyrdom. Seventeenth-century Jesuit missionary Andrés Pérez de Ribas recounted a detail about the death of Father Gonzalo de Tapia at the hands of natives of Tovoropa (near San Luis de la Paz, Guanajuato) that he took to be a heavenly sign. Tapia's headless body was found

> stretched out in front of a Cross, with the right arm, which had been left by the killers in an amazing position. When the trunk of the body landed face down (I mean, with the chest facing the ground), the right arm was elevated above the elbow and the thumb and index finger were making the sign of the Cross; the remaining fingers were tightly closed. Although dead, the priest's arm and hand raised high the standard of the holy Cross.[20]

Even as a symbol, the cross's mystique required a certain presentation and regard. The wooden cross was a metaphorical tree of life, as Christ was the redeemer and source of eternal life, and it must be treated as such.[21] Recalling Christ's crucifixion on the hill of Calvary, it needed to be displayed "en alto," in an elevated place, because, as a sermonizer put it in 1630, "He died on high."[22] In the words of the prelates attending New Spain's Fourth Synod in 1771,

> the Holy Cross is the cross of our redemption, and we should worship it [*dar adoración de Latria*] as we do Jesus Christ. Accordingly, it should not be placed on anything profane, such as figures made of sugar or other edibles, nor should it be used on jewelry or carved or painted on boxes and coffins, or placed on the ground

where it might be trampled. Nor should it be used as a brand for livestock. Rather, it should always be placed in an elevated and decent location where it will not be treated irreverently.[23]

As the universal Christian symbol, crosses had a spatial dimension. Citing St. Jerome, among other authorities, Juan de Solórzano Pereira, a seventeenth-century Spanish commentator on the laws of the Indies, wrote: "the said four [cardinal] directions are represented by the ends of the Cross in which the mystery of our Redemption was achieved: the East shines forth at the top; the south in the left arm; the north in the right arm; and in the west the base of the trunk sinks into the earth below the feet of Christ."[24]

European and Mesoamerican ideas about trees and crosses sometimes converged as symbols, myths, and consolations. Sacred trees were shared symbols of life and sustenance, of the cycle of death and rebirth in nature and the majestic sweep of sacred time, "with the yearly shedding of its leaves in autumn and its renewal in spring time" or in the evergreen trees that remain green throughout the year.[25] Broadly speaking, European and Mesoamerican cultures embraced World Tree motifs. There is the tree of life/tree of the knowledge of good and evil in the Garden of Eden where, in St. Augustine's words, "man was furnished with food against hunger, with drink against thirst, and with the tree of life against the ravages of old age," the body and blood of Christ eventually regarded as its fruit.[26] In the meetings of cultures in New Spain, the Christian cross became closely associated with trees from both perspectives. On the Spaniards' part, there were splinters of the True Cross that brought the dead to life, the reading of Christ into the tree of life in the Garden of Eden,[27] the trees that stood for the Virgin Mary of the Immaculate Conception and her divine son, and the great wooden crosses they erected in the early colonial landscape. The first Spanish proselytizers took the cross-like native representations of sacred trees as proto-crosses that promised conversion if not prior experience of Christianity. In turn, according to Torquemada, natives embraced the Christian cross as itself a sacred tree, *Tonacquahuitl*, "which means wood that nourishes our life, . . . 'our flesh'; that is to say 'the thing that feeds our body.'"[28] More than a few colonial crosses were found in living trees in the local landscape. Spaniards' attachment to trees, too, was more than symbolic. In his visit to Sonsonate (in modern El Salvador) in 1595, young Florentine traveler, Francesco Carletti, noticed that early Spanish settlers had organized their town around the graceful, spreading branches of a huge tree that cast a shadow some sixty paces in all directions when the sun was high: "When in its shadow, the inhabitants of that city could be very comfortable in cool air. But do not think that this tree gave good fruit, either for eating or of any other kind; it was there entirely for comfort and beauty."[29] Part of the mystique of great trees in these cultures

Figure 8.1 Here in the Codex Fejervary-Mayer from central Mexico, perhaps painted in the 1510s or 1520s, cosmic order is depicted as four quarters, each supported by a cross-like celestial tree. Courtesy of the National Museums Liverpool.

came from the fact that they were older than any living thing. Their origins were obscure and they endured. As Baron Wormser writes, trees "lived slowly; they grew slowly. ... Most of what happened to them couldn't be watched or known."[30]

Cross-like forms were potent signs in Mesoamerican ritual symbolism, too, invested with cosmic significance. They described the sacred landscape that connected a deep, ancestral past with the present. Often, the cosmos was divided into four quarters, extending north, south, east, and west, with a great silk cotton (*ceiba*) tree on each side, supporting the heavens above. At the intersection of these four quarters in some representations was the World Tree of origin (*Tamoanchan*) on a hill that covered a cave and spring. This was the navel of the universe, a spatial and temporal pivot point of creation, death, and divine power connecting the sky to the underworld inhabited by spirits, including community ancestors.[31] In the 1940s when Maud Oakes asked one of the *chimanes* (shamans, spiritual leaders, and healers) of the town of Todos Santos Cuchumatán in western Guatemala what the cross signified, he responded, "The world; it [the cross] has existed since the world was born." Another chimán told her: "God said, 'This pueblo is the center of the world; it is the heart of the world.' [He] spread his arms out like a cross and turned halfway around so that he covered the four directions."[32]

Natural features, especially trees, water sources, hills, and mountains, are prominent in this cruciform cosmos. For modern Totonacs of Veracruz and Mayas of Yucatán past and present, among others, trees are "the living thing where sanctity par excellence resides," the source of sustenance, as Alfredo López Austin puts it.[33] They are associated with life-giving water and Tlaloc, lord of moisture and fertility.[34] Rain, rivers, and lakes are, in turn, paired with hills and mountains.[35] As early colonial chroniclers understood, mountains and hills were treated as living entities and exalted symbols of place and creation in Mesoamerican conceptions of the cosmos.[36] In describing the importance of hills in the Mesoamerican sacred landscape, Dominican friar Diego Durán pointed to Tlalocan, the primordial place of Tlaloc "where the clouds gather and storms with thunder, lightning and hail form."[37] Torquemada – who has much to say about colonial crosses and their sacred places – also remarked on the association of mountains with the life force and celestial power in native lore. The mountains were, he said, understood to be the dwelling places of fire, clouds, fog, rain, and earthquakes. Their caves were veritable storehouses not only of life-giving crops, deer, and water, but also of monsters and spirits. And their rocky outcroppings and stones were petrified ancestors.[38]

Just how European and Mesoamerican understandings of crosses came together in the colonial period resists easy generalization. There are always local variations, signs of change, and silences in the documentation. The symbolic meanings of the cross form were different in Europe and precolonial America – being especially about the shape of cosmic order in Mesoamerica and the symbol of Christ's redemption of humanity in Christian Europe – but even at the symbolic level there was mutual intelligibility. For both, the cross form was associated with trees – the "tree of life" for Christians;[39] the living vector of sacred time and space for Mesoamericans. And in both cases sacred trees or wooden crosses had a spatial dimension, situated at the axis mundi, on high, visible to all.[40]

Colonial Patterns

Crosses came to have an unusually important presence in colonial Mexico that goes beyond these original meanings enduring, opposing, disappearing, and combining, but few of the obvious aspects of devotion to the cross in the colonial period were uniquely American. In both Europe and America, crosses were associated with fertility, the agricultural cycle, protection, and cosmic order. What was different about American crosses was, first, the extent of their presence in the landscape.[41] (At least 21 of roughly 240 miraculous images depicting or directly referring to Christ in New Spain were simple crosses, compared to only two or three of the 104 miraculous images listed by Roque Alberto Faci for the Kingdom of Aragón in 1739.) And, second, 9 of the 21 were said to be natural crosses discovered in living trees and rocks.

Throughout the colonial period, missionaries, pastors, and bishops demonstrated their devotion to the Holy Cross and actively promoted it as an emblem of Christian practice and protection. They used it as the great symbol of providential Christianity. For early mendicant pastors, the cross was a central symbol and instrument of their evangelizing mission and struggle against the devil, whose handiwork seemed to be everywhere. For them, crosses stood for conversion and redemption, fulfilling a biblical injunction to raise high the sign.[42] Idol smashing became an early ritual practice of the friars, calling on their newly baptized flock to bring in their effigies to be destroyed in a public spectacle and replaced them with crosses.[43]

The first generations of missionaries encountered cruciform shapes in Mesoamerican imagery often enough to imagine that an earlier Christian evangelization had paved the way for their mission. Seventeenth-century Dominican chronicler Francisco de Burgoa understood natives of the Huatulco region in Oaxaca to tell him that their famous wooden cross originally had been planted by one of Christ's apostles, perhaps St. Thomas.[44] A similar story of precolonial evangelization circulated in Tlaxcala and was enthusiastically endorsed by Tlaxcalan leaders as proof that their province enjoyed special divine favor.[45] Another providential colonial narrative developed around a legendary cross on the island of Cozumel off the coast of Yucatán. In Torquemada's telling, the first Spaniards to reach the island found a cross of stone and mortar about seven feet high (10.5 *palmos*) in a very fine, fortified patio next to an imposing temple. A few years before they arrived, a priestly lord of the island was said to have prophesied that bearded white men would soon arrive from the east carrying the sign of the cross, which would vanquish the native gods. The lord ordered a stone cross for the temple precinct, saying that it was the true tree of the world. The new object supposedly attracted considerable attention and veneration.[46]

But indigenous symbols rarely were viewed in such a favorable light. More often, Catholic pastors regarded the deep connections between indigenous conceptions of nature and the sacred as threatening, misguided, or ridiculous, and attributed them to diabolical direction.[47] Early missionaries

Figure 8.2 Native demons are vanquished as the first twelve Franciscans in New Spain pray before the great wooden cross of Tlaxcala, ca. 1585. Ink drawing from Diego Muñoz Camargo, "Historia de Tlaxcala," Ms Hunter 242 f.239v, "The Erection of the First Cross." Courtesy of the Glasgow University Library, Scotland/Bridgeman Images, copyright holders.

peppered the colonial landscape with crosses as the symbol of Christian presence and protection wherever "idolatry" was suspected. Torquemada explained, "the friars ordered them to make many crosses and place them at all the intersections and entrances to their towns, and on some high hills," and then he offered a personal story from his time as warden of the Franciscan convent at Zacatlán in the Sierra Norte of Puebla.[48] Hearing about a stone draped in cloth and other offerings in the nearby mountains, he went to inspect. The mountain was shrouded in a dense fog that day, and it started to rain hard as they ascended. He came upon a large, faceless stone on a heap of smaller stones, with offerings of *copal* (incense) and small blankets. He and his companions pushed the stone off the mountain; then they cleaned the site. "We made a cross from the tallest tree we could find, and singing the hymn 'Vexilla Regis prodeunt, fulget Crucis Mysterium' ('Abroad the royal banners fly, And bear the gleaming Cross on high'), we raised it up on the spot where the idol had been," and the skies cleared. He assured his early seventeenth-century readers that the cross was still there, visible from a great distance.[49]

Colonial Indians often embraced the Christian cross and its meanings in ways that also echoed the importance of great trees in the Mesoamerican cosmic landscape and the idea that natural features and objects could attract and contain divine presence.[50] They honored and maintained the crosses placed by their Catholic pastors in the hills and mountains, on the outskirts of their settlements, on their churches, and in their cemeteries, even when a cross had originally been erected as a symbol of conquest more than of divine love and redemption;[51] and they added others to complete the sacralization of a landscape of boundaries, planted fields, springs, caves, and wondrous signs. Borrowing a phrase from the liturgy of the Mass, one colonial Indian text called the miraculous stone cross of the town of Querétaro "Our boundary marker forever and ever."[52] Crosses also came to mark the order inside colonial settlements and dwellings. Sometimes, as at Tlayacapan, Morelos, protective crosses were placed at cardinal points of the community, forming lines that crossed at the principal church.[53] Crosses were also placed at intersections of other pathways through the community, on every church and chapel, on houses, sometimes at each corner of a house, and on an altar table inside the house to signify the cosmic order of the five directions at home.[54]

Crosses also traversed and blessed the local landscape and its bounty – transported in processions into the fields and hills, to or from a particular church or shrine, or tracing the community's boundaries.[55] Torquemada remarked, "the crosses they display and carry through the streets and on the roads during Holy Week are something to behold. They take great care to decorate them with greenery and strings of roses and other flowers."[56] He went on to describe an early (1536) colonial procession during the feast of Corpus Christi at Tlaxcala in which the Christian cross became a key feature in a ritual enactment of sacred space bounded by mountains. Crosses were carried along a route strewn with sedge, cattails, and flowers of all kinds through bowers, to the accompaniment of singing and dancing. The crosses passed through one intersection with artificial mountains installed at the four corners. Each of these miniature mountains teemed with natural life – carpets of grass and flowers, various trees in leaf and bloom, mushrooms, snakes, birds, even live falcons, owls, deer, hares, rabbits, and coyotes, and men on the hunt, hiding in the vegetation with their bows and arrows. One of the mountains featured Adam and Eve; another, the Temptation of Christ; a third, St. Jerome; and the fourth, St. Francis.[57]

Great wooden crosses were erected at the friars' behest soon after the conquest. As Torquemada put it, "It is God's desire that not only should His Most Holy Son Jesus Christ, Our Lord, be worshiped and known as our Redeemer, but that the wood [of the Cross] where this great benefit of our Redemption was achieved be held in the highest esteem and regard."[58] Several of the early wooden crosses were famous in their own right as numinous objects. The earliest of these most celebrated crosses, in Torquemada's telling, was at the site where the Tlaxcalan lords first received Cortés and his men (Figure 1.1, in Chapter 1). Cortés noticed this cross the night after that meeting, and no one could say how it got there. That same night a bright light in the form of a cross could be seen over Tenochtitlan all the way from Tlaxcala, and a native Tlaxcalan priest saw the devil in the form of a pig scurry from a nearby temple. According to other early colonial accounts of the legend, a cloud descended on this cross while the Tlaxcalan lords deliberated over whether to ally with the Christians, and they took it to be a sign.[59]

Also in the 1520s a huge cross, "taller than any tower in Mexico,"[60] was erected in the patio of the first Indian chapel in Mexico City, San José de los Naturales. It was made from an ancient tree harvested in the woods of Chapultepec, the royal retreat where Moctezuma's collection of wild animals was kept. Torquemada, citing native elders, says "the Mexicans took it to be a deified thing; in the time of their heathendom, they cleaned and pruned it often and with the greatest care. And after the friars came and settled, they cut down this ... tree and raised a cross made from it in the middle of the [chapel's] patio."[61] The placement of this great tree-cross recalls the precolonial festival to Tlaloc, the god of water, in which a small forest was erected in the patio of the temple; the tallest of the trees, called *tota* (our father), was considered lord of the mountains, forests, and waters.[62] This cross apparently was treated as a cult object even after it fell over during a storm in 1571. Splinters from it were widely distributed as relics.[63] Early Franciscan chroniclers Motolinía and Torquemada also singled out a cross at Cholula for a special place in the drama of evangelization and celestial struggle during the sixteenth century. The first friars destroyed the temple on top of Cholula's great pyramid and replaced it with a "very tall" cross, which would later be replaced by a chapel to Our Lady of los Remedios, much visited and revered by local Indians. The first cross was struck by lightning, as was its replacement. The friars took this as a sign that the devil was trying to defend his place at all costs.[64]

Maud Oakes's account of the two crosses in the churchyard of the western Guatemalan town of Todos Santos Cuchumatán provides an ethnographic perspective on why large wooden crosses were enthusiastically received by colonial Indians, building on the precolonial symbolism of great trees, cosmic order, and time. Oakes asked the Chief Prayermaker of the community why there were two crosses, one "tall and commanding in appearance, made of ancient wood, the other one made of stone and much smaller." He told her that a few years earlier the *intendente*, a Guatemalan outsider appointed by the state government to oversee local affairs, ordered that the venerable wooden cross be pulled down and replaced with a smaller one made of cement. The Prayermaker told him the people did not want the new cross and begged him not to remove the great wooden cross because it belonged to the ancestors. But the intendente ignored him and replaced the old cross with the new one. Soon an ill wind blew in, the weather turned very cold, and the rains ceased. There was no maize harvest that year; animals and people were starving. The prayermakers went to the mountaintops to pray for rain, but to no avail. Then the people went to the *chimanes* (shamans) and asked them to perform their rituals for rain. The chimanes

Figure 8.3 The two crosses of Todos Santos Cuchumatán, Guatemala, photograph by Hans Namuth. Courtesy of the Center for Creative Photography, University of Arizona.

consulted the *dueño del cerro* (the spirit of the mountain) to find out why the people were being punished. The *dueño* answered: "You have cast down the big cross ... that came with the creation of the world. ... Put the big cross up again in the same place. Otherwise all the people and all the animals will die." While they were re-erecting the ancient cross a new intendente threatened to arrest them for using wood without permission. They explained why they had to replace the cross, and added, "If you imprison us, you will win and we will win. Send us to prison; we have no fear." The intendente let them proceed, but insisted that the new cement cross be left in place; and so there are two crosses.[65] The wooden cross was understood to embody the ancestors and represent the world order both in its form and in its antiquity.[66]

The crosses celebrated as wonder-working objects of devotion often were said to appear fully formed in the forests and wooded hilltops, not crafted by human hands. Trees shaped like crosses were especially revered, such as the Cruz de Maye near Ixquilipan, Hidalgo, the cross of Teccistlan near Jocotepec, Jalisco, the Señor del Encino of Yahualica, Jalisco, the providential cross celebrated in the Nahuatl "Códice Municipal" of Cuernavaca, which appeared when a black zapote tree was cut open, the cross of Jacona, Michoacán discovered inside a guayabo tree, the cross of Tamazula, Jalisco, found in the root of a huizache bush, or the cross in front of the new shrine church of Our Lady of Guadalupe at Tepeyac in 1709, with its inscription, "This cross was found on a mountain in the form you see it here."[67] Other reports of natural crosses discovered inside logs and rocks were celebrated even in the late colonial period, when official policing of miracles and miraculous images intensified.[68] If not discovered under mysterious circumstances, they were said to tremble or show other signs of vitality and resist destruction.[69] Celebrated crosses sometimes were painted green, apparently as a sign that they were alive with the sacred in the present and remote past as well as symbolizing resurrection and the promise of life everlasting.[70] Examples of natural and animated crosses come from various parts of Mexico and different times during the seventeenth and eighteenth centuries, but they were most often reported in Hidalgo, Querétaro, Yucatán, Morelos, Michoacán, and Jalisco. Augustinian pastors were prominent in most of these areas, and their order was especially devoted to the cross, but there was no Augustinian *deus ex machina* at work in this clustering of living crosses. All the orders, as well as the diocesan clergy, were devoted to the cross; Yucatán was a Franciscan, not an Augustinian, pastoral preserve;[71] and local enthusiasms were always a shaping, if not determining, consideration.[72] Natural crosses have had a very important place in Maya ritual life, and the fact that that they are often clothed and painted green suggests that they are more than liturgical symbols. They have long been prized in Yucatán and

Figure 8.4 A living cross depicted on the cover of an Indian confraternity book from Rancho Santa Bárbara, a small settlement near Dolores Hidalgo, Guanajuato in the late eighteenth century. It shows a draped cross with jaguar markings, sprouting vines and flowers from its base. AGN Tierras 1332. Courtesy of the Archivo General de la Nación, Mexico.

Chiapas, but whether colonial-era devotees thought they spoke or were animated in other ways is not clear. The literature on the famous speaking crosses of the Caste War period after 1847 suggests that their fame as conveyors of spoken messages dates from that period.[73]

Miraculous crosses made of wood predominate, and wooden ceremonial objects were much esteemed in precolonial times, particularly in Yucatán,[74] but they are more perishable than stone crosses and few that were left outdoors lasted long. The carved stone crosses that were placed in church courtyards early in the colonial period survive in greater number, and their survival speaks both to the durability of the material and to the care taken to preserve them. Some clearly were treated as cult objects, such as the stone cross of Querétaro featured in the next section. Whether all or most of the early atrium crosses were regarded as numinous in themselves more than symbols of Christ's Passion is not clear. María de los Ángeles Rodríguez Álvarez thinks not. She suggests that they had two functions: as symbols of faith, and as the special insignia of cemeteries.[75] And a directive from a council of Mexican prelates in 1539 that crosses should be smaller, expertly crafted, and made of stone, if possible, suggests that they were encouraged by the clergy as a substitute for the monumental wooden crosses of the first years.[76] Samuel Edgerton and Jaime Lara, on the other hand, posit that the function and symbolism of these churchyard crosses was as much indigenous as Christian, representing the precious center of creation in a schematic quincunx framed by the four-cornered walled courtyard.[77]

Carol Callaway also found parallels between these symbol-studded stone crosses and precolonial understandings of space, time, and sacrifice that may suggest they were treated as cult objects. Callaway's most compelling examples have to do mainly with precolonial conceptions transposed into Christian terms of sacrifice and salvation. In an unusual cross from Topiltepec, Oaxaca, precolonial forms are used to represent Christ's death as the arrow sacrifice of a figure dressed as Xipe Totec, "an earth god associated with the moon, young corn, rain, and fertility."[78] Her other example is a cross from Tepeapulco, Hidalgo with a crown of thorns at the intersection that looks "like the rays of a pre-Columbian image of the sun," with a recessed center that may have held an obsidian disk, "a characteristic of atrium crosses that follows a pre-Columbian custom of adding such a stone to give them the force of life."[79] As with many of these early atrium crosses, since the body of Christ is not represented, blood appears to spurt from the arms and base of the cross, so that the stone itself bleeds. Tepeapulco was the home of at least four early stone crosses of this kind. The fact that one of the Tepeapulco stone crosses was sent to Mexico City in 1648 to be displayed in the cemetery of the cathedral facing the front entrance may suggest some special devotional status of the object in itself since it was mentioned then as "this wondrous cross." But apparently this cross was in poor repair when Archbishop Mañozca found it in Tepeapulco's cemetery during his pastoral visit, and in its new location it seems to have served more as a fittingly imposing symbol and beautiful curiosity than as a cult image.[80] If these striking, symbol-laden stone crosses in rural communities *were* important objects of devotion, it is puzzling that some of the many others displayed in church atriums were not described as such in colonial documentation, in contrast to other kinds of stone and wooden crosses that were said to be numinous. Perhaps those early sculptural crosses were rarely mentioned as treasured objects of devotion because their appeal was rooted in a particular community, expressing a very localized sense of being situated at the axis mundi. In any event, we know little about how they were regarded and used, whether in their original locations or transplanted.

To one side of the cathedral in Mexico City, across from the palace of the Marqueses del Valle (which became the offices of the Monte de Piedad pawnshop founded by the Conde de Regla in the 1770s), was another celebrated cross, a large wooden one on a stone pedestal that was a gathering place for annual observances on the May 3 feast of the Holy Cross beginning in the early seventeenth century.[81] By 1640 celebrations at what was by then known as the Cruz de los Talabarteros had been institutionalized with a confraternity, indulgences, and a procession featuring a "splendidly outfitted infantry company." Licenses were issued to collect alms in the neighborhood and celebrate Mass at the site on May 3, even though ecclesiastical authorities at the time were of two minds about whether to promote this feast day because of the way crosses were being put to use.[82] Then in 1643 a fire in the adjacent palace that consumed the legal records, theater set (including a "Cielo" or depiction of heaven, possibly painted on canvas), and other props for the May 3 observances led to decisive action by members of the cathedral chapter to promote the devotion rather than letting it lapse. With authorization by the city council, the cathedral chapter, and the Marqués del Valle, the pedestal and cross were covered with a peaked roof supported by six stone pillars, forming a hexagon roughly thirty feet across. While the sides of the structure were still open, the intent was both to give the site a more imposing presence, to guard against the "indecency" of food vendors setting up shop next to the cross, and to prevent others from tying their horses, mules, and burros to the open-air posts that had protected the cross. At the same time, key documents were collected, including the confraternity's constitution, account books, and papal indulgences for those participating in the May 3 festivities; and a strongbox was added for the safekeeping of donations and other income. In 1651 the cathedral authorized one low Mass to be celebrated there on May 3 as long as no other crosses from other parts of the city were brought to the site.

By the 1680s promotion of the Cruz de los Talabarteros site was in full swing, with the cathedral's cantor urging officers of the confraternity to expand their membership and devotion to the Holy Cross, and the confraternity seeking permission to enclose the spaces between the pillars in order to make the structure an *oratorio* or minor chapel where Mass could be celebrated weekly rather than just once a year. Archbishop Aguiar y Seixas gladly acceded to their request, granting a license in 1688 for Masses on Mondays, on Fridays during Lent, and during the eight-day All Souls observances at the beginning of November, as long as the chapel remained a dignified and well-maintained place. The cult of the Holy Cross continued to expand there in the early eighteenth century, with Masses celebrated almost daily, often accompanied by sermons and religious instruction. The old chapel burned to the ground in 1748, but it was rebuilt, this time with a taller, more imposing domed structure made of stone and tezontle blocks that repeated the hexagonal footprint of the original. It was completed and dedicated in 1757. But the Cruz de los Talabarteros and its chapel apparently did not develop a following that drew devotees from distant places with news of miracles. The usual material culture of colonial-era shrines was also lacking for this cross – replicas, *medidas*, printed devotional literature that recounted a heavenly origin story and personal miracles of healing and rescue. Perhaps being so close to the cathedral and oversight by cathedral dignitaries increasingly suspicious of rumors of enchantment made for more conventional, liturgical uses even after the chapel was rebuilt on a grander scale in the 1750s.

In general, however, crosses were as compelling and present in the landscape at the end of the colonial period as they had been earlier. What seems to have changed most by the late eighteenth century was the official view of where crosses belonged and how they should be honored. For the most part, news of animated, wonder-working crosses was viewed with suspicion by ecclesiastical authorities in the late eighteenth century,[83] and there were moves to confine the display of crosses to urban settings, preferably indoors. The pastoral visitor for the archdiocese of Mexico in 1792 called for Indian parishioners to bring into the parish church the crosses they kept out in the open, in the mountains and other remote places.[84] But this was bound to be a fruitless campaign. Places of the cross and open-air ceremonies had become too important to be removed from a community's territorial landscape without inviting trouble.

Three Renowned Crosses

Three crosses – the wooden cross of Huatulco, the stone cross of Querétaro, and the verdant cross of Tepic – were more renowned than others thanks to some strategic support and publicity from bishops and friars. Their legendary beginnings, woven into the fabric of missionary evangelization and providential imperialism, were in place by the early

The Cross of Huatulco

The cross of Huatulco, apparently the most famous of the three in the seventeenth century,[85] was also the most European in its Counter-Reformation story of a relic resisting sacrilegious attack by Protestant heretics and protecting ships at sea. In 1579 or 1587 (the early chroniclers aren't agreed), English pirates sacked the west coast port of Huatulco on the coast of Oaxaca and tried to destroy the settlement's large, sweet-smelling wooden cross.[86] They pulled it down, covered it with tar, and set it aflame. The tar burned, but not the cross. Failing in their attempt to destroy the cross, the pirates left Huatulco, and the news of this miracle caused an immediate stir in the region. Ships calling at the port took slivers of the cross to cast into the sea for protection during violent storms.[87] Local people considered the tiniest bits of wood from the cross to be efficacious medicine, mixing it in water for the sick to drink. They were so much in demand for these purposes in the early years that it soon dwindled to a height of five feet.[88] At that point, Bishop Juan de Cervantes (1608–14) ordered it sent to Antequera for safekeeping and public display in a special chapel inside the cathedral. And there it remained, working more wonders of healing and rescue. "Of this kind, the numbers are infinite," wrote Torquemada before 1615.[89] Substantial pieces of the original cross also went to Pope Paul V before his death in 1621,[90] and to the Carmelite convent in Puebla,[91] but one piece evidently remained in Huatulco. A mid-eighteenth-century source reported that a chapel about two leagues from Huatulco displayed a small cross made from "the one to which the great marvel happened,"[92] and the parish church of Huatulco still advertises such a cross. Although widespread popular devotion to the cross of Huatulco declined from the eighteenth century,[93] its fame and devotion lingered in Oaxaca thanks to the printed accounts, the removal of the largest fragment to the cathedral, and a famous seventeenth-century painting there of the foiled sacrilege. (Figure 8.5)

The Stone Cross of Querétaro

The stone cross of Querétaro had the earliest following of the three and was the most closely related to Indian evangelization in the sixteenth century, but its beginnings are obscure. Surviving written sources and active promotion date from the seventeenth and eighteenth centuries. Apparently formal investigations into the creation of this cross and miracles associated with it were made in 1639 and 1650 on orders of

Figure 8.5 This anonymous seventeenth-century painting in the cathedral of the Archdiocese of Antequera (Oaxaca) depicts the foiled attempt by English pirates to destroy the Cruz de Huatulco by fire in 1587. Photograph courtesy of Jaime Cuadriello; permission courtesy of the Archdiocese of Oaxaca.

the bishop of Michoacán, and sixteen witnesses were summoned in 1650.[94] Unfortunately, the records of these investigations have not been found. The earliest dated reference comes from the Franciscan chronicler Alonso de la Rea's 1639 history of his province.[95] He admitted that "the origin of this relic is not known because over time [memory of] it has been erased,"[96] but he extolled it as a "tree of life in the middle of Paradise" (*Lignum vitae in medio Paradysi*), famous for its miracles, situated on the brow of the Sangremal hill just outside the city of Querétaro, housed in a richly furnished chapel. De la Rea proceeded to mention several exemplary miracles "so that they are not erased from memory." They included the cross growing in size and trembling, especially on Fridays; a moribund girl brought back to life; a string of rosary beads that miraculously stuck to the cross; and a gentleman of the city who took a mortal fall from his horse yet survived unscathed.[97] Clearly the devotion was growing when the investigations were undertaken and de la Rea wrote about it. The witnesses in 1650 were said to have urged the bishop and the crown to support the cult;[98] in 1654 an impressive new church was completed on the site; and the devotion continued to grow with news of miraculous healings, an institutionalized feast day,[99] and tireless alms collections by the local Franciscans.[100]

In 1694, in the aftermath of the notorious Mexico City riots of 1692, the archbishop of Mexico would not allow the people of Querétaro to celebrate their great public feast in honor of the stone cross. The city fathers and other prominent citizens, totaling forty-seven signators, seven of them *dones,* appealed to the viceroy to overrule the archbishop's order because the celebration was "so deeply rooted and such an ancient custom among the residents." They claimed that the fiestas began in 1614, that the city's cross was said to date from the time of the conquest, and that the solemn festivities were urgently needed because of present calamities. They added that those of them who had participated in past fiestas enjoyed remarkably good health, but were now ill. Unmoved, the archbishop again prohibited the celebrations, with a penalty of 500 pesos for violators, and he urged the viceroy to punish the petitioners for their insolence. The viceroy ordered his representative in Querétaro to call these men together and warn them sternly about how provocative their words and actions had been and to order them to obey the archbishop's decree and acknowledge their ignorance.[101] This tough stand by the highest colonial authorities could have been the beginning of a steep decline in the popularity of Querétaro's stone cross, but it was not. In addition to the depth of popular devotion, the establishment of a new missionary college – a *colegio de propaganda fide* named for the cross, El Colegio de la Santa Cruz – on the site in 1683 by Spanish Franciscan reformers with a new evangelical fervor contributed to its staying power.[102] Members of this college were active promoters of the devotion during the eighteenth century, searching for historical records to fill out its legendary past, embellishing the church, and publicizing the cross in their chronicles, devotional histories, and sermons. Later chroniclers of the order mentioned additions to the physical plant by the missionary friars during those years, including a "famous library" of some

7,000 volumes.[103] And in 1702 a sermon by Fr. José de Castro celebrating the stone cross and the rebuilding of the church was published.[104]

What may be the earliest written account of this cross is known in a 1717 manuscript from the library of the Querétaro college.[105] The warden of the convent and colegio at the time attached a note to the 1717 document that the original record was in poor condition and a copy was needed in order to preserve its contents. If the original document was, in fact, composed before 1639,[106] de la Rea did not consult it when he wrote about the cross, and the document gives no indication that it drew from his history. The author identified himself as don Nicolás Muntáñez, an Otomí lord from Tula and one of the Christian captains who led the conquest of Querétaro against Chichimec heathens in 1551. His rambling narrative set out the origin story for the stone cross as it would be recounted after 1722, placing the symbol of the cross at the center of the story of conquest. He described the heavenly apparition of St. James and a refulgent cross during the decisive battle; then, at the beginning of July 1552, a great pine cross nearly thirty-five feet high was raised on the hill where the battle had been fought and the peace made. But when the Chichimecs objected that it was not the kind of cross they wanted, the Franciscan pastor promised that within twenty-four hours the Chichimecs would have their cross. On July 3 stones for the cross were brought from a quarry more than ten miles away "by 1,000 men," and Mass was celebrated for the Chichimecs, as promised. The text says that it was a miracle to find such excellent, multicolored, sweet smelling stones that fit together perfectly in the form of the cross (see Chapter 7, Figure 7.7). The author repeated that this cross itself was a miracle, but he made no mention of it growing or trembling, as de la Rea did.[107]

Whenever the original text was composed, the 1717 date of the copy is significant. It opens a period of very active promotion by Franciscans of the Holy Cross college as part of their efforts at a spiritual awakening in urban and rural parishes that set the stage for an official story of origin, one that would circulate without much variation thereafter. This streamlined story of origin and devotion, informed by Muntáñez's text, was written by Fr. Francisco Xavier de Santa Gertrudis, chronicler of the college, and sponsored by its warden, Fr. Isidro Félix de Espinosa. Santa Gertrudis's little book was published in 1722 with a long, suitably descriptive title, *Cruz de piedra, imán de la devoción, venerada en el Colegio de Misioneros Apostólicos de la Ciudad de Santiago de Querétaro. Descripción panegírica de su prodigioso origen y portentosos milagros*. Santa Gertrudis summarized the providential apparition of the cross and Santiago in the heat of battle described by Muntáñez, elaborated on the search for the right stones, and placed the Querétaro cross into the wider context of the Christian cross as "glorious conqueror of the universe," alluding to various visions of the True

Cross in battles for Christianity, including Constantine's vision and others from the Reconquista. He also mentioned several miraculous crosses and apparitions in New Spain. Taking a page from de la Rea, Santa Gertrudis highlighted among its miracles trembling movements that traced the sign of the cross "like a tree in the wind." These movements were often detected on Fridays, he said; then he noted two occasions when the movements were more pronounced – once in 1680 when the Pueblo Indians of New Mexico rose up in rebellion and killed their Franciscan pastors; the other in 1683 when the Spanish Franciscans who would found the Missionary College of the Holy Cross reached the shores of Veracruz. America was, he added, "the land of the cross" and true "magnet" of souls.

Other promotional works followed before the end of the colonial period. In his discussion of miraculous images in Querétaro in 1739, Francisco Antonio Navarrete, SJ, turned first to the stone cross, marvelous because of its propensity to grow and the many wonders it had worked for devotees, so many that to count them would be like "counting the rays of the sun."[108] Isidro Félix de Espinoza included a chapter in praise of the miraculous stone cross of Querétaro in his history of the college published in 1746, although he suggested that the Christian Otomí conqueror was Hernando de Tapia and the miracles happened in 1531 rather than 1550.[109] The late eighteenth-century history of holy people and miraculous images in Mexico by José Díaz de la Vega, OFM, which circulated in manuscript copies, also devoted a chapter to the Querétaro cross, and concluded that "this is the most prodigious relic and the most estimable treasure with which Divine Providence enriched the Most Noble city of Querétaro."[110] A sermon to the Exaltation of the Cross by Antonio Ruiz Narváez delivered on the day of the feast in 1801 was published in 1802, and José María Zeláa e Hidalgo's *Glorias de Querétaro* (1804) also described and praised the stone cross.[111]

During the course of the eighteenth century, other references to this stone cross suggest continuing popularity, as well as promotional activity. The cross was celebrated in an article published in the May 1730 issue of the *Gazeta de México* to mark the great May 3 fiesta. The origin story of the signs in the sky and the miraculous discovery of five beautiful white and red stones for the cross were briefly recounted; then the article emphasized the movements of the cross and its remarkable growth, from about eight feet in 1639 to a full eleven feet in 1730.[112] The *relación geográfica* for Querétaro in 1743 described the cross on the main altar of the Franciscan College of the Holy Cross, encased in silver and glass with a beautiful and capacious alcove (*camarín*) behind. The reporter spoke of the movement of the cross and the many miracles of healing, both physical and spiritual. This cross was treated, he said, "as if it was sent from Heaven."[113]

The Green Cross of Tepic

Chroniclers' accounts of the tradition of the verdant cross of Tepic, Nayarit in western Mexico share with the cross of Huatulco a providential pre-colonial origin story: both were said to have been planted by one of Christ's apostles. In other respects, their histories are quite different.[114] Tepic's cross was a patch of unusual grass in the form of a cross about forty feet long and twenty-two feet across the arms that remained green year around and was said to regenerate itself endlessly. The first brief mention of this cross was written in 1621 by Domingo Lázaro de Arregui, a priest born in Spain but long resident in the Diocese of Guadalajara, most recently in the small town of Tepic. According to his account, a young man was driving his mules near Tepic in 1619. The animals suddenly halted and would not move further in the direction of the unseen cross, which the young man soon discovered.[115] Later chronicles embellished the story. One added that the outline of the cross was caused by an ancient wooden cross having fertilized the ground where it fell; others described miracles associated with this cross. Antonio Tello, the mid-seventeenth-century chronicler of the Franciscan Province of Xalisco, located the cross one-quarter league (about half a mile) from Tepic and added that after the young man told everyone in town, there was a rush of people to see for themselves and pray there, and they began to take bits of the grass as relics for medicinal use.[116] The great Jesuit chronicler of miraculous images, Francisco de Florencia, picked up the story in his *Origen de dos célebres santuarios de la Nueva Galicia, Obispado de Guadalajara en la América septentrional,* published in 1692.[117] He added nothing new, but his publications circulated more widely than Arregui's or Tello's then-unpublished chronicles, and he included a visually striking engraving of the verdant cross that included a set of purported footprints impressed in stone from another part of the province of Jalisco that were thought to have been made by Christ or one of his apostles.[118] This engraving served as the model for several runs of prints that circulated in western Mexico as devotion to the Tepic cross grew during the eighteenth century. (See Figure 8.6) As the parish of Tepic grew to nearly 3,000 inhabitants, the small shrine maintained at the site by Franciscans from their convent in the town of Xalisco during the seventeenth century was enlarged in the eighteenth century with a hospice of ten cells to accommodate visitors.[119] As the shrine grew more popular and the Franciscan hospice gained importance in the 1760s,[120] the Bishop of Guadalajara, undeterred by the first signs of skepticism about the truth of the self-restoring grass and earth of the Tepic cross, petitioned the crown to elevate the shrine with the establishment of convent there, with resident friars. The church was rebuilt in 1777, and the royal order granting the establishment of a Franciscan convent was made in 1784. Also in the

Figure 8.6 Loose print of the "Prodigious Cross of Tepique" from unsigned engraving, collected by Francisco de Ajofrín in the 1760s. Courtesy of the Real Academia de la Historia, Madrid.

mid-eighteenth century several short texts about this cross were written but not published, including Jesuit Segismundo Taraval's "El milagro más visible: o el milagro de los milagros más patentes. La Santíssima Cruz de Tepique" ("The Most Visible Miracle; or, the Miracle Among the Most Certain of Miracles: the Most Holy Cross of Tepic"),[121] and Fernando Bustillos Varas y Gutiérrez's "Representación hecha al Rey Nuestro Señor Don Fernando Sexto, por los indios de la Nueva España sobre que Su Magestad les funde un colegio privativo a su nación" (ca. 1752).[122]

Including the print from Florencia as a kind of talisman, Bustillos enlarged upon Arregui's story by focusing on the cross itself and its miraculous regeneration in the face of incessant harvesting by relic seekers:

> Faced with the vagaries of the weather, that wondrous grassy cross remains evergreen and beautiful even when the surrounding land is bone dry. And it is so prolific that almost as soon as some of it is cut for relics – which happens every day and in great amount – the next day it is whole again. This is not an end to its wonders, for part way down the vertical member of the cross there is a hole like a wound corresponding to the one in Our Divine Lord's side, with a seemingly inexhaustible supply of whitish earth. Much of it is taken away for relics and medicine yet it is always full. Even more marvelous, even though many attempts have been made to put a roof over the chapel that encloses [the cross], it has never lasted, ... as if this wondrous sign wanted only the canopy of heaven.[123]

A Closer View of Two Places in Time

A less famous miraculous cross was investigated very soon after it reportedly came to life, before a polished summary account like those for the crosses of Querétaro, Huatulco, and Tepic could smooth over doubts, loose ends, and local interests.[124] It merits some attention as another kind of historical record of devotion as well as a late colonial example of a living cross.

On May 3, 1728, the parish priest of Tlayacapan, Morelos, about forty miles east of Cuernavaca, wrote to the Archbishop of Mexico with sensational news.[125] The day before – the eve of the feast of the Invention of the Holy Cross – parishioners in the Tepetenchi neighborhood had urged him to come see something amazing. As they were cleaning and decorating a large stone and mortar roadside cross, it had begun to sway.[126] The priest reported that from about 2:30 that afternoon until vespers, he and many others witnessed this marvel. The archbishop immediately dispatched the ecclesiastical judge of Chalco (*juez eclesiástico*) to investigate and, if possible, discreetly transfer the cross to the parish church. The judge recognized that he would not be able to take possession of the cross without an uproar when a crowd of people – Indians, Spaniards, and other non-Indians – met him at the nearby Santa Ysabel chapel, where the cross was being guarded around the clock. In the company of the district governor, the resident Augustinian friars, and local Indians he went to the place where the cross had been, then adjourned to the friary to begin to inform himself about the reported marvel and why the cross had been moved.

On May 17 the judge forwarded to the archbishop a petition by five Indian elders of Tepetenchi. In it they earnestly explained that the cross had been moved to the chapel as a place for proper veneration, at least until the pedestal at the original location was rebuilt. The villagers were becoming disconsolate, the elders said, because the cross was "of our very being" and they "feared being deprived of what we consider an inestimable relic to ward off storms and what lurks outside after dark." This marvelous cross had renewed their faith and they were eager to build a fitting chapel on the spot and sponsor an annual fiesta on its May 3 feast day in order to "celebrate the triumph of our redemption," and "promote devotion in this barrio and in the whole community ... as a witness to our conversion." They shrewdly observed that the famous shrines to the images of Our Lady of Guadalupe and Our Lady of Los Remedios had been built on the sites of the Virgin's apparitions, not moved elsewhere.

Meanwhile, the judge proceeded with his investigation, interviewing the parish priest and thirteen other Spaniards living in the community. He also received an inspection report from the local royal governor.[127] Everyone testified to having seen the cross move for the better part of three days – shaking back and forth, then side to side, as if making the sign of the cross. They were also of the opinion that the people of Tepetenchi were deeply moved by this portent and eager to build a chapel on the spot. Their testimony effectively confirmed everything the elders had said in their petition.[128] And the prior of the Augustinian convent offered an acceptable explanation for why he had ordered the removal of the cross and had the pedestal unearthed. He said the site needed to be excavated in order to determine whether there was some natural or diabolical cause for the movement – whether some individuals had hidden themselves under the pedestal and manipulated the cross, as had happened at Atlixtac (near Iguala, Guerrero, southwest of Tlayacapan); or whether there was a cavity underneath the pedestal that might be causing the ground to shift and the cross to move; or whether idols were hidden there.

Pleased with his own forensic methods, the district governor submitted an unusually favorable report. When he and two acquaintances arrived at the scene on the afternoon of May 2 a crowd had gathered, speaking out all at once about the holy cross's movements. Ordering everyone back from the pedestal so he could see for himself, he touched the arms of the cross with a branch and could see definite movement from time to time – forward and back, side to side. He then ordered a ladder brought to the pedestal so he could climb up for a closer inspection. At that point, the movement of the cross became so violent he thought it would fall over. The onlookers came closer – "everyone in this populous town, people of all kinds and both sexes" – to see it move. He and all the witnesses concluded that there was no external, natural explanation. The case record ends with the opinion of the archbishop's legal adviser (*promotor fiscal*) that the movement of this cross was a genuine miracle – that the ground underneath the pedestal was solid and that many people had seen the cross move. "Considering that [this cross] can be a most efficacious instrument of yet greater wonders," he wrote, it should be declared miraculous and kept in the Santa Ysabel chapel for proper devotion, veneration, and display. On August 2, 1728, the vicar general of the archdiocese concurred, certifying the cross of Tepetenchi to be "miraculous and wondrous."

Five months later Mexico City's monthly newspaper, the *Gazeta de México*, reported that devotion to the cross of Tepetenchi was on the rise. The cornerstone of a chapel to house the cross at its original site had been placed on Christmas day with all the proper licenses, sponsored by the local royal governor who had made the fulsome endorsement the previous May, and the town's sixteen barrios had promised to support the building project.[129] Eight years later another item in the *Gazeta de México* announced that a glorious procession through Tlayacapan had taken place on May 28, 1737, to celebrate completion of one of the vaulted sections of the chapel. The festivities were meant to elicit more donations to finish the chapel. As the reporter put it, "it is hoped that the devotion of the townspeople and neighbors will carry the project to completion."[130] Apparently it eventually did, or so the chapel of Santa Cruz de Altica with its plain stone cross at the altar and May 3 feast day would suggest.[131]

This story of the swaying cross of Tepetenchi contrasts with another emergent cult to a stone cross nearly a century later, in 1809, at Huaquechula, Puebla.[132] There the enthusiastic popular devotion to an unremarkable cross marking on a small boulder was spreading spontaneously to distant parts of the Diocese of Puebla without much ecclesiastical supervision. That would have been a problem in any event, but the bishop's response in 1809 was stunning. He ordered the boulder smashed to bits and the chapel housing it destroyed. The time was different. Regalist bishops in the late eighteenth and early nineteenth centuries were more reluctant to endorse new shrines and miraculous images, and were quicker to contain what Durkheim called "the contagiousness of the sacred" in the name of episcopal authority and decorous faith.

As close in time as this record of Tepetenchi's cross is to the events it describes, and as welcome as the local voices in it are to a historian, questions we would want to ask of its devotees and promoters go unanswered. How was the cross venerated and remembered? How was the devotion organized and how did it develop after May 1728? What stories of divine presence and favor were told, by whom and when? To suggest that recent practices and memories can be projected back in time is a doubtful proposition, but ethnographies and oral histories that have not been tailored to demonstrate continuities between the present and the precolonial or colonial past sometimes suggest meanings of devotion or connections and developments that historians can only guess at otherwise. For this subject of devotion to the True Cross and particular crosses, Bibiana Ugalde Mendoza's *Xitaces con sentimiento y tradición: Historia del culto a la cruz verde de Tequisquiapan en la voz de un pueblo creyente* (History of the Cult of the Green Cross of Tequisquiapan in the Words of a Believing Community) is an inviting source. In 1995 and 1996, the author surveyed more than 100 families and interviewed thirty-eight adults from seven settlements in and near Tequisquiapan, Querétaro, who had jointly participated in the feasts of the Holy Cross for many years.[133] Her informants ranged in age from thirty-five to ninety-seven years old, more than half of them over seventy. Most had helped to sponsor the devotions and had participated in the processions and dances or supplied the fireworks and refreshments. In their reminiscences they said remarkably little about the role of priests in the devotion, other than to mention a Father Concha who had been the pastor some decades earlier and was remembered as an enthusiastic participant and promoter of the annual celebrations.

Their stories about the devotion and special rites revolve around a "cruz aparecida" – a tree cross that suddenly appeared – and celebrations of the Holy Cross going back to the 1770s. Most of Ugalde Mendoza's informants spoke of an oak tree in the shape of a cross appearing on the Cerro Grande, a hill above the town. Local people went to see the cross and pray, and the site became known as Cruz Verde – Green Cross, living cross. But the rancher who owned the hill eventually closed the site to visitors, and his foreman cut down the tree and dragged it into town as far as the San Juan barrio where it either became too heavy to move further, or his horse died and he abandoned his burden, or he was thrown from his horse and died on the spot. Several informants from San Juan emphasized that however the cross came to rest there, this was a sign that it "wanted this place for its chapel." Everyone who commented on the provenance of various crosses associated with the devotion agreed that San Juan has the largest piece of the famous tree cross. The San Juanino informants call theirs "the original and principal cross,"[134] but they also recognize that the natural cross was claimed by the people of Magdalena, San Francisco, and Santa Rosa Xajay, as well as San Juan, and that this dispute was finally settled by cutting enough wood from the original cross for three more smaller crosses, one for San Francisco, one for Santa Rosa, and another one for San Juan; and that Magdalena received a stone cross made from the rock that was displaced when the tree suddenly sprouted from the hilltop. Some of the informants spoke of later miracles with crosses cut from the original tree or other crosses that touched them during the fiestas. The miracles they described were healings and supernatural punishment of those who were disrespectful to the cross or shirked their fiesta duties. Others added a detail or two not mentioned by anyone else – that the first cuts on the tree healed overnight, for instance, or that the cherub companions of the true cross turn pale when they are angry.

No official origin story for this natural cross was published or accepted in a way that has silenced local variations. Informants from several of the communities did not agree on whose ancestors first noticed and venerated the cross. According to some, strange lights and celestial music marked the place of the tree cross; for another, the first sign of divine presence was that the tree bled when it was cut; still others mentioned no supernatural signs other than the shape of the tree itself and its sudden appearance. Beyond telling their version of the origin story, many of the informants spoke of their personal participation in the annual celebrations, especially as children; how their participation sometimes faltered; and the portents and miracles they or their relatives and neighbors experienced. With their proprietary claims to being the keepers of the real cross and its chapel, people of San Juan were especially eager to talk to the author about their leading role in the history of the devotion, while devotees from other places sometimes expressed a more theological interest in purification rites like the cleaning of the chapel and cherubim or how the bleeding tree dragged into town reenacted Christ's Passion, and how the tree cross triumphed in the end.

Some of the informants noticed changes in the devotion. Apparently one mayordomo had been in charge of the festivities at the Cerro Grande, but now different groups participated largely on their own. May 3 remains an important feast day in San Juan, but it does not attract as many crosses from neighboring towns as before. September 13–14 has become an important occasion, when devotees, led by the people of Santa Rosa, ascend the Cerro Grande with their crosses for special services, dances, and feasting. But participation in the September celebrations has its complications. One informant from the El Cerrito barrio said the celebrations on the hill in September were not so well attended in recent years and that four communities no longer go there to sing the night before the feast day as they once did; and villages with many Protestants no longer participate. For a time, people from San Joaquín, San Francisco, and Panhe stopped going, but recently they began again, bringing flowers and candles "so that the Lord might return" and favor them again. Other communities used to gather with their crosses at Magdalena's September fiesta, but were no longer invited. People of San Juan still attended the fiesta at Magdalena in September, but without their great green cross. As one San Juanino put it, the last time they tried to take the great cross there a thunderclap halted them in their tracks and the cross grew very heavy when they tried to go forward. Now they take a smaller "traveling" (*peregrina*) cross to Magdalena and take the great cross with them only on the September 14 procession to the Cerro Grande. Some informants lamented a general decline of devotion and respect for the Holy Cross, especially among young people who attended just to clown around.[135]

But for all their differences in perspective, these devotees of Tequisquiapan's *cruz aparecida* and participants in the May and September festivals have not lost sight of *place* in the story of their Holy Cross. Despite San Juan's claim to have the largest piece of the great cross, people from other communities considered their local cross to be the most important relic.[136] And the hilltop site of the apparition has been as important to the devotion and the regeneration of divine presence and favor as possession of a piece, large or small, of the original tree cross. The other common thread in the informants' words also returns to place: the original cross was natural, a living cross, and it appeared right here.

Conclusion

These personal and collective stories of the Green Cross of Tequisquiapan recall for one place in the recent past the main patterns of devotion to the cross during the colonial period discussed in this chapter. Here is the deep appeal of crosses in themselves, alive with the sacred, many of them natural crosses. May 3 remains a principal day of the Holy Cross there and in much of Mexico, even with the growing importance and promotion of September 14. And this is not just a history of Indians and early mendicant missionaries. All kinds of people – elites and *plebe*, people of different ethnic designations, priests and laity – participated enthusiastically, and "Spaniards" and "Indians" had become porous categories. Over the long run, diocesan authorities and many parish priests allowed and attempted to direct these devotions even though there were times and places where they were officially discouraged.[137] While standing for the story of Christ in the Gospels, colonial crosses had other, latent meanings that could be equivocal if not contradictory – as symbols of both domination and liberation; representing both a Mesoamerican cosmovision and a Christian, colonial ideology; little homelands and the universal church; and holding out the possibility of salvation and protection in the face of the palpable presence of evil in the world. The meanings and variations were both American and deeply clerical and Spanish colonial. Crosses protected in ways long familiar to European Christians, warding off evil, moving Satan aside, but here in Mesoamerica crosses virtually saturated the colonial landscape, more often springing from it, green and pulsating with divine presence.

In the long run, it was more important to the devotional history of these crosses where devotees were from than what ethnicity they claimed or accepted, which leads to the most basic shared pattern of all – that the history of miraculous crosses is especially about presence in place, in a localizing way. They belong to a sacred landscape visible from a particular place of origin and settlement at the center. They are located all over what had been New Spain, but none, not even the most celebrated, became the site of a great regional or national shrine. As at Tequisquiapan, the tradition, whether oral or written, called attention to the place of origin or where the cross chose to remain. And that is where it was celebrated. The cross of Tequisquiapan sprang from that soil and is nestled in place, much as the sixteenth-century crosses planted at the urging of the early missionaries marked a visible landscape and the cruciform symbol described a local vision of the shape of the cosmos, with "the people" and their settlement at the navel of a universe spreading out in the cardinal directions, each with a great tree of life at its margin. This rootedness has been more characteristic of prized crosses and crucifixes than of images of Mary and the infant Jesus, some of which continue to be sighted in apparitions far from home or are famous for the wet or muddy hems of their dresses from having traveled afar during the night. The planted and natural crosses rarely are said to have moved from their place of origin, as if their meaning and power were confined to the local landscape.

Notes

1. The feast of the Invention of the Cross was favored in New Spain, but the feast of the Exaltation of the Cross was also celebrated, as it had been in Europe for centuries. Genoese bishop Jacobus de Voragine's thirteenth-century hagiography of saints, which circulated in New Spain, featured both devotions, *The Golden Legend: Readings on the Saints*, trans. William Granger Ryan, Princeton: Princeton University Press, 1993, I, 277–284 (Invention of the Cross), and II, 168–173 (Exaltation of the Cross).
2. As Yolanda Lastra, Joel Sherzer, and Dina Sherzer note, crosses in the greater Bajío region of Guanajuato, Querétaro, and much of the adjacent state of Hidalgo are still honored "like a saint," and in some communities "the entire month of May is dedicated to the fiesta de Santa Cruz," *Adoring the Saints: Fiestas in Central Mexico*, Austin: University of Texas Press, 2009, pp. 52, 188. For the central importance of May 3 in Otomí observances, *Crónica otomí del Estado de México: narrativa oral tradicional*, ed. Margarita de la Vega Lázaro, Toluca: Gobierno del Estado de México, 1998, pp. 48–53.
3. The cross often remains long after the building project ends. As Brian Connaughton wrote in a personal communication: "Epifanio decorates our construction cross in Nepantla every year (on May 3) without saying anything to him [even though] the house has been done for three or four years." A YouTube video records the gathering of *albañiles* and construction workers in the cathedral square of Puebla on May 3, 2010, with their crosses and crucifixes fashioned out of reinforcing steel bars and other building materials In the words of one of the *albañiles*, the crosses "guard the site" – *cuidan la obra* (accessed December 6, 2010, www.youtube.com/watch?v=Pqsdtj9pUV4).

    I have not been able to document when and how May 3 observances became so closely connected to the building trades. There may be no surprise in the eventual answer.

The cross as protective sign was a natural, and May 3 was the principal day of the Holy Cross in Mexico. Even after 1960 it was the only day of the Holy Cross celebrated in many communities. For example, the festive calendar for Chignautla, Puebla, in 1971 listed a great feast on May 3 and daily rosaries and neighborhood celebrations of the cross throughout May, but no observances on September 14, Doren L. Slade, *Making the World Safe for Existence: Celebration of the Saints among the Sierra Nahuat of Chignautla, Mexico*, Ann Arbor: University of Michigan Press, 1992, pp. 223–226.

The deeply rooted appeal of the May 3 feast day is also related to this date being the feast day of some famous shrines to miraculous images of Christ on the cross; for example, the shrine of Otatitlán, Veracruz. See José Velasco Toro, "Imaginario cultural e identidad devocional en el Santuario de Otatitlán," in *Santuarios, peregrinaciones, y religiosidad popular*, ed. María Rodríguez-Shadow and Ricardo Ávila, Guadalajara: Universidad de Guadalajara, 2010, pp. 183–205.

4. AGN Inquisición 366 exp. 16. This inquiry had no resounding conclusion since the offenders were not identified.

5. AGN Edictos Inquisición 1 exp. 15, March 30, 1691. AGN General de Parte 17 exps. 34–35 records the archbishop's opposition in 1694 to traditional festivities on the Day of the Holy Cross at Querétaro, which included a Moors and Christians pageant "and various other profane diversions" such as bullfights and farces. An earlier Inquisition decree meant to stop improper display of crosses in public places was issued on October 20, 1626, "para obviar el abuso de poner y pintar cruzes en rincones públicos y otros lugares indecentes," UND Harley L. McDevitt Inquisition Collection, document #223.

6. For example, AGN Clero Regular y Secular 192 exps. 11–12. There are also incidental references in criminal trials. Judging by the pastoral visit records of the Archdiocese of Mexico, confraternities dedicated to the Holy Cross were common in rural central Mexico after 1684.

The association of hilltop crosses with Via Crucis processions was actively promoted by bishops in the seventeenth and eighteenth centuries. For example, in the early 1640s, when Bishop Juan de Palafox y Mendoza began to promote a shrine at the site of the apparition of St. Michael to Diego Lázaro near Nativitas, Tlaxcala, he noted that "para maior devoción se han puesto a trechos cruces grandes conforme a los pasos de la Via Crucis del Santo Calvario, desde la yglesia parroquial del pueblo" up to the hilltop chapel, AGN Historia 1 exp. 7, fol. 160r.

7. At several points in this chapter and others, I use ethnographies to imagine what remains hidden or just suggested in my colonial-era sources, while remembering Inga Clendinnen's approach to colonial religious studies in "Ways to the Sacred: Reconstructing 'Religion' in Sixteenth-Century Mexico," in her *The Cost of Courage in Aztec Society: Essays on Mesoamerican Society and Culture*, New York: Cambridge University Press, 2010, pp. 116–155; David Carrasco's call for a "borderlands" approach to "hybrid-thinking spaces, contact zones, and cultural creativity" in which European, African, Asian, and native American cultural streams meet and transform, "Borderlands and the 'Biblical Hurricane': Images and Stories of Latin American Rhythms of Life," *Harvard Theological Review* 101: 3–4 (July–October 2008), 353–376; Carrasco's "Jaguar Christians in the Contact Zone: Concealed Narratives in the Histories of Religions in the Americas," in Jacob K. Olupona, *Beyond Primitivism: Indigenous Religious Traditions*

and Modernity, New York: Routledge, 2004, pp. 128–138; and the approach I outlined in Chapter 3 of *Magistrates of the Sacred: Priests and Parishioners in Eighteenth-Century Mexico*, Stanford, CA: Stanford University Press, 1996. William F. Hanks's *Converting Words: Maya in the Age of the Cross*, Berkeley: University of California Press, 2010, is exemplary in combining ethnographic and historical materials to reckon with cultural change during the colonial period; and Jaime Lara combines colonial pictorial and liturgical materials with scholarship on precolonial culture and medieval Christian theology and practice for another suggestive rendering of visual imagination and worship in sixteenth-century central and southern Mexico, *City, Temple, Stage: Eschatological Architecture and Liturgical Theatrics in New Spain*, Notre Dame: University of Notre Dame Press, 2004, and *Christian Texts for Aztecs: Art and Liturgy in Colonial Mexico*, Notre Dame: Notre Dame University Press, 2008. Among more historical studies, see Nancy M. Farriss, *Maya Society under Colonial Rule: The Collective Enterprise of Survival*, Princeton: Princeton University Press, 1984, and John K. Chance, *Conquest of the Sierra: Spaniards and Indians in Colonial Oaxaca*, Norman: University of Oklahoma Press, 1989.

8. Octavio Hernández Espejo, "La fiesta de la Santa Cruz en San Francisco Ozomatlán," *México Desconocido* 23: 267 (May 1999), 52–60. Ozomatlán is located in the municipio of Huitzuco, Guerrero (about 22 miles east of Highway 95 after traveling south of Iguala 28 miles) which is featured in several YouTube videos of May 3 festivities showing religious ceremonies including prayers before crosses covered with paper flowers. In one video, a priest speaks of the rain not yet arriving and invites those assembled to "pray for favors" (*pedir beneficios*) from God, and remember that through the Cross Jesus saved his followers. In another video, several Huitzuco men visited a hilltop spring on May 3 ("el día de la Cruz del albañil") to shoot off rockets and appeal for rain.

9. Robert Haskett, citing a 1743 report of the alcalde mayor for Cuernavaca, "Conquering the Spiritual Conquest in Cuernavaca," in *The Conquest All Over Again: Nahuas and Zapotecs Thinking, Writing, and Painting Spanish Colonialism*, ed. Susan Schroeder, Brighton, UK: Sussex Academic Press, 2010, p. 242. In a recent, deeply researched book on the Mixteca Baja of Oaxaca, *The Roots of Conservatism in Mexico: Catholicism and Politics in the Mixteca Baja, 1750–1962*, Albuquerque: University of New Mexico Press, 2012, Benjamin T. Smith calls his chapter on the colonial period "The People of the Cross" with good reason, since miraculous crosses were common there, as was "the region's Christocentric religious culture." One cross in particular, the Sacred Cross of Santo Domingo Tonala, gained a regional following and spawned "countless community Christ cults."

10. Gilberto Giménez, *Cultura popular y religion en el Anáhuac*, Mexico: Centro de Estudios Ecuménicos, 1978, p. 77. In the Chiapas highlands, each of the barrios of San Juan Chamula has a nearby hill with one or more tall wooden crosses painted green at the base and summit – the threshold and the center – that serves as its cemetery and the sacred place to which processions are made throughout the year, including Holy Week and May 3, David Freidel, Linda Schele, and Joy Parker, *Maya Cosmos: Three Thousand Years on the Shaman's Path*, New York: William Morrow, 1993, pp. 53, 118, 124. Enrique Marroquín described in some detail "the insistent and ubiquitous presence of the cross" in the landscape and ceremonial life of rural communities of Oaxaca, *La cruz*

mesiánica: Una aproximación al sincretismo católico indígena, Oaxaca: Universidad Autónoma "Benito Juárez," 1989, especially pp. 41–42. Crosses also dot the landscape along pilgrimage routes to Talpa, Jalisco. According to Ricardo Ávila and Martín Tena, they mainly commemorate departed devotees who were unable to reach the shrine before they died, "Morir peregrinando a Talpa," in *Santuarios, peregrinaciones, y religiosidad popular*, ed. Rodríguez Shadow and Ávila, p. 234.

11. For examples from the Sierra de Puebla and the district of Huizquilucan, near the Valley of Mexico, see "Espacios, territorios y santuarios en las comunidades indígenas de Puebla," coord. Elio Masferrer Kan, in Barabás, *Diálogos con el territorio*, II, 73–75; and H. R. Harvey, "Pilgrimage and Shrine: Religious Practices among the Otomí of Huixquilucan, Mexico," in *Pilgrimage in Latin America*, ed. E. Alan Morinis and N. Ross Crumrine, New York: Greenwood Press, 1991, pp. 95–102. Fr. Diego Durán, OP, *Historia de las Indias de Nueva España e islas de Tierra Firme*, Mexico: CONACULTA, 1995, II, 90–91 (tratado 2, chapter 8), described the main hill of Tlaloc surrounded by smaller hills – "little brothers" – all of them with names. Diego Prieto Hernández et al., "Mahets'I jar hai (el cielo en la tierra). Los territorios de lo sagrado entre los Ñaño de Querétaro," in Barabás, *Diálogos con el territorio*, II, 235–249, note that the crosses on hills in San Pablo in the municipio de Tolimán have *padrinos* on other hills to which the faithful of the first hill go with offerings.

12. While crosses in the landscape are the focus of this chapter, I can think of a miraculous cross with a different kind of history, attached to its town more than the surrounding landscape. The Cross of Totolapan, located in the *pueblo de indios* of the same name just outside the Valley of Mexico in the modern state of Morelos, was originally part of a celebrated crucifix that mysteriously came into the possession of the famed early Augustinian evangelizer, Fr. Antonio de Roa. In 1583 the corpus was separated from the cross and removed to the Augustinians' convent church in Mexico City, but both parts of the crucifix continued to be celebrated by local devotees for miracles of healing, rainfall, and protection from fierce storms. For references to miracles associated with the "cruz aparecida" that remained in Totolapa, see Antonio de Robles, *Diario de sucesos notables (1665–1703)*, Mexico: Porrúa 1946, I, 211 (1677) and II, 223 (1691). See also the cross of Tepetenchi discussed later in this chapter.

13. One of many examples is Diego Basalenque's *Historia de la Provincia de San Nicolás de Michoacán del Orden de N.P.S. Agustín* [1644], ed. José Bravo Ugarte, Mexico: Editorial Jus, 1963. The juxtaposition of crosses and Satan runs throughout this chronicle. Basalenque's theme is summarized in his narrative of the life of Fr. Diego de Villarrubia on p. 353 where the friar took up a cross and pointed it in all directions, saying "Ecce Crucem Domini, fugite partes adversae, vicit Leo de tribu Iuda" (which Basalenque translates as "Here is the cross with which my Lord Jesus Christ conquered you; flee, demons, for I am displaying the sign of the cross of my Redeemer").

14. *Colección de las ordenanzas, que para el gobierno de el obispado de Michoacán hicieron y promulgaron con real aprobación . . .*, Mexico: Zúñiga y Ontiveros, 1776, p. 225 decried cases of priests not going out with a cross to receive the dead for burial. Pastors were ordered to go out with *capa y cruz* irrespective of the social standing of the deceased. Examples of the mystique of signing the cross are virtually endless. According to Francisco de Florencia, when Diego Lázaro (the Indian from Nativitas, Tlaxcala, who saw St. Michael and the miraculous spring in 1631) made the sign of the cross it would

leave a permanent mark, and those favored by this miracle became devotees of the Holy Cross, *Narración de la marabillosa aparición que hizo el archangel San Miguel a Diego Lázaro de San Francisco* ..., Sevilla: Impr. de las Siete Revueltas, 1692, p. 141.

15. Felipe Pereda, *Las imágenes de la discordia: Política y poética de la imagen sagrada en la España del 400*, Madrid: Marcial Pons, 2007, p. 300.

16. Francisco Xavier de Santa Gertrudis, *Cruz de piedra: Imán de la devoción venerada en el Colegio de Misioneros Apostólicos de la ciudad de Santiago de Querétaro descripción panegírica de su prodigioso origen y portentosos milagros* [1722], Querétaro: Ediciones Cimatario, 1946, pp. 14–15.

17. Kevin Sheehan, "Iberian Asia: The Strategies of Spanish and Portuguese Empire Buiding, 1540–1700," Ph.D. dissertation, University of California, Berkeley, 2008, chapter 2. Mónica Domínguez Torres explores crosses as emblems in a convergence of elite martial cultures in New Spain in *Military Ethos and Visual Culture in Post-Conquest Mexico*, Farnam, Surrey, UK and Burlington, VT: Ashgate, 2013, chapter 2. William Christian's *Local Religion in Sixteenth-Century Spain, and Apparitions in Late Medieval and Renaissance Spain*, both published by Princeton University Press in 1981, remain touchstones for the devotional history of Spain in the early modern period.

18. Roque Alberto Faci, *Aragón, Reyno de Christo y dote de María Ssma* ... [1739], facsimile edition, Zaragoza: Diputación General de Aragón, 1979, pp. 43, 134, 151–152.

19. Torquemada, *Monarquía Indiana*, Mexico: Porrúa, 1986, III, 298–299 (libro 18, cap. 7).

20. Andrés Pérez de Ribas, *History of the Triumphs of Our Holy Faith amongst the Most Barbarous and Fierce Peoples of the New World* [1645], ed. Daniel T. Reff, trans. Daniel T. Reff, Maureen Ahern, and Richard K. Danford, Tucson: University of Arizona Press, 1999, pp. 124–126.

21. For examples of the Christian tree of life, Nelly Sigaut, "El árbol de la vida en el convento de Meztitlán," *Relaciones. Estudios de Historia y Sociedad* 47 (verano 1991), 7–29; Isidro Félix de Espinosa, *El cherubín custodio de el árbol de la vida, la Santa Cruz de Querétaro*, Mexico: Joseph Bernardo de Hogal, 1731, based on Alonso de la Rea's *Crónica de la orden de N. Seráfico P.S. Francisco, Provincia de San Pedro y San Pablo de Mechoacan en la Nueva España* [1639], Mexico: J.R. Barbedillo, 1882; Roque Alberto Faci, *Aragón, Reyno de Christo y Dote de María Ssma*, Zaragoza: Joseph Fort, 1739, p. 43, Christ as eternal life; and Samuel C. Chew, *The Pilgrimage of Life*, New Haven: Yale University Press, 1962, p. 252 on an engraving by Robert Vaughan in the 1650s depicting a pilgrim carrying a cross up a steep mountain, away from the tree of knowledge of good and evil. On top of the mountain is the Tree of Life, with a Latin inscription meaning "from the wood of life flows the balm that brings health to every wound."

22. Pedro de Avendaño, *Sermones para las festividades de Christo Nuestro Señor*, Madrid: Viuda de I. Gonçalez, 1634.

23. *Concilio provincial mexicano IV celebrado en la Ciudad de México el año de 1771*, Querétaro: Imprenta de la Escuela de Artes, 1898, p. 167(3–21-9).

24. Juan de Solórzano Pereira, *Política indiana* ....., Madrid: Atlas, 1972, I, 72, libro 1, cap. VII, num. 5.

25. Joseph L. Henderson and Maud Oakes, *The Wisdom of the Serpent: The Myths of Death, Rebirth, and Resurrection*, New York: George Braziller, 1963, p. 99.

26. St. Augustine, *The City of God against the Pagans*, ed. and trans. R. W. Dyson, Cambridge, UK and New York: Cambridge University Press, 1998, pp. xiv, 26.

Placing the Cross in Colonial Mexico 489

27. Mircea Eliade, *Patterns in Comparative Religion*, Rosemary Sheed, trans., London and New York: Sheed & Ward, 1958, pp. 292–294.
28. Torquemada, *Monarquía Indiana*. Eleanor Wake concludes that "native perception of the cruz did not change; it remained very much a tree," in *Framing the Sacred: The Indian Churches of Early Colonial Mexico*, Norman: University of Oklahoma Press, 2010, p. 217.
29. Francesco Carletti, *My Voyage around the World*, Herbert Weinstock, trans., New York: Pantheon Books, 1964, p. 54.
30. For Baron Wormser on trees, *The Road Washes Out in Spring: A Poet's Memoir of Living Off the Grid*, Hanover, NH and London: University Press of New England, 2008, pp. 74, 76, 174.
31. For Nahuas of central Mexico, Alfredo López Austin *Tamoanchan, Tlalocan: Places of Mist*, trans. Bernardo R. Ortiz de Montellano and Thelma Ortiz de Montellano, Boulder: University Press of Colorado, 1997, pp. 108, 223; and David Carrasco, *Religions of Mesoamerica*, New York: Harper & Row, 1990, pp. 51–52. For a similar conception among Otomíes, see Sergio Sánchez Vásquez, "La Santa Cruz: Culto en los cerros de la region Otomí Actopan-Ixmiquilpan," in *La montaña en el paisaje ritual*, ed. Johanna Broda, Stanislaw Iwaniszewski, and Arturo Montero, Mexico: CONACULTA-INAH, 2001, pp. 444–447, who also notes the relationship of hills and crosses with ancestors, their bones transformed into numinous stones. Alejandro Vázquez Estrada notes that in the San Pedro Tolimán area souls of the ancestors are still represented by wooden crosses, and are connected to devotional practices for souls in purgatory, in "Territorio e identidad étnica. La peregrinación a El Divino Salvador," in *Santuarios, peregrinaciones y religiosidad popular*, ed. Rodríguez-Shadow and Ávila, p. 170. And for Mayas in southern Mexico, see Freidel, Schele, and Parker, *Maya Cosmos*, pp. 53–55, 124, 251, 254, 457.
32. Maud Oakes, *The Two Crosses of Todos Santos: Survivals of Mayan Religious Ritual*, Princeton, NJ: Princeton University Press, 1951, pp. 54, 138, 234.
33. López Austin, *Tamoanchan*, p. 154; Carol H. Callaway, "Pre-Columbian and Colonial Mexican Images of the Cross: Christ's Sacrifice and the Fertile Earth," *Journal of Latin American Lore* 16: 1990, 208.
34. Harvey, "Pilgrimage and Shrine," p. 99.
35. As James Lockhart explains, a Nahua community with its territory was known as an *altepetl* – water and mountain, *The Nahuas after the Conquest: A Social and Cultural History of the Indians of Central Mexico, Sixteenth through Eighteenth Centuries*, Stanford, CA: Stanford University Press, 1992, p. 14.
36. In various publications, Johanna Broda has explored the importance of hills and mountains in Mesoamerican cosmovisions; for example, "The Sacred Landscape of Aztec Calendar Festivals: Myth, Nature, and Society," in *To Change Place: Aztec Ceremonial Landscapes*, ed. David Carrasco, Boulder: University Press of Colorado, 1991, pp. 74–120.
37. Durán, *Historia de las Indias*, II, 90 (tratado 2, chapter 8).
38. Torquemada, *Monarquía Indiana*, II, 617–619 (libro 14, cap. XLI).
39. Haskett, "Conquering the Spiritual Conquest," p. 243, citing Sahagún's *Psalmodia Christiana*; Sigaut, "El árbol de la vida."
40. On cosmogonic centers being located on elevated sites in precolonial and modern Mesoamerican communities, Mercedes Guadarrama Olivera, "El espacio y el tiempo

sagrados en tres comunidades totonacas de la Sierra de Papantla," in *Procesos rurales e historia regional (sierra y costa totonacas de Veracruz)*, coord. Victoria Chenaut, Mexico: CIESAS, 1996 p. 185.

41. In this chapter, I am mainly concerned with prodigious crosses in rural places and smaller towns, but crosses were as ubiquitous and visible in provincial centers and Mexico City. As Miguel Sánchez resoundingly affirmed in his famous 1648 text about the Virgin of Guadalupe, *Imagen de la Virgen María Madre de Dios de Guadalupe, milagrosamente aparecida en la Ciudad de México* ..., Mexico: Vda. de Bernardo Calderón, 1648, fol. 13r, "no ay calle, esquina, plaça, y barrio en que no tenga la Santa Cruz en mucho número y santa veneración, y en estos años con singular esmero." Sánchez was referring to the campaign of the Inquisition in the 1640s "against enemies of Christ's Cross" ("enemigos de la Cruz de Christo, por ser ella el Estandarte de su Fe").

42. Torquemada, *Monarquía Indiana*, III, 143 (libro 16, cap. 2) quotes Isaiah, ch. 11: "sobre el Monte oscuro y caliginoso, levantad el Signo, levantad la voz, y no temáis."

43. Torquemada, *Monarquía Indiana*, III, 143 (libro 16, cap. 2).

44. Francisco de Burgoa, *Geográfica descripción de la parte septentrional del Polo Ártico de la América* [1674], Oaxaca: Instituto Oaxaqueño de las Culturas, 1997, fols. 343r–352r. Burgoa and Isidro de la Asunción (*Itinerario a Indias (1673–1678)*, Mexico: CONDUMEX, 1992, p. 108) speculated that it was St. Thomas; Torquemada, *Monarquía Indiana*, III, 205 thought it might be St. Andrew (although he thought it more likely that Martín de Valencia, leader of "the Twelve" Franciscans who arrived together in 1523, planted this cross); and Gil González Dávila, *Teatro eclesiástico de la primitiva Iglesia de las Indias Occidentales*, facsimile edition, Chimalistac, Mexico: CONDUMEX, 1982, p. 79, opted for St. Matthew.

45. Jaime Cuadriello, *Las glorias de la República de Tlaxcala, o la conciencia como imagen sublime*, Mexico: Instituto Nacional de Bellas Artes/Instituto de Investigaciones Estéticas, 2004, pp. 333–337.

46. Torquemada, *Monarquía Indiana*, III, 132 (libro 15, cap. 49).

47. This is a common theme in Torquemada, *Monarquía Indiana*. See also Pérez de Ribas, *History of the Triumphs*, p. 755, for forty index entries about demonic intervention.

48. Torquemada, *Monarquía Indiana* II, 62 (libro 15, cap. 23). Writing his treatise before 1656 to combat idolatry, Dr. Jacinto de la Serna (who had been the pastor of Tenancingo, Estado de México, in 1626) took a dimmer view of what was achieved by planting crosses in the mountains. Before describing in chapter 15 how Indians of the Valley of Toluca regarded trees as imbued with souls and having been humans in an earlier incarnation, he acknowledged in chapter 2 that "there are some crosses there today," but that they served as cover for "bad behavior in other ways" ("obrar mal en las demás cosas"), "Manual de ministros de indios para el conocimiento de sus idolatrías, y extirpación de ellas," in *Colección de documentos inéditos para la historia de España*, Madrid: Academia de la Historia, 1892, 104: 41. On Serna and his text, see José Luis González M., "Sincretismo e identidades emergentes: El *Manual* de Jacinto de la Serna (1630)," *Dimensión Antropológica* 13: 38 (sept.–dic. 2006), 87–113.

49. *Monarquía Indiana*, III, 204 (libro 16, cap. 28). The Vexilla Regis hymn, composed by Venantius Fortunatus, Bishop of Poitiers, was first sung in 569 in the procession from Tours to Poitiers with a relic of the True Cross. It became a part of the Divine

Office during Holy Week, *Catholic Encyclopedia*, entry for "Vexilla Regis" (online at www.newadvent.org/cathen/15396a.h).

The early Spanish evangelizers in New Spain evidently were in the habit of erecting giant wooden crosses in the churchyards they designed in Indian communities to signal the greatness and power of Christianity. In 1539 the First Synod of bishops issued a stern warning about these crosses being made too large – "like the masts of a ship" – not in the spirit of Christ's "humility, patience, and gentleness" (*humildad, y paciencia y mansedumbre*) and a danger to public safety because they drew lightning strikes and rotted at the base. The bishops cited the example of Taximaroa where a great cross toppled over, crushing the Indians who were dancing in its shadow: "no es razón que la Imagen de la vida sea ocasión de la muerte corporal." They ordered that henceforth crosses in church courtyards be smaller and preferably made of stone, "Apéndice a los concilios primero y segundo mexicanos," in *Bibliografía mexicana del siglo XVIII*, ed. Nicolás León, Mexico: J.I. Guerrero y Cia., 1903, part 4, p. 329.

50. Gerónimo de Mendieta, OFM, *Historia eclesiástica indiana*, Mexico: CONACULTA, 1997 [ca. 1597], I, chapter 49 (pp. 473–476): "De la gran devoción y reverencia que los indios cobraron y tienen a la santa cruz del Señor, y cosas maravillosas que cerca de ella acaecieron"; Torquemada, *Monarquía Indiana*, III, 200 (libro 16, cap. XXVI), speaks of "la mucha devoción que los Indios desde el principio de su conversión tomaron a la Imagen o Figura de la Santa Cruz," and on their own began to place crosses in the landscape: "Tomaron esto los Indios tan de gana que levantaron muchas Cruces en las Cumbres de las Sierras y Mogotes de los cerros y en otras muchas partes." On rocks and trees as numinous, Durán noted the dressing and ornamentation of stone images, *Historia de las Indias*, III, 90. Crosses were "dressed" during colonial period and beyond, especially in Yucatán.

This chapter centers on the materiality of crosses and their spiritual geography. Another approach is taken by anthropologist-linguist William Hanks in his study of colonial texts and the cultural significance of linguistic changes in Yucatec Maya during the colonial period. In *Converting Words*, pp. 133, 251, he notes extensive use of the Spanish term *cruz* in colonial Maya texts. The cross was routinely invoked in prayers, and to this day is signed at the beginning of all prayers and rituals, including curing ceremonies.

51. Marroquín, *La cruz mesiánica*, pp. 46–49, notes the polysemic possibilities of crosses planted in the sixteenth century – as symbols of Spanish domination and messianic promise conveyed by early settlers and evangelizers, and embraced by native Christians as symbols of resistance, protection, and a different kind of providential messianic significance.

52. Nicolás Muntáñez, *Relación histórica de la Conquista de Querétaro* [pre-1722], ed. Rafael Ayala Echavarri, Mexico: Sociedad Mexicana de Geografía y Estadística, 1948, p. 151. For extensive use of crosses as boundary markers in the Valley of Mexico, see the record of inspection of Mexico City's *ejidos* in 1608, Bancroft M-M 272.

53. For a brief consideration of chapels and sacred space at Tlayacapan in the sixteenth century, see Clara Bargellini, "Representations of Conversion: Sixteenth-Century Architecture in New Spain," in *The Word Made Image: Religion, Art, and Architecture in Spain and Spanish America, 1500–1600*, ed. Jonathan Brown, Boston: Isabella Stewart Gardner Museum, 1998, p. 98. She suggests that lines from two pairs of barrio chapels

dating from the sixteenth century intersect at the great Augustinian convent church to form a cross.
54. Torquemada, *Monarquía Indiana*, III, 200 (libro 16, cap. 26); Mercedes Guadarrama Olivera, "El espacio y el tiempo sagrados," p. 187 describes the pattern for three Totonac communities in Veracruz: "Hay una cruz en cada 'esquina' del pueblo, es decir, en cada punto cardinal, de tal manera que forma una cruz invisible sobre éste que 'ataja las enfermedades y los malos espíritus.'" Other domestic uses described in contemporary Oaxaca villages echo the blessings and appeal for protection and fertility. Marroquín, *La cruz mesiánica*, p. 41, mentions the placement of ceramic "police" crosses by Zapotecs on the roofs of newly completed houses; forming the cross with plates or bits of tortilla and salt at the end of a meal; making offerings to crosses formed from corn stalks at the end of the harvest season; and burning Palm Sunday straw crosses if the spring rains have not yet come. There he also notes other locations for protective crosses, and he suggests that the "fifth direction" at the intersection of the four points could represent Venus and amount to a mapping of the heavens onto the land, pp. 42–45.
55. Alicia Barabás, "Etnoterritorialidad sagrada en Oaxaca," in *Diálogos con el territorio*, ed. Barabás, I, 113, describes processions as rites tracing the boundaries and enclosing the pueblo or municipio in order to keep dangerous forces from entering, especially on May 3.
56. Torquemada, *Monarquía Indiana* III, 200 (libro 16, cap. 26), and 224 (libro 17, cap. 7); William B. Taylor, *Shrines & Miraculous Images: Religious Life in Mexico Before the Reforma*, Albuquerque: University of New Mexico Press, 2011, pp. 85–86; Sánchez Vásquez, "La Santa Cruz," p. 447, in the Otomi region of Ixmiquilpan-Actopan crosses are taken to the hilltop annually and replanted there before returning home.
57. Torquemada, *Monarquía Indiana*, III, 230–232 (libro 17, cap. 9).
58. Torquemada, *Monarquía Indiana*, III, 200 (libro 16, cap. 27).
59. Rodrigo Martínez Baracs, *La secuencia tlaxcalteca: Orígenes del culto a Nuestra Señora de Ocotlán*, Mexico: INAH, 2000, p. 93, citing Tadeo de Niza, Fernando de Alva Ixtlilxóchitl, and Diego Muñoz Camargo. A related story of a miraculous cross is told in the Mapa de Cuauhtlantzinco (Tlaxcala) and other sources, studied by Stephanie Wood. The "mapa" has a striking image of this cross as a living plant with a sword as the cross member, Wood, *Transcending Conquest: Nahua Views of Spanish Colonial Mexico*, Norman: University of Oklahoma Press, 2003, pp. 88, 89, 97, and 104. Minatory Indian miracles that the early seventeenth-century Nahua chronicler Chimalpahin associated with colonial crosses are mentioned by Lockhart, *The Nahuas After the Conquest*, p. 245. See also the discussion of Tequisquiapan at the end of this chapter.
60. Fr. Agustín de Vetancurt, *Teatro mexicano. Descripción breve de los sucesos ejemplares históricos y religiosos del Nuevo Mundo de las Indias; Crónica de la Provincia del Santo Evangelio de México* [1698], Mexico: Porrúa, 1982, facsimile edition, part. 4 trat. 2 ("de los sucesos religiosos"), p. 41; Torquemada, *Monarquía Indiana*, I, 303 (libro 3, cap. 26).
61. Torquemada, *Monarquía Indiana*, I, 303 (libro 3, cap. 26).
62. Solange Alberro, *El águila y la cruz: Orígenes religiosos de la conciencia criolla. México, siglos XVI–XVII*, Mexico: Fondo de Cultura Económica, 1999, p. 61, drawing on Durán.
63. Alberro, *El águila y la cruz*, pp. 62–63, citing Torquemada and Vetancurt.

64. Guy Rozat Dupeyron, *América, imperio del demonio: Cuentos y recuentos*, Mexico: Universidad Iberoamericana, 1995, p. 90. Torquemada recounted another struggle between the cross and the devil at the chapel of San José de los Naturales in Mexico City, *Monarquía Indiana*, I, 303 (libro 3, cap. 26).
65. Oakes, *Two Crosses of Todos Santos*, pp. 23–25. According to Ronald Wright and his American informant, the wooden cross was removed again and then reinstalled in the 1980s during the height of Guatemala's bloody civil war, "and people told me that from then on things began to improve," *Time Among the Maya: Travels in Belize, Guatemala, and Mexico*, New York: Grove Press, 2000, pp. 225–226.
66. Crosses, trees, and ancestors are linked by Freidel, Schele, and Parker in *Maya Cosmos*, pp. 124, 457.
67. For the Cruz de Maye as originally a tree, Sergio Sánchez Vásquez, "La Santa Cruz: Culto en los cerros de la región Otomí Actopan-Ixmiquilpan," in *La montaña en el paisaje ritual*, ed. Broda, Iwaniszewski, and Montero, pp. 442, 447. Sánchez Vásquez recounts the legend that giant ancestors carrying the Cruz de Maye stopped there and got drunk. While they were in a stupor the cross grew and could not be moved again. For the Cuernavaca cross, see Haskett, "Conquering the Spiritual Conquest," pp. 242, 253–254; for Jacona, in 1662, the addition to Basalenque, *Historia de la Provincia de San Nicolás Toletino de Michoacán*, p. 174; for Teccistlan, CAAG, unclassified 1721 expediente, "Autos pertenecientes a la cofradía del Santo Cristo de la Expiración del pueblo de Jocotepec"; for Tamazula and Yahualica, Higinio Vásquez, *Cristos célebres de México*, Mexico: n.p., pp. 69–72. The cross at Tepeyac is depicted in José de Arellano's 1709 painting of the new shrine to Guadalupe on the occasion of its dedication, examined at the Los Angeles County Museum of Art, September 2007. In addition to the crosses of Jacona, Tamazula, and Jocotepec, Matías de Escobar, *América thebaida: Vitas patrum de los religiosos hermitaños de N.P. San Agustín de la provincia de San Nicolás Toletino de Mechoacán* [1729], Morelia: Balsal Editores, 1970, pp. 464–466, lists six other miraculous natural crosses and crucifixes at San Pedro Piedra Gorda, Santiago Ocotlán, San Miguel de Atotonilco, Villa de León, Tupátaro, Ziragüen, and in the Santuario de Guadalupe of Valladolid.
68. For example, in a piece of mulberry split for firewood in the home of D. Felipe Yestes, barrio Santiago, Querétaro reported in the *Gazeta de México* issue of October 20, 1784; inside a rock that was split open at San Cristóbal Ecatepec reported in the *Gazeta de México* issue of March 20, 1792, "formó la Naturaleza"; and in Campeche in January 1815 Arturo Alvarez reported "two perfect crosses" discovered by Arturo Álvarez inside a log he was splitting for firewood, Terry Rugeley, "Origins of the Caste War: A Social History of Rural Yucatán, 1800–1847," Ph.D. dissertation, University of Houston, 1992, p. 271. Sánchez Vásquez notes that the crosses most revered in Otomí communities of Hidalgo are understood to be "cruces vivas" and "naturales," "La Santa Cruz," p. 447.
69. See the discussion later in this chapter of particular crosses that reportedly trembled; also the wooden cross of Rosario, Sinaloa which reportedly shook for several days in 1683 and became the object of ardent veneration, mentioned in a note to Francisco Sedano, *Apéndices a la obra Noticias de México*, Mexico: Barbedillo, 1880, tomo 1 pp. 166–168; the trembling stone crossroads cross at Totolapa in 1728, Melgar in Barabás, *Diálogos con el territorio*, 2: 323–324; the trembling stone cross of

494 Part II Soundings: Divine Presence, Place, and the Power of Things

Zapotla in the jurisdiction of Tacuba in 1741, AGN Bienes Nacionales 749 exp. 16; and the Cross of Sayula, Jalisco, that was said to have trembled in 1632, Sigismundo Taraval, *El milagro más visible o el milagro de los milagros más patentes. La santísima cruz de Tepique*, Guadalajara: El Colegio de Jalisco, 1992 printing of mid-eighteenth century text, p. 24.

70. Taylor, *Shrines & Miraculous Images*, p. 75; Harvey, "Pilgrimage and Shrine," pp. 95–96; Lara, *Christian Texts for Aztecs*, pp. 251, 252; Bibiana Ugalde Mendoza, *Xitaces con sentimiento y tradición: Historia del culto a la cruz verde de Tequisquiapan en la voz de un pueblo creyente*, Querétaro: Hear Taller Gráfico, 1997, *passim*; a "cross painted green" inventoried at the shrine of Mapethé, Hidalgo, in 1748, AGN Civil 1384 exp. 11; and the green cross of Tepic, discussed later in this essay. On green crosses in Yucatán and Chiapas, see Freidel, Schele, and Parker, *Maya Cosmos*, pp. 55, 174, 254, 401. A green cross associated with an apparition of Christ was prominent in the revitalization movement in Tlacoxcalco, Oaxaca, in 1911, Edward Wright-Ríos, "Envisioning Mexico's Catholic Resurgence: The Virgin of Solitude and the Talking Christ of Tlacoxcalco, 1908–1924," *Past and Present*, 195 (May 2007), 197–239, especially pp. 222, 225, 239.

71. Augustinians were, however, bishops of the Diocese of Yucatán from 1608–1636, 1696–1698, and 1753–1760.

72. For other numinous crosses, see Luis Weckmann, *The Medieval Heritage of Mexico*, trans. Frances M. López-Morillas, New York: Fordham University Press, 1992, p. 291 (cross near Paso del Norte, Chihuahua alleviated physical pain; Moqui, New Mexico, cross, given by the Lady in Blue, restored a girl's sight); *Gazeta de México* for July 1732, BIBM 4, pp. 334–335 reported a prodigious black cross at Mizquic in the Valley of Mexico; the miraculous cross of Rosales, Chihuahua reportedly survived a fire and other vicissitudes, Jesús José Lerma Almanza, *Santa Cruz: Símbolo, misión, y pueblo de Rosales, Chihuahua*, Chihuahua: Doble Hélice, 2006; and miraculous crosses at Sayula, Autlán, Ahuacatlan, and Zacoalco, Jalisco mentioned in William B. Taylor, *Magistrates of the Sacred: Priests and Parishioners in Eighteenth-Century Mexico*, Stanford, CA: Stanford University Press, 1996, pp. 268–269, 263 n. 134, and 669 n. 13, and Sigismundo Taraval's mid-eighteenth-century chronicle, *El milagro más visible*, p. 24. More recent cases of living crosses in Oaxaca are mentioned in Marroquín, *La cruz mesiánica*, p. 42.

73. Terry Rugeley, *Rebellion Now and Forever: Mayas, Hispanics, and Caste War Violence in Yucatan, 1800–1880*, Stanford: Stanford University Press, 2009, pp. 3, 5, and chapter 3; Victoria Reifler Bricker *The Indian Christ, the Indian King: The Historical Substrate of Maya Myth and Ritual*, Austin: University of Texas Press, 1981, pp. 102–103, and the cross's instructions to the governor in 1851, pp. 208–218. Miguel Ángel Astor Aguilera, *The Maya World of Communicating Objects, Quadripartite Crosses, Trees and Stones*, Albuquerque: University of New Mexico Press, 2011, suggests that oracular natural objects such as speaking crosses have a long history in Yucatán.

74. Fr. Diego de Landa, *Yucatán Before and After the Conquest* [1566], trans. William Gates, New York: Dover Publications, 1977, p. 47.

75. María de los Ángeles Rodríguez Álvarez, *Usos y costumbres funerarias en la Nueva España*, Zamora: El Colegio de Michoacán/El Colegio Mexiquense, 2001, p. 60.

76. "Copia de un original muy precioso de la junta que se hicieron en la ciudad de Thenuxtitlan México," appendix to Francisco Antonio de Lorenzana, ed., *Concilios provinciales primero, y segundo, celebrados en la muy noble, y muy leal ciudad de México* ...,

Mexico: Imprenta de el Superior Gobierno de Joseph Antonio de Hogal, 1769, p. 329 (April 27, 1539).
77. Samuel Y. Edgerton, *Theaters of Conversion: Religious Architecture and Indian Artisans in Colonial Mexico*, Albuquerque: University of New Mexico Press, 2001, chapter 2, and "Christan Cross as Indigenous 'World Tree' in Sixteenth-Century Mexico: The 'Atrio' Cross in the Frederick and Jan Mayer Collection," in *Exploring New World Imagery: Spanish Colonial Papers from the 2002 Mayer Center Symposium*, ed. Donna Pierce, Denver: Denver Art Musuem, 2005, pp. 11–40; Lara, *City, Temple, Stage*, chapter 5. Eleanor Wake's *Framing the Sacred: The Indian Churches of Early Colonial Mexico*, Norman: University of Oklahoma Press, 2010, another ambitious book on sixteenth-century churches, is even more insistent on indigenous roots and branches of the symbol-studded stone atrium crosses: "a greater part of the religious art and architecture of Indian Mexico expressed not only native religious responses to the conversion program but also native cultural responses to its introduction and imposition," p. 3. Like Lara, Edgerton, and other authors who recognize native conceptions in early colonial architecture, she highlights the orientation of new construction according to sacred features in the landscape and the five-part precolonial conception of the cosmos (with an even greater emphasis on the great central tree of Tamoanchan), but she criticizes Edgerton for viewing this organization of space as mainly an opportunistic strategy of the early mendicant evangelizers, thereby denying "any autonomy of native thought and action," pp. 4, 228–232. See Marroquín, *La cruz mesiánica*, pp. 42–45 for another work that emphasizes the precolonial quincunx and associates the planet Venus with the central direction.

All of these recent works by art historians focus on the visual, including the iconography of the symbols on the stone crosses, with less attention to the ever-present plain wooden crosses. Within her emphasis on precolonial continuities and crosses as "ritualized cosmic trees" (p. 229), Wake sees the symbol-studded early stone crosses as an example of native *horror vacui*. If that is so, what is one to make of the many crosses in the colonial landscape with little or no decoration permanently fashioned on them? If the plain crosses are new, and the opposite of a preference for inscribing the entire surface, could this be evidence of Christian conceptions of the cross finding their way into colonial Indian practice, reworked, in ways similar to the incorporation of the word "cruz" into colonial Maya texts discussed in Hanks's *Converting Words*? Wake seems to close off this possibility, suggesting that while the word "cruz" was adopted in Nahuatl, "native perception of the cruz did not change," from its precolonial meanings, p. 217.
78. Callaway, "Pre-Columbian and Colonial Mexican Images," p. 213. For her understanding of Xipe Totec, she relies on the work of Eduard Seler.
79. Callaway, "Pre-Columbian and Colonial Mexican Images," p. 222.
80. In a dedication booklet that regarded this cross as an early missionary creation, Miguel de Bárcena described it as an "hermosísima cruz de piedra de cantería colorada ... grabada con mucho primor de arte que plantaron los primeros religiosos," in Miguel de Bárcena, *Relación de la pompa festiva y solemne colocación de una santa y hermosa cruz de piedra, que el ilustrísimo señor don Juan de Mañozca, arzobispo de México ... trasladó al cementerio de esta Iglesia Cathedral de México ...*, Mexico: Hipólito de Rivera, 1648. According to Bárcena, Archbishop Mañozca found it in pieces in the atrium/cemetery of

the church complex during his pastoral visit to Tepeapulco. Before long, Indians from the town paid a visit to the archbishop in Mexico City and ceded the cross to him "a pesar de que la estimaban en mucho, pues creían que la había levantado el famoso Fr. Francisco de Tembleque." He sent them on their way with expense money and 100 pesos to repair their church. The cross was placed in the cemetery, facing the main door of the cathedral, covered with flowers and sedge for the dedication ceremony on the Day of the Exaltation of the Cross, September 14, 1648. Later known as the "cruz de Mañozca," it was moved again in 1792 during the reconstruction of the Zócalo, after being reworked into a plain cross, its low-relief carvings obliterated. Information about this cross after 1648 comes from the archdiocesan website www.arquidiocesismexico.org.mx/Hist Fabrica Material La Cruz.html accessed December 14, 2010.

81. Details about the history of the Cruz de Talabarteros in this paragraph come from UT Benson G-97 "Testimonio de los papeles e instrumentos en que consta la fundasión de la capilla de la Santa Cruz de los Talabarteros."

82. In 1641 the Inquisition issued an edict forbidding fiestas de la Santa Cruz because crosses were being placed and painted in "indecent locations," AGN Edictos de la Inquisición vol. 1, fol. 16. If this edict was enforced, it was only for a short time. However, fiestas on the Day of the Holy Cross were suspended from time to time during emergencies; for example in the Archdiocese of Mexico in 1694 because of famine, AGN General de Parte 17 exp. 34, fols. 29v–30.

83. Examples of surveillance and restriction, and in one case removal, include the cross of Huaquechula in 1806, discussed in note 130; the found cross of Teccistlán, Jalisco in 1721, CAAG, unclassified 1721 expediente, "Autos pertenecientes a la cofradía del Santo Cristo de la Expiración del pueblo de Jocotepec"; and the "cross of justice" at San Francisco Galileo, Querétaro in 1817, AGN Inquisición 1465 exp. 7, fols. 85–87. Found crosses were reported again in the nineteenth and twentieth centuries. The example of El Señor de la Misericordia in Tepatitlán (in the Altos de Jalisco), a cross that appeared in an oak tree to a campesino from the El Durazno rancho in 1839 is discussed in Kinga Novak, "Of Gratitude and Sorrow: A Visual History of Everyday Mexican Spirituality, 1700–2013," Ph.D. dissertation, University of California, Berkeley, 2013, pp. 76–77.

84. AHM L10B/28, fol. 107.

85. Weckmann, *Medieval Heritage*, pp. 289–290.

86. Sources consulted for the Huatulco cross include Torquemada, González Dávila, Burgoa, Isidro de la Asunción, Alcedo, Alegre, Juan Antonio Rivera, Villaseñor y Sánchez, Weckmann, Cuadriello, and Callaway. I am drawing especially from Torquemada, the earliest printed source, *Monarquía Indiana*, III, 203–206 (libro 16, cap. 28). Other particularly helpful secondary sources are the essays in ed. Jaime Cuadriello, *Ciclos pictóricos de Antequera-Oaxaca, siglos XVII-XVIII: Mito, santidad e identidad*, Mexico: Instituto de Investigaciones Estéticas, UNAM, et al., 2013. For the history of the settlement of Huatulco after the pirate raids, there is Nahui Ollin Vásquez Mendoza's "Huatulco, Oaxaca: Fragmentos de una historia colonial de abandonos y melancolías," *Relaciones: Estudios de Historia y Sociedad* 134 (primavera 2013), 159–192. Two other miraculous crosses from western Mexico with similar stories at about the same time are associated with Colima and Autlán (Jalisco), Weckmann, *Medieval Heritage*, pp. 289–290.

Placing the Cross in Colonial Mexico 497

87. On the connection to ocean travel and the port of Huatulco, several late seventeenth-century sources appeal to the cross of Huatulco to protect the port and ships against the "perfidious heretic": Nicolás Gómez de Cervantes, *Sermón de la Exaltación de la Cruz Sacrosanta, en la solemnidad que esse día celebra la Iglesia Cathedral de la Ciudad de Antequera Valle de Oaxaca, en memoria del triumpho, y Victoria del milagroso y Santo Madero del Puerto de Guatulco contra el pérfido herege*, Mexico: Francisco Rodríguez Lupercio, 1671; for 1685 news of pirates burning the port of Huatulco again, Juan Antonio Rivera, *Diario curioso del capellán del Hospital de Jesús Nazareno de México*, Mexico: Vargas Rea, 1953, I, 40; and for prayers offered to the cross for some years thereafter when news arrived of the annual fleet's safe travels to Spain arrived, Fr. Angel Maldonado, *Oración evangélica en la solemnidad que a la Santa Cruz de Huatulco dedica todos los años la Santa Iglesia Cathedral de la Ciudad de Antequera, Valle de Oaxaca, día de la Exaltación de la Cruz. En ocasión que llegaron de España las noticias de la flota*, Mexico: Francisco de Rivera Calderón, 1703.
88. One *braza* (about 5.47 feet).
89. Torquemada, *Monarquía Indiana*, III, 205.
90. Jacobo Dalevuelta [pseud.], *Oaxaca, de sus historias y sus leyendas*, Mexico: Andrés Botas e Hijo, 1922, p. 71.
91. González Dávila, *Teatro eclesiástico*, p 79. Isidro de la Asunción, *Itinerario*, p. 108 said it made a complete cross roughly sixteen inches tall (said to be a palmo y medio high; a palmo being about 8.22"). He also claimed to have "un pedazo muy grande envajado en una cruz" to ward off lightning strikes and exorcise demons. Yet another fragment went to the Mercedarian church in Mexico City and eventually to the Colegio de San Pedro Pascual de Belén (founded in 1784). It was said to be large enough to fashion into a small cross, Dalevuelta, *Oaxaca*, p. 71.
92. Antonio de Alcedo, *Diccionario geográfico histórico de las Indias Occidentales o América*, 4 vols. (1786–1789), Madrid: Ediciones Atlas, 1967, II, 207, drawing from Villaseñor y Sánchez.
93. Judging by the sparse documentation after the late seventeenth century, this devotion has declined since then. Jaime Cuadriello notes its virtual disappearance in the twentieth century, *Las glorias de la República de Tlaxcala*, p. 396.
94. Santa Gertrudis, *Cruz de piedra*, pp. 23–24, 33–34. Antonio Rubial García, "Santiago y la cruz de piedra. La mítica y milagrosa fundación de Querétaro, ¿Una elaboración del Siglo de las Luces?" in *Creencias y prácticas religiosas en Querétaro, siglos XVI–XIX*, ed. Juan Ricardo Jiménez Gómez, Mexico: Plaza y Valdés, 2004, pp. 27–28, cites a notarial record for de la Rea from May 3, 1649 that refers to the chapel there being built forty years before and attracting both Spaniards and Indians.
95. De la Rea, *Crónica de la orden de N. Seráfico P.S. Francisco*, pp. 287–295.
96. In the 1649 notarial record he also does not mention miraculous apparitions or a founding battle, Rubial García, "Santiago y la cruz," p. 28.
97. De la Rea, *Crónica de la orden de N. Seráfico P.S. Francisco*, pp. 287–292 mentions that this fallen horseman also survived another accident that should have killed him. The growth and movement of this cross are recurring themes in this literature. Writing in 1680, Carlos de Sigüenza y Góngora understood that the growth was continual but that the trembling had lapsed for many years until May 5, 1680, at 3 p.m. He regarded the new movement as an "obsequio cariñoso de su amante Madre," and that the cross "pretendía festejar a la inmaculada Reina del Universo" at the time of the dedication of Querétaro's

church of the Virgin of Guadalupe, *Glorias de Querétaro (1531–1680)*, Querétaro: Gobierno del Estado, 1985, pp. 29–31.
98. Santa Gertrudis, *Cruz de piedra*, p. 23.
99. Judging by the urgent application by Querétaro's leaders in April 1694 for permission to hold their annual feast of the Holy Cross, and responses by the archbishop and viceroy before the end of the month, the feast day in the seventeenth century would have taken place on May 3, AGN General de Parte 17 exps. 34–35, fols. 29v–32. If so, it had shifted to September 14 by the turn of the nineteenth century, Antonio Ruiz Narváez, *Sermón de la exaltación de la Cruz* ..., Mexico: Zúñiga y Ontiveros, 1802, or perhaps this cross was honored on both days of the Holy Cross.
100. Santa Gertrudis, *Cruz de piedra*, p. 23. For completion of a more capacious church in 1654 and a new convent in 1666, see Joseph María Zelaá e Hidalgo, *Glorias de Querétaro y sus adiciones* [1803], introduced by Jaime Septién, Querétaro: Gobierno Constitucional del Estado, 2009, pp. 37–39. Carlos de Sigüenza y Góngora, *Glorias de Querétaro (1531–1680)*, pp. 29–31, spoke of the new construction and growing devotion, crediting Fr. José Santos, the *guardián* in 1680, with collecting 120,000p in alms over the course of twelve years of travel in the province.
101. AGN General de Parte 17 exps. 34–35, fols. 29v–32.
102. The celebrated Fr. Antonio de Llinaz established the new college, with the help of his twenty-seven Franciscan companions. Rubial García, "Santiago y la cruz," pp. 30–37 also emphasizes the role of the Franciscan missionary college in the development and promotion of the miracle stories.
103. Zeláa e Hidalgo, *Glorias de Querétaro*, pp. 37–39.
104. José de Castro, *Sermón que en el día primero de su celebridad, en la mui plausible fiesta de la ampliación de el Cruzero y reedificación del Templo de la milagrosa Santíssima Cruz de Piedra de la Ciudad de Querétaro*, Mexico: Francisco Rodríguez Lupercio, 1702, sponsored by Isidro Félix de Espinosa.
105. Nicolás Muntáñez (?), *Relación histórica de la Conquista de Querétaro*, ed. Rafael Ayala Echavarri, Mexico: Sociedad Mexicana de Geografía y Estadística, 1948. A different reading of the text is given by Serge Gruzinski, "Mutilated Memory: Reconstruction of the Past and the Mechanisms of Memory Among Seventeenth-Century Otomis," *History and Anthropology* 2 (1986), 337–351.
106. Rubial García infers that the Montáñez narrative was written in the late seventeenth century, drawing from earlier indigenous oral tradition, "Santiago y la cruz," pp. 42–43. Another possibility is that the text was created by or for the Franciscans from oral tradition and other sources in 1717.
107. *Relación histórica de la Conquista de Querétaro*, ed. Ayala Echavarri, pp. 139, 142, 143.
108. Francisco Antonio Navarrete, SJ, *Relación peregrina de la agua corriente* ..., Mexico: José Bernardo de Hogal, 1739, pp. 17ff.
109. These two versions of the founding miracles – Tapia in 1531 and Montáñez in 1550 – are juxtaposed by Rubial García in "Santiago y la cruz," pp. 25–58. He attributes both to native traditions, but places their narrative formulation and promotion in the late seventeenth and eighteenth centuries, composed by Franciscans of the Santa Cruz college.
110. Bancroft M-M 240, part 3 ("Memorias piadosas de la nación indiana," 1782), p. 83.

111. Ruiz Narváez, *Sermón de la exaltación de la cruz* . . .; Zeláa e Hidalgo, *Glorias de Querétaro*, pp. 41–44. Two unpublished sermons by members of the Colegio de la Santa Cruz at Querétaro in the early 1740s suggest that Franciscans there were already promoting the devotion and feast day of the Exaltation of the Cross, perhaps at the expense of the feast of the Invention of the Cross, untitled volume of thirty-four Mexican manuscript sermons and "pláticas religiosas" dating from the mid-eighteenth century, deaccesioned from the St. Francis Xavier College Library, New York City and purchased by the University of Dayton Marian Library in 1970, no call number, fols. 4–10 (sermon preached by Fr. Tomás de Urive Larrea in 1741) and fols. 11–14.
112. *Gazeta de México*, May 1730, BIBM 4, pp. 182–183.
113. *Relaciones geográficas del Arzobispado de México. 1743*, ed. Francisco de Solano, Madrid: C.S.I.C., 1988, I, 261–262.
114. The available documentation on this tradition is digested in Pedro López González, *Álbum histórico del ex-convento de la Cruz de Zacate*, 2nd ed., Tepic: Ayuntamiento de Tepic, 2000, and Guillermo García Mar, "La Santísima Cruz de Tepic. Construcción, difusión, amplitud, y permanencia en el occidente de la Nueva España, 1619–1812," M.A. thesis, Universidad de Guadalajara, 2011.
115. Domingo Lázaro de Arregui, *Descripción de la Nueva Galicia*, Sevilla: Escuela de Estudios Hispanoamericanos, 1946, p. 94. In the 1760s Francisco de Ajofrín reported having heard that on the site of this relic a wooden cross had long before fallen over and decayed, but that excavations beneath the grass had not produced evidence that a wooden cross had served as its original seedbed, *Diario del viaje que hizo a la América en el siglo XVIII el P. Fray Francisco de Ajofrín*, Mexico: Instituto Cultural Hispano Mexicano, 1964, I, 220–221.
116. *Crónica miscelánea de la Santa Provincia de Xalisco*, III, 45.
117. Francisco de Florencia, *Origen de dos célebres santuarios de la Nueva Galicia, Obispado de Guadalajara en la América septentrional*, Mexico: Impr. de Juan Joseph Guillena Carrascoso, 1694, pp. 6–8.
118. In the mid-eighteenth century, another Jesuit, Francisco Javier Alegre, added to the idea of a prior Christian evangelization in the region by noting that there were precolonial crosses in the region and an ancient image of Christ carved into a local rock face, *Historia de la Compañía de Jesús en Nueva España, que estaba escribiendo el P. Francisco Javier Alegre al tiempo de su expulsión*, Mexico: Imprenta de J. M. Lara, 1841–1842, I, 201.
119. Beginning in the 1720s the verdant cross attracted attention outside its home area. In 1722 Santa Gertrudis referred to it in his devotional history of the stone cross of Querétaro, and in the December 1729 issue the *Gazeta de México* reported that the Bishop of Guadalajara made a point of visiting the shrine during his pastoral visit to Tepic, adding that the site was celebrated for its perennially green cross of grass in an arid spot, even during the winter, BIBM 4, p. 154.
120. In a 1770 treatise, Canon Mateo José de Arteaga y Rincón Gallardo questioned the truth of the miracle of perpetual verdure but acknowledged that the Cross of Tepic enjoyed widespread veneration "among all the towns in the area," García Mar, "La Santísima Cruz de Tepic," p. 322.
121. This text is known only in a manuscript copy in the BN, Madrid, cited by López González, *Álbum*, pp. 72–73. Francisco Xavier Alegre added a little to the aura of

crosses in the Tepic area in his *Historia de la Compañía de Jesús en Nueva España*, which was still in manuscript when he and other Jesuits left Spanish America in 1767. Speaking of Tepic as "famoso por el prodigio de la Santa Cruz que allí se venera," Alegre mentioned that ancient crosses and a Christ sculpted on a rock outcropping had been found (citing a 1615 report of fellow Jesuit Rodrigo de Cabredo), and that in April each year beautiful sounds of a bell coming from that same mountain (Sierra de Chacala) are heard throughout the valley, Alegre, *Historia*, I, 201.

122. Bancroft MSS 99/374m, fols. 48v–49r. A printed description of the Tepic cross and its mystique, from 1756, appears in Joaquín Osuna's *Peregrinación Christiana por el camino real de la celeste Jerusalén*, Mexico: Bibliotheca Mexicana, 1756, paragraph 3 no. 6:

En un lugar de este Reyno llamado Thepique, perteneciente a Guadalaxara, se ve tendida en la tierra una cruz grande, y ancha, naturalmente formada del mismo heno o sacates que allí nacen, todos de igual color y altura como si a mano emparejassen (salvo en los lugares correspondientes a los clavos, que aquí sobresalen un poco más) y todo sin cultivo alguno permanecen todo el año verdes, sin secarse ni desminuirse, pues aun cuando estaba del todo descubierta, y estando en el campo jamás se atrevieron las bestias a hoyar ni comer su zacate; y quando la devoción le arranca algún manojo, brevemente crece y se empareja con el demás.

123. Bancroft MSS 99/374m, fol. 48v. Francisco de Ajofrín, also writing in the mid-eighteenth century, muffled the story of discovery in 1619, saying "there is no memory from the time this prodigy appeared." He also described the size and nature of the grassy plot: The grass was half a vara high (about 16 inches), twenty-one and two-thirds feet wide (8 1/8 varas), and forty feet long (15 varas), with arms extending twelve and a third feet on each side (4 5/8 varas). The grass was unlike any that grew in the area and was always green even though the site was naturally arid. Like Bustillo, he stressed that much grass was taken away as relics, yet the cross somehow was not diminished, *Diario del viaje*, I, 220–221, 280.

124. AGN Clero Regular y Secular 215 exp. 29, and UT Benson, García Collection folders 74, 75.

125. AGN Clero Regular y Secular 215 exp. 29, and UT Benson, García Collection folders 74, 75. The AGN case is summarized with a different purpose in mind by Edward Osowski, "Passion Miracles and Indigenous Historical Memory in New Spain," *Hispanic American Historical Review* 88: 4 (2008), 607–638.

126. The cross was said to be two and three-quarters *varas* tall – about seven and a half feet.

127. The "teniente general del partido," appointed by the *alcalde mayor*.

128. According to the pastoral visit records of the Archdiocese of Mexico, the "Spaniards" of Tlayacapan had their own confraternity dedicated to the Holy Cross as early as 1716. It was still in place in 1757. This pattern of popular beliefs and practices being widely shared across classes and ethnic groups in Tlayacapan is taken up in John M. Ingham, *Mary, Michael & Lucifer: Folk Catholicism in Central Mexico*, Austin: University of Texas Press, 1986, p. 38. In 1743, about 10 percent of Tlayacapan's families were Spaniards and mestizos. The social gulf between them and the majority Indian population was reduced by the fact that few of the non-Indians were large landowners. Many were shopkeepers and artisans, and most of those who farmed and raised livestock were

renters. They had an interest in protecting village lands, and although they acted to perpetuate ethnic distinctions, they were rarely in open conflict with their Indian neighbors.

Other examples of devotion to miraculous crosses and figures of Christ across ethnic lines for the Mixteca Baja of Oaxaca in the eighteenth and nineteenth centuries are mentioned in Smith, *Roots of Conservatism in Mexico*, chapters 1, 2.

129. *Gazeta de México* for January 1729, BIBM 4, p. 91.

130. "se espera finalize la devoción de los vecinos y comarcanos," reported the article, *Gazeta de México* for May 1737, BIBM 4, p. 698. This cross and its wondrous movement also merited mention by the author of the *relación geográfica* for the Chalco Tlalmanalco district in 1743, who summarized the judicial record in two paragraphs, *Relaciones geográficas . . . . 1743*, I, 46.

131. Tlayacapan is famous for its many neighborhood "chapels," some of them substantial little churches. The most detailed study is by Claudio Favier Orendáin, *Ruinas de utopia: San Juan Tlayacapan; espacio y tiempo en el encuentro . . .*, Cuernavaca: Gobierno del Estado, 1998. In addition to the sixteenth-century Augustinian church, there are reported to be twenty-six chapels, eighteen of them still in use. No barrio chapel today is called Santa Ysabel, nor is Tepetenchi the name used for a barrio.

132. See Taylor, *Shrines & Miraculous Images*, pp. 49–51.

133. Barrio San Juan, Barrio Magdalena, Barrio El Cerrito, Santa Rosa Xajay, San Francisco Hidalgo, San Joaquín, and Maguey Verde. Other communities that participated in the fiesta cycle are mentioned. Informants from the barrio of San Juan predominate in Ugalde Mendoza's array of informants.

134. Not surprisingly, the informants from San Juan have the most elaborate stories to tell about the legendary beginnings, including members of the local Bárcenas family coming out as the overseer dragged the cross past their house crying "Ahí va mi papacito," and pleading with him to leave it with them.

135. "pura payasada," as one put it.

136. Donancio González from Santa Rosa Xajay averred that while San Juan's cross is the main one (*la principal*), theirs is the most important to them: "nosotros tratamos como principal la que tenemos, aunque sea una peregrina," Ugalde Mendoza, *Xitaces*, pp. 69–70.

137. For discussion of an "ongoing accord" between priests and parishioners over perspiring Christs and other reports on divine immanence in the Mixteca Baja during the late nineteenth century, see Smith, *The Roots of Conservatism in Mexico*, chapter 4. Pragmatic accommodations of bishops and parish priests to local devotional practices are also discussed in Taylor, *Magistrates of the Sacred*, and chapters 1 and 6 of *Shrines and Miraculous Images*.

9
Pilgrims, Processions, and Romerías

What most distinguishes a shrine from other churches is that it is the object of pilgrimage; it draws people from beyond the immediate vicinity to a sacred place where devotees believe that God has shown His presence and special favor.[1] But the meaning of pilgrimage and cognate terms in other languages is not as straightforward as "leaving home on a spiritual journey"; and even when scholars share an interest in large-scale journeys to a Christian sacred place, they have disagreed about what is going on. Beyond the many meanings of "pilgrimage" in our time, the ways people used the term hundreds of years ago also varied. And we rarely know exactly what pilgrims did and thought on their journeys.

Nearly all the colonial pilgrimages I can identify were short in duration and distance, directed to a nearby image shrine or other sacred place. They were not much like the great medieval and early modern Christian journeys of personal atonement along an established route of shrines leading to one of the great destinations – Compostela, Rome, or Jerusalem.[2] From my early readings, including Victor Turner and the vast devotional literature for Our Lady of Guadalupe at Tepeyac, this was a surprise.[3] Distant journeys of faith may have been a larger part of the story of pilgrimage in New Spain than I could document from the paper trail since ecclesiastical and civil authorities focused on regulating what went on at shrines more than on transit to and from them. On the other hand, colonial officials had good reasons to track long-distance commerce and what they regarded as vagrancy, and they did so without much attention to pilgrims.

After a few lines about the state of play in Christian pilgrimage studies and how the term pilgrimage is used, this chapter centers on how and why short journeys to sacred places were so important in the territory of New Spain until the mid-nineteenth century, and closes with an approach to further study. Again, sources and their uses are as much at issue as the patterns in sacred journeys over time that can be found in them.

The Idea of Pilgrimage

Beyond medieval Europe and a few great destinations in more recent times or other traditions, including Lourdes, Knock, Tepeyac, Mecca, Varanasi, Buddhist sites in South Asia, and Shikoku in Japan, pilgrimage was not much studied before the late 1970s, when anthropologists and geographers took the lead, sharpening the focus on processes, structures, spatial relations, and group dynamics. This recent scholarly interest coincided with the growing popularity of journeys described as pilgrimages (about 200 million pilgrims a year in one geographer's estimation, most of them Christians, although Mecca alone is said to draw at least 15 million pilgrims) and of religious and cultural tourism to Compostela, the Christian holy lands, Civil War battlefields, Holocaust sites and museums, the Vietnam Veterans Memorial, the Red Rocks of Sedona, Arizona, and Elvis Presley's Graceland, among the many destinations.

Among anthropologists, no one has influenced the study of pilgrimage in our time more than Victor Turner. Drawing on Arnold Van Gennep's *The Rites of Passage* and what Turner understood from field experience in Africa and Mexico and his reading about long-distance pilgrimage in medieval Europe and elsewhere, he and Edith Turner proposed in 1978 that pilgrimages are phased spiritual journeys in which there is a liminal release from the structures and constraints of everyday social life, toward a cathartic burst of subversive bliss in the shared experience of the journey away from home: a communion of transcendent feeling across classes and communities.[4] "A bout of nomadism," Victor Turner once called it, usually directed toward sacred places "out there," far from the centers of institutional life.[5] Mexico was one of the Turners' examples of "a pilgrimage system." In their view, the image of the Virgin of Guadalupe and its shrine at Tepeyac in the Valley of Mexico stands as a timeless "dominant symbol" at the apex of a hierarchy of lesser shrines connected by well-established pilgrimage routes. By dominant symbol they mean "a relatively fixed point in both the social and the cultural structure," a symbol that "presides over ... the total symbolic system."[6] In taking a performance approach to pilgrimage, the Turners emphasized the journey over the destination, and time over place. The destinations interested them less, perhaps because they represented a return to more structured, prescribed activity.

The Turners' work has met a mixed reception, especially among anthropologists and sociologists. They have been sharply criticized for stressing social communion, spontaneity, and liminality where others find social divisions, conflict, and structures orchestrated by elites.[7] From this present-oriented perspective, the activities the Turners described were not so much a break from ordinary life and relationships as an expression of it, another of many "forms of motion" in a world of "fluid physical and social processes."[8]

This view leads to broad definitions that downplay religiosity: pilgrimage is "physical movement through a terrain of culturally constructed symbols,"[9] directed toward something extraordinary and perhaps cathartic, but rooted in social distinctions, orchestration, and the everyday.[10] This view suits the popular use of the word pilgrimage in our time for all sorts of literal and figurative exercises in self-expression and personal identity, not only long distance journeys toward spiritual enlightenment and transcendence. The catharsis might come from John Denver's Rocky Mountain high, or from a trip to Stonehenge or New Orleans in the wake of Hurricane Katrina, or as a metaphorical journey of discovery and self-improvement, as suggested by recent book titles like *A Pilgrimage Toward Self Mastery* and *My Pilgrim's Heart: A Woman's Journey Through Marriage and Other Foreign Lands*; or an homage to the taste buds, such as *Barbecue America: A Pilgrimage in Search of America's Best Barbecue*.

The other great debate in pilgrimage studies is over space and place, and brings in geographers and philosophers. As I have written elsewhere, the articulation of space and place, or often space *versus* place, is an ongoing conundrum for geographers.[11] Yi-fu Tuan and other "humanistic" geographers and anthropologists have given primacy to place and intersections of activity in describing location for many world cultures, while the more calibrated approaches of "scientific" geographers tend to emphasize space and mathematical modeling. Philosopher-phenomenologist-intellectual historian Edward Casey has given the humanistic geographers' perspective a more polemical and historical edge with his project of "recovering" place as the most fundamental form of embodied experience,[12] arguing against the idea of space as having an objective, *a priori* existence as a void to be filled in. Casey considers such a view of space to be distinctly Western and modern, epitomized by Newton's view of places as compartmentalized parts of space, which, Casey says, is the common sense of our time and culture.[13]

I am less interested in debates over the conceptual primacy of space or place than in place making and circulation of people, things, ideas, and sacred energy that are not marked only by buildings and other enclosures and visible boundaries.[14] Places get made when people occupy them, physically and imaginatively, when the activity around and through them makes them "inside."[15] In any event, space and place are not neutral, self-evident concepts. They express how people perceive and encounter location and territory. Take burial places. Whether located within or beyond a residential community, burial places express remembrance, continuity, ancestry, and home. During the colonial period, the settlements and burial sites of rural central and southern Mexico were part of a symbolic landscape of social, moral, and cosmic order. The saints, like the dead, were present there, if approached in the right way.[16] The late sixteenth-century

Indian resettlement program in central and southern Mexico had mixed results in large part because people would not willingly abandon these dwelling places of their ancestors and transcendent patrons, even for better farmlands.

As a way to go beyond the place and space divide, and sidestep the Turners' accent on center-periphery distinctions and a nested hierarchy of places, I am thinking about sacred travel and being in terms of devotional landscapes, which in Mexico are usually framed by mountains. J. B. Jackson characterized landscapes as "the various ways humans had come to terms with their environment, specifically how we created landscapes as places where we could live and work and celebrate together."[17] Speaking of landscapes invites a view of place that is marked by movement without jumping into the void of space or insisting on the journey as the destination. The experiences of sacred place and territory in New Spain seem to me to be not only about fixed location, but also about dwelling, proximity, comings, and goings – made and re-made through the experience of arriving, encompassing, seeing, touching, hearing, smelling, tasting, and sounding off. In short, the landscapes of colonial shrines were restless and repeatedly traversed, with devotees reaching for communication with the divine where it was understood to be powerfully available, often in and of nature.[18] During the colonial period, this movement usually was accomplished on foot – an extended, tactile experience, marking and taking in surroundings. In other words, processions and short journeys to a shrine, often with a sacred image, by groups of devotees were extended place making, inspiriting rituals that renewed a link between the divine patron and the places and territory protected. Within this kind of landscape, the world could become ordered and made complete, while what remained outside was unfinished, wild and, in a sense, off the spiritual map.

There are faint echoes of the debates about space, place, *communitas*, and conflict in the scholarship on Mesoamerica, but the merging of pilgrimage with movement in general as a category of analysis has barely been noticed. Mainly, the Turners' work on pilgrimage continues to be cited approvingly in ethnographic and ethnohistorical studies for its themes of antistructure, crossing thresholds, rites of passage, the journey, *communitas*, and dominant symbols, rather than closely examined as a line of interpretation with historical underpinnings. The discussion of Mesoamerican pilgrimages has been shaped more by a long-standing disagreement over whether pilgrimage in the colonial period was largely a continuation of precolonial practices in the guise of the Catholic cult of saints or whether long-distance pilgrimages were introduced by Europeans and shaped by European practices.[19]

Mexican scholarship, especially by anthropologists and ethnohistorians working in precolonial studies, has treated pilgrimage as a great arc of continuity between the aboriginal past and present-day communities where indigenous languages are or were until recently spoken. Migration and processions certainly appear as leading themes in precolonial and early colonial texts, especially as ritual processions that punctuated the ceremonial calendar.[20] But the legendary long-distance travels described in indigenous pictorial sources from the early colonial period are mostly one-way journeys by a whole people to a promised land or the ceremonious travels of state traders in luxury goods.[21] Evidence of a precolonial culture of pilgrimage in the European Christian sense of popular, penitential journeys to and from a great shrine "out there" is less clear. Cholula, with its great temple-pyramid, market, and sixteenth-century testimony that ritual visits were made there, seems to come closest. Early Spanish commentators were quick to call Cholula a native pilgrimage center; and Geoffrey McCafferty, relying on a late sixteenth-century *relación geográfica* written by the Spanish alcalde mayor of Cholula, suggests that "nobles from central Mexico came to Cholula to offer tribute to these priests and in exchange receive legitimation of their authority." David Carrasco and Scott Sessions agree about this function and add that Cholula "was accessible and prized by the wider populace."[22] But who went and how do we know? Was it mainly elites? When did they go? Where were they from? And where else did they go? The only attempt to survey precolonial pilgrimages, which relies heavily on colonial chronicles, lists eighteen pilgrimage sites in central and southern Mexico, most of them situated near mountains, caves, and springs; but ritual journeys to most of these places seem to have been short and focused on propitiation, more like penitential processions than like the famous medieval European pilgrimages.[23]

George Kubler, art historian extraordinaire, offered a different view of precolonial and early colonial pilgrimage in Mesoamerica.[24] Because of chronic warfare, inter-regional pilgrimages of any kind were rare before the arrival of Europeans and were mainly undertaken by groups of merchants, he suggested. Spanish conquest and colonization ushered in "new and very inviting European-style [long-distance] pilgrimages" to Christian shrines, quickly displacing "the harsh, native American eschatological" journeys. Rather than sited at major precolonial holy sites, these "huge new pilgrimages of peoples" developed elsewhere, at "such places as Guadalupe ..., Chalma ..., and Esquipulas" (both he and the Turners imagined that the great modern pilgrimages to Tepeyac extended back into the early colonial period).[25] For Kubler, as well as the Turners, Mesoamerica and the central Andes breathed new life into a medieval Christian mode of pilgrimage.

In spite of their considerable differences, anthropologists, sociologists, geographers, and historians of medieval Europe and Mesoamerica have assumed that Christian pilgrimages mainly meant long-distance journeys to a few great shrines. Only recently have several scholars – James Bugslag, Eamon Duffy, William Christian, and Marc Forster especially – considered that most journeys of faith and atonement in Europe during the late Middle Ages and early modern period were made closer to home, in a local landscape of sacred springs, rocks, and trees "in response to vows undertaken when the commune was endangered by disease or disaster," or noticed that Spanish monarchs by the late sixteenth century were not encouraging long-distance pilgrimages to the great shrines, especially Santiago de Compostela, for fear of vagabondage.[26] As Bugslag notes, local shrines and visits to them are poorly documented because they "lacked the institutional basis of the great shrines" and, unlike their counterparts in Mexico, many have "all but disappeared from the mechanized world of the twenty-first century."[27]

In Spain and Spanish America, as well as Catholic Europe more generally during the early modern period, pilgrimage (*peregrinación*) was defined especially as a long journey to a shrine or other dwelling place of the divine. This idea of a long journey toward a sacred destination invited other meanings. One was life as an arduous spiritual journey toward salvation. As Dr. Juan Ubaldo de Anguita Sandoval y Roxas put it in a 1727 funeral sermon he called The Prudent Pilgrim (*El prudente peregrino*), "pilgrimage means a journey beyond one's homeland; therefore, one who lives absent from one's homeland carries the name of pilgrim. For that reason the people's apostle, St. Paul rightly calls our life a prolonged pilgrimage because, absent from the homeland which we anxiously desire, we travel as pilgrims along the painful path of life."[28] In 1700, Basque merchant Tomás de Urdiñola had written less spiritually about his difficult ocean passage from Spain to Peru of nearly two years as "a prolonged and difficult pilgrimage."[29] Pilgrimages in both these meanings were extensions of the common sense of the time, registered in the dictionary of the Castilian language compiled by Sebastián de Cobarrubias for publication in 1611: long journeys to a sacred destination beyond one's homeland. But Cobarrubias's definition of the verb *peregrinar* – to go on a pilgrimage – introduced another term, *romería*, for a second kind of religious journey. To make a pilgrimage was "to go walking en romería or [emphasis added] beyond one's homeland," suggesting that pilgrimages were either distant journeys or romerías close to home. Benito Jerónimo Feijóo y Montenegro highlighted this distinction in his *Teatro crítico universal* (1726–1739). He started with the usual definition of pilgrimage as "the act of visiting sacred places far from the region or town where one lives in order to adore saints' relics or those images of them that became famous as the most miraculous."[30] Journeys to "very distant" shrines such as Compostela were, Feijóo wrote, the "real pilgrimages." He called romerías another "type of pilgrimage ..., to a shrine, church, or chapel nearby" especially during the

VIDA
DEL VENERABLE
SIERVO DE DIOS
FR. FRANCISCO
DE LA CRUZ,
RELIGIOSO DE VIDA ACTIVA
del Orden de Nueſtra Señora del Carmen,
de Antigua, y Regular Obſervancia.

EL PRIMER HIJO DE LA IGLESIA, QUE HIZO
peregrinacion à los Santos Lugares de Jeruſalèn, Roma, y
Santiago de Galicia con Cruz acueſtas : Por quien nueſtro
Señor ha obrado grandes, y extraordinarios prodigios en vida, y en muerte.

ESCRITA
POR EL LIC. DON SEBASTIAN MUÑOZ SUAREZ,
Presbytero, Comiſſario del Santo Oficio.

ADDICIONADA
POR EL M. R. P. M. FR. MARCELINO FERNANDEZ
de Quiròs, Doctor en Sagrada Theologia por la Univerſidad
de Salamanca, y Cathedratico de Philoſophia en ella, Exa-
minador Synodal de eſte Arzobiſpado, Prior que ha ſido de
ſu Convento de Toledo, y Difinidor Mayor de la Provincia de Caſtilla, de dicho Orden.

QUARTA IMPRESSION.

Con licencia : En Madrid, en la Imprenta de PANTALEON
AZNAR, calle del Arenal. Año de 1768.

Figure 9.1 Title page and print from a popular seventeenth-century Spanish text reprinted twice in the eighteenth century that celebrates the heroic pilgrimage in the 1640s on foot to Rome, the Holy Land, and Compostela by Fray Francisco de la Cruz, an elderly Carmelite friar from Castile. Publication of this kind of edifying story and illustration representing long-distance pilgrimage is conspicuously missing for New Spain. Author's copy.

annual feast of the patron saint.[31] Feijóo dismissed romerías as occasions for mundane distractions ("innumerables relajaciones") rather than true pilgrimages, a sentiment echoed in the popular saying included in the Real Academia de la Lengua's definition of *peregrinación*: "romería de cerca, mucho vino y poca cera" (romerías close to home mean much wine and few candles). This distinction between long and short pilgrimages appears in colonial records, too, although not always so unequivocally. Journeys to American shrines within a few days walk were usually called romerías, but visitors to nearby shrines might be called *peregrinos*, and extended journeys to the regional shrine of Chalma sometimes were called romerías.

Other than a few hermits – most of them Spanish immigrants – who journeyed to a distant sacred place and took up residence there rather than returning home, and the distant travels of solitary alms collectors representing a shrine that performed a kind of pilgrimage in reverse, with the shrine venturing out to devotees,[32] there seems to have been little in the way of long religious pilgrimages for authorities in New Spain to monitor.

Religious tracts published in Spain in the eighteenth century, such as Francisco Lárraga's *Promptuario de la theología moral*, describe the legal standing of pilgrims in some detail, which was uncommon in works produced in New Spain. Lárraga's book circulated in New Spain, but I have not seen its passages about pilgrims cited in colonial records. Laws to protect pilgrimage routes and hostels that were common in Europe but I have found none for New Spain.[33] Nor have I found pilgrims' guidebooks and accounts like those circulating in Europe at the time or the debates over the comparative merits of different shrines, or characters like the wife of Bath or Margery Kempe who devoted years to visiting distant shrines,[34] or casual mention of pilgrims in literary works like Rabelais's Gargantua pulling up a handful of pilgrims with the garden lettuce for his dinner salad. Nor do the decrees and minutes of the four Mexican synods of prelates meeting during the colonial period mention long-distance pilgrimage.[35] Yet the same colonial authorities who were silent about pilgrimage were busy tracking vagabonds and licensing alms collectors, traders, and others who plied the colonial roadways.[36] Even for the shrine of Our Lady of Guadalupe, which is widely regarded as Mexico's supreme pilgrimage destination from the beginning of Spanish colonization, we are left with few traces of this kind of long-distance journey until the nineteenth century. The image of Guadalupe was revered throughout the viceroyalty by the 1750s, but few devotees from distant places seem to have traveled to the shrine at Tepeyac. Visitors mainly came from nearby Mexico City and its vicinity, and occasionally from rural communities in central Mexico during the *fiestas de indios* at the shrine in September.[37] But in the late colonial period, even rural devotees near the Valley of Mexico, who left their villages on the Day of Guadalupe, December 12, might go to a chapel or church altar dedicated to Guadalupe at Texcoco or another head town rather than continue on to Tepeyac.[38] And when a colonial aristocrat from the far northern town of Monterrey vowed to visit the shrine to Guadalupe at Tepeyac in 1758 (soon after official papal recognition of the Virgin of Guadalupe as patroness of New Spain), her bishop substituted a different penance.

This is not to say that the idea of pilgrimage as a long, arduous, penitential journey to a sacred place or a metaphorical journey of the Christian body and soul through life's perils was forgotten in New Spain. On the contrary, pilgrimage was a common trope in colonial sermons, correspondence, and prints[39]; bishops encouraged virtual pilgrimages to iconic shrines as devotional exercises by issuing indulgences and publishing promotional texts for them; a chronicle about Holy Year celebrations in 1750 by a Mexican priest declared that while the ideal pilgrimage on this occasion would be to Rome, a virtual pilgrimage of special spiritual exercises for those who must stay home was good, too;[40] and the chief chronicler of Mexican shrines and miraculous images in the late seventeenth century, Francisco de Florencia, SJ, held pilgrimage up to his Mexican readers as an especially worthy practice by suggesting that devotees who traveled farther to reach the shrine of San Miguel del Milagro would find the healing waters there more efficacious "because of the greater faith required of them and the greater devotion."[41]

Officials in Spain may have disparaged romerías, but they remained popular there and became the chief type of sacred journey in New Spain. Accordingly, my main historical questions are why that was, what romerías amounted to, and how several shrines rose to greater prominence. A dozen or so well-known colonial shrines developed something of a pilgrimage infrastructure during the seventeenth and eighteenth centuries (see Appendix 1); and as far as possible, I have woven their development into the chapters in Part I. For this chapter, it is enough to touch on the four long-lived regional shrines that developed during the seventeenth and eighteenth centuries at Tepeyac, Chalma, San Juan de los Lagos, and Esquipulas, to suggest how they came to attract more attention and more pilgrims than other colonial shrines. But even these were not much like the celebrated European destinations of Jerusalem, Rome, or Compostela with their elaborate networks of secondary shrines, routes, hospitality, regulation, and reward. They developed in different ways, for somewhat different reasons, over a shorter span of time. Briefly, the Virgin of Guadalupe at Tepeyac was closely associated with nearby Mexico City during the colonial period and drew most of its visitors from the city and nearby districts, especially after the great epidemic of 1737 and papal certification in 1754 of the Guadalupan apparitions. The shrine of the Lord of Chalma in the mountainous western section of the modern Estado de México was the most popular destination for rural Indians in central Mexico by the mid-seventeenth century, especially for Otomí peoples who were dispersed in villages of what are now the states of México, Hidalgo, and Morelos. But it was always more, a destination for *castas* and some residents of Mexico City, and a favorite retreat for hermits and Augustinians. As interest in the Christ of Chalma grew in the late eighteenth century, the Augustinians and civic leaders in Mexico City sought special royal recognition and privileges for the shrine.[42] The shrine of Our Lady of San Juan de los Lagos in the Altos de Jalisco, near heavily traveled routes between northern and western New Spain and the silver mines of Guanajuato and Zacatecas, became an important pilgrimage destination in the eighteenth century when its annual trade fair developed. Of these four regional shrines, colonial Esquipulas in Guatemala near the Honduras border most closely resembles on a smaller scale a cosmopolitan European pilgrimage site in its geographical and ethnic reach – attracting Caribbean sailors, recent arrivals from Europe, coastal Central Americans of Spanish and African descent, and highlanders of all kinds from Guatemala, Honduras, El Salvador, Nicaragua, Chiapas, and Oaxaca. A late eighteenth-century novena booklet for the shrine of Our Lord of Esquipulas is unusual in emphasizing long-distance travel to the site by specifying the homeland of devotees who were favored with miracles. Of the twenty-five devotees mentioned in this booklet, two came to the shrine from the Caribbean islands, one from Mexico City, one from Oaxaca, and the rest from various places in Central America.[43]

Romerías in Colonial Mexico

Romerías usually were passed over by authorities, neither much encouraged nor viewed with disfavor unless their destinations were caves, mountains (other than Calvary sites), or other places where idolatry was suspected, or unless local shrines suddenly began to draw crowds of curious visitors from farther away or seriously disrupted the local labor supply.[44] Much as the movement of devotees from Mexico City to the nearby shrine of the Virgin of Guadalupe at Tepeyac was called a "devota romería" by the city's chronicler Juan de Viera in the 1770s, the journeys to most shrines were short, usually no more than two or three days' travel.[45] Although there would have been a steady trickle of supplicants, crowds gathered at these shrines a few times a year, on market days if they were located in or near communities that hosted periodic markets, or on special feast days. Until the late eighteenth century these romerías were documented by chance. For instance, an investigation into the shocking murder of a pregnant Zapotec woman from Santiago Lalopa in the Sierra Norte region of Oaxaca by her husband in 1657 revealed that he had persuaded her to go with him alone on what the scribe recorded as a "romería" to the nearby shrine of Nuestra Señora de la Hermita to pray for a safe birth and then strangled her on the way.[46] This is the only mention I have seen of the shrine of Nuestra Señora de la Hermita. Many of the colonial shrines to celebrated images of Christ or Mary are better known, but, like this one, most attracted devotees from the vicinity, usually not much beyond twenty miles away. The shrine to an image of Jesús Nazareno in San Bernardino Contla, Tlaxcala, for example, was described in alms collection records as having a districtwide appeal, with "all those pueblos professing their particular devotion to it [as] very miraculous"[47]

In the spirit of the Bourbon program for "greater vigilance" (*mayor vigilancia*) and regulation, late colonial governors showed more interest in collecting information about romerías. In 1743, the crown called for reports from districts in its American colonies, as it occasionally had done before. But now, for the first time, one of the questions had to do with miraculous images, suggesting an interest in surveillance.[48] The responses from districts in the Archdiocese of Mexico provide one of the few colonial surveys of shrines and miraculous images for a substantial part of New Spain. The focus in these reports was more on the shrines and images than on travels to them, but they occasionally included a remark about pilgrimages. For the scores of shrines identified, only one mentioned visitors from "distant lands." That was for Chalma. Five other reports mentioned journeys from "neighboring jurisdictions," "throughout the district," or "in and near the city."[49] Half a century later, in 1796, a complaint filed by a parish priest serving in Tzompantepec, Tlaxcala that unseemly processions with statues of Christ and the saints were taking place in his parish led the bishop of Puebla and the viceroy to solicit a round of reports from prelates and provincial governors.[50] Most of the reports were perfunctory – either the governors and church officials were poorly informed or they saluted to the broad hint in the instructions that royal authorities wanted to restrict romerías and processions, whether or not there was evidence of local abuses.[51] But several reports for the Diocese of Michoacán in western Mexico were more detailed, describing what amounted to three kinds of short pilgrimages in the company of cherished local images of the saints and Christ: to a district shrine, especially during harvest celebrations and the octaves of Corpus Christi and Holy Week; to a neighboring community for special ceremonies centered on the images; or to the fields or a nearby site sacred to the community, often a hill, cave, or spring that may have been regarded as the community's place of origin and renewal. Most often the site was a hill or accessible mountain surmounted by a cross.[52]

At the time of the colonial period, community members visited these sites during Holy Week and the May 3 feast of the Invention of the Holy Cross with springtime rituals of renewal to honor the death and resurrection of Christ and appeal for abundant crops.[53] A few earlier regional reports from the late 1570s relying on Indian noble informants mention short pilgrimages of the third kind. In one case from the report for Teotitlán del Camino, Oaxaca, the informants described some of the eighteen monthly feast days that were celebrated during the solar year. In the sixteenth feast (Tititl, dedicated to the deceased, including women who died in childbirth), *macehuales* (commoners) went out to hunt game for their lords. They would hang what they caught from a large tree in the mountains. Later, the tree was uprooted and carried with the game still dangling from its branches to a place associated with female spirits, usually represented either as Cihuacoatl (snake woman) or the old goddess Ilamatecuhtli (star garment), cocreator of the stars. Along the way the hunters sang to the accompaniment of drums and other instruments. When they reached the destination they fell to their knees, burned the tree and game, and sang and danced until the fire turned the offerings to ashes.[54]

Whether to a districtwide shrine or to a sacred site nearby, many colonial romerías, like those described in 1796 for Michoacán, were prolonged processions more than long pilgrimages: synchronized excursions on foot, often carrying the community saints to a nearby town to visit a host saint. Romerías and processions merged in other ways, too, since sacred movement of all kinds in Mexico was directed toward a destination, where circumambulation and other choreographed acts of place making, salutation, and renewal were performed. At Amecameca, near the snow-capped volcanoes above Mexico City, for example, people traveled on romerías several times a year to participate in processions carrying the renowned figure of Christ from its hillside shrine of the Sacromonte to the community's principal church of the Assumption.[55] And celebrated images from shrines near colonial cities were ceremoniously carried to the city for novenas and local processions: Our Lady of El Pueblito and the city of Querétaro; Our Lady of Zapopan and Guadalajara; Our Lady of Los Remedios and Mexico City; and the image of Our Lady of Guadalupe in its shrine outside the city of San Luis Potosí. Where does a local pilgrimage end and a procession begin? The distinction can seem contrived. Processions at a shrine destination often were regarded as the most important part of a romería; for the moment, at least, a transcendent act.

Processions in Colonial Mexico

Whether in Mexico City or a rural pueblo, processions with images were an especially popular way to spread divine grace in desperate or fortunate times.[56] Authorities paid little attention to romerías until the late eighteenth century but they actively encouraged and regulated pious processions, leaving behind an ample prescriptive and descriptive record about them. In this, they rehearsed a pattern in early modern European Catholic practice that generally encouraged processions more than pilgrimages, long or short.[57] In processions at or near shrines, devotees approached the divine presence formally, together, often in song and prayer, perhaps circling the building with their banners waving and the statues they brought lifted high on litters, with fragrant *copal* smoke rising from handheld braziers. In effect, processions were a special form of dance.[58] An example from the eighteenth century is Mapethé, Hidalgo, the celebrated place where a crucified Christ came to life and was restored to fine condition. Otomí villagers marched in groups from neighboring districts during the week before Palm Sunday, usually staying for a full novena of prayers and community processions with their crucifixes, as if to charge them with sacred energy at the place of the miraculous renovation.[59]

Colonial record keepers were inclined to treat processions as a separate event, but an array of customary rituals of public worship went on together at the shrines for feast day observances – processions bearing statues of Christ and the saints, dances, sacred theater, Masses, tableaux of images, singing, and prayer – in addition to more profane pleasures, including festive meals, drinking, mock battles, fireworks, gambling, and bullfights.[60] Fray Juan de Mendoza, OFM, chronicler of the burgeoning shrine of Nuestra Señora de Tecaxic near Toluca in the 1680s, was especially taken with the pageantry and dances performed there by Indian maidens from surrounding communities before entering the shrine:

> ... There come groups of eight ten, and sometimes twelve young girls clothed, in their manner, in rich blouses (*huipiles*), in costly blankets that are elegantly arranged, their hair in tufts tied with variously-colored ribbons; they wear a dance (*mitote*) costume; they carry in their left hand a very large and thin feather and a little bell or *ayacastle* in their right hand, and on their forehead they wear a large headband they call *copili* in their language, decorated with green stones that are the baubles these people use. The parents bring them, and musicians accompany them with harps and guitars during the dances they have prepared and studied. ... All bring their distinctive emblem, placing it in the middle of where they dance: for example, a palm leaf mounted with a terrestrial globe that slowly opens as the dance goes on and in which the Most Holy Virgin of Tecaxique appears,to whom they offer their poor wax candles, incense, copal, flowers and fruits. ...
>
> With this device and in this manner they enter the shrines, and after praying devoutly to Our Lady they dance with exceedingly great modesty and sing to her in their manner and in their language sweet songs. It is deeply moving to see and hear them, and it should be a source of edification and example to those people who live in ways that are forgetful of the things of God. ... They spend nine days in these offerings to Our Lady, and other dance troops from various places often come at the same time, so that the precinct is filled with different dances .....[61]

The processions, dances, music, and other acts of worship were part of the process of preparation and approach, calling upon the divine presence in a particular location.[62] More than elective acts of courtesy, joy, and supplication, they were offerings vital to well-being and divine favor. As Mercedes Guadarrama Olivera learned in her study of mountain Totonac communities near Papantla, Veracruz, some of the saints were said to have abandoned the community when the people stopped celebrating their feast days and traditional dances.[63] For 300 years, Spanish colonial officials gave a wary endorsement to these activities, alert to the possibility of improper, if not pagan and satanic, content in colonial Indian dances, songs, and processions. As early as 1539, Mexican prelates called for more restrained and decorous behavior pleasing to God. Indian fiestas and processions were to dispense with native dances, banquets, alcoholic beverages, flowered arches, and swept paths on processional routes when the

Celebra Regozijada Mexico, la Beatificacion de su
Esclarecido hijo el Bienaventurado Felipe de Jesus

Figure 9.2 1801 print of a celebration in Mexico City's great square for the beatification of native son Felipe de Jesús, showing rockets exploding in the sky, an elaborate fireworks display ("castillo") in the foreground, a procession in progress in front of the row of buildings and spectators on the left, food vendors under their sunshades, and several carriages to suggest that leading families of the city took part. From the book of engravings by José María Montes de Oca, Vida de San Felipe de Jesús protomártir de Japón y patrón de su patria México. Se gravó el año de 1801. Montes de Oca la inventó i grabó en Mexco. Calle del Bautisterio de S. Catalina Mr no. 3, 27th engraving in this volume. Courtesy of Bridwell Library, Southern Methodist University.

bishop arrived. People from different communities were not to cluster together on these occasions, or beat their chests or sound the call to Mass with spectacles such as mock battles or traditional songs and dances that turned hearts and minds from God.[64] A century later, Bishop Juan de Palafox y Mendoza of Puebla, often a defender of Indian interests and local traditions, ordered that cross dressing in Indian dances be forbidden, along with songs in native languages and the pole flyers spectacle, because they might be idolatrous.[65]

If there is an enduring thread of precolonial practice in colonial journeys, then romerías to mountains, caves, and springs, and danced processions in and beyond Indian communities, are likely candidates. In several ways they seem remarkably like practices described in very early colonial reports that look back to precolonial traditions of lavish ceremony: masked teams (*quadrillas*) of dancers in fancy dress moving together slowly along swept pathways strewn with vegetation, under arches made of branches thick with foliage and fragrant flowers, perhaps with live snakes and insects in the woven boughs,[66] the travelers bearing sacred bundles and seeking protection, abundance, and appeasement with precious offerings.[67] The masks, feathered regalia, arches, profusion of flowers and greenery, throbbing drumbeats, and copal incense were distinctive. In their own community celebrations the dancers were likely to be dismissed by colonial authorities as "disguised with masks and very ridiculous apparel,"[68] but viceroys included them in their festivities, and in some ways colonial Indian festivals were not so different from Spanish liturgical spectacles of the fifteenth and sixteenth centuries, mixing gravitas and merrymaking in the grand processions, papier-maché dragons and giants as well as images of Christ and the saints in the line of march.[69]

The late sixteenth-century Franciscan chronicler Gerónimo de Mendieta was especially taken by the scale of the stately processions staged with the Blessed Sacrament in central Mexico, in which 3,000–8,000 penitents, some carrying crosses and crucifixes, marched to the sound of trumpets, drums, and bells before a sea of spectators. In one of these processions, temporary chapels were erected at the four corners of the route, covered with carpets of flowers and images. At each one the lead priest stopped to pray and the richly attired young Indian dancers performed or a biblical event was enacted.[70]

How did old and new traditions of procession come together? There is no one answer, but here is how Diego de Soto, a Tlaxcalan Indian noble testifying apparently in 1582, presented the process as an event: One parched spring in the 1520s, Tlaxcalans went to their Franciscan pastors saying that in former times when the rains were late, they swept the roads, went to war, and made sacrifices to appease their gods. Now that they were Christians, what should they do? Father Martín de Valencia promised them a procession – "we will perform a penitential scourging and implore God and his mother to hear us." And he did so, bringing out the image of the Virgin Mary called *la conquistadora* that Cortés had given to the native lord Don Gonzalo Alxotecatcocomitzi of Atlihuetzian for his loyal service. Valencia stripped to the waist and whipped himself in the procession, and the rains came before the procession ended.[71] Although Soto did not mention native processions, by highlighting processions as a legitimate Christian practice he validated an indigenous tradition.

Nearly 200 years later, the lavish processions with a celebrated painting of Our Lady of Guadalupe from her shrine outside the city of San Luis Potosí to the city center in December 1771 to celebrate papal recognition of the apparitions of the Virgin in 1531 incorporated native participants, dances, instruments, and decorative touches into proceedings that Iberian Catholics of the time would have recognized as conventional in other respects, from the carefully ordered hierarchy of marchers and chanting of the Loretan Litany to the fireworks and the allegory of angels defeating the devil. Troops of colorfully costumed Indians from the "ranchos" and outlying neighborhoods of the district marched and performed the *danza de pluma* and *danza de matachines*, displaying their agility "in orderly leaps" to the sound of native whistles and log drums (*música de teponastle*) along routes strewn with sweet-smelling flowers. Many wore native cloaks (*tilmas*), and some of the caciques and young boys in the line of march dressed as Juan Diego.[72] Was this spectacle little more than an eighteenth-century version of the *Ballet Folklórico*? In a way, yes, but the performers were not professional dancers and musicians but local farmers, artisans, and laborers, many of whom would have understood the performance in local terms, with local meaning, in the spirit of their ancestors.

Carrying images in processions and romerías was a widespread practice in Spain before the conquest of Mexico, which was embraced on a grand scale in New Spain – in short pilgrimages to shrines and places of origin; on feast days of all kinds including Good Friday processions with images of Our Lady of Sorrows and Christ crucified; the famous processions of hundreds of crosses and crucifixes for Corpus Christi, Jueves Santo, and the Day of the Holy Cross (May 3 and sometimes September 14); and in penitential processions of supplication during natural disasters.[73] Especially in Indian communities, these traveling images did not stand for something absent. They were understood to represent a living presence that embodied community identity. As this book begins to establish, images coming to life are reported hundreds of times in colonial records, but the sense of their living presence in processions and romerías is better documented in ethnographic descriptions than in colonial records, although images taken out on alms-collecting tours or in processions to shrines often were called pilgrims, *peregrinas*. In his pioneering 1978 study of contemporary pilgrimages to Chalma from villages in the Estado de México and neighboring states, Gilberto Giménez found that groups of pilgrims spoke of the images they carried (some of them statues weighing about ninety pounds) as the pilgrims, going to visit the great father, the prodigious Christ of Chalma. People on the way from San Pedro Atlapulco told Giménez that they were merely escorting their patron saints, San Pedrito and the Divino Salvador.[74] The rituals of the journey centered on these local images, and they were understood to return from the shrine recharged with sacred energy.[75]

In colonial records there are glimpses of this sense of the image becoming the living protagonist of special journeys of obligation and regeneration or encounters with other patron saints in a neighboring community, again accompanied by devotees rather than borne by them as a symbol.[76] The early seventeenth-century Nahua chronicler Chimalpahin provided an example in his entry for July 31, 1610, describing the dedication of the Jesuit church in Mexico City, which included a procession from the cathedral with the Blessed Sacrament: "San Ignacio [by which he meant the statue of St. Ignatius] did not ... go to the said procession. San Ignacio only came to meet the sacrament outside the church.... His children [the Jesuits] brought him out of his home, the Casa Profesa, on a carrying platform. When he had come to meet the Sacrament, he led it, taking it into his home, the new church."[77] And José Manuel Ruiz y Cervantes mentioned pilgrim images in his 1791 text about the image and shrine of Our Lady of Xuquila (Oaxaca) when he observed that some communities "bring images of the admirable Lady to be blessed there."[78]

Reformers, Local Pilgrims, and Their Discontents

The eighteenth-century campaign to eliminate or at least restrain some popular devotional practices began in earnest in the 1750s when episcopal courts and pastoral visitors issued orders that processions be held during daylight hours and travel directly to their destination without stopping, and that images of Christ and the saints not be carried in Corpus Christi processions.[79] Then, in 1769, Archbishop Francisco Antonio de Lorenzana (1766–1772) ordered an end to various Indian dances and spectacles on feast days, and the Fourth Synod of prelates in New Spain meeting under his direction in 1771 proposed to reduce the number of mandatory feast days in Indian communities and called for less extravagant galas and costumes, and an end to drunkenness and self-mortification by revelers.[80] By the 1780s Bourbon administrators brought into their reforming, standardizing efforts various acts of public worship including fiestas, processions, dances, mock battles, and groups of the faithful carrying images outside their communities. Not surprisingly, the Corpus Christi processions and Holy Week observances received special attention. From the beginning of the colonial period, Holy Week and Corpus Christi in the cities and other head towns stretched over eight days and were the most spectacular and elaborately staged celebrations in the liturgical calendar, including Calvary romerías as well as the whole array of other sacred and profane activities.[81] The great processions of Holy Week were staged on Maunday Thursday, Good Friday, and sometimes Holy Saturday.[82] For Mexico City, Mendieta described a Good Friday procession in which 3,000 Indian penitents marched with 230 images of Christ and saints on gilded litters along designated routes, passing through hundreds of flowered arches, before more than 20,000 spectators.[83] Even if the round numbers here are inflated, these were impressive spectacles that continued throughout the colonial period.[84]

Giovanni Francesco Gemelli Careri, Italian world traveler, visited New Spain in 1697 and left the following description of the Corpus Christi procession in Mexico City that year:

All the streets of the city and the balconies and windows of the houses were richly decorated with valuable objects, rugs, and tapestries that, with the green of the vegetation and the beauty of the flowers, made an attractive sight. On Plateros street there was a well-painted history of the Conquest of Mexico, with the houses as they were in those days and the Indians dressed as they were then. The procession began with about 100 flower-bedecked statues, followed by the confraternities, then all the religious orders except for the Jesuits and Carmelites, then the canons carrying the Blessed Sacrament on a litter. The pageantry ended with the archbishop, the viceroy and the government ministers, without capes, the city council, and the nobility. Along the entire length of the processional route, dancing was to be seen and occasionally monsters and masked participants in different costumes, as one often finds in Spain.[85]

While the number of participants and spectators in these Mexico City festivities was always large,[86] the Corpus Christi and Holy Week events differed somewhat from each other. There were high spirits and potential for disorder in both, but the Holy Week festivities were expected to be more solemn, sometimes including penitential processions with scourging, and participation in processions was more selective than at Corpus Christi, when people of all stations were permitted to march as members of the social body united in the living body of Christ. Holy Week processions were sponsored by confraternities, including those with Indian and black members and the less prestigious trades, including chandlers, pastry makers, shoemakers, tailors, building trades, porters, water carriers, butchers, and oarsmen. But in the Holy Week processions, except for the Via Crucis pageantry on Good Friday, it was the clergy and dignitaries of the state who were featured.

From personal experience, Torquemada described Indian Holy Week fiestas and processions in Mexico City in some detail near the turn of the seventeenth century:

The Indians celebrate with much rejoicing and solemnity on the high holy days [Holy Week, Christmas, Pentecost, and Epiphany] and feast days of Our Lord, his Mother, and patron saints of their communities. ... They adorn their churches very attractively, decorating them with what they have available; and what they lack in tapestries [to hang from their windows and doorways] they make up for with greenery and flowers of many kinds that grow abundantly in this land .... These sweet-smelling plants, along with reeds and sedge, are spread out on the floor of the church as well as the roadways along which the procession is to travel; and on top of this greenery they scatter flowers. This processional route has bowers [archways made of branches and plants] here and there. ..... The route has three lanes. In the widest middle lane go the priests, crosses, litters, and other processional pomp; on one of the side lanes go the men; and on the other go the women, although this separation of the sexes is no longer usually practiced now that Spaniards have mixed into the processions. ... There have been processions of the Blessed Sacrament with more than a thousand [arches] ... covered with branches and flowers of various kinds and colors.[87]

Always grand in scale and charged with emotion, Holy Week and Corpus Christi processions were the most closely watched and regulated processional feasts, especially during the late eighteenth-century reforms. The usual worries about high spirits, masks, drunkenness, and violence were magnified by the expectation of solemnity and decorum during Holy Week and Corpus Christi, which combined the miracle of transubstantiation with the symbolic representation of transcendent unity in society within and through hierarchy. Officials were alert to anything that diminished these occasions. With its popular participation and complex message of unity and division, Corpus Christi was always hard to contain, spinning out of control in Valladolid in 1629, Mexico City in 1692, and Querétaro in 1694 and 1799. In his directive that Corpus Christi be celebrated for only one day rather than a full octave and then only during the daytime, Archbishop Rubio y Salinas warned in 1752 that allowing crowds of all sorts of people to gather after dark led to "the gravest sins, scandals and even deaths."[88] He could have given many examples.[89] But the more privileged participants in the great procession frequently were willing collaborators in government regulation. The religious orders, in particular, frequently appealed to the viceroy and archbishop to protect their customary place of precedence in the order of march.

Correspondence in 1790 between the viceroy and archbishop of Mexico about Corpus Christi and Holy Week points up the official worries, and also documents the rationale for the reforms at this time.

The viceroy fumed to his ecclesiastical colleague about "the many excesses caused by abuses committed in former times during Holy Week along the routes of their processions when every church, plaza, and street should breathe silence and pious devotion." Instead, he wrote, there are "detestable irreverences" such as curbside sale of all kinds of food and drink along the routes. He asked the archbishop to exercise his "pastoral zeal" against the abuses and excesses. The archbishop concurred wholeheartedly and informed the viceroy that he was using the ecclesiastical prison to detain violators. With respect to Corpus Christi, their exchange focused more on the need for greater decorum in the procession, especially that none of the marchers should be dressed indecently or nearly naked. The archbishop asked the viceroy to order troops along the route to remove poorly clothed marchers. The viceroy ordered the confraternities of the guilds of porters, butchers, and water carriers, and the confraternities of the Indian districts of the city, to provide decent uniforms for their participants and to keep the races and guilds apart from each other. He also called for constables to patrol the processional line up to where the clergy were arrayed.[90] That the new surveillance was driven as much by reasons of state as by religious reforms[91] is apparent in the growing role of state officials documented in local archives. For example, the intendant of Guadalajara instructed his district governor (*subdelegado*) and lieutenants in central Jalisco in 1796 to insure that in Acatlán only the feasts of Corpus Christi and the patron saint were permitted and only ten pesos toward expenses could come from the community chest unless the district governor expressly permitted more. His justification was that expensive religious feasts were the main cause of the town's "ruin."[92]

The reforming bishops and royal governors imagined shaping a world of dignified moderation – purifying the sacred, promoting a simpler, more decorous piety, eliminating what they called "ridiculous" plebeian "excesses," and fostering public tranquility.[93] Decrees were issued against lavish spending on costumes and accessories, against vendors selling food and drink in the streets during the processions, against residents throwing scented or colored water, doves, eggshells filled with confetti, and paper balls filled with flower petals from their balconies as the processions passed by. Fireworks and candles were restricted on the ground that they contributed to the general disorder and excess, caused fires, and too often were accompanied by profane behavior.[94]

Lic. Miguel Domínguez, the royal governor (*corregidor*) of Querétaro and husband of Mexico's future heroine of national independence Josefa Ortiz de Domínguez, summed up the Bourbon reformers' dim view of Indian fiestas when he banned the local custom of a Moors-and-Christians mock battle during the feast of the Immaculate Conception at Tequisquiapan in

1802. It was, he said, a source of "all sorts of dangerous and disorderly conduct" among the Indians, and the cost of supplying horses and ridiculous costumes, food, and drink for the actors amounted to a great financial burden to the plebeian sponsors.[95] The laborers who took part lost their wages while the festivities lasted, their employers lost valuable time and labor, and the whole community was distracted from more productive activity to watch the dancing and antics (*monadas*) of the drunken teams of marchers. The fighting, he said, could escalate beyond simulated combat and lead to serious injuries because some of the combatants were on horseback and many others were armed with cudgels and sharp swords.

Devotion to the Blessed Gonzalo de Amarante, a thirteenth-century Dominican pastor who was promoted in a limited way by members of his order in New Spain at the end of the colonial period, provides a glimpse of the official suspicion about dancing then. San Gonzalo was said to have left his parish in Portugal on a fourteen-year pilgrimage to the Holy Land. When he returned, members of his congregation reportedly danced for joy. Thereafter he became famous for receiving visits from the Virgin Mary and bringing forth wine from rocks and fish from the sea in times of need. He was beatified in 1560. Devotees of the Blessed Gonzalo de Amarante in the great Dominican church in Mexico City in 1816 became known for dancing in front of an image of the saint, inspired by the story of his homecoming. Had the events described then occurred in the seventeenth century, they would probably not have received much attention from royal authorities or more than passing notice from the cathedral clergy. But in 1816, officials of the cathedral chapter, represented by the vicar general and a leading canon, the prolific sermonizer and sharp-tongued public intellectual Father José Mariano Beristáin y Sousa, preferred the lofty austerity of neoclassicism to exuberant, boisterous movement, and they regarded this dancing as "an exotic and extravagant devotion" that should not be encouraged. It was a recent innovation, Beristáin said, and "the novelty of it also arouses suspicion."[96] They took no comfort in the Dominican provincial's assurance that the dancing was restrained, devout, and not so new. For Beristáin, the practice was irredeemably indecorous, trance-like, and wanton, a product of crass motives on the part of both devotees seeking the saint's favor for their health and wealth and Dominican promoters who, he intimated, had moneymaking in mind. The record of the dispute ended with the vicar general reaffirming his decision to forbid the dance.[97]

Dancing and processing by "miserable" Indians in their communities on feast days and at shrines always worried colonial authorities.[98] The endlessly repeated steps of masked dancers in feathered costumes before murmuring crowds of onlookers[99] was strange and possibly threatening, especially in the political climate of the late eighteenth century. Yet, even at the height of the Bourbon reforms, Indian dancers were still prized by imperial authorities and city fathers as exotic performers and included in their own grand processions.[100] A description of the festivities in the city of San Luis Potosí on December 13, 14, and 15, 1771, in honor of Our Lady of Guadalupe enthused over the participation of Indian feathered dancers in the great procession of the region's celebrated replica of the image from its shrine to the parish church. The contingent of marchers from the Barrio de Guadalupe performed a toned-down *matachines* dance, which the chronicler praised for "the good taste of their costumes, the array of colors, their nimbleness, mastery, and new figures with leaps of pure pleasure."[101]

Late colonial reformers looked more favorably on the long-standing tradition of processions of supplication and penitence (*procesiones rogativas*) – which were increasingly meant for the benefit of Spain and the royal family in wartime as much as for the local community in time of crisis – perhaps because they were less likely to mix with gambling, drunkenness, and other profane behavior.[102] A nine-day round of prayers and processions of this kind in Orizaba (Veracruz) was described by a local chronicler in 1819:[103]

Vexed by the inhabitants of this Villa for their many sins, the Divine Judge menaced them with earthquakes, plague, drought, and hunger. The people resolved to hold a novena dedicated to the Miraculous Image of the Lord of Calvary and their patron saint, St. Michael, appealing to the Lord for mercy through his son and the Prince of the Celestial Militia. A solemn Mass was said in every church; the Host was carried in procession accompanied by the singing of the litany of the saints. All the residents whose homes were on the procession route strove to adorn their streets with imaginative triumphal arches, hangings on the doors and windows, bunches of flowers fastened to various trees marking the way, and sweet-smelling leaves and flowers strewn on the ground. Many devotees sang the *Miserere*,[104] especially those from the Yxguatlan neighborhood.

At night, throughout the novena, the *Via Sacra*,[105] the litany of the saints, a hymn to the Blessed Sacrament or The Loving Jesus was prayed, always ending with a vigorous scourging. Sunday the 23rd [of April 1819], the last day of the novena, our parish priest, don Joaquín de Palafos y Hacha, preached a sermon admonishing us to do penance because the Lord had raised his hand of Justice. That afternoon the Lord was carried to his temple in a penitential procession.

The accent here was on contrition, and even most of the homemade street decorations were understood to be a devout offering that did not diminish the solemnity of the occasion or the authority of the archbishop and the king. But in chanting and marching together to lift the spirits as no private prayer could, the *orizabeños* pushed the limits of decorum. The scourging, exuberant displays of flowered arches, and streets covered in ferns and other vegetation would have been frowned upon by higher authorities of the time in Mexico City. Even though such a display spilled beyond official expectations and expressed a kind of community identity and even autonomy, there was always a dark side to such collective movement. It expressed also the fears and hardships that made it necessary, as well as official demands for conformity that Foucault called "the disciplined body."[106] Still, as orderly as it was, this procession was more than the archbishop would have wanted and less than a model of what late colonial reformers intended.

The balance between sacred and profane in the festivities could tip toward irreverent behavior, violence, and falling-down drunkenness, especially when the formal observances ended and nighttime revelry fueled by music and alcohol took over. But the mounting view of spirited public displays in Indian communities as unbridled and chaotic was belied by the elaborate organization of processions even in many small pueblos, for example in the district of Tangancícuaro, Michoacán, in 1789.[107] According to reports for four small Purépecha communities in the district, local confraternities elected a slate of officers who sponsored the festivities and led the processions. For the feast of the Immaculate Conception, the community of Nuestra Señora de la Asunción Tangancícuaro elected a *prioste* who paid for the Mass and candles needed in the events. They also elected eight women to organize and lead the procession in fancy dress, including two *capitanas* (who in other communities were called *madres fiesteras* or *madres mayores*), four young women (*guananchas*, festival participants) to carry the processional statue of Our Lady, and two flower bearers (*chuchilparis*). For the feast of the patron saint, a mock battle was added with a standard bearer and the elected captains and sergeants of the Moors and Christians as the lead actors. These men also covered the substantial costs of renting costumes and horses, and paid for fireworks, meals, and liquor for the dancers, who were called *quadrilleros* to emphasize that they danced as a unit. The other three communities elected processional officers of their own, including *capitanes; fiscalitos/fiscalitas* (managers); banner bearers; women who carried special vestments, the incense brazier, and candles; plus the Great Turk and the Ambassador for the Moors. During Holy Week, in one of the communities men were chosen to act as Christ's apostles and, again, a mock battle of Moors and Christians was staged, plus a special procession was undertaken on Good Friday with Our Lady of Sorrows, which was led by the "main mother" (*madre mayor*) and her three cosponsors.

Colonial Accommodations

In the late colonial campaign to legislate good order by scaling back romerías, religious feasts, processions, dances, fireworks, and alms-collecting missions for shrine images, there was a wide gap between policy and practice. As a recently arrived Spanish Franciscan complained in 1810, many pastors, including his fellow friars, turned a blind eye to "abuses and ceremonies that are nearly superstitious" in processions and other feast day celebrations.[108] It was not unusual for Spanish priests to recoil from religious practices they found in America and call for reform. For example, Archbishop José Manuel Rubio y Salinas's vicar general, acting as pastoral visitor in 1752, expressed his disapproval to the Franciscans' headquarters convent in Mexico City about the Corpus Christi festivities there: "Since I arrived from Spain it has caused me some religious dissonance to see the solemnity of the Corpus Christi procession tainted by displaying images of the saints along with the Blessed Sacrament." He directed Indians not to carry their images in this procession so that only the consecrated Host – the living body of Christ – would be held aloft. But a marginal comment by archivist Fr. Francisco de la Rosa Figueroa on the vicar general's letter filed in the Franciscan archive made the tart observation that "the plans in this letter have never been realized. The annual Corpus Christi procession leaving from this convent has always gone out with images and confraternity members, without interruption."[109] And four years later the archbishop, himself, while on pastoral visit to the Indian town of Otumba, left the traditional processions undisturbed as long as they were held in the daytime.[110]

This was the usual trajectory of late colonial fiesta reform. During another pastoral visit in 1774, Archbishop Alonso Núñez de Haro y Peralta called for restraint in Indian celebrations when he arrived. He instructed the communities on his route not to receive him with "fireworks, triumphal arches, dances or any other type of amusement or profane festivity"; nor should confraternities, "even the Indian ones, meet me with their crosses, statues, flags or any other insignia until I am near the church."[111] But thirty years later, his successor was still being received with the old pageantry and high spirits. At Huehuetoca in 1803, the Indian faithful greeted the archbishop on the outskirts of town with flowered arches, drums, flutes (*chirimías*), and a portable tower with a bell that they rang vigorously – "con mucha violencia."[112]

In most circumstances, colonial authorities lacked the means or will to eradicate local memories and customs associated with religious images, places, and shrines. Selectively they might impose their directives, but local circumstances often bid otherwise. There is no single explanation of how and why accommodations were reached, but expediency usually trumped principle. In some places imperial officials learned the hard way that reforming festive practices came at a high price, when it could be achieved. In 1797, the district governor of Zapotlán el Grande (modern Ciudad Guzmán, Jalisco) wrote to the high court in Guadalajara that he was worried about the parish priest's interference with local Indian customs during their Holy Week processions. He spoke from personal experience, having himself touched off an uproar there several years before by ordering that the processions take an alternate route.[113] Both he and the priest feigned ignorance of earlier failed attempts at reforming religious festivities in their district, but in 1774, when the vicar general, acting on the advice of three interim pastors of Zapotlán, ordered the length of the Holy Week processions reduced by six blocks, an angry crowd gathered, occupied the parish church, and menaced the priests. The customary route was quickly reinstated.[114] Then in 1782 another parish priest of Zapotlán, Bernardino Antonio de Lepe y Rivera, wrote to the audiencia to decry the local Holy Week processions as exceedingly expensive and disorderly. The drunkenness, bloody flagellations, and masked dancing scandalized him, but he was especially troubled by the errant pride his parishioners took in their flowered arches. When the flowers they wanted were out of season locally, they would go to distant towns to buy them at a premium. With this expense, the monumental size of the arches (requiring fifteen to twenty carriers each) and the intricate work of interweaving the branches and flowers, the cost for one arch typically rose to 50 pesos. He estimated that the community was spending at least 1,500 pesos a year on the thirty or more arches that were constructed, roughly the annual income of a hundred families. Worse yet, the arches were assembled at night on private property by exuberant crowds, "a multitude [of people]," wrote the priest – men and women of all stations in society – with much drinking, loud noise, and lewd and risky behavior. It all seemed highly irregular and scandalous to Father Lepe, but little changed thereafter, in part because the high court concluded that Lepe was a source of the conflict by "insinuating himself into what is not his business and seeking to suddenly eliminate those practices and customs that are second nature to these Indians." He was ordered "to change nothing for now."[115] In 1786 the viceroy received an anonymous letter – probably from Father Lepe again – denouncing the district governor for allowing the Indians free rein, to live "as Moors without a lord."[116] Finally, in 1792 and 1793, an assistant pastor there filed complaints with the Inquisition that his predecessor, Father Lepe, had been too lenient! – that men of Zapotlán displayed obscene or blasphemous figures on their arms and legs, and that a great number of crude and ugly images of Christ were processed through town on Good Friday.[117]

Sometimes colonial judges could resolve conflicts over local spectacles in a way that respected tradition and satisfied the contending parties. A dispute in Teocaltiche, Jalisco, in 1671 pitted non-Indian residents against local Indians over the Good Friday procession featuring the Virgin of Sorrows. The Indians claimed that for many years they had staged the procession, "founded by our ancestors." Sometimes Spanish residents of the town joined them, they said, but now they were having "great differences." The Spaniards had acquired their own statues of the Virgin of Sorrows and St. John, and had taken over this year's procession. They would not permit the Indians to participate as a group or carry their own "time-honored" (*antigua*) image of the Virgin. The Indians appealed to the parish priest, but he declined to intervene, so "we retired to the hospital chapel with heavy hearts to put our statue and trumpets back in their places." According to the Indians' petition to the bishop of Guadalajara, the Spaniards then demanded their statue and musical instruments for the procession. When they refused to provide these, the priest came in person with the Spaniards and took these things and more, including the Indians' drum and their figure of death. Now they appealed to the bishop to order the priest to let them stage this procession in the future and keep the Spaniards from interfering. The Indians offered the Spaniards something of an olive branch – that they could hold their own separate procession as long as it did not prejudice the Indians' interests. The bishop agreed, specifying that the Indians be allowed to hold their customary procession at 2:00 p.m. without interference. If the Spaniards wished to have their own procession, it could take place afterwards.

There was less room for this kind of legal remedy in the late eighteenth century, when imperial officials no longer routinely supported the separation of races as a legal principle.[118] But communities continued their customary spectacles in spite of the reformers' decrees. In 1763, for example, the pastor of Temoac (parish of Zacualpa in the modern state of Morelos) thought his word was enough to end the local Indians' version of the Santiagueros dance that recently had been banned by the archbishop. To his dismay, the community retaliated the following year by moving the festivities to the cemetery, including bullfights and fireworks, and refusing to pay him for special Masses and other feast day services.[119]

Despite their own decrees, royal officials had financial and institutional reasons to encourage some of the festive activities. Even as a flurry of decrees called for fewer feast days and less extravagant spectacles, complaints were received in the audiencia and episcopal courts from parishioners against their pastors for establishing new fiestas and demanding contributions to support them, or for imprisoning Indian parishioners who would not allow a beloved image to go out on procession.[120] Royal orders to restrict excessive use of fireworks and candle wax in religious rituals inevitably led to complaints and requests for exemptions by fireworks makers and chandlers that carried weight with royal governors because the royal treasury collected license fees and taxes on this commerce.[121] Even if there was not an obvious economic motive, restrictions of this kind were not likely to be sanctioned with much alacrity by the high courts. The parish priest of Alahuistlan in the district of Sultepec caught the new spirit of devotional restraint and in 1798 requested that the audiencia order an end to the costly local practice in Totomaloyan of *mayordomos de santos* (individuals who sponsored the cult of a particular saint in the community) being required to burn candles before their saint's image in church every day. The judges were sympathetic, but ordered further investigation because, they said, local customs were not to be overturned lightly.[122]

Again and again, experienced royal and ecclesiastical judges sounded the same warning and hesitated to vigorously enforce the orders of the Council of the Indies, viceroys, and audiencias to reform practices of public worship in Indian communities. In 1796, the archbishop of Mexico was wary of the sweeping viceregal order that Indian romerías not include images of the saints or venture more than one league (roughly 2.6 miles) from the edge of town. He warned that indiscriminate enforcement of the order could be dangerous: "the Indians are very tenacious in keeping their customs, and they love to carry images and the rest to distant places to the sound of rockets and musical instruments."[123] The archbishop's note of caution was not heeded when the audiencia responded ten years later to a complaint by the pastor of Amecameca, Br. Ygnacio de Castañeda y Medina, about unruly romerías to the shrine of the Sacromonte there from neighboring towns. The judges summarily banned the romerías altogether and called for all festivities to end by sundown, as Father Castañeda requested. But the pastor was back in court the next year, complaining now that the romerías continued in spite of the prohibition and were even more disorderly than before. Local merchants counterargued, unhappy with the restrictions on sale of food after 6:00 p.m. They noted that participants in the romerías were mainly poor people who came to Amecameca directly from their labors in the fields, usually long after the 6 o'clock curfew.[124]

In 1796, Zacatecas's lieutenant governor ruefully reported to the viceroy that "the government here tolerates [abuses in processions with images] in order to avoid worse harm to religion and the state," but there was little a viceroy or anyone else could accomplish in the way of cultural reprogramming through decrees and exhortations. As the provincial governor of Nueva Galicia had observed eighteen years earlier, there were not enough district judges and governors to enforce the proposed changes "in the ridiculous feast day spectacles to which the Indians are prone." He, like others, advised caution in trying to impose sudden changes in local customs.[125]

Conclusion

Looking for long-distance pilgrimages, I found romerías and processions.[126] Does the near silence about long-distance pilgrimage suggest that it was not there? Or is it fair to say that as a rule the written record of colonial Latin America captures in one way or the other what imperial authorities approved or disapproved of and only rarely documents activity they simply let pass? The vagrancy laws suggest that colonial authorities would have been alert to and concerned about pilgrimages, yet there is hardly any record of such journeys, prescriptive or otherwise, beyond the occasional late colonial note from a bishop excusing a devotee from a pilgrimage vow or petition for permission to visit a distant shrine. So, I doubt that a tradition of long-distance pilgrimages similar to the European ones has somehow slipped through the documentary cracks for New Spain. In contrast, processions appear often in colonial records, sometimes in detailed descriptions and prescriptions. But, for the most part, colonial authorities largely overlooked the romerías of commuter pilgrims until the late eighteenth century, making the occasional mention of them in earlier written records especially noteworthy.

Why was there so little pilgrimage of the kind the Turners and Kubler imagined? Beyond the geographical impediments to distant travel on foot or muleback through much of New Spain, three considerations stand out: (1) the nature of the miraculous as understood at the time; (2) the attraction of the local; and (3) government policies. The least obvious of these considerations is the nature of the miraculous, especially the capacity of copies of a celebrated image and things that had touched it to somehow contain and transmit the matrix image's divine presence. The reach of Christianity in colonial Mexico depended on the proliferation and distribution of sacred images more than on the circulation of the laity to distant places and images regarded as especially numinous. In other words, the cherished copy, whether a reasonable facsimile painting, statue, or print, or a relic, invited the divine presence, especially if it had touched the matrix image. This helps to explain the Guadalupan paradox – that the image of Our Lady of Guadalupe was very widely known, promoted, and beloved in the late colonial period before the shrine at Tepeyac became a great, long-distance pilgrimage destination. Shrine images and a site such as Tepeyac could retain their central importance without requiring devotees to visit the shrine itself.

Potentially numinous copies that obviated the need to visit the original shrine also contributed to local identities.[127] For the most part, the traditional festival cycle and confraternities in Mexican communities followed general practices in Europe and most of New Spain, yet they had a distinctly local quality as well, treated as "our way." Romerías to caves, mountains, and other places of origin, and the lavish processions with images to appeal for protection, fertility, and mercy from divine beings suggest some (though not unaltered) continuities from precolonial times, perhaps especially in the taste for masked dancers and flowered archways.

Local affiliations, customs, and lore about miracles and images of Christ and the saints often were encouraged by elites who mediated between their communities and colonial authorities (including the parish priest), gaining prestige and favor from both by identifying with the colonial hierarchy of authority and power. At the same time, in the name of age-old traditions, they validated local ritual practices and could lead to struggles with authorities over changes in fiestas and processions.[128]

Government policies, the third consideration, were the other face of the lure of the local, discouraging unauthorized long-distance travel of the crown's subjects and favoring devotion to images over visits to shrines, even to the Virgin of Guadalupe at Tepeyac, the one image and shrine that was consistently embraced and actively promoted by the highest civil and ecclesiastical officials in the eighteenth century. As often as not, local practices were condoned, if not promoted, by imperial elites. Parish priests were particularly active in promoting shrines and encouraging providential localism as a means to spiritual revival and revenue.[129] In this way, official policy and compliance went hand in hand. However, the issue of local compliance with the late colonial restrictions on processions, dances, and romerías more often was fraught with friction and the risk of protest.

The Turners may have been wrong about Mexico's early history of pilgrimage and they may have focused too much on *communitas* and the journey, but Victor Turner's wide-ranging performance approach to sacred travel, looking for piety in motion, and approaching what people understand through what they do is helpful to historians who find tracks of activity in written records and material culture but cannot accompany their actors on the journey.[130] For New Spain, at least, the key may be to look more closely at what the Turners slighted – the destination and the organization, protocol, and orchestration of inspiring activity there. And for sacred travel in Mexico, although *communitas* merits a prominent place, as Mexican ethnographers have repeatedly shown, that place was and is more hemmed in and structured than the Turners imagined.

For more than a generation, social science and humanities disciplines have made a special point of delving into the ideological underpinnings of terms and concepts used to describe and explain reality. Among other terms, space, dance, pilgrimage, religion, and Church in modern academic and popular parlance have been scrutinized as social constructions rooted in Western Enlightenment thought during an age of hegemonic imperialism, expressing the logic of power rather than objective, universal verities. A result is that a familiar stand-alone category such as pilgrimage is being merged into others that are more inclusive and presumably less charged, or at least more in line with patterns of behavior in our time. The lesson for scholars who write about pilgrimage is that drawing tight boundaries around particular kinds of inspiring movement is a doubtful, if convenient, practice. At least for Europe and North America, since the nineteenth-century, pilgrimage is not easily separated conceptually from tourism and some other kinds of travel, although the recipes for a more inclusive conceptual approach to pilgrimage studies usually have been honored in the breach. Few who recommend them have been so comprehensive and ecumenical in their own research. More importantly for historians, merging pilgrimage with all kinds of travel, especially tourism, and defining pilgrimage in a way that makes religiosity a secondary matter can muffle what pilgrims in other times and places understood themselves to be doing. I do not find a definition of pilgrimage like "physical movement through a terrain of culturally constructed symbols" of much help in understanding early modern Christian shrines and their visitors. Still, the habits of questioning, historicizing, and combining categories that have come to be widely accepted as natural and innocent can be useful, provided that we do not see the ways in which people in other times and places used those categories and terms only as mystifications and false consciousness.

My intention in the last part of this chapter was to suggest the value of blurring widely accepted categorical lines between pilgrimage and other kinds of synchronized movement – in particular, the lines separating romerías, processions, and dancing. In practice, these activities merged in a multisensory experience of sight, smell, sound, touch, heart-pounding exertion, and exhilaration that was understood to open the way to a spiritual transformation in which "men and gods are held to be transparent to one another."[131] As synchronized movement, romerías folded into processions, and processions sometimes were said to be "danced,"[132] with sacred images of Christ and saints bobbing in line to the thump, boom, and crackle of fireworks, drums, trumpets, and hands clapping; the pad of feet and rhythmic movement of participants; the heavenly sounds of hymns, prayers, and bells; blessed tears; and the colors and sweet smells of flowered arch thresholds and incense,[133] together "levantando los espíritus," as Mendieta put it, elevating the spirit and inviting a miracle.

Notes

1. Michael Carroll, *Madonnas that Maim: Popular Catholicism in Italy Since the Fifteenth Century*, Baltimore: Johns Hopkins University Press, 1992, p. 23.
2. Early modern long-distance Christian pilgrimages in Europe have been less studied, but see *Pèlerins et pèlerinages dans l'Europe moderne*, ed. Philippe Boutry and Dominique Julia, Rome: École Française de Rome, 2000 for essays on seventeenth- and eighteenth-century pilgrimages to Rome and Compostela from France, Portugal, Germany, and the Low Countries along routes sprinkled with lesser shrines and notable relics. There seems to have been more of a system of satellite shrines in Spain than in New Spain. See

William A. Christian, Jr., *Local Religion in Sixteenth-Century Spain*, Princeton: Princeton University Press, 1981, p. 87.
3. Distant journeys of faith possibly were a larger part of the story of pilgrimage in New Spain than I could establish since the paper trail is weighted toward the destination and what went on there. That is, ecclesiastical and civil authorities focused on regulating what went on at the shrine more than transit to and from it. On the other hand, colonial officials had good reasons to track long distance travel and commerce and what they regarded as vagrancy. And they rarely mentioned pilgrims.
4. Victor Turner and Edith Turner, *Image and Pilgrimage in Christian Culture: Anthropological Perspectives*, New York: Columbia University Press, 1978.
5. Victor Turner, "The Center Out There, Pilgrim's Goal," *History of Religions* 12: 3 (February 1973), 195.
6. Turner and Turner, *Image and Pilgrimage*, p. 245.
7. On pilgrimages as institutions in which ideological beliefs are imposed and reiterated, see, for example, Mart Bax, *Medjugorje: Religion, Politics and Violence in Rural Bosnia*, Amsterdam: Vrij Universiteit Uitgeverji, 1995; Glenn Bowman, "Anthropology of Pilgrimage," in *Dimensions of Pilgrimage: An Anthropological Appraisal*, ed. M. Jha, New Delhi: Inter-India, 1985, pp. 1–9; and *Contesting the Sacred: The Anthropology of Christian Pilgrimage*, ed. John Eade and Michael Sallnow, Urbana: University of Illinois Press, 2000. By contrast, much of the literature on religious pilgrimage in Mexico by anthropologist-ethnohistorians continues to emphasize *communitas* and the journey. See, for example, *Peregrinaciones ayer y hoy: Arqueología y antropología de las religiones*, ed. Patricia Fournier, Carlos Mondragón, and Walburga Wiesheu, Mexico: El Colegio de México, 2012.
8. *Reframing Pilgrimage: Cultures in Motion*, ed. Simon Coleman and John Eade, New York and London: Routledge, 2004, pp. 2–3.
9. Simon Coleman and John Elsner, *Pilgrimage: Past and Present in the World Religions*, Cambridge, MA: Harvard University Press, 1995, p. 167. Coleman and Eade have gone a step beyond this definition to narrow the focus on movement and organization. They treat pilgrimage as "involving the institutionalization (or even domestication) of mobility," *Reframing Pilgrimage*, p. 17. This is a present-oriented approach to pilgrimage, as "just one of the twenty-first century's many forms of cultural mobility," in a world "constantly en route," *Reframing Pilgrimage*, abstract inside the front cover and p. 5. They do acknowledge that theirs is not "the only means of encapsulating pilgrimage" (p. 18), and they open the study of pilgrimage to what takes place at shrines as well as journeys to shrines (p. 3), but their call for attention to the return journey tends to downplay the destination, and their criticism of the Turners as too "place-centred" is surprising (p. 2). Unlike Coleman and Eade, James Clifford, *Routes: Travel and Translation in the Late Twentieth Century*, Cambridge, MA: Harvard University Press, 1997, does not fold pilgrimage into his overarching category of modern travel ("people going places") because pilgrimage's "sacred meanings tend to predominate," p. 39.
10. Of the many works in this vein, see *From Medieval Pilgrimage to Religious Tourism*, ed. William H. Swatos and Luigi Tomasi, Westport CT: Praeger, 2002 (especially Tomasi's "Homo Viator: From Pilgrimage to Religious Tourism Via the Journey"); Ellen Badone and Sharon R. Roseman, *Intersecting Journeys: The Anthropology of Pilgrimage and Tourism*, Urbana: University of Illinois Press, 2004; and Nelson Graburn,

The Anthropology of Tourism, New York: Pergamon Press, 1983. An especially rich inquiry into the interface of tourism and religion in one place is Thomas S. Bremer's *Blessed with Tourists: The Borderlands of Religion and Tourism in San Antonio*, Chapel Hill: University of North Carolina Press, 2004.
11. William B. Taylor, *Shrines & Miraculous Images: Religious Life in Mexico Before the Reforma*, Albuquerque: University of New Mexico Press, 2010, pp. 132–135.
12. "Where self, space, and time blend." Casey's writings on phenomenology of place include, among others, *Representing Place: Landscape Painting and Maps*, Minneapolis: University of Minnesota Press, 2002, *The Fate of Place: A Philosophical History*, Berkeley: University of California Press, 1997, and two interventions in the "Place Matters" forum published in the *Annals of the Association of American Geographers* 91: 4 (2001): "Between Geography and Philosophy: What Does It Mean to Be in the Place-World," pp. 716–723, and "On Habitus and Place: Responding to My Critics," pp. 716–723. In his reflections on non-Western conceptions of location and territory, anthropologist Edward Hall anticipated Casey's argument about the *a priori* existence of place. See *The Hidden Dimension*, Garden City, New York: Doubleday, 1966. Hall noted that European languages refer to space/spaces more than most languages do, and that some languages – Hopi is his main example – have no vocabulary for space except in terms of time, and no conception of abstract space that gets filled with objects. Keith Basso makes a similar point for Western Apaches' "place-centered view of time and human endeavor" in the local landscape, *Wisdom Sits in Places: Landscape and Language Among the Western Apache*, Albuquerque: University of New Mexico Press, 1996, pp. 60, 62–63, 74. See also J. B. Jackson, *A Sense of Place, a Sense of Time*, New Haven: Yale University Press, 1994, p. 32.
13. As Casey points out, place was more immediately apprehended by early Europeans than a Newtonian sense of space, and place-centered thinking was fundamental to at least some non-Western cultures, including Mesoamerica. In colonial Mexico, the Catholic Church and other Spanish colonial institutions introduced new and larger bounded spaces – dioceses and high court districts among them – and standard units of measurement, including the vara (about 33 inches long), but notions of greater distance were not yet so measured and fixed. Beyond a town's limits or the dimensions of a land grant, distance was still relational, more attached to time and place. A league was commonly understood to be the distance a mule could travel in one hour over local terrain; and territories like dioceses and audiencias were defined by the settlements located within them rather than by hypothetical boundary lines traced on the ground.
14. See Jackson, *A Sense of Place, passim*, and Christian Norberg-Schulz, *Genius Loci: Towards a Phenomenology of Architecture*, New York: Rizzoli, 1980.
15. For a more sustained discussion of this point, see Tim Ingold, *Being Alive: Essays on Movement, Knowledge and Description*, London and New York: Routledge, 2011, p. 148, "My contention is that lives are led not inside places but through, around, to and from them, from and to places elsewhere. I use the term wayfaring to describe the embodied experience of this perambulatory movement."
16. Perhaps an echo of this geographical importance of burial places may be found in the contemporary practice in Tepoztlán, Morelos, of groups of pilgrims to shrines in other parts of Morelos leaving from the town cemetery, in the presence of other members of their community, Françoise Odile Neff Nuixa, "De un lado al otro del cerro:

Peregrinaciones tepoztecas," in *Peregrinaciones ayer y hoy*, ed. Patricia Fournier, Carlos Mondragón, and Walburga Wiesheu, Mexico: Colmex, 2012, p. 55.
17. J. B. Jackson, foreword to *The Evolving Landscape: Homer Aschmann's Geography*, ed. Martin Pasqualetti, Baltimore: Johns Hopkins University Press, 1997, pp. vii–viii.
18. I have suggested that this was less the case in the more dualistic European Christian traditions, "Placing the Cross in Colonial Mexico," *The Americas* 69: 2 (October 2012), 145–178.
19. The Turners' view of pilgrimage in Mexican history as an extension of medieval European great pilgrimages rarely comes up in this literature. This is not the place for a survey of the secondary literature, but for a recent collection of scholarly essays on pilgrimage in Mexico by anthropologists and archaeologists that largely follows the Turners' approach, see *Peregrinaciones ayer y hoy: Arqueología y antropología de las religiones*, ed. Fournier, Mondragón, and Wiesheu.
20. Sahagún's *Florentine Codex, Book 2* on ceremonies mentions pre-colonial processions in the form of circumambulations of great pyramid temples, *Florentine Codex: General History of the Things of New Spain*, ed. and trans. Arthur J. O. Anderson and Charles E. Dibble, Salt Lake City: University of Utah Press, 1982, II, 115, 136. The *relaciones geográficas* of 1579–81 from districts throughout central and southern Mexico describe processions and short pilgrimages, but have little to say about longer journeys to sacred places; e.g., for the Archdiocese of Mexico, *Papeles de Nueva España*, Madrid: Tip. Sucesores de Rivadeneyra, 1905, VI, 73, Chimalhuacan-Atenco; VI, 118 Coatepec de Guerrero; VI, 216–217, Acolman; VI, 276–277 minas de Tasco; and IV for the Diocese of Antequera (Oaxaca), p. 220, Teutitlan del Camino.
21. On rituals associated with the dangerous journeys of the *pochteca* (merchants for the Mexica state), see the descriptions of leaving and returning in David Carrasco and Scott Sessions, *Daily Life of the Aztecs*, 2nd edition, Santa Barbara: Greenwood Press/ABC-CLIO, 2011, pp. 156–159.
22. Geoffrey McCafferty, "Mountain of Heaven, Mountain of Earth: The Great Pyramid of Cholula as Sacred Landscape," in *Landscape and Power in Ancient Mesoamerica*, ed. Rex Koontz, Kathryn Reese-Taylor, and Annabeth Headrick, Boulder, CO: Westview Press, 2001, p. 281, relying on the late sixteenth-century *relación geográfica* written by the Spanish *alcalde mayor* of Cholula. For a summary of the scholarship on pilgrimage to ancient Cholula as religious capital city, see David Carrasco and Scott Sessions, "Middle Space, Labyrinth, and Circumambulation: Cholula's Peripatetic Role in the *Mapa de Cuauhtinchan No. 2*," in *City, Cave, and Eagle's Nest: An Interpretive Journey through the Mapa de Cuauhtinchan No. 2*, ed. David Carrasco and Scott Sessions, Albuquerque: University of New Mexico Press, 2007, pp. 427–454, especially pp. 436–440. They suggest that Cholula was visited by elites from other cities to sanctify their rule and that "it was accessible and prized by the wider populace."
23. Carlos Martínez Marín, "Santuarios y peregrinaciones en el México pre-hispánico," in *Mesoamérica. XII Mesa Redonda. Sociedad Mexicana de Antropología*, Mexico: UNAM, 1972, pp. 161–179. Curiously, Fr. Juan de Torquemada, the early seventeenth-century Franciscan chronicler, does not mention Cholula as a "pilgrimage" site, but he does mention three other sites: Matlalcueye in the foothills of the Sierra Grande of Tlaxcala, dedicated to the goddess Toci, "our grandmother"; Tianguismanalco, dedicated to the

god Telpuchtli; and Tepeyac, dedicated to "our precious mother." Of these, only Tepeyac was a major Christian shrine in the colonial period.

For mountains, caves, and bodies of water as "topographic shrines," where "gods" resided and rituals were performed in precolonial Mesoamerica, see also Andrea Stone, "From Ritual in the Landscape to Capture in the Urban Center: The Recreation of Ritual Environments in Mesoamerica," *Journal of Ritual Studies* 6: 1 (winter 1992), 109–132. Stone suggests that these natural shrines were "intensely personal," more than social, and that pilgrims to them focused on propitiation, p. 115.

24. George Kubler, "Pre-Columbian Pilgrimages in Mesoamerica," *Diogenes* 32: #125 (1984), 11–23; and "Peregrinajes antes y después de la Conquista Española en América," in *La ciudad, concepto y obra (VI Coloquio de Historia del Arte)*, Mexico: UNAM, 1987, pp. 221–249, with commentary by Carlos Martínez Marín, pp. 250–256.
25. Kubler, "Pre-Columbian Pilgrimages in Mesoamerica," p. 21.
26. James Bugslag, "Local Pilgrimages and Their Shrines in Pre-Modern Europe," *Peregrinations: Journal of Medieval Art & Architecture* 2: 1 (2010), 1–26, especially pp. 1–2, 12–13; Eamon Duffy, "The Dynamics of Pilgrimage in Late Medieval England," in *Pilgrimage: English Experience from Becket to Bunyan*, ed. Colin Morris and Peter Roberts, Cambridge, UK and New York: Cambridge University Press, 2002, pp. 164–177. Philip M. Soergel, *Wondrous in His Saints: Counter-Reformation Propaganda in Bavaria*, Berkeley: University of California Press, 1993, p. 167, noted that Bavarian Catholic propagandists in the seventeenth and eighteenth centuries were promoting shorter, more regulated "pilgrimages"; and Marc Forster recognized the importance of short journeys in his *Catholic Revival in the Age of the Baroque: Religious Identity in Southwest Germany, 1550–1750*, Cambridge, UK and New York: Cambridge University Press, 2001. For an earlier appreciation of the importance of local pilgrimages in France, see Marie Hélène Froeschlé-Chopard, *La religion populaire en Provence Orientale au XVIIIe siècle*, Paris: Beauchesne, 1980, pp. 294ff.

By the 1590s, the Spanish Hapsburgs no longer promoted long distance pilgrimages on the peninsula by their Spanish subjects for fear of vagabondage, but they were less inclined to discourage foreign Catholics from making the long trek across northern Spain to Compostela, William A. Christian, Jr., *Divine Presence in Spain and Western Europe, 1500–1960*, Budapest-New York: Central European University Press, 2012, p. 34.
27. Bugslag, "Local Pilgrimages," pp. 1–2.
28. Juan Ubaldo de Anguita Sandoval y Roxas, *El prudente peregrino: Oración fúnebre que en las honras de el Sr. Dr. d. Antonio Villaseñor y Monroy* ..., Mexico: Vda. de F. Rodríguez Lupercio, 1727.
29. "una peregrinación bien penosa y dilatada," Juan Javier Pescador, "'Thio Señor y Muy dueño Mio': Cartas de Indias de la familia Urdiñola del Valle de Oyarzun, 1700–1708," *Boletín de la Real Sociedad Bascongada de Amigos del País* 52: 2 (1996), 503–518, especially pp. 506–507, letter from Tomás de Urdiñola to his uncle, Sarxento Mayor Don Antonio de Urdiñola, dated Lima, September 9, 1700. The trip, wrote Urdiñola, took 21 months, 14 days.
30. Benito Jerónimo Feijóo, *Teatro crítico universal*, Madrid: Atlas, 1961, 3, 51–56.
31. "muy distantes"; "propiamente tales." Feijóo dismissed romerías as occasions for "innumerables relajaciones" rather than true pilgrimages, a sentiment echoed in the

popular saying included in the Real Academia de Lengua's definition of *peregrinación*: "romería de cerca, mucho vino y poca cera" (romerías close to home make for much wine and few candles).

32. Called *demandantes* or *demandadores*, and sometimes *peregrinos* (pilgrims), the alms collectors' purpose was less penitential than pecuniary. Their travels required episcopal licenses, which were routinely granted in the seventeenth century. In the late colonial period they were more closely regulated and usually confined to local collections that roughly coincided in time with the late colonial restrictions on public celebrations and processions with images outside the community. For a singular ex-voto painting that depicts demandantes escaping an attack by Chichimecs in 1710, see Sergio Sánchez Vázquez, "Peregrinaciones, espacios sagrados y santuarios: El ámbito nacional, regional y local en la cosmovisión otomiana del Valle del Mezquital," in *Peregrinaciones ayer y hoy*, ed. Fournier, Mondragón, and Wiesheu, p. 138.

On the long-standing presence of hermits at the Chalma shrine, see Gonzalo Obregón, "El Real Convento y Santuario de San Miguel de Chalma," in *Estudios históricos americanos: Homenaje a Silvio Zavala*, Mexico: El Colegio de México, 1953, pp. 124–129; also Pierre Ragon, *Les saints et les images du Mexique (XVIe-XVIIIe siècle)*, Paris: L'Harmattan, 2003, pp. 48–54. There were others, elsewhere.

33. See Francisco Lárraga, *Promptuario de la theología moral ...*, 32nd printing, Madrid: Herederos de Don Joseph Horta, 1751, pp. 194 and 370 on the privileges and duties of passing pilgrims, the prosecution of those who attack or rob them, and who may confess them. Lárraga was drawing upon a body of formal law in Christian Europe regarding pilgrims and pilgrimage that was emerging in the eleventh century.

34. Francisco de Ajofrín, the Spanish Capuchin alms collector who visited many shrines in New Spain during his sojourn there in the 1760s and collected prints of their miraculous images, is exceptional. See his *Diario del viaje que hizo a la América en el siglo XVIII el P. Fray Francisco de Ajofrín*, 2 vols., Mexico: Instituto Cultural Hispano Mexicano, 1964.

35. In the same vein, it is curious that the Franciscans, who were so prominent in the early colonial evangelization, pastoral service, and spiritual missions of the eighteenth century, were not promoters of pilgrimages as they knew them in Europe since they had been chosen to take up residence in the Holy Land from the late Middle Ages to guide, instruct, and care for Latin pilgrims and oversee the Catholic shrines in the area, Annabel Jane Wharton, *Selling Jerusalem: Relics, Replics, Theme Parks*, Chicago: University of Chicago Press, 2006, p. 109.

36. Sixteenth-century colonial officials attempted to restrict movement of native peoples to distant places; for Yucatán, Amara Solari, *Maya Ideologies of the Sacred: The Transfiguration of Space in Colonial Yucatan*, Austin: University of Texas Press, 2013, p. 148.

37. Florencia mentioned that an Indian from the mines of Zacualpan undertook a personal pilgrimage to the shrine during the September fiestas in 1678, *Las novenas del santuario de Nuestra Señora de Guadalupe de México, que se apareció en la manta de Juan Diego*, Madrid: Imprenta de Lorenzo de San Martín, 1785, pp. 13–15; and Antonio de Ulloa, during his visit to New Spain in 1776–1778, was impressed that Indians "came from great distances" for the annual fiestas at Tepeyac. Just where they came from is not clear, Francisco de Solano, *Antonio de Ulloa y la Nueva España*, Mexico: UNAM, 1979, p. 116.

38. A similar pattern of devotees visiting a copy of a revered image nearby rather than journeying to the shrine of the matrix image is mentioned by Ruiz y Cervantes (1791) for Our Lady of Xuquila. After saying that some pilgrims traveled to the shrine from the city of Antequera, he noted that many from Antequera visited a copy of the Virgin of Xuquila at Zaachila instead, José Manuel Ruiz y Cervantes, *Memorias de la portentosa imagen de Nuestra Señora de Xuquila* . . ., Mexico: Zúñiga y Ontiveros, 1791, p. 64.
39. The classic study of life understood as a pilgrimage in late medieval and early modern Europe is Samuel C. Chew's *The Pilgrimage of Life*, New Haven: Yale University Press, 1962. Chew drew suggestively on an array of prints from the time.
40. Spanish and Italian guidebooks to the Holy Land were reprinted in Mexico City and circulated especially among priests. For example, Antonio del Castillo's *El devoto peregrino y viaje de tierra santa,* various editions, different publishers, Madrid and Barcelona, 1656–; 1785. Tulane University's copy belonged to Miguel Hidalgo and includes at the back of the volume account records for a few of his estate workers in the early nineteenth century, some of whom purchased *bulas de la Santa Cruzada* (Tu RBC DS106 C38 LAL). Other texts exhorted devotees to undertake *romerías interiores* or virtual pilgrimages to the holy lands; for example, Pedro Joseph Rodríguez de Arizpe, *Relación de lo acaecido en la celebridad de el jubileo de el año santo* . . ., Mexico: Bibliotheca Mexicana, 1753, Joaquín Osuna, *Peregrinación Christiana por el camino real de la celeste Jerusalén*, Mexico: Bibliotheca Mexicana, 1756 (divided into nine journeys); and *Colección de noticias de muchas de las indulgencias plenarias y perpetuas que pueden ganar todos los fieles de Christo que . . . visitaren en sus respectivos días las iglesias que se irán nombrando* . . ., Mexico: Zúñiga y Ontiveros, 1787.
41. Francisco de Florencia, *Narración de la marabillosa aparición que hizo el archángel San Miguel* . . ., Seville: Impr. de las Siete Revueltas, 1692, pp. 98–99: "esta agua milagrosa haría más operación en los que vendrían de lexos por la mayor fee con que bendrían y la mayor devoción." He also advised devotees of Our Lady of Guadalupe to "visit the Virgin in her celestial image" at Tepeyac ("se ha de ir con fin de visitar a la Ssma Virgen en su celestial Imagen"), *Las novenas del santuario de Nuestra Señora de Guadalupe de México* . . ., Mexico: Edit. Cultura, 1945, pp. 7–8.
42. TU VEMC leg. 41 exp. 2, 1776–1780. There was some historical basis for this proposal. At least one earlier viceroy had demonstrated his devotion to the Lord of Chalma by visiting the shrine. Diarist Juan Antonio Rivera recorded on January 1686 that the viceroy and two audiencia judges had just returned from the shrine, *Diario curioso del capellán del Hospital de Jesús Nazareno de México*, Mexico: Vargas Rea, 1953, II, 7.
43. Including León, Granada, Trujillo, Tegucigalpa, San Salvador, Sonsonate, Valle del Dorado, Villa de San Vicente de Austria, the city of Guatemala, and the Valley of Esquipulas. An example of a long journey to Esquipulas to fulfill a promise is documented in AGCA A1.15 Leg. 66 exp. 810. 1791: Doña Casilda de Arada, mulata, petitioned the commander of Omoa (Honduras) for a license to go by boat to Zacapa and then overland to Esquipulas: "tengo hecha promesa por mi enfermedad pasada de hir a dho Santuario a cumplirla" ("I made a vow to go to the said Shrine during my recent illness"). My thanks to Rus Sheptak for this reference.
44. For one of many examples of authorities expressing concern about evidence of offerings made on hilltops and in caves, see the pastoral visit of Archbishop Rubio y Salinas to

Tlaquiltenango, Morelos in 1759, AHM L10A/7–8 fol. 163r ". . . sacrificio en los cerros y alturas y en otros parajes sospechosos e indecentes, formando para ello enrramadas y siguiéndose de ellos gravíssimos inconvenientes." For the example of burgeoning interest in a recently discovered cross at Huaquechula, Puebla being suppressed by the bishop in 1810, see AGN Clero Regular y Secular 215 exp. 26, fols. 604–638.

45. Juan de Viera, *Breve compendiossa narración de la ciudad de México* [1777] Mexico: Edit. Guaranía, 1952, pp. 81–82. Having called travel to Tepeyac a "devota romería," he added that the shrine was "much visited by all the patricians of this city and all the communities and settlements nearby."

 To the extent that colonial romerías in central Mexico were nested in a pilgrimage "system," it may have resembled the kind of network described by Andrés Medina Hernández for the Milpa Alta area (in the southeast corner of the Distrito Federal, in the mountainous fringe above the Valley of Mexico) in recent years. Villagers undertake "promesas" or short pilgrimages to shrines in neighboring communities to fulfill a vow. They may also make an annual visit to Chalma, Amecameca, and/or Tepeyac, "Los pueblos originarios del sur del Distrito Federal: una primera mirada etnográfica," in *La memoria negada de la Ciudad de México: sus pueblos originarios*, ed. Andrés Medina Hernández, Mexico: UNAM/UAM, 2007, pp. 53–56.

46. AGN Criminal 590 exp. 2, trial record of Jasintho Manzano for the murder of María de Vargas. After Manzano's execution by hanging, his body was subjected to a gruesome desecration that ancient Romans had practiced in cases of parricide. His body was placed in a large sack with a live dog, a snake, a female monkey, and a castrated rooster. Once the sack was sewn closed, it was thrown into the deepest river nearby.

47. People came from Contla and vicinity "alentados con la experiencia de haver visto mil marabillas," AGN Civil 1557 exp. 8, 1790.

48. Dated July 19, 1741, the royal cédula called for "informes sobre núcleos urbanos, demográficos, económicos y eclesiásticos de todos los territorios de Indias." Royal governors at the district level (alcaldes mayores and *subdelegados*) were to carry out the assignment under the direction of higher authorities. Three of the eight questions dealt with ecclesiastical and religious affairs: #5 "¿Por qué sujetos y doctrineros están administrados en lo espiritual? Si hay falta de ellos. Las imágenes milagrosas y su origen; #6 ¿Qué misión o misiones se hallan en la propagación de nuestra Santa Fe Católica? las que son ya establecidas, y las que son nuevas reducciones; #7 ¿Qué misioneros asisten en ellas a la dilatación del Santo Evangelio, sus idiomas, y su Estatuto?"

49. *Relaciones geográficas del Arzobispado de México. 1743*, ed. Francisco de Solano, Madrid: C.S.I.C., 1988, I, 143ff, Tecaxic; I, 157, Tenancingo; I, 164, Chalma; II, 306, Amatepec; II 491–517, Toluca; II, 309, Temascaltepec (hacen romerías todos los de las jurisdicciones comarcanas). Six years later, witnesses testifying in support of a newly celebrated miraculous image, El Señor de las Suertes, a crucifix in the Carmelite convent church of Orizaba, noted that devotees were coming from throughout the diocese of Puebla. The testimonies of the seven Spanish and creole witnesses were brief and virtually identical, SMU Bridwell, manuscript AFB 5361, Orizaba, 1749. Some of these romerías may well have connected the sending and receiving communities in ritual hospitality, as they do today in the Valle del Mezquital, among other places, but the written record I know is silent on the subject. See Fernando López Aguilar and

Patricia Fournier, "Peregrinaciones otomíes. Vínculos locales y regionales en el Valle del Mezquital," in *Peregrinaciones ayer y hoy*, ed. Fournier, Mondragón, and Wiesheu, p. 94.
50. AHM Fondo Catedral Colonia, 1796.
51. The move to restrict longer processions with images reached beyond districts that were reported on in that 1796 inquiry. The files of the Audiencia of Nueva Galicia include a September 24, 1796 decree by this court at the recommendation of the fiscal "que no bayan de los pueblos a las cabeceras por los abusos que se cometen," BEJ MS300 Papeles de Derecho, II, fs. 263v–264v.
52. Corpus Christi processions were held even in small towns in the Diocese of Michoacán in the late seventeenth century. See Alberto Carrillo Cázares, *Michoacán en el otoño del siglo XVII*, Zamora: El Colegio de Michoacán, 1993, pp. 251–269.
53. For a 1570s example of a precolonial ceremonial site converted into a chapel dedicated to the Holy Cross, see *Papeles de Nueva España*, VI, 54, Coatepec-Chalco *relación*.
54. The report for Taxco mentions that community members would visit a prominent rock or tree in the countryside and cover it with native paper, then they would bathe at midnight in the deepest river some distance from their settlement, then gather small stones and dried maize stalks that they brought to the rock or tree as offerings, and humbled themselves there, *Papeles de Nueva España*, VI, 276–277; at Coatepec de Guerrero, veneration of stone idols placed on hilltops and offering of incense and blankets was reported, *Papeles de Nueva España*, IV, 188; and in one fiesta (*quahuitlegua*) *caciques* led commoners to the top of a hill where sheafs of native paper and incense were offered to the gods, and cotton mantles were placed on the "idols" and left there to disintegrate, *Papeles de Nueva España*, VI, 217. Juan de Torquemada also described offerings of cloaks at a hilltop site, *Monarquía Indiana*, Mexico: Porrúa, 1986, III, 132 (libro 15, cap. 49).
55. AGN Criminal 71 exp. 6 fol. 167r, cave; Edward Osowski, "Passion Miracles and Indigenous Historical Memory in New Spain," *Hispanic American Historical Review* 88: 4 (2008), 607–638; Ragon, *Les saints et les images*, pp. 61–67.
56. Cayetano Cabrera y Quintero, *Escudo de armas de México: Celestial protección de esta nobilíssima ciudad, de la Nueva España, y casi todo el Nuevo Mundo*, Mexico: Vda. de Joseph Bernardo de Hogal, 1746, *passim*; Gómez, "Diario de México," Bancroft M-M 105, entry for November 17, 1796.
57. Charles Zika, "Hosts, Processions, and Pilgrimages: Controlling the Sacred in Fifteenth-Century Germany." *Past & Present* 118 (February 1988), 25–64.
58. Gerardus Van der Leeuw made this point about processions as a kind of dance: "A pure and universally preserved relic of the cultic dance is the procession. In all cultures, a parade is a kind of social mobilization in which all the people involved appear in a fixed order, to show themselves to the spectators. Especially in processions we find a latent awareness of the rhythmic background of life; when things are serious, we do not simply run to and fro in confusion, but group ourselves according to a definite, conventional order," *Sacred and Profane Beauty: The Holy in Art*, trans. David E. Green, New York: Holt, Rinehart and Winston, 1963, p. 39. An especially helpful study of the forms and meanings of dance in central Mexico before and after the Conquest is Paul A. Scolieri's *Dancing the New World: Aztecs, Spaniards, and the Choreography of Conquest*, Austin: University of Texas Press, 2013. An especially suggestive

ethnographic study of processions in two local pilgrimages is Françoise Odile Neff Nuixa's "De un lado al otro del cerro: Peregrinaciones tepoztecas," in *Peregrinaciones ayer y hoy*, ed. Fournier, Mondragón, and Wiesheu, pp. 59-79. For details about the sights, sounds, and protocol of processions and dances in patron saint fiestas in two towns of Guanajuato in the recent past, see Yolanda Lastra, Joel Sherzer, and Dina Sherzer, *Adoring the Saints: Fiestas in Central Mexico*, Austin: University of Texas Press, 2009.

59. Taylor, *Shrines & Miraculous Images*, pp. 75–81. Perhaps because devotees could show that they did not engage in unruly activity, appeals in the 1790s by owners of mines about scandalous behavior by their workers and lost production did not move the archbishop or viceroy to restrict the romerías to Mapethé and processions at the site or otherwise discourage the devotion. The 1769 Tututepec millenarian uprising nearby and the fact that in 1792 local people ignored the alcalde mayor of Zimapán's order not to visit Mapethé may have prompted this apparent leniency.

60. As Higinio Vásquez put it, pilgrims to the shrine of the Santa Cruz de los Milagros at San Juan Parangaricútiro "entered dancing" (entrar bailando), *Cristos célebres de México*, Mexico: n.p., 1950, entry no. 14. For examples of lavish celebrations with fireworks and processions, see the descriptions of dedications of new altars in the Mexico City churches of the Jesuits' Colegio Máximo and the shrine of the miraculous image of the Mater Dolorosa in the church of the Augustinian nuns published in the February and March 1729 issues of the *Gazeta de México*, BIBM 4, pp. 819–820, 828. The latter included a particularly elaborate fireworks display.

61. Juan de Mendoza, *Relación de el santuario de Tecaxique, en que está colocada la milagrosa Imagen de Nuestra Señora de los Ángeles . . .*, Mexico: J. de Ribera, 1684, fols. 17–18. The first paragraph is translated in Serge Gruzinski, *Images at War, From Columbus to Blade Runner*, Durham: Duke University Press, 2001, p. 195; the second paragraph is my translation. Gruzinski regards this spectacle at Tecaxic as an epitome of *lo barroco* that reached beyond Spanish colonial cities into the countryside.

62. For clues to meanings of dance, music, and procession as religious expression – as "motion-magic" and holy sounds and sights – there is Van der Leeuw, *Sacred and Profane Beauty*, especially pp. 15, 36, 39, 213, 215. Although Van der Leeuw treats dance, procession, music, poetry, drama, architecture, and theological aesthetics in separate sections, his is one of the few studies that have all of them in mind, together.

63. Mercedes Guadarrama Olivera, "El espacio y el tiempo sagrados en tres comunidades totonacas de la Sierra de Papantla," in *Procesos rurales e historia regional (sierra y costa totonacas de Veracruz)*, ed. Victoria Chenaut, Mexico: CIESAS, 1996, p. 186.

64. "Apéndice a los concilios primero y segundo mexicanos," in Nicolás León, *Bibliografía mexicana del siglo XVIII*, BIBM 4: 314–315, April 27, 1539. "Decoro" – decorum – was also the watchword for liturgical events, women's attire, and the practice of confessing women in the Diocese of Michoacán during the seventeenth century. See *Colección de las ordenanzas, que para el gobierno de el obispado de Michoacán hicieron y promulgaron . . .*, Mexico: Zúñiga y Ontiveros, 1776, especially pp. 23 and 15–16: "se le debe guardar mucho decoro"; "sean honestos."

Reflecting on the dancing figures in full body animal costumes depicted in the Codex Tlatelolco (1560s?), Barbara Mundy speculates that indigenous audiences would have understood the dance costumes as "battle gear of elite [Mexica] warriors" and political representations of "liminal states and transitions," "Indigenous Dances in Early

Pilgrims, Processions, and Romerías 541

Colonial Mexico City," in *Festivals & Daily Life in the Arts of Colonial Latin America, 1492–1850*, ed. Donna Pierce, Denver: Denver Art Museum, 2014, pp. 24, 28. Whether or not this was so, it is a further stretch to assume the dances in animal costumes were understood in these terms in the late colonial period. Max Harris comes to the timeless conclusion that dances by "indigenous performers" during the colonial period and beyond, including Corpus Christi festivities, represent "communal expressions of dissent" and paganism, a "reconquest, the expulsion of invading foreigners by the owners of the land, an eviction," *Aztecs, Moors, and Christians: Festivals of Reconquest in Mexico and Spain*, Austin: University of Texas Press, 2000, back cover, and *Carnival and Other Christian Festivals: Folk Theology and Folk Performance*, Austin: University of Texas Press, 2003, pp. 7, 10.

One of the earliest printed works in Mexico was a Spanish translation of a minatory text on processions by a fifteenth-century Carthusian monk, Dionicio Richel ("Denis the Carthusian"), *Éste es un compendio breve que tracta de la manera de cómo se han de hazer las pcessiones* [sic], Mexico: Juan Cromberger, 1544. Like the prelates of the First Provincial Synod, Richel was preoccupied with "malos usos" – "dissolute behavior," "disorderly conduct," "licentiousness," dancing, drinking, feasting, and gambling that could provoke God's ire. To the extent that the handling of sacred things in processions was an issue for Richel, relics were his focus. "Idolatries" (by Turks and Moors) were another of his concerns. Establishing good order (*regimiento*) was the underlying motive of this text, but the author's approach was negative – eliminating what was not in good order. He had little to say about how a proper procession should be organized.

The Third Provincial Synod in 1585 picked up on the language of Richel with a predictable American twist: native dances and fiestas were regarded as going hand in hand with "the vomit of idolatry" and songs that recalled the indigenous past, *Concilio III provincial mexicano: celebrado en México el año de 1585* ..., ed. Mariano Galván Rivera, Mexico: Eugenio Maillefert y Compañía, 1859, p. 23 (libro 1, título 1). The descriptions of frequent native feasting in the *relaciones geográficas* (1579–81) often mention processions, dancing and singing to musical instruments, and copal smoke that the reporter associated with sacrifices and drunkenness; e.g., *Papeles de Nueva España*, VI, 9, Totolapan; VI, 139 Cuezala; VI, 146, Teloloapan; IV, 101 Macuilxóchitl; VI, 128, Miahuatlan; IV, 149, Mitla; VI, 179, Talistaca; IV, 217, Teutitlan del Camino. Sometimes the report conflated the processions and dancing, as in the description of five or six children who "andavan bailando en quadrillas" during the Mesalqualisstli feast in Acolman, VI, 216. Later compilations of episcopal edicts continued to connect native dances with idolatry, drunkenness, and sacrifice. For example, *Colección de las ordenanzas* ... *Michoacán*, pp. 192–193.

65. FHA roll 102 exp. 1 fol. 153v, 1653 pastoral letter. In his pastoral visits in 1687, Archbishop Aguiar y Seixas worried about too much profane celebrating during what should be solemn liturgical occasions, LC Monday Collection, microfilm roll 11 fol. 155ff. Were dances and other spectacles that seemed strange to Spanish eyes necessarily precolonial and non-Christian? Several of the forbidden dances appear to have been Spanish and Christian in origin – the Santiagueros, Moors-and-Christians, and Los Negritos, to mention three. Perhaps the strangeness made them seem like perversions of true Christianity, which could have been judged worse than idolatrous. The popularity of fancy dress continued in the colonial period, but now more often it

was centurion outfits, and they were usually rented. Perhaps they were still transformative even if not made by native specialists or used in the same ritual contexts? Spanish practices are discussed in Lynn Matluck Brooks, *The Art of Dancing in Seventeenth-Century Spain: Juan de Esquivel Navarro and His World*, Lewisburg, PA: Bucknell University Press, 2003, pp. 22–26, and Susan Verdi Webster, *Art and Ritual in Golden Age Spain; Sevillian Confraternities and the Processional Sculpture of Holy Week*, Princeton: Princeton University Press, 1998.

For a ban on the Santiagos dance, see Archbishop Lorenzana's February 11, 1769 pastoral letter and AGN Criminal 12 exp. 25 (1769); for the Tlaxcaltecos o Huehuentriz dance, AGN Criminal 25 exp. 23 (1773); for the *ahorcado* ceremony and *huehuenches* dance forbidden as pagan rites, AGN Civil 194 exp. 3 (1780); for the *matachines* dance, AJANG Civil 231-1-3008 (1804, Ocotlán, Jalisco); for concern about *mogigangas*, masked dancing and processions with drunkenness and flagellation, (1782 Zapotlán el Grande, Jalisco); for restrictions on *moros y cristianos* pageantry, AGN Consulado 150 exp. 13 (1802, Tequisquiapan, Querétaro).

66. According to the cathedral chapter of Michoacán in 1685, *Colección de las ordenanzas*, pp. 192–193. According to Alfredo López Austin, the arches were, and still are, generally understood to represent the cosmos, the celestial canopy (personal communication to David Carrasco, June 28, 2012), and snakes were emblematic of the earth; the combination of heavens and earth in the arches may suggest a more widespread pattern in which passing under the arches was a kind of threshold rite, like entering a cosmic cave of origin.

67. Guilhem Olivier has noted in the Mapa de Cuauhtinchan II and other precolonial and early colonial pictorial records that "god bearers" are depicted carrying from their place of origin to their providential homeland cloth bundles containing the bones or other artifacts of a people's totemic ancestor and tutelary deity. The bundle, writes Olivier, "represented their collective identity," "Sacred Bundles, Arrows, and New Fire Foundation and Power in the *Mapa de Cuauhtinchan No. 2*," in *Cave, City, and Eagle's Nest*, ed. Carrasco and Sessions, pp. 286, 288, 301.

68. AGN Clero Regular y Secular 84 exp. 5, Azcapotzalco; and AGN Historia 319 exp. 18, Zapotlan. In the aftermath of the Tzeltal rebellion of 1712, Fr. Gabriel de Artiga, OP, decried the "bailes supersticiosas con máscaras de demonios y plumas" used by Indians there, *La guerra de las dos vírgenes: La rebelión de Los Zendales (Chiapas, 1712) documentada, recordada, recreada*, ed. Jan de Vos, Mérida: UNAM/Universidad de Ciencias y Artes de Chiapas, 2011, p. 215.

69. Matluck Brooks, *The Art of Dancing*, pp. 22–26; Verdi Webster, *Art and Ritual*, passim. St. Augustine's *The City of God*, a text widely cited in colonial ecclesiastical writings and familiar to seminarians, offers a key to this paradoxical combination of monsters and saints in authorized religious processions: "He foreknew that, in their pride, some of the angels would indeed wish to be self-sufficient for their own blessedness, and hence forsake their true Good. Yet he did not deprive them of the power to do this; for He judged it an act of greater power and goodness to bring good even out of evil than to exclude the existence of evil," *The City of God Against the Pagans*, ed. and trans. R. W. Dyson, Cambridge, UK and New York: Cambridge University Press, 1998, pp. 1107–1108 (Book XXII chapter 1). The monsters had their place, but it was usually at the back of the procession.

70. Gerónimo de Mendieta, *Historia eclesiástica indiana*, Mexico: CONACULTA, 1997, II, chapters 19 and 20. Also according to Mendieta, *Historia eclesiástica indiana,* II, chapter 20, Christian Indians from the chapel of San José de los Naturales carried some 230 litters with images of Christ, Mary, and the saints in a procession through the streets of Mexico City on Easter Sunday. It is not clear whether Mendieta's claim that similar processions took place in all the large Indian settlements in New Spain at the time can be trusted.
71. *Información jurídica recibida en el año de 1582 con la que se acredita que la Imagen de María Santísima baxo la advocación de Conquistadora . . .*, Puebla: Oficina de D. Pedro de la Rosa, 1804, said to have been first printed in 1666, here from the 1804 printing, first witness, August 29, 1582, Diego de Soto, indio principal; "y haremos una disciplina y rogaremos a Dios y a su madre que nos oyga."
72. The ceremonies at San Luis Potosí in December 1771 are described in considerable detail in AGN Civil 494, fs. 422–444.
73. The large-scale processions with crosses and crucifixes in major towns are the best known, but many more such events in smaller, remote communities passed unmentioned in colonial records or have not yet been found. Ajofrín, for example, mentions witnessing Jueves Santo observances in Theutila, Oaxaca in which Cuicatec people processed with "10 or 12 crucifixes of all sizes," *Diario del viaje* [1964 ed.] II, 50–51. Images also traveled on missions of healing to the sick and injured. For example, Ajofrín, *Diario del viaje* [1964 ed.], I, 46 for San Francisco del Milagro in the city of Puebla. The statue of Nuestra Señora del Patrocinio was conveyed to the homes of sick devotees in Mexico City in 1743, William B. Taylor, *Marvels & Miracles in Late Colonial Mexico*, Albuquerque: University of New Mexico Press, 2011, pp. 106–118.
74. Gilberto Giménez, *Cultura popular y religión en el Anáhuac*, Mexico: Centro de Estudios Ecuménicos, 1978, p. 103, "El pueblo sólo les sirve de cortejo." This point about the *santos* – the cherished images of holy personages – being regarded as the pilgrims and protagonists on the journeys is also made by Isabel Hernández, "El Catolicismo popular en San Mateo Atenco," in *Historia de la religión en Mesoamérica y áreas afines*, ed. Barbro Dahlgren de Jordán, Mexico: UNAM, 1987, p. 219.
75. Giménez, *Cultura popular*, pp. 103–104, 158. The processional entrance to the shrine precinct is described on pp. 119–120.
76. Colonial records occasionally mention processions with images in these terms, but miss the preparations that could be said to activate the image. Kay Turner offers a suggestive ethnographic description for the image of Our Lady of San Juan de los Lagos: "The lowering of the Virgin from the altar and her subsequent exhibition before the procession is a time of intense iconic display. Bringing the icon down is an iconicizing gesture in itself: the Virgin is transformed in this moment from a static, representational church image to an active, present personification of deity," Kay Turner, "The Cultural Semiotics of Religious Icons: La Virgen de San Juan de los Lagos," *Semiotica* 47: 1 (1983), 351.
77. Don Domingo de San Antón Muñón Chimalpahin Quauhtlehuanitzin, *Annals of His Time*, trans. James Lockhart, Susan Schroeder, and Doris Namala, Stanford: Stanford University, 2006, p. 165. Criminal and civil records sometimes refer incidentally to individuals "visiting the saints," meaning visiting chapels dedicated to them and images of them. For example, in an 1807 criminal trial before the Audiencia of

Nueva Galicia of drunken men accused of assaulting town officers of Jocotán, one of the accused, Pedro de la Cruz, testified he stopped by a local tavern on the night of the feast of the Purification of the Virgin (Candlemas) after "visiting the saints in church" ("salió de la iglesia de visitar a los santos"), AJANG Criminal, bundle labeled "1808 leg. 1 (74)."

78. Ruiz y Cervantes, *Memorias de . . . Nuestra Señora de Xuquila,* p. 63.
79. BNM Fondo Franciscano, caja 142 doc 1736, April 16, 1752, on images in Corpus Christi processions; AHM L10A/7–8 pastoral visit book of Rubio y Salinas, entry for March 11, 1753 at Pachuca; AJANG 80-2-982, no stops allowed during funeral procession in Sierra de Pinos, 1772. Archbishop Rubio y Salinas in his pastoral visit to Otumba in November 1756 encouraged the community's procession with the statue of Jesús Nazareno but stipulated that it had to end before dark, AHM L10A/7–8.
80. In Lorenzana's published pastoral letter of February 11, 1769 (included in *Cartas pastorales y edictos del Illmo. Señor D. Francisco Antonio Lorenzana y Butrón . . .*, Mexico: Joseph Antonio de Hogal, 1770), the Fourth Provincial Synod in New Spain proposed that only simulated mortification of the flesh should be permitted in processions, *Concilio provincial mexicano IV*, p. 161 (decree 3-18-16).
81. Corpus Christi festivities are often listed among the financial records of district seats, as well as the major cities. Also, judging by reports from parish priests in the Diocese of Michoacán in 1680–1681, Corpus Christi processions were held even in smaller towns, Carrillo Cázares, *Michoacán en el otoño del siglo XVII,* transcriptions of the reports are included in pp. 327–486. Confraternities of the Blessed Sacrament, the most common kind of colonial confraternity, sponsored many of the Corpus Christi festivities.
82. Torquemada (1615), among others, singled out *jueves santo* and *viernes santo* as the centerpieces of Semana Santa festivities in Mexico. And so it remained. In the early decades after Mexican independence in 1821, when Catholicism was still the official state religion, two of the five official religious holidays of the new nation were *jueves santo* and *viernes santo* (along with Corpus Christi, the feast of Our Lady of Guadalupe, and the feast of the Blessed Felipe de Jesús, Mexico's first native saint, beatified in 1627 and canonized in 1862), *Guía de forasteros en Jalisco para el año de 1828,* Guadalajara: Impr. del C. Úrbano Sanromán, 1828, p. 39.
83. Mendieta, *Historia eclesiástica indiana*, II, chapter 20. Many more Indian penitents were said to process in the Holy Week processions in Tlaxcala, some 15,000–20,000 by Mendieta's estimate; and a penitential procession in Mexico City during the flood of 1604 reportedly drew some 24,000 participants, including 4,000 flagellants.
84. 4,000 lighted candles for the *lunes santo* procession in Mexico City in 1689, Rivera, *Diario curioso,* II, 23; at Querétaro in 1799, 8,000 Indians and 300+ images of Christ were said to have processed through the city's streets, AGN Arzobispos y Obispos 2, fs. 308–315; and some 297 arches were still being erected in the late 1770s for the Corpus Christi procession in Mexico City by members of some 292 Indian communities within a roughly 50 mile radius of the city (compiled from information in AHACM Num. de inventario 3712). Edward Osowski estimates that about 1,000 Indian builders worked on these arches annually, *Indigenous Miracles: Nahua Authority in Colonial Mexico,* Tucson: University of Arizona Press, 2010, p. 165.

The Italian Capuchin visitor Ilarione da Bergamo offered a detailed description of Holy Week processions at Real del Monte in 1764, including a great procession of

many crucifixes by Indians of the district on Maundy Thursday (in which few women participated), the procession of the "three falls" on Good Friday, and the women's procession of Solitude on Holy Saturday when a statue of the Blessed Virgin dressed in mourning was carried through the streets, *Daily Life in Colonial Mexico: The Journey of Friar Ilarione da Bergamo, 1761–1768*, ed. Robert Ryall Miller and William J. Orr, Norman: University of Oklahoma Press, 2000, pp. 184–187.
85. Juan F. Gemelli Carreri, *Viaje a la Nueva España: México a fines del siglo XVII*, Mexico: Libro Mex, 1955, II, 179–180. Rugs and tapestries were a common household item of rich and aspiring families in the seventeenth and eighteenth centuries, Jorge F. Rivas Pérez, "Domestic Display in the Spanish Overseas Territories," in *Behind Closed Doors: Art in the Spanish American Home, 1492–1898*, ed. Richard Aste, Brooklyn: Brooklyn Museum and The Monacelli Press, 2013, p. 55.

For the Corpus Christi tradition in early modern Spain, see Teófilo Ruiz, *A King Travels: Festive Traditions in Late Medieval and Early Modern Spain*, Princeton: Princeton University Press, 2012, pp. 266–284. One of the "monsters" Gemelli Carreri referred to would have been a "tarasca" – the fearsome dragon-devil that fought against God and was cast out and chained for a thousand years – a common feature of Corpus Christi processions in Spain and America. Officials may have been worried about unseemly disorder and revelry around the *tarasca* and other grotesque figures in the parade line, but they needed the monster to signify the triumph of Christ and good order over the devil and chaos, an ongoing theme in colonial pageantry. The theological underpinning for this presence of the devil and the drama of good v. evil was described by St. Augustine. See note 69.
86. Indians participated by the thousands in the Mexico City pageantry throughout the colonial period, but their participation followed from orders, organization, and custom as much as – or more than – from spontaneous enthusiasm. Indian dancers sometimes were enlisted to perform and, given the opportunity, some villages responsible for constructing flowered arches and decorating the streets of the city center for Corpus Christi preferred to stay home and pay surrogates to do the work. However, city officials generally were more concerned about too many poorly paid villagers traveling to Mexico City to build the arches and revel in the festivities than they were about absentees, AHCM núm. de inventario 3712, exp. 7, 1776–1778.
87. *Monarquía indiana*, III, 224 (libro 17 cap. 7). Torquemada sometimes is criticized by modern scholars for plagiarism – copying passages from other sources without attribution. Just before this quotation, he inserted a passage from Mendieta about Indian processions with crosses. Nevertheless, there is much in the *Monarquía indiana* that is not found in Mendieta or other early Franciscan chronicles.

Nearly a century later another Franciscan, Agustín de Vetancurt, described fiestas of the communities of Xochimilco in similar terms, featuring flowered arches and masked dancers, *Teatro mexicano. Descripción breve de los sucesos ejemplares históricos y religiosos del Nuevo Mundo de las Indias; Crónica de la Provincia del Santo Evangelio de México* [1698], Mexico: Porrúa, 1982, facsimile edition, 156–157.
88. AHM L10A/7-8 pastoral visit book of Archbishop Rubio y Salinas, entry for December 24, 1752, "gravísimos pecados, escándalos y aun muertes."
89. There are many cases in the audiencia criminal files of AGN Criminal and AJANG Criminal.

90. TU VEMC 73 exp. 41.
91. As was true of the changing activities of the Mexican Inquisition in the late eighteenth century. See Monelisa Lina Pérez Marchand, *Dos etapas ideológicas del siglo XVIII en México a través de los papeles de la Inquisición*, Mexico: El Colegio de México, 1945, and Richard E. Greenleaf, "The Inquisition in Eighteenth-Century Mexico," *New Mexico Historical Review* 60 (1985), 29–60 and "The Mexican Inquisition and the Enlightenment," *New Mexico Historical Review* 41 (1966), 181–191.
92. AHJ, collection of records for Acatlán de Juárez, paquete 8, 1796.
93. Pilar Gonzalbo Aizpurú, "Auge y ocaso de la fiesta. Las fiestas en la Nueva España. Júbilo y piedad, programación y espontaneidad," in *Fiesta y celebración: Discurso y espacio novohispanos*, ed. María Águeda Méndez, Mexico: El Colegio de México, 2009, p. 72.
94. For example, AGN Bandos 28, exp. 35, 1815; AGN Bandos 31 exp. 45 fol. 45, 1812; AGN Bandos 25 exp. 129, 1810; AHACM núm. de inventario 3712, exp. 30, 31, 1807–1809.
95. "Especies tumulturarios y peligrosos . . .," AGN Consulado 150 exp. 13, fol. 303.
96. Even as Bourbon authorities pressed for reforms, they wrapped themselves in the cloak of tradition and earlier law when they could, decrying "novelties" and abjuring "innovations."
97. The dispute is documented at length in the Ayer Collection, 1816, of Chicago's Newberry Library. I am grateful to Ethelia Ruiz Medrano for obtaining a copy of the Ayer Collection file for me. See also Julio Jiménez Rueda, "Nadie se engaña si con fe baila," *Boletín del Archivo General de la Nación* 16:4 (1945), 525–586, and José Antonio Robles Cahero, " 'Nadie se engaña si con fe baila': entre lo santo y lo pecaminoso en el baile de San Gonzalo, 1816," in *De la santidad a la perversión, o de por qué no se cumplía la ley de Dios en la sociedad novohispana*, ed. Sergio Ortega, Mexico: Grijalbo, 1985, pp. 93–127. The manuscript record amounts to arguments for and against the practice by two Dominican representatives, in addition to rebuttals by Beristáin and the vicar general. The dancing itself is not described at any length. The vicar general's decree seems to have succeeded in discouraging widespread dancing to San Gonzalo in the archdiocese, but Englishman G. F. Lyon mentioned the practice in Zacatecas or Guadalajara during his travels in north-central Mexico in 1826 (his article says Zacatecas, but the chapel in question to San Gonzalo seems to have been in Guadalajara) and provided more detail about the dance than does the Ayer file: "We stopped for a time at the chapel of San Gonzalo de Amarante, better known by the name of El Baylador. Here I was so fortunate as to find three old women praying rapidly and at the same time very seriously dancing before the image of the saint, who is celebrated for his miraculous cures of 'frios y calenturas' (colds and agues). These grave and venerable personages, who were perspiring profusely at every pore, had selected for their figure that so well known in the country as the 'Guajolote,' or turkey dance, from its resemblance in dignity and grace to the enamoured curvettings of those important birds; and ever and anon these faithful votaries murmured forth the following invocation, in a mingled tone of singing and moaning: 'San Gonzalo de Amarante, que sacas pescado del mar, sácame de este cuidado, que y ate vengo baylar.' [San Gonzalo de Amarante, you for whom fish jump out of the sea, free me from my present woe, for I come to dance for you.] Which ended, they began pirouetting with renewed energy. . . . Inspired by faith, the votary performs that which no other power could

Pilgrims, Processions, and Romerías 547

induce her to undertake and dances unceasingly during six or eight hours." Published as "Lyon's Mexico (Fifth Notice)," *The London Literary Gazette and Journal of the Belles Lettres, Arts, Sciences, etc.*, 487 (April 19, 1828), 246.

The chapel in Guadalajara was said to be located behind the Dominican convent (later the church of San José), www.guadalajara.net/html/tradiciones/03.shtml. It no longer exists, but there is still a chapel to San Gonzalo in Salamanca, Guanajuato, www/vamosalbable.blogspot.com/2009/01/san-gonzalo.shtml.

98. As the *comandante gobernador* of New Galicia put it, Indians wanted dancing and drink in their fiestas while Americans of other kinds wanted bullfighting and gambling, BEJ MS 300, Papeles de Derecho, IV, fol. 607, October 16, 1778.

99. Diego Valadés, the sixteenth-century *mestizo* Franciscan who wrote on Christian evangelization in Mexico and missionary encounters with native peoples, included an observation about their dance tradition: "Todos bailaban en esos bailes con agilidad y donosura . . . siendo tanta la gente reunida, sin embargo todos cantaban y bailaban siguiendo a un tiempo los ritmos y sones y no eran obstáculo alguno los diversos cambios de son," *Retórica cristiana*, trans. Tarsicio Herrera Zapién, Mexico: UNAM/Fondo de Cultura Económica, 1989, pp. 380–381.

100. Viceroys, bishops, and city councils continued to call for their participation in special festivities, at least in Mexico City, José Gómez, "Diario de México," Bancroft M-M 105 p. 651, July 20, 1795; Natalia Silva Prada, *La política de una rebelión. Los indígenas frente al tumulto de 1692 en la ciudad de México*, Mexico: El Colegio de México, 2001, p. 137, spectacles in the church courtyard included a "mitote del emperador Moctezuma," with dancing and indigenous instruments; AGN General de Parte 13 exp. 180, 1673, the viceroy called upon Indians of the San Juan and Santiago districts in Mexico City to dance in celebration of San Fernando Rey. For masked Indian dancers in the dedication ceremony of the church of Our Lady of Guadalupe at Querétaro in 1680, see Joseph María Zelaá e Hidalgo, *Glorias de Querétaro y sus adiciones*, introduced by Jaime Septién, Querétaro: Gobierno Constitucional del Estado, 2009, chapter 7 pp. 151–172, quoting Carlos de Sigüenza y Góngora. For Indian dancers summoned to a procession for Nuestra Señora del Patrocinio in the city of Zacatecas in 1795, see José Rafael Oliva, *El blazón zacatecano Coronado por el cielo . . .*, Mexico: Zúñiga y Ontiveros, 1797, p. 8.

101. AGN Civil 494 fs. 422–444.

102. For example, in 1786 the Archbishop of Mexico distributed a circular recommending such penitential processions "to placate the ire of God manifest in epidemics and other plagues and to plea to the Lord with a contrite and humble heart to bless the fruits of the land," AGN Indiferente Virreinal caja 2219 exp. 7. An especially striking case is the many processions with images in Mexico City during the great epidemic of 1737, which is described in some detail by Cabrera y Quintero, *Escudo de armas de México, passim*.

103. "Libro noticioso que contiene algunos apuntes particulares, acaesidos en esta villa de Orizava y otras noticias que an yegado aquí de sujetos fidedignos, 1812–1821," Bancroft M-M 178, pp. 143–145.

104. Song set to Psalm 52, which begins "Miserere mei, Deus" (Have mercy on me, O God).

105. Prayers for stations of the Cross at designated locations.

106. Michel Foucault, *Discipline and Punish: The Birth of the Prison*, trans. Alan Sheridan, New York: Random House, 1975. Foucault was especially concerned with how disciplinary power conditions society and creates "docile bodies" for industrialization and rise of a bourgeoisie in the eighteenth and nineteenth centuries.
107. Drawn from reports on the financing of processions presented to the intendant of Michoacán that year, AGN Historia 578A.
108. TU VEMC leg. 70 exp. 64, 1810, "abusos y ceremonias casi supersticiosas." He was especially critical of the Franciscan guardian of the Churubusco convent.
109. BN Archivo Franciscano caja 142, doc. 1736, fol. 1.
110. AHM L10A/7–8 Archbishop Rubio y Salinas's pastoral visit books, entry for November 1756.
111. AHM L10A/11 fol. 4 *carta circular de aviso*.
112. AHM L10B/32 fol. 2.
113. AJANG Civil 143–5-1564. He added that the *gente de razón* had to lock themselves in their homes for safety.
114. AGN Historia 319 exp. 18 fols. 1r–4r.
115. AGN Historia 319 exp. 18, the fiscal's judgment dated April 28, 1782.
116. AGN Historia 132 exp. 22. Apparently, no action was taken at the time by higher authorities. Tensions between Father Lepe and the district governor, D. Vicente Leis y Oca, were running high just then, in ways Lepe could not avoid. In May 1786, Father Lepe was commissioned by the viceroy to inform him about charges that Leis y Oca was extorting money and crops from local farmers, was drunk in public, and did not attend church services. Then, in his role as the local notary for the Inquisition, Lepe was instructed in December 1797 to investigate the accusation of a visiting Franciscan that Leis y Oca had tried to sodomize him, AGN Inquisición 1297 exp. 9.
117. AGN Inquisición 1318 exp. 5. According to this priest, Father Lepe had died by then. AGN Inquisición 1318 exp. 15 added various complaints about residents of neighboring Zapotiltic. The pastor denounced them for keeping a great many ugly images of Christ, the Virgin Mary, and saints that "más probocan a murmuración que a deboción y respeto," and complained that Father Lepe had been lenient with an Indian woman who hid in her shawl the consecrated wafer she received at communion rather than ingesting it. The Inquisition chose to pass these complaints on to the archbishop's vicar general rather than investigate them.
118. Magnus Mörner, *La corona española y los foráneos en los pueblos de indios de América*, Stockholm: Almquist & Wiksell, 1970.
119. AGN CRS 156 exps. 2, 3, and 9. The pastor claimed the dance had been eliminated elsewhere. See also 1802 unsorted Guadalajara cathedral records of the Cofradía del la Purísima Concepción for Ixtlahuaca: February, 1802, Indians ignoring the order not to undertake unsupervised processions called "visits" or "demandas" through the streets and fields in which women carried the images "with notable indecency."
120. Also AGN Templos y Conventos 25 exp. 4, 1769 Tlayacapan complaint against the parish priest for demanding fiesta contributions; AGN Indios 65 exp. 109, 1776 parish priest of Teotihuacan imprisoned Indians for not allowing the image of Our Lady of the Rosary to be carried in procession. Such complaints were encouraged by royal edicts that reduced the number of mandatory fiestas: AGN Historia 578A

no. 229, 1793 Intendant of Valladolid (Michoacán) Juan Antonio de Riaño objected to the numerous fiestas he said were recently established by priests to boost their personal income; AGN CRS 25 exp. 4, 1793–1803 Indians of Huiciltepec complained that the priest was charging extra for fiestas and adding new ones.

121. Edicts against fireworks, the number of mandatory feast days, and lavish expenditures for them in the 1780s are mentioned in Dorothy Tanck de Estrada, *Pueblos de indios y educación en el México colonial, 1750–1821*, Mexico: El Colegio de México, 1999, pp. 293–295, and in AGN Bandos 15 exp. 30, and AGN Reales Cédulas Originales 134 exp. 28. But the crown also promoted fireworks; e.g., AGN Bandos 11 exp. 63, June 28, 1780 viceregal decree calling upon district officials to encourage the continued use of fireworks in local celebrations because this industry supported many Indians and poor people who live by "el arte de formar semejantes fuegos." For similar complaints by chandlers against a 1782 prohibition of "exceso de luces en los altares por su alto precio," see AGN Industria y Comercio 32 exp. 1, 1790.

122. AGN Clero Regular y Secular 206 exp. 3.

123. AHM Fondo Catedral Colonia, 1796. The viceroy added that images could be processed within the confines of the community as long as the spectacle was decorous. This verdict was pointedly regarded as law in the Audiencia of Nueva Galicia, BEJ MS 300, Papeles de Derecho, II, fols. 263v–264v.

124. AGN Criminal 71 exp. 6.

125. AHM caja 1 1796 report for Zacatecas; for the comandante general's appraisal, BEJ MS 300, Papeles de Derecho, IV, fols. 6–7, October 16, 1778.

126. By contrast, the long-distance journeys of colonial dignitaries often are extensively documented, in the pastoral visit books of bishops and chronicles of the travels of new viceroys. For the 1755 journey of arrival of the Marqués de Amarillas from Veracruz to Mexico City, see Diego García Panes, *Diario particular del camino que sigue un virrey de México desde su llegada a Veracruz hasta su entrada pública en la capital*, Madrid: CEHOPU/CEDEX, 1994.

127. Robert Maniura, "The Image and Miracles of Santa Maria delle Carceri," in *The Miraculous Image in the Late Middle Ages and Renaissance Rome*, ed. Erik Thunø and Gerhard Wolf, Rome: "LeErma" di Bretschneider, 2004, p. 91.

128. Edward Osowski demonstrates in detail the interests – especially political interests – of Indian elites and their central Mexican communities in meeting their obligations to construct the flowered arches for Corpus Christi festivities in Mexico City toward the end of the colonial period, *Indigenous Miracles*, chapters 5 and 6, especially pp. 156–158. This was more than a straightforward story of Spanish demands and Indian compliance.

129. See, for example, "Our Lady in the Kernel of Corn," in Taylor, *Marvels & Miracles*, pp. 53–70. The abundant documentation of petitions for licenses to carry out alms-collecting missions for shrines and celebrated images often features local pastors and chaplains. For example, see the promotion of the shrine of the Lord of Calvary at Coatepec Amilpas discussed at the end of the Introduction.

130. For Inga Clendinnen's engagement with Victor Turner's writings on the performance of "root metaphors," see *Aztecs, An Interpretation*, Cambridge, UK and New York: Cambridge University Press, 1991, pp. 5, 143. This approach is more akin to phenomenology than to "performativity," with its focus on identity and authoritative

speech and its home in gender studies. On performativity, see Judith Butler, *Excitable Speech: A Politics of the Performative*, London and New York: Routledge, 1997. Although she prefers "performatic" to "performative" in order to emphasize performance more than discourse, Diana Taylor's *The Archive and the Repertoire: Performing Cultural Memory in the Americas*, Durham: Duke University Press, 2003, has much in common with Butler's approach. On pilgrimage and icons as "performative sites" in the Americas, see Silvia Spitta's *Misplaced Objects: Migrating Collections and Recollections in Europe and the Americas*, Austin: University of Texas Press, 2009.

131. Jonathan Z. Smith, *Imagining Religion: From Babylon to Jonestown*, Chicago: University of Chicago Press, 1982, p. 54. This multisensory experience of divine presence is similar to South Asian *darsan* as Diana Eck described it in *Darsan: Seeing the Divine Image in India*, Chambersburg, PA: Anima Books, 1981.

132. Deidre Sklar memorably describes dances in the Guadalupan festival in Tortugas/Las Cruces, New Mexico, as prayer and an experience of spiritual knowing and belonging through choreographed, stately movement. Her informants spoke of dancing for and *with* the Virgin, as a way of "talking with the Virgin," *Dancing with the Virgin: Body and Faith in the Fiesta of Tortugas, New Mexico*, Berkeley: University of California Press, 2001.

133. On ornamentation as a way to approach the study of reception of sacred images, see Richard Trexler, "Being and Non-Being: Parameters of the Miraculous in the Traditional Religious Image," in *The Miraculous Image in the Late Middle Ages and Renaissance*, ed. Thunø and Wolf, pp. 15–27, especially pp. 19–27. Not surprisingly, colonial officials routinely dismissed the decoration of images of holy figures in Indian communities as indecent and ridiculous. See, for example, Archbishop Rubio y Salinas's opinion and order during his pastoral visit to Atlatauca in 1759, AHM L10A/7–8 fols. 86r–87r.

Conclusion

By the turn of the seventeenth century, Catholic institutions, beliefs, and practices were ingrained features of everyday life and ceremonial occasions in New Spain, as imperial authorities and evangelizers intended. Christianity provided an increasingly diverse populace with an outlook on life and practices that complemented, but proved more durable than, the hierarchy of colonial political offices and administrators. A lasting sense of enchantment, of divine immanence in the present, was part of what most people shared as New World Catholics, along with a hunger for epiphanies in daily life and personal salvation. A great many shrines would come to feed this hunger as long-lived sites of shared devotion and contestation across social groups in many places. Shrines were understood to be havens of divine protection and sources of well-being – "Little heavens on earth," Francisco de Florencia called them[1] – but this was not the sunlit enchantment of the Garden of Eden before the Fall. Satan was immanent, too. For Spaniards in America, he and his demon minions were fully present, deceiving the native population into idolatry and corrupting the ignorant, gullible, and devious of all classes, at every turn. Native Mesoamericans' monistic views of divine power and presence as simultaneously nurturing and destructive could lead them to propitiate Satan as well as Christ and the saints, for the superhuman powers attributed to him by Catholic pastors and local adepts. And people labeled "castas," often without a secure place in the social and legal order, were especially likely to be suspected of pacts with the devil and overrepresented for that reason in the Inquisition's investigations into satanic worship. Not surprisingly, exorcisms remained a familiar feature of Catholic practice throughout the colonial period.

The hold of miracles on the imagination settled on sacred things, especially images of Christ and the Virgin Mary, and the patina of time usually added to their store of wonder.[2] Through age, use, and reputation, they were rooted in local time that transcended chronology in the marks of loving devotion by untold numbers of forebears, legendary origins in a distant past, and miracles both remote and recent. Catholicism's ways of expressing faith in an incarnate God were wellsprings of the charisma of shrine images and sites, valorizing intense feelings of contrition and love and embracing the power and uses of things. This embodied, participatory, atmospheric devotion kept images and structures alive in the present. All the senses were in play. Sight and light stood out as metaphors and means of sensing divine presence: seeing celestial lights and votive candles flickering on an altar; beholding a beautiful statue or painting inside a richly furnished temple; watching the sacred image transform before one's eyes; witnessing a miracle of healing or protection; Christ as the light of the world. But the unseen was sensed also in more active movement and gestures of faith – in processions, dance, postures of prayer and penitence, the feel of a sacred object, and the act of dressing or cleaning an image. "I see only what I touch," wrote Sor Juana Inés de la Cruz.[3] The unseen was sensed in the smell and sight of clouds of incense and offerings of flowers, in sweet odors of sanctity and the stench of decay. It was heard in heavenly music from a choir or organ or ensemble of instruments, and in the uttered words and sounds of the Mass and the Rosary. When Father Juan Francisco Domínguez was called upon to describe his accomplishments as parish priest of Singuilucan (Hidalgo) in 1760, he thought first of sacred sights and sounds: "he finished and dedicated a beautiful temple, and furnished the shrine [of the miraculous Christ] in ways that promote devout worship with new sacred ornaments and vestments, holy images, and choir music, greatly enhanced by a new organ."[4]

These overarching features of enchantment are clear enough, but generalizations about development – how twenty or so shrines and shrine images gained wider, regional fame over the course of many years – are checked by local circumstances and poorly documented variables. Several patterns stand out, but the main lines of interpretation that have been proposed float above what can be said with some assurance from the historical record. There is little to support George Kubler's idea that a colonial Pax Hispanica allowed long distance pilgrimages and led to networks of regional shrines. Precolonial Mesoamerican associations, if not origins, of leading colonial shrines also have been proposed, but rarely demonstrated. A compelling case could be made for precolonial underpinnings of some, perhaps many local shrines, but evidence of large-scale, long-distance pilgrimage to Mesoamerican shrines before Spanish colonization is thin and equivocal, and the sites mentioned as precolonial magnets for sacred journeys rarely were the places where regional shrines were found in the colonial period. Since virtually every hill and spring tingled with divine power in Mesoamerican terms, and ceremonial structures were located near most of them, the fact of association with precolonial worship does not go far toward explaining how some became regional shrines in the colonial period. The precolonial association seems to have been strongest for regional shrines when Catholic evangelizers chose to promote them on sites of Mesoamerican sacred centers that already had something of a regional reputation. An example is the ceremonial center of Izamal in Yucatán, about fifty miles east of Mérida, where the remains of several precolonial ceremonial structures are still visible and devotees entered the colonial sanctuary by climbing an ancient platform. Sixteenth-century Franciscans turned Izamal into a monastic-church complex, regional center of Christian instruction, and shrine to a miraculous statue of Our Lady that was acquired by local Mayas in a bargain to keep their settlement close to an ancient temple.[5]

Early friars and bishops guided some other image shrines into regional prominence, too, but the Virgin of Guadalupe at Tepeyac is a prime example of a devotion promoted and guided by cathedral clergy of the Archdiocese of Mexico, and eventually by viceroys and audiencia judges. Equally important in the case of Guadalupe, and even more important for about half of the image shrines with regional followings, was their location or base of support in a colonial city: Nuestra Señora de los Remedios and Mexico City; La Conquistadora and Puebla; Nuestra Señora del Pueblito and Querétaro; Nuestra Señora de Guanajuato; Nuestra Señora del Patrocinio and Zacatecas; Nuestra Señora de Zapopan and Guadalajara; Nuestra Señora de la Soledad and Antequera; Nuestra Señora de Ocotlán and Tlaxcala; and Nuestra Señora de Izamal and Mérida after the mid-seventeenth century. This connection between cities and shrines with a regional following is not surprising. Leaders in every colonial city sought legitimacy and divine protection to make their city more than a center of population, production, commerce, administration, and patronage; and cities were centers of communications and diffusion of authority and local knowledge. Priests, convents, and monasteries were concentrated in cities, and if a city was the seat of a diocese with a seminary (as were Mexico City, Puebla, Valladolid, Guadalajara, Antequera, San Cristóbal, Mérida, and Guatemala), priests trained there were likely to carry urban devotions with them into pastoral service, their preaching, and the confessional. Cities also were more likely to have rich confraternities and wealthy patrons to sponsor new construction and fine furnishings that boosted a shrine's fame and grandeur. Mexico City – with the Virgin of Guadalupe, the Virgin of Remedios, and its scores of other image shrines – stood out in this regard, but it was not unique.

Cities were not the only centers of regional devotions to shrine images. Several of the most popular image shrines were located "out there," as Victor Turner put it, in remote places with small resident populations. And judging by the shrines and images of the Virgin of San Juan de los Lagos and the Christs of Chalma and Esquipulas, they could develop in different ways. The shrine of Nuestra Señora de San Juan de los Lagos in the Altos de Jalisco was strategically located near the main corridor of travel and trade from central Mexico into the mining zones of Guanajuato, Zacatecas, San

Luis Potosí, and the far north, and the farming and ranching regions to the west and north that supplied the mines with food, draft animals, leather and wood products, and other provisions. This shrine drew its crowds of visitors and devotees of diverse backgrounds mainly during the great trade fair in early December. The shrine of Nuestro Señor de Chalma in the mountains of the Estado de México near Malinalco was off the beaten path of commerce in an area of mountains and caves and attracted different devotees. Founded by Augustinian friars as a sacred center of evangelization and divine protection for Indian neophytes, it drew Otomí, Nahua, and Mazahua speakers from pueblos mainly in what are today the states of México, Hidalgo, and Morelos and may have been a significant precolonial sacred site. But by the mid-eighteenth century, Chalma gained recognition as a royal shrine and was visited by people from various social and ethnic origins in Mexico City and the Valley of Mexico. Nuestro Señor de Esquipulas, the preeminent regional shrine for Central America and Chiapas, located in eastern Guatemala near the border with modern Honduras and El Salvador, also was strikingly present in parts of western and northern Mexico in the eighteenth century, thanks to the tireless Franciscan missioner Antonio Margil de Jesús, a leading figure in the development of the Franciscans' *colegios de propaganda fide* in Guatemala, Querétaro, and Zacatecas. The Esquipulas devotion took hold mainly in the parts of Mexico Margil and his associates had served – or trade networks connected with them – in Querétaro, Jalisco, Michoacán, Colima, Zacatecas, Durango, and New Mexico. Shrines with a more confined reach developed in yet other, less orchestrated ways. For example, the shrine to the statuette of Our Lady of Xuquila in a hilly coastal region of southwestern Oaxaca, about 125 miles south of the city of Antequera, started in a family oratory in Amialtepec and was transferred to the village church there, apparently in the 1630s after its reputation for divine favors attracted devotees from nearby villages. The statue's fame increased after a fire destroyed the church but left the image unmarked except for darkening it. It was moved again, to the parish seat of Xuquila in 1719, as pilgrims from more distant places, including Antequera, began to come.[6]

Shrines by definition reached beyond the local, but the history of image shrines in New Spain is less about a few central places interlocking with secondary shrines than it is about hundreds of clusters of communities with more parochial loyalties and sacred landscapes, where one devotion seldom eclipsed all others. Widening webs of circulation developed in the colonial period with the mining economy, labor drafts and seasonal labor, tax demands, markets, trade routes, urban administration, and some famous shrines, but long-distance devotional travel was limited by the mountainous terrain, laws restricting travel, the power of copies of celebrated images, and the seasonal demands of life in dispersed agricultural communities that in central and southern Mexico often go back to precolonial villages and ministates. Where the webs of communication and circulation for regional image shrines can be traced, they show more movement of things and information about celebrated images and shrines than of people traveling to and from them.[7] During the seventeenth century, shrine images themselves sometimes visited prospective devotees on alms-collecting tours and revival missions; or surrogate "peregrina" images (small, portable copies, often renowned for wonders in their own right) traveled for the same reasons. Many painted and sculpted copies of shrine images of various sizes and uses were found in homes and churches far away, and inexpensive prints were sprinkled everywhere. Images in private hands that gained a reputation for miracles and attracted crowds of visitors were often appropriated for the parish church, but rarely did colonial authorities succeed in relocating emergent miraculous images to their cities and distant shrines. The protests by people of Hueyapan, Oaxaca, in the seventeenth century to the efforts by cathedral authorities in Antequera to appropriate their crucifix after it showed signs of life are just one example of the resistance colonial officials were likely to face when they tried.

Local variations, changes, and the tailoring of written records to administrative and pious ends from an urban perspective also complicate the perennial question of how official promotion and lay devotion combined in the development of an image shrine. Were performative faith and the thrill of spectacles in small communities mainly the effect of orchestration by the clergy, especially the Jesuits and mendicants? The laity almost everywhere regarded priests as indispensable, but ritual life was also a site of tension and struggle. People danced in the courtyard and murmured during services whether church authorities liked it or not. But where it can be traced, the power of the local in the history of miraculous images is rarely explained simply by limited communications or concerted resistance to outside pressure by self-defined communities, any more than bishops and missionary priests had full control over the development of shrines. In any event, priests and colonial governors rarely were adamantly opposed to unconventional local habits, for it was usually in their interest to encourage local affiliations that did not challenge the political order.

For image shrines, one inevitable, though not always central, issue in the development of colonialism and Christianity in the New World is the relationship between imperial initiatives and indigenous politics and culture. Can this history of faith be reduced to a "war of images" across cultures? Was it a "spiritual conquest" over native beliefs and practices? Was it marked by exalted resistance to evangelization or abject submission? Can it be described as a mixing of faiths and practices that largely preserved or largely displaced indigenous cosmovisions? While these questions are important to the cultural history of the colonial period, they have little to do with the development of most colonial shrines and the popularity of miraculous images. For the history of image shrines, there is more than a story of Spaniards and Indians or elites and plebeians. Shrine devotions were often shared across classes; elites participated in vernacular cultures of enchantment (consulting peyote shamans, commissioning ex-voto paintings, and purchasing *medidas, panecitos,* and *milagritos,* for instance); and devotees who did not read or write were more informed by elite teachings than might be supposed.

The long, largely undiminished life of enchantment and many image shrines in this history is clear enough, while other plotlines that have been proposed, such as crystallization and declension, are interrupted, if not undermined, by local developments and circumstantial evidence. Nevertheless, there are signs of change and new challenges in a middle range, across three fairly distinct periods. From the beginning of colonization in the 1520s, Spanish priests and other colonists introduced and encouraged the use of Christian images, especially of Christ and the Virgin Mary. Several image shrines, mostly dedicated to Mary, began before the 1580s and were associated with Iberian conquest, both military and spiritual, but apparitions were more prominent than miraculous images in the culture of enchantment recorded for New Spain at that time. Then during a long seventeenth century, from the 1580s to the 1710s, most of the hundreds of colonial image shrines were established. Shrines to images of Christ became more common but, with the exception of the Lord of Chalma, they attracted a more parochial following than nearly a dozen Marian shrines. In broad outline, the growing number of christocentric shrines, interest in images of the Mater Dolorosa, paucity of apparitions in shrine miracle stories, and publication of devotional histories for image shrines followed similar European developments. During the eighteenth century, from the 1720s to 1810s, there were fewer new shrines, and colonial officials were less inclined to encourage the growth of existing shrines. Indeed, regalist bishops and royal governors made some moves to rein in popular religiosity and restrict confraternities and alms collecting, suppressed a few shrines and reputedly miraculous images, and expelled the Jesuits, who were leading promoters of image shrines. Nevertheless, image shrines continued to grow in number and reach. Interest in the Virgin of Guadalupe at Tepeyac throughout the viceroyalty at this time was extraordinary, with official promoters in the lead, but this was rarely at the expense of other image shrines outside the Valley of Mexico.

Comparisons and Connections

Drawing out connected similarities and differences between Spain and New Spain in this history of miraculous images is an inviting way to reckon with how Catholicism was becoming an American religion, but the exercise is filled with traps. Connected similarities over time originating from Spain inevitably stand out because colonial records usually highlight the activities of Spanish and Hispanophone authorities. Furthermore, neither Spain nor New Spain can be treated as firm and fixed without distortions creeping in. There are regional, local, and temporal particularities to account for, both in Europe and America, and European Christianity underwent great changes in the early modern period and broke in on the Western Hemisphere repeatedly, in many ways, not just once or always to the same effect. Latin Americanists are quick to recognize the many languages, subregions, and local affiliations and markets within the cultural area of Mesoamerica and places to the north that made up New Spain, but differences within Iberia are no less remarkable.

Still, many Christian institutions, practices, and beliefs that developed in New Spain were already well established in Iberia and the rest of European Christendom before Iberians began to colonize mainland America in the early sixteenth century. Among them were dioceses, parishes, religious orders, the cult of saints and their intercessory powers, relics, Marian devotion, indulgences, lay confraternities, pious hermits, liturgical practices, shrines, miracles, some association of divine immanence with images, and ideas about purgatory and the presence of evil in the guise of Satan. In New Spain, immigrant bishops were more inclined to endorse long-standing European traditions than to institute major reforms in devotion. Among other traditions the bishops reaffirmed were the cult of saints and relics, processions and festive splendor, expectation of miracles, Satan's perennial presence in daily affairs, the doctrine of works, use of Latin in the liturgy, and confraternities. Images of Christ on the cross and in other guises were increasingly featured in Catholic Europe and America after the Council of Trent as illustrations of the theology in the Savior's life story and his salvific suffering, but the Virgin Mary, too, was in the forefront of Counter-Reformation imagery, politics, and mystique, as she had long been.

For New Spain, connected similarities originating in the Old World are described in the opening chapters: the special renown and attributes of miraculous images of the Virgin Mary and Christ; similar stories about images that came alive and worked wonders for the faithful; prayers, processions, and other rituals; the financing and administration of shrines through confraternities, alms-collecting missions, bequests, and endowments; church architecture and furnishings; and a shared material culture of devotion, including votive offerings, milagritos, ex-voto paintings, brandea, novena booklets, devotional prints, and published sermons. The development of image shrines and various aspects of shrine culture in New Spain during the long seventeenth century followed similar developments in Spain and much of Europe into a "a great century of miracles" in which "hundreds, perhaps thousands, of miracle-working shrines were established" in Catholic Christendom.[8] During the eighteenth century, both Spain and New Spain experienced similar regalist reforms and currents of change in religious outlook, if not always to the same effect or with the same intensity. There was more surveillance, regulation, and fiscal efficiency and more attention to reform of public piety. But there was also an underlying hesitation that stopped short of proposing to separate church and state or openly questioning God's hand in the course of human events.

Spanish messengers and agents were in a position to introduce, encourage, and supervise shrines and ideas about the miraculous, from prelates such as Palafox and Aguiar y Seixas to parish priests and ardent Marianists among the orders, especially Franciscans and Jesuits. Some of the more important image shrines and Marian advocations might have remained only locally known without them. But the many similarities between Spanish and American image shrines are not by themselves conclusive evidence of cause and effect. Similar devotions centering on fertility and life-giving moisture, for example, were as much about universal hopes and fears as about imperial introductions. And extrapolating causal relationships from similar practices and expressions of faith assumes, rather than demonstrates, that they had the same meaning and uses everywhere. For the history of colonial Latin America, this kind of straight-line thinking led some leading twentieth-century North American and European scholars to treat colonial Latin America as a much simplified, crystallized version of medieval or Tridentine Mediterranean ways, little different from a corner of life in Europe during the Middle Ages or Counter Reformation. Among Mexican scholars and recent Anglophone scholars it led in a different direction, toward an emphasis on indigenous resistance that blunted the imposition or embrace of Christianity.

Connected Differences

At almost every turn, Spain – and Europe more generally – is woven into the history of image shrines and the culture of enchantment in New Spain, but often in ways that made for differences more than replication.[9] Sometimes the intentions and practices of imperial officials counted most in this process, as when their management of record keeping and publications enabled them to limit in America a practice that was well established in Spain. For example, to guard against uncritical exuberance of American Christians, the thick shrine registers of reported miracles that were familiar in Spain from the fifteenth century rarely, if ever, were encouraged, and the published devotional histories for shrines in New Spain usually included far fewer miracle stories. But it is the mutual devotion to images that stands out, and that devotion was less about Spanish agents than about convergences and commensurables across cultures in sustained engagement on unequal, local terms, and the resulting new uses and misunderstandings. Even where there seems to be a direct line from a European practice to an American one, devotees were unlikely to understand their beliefs and practices as European unless they were immigrant Spaniards.[10] Locals thought about their images in local terms: "our santo," "she is ours," "this is the place."

Christianity was new to the Western Hemisphere in the sixteenth century, introduced suddenly, although not all at once, and not in all its splintered European variety and ongoing permutations. Protestant Christianity, for instance, was hardly a factor in Spanish America; and some developments in the history of shrines in Spain predictably lagged or differed in intensity in New Spain: there were few image shrines in New Spain during the sixteenth century and no published devotional histories for any of them before the 1620s; a transition from apparitions to numinous images happened later in New Spain, during the seventeenth century; resident hermits at shrines in New Spain arrived in the late sixteenth and seventeenth centuries, after their counterparts had been rousted out of shrines in Spain; and a shift toward images of Christ and the Mater Dolorosa came a generation or two later than in Spain, again mainly in the seventeenth century.[11] But most differences in the transition to image shrines in Spain and New Spain amounted to more than a lag in time. Europe's ongoing attachment to bone relics made the transition to image shrines less complete there. (For example, St. James's mortal remains continued to be the main attraction for pilgrims to Compostela, as were the relics of the Magi in Cologne's cathedral.) Choice bone relics of the iconic saints and second-class relics of Christ and Mary were monopolized by European shrines, and none of the many other bone relics imported became the focal point of a leading shrine in New Spain. Even the reputed splinters of the True Cross and thorns from Christ's crown failed to become shrine centerpieces in their own right, at least in part because they were not actively promoted to a popular audience by the church hierarchy.[12] The apparition stories that were so prominent in the chronicles and annals of New Spain during the sixteenth century – which may have been muffled more than displaced by the later emphasis on sacred images – speak to the leading role of Observant Franciscans in the early evangelization and spiritual revivals undertaken by members of their Propaganda Fide colleges, as well as to the importance of dreams and visions in indigenous divination. Franciscans, like Jesuits and some seventeenth-century bishops, were also deeply invested in the mystique of images and Baroque religiosity in ways that contributed to the rise of image shrines.

Less certain is whether some representations of Mary and Christ – especially of Mary Immaculate and the cross – were more popular in New Spain and understood somewhat differently there. Our Lady of the Immaculate Conception was an especially beloved and frequently depicted representation of the Blessed Mary in both Spain and New Spain, but statues of her placed in scores of Franciscan hospital chapels in New Spain during the sixteenth century were the nursery for many local Marian shrines during the seventeenth and eighteenth centuries, in contrast to the longer, slower, earlier development of Marian shrines in Spain with their greater variety of images, advocations, and origins. Outdoor crosses were common in both Spain and New Spain, especially on hilltops where the Passion of Christ was commemorated each year during Semana Santa, but did Spain have virtual forests of protective crosses to match those planted by early missionaries wherever Mesoamerican ceremonial sites had been located? Did Spain have as many crosses that trembled or otherwise came to life as New Spain did during the seventeenth and eighteenth centuries? In contrast to some parts of Europe, image shrines in New Spain during the late eighteenth and nineteenth centuries were growing in popularity in spite of official restrictions, and many remain vibrant places of devotion today. Less certain, again, was whether Spain was more like New Spain than, say, France, in this regard. If more like New Spain, did Spain match the popularity of novena booklets and cheap prints of sacred images in New Spain (which had been introduced from Spain and were sometimes produced there)?

Five differences within broad similarities distinguish the mystique, practice, and material culture of the miraculous in New Spain. First, the iconic origin stories for image shrines in Reconquista Spain – of a long-forgotten statue of the Virgin Mary hidden away from infidel enemies in some remote place, usually revealed to a humble herdsman by a bull or some other wandering animal – were uncommon in New Spain. Instead, most shrine images in New Spain were already in place in a chapel or church when they began to show signs of divine presence, coming to life or curing the hopelessly ill and disabled. And when sacred images were fortuitously discovered in New Spain, they were more likely to be found growing in living trees, or in one case a patch of grass, than to have been hidden from enemies of the faith.

Second, considering how important the Reconquista context was for many celebrated shrine images of the Virgin Mary in Spain and how powerfully present the Conquest of Mexico was in the historical imagination of early Spanish authors and colonizers (as it remains for historians and many Mexican citizens), surprisingly few of the miraculous images of Mary in New Spain were identified as warrior Virgins, *conquistadoras*. The La Conquistadora shrine images of Puebla, Zacatecas, and New

Mexico were unusual, which is not to say that the Virgin Mary was not understood as an agent and providential symbol in wartime. Many New World images of the Virgin – the Virgin of Guadalupe, Our Lady of Remedios, and Our Lady of El Pueblito among them – were invoked in Spain's European wars during the eighteenth century and in Mexico's War of Independence. But that there were few warrior Virgin images is not simply a function of the sixteenth-century scarcity of miracle-working images and image shrines in general. Rather it reflects the fact that Mary was usually introduced to neophyte Christians and revered by colonists and their descendants as Mary Immaculate and the Mater Dolorosa – the loving mother, healer, and all-purpose intercessor with her Son of God. It is not surprising, then, that as image shrines developed in the seventeenth century, most stories of divine intervention focused not on combat or on stern moral lessons, with threats of divine retribution, but on acts of personal and collective protection in natural disasters and everyday circumstances.

Third, while regional image shrines in Spain were more numerous, older, and more developed than their counterparts in New Spain, nothing in early modern Spain compared to the emergence and growth of devotion to the miraculous American image of Our Lady of Guadalupe across regions and social groups during the seventeenth and eighteenth centuries. The fame of the American Guadalupe (in Spain as well as New Spain) depended less on pilgrimage networks and visitors to the shrine at Tepeyac from outside the Valley of Mexico than on the circulation of meticulous painted copies and prints of the image during the late seventeenth and eighteenth centuries, reproductions that were promoted and embraced locally as places of the Virgin's presence in their own right. Following the lead of viceroys, archbishops, and priests in the Archdiocese of Mexico, bishops and civic leaders elsewhere actively encouraged interest in the Virgin of Guadalupe by authorizing special chapels, altars, confraternities, and regular observances in her honor in hundreds of parishes that were more than receptive. And Guadalupe was unique in gaining papal recognition as an authentic Marian apparition (1754). Could any one shrine or image have developed like this in early modern Spain? The hold of more than a dozen great regional shrines there dating back to the Middle Ages made it unlikely. In this sense, New Spain was a more open field.

Fourth, differences in pilgrimage traditions went well beyond the singular history of the shrine of Guadalupe at Tepeyac. The networks of shrines and hostels feeding into the great regional shrines in Spain were not duplicated in New Spain. Tepeyac was not yet the great pilgrimage destination it would become in the late nineteenth century with the advent of railroad travel to Mexico City from several directions. The shrines at San Juan de los Lagos, Chalma, and Esquipulas drew devotees from more distant places, but most Mexican shrines traced smaller catchment areas, within a few days' travel, and had not yet developed the institutional foundations that supported many Spanish shrines. Satellite shrines were not unknown in New Spain, but they appealed to local audiences rather than comprising networks of devotees motivated to visit the mother shrine – for example, the shrine of Guadalupe in San Luis Potosí, or the images, altars and chapels dedicated to the Christ of Esquipulas in western and northern Mexico during the eighteenth century. The pull of local affiliation and livelihood limited pilgrimage in New Spain, as did colonial officials' campaigns against vagrancy and surveillance of people otherwise out of place.

One last difference – the number of dark Christs and green crosses, many of them naturally formed – stands out as an American variation that was likely rooted in Mesoamerican traditions. There were some notable black or dark images on both sides of the Atlantic, but in Europe they were mostly of the Virgin Mary. In New Spain there were few dark images of Mary, but twenty or so celebrated Christs were black or very dark, and crosses were sometimes green. Most of the dark Christs were located in rural, Indian parishes and about a third of them were fashioned in nature, not just discovered in natural settings. There is a difference here between cherished images made from inert matter – a divinely inspired perfection achieved by human hands that transcended the material – and images whose breath of divine life came at least as much from the material itself, the wood, stone, or maize plant, as from its reshaping and signs of use. Here is a glimpse into the vast question of how Mesoamerican cosmovisions, animism, and ancestor veneration, as well as Catholic Holy Week traditions, shaped the reception of Christianity and the meaning of images. Perhaps the symbolism of the color black in Mesoamerican spirituality, recalling Tezcatlipoca and shamanic powers, is behind some of the dark Christs; or perhaps it was more a colonial association of "dark like us," "He suffered as we do." I have suggested another possibility, associating these dark Christs with age, ancestral uses, death and rebirth, and the color of old wood lovingly handled and once alive, the material from which most of these crucifixes were made.

******

Hermann Hesse famously called Catholic Christianity "a religion that through the centuries had so many times become unmodern and outmoded, antiquated and rigid, but repeatedly recalled the sources of its being and thereby renewed itself."[13] The salient long-term patterns traced by image shrines during the colonial period do not make for a grand narrative of conquest and resistance or ascendance and declension, but they do represent remarkable durability and resilience. There were more shrines in the eighteenth century than before, regional shrines were growing, and many of them appealed to a cross-section of society, but this had not been a smooth, upward trajectory. Most image shrines remained local and disconnected, a few were suppressed, and the fortunes of many were affected as much by short-term crises, seasonal devotions, and local circumstances as by long-term patterns of rise or fall.

That Christianity, especially Catholic Christianity, thrived in different cultural settings during the early modern period depended less on systematic conversion and indoctrination as evangelizers and pastors imagined it than on a measure of flexibility at the margins of the faith, tolerating local "aberrations" as long as they were kept under the umbrella of the Church. There was also more flexibility in canon law and the practice of ecclesiastical justice than is generally assumed, although not endlessly so since Catholicism was a creed, with commandments and fundamental beliefs. This was relativism and flexibility of a hierarchical kind, suspicious of mystics, seers, and other spiritual free agents. Some of them might be treated as heroes of the faith after they were gone, but not when they operated beyond administrative oversight.

Administrative flexibility in matters of image shrines and enchantment in this colonial setting was particularly tested during the eighteenth century by Bourbon reformers and the regalist bishops they placed in American dioceses. In the last decades of Spanish rule, there were fewer new shrines, stricter regulation of confraternities, and formal restrictions on alms collecting for numinous images, public celebrations, and the presentation of sacred images; but colonial officials also continued to temporize in the name of public tranquillity, and fewer confraternities were disbanded in New Spain for lack of proper titles and formal constitutions than is sometimes thought, especially among those attached to image shrines. Even the most reform-minded prelates of the late eighteenth century rarely waged campaigns against news of miracles or established shrines in New Spain, and in Mexico City, where the Virgin of Guadalupe and the Virgin of Remedios were officially favored, some other image shrines continued to flourish. In the end, religious life in general, and image shrines in particular, were less important to the eighteenth-century reformers than protecting revenues and maintaining good order under the nominal direction of the royal bureaucracy. If the politics of religion in the eighteenth century diminished the prosperity and popularity of image shrines, this was more evident in parts of Europe than in New Spain, although enchantment did not simply melt away in Europe either, perhaps especially not in Spain.[14]

As profoundly disruptive and destructive as Spanish imperialism was in the Americas, colonial authorities lacked the means and arguably the intention and will to eradicate local memories and customs, including the meaning and uses of religious images and shrines. Authorities issued some directives for reform and their subordinates might attempt to impose them, but local circumstances often bid otherwise or led to unwanted consequences – as they did in the city of Querétaro, where, after authorities enforced a ban on raucous Indian processions with images of Christ during Semana Santa in 1799, other processions for the feasts of the Holy Cross on May 3 and September 14 became more popular and unmanageable than ever.[15] There is no single explanation for how and why accommodations were reached, but on the administrative side expediency and forgiveness of a kind usually trumped other principles. Bishop Palafox's advice to young seminarians in Puebla in the mid-seventeenth century echoes through the late colonial church record, even when it was honored in the breach: "Take with a grain of salt and Christian prudence your zeal to correct the customs of others and to speak truth."[16] Zeal and prudence, passion and order. Hesse might say it was ever so.

Notes

1. "cielos abreviados en la tierra," Francisco de Florencia, *Narración de la marabillosa aparición que hizo el archángel San Miguel a Diego Lázaro de San Francisco, indio feligrés del pueblo de S. Bernardo* ..., Sevilla: Imprenta de las Siete Revueltas, 1692, p. 35.
2. On the charisma of images and works of art, see C. Stephen Jaeger, *Enchantment: On Charisma and the Sublime in the Arts of the West*, Philadelphia: University of Pennsylvania Press, 2012, pp. 22–23. Fernando Bouza underscores the expectation in early modern Spain that a representation such as a painting or statue could materialize as a real presence animated by a mysterious power; see his *Communication, Knowledge, and Memory in Early Modern Spain*, trans. Sonia López and Michael Agnew, Philadelphia: University of Pennsylvania Press, 2004, p. 21.
3. Sor Juana Inés de la Cruz, *Obras selectas*, ed. Georgina Sabat de Rivers and Elías L. Rivers, Barcelona: Noguer, 1976, p. 630.
4. *Relación de méritos y servicios* of Br. Juan Francisco Domínguez, The John Carter Brown Library, B760 A973i.
5. See also Amara Solari, *Maya Ideologies of the Sacred: The Transfiguration of Space in Colonial Yucatan*, Austin: University of Texas Press, 2013, pp. 149–150. Linda K. Williams, "Modalities of Representation: Symbol and Narrative in 16th-Century Murals at the Convent of Izamal, Yucatán," *Colonial Latin American Review* 22: 1 (April 2013), 98–126 discusses the late sixteenth-century murals in the passageway from the church to the cloister at Izamal that seem to be in this spirit of evangelization, recognizing the ancient sacrality of Izamal, now reconsecrated through the presence of the Virgin Mary. It features a figure of Mary Immaculate and includes a struggle in which demons seem to be under attack while friars gather fruit from a large tree.
6. Joseph Manuel Ruiz de Cervantes, *Memorias de la portentosa imagen de Nuestra Señora de Xuquila* ..., Mexico: Zúñiga y Ontiveros, 1791, pp. 6–22. Ruiz y Cervantes wrote that he finished the text on July 2, 1786.
7. The most dynamic zone of migration and movement of goods in New Spain during the late colonial period, the area north of the Valley of Mexico from Querétaro north and west

into the silver centers and the areas that supplied them, was the home of one of the most visited shrines, to Our Lady of San Juan de los Lagos, but surprisingly was not the seedbed of other major shrines or pilgrimages to Tepeyac until the nineteenth century. Also surprisingly, the heavily traveled corridor from Mexico City to Veracruz did not give rise to regional shrines.

8. Craig Harline, *Miracles at the Jesus Oak*, 2nd ed., New Haven: Yale University Press, 2011, p. v. Harline added on p. 4: "Among the golden ages and places of miracles in Christian history, here was one of the brightest. For although the Middle Ages are most often associated with miracles and saints and God, in fact more miracle-commemorating shrines were born in Europe's seventeenth century than in any other."

9. For a general view of Spain, England, and religious transformation in the New World, see J. H. Elliott, "Religions on the Move," in *Religious Transformations in the Early Modern Americas*, ed. Stephanie Kirk and Sarah Rivett, Philadelphia: University of Pennsylvania Press, 2014, pp. 25–45.

10. As Francisco Rojas González understood in his story, "Nuestra Señora de Nequetejé," *El diosero y todos los cuentos*, Mexico: Fondo de Cultura Económica, 2006, pp. 296–303.

11. William A. Christian, Jr., *Divine Presence in Spain and Western Europe, 1500–1960*. Budapest-New York: Central European University Press, 2012, p. 71.

12. The piece of the True Cross at Pachuca in the late eighteenth century is something of an exception. And the remains and belongings of local holy men and women were coveted, if not promoted as shrine relics, as Antonio Rubial García has shown in *La santidad controvertida: Hagiografía y conciencia criolla alredededor de los venerables no canonizados de Nueva España*, Mexico: UNAM/Fondo de Cultura Económica, 1999 and *Profetisas y solitarios. Espacios y mensajes de una religión dirigida por ermitaños y beatas laicos en las ciudades de Nueva España*, Mexico: UNAM/Fondo de Cultura Económica, 2006.

13. Hermann Hesse, *The Glass Bead Game*, New York: Holt, Rinehart and Winston, 1969, p. 174.

14. For belief in evil spirits active in the world and fierce debates in Germany about them in the eighteenth century, see H. C. Erik Midelfort, *Exorcism and Enlightenment: Johann Joseph Gassner and the Demons of Eighteenth-Century Germany*, New Haven: Yale University Press, 2005. Pope Benedict XIV (1740–58) embraced enchantment in the world, authorizing new canonizations and recognizing miracles. Considerable interest in new or newly introduced European devotions in New Spain includes the Divina Pastora, Nuestra Señora del Refugio, Nuestra Señora de la Luz, and the Sacred Heart of Jesus. The eighteenth century was also the peak period of the Franciscan missionary colleges.

15. AGN Arzobispos y Obispos 2 fols 308–315; José Rodolfo Anaya Larios, *Los cristos de Querétaro*, Querétaro: El Peregrino, 2002, p. 28.

16. Manuel de Palafox y Mendoza, *Manual de sacerdotes*, Mexico: Vda. de Bernardo Calderón, 1664, fol. 9v.

Appendix 1
Colonial Image Shrines

Readers of this appendix may be surprised to find so many colonial-era shrines and miraculous images listed; 498 in all: 238 sited images of Christ or the cross; 240 sited images of the Virgin Mary; and 20 sited images of other saints. By any reckoning, since the mid-seventeenth century there have always been many shrines and images that enjoyed more than neighborhood fame, but, as I suggest below, this is not a fixed and finished count. The more localized shrines and miraculous images are elusive in the written record, and some that are better documented were not necessarily more popular than others that are not. Most are little known because they were not heavily promoted beyond the parish (which Spanish visitors sometimes noted could be as large as an Iberian diocese), and they might attract more distant devotees only once or twice a year or during a time of crisis. While the territorial reach and number of devotees of many colonial shrines over time remains uncertain and may have fluctuated considerably, their longevity compared to shrines in various parts of Europe has been remarkable.

Even though colonial references to shrines may seem straightforward, and many have a continuous history since the seventeenth century, they are moving targets rather than unchanging monuments of faith. Beyond the fifty-eight starred (*) shrines and images on this list that enjoyed documented fame well beyond their immediate vicinity, usually over many years, there are bound to be questions about why some particular places are included in or excluded from this list.[1] And there are distortions of commission as well as omission in the record. For larger cities, especially Mexico City, Puebla, Guadalajara, and Querétaro, every possible image shrine is likely to be recorded and extolled in some fashion by local chroniclers and promoters. And some modern Mexican states are unusually well served by histories of the Church and religious life, especially Jalisco, Querétaro, and Puebla. Their colonial shrines were well known, if not necessarily more popular than shrines in other places, and there is probably a tendency in these sources to exaggerate their appeal beyond the local.

Here is how I dealt with the less intractable uncertainties in individual cases. Excluded are those miraculous images that, from the colonial record, seem to have remained little known outside their neighborhood or precinct. But I have included those that had at least one burst of wider fame – usually, during an epidemic, famine, or other local crisis, or in a flush of news of marvelous cures and rescues. More than thirty places are excluded because I know of them only from a single mention in a journal or promotional source such as a petition to collect alms, or an indulgence, or a novena booklet, or a rumor of a miracle, or because they were repudiated by authorities soon after they began to attract a following and are not documented thereafter, or because the devotion does not clearly date from the colonial period. I have also left out all of the various eighteenth-century Mexican images and altars to the Lord of Esquipulas, the famous Guatemalan crucified Christ, even though together they attest to the remarkable territorial reach of the Guatemalan image. As far as I can tell, none of these images (except perhaps the one in Colima) had become a notable colonial shrine in the way that copies of the Virgin of Guadalupe in the cities of San Luis Potosí, Querétaro, Guadalajara, and Valladolid did, and their wider appeal may, like that of the Lord of Esquipulas in the Santuario de Chimayó in New Mexico, date from the nineteenth century. Local devotions to a coveted image that are documented only in a dispute over possession, a robbery, or an investigation into abuse of the image are also left off the list. However, I included several shrines for which the main evidence is a published print of their miraculous image, because these prints often became devotional objects in themselves that joined promotion and popular devotion more definitely and circulated more widely than did other promotional materials such as sermons or novena booklets.[2] Additional research may well establish that some of my omissions ought to be included in the list at particular times and that some of the devotions with a printed image were more localized than I thought.

Although it is clear from the scattered record of many shrines that most of those that can be dated began in the seventeenth century and matured during the eighteenth century into "sweet magnets" of faith, I have not assigned dates of origin in the appendixes. This would require reckoning with (1) whether to assign sixteenth-century origins to shrines that have no historical record of their beginnings other than a later devotional text or oral tradition and (2) whether to posit that a devotional tradition began when a celebrated image apparently was made or acquired. The problem with indirect inferences about early origins is that every image of Christ or a saint was a potential medium of the miraculous, but only some gained this public reputation, often many years after the image was in place. These and other thorny matters of chronology are taken up for particular shrines and images in Chapters 1–9 and some of my earlier essays.

Sources

Information about the shrines on this list comes from scattered colonial records that mounted up as the research proceeded. Dedicated shrine archives are rare for colonial Mexico, even for great *santuarios* such as San Juan de los Lagos, Chalma, or Zapopan, but an array of documentation for most of the more localized shrines is rarer still. It usually takes the form of an inquiry into a reported miracle, surveillance of a sudden surge of popular interest or a controversial practice, disputed possession of a coveted image, confraternity activities, financial records, special promotional initiatives, mention in a pastoral visit record or commissioned report (such as the 1743 *relaciones geográficas* for the Archdiocese of Mexico), ex-votos of various kinds, devotional prints, or brief references in wills and litigation records.

Compilations made by colonial chroniclers and postcolonial scholars have been useful, too, especially when they discuss particular shrines or provide eyewitness accounts. But mainly they have been helpful in confirming entries that are documented in other ways and clarifying whether or not a particular devotion dates from the colonial period. Colonial compilations include the following six titles:

1. The *Zodíaco mariano*, which Francisco de Florencia, SJ, began in the 1690s and his fellow Jesuit, Juan Antonio de Oviedo, completed in the 1750s[3] identifies eighty-four Marian shrines from published chronicles and personal observation. Several statues and paintings in Jesuit churches of Mexico City listed by Florencia and Oviedo are not mentioned elsewhere in colonial sources I consulted and are excluded here.
2. The 1743 *relaciones geográficas* for districts in the Archdiocese of Mexico identify forty shrines (sixteen to images of Christ, sixteen to images of Mary, and eight to images of other saints).[4]
3. Cayetano de Cabrera y Quintero's chronicle of the great epidemic of 1737 in Mexico City identifies thirty-nine renowned images (eighteen of Mary, sixteen of Christ, and five of other saints) that were processed through the city that year with pious appeals for the sickness to end.[5]
4. José Antonio Villaseñor y Sánchez's *Theatro Americano* of 1746 offers a somewhat eccentric list of thirty shrines in New Spain that passes over some of the better-known images and shrines and includes several that are not described at any length elsewhere. Villaseñor y Sánchez includes seventeen miraculous images of the Virgin Mary and eleven to images of Christ.

5. Capuchin alms collector and Marian devotee Francisco de Ajofrín's journal of his travels in central Mexico, Michoacán, Jalisco, the Bajío, Oaxaca, and Veracruz in 1763–1767 identifies twenty-three celebrated Marian images, fourteen images of Christ, and three of other saints, for a total of forty. And he alludes to many more.[6]
6. José Joaquín Granados y Gálvez's *Tardes americanas* of 1778 identifies twenty of the leading Marian shrines.[7]

The most extensive compilation published since the colonial period is *La ruta de los santuarios en México* (1994), which mentions 192 shrines, of which 89 are dedicated to images of Christ and 70 to images of Mary.[8] Many of the 151 Marian and Cristo shrines listed below as postcolonial or of uncertain date of origin come from the listings in this source. Luis Mario Schneider's *Cristos, santos y vírgenes* (1995) treats sixty-eight shrines, including forty to images of Christ, twenty to images of Mary, six to other saints, and two to "santos laicos" (Jesús Malverde and Juan Soldado). This book, too, is useful for distinguishing colonial from postcolonial shrines. Higinio Vásquez's compendium of twenty-five Mexican shrines dedicated to images of Christ is weighted toward the western and northern parts of the country but provides valuable early references for several shrines that are not available elsewhere.[9] Vicente de Paula Andrade's *Mes histórico de la Preciosa Sangre* (1908) lists sixty-eight miraculous Christs, some not mentioned elsewhere, refers in passing to fifteen others, and includes some useful historical references.[10] Luis Enrique Orozco's exhaustive study of Marian images and shrines in the Archdiocese of Guadalajara in five stout volumes contains historical references for fifty-two images not found elsewhere.[11] Scores of colonial shrines up to about 1650, including some local ones, drawn from ecclesiastical chronicles are mentioned in Luis Weckmann's *The Medieval Heritage of Mexico* (New York: Fordham University Press, 1992, chapter 18). Ignacio Campero Alatorre, *Santuarios marianos en México* (Guadalajara: Populares, 1999) identifies seventy-five Marian shrines but offers little information about their historical development. Guadalupe Pimentel, *México mariano* (Mexico: Progreso, 1995), includes seventeen well-known Marian shrines. The most extensive listing of shrines thought to have developed in the colonial period is Félix Baez-Jorge's *Entre los naguales y los santos*. Of the 168 shrines listed, 133 are said to date from the colonial period. Of these, seventy-four were dedicated to images of Mary, seventy-three to images of Christ, and twenty-one to images of other saints. Unfortunately, Baez-Jorge's sources of information for most of these shrines are not identified, and some of the attributions, especially to early colonial origins, seem to be based only on much later traditions.

They are included when I could corroborate their development in the colonial period. No doubt some others could be added to the following list with further research. Mary Lee Nolan offers some aggregate figures and historical patterns for Latin American image shrines including Mexico, but it is not clear which shrines are included or how she established date of establishment, physical appearance, and origin stories during the colonial period.[12]

Colonial Shrines, Chapels, and Altars Dedicated to a Renowned Image and/or Apparition of the Virgin Mary (240)

Mexico City and Environs of the Valley of Mexico (55)

*Nuestra Señora de Guadalupe, Tepeyac
*Nuestra Señora de los Remedios, Naucalpan
*Nuestra Señora de los Ángeles, Tlatelolco
*Nuestra Señora de la Piedad
*Nuestra Señora de la Bala, a.k.a. Nuestra Señora de Ixtapalapa, church of San Lázaro
Nuestra Señora de la Macana, Franciscan church of Tlalnepantla
Nuestra Señora de Consolación, a.k.a. Nuestra Señora del Valle, church of the Recollect Franciscans at San Cosmé
Nuestra Señora de Campo Florido, parish church of San José
Nuestra Señora de las Maravillas, Hospital de Jesús (same as Nuestra Señora de los Milagros mentioned in *Gaceta de México*, 1728, p. 238?)
Nuestra Señora de las Angustias, Hospital del Amor de Dios, later moved to the church of La Merced
Nuestra Señora de Santa María, parish church of Santa Isabel
Nuestra Señora de la Merced, church of La Merced
Nuestra Señora del Rosario, church of Santo Domingo
Nuestra Señora de Copacabana, church of La Merced
Nuestra Señora de la Balvanera, convent church of La Balvanera
Nuestra Señora de Monserrate
Nuestra Señora del Refugio, convent church of Espíritu Santo
Nuestra Señora del Carmen, church of El Carmen
Nuestra Señora de la Barca, church of San José de Carmelitas
Santa María de la Redonda, parish church of Santa María de la Redonda
Nuestra Señora del Tránsito, church of the Augustinian Colegio de San Pablo
Nuestra Señora de la Paz, church of San Agustín
Nuestra Señora del Coro, convent church of Santa Catharina de Sena
Nuestra Señora de Santa Clara, church of Santa Clara
Nuestra Señora de las Lágrimas, cathedral church
Nuestra Señora del Perdón

Nuestra Señora de la Candelaria, church of the Augustinian doctrina of Santa Cruz
Nuestra Señora de la Asunción, Milpa Alta
Nuestra Señora de la Concepción, cathedral church
Nuestra Señora de la Concepción, convent church of La Concepción
Nuestra Señora de la Concepción, Jesuit Colegio de San Pedro y San Pablo
Santa María la Mayor, church of the Jesuit Colegio de San Pedro y San Pablo
Nuestra Señora de los Dolores, church of the Jesuit Colegio de San Pedro y San Pablo
Nuestra Señora de la Concepción, Franciscan convent church
Nuestra Señora de la Concepción, parish church of Salto del Agua
Nuestra Señora de la Concepción, barrio chapel of Tlaxcuac
Santa María de Gracia, convent church of San José de Gracia
Nuestra Señora del Sagrario, novices' chapel of the Franciscan convent church
Nuestra Señora del Buen Suceso, convent church of San Bernardo
Nuestra Señora de la Charidad, church of the Escuela de Christo
Nuestra Señora de la Salud, church of Santísima Trinidad
Nuestra Señora de los Dolores, chapel of San José de los Naturales
Nuestra Señora de los Dolores, church of the Franciscan convent grande
Nuestra Señora de los Dolores, parish church of Santa Ana
Nuestra Señora del Socorro (an image of Dolores), church of the Franciscan convento grande
Nuestra Señora de la Antigua, church of the Jesuit colegio
Nuestra Señora de la Antigua, Carmelite church of San José
Nuestra Señora de la Luz, church of the Jesuit colegio
Nuestra Señora de Loreto, church of the Jesuit colegio
Madonna and child, Jesuit Casa Profesa church
Nuestra Señora de la Asunción, golden image in cathedral church
Nuestra Señora de la Plata, cathedral church
Nuestra Señora de los Ángeles, marble image in cathedral church
Nuestra Señora de Covadonga, church of Santo Domingo
Nuestra Señora de Loreto, Jesuit church of Tepotzotlan
Others without definite colonial references or of more recent origin:
Nuestra Señora del Rayo, parish church of Santa Catarina Mártir
Nuestra Señora de la Candelaria, barrio church of la Candelaria de los Patos
Nuestra Señora de la Concepción, parish church of Santa Cruz y Soledad
Nuestra Señora de la Fuente, convent church of Regina Coeli
Nuestra Señora del pie de la cruz
Nuestra Señora de los Dolores, Xaltocan barrio
Nuestra Señora del Carmen, San Angel, D.F.
Nuestra Señora de los Dolores, Xochimilco, D.F.
Nuestra Señora del Carmen, Tacubaya, D.F.
Nuestra Señora de la Guía, Culhuacan

Nuestra Señora del Pópulo, Jesuit church of Tepotzotlan
Nuestra Señora de la Escalera, Jesuit church of Tepotzotlan
Nuestra Señora de la Purificación, Ayotzingo (Chalco)
Nuestra Señora de Chepinque

Jalisco (27)

Nuestra Señora de la Soledad, Guadalajara
Nuestra Señora del Rosario, church of Santa Mónica, Guadalajara
Nuestra Señora de la Salud, Analco
Nuestra Señora del Refugio, Analco
Nuestra Señora de Aranzazú, Guadalajara
Nuestra Señora del Carmen, church of Santa Teresa, Guadalajara
Nuestra Señora de la Soledad de Capuchinas, Guadalajara
Nuestra Señora del Refugio, Guadalajara
Nuestra Señora de Mexicaltzingo
Nuestra Señora del Rayo, Guadalajara
Nuestra Señora de los Ángeles, convent church of Observant Franciscans, Guadalajara
*Nuestra Señora de Zapopan
*Nuestra Señora de San Juan de los Lagos
*Nuestra Señora de Talpa
Nuestra Señora de Mexticacan
Nuestra Señora de Sentispac
Nuestra Señora de Mezquititlan
Nuestra Señora de Santa Anita, Santa Ana Tistac
Nuestra Señora de la Candelaria de Acatic
Nuestra Señora de Moya
Nuestra Señora de la Asunción, Jalostotitlan
Nuestra Señora de la Concepción, Amatitlan
Nuestra Señora de la Concepción, Ixtlan
Nuestra Señora de los Dolores, San Pedro Tlaquepaque
Nuestra Señora del Rosario, La Barca
Nuestra Señora del Rosario, Tezoatlan
Nuestra Señora del Rosario, Tecolotlan
Others without definite colonial references or of more recent origin:
Nuestra Señora del Favor, Hostotipaquillo
Nuestra Señora del Sagrado Corazón, Guadalajara

Estado de México (24)

Nuestra Señora del Rosario, Totolapa
Nuestra Señora del Rosario, Necaltitlan
*Nuestra Señora de Tulantongo, Texcoco
Nuestra Señora de la Concepción, Cuauhtitlan
Nuestra Señora de la Paz, Chalco

Nuestra Seõra del Socorro, Chalco
Nuestra Señora de los Remedios, Tepepan
*Nuestra Señora de los Ángeles, Tecaxic (Toluca)
Nuestra Señora del Rosario, parish church of Toluca
Nuestra Señora de la Merced, parish church of Toluca
Nuestra Señora de los Remedios, Sultepec
Nuestra Señora de la Natividad, Sultepec barrio la Cuadrilla
Nuestra Señora de la Concepción, Teziutlan y Atempa
Nuestra Señora de la Soledad, Teziutlan y Atempa
Nuestra Señora de la Candelaria, Ocuila, Malinalco district
Nuestra Señora, Temascalcingo
Nuestra Señora de Xocotitlan, Metepec district
Nuestra Señora del Calvario, Metepec
Nuestra Señora de la Purificación, Zinacantepec
Nuestra Señora de la Concepción, Tonatico, Zacualpan district
Nuestra Señora de los Dolores del Calvario, Tenancingo
Nuestra Señora de la Candelaria Totalasito, Chalma
Nuestra Señora del Rosario de Tonaltico, Zumpahuacan
Nuestra Señora del Rosario, Zacualpa Amilpas
Others without definite colonial references or of more recent origin:
Virgen de la Piedrita, Canalejas
Nuestra Señora de Buen Suceso, Tianguistengo

Puebla, City and State (20)
*La Conquistadora, Franciscan convent church, city
*Nuestra Señora de la Defensa, city
Nuestra Señora del Buen Suceso, city
Nuestra Señora de la Soledad, Carmelite church, city
Nuestra Señora de la Soledad, Hospital de San Pedro, city
Nuestra Señora de Guadalupe, santuario, city
Nuestra Señora de la Manga, Dominican convent church, city
Nuestra Señora de los Remedios (a.k.a. Nuestra Señora de la Rosa), santuario-church of the Discalced Carmelitess, city
Nuestra Señora del Carmen, Concepcionist convent church, city
Nuestra Señora del Pópulo, Jesuit Colegio del Espíritu Santo church, city
Nuestra Señora de la Luz, city
Nuestra Señora de Loreto, Jesuit Colegio del Espíritu Santo church, city
Nuestra Señora del Rosario, Dominican church, city
Nuestra Señora del Nicho (a.k.a. Belem), city
Nuestra Señora de los Gozos, city
La Incorporada, city
*Nuestra Señora de los Dolores, Acatzingo
*Nuestra Señora de los Remedios, Cholula

Nuestra Señora de Tzocuilac
Nuestra Señora de la Soledad, Atlixco
Nuestra Señora de los Dolores, Tepeaca
Others without definite colonial references or of more recent origin:
Nuestra Señora del Carmen, Teziutlan

Yucatán (14)
*Nuestra Señora de Izamal
Nuestra Señora de la Laguna
Nuestra Señora de la Concepción, Valladolid
Nuestra Señora de la Concepción, Calatamul
Nuestra Señora de la Soledad, Mérida
Nuestra Señora del Rosario, Mérida
Nuestra Senora de la Concepción, Colomul, Valladolid district
Nuestra Señora de la Candelaria, Tibolon
Nuestra Señora, Becal, Kalkiní district
*Nuestra Señora de la Asunción (a.k.a. La Virgen Pobre de Dios), Tetiz
Nuestra Señora de la Concepción, Mani
Nuestra Señora, Tabi
Nuestra Señora, Zetuna
Madonna and child, Vaimas, Valladolid district
Others without definite colonial references or of more recent origin:
Nuestra Señora de la Asunción, Pustunich
Nuestra Señora del Perpetuo Socorro, Itzinmá
Nuestra Señora de la Concepción, Buctzotz

Querétaro (14)
*Nuestra Señora del Pueblito, San Francisco Galisteo near city
Nuestra Señora de los Remedios, Recollect Franciscan church of San Antonio, city
Nuestra Señora del Refugio, Franciscan Colegio de la Santa Cruz, city
Nuestra Señora del Rosario, church of Santo Domingo, city
Divina Pastora, San Francisquito barrio, city
Nuestra Señora de los Dolores, Jesuit church, city
Nuestra Señora de la Merced, city
Nuestra Señora de Loreto, Jesuit church, city
Nuestra Señora de la Cueva Santa, in Franciscan Colegio de la Santa Cruz, city
Nuestra Señora de la Concepción, church of Hospital de la Limpia Concepción, city
Nuestra Señora de la Concepción, church of the Santa Clara convent, city
*Nuestra Señora de los Dolores de Soriano, Villa Corregidora
María Santísima del Sagrario, Cadereyta
Nuestra Señora de los Dolores, San Francisco Tolimanejo

Others without definite colonial references or of more recent origin:
Nuestra Señora de los Dolores, Colón

Oaxaca (13)
*Nuestra Señora de la Soledad, Antequera
Nuestra Señora de la Merced, Antequera
Nuestra Señora del Patrocinio, Antequera
Nuestra Señora del Socorro, Antequera church of Vera Cruz
Nuestra Señora de la Piedad, Antequera
Nuestra Señora del Rosario, Antequera church of Santo Domingo
Santa María la Mayor, Antequera Jesuit church
Nuestra Señora del Rosario, Xuchitepec, Villa Alta district
Nuestra Señora del Rosario, Tlapaltepeque
Nuestra Señora, Teotitlan del Valle
Nuestra Señora de las Nieves, Ixpantepec
Nuestra Señora de la Concepción, Mialtepec, Xicayan distrct
*Nuestra Señora de Xuquila

Michoacán (11)
Nuestra Señora de los Urdiales, Valladolid
*Nuestra Señora del Socorro, Valladolid
*Nuestra Señora de los Remedios, Zitácuaro
*Nuestra Señora de la Salud, Pátzcuaro
Nuestra Señora de Acahuato, Apatzingán district
Nuestra Señora del Buen Suceso, Zamora
*Nuestra Señora de la Raiz (a.k.a. Nuestra Señora de la Esperanza), Jacona
Nuestra Señora de la Candelaria, Maravatío
Nuestra Señora del Carmen, Tlalpuxajua
Nuestra Señora de los Remedios, Totolan, Jiquilpan district
Nuestra Senora, Santa Fe del Río, near Santa Fe de la Laguna
[Virgin of Tiripitío, Weckmann 285]
Others without definite colonial references, or of more recent origin:
Nuestra Señora de la Candelaria (a.k.a. Virgen de San Lucas, "la Reina de Tierra Caliente"), Cuitzeo district
Nuestra Señora del Rosario, Morelia (Valladolid)
Nuestra Señora de la Asunción, Tinguindin

Guanajuato (9)
*Nuestra Señora de Guanajuato, city
Nuestra Señora de Rayas, city
Nuestra Señora del Rosario, city
Nuestra Señora de la Purísima Concepción, Celaya
Nuestra Señora de Salvatierra
Nuestra Señora del Refugio, Acámbaro

Nuestra Señora de la Merced, Valle de Santiago
Nuestra Señora de los Dolores, San Pedro de los Pozos, San Luis de la Paz district
Nuestra Señora de la Purisima Concepción, León
*Nuestra Señora de la Luz, León
Others without definite colonial references or of more recent origin:
Nuestra Señora de la Luz, Salvatierra
Nuestra Señora de la Soledad, León

Zacatecas (9)
*Nuestra Señora del Patrocinio [Santuario de la Bufa], city
*Nuestra Señora de Zacatecas, cathedral church
Nuestra Señora de Loreto, Jesuit church, city
Nuestra Señora del Refugio, Villa de Guadalupe
Nuestra Señora de Guadalupe, Villa de Guadalupe
Nuestra Señora de Tlaltenango
*Nuestra Señora de la Soledad, Jerez
Nuestra Señora de la Concepción, Sombrerete
Nuestra Señora de la Soledad, Sombrerete
Others without definite colonial references or of more recent origin:
Nuestra Señora del Refugio, Moyahua
Nuestra Señora de Toyahua, Nochistlan
Nuestra Señora de Guadalupe, Calera
Nuestra Señora del Rosario de Talpa, Colotlan-Tlaltenango
Nuestra Señora de la Purificación, Fresnillo
Nuestra Señora del Carmen de la Encarnación, Jalpa Villanueva
Nuestra Señora del Refugio, Huejúcar
Nuestra Señora de Aranzazú, Norte, El Cobre
Nuestra Señora de los Milagros, Ojocaliente
Nuestra Señora de la Purísima Concepción, Sierra de Pinos
Nuestra Señora de Lourdes, Plateros
Nuestra Señora María Auxiliadora, Huejuquilla

Veracruz (9)
La Divina Pastora, city
Nuestra Señora de la Escalera, city
Nuestra Señora del Chico, Jalapa
Nuestra Señora de la Concepción, Papantla
*Nuestra Señora de los Dolores, Cosamaloapan
Nuestra Señora de Catemaco
Nuestra Señora de Tecpan, Zacatlan district
Nuestra Señora de la Inmaculada Concepción, Alvarado

Nuestra Señora de la Inmaculada Concepción, Chinamecas, district of Acayucan
Others without definite colonial references or of more recent origin:
Nuestra Señora de la Candelaria, Tlacotalpan

Hidalgo (8)
Nuestra Señora del Carmen, Ixmiquilpan
*Nuestra Señora de la Asunción, Zoquizoquipan
Nuestra Señora del Rosario, Molango
Nuestra Señora de la Purificación, Ayozingo
Nuestra Señora de las Lágrimas, Tetepango
Nuestra Señora de los Dolores, Tolcayuca
Nuestra Señora de la Esperanza, Pachuca
Nuestra Señora de la Merced, Pachuca
Virgin of El Cardonal
Others without definite colonial references or of more recent origin:
Nuestra Señora de los Ángeles, Tulancingo
Nuestra Señora de Cosamaloapan (moved to Tizayuca)

Morelos (7)
*Nuestra Señora de los Milagros, Tlaltenango
Nuestra Señora de la Concepción, Cuernavaca
Nuestra Señora del Alma de la Virgen, Miacatlan
*Nuestra Señora del Monte, Xomultepec (Jumiltepec)
Nuestra Señora de la Inmaculada Concepción, Tlayacapan
Nuestra Señora, Huautla
Nuestra Señora, Ocuituco
Others without definite colonial references or of more recent origin:
Nuestra Señora, Amatitlan

Chiapas (4)
Nuestra Señora del Rosario, Josozoltenango
Nuestra Señora del Rosario, Tlacuazintepec
Nuestra Señora del Rosario, Ciudad Real
Nuestra Señora de Cancuc
Others without definite colonial references or of more recent origin:
Nuestra Señora de la Concepción, Mazatlan, Tapachula district
Nuestra Señora de la Candelaria, Comitán
Nuestra Señora de la Candelaria, Socoltenango

Durango (4)
Nuestra Señora del Rayo, city of Durango
*Nuestra Señora del Zape, city of Durango
Nuestra Señora, Valle de Suchil
Nuestra Señora del Buen Suceso, Guadiana

Others without definite colonial references or of more recent origin:
Nuestra Señora de los Remedios, city of Durango

Tlaxcala (3)
*Nuestra Señora de Ocotlán
Nuestra Señora de la Guía
Nuestra Señora de Loreto, Españita
Others without definite colonial references or of more recent origin:
Nuestra Señora de la Caridad, Huamantla
Nuestra Señora de la Defensa, near Pantla
Nuestra Señora de la Misericordia, Apizaco

Guerrero (3)
Nuestra Señora de la Soledad, Acamixtla
Nuestra Señora, Atoyac, near Tecpan, Zacatula district
Nuestra Señora del Rosario, Coaguayutla
Others without definite colonial references or of more recent origin:
Natividad de la Virgen, Tixtla
Nuestra Señora de la Soledad, Acapulco
Nuestra Señora de los Remedios, Acatepec, Ometepec district
Nuestra Señora de Schoenstad, Chilapa
Nuestra Señora de Coronillas, Ajuchitlan

San Luis Potosí (3)
*Nuestra Señora de Guadalupe, city of San Luis
Santa María de las Charcas, Charcas
Nuestra Señora de los Dolores, San Pedro de los Pozos, San Luis de la Paz district

Aguascalientes (2)
*Nuestra Señora de la Purísima Concepción, city
Nuestra Señora de la Encarnación, Villa Encarnación
Others without definite colonial references or of more recent origin:
Nuestra Señora de la Asunción, city

Nayarit (2)
Nuestra Señora de Huajicori
Nuestra Señora de Xala

Nuevo León (1)
*Nuestra Señora del Roble [a.k.a. Nuestra Señora del Nogal], Monterrey
Others without definite colonial references or of more recent origin:
Virgen Chiquita, Monterrey
Nuestra Señora de Agualeguas

Chihuahua (1)
Nuestra Señora del Rayo, Parral

New Mexico (1)
*La Conquistadora, Santa Fe

Tabasco
Without definite colonial references
Of more recent origin:
Nuestra Señora de Cupilco, Comalcalco district

Colima
Without definite colonial references
Of more recent origin:
Nuestra Señora de la Candelaria, Tecoman

Sonora
Without definite colonial references
Of more recent origin:
Nuestra Señora de Guadalupe, Cananea
Nuestra Señora de Balvanera, Álamos

Sinaloa
Without definite colonial references
Of more recent origin:
Nuestra Señora de Quilá
Nuestra Señora del Rosario, Guasave
Nuestra Señora de Loreto, San Miguel Zapotitlan

Coahuila
Without definite colonial references
Of more recent origin:
Nuestra Señora de Guadalupe, Saltillo

Colonial Shrines and Altars to a Renowned Image of Christ or the Cross (238)

Mexico City and Valley of Mexico (49)
Santa Cruz de Tepeapulco, cathedral church precinct
Santa Cruz de Talabarteros
Santo Cristo de Totolapa
Santa Cruz de Tepexpan
Señor del Cerrito, Tepexpan
Cruz de Zapotla, Tacuba district
Cristo Negro de Mizquic
Cruz de San Cristóbal Ecatepec
Señor del Buen Despacho, cathedral church

Señor del Socorro, cathedral church
Señor del Veneno, cathedral church
*Santo Cristo del Noviciado, convent church of Santo Domingo
Santo Cristo del Noviciado, convent church of San Agustín
Santo Cristo de los Desagravios, cathedral church
Crucifijo de la Condesa del Valle, transferred to cathedral church
*Cristo Renovado de Santa Teresa [transferred from Mapethé, Hidalgo]
Cristo Renovado de la Balvanera, church of la Balvanera
Señor de la Santa Veracruz [a.k.a. Señor de los Siete Velos] parish church of Santa Veracruz
Santo Cristo de la Columna, parish church of Santa Catarina Mártir
Señor de la Misericordia, parish of Santa Veracruz church of the recogimiento de la Misericordia
Señor Crucificado, choir of the Franciscan convento grande
Santo Cristo, Conceptionist convent church
Santo Cristo, church of San José
Santo Cristo, cofradía del Santísimo Sacramento, cathedral church
Cristo Crucificado, convent church of Jesús María
Cristo Renovado, church of the Hospital de San Juan de Dios
Santo Cristo de la Salud, hospital church of Santísima Trinidad
Santo Cristo del Balazo, San Lázaro church
Divino Salvador, parish church of Santa Cruz Acatlan
Ecce Homo, convent church of La Balvanera
Ecce Homo, convent church of Regina Coeli
Santo Ecce Homo del Portal, a.k.a. Ecce Homo de los Mercaderes
Jesús Nazareno, convent church of San Lorenzo
Cristo Crucificado, Tlatelolco
Señor de la Cuevita, Iztapalapa, transferred from Etla, Oaxaca
Señor de Nextengo, Azcapotzalco
Santo Cristo de Tepotzotlán
Santo Cristo del Claustro, Tacuba
Señor de las Misericordias, Tlalnepantla
Jesús Nazareno de los Desagravios
Santo Cristo de la Expiración, a.k.a. Señor del Rebozo, church of Santa Catalina de Sena
Jesús Nazareno, Hospital de la Purísima Concepción
Jesús Nazareno, convent church of San Lorenzo
Rostro de Cristo
Jesús de la Caridad, Capuchin convent church
Niño Jesús, Capuchin convent church
Niño Jesús, San José de Gracia convent
*Niño Jesús of convent church of San Juan de la Penitencia
Niño Jesús, parish church of Santa Cruz Acatlán

Others without definite colonial references or of more recent origin:
Señor del Cerrito, Tepexpan
Divino Redentor, Teotihuacan
Ecce Homo, Santa Cruz y Soledad parish church
Niñopan (Niño Jesús), Xochimilco
Niño Perdido a.k.a. Santo Niño de las Suertes, Tacubaya

Jalisco (31)
Santa Cruz de Sayula
Santa Cruz del Astillero, Autlán (brought from Barra de Navidad)
Santa Cruz de Ahuacatlán
Señor de las Aguas, cathedral church, Guadalajara
Señor de la Penitencia, santuario, Guadalajara
Señor del Rescate, Guadalajara
Santo Cristo del Dulce Nombre de Jesús, Aranzazú church, Guadalajara
Señor de la Penitencia, Mexicaltzingo
Señor de la Misericordia, Tonalá
Señor de la Asención, San Pedro Tlaquepaque
Señor de la Salud, Zacoalco
Señor del Mesquite, Zacoalco
Santo Cristo del Dulce Nombre de Jesús, Amacueca
Santo Cristo del Dulce Nombre de Jesús, La Magdalena
Señor de la Misericordia, Etzatlán
Señor de las Maravillas, a.k.a. Santo Cristo de la Expiración, Ahualulco
Cristo Crucificado, Tamazula
Señor de la Misericordia, Tepatitlán
Santo Cristo de Tizapan
Cristo aparecido, Teccistlan, Jocotepec district
Señor del Perdón, Cocula
*Señor de los Rayos, Temastián
Señor de Ocote, Tapalpa
Señor Grande, Ameca
Señor del Encino, Yahualica
Señor del Perdón, Tuxpan
Señor de la Misericordia, Amula
Señor de la Salud, Tototlán
Señor del Perdón, a.k.a. Santo Cristo de la Expiración, Zapotiltic
Señor de la Misericordia, Compostela
Señor del Encino, Santa María Lagos
Others without definite colonial references or of more recent origin:
Señor de la Misericordia, Ocotlán
Señor de las Maravillas, Teocaltiche
Señor del Ocote, Atemajac

Señor del Mezquitito, Ciénega
Señor de la Misericordia, Encarnación

Michoacán (21)
Señor de la Sacristía, Valladolid
Crucifixo de raíces, church of Guadalupe, Valladolid
Santo Cristo de Jacona
Cristo Vida Nuestra, San Pedro Piedra Gorda
Cristo de los Trapiches, San Miguel de Atotonilco
Cristo Crucificado, Tupátaro
Crucifixo de la Expiracion, Zirahuén
Santo Cristo, Carácuaro
Cristo de Tarecuato
Cristo de la Salud, Zamora
Santo Cristo de los Zapateros, Tlalpujahua
Señor de la Misericordia, Indaparapeo
Señor del Perdón, Villa Morelos
Santo Cristo, Amatlán, Tancítaro district
Santo Cristo, La Piedad
Señor de Araró
Señor de la Lámpara, Charo
Cristo Crucificado, Tziritzícuaro
Señor del Socorro, Jiquilpan
Señor de Zinapécuaro
Niño Jesús, in Mercedarian convent church, Valladolid
Others without definite colonial references or of more recent origin:
Señor del Rescate, Tzintzuntzan
Señor de los Milagros, San Juan Parangaricutiro
Niño Jesús de la Salud, Morelia (Valladolid)
Niño Jesús, Santa Ana Pacueco
Santo Niño de Numaran

Estado de México (17)
Señor de la Santa Veracruz, Sultepec
Señor de la Veracruz o de los Labradores, Toluca
Santo Cristo, San Juan de Dios church, Toluca
*Señor de Chalma
*Señor del Sacromonte, Amecameca
Santo Cristo de Burgos, Culhuacan
Santo Cristo de Capultitlan, Toluca district
Señor del Perdón, Ixtapan de la Sal
Santo Cristo de la Escalera, Malinalco
Señor del Calvario, Coatepec Harinas
Señor del Perdón, Temascaltepec

Señor del Perdón, Ixtapan de la Sal
Señor de Ocotitlan, Xocotitlan, district of Metepec
Santo Cristo, Tescaliacac, Tenango del Valle district
Señor del Huerto, Atlacomulco
Niño Jesús, Toluca
Niño Jesús, San Bartolomé Hueypoxtla
Others without definite colonial references or of more recent origin:
Señor de Zacualpilla, Zacualpan
Señor del Cerrito, Ixtlahuaca (Cristo Crucificado de la Expiración?)
Señor de Santa María, Valle de Bravo
Señor del Santuarito, San Salvador Atenco
Señor de las Agonías, Juchitepec
Señor de la Capilla, Tequixquiac
Señor de la Salud, Villa Cuauhtémoc
Señor de la Cañita o de las Burlas, Lerma
Nuestro Padre Jesús, Tenango del Valle
Señor de Jiquipilco
Niño de Atocha, Coatepec Harinas
Señor de Zacango, Tecualoya district
Señor de Chiautla

Querétaro (16)
*Cruz de Piedra, Franciscan Colegio de la Santa Cruz, city
Cruz Verde, Tequisquiapan
Santo Cristo de la Esclavitud, city
Santo Cristo de San Benito, city
*Santo Cristo de los Trabajos, city
Señor de Santa Teresa, Carmelite convent church, city
Señor de la Portada, Augustinian convent church, city
Señor del Mesquite, barrio of city
Santo Cristo de Marfil, church of La Cruz, city
Señor de las Maravillas, Franciscan convent church, city
Señor de la Ermita, city
Cristo aparecido, San Juan del Río
Jesús Nazareno de los Terceros
*Señor de la Huertecilla, taken to church of the Congregación de Nuestra Señora de Guadalupe
Ecce Homo, church of the Franciscan Colegio de la Santa Cruz, now lost
Niño Jesús de bulto, city

Puebla (16)
*Cruz de Huaquechula
Santo Cristo, Carmelite convent church, Puebla city
Santo Cristo de los Trabajos, Augustinian convent church, Puebla city

Jesús Nazareno, parish of San José church, Puebla city
Santo Entierro, church of the Hospital Real del Sr. San Pedro, Puebla city
Santo Cristo de Burgos, Puebla city
Señor de las Maravillas, Santa Mónica convent church, Puebla city
Jesús Nazareno, Santa Clara convent church, Puebla city
Santo Cristo de la Buena Muerte, Santuario de los Gozos, Puebla city
Santo Cristo de Atlixco
Señor de los Desconsolados, Tehuacan
Jesús Nazareno, Tecali
Ecce Homo, convent church of San Juan de la Penitencia, Puebla city
Señor del Rescate, Mercedarian convent church, Puebla city
Cristo Yacente, Huauchinango
Santo Niño, Atlixco
Cristo de la Columna, Huamantla
Others without definite colonial references or of more recent origin:
Santo Cristo, capilla de San Miguel, Jesuit Colegio de Espíritu Santo, Puebla city
Señor de los Trabajos, Puebla city
Señor del Desmayo, Tecamachalco
Jesucristo Crucificado, Tochimilco
Señor del Calvario, Tlacotepec
Señor de la Buena Muerte, Texocuixpan
Señor de las Agonías, Zinacantepec
Señor de Coculco, Ajalpan, Tehuacan district
Señor del Honguito, Chignahuapan
Señor de las Misericordias, Caltepec
Señor de la Paz, San Pablo Anicano
Santo Niño Cieguito, Puebla city
Santo Niño Doctor de los Enfermos, Tepeaca

Guanajuato (13)

Santísima Cruz, Celaya santuario
Señor de la Conquista, San Felipe Torres Mochas
Santo Cristo de Burgos, city
Señor de Villaseca, city
Santo Cristo de Escamilla, León
Santísimo Cristo, Celaya
Señor del Socorro, Salvatierra
Cristo del Pueblo, a.k.a. de la Piedad, Piedad
Señor de la Veracruz, Silao
Señor de la Conquista, San Miguel el Grande
Señor del Hospital, Salamanca
Jesús Nazareno, Atotonilco, near San Miguel el Grande

Ecce Homo, San Miguel el Grande
Others without definite colonial references or of more recent origin:
Santo Cristo de la Columna, Purísima del Rincón
El Divino Pastorcito de la Cañada de Corralejo

Hidalgo (13)
Santa Cruz de Ayotusco, Huizquilucan district
Ligno Crucis, Pachuca
Cruz de Maye
Cruz de Tepeapulco
[Cristo Renovado de Mapethé, listed above under Mexico City, Cristo Renovado de Santa Teresa]
Señor de las Misericordias, Actopan
Cristo Viejo, Xichú
Señor de las Maravillas, El Arenal
Cristo del Milagro, Zinguilucan
*Cristo de Zerezo, Pachuca
Rostro de Cristo, Pachuca
Santo Entierro, Apasco, Tetepango Huepustla
Niño Jesús, Cayuca, district of Tulancingo
Niño Jesús, Actopan
Others without definite colonial references or of more recent origin:
Señor de Jalpan, Ixmiquilpan
Señor de la Salud, Mezquititlan de la Sierra
Señor de la Salud, Huejutla
Señor de la Preciosa Sangre, Tezontepec
Señor del Calvario, Huichapan
Señor de las Tres Caídas, Huichapan
Señor de la Buena Muerte, Alfajayucan
Señor de Zelonta, Real del Monte
Señor de los Trabajos, Pemusco, Tianguistengo district
Señor de las Tres Caídas, Tepetitlan
Señor de la Humildad, Jilotepec
Santo Niño de Actopan
Santo Niño, Hueypustla

Oaxaca (13)
*Cruz de Huatulco (moved to cathedral in Antequera)
Señor del Consuelo, Mercedarian church, Antequera
Señor del Rayo, Antequera
Santo Cristo de Juxtlahuaca
*Señor de las Batallas, Tlacolula
Señor de los Corazones, Huajuapan

Señor de Hueyapan
Señor de las Peñas, San Pablo Etla
Santo Cristo de Teotitlán del Valle
Señor del Desmayo, Tamazulapan
Señor de la Capilla, Tezoatlan
Señor de las Tres Caídas, Teutila
Santa Cruz, Santo Domingo Tonala
Others without definite colonial references or of more recent origin:
Señor de Etla
Señor de las Llagas, Santiago Miltepec
Señor de las Tres Caídas, Ixcatlan

Morelos (7)
Santa Cruz de Tepetenchi, Tlayacapan
Señor del Espino, Xoxutla
Jesús Nazareno, Xonacatepec
Jesús Nazareno, Cuauhtla
*Jesús Nazareno, Tepalcingo
Jesús Nazareno, Jalacingo
Santo Cristo de la Columna, Jiutepec
Without definite colonial references or of more recent origin:
Señor del Calvario, Mazatepec

Veracruz (7)
Señor del Calvario, Orizaba
Señor de las Suertes, Carmelite church, Orizaba
Padre Jesús, Jalacingo
Señor de la Antigua Veracruz
Señor del Buen Viaje, Veracruz city
*Cristo Negro, Otatitlan
Niño Jesús, Cosamaloapan
Niño Perdido, Orizaba
[Niño Perdido, Jalapa Weckmann 288]
Without definite colonial references or of more recent origin:
Señor de las Misericordias, Tampico Alto

Zacatecas (5)
Santo Cristo de Zacatecas, city
Santo Cristo, parish of San Pedro, city
Cristo de Rajapeñas, Tarascan barrio of San José, city
Cristo de Plateros, Fresnillo
Cristo de Tlacuitlapan
Others without definite colonial references or of more recent origin:
Señor Crucificado, Tlaltenango

Santo Niño de Atocha, Plateros, Fresnillo
Niño de las Palomitas, Tacoaleche

Tlaxcala (3)
Cruz de madera, city of Tlaxcala
Señor del Calvario, Apizaquito
Jesús Nazareno, Apetelatitlan
Others without definite colonial references or of more recent origin:
Señor del Coro, Santa Cruz, Tlaxcala
Niño Milagroso de Tlaxcala

Guerrero (4)
Santo Cristo de Zumpango, Tixtla district
Señor de Cuetzala, Ichcateopan district
*Santo Niño de Cebu, San Miguel Azoyú (Costa Chica)
Padre Jesús de Petatlán (Costa Grande)
Others without definite colonial references or of more recent origin:
Cristo de Colotlipa
Señor de Petatlan
Padre Jesús de Tecalpulco
Señor del Perdón [Ruta]
Señor de la Veracruz, Taxco
Señor de Oxtotitlan
Santo Entierro, Xalpatlahuac

San Luis Potosí (3)
*Señor del Saucito, a.k.a. Nuestro Señor de Burgos del Saucito, city
Cristo de Matehuala
Señor del Jovo, Tamazunchale

Campeche (2)
Cruz refulgente en el cielo
*Nuestro Señor de San Román

Nayarit (2)
*Cruz de Zacate, a.k.a. Cruz Verde de Tepic
Señor de la Asención, Ixcuintla

Colima (2)
Señor de la Expiración, a.k.a. Señor del Rancho de Villa
Santo Cristo de la Sacristía de "El Platanal," Tuxpan

Coahuila (2)
Cristo Crucificado, Saltillo
Rostro de Cristo, Parras
Others without definite colonial references or of more recent origin:

Santo Cristo de la Capilla, Saltillo
Santo Cristo del Ojo de Agua

Nuevo León (3)
Señor de Tlaxcala de Bustamante
Señor de la Expiración, Guadalupe
Jesuchristo Crucificado, San Miguel Aguayo

Tamaulipas (2)
Santa Cruz del Milagro, Ozuluama
Santo Cristo de Tampico, Tampico el Alto

Aguascalientes (1)
Señor del Encino, city
Others without definite colonial references or of more recent origin:
Señor de los Rayos, city
Señor de las Angustias, Rincón de Romos
Señor de Tepozan, Asientos
Santo Niño de Peyotes, Villa Unión

Durango (1)
Señor de Mapimí, Cuencamé
Others without definite colonial references or of more recent origin:
Señor de los Guerreros, San José del Tizonazo
Señor del Santo Entierro, Durango city

Chihuahua (1)
Niño Jesús, Cayuca

New Mexico (1)
Cruz de Moqui

Chiapas (1)
*Cristo de los Desagravios, aka Señor de Tila, Chapultenango district
Without definite colonial references or of more recent origin:
Señor del Pozo

Yucatán (1)
*Cristo de las Ampollas, Mérida

Tabasco
Without definite colonial references or of more recent origin:
Señor de la Salud, a.k.a. Señor de las Teresitas

Quintana Roo
Without definite colonial references or of more recent origin:
Cruz parlante, Chan Santa Cruz

Colonial Shrines, Chapels, and Altars Dedicated to a Renowned Image of a Saint Other than the Blessed Mary (20)

Querétaro (5)
Santiago, parish church, city
San Francisco Javier, Jesuit colegio church, city
San Antonio de Padua, church of Santa Clara, city
San José, church of Santa Clara, city
San Vicente Ferrer, Santo Domingo church, city

Mexico City and Valley of Mexico (3)
San Antonio el Pobre (San Antonio de Padua), Tlatelolco
San Antonio de Padua, Franciscan Convento Grande church
San Antonio de Padua, Tultitlan

Tlaxcala (2)
*San Miguel del Milagro, near Nativitas
San Antonio de Padua, Calpulalpan

Guerrero (2)
San Nicolás Tolentino, Costa Chica area and Zitlalá
San Antonio de Padua, Acapulco

Estado de México (2)
Santa Ana, Amatepec
San Nicolás Obispo, Malinalco

Morelos (1)
San Juan Bautista, Yecapixtla

Puebla (1)
San Francisco del Milagro, Franciscan convent, city of Puebla

Oaxaca (1)
San Antonio de Padua, Ixtepeji

San Luis Potosí (1)
San Antonio de Padua, Villa del Dulce Nombre de Dios de Rioverde

Sonora (1)
San Francisco Javier, Magdalena de Kino

Veracruz (1)
San Joseph, Córdoba

Notes

1. For example, Luis Enrique Orozco, in his *Iconografía mariana de la Arquidiócesis de Guadalajara*, Guadalajara: n.p., 1954, claims fifty-two Marian shrines in Jalisco while my list totals seventeen for the colonial period. Matías de la Mota Padilla's chronicle for Nueva Galicia in 1742 mentions ten miraculous images of the Virgin Mary (but does not include Talpa) and "many santuarios," *Historia de la conquista de la Nueva-Galicia* [1742], Guadalajara: Tipografía del Gobierno, 1856.
2. For example, the record of an *estampa* of "Jesús de Petatlán" (the still regionally famous Padre Jesús de Petatlán, El Rey de la Paz) from the Costa Grande of Guerrero displayed on a home altar in San Miguel Azoyú, far to the south on the Costa Chica, in the 1780s leads me to include this shrine image, AGN Inquisición 1223 exp. 14, fols. 209–210.
3. Francisco de Florencia and Antonio de Oviedo, *Zodíaco mariano*..., Mexico: Colegio de San Ildefonso, 1755. How many of the eighty-four shrines and images included in its pages were added by Oviedo and reflect eighteenth-century developments? It is not always clear. A more serious problem with relying on the *Zodíaco mariano* is that Florencia and Oviedo favored images and shrines that their order sponsored or otherwise promoted. These included images in urban Jesuit churches that may not have had a large following or qualified as shrines in other ways.
4. *Relaciones geográficas del Arzobispado de México. 1743*, ed. Francisco de Solano, 2 vols., Madrid: C.S.I.C., 1988.
5. Cayetano de Cabrera y Quintero, *Escudo de armas de Mexico: Celestial protección de esta nobilíssima ciudad, de la Nueva España, y de casi todo el Nuevo Mundo*..., Mexico: Vda de Joseph Bernardo de Hogal, 1746.
6. *Diario del viaje que hizo a la América en el siglo XVIII el P. Fray Francisco de Ajofrín*, 2 vols., Mexico: Instituto Cultural Hispano Mexicano, 1964, *passim*.
7. *Tardes americanas: Gobierno géntil y católico. Breve y particular noticia de toda la historia Indiana*..., Mexico: Zúñiga y Ontiveros, 1778.
8. *La ruta de los santuarios en México*, Mexico: Secretaría de Turismo, 1994. Schneider refers to a list of 253 shrines compiled by Mexico's Comisión Episcopal de Evangelización y Catequesis in the 1980s, but, to my knowledge, this list has not been published and I have not been able to consult it on site.
9. *Cristos célebres de México*, Mexico: n.p., 1950.
10. Mexico: Tipografía de "Artes Gráficas," S.A., 1908.
11. *Iconografía mariana, passim*.
12. "The European Roots of Latin American Pilgrimage," in *Pilgrimage in Latin America*, ed. N. Ross Crumrine and Alan Morinis, Westport, CT: Greenwood Press, 1991, pp. 19–49.

Appendix 2
When Shrines Began

When did a miraculous image become established and gain fame and a following beyond the immediate vicinity? When was it regarded as a shrine? The answer is uncertain for most of the many celebrated images and shrines in colonial Mexico. Even colonial era chroniclers of shrines lamented a lack of evidence about their early years beyond reputation – *la voz pública y fama*, as they called it.

Sources used to compile the lists in Appendix 1 are used again here, although more selectively. Published provincial chronicles and compendia by Florencia and Oviedo, Vetancurt, Torquemada, Lizana, Tello, Burgoa, Veytia, Mota Padilla, Escobar, Cabrera y Quintero, and other colonial authors were helpful starting points, but more certain dates come from early devotional histories of particular shrines, novena booklets published mainly in the eighteenth century, a group of formal investigations into miracle traditions conducted during the seventeenth and eighteenth centuries,[1] pastoral visit books, colonial gazettes and diaries of public events (*efemérides*), and scattered administrative and judicial records across three centuries. The lack of serial records for most shrines and the selective, hagiographical nature of nearly all the narrative sources make dating a difficult, often frustrating endeavor. The challenges of tracking particular shrines over time are evident in the chapters of this book. Here, briefly, are two examples of how establishing when a shrine began is confounded by fragmentary and fugitive evidence.

The image of Nuestra Señora de los Rayos of Temastián, Jalisco, may well have been made and then acquired by the community of Temastián before the end of the sixteenth century, and the image was later housed in a chapel built during the early seventeenth century, but popular devotion is more clearly documented later, in the late eighteenth century. As a shrine, should it be included in the sixteenth, seventeenth, or eighteenth-century list of beginnings?

The testimony of local residents, when it is recorded in colonial records, usually is not much help in dating unless the devotion had begun recently. For example, in 1776, when the ecclesiastical judge for

Tlalpujahua (in Michoacán near the Estado de México border) queried residents about the antiquity of the miraculous image of Nuestra Señora del Carmen and devotion to her in a chapel on the edge of town, no one could say more specifically than that it had been there "from time immemorial," when a miner built a chapel. The story was that the chapel was later abandoned and fell to ruins, but somehow the statue of the Virgin had been left behind and remained in perfect condition. The ecclesiastical judge reported that at the time of his investigation, people came from distant places to see the image and pray for special favors and that Indians came to dance before the Virgin. So the devotion was well established by the 1770s, but what was it like earlier in the eighteenth century or in the seventeenth century?

Fewer than half of the shrines and images listed in Appendix 1 are included here – 205 of 498. While 205 is a large enough number to describe with some confidence several chronological patterns in the founding and development of shrines, uncertainties abound. Grouping by centuries is a necessary convenience that obscures the occasional clustering of new activity at the turn of the seventeenth and eighteenth centuries. A long seventeenth century, from about 1580 to 1720, was the span of time in which the early years of most shrines fit, but there are two reasons to group the beginnings in the conventional way, by century. It is faithful to the fact that the first years of shrines are often impossible to locate with precision, in good part because a loyal following and physical facilities did not come into existence suddenly; and some striking patterns in the history of colonial shrines do roughly conform to the rhythm of open-ended centuries.

Patterns and Distortions

That only 22 of the 205 shrines listed here probably began in the sixteenth century may come as a surprise since it has been customary to highlight the first decades of colonization as the formative time for many Mexican shrines.[2] Most of those sixteenth-century attributions depend on legendary beginnings that were registered a century or two or three later or on the fact that the image in question probably was made in the sixteenth century. Working against early attributions based on the age of the image is a distinctive pattern in the emergence of Mexican shrines: the founding stories often highlight a miracle associated with an image that had long been present in a particular church, chapel, or home without attracting special attention. Unless I found other sources that confirm early devotion and promotion (and especially when the earliest evidence of popular devotion I could find was much later), I have not classified a shrine as "sixteenth-century" only because of the age of the image or because a founding legend says so. Early attributions that depend on dating a chapel (*hermita*) where the image was kept also are problematic. The early colonial record is filled with references to hermitas as local places of worship – public or private – that inevitably would have had one or more images of Christ and saints, but most of these references do not draw attention to the miraculous reputation of a particular image.

Another surprise is that quite a few new shrines developed during the eighteenth century, especially shrines dedicated to images of Christ – albeit on a smaller scale than in the seventeenth century. Many of these shrines began between 1700 and 1730 and could be regarded as an extension of the seventeenth-century peak, but others developed in the second half of the eighteenth century. Equally strikingly, many more shrines and miraculous images than are listed here are documented only in eighteenth-century records. No doubt some of these late colonial devotions were new or newly popular, but unless there is evidence that they were, in fact, just beginning, I have not included them as eighteenth-century foundings. For better or worse, the eighteenth century is simply more abundantly documented for almost any subject imaginable, and some established but less actively promoted image devotions inevitably rose to the surface of the written record then for the first time. This documentation of old and new shrines during the eighteenth century *does* suggest a historical pattern that is more than a reflection of distortions of the written record: the eighteenth century was a time of further development and deepening interest in many already established shrines and images. Fewer new foundings does not make the eighteenth century a time of decline or even much retrenchment, thanks in part to the imperial government's limited ability to choke off new or nominally unacceptable devotions, as it sometimes wished to do.

Several patterns apparent in this register of shrine beginnings are more apparent than real, or at least not quite what they seem to be. The proportion of Marian images in Appendix 2 (66 percent compared to 51 percent in Appendix 1) would seem to be mainly the result of more Marian shrines being extensively documented because they appealed to a larger audience than the often more localized shrines dedicated to images of Christ. On the other hand, the very large proportion of Marian shrines represented in seventeenth-century beginnings (nearly 75 percent) compared to the eighteenth century (42 percent) suggests a real change – that belief in Mary's presence and protection was especially compelling in the seventeenth century, or at least not so concentrated in a few images and shrines then.

The prominence of urban shrines and images in this list may also be mainly a function of colonial cities being more extensively documented than provincial and rural places, especially for shrines. The *Zodíaco mariano*, for example, overrepresents early colonial city shrines. Over half of the eighty-two miraculous images and their shrines listed there for the sixteenth and seventeenth centuries were located in three cities: Mexico City, Puebla, and Guatemala, with Mexico City alone accounting for 39 percent of the sixteenth-century shrine foundings in this source, and 30.7 percent of those listed for the seventeenth century. These figures may seem inflated, but Mexico City is far and away the most extensively documented population center in New Spain, and even minor shrines would have been noticed in writing there whereas similar local shrines in out-of-the-way places were not.[3] But if this particular distortion in the documentation for Mexico City was more or less stable over time, there was a real proportional decline in new shrines in Mexico City during the eighteenth century – down to 16.1 percent, about half the proportion for the rest of the colonial period. Dramatic growth in promotion of and devotion to Our Lady of Guadalupe at the expense of other shrines in and near Mexico City helps to explain this shift.

Finally, some regions of Mexico may well be overrepresented or underrepresented. Jalisco, in particular, has long been blessed with Catholic historians interested in the state's religious traditions. For whatever reason, neighboring Michoacán has been less favored, even though popular piety is a prominent – if more contentious – theme in that state's history, too. Northern Mexico is less present here than the west, center, or south. A thinner historical record for the north is partly the reason, but there just were not many image devotions in the far north that came to be regarded as shrines during the colonial period.[4]

Shrine Beginnings: Sixteenth Century (twenty-two probable cases: eleven images of the Virgin Mary; ten images of the Cross or Christ; one image of another saint)

Mexico City and vicinity (three images of the Virgin Mary; four images of Christ or cross)

Nuestra Señora de los Remedios
Nuestra Señora de Guadalupe
Santa María la Mayor, Jesuit College
Wooden ahuehuete cross of San Jose de los Naturales chapel
Cristo de los Siete Velos, Santa Veracruz parish
Santo Cristo de Totolapan, Augustinian convent church
Cristo de Nextengo, Azcapotzalco

Puebla (three images of the Virgin Mary)
Nuestra Señora de los Remedios, Cholula
La Conquistadora, Puebla city
Nuestra Señora del Pópulo, Puebla city

Tlaxcala (one image of the Virgin Mary; one image of Christ)
Nuestra Señora de Ocotlán
The great wooden cross erected by Hernán Cortés

Querétaro (one image of the Holy Cross; one image of another saint)
Cruz de piedra
Santiago, parish church of Querétaro city

Guanajuato (one image of the Virgin Mary)
Nuestra Señora de Guanajuato

Zacatecas (one image of the Virgin Mary; one image of Christ)
Nuestra Señora de los Zacatecas
Santo Cristo de la Parroquia

Jalisco (one image of the Virgin Mary)
Nuestra Señora de la Asunción, Xalostotitlan

Estado de México (one image of Christ)
Cristo del Sacromonte, Amecameca

Oaxaca (one image of the cross)
Cruz de Huatulco

Yucatán (one image of the Virgin Mary)
Nuestra Señora de Izamal

Shrine Beginnings: Seventeenth Century (ca. 140 cases: 101 or 102 images of the Virgin Mary; 35 images of Christ; 3 images of other saints)

Mexico City and Immediate Vicinity (thirty-four images of the Virgin Mary; ten images of Christ; two images of other saints)
Nuestra Señora de la Piedad
Nuestra Señora de la Bala
Nuestra Señora de Santa María
Nuestra Señora de la Merced, Mercedarian convent church
Nuestra Señora del Rosario, Dominican convent church
Santa María la Redonda parish church
Nuestra Señora de la Consolación, Franciscan church of San Cosmé
Nuestra Señora del Tránsito, Augustinian Colegio de San Pablo chapel
Nuestra Señora de la Paz, Augustinian convent church
Santa María de Gracia, convent church of Santa María de Gracia
Nuestra Señora del Buen Suceso convent of San Bernardo
Nuestra Señora de la Asunción, cathedral
Nuestra Señora de la Plata, silver Immaculate Conception, cathedral
Nuestra Señora de la Asunción de oro, cathedral
Nuestra Señora de las Lágrimas, cathedral

Nuestra Señora de las Maravillas, hospital church of Jesús Nazareno
Nuestra Señora del Sagrario, Capilla del Noviciado, Franciscan convent
Nuestra Señora de Guadalupe, convent church of San Gerónimo
Nuestra Señora de las Angustias, hospital church of Amor de Dios
Nuestra Señora del Coro, convent church of Santa Catharina de Sena
Señor de la Columna, parish church of Santa Catharina Mártir
Nuestra Señora del Socorro, convent church of San Juan de la Penitencia
Nuestra Señora de los Dolores, Jesuit church of the Colegio Máximo
Virgen Dolorosa, Jesuit church of the Colegio Máximo (a second image)
Nuestra Señora de la Antigua, Jesuit church of the Colegio Máximo
Immaculate Conception, Jesuit church of the Colegio Máximo
Nuestra Señora de Loreto, Jesuit church of the Colegio Máximo
Nuestra Señora de Loreto, Jesuit church of the Colegio de San Gregorio
Nuestra Señora de Loreto, Jesuit Casa Profesa
Nuestra Señora de Loreto, Tepotzotlán
Immaculate Conception brought by Jesuits from Xalmolonga
Nuestra Señora de Tepepan
Niño Jesús, Jesuit Casa Profesa
Cristo Renovado de Santa Teresa, Carmelite convent church
Cristo de la Humildad, church of Santísima Trinidad
Cristo del Balazo, San Lázaro church
Ecce Homo, convent church of Regina Coeli
Ecce Homo, convent church of San Juan de la Penitencia
Cristo de la Columna, Franciscan Third Order chapel
Cristo Augustinian novitiates' chapel
Santo Cristo de Tlatelolco
Santo Cristo de Tlalnepantla
San Antonio el Pobre, Tlatelolco
San Antonio de Padua, Franciscan convent church

Estado de México (four images of the Virgin Mary; two images of Christ)
Nuestra Señora de los Angeles, Tecaxic
Nuestra Señora de Tonatico
Nuestra Señora de Tulantongo
Nuestra Señora del Rosario, Toluca
Santo Cristo de la Cofradía de la Veracruz, Toluca
Santo Niño, Toluca

Hidalgo (two images of the Virgin Mary; one image of Christ)
Nuestra Señora de Zoquizoquipan, Meztitlán district
Immaculate Conception of El Cardonal
Santo Niño de Cayuca, Tulancingo district

Querétaro (two images of the Virgin Mary)
Nuestra Señora del Pueblito
Nuestra Señora de Guadalupe image in city church dedicated to Guadalupe

Guanajuato (three images of the Virgin Mary; one image of Christ)
Nuestra Señora de Salvatierra
Immaculate Conception, Celaya
Immaculate Conception, León
Señor del Hospital, Salamanca

Michoacán (seven images of the Virgin Mary; three images of Christ)
Nuestra Señora de la Salud, Pátzcuaro
Santa María la Mayor, Jesuit college, Pátzcuaro
Nuestra Señora de Santa Clara, near Pátzcuaro
Nuestra Señora de Guaniqueo
Nuestra Señora de Belén, Tarímbaro Franciscan convent
Nuestra Señora de los Remedios, Zitácuaro
Nuestra Señora de la Esperanza (Nuestra Señora de la Raíz), Jacona
Santa Cruz del Guayabo, Jacona
Cristo de La Piedad
Cristo de las Monjas, Valladolid

Jalisco (four images of the Virgin Mary; four images of Christ)
Nuestra Señora de Zapopan
Nuestra Señora de San Juan de los Lagos
Nuestra Señora de Santa Anita
Nuestra Señora de Talpa
Cristo de Cocula
Señor de la Penitencia, Guadalajara
Cristo de La Magdalena
Cruz Grande de Ameca

Nayarit (two images of Christ or the Holy Cross)
Cruz Verde, Tepic
Señor de la Misericordia, Compostela

Zacatecas (one image of Christ)
Santo Cristo de la Parroquia, city

San Luis Potosí (one image of the Virgin Mary)
Nuestra Señora de Guadalupe, outside the city

Durango (one image of the Virgin Mary)
Nuestra Señora de Zape

Coahuila (two images of Christ)
Señor de la Capilla, Saltillo
Santo Niño de Peyotes, Villa Unión

Nuevo León (one image of the Virgin Mary)
Nuestra Señora del Roble, Monterrey

New Mexico (one image of the Virgin Mary)
La Conquistadora

Morelos (one image of the Virgin Mary; one image of Christ)
Nuestra Señora del Sacromonte, Jumiltepec
Señor de Tepalcingo

Tlaxcala (two images of the Virgin Mary; one image of another saint)
Nuestra Señora de la Guía
Nuestra Señora de Loreto, Españita
San Miguel del Milagro

Puebla (nine images of the Virgin Mary)
Nuestra Señora de la Defensa, city
Nuestra Señora de la Soledad, Dominican convent church, city
Nuestra Señora de la Soledad, Carmelite convent church, city
Nuestra Señora del Rosario, Dominican convent church, city
Nuestra Señora del Carmen, Conceptionist convent, city
Nuestra Señora del Pópulo, Jesuit Colegio del Espíritu Santo, city
Nuestra Señora de Loreto, Jesuit church, city
Nuestra Señora de los Dolores, Acatzingo
Immaculate Conception of Tecamachalco

Guerrero (one image of Christ)
Señor de Tlacotepec

Oaxaca (five images of the Virgin Mary; three images of Christ)
Nuestra Señora de la Soledad, Antequera
Nuestra Señora del Socorro, church of Vera Cruz, Antequera
Nuestra Señora de las Nieves, Ixpantepec
Nuestra Señora del Rosario, Xuchitepec, Villa Alta district
Nuestra Señora de Xuquila (first chapel at Amialtepec, 1663; moved to Xuquila in early eighteenth century)
Cross of Santo Domingo Tonala
Señor de los Corazones, Huajuapan
Cristo de Hueyapan

Chiapas (five images of the Virgin Mary)
Nuestra Señora del Rosario, Ciudad Real
Nuestra Senora de Sosozoltenango

Nuestra Señora de la Purificación, Tlacuazintepeque
Nuestra Señora del Rosario, Chipacaque, Soconusco district
Nuestra Señora de la Merced, Chiantla and Ostuncalco

Veracruz (two images of the Virgin Mary; one image of Christ)
Nuestra Señora de la Escalera, port of Veracruz
Nuestra Señora de Cosamaloapan
Señor de Otatitlán

Campeche (one image of the Virgin Mary; one image of Christ)
Nuestra Señora de Guadalupe, city
Cristo de San Román, city

Yucatán (thirteen images of the Virgin Mary; one image of Christ)
Immaculate Conception of Tix
Immaculate Conception of Zetuna
Immaculate Conception of Calatamul
Immaculate Conception of Colomul
Immaculate Conception of Sotuta
Nuestra Señora de la Laguna
Nuestra Señora de Mani
Nuestra Señora de Becal
Nuestra Señora de Tizimin
Nuestra Señora de Vaimas
Nuestra Señora del Rosario, Mérida
Nuestra Señora de la Soledad, Mérida
Immaculate Conception, Valladolid
Santo Cristo de las Ampollas, Mérida

Guatemala (three images of the Virgin Mary; one image of Christ)
Nuestra Señora del Socorro, cathedral, city
Nuestra Señora de Loreto, Franciscan church, city
Nuestra Señora la Pobre, Franciscan church, city
Señor de Esquipulas

Shrine Beginnings: Eighteenth and Early Nineteenth Centuries (forty-six cases: eighteen images of the Virgin Mary; twenty-six images of Christ; two images of other saints)

  Mexico City and Vicinity (four images of the Virgin Mary; three images of Christ)
Nuestra Señora de los Dolores, Mercedarian church
Nuestra Señora de la Macana (brought by Franciscans to Tlalnepantla after 1680; later moved to the Convento Grande)
Nuestra Señora de la Fuente, Regina Coeli church
Nuestra Señora del Socorro, Chalco district

Ecce Homo, Balvanera convent church
  Zapotla stone cross, Tacuba district
  Cristo del Claustro, Tacuba

Hidalgo (two images of Christ)
  Señor de las Maravillas, Arenal
  Santo Cristo de Singuilucan

Guanajuato (two images of Christ)
  Ecce Homo, San Miguel el Grande
  Cristo Negro de Villaseca

Michoacán (three images of Christ)
  Cristo de Araró
  Cristo de Amatlán, Tancítaro district
  Niño milagroso, Mercedarian convent church, Valladolid

Jalisco (three images of the Virgin Mary; two images of Christ)
  Nuestra Señora de las Aguas, convent church of Jesús María, Guadalajara
  Nuestra Señora del Rayo, convent church of Jesús María, Guadalajara
  Nuestra Señora de la Encarnación, Villa Encarnación
  Cristo del Encino, Santa María Lagos
  Señor de los Rayos, Temastián

Colima (one image of Christ)
  Señor de la Expiración, Colima

Aguascalientes (one image of Christ)
  Señor del Encino, Aguascalientes city

Zacatecas (three images of the Virgin Mary; one image of Christ)
  Nuestra Señora de la Soledad, Jerez
  Nuestra Señora del Patrocinio, city
  Nuestra Señora de Huejúcar
  Señor de Plateros, near Fresnillo (turn of the eighteenth century)

Coahuila (one image of Christ)
  Santo Cristo, Jesuit college church, Parras

Nuevo León (two images of Christ)
  Señor de Tlaxcala, Bustamante
  Señor de la Expiración, Guadalupe

Tamaulipas (one image of Christ)
  Señor del Jovo, Tamazunchale

New Mexico (one image of Christ)
  Señor de Esquipulas, Chimayó

Morelos (one image of the Virgin Mary; two images of Christ)
  Nuestra Señora de Tlaltenango
  Señor de Tula, Jojutla
  Cruz de Tepetenchi, Tlayacapan

Puebla (three images of the Virgin Mary; one image of the Holy Cross; two images of another saint)
  Nuestra Señora del Refugio, Puebla city
  Nuestra Señora del Nicho, Puebla city
  Nuestra Señora de los Angeles (Santuario de Tzocuilac), Cholula
  Cruz de Huaquechula
  San Francisco del Milagro, Puebla city
  Señor San José, San José Chiapa, Nopalucan district

Guerrero (one image of Christ)
  Santo Niño de Sibuu, San Miguel Azoyu

Oaxaca (one image of the Virgin Mary; one image of Christ)
  Nuestra Señora de Teotitlán del Valle
  Jesús Nazareno de las Tres Caídas, Teutila

Veracruz (one image of Christ)
  Señor de las Suertes, Orizaba

Yucatán (one image of the Virgin Mary)
  Nuestra Señora de Tetiz

Guatemala (two images of the Virgin Mary)
  Nuestra Señora del los Dolores, Jesuit colegio chapel of San Francisco Borja, city
  Nuestra Señora de los Pobres, Franciscan church, city

Notes

1. Fifteen of these *investigaciones jurídicas*, dating from 1582 to 1755, are mentioned in colonial sources. Nine of the fifteen reportedly date from 1639 to 1670. (La Conquistadora, Puebla, 1582, published 1666; Nuestra Señora de la Piedad, Valley of Mexico, 1614; Nuestra Señora de Izamal, Yucatán, 1633; Cruz de Piedra, Querétaro, 1639, 1650; Zapopan, Jalisco, 1641, 1653 authorized but not completed; San Miguel del Milagro, Tlaxcala, 1643–1644, excerpted in Florencia, 1675; El Pueblito, Querétaro, 1649 not completed; Nuestra Señora de la Laguna, Yucatán, 1649; Nuestra Señora de Tix, Yucatán, 1650; Nuestra Señora de Guadalupe, Tepeyac, 1666; Nuestra Señora de San Juan de los Lagos, Jalisco, 1634 *visita* to investigate, 1668, 1734; Nuestra Señora de Talpa, Jalisco, 1670 in 1732 copy; Cristo Renovado de Santa Teresa, Mexico City, 1689; Nuestra Señora de la Salud, Pátzcuaro, Michoacán, 1739; Nuestra Señora de Ocotlán, Tlaxcala, 1754–1755.) Four were published in the seventeenth century and five others apparently were incorporated into devotional histories of the shrine.

2. See Rubén Vargas Ugarte, *Historia del culto de María en Ibero-América: y de sus imágenes y santuarios más celebrados*, 3rd ed., 2 vols., Madrid: Talleres Gráficos Jura, 1956; Félix Báez-Jorge, *Entre los naguales y los santos: Religión popular y ejercicio clerical en el México indígena*, Xalapa: Universidad Veracruzana, 1998; and Luis Mario Schneider, *Cristos, santos y vírgenes: Santuarios y devociones de México*, Mexico: Grupo Editorial Planeta. Other helpful secondary sources include Luis Weckmann, *The Medieval Heritage of Mexico*, trans. Frances M. López-Morillas, New York: Fordham University Press, 1992; Higinio Vásquez Santa Ana, *Cristos célebres de México*, Mexico: n.p., 1950; Luis Enrique Orozco, *Iconografía mariana de la Arquidiócesis de Guadalajara*, 5 vols., Guadalajara: n.p., 1954, and *Los cristos de caña de maíz y otras venerables imágenes de Nuestro Señor Jesucristo*, Guadalajara: n.p., 1970; *La ruta de los santuarios en México*, Mexico: Secretaría de Turismo, 1994; *La pastoral de santuarios en México*, Mexico: Comisión Episcopal de Evangelización y Catequesis, 1988; and various studies of particular shrines and images cited in the notes.
3. This spotlight on Mexico City still holds true. Take the stain on the Hidalgo subway station floor widely regarded as a depiction of the Virgin Mary. It created a considerable stir when first reported in 1997 and has continued to be the subject of occasional newspaper and television stories. Similar sightings elsewhere rarely receive the same media coverage.
4. In well-documented local studies, Israel Cavazos Garza demonstrates that at least three image shrines developed in and near Monterrey, Nuevo León during the seventeenth and eighteenth centuries.

Appendix 3
Other Saints

Few images of saints other than the Blessed Mary became widely renowned as miraculous in New Spain. Of course, virtually every saint – and some exemplary Christians not destined for sainthood – had followers, and every image of a saint might take on the aura of immanence since miraculous power was by definition an attribute of sainthood. A few shrines and images of saints did gain fame beyond the local community, and even an obscure saint like San Félix Papa could become the outstanding divine protector of an important town.[1] But only the colonial shrine of San Miguel del Milagro in Tlaxcala gained a regional following comparable to Marian shrines like Zapopan, Xuquila, Izamal, and El Pueblito; and it fell short of the reach of the great shrines to the Virgin of Guadalupe at Tepeyac, the Virgin of the Immaculate Conception at San Juan de los Lagos, the Christ of Chalma, and the Christ of Esquipulas.

How and when the saints and their images became widely known and venerated during the colonial period is not altogether clear. While emphasizing that "no other aspect of Christian belief and ritual had a remotely comparable impact on the broad range of [Nahua] activity" in central Mexico during the colonial period, James Lockhart suggests that the saints only gradually "seeped" into Nahuas' devotions, mainly through the influence of Spanish lay settlers beginning in the late sixteenth century.[2] However, European influences by and large favored earlier promotion and enthusiasm for saints despite some constraints in the first generations of colonization. Devotional reforms of the time, both before and after the Council of Trent decrees (1546–1563), tended to promote episcopal and papal authority and universal features of the faith at the expense of the local and eccentric, inevitably affecting the cult of saints, which was so important to Christian devotion in Europe during the late Middle Ages. The calendar of saints was pruned back by the reformers, and no new saints were recognized between 1523 and 1588, but the cult of saints and their images still flourished within a more restricted, hierarchical order that featured canonized heroes of the New Testament and the leading religious orders, and early Christian martyrs.[3] After canonizations resumed in 1588, some new saints who brought to life the spirit of the sixteenth-century reforms were recognized, among them San Ignacio de Loyola, San Francisco Javier, Santa Teresa de Ávila, San Felipe Neri, and the first New World saint, Rosa de Lima.[4] Some ancestral community saints in Spain came into their own again near the turn of the seventeenth century as mainstays of local spiritual fervor, and the cult of saints entered its "golden age" both in Mediterranean Europe and Spanish America during the seventeenth century.[5]

Within the countercurrents of devotion in the sixteenth century, a select group of saints were introduced and promoted into America by early evangelizers as well as laymen. The Virgin Mary was only the most prominent of them.[6] Colonial towns had their patron saints from the beginning; images of saints were placed in churches; individuals were christened with the names of saints; and the mendicants made their founders and other favorite saints well known – San Francisco, San Antonio de Padua, and San Buenaventura, among others, for the Franciscans; San Nicolás de Tolentino and San Agustín for the Augustinians; Santo Domingo for the Dominicans; and San Pedro Nolasco for the Mercedarians. Once the Jesuits reached New Spain in the 1570s, the names and images of Francisco Javier, Francisco de Borja, and Ignacio de Loyola became familiar. By far the favorite community patron saints during the colonial period were María, Juan, Miguel, Santiago, Francisco, and Pedro, while the most common baptismal names included María (with the addition of special advocations of the Blessed Mary such as María del Carmen and María del Rosario by the late seventeenth century), José/Joseph, Juan, Pablo, Antonio, Miguel, Santiago, Francisco, Pedro, Ana, Andrés, Nicolás, Sebastián, Bartolomé, Agustín, Lucas, and Mateo – again, for the most part figures from the New Testament or members of the evangelizing orders.[7] The appeal of the saints ran deeper than just the hope for personal and collective favors. Community devotions to the saints often revolved around *cofradías* and other confraternities.

Colonial records attest to a broad scattering of miracles associated with patron saints other than the Virgin Mary in particular places, sometimes said to be worked "by means of" their images – among them San Juan Bautista, San Homobono de Cremona, San Sebastián, San Nicolás Obispo, San Martín, San Rafael, San Juan de Dios, San Francisco, San Antonio de Padua, San Diego de Alcalá, San Pedro, Santa Bárbara, San Vicente Ferrer, San Dimas, and Santa Ana, to mention a few who are not discussed here.[8] Some of their wonders were duly noted throughout the seventeenth, eighteenth, and nineteenth centuries, but for the most part images of these and other saints were shooting stars of notoriety or focal points of localized devotions. Some saints who were popular in the colonial period are barely remembered now, including those associated with the old craft guilds, such as San Eloy for silversmiths, San Homobono for tailors, and Santa Cecilia for musicians and makers of musical instruments.[9] And towns might replace their patron saint with a new one, as Santiago Nuyoo in the Mixteca Alta region of Oaxaca did in 1873.[10]

Other canonized saints and folk saints have come into their own more recently, such as San Judas Tadeo, the patron saint of lost causes who is especially popular with outlaws, policemen, and the unemployed.[11] Still other contemporary devotions favor figures with little or no standing in the church, such as Jesús Malverde, Juan Soldado, and the Santa Muerte.[12] The Santa Muerte skeleton figure is more than a contemporary folk saint in Mexico, and more ambiguously so than Juan Soldado or Jesús Malverde. As in Spain, the skeleton figure has long had a place in the Easter liturgy, especially in Good Friday processions, representing human mortality and impending eternal judgment. Known as the Santa Muerte, "Angelina," or El Justo Juez ("The Just Judge"), these wooden skeleton figures could become cult objects in themselves, especially during epidemics.[13] In one early nineteenth-century case from the mining community of Real del Monte (in modern Hidalgo), an Angelina-Muerte figure was said to be the object of "gran afecto y deboción," offered candles, flowers, and incense during Semana Santa and appealed to for special favors in times of personal and collective crisis. Devotees were said to be mostly non-Indians. The Franciscan friar commissioned to undertake an extrajudicial investigation was reluctant to probe too deeply because his main informant, José Gregorio Pérez, said that there were many devotees, some even in Mexico City. This file also alludes to an earlier case of devotion to a Santa Muerte figure in "tierra adentro" – in the interior north.[14] The judges of the Inquisition contented themselves in this case with an order for the parish priest of Real del Monte to warn his parishioners from the pulpit not to make offerings of any kind to the skeleton and to adore only God and his saints.[15]

It is tempting to single out a particular saint as the most important one in early modern Spain and Mexico, and a case either has been or could be made for at least four of them: San José, Santiago, San Miguel, and San Juan Bautista.[16] But if the many saints, shrines, and images that attracted devotees and promoters in colonial Mexico are considered together rather than separately, no one saint overshadowed the others, except in particular places and situations. If a sweeping generalization is in order, it is that none of the saints approached the popularity of the versatile Blessed Mary. Some saints do seem more present than others in the faith and daily affairs of colonial Christians, but they rarely enjoyed the audience and staying power of the miracle shrines and images of Mary and Christ. They appealed for some purposes, but not others; some were common baptismal names, but not among the leading community saints; and they often joined other saints as local patrons and defenders.

San José, Santiago, and San Miguel

Mary's husband and Christ's foster father, San José, is an especially important, if elusive, saint in Mexico's devotional history. He was present in paintings, statues, personal devotional objects, religious literature, place names, and baptismal names almost everywhere, especially in the seventeenth and eighteenth centuries, for women as well as men of all social groups.[17] Altars were dedicated to him in many churches, and he was a patron saint and divine protector of more than one important city, often as a specialist against lightning strikes and storms.[18] In Mexico City, devotion to him was formally encouraged with plenary indulgences in thirteen churches and chapels on the nineteenth of every month.[19] And he was a patron of the early evangelization, a status evidenced by the dedication to him of the first Indian chapel in Mexico City to him (San José de los Naturales) and his designations as patron saint of the Archdiocese of Mexico and nominal patron saint of the viceroyalty.[20]

As Charlene Villaseñor Black and Gabriela Sánchez Reyes observe in their studies of Josephine imagery in early modern Spain and New Spain, Mary's consort gained new visibility and importance in the seventeenth and eighteenth centuries as "the Glorious Patriarch" of the Holy Family and model father.[21] He also had special standing as "refuge of the dying" (*refugio de agonizantes*). See Figure A3.2.

Promotion of Josephine devotion culminated in a wave of local coronations of the saint, in Puebla in 1788, and in the Bajío and Michoacán beginning in 1790, with the encouragement of Carmelites as well as royal authorities and bishops.[22] Rarely adopted as a baptismal name in the sixteenth century, José/Joseph became the second most common male Christian name – after Juan – in the Sagrario parish of Mexico City by 1640 and was the most popular baptismal name of all by 1700. By 1740, when the Holy Family enjoyed even greater popularity, José was by far the most popular name for boys and remained so in the nineteenth century. By then Josefa/Josepha was also the second most common girl's name, as well, albeit a distant second to María.[23] During the eighteenth century, San José was often depicted without the Blessed Mary, holding the hand of the Christ Child – a strapping young father rather than the tired old man relegated to the background of medieval paintings of the Holy Family.[24] And Francisco de Ajofrín, the Spanish Capuchin traveler in Mexico in the 1760s, observed that San José was "the Patron of the whole realm, and beloved by all the Indians," who never spoke his name without the honorific "señor" – Señor San José.[25]

Figure A3.1 San José with the Christ Child, on a globe held up by allegorical figures representing the four continents. Loose print collected by Francisco de Ajofrín in the 1760s. He has written on it "Patron of Mexico [City] and all of New Spain." Courtesy of the Real Academia de la Historia, Madrid.

Figure A3.2 This eighteenth-century devotional print of San José as Refuge of the Dying includes a prayer beseeching his aid in the tortuous journey toward eternal life. His presence at the deaths of Christ and the Virgin Mary is said to have established this role. Courtesy of the Getty Research Center.

But it is doubtful that Joseph's was "the central saint's cult of the early modern period" and that the Virgin Mary (other than as the Virgin of Guadalupe) was marginalized as an "untouchable icon of purity" after images of the Immaculate Conception became especially popular in the seventeenth century.[26] Mary's maternal love remained alive to the laity as well as frequently projected by preachers and authors of devotional histories of Mary Immaculate, the Assumption, the Madonna and Child, and the Mater Dolorosa throughout the colonial period; images of Mary Immaculate were associated with healing miracles; and María remained overwhelmingly the most popular baptismal name for girls of all social groups.[27] Furthermore, there were new devotions to the Madonna and Child in the eighteenth century that became widely known and celebrated, especially Nuestra Señora de la Luz, Nuestra Señora del Refugio, and La Divina Pastora. Even though Joseph was associated with protection and cures,[28] few of the many images of him had such widespread, magnetic appeal. One of the few was a statue of Joseph and the Christ Child in the Villa de Córdoba (Veracruz) that was first displayed in 1675 and became the principal patron of the community in 1685. Prints of this image from an engraving by José de Nava (1735–1817) circulated in the late eighteenth century.[29] Other miraculous images of San José include the ones located in the Santa Clara convent of the city of Querétaro and mentioned in its 1743 *relación geográfica*; in the convent church of San Bernardo, Mexico City, mentioned by Cayetano Cabrera y Quintero in his account of the great epidemic of 1737;[30] at Pachuca; and at San José Chiapa in the district of Nopalucan east of the city of Puebla between 1783 and 1809.[31]

To say that San José was patron saint of Mexico City – the viceregal capital and most populous New World city during the eighteenth century – or a provincial city is not as simple and straightforward as royal decrees or formal oaths at a particular time would make it seem. Patronage was rarely exclusive, whether in a humble village home or a metropolitan center. In effect, San José was first among equals in New Spain's metropolis. He shared billing as all-purpose divine protector there with at least eight other saints and venerables in the late eighteenth century: San Antonio Abad, the Blessed Felipe de Jesús, San Bernardo, San Nicolás, San Isidro, San Francisco Javier, Santa Teresa de Jesús, and San Hipólito, not to mention the shrine images of Remedios and Guadalupe. At other times, Santo Domingo, San Miguel Arcángel, and Santa Margarita were designated patron saints of the city for special purposes, such as protection from fires, earthquakes, storms, and lightning strikes.[32] San José was also named patron saint of the viceroyalty in the late seventeenth century and "patrón general de la provincia" by the Fourth Provincial Synod of prelates in 1771,[33] but, other than many new images and José/

Retrato de la Milagrosa Imagen de Sr. San JOSEPH, expuesta à la veneracion de la Iglesia, año de 1675. en la Villa de Cordova, y la Juró por su principal Patron el año de 1686.

Figure A3.3 Undated eighteenth-century print from engraving by "Nava" of the Villa de Córdoba's miraculous image of San José, published in José Antonio Rodríguez y Valero, *Oración evangélica del sacro triumpho de Jerusalen en la solemne dominica de palmas . . .*, Puebla: Colegio Real de San Ignacio, 1765. Courtesy of the Bancroft Library, University of California, Berkeley.

Josefina as the given name for boys and girls (both of these trends well underway before the late seventeenth century), these sweeping designations do not seem to have had much effect on popular devotion before the wave of local coronations of San José in the 1790s, any more than the designation of

Santa Rosa de Lima as Patrona General de las Américas in 1771 (to mark the centennial of her canonization) made her a towering devotional figure in New Spain thereafter.[34] And San José's popularity and patronage in a town or city was rarely fixed once and for all. He was Puebla's primary protector against storms before 1580, but by 1611 he had been displaced in that role by Santa Bárbara.[35]

San José as vigorous young father was promoted by imperial authorities in the late colonial period as a model of benevolent rule, and the coronation ceremonies for him in the 1790s were meant to add to the legitimacy of the Bourbon dynasty, but whether he was embraced wholeheartedly and preeminently by most colonial subjects is a question that cannot be answered by studying only the surviving pictorial representations or events and messages orchestrated by the state. If San José had become the leading saint for divine protection in New Spain, it is surprising that there were few miracle shrines associated with his images, comparatively few reports of miracles attributed to him, and few confraternities dedicated to him (fourteen recorded in the pastoral visit records of the Archdiocese of Mexico in the 1680s, 1717, the 1750s, 1766–1768, and 1774, compared to hundreds of confraternities dedicated to various advocations and images of the Virgin Mary and Christ).[36]

Santiago has been described similarly as "the most widespread devotion in Mexico after the Virgin of Guadalupe," and Mexico is said to be the country with the most churches dedicated to Santiago.[37] Both claims may be true but, again, they tell only part of the story. There is no doubt that arresting images of Santiago were common in New Spain, but, unlike San José, he was a compelling figure mainly to Indians and Spaniards, and his popularity seems to have declined toward the end of the colonial period. Almost always depicted as a warrior on a white horse with a sword raised in his right hand to vanquish the turbaned enemies arrayed beneath him, Santiago was a central figure in conquest iconography from the beginning. For early colonial Spaniards, he was a satisfying, providential symbol of militant Christianity's destiny to reconquer the Iberian Peninsula from Islam and extend their dominion overseas.[38] His exploits in the conquest were described by several sixteenth-century chroniclers and spread by the first generations of colonists and evangelizers. Santiago was also widely accepted then by Indians as a powerful force to be propitiated. Even in the late colonial period there were Spaniards in America who continued to herald Santiago as *Patrón de las Españas*, support confraternities in his honor, and sponsor sermons dedicated jointly to the king and the saint.[39] This was especially true of immigrants from Galicia in northwestern Spain, where the great pilgrimage shrine to Santiago and his relics was located. They founded a new *congregación* to him in Mexico City by royal cedula in 1741, formalized with the republication of their original seventeenth-century constitution in 1768.[40]

Because Santiago was so conspicuous in sixteenth-century American iconography and in long-lived devotional practices, such as the Dance of the Santiaguitos and the Moors and Christians pageants, he is often regarded as the permanent symbol of conquest and subjugation of native peoples to Spanish rule – "Santiago Mataindios." For example, the catalogue for the great 2006–2007 art exhibition, "The Arts in Latin America, 1492–1820," made the following comment in the caption for an unusual Mexican image of Santiago with Indians below his horse's hooves: "In the Americas he appeared again, siding with the Christian conquerors against the indigenous insurgents, newly minted as Saint James, killer of Indians."[41] And a few years earlier the authors of a book on Christian devotions in Mexican history assured readers, "the truth is that whenever Santiago appeared in Mexico, it was to conquer natives who fought against the Spaniards."[42] But some tantalizing documentation for Indian communities during the seventeenth and eighteenth centuries suggests that veneration of Santiago was neither so fixed nor so easily characterized and that Indian devotion to him could amount to more than propitiating the divine agent of their submission. Elsewhere I have suggested other, local meanings of Santiago for late colonial Indians of central and western Mexico.[43] These meanings were rooted not only in official Spanish cues about conquest and conversion but also in native understandings of animals as powerful benefactors as well as agents of havoc, and in adjustments to colonial rule that invited devotees to regard Santiago as the potential protector of all Christians. Even when he was not the community's patron saint, his protective power was being harnessed to local purposes, and native shamans invoked his aid in healing and conjuring rain.[44]

The literature about Santiago in New Spain has recently been enriched by Araceli Campos's and Louis Cardaillac's ambitious *Indios y cristianos: Cómo en México el Santiago español se hizo indio*. Their research strategy was to visit many places where images of Santiago are still venerated, study ex-voto paintings, collect oral accounts of personal miracles and local traditions, and consider the available secondary literature. The great virtue of their study is the breadth of geographical coverage and the conviction that generalizations should follow from comparative study of many places. Within their regional chapters they follow several features of the devotion, including the saint's horse, that lead to some comparisons across different regions in Mexico as well as with Spain. The armed frontier areas of Nueva Galicia in western Mexico emerge from this study as having the greatest number of images of the saint. The early chapters elaborate on and complicate the sixteenth-century narrative of Santiago as patron saint of conquest and draw attention to the role of priests, especially the various religious orders, in promoting the devotion. Franciscans were leading promoters, not only introducing images of Santiago but also contributing to the strength and longevity of the devotion in Yucatán, among other places, by establishing *gremios* to the saint – sodalities to him associated with a particular occupational or social group in the community.[45] The authors' main interest is "religiosidad indígena" and Indian agency. They eschew the *mataindios* line of interpretation in favor of its opposite – "indigenization" in which the saint was appropriated to native ends and means. The evidence for this is both allusive and elusive, but they conclude that the cult of saints, especially of Santiago and Mary, was "at the heart of indigenous religiosity."[46]

Santiago was a leading saint throughout the colonial period, and his images may well have conveyed a sense of divine presence more often than those of other saints. But this significance seems to have changed in the seventeenth century, and – with many local exceptions – he was less promoted by colonial authorities during the eighteenth century. From a symbol of military might and Spanish conquest in the sixteenth century, he became a local protector, more an independent, telluric force to be propitiated and embraced than a militant messenger of God. He remained an armed protector and avenger, but not just for Spanish conquerors and rulers. Whether or not Santiago was widely Indianized in the way Campos and Cardaillac suggest, he remained a local saint of great power in many places even in the eighteenth century, as he still is, a man of the pueblo dressed in *calzones* (homespun pants) and a straw hat, or a charro outfit, sometimes celebrated as much for the horse as for the rider.[47] But none of his images became the focal point of a major shrine or the magnet for a regional devotion.

San Miguel – the Archangel Michael – was the patron saint and protector of many communities in New Spain and another popular baptismal name.[48] Like Mary, Christ, and Joseph, he attracted followers from many social groups and places (although confraternities dedicated to him were most common in Indian communities), and he was associated with the single most renowned miracle site to a saint other than the Virgin Mary – the Santuario de San Miguel del Milagro near the town of Nativitas, Tlaxcala. Usually depicted as a winged warrior with his sword unsheathed, he was associated with the Virgin Mary as the supreme enemy of Satan in the Book of Revelation, vanquishing the dragon that menaced the pregnant woman of the crown of twelve stars and her unborn son.[49] Miguel Sánchez, whose 1649 book *Imagen de la Virgen María* became the key text for the apparitions of the Virgin of Guadalupe to Juan Diego, identified the cherub beneath Guadalupe's feet as San Miguel, and some later depictions of the Guadalupana image replaced the cherub with the archangel in his classic martial pose.[50] Printed sermons also connected San Miguel and Guadalupe;[51] Indian shamans in the Valley of Toluca reportedly appealed to him in particular to lend his strength to their prayers for rain and healing;[52] and chapels and confraternities dedicated to him were common in communities of the Diocese of Puebla and beyond.[53] In the case of San Miguel de las Tetillas (modern Villa Progreso, in the municipio de Zimapán, Hidalgo, about 45 miles east of the city of Querétaro), the founding of the town by viceregal land grant in 1676 followed an apparition of San Miguel to a muleteer at a spring near a prominent hill, the Cerro Grande, instructing the man to have the people build him a temple there.[54]

Among Old World Christians, San Miguel also had long been celebrated as a healing angel, associated with wondrous medicinal springs that appeared out of nowhere in barren, rocky places. The "Miracle of the Archangel Michael at Chonae" in which the saint appeared in the fourth century to the people of Colossae (an ancient city in Phrygia near modern Honaz, Turkey) and split a rock with a lightning bolt to divert life-giving water to the city is the most famous and perhaps the earliest. Hot springs elsewhere in Asia Minor were also dedicated to him. According to tradition, the archangel appeared for the first time in Western Europe a century later to take on the role of warrior-protector foretold in the *Book of Daniel* 12:1. This apparition story, as related in the thirteenth-century *Golden Legend,* tells of a rich man from the town of Sipontus in southeast Italy around 490 searching on Mount Gargano for his lost bull. Finding the animal at the entrance to a cave, he "aimed a poison arrow at him, but at once as if blown by the wind, the arrow returned and struck down him who had shot it."[55] Townsfolk hurried to the bishop for his advice. The bishop understood this to be a miraculous sign and ordered three days of prayer and penance. On the third day, the archangel appeared, pronounced himself the protector of the cave, and asked the bishop to honor him at that place. The bishop demurred, worried that drawing attention to the cave would rekindle pagan worship at the site. The archangel appeared to the bishop again when Sipontum was besieged by pagan armies and promised to do battle with the enemy and protect the city. In gratitude, the bishop consecrated the cave to St. Michael as protector of the province and had a shrine built on the site. The Golden Legend also recounted four later apparitions of the archangel and four "victories" that cemented his credentials as Christ's standardbearer, warrior against the devil, and protector and healer, especially in epidemics.[56]

The celebrated shrine to San Miguel in Tlaxcala, with its story of the archangel's appearance to a local Indian, Diego Lázaro, and a healing spring revealed to the seer by a bolt of lightning, effectively Mexicanized this saint's association with both healing springs and protection against Satan. As Francisco de Florencia would note near the end of the seventeenth century, San Miguel healed the sick with water from his well and chose this particular place in order to aid and encourage the Tlaxcalans, those indispensable allies of the Spanish crown in winning "this whole kingdom to the faith and obedience of the King of Kings."[57]

Tlaxcala's San Miguel del Milagro was part of the first wave of miracle shrines that were formally recognized with episcopal and audiencia encouragement through devotional texts, inquests, and construction projects during the seventeenth century. An early *información jurídica* apparently was undertaken by a canon of the Puebla cathedral soon after the celebrated apparition of the archangel in 1631, when Franciscans were the pastors there,[58] but Bishop Juan de Palafox y Mendoza was the essential early advocate. In 1643, he ordered another formal investigation into the apparition and reports of healing miracles and authorized Lic. Pedro Salmerón to compose a narrative account of the founding apparition.[59] After his visit to the site on July 18, 1644, Palafox ordered construction of a suitable temple and maintenance of the sacred spring discovered by the saint, and the audiencia supported the project by authorizing regular labor service at the shrine by Tlaxcalan Indians.[60] A third investigation into the origins of the devotion and reported miracles was conducted in 1675 to conform more fully to proper notarial form and the practices of the Roman Curia.[61] Then, in 1692, a full-fledged devotional history by Francisco de Florencia, the prolific Jesuit creole chronicler of miraculous images and shrines in New Spain, was published in Seville (*Narración de la maravillosa aparición, que hizo el archángel San Miguel a Diego Lázaro de San Francisco*). It highlighted the continuing succession of individual miracles that occurred after the first inquest.[62]

According to Florencia, by the time his devotional history was published in 1692 the shrine and apparition of San Miguel del Milagro were widely known and celebrated throughout the Diocese of Puebla, above all in the provincial capital of Puebla. In one of his sweeping generalizations about popular devotion, Florencia claimed that "there is hardly a home or Indian family chapel that lacks an image of San Miguel," and the same was true of "Spanish homes, whether of the rich or poor," and "there is not a church or chapel in the whole diocese without one or many images of this sainted archangel."[63] Other centers of devotion to San Miguel del Milagro included the city of Tlaxcala, Texmelucan, Huejotzingo, Tepeaca, Atlixco, and Nativitas. And the devotion extended beyond the Diocese of Puebla, with cofradías and altars in the cathedral of Mexico, the Encarnación convent in the capital, and the Jesuit Colegio de San Pedro y San Pablo there. In 1752, collections of alms for the Tlaxcalan shrine even were granted to a village dedicated to the saint in Querétaro, San Miguel de Guimilpa; and testators in Mexico City left bequests to the shrine.[64] Water from the spring was collected and distributed to various parts of New Spain as early as the 1640s, and

Salmerón assured his readers that a priest devotee in Mexico City at that time kept a supply on hand for sick communicants.[65] The soil at the spring also was coveted for its healing properties. If we can believe Florencia and Salmerón, little cakes and "pills" molded from it and stamped with the archangel's image circulated from the 1640s to Sevilla and throughout New Spain, including Guatemala.[66]

The accounts of miracles and the spiritual geography of this shrine cross ethnic lines and places,[67] but, with Bishop Palafox's encouragement, it apparently began as a special place of divine immanence for Tlaxcalan Indians. Not only was the seer, Domingo Lázaro, a local Tlaxcalan, but the shrine and the miracle of the spring were situated only a mile or so east of Xochitécatl, a large ceremonial site dating back more than a thousand years, dedicated to female divinity and fertility, that served the ancient city of Cacaxtla. Mari Carmen Serra Puche and John B. Carlson posit a connection between Xochitécatl as a place of female divinity and the nearby colonial shrine of San Miguel through the archangel's role as protector of the Virgin Mary. They point to the fact that each year on September 28 – the day before the annual feast of San Miguel at the colonial shrine – the sun, as seen from the Pyramid of the Flowers at Xochitécatl, rises through the mouth of the female profile outlined on the summit of La Malinche mountain.[68]

Celebrated Saints of the Orders and a Homegrown Saint-in-the-Making

Other saints especially celebrated for their favors and protection in New Spain were San Antonio de Padua, San Nicolás de Tolentino, and San Francisco Javier. Each of them was a favorite of one of the religious orders active in evangelization and pastoral care during the colonial period.[69]

San Antonio de Padua's reputation for his "extraordinary gift of miracles"[70] was well established before the colonization of America, as Titian's 1511 frescoes *Scenes from the Life of St. Anthony of Padua* in the Scuola del Santo, Padua, Italy, attest. This Portuguese Franciscan, contemporary of St. Francis, usually was depicted with the infant Jesus in his arms, an allusion to an apparition of Christ experienced by the saint. Known as "the greatest thaumaturgist," he had a reputation for healing the sick and lame. Images of San Antonio de Padua were common in Mexican churches, especially those founded by the Franciscans, and an unusual number of them were called miraculous ("milagrosas") in colonial sources. San Antonio de Padua seems to have been universally popular in central and southern Mexico, although the cofradías to him tended to be concentrated in Indian communities. Fr. Agustín de Vetancurt, the late seventeenth-century Franciscan chronicler of the central Mexico Province of the Holy

Gospel, described two images of San Antonio de Padua in Mexico City's great Franciscan convent as famously miraculous, as well as the image known as San Antonio el Pobre in the Indian chapel to San Antonio at Tlatelolco.[71] During the eighteenth century, other numinous images of San Antonio de Padua made news as wonder workers in far-flung places, including Acapulco in 1729, where a statue of San Antonio reportedly perspired; Ixtepeji, Oaxaca in 1794; and the Villa del Dulce Nombre de Jesús de Rioverde, San Luis Potosí, in 1797.[72] At Ixtepeji, a Zapotec girl, Anastasia de Paz, escaped certain death by invoking the saint's name when she fell into a turbulent river and was swept over a waterfall. At Rioverde, local devotees secured a license to collect alms to rebuild a chapel to their San Antonio, a statue reported to be "amazing in its miracles" ("portentosa en sus milagros"). And at Tultitlán (at the northern tip of the Distrito Federal) in 1774, a celebrated statue of the saint was accompanied by eight paintings of miracles he had worked.[73] Perhaps the most renowned of the miracle-working images of San Antonio was the statue in Calpulalpan, Tlaxcala. Inexpensive prints depicting this one circulated during the nineteenth century, if not before, and it made headlines during the Independence War when Tlaxcalan soldiers seized the statue following a royalist assault on the town in 1812. Elders of Calpulalpan quickly appealed to the viceroy for the return of their priceless protector, and he complied.[74]

San Nicolás de Tolentino (canonized in 1466) is said to have been of limited importance worldwide, but he became a favorite divine protector in New Spain. At least initially, the prominence of this saint depended on the Augustinian order's evangelizing ministry. Himself a late thirteenth-century Augustinian from Sant'Angelo in Pontano near Ancona, Italy, Nicolás claimed that angels visited him in a dream a few years after his ordination. He followed their instructions to go minister in Tolentino in the nearby province of Macerata, and there he became famous for healings and more visions, especially of souls in purgatory who beseeched him for prayers on their behalf. He reported another vision in which the Virgin Mary, St. Anne, and St. Monica came to him during an illness and recommended a certain type of bread dipped in water. He followed their instructions, ate the bread, recovered, and began to distribute rolls of this kind as medicine for the sick. (In Spain and America, they were known as *panecitos de San Nicolás*.[75]) His reputation as a healer of the sick is amply documented in personal testimonials and penitential processions from the colonial period.[76] And his fame for worldly favors reached further, with some local twists. As the Nahua chronicler Chimalpahin observed, after a Spanish woman and her children, buried in the rubble of an earthquake in Mexico City in 1611, called upon San Nicolás for protection and they miraculously survived, he became a general patron of the city's residents.

Later he gained fame particularly for extinguishing raging fires, apparently transferring his association with protecting souls from the flames of purgatory to the world of the living.[77]

San Nicolás is mentioned early and often in the colonial record, perhaps first as patron of the Augustinian monastery-church pastoral complex at Actopan, Hidalgo (founded in 1546). He was the patron saint of many towns and villages, including an eponymous town in San Luis Potosí founded in 1614, and his statues appear in colonial church inventories, not only where Augustinians had ministered. Above all, he was a favorite saint of confraternities dedicated to the relief of souls in purgatory.[78] Even when they were not dedicated to him, these confraternities drew him in as a favorite intercessor.[79] Chimalpahin's Nahuatl annals from 1611 recount that "the cofradía dedicated to the Souls of Purgatory, where people are purified by fire, organized this procession. And as they went in procession they brought out San Nicolás Tolentino so that it would be seen that he is the helper of the said souls; he redeems them from the said purgatory by order of our lord God."[80]

San Nicolás de Tolentino was also a favorite patron of black and mulatto cofradías and settlements.[81] One *afromestizo* area on the Costa Chica of Guerrero has long been linked to the upland Indian pueblo of Zitlalá some 200 miles away on the old road from Puebla to Acapulco by their mutual devotion to San Nicolás and a particular image of him. Zitlalá's version of the connection dates from the mid-eighteenth century, if not earlier. It recounts how black devotees of the saint from coastal farms went to the city of Puebla to collect a statue of San Nicolás that they had commissioned from an Augustinian sculptor there. When they reached the town of Zitlalá on their way home with the statue, it became too heavy to move. After several failed attempts to move the statue, they decided to leave it with the Indians of Zitlalá and promised to visit him every year and enter the church on their knees. These eighteenth-century accounts speak of many miracles associated with this image.[82] The story told to Laura Lewis in the 1990s by people of the coastal community of San Nicolás de Tolentino emphasizes that the miraculous image was "born" in their village, not in Puebla, and that it was taken from them long ago. They now have another, whiter image of San Nicolás in their church that they say is "not from here."[83] A delegation of devotees from the coast usually goes to Zitlalá at the end of the annual festival cycle to the saint there,[84] but the people of San Nicolás say that the original image returns home to visit them on his saint's day and that on that day the doors of the Zitlalá church won't open. He returns to Zitlalá at nightfall with sandy feet, Lewis was told. Bound by their differences, the two towns remain devoted to San Nicolás de Tolentino through their miraculous statue of the saint.[85]

Among the male orders in New Spain, the Dominicans and Mercedarians seem to have been less devoted than others to miracle-working saints and their images, beyond their special associations with an advocation of the Blessed Mary – Our Lady of the Rosary for the Dominicans, Our Lady of Mercy for the Mercedarians. As the Order of the Blessed Virgin Mary of Mercy, the Mercedarians were prominent Marian devotees, and they regarded Mary as their founder. Two favorite thirteenth-century Spanish saints of the order – the earthly founder San Pedro Nolasco (to whom Mary appeared with instructions to establish an order committed to the redemption of captives), and his student San Raymundo Nonato ("not born," because he was recovered from his dead mother's womb) – were known in New Spain, and their images occasionally appear in church inventories, but they were less popular among the laity than San Antonio de Padua or San Nicolás de Tolentino, in part because (except perhaps in Guatemala) the Mercedarians were not in a position to promote them in the ways central and southern Mexico's pastoral orders could.

As active pastors, especially in Oaxaca and Chiapas, the Dominicans were in a better position to promote saints of their order as healers and protectors, but they were less inclined to do so than the Franciscans, Augustinians, and Jesuits. Santo Domingo, the order's Spanish founder, was a familiar figure in colonial churches, but no image of him became the focal point of a great healing shrine. San Vicente Ferrer (1350–1419; canonized in 1455), a famous Spanish missionary and preacher of penance, would have been an attractive candidate because of his miraculous recovery from a grave illness after Christ, St. Dominic, and St. Francis appeared to him, and he was known to have worked healing miracles in Spain; but, again, no images of him became widely known in New Spain for their association with wondrous favors. Other famous Dominican saints – San Raymundo de Peñafort and Santa Catarina de Sena – were better known for their writings and erudition than for worldly wonders. Santa Rosa de Lima, the first American saint, who became a Dominican tertiary at twenty years of age, was well known in Mexico in the late seventeenth and early eighteenth centuries, and statues and paintings of her were popular objects of devotion, but, again, none became the "sweet magnet" of a regional shrine.

Dominican saints may have been less renowned as miracle workers than others, but this is not to say they went unnoticed. News of a beautiful painting of St. Dominic brought to the Dominican convent church of Calabria, south of Naples, in 1510 by the Virgin Mary, Mary Magdalene, and St. Catherine of Siena became part of the devotional history of New Spain, as well. The first Dominican convent in Oaxaca was dedicated to this image, known as Santo Domingo en Soriano, in 1529, and painted copies were displayed in other Dominican churches, such as the altarpiece of the Virgen del Camino in the Dominican church in Mexico City and in Zacatecas. Around 1640 an alcalde mayor in the Sierra de Juárez of Oaxaca, a devotee of Santo Domingo en Soriano, founded a chapel, cemetery, and endowment to the devotion in his district seat of Villa Alta. It eventually lost favor, only to be revived by another district governor in the 1780s with the help of the bishop of Oaxaca and the parish priest.[86] But, again, no particular shrine or image of Santo Domingo en Soriano seems to have attracted a wider constituency.[87] Members of the order in the early nineteenth century encouraged public devotion to Gonzalo de Amarante, OP, who was beatified in 1560.[88] Whether mainly responding to a growing devotion to San Gonzalo or promoting it, three printings of a novena booklet dedicated to him, sponsored by an anonymous devotee, were published in 1816,[89] and devotees of the saint in the great Dominican church in Mexico City were noticed that year mainly for dancing in front of an image of the saint, a tradition inspired by the story of his homecoming after a great pilgrimage. Officials of the cathedral chapter took a dim view of "such an exotic and extravagant devotion" and banned the practice in 1816.

The most popular Jesuit saint, celebrated in paintings, statues, and miracle stories, was Francisco Javier (Francis Xavier), cofounder of the order in the sixteenth century. He was also known as "the apostle of the Indies," having served as a missionary in Portuguese Asia, especially India.[90] Francisco Javier's fame was perhaps greatest in the areas of northern Mexico missionized by the Jesuits, judging by their seventeenth- and eighteenth-century chronicles. Writing after 1669, Francisco Javier Alegre, SJ, praised this saint's patronage in Nueva Vizcaya (in northern Mexico), especially for his role in defeating the hostile Tobosos and Cabezas people and for working "almost miraculous cures," including the uneventful birth of a surprisingly healthy child to an older elite Spanish couple who had been unable to conceive until the wife appealed to San Francisco Javier.[91] This saint was famous also in Mexico City for an array of marvelous interventions, beginning with the survival of a young nobleman who was attacked and nearly killed by a rival in the 1670s.[92] Sometime before 1725 a painting of the saint in the Jesuits' Mexico City Colegio de San Ildefonso reportedly perspired and turned pale, manifestations later taken to be a premonition of the imminent martyrdom of Father Diego Luis de Sanvitores in the Mariana Islands.[93] Another image of Francisco Javier, in the Mexico City parish of Santa Veracruz, was reputed to be a "miracle-worker and almost miraculous in its form," changing expression from sad to happy and pallid to rosy according to the circumstances. During a procession in a downpour in 1659 only this statue escaped a drenching. And in keeping with Francisco Javier's reputation as a special advocate in epidemics, it was processed again in 1737 in hopes of abating the sickness that was spreading in the city that year.[94] He was also reported to be a helping saint in other places, including Choapa in the district of Villa Alta, Oaxaca, where in 1668 the entire community invoked his protection in an epidemic and was spared. In thanks, parishioners built a chapel and altarpiece to him.[95]

One early eighteenth-century chapel to San Francisco Javier that has flourished in an unusual way since the 1830s is located at Magdalena de Kino, Sonora.[96] Dedicated in 1711 by the pioneer Jesuit missionary of the Pimería Alta, Eusebio Kino, SJ, to his personal patron saint, the chapel and its statue of Francisco Javier became part of the Franciscan mission system after the expulsion of the Jesuits from Spanish America in 1767. Until at least 1832 the annual fiesta took place on this saint's day, December 3. Later in the nineteenth century, perhaps before Franciscans left the region in 1843, the feast day was changed to October 4, the day of San Francisco de Asís. As Magdalena de Kino became an important regional pilgrimage site during the second quarter of the nineteenth century – drawing devotees from the vicinity, from the north into southern Arizona, and as far away as Guadalajara to the south and the Sierra Madre Occidental to the east – the beloved, wonder-working recumbent statue has come to combine aspects of both Francisco Javier and Francisco de Asís and also of the saintly missionary Kino, who is buried there. The figure is known simply as "San Francisco."

New Spain did not have a native-born canonized saint, but Felipe de Jesús, a creole Spaniard from Mexico City and one of the martyrs of Nagasaki in 1597, was beatified in 1627. In a way, Felipe de Jesús became more than another martyr saint-in-waiting associated with the Franciscans. Viceroys and archbishops of Mexico encouraged his cause, especially during the late eighteenth century, and the devotion to him became closely connected to Mexico City.[97] His popularity was never widespread or very intense, even after a royal cedula of 1689 directed all tribunals in the viceroyalty to celebrate his feast and honor him "as a Mexicano" (with a possible double reference to both the capital city – Mexico – and its high court jurisdiction, covering much of central Mexico); a special liturgical office was granted by the pope in 1779; and he was eventually canonized (in 1862). Although a striking wooden statue of Felipe de Jesús with a spear protruding from both shoulders is well known to art historians and was a familiar processional figure in Mexico City, no particular image of him became a focal point of devotion or was widely acclaimed for miracles, and his devotees rarely reached much beyond imperial officials and creoles in the capital, where as early as 1629 a solemn procession and feast attended by members of the city council and judges of the audiencia and other tribunals was celebrated every February 5.[98] When the viceroy and archbishop in 1797 called for donations to launch a new campaign in Rome to complete Felipe de Jesús's elevation to sainthood, the response was disappointing except from parishes in Mexico City and the Indian town council of Tlaxcala, where the collections were punctual and substantial. District officials elsewhere in the viceroyalty reported grudging and meager donations, even in San Luis Potosí, where the intendant was an enthusiastic promoter, exhorting his *subdelegados* to call upon wealthy miners, merchants, and landlords for contributions and to encourage the parish priests to collect what they could from their congregations.[99] Lasting enthusiasm for the Blessed Felipe de Jesús proved hard to sustain even among members of the *ayuntamiento* in Mexico City. In 1815, one of the cathedral dignitaries appealed to the city councilors to participate in the annual celebration and procession. That year apparently only a few agreed to march.[100]

European Catholic reforms before and after the Protestant Reformation both encouraged and constrained the cult of saints. In retrospect, the constraints did not much dampen devotion to the saints in the New World, even in the sixteenth century, except to focus more attention on the universal saints of the New Testament and some canonized heroes of the missionary orders. Authenticated relics of saints' remains were also destined to be less prominent in popular devotion to saints in America than they were in Europe, in part because relics of the leading saints were rarely available in America, and there were few officially recognized local saints and venerables. Other than Santa Rosa de Lima, they did not attract a panregional following that included New Spain; and Mexico's one prospective saint from the colonial period, Felipe de Jesús, had limited appeal despite active promotion by authorities in Mexico City and images of him found in churches elsewhere.

Paintings, statues, or prints were often available nearby for most of the favored saints, who might make their presence felt in association with or "by means of" (*por medio de*) those images. But the cult of saints other than the Blessed Mary was less about particular images than about the saint's reputation for presence in a place – in a foundational dream vision or apparition like San Miguel del Milagro, and in special favors known to local devotees. Few of the stories of apparitions and supernatural cures and rescues for these other saints circulated widely to regional audiences (San Miguel del Milagro since the mid-seventeenth century, the dual San Francisco at Magdalena de Kino in the nineteenth and twentieth centuries, and La Santa Muerte more recently being outstanding exceptions). In all the places of the saints, devotion to them offered ample room for what Aviad Kleinberg calls "creative consumption." While saints of the New Testament and the religious orders were the most familiar, more obscure divine patrons also found their way into the homes and prayers of colonial Christians, whether the images were American made or imported, and all of them could take on distinctive meanings, shaping and shaped by local circumstances, reinforcing and sometimes bridging different occupational and ethnic groups.

Notes

1. Villa de Carrión (Atlixco, Puebla), settled by Spanish farmers in the late 1570s, adopted San Félix Papa as its patron saint in 1580 after entreaties to him were followed by a wheat crop free of the worm infestations and storm damage of earlier years. A formal inquiry into the miracles of San Félix Papa was undertaken by the town council's *escribano* in 1614. Witnesses testified to the 1580 events, including how this saint came to be their patron in the first place. They spoke of a child chosen to pick a slip of paper with a saint's name written on it from a bowl filled with such slips repeatedly picking the one with "San Félix Papa" written on it. Witnesses also testified to bumper crops in the years since San Félix Papa was chosen. An eighteenth-century copy of the 1614 *información*, edited by Pedro Angel Palou, was recently published as *San Félix Papa: Patrono espiritual de la Villa de Atlixco*, Puebla: Edit. Nuestra República, 1997. The events of 1580 were recounted in a 1792 report in words that repeat this información, Lourdes M. Romero Navarrete and Felipe I. Echenique March, eds., *Relaciones geográficas de 1792*, Mexico: INAH, 1995, p. 123.

   Still, Villa de Carrión townspeople looked to other saints, as well. For example, its fine chapel to San Miguel Arcángel is mentioned by Francisco de Florencia, *Narración de la maravillosa aparición, que hizo el archangel San Miguel a Diego Lázaro de San Francisco . . .*, Sevilla: Impr. de las Siete Revueltas, 1692, p. 163.

2. James Lockhart, *The Nahuas after the Conquest: A Social and Cultural History of the Indians of Central Mexico, Sixteenth through Eighteenth Centuries*, Stanford: Stanford University Press, 1992, pp. 243–244.

3. On the popularity of martyred saints and vogue of paintings of virgin martyrs in seventeenth-century Spain, see Cécile Vincent-Cassy, *Les saintes vierges et martyres dans l'Espagne du XVIIe siècle: Culte et image*, Madrid: Casa de Velásquez, 2011.

4. There were eleven canonizations and eighteen beatifications between 1588 and 1665.

5. In an essay about San Julián of Cuenca as a case of such a revival of devotion to a local saint in the sixteenth century, Sarah Nalle offers other Spanish examples, including San Segundo of Ávila, San Frutos of Segovia, San Froylan of León, San Isidro Labrador of Madrid, and Santa Leocadia of Toledo. Nalle suggests that devotion to San Julián in Cuenca was barely apparent during the reform period even though local priests promoted it but that after 1591 it gained great popularity and spread to neighboring dioceses, with the support of canons of Cuenca's cathedral, the city fathers, and the poor and sick, Nalle, "A Saint for All Seasons: The Cult of San Julián," in *Culture and Control in Counter-Reformation Spain*, ed. Anne J. Cruz and Mary Elizabeth Perry, Minneapolis: University of Minnesota Press, 1991, pp. 25–50.

   In his study of the cult of saints in Naples during the sixteenth and seventeenth centuries, Jean-Michel Sallmann posits an "extraordinary" growth in the popularity and promotion of the saints during the seventeenth century and develops this hypothesis in

rich detail, *Naples et ses saints à l'âge baroque, 1540–1750*, Paris: Presses Universitaires de France, 1994, *passim* and p. 371. One can describe a similar "golden age" in seventeenth-century New Spain without denying the place of saints in sixteenth-century devotional practices or its limitations later.
6. On early enthusiasm for Marian devotion among Franciscans and other leading evangelizers, see Ernesto de la Torre Villar, "El culto mariano en la catequesis novohispana del siglo XVI," *Anuario de Historia de la Iglesia* 3 (1994), 233–243.
7. The list of baptismal names is based on the index in Dorothy Tanck de Estrada and others, *Atlas ilustrado de los pueblos de indios: Nueva España, 1800*, Mexico: El Colegio de México, 2005 and my earlier work with baptismal records. On favorite saints' names for communities in Oaxaca, see Enrique Marroquín, *La cruz mesiánica: Una aproximación al sincretismo católico indígena*, Oaxaca: Universidad Autónoma "Benito Juárez," 1989, p. 78.
8. Miracles associated with images of these saints are mentioned in Cayetano Cabrera y Quintero, *Escudo de armas de Mexico: Celestial protección de esta nobilíssima ciudad, de la Nueva España, y de casi todo el Nuevo Mundo* . . ., Mexico: Vda. de Joseph Bernardo de Hogal, 1746, pp.174, 177, 260 (San Sebastián, Santa Clara, San Vicente Ferrer); Antonio de Robles, *Diario de sucesos notables (1665–1703)*, Mexico: Porrúa, 1946, III, 54 (San Sebastián); untitled volume of manuscript Mexican sermons, post 1763, in the University of Dayton Marian Library, fols. 102–107 (Santa Margarita); *Gazeta de México,* issue for February 1722, BIBM 5, p. 958 (San Pedro, Puebla cathedral); BNM fondos reservados MS357 (manuscript novena for San Homobono, "Vida y milagros de este santo"); Antonio de Alcedo (1735–1812), *Diccionario geográfico de las Indias Occidentales o América*, Madrid: Atlas, 1967, IV, 193 (San Juan Bautista of Yecapixtla); Francisco de Ajofrín, *Diario del viaje*, Madrid: Real Academia de la Historia, 1958–1959, II, 118 (San Dimas, convent church of the Augustinians, Mexico City; San Francisco del Milagro in the Franciscan convent in Puebla, which was reputed to have changed posture and saved the building in an earthquake); *La estampa religiosa popular mexicana, siglos XVIII y XIX*, Mexico: Claustro de Sor Juana, 1981, unnumbered page with *estampa* of San Pablo "que se venera en el Convento de San Gerónimo"; Luis Weckmann, *The Medieval Heritage of Mexico*, trans. Frances M. López-Morillas, New York: Fordham University Press, 1992, p. 292 (San Diego de Alcalá of Tekax, Yucatán); *Relaciones geográficas del Arzobispado de México. 1743*, ed. Francisco de Solano, Madrid: C.S.I.C., 1988, I, 198, 56, 147, 254, 266; II, 306, 466 (San Nicolás Obispo at Malinalco, San Vicente Ferrer in the Dominican church of Querétaro, San Antonio in the church of the discalced Franciscans at Querétaro, and Santa Ana at Amatepec); Francisco Antonio Navarrete, SJ, *Relación peregrina de la agua corriente, que para beber, y vivir goza la muy noble, leal, y florida ciudad de Santiago de Querétaro* . . ., Mexico: José Bernardo de Hogal, 1739, p. 18 (images of San Francisco and San Antonio de Padua in the Franciscan Recollect convent church); and *Gazeta de México* for 1786, issue #10, and 1787, issue #37 (images of San Rafael and San Juan de Dios in Pachuca). For an especially satisfying introduction to San Vicente Ferrer in Spanish America as well as early modern Europe, especially in the Dominicans' province of San Hipólito Mártir (Oaxaca), see Laura Ackerman Smoller, *The Saint and the Chopped-Up Baby: The Cult of Vincent Ferrer in Medieval and Early Modern Europe*, Ithaca and London: Cornell University Press, 2014, pp. 274–297.

A few postcolonial shrines to other saints celebrated for their healing wonders are mentioned in *La Ruta de los santuarios en México*, Mexico: Secretaría de Turismo, 1994, appendix following p. 187: San Francisco Javier Biaundó, San Pascualito, San Caralampio, San Judas Tadeo, San Juan Bosco, Sebastián de Aparicio, and San Juanito. A well-documented devotion of this kind at its beginning is recorded for San Caralampio among *ladinos* of Comitán, Chiapas, in the 1850s. Caralampio is still regarded as "el santo más milagroso" there, Carlos Navarrete, ed., *Documentos para la historia del culto a San Caralampio, Comitán, Chiapas*, Tuxtla Gutiérrez: Gobierno del Estado de Chiapas, 1990. According to Alicia Barabás, "Los santuarios de vírgenes y santos aparecidos en Oaxaca," *Cuicuilco*, no. 36 (enero–abril 2006), p. 237, San Pedro reportedly appeared at Quiatoni, Oaxaca, in the twentieth century.

9. These three artisans' saints are identified by Mariano Monterrosa Prado and Leticia Talavera Solórzano, *Las devociones cristianas y México en el cambio del milenio*, Mexico: Plaza y Valdés/CONACULTA/INAH, 2002, pp. 44, 56, 58–61.

10. John Monaghan, *The Covenants with Earth and Rain: Exchange, Sacrifice, and Revelation in Mixtec Sociality*, Norman: University of Oklahoma Press, 1995 discusses the change in patron saint from Santiago to La Misericordia, a crucifix that appeared mysteriously at the church door in 1873. Barabás mentions that in Oaxaca other "'appeared' saints became the new patron saints and have taken over the role of founder and protector of the pueblo they have chosen and its surrounding territory," "Los santuarios de vírgenes," p. 231.

11. Mary Jordan, "'Outlaws' Patron Is Popular with Police, Too," *Washington Post*, November 29, 2002; and Victor Campa Mendoza, *Santuarios y milagros*, Mexico: CONACYT, 2002, pp. 331–360.

12. Paul J. Vanderwood, *Juan Soldado: Rapist, Murderer, Martyr, Saint*, Durham: Duke University Press, 2004; J. Katia Perdigón Castañeda, *La Santa Muerte, protectora de los hombres*, Mexico: INAH, 2008. For a present-oriented treatment in English, R. Andrew Chestnut, *Devoted to Death: Santa Muerte, the Skeleton Saint*, Oxford, NY: Oxford University Press, 2012.

13. Perdigón, *La Santa Muerte*, pp. 31–32, includes two passing references in colonial sources for seventeenth-century Guatemala and the Archdiocese of Mexico in 1754 to skeleton figures as objects of devotion. The recent surge in interest in the Santa Muerte builds on an older, if less flamboyant, base of popularity in rural Mexico. See, for example, the devotional leaflets collected by Guido Munch Galindo for his ethnographic study of southern Veracruz published in 1983, *Etnología del istmo veracruzano*, Mexico: UNAM, 1983. Following page 127, Munch includes photographs of various leaflets of prayers and prints to a particular saint that were used for exorcisms and curing ceremonies. Several depict the Santa Muerte. One is called "El secreto de la Santa Muerte."

14. This mention of an earlier incident with a Santa Muerte figure may refer to one or both of the following occasions to document the practice: a denunciation to the Inquisition in 1793 by the Franciscan pastor of Amoles, Querétaro, against local Indians placing "an idol named the just judge, in the form of the full-length skeleton . . . carrying a bow and arrow in its hands" on the altar before Mass; and a 1797 report on superstitions among Indians of San Luis de la Paz, Guanajuato, that mentions a practice of whipping crosses and "a figure of death that they call Santa Muerte," menacing it with the whip if

it did not perform a miracle, Perdigón, *La Santa Muerte*, pp. 33–34, summarizing records from AGN Inquisición and the Casa de Morelos in Morelia.
15. This would have been one of the last cases of any kind brought before the Mexican Inquisition, LC, Monday Collection, container 17 (microfilm reel 13), "Real del Monte, 1819. Expediente formado con motivo de haberse denunciado que en el Rl del Monte tenían gran afecto y debocíon a un esqueleto de madera que comunmente se llama Muerte y en dho Rl le nombran Angelina."
16. For San José, see Charlene Villaseñor Black, *Creating the Cult of St. Joseph: Art and Gender in the Spanish Empire*, Princeton: Princeton University Press, 2006; for Santiago, Araceli Campos and Louis Cardaillac, *Indios y cristianos: Cómo en México el Santiago español se hizo indio*, Mexico: El Colegio de Jalisco/UNAM/Editorial Itaca, 2007, and Rafael Heliodoro Valle, *Santiago en América*, Mexico: Editorial Santiago, 1946; and for San Miguel, Florencia, *Narración*, p. 163. San Juan Bautista and San Juan Evangelista have yet to find their New World historian, but "Juan" was an especially common baptismal name, and images of these two most celebrated Juans were to be found in many colonial churches.
17. For a sense of the many devotional publications dedicated to San José, especially during the eighteenth century, see José Toribio Medina, *La imprenta en México (1539–1821)*, facsimile edition, 8 vols., Mexico: UNAM, 1989–1990; WorldCat; or the online catalogues of the great libraries of early printed matter in Latin America such as the John Carter Brown Library, the Lilly Library of Indiana University, and the Bancroft Library of the University of California at Berkeley. Evidence of devotion to San José appears often in administrative and judicial records as well as in the discourse of colonial authorities. For example, an investigation of *afromestizo* residents of a rancho in the jurisdiction of El Venado, San Luis Potosí, in 1774 revealed that women there were devotees of "el Patriarca San José" and performed a rosary procession in his honor on the nineteenth of every month, UND Inquisition document 123. And traces of devotion to him sometimes are found in the material record. The Sutro Library's copy of the 1843 printing of José Manuel Sartorio's *Novena en honor de la augustísima María de Guadalupe . . .*, Mexico: Imprenta de las Escalerillas, has a print of San José laid in by a previous owner, Sutro BX2162.G8 S27 1843.

Nevertheless, San José was not among the most common community patron saints. He was three or four times less common than Santa María, San Juan, San Miguel, Santiago, San Francisco, and San Pedro – the Blessed Mary, the three apostles closest to Christ, and the founding saint of the leading religious order in the early evangelization and pastoral work of the colonial period.

Villaseñor Black, *Creating the Cult of St. Joseph*, pp. 31–32, posits a connection between representations of Tlaloc – the precolonial divinity of water sources, fertility, storms, lightning, and earthquakes – and San José, suggesting that colonial Indians and others in central Mexico turned to Joseph for protection against these dangers, whereas peninsular Spaniards did not. She also speculates on a connection between the precolonial divinity Toci and veneration of St. Anne in Tlaxcala. See "St. Anne Imagery and Maternal Archetypes in Spain and Mexico," in *Colonial Saints: Discovering the Holy in the Americas*, ed. Allan Greer and Jodi Bilinkoff, New York and London: Routledge, 2002, pp. 3–29, and "Inquisitorial Practices Past and Present: Artistic Censorship, the Virgin Mary, and St. Anne," in *Art, Piety, and Destruction in the Christian West,*

1500–1700, ed. Virginia Chieffo Raguin, Burlington, VT: Ashgate, 2010, pp. 173–200.

On St. Joseph in New Spain, see also John McAndrew, *The Open-Air Churches of Sixteenth-Century Mexico: Atrios, Posas, Open Chapels, and Other Studies*, Cambridge, MA: Harvard University Press, 1965, pp. 393–397, and Pierre Ragon, *Les saints et les images du Mexique (XVIe-XVIII siècle)*, Paris: L'Harmattan, 2003, pp. 265–273.

18. For Mexico City, AHACM num. del inventario vol. 3604 labeled Patronatos y Santos Patronos, 1581–1824; for Puebla, Nicolás Carrasco Moscoso, *Sermón de el patrocinio que contra los rayos y tempestades goza dichosa la ciudad de Puebla en el esclarecido patriarca San Joseph*, Puebla: Impr. de Diego Fernández de León, 1688. San José was Puebla's patron and defender against lightning strikes by the time Fr. Juan de Torquemada wrote his *Monarquía Indiana* in the early seventeenth century, Mexico: Porrúa, 1986, I, 315. Frances L. Ramos tracks Joseph's important role as patron saint in Puebla during the colonial period, "Celebrating the Patriarch(s) of Puebla: The Municipal Council and the Cult of Saint Joseph," in *Festivals & Daily Life in the Arts of Colonial Latin America, 1492–1850*, ed. Donna Pierce, Denver: Denver Art Museum, 2014, pp. 73–96.

19. José de Ávila, *Colección de noticias de muchas de las indulgencias plenarias y perpetuas que pueden ganar todos los fieles de Christo que . . . visitaren en sus respectivos días las iglesias que se irán nombrando . . .*, Mexico: Zúñiga y Ontiveros, 1787. See entries for January 19, March 19, and July 20, which list the churches privileged with these plenary indulgences for honoring San José: San Juan de Dios, San Bernardo, San Gregorio, la Enseñanza, Merced, Carmen, Belén, San José de Gracia, the Colegio de Doncellas de San Miguel de Belén, the Colegiata church of Our Lady of Guadalupe, the Augustinian Third Order chapel, the chapel of San José el Real, and the cathedral's Sagrario church.

20. On the designation of San José as patron saint of the Archdiocese of Mexico in 1555, see Mariano Galván Rivera, ed., *Concilio III provincial mexicano celebrado el año de 1585 . . .*, Mexico: Eugenio Maillefert y Cia., 1859, libro 2 título III, paragraph ii.

21. Villaseñor Black, *Creating the Cult of St. Joseph*, passim; Gabriela Sánchez Reyes, "Su oficio fue criarlo, sustentarlo y traerlo en brazos: Reflexiones sobre la imagen de San José y el niño Jesús como ideal del amor paterno," in *Amor e historia: La expresión de los afectos en el mundo de ayer*, ed. Pilar Gonzalbo, Mexico: El Colegio de México, 2013, pp. 319–341.

22. Villaseñor Black, *Creating the Cult of St. Joseph*, p. 147. Local coronation celebrations with processions featuring a statue of San José and the Christ Child were reported in the *Gazeta de México* on April 23, 1790 for Zacatecas; on May 18, 1790 for Valladolid, with Carmelite friars heading the procession; for the Valle de Santiago on July 20, 1790, with Mercedarians in the lead and Our Lady of Mercy as "godmother of the coronation" (*madrina de la coronación*); on August 10, 1790 for the city of Guanajuato; on October 19, 1790 for Salvatierra (Guanajuato); on March 21, 1791 for Dolores (Guanajuato), with San Miguel and Nuestra Señora de los Dolores as godparents; and on June 17, 1797 for Sierra de Pinos, with San Matías and Nuestra Señora de Tlaxcala as godparents. For Puebla, see Ramos, "Celebrating the Patriarch(s) of Puebla," pp. 86, 88, 91–92. The special attachment of the Carmelite Order to the cult of San José is mentioned by Stephen Wilson (ed.) in *Saints and Their Cults: Studies in Religious Sociology, Folklore and History*, Cambridge, UK: Cambridge University Press, 1983, p. 31.

23. More images of San José also are recorded in mid-eighteenth-century pastoral visit books. Peter Boyd-Bowman, "Los nombres de pila en México desde 1540 hasta 1950," *Nueva Revista de Filología Hispánica* 19: 1 (1970), 12–48 presents patterns of naming in Mexico City's Sagrario parish, 1540–1950, and Mérida, Yucatán, 1570–1606. José/Josefa was not among the top ten names for boys and girls until 1620.
24. Pamela Sheingorn, "Joseph the Carpenter's Failure at Familial Discipline," in *Insights and Interpretations: Studies in Celebration of the Eighty-Fifth Anniversary of the Index of Christian Art*, ed. Colum Hourihane, Princeton: Princeton University Press, 2002, pp. 156–167.
25. Francisco de Ajofrín, *Diario del viaje que hizo a la América en el siglo XVIII el P. Fray Francisco de Ajofrín*, Mexico: Instituto Cultural Hispano Mexicano, 1964, I, 83. Despite Ajofrín's remark, Joseph apparently was more promoted and popular among non-Indians. The 1771 synod of prelates listed the feast of San José (March 19) as a day of obligation for Spaniards and castas, but not for Indians. New World Franciscans more generally were prominent devotees of Joseph, as Jaime Cuadriello notes in describing a fine ex-voto painting in the Santuario de la Asunción de María in Milpa Alta (in the southeast corner of the Distrito Federal) that depicts the saint rescuing Franciscans from a 1700 shipwreck, "Tierra de prodigios: La ventura como destino," in *Los pinceles de la historia: El origen del reino de la Nueva España, 1680–1750*, Mexico: Museo Nacional de Arte, 1999, p. 181.
26. Villaseñor Black, *Creating the Cult of St. Joseph*, pp. 110, 117. The Immaculate Conception gained new popularity in New Spain after 1662 when news of a papal bull approving the devotion arrived. Even the Dominicans, longtime critics of the belief, joined in the celebrations that year, Antonio Rubial García, "Presencias y ausencias: La fiesta como escenario político," in *Fiesta y celebración: Discurso y espacio novohispanos*, ed. María Águeda Méndez, Mexico: El Colegio de México, 2009, pp. 29–30.
27. Boyd-Bowman, "Los nombres de pila," pp. 14–17, 23–26. Particular advocations of María, such as María de la Concepción, María del Rosario, etc. did not enter the baptismal record of Mexico City's Sagrario parish until around 1675, some sixty years after they appeared in Spanish parish registers following the theological campaign by Carmelites of Sevilla to defend the doctrine of the Immaculate Conception, Boyd-Bowman, "Los nombres de pila," p. 19. José María and Mariano were also popular names for boys at the time.

    Among the cherished statues and paintings of Mary Immaculate that were famously associated with miracles and personal favors in the seventeenth and eighteenth centuries were those of Teuzitlan y Atempa (Estado de México), Xalmolonga (district of Malinalco), Cuernavaca (in the Third Order Chapel of the Franciscan church), Zitácuaro (Michoacán), Amatitlán (Jalisco), Zapopan (Jalisco), Aguascalientes, Calatayud (Yucatán), Tibolón (Yucatán), and various images in the hospital chapels of western and central Mexico.
28. For a late colonial compendium of personal miracles associated with San José, see Ignacio de Torres, *Salud, y gusto para todo el año, o, Año Josephino, a los fieles que gustan leer las virtudes, y excelencias, con que Dios favoreció a su padre putativo, y esposo de su madre . . .*, 3 vols., Mexico: Imprenta de la Bibliotheca Mexicana, 1757–1793.

29. Neither this image nor a church dedicated to San José was mentioned by Juan de Palafox y Mendoza in his pastoral visit to Córdoba in 1644 (*Relación de la visita eclesiástica del Obispo de Puebla, 1643–1646*, ed. Bernardo García Martínez, Puebla: Secretaría de Cultura, Gobierno del Estado, 1997, pp. 36–38). The church of San José in Córdoba is no longer featured as a pilgrimage destination.

San José has remained a popular saint in Mexico, and at least one important regional shrine to him developed in the late nineteenth century, at San Luis Potosí, Rafael Montejano y Aguiñaga, *Primer centenario del Santuario del Señor San José, 1885–1985*, San Luis Potosí: n.p., 1985. The continuing popularity of San José has been enhanced by representations of him as the Señor de los Trabajos, a patron saint of carpenters and construction workers.

Art historian Elizabeth Wilder Weismann suggested more than sixty years ago that images of Mary Immaculate in late colonial Mexico were not always aloof, idealized pin-ups, but could be welcoming diminutive figures of more ordinary women, *Mexico in Sculpture, 1521–1821*, Cambridge, MA: Harvard University Press, 1950, pp. 172–173. New representations of Mary in the eighteenth century, such as the Divina Pastora, also had a sweetness and approachability. And the many miracle shrines to more idealized, conventionally beautiful images of Mary Immaculate suggest that devotees regarded them, too, as loving, approachable figures.

Villaseñor Black, *Creating the Cult of St. Joseph*, p. 97, suggests that "beginning in the seventeenth century, miracles worked by the saint were reported in great numbers" and that he was especially renowned for aid to lost travelers, rescues from drowning and shipwreck, and protection against earthquakes and storms. She adds (p. 31) that many primary sources document colonial-period Mexicans seeking Joseph's protection as protector in rainstorms and lightning strikes, but her source for 132 Josephine miracles in Spain and the New World was authored by a late seventeenth-century Dominican devotee from Peru who identified few of his miracle stories by place or date, none of them for New Spain, Charlene Villaseñor Black, "Las imágenes milagrosas de San José en España y Sudamérica. Las teorías del arte y el poder de la imagen en el siglo XVII," *Estudios Josefinos: Revista Dirigida por Carmelitas Descalzos*, XLVIII: num. 95 (enero–junio 1994), 27–46. Her source for the miracle stories is Antonio José de Pastrana, *Empeños del Poder y Amor de Dios, en la Admirable, y prodigiosa Vida de Sanctíssimo Patriarca Joseph, Esposo de la Madre de Dios*, Madrid: Francisco Nieto, 1696.

30. *Relaciones geográficas del Arzobispado de México*. 1743, I, 241–286; Cabrera y Quintero, *Escudo de armas*, p. 142; *Gazeta de Mexico* 1786, issue #10, for Pachuca.
31. AGN Tierras 1091 exp. 5; AGN Indios 71 exp. 181.
32. These various patron saints of colonial Mexico City are documented in AHACM, vol. 3604 del inventario, labeled Patronatos y Santos Patronos, 1581–1824.
33. Villaseñor Black, *Creating the Cult of St. Joseph*, p. 157; proceedings of the IV Concilio Provincial Mexicano, Bancroft M-M 69–70, I, 117.
34. Bancroft M-M 69–70, I, 117. Santa Rosa was a popular saint in New Spain from the time of her beatification and canonization in 1667/1671 to the 1740s. Devotional texts published in the run up to canonization served to promote her popularity throughout Spanish America. The license for one of them to be published in New Spain is recorded in AGN General de Parte 13 exp. 10, 1670 (*Estrella de occidente. La Rosa de Lima, vida y milagros*). Paintings of her from the first half of the eighteenth century could be found

in many churches of central Mexico, but the cult of Santa Rosa in New Spain was eclipsed by the Virgin of Guadalupe at least twenty years before the 1771 designation of Rosa as Patrona de las Américas.

35. Pierre Ragon, "Los santos patronos de las ciudades del México central (siglos XVI y XVII)," *Historia Mexicana* LII: 3 (2002), 371, 377–378.
36. The lack of a confraternity dedicated to St. Joseph did not necessarily mean there were no observances in his honor. For example, in the mid-1770s the confraternity of souls in purgatory of the parish of San Salvador Tisayuca in Hidalgo near the Valley of Mexico sponsored an annual fiesta to him, TU VEMC leg. 7 exp. 5.
37. Campos and Cardaillac, *Indios y cristianos,* pp. 12–13; Valle, *Santiago en América, passim.*
38. William B. Taylor, *Magistrates of the Sacred: Priests and Parishioners in Eighteenth-Century Mexico*, Stanford, CA: Stanford University Press, 1996, pp. 272–277, 297–298; "Santiago's Horse: Christianity and Colonial Indian Resistance in the Heartland of New Spain," in *Violence, Resistance and Survival in the Americas*, ed. William B. Taylor and Franklin Pease G. Y., Washington: Smithsonian Institution Press, 1994, pp. 153–189.

    The ongoing importance of Santiago in Spanish ideology was highlighted in 1679 when Charles II's proposal to declare San José patron of all Spanish dominions was rejected because Santiago should not be displaced from that honor, Villaseñor Black, *Creating the Cult of St. Joseph*, p. 157.
39. Dr. Agustín de Quintela, *Oración gratulatoria, que en la primera función, que celebró la Real Congregación de los Naturales, y Originarios del Reyno de Galicia: en el día del patrón de las Españas señor Santiago ...*, Mexico: Zúñiga y Ontiveros, 1769; Dr. Luis Carrasco y Enciso, OP, *Sermón panegírico de Santiago el Mayor, que en la solemne función que le hace anualmente la Real Congregación de los naturales y originarios del reyno de Galicia ...* (July 25, 1809), Mexico: Arizpe, 1809.
40. *Constituciones de la cofradía del apóstol Santiago en la ciudad de México*, Mexico: [title page with publisher information missing], 1768 (Bancroft Library Folio fF1207.C513).
41. *The Arts in Latin America, 1492–1820*, ed. Suzanne Stratton-Pruitt, Philadelphia: Philadelphia Museum of Art, 2006, p. 267.
42. Monterrosa Prado and Solórzano, *Las devociones cristianas*, p. 133. The photograph associated with this text is a statue from Yautepec, Morelos displaying Moors rather than Indians at the horse's feet.
43. Taylor, *Magistrates of the Sacred*, p. 277.
44. For more on the saints in Indian communities discussed in suggestive ethnographic terms, see Mario Humberto Ruz, ed., *De la mano de lo sacro. Santos y demonios en el mundo Maya*, Mexico: UNAM, 2006, especially the essays by Perla Petrich and Pedro Pitarch which examine saints and their images as miracle-workers, their physical condition, rituals associated with them, and their standing as "the heart of the pueblo," pp. 67–90, 225–256.
45. Campos and Cardaillac, *Indios y cristianos*, pp. 340–341.
46. Campos and Cardaillac, *Indios y cristianos*, pp. 425, 429.
47. Monterrosa Prado and Talavera, *Las devociones cristianas*, p. 136, gives the example of Santiago of Huizquilucan. In my visits to Tlajomulco, Jalisco over the years, the mounted figure of Santiago there has always been dressed in fresh *calzones* and a cowboy hat of some kind. Edward Weston, *Daybooks*, New York: Aperture, 1961, I, 176, described the statue of Santiago as he found it in Tupátaro, Michoacán, in 1926:

Santiago was a childlike expression. They must feel more than mere reverence for a saint. He must be like them – one of them. So Santiago was. He could have been displayed in any American department store amongst the toys – a super toy. All details had received careful, tender attention. He was booted and spurred, over his neck hung a little sarape, around the waist a real faja, and his spirited hobby horse had been branded!

48. One early nineteenth-century source centered on San Miguel claimed that his was the most popular devotional image in New Spain after Christ and Mary, "Libro noticioso que contiene algunos apuntes particulares acaesidos en esta villa de Orizava y otras noticias que an yegado aquí de sujetos fidedignos, 1812–1921," Bancroft M-M 178, p. 163. Recently, María Teresa Jarquín Ortega noted that since the early seventeenth century San Miguel has been an unusually popular patron saint, especially for Indian pueblos in the western part of the Estado de México, *Los santos del corazón de Metepec: San Isidro Labrador y San Miguel Arcángel*, Toluca: Instituto Mexiquense de Cultura, 2011, p. 78.

49. A graphic sixteenth-century Mexican depiction of the archangel Michael defeating Satan appears in relief on one of the *posa* chapels of San Andrés Calpan, near Huejotzingo, Puebla. The martial aspect of "spiritual conquest" in the Spanish colonization in mainland America no doubt reinforced the representation of Michael as warrior in the struggle against Satan, but his reputation for "wondrous power" as a kind of right hand of God, especially in battle, was well established long before, as in Jacobus de Voragine's thirteenth-century compendium of hagiographies, *The Golden Legend: Readings on the Saints*, trans. William Granger Ryan, Princeton: Princeton University Press, 1993, II, 201–211.

50. David Brading mentions the learned speculation by Sánchez and others about the Archangel Michael and Guadalupe's cherub in *Mexican Phoenix. Our Lady of Guadalupe: Image and Tradition Across Five Centuries*, Cambridge, UK: Cambridge University Press, 2001, pp. 57, 69, 110, 128–129, 152, 164. On p. 174, he includes an eighteenth-century print by Troncoso depicting Michael in place of the cherub.

51. E.g., Alonso Francisco Moreno y Castro, *La vida instantánea del Archi-Seraphin Santíssimo Señor San Miguel*, Mexico: Vda. de J. B. Hogal, 1750, Eduardo Báez Macías, *El arcángel San Miguel: Su patrocinio, la ermita en el Santo Desierto de Cuajimalpa y el santuario de Tlaxcala*, Mexico: UNAM, 1979, p. 175, and Antonio Claudio de Villegas, *La mayor gloria del máximo de los celestes espíritus, del primero de los mayores príncipes el archiseraphin señor San Miguel . . .*, Mexico: Vda. de J. B. Hogal, 1751.

52. Jacinto de la Serna, "Manual de ministros de indios para el conocimiento de sus idolatrías, y extirpación de ellas," in *Colección de documentos inéditos para la historia de España*, Madrid: Academia de la Historia, 1892, 104, 65.

53. San Miguel was especially popular in Metepec and other communities in the western part of the Estado de México even when he was not the patron saint, according to Jarquín Ortega, *Los santos del corazón de Metepec*, p. 78. Guadalajara is mentioned in the *Gazeta de México*, October 18, 1785; Guimilpa, Querétaro, AHM L10A/5 pastoral visit book of Archbishop Rubio y Salinas, fol. 116v, November 24, 1752; El Oro (Edo de Mexico), *La ruta de los santuarios*, p. 189; parish of San Miguel, Mexico City, *Constituciones de los señores de la ilustre Archicofradía del Señor San Miguel fundada en la parroquia del mismo santo arcángel de esta capital de México*, Mexico: Abadiano y Valdés,

1838; Orizaba, 1812 Bancroft M-M 178; chapel in Sierra de Cuajimalpa near Mexico City, Báez Macías, *El arcángel San Miguel*, pp. 7–8; San Miguel de las Tetillas, Querétaro, in *Diálogos con el territorio*, ed. Alicia Barabás, Mexico: INAH, 2003–2004, III, 249–263. A prominent Indian community in the Diocese of Puebla dedicated to San Miguel from the early colonial period is Huejotzingo.

54. Eduardo Solorio Santiago, "Redescubriendo el territorio en San Miguel de las Tetillas," in *Diálogos con el territorio*, ed. Barabás, II, 249–263. The fame of the image of St. Michael in this church has attracted visitors from nearby communities in Hidalgo and Querétaro, and some from more distant places (presumably from families that had once resided in the area) for the feast of the patron saint on September 29.

55. *The Golden Legend of Jacobus de Voragine*, ed. and trans. Ryan Granger and Helmut Ripperger, London, New York, and Toronto: Longmans, Green and Co., 1941, pt. 2, p. 579.

56. *Golden Legend*, pt. 2, pp. 578–582.

57. Florencia, *Narración*, pp. 98–99. The quotation was used by Jaime Cuadriello, "Tierra de prodigios: La ventura como destino," pp. 200–201. Painted depictions at the shrine are discussed by Fernando E. Rodríguez-Miaja, "Una maravilla en San Miguel del Milagro," in *Imágenes de los naturales en el arte de la Nueva España, siglos XVI al XVIII*, ed. Cándida Fernández Calderón, Mexico: Banamex, 2005, pp. 355–383.

58. Undertaken by canon Alonso Herrera, according to José Rojas Garciduéñas, "San Miguel del Milagro," *Anales del Instituto de Investigaciones Estéticas*, núm. 4 (1939), 56.

59. Pedro Salmerón, "Relación de la aparición que el soverano arcángel San Miguel, defensor y patrón de esta yglesia militante y de la monarquía de España hizo en un lugar del Obispado de la Puebla de los Ángeles, llamado de nuestra señora de Nativitas el año de 1631." A nineteenth-century copy is in AGN Historia 1 exp. 7, fols. 152–170. Also in 1643, a lengthy text celebrating devotion to San Miguel and his apariciones and other miracles in Europe, written by the Jesuit Juan Eusebio Nieremberg, was published both in Spain and Mexico, *De la devoción y patrocinio de San Miguel, príncipe de los ángeles* ... The Mexican edition was printed in the shop of the widow of Bernardo Calderón.

60. Palafox, *Relación de la visita*, ed. García Martínez, pp. 70–71, "A la tarde fui a la ermita de San Miguel, que está del pueblo media legua, donde el ángel se apareció y despues ha hecho muchos milagros. Di orden para que se hiciese un santuario para conservación de una fuente de agua que el santo arcángel descubrió." In 1685, the audiencia ordered two Indians from the communities of San Bernabé Capula and San Miguel to serve the shrine every week. In return, these communities were exempted from other labor service for the church, AGN Indios 28 exp. 221, September 3, 1685.

61. Florencia, *Narración*, pp. 100–120.

62. Florencia, *Narración*, especially pp. 100–152. The popularity of the shrine and healing miracles of the water in the late seventeenth century were mentioned also by Fr. Agustín de Vetancurt, OFM, *Teatro mexicano. Descripción breve de los sucesos ejemplares históricos y religiosos del Nuevo Mundo de las Indias; Crónica de la Provincia del Santo Evangelio de México* [1698], facsimile edition, Mexico: Porrúa, 1982, p. 69: "es de mucha devoción por los milagros del Santo Archángel y de las aguas de un pozo milagroso que sanan de enfermedades; ... avía cofradías de Españoles y de los Naturales."

63. Florencia, *Narración*, pp. 162–164.
64. Pastoral visit book of Archbishop Rubio y Salinas, AHM L10A/5, fol. 116v, November 24, 1752; Bancroft M-M 144, 1714 will of Juan Félix Ramírez Ponce de León.
65. AGN Historia 1 exp. 7, fols. 152–170.
66. Florencia, *Narración*, pp. 164–165; AGN Historia 1 exp. 7, fols. 152–170.
67. Nineteen miracles are recounted in Salmerón, AGN Historia 1 exp. 7; and many of the additional miracles in Florencia, *Narración*, cross ethnic lines.
68. Mari Carmen Serra Puche, "The Concept of Feminine Places in Mesoamerica: The Case of Xochitécatl, Tlaxcala, Mexico," in *Gender in Pre-Hispanic America*, ed. Cecilia F. Klein, Washington: Dumbarton Oaks, 2001, pp. 274, 277, and personal communication from John B. Carlson, March 22, 2000. The providential origin story of the town of San Miguel de las Tetillas, Hidalgo also has a precolonial resonance in its association with water and mountain – the *altepetl*, which represented a community's territorial home, Solorio Santiago, "Redescubriendo el territorio," pp. 252–255.
69. The cult of San José was a favorite of the Carmelites, but it seems to have depended less on clerical sponsorship.
70. As described on the New Advent Catholic Encyclopedia website, "Saint Anthony of Padua" (www.newadvent.org/cathen/01556a.h).
71. Vetancurt, *Teatro mexicano*, p. 134. These images are also mentioned in Cabrera y Quintero, *Escudo de armas*, pp. 149–150, and *Gazeta de México,* November 1733, BIBM 4, p. 428.
72. AGN Bienes Nacionales 992 exp. 36, Acapulco; *Gazeta de México,* October 21, 1794, Ixtepeji (the report added "podemos piadosamente creer que el santo quiso añadir ésta a las muchas maravillas que ha obrado en favor de los que lo invocan"); AGN Clero Regular y Secular 27 exp. 4, Rioverde. Another statue of the saint that was honored and promoted with its own chapel was located in the city of Querétaro's cemetery, AHM L10A/5 pastoral visit book of Archbishop Rubio y Salinas, fols. 198–199, January 2, 1753, as well as a painting of the saint in the church of the discalced Franciscans and another statue in the convent church of Santa Clara, both at Querétaro, in 1743, *Relaciones geográficas del Arzobispado de México.* 1743, I, 260, 269.
73. AHM L10A/11 pastoral visit book of Archbishop Núñez de Haro y Peralta, fol. 84v, November 1, 1774.
74. William B. Taylor, *Shrines & Miraculous Images: Religious Life in Mexico Before the Reforma*, Albuquerque: University of New Mexico Press, 2011, pp. 16–17. The major annual fiesta in Calpulalpan (documented in several YouTube videos from 2009) still celebrates San Antonio de Padua and this statue.
75. Panecitos de San Nicolás used for healing are mentioned in AGN Inquisición 278 exp. 7, Celaya, 1624. Nicole Von Germeten reports that the members of the cofradía de San Nicolás de Tolentino baked "buns for the brothers" – perhaps the *panecitos* referred to here, *Black Blood Brothers: Confraternities and Social Mobility for Afro-Mexicans*, Gainesville: University Press of Florida, 2006, p. 64.
76. For example, Don Domingo de San Antón Muñón Chimalpahin Quauhtlehuanitzin, *Annals of His Time*, ed. and trans. James Lockhart, Susan Schroeder, and Doris Namala, Stanford: Stanford University, 2006, pp. 193, 1611; AGN Inquisición 278 exp. 7,

Celaya, 1614; *Gazeta de México*, January 14, 1784, procession for the *dolor de costado* epidemic; *Gazeta de México*, September 26, 1786, Guanajuato epidemic; José Antonio de Villaseñor y Sánchez, *Suplemento al Theatro Americano: La Ciudad de México en 1755*, Mexico: UNAM, 1980, p. 123, 1755 Mexico City.

An extensive discussion of colonial paintings in Oaxaca depicting San Nicolás Tolentino, especially in his role as rescuer of souls in purgatory is in Selene García Jiménez, "Entre el bien morir y el rescate de las ánimas: las pinturas tolentinianas de Isidro de Castro, 1701–1732," in *Ciclos pictóricos de Antequera-Oaxaca, siglos XVII-XVIII: Mito, santidad e identidad*, ed. Jaime Cuadriello, Mexico: Fundación Harp Helú/Instituto de Investigaciones Estéticas, UNAM, 2013, pp. 65–107.

77. Villaseñor y Sánchez, *Suplemento*, p. 123.
78. Late seventeenth- and eighteenth-century pastoral visit books in AHM record at least fifty-two confraternities dedicated to San Nicolás. Many (but not most) noted that they were founded by, and intended for, a particular group – Indians, Spaniards, or blacks and mulattoes. One in Zacualpan in the late seventeenth century was for Spaniards and mulattoes; rather than leaving racial qualifications unspecified, another (in Coatepec, Malinaltenango parish), was said to be for Spaniards, mestizos, mulattoes, and Indians.
79. In at least one case a cofradía was dedicated to both San Nicolás and the souls in purgatory, AHM L10A/1, pastoral visit book for Archbishop Aguiar y Seixas, fols. 679–684, Tacuba, June 9, 1685.
80. Chimalpahin, *Annals*, p. 215.
81. Von Germeten discusses mulatto cofradías to San Nicolás in Acapulco, Parral, Salvatierra, Taxco, and Valladolid, *Black Blood Brothers*, pp. 15, 63, 64, 66–68, 164–166, 199–202. Another in the Tlaxocotla sugar mill (Tololoapan parish) is mentioned in 1685 in the pastoral visit book of Archbishop Aguiar y Seixas in AHAM L10A/1. Most were established in the mid-seventeenth century, but perhaps the earliest one was founded in Mexico City in 1560 in the church of Santa Veracruz, Alicia Bazarte Martínez, *Las cofradías de españoles en la Ciudad de México (1526–1860)*, Mexico: UAM-Azcapotzalco, 1989, p. 42.
82. The rudiments of the story from Zitlalá's point of view, referring to the beginning of the devotion in the past tense are included in a *relación geográfica* of 1743, *Relaciones geográficas del Arzobispado de México, 1743*, I, 56, and enlarged upon by Danièle Dehouve from documentation in the Archivo General de Indias and oral tradition in Zitlalá, *Entre el caimán y el jaguar: Los pueblos indios de Guerrero*, Mexico: CIESAS, 1994, pp. 71–72, 158–159. An Indian cofradía for San Nicolás and this image was founded at Zitlalá in 1766, so perhaps the organized devotion may not date from much before the 1740s, Dehouve, *Entre el caimán*, p. 158.
83. Laura A. Lewis, "Of Ships and Saints: History, Memory, and Place in the Making of Moreno Mexican Identity," *Cultural Anthropology* 16: 1 (2001), 62–82. For Lewis's full-scale ethnographic study, see *Chocolate and Corn Flour: History, Race and Place in the Making of "Black" Mexico*, Durham: Duke University Press, 2012, especially pp. 90–106.
84. Dehouve, *Entre el caimán*, p. 72.
85. Lewis, "Of Ships and Saints," p. 72. In addition to Zitlalá's, statues of San Nicolás de Tolentino that were celebrated as miracle-workers include the one in the Augustinian convent church in Mexico City which Villaseñor y Sánchez described in 1755 as well

known for its "prodigiosos milagros en incendios y pestes," *Suplemento*, p. 123; and another in Guanajuato where San Nicolás was patron saint, mentioned in *Gazeta de México*, September 26, 1786.
86. AGN Clero Regular y Secular 188, exp. 12. In 1793, a new *subdelegado* reportedly discouraged the devotion.
87. Interest in this image may have revived sometime after 1871 when Rome circulated news that a statue in the Dominican church in Calabria was seen to move forward and back, raising and lowering its right arm, with a furrowed brow and a menacing look, then changing to a sad and tender expression as it turned toward the Virgin of the Rosary. AHM, Sección Acuerdos caja abril–junio 1871.
88. For more on the case of Gonzalo de Amarante, see Chapter 9.
89. *Novena a el Glorioso Señor San Gonzalo de Amarante, del Orden de Predicadores, dispuesta por un devoto suyo*, Mexico: Oficina de Da. María Fernández de Jáuregui, 1816. This tiny booklet, about 3" × 4.5", was reprinted from a text first published in Mexico in 1811 and reprinted in 1812, 1817, and 1820, as well as the three printings from different printers in 1816. The contents are unremarkable except that the novena exercises in it were intended for personal devotion rather than an organized public event: "esta novena se podrá hacer en qualquier tiempo del año."
90. On the many colonial Mexican paintings of Francis Xavier and their symbolism, see Jaime Cuadriello, "Xavier indiano o los indios sin apóstol," in *San Francisco Javier en las artes: El poder de la imagen*, Navarre: Fundación Can/Gobierno de Navarra, 2006, pp. 200–233.

San Ignacio – Ignatius of Loyola – was also depicted in many colonial paintings and statues, especially in Jesuit churches, but miracles associated with him and his images are less common in the written record than for Francisco Javier. Francisco Javier Alegre identified several healing miracles associated with ("por medio de") images and relics of the saint from the early seventeenth century, *Historia de la Compañía de Jesús en Nueva España, que estaba escribiendo el P. Francisco Javier Alegre al tiempo de su expulsión*, Mexico: Imprenta de J. M. Lara, 1841–1842, I, 359, 415, and II, 8, 42–44. An unusual miracle story of resistance to disenchantment associated with the chapel, altar, and image of San Ignacio in the cathedral of Puebla was recorded in 1747. It is discussed in Chapter 2.
91. Alegre, *Historia*, II, 451 and III, 23.
92. Alegre, *Historia*, II, 421.
93. *Breve noticia de la milagrosa imagen de San Francisco Xavier, que se venera en el Colegio de San Ildefonso . . .*, Mexico: Impr. de J. M. Lara, 1864. The painting was said to have been moved to the Jesuit Colegio Máximo of San Pedro and San Pablo where it worked healing wonders. Eventually it was returned to a beautiful new chapel of its own in the Colegio de San Ildefonso.
94. Cabrera y Quintero, *Escudo de armas*, pp. 171–174, "su milagrosa celebrada imagen . . . casi milagro en la escultura." A statue of this saint in the Jesuit collegiate church in Querétaro was also said to be "prodigiosa," *Relaciones geográficas del Arzobispado. 1743*, I, 266.
95. AGN Indios 24 exp. 257, fols. 163v–164.
96. This paragraph is based on James S. Griffith, *Beliefs and Holy Places: A Spiritual Geography of the Pimería Alta*, Tucson: University of Arizona Press, 1992, chapter 3; Eileen Oktavec, *Answered Prayers: Miracles and Milagros Along the Border*,

Tucson: University of Arizona Press, 1995; and Henry F. Dobyns, "Do-It-Yourself Religion: The Diffusion of Folk Catholicism on Mexico's Northern Frontier, 1821–1846," in *Pilgrimage in Latin America*, ed. N. Ross Crumrine and Alan Morinis, Westport, CT: Greenwood Press, 1991, pp. 53–67.

97. Two confraternities to Felipe de Jesús outside the capital, both in the modern state of Hidalgo, were identified in eighteenth-century pastoral visit records: among *españoles* of Huichapan in 1774, and in Tecosautla in 1755, AHM L10A/11 Archbishop Núñez de Haro y Peralta's visit book, fols. 190v–192v, December 13, 1774, and AHM L10A/5 Archbishop Rubio y Salinas's pastoral visit book, fol. 42, January 13, 1755.

98. The annual celebrations in Mexico City are described in *Gazeta de México*, February 1722, BIBM 5, pp. 965–966; *Gazeta de México*, issue for February 1729, BIBM 4, p. 93 (mentions the first procession in 1629 honoring him as a patron of the city); and *Gazeta de México*, February 11, 1784, and March 10, 1801 (which described an especially "magnificent" event, with fireworks, the city well decorated, and ample participation by the city's craft guilds, cofradías, Indian districts, and Franciscans). In Manuel de Arellano's famous 1709 painting of the grand procession carrying the image of Our Lady of Guadalupe into her new church at Tepeyac shows a statue of Felipe de Jesús as the only other holy image included, García, "Presencias y ausencias," p. 27.

99. AGN Correspondencia de Virreyes 188, fol. 51 and, especially, AHM legajo for 1797 concerning the canonization campaign that year. In his doctoral dissertation, Cornelius B. Conover documents Felipe de Jesús as a hero of the empire, embraced more by royal officials than creole patriots, "A Saint in the Empire: Mexico City's San Felipe de Jesús, 1597–1820," University of Texas at Austin, 2008. Antonio Rubial García briefly makes a case for Felipe de Jesús as a creole hero, "Icons of Devotion: The Appropriation and Use of Saints in New Spain," in *Local Religion in Colonial Mexico*, ed. and trans. Martin A. Nesvig, Albuquerque: University of New Mexico Press, 2006, pp. 56–57.

100. AHCM núm. del inventario vol. 3712, exp. 33, 1815.

Index

abuse of images. *See* images, use and abuse of; prints, abuse of
Acapulco, 618
Acatlán (Jalisco), 521
Adorno, Rolena, 24n21
Aguiar y Seixas, Francisco de, 68, 72, 74, 96, 182, 432–433, 470, 541n65
Aiohuizcuauhtla, 132–136
Ajofrín, Francisco de, 60, 150n20, 297n75, 407, 420, 427–428, 499n115, 500n123, 536n34, 543n73, 570, 607
Alahuistlan, 527–528
Alcedo, Antonio de, 333
Alcivia, José María Guadalupe, 282
Alcocer, José Antonio, 147n2, 280, 283–284, 304n123
Alegre, Francisco Xavier, 347n20, 354n78, 363, 499n118, 500n121, 621, 636n90
Almeida, Theodoro de, 429–434, 451n103
alms collection. *See demandas*
altars, home, 60, 118, 143–144, 407, 427–428, 449–450n91
Alva, Bartolomé de, 348n26
Álvarez de Abreu, Domingo Pantaleón, 276
Amacueca, Christ of, 203
Amadeus, Blessed, 4
Amecameca, 513, 528. *See also* Sacromonte
ancestor veneration, 21, 140, 142, 167n167, 361, 562
Ancona, Our Lady of, 405–407
Andrade, Alonso de, 59
Ángeles, Our Lady of los (Tlatelolco), 92n131, 117, 183–186, 404
Anguita Sandoval y Roxas, Juan Ubaldo de, 507
Antequera, 56, 87n95, 90n118, 172, 178, 206, 235n68, 253, 289n21, 440n24, 471, 537n38, 555

Antonio (as baptismal name), 605
Anunciación, Domingo de la, 374
Aparicio, Sebastián de, 119, 363, 372, 377
apparitions and visions, 17, 39, 40, 43–45, 59, 68, 81n36, 163n144, 353n72
Aquino, Marcos de, 72
Aragonese, 259–261
Arantzan, 155
Aranzazú, Our Lady of, 259, 261, 265, 284, 293n46, 294n54–55
Arce y Miranda, Andrés de, 171, 248
arches, processional, 110, 364, 514, 516, 519, 520, 523, 525–526, 542n66
Arregui, Domingo Lázaro de, 476
Astor Aguilera, Miguel Ángel, 159n108, 494n73
astrology, 144, 166n159
astronomy, 144, 166n159
Asturias, 261
Asunción, Isidro de la, 177, 187
Atlatlahuca, 110
Atlas Marianus, 59, 314, 342
Atlixco, 117–118, 144–145, 445n60
Atocha, Our Lady of, 214, 292n43
Atonal, Juan, 131–132
Atotonilco, Jesús Nazareno, 99, 213–214
Augustinians, 3–4, 39, 40, 46, 61–62, 78n11, 81n37, 94n154, 252–253, 261, 265–266, 326–328, 466, 478, 479, 487n12, 494n71, 510, 554. *See also* individual Augustinian chroniclers such as Juan de Grijalva
and miracles, 4, 327–328, 365, 370
and crosses and figures of Christ, 46, 61–62, 124–125, 198, 209, 265–266, 326–327, 367–368, 466, 478–479, 510, 554
Avencerraje, Calixto, 394n84
Ávila, José de, 105
Aynsa, 457

639

Báez Jorge, Félix, 94n155, 158n107
Bajío, 103, 359, 564–565n7
Bala, Our Lady of la, 172, 183, 216, 240n131, 420, 423
Balazo, Christ of El, 216–217
Baldinucci, Antonio, 281, 282
Balvanera, Our Lady of la, 259, 261
Baptista, Juan, 390n60
Barabás, Alicia, 492n55, 626n10
Bárcena, Miguel de, 495n80
Bargellini, Clara, 438n13, 443n40, 491–492n53
baroque, 4–9, 10, 24n18, 24n19, 24n20–21, 25n28, 26n37, 141
Barragán Álvarez, José Adrián, 356n93
Barrio y Sedano, Manuel del, 104
Bartlett, Robert, 354n79
Basalenque, Diego de, 94n154, 355n82, 487n13
Basques, 259–260, 507. See also Aranzazú
Basso, Keith, 533n12
Baxandall, Michael, 24n19, 436–437n3, 439n20, 453n117
beauty, 8–9, 27n42, 379–380, 395n99
Becerra Tanco, Luis, 323, 330, 331, 355n85, 418, 451n104
bells, church, 9, 26n38, 201, 324, 352n67, 378, 417
Belting, Hans, 437n3
Benedict XIV, 157n100, 565n14
Bergamo, Ilarione da, 544n84
Beristáin y Sousa, Mariano, 522
bishops. See also individual bishops by name
 and image shrines, 101, 145, 148n6, 168n183, 394n93, 444n50, 557
 encourage local religious heroes, 389n54
blind, 204, 309–311, 315, 322, 323, 332, 333, 344n3, 345n9, 388n44
Bonavía, Bernardo, 135
Books of Chilam Balam, 141
Boone, Elizabeth, 159n112, 168n178
Borah, Woodrow, 85n69
Borromeo, Carlo, 408
Bourbon reforms, 95–97, 108–117, 119–123, 148n13, 518–523, 546n96
Bouza, Fernando, 564n2
Brading, David, 632n50
Branciforte, Marqués de, 116, 117, 155n78
brandea, 59, 87n91, 176, 316, 332, 369, 370, 372, 378, 380, 396n103
Brentano, Robert, 12

Brihuega, 54, 295n61
Broda, Johanna, 159n107, 489n31, 489n36
Brooks, Timothy, 437n6
Bugslag, James, 507
bundles, sacred, 361, 384n2, 516, 542n67
Burgoa, Francisco de, 65, 67, 90n118, 355n82, 461, 490n44
Burgos, Christ of, 259, 265–266, 297n69–70, 433, 452n110
Burgos, Pedro de, 313, 342
Burkhart, Louise, 82n43, 353n72, 360n123
Bustamante, Carlos María, 92n139, 390n56
Bustamante, Francisco, 46
Bustillos Vara y Gutiérrez, Fernando, 477–478

Cabrera, Miguel, 74–75, 108, 125, 180, 266, 272, 273
Cabrera y Quintero, Cayetano, 8–9, 11, 233n50, 240n131, 257, 299n86
Cacaxtla, 617
Calatayud, Our Lady of, 65, 295n61
Calendar Stone, 143
Callaway, Carol, 468
Calpan, 257
Calpulalpan, 117, 381, 618, 634n74
Calvary, 19–21, 116, 200, 252, 256, 318, 455, 457, 519, 523
Calvary, Christ of (Tochimilco), 114–115
Calvary, Lord of (Edo. de México), 19–21, 322
Camacho, Joachin, 334–335
Camaxtle, 50
Camillians, 264
Camós, Narcís, 59, 87n89, 360n121
Campeche, 64, 87n95
Campos, Araceli, 613–614
candles, 7, 18, 19, 25n30, 66, 69, 105, 142, 168n176, 242n147, 303n117, 304n127, 356n90, 396n103
Canisius, Peter, 73, 267
Cántigas de Santa María, 342
Cappannari, Stephen C., 224
Capuchins and la Divina Pastora, 272, 275, 285, 300–301n95, 301n97, 301n99
Carbajal López, David, 154n68
Cardaillac, Louis, 613–614
Cárdenas Valencia, Francisco de, 64–65, 314, 321, 322, 329
Carletti, Francisco, 458
Carlson, John B., 617
Carmelites, 7, 72, 74, 210, 245, 266, 268, 362, 363, 365, 369, 370, 457, 471, 508, 591

Carmen, Our Lady of, 245, 286n2, 297–298n75
Carpentier, Alejo, 6
Carrasco, David, 485n7, 506, 534n22
Carrión, Villa de, 624n1
Casey, Edward, 504, 533n12, 533n13
Castañeda, Carmen, 358n107
Castro, José de, 498n104
caves, 126, 131, 137, 144, 146, 325, 455, 460, 511, 529, 535n23, 538n44
Ce Cuautli Tovar (Ceteutli), Juan, 45, 47, 365
cemeteries, 108, 118, 463, 468, 496n80, 527, 533n16, 634n72
Cervantes, Juan de, 471
Chalma, Christ of, 178, 208–209, 222, 227, 310, 332, 356n93, 377–379, 388n44, 393n83, 455, 510, 512, 518, 537n42, 554, 556
Chamula, San Juan, 394n85, 486n10
Charo, Our Lady of, 349n35
Chiapa, San José, 610
Chiapas, 131–132
Chew, Samuel, 488n21, 537n39
Chichimecs, 49, 474, 536n32
Chimalpahin, Domingo de San Antón Muñón, 259, 288n14, 354n78, 387n36, 492n59, 518, 618, 619
Chínipas, 375
Chirinos, Pedro, 363–364
Choapa, 622
Cholula, 464, 506, 534n22, 534n23
Christ. *See* crucifixes and other celebrated images of Christ; crosses; crown of thorns
Christ of the Oak (Cáceres), 353n68
Christian, William A., Jr., 16–17, 30n72, 59, 238n108, 313, 507
Cihuacoatl, 140, 512
Cisneros, Luis de, 4, 47, 64, 318–319, 321, 324, 329, 387n32, 395n99
cities of the sacred, 103, 119–120, 166n159, 513, 553. *See* individual cities, especially Mexico City, Puebla, Querétaro, Guadalajara, Mérida
Ciudad Jiménez, Chih., 296n68
Clendinnen, Inga, 159n107, 485n7, 549n130
Clifford, James, 532n9
Clifton, James, 9
Coatepec Harinas, 19
Cobarrubias, Sebastián de, 507
Cocentayna, Our Lady of the Miracle of, 293n43
Codex Calixtinus, 342
cofradías. *See* confraternities

Colegiata of Our Lady of Guadalupe, 178–179, 232n39, 234n59
Colegio de San Gregorio, 267, 268, 271, 272, 299n80, 299n84–86, 300n90, 300n92–93, 349n35
Coleman, Simon, 532n9
Cologne, 43
color, 399, 438n11
communitas, 505, 530, 532n7
Compostela, 387n34, 502, 503, 507, 559
Concilio Provincial I, 44, 468, 514–515, 541n64
Concilio Provincial II, 44
Concilio Provincial III, 44, 55, 130, 361, 362, 377, 384n5, 541n64
Concilio Provincial IV, 111, 137, 154n65, 164n146–147, 377, 544n79, 610
Conde de la Laguna, 49
Conde de Orizaba, 433–434
confraternities, 5, 39, 42, 47, 48, 58, 62, 65, 72, 73, 88n103, 95, 96, 111–112, 124, 131, 139, 142, 146, 154n68–69, 175–177, 187, 218, 252, 257–258, 259, 261, 266–268, 278, 294n54, 366, 400, 402, 403, 407, 420, 485n6, 519, 521, 524, 525, 529, 553, 556, 557, 563, 605, 612, 614, 615, 619, 631n36, 635n78, 637n97
Conicari, 375
Conover, Cornelius, 229n19, 637n99
Conquistadora, La (Puebla), 46, 48, 83n57, 89–90n113
Consolación, Our Lady of La, 334–336
Constantine, 456
Constanzó, Miguel, 101
Contla, San Bernardino, 114, 511, 538n47
copperplate engravings, 404, 441
Corpus Christi, 75, 109, 110, 200, 201, 219, 369, 434, 512, 517–521, 525, 539n52, 541n64, 544n79, 544n81–82, 544n84
Correa, Juan, 259
Cortés, Fernando, 40, 46–48, 51–52
Cortesero, Hernando, 374
Cosamaloapan, Our Lady of, 65, 66, 152n50
Council of Trent, 5, 6, 38, 39, 41, 42, 44, 55, 79n21, 79n23, 248, 314, 348n23, 394n93, 396n108, 408, 444n48
Covadonga, Our Lady of, 97, 245, 261–263, 284, 295n59
creole patriotism, 145, 175, 229n19
crisis, seventeenth century, 85n69–72
Cristo de San Benito (Querétaro), 201
Cristo del Noviciado (Mexico City), 311

Cristo del Veneno, 223
Cristo Renovado de Santa Teresa (Ixmiquilpan; Mapethé), 72, 74, 92n139, 105, 145, 183, 205, 210–211, 238n111, 331
crosses, 19, 45–46, 50–52, 66, 72, 75, 124–125, 130, 142, 143, 200–203, 226, 322, 332, 365–369, 409, 454–501, *passim*, 516, 517, 525. *See also* Augustinians; particular crosses, such as the Cross of Huatulco
crown of thorns, 202, 365–366, 368, 468, 559
crucifixes and other celebrated images of Christ, *passim*, and especially 42, 103, 120–123, 198–228, *passim*, 456, 562. *See also* Augustinians; individual Christocentric shrines and images; Augustinians; and Kempis, Thomas à
Cruz, Mateo de la, 73, 93n142
Cruz de Maye, 466
Cruz de Piedra (Querétaro), 52, 125, 143, 332, 420, 471–475, 495n80, 497n96–97, 498n100, 498n102, 499n111
Cruz González, Cristina, 92n131, 149n16, 443n43
crystallization (of culture), 1–2, 556
Cuadriello, Jaime, 222, 234n58, 239n120, 497n93, 629n25
Cuchumatán, Todos Santos, 460, 465–466
Cueva Santa, Our Lady de la, 103, 246, 261, 263–264, 281, 284
curandero, 128. *See also* maestro de enseñanza; shaman
Czestochowa, Our Lady of, 226, 399

dance, 514, 516, 522–523, 531, 539n58, 540n60, 540n64, 542n68, 547n98–100
darsan, 550n131
Davies, Drew, 77n7
Dávila Padilla, Agustín, 63, 289n21, 330, 354n78, 379
Deans-Smith, Susan, 302n99, 442n38
decorum, 6, 44, 96, 100, 110, 111, 120, 292n41, 380, 381, 408, 444n51, 480, 514, 520–523, 540n64, 549n123
Defensa, Our Lady of La, 331–332
Delgado Loria, Pedro, 218
demandas, 19–21, 67, 71, 112–117, 154n72, 155n78, 156n79, 536n32, 548n119
demons. *See* Satan
desacatos. *See* abuse of images
Desagravios, Christ of (Mexico City), 431, 433, 434, 452n114
Desamparados, Our Lady of the, 294n55, 296n61

Desconsolados, Christ of the (Tehuacán), 347n17, 402, 418, 448n79
Destefano, Michael, 391n64
devil. *See* Satan
demons. *See* Satan
devotional histories, 59, 65. *See also* individual authors
Díaz de la Vega, José, 475
Dickinson, Emily, 16, 23n14, 398
disenchantment, 10, 95, 96, 97, 106, 157n100, 340. *See also* enchantment
distance, as relational, 533n13
Divina Pastora, La, 266, 272–277, 284, 285, 301n96–99, 305n132
divine presence, 8, 17, 39, 41, 44, 50, 52, 55, 56, 70, 75, 76, 108, 110, 124, 130, 140, 144, 173, 180, 182, 209, 245–246, 248, 309, 313–315, 319, 324–326, 339, 361–362, 379, 402, 416–418, 421–422, 430, 456, 463, 481–482, 513, 514, 517, 529, 551–552, 562, 604, 623–624. *See also* enchantment
dolor, 290n25
Dolores, Our Lady of. *See* Mater Dolorosa
dominant symbols, 503
Domínguez, Juan Francisco, 552
Domínguez, Miguel, 521
Domínguez Torres, Mónica, 488n17
Dominicans, 39, 45, 213, 245–247, 262, 267, 268, 275, 362, 363, 369, 374, 382, 605, 620–621. *See also* Rosary, Our Lady of the; particular Dominican chroniclers such as Francisco de Burgoa
and miracles, 63, 65, 309, 321, 330, 333–334, 374, 461, 522
and image shrines, 67, 186, 213, 246, 252, 321
and *Mater Dolorosa*, 252–253
and Covadonga, Our Lady of, 261
and Loreto, Our Lady of, 267, 268
Donahue-Wallace, Kelly, 439n16, 440n24, 443n43
dreams, 16, 81n36, 353n74, 559
dualistic religious traditions, 222, 534n18
Duffy, Eamon, 31n75, 507
Durán, Diego, 128, 130, 460, 487n11, 491n50
Durkheim, Émile, 480

Echave Ibía, Baltasar de, 250, 287n13, 288n13
Eck, Diana, 166n159
Eden, Garden of, 548

Edgerton, Samuel, 468
Eguiara y Eguren, Juan José, 401
eighteenth-century developments, 95–123, *passim*, 178–185, 190, 193–195, 197, 260, 266–284, 285–286, 319, 337, 338–339, 378, 518–524, 556
Elkins, James, 379
Elsner, John, 532
enchantment, 43, 54–55, 76, 97, 102–103, 120, 124, 130, 226, 285–286, 326, 333, 334, 338, 434, 470, 528–529, 552, 555, 558, 563. *See also* disenchantment; divine presence
Enlightenment, 95, 124, 147n3, 275, 276, 432, 530
Enríquez, Martín, 46
Enríquez de Rivera, Payo, 371
epidemic of 1737, 104, 106, 178–179, 258, 268, 316, 323, 333, 338, 480, 510
Escobar, Matías de, 94n154, 355n82
España, Our Lady of (Españita, Tlaxcala), 299n89
Espinosa, Isidro Félix de, 427, 474
Esquipulas, Christ of, 209–210, 220, 223, 239n123, 242n148, 312, 336, 388n44, 511, 537n43, 554, 562
Eucharist, 124, 130, 200–201, 432
Europe and New Spain, 5, 6, 10, 11, 35–52, *passim*, 54, 58, 59, 63, 73, 95–97, 111, 113, 139, 143, 145, 170–172, 198, 200, 202, 219–220, 224–226, 245–286, *passim*, 311, 312, 316, 321, 324–325, 328, 337, 339–342, 349n31, 349n35, 352n64, 354n79, 400, 456–458, 460–461, 471, 503, 505–507, 509–511, 513, 529, 531n2, 535n26, 536n33, 537n39, 556–563, 604, 605, 615, 617–618, 623. *See also* Spain; Council of Trent
exorcism, 40, 56, 309, 316, 319, 323, 340, 344n3, 374, 456, 457, 551
extirpation, 132, 146
ex-voto paintings, 316–319, 331, 349n31, 349n35

Fabián y Fuero, Francisco, 258, 276, 288n16, 292n41
Faci, Roque Alberto, 238n114, 457
Feijóo, Benito Jerónimo, 507–508, 535–536n31
Feria, Pedro de, 131–132
Fernández de Lizardi, Joaquín, 378
Fernández Echeverría y Veitia, Mariano, 346n16, 365

Ferrero de Caldecebro, Andrés, 9
fiestas, 446n65, 516, 518, 520, 521, 525, 528, 530, 545n86–88, 547n98, 547n100, 548n119–120
fireworks, 7, 42, 481, 514, 515, 518, 521, 524, 525, 527, 531
Flanders, 400, 442n38
Flon, Manuel, 117–120, 156n94
flood of 1629, 176–177, 331
Florencia, Francisco de, 4, 11, 17, 62, 72, 94n154, 98, 99, 102, 125, 150n18, 179, 187, 234n64–65, 239n120, 267, 314–316, 321, 323, 332–333, 350n35, 357n96, 407, 442n38, 476, 510, 551
flowers, 7, 16, 18, 87n91, 121, 145, 166n157, 202, 374, 380, 389n55, 332, 396n105, 427, 455, 463, 467, 482, 496n80, 514, 516, 517, 519, 520, 523, 526, 617
Folgar, Manuel de, 74
Forster, Marc, 507, 535n26
Foster, George, 38
Foucault, Michel, 524, 548n106
Franciscans, 39–41, 45, 48, 50, 75–76, 78n18–19, 80n30, 130, 248–249, 259, 261, 278, 282–284, 323, 326, 336–337, 348n21, 372, 381, 407, 409, 434, 498n102, 499n111, 524, 553, 605, 606, 613–614, 617–618, 622. *See also* individual Franciscans such as Juan de Torquemada; particular shrines administered by Franciscans such as Tecaxic, Our Lady of
and devotional images and miracles, 4, 61, 63, 67–68, 81n37, 88n101, 103, 104, 183–185, 190, 245–286, *passim*, 312–314, 323, 326, 336, 338, 372–373, 454–484, *passim*
and pilgrimage, 517, 536n35
and Mary Immaculate, 245, 248, 287n12, 560
and Jesuits, 55, 61, 252, 271, 278, 280–281, 284, 286, 313–314, 340, 558–559, 622
and Dominicans, 39–40, 45, 247, 311, 325, 362, 409, 620
and relics, 119, 362–363, 365, 366, 369
and revival missions, 190, 210, 263–265, 277–278, 426–427, 448–449n84–85, 473
Francisco (baptismal name), 605
Franco, Alonso, 44, 321, 330, 351n58, 374, 442n39
Freedberg, David, 399, 437n4
Froeschlè-Chopard, Marie Hélène, 535n26
Fuente, Our Lady of la, 407

Furet, François, 13–14
furta sacra, 81n41

Galarza, Pedro de, 374
Galicia y Castilla, Julián Cirilo de, 300n92
Garibay y Zamalloa, Esteban de, 78n11
Gemelli Careri, Giovanni Francesco, 519
Genovesi, Antonio, 277–278
Giffords, Gloria, 349n34
Gil, Gerónimo Antonio, 364
Giménez, Gilberto, 455, 518
Giuca, Juan José, 282
Glassie, John, 398
Gombrich, E.H., 29n62
Gómez, José, 105, 297n70, 303n120, 389–390n56
Gómez de Parada, Juan, 193
González, Juan, 377
González Dávila, Gil, 369
Gosner, Kevin, 162n133, 162n135
Gospels, miracles in, 309, 344n3
Granados Salinas, Rosario Inés, 81n38, 83n54, 147n3, 198
Gregory XIII, 362
green, 287n13, 288n14, 380, 458, 466, 476–478, 481, 483, 486n10, 494n70, 499n119, 500n123, 514, 519–520, 562
Greenblatt, Stephen, 23n12
Grijalva, Juan de, 60, 80n29, 81n37, 198, 365, 387n32
Gruzinski, Serge, 147n1, 163n140, 498n105, 540n61
Guadalajara, 101, 104, 172, 178, 180, 219, 241n135, 257–259, 261, 285, 291n33, 358n107, 364, 407, 440n24, 546n97. *See also* Zapopan, Our Lady of
Guadalupe, Our Lady of (Spain), 65, 224, 265, 313, 334–335, 342
Guadalupe, Our Lady of (New Spain), xxi, 45–47, 60, 63–64, 65, 67, 73, 74, 76, 98, 99, 101, 105–106, 113, 117, 145, 173–183, 224–226, 265, 322–323, 330–331, 334, 338, 418–419, 421, 502, 510–511, 517, 523, 529, 556, 561. *See also* Tepeyac
Guadarrama Olivera, Mercedes, 144, 492n54, 514
Guanajuato, Our Lady of, 45, 49, 171, 310, 341, 352n67, 553
Guazápares, 375
Guevara, Miguel Tadeo de, 180
Guimilpa, San Miguel de, 616
Gumppenberg, Wilhelm, 59, 87n93, 298n76

haciendas, 54
Hall, Edward, 533n12
Hanks, William F., 141, 167n163, 486n7, 491n50
Harline, Craig, 359n119, 565n8
Harris, Max, 541n64
Hartz, Louis, 38
Heal, Bridget, 43
hearing, 9, 309, 315, 359n114, 505. *See also* reception, *voz pública y fama*
heart, 7, 50, 57, 140, 142, 174, 245, 252, 278, 281, 283, 322, 348n26, 389n56, 400, 426, 430, 432, 460, 527, 531, 547n102
Hermita, Our Lady of the, 511
hermits, 18, 43, 59, 64, 80, 119, 209, 375–378, 392n77, 394n84, 508, 510, 559
Herrera, Rafael, 8
Hesse, Hermann, 562
historical approach, xxi–xxii, 1–3, 10–16, 21, 35–45, 139–147, 339–344, 453n117, 555–562. *See also* synoptic study; narrative
Hobsbawm, Eric, 146
Holy Child figures, 65, 103, 106–108, 142, 153n58, 204–205, 238n116–117, 305n130, 382, 420, 422
Holy Cross, Feast of the Exaltation (Sept. 14), 369, 454, 482, 483, 484n1, 496n80, 499n111
Holy Cross, Feast of the Invention (May 3), 369, 454–456, 469, 475, 478, 483, 484n1, 484n3, 485n5, 486n8, 498n99
Holy Cross, Franciscan missionary college, 5, 210, 264, 284, 473–474
Holy Land pilgrimages, 537n40
Horta, Lorenzo de, 375
hospitals, 49, 72, 104, 218, 248, 258, 264, 291n33, 363
Huamantla, 317–318, 403
Huaquechula, cross of, 106, 397n116, 409, 410, 445n55, 480
Huatulco, cross of, 75, 81n41, 93n144, 369, 461, 471, 472, 497n87
  other crosses in western Mexico with a similar tradition, 496n86
Huecholan, 378
Huehuetoca, 525
Hueyapan, crucifix, 65, 67, 355n82, 555
Huixquilucan, 352n67, 487n11

Ibarra, Diego, 49
Ibarra, José de, 74, 108

Index

idolatry, 45, 59, 76, 128–138, 145, 161n120, 164n147, 461, 516, 539n54
idols behind altars, 165n154, 167n165
Ilamatecuhtli, 512
images (of Christ, Mary and other saints), *passim*, and especially, 39, 43, 54, 61. *See also* reception; processions, with images; image shrines; seventeenth-century developments; eighteenth-century developments; "santos"; and individual image and shrine entries
   conception of, 3, 401
   as living presence, 55–56, 58, 66, 140, 219, 343, 400–401, 412, 416–418, 420, 426, 433–434, 456, 463, 483, 551, 621, 623
   as evolved objects, 16, 172–173, 399
   and agency, 23n17, 89n106, 417. *See also* images as living presence
   as places, 3
   relocated, 381–383. *See also furta sacra*
   as relics, 379–383
   vital to wellbeing, 21, 381–382, 397n111
   of nature, 202–204, 220, 226, 241n137, 244n164, 325, 329, 341, 461, 466–467, 481, 505
   as pilgrims, 151n44, 219, 298n75, 397n118, 482, 518, 543n74, 543n76
   self-restoring, 202, 205, 238n112, 241n135
   damage, adds to evocative power, 448n82
   decoration of, 550n133
   ambivalence about, 4–5, 16
   conflict over, 382–383, 397n113
   policing of, 153n63
   from Ecuador, 382–383, 397n118
   use of, 16, 18, 55, 58, 110–111, 143–144, 215–216, 253, 326, 339, 381, 398–400, 401, 408–409, 418, 427, 432–436, 456–458, 469
   abuse of, 120, 218, 397n112, 409, 417–419
image shrines, New Spain, *passim. See especially* cities; images; origin stories; promotional activity; prints, and promotion of shrines; regulations; shrines listed individually on Map 1.1 (6–7)
   as "little heavens on earth," 551
   promotion, 624n5
   and politico-economic change in the eighteenth century, 148–149n13
   and diocesan clergy, 151n31, 624–625n5
   appeal across social groups, 56–58, 124, 141, 146, 175–176, 245, 458, 503, 551, 555, 616–619, 624. *See also* regional shrines

immanence. *See* divine presence; enchantment
Immaculate Conception, Our Lady of the, 41, 65, 245, 247–251, 284, 286n2, 287n13, 288n14, 629n26–27, 630n29
immigration, 54, 85n72, 124, 400
incense, 7, 9, 71, 128, 133, 144, 145, 223, 378, 380, 463, 513, 514, 516, 524, 531, 539n54, 552, 606. *See also* smell
indulgences, papal, 39, 41, 44, 47, 72, 83n52, 96, 105, 142, 145, 177, 193, 206, 294n52, 366, 400, 403, 408, 426, 469, 509, 607
informaciones jurídicas and other formal inquiries, 17, 45, 48, 62, 65, 312–313, 331
Ingold, Tim, 533n15
Inquisition, 10, 44, 56, 59, 106, 108–109, 111, 117–120, 132, 142, 162n128, 162n138, 327–328, 343, 371, 377, 380, 400, 408–409, 411–418, 427, 443n44, 444n50, 446n70, 449n89, 454–455, 496n82, 546n91, 606
Inquisition, episcopal, 162n128
ixiptla, 129
Ixtepeji, 357n99, 378, 618
Izamal, Our Lady of, 49, 50, 61, 65, 84n63, 190, 197, 314, 315, 329, 553, 564n5

Jackson, J.B., 505
Jacona, cross of, 94n154, 355n82
Jalisco, 258. *See also* Zapopan, Our Lady of; San Juan de los Lagos, Our Lady of; Talpa, Our Lady of; Guadalajara
Jansenist, 102, 111, 275, 434
Jerusalem, 502, 510
Jesuits, 6, 9, 55, 59, 72–73, 102–103, 140, 201, 245, 248, 284–285, 329, 344n3, 348n21, 418, 438n13, 450n100, 457, 499n118, 555. *See also* Francisco de Florencia; Juan Antonio Oviedo; Andrés Pérez de Ribas
   and devotional images and miracles, 61, 72–73, 93n143, 102, 151n33, 310, 323, 340, 348n21, 443n40, 457
   and Marian devotion, 59, 72–73. *See also Zodíaco mariano*
   and *Mater Dolorosa*, 245, 252–253, 257, 289n22
   and Our Lady of Loreto, 73, 96, 224, 226, 267–271, 298–299n76–81, 299n84–86, 300n92–93
   and Our Lady of La Luz, 277–280
   and Our Lady of El Refugio, 280–284

646　　　　　　　　　　　　　Index

Jesuits (cont.)
  and relics, 362–363, 365, 371, 375–376, 386n22–23
  revival missions, 102, 286, 305n131, 427, 448–449n84. *See also* Jesuits and Our Lady of Loreto; Jesuits and Our Lady of Luz; Jesuits and Our Lady of El Refugio
Jiménez de Cisneros, Francisco, 44, 78–79n19, 81n36
Jones, Pamela M., 438n8
José (baptismal name), 605
Juan (baptismal name), 605

Kempe, Margery, 509
Kempis, Thomas à, 200
Kino, Eusebio, 622
Knab, Timothy, 158n104
Kubler, George, 38, 165n151, 436n1, 506, 529, 552

laicization, 122
Lalopa, Santiago, 511
Landa, Diego de, 49–50, 162n128
landscape, 2, 7, 12, 52, 65, 75, 98, 126, 325, 455, 459, 460, 462, 463, 484, 504, 505, 533n12
Lara, Jaime, 468, 486n7
Larkin, Brian, 147n1, 452n114
Lárraga, Francisco, 290n25, 449n89, 509, 536n33
Lasso de la Vega, Luis, 177, 229n20, 232n40, 331
Lastra, Yolanda, 484n2
Lazcano, Francisco Javier, 200
Leavitt-Alcántara, Brianna, 290n28
Leis y Oca, Vicente, 548n116
León, Villa de, 278
León-Portilla, Miguel, 167n168
Lepe y Rivera, Antonio de, 526, 548n116
Levi D'Ancona, Mirella, 287n13
Leviathan, 273, 278, 280, 285, 303n112
Lewis, Laura, 619
Lezama Lima, José, 6
libros de magia, 411–414
libros de milagros, 16, 43, 63, 313–314, 342, 558
light, 7, 9, 69, 70, 103, 144, 200, 218, 222, 243n155, 248, 250, 277–280, 287n13, 309, 321, 323, 324, 343, 353n69, 356n90, 396n103, 412, 552. *See also* candles; lightning; Luz, Our Lady of La

lightning, 25n28, 102–103, 126, 193, 247, 284, 296n61, 310, 333, 351n52, 420, 427, 457, 460, 464, 497n91, 615, 627n17, 628n18
Ligno Crucis, 365–369, 387n39, 416–417, 446n68
Liguori, Alphonsus, 228n9
Litany of the Blessed Virgin, 250, 283, 288n13, 517
Lizana, Bernardo de, 49–50, 61, 311, 315
Loaizaga, Manuel, 323, 338, 347n16, 447n79
Lockhart, James, 165n152, 489n35, 492n59, 604
López, Gregorio, 64, 375, 377
López Austin, Alfredo, 142, 159n107, 168n180, 384n2, 460, 542n66
Lorenzana, Francisco Antonio de, 111, 115, 137, 164n147, 182, 225, 276, 333, 518, 542n65, 544n80
Loreto, Our Lady of, 72, 73, 96, 102, 103, 109, 145, 224, 226, 245, 266–272, 284, 285, 298n77, 332, 356n94, 438n10
Loreto López, Rosalva, 390n60
Luz, Our Lady of La, 102, 245, 250, 277–280, 285, 302n111, 303n112–115, 303n119–120, 304n122

Macana, Our Lady of la, 62–63, 172, 345n8, 448n82
maestro de enseñanza, 127
Magdalena de Kino (Sonora), 351n51, 622
Maine, 12
Malinaltenango, 19
Malinche, La (mountain), 617
Maniura, Robert, 399
Mañozca y Zamora, Juan de, 66, 388n46, 396n103, 496n80
Maravall, José Antonio, 24n20
Margil de Jesús, Antonio, 210, 232n40, 554
María (baptismal name), 605, 607, 610
María Anna Águeda de San Ignacio, 276, 373
María de Jesús, Madre, 390n60
Marroquín, Enrique, 486n10, 491n51, 492n54, 494n72
Marshall, Peter, 360n119
Martínez, María Elena, 244n163
Martagon, Fernando, 434, 435, 452n114, 453n115
Martínez Baracs, Rodrigo, 50, 84n66
martyrs, 362–364, 372, 376, 377, 457, 604, 621, 624n3

Index

Mary, Blessed, passim, but especially 42–43, 62–63, 170–308, *passim*, 286n1, 360n123, 610. *See also* individual Marian shrines and images, e.g. Guadalupe, Our Lady of
  As warrior, 45, 62–63, 97, 341
  As theotokos, 228n2
  Shares an image shrine with miraculous Christ, 216–218, 240n132
  Made of precious metal, 89n111
  Whiteness, 223–225, 243n155
Mater Dolorosa, 63, 73, 140, 245, 252–258, 284, 288n16–17, 289n20, 290n23, 290n26, 290n28, 291n33, 291n35, 292n40–41, 312
material culture, 7, 18–19, 59, 62, 73–74, 98, 316–322, 339, 361–384, *passim*, 398–436, *passim*, 557–558, 560
Material Religion (journal), 438n9
Matlalcueye, 534n23
mayordoma, 300n93
McCafferty, Geoffrey, 506
medidas, 59, 62, 67, 74, 176, 230n25, 339, 380, 396n102, 402, 470, 556
medieval, 10, 28n49, 31n80, 38, 39, 43, 54, 141, 224, 250, 254, 303n112, 316, 324, 328, 353n72, 379, 486n7, 502, 506, 558
Medina, Baltasar, 185, 187, 355n82, 385n15, 390n60
medio de limosna, 405, 436
Megged, Amos, 162n132
memory, mediums of, 21, 31n79
Mendieta, Gerónimo de, 44, 78n18, 213, 257, 314, 325, 353n70, 354n78, 387n42, 516, 519, 531, 543n70, 544n83, 545n87
Mendoza, Juan de, 69–71, 91n128, 125, 225, 293n46, 314, 332, 350n44, 351n52, 514
Mercy, Our Lady of, 245, 287n3, 297n75
Mérida (Yucatán), 60, 61, 65, 87n95, 197, 220, 237n91, 257, 267, 291n33
mesa. *See* altars, home
Mesoamerica, pre-colonial, 10, 12, 104, 125, 126, 128–129, 140–145, *passim*, 224, 361, 458–461, 463, 483, 505, 506, 551, 552, 560, 562
Mesoamerican religiosity and Christianity, 139–144, 146, 224, 226, 361, 458, 460, 461, 463, 483, 505, 506, 551–553, 558–559, 562
Mexicalcingo, 111, 143
Mexico City, 35, 44–46, 50, 54, 57, 60–64, 66, 73–76, 88n96, 97, 103, 105–106, 114, 117, 125, 145, 172, 173, 175–187, 193, 197, 204–205, 209–212, 220, 227, 248, 259, 261–262, 264–265, 267–271, 278–280, 282, 285, 321, 326, 330–333, 335, 363–366, 369–371, 373, 374, 376, 401–407, 427, 430–434, 440n24, 454–455, 464, 468, 509–511, 518–520, 525, 606–608, 610, 612, 617–619, 621–623. *See also* Guadalupe, Our Lady of; Remedios, Our Lady of; Cristo Renovado de Santa Teresa; and other shrines in and near Mexico City
Michoacán, 512
Miedes, 457
Miguel (baptismal name), 605
milagritos, 18, 59, 62, 74, 98, 105, 121, 321, 322, 329, 339, 343, 351n51, 396n105, 556, 557
mirabilia, 55
miracles, 4, 16, 17, 40, 42–43, 45–50, 55–56, 58–59, 63–65, 67–68, 70, 72–75, 95–96, 104–106, 109, 125, 140, 145, 166n157, 247, 257–258, 268, 275, 291–292n35–36, 309–360, *passim*, 369, 370, 372, 374, 378, 405–406, 418, 433, 457, 471, 474–475, 479–480, 510–511, 518, 520, 531, 551–552, 558–559, 605, 612, 614–618, 621–623. *See also libros de milagros*; enchantment, divine presence; origin stories
Mitchell, Nathan, 54
Mittermaier, Amira, 353n74
modernity and religion, 11–12, 53
Molango, 417
Molina, J. Michelle, 450n100
Monaghan, John, 626n10
monistic religious traditions, 126–127, 144–145, 551
Montserrat, Our Lady of, 39, 73, 224, 245, 259, 293n44, 313, 342
Montúfar, Alonso de, 46–47, 175–176
moon, 126, 166n159, 171, 198, 245, 248, 250, 287n9, 288n13–14, 411–412, 414, 468
Moro Romero, Raffaele, 445n56
Moss, Leonard W., 224
Mota Padilla, Matías de la, 252, 591n1
Motolinía, 373, 378, 464
mountains, 75, 126–127, 137–138, 140, 144, 146, 340, 411, 460, 462–466, 470, 488n21, 490n48, 506, 511–512, 516, 529
Moxica, Manuel Antonio, 311
Moya de Contreras, Pedro, 47, 377

mulato (and *casta*), 53, 56–57, 61–62, 64, 87n83, 104, 107, 118, 130, 142, 310, 315, 331, 428, 510, 551
Muntáñez, Nicolás, 474
music, 9, 26n40, 27n41, 69–70, 77n7, 218, 324, 340, 482, 540n62, 552

nagual, 127, 129
Nalle, Sarah, 624n5
narrative, 1, 10–14, 17, 21, 27n44, 28n51, 29n61, 46, 75, 339, 461, 474, 562
Nativitas Tepetlatcingo, 106, 336–337
Nava, José de, 610
Navarrete, Carlos, 223, 242n148
Navarrete, Francisco Antonio, 254, 333, 436, 475
networks, 2, 73, 107–108, 212–213, 261, 455–456, 510, 552, 555, 561–562
New Mexico, 252, 443n43
Nican mopohua, 81n39, 82n43, 229n20
Nicholas V, 40
Nieto de Salmerón, Miguel, 373
Niño Cautivo, Santo, 305n130
Niño de Atocha (Plateros), 204, 214
Niño de San Juan de la Penitencia, 204–205, 238n117, 357n97, 396n104, 422
Nora, Pierre, 13, 21, 28n50, 31n79
novena booklets, 4, 17, 59, 62, 73–74, 97, 99, 104–105, 177–180, 190, 193, 195, 198, 209, 212, 220, 257, 259–260, 264, 271, 283, 294n52, 450n94
Nueva Galicia, 90n114
Núñez de Haro y Peralta, Alonso, 112, 115, 303n120, 525
Núñez de Miranda, Antonio, 371

Oakes, Maud, 460, 465
Oaxaca, 136–137. *See also* Antequera; and individual shrines in Oaxaca
Obrajes, 54, 85n72, 447n73, 449n88
Ocaña, Diego de, 265
Ockham, William of, 40
Ocotlán, Our Lady of (Tlaxcala), 45, 46, 50, 61, 66, 84n66, 235n68, 276, 323, 338, 350n35, 378, 388n44
offerings, 7, 9, 59, 62, 118, 128, 144, 271, 282–283, 316–322, 329, 380, 416, 436, 453n117, 516, 539n54
O'Gorman, Edmundo, 46
Oleszkiewicz-Peralba, Malgorzata, 243n154
Olivier, Guilhem, 361, 542n67

ololiuhqui, 142–143
O'Malley, John W., 79n21
oral sources validated in colonial chronicles, 27n47. *See also* reception, *voz pública y fama*
Oratorians, 55, 74, 213, 429, 432, 433, 450n100, 451n102, 451n104
origin stories, providential, 81n39, 81n42, 149n16, 152n46, 313, 323–325, 341, 352n66–67, 482, 624n1
Oroz, Pedro (Oroz Codex), 44, 80n30, 166n157, 325–326, 353n74, 365
Orsi, Robert, 170
Ortega y San Antonio, Joaquín de, 171
Osowski, Edward, 500n125, 544n84, 549n128
Otatitlán, Christ of, 22n10, 104, 152n45, 485n3
Otomí, 70, 124, 182, 193, 212, 234n59, 474–475, 484n2, 510, 513, 554
Otumba, 525, 544n79
Oviedo, Juan Antonio de, 17, 62, 98, 99, 102, 200, 272, 274, 282–283, 302n102, 304n125–126, 314, 316, 348n28
Ozomatlán (Guerrero), 455, 486n8

Pablo (baptismal name), 605
Pacheco, Francisco, 287n9
Pachuca, 220, 278, 366, 368–369, 387n39, 426, 449n85, 610
Páez, José de, 75, 272, 301n99, 309
Palafox y Mendoza, Juan de, 66, 76, 96, 346n16, 388n46, 439n22, 449n89, 485n6, 516, 558, 564, 616–617, 633n60
panecitos, 370–371, 388n44, 442n40, 552, 618, 634n75
Parker, Geoffrey, 85n69
Parras (Coahuila), 331, 418
parricide, 538n46
Parshall, Peter, 400
Pasztory, Esther, 25n24, 436n3
Patentes, 402, 403
Patiño, Pedro Pablo, 348n23, 371, 401
Patrocinio, Our Lady of El, 106, 172, 184, 336, 420, 543n73
Pátzcuaro, 98, 104, 203, 258, 267, 313
Pedro (as baptismal name), 605
peninsular patriotism, 263, 284
Peñaloza, Diego de, 274, 276
Perdigón Castañeda, J. Katia, 626n13
Pereda, Felipe, 296n67, 456
peregrina images, 151n44, 219, 298n75, 397n118, 482, 501n136, 517, 555
Pérez de la Serna, Juan, 176, 211, 230n23

Index

Pérez de Ribas, Andrés, 310, 344n3, 345n5, 355n82, 375–376, 390n60, 391n67, 392n68, 457
Pérez de Velasco, Andrés Miguel, 240n133
performativity, 549n130
Pescador, Juan Javier, 261
Petatlán, Christ of, 407, 428, 450n92
Peterson, Jeannette Favrot, 222–223, 243n155
Petrich, Perla, 631n44
peyote, 142, 167n170, 168n176, 353n74, 556
Phelan, John L., 78n18, 353n70
phenomenology, 22n9, 533n12, 549n130
Philip II, 13, 41, 42, 49, 362
Phillips, Miles, 82n48
Piazza, Rosalba, 146, 353n74
Picazo, Andrés, 195, 333
Piedad, Our Lady of La, 30n74, 110, 183, 214
Pietà, 252, 254
Pilar de Zaragoza, Our Lady of, 61, 103, 154n72, 245, 259–261, 284, 442n38
pilgrimage, 502–550, *passim*. See also *romería*
 sources, 532n3
 distinguished from romería, 532n3, 535n31, 537n41
 restrictions, 536n36
 and modern travel, tourism 532n9–10
 as institution, 532n7, 532n9
Pío Álvarez, Juan, 109, 153n61
Pitarch, Pedro, 631n44
Pius V, 363
place, concept of, 3, 96, 276, 483–484, 504, 530, 533n12–13
Poblete, Doña María de, 343, 370–371
pochteca, 534n21
Polo, Joseph Patricio, 317–318
Poole, Stafford, 82n43, 83n52
Pópulo, Our Lady of El, 46, 293n43
Portús, Javier, 400
Priego Velarde, Pedro de Jesús María, 335
Prieto, Guillermo, 143, 290n26
print, printing, printers, 11, 17–18, 43, 44, 73, 97, 105, 180, 264, 328, 334, 371, 398–436, *passim*
prints of shrine images, 4, 16, 74, 96, 103, 145, 178, 198, 202, 205, 212, 219, 227, 250, 257, 260, 274, 278, 282–283, 318, 331, 334, 369–370, 379, 398–436, *passim*, 438n13, 439n18, 441n33, 441n37, 442n38, 442n40, 443n43, 450n94–95, 618. See also the figures of colonial era prints and their captions listed on pp. xiii–xvii
 come to life, 418, 420, 447n75, 448n81
 on theses announcements, 219, 278, 440n27
 and Inquisition, 417, 443n44, 444n47, 444n50
 from Europe, 400, 442n38–39
 commerce in, 401–410, 416, 443n41–42
 and alms collecting, 409, 436, 443n42
 censored, 409, 444n52–53, 445n55
 abuse of, 409, 418, 446n72–73
 and healings, 416, 418, 420, 447n79
 and promotion of shrines, 398–436, *passim*, 442n39–40
probabilism, 102, 151n32
processions, 75, 257, 272–274, 454, 492n55, 511–512, 513–518, 522–523, 524–527, 529, 531, 539n51, 539n58, 540n59–60, 540n64, 542n69, 543n75, 544n79, 548n120. See also Corpus Christi; Semana Santa
 with images, 434, 513, 518, 528, 531
 with sacred bundles, 516
promesas, 348n30, 537n43, 538n45
promotional activity. See Franciscans; Jesuits; Augustinians (and other religious orders); Oratorians; bishops (and individual bishops and priests); publications include devotional histories (especially *Zodíaco mariano*); chronicles; indulgences; novena booklets; prints; *medidas*; *informaciones jurídicas*; confraternities; image shrines (and individual image shrines, especially Tecaxic for blurred lines between promotion and devotion); cities (and particular cities, especially Mexico City, Puebla, Querétaro, Guadalajara, and Tlaxcala); and regulations, conflict, and pragmatic accommodations
Puebla, 45, 48, 54, 60, 66, 87n95, 98, 102–104, 117, 119–120, 172, 205, 218, 220, 258, 259, 266–268, 272, 276, 280–282, 332, 334–335, 338, 340, 363–366, 369–370, 372–374, 376–377, 401, 407, 411, 432, 440n24, 471, 564
Pueblito, Our Lady of el, 5, 125, 164n148, 171, 190, 193–195, 318, 333, 352n59
Puerto de Santa María, Christ Child 'El Enfermero', 296n66
Purgatory, 47, 619

Querétaro, 125, 139, 178, 205, 236n81, 239n119, 485n5, 497n94, 498n100, 499n111, 564, 610
Quiroga, Domingo de, 74

Rabelais, François, 509
race and color, 224–226
Ranger, Terence, 146
Rea, Alonso de la, 315, 330, 472–474
Real del Monte, 544n84, 606
reception, 9, 312–313, 399, 410–436. *See also* images, use of; beauty
voz pública y fama, 11, 27n47, 343, 592
recogimientos, 450n98
Reconquista, 45, 49, 63, 77n6, 263, 341, 342, 352n67, 456, 457, 475, 560, 612
Refugio, Our Lady of El, 96, 172, 246, 280–284, 304n126, 305n129–130, 311, 351n45
regional shrines, 3–4, 20, 39, 44, 49, 60–61, 64, 66, 72–73, 98–99, 104, 106, 124–125, 145, 170, 172, 190, 197, 208, 210, 212, 219, 259, 284–285, 331, 354n78, 407, 483–484, 510, 552–555, 561, 604. *See also* Guadalupe, Our Lady of; San Juan de los Lagos, Our Lady of; Chalma, Christ of; Esquipulas, Christ of; Zapopan, Our Lady of; Sacromonte (Amecameca); San Miguel del Milagro; Ocotlán, Our Lady of; Pueblito, Our Lady of; Remedios, Our Lady of (Totoltepec); Izamal, Our Lady of; Xuquila, Our Lady of; *Mater Dolorosa* (Our Lady of La Soledad, Oaxaca)
Regulations, conflict and pragmatic accommodations, 59, 96, 105, 106, 108–117, 120, 136–137, 140, 145, 314, 327–328, 343, 377, 380–383, 407–409, 418, 454, 470, 473, 496n83, 501n137, 521–523, 524–528, 536n36, 537n44, 538n48, 539n51, 540n59, 540n64, 541n65, 545n86, 547n100, 547n102, 548n120, 549n121, 549n123, 550n133, 606. *See also* Inquisition; bishops; decorum
relics, 361–384, *passim*, and in notes *see* bone, 384n4, 384n6, 385n7, 385n12–13, 386n22–25
  first class, 385n12, 385n15, 395n98
  of local spiritual heroes, 390n56, 391n62, 391n67
Remedios, Our Lady of (Totoltepec), 16, 44, 45, 47–49, 60, 63, 64, 72, 75, 81n38, 83n53, 97, 104, 105, 117, 125, 150n18, 171, 173, 176, 177, 183, 185, 187–190, 193, 197, 214, 216, 234n62, 290n22, 299n81, 312, 318–319, 321, 324, 326, 332, 341, 354n78, 365, 377, 395n99, 402, 479, 553, 561

Remedios, Our Lady of (Cholula), 45, 81n42, 171, 464
Remedios, Our Lady of (Tepepan), 394n84
Remedios, Our Lady of (Tzitácuaro), 190, 197, 198, 315
Remensnyder, Amy, 77n6
Revillagigedo II, Conde de, 113, 114, 117, 147n5, 155n78
revival missions, 73, 152, 245–246, 266, 275, 276, 278, 281–282, 284–286, 426, 530, 555, 559
Ricard, Robert, 38
Ricci, Scipio, 111
Richardson, Miles, 222–223
Richel, Dionicio, 541n64
Rioverde (San Luis Potosí), 618
Roa, Antonio de, 487n12
Robles, Antonio de, 229n19, 257
Rocha Manrique de Lara, José Francisco de la, 195
rocks, 126, 461, 491n50, 539n54
Rodríguez Álvarez, María de los Ángeles, 468
Rome, 502, 510
romería, 511–514, 528–529, 531, 537n38, 538n45, 538n49, 539n51
Rosa Figueroa, Francisco de la, 183–184, 336, 420, 427, 525
rosary, 5, 7, 9, 20, 66, 177, 182, 198, 245, 252, 274–275, 283, 369, 370, 374, 415, 416, 433, 455, 473, 627n17
Rosary, Our Lady of the, 25n33, 42, 246–247, 266, 268, 277, 287n3, 310, 317–318, 382–383, 438n10, 548n120, 620
Rúa, Juan de, 56–58, 86n81
Rubial García, Antonio, 24–25n24, 90n113, 149n14, 371, 372, 385n11, 392–393n77, 394n84, 441n32, 498n102, 498n106, 498n109, 565n12, 637n99
Rubio y Salinas, Manuel José, 110, 136, 164n145, 322, 520, 525
Ruiz Narváez, Antonio, 475
Ruiz y Cervantes, José Manuel, 234n56, 243n154, 349n35, 396n105, 441n29, 448n82, 518, 537n38, 564n6

Sacromonte (Amecameca), 99, 101, 208, 212–213, 244n166, 513, 528
Sahagún, Bernardino de, 166n157, 534n20
Sahlins, Marshall, 146, 169n185
Saigneux, Joel, 275–276
Saint-Charles Zetina, Juan Carlos, 139

Index

saints, images (other than the Blessed Mary), 43, 65, 604–624, *passim*. *See also* individual saints, such as San Antonio de Padua
   miracles of, 170–228, *passim*, 625, 631n44
Salgado de Somoza, Pedro, 331–332
Sallmann, Jean-Michel, 624–625n5
Salmerón, Pedro, 616–617, 634n67
Saltillo, Christ, 207
Salud, Our Lady of la, 99, 101, 102, 104, 151n43–44, 289n22, 313, 346n16
Salvatierra, Juan María, 73, 268, 299n84
Salvucci, Richard, 85n72
San Antonio de Padua, 349n34, 357n99, 363, 381, 605, 617–618, 620
San Felipe de Jesús, 372, 622–623, 637n97–98
San Felipe Neri, 451n102
San Félix Papa, 411, 445n60, 604, 624n1
San Francisco de Asís, 622
San Francisco de los Conchos, 178, 331
San Francisco Javier, 621, 636n90
San Francisco Solano, 365, 372
San Gonzalo de Amarante, 522, 546n97, 621, 636n86–87, 636n89
San Gregorio, Colegio de, 267–268, 271–272, 299n84–86, 300n90, 300n92, 349n35
San Gregorio Thaumaturgo, 64, 230n26
San Hipólito hospitallers, 88n101
San Ignacio de Loyola, 73, 93n143, 102–103, 354n78, 447n79, 605, 636n90
San Isidro Labrador, 411, 445n60
San José, 365, 607–612, 627n17, 628n20, 628n22, 629n23, 629n25, 630n29, 631n36, 634n69
San José de los Naturales, chapel, 46, 52, 369, 394n88, 493n64, 543n70, 607
San Juan Bautista, 606
San Juan de la Penitencia, Holy Child of, 204–205, 238n117, 240n132, 357n97, 358n110, 396n104, 420, 422
San Juan de los Lagos, Our Lady of, 3, 21, 61, 65–67, 72, 98–99, 101–102, 148n13, 150n18, 172, 190–191, 197, 219, 310, 313, 332, 396n102, 451n101, 543n76, 553–554, 565n7
San Judas Tadeo, 606
San Julián (Cuenca), 624n5
San Lorenzo Huitzizilapan, 138
San Luis Potosí, 60, 103, 178, 282, 377, 517, 523, 568
San Miguel Arcángel, 113, 156n90, 380, 632n49, 632n53, 633n53–54, 633n59

San Miguel de Tetillas, 615, 634n68
San Miguel del Milagro (Tlaxcala), 27n46, 113, 323, 604, 615–617, 623, 633n59–60, 633n62
San Nicolás de Tolentino, 64, 363, 370, 605, 617–620, 635n76, 635n85
San Pedro de la Cañada, 380
San Pedro Nolasco, 297n75, 605, 620
San Raymundo Nonato, 620
San Román, Christ, 64, 310, 312, 321, 329
San Vicente Ferrer, 620, 625n8
Santa Catarina de Sena, 621
Sánchez, Joan, 73
Sánchez, Miguel, 73, 125, 175, 177, 229n20, 322–323, 451n104, 490n41
Sánchez de Aguilar, Pedro, 329–330, 355n81
Sánchez Salmerón, Marcos, 388n44, 390n60
Sánchez Reyes, Gabriela, 371, 384n4, 388n43, 446n68, 607
Sánchez Vásquez, Sergio, 489n31
Sandstrom, Alan R., 146, 244n165
Santa Ana, 141, 247, 365, 627n17
Santa Ana Xilotzingo, 137
Santa Bárbara, 612
Santa Gertudis, Francisco Xavier, 332, 474–475, 499n119
Santa María de la Redonda, Our Lady of, 331, 407
Santa Muerte, 606, 623, 626n13
Santa Rosa de Lima, 372, 612, 623
Santa Veneranda, 364, 387n26
Santa Veracruz, La, Christ of (Toluca), 153n60
Santiago, 143, 164n146, 605, 612–614
Santiago y León Garabito, Juan de, 190
Santiagos dance, 164n146, 542n65
Santíssimo Sacramento, Lorenzo del, 347n17, 402, 418, 448n79
Santo Domingo en Soriano, 88n103, 292n40, 321, 330
Santo Toribio de Mogrovejo, 372
"santos," images of Christ and Mary as, 143, 218, 240n134, 379, 384, 395n96
Sardo, Joaquín, 356n93
Sariñana y Cuenca, Isidro, 371
Sarmiento, Pedro, 104
Satan, 22n11, 39, 42, 44, 50, 55, 61, 75–76, 84n63, 89n105, 94n155, 124, 130, 136, 144, 145, 149n14, 160n120, 161n121–122, 175, 200, 209, 248, 273, 303n112, 309–311, 314, 316, 323, 326, 330, 332, 340–341, 353n69, 353n74, 355n82, 412, 414, 415, 417, 456,

461–462, 464, 483, 487n13, 490n47, 493n64, 514, 517, 551, 557, 614, 615, 632n49
Sayula, Cross of, 89n106, 494n69
Scheer, Monique, 223, 225, 226, 243n158
Scolieri, Paul, 539n58
Scott, Robert A., 344n2
Seers, 45, 58, 64
Segura, Nicolás de, 225
Seitz, Jonathan, 59, 86n78
Semana Santa, 75, 201, 222, 254, 288n16, 544n82–84, 560, 564, 606
Señor del Jovo, 120–123
Señor de las Suertes (Orizaba), 538n49
sermons, 233n50, 243n157, 357n97
Serna, Jacinto de la, 169n186, 375, 490n48
Serra Puche, MariCarmen, 617
Servites of Mary, 252
Sessions, Scott, 506, 534n21–22
seventeenth-century developments, 52–76, 175–178, 186–193, 197, 198, 200–201, 328, 331, 339, 341, 360n124, 377, 551, 556
shamans, 59, 127–128, 134–135, 141, 160n113, 163n140, 169n186, 226, 378, 459, 556, 613–615
Shils, Edward, 165n156
Shrines. *See also* image shrines; images; Spain; and individual shrines by name
  Defined, 1, 554
  Spain, Marian, 78n10
Siete Velos, Christ of, 46, 84n68
sight, 4–5, 9, 68, 138, 309, 311, 315, 322, 344n3, 345n9, 435, 439n20, 531. *See also* light
signs, miraculous, 353n69, 353n71
sixteenth-century developments, 35–52, 173–175, 185, 200–201, 325–328, 341
Sklar, Deidre, 550n132
smell, 9, 104, 143, 171, 372, 380, 390n60, 391n67, 471, 474, 505, 517, 520, 523, 531, 552. *See also* incense
Smith, Benjamin T., 486n9, 501n128
Soergel, Philip, 535n26
Soledad, Our Lady of La. *See* Mater Dolorosa
Solórzano y Pereyra, Juan de, 458
Sonsonate, 458
Sor Juana Inés de la Cruz, 552
Soterraña de Nieva, Our Lady of, 295n61, 418, 445n60

sources, 14–19, 63, 65, 175–176, 312–323, *passim*, 329, 337, 339, 407, 471–473, 506, 604–606
space, 504, 533n12–13
Spain, compared and connected to religious life in New Spain, 12, 16–17, 38–44, 47, 49, 53–54, 56, 58–61, 63, 87n89, 95–97, 105, 112–113, 124, 139, 145, 154n68, 170, 172, 185, 197–198, 201–204, 214, 219–220, 224, 227, 238n116, 245–308, *passim*, 292n43, 295n61, 296n66–68, 297n69–71, 313, 316, 325, 328, 334, 337, 340–342, 359n113–114, 361–362, 365, 376–377, 400, 407, 418, 420, 433, 456–457, 471, 473, 507–510, 517, 519, 523, 529, 556–563, 605–607, 612, 614, 618, 621, 624n5. *See also* particular Spanish shrines and devotions, such as Burgos, Christ of, and Covadonga, Our Lady of
spiritual geography, 20. *See also* chapters 1, 2, 3, 8, 9, and Conclusion, *passim*
St Augustine, 44, 89n106, 365, 387n32
  City of God, 310, 458, 542n69
St. Bonaventure, 40
St. Francis Borgia, 103
St. Francis Xavier, 103
St. Jerome, 143, 458, 464
St. Ursula, 362–363
star, 4, 126, 134, 144, 166n159, 171, 172, 179, 196, 197, 248, 250, 267, 287n9, 288n13–14, 315, 316, 352n62, 512, 614
Stone, Andrea, 535n23
Stradanus, Samuel, 176, 316, 319–320, 330–331
sun, 126, 139, 144, 166n159, 248–250, 278, 287n9, 288n13, 379, 412, 475, 617
symbols for images, 170–228, *passim*, 245–286, *passim*, 438n10
synesthesia, 9, 26–27n40–41, 551–552
synpotic study, xxii, 15, 453n117

Taggart, James M., 157n104
Talabarteros, Cross of los, 469–470
Talpa, Our Lady of, 30n74, 99, 101–102, 241n135, 346n16, 487n10
Tamayo de Vargas, Tomás, 64
Tamazunchale, 120–123
Tanck de Estrada, Dorothy, 441n28, 549n121, 625n7
Tangancícuaro, 524
Tapia, Gonzalo de, 376, 457
tarasca, 519, 545n85

Index

Taraval, Segismundo, 477
tattoos, 22n11
Tavárez, David, 125–126, 130, 140, 169n188
Taylor, Charles, 147n3
Tecaxic, Our Lady of, 61, 68–71, 91n128, 92n131, 149n16, 284, 314, 321, 332, 345n6, 351n52, 514
Tello, Antonio, 44, 80n30, 89n106, 90n114, 166n157, 235n70, 323, 330, 355n82, 476
Temastián, Señor de los Rayos, 310, 592
Tembleque, Francisco de, 496n80
Temoac, 527
Tenancingo, 20, 263, 375
Tenochtitlan, 47, 61, 250, 464
Teocaltiche, 526–527
Teotitlán del Camino, 512
Tepalcingo, Christ of, 98–99, 106
Tepeapulco, 66, 468, 496n80
Tepemajalco, 178
Tepetenchi, cross of, 478–480
Tepeyac, 2, 45–47, 50, 63–64, 67, 72, 103, 113, 117, 127, 150n18, 173–182, 229–230n19–23, 265, 271, 316, 330–331, 394n87, 466, 493n67, 503, 506, 509–511, 529–530, 535n23, 536n37, 538n45, 553, 556, 561
Tepic, green cross, 99, 102, 380, 476–478, 500n121
Tepoztlán, 382–383
Tequisquiapan, 220, 481–483, 521–522
Tequixquipan, 259
Tesoro de paciencia, 429–435
Teyolia, 142
Tianguismanalco, 534n23
Tila, Christ of, 242n147
time immemorial (*de tiempo inmemorial*), 146
Tlacolula, Christ of, 206
Tlaloc, 460, 464, 487n11, 627n17
Tlalocan, 157n104, 460
Tlaltenango, 8
Tlamacazapa, 106
Tlatelolco, 75, 187, 540n64, 618
Tlatlauqui, 375
Tlaxcalans, 51–52, 61, 178, 302n107, 381, 462, 463, 615–617. *See also* Ocotlán, Our Lady of; San Miguel del Milagro; crosses
Tlayacapan, 66, 463, 491n53, 500n128, 501n131, 548n120
Tlayacapan, trembling cross, 478–480, 500n126, 500n128, 501n130–131
Toci, 140, 534n23, 627n17

Toluca, 60, 61, 69, 71, 87n95, 108, 205, 351n52, 380, 447n73
Tonalismo, 127, 143
Tonantzin, 127, 140, 165n154, 244n165
Topiltepec, 468
Torquemada, Juan de, 48, 52, 75, 94n150, 257, 322, 325, 343, 353n69, 354n78, 372–373, 457–458, 460–464, 471, 491n50, 493n64, 520, 534n23, 544n82, 545n87
Totolapan, Christ and cross, 81n37, 326–328, 343, 354n76, 487n12
Totomaloyan, 528
touch, mystique of, 3, 7, 9, 18, 40, 59, 87n91, 92n137, 206, 223, 240n133, 268, 299, 331–332, 344n3, 369–370, 372, 374, 378, 383, 390n56, 396n102, 420–421, 436, 481, 529, 531, 552
Trabajadores, Christ of the (Toluca), 61, 108–109, 380
travel, long distance by officials, 549n126
tree root Virgin Mary, 56–58
trees, 2, 52, 56, 84n63, 94n154, 120, 126, 140, 157n104, 166n157, 171, 202, 219–220, 226, 228n6, 250, 288n13–14, 324, 365, 457–460, 463–466, 473, 481–482, 484, 489n28, 490n48, 491n50, 495n77, 512, 539n54
Trexler, Richard, 437n7
triduo booklets, 294n52, 334, 358n111
Tuan, Yi-fu, 504
Tudge, Colin, 1
Tulantongo, Our Lady of, 27n46
Tultitlán, 618
Turner, Edith, 503, 532n9
Turner, Kay, 543n76
Turner, Victor, 22n6, 503, 505–506, 529–530, 534n19, 549n130, 553
Tzompantepec, 512

Ugalde Mendoza, Bibiana, 481
Ulloa, Antonio de, 536n37
university theses, 241n136

vagrancy, 377–378, 502, 529, 532n3, 562
Valadés, Diego de, 547n99
Valderrama, Pedro de, 390n60
Valencia, Martín de, 166n157, 213, 373, 377, 490n44, 516–517
Valencia Cruz, Daniel, 139
Valeriano, Antonio, 46, 82n43

Valladolid (Michoacán), 178, 198, 205, 220, 295n61, 363, 454, 520, 549n120
Valladolid (Yucatán), 60, 65, 353n71, 355n81
Vallejo, Francisco Antonio, 75
Van der Leeuw, Gerardus, 27n41, 539n58, 540n62
Vásquez Estrada, Alejandro, 489n31
Vega, Jesusa, 400
Velasco, Alonso Alberto de, 92n139, 211, 212, 332, 346n16, 401, 432–433, 451n104
Vélez, Karin, 298n77
Venegas, Miguel, 242n151, 268
Venus, 144, 492n54, 495n77
Veracruz, 87n95, 267, 272–277, 363
Vetancurt, Agustín de, 68, 70, 75–76, 91n125, 94n154, 259, 261, 362, 545n87, 617–618
Via Crucis processions, 485n6
Viera, Juan de, 157n102, 511, 538n45
Vilaplana, Hermenegildo, 5, 195, 236n83, 344n1
Villa Alta, 109–110
Villa Sánchez, Juan, 268
Villafañe, Juan de, 96, 342
Villalobos, Joachin, 373
Villalpando, Cristóbal de, 290n26, 293n46
Villaseñor Black, Charlene, 27n43, 607, 629n26, 630n29, 631n38
Villaseñor y Sánchez, José Antonio, 98, 104, 152n46, 235n77, 297n75, 569
Virgin Mary. *See* Mary, Blessed
Vizarrón y Eguiarreta, Juan Antonio de, 178–179, 184
Von Germeten, Nicole, 634n75
Voragine, Jacobus de, 484n1, 632n49

Wake, Eleanor, 489n28, 495n77
Weckmann, Luis, 77n6, 386n22, 570
Weismann, Elizabeth Wilder, 317–318, 630n29
Weston, Edward, 631n47
Wharton, Annabel, 361
Williams, Linda K., 84n63, 564n5
Winckelmann, Johan Joachim, 5
witchcraft, 76, 130, 132, 136–137, 160n114, 161n126, 172
women and Catholic faith and practice. *See also* Blessed Mary; individual shrines devoted to images of Mary
  as participants, 19, 70, 106, 118, 124, 125, 131, 142, 153n63, 218, 252, 254, 258, 271, 290–291n28, 300n93, 327, 370–371, 429–435, 450n98, 455, 521, 524, 526, 540n64, 545n84, 546n97, 548n119, 607, 627n17, 630n29
  and miracles, 315, 319, 321, 327, 328, 337, 354n78, 374, 387n42, 618
  and Mater Dolorosa, 106, 218, 252, 254, 258, 417
  Holy women, 372–375, 383, 392n77, 435, 429, 565n12
Wood, Stephanie, 492n59
woodcuts, 404, 426, 439n14
Woodward, Kenneth, 312, 344n1
Wright, Ronald, 493n65

Xichú, 378
Xipe Totec, 468
Xmalana Tiyat, 126
Xochiquetzal, 50, 617
Xuquila, Our Lady of, 90n118, 98, 243n154, 245, 322, 396n105, 441n29, 448n82, 518, 537n38, 554

Yucatán, 49, 50, 60, 61, 64, 87n95, 141, 162n128, 197, 200, 220, 245, 257, 267, 315, 329, 353n71, 466, 468, 491n50, 536n36, 614. *See also* Izamal, Our Lady of; Mérida; Valladolid

Zacatecas, 103, 148n13, 172, 210, 278, 281–283, 285, 294n55, 304n126, 528, 547n100
Zacatecas, Our Lady of, 45, 46, 49
Zacatlán, 462–463
Zacoalco, 178
Zacualpan, 536n37, 635n78
Zape, Our Lady of El, 62
Zapopan, Our Lady of, 61, 172, 190, 192, 193, 235n70, 311, 346n16, 407, 446n73
Zapotlán el Grande, 525–526, 542n65, 548n116
Zappa, Juan Bautista, 73, 268, 269, 271, 272, 299n84–85
Zeláa e Hidalgo, Joseph María, 357n98, 475
Zetuna, Our Lady of, 352n67
Ziegler, Joanna, 399
Zitlalá, 619
Zodíaco mariano, 17–18, 27n47, 49, 92n140, 98, 102, 104, 219, 226, 272, 282, 311, 314–316, 323, 328, 332, 348n28, 569
Zumárraga, Juan de, 175, 314, 348n23, 362, 373
Zúñiga y Ontiveros family, 402